8th International Operational Modal Analysis Conference (IOMAC 2019)

Copenhagen, Denmark
13-15 May 2019

Editors:

Sandro D. R. Amador
Rune Brincker
Evangelos I. Katsanos
Manuel López Aenlle
Pelayo Fernández

ISBN: 978-1-5108-8833-3

Printed from e-media with permission by:

Curran Associates, Inc.
57 Morehouse Lane
Red Hook, NY 12571

Some format issues inherent in the e-media version may also appear in this print version.

Copyright© (2019) by International Operational Modal Analysis Conference (IOMAC)
All rights reserved.

Printed by Curran Associates, Inc. (2019)

For permission requests, please contact International Operational Modal Analysis Conference (IOMAC) at the address below.

International Operational Modal Analysis Conference (IOMAC)
University of Oviedo
Department of Construction and Manufacturing Engineering
C/ Pedro Puig Adam
Edificio Oeste. Módulo 7
Campus de Gijón
33204, Gijón
Spain

Phone: +34 985 182057
Fax: +34 985 182033

iomac@uniovi.es

Additional copies of this publication are available from:

Curran Associates, Inc.
57 Morehouse Lane
Red Hook, NY 12571 USA
Phone: 845-758-0400
Fax: 845-758-2633
Email: curran@proceedings.com
Web: www.proceedings.com

8th IOMAC INTERNATIONAL **OPERATIONAL MODAL ANALYSIS** CONFERENCE

Proceedings

Copenhagen - Denmark
13-15 May 2019

Editors: Sandro D. R. Amador, Rune Brincker, Evangelos I. Katsanos, Manuel López Aenlle and Pelayo Fernández

iomac

International Operational
Modal Analysis Conference

DTU Technical
University of
Denmark

DTU Civil Engineering
Department of Civil Engineering

SPONSORS IOMAC 2019

Brüel & Kjær

BEYOND MEASURE

Structural Vibration Solutions

SIEMENS

Ingenuity for life

gfai tech

PUBLISHING INFORMATION

Editors:
Sandro D. R. Amador
Rune Brincker
Evangelos I. Katsanos
Manuel López Aenlle
Pelayo Fernández

Title: Proceedings of the 8th International Operational Modal Analysis

All rights reserved
© 2019 INTERNATIONAL GROUP OF OPERATIONAL MODAL ANALYSIS
© 2019 S. D. R. Amador, R. Brincker, E. I. Katsanos, M. López-Aenlle and P. Fernández

INTERNATIONAL GROUP OF OPERATIONAL MODAL ANALYSIS
Campus de Gijón
C/ Pedro Puig Adam s/n, Edificio 7
33204, Gijón, Spain
Email: iomac@uniovi.es
www.iomac.eu

All rights reserved. No part of this publication may be reproduced or transmitted, in any form or by any means, without the prior written permission of the editors.

ACKNOWLEDGEMENTS

The local organizing committee acknowledges the support provided by:
Alejandro L. Caballero
Bruna S. Nabuco
Danny Grydholt
Line L. Christiansen
Pernille L. Andersen
Salihi Lirije
Tobias Friis

8th IOMAC INTERNATIONAL **OPERATIONAL MODAL ANALYSIS** CONFERENCE

Proceedings

Copenhagen - Denmark
13-15 May 2019

Editors: Sandro D. R. Amador, Rune Brincker, Evangelos I. Katsanos, Manuel López Aenlle and Pelayo Fernández

PREFACE

Just like in the occasion of the first two editions of the International Operational Modal Analysis Conference (IOMAC), Copenhagen again hosted the 8th IOMAC. This year's edition of the IOMAC was held in May, from Monday 13 to Wednesday 15, during the colourful Danish spring of 2019, and was organized by the Technical University of Denmark (DTU) and the International Group of Operational Modal Analysis with the sponsorship from Brüel & Kjær, Gfai Tech, Siemens, Structural Vibration Solutions. The local organizing committee thanks all who, directly or indirectly, contributed to the organization of the 8th IOMAC.

The local organizing committee is also proud to contribute to the consolidation of Operational Modal Analysis (OMA) as alternative to the traditional Experimental Modal Analysis (EMA) in experimental structural dynamics. Since the first edition of the IOMAC conference held in Copenhagen, in 2005, OMA has experienced an enormous progress in terms of development of new reliable techniques suitable for solving a broad range of engineering problems in the real world. This achievement can be quantified by the substantial number of papers published in journals and Conferences, as well as by the publication of new books related to OMA background theory and applications.

Similarly to the previous IOMAC editions, the IOMAC'19 conference covers all major aspects related to OMA by focusing on the following topics: Applications in Civil Structures, Damage Detection under Changing Operational Conditions, FEM Updating Using Operating Responses, Identification Techniques & Related Topics, Measurement Techniques and Virtual Sensing, Rotatory Machinery & OMA, Special Applications, Structural Health Monitoring, and Test and Monitoring of Wind Turbines. Apart from the considerable number of interesting papers on these topics, presented by researchers, engineers and students, the conference hosts two Keynote Lectures given by Professor Ph.D. Camelo Gentile and M.Sc. Svend Gade who are prestigious members of the OMA community.

As in the previous editions of the IOMAC held in Denmark (2005 and 2007), Ancona, Italy (2009), Istambul, Turkey (2011), Guimaraes, Portugal (2013), Gijón, Spain (2015) and in Ingolstadt, Germany (2017), scientists, applicants, vendors, engineers and students had the opportunity to share and improve their knowledge and skills in the field of OMA. The local organizing committee wishes that IOMAC'19 enabled fruitful scientific discussions and offered the participants the opportunity to have a pleasant time in Copenhagen.

Lyngby, Denmark, May 2019
The local organizing committee

LOCAL IOMAC ORGANIZING COMMITTEE

Rune Brincker (Chair)
Technical University of Denmark (DTU)
Evangelos Katsanos (Vice chair)
Technical University of Denmark (DTU)
Sandro Amador (2nd Vice chair)
Technical University of Denmark (DTU)
Ilmar Santos
Technical University of Denmark (DTU)
Christos Georgakis
Aarhus University
Anders Brandt
University of Southern Denmark (SDU)
Niels-Jørgen Jacobsen
Brüel & Kjær
Palle Andersen
Structural vibration Solutions A/S (SVS)
Ulf Tyge Tygesen
Ramboll A/S

PERMANENT IOMAC COMMITTEE

Manuel López Aenlle (Chair)
University of Oviedo
Marián García Prieto (Secretary)
University of Oviedo
Niels-Jørgen Jacobsen
Brüel & Kjær
Antonino Morassi
University of Udine
Pelayo Fernández Fernández (Vice-Chair)
University of Oviedo
Carlos Ventura (Interim Chair)
University of British Columbia
Palle Andersen
Structural Vibration Solutions

INTERNATIONAL SCIENTIFIC COMMITTEE

Manuel L. Aenlle, Spain
Joerg Bienert, Germany
Rune Brincker, Denmark
Javier Cara Cañas, Spain
Álvaro Cunha, Spain
Guido De Roeck, Belgium
Spilios Fassois, Greece
Pelayo Fernández Fernández, Spain
Svend Gade, Denmark
Carmelo Gentile, Italy
Niels-Jørgen Jacobsen, Denmark
Filipe Magalhães, Portugal
Simon Marwitz, Germany
Antonio Morassi, Italy
Bart Peeters, Belgium
Luís Ramos, Portugal
Julie Regnier, France
Thomas Schmidt, Germany
Yukio Tamura, China
Ulf Tyge Tygesen, Denmark
Håvard Vold, USA
Palle Andersen, Denmark
Anders Brandt, Denmark
Reto Cantieni, Switzerland
Giuliano Coppotelli, Italy
Eddy Dascotte, Belgium
Michael Döhler, France
Alfonso Fernández Canteli, Spain
Dora Foti, Italy
Marián García Prieto, Spain
Jacek Grosel, Poland
Thomas Lagö, USA
Nuno Maia, Portugal
Laurent Mevel, France
Miguel Muñiz-Calvente, Spain
Carlo Rainieri, Italy
Carlos Rebelo, Portugal
Paul Reynolds, United Kingdom
Piotr Sitarz, Poland
Dmitri Tcherniak, Denmark
Carlos Ventura, Canada

CONFERENCE SECRETARIAT

Line Leth Christiansen
DTU Civil Engineering
Melena Schjøth
DIS Congress Service A/S

TABLE OF CONTENTS

KEYNOTE LECTURES

KEYNOTE LECTURE

Carmelo Gentile
Professor of Structural Engineering
Politecnico di Milano Milan, Italy

OMA-BASED STRUCTURAL HEALTH MONITORING OF HISTORIC STRUCTURES

Structural Health Monitoring (SHM) is generally defined as a multi-disciplinary process involving: (a) the repeated or continuous measurement of the response of a structural system through arrays of appropriate sensors; (b) the extraction from measured data of features, which are representative of the health condition and (c) the statistical analysis of these features to detect any novelty or abnormal change in the investigated system. Among the different SHM strategies, the fully non-destructive nature and the minimum impact of the vibration monitoring makes the OMA-based approach especially suitable to address the preservation of Cultural Heritage structures and also to avoid, in some cases, inappropriate strengthening interventions. The main ideas of OMA-based SHM of historic structures are presented and exemplified through the application to ancient towers and complex historic buildings. For ancient towers, exhibiting cantilever-like dynamic behavior, few accelerometers installed in the upper part of the building allow a successful monitoring of the dynamic characteristics and, most important, the assessment of the effects of changing temperature on natural frequencies and the detection of small damages from frequency shifts. Subsequently, the focus is moved to the vibration monitoring of complex Cultural Heritage buildings, involving the installation of a large number of sensors and more complex SHM strategies. The main expectations are exemplified by using data collected in the first months of continuous monitoring of the Milan Cathedral.

***CV. CARMELO GENTILE** received his MSc and PhD degrees at the Politecnico di Milano (PoliMI), Milan, Italy.*
ACADEMIC CAREER: 1987-1990: PhD student, PoliMi. 1991-2001: Assistant Professor at the Department of Structural Engineering, PoliMi. 2001-2006: Associate professor at the Department of Structural Engineering, PoliMI. 2006-2012: Associate professor at the Department of Structural Engineering, PoliMI; Head of the Laboratory of Vibration Testing and Monitoring of Structures, PoliMI. 2013-2018: Associate professor at the Department of Architecture, Built environment and Construction engineering, PoliMI. 2018–present: Professor at the Department of Architecture, Built environment and Construction engineering, PoliMI; Coordinator of the joint research between PoliMI and the Veneranda Fabbrica del Duomo di Milano on the condition-based structural maintenance of the Milan Cathedral. PROFESSIONAL EXPERIENCE: Committed as consultant or check engineer in the structural assessment of more than 100 bridges. BOARDS and CHAIRS: Member of the Scientific Committee of several international conferences (such as EVACES, IOMAC, EURODYN, etc.). He has been the co-chair of the Organizing Committee of IOMAC 2009 and EVACES 2011.

LECTURE OF HONOR

Svend Gade
Gade S&V Consultant
Denmark

35 YEARS OF MODAL ANALYSIS

The modern era of structural measurements began in the early 1980s. The first international modal analysis conference IMAC I in Orlando, Florida, USA was held in 1982. At that time, modal analysis changed from being a pure scientific concept to be a practical engineering tool. Many tests were then limited to single-input/single-output (SISO) measurements. In 1983 the first dual channel signal analyser was released by Brüel & Kjær. Today dual-channel FFT analysis is the established method of performing frequency response function measurements used for what we might call classical mobility based modal testing and analysis. Over the years, progress and development in all fields of the measurement chain has occurred. Developments include the input vibration transducers via signal conditioning to the analogue to digital conversion, real-time and post-processing of functions followed by modal parameter estimation and applications of the modal model. This paper deals with some of the most important steps achieved in this progress. Today it is not unusual that modal analysis is performed using several hundred high dynamic range measurement channels connected to dedicated smart modal accelerometers. These have built-in transducer electronic data sheets (TEDS) doing multiple-input/multiple output (MIMO) measurements or output only measurements with automated modal parameter estimation and model correlation with large finite-element models.

CV. SVEND GADE *received his MSc degree at the Technical University of Denmark.*
PROFESSIONAL EMPLOYMENT: 1973-1980: Lecturing at various danish locations. DTU. 1980-2017: Associate professor and Application Engineer at Brüel & Kjær University, Brüel & Kjær Measurement A/S. 2010–present: Gade runs his own one man consulting company, Gade S&V. INVENTIONS: Gade was first to identify errors of modal parameter estimation when using Impulse Response Functions calculated via the inverse Fourier Transform of Frequency Response Functions. Published in various magazines as well as a B&K Technical Review. Gade described and introduced worldwide the theory of Sound Intensity Measurements in the early 1980es. Gade published an easy to understand description of FFT-analysis similar to analog filters in 1987. BOARDS and CHAIRS: Gade has been is 2nd chair of the IOMAC conference between 2009 to 2017. Has also been chairman at several conferences (IMAC, IOMAC, Inter-Noise, ICSV…). PAPERS and ARTICLES: Gade has presented more than 150 papers at conferences such as SAE, JSAE, Inter-noise, ICSV, IMAC, ISMA and IOMAC. Gade has written more than 50 major articles including 20 articles in Sound & Vibration Magazine and 20 Brüel & Kjær Technical Reviews and a chapter in "Handbook of Noise and Vibration Control" (John Wiley & Sons, Inc.). LECTURING: Gade has lectured extensively throughout the world including Japan, Korea, China, India, Australia, Brazil and USA.

APPLICATIONS IN CIVIL STRUCTURES

IOMAC'19

8th International Operational Modal Analysis Conference

2019 May13-15 Copenhagen

BAYESIAN OMA OF OFFSHORE ROCK LIGHTHOUSES: SURPRISES WITH CLOSE MODES, SYMMETRY AND ALIGNMENT

James Brownjohn[1], Alison Raby[2], Siu-Kui Au[3], Zuo Zhu[4], Xinrui Wang[5], and Alessandro Antonini[6]

[1] Professor of Structural Dynamics, University of Exeter, j.brownjohn@exeter.ac.uk
[2] *Professor of Environmental Fluid Mechanics, University of Plymouth*, alison.raby@plymouth.ac.uk
[3] Chair of Uncertainty, Reliability and Risk, University of Liverpool, siu-kui.au@liverpool.ac.uk
[4] PhD Student, University of Liverpool, zuo.zhu@liverpool.ac.uk
[5] PhD Student, University of Liverpool, sgxwan25@student.liverpool
[6] Assistant Professor in Coastal Structures, Delft University of Technology, a.antonini@tudelft.nl

A set of seven rock lighthouses around the British Isles was studied by a combination of forced and ambient vibration tests executed with some extreme logistical constraints. Forced vibration testing of the circular section masonry towers combined with experimental modal analysis identified modes with alignment assumed the same as the shaker as well as some interesting effects of helideck retrofit, whereas operational modal analysis revealed the considerable degree of uncertainty in mode shape alignment. Hence Bayesian operational modal analysis was used to characterise the uncertainty and find the best representation of mode shape direction. While perfectly axisymmetric towers would show a single frequency omnidirectional mode, OMA reveals the split modes and allows un unbiased view of directionality. The variability and uncertainty of these mode shape directions are further revealed using Bayesian OMA.

Keywords: lighthouse, condition, assessment, system, identification, Bayesian, OMA

1. INTRODUCTION

Lighthouses are iconic structures that provide visual navigational aids to protect mariners and preserve vital maritime trade. Some of the most spectacular examples are the masonry towers constructed in the Victorian era (1837-1901) on rock outcrops (reefs) around the British Isles. A collaborative research project was established in 2016 to examine the performance of a set of these structures, evaluate the wave loads they experience and provide guidance for their future management. A significant component of this project has been evaluation of the lighthouse dynamic characteristics i.e. their modal properties, since these provide insight into the way the structures resist wave forces as well as the means to infer the distribution of extreme wave loads through extended monitoring of dynamic response. To this end an experimental programme of dynamic investigation was organised to provide sufficient information to calibrate finite element simulations and to infer wave loads [1] on a set of seven lighthouses.

This programme focused on a sequence of modal tests primarily relying on a 180 N electrodynamic shaker to produce input-output data for experimental modal analysis (EMA) using classical frequency domain methods (circle fit and GRFP). For five of the lighthouses topped by a steel helideck there were obviously two fundamental modes, rather similar to a tuned mass damper, with alternating phase angle of the lightweight steel helideck. Additionally, each of these modes was in fact a pair of modes occurring at very close frequencies, and EMA was unable adequately to identify these distinct modes in terms of likely slightly different frequencies and roughly orthogonal 'principal' directions.

As a complement to the shaker testing, the secondary ambient vibration exercise is described, the singular value spectra of acceleration responses presented and the Bayesian operational modal analysis (BAYOMA) process introduced, that allows identification and quantification of most probable values (MPV) and coefficients of variation (COVs) of natural frequency, damping ratio and mode shape.

Seven lighthouses were studied, but a sample of three of these, all with helidecks, is chosen for this paper. All three lighthouses masonry towers are 'concave elliptic frustums' following Smeaton's classic design on Eddystone Rocks (south of Plymouth), and have helidecks fixed to the crown of the masonry structure and straddling the lantern. Wolf Rock lighthouse was the first rock lighthouse to be equipped with a helideck, in 1973, to simplify, render safer and less costly access for lighthouse keepers and (when the lighthouses were automated) by maintenance crews. The three examples are operated by Trinity House, one of the three General Lighthouse Authorities of the British Isles.

Table 1: Lighthouse details

Lighthouse	Location	Built	Designer	Tower height	Modal test date
Les Hanois (TH)	Guernsey west coast 49°26′06.2″N 2°42′08.4″W	1860-1862	James Douglass	36 m	2/6/2016
Wolf Rock (TH)	15 km west of Land's End 49°56.72′N 5°48.50′W	1861-1869	James Walker	41 m	18/7/2016
Eddystone (TH)	21 km southwest of Plymouth 50°10′48″N 4°15′54″W	1879-1882	James Douglass	49 m	1010/2017- 11/10/2017

Design of British lighthouses evolved by trial and destruction. Smeaton's Tower on Eddystone Rocks (completed in 1759) was the classic design with multiple circular masonry courses comprising shaped and dovetailed granite blocks. Lighthouse construction technology evolved fast during the last half of the 19th century and Les Hanois Lighthouse was the first new lighthouse to employ dovetailed connections to blocks above. The construction method was used in all subsequent structures.

Detail at the foundation level is particularly important as it affects lighthouse axisymmetry. Fixing to the rocks for Wolf Rock [2] and Eddystone Lighthouses [3] was by metal bolts sunk into the foundation rock and 'fox-wedged' at each end. Such mechanical connections extend into lower courses and with the dovetailing and grouting, the lighthouses should act as monolithic granite towers continuous with the foundation rock. This was designed to prevent strong vibrations observed on earlier lighthouses, but which are still known to occur on Wolf Rock, due to its very exposed location. A major objective of the test programme was to identify the modal parameters through forced and ambient vibration measurements in order to evaluate their vulnerability to extreme breaking wave impact loads and to observe the response during long term monitoring of two lighthouses, one being Wolf Rock. Hence Wolf Rock modal parameters are particularly interesting.

2. RELEVANT RESULTS FROM EMA

The most important modes relating to loads from breaking wave impact are the fundamental modes that have lowest modal masses corresponding to mode shape scaling at the effective point of impact, which is usually about one third up the tower height. Modal mass normalised to unity at the crown of the masonry tower is a good proxy as mode shapes in the tower are similar between lighthouses.

Figure 1 shows the three lighthouses and their (two) fundamental mode shapes from EMA in one axis. Modal masses as described but the mode shapes are shown with unity overall maximum value.

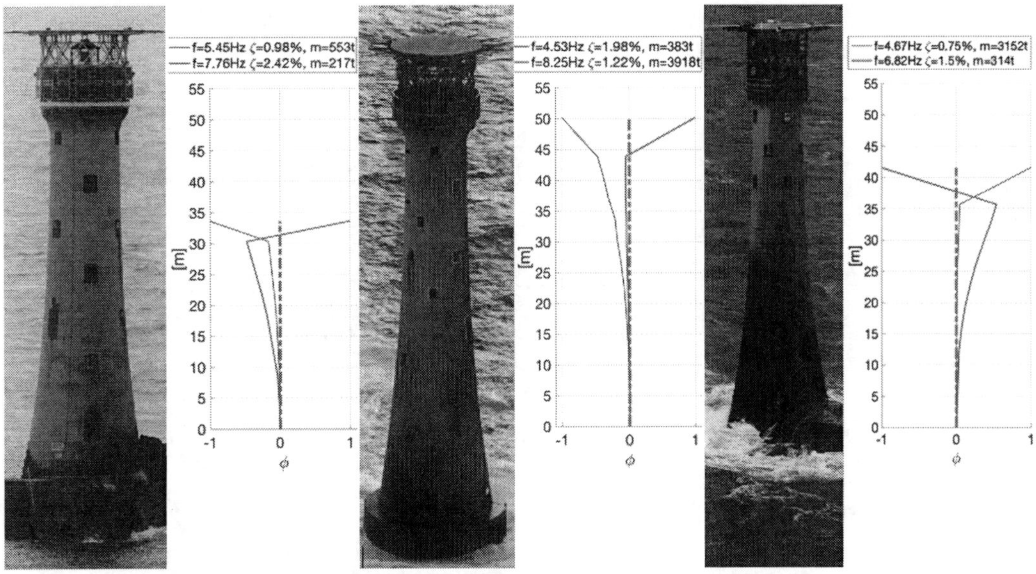

Figure 1 Rock lighthouses and their fundamental modes shapes from shaker testing. Left to right: Les Hanois, Eddystone and Wolf Rock. Photos by Emma Hudson, Trinity House and James Bassitt.

For Eddystone the second mode, and for Wolf Rock the first mode of the pair have very high modal mass due to the high valued helideck mode shape ordinate compared to the crown of the masonry tower. The modal parameters were extracted using the shaker aligned to a direction chosen for logistical convenience, usually to allow more accurate and consistent alignment of accelerometers at different levels within the lighthouse. Compared to buildings and bridges that have obvious cues to aid alignment, in lighthouses the steeply curved inner walls with irregularly spaced features such as windows, the various metallic fittings and electrical equipment, and the spiral staircases all conspire to confound accurate and consistent accelerometer alignment. Shaking in orthogonal direction generally identified almost identical modal parameters, the exception being Fastnet Lighthouse (not described here).

3. SINGULAR VALUE SPECTRA AND BAYESIAN

Power spectral densities (PSDs) of ambient response are the usual way to investigate modal properties. These are obtained as the diagonals of the cross-spectral density (CSD) matrix of all acceleration response channels obtained using the Welch procedure. The number of averages for fixed data length goes inversely with frequency line spacing and there is a trade-off between variance of spectral (line) variance error and bias in modal parameter estimates using some operational modal analysis (OMA) techniques. For stationary systems with stochastic stationary modal forces, the relationship of record length with uncertainty in modal parameter estimates has more recently been established [4], although it is well known that the longest possible duration recordings of stationary data should be used.

Due to logistical constraints (time, helicopter freight capacity) data for OMA (as well separately for EMA) comprised two setups to cover all levels in the lighthouse, there being 9 levels for Wolf Rock, 10 for Les Hanois and 11 for Eddystone, including helideck. Honeywell QA 750s were used, with sets of four (coloured) signal cables feeding drummed multicore signal cables from (Data Physics SignalCalc) analyser via power supply and connection boxes, with the acquisition set up in the service or battery room at the top of the tower. Cables were run externally up the helideck structure to the flat helipad level. Les Hanois and Wolf Rock used two setups of biaxial pairs, Eddystone used biaxial pair references and other accelerometers rotated 90° between setups, which was a more efficient approach.

The whole operation of cabling was time consuming despite preparations based on limited Trinity House photographs, so time on station for Wolf Rock and Les Hanois between inbound and outbound daylight helicopter flights reduced available acquisition time, even before bug-chasing. Modal tests were only possible during visits of maintenance crew who took priority for accommodation, but for the larger Eddystone Lighthouse an overnight stay was possible allowing more time to work and longer to acquire data. The OMA data set details for the three lighthouses are given in Table 2.

Table 2: Ambient vibration data sets used

Lighthouse	Set	Levels and directions	Duration (s)	Sample rate (Hz)
Les Hanois	1	1,2,5,6,9,10 x+y;	940	204.8
	2	3,4,7,8,9,10 x+y;	340	204.8
Wolf Rock	1	1,2,5,6,8,9 x+y;	960	256
2017	2	3,4,7,6,8,9 x+y;	64	256
2019	3	1,5,7,8 x+y;	28800 (8 h)	256
Eddystone	1	1-6y, 7-11x+y;	35968 (10 h)	128

CSD matrices for response data in each set used default rectangular windowing and zero overlap over multiple averages, with PSDs prepared using CSD diagonals, for inspection on site to choose shaker bandwidth for EMA. PSD plots cannot identify identify number of modes in a band, so singular value decomposition (SVD) was applied to CSD matrices, (frequency) line by line. Near the resonance bands of modes the rank of the CSD matrix at any frequency line should equal the number of contributing modes in the band, but in practice practice the rank is usually identified by a sudden reduction of singular values to noise. Hence SVD of the ambient response CSD matrix indicates the number of modes clearly through traces of singular values (SVs) peaking in a frequency band. SVD plots for the the three lighthouses (using the longer recordings when available) are shown in Figure 2.

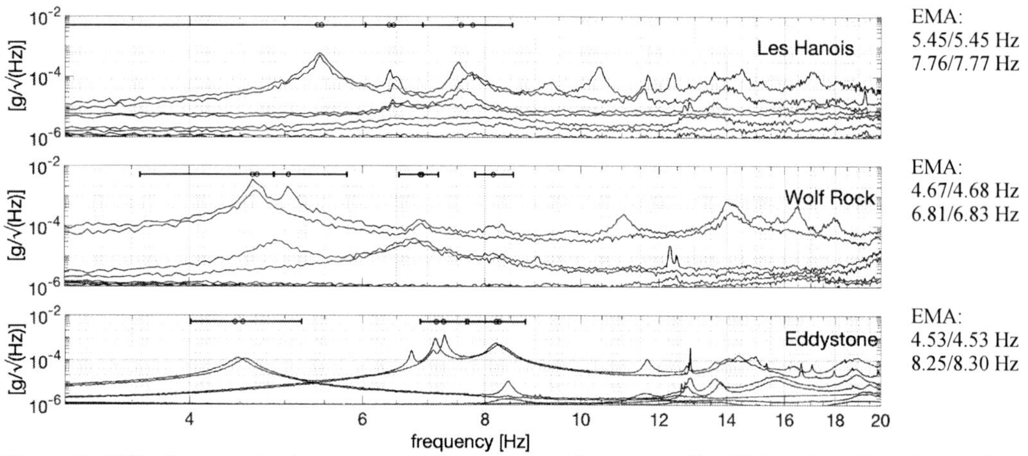

Figure 2: SVD of averaged ambient response data spectra, with corresponding EMA values. Error bars indicate chosen frequency bands and initial estimates for BAYOMA identification.

Les Hanois SVD clearly shows two modes at 5.45 Hz and at least two modes around 7.76 Hz. A generator was running (at the standard 1500 revolutions/minute, with about 10% variation depending on load) and a subharmonic around 6.2 Hz was the suspected cause of PSD peaks, but presence of two SVD peaks suggests otherwise. For Wolf Rock, modes around 4.7 Hz and 6.8 Hz correspond to EMA estimates but there are also additional peaks e.g. at 5 Hz and 8 Hz not identified using EMA. Eddystone Lighthouse benefitted from much better understanding of the modal properties of the structural type, the largest set of (16) accelerometers including many biaxial pairs and an overnight stay that allowed for more comprehensive and long duration measurements. Hence the SVD shows clear mode pairs in bands around 4.3 Hz and 8.2 Hz, plus extra modes which remain mysterious.

As a possible complement to the EMA and specifically to provide some information on mode direction in the absence of forcing, OMA of the ambient response data was initially attempted using a conventional second generation technique i.e. NExT/ERA [5]. Compared to the clean shapes produced by EMA, OMA mode shapes were rather disappointing, with unclear alignment and non-smooth shapes, particularly for Wolf Rock. A significant problem with NExT/ERA is that results depend on operator heuristics i.e. preparation of the CSDs and choice of parameters such as Hankel matrix block size. Compared to EMA there is a high degree of judgement involved in deciding what is a convincing result and the process is complicated by small changes in environmental conditions between setups.

Bayesian operational modal analysis (BAYOMA) [6][7] yields the probability density function of modal properties using the FFT of ambient (vibration) time series, with preselected mode frequency estimates in frequency bands, both chosen based on singular value spectra. Using Bayes' theorem, given the data, the most probable value (MPV) of the set of modal parameters Θ is found by minimising a likelihood function (the 'negative log of the likelihood function' or NLLF) for the given data while the curvature (of NLLF) at the minimum point provides the covariance of Θ. In BAYOMA, the modes are assumed to be classically damped while the noise and modal force are assumed to be independent and to have constant PSDs within the frequency bands (e.g. those shown in Figure 2). BAYOMA identifies mode shapes (not operating deflection shapes), but these need not be orthogonal in the measured DOFs.

In the case of multiple data sets, mode shape pieces are glued using a global least square method [8], but for challenging cases where the signal to noise ratio is low in some sets, a multi-set Bayesian algorithm may be adopted, although presently it only works efficiently when the modes are well-separated. Neither requirement held for the lighthouse data: for Wolf Rock the very short second measurement set was rescued from the end of using a shaker measurement due to lack of time on station.

4. BAYOMA RESULTS

4.1. Mode shapes

Results are presented as mode shape plots for Les Hanois, Wolf Rock and Eddystone lighthouses in Figure 3, gluing sets (as described) to obtain the full mode shapes in elevation and plan. For the plan views the accelerometer x axis is at 0°, and for the elevation views the best fit vertical plane of each mode is identified and the mode is rotated through the plane angle with respect to the x axis to provide a common view. Mode shapes for Les Hanois and Eddystone appear smooth whereas those for Wolf Rock are, unexpectedly, not smooth, most likely due to the very short data duration of set 2.

Three closely spaced mode pairs are identified for Les Hanois. The first and last pair correspond to the EMA pairs but the second pair (at the previously mentioned generator subharmonic frequency) was not clear enough for identification in the FVT. All damping estimates are believable and the modes in each pair are approximately orthogonal within the pair but at different alignments for different pairs. Eddystone data are good quality and like Les Hanois there are three mode pairs, with the second unclear in and missed by EMA, and all three pairs are (self) orthogonal.

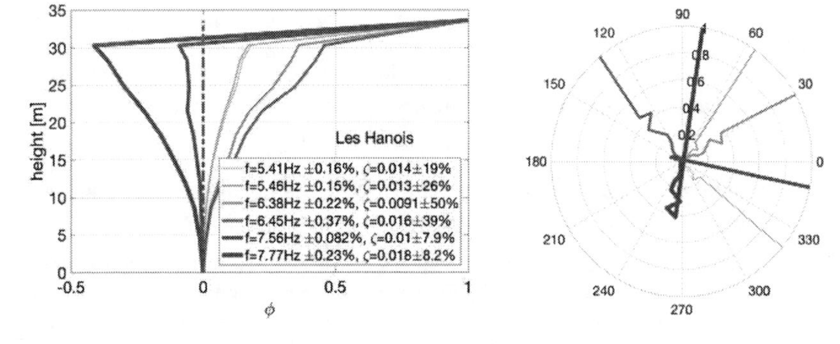

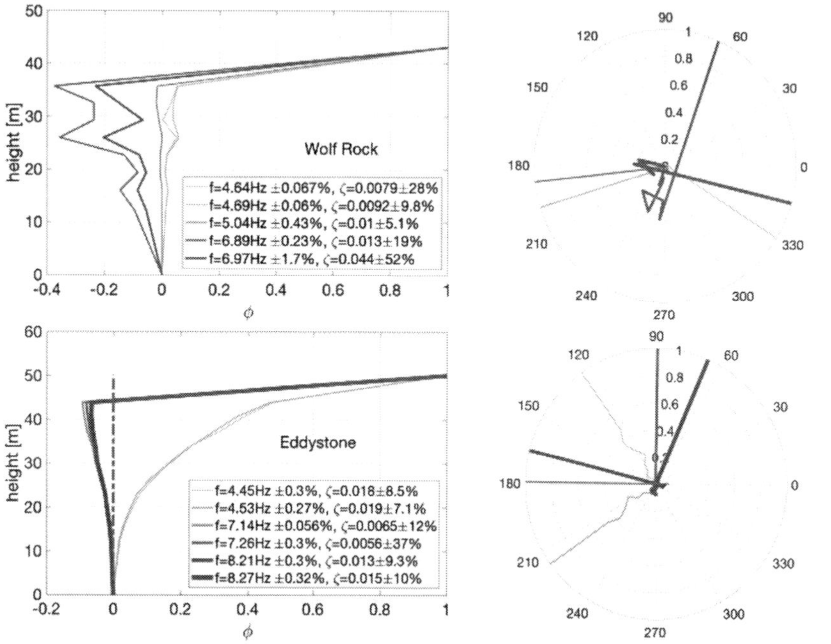

Figure 3: BAYOMA modes. Left elevation, rotated to the same plane; right in plan.

4.2. Mode directionality

Usually modal tests for identifying sway and torsional modes of buildings are planned with a specific orientation and aligned with e.g. core walls, rectangular columns or building envelope [9]. For buildings with square or rectangular section, modes are expected to align with the two symmetry axes. Even with clear symmetry this is not guaranteed, and directions need not align precisely with geometric symmetry axes, neither do the directions need to be at exact right angles at any level.

For structures like lighthouses with circular section there may be no expected alignment which begs questions of whether modes have predominant directions, and how they reflect variation of structural stiffness and mass. Few full-scale tests on supposedly axisymmetric structures have been reported, the closest analog to the studied lighthouse being industrial chimneys. Studies rarely report full-height mode shapes or their alignment, although some papers e.g. [9] do report very close modal frequencies.

The BAYOMA mode shape alignment variability for Wolf Rock is presented in Figure 4. The MPV of mode shapes are illustrated as vectors originating from the vertical axis through the lighthouse. Being vector-valued the dominant uncertainty of each mode shape is obtained from the eigenvector (maximum eigenvalue) of its posterior covariance matrix multiplied by the square root of the eigenvalue. This $\pm 1\sigma$ uncertainty is shown as dashed lines that are roughly perpendicular to the vector tip with thicker lines for second mode of the pair and estimates from both sets are shown. Set 2 duration was approximately one third of set 1 duration and this is reflected in the larger variance for the first mode pair. While mode pairs are self-orthogonal, directions of the three mode pairs do not correlate.

The first (slightly lower frequency) mode of the pair seems to align with brickwork landing. FEM mode alignment is rotated a little anticlockwise for the first pair but is inconsistent with that for the second pair. The FEM mode frequencies are a good match with the experimental modes and a curious result is that the first mode frequency of the helideck alone is remarkably close to the frequency of the additional mode at ~5 Hz identified by both BAYOMA (Figure 3).

mode 1 set1 f=4.640 Hz± 0.06%
mode 1 set2 f=4.630 Hz± 0.23%
mode 2 set1 f=4.697 Hz± 0.07%
mode 2 set2 f=4.698 Hz± 0.20%

mode 4 set1 f=6.886 Hz± 0.07%
mode 4 set2 f=6.901 Hz± 0.28%
mode 5 set1 f=6.910 Hz± 0.18%
mode 5 set2 f=7.025 Hz± 2.12%

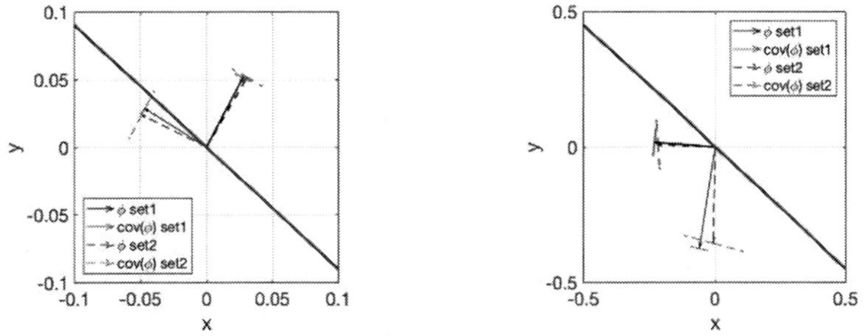

Figure 4: Wolf Rock first (left columns) and second (right columns) mode pairs at Level 8, normalised to unit at helideck. Blue lines are in direction of landing platform and entrance.

4.3. Mode stationarity

Non-stationarity of MPs has already been mentioned. Various factors such as wind speed, temperature and internal live loading can affect structure mass, stiffness and energy dissipation. Modal parameter variation and correlation with such factors is sometimes very clear [11][12] but it can sometimes be challenging to identify beneath the uncertainty in the modal parameter estimation. This is a particularly pertinent problem for the significant bodies of research concerned with diagnosing structural condition via MP changes [12] and inverse identification (of loading and/or structure) [13].

Following a maintenance visit to Wolf Rock in 2019 extended recordings of multiple accelerometer array are available. Estimates shown in Figure 5 are from 5-minute segments; for frequencies as error bars representing $\pm 1\sigma$ identification uncertainty about MPVs and for mode shapes as circles with diameter proportional to uncertainty. Using the same frequency range among the plots highlights the differing frequency 'closeness' as well as the inherent MP variation. The segment length is a trade-off between controlling identification uncertainty (the longer the better) and modelling error arising from potential MP variation between segments (the shorter the better). The mode shape uncertainty and variation indicate a clear link with closeness of frequencies

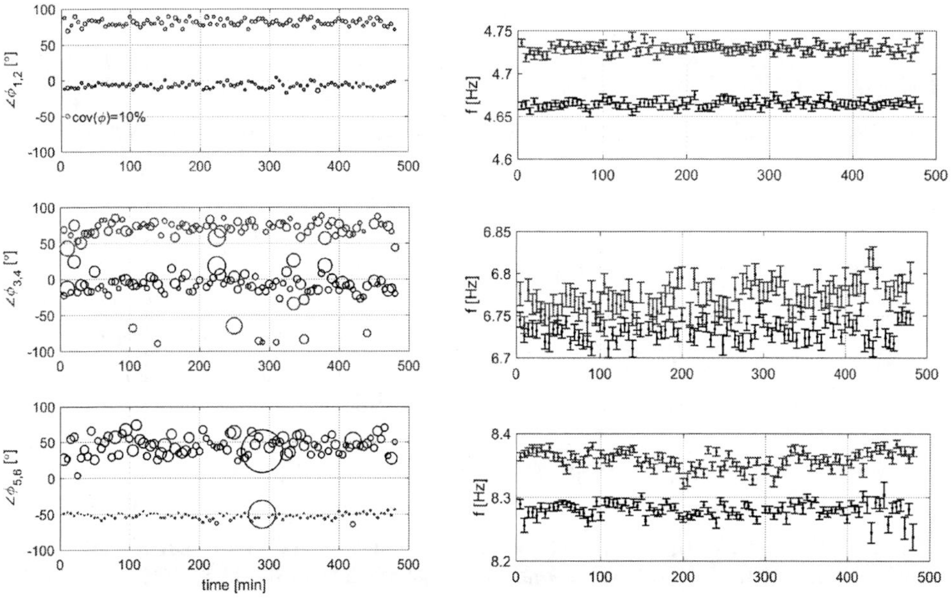

Figure 5: Mode pair mode shape (left) and frequency (right) variation for overnight recording at Wolf Rock Lighthouse.

5. CONCLUSIONS

The dynamic properties of this set of iconic rock lighthouses are important to study for the purpose of vulnerability assessment but the results are useful for studying the problem of distinguishing and aligning very close modes. Mysteries remain about the structural origins of some of the modes but the outcomes are very useful for further development of BAYOMA.

ACKNOWLEDGEMENTS

The research was supported by EPSRC grants EP/N022947/1, EP/N022955/1, EP/NO23285/1 EP/N017803/1 and EP/N017897/1 and by the General Lighthouse Authorities. We are very grateful to James Bassitt, Ian Moon, Emma Hudson, Vincent Ao and Alex Pavic for help with field testing.

REFERENCES

[1] J. M. W. Brownjohn, A. Raby, J. Bassitt, A. Antonini, E. Hudson, and P. Dobson, "Experimental modal analysis of British rock lighthouses," *Mar. Struct.*, vol. 62, pp. 1–22, Nov. 2018.

[2] J. N. Douglass, "The Wolf Rock Lighthouse. (Includes Plates).," *Minutes Proc. Inst. Civ. Eng.*, vol. 30, no. 1870, pp. 1–16, Jan. 1870.

[3] W. T. Douglass, S. Webb, G. W. Owen, J. B. Redman, M. Beazeley, L. F. V Harcourt, P. Williams, J. C. Inglis, S. R. Rawlinson, R. H. Brunton, J. W. Barry, E. C. Allam, and J. Douglass, "Discussion. The new Eddystone Lighthouse.," *Minutes Proc. Inst. Civ. Eng.*, vol. 75, no. 1884, pp. 37–56, Jan. 1884.

[4] S. K. Au, "Uncertainty law in ambient modal identification - Part I: Theory," *Mech. Syst. Signal Process.*, vol. 48, no. 1–2, pp. 15–33, Oct. 2014.

[5] J. M. Caicedo, "Practical guidelines for the natural excitation technique (NExT) and the eigensystem realisation algorithm (ERA) for modal identification using ambient vibration," *Exp. Tech.*, vol. 35, no. 4, pp. 52–58, Jul. 2011.

[6] S. K. Au, "Fast Bayesian ambient modal identification in the frequency domain, Part I: Posterior most probable value," *Mech. Syst. Signal Process.*, vol. 26, pp. 60–75, Jan. 2012.

[7] S. K. Au, *Operational Modal Analysis: Modeling, Bayesian Inference, Uncertainty Laws*. Springer, 2017.

[8] S. K. Au, "Assembling mode shapes by least squares," *Mechanical Systems and Signal Processing*, vol. 25, no. 1. pp. 163–179, 2011.

[9] Y. Tamura, A. Yoshida, L. Zhang, S. Ito, S. Nakata, and K. Sato, "Examples of modal identification of structures in Japan by FDD and MRD techniques," in *Proceedings of 1st International Operational Modal Analysis Conference, Copenhagen*, 2005, pp. 237–248.

[10] G. Diana, F. Cheli, A. Zasso, A. Collina, and J. M. W. Brownjohn, "Suspension bridge parameter identification in full-scale test," *J. Wind Eng. Ind. Aerodyn.*, vol. 41, pp. 165–176, 1992.

[11] G. R. Darbre, C. A. M. De Smet, and C. Kraemer, "Natural frequencies measured from ambient vibration response of the arch dam of Mauvoisin," *Earthq. Eng. Struct. Dyn.*, vol. 29, no. 5, pp. 577–586, 2000.

[12] S. Das, P. Saha, and S. K. Patro, "Vibration-based damage detection techniques used for health monitoring of structures: a review," *J. Civ. Struct. Heal. Monit.*, vol. 6, no. 3, pp. 477–507, 2016.

[13] J. D. Collins, G. C. Hart, T. K. Hasselman, and B. Kennedy, "Statistical identification of structures," *Am. Inst. Aeronaut. Astronaut. J.*, vol. 12, no. 2, pp. 185–190, 1974.

IOMAC'19

8th International Operational Modal Analysis Conference
2019 May13-15 Copenhagen

DEVELOPMENT AND APPLICATION OF AUTOMATED OMA ALGORITHMS

Gabriele Marrongelli[1], and Carmelo Gentile[2]

[1] PhD candidate, Politecnico di Milano, Milan, Italy, gabriele.marrongelli@polimi.it
[2] Professor, Department ABC, Politecnico di Milano, Milan, Italy, carmelo.gentile@polimi.it

ABSTRACT

Within the contest of vibration-based monitoring, the paper summarizes the conceptual development of automated procedures of modal parameter estimation (MPE) and modal tracking (MT). The performance of the proposed algorithms is demonstrated using data collected both in single data-sets and over a period of continuous monitoring. The MPE process, based on the automated interpretation of the stabilization diagram associated to any parametric identification methods, is exemplified by using the SSI-Cov technique and consists of three key steps: (1) filtering a high number of spurious poles in the stabilization diagram (2) clustering process and (3) improving the accuracy of the estimates. Eventually, the mean modal parameters are computed for each clustered mode. The MT task is based on the definition of: (a) a pre-selected list of baseline modes with adaptive thresholds and (b) a dynamic reference list of modes associated to fixed thresholds.

Keywords: Automated OMA, Masonry tower, Modal parameter estimation, Modal tracking

1. INTRODUCTION

The development of efficient strategies of Structural Health Monitoring (SHM), aimed at assessing the health condition of structural systems, is still a research topic of utmost importance and is receiving increasing attention from different disciplines. Among the SHM approaches, one of the most popular is based on Operational Modal Analysis (OMA) techniques and the use of modal parameters as damage-sensitive features [1-3]. Moreover, the technological advances and the consequent easier installation of dynamic monitoring systems on both large infrastructures [1-2], [3-6] and Cultural Heritage structures [3], [6-10] have favored the studies on vibration-based SHM.

In vibration monitoring, it is essential to combine state-of-art sensors and robust algorithms in order to manage the huge amount of continuously collected data and to automatically identify the modal parameters at pre-selected time intervals. Among the different OMA methods available in the literature, the FDD [11] is very popular in the application to the time series collected in a single test (single set-up or multiple set-ups) but it is less used within continuous monitoring projects because its difficulty to be automated. On the contrary, SSI procedures [12] are widely used for automated OMA because the SSI techniques are suited to be automated and are capable to identifying weakly excited and closely space modes [13-15].

The focus of the present paper is a series of robust tools that allow fully automated OMA avoiding any user interaction and mimicking the choices of an expert user during the modal identification task. As usual, the implemented approach consists of two different procedures: (a) the automated Modal Parameter Estimation (MPE) procedure, aimed at extracting the modal parameters from the stabilization diagram [12-15] of each single data-set; (b) the Modal Tracking (MT) procedure developed to automatically provide the evolution in time of the dynamic characteristics.

The MPE task consists of three key steps, which are subsequently applied in order to: (1) identify and remove a high number of spurious poles, (2) estimate the modal parameters through a clustering procedure and (3) improve the accuracy of the obtained estimates through the application of simple statistical tools. It should be noticed that the noise modes removal and the clustering are based on previously developed algorithms [13-15], whereas the post-processing, aimed at improving the accuracy of the modal estimates, is one distinctive aspect of the proposed procedures.
The automated MT is mainly performed by: (i) exploiting the consistency of the modal parameters, (ii) adopting a reference list of structural modes and (iii) enduring the correct tracking with self-adaptable thresholds. It is worth noting that the definition and the appropriate management of the self-adaptive thresholds characterizes the proposed MT algorithm.

The organization of this paper is as follows. The developed MPE and MT procedures are presented in section 2 and both the cleaning action exerted by each step of the MPE tool and the distinctive aspects characterizing the proposed MT approach are discussed. Section 3 exemplifies the application of the MPE algorithm to a single dataset obtained during the continuous monitoring of the *Gabbia* tower [3], [16] in Mantua, Italy. In section 4, the implemented procedures have been applied to a evaluate the time evolution of the resonant frequencies of the same tower over a period of six months and validation of the results is demonstrated through the comparison with the modal frequencies obtained by manual application of the commercial software ARTeMIS [17].

2. THE PROPOSED AUTOMATED OMA TOOLS

2.1. Modal Parameters Estimation

The procedure implemented to automatically identify the modal parameters consists of a series of subsequent tasks applied to the stabilization diagram [12-15] obtained from a single dataset. In the presented applications, the vibration data measured in operational conditions have been processed using the covariance-driven Stochastic Subspace Identification (SSI-Cov) method [12]. As previously stated, the MPE approach is composed by three steps:

1) Pre-filtering, i.e. the removal of certainly spurious poles that are detected by applying three single-mode validation criteria. As usual [12-15], validation criteria considering the physical consistency of damping ratios and the complexity of mode shape components have been adopted;
2) Clustering, i.e. the process of detecting and grouping all the poles of the stabilization diagram sharing the same characteristics in terms of modal parameters. This step ideally corresponds to the inspection of the stabilization diagram, carried out by an expert user in a manual approach, to identify the alignments of stable poles;
3) Post-processing, i.e. the removal of possible replications of the structural modes and outliers in order to conceivably increase the accuracy of the modal estimates.

The pre-filtering and clustering tasks are exemplified in Fig. 1 and Fig. 2, respectively.

Figure 1a schematically shows the results obtained by applying the SSI method for different model orders (from 4 to 30). Each pole is defined in terms of eigenvalue and eigenvector, with the eigenvalue being associated to modal frequency and damping ratio and the eigenvector being used to estimate the corresponding mode shape. Therefore, possible measures of the mode shape complexity are the Modal Phase Collinearity [14-15] (MPC, which provides an estimate of the correlation between the imaginary and real part of the mode shape components and tends to unity for real modes) and the Mean Phase Deviation [14-15] (MPD, which measures the phase angle of the mode shape vector in the complex plane and tends to 0 for real modes). The action exerted by the pre-filtering step is illustrated in Figs. 1b-d. As shown in Fig. 1b, discrimination between certainly spurious poles and the physical ones is firstly performed by removing the poles associated to negative damping ratio or high damping (i.e., damping exceeding a 10% threshold, which seems a conservative value for civil engineering structures under ambient or operational excitations). Subsequently and shown in Figs. 1c-d, the complexity of the mode shapes is checked by using both the MPC and the MPD validation criteria, as the complexity measure given by the two indices is not completely equivalent [15]. This choice aims to guarantee the removal of a large amount of spurious poles.

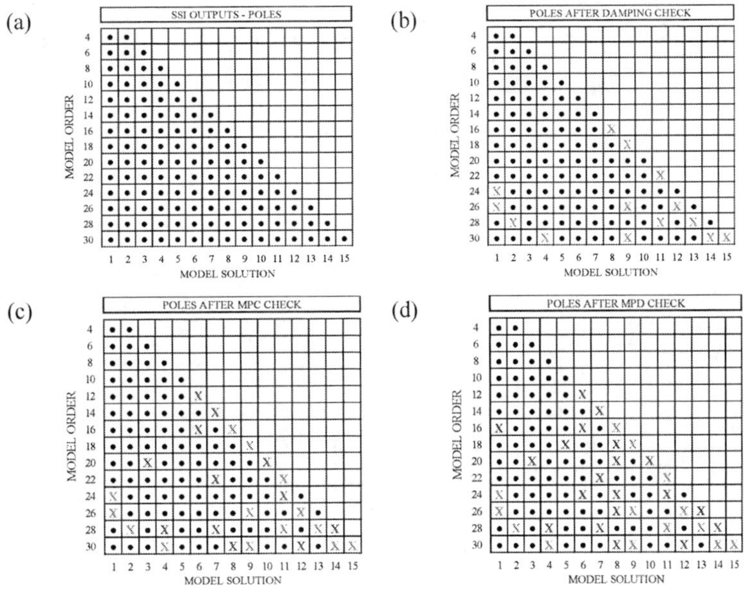

Figure 1. Action exerted by the pre-filtering: (a) SSI output; (b) after the damping check; (c) after the MPC check and (d) after the MPD check (the "X" mark indicates the removed poles).

After cleaning the stabilization diagram from noise and spurious poles, a clustering procedure is used to group all the poles that share same characteristics in terms of modal parameters. In the context of OMA, the most popular way to group stable poles is to measure the distance of all pairs of estimated poles: this operation can be performed because stable poles are generally grouped in high density areas whereas noise modes are much more scattered. According to [12-13], the distance between pair of estimates is calculated checking the similarity between natural frequencies and mode shapes and adopting a hierarchical clustering approach. This approach turned out to be very effective for modal identification of recent constructions using monitoring system with diffused sensors: in such instances, the generation of a high quantity of noise modes is avoided and an easier detection of the structural ones. On the other hand, applying the same strategy to ancient buildings and masonry constructions, in which the monitoring process is usually carried out using a limited number of sensors, could not be always straightforward. For this reason, the metric described in [15] is herein adopted and the clustering approach is based on the definition of one reference point inside each cluster; in other words, the clustering process herein presented uses the concepts of reference pole and fixed reject distance (see e.g. [13], [15]) to group all those poles that share the same characteristics in terms of modal parameters (i.e., natural frequencies and mode shapes). The metric used in the clustering procedure is the following:

$$d_{i,ref} = \frac{|f_{i,ref} - f_{i,j}|}{f_{i,ref}} + 1 - \frac{|\varphi^H_{i,ref} \cdot \varphi_{i,j}|^2}{\left[\left(\varphi^H_{i,ref} \cdot \varphi_{i,ref}\right) \cdot \left(\varphi^H_{i,j} \cdot \varphi_{i,j}\right)\right]} \quad (1)$$

where:

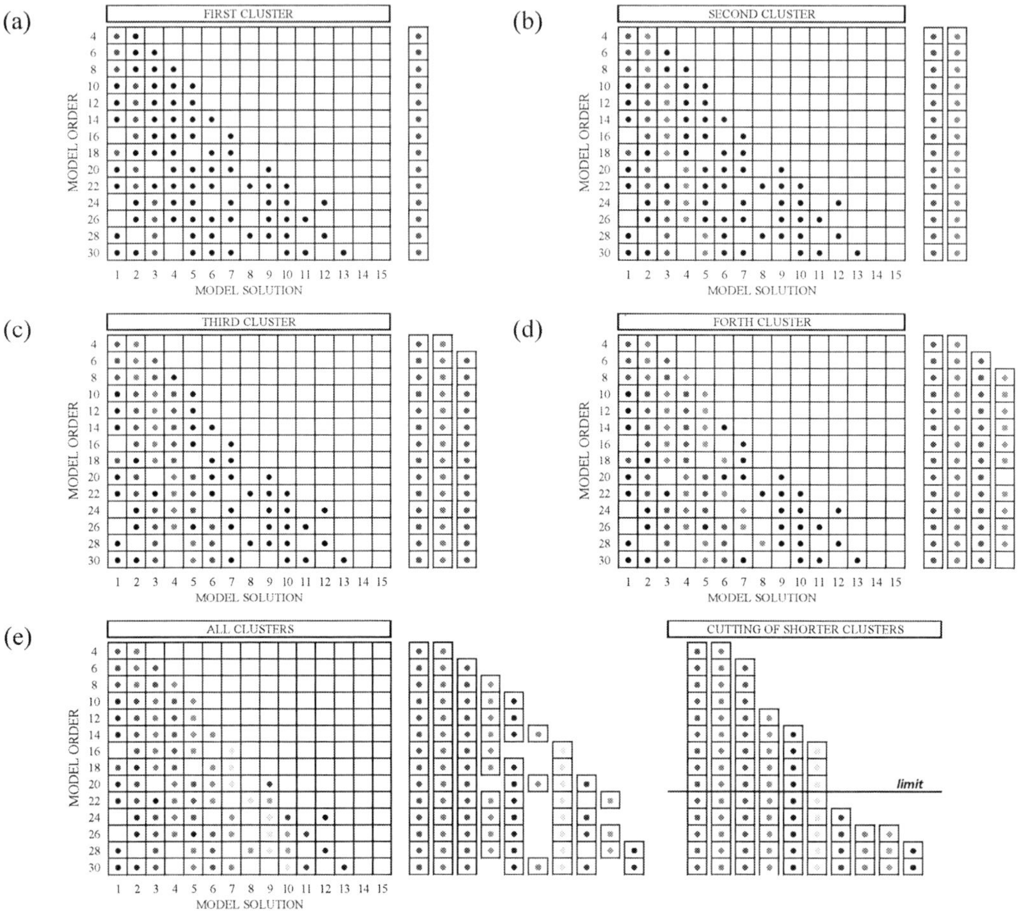

Figure 2. Schematic representation of the clustering process: (a)-(d) construction of the first clusters; (e) allocation of all poles in the clusters and cutting of the shorter clusters.

- $d_{i,ref}$ represents the inter-cluster distance, defined as the distance between each candidate pole and the reference pole of the cluster;
- $f_{i,ref}$ and $\varphi_{i,ref}$ are the mean frequency and mean mode shape of the reference pole, which are updated with the icreased dimension of the cluster;
- $f_{i,j}$ and $\varphi_{i,j}$ are the modal parameters corresponding to the current pole..

The procedure is repeated in order to scan all available poles and it is stopped only when all poles have been scanned and grouped into clusters. The clustering procedure consists of the following steps (Fig. 2):

1) Starting from the lowest model order, the reference point of the first cluster is associated to the pole with the lowest natural frequency;
2) The similarity between the reference point and the poles obtained for increased orders is evaluated using eq. (1) and if the distance does not exceed a pre-selected inter-cluster threshold, the current pole is kept on;
3) Detection of the closest pole among the previously detected ones;
4) Selection and inclusion of the closest pole into the cluster;
5) Definition of the new reference cluster point (in terms of mean natural frequency and mean modal shape) using all poles present into the cluster;
6) Repetition of the points 2)-5) until the poles belonging to the highest model order are reached.

A schematic representation of the main steps constituting the clustering procedure is shown in Fig. 2 When the highest model order is reached, the first cluster is completed (Fig. 2a) and all poles already assigned to the cluster are no more considered. Subsequently, the above steps 1)-6) are repeated in the same way to group poles with same characteristics into another representative cluster (Figs. 2b-d). When all poles have been considered and grouped, as it is customary, the shorter clusters (i.e., the clusters containig a number of elements lower than one third of those present in the largest cluster) are considered as noise modes and deleted (Fig. 2e).

In the end of the clustering procedure, only the clusters standing above the limit are not removed and saved for the next subroutine. Moreover, the mean values in terms of natural frequencies, mode shapes and modal damping ratios become the set of reference modes used in the subsequent post-processing, aimed at checking the results provided by the clustering process and at improving the accuracy of the previous modal estimates by applying simple statistical rules. The post-processing is composed by three different *checks*:

a) The first check is a new clustering process, which is now agglomerative and scans the previously clustered poles. The reference points associated to each previously defined cluster are used as centroids and the inter-cluster distance is now defined by the real distribution of poles inside each previously defined cluster. The present check is performed to amend possible inaccuracies (such as lost of poles belonging to the cluster or, conversely, outliers fallen in the cluster) occurred at the beginning of the cluster generation and to conceivably reduce the dependence of the identified modes on user parameters (i.e. inter-cluster threshold) that needs to be tuned before the identification. The new clustering process often results in slight changes of the estimated mean values, with the accuracy improvement being highlighted by the decrease of standard deviations. It is further noticed that, since the reference values have been already defined, the computational cost of the second clustering is drastically reduced;
b) The second check is introduced to remove any possible replication of structural modes;
c) Finally, possible outliers affecting the damping estimates are detected and removed by applying a simple statistical tool based on the box-plot rule.

The final outputs of the MPE procedure are the mean values of the modal estimates (mean natural frequency, mean mode shape and median modal damping ratio) and the geometric mean value extracted considering the distribution of the MPC and MPD values associated to each pole of the cluster.

2.2. Modal Tracking

Within the context of OMA-based SHM, the tracking process deserves a special attention because it directly provides the input for the statistical tools adopted to detect any novelty or abnormal change in the investigated system [1-3], [9-10]. based-OMA damage detection strategies. Despite the MT represents the very initial step of any OMA-based strategy of SHM, a few strategies have been developed in the literature for the full automation of this phase. A common approach [13] adopted to link the currently identified modes to a baseline list is based on similarity of the modal parameters in terms of natural frequency and mode shape (using MAC index).

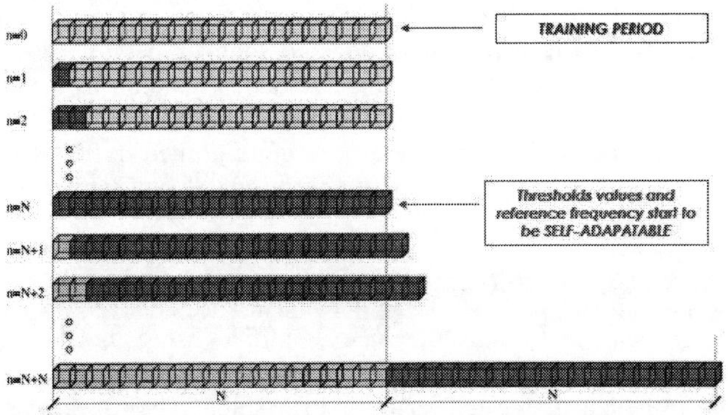

Figure 3. Schematic of the Modal Tracking procedure: training period (grey cubes) and tracking window used for the definition of adaptable thresholds (blue cubes).

The main improvements of the MT procedure herein proposed can be summarized in four aspects: (a) exploiting the consistency of the modal parameters over time, (b) adopting a short training period to make the process fully automated; (c) using a dynamic set of reference modes together with self-adaptable thresholds in order to account for the variations associated to the thermal effects. It should be noticed that the training period plays an important role because it is used to define the adaptive reject thresholds and the complete automation of the process. Figure 3 shows a graphical scheme to better understand the main feature of the developed MT strategy As shown in Fig. 3, the procedure works in two different stages: in the training period (grey slots) and after the raining period (blues slots).

During the training period, the current modal estimates are linked to a pre-selected list of reference modes if two conditions are satisfied. The two conditions involve the computation of the euclidean distance, defined in term of both frequency and MAC variation, between the current modal estimates and two sets of reference modes: the pre-selected list of baseline modes and a dynamic list of modes, which is formed and continuously updated after each MPE. As usual, the current modal estimates are retained (i.e., are linked to the reference ones) if all the distances are lower than pre-defined tolerances. It is worth noting that the dynamic references allow a correct tracking also when the tracking zones between different modes overlap (even if this performance is more evident when training phase is expired).

The training period expires when a limited number, say *N*, of modal parameters estimates has been completed. During this period: (a) a dynamic set of reference modes has been formed and (b) adaptive thresholds have been defined:

$$d^f_{i-ref,j} = \sqrt{std\left(d^f_{i-ref,j}\right)} \qquad d^{MAC}_{i-ref,j} = \sqrt{std\left(d^{MAC}_{i-ref,j}\right)} \tag{2}$$

where $std(d^f_{i,ref\text{-}j})$ and $std(d^{MAC}_{i,ref\text{-}j})$ are the standard deviation of the distance – computed in terms of natural frequency and MAC, respectively – between the *j-th* estimates ($j=1 \ldots N$) related to *i-th* reference mode, collected into each representative group.

Herein after, the *tracking window* (see blue cubes in Fig. 3) shifts one position when each new dataset of modal estimates is considered and the MT process is again performed by checking the distances between the current modal estimates and the two series of reference modes (the baseline list and the dynamic one). The first check (with the distances being computed with respect to the static reference modes) is carried out by using the adaptive thresholds (2), whereas the second one (with the distances being computed with respect to the dynamic reference modes) refers to pre-selected thresholds. At each shift of the tracking window, both the thresholds (2) and the dynamic reference modes are updated by using the last available *N* sets of linked modes.

The proposed MT approach has the objective of modifying the reject thresholds (2) in order to cover the normal fluctuation of the modal parameters but also possible high variations induced by any environmental phenomena. The reliability of the MT approach will be highlighted by the results obtained for the case study presented in sections 3-4, where the resonant frequency of one (local) mode changes dramatically between the winter and the summer period. As it will be shown, the algorithm does not suffer any significant failure and automatically performs the correct tracking of the detected modes using a short period of training. Another important advantage obtained adopting this strategy is referred to the computational cost, that it is quite limited due to the minimal quantity of allocated memory continuously used in the definition of the adaptive distance thresholds.

3. APPLICATION TO A SINGLE DATASET

The validation of the developed tools is herein exemplified using the data collected during the continuos dynamic monitoring of the *Gabbia* tower in Mantua, Italy [3], [16]. The investigated tower (Fig. 4), with its 54.0 m height, is the tallest tower in Mantua. The tower was erected in the 13th century by the Bonacolsi family (i.e. the Lords governing Mantua at that time) for defensive purposes.

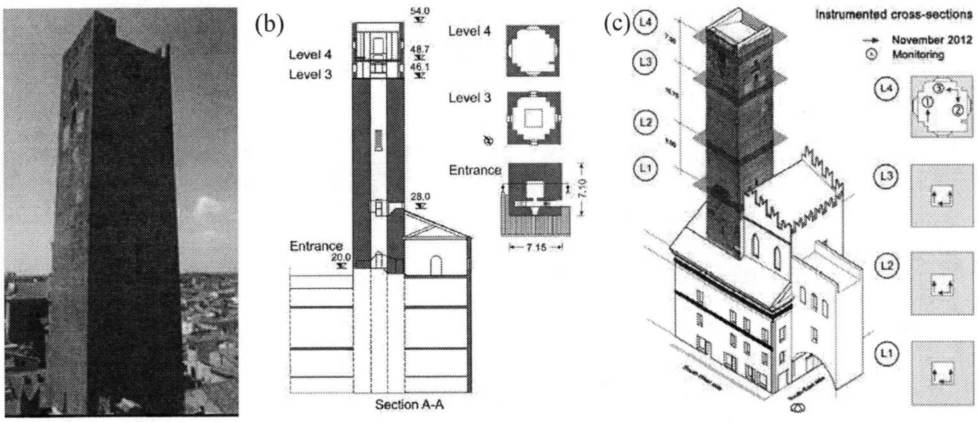

Figure 4. (a) View of the *Gabbia* tower (Mantua, Italy); (b) Sections of the tower (dimensions in m); (c) Instrumented cross-sections and layout of the accelerometers during the preliminary tests (November 2012) and the continuous dynamic monitoring.

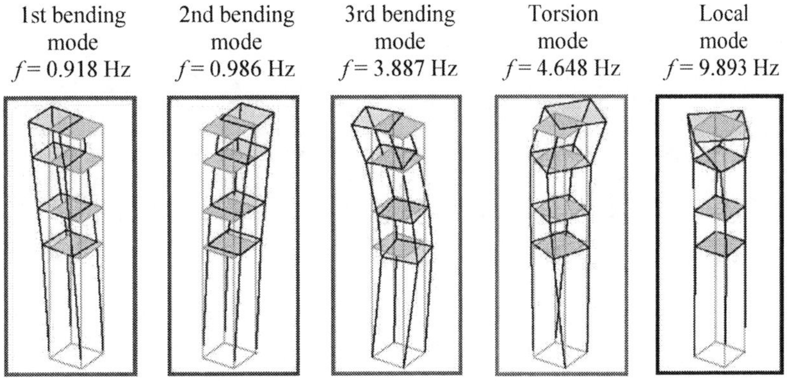

Figure 5. The *Gabbia* tower: vibration modes identified in the preliminary dynamic test [4] (SSI-Data, 27/11/2012).

The structure is built in solid brick masonry and the load-bearing walls are about 2.4 m thick, except in the upper levels, where the walls thickness decreases to about 0.7 m. As shown in Fig. 4, the tower is nowadays part of an important palace, whose load-bearing walls seem to be not effectively connected to the tower, whereas various vaults and floors of the palace are directly supported by the tower. While the main part of the building, below the height of about 46.0 m from the ground level, did not exhibit any evident structural damage (with the materials being only affected by superficial decay), the upper part of the tower turned out to be in a poor state of preservation [4].

An ambient vibration test, preparatory to the continuous dynamic monitoring of the tower, was performed on November 27th, 2012 (Fig. 4c) [4], [16]. The modal identification was performed considering time windows of 3600 s and applying the datadriven Stochastic Subspace Identification algorithm (SSI-Data) [12] available in the commercial software ARTeMIS [17]. Figure 5 summarizes the identified dynamic characteristics of the tower [4] and allowed to confirm that the installation of only 3 accelerometers in the upper available level is in principle sufficient to identify the vibration modes that are normally excited at the low amplitude of ambient vibration detected in the structure. In addition, one local mode was identified at 9.89 Hz (Fig. 5) and involved torsion of the upper part of the tower: the presence of a local mode provided further evidence of the structural effect of the change in the masonry quality and morphology (including un-toothed opening infillings and discontinuities) observed in the upper part of the tower during the visual inspection.

Figure 6 summarizes the results of the application of the newly developed MPE procedure to one single dataset recorded on 17/12/2012, during the continuous monitoring of the tower. The analyzed dataset includes three time series of 3600 s.

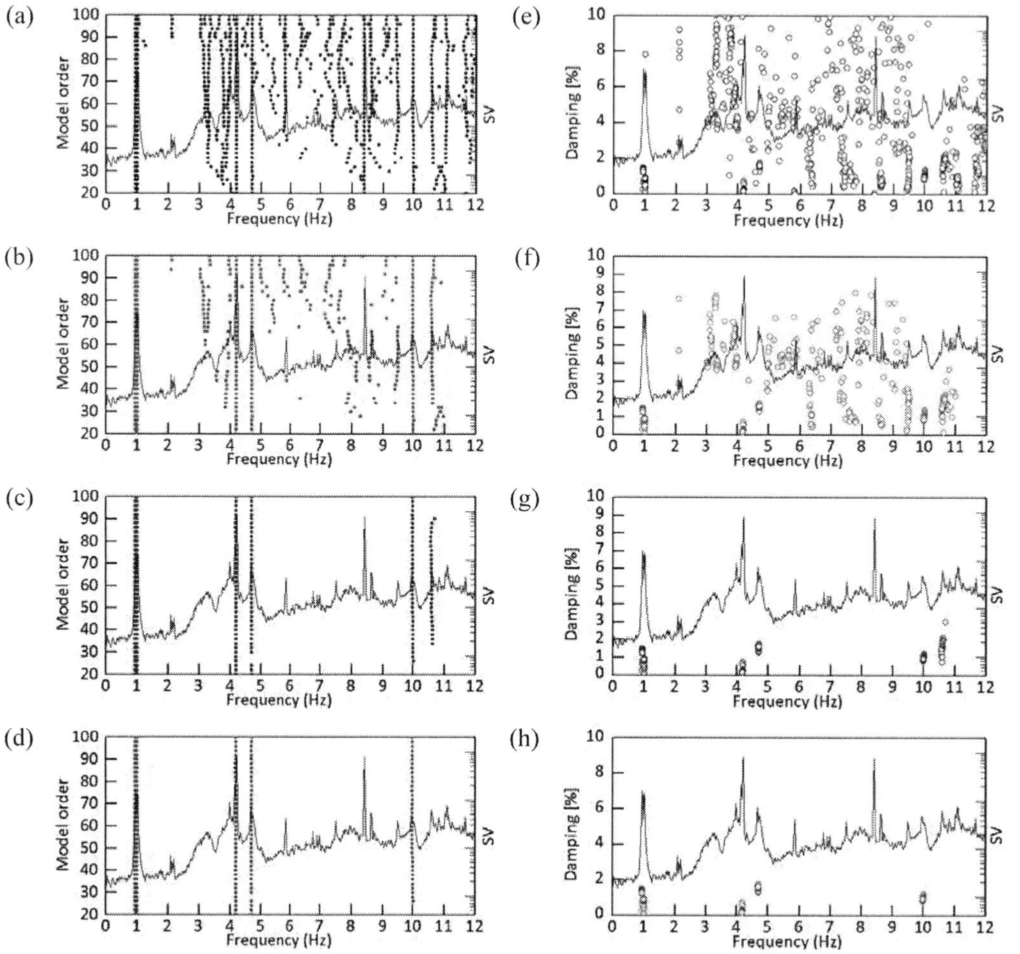

Figure 6. Stabilization diagrams frequency-damping plots: (a) after the SSI-COV run; (b) after the pre-filtering (check on damping ratios and modal complexity); (c) after clustering; (d) after the post-processing to improve accuracy (final results).

Figure 6 shows the typical cleaning action exerted by the different steps of the MPE procedure on the stabilization diagrams. In more details: (a) Fig. 6a shows the SSI outputs obtained for increasing model order; (b) Fig. 6b shows the results obtained after the pre-filtering step; (c) Fig. 6c shows the stable alignments obtained by the clustering process and (d) Fig. 6d contains the final alignments of stable poles corresponding to physical modes performed after the removal of a replicating mode and some outliers provided in the previous step. All plots in Fig. 6 also show the first Singular Value (SV) line of the spectral matrix, which is the mode indication function used in the FDD method [11] to highlight the resonant frequencies.

Figure 6 highlights the robust performance provided by the MPE procedure, with all modes of the tower (Fig. 5) being clearly detected, notwithstanding the low level of measured acceleration (which is testified by the large number of spurious poles in Fig. 6a as well as by the inspection of the first SV line) and the limited number of available sensors.

4. APPLICATION TO CONTINUOUS MONITORING

In order to demonstrate the reliability of the developed tools in the application to dynamic monitoring, six months of data collected on the *Gabbia* tower were considered and the automatically identified natural frequencies are compared with the modal estimates obtained by manual runs [16] of the SSI-data method available in the commercial software ARTeMIS [17]. The investigated monitoring period spans from 12/12/2012 to 30/06/2013 and includes 4651 1-hour datasets of three acceleration time series.

Figures 7a and 7b shows the variations of the modal frequencies versus time, obtained from the manual and the automatic approach, respectively. Inspection of Figs. 7a and 7b provides clear evidence of the correspondance between the results. Moreover, the time evolution of the local mode (described by the blue line in Fig. 7) confirms the robustness of the implemented MT strategy when modal frequencies exhibit significant change.

It is worth noting that the dark red vertical line drawn in Fig. 7b indicates the end of the training period, that was set equal to 4 days (96 estimates). During this period, to ensure the tracking of the modes the rejection distances for all natural frequencies and MAC values were set equal to $d_{fi,max}$=0.20 Hz and $d_{MACi,max}$=0.30, respectively.

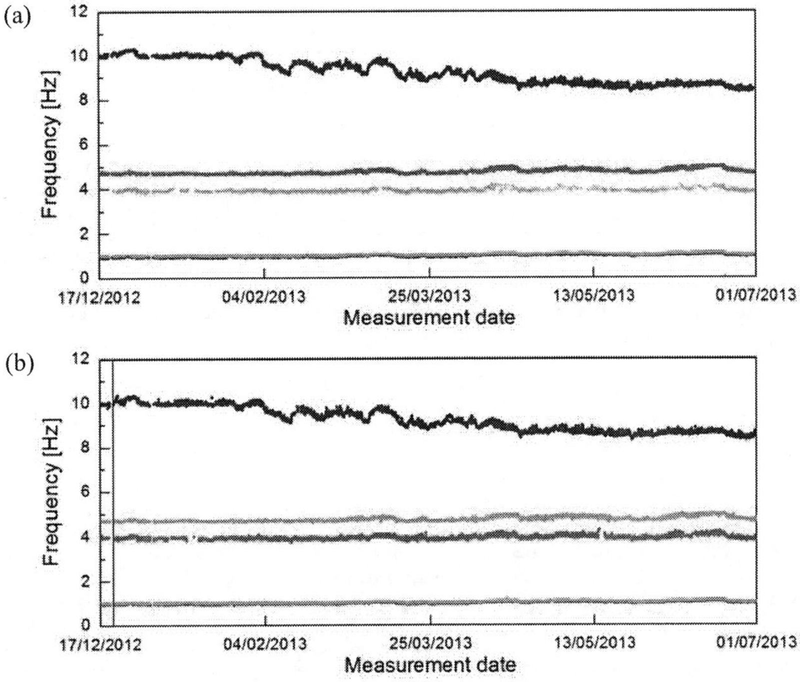

Figure 7. Time evolution of the identified natural frequencies from 17/12/2012 to 30/06/2013: (a) Manual results; (b) Automatically identified results.

In order to better exemplify the efficiency of the developed tools, more details on the evolution of the natural frequencies and the variation of the mode shapes (using the MAC index), related to six months of continuous monitoring, are given. Figure 8 shows the automatically identified modal frequencies and the evolution of the corresponding adaptive thresholds for: (a) the first bending mode, (b) the torsion modes and (c) the local mode. It is worth highlighting as after a short period of training, the continuous updating of the adaptive thresholds enables a correct tracking and prevents the failure of the automatic process (avoiding any intervention of the user and conceivably limiting the comparison of outliers). Similarly to the frequency thresholds also the MAC threshold is updated during the tracking phase, as shown in Fig. 9 for the same modes considered in the previous Fig. 8.

In conclusion, Table 1 compares the performance of manual and fully automated. In more details, the first column of Table 1 identies each vibration mode, the second and third column reports the success rate associated to manually and automatically extracted frequencies, respectively; in the last column, the percentage of commonly identified values – within a frequency tolerance lower than 0.02 Hz – is reported.

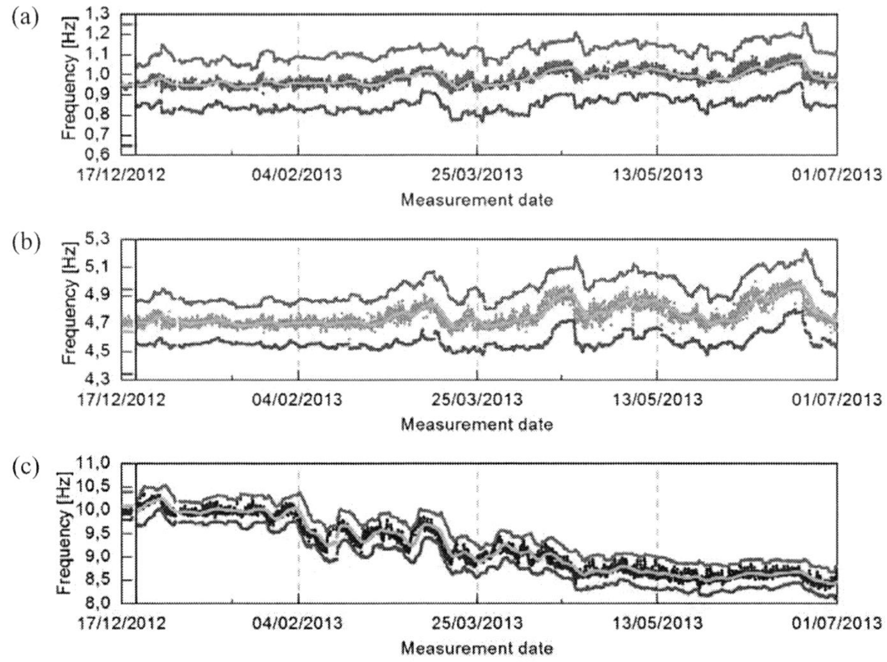

Figure 8. Time evolution (from 17/12/2012 to 30/06/2013) of the identied natural frequency and the corresponding adaptive threshold: (a) First bending mode; (b) Torsion mode; (c) Local mode.

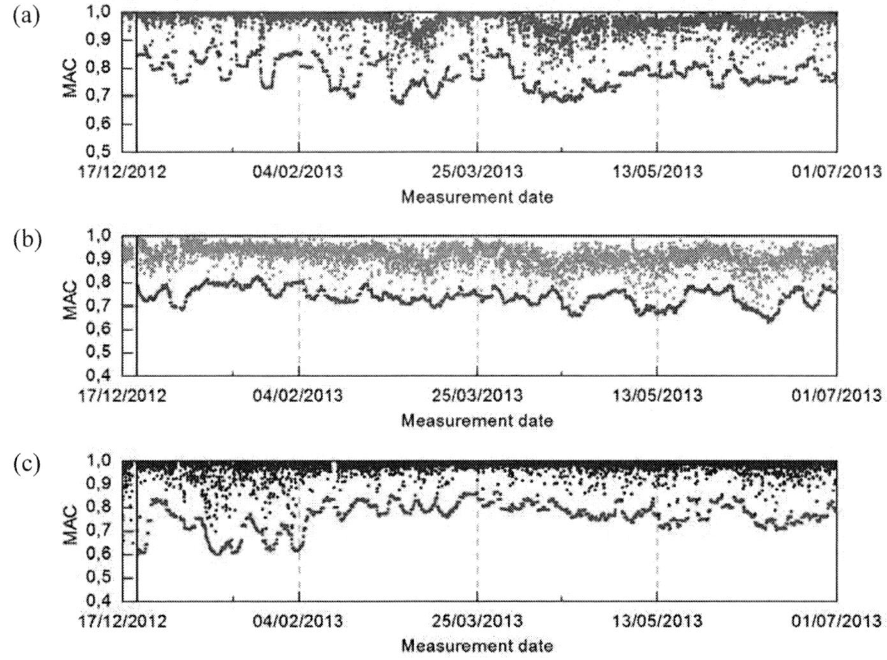

Figure 9. Time evolution (from 17/12/2012 to 30/06/2013) of the MAC value and the corresponding adaptive threshold: (a) First bending mode; (b) Torsion mode; (c) Local mode.

Table 1. Comparison between manually and automatically identified natural frequencies.

Mode Type	Manual identification rate [%]	Automated identification rate [%]	Correspondences with Δf<0.02 Hz [%]
1st bending	80.97	95.16	95.43
2nd bending	80.56	88.11	94.22
3rd bending	31.25	69.98	47.21
Torsion	76.53	93.18	91.06
Local	78.89	91.96	92.19

5. CONCLUSIONS

An automated modal identification procedure, based on parametric methods and the construction of stabilization diagrams, has been presented in the paper. The developed approach is based on the combination of two different procedures: (a) the MPE algorithm, that automatically extracts the modal parameters from a single recorded dataset and (b) the MT algorithm used to evaluate the evolution in time of the natural frequencies and the mode shapes. The validation of the developed tools was exemplified using real data continuously collected during the dynamic monitoring of the historic *Gabbia* tower (Mantua, Italy) [4]. [16].

The application of the proposed algorithms allowed to accurately identifying and tracking the evolution in time of 5 normal modes of the tower; in addition, accurate tracking of the structural modes turns out to be obtaoned even in the case of high variations induced the environmental conditions.

ACKNOWLEDGEMENTS

The co-operation of Prof. Antonella Saisi, who was the responsible of the continuous monitoring of the *Gabbia Tower*, is gratefully acknowledged.

REFERENCES

[1] Peeters, B., & De Roeck, G. (2001). One-year monitoring of the Z24-Bridge: environmental effects versus damage events, *Earthquake Engineering and Structural Dynamics* 30(2), 149-171.

[2] Magalhães, F., Cunha, Á., & Caetano, E. (2012). Vibration based structural health monitoring of an arch bridge: from automated OMA to damage detection. *Mechanical Systems and Signal Processing* 28, 212-228.

[3] Gentile, C., Guidobaldi, M., & Saisi, A. (2016). One year of monitoring of historic tower: damage detection under changing environment, *Meccanica* 51, 2873-2889.

[4] Wenzel, H. (2009). *Health monitoring of bridges*. John Wiley & Sons.

[5] Cross, E.J., Koo, K.Y., Brownjohn, J.M.W., & Worden, K. (2013). Long-term monitoring and data analysis of the Tamar Bridge, *Mechanical Systems and Signal Processing* 35, 16-34.

[6] Gentile, C., & Saisi, A. (2015). Continuous dynamic monitoring of a centenary iron arch bridge for structural modification assessment, *Frontiers of Structural and Civil Engineering* 9, 26-41.

[7] Ramos, L.F., Aguilar, R., Lourenco, P.B., & Moreira, S. (2013). Dynamic structural health monitoring of Saint Torcato Church, *Mechanical Systems and Signal Processing* 35, 1-15.

[8] Elyamani, A., Caselles, O., Roca, P., & Clapes, J. (2017). Dynamic investigation of large historical cathedral, *Structural Control and Health Monitoring* 24(3), 1-25.

[9] Azzara, R.M., De Roeck, G., Girardi, M., Padovani, C., Pellegrini, D., & Reynders, E. (2018). The influence of environmental parameters on the dynamic behaviour of the San Frediano bell tower in Lucca, *Engineering Structures* 156, 175-187.

[10] Ubertini, F., Cavalagli, N., Kita, A., & Comanducci, G. (2018). Assessment of a monumental masonry bell-tower after 2016 Central Italy seismic sequence by long-term SHM, *Bulletin of Earthquake Engineering* 16(2), 775-801.

[11] Brincker, R., Zhang, L., & Andersen, P. (2001). Modal identification of output-only systems using Frequency Domain Decomposition, *Smart Materials and Structures* 10, 441-445.

[12] Peeters, B., & De Roeck, G. (1999). Reference-based Stochastic Subspace Identification for output-only modal analysis, *Mechanical Systems and Signal Processing* 13, 855-878.

[13] Magalhães, F., Cunha, Á., & Caetano, E. (2009). Online automatic identification of the modal parameters of a long span arch bridge, *Mechanical Systems and Signal Processing* 23, 316-329.

[14] Reynders, E., Houbrechts, J., & De Roeck, G. (2012). Fully automated (operational) modal analysis, *Mechanical Systems and Signal Processing* 29, 228-250.

[15] Cabboi, A., Magalhães, F., Gentile, C., & Cunha, Á. (2017). Automated modal identification and tracking: application to an iron arch bridge, *Structural Control and Health Monitoring* 24(1), e1854.

[16] Guidobaldi, M. (2016). *Vibration-based structural health monitoring for historic masonry towers*. Ph.D. Thesis, Politecnico di Milano, Italy.

[17] SVS (2011) ARTeMIS Extractor 2011. http://www.svibs.com/

IOMAC'19

8th International Operational Modal Analysis Conference
2019 May13-15 Copenhagen

EXPERIMENTAL ASSESSMENT OF THE EXPECTED IMPACT OF A BRIDGE SEISMIC RETROFIT THROUGH AMBIENT VIBRATION TESTS

Lucia Minnucci[1], Marco Regni[2], Elisa Speranza[3], Sandro Carbonari[4], Fabrizio Gara[5]

[1] PhD Student, Department of Construction, Civil Engineering and Architecture - DICEA, Università Politecnica delle Marche, 60131 Ancona, Italy, l.minnucci@pm.univpm.it.
[2] PhD Student, Department of Construction, Civil Engineering and Architecture - DICEA, Università Politecnica delle Marche, 60131 Ancona, Italy, m.regni@pm.univpm.it.
[3] PhD Student, Department of Construction, Civil Engineering and Architecture - DICEA, Università Politecnica delle Marche, 60131 Ancona, Italy, e.speranza@pm.univpm.it.
[4] Assistant Professor, Department of Construction, Civil Engineering and Architecture - DICEA, Università Politecnica delle Marche, 60131 Ancona, Italy, s.carbonari@staff.univpm.it.
[5] Associate Professor, Department of Construction, Civil Engineering and Architecture - DICEA, Università Politecnica delle Marche, 60131 Ancona, Italy, f.gara@staff.univpm.it.

ABSTRACT

This paper presents and discusses results of ambient vibration tests performed on the Moscosi Bridge in Cingoli (Italy) before and after the execution of seismic retrofitting works. The aim of the first tests is to evaluate the dynamic parameters of the bridge, such as the eigenfrequencies, the mode shapes and the relevant modal damping ratios, in order to build up a numerical model and, through it, to predict the behaviour of the bridge after the interventions. The dynamic characterization of the bridge is obtained through the measurements of ambient vibrations, which are processed with the Covariance-driven Stochastic Subspace Identification. The information derived by the calibrated model are compared with the results of a second ambient vibrational measurement campaign, and the effectiveness of the retrofit is assessed.

Keywords: Operational Modal Analysis, SSI-Cov, Bridges, Calibrated FEM Models, Retrofit

1. INTRODUCTION

In structural dynamics, modal parameter estimation is the most widespread method to identify and monitor the dynamic behaviour of structures. The system is characterized through modal parameters, namely natural frequencies, vibration modes and damping ratios, which can describe any type of system under various types of input and input ranges. Vibration-based structural monitoring methods are divided into two groups: using controlled excitation, that leads to the Experimental Modal Analysis (EMA) [1], or using random exciting loads, also called Operational Modal Analysis (OMA) [2]. In the first case, the method offers a high accuracy and low difficulties for the identification of the modal parameters; however, its application is onerous especially in case of large scales structures such as viaducts, bridges or dams. In the second case, despite the difficulty to measure the external force, random excitation, constituted manly by wind and traffic loads, is well applicable to the identification of the modal parameters and provides good results for massive structures or big constructions.

In case of bridges, the results of the structural monitoring are slightly affected by the presence of secondary or non-structural elements, so that the modal identification could be efficiently employed to calibrate Finite Element (FE) models through which it is possible to predict the behaviour of the structure in case of damaging (due to earthquakes or degradation phenomena over time) or in case of execution of retrofitting works. The combined use of numerical models and experimental data allows a full evaluation of the structure in every step of its life.

In this paper, the results of the dynamic structural characterization of the Moscosi Bridge, located in Cingoli, in the centre of Italy, are presented and discussed. First, the main structural characteristics of the viaduct are described; then, tests and data processing methods are presented. A first experimental campaign (*ante-operam*) led to the identification of the bridge's modal parameters before some retrofitting works, necessary to restore the integrity of the structure after the seismic events in centre Italy started on 24th August 2016. Then, a second experimental campaign (*post-operam*) took place to evaluate the modal properties after the interventions. The global dynamic response of the structure is checked by means of different placement configurations of accelerometers with the aim of highlighting the flexural-torsional behaviour and the transverse one of the bridge deck under ambient vibrations. The processing of the tests data both before and after the interventions is carried out with the SSI-Cov method [3-5], then the PoSER technique [6] is adopted to merge results of different configurations and to finally identify the global behaviour of the structure. A numerical model of the bridge is developed and calibrated basing on the first OMA results. Then, the FE model is updated according to the retrofitting interventions, in order to predict the structural behaviour of the bridge after the execution of the works, and the numerical data from the second OMA results are compared to the modal analyses ones. The results show the reliability of the numerical model and the goodness of the retrofitting works.

2. DESCRIPTION OF THE MOSCOSI BRIDGE

The Moscosi bridge is a roadway viaduct located in centre Italy, in Cingoli (MC). The viaduct has a total length of about 440 m, formed by 14 spans of 31.6 m (except for the first and the last ones, which are 30.6 m) developed in a curved shape. The bridge deck is constituted by 3 simply-supported prestressed concrete box girders, of 3.6 m spacing, 1.8 m height, with a superior width of 3.09 m, an inferior width of 0.85 m and a web thickness of 0.14 m. The girders are separated by structural joints at each edge of the bridge deck that allow thermal expansion. The box girders are connected by end cross beams. The slab is 0.2 m thick, with a total width of 10.7 m under a 8.6 m carriageway. The bridge deck is supported by 84 fixed both mono and multi-directional bearings of 0.8x0.8 m (6 on each pier and 3 on each abutment) on 13 reinforced concrete circular piers of variable heights. The pier bents have rectangular cross sections of 3 m width, 9 m total length and variable height from 0.8 m to 1.55 m. The piers circular cross section presents a variable diameter from 2.6 m to 4.0 m from the top to the base. The foundation is constituted by squared-plan plinths of 1.8 m height with variable dimensions (7.6x7.6 m, 8.5x8.5 m, 9.3x9.3 m), while the abutments are 4.2 m high, 1.2 m thick, based on a 1.2 m height foundation. The aerial and prospective views of the Moscosi Bridge are reported in Figure 1.

3. TESTS AND MEASUREMENTS

3.1. Measurement instrumentation

To measure the vibrations derived from ambient source 10 accelerometers with high sensibility and low noise are employed. The sensors are connected through coaxial cables to a 3 4-channel acquisition units. In detail, the measuring chain is composed by:

Figure 1. From the top: aerial view of the Moscosi Bridge deck (from Google Maps) and before-retrofitting-works state of the Moscosi Bridge.

- 10 single-axis piezoelectric accelerometers PCB model 393B31 characterized by a sensitivity of 10 V/g, a measurement range of ± 0.5 g, a frequency range 0.07÷300 Hz and a broadband resolution of 1 μg r.m.s.,
- 1 USB chassis NI cDAQ 9178 equipped with 3 NI 9234 4-channel dynamic signal acquisition modules (24-bit),
- 1 laptop,
- coaxial cables.

The air humidity and temperature conditions were stable, within a range of ±3 °C around the average temperature (27 °C), so that perceptible collateral effects on the measurements due to temperature or humidity variations can be excluded.

3.2. Tests configurations

In order to monitor the effects of the ambient excitations on the bridge deck, eight different test configurations were adopted, involving both the edges of the carriage way corresponding to the structural joints between adjacent spans, over both their left and right side. The configurations are described below:

- in P2, P3, P7 and P8 the accelerometers were positioned only on one side of the bridge deck, to evaluate the transverse behaviour of the bridge;
- in P1, P4, P5 and P6 the accelerometers were located on both the bridge deck sides to measure the vertical response due to the flexural and torsional behaviour of the deck.

The numbering and the position of sensors in all the eight configurations are illustrated in Figure 2. The response was registered with a sampling rate of 2048 Hz (the minimum for the used equipment). The total recording length of 2800 s provides a good accuracy in the modal parameter estimates [7].

4. ANTE-OPERAM TESTS AND FEM MODEL

4.1. Experimental data elaborations (ante-operam)

The identification of the modal parameters is performed with the Covariance-driven Stochastic Subspace Identification (SSI-Cov) technique, processed with routines implemented in a Matlab® code. The application of SSI-Cov method for the analysis of ambient vibrations on bridges is common in the literature [8-12].

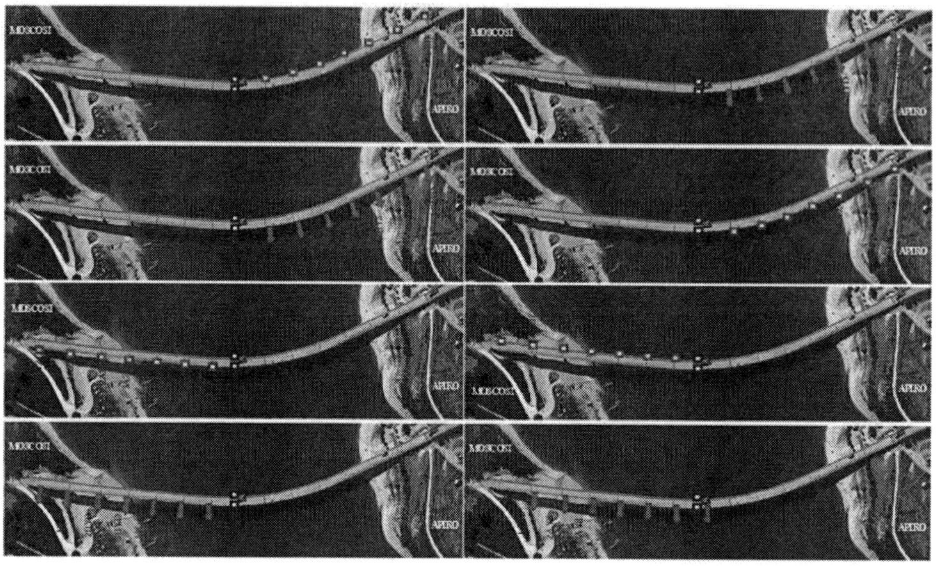

Figure 2. Sensors placement configuration for the vibration tests.

In order to obtain the most accurate modal shapes from the different configurations, the PoSER technique is adopted, a data merging procedure that, for the actual case, is set on the measurement points highlighted in dark red in Figure 2, which were left in the same position for all the tests period. The modes are selected by peak picking from the Singular Value Decomposition (SVD) of the spectral density matrices and for each mode a frequency band surrounding the peak is selected by means of the evaluation of the Modal Assurance Criterion (MAC) [13]. Table 1 shows the average values of resonance frequency and damping ratios, with the relevant standard deviations, while Figure 3 shows the Auto-MAC matrix of the first 6 identified modes.

Table 1. Frequencies and damping ratios of the identified vibrational modes.

Mode	f [Hz]	Δf [%]	ξ [%]	$\Delta\xi$ [%]
1°	0.91	2.74	3.65	1.51
2°	0.99	1.66	1.95	6.85
3°	1.13	4.06	1.85	5.94
4°	1.34	1.73	1.16	1.19
5°	1.64	1.50	1.95	0.99
6°	1.70	1.42	2.21	0.86

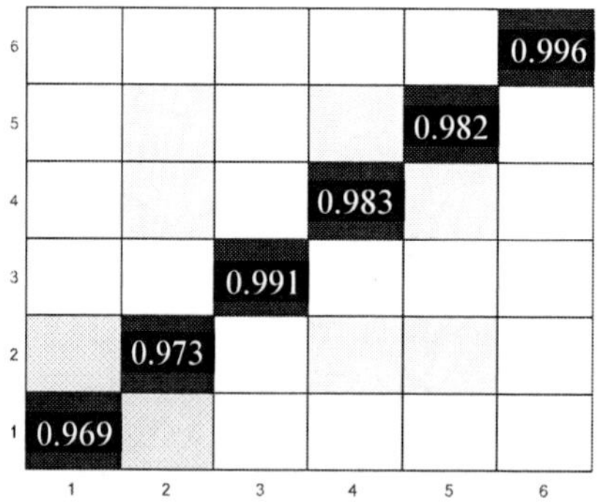

Figure 3. AutoMAC matrix of the first 6 identified vibrational modes.

4.2. FEM model of the Moscosi Viaduct

A numerical model of the bridge before retrofitting is developed with SAP2000 v20.2.0 software. The structural elements are modelled with elastic beam and shell elements. The mono and multi-directional behaviour allowed by the bearings is realized through link elastic elements connecting the deck to the supports. The geometry of the model, described in Chapter 2, is obtained from design drawings, while the properties of the materials are chosen starting from the characterization measurements relating to technical surveys carried out in 2007. A 3D view of the numerical model is illustrated in Figure 4, whereas Table 2 summarizes its main geometrical features and the adopted material characteristics. The value of the elastic modulus e and shell mesh dimensions that allow to reproduce at best the real dynamic behaviour of the viaduct are obtained through an iterative procedure on the vibration frequencies and the relevant mode shapes from the eigenvalue analyses.

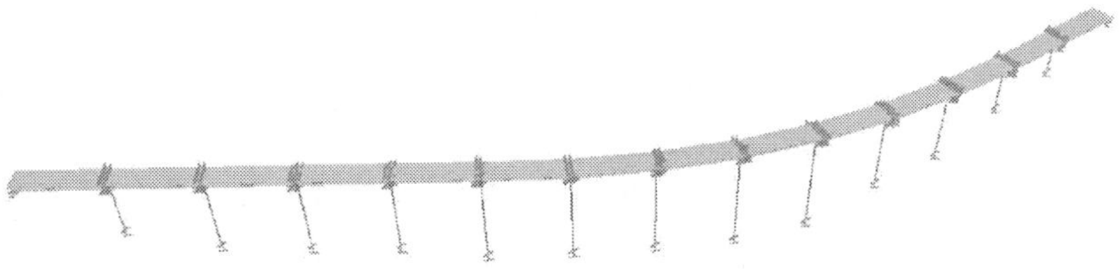

Figure 4. SAP2000 model of the Moscosi Bridge (ante-operam configuration).

Table 2. Materials and geometical properties of the Finite Element model (ante-operam).

Structural element	Geometry	Material
Piles	d = 2.60÷4.00 m	Reinforced concrete: Rck = 30 MPa, E = 3.14e4 MPa
Pier bents (rigid behaviour)	b = 3.00 m, l = 9.00 m, h = 0.80÷1.50 m	Reinforced concrete: Rck = 30 MPa, E = 3.14e7 MPa
Bearings	d = 0.24 m, h = 0.10 m	Reinforced concrete: Rck = 30 MPa, E = 3.14e7 MPa
Prestressed box girders (shell elements)	B=3.09 m, b=0.85 m, h=1.80 m, t=0.14 m	Prestressed concrete: Rck = 55 MPa, 3.63e4 MPa
Slab (shell elements)	b = 10.70 m, t = 0.20 m	Reinforced concrete: Rck = 35 MPa, E = 3.23e4 MPa
Structural joints	t = 0.07 m	Rubber: E = 3 MPa, K = 5e4 kN/m

4.3. Comparison between experimental and analytical results

Comparisons between experimental and eigenvalue analysis results are expressed in the form of percentage of error in Table 3. The MAC values related to the first 6 modal displacements attest a good agreement between experimental and numerical values of natural frequencies.

5. TESTS AND FEM MODEL IN THE POST-OPERAM CONFIGURATION

5.1. Damages and degradation assessment

Since August 2016 the centre Italy was affected by numerous earthquakes, with the main shocks occurred in 24th August, 26th and 30th October. After these seismic events, new technical surveys took place on the Moscosi Bridge on 9th November 2016 to assess the health state of the structure.

Table 3. Comparison between experimental and numerical results (ante-operam).

Mode	Frequency			MAC
	Experimetal [Hz]	Numerical [Hz]	Error [%]	
1	0.91	0.91	0.1	0.997
2	0.99	1.00	1.0	0.971
3	1.13	1.17	3.4	0.982
4	1.34	1.36	1.5	0.994
5	1.64	1.64	0.2	0.955
6	1.70	1.98	14.1	0.977

In detail, the main vulnerabilities highlighted by the investigations were:

- widespread presence of cracks on the bridge piers stems;
- widespread corrosion state of the reinforcement bars on the piers and the pier bents;
- cover detachment on piers and abutments;
- plastic deformation of the majority of the studs constituting the supports.

In Figure 5 photos of damages found during the inspections are reported.

Some retrofitting works needed to restore the bridge integrity after the seismic events of 2016 took place during 2017. Among the interventions, the retrofit provides for:

- the strengthen of piers through an external concrete enlargement, realized with steel jackets and carbon fiber bandages;
- the removal of the existent structural joints, the execution of a continuous slab and the connection of the beams through longitudinal diaphragms in order to change the static scheme from simply supported to semi-continuous;
- the substitution of fixed mono and multi-directional bearings with friction pendulum isolators;
- the restoration of the damaged concrete cover on the entire structure.

5.2. Update of the FEM model

A second FE model is realized to reproduce changes of the viaduct geometry and improved giving a detailed material characterization after the second campaign of technical surveys in 2016. Table 4 describes the interventions for each structural element and lists the most important changes in the model parameters, while Figure 6 shows the new structural configuration, where the inclusion of the diaphragms makes the slab continuous.

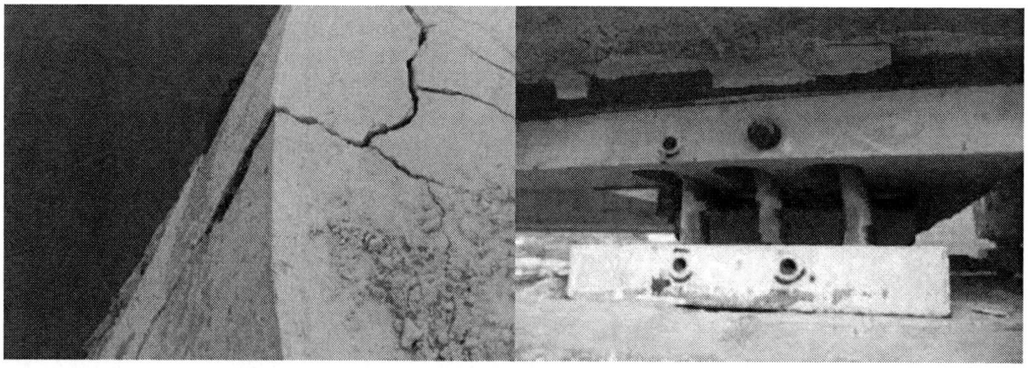

Figure 5. Damaging state of the Moscosi viaduct after the technical survey of November 2016: cracks on one pier base and plastic deformation of the supports.

Table 4. New material and geometry parameters due to the interventions.

Structural element	Description of the interventions	Geometry	Material
Piles	External reinforcement	d = 2.90÷4.00 m	Reinforced concrete: Rck = 45 MPa, E = 3.85e4 MPa
Bearings	Substitution with friction pendolum isolators	d = 0.30 m, h = 0.10 m	*as ante-operam*
Prestressed box girders	Connection of the spans through U-shaped diaphragms and longitudinal bars; removal of structural joints	*as ante-operam*	*as ante-operam*
Diaphragms	Insertion of connection elements in the deck structure	t_{diaph} = 0.50 m, l_{diaph} = 8.70 m	Reinforced concrete: Rck = 45 MPa, E = 3.41e4 MPa
Slab	Construction of a continuous slab	*as ante-operam*	Reinforced concrete: Rck = 35 MPa, E = 2.97e4 MPa

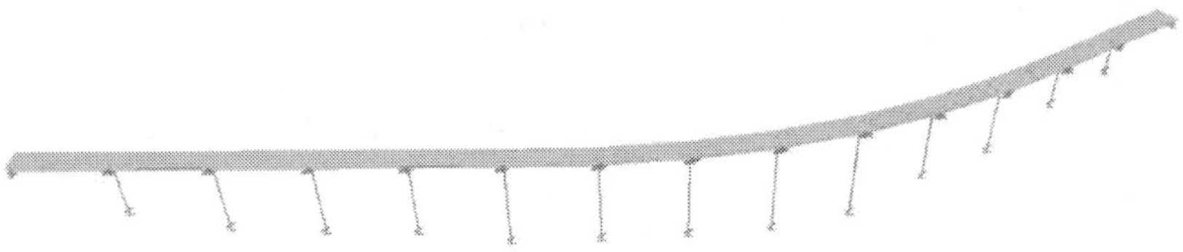

Figure 6. SAP2000 model of the Moscosi Viaduct (post-operam configuration).

5.3. Post-operam tests and comparisons

The eigenvalue analysis results reported in Table 6 allow to predict the behaviour of the structure after the interventions. The numerical model is assessed after a second test campaign, developed with the aim of characterizing the viaduct's modal parameters after the retrofitting works. The results of this second experimental data elaborations are illustrated in a comparison form with the numerical elaborations in Table 6. It is worth noticing that, as expected, the retrofitting works improved the global stiffness of the bridge, causing an increase of the resonance frequency values. The accuracy of the model reflects in the high values of the MAC results relatively to the measured and the new FE model modal displacements. In conclusion, the good accordance between the numerical model and the in-situ behaviour of the bridge is clear evidence of the retrofit efficiency.

Table 6. Comparison between experimental and numerical results (post-operam).

Mode	Frequency			MAC
	Numerical [Hz]	Experimetal [Hz]	Error [%]	
1	1.05	1.05	0.1	0.988
2	1.19	1.24	4.0	0.947
3	1.43	1.43	0.1	0.959
4	1.83	1.84	1.2	0.994
5	2.37	2.39	0.8	0.995
6	2.98	2.99	0.3	0.985

6. CONCLUSIONS

The dynamic characterization of the Moscosi Bridge is described and commented in this paper. Ambient vibration tests carried out during two consecutive experimental campaigns are oriented at determining the modal parameters of the bridge before and after the execution of some required restoration works. The first experimental data provide useful information for the development of the ante-operam numerical model, from which, according to the design interventions, a second post-operam FE model is developed, as a benchmark for the evaluation of the retrofit effectiveness. Through the Covariance-driven Stochastic Subspace Identification (SSI-Cov) technique, in conjunction with the PoSER method to merge results of different configurations, fundamental periods, mode shapes and the relevant damping ratios are identified, processing results of different sensor configurations to capture both flexural-torsional and transverse displacements of the bridge induced by ambient vibrations. The MAC matrix reveals that the first 6 vibrational modes of the structure are properly identified both in ante- and in post-operam layouts. The good correspondence between numerical models and data elaboration results highlights (i) the accuracy of the developed FE models, (ii) the possibility of predicting the real structural behaviour from eigenvalue analyses performed on the upgraded model after the intervention and (iii) the retrofitting works effectiveness.

REFERENCES

[1] D. Ewins, D. (2000) *Modal Testing*, second ed., Research Studies Press, Baldock.

[2] Peeters, B. (2000) *System identification and damage detection in civil engineering*, Ph.D. Thesis, Katholieke Universiteit Leuven.

[3] Juang, J.-N. (1994) *Applied System Identification*, Prentice Hall, Englewood Cliffs, NJ.

[4] Peeters, B., & G. De Roeck, G. (1999). Reference-based stochastic subspace identification for output-only modal analysis. *Mechanical Systems and Signal Processing*, 13(6), 855–878.

[5] Peeters, B. & De Roeck, G. (2001). Stochastic System Identification for Operational Modal Analysis: A Review. *ASME Journal of Dynamic Systems, Measurement, and Control*, 123, 659-667.

[6] Dohler, M., Reyndners, E., Magalhaes, F., Mevel, L., De Roeck, G., & Cunha, A. (2010). Pre-and Post-identification Merging for Multi-Setup OMA with Covariance Driven SSI. In: *Proceedings of the IMAC-XXVIII*, Jacksonville, Florida USA.

[7] Cantieni, R. (2005). Experimental methods used in system identification of civil engineering structures. In: Proc. *1st Int. Operational Modal Analysis Conf.* (pp. 249-260), Copenhagen, Denmark.

[8] Farrar, C. R., & James III, G. H. (1997). System Identification from Ambient Vibration Measurements on a Bridge. *Journal of Sound and Vibration*, 205(1), 1–18.

[9] Peeters, B., & Ventura, C. E. (2003). Comparative Study of Modal Analysis Techniques for Bridge Dynamic Characteristics. *Mechanical Systems and Signal Processing*, 17(5), 965–988.

[10] Brownjohn, J. M. W., Magalhaes, F., Caetano, E., & Cunha, A. (2010). Ambient vibration re-testing and operational modal analysis of the Humber Bridge. *Engineering Structures*, 32(8), 2003–2018.

[11] Ubertini, F., Gentile, C., Materazzi, A. L. (2013). Automated modal identification in operational conditions and its application to bridges. *Engineering Structures* 46, 264–278.

[12] Dezi, L., Gara, F., Roia, D. & Leoni, G. (2016). Experimental and numerical modal analysis of a historical masonry bridge. In: *16th Int. Brick and Block Masonry Conference*, Padova, Italy.

[13] Pastor, M., Binda, M., Harþarik, T. (2012). Modal Assurance Criterion. *Procedia Engineering*, 48, 543–548.

IOMAC'19

8th *International Operational Modal Analysis Conference*

2019 May 13-15 Copenhagen

MODAL IDENTIFICATION OF CONCRETE DAMS WITH DIFFERENT TYPOLOGIES UNDER NATURAL EXCITATION

Sérgio Pereira[1], *Filipe Magalhães*[2], *Álvaro Cunha*[3]

[1] PhD Student, Faculty of Engineering of the University of Porto (FEUP), pereira.sergio@fe.up.pt

[2] Assistant Professor, Faculty of Engineering of the University of Porto (FEUP), filipema@fe.up.pt.

[3] Full Professor, Faculty of Engineering of the University of Porto (FEUP), acunha@fe.up.pt.

ABSTRACT

The Laboratory of Vibrations and Structural Monitoring (ViBest) of FEUP is presently responsible by the development of the research project DAM_AGE (Advanced Online Dynamic Structural Health Monitoring of Concrete Dams).

One of the first tasks of this project consists on the performance of ambient vibration tests on concrete dams with different typologies and stiffness characteristics and on the application of state of art output-only modal identification methods, getting better sensitivity to the problems raised by the very low collected signals (of the order of micro g) when dealing with such massive structures.

In this context, this paper describes a set of ambient vibration tests performed on different Portuguese concrete dams and presents the most relevant modal estimates obtained with the application of modern output-only modal identification techniques, stressing the good level of accuracy in general achieved, despite the very unfavourable signal-to-noise ratio in comparison with other civil engineering applications.

Keywords: Operational Modal Analysis, Concrete Dams, Ambient Vibration Tests

1. INTRODUCTION

The modal identification of dams is historically associated to experimental modal analysis, which has been widely used to identify the most relevant dynamic parameters of large civil structures, with the main purpose of establishing correlations with numerical predictions or in some cases developing the updating of finite element models [1]. In this sense, many forced vibration tests have been performed on dams in the past and continue to be performed nowadays [2] [3].

However, the technological progress that occurred in the field of data acquisition systems during the past few decades promoted the emergence of operational modal analysis as a reliable alternative that gradually became more frequent. Even though operational modal analysis today is more common in bridges, wind turbines, towers and other lighter structures, there are already some successful examples of the application of such modal identification techniques to dams, both through the performance of ambient vibration tests [4] [5] and through the installation of vibration-based health monitoring systems [6] [7]. Nevertheless, when compared to forced vibration tests, much lower levels of vibration and much lower signal to noise ratios should be expected under natural excitation [8], thus very sensitive sensors and high-resolution digitizers are required to obtain good results.

In this context, this work refers a set of ambient vibration tests performed on six Portuguese concrete dams with different typologies and stiffness characteristics, with the aim of getting better sensitivity to the problems raised by such very unfavourable signal-to-noise ratios, as well as to better understand the level of accuracy that can be achieved in such applications. More specifically, the results from the application of operational modal analysis to three of the tested arch dams, which vary from 39 to 110 meters of height, are presented and analysed.

1.1. Overview on performed tests

The Laboratory of Vibrations and Monitoring (ViBest) of FEUP has tested a set of six concrete dams with different characteristics during the last couple of years. This group is composed by four arch dams with very different heights (Alto Lindoso dam, Santa Luzia dam, Bouçã dam and Caldeirão dam), an arch-gravity dam (Castelo do Bode dam) and a multiple arch dam (Aguieira dam). Pictures of the six dams are presented in Figure 1.

Figure 1. Pictures of the six tested dams [9]

The tests performed consisted of ambient vibration tests executed during the day with normal operational conditions, which periodically included the rotation of electricity production turbines since all the dams are part of hydroelectric developments. Even though a few measurements have been conducted in visit galleries, the bulk of the tests were performed in the dam crowns, which are generally accessible and mostly consist of road connections between the two river margins. The exception was Bouçã dam, whose crown constitutes the dam main spillway, in which the test was performed inside the upper visit gallery. A sampling frequency of 100 Hz was used in every test.

1.2. Equipment used during ambient vibration tests

Two different sets of equipment have been used, depending on the dam's dimensions and characteristics. The first system consisted of uniaxial force balance accelerometers connected to a central acquisition unit with electric cables. Cables with different lengths were used, the longest one being just 75 m long, in order to guarantee good quality signals. Therefore, this equipment was used to test just three dams (Bouçã, Caldeirão and Santa Luzia) since it can only cover a maximum length of roughly 150 m.

The second system consisted of a set of tri-axial force balance accelerometers with internal acquisition units and batteries, whose synchronization is achieved through GPS. This system was used to test the larger dams (Alto Lindoso, Castelo do Bode and Aguieira) and it was used simultaneously with the first system in Caldeirão dam and Santa Luzia dam, so that the results from both systems could be compared. Bouçã dam is the only one where the second system could not be used, since the test had to be performed inside the upper visit gallery where there is no GPS signal, so the sensors would not be synchronized.

Figure 2 presents pictures of both the uniaxial (on the left) and the tri-axial (on the right) accelerometers used. The first one is connected to the acquisition system through an orange cable, while the second is connected to a GPS antenna.

Figure 2. Sensors positioned during tests: uniaxial accelerometer with cable (on the left); tri-axial recorder with GPS antenna (on the right)

2. GENERAL RESULTS

Even though different test layouts and durations had to be considered for each case, all the tests were successfully executed and time series of accelerations were collected for the whole set of dams.

The intensity of the recorded accelerations mainly varies according to the operation conditions, namely the rotation of turbines in power plants whose operation may increase vibration levels by a factor of 100 to 1000, depending on the proximity of the plant to the dam. Apart from Santa Luzia dam, whose respective power plant is not located in its vicinity, the effect of the production complex operation on vibration levels was felt in every dam during the entire test or just part of it, depending on the case.

In order to compare the extremely low vibration levels recorded in the different dams, time series of accelerations recorded by the sensors positioned in the central part of each of the tested structures are presented in Figure 3. Time series were chosen taking into account operation conditions, so that electricity production turbines were stopped, and only ambient vibration was exciting the dams during these periods. In the case of Castelo do Bode dam, the power plant was operating during the entire test, thus it was not possible to record any period during which the dam was being excited solely by ambient vibration. Generally, the vibration levels recorded go from a few micro g in quiet conditions to many tens of micro g when traffic crosses the dam or human activities with machinery occur nearby. In the case of Castelo do Bode, which had the power plant fully operating, vibration levels are constantly close to milli g.

To complement this analysis, the time series presented in Figure 3 were used to obtain auto-spectra, which are represented in Figure 4 with the same colour codes. Figure 4 is very interesting in the sense that it exposes the minimum signal amplitude needed to assure adequate characterization of the auto-spectra from the whole set of tested dams, which is between 10^{-13} and 10^{-14} g^2/Hz.

It is also interesting to notice that the auto-spectra from the time-series measured in Castelo do Bode, though being the ones with more energy associated, present poorly defined peaks, suggesting higher vibration intensities do not necessarily imply better results. Even though it is not represented in Figure 4, the same was observed at Aguieira dam (whose power plant is also very close), with time series measured when the turbines were operating.

Additionally, it may be concluded that the frequency of the first vibration mode of dams can vary significantly in the range 3-12 Hz, depending on the structure's geometry.

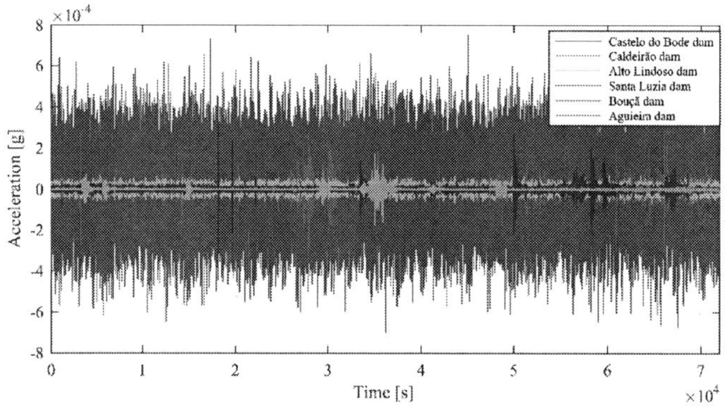

Figure 3. Time series of accelerations collected in the whole set of tested dams

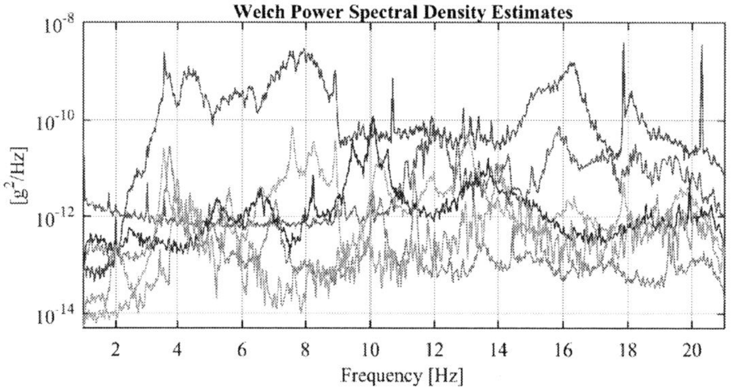

Figure 4. Auto-spectra obtained from each of the time series presented in **Figure 3**

3. AMBIENT VIBRATION TEST OF ALTO LINDOSO DAM

Alto Lindoso dam is an arch dam embedded in a narrow valley zone in the Lima River, in the north of Portugal. The dam is 110 meters high and its 297 meters long crest constitutes a road link between the two banks of the river. A hydroelectric power plant was built close to the dam left abutment, where two vertical Francis turbines operate at 214.3 rpm.

The ambient vibration test of Alto Lindoso dam was performed on the 22nd of February 2017 and it was based on the use of ten GSR-24 recorders from Geosig equipped with internal tri-axial force-balance accelerometers. With the purpose of identifying as many vibration modes as possible, and taking into account the large dimensions of the structure, a test grid was prepared considering 21 measuring points, corresponding to the dam's 21 concrete blocks. To assure the measuring of accelerations in every point of the defined grid, four setups were considered, during which 6 recorders acted as references, and the other 4 recorders as mobile sensors. The six points marked with red dots in **Figure 5** were used as references, while the other 15 points (blue dots) were measured by the mobile recorders. The water level in the reservoir during the test was 322 m (elevation above sea level).

The SSI-cov method was applied to obtain accurate estimates of natural frequencies, modal damping ratios and mode shapes. This method was applied to each setup, and model orders between 20 and 80 were considered. The first 7 vibration modes were identified, and their modal properties are presented in **Table 1**. The results presented correspond to the average of each of the values identified across the several setups. In the case of the first symmetric mode (mode 2), two different frequencies that are associated with the same mode shape were identified, depending on the structure vibration level.

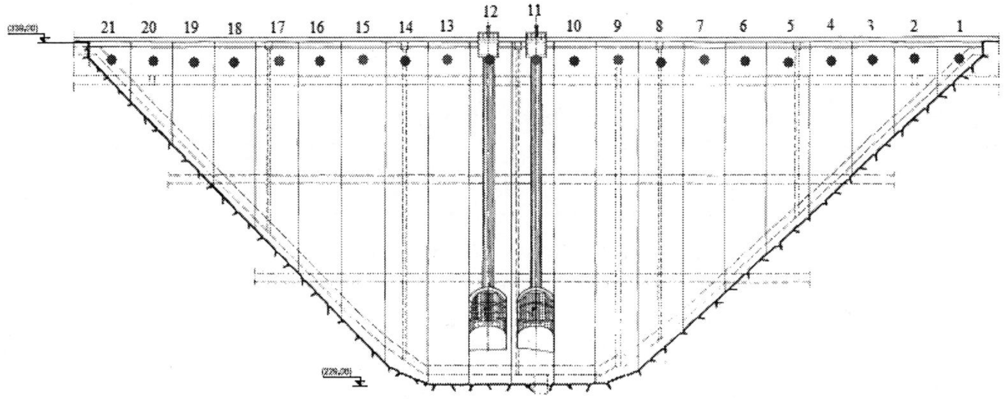

Figure 5. Alto Lindoso dam: test layout

Table 1. Modal parameters for Alto Lindoso dam first 7 vibration modes

Mode	f_{mean} [Hz]	ξ_{mean} [%]	Description
1	3.547	1.259	Antisymmetric
2	3.752 / 3.963	2.850 / 2.164	Symmetric
3	5.004	1.593	Symmetric
4	6.564	1.305	Antisymmetric
5	8.256	1.336	Symmetric
6	9.972	1.291	Antisymmetric
7	11.863	1.497	Symmetric

Very clear and well-defined modal shapes were achieved for the seven identified modes, which are presented in **Figure 6**. In order to facilitate the observation of modal configurations of higher order modes, splines were adjusted to the identified modal ordinates. The first mode is antisymmetric and the second one is symmetric. From the third to the seventh mode, the configurations are alternatively symmetric and antisymmetric.

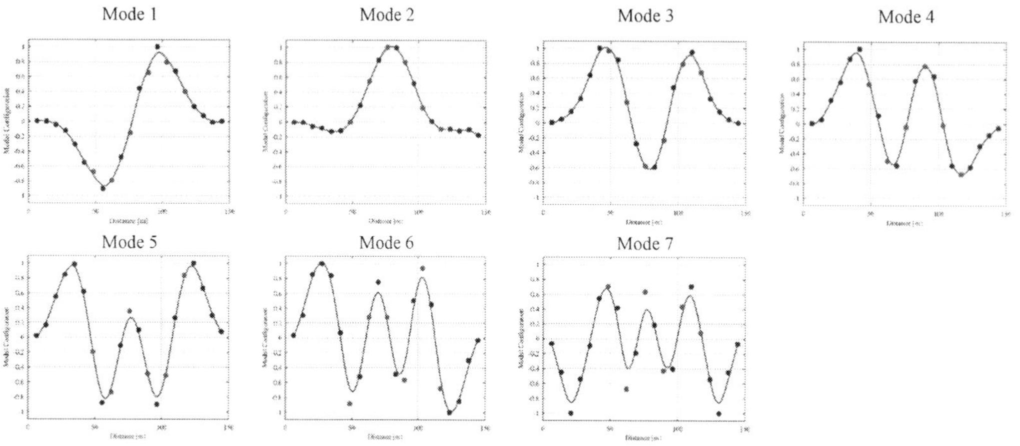

Figure 6. Modal shapes of the first 7 modes of Alto Lindoso dam

4. AMBIENT VIBRATION TEST OF BOUÇÃ DAM

Bouçã dam is an arch dam located in Zêzere river, a tributary of Tagus river in central Portugal. The dam, which started operating in 1955, is 63 meters high and its 175 meters long crest mostly constitutes the structure spillway. The hydroelectric power plant that was built downstream is installed with a capacity of 44 MW, assured by two Francis turbines that operate at 214.3 rpm.

The ambient vibration test of the Bouçã dam was performed on the 12th of June 2018 and it was based on the use of nine uniaxial force-balance accelerometers that were radially disposed along the dam's upper visit gallery. Since the dam crown is constituted by its main spillway, the test had to be performed inside the upper visit gallery, precluding the utilization of the GPS based system. Therefore, the acquisition system using cables was used and every measuring point had its own fixed sensor. The test grid prepared considered 9 measuring points on the dam's 9 central concrete blocks, which correspond to the group of blocks that are crowned by the spillway, and the farthest sensor was nearly 65 m away from the acquisition unit. To assure a good characterization of the structure's dynamic behaviour several similar setups were developed with a sampling rate of 100 Hz. The level in the reservoir during the test was 174.7 m (elevation above sea level).

To assure accurate estimates of modal properties, the SSI-cov method was applied considering model orders between 20 and 80. The first 8 vibration modes were identified and their modal properties, including natural frequencies and damping values, as well as the description of mode shapes, are presented in Table 2. The results shown correspond to the average of each of the values identified across the several setups.

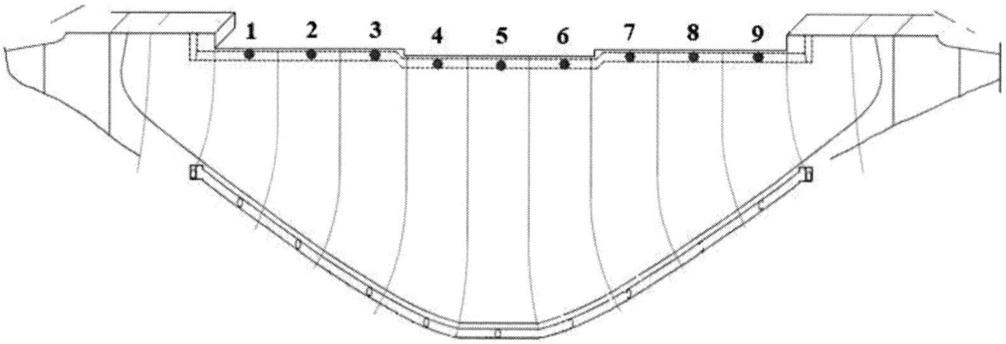

Figure 7. Bouçã dam: test layout

Table 2. Modal parameters for Bouçã dam first 8 vibration modes

Mode	f_{mean} [Hz]	ξ_{mean} [%]	Description
1	3.298	1.500	Antisymmetric
2	3.737	1.363	Symmetric
3	5.063	2.631	Symmetric
4	5.678	1.808	Antisymmetric
5	6.874	1.802	Symmetric
6	8.452	1.562	Antisymmetric
7	10.302	1.055	Symmetric
8	11.394	1.936	Antisymmetric

Very clear and well-defined modal shapes were achieved for the 8 identified modes, which are presented in **Figure 8**. The first mode is antisymmetric and the second one is symmetric. From the third to the eighth mode, the configurations are alternatively symmetric and antisymmetric.

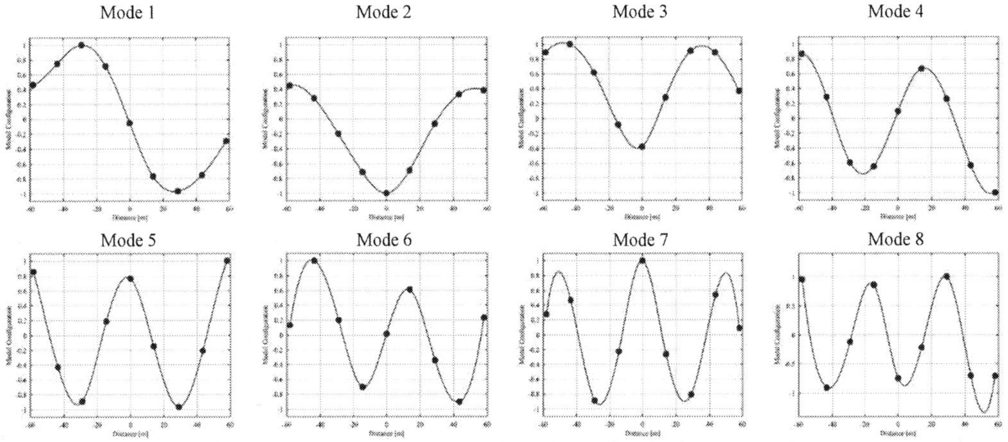

Figure 8. Modal shapes of the first 8 modes of Bouçã dam

5. AMBIENT VIBRATION TEST OF CALDEIRÃO DAM

Caldeirão dam is a stiff double-curvature arch dam located in the interior of Portugal, just 50 km away from the border with Spain. The dam is just 39 meters high and its 122 meters long crest is mostly constituted by the dam spillway, even though there is a viaduct over the dam that allows to cross the Ribeira do Caldeirão river by car. The hydroelectric power plant associated with Caldeirão dam has a total installed capacity of 40 MW, assured by vertical Francis turbines that operate at 333.3 rpm.

The ambient vibration test of Caldeirão dam was performed on the 2nd of June 2017 and it was based on the use of both the acquisition systems presented before, with the purpose of comparing the results obtained from the two procedures. Therefore, since GPS signal was needed for synchronization when using the seismographs, the test could not be performed on the dam gallery and thus seven uniaxial force-balance accelerometers and six GSR-24 recorders from Geosig (equipped with internal tri-axial force-balance accelerometers) were radially disposed, side by side, along the dam's top viaduct. The test grid prepared considered 7 measuring points corresponding to the position of the walls connecting the dam to the viaduct, which in the case of the tri-axial recorders were covered in two setups, and a sampling rate of 100 Hz was used during the acquisition with both the used systems. Additional measures were performed with two tri-axial recorders in the dam's upper visit gallery. The position of the 7 measuring points is marked with blue dots in the picture of the structure presented in **Figure 9**. The level in the reservoir during the test was 655.08 m (elevation above sea level).

Figure 9. Caldeirão dam: test layout

Modal identification was developed using the measured time series of accelerations, through the application of the SSI-cov method. Model orders between 20 and 80 were used and the stabilization diagram presented in **Figure 10** was obtained. A few well-defined vertical alignments appear between 9 and 16 Hz, whereas from 16 to 20 Hz many disperse poles appear, creating a couple of poorly-defined vertical alignments.

However, this analysis suggested that besides the vibration modes of the dam, vibration modes of the viaduct are being identified as well, creating uncertainty in the identification process. In order to clarify which modes were really vibration modes of the dam, separating those of the viaduct, auto-spectra were calculated using time series measured by the two sensors that had been placed in the upper visit gallery, thus not suffering direct influence from the viaduct dynamic properties.

Two calculated auto-spectra, from measures in the gallery (on the left) and from measures in the viaduct (on the right), are represented in **Figure 11** for comparison. Even though not being entirely clear, the auto-spectra obtained from the data recorded in the visit gallery show a couple of distinct peaks around 12.2 and 15.7 Hz, frequencies that are present in the auto-spectra from the viaduct as well, and therefore must correspond to vibration modes of the dam. Also around 14.1 Hz, a smaller peak may correspond to a different vibration mode. Nevertheless, this can still be due to the influence of the viaduct, therefore this frequency ends up being discarded, along with all the other frequencies that had been previously identified, since neither of them may be assuredly associated to either the dam or the viaduct.

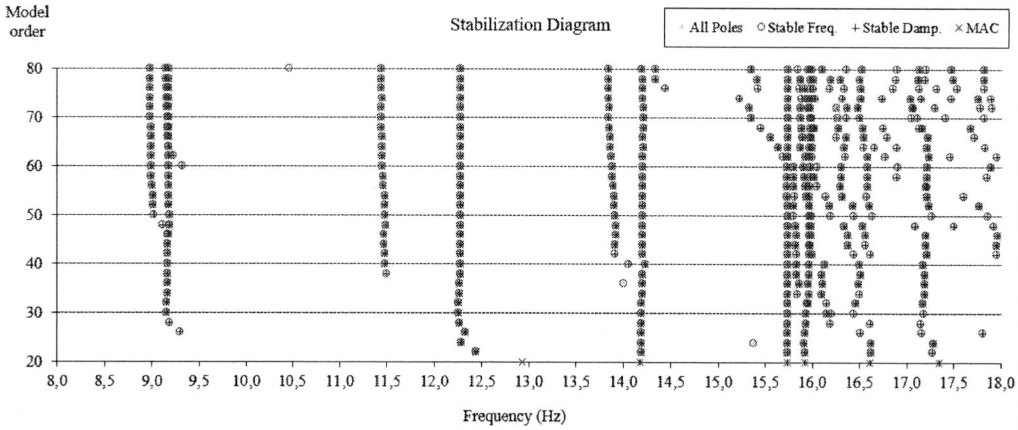

Figure 10. Stabilization diagram obtained after the application of SSI-cov method to data from Caldeirão dam

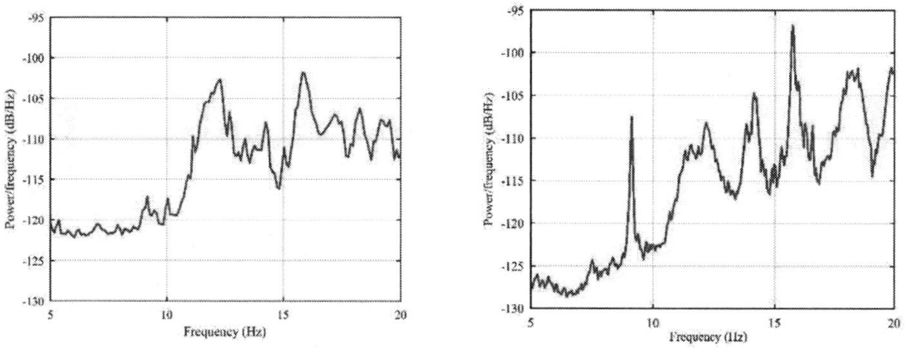

Figure 11. Auto-spectra from time series recorded inside the upper visit gallery (on the left) and from time series recorded in the top viaduct (on the right)

Finally, natural frequencies and damping ratios associated to the two identified vibration modes are presented in **Table 3**. The mode shapes of the two identified modes are presented in **Figure 12**. These modes are antisymmetric and symmetric, respectively.

Table 3. Modal parameters for Caldeirão dam identified vibration modes

Mode	f_{mean} [Hz]	ξ_{mean} [%]	Description
1	12.265	2.074	Antisymmetric
2	15.759	0.336	Symmetric

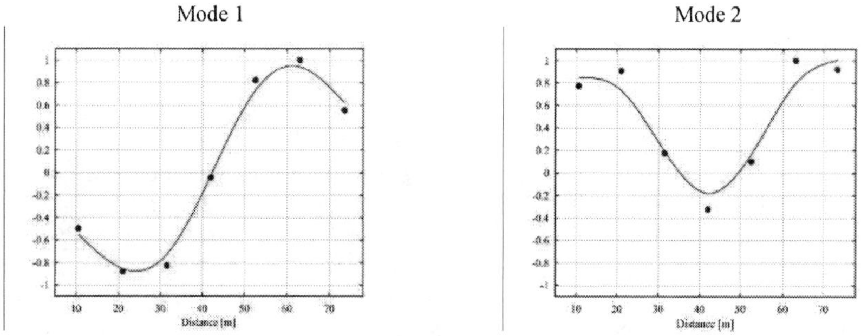

Figure 12. Mode shapes of the identified modes of Caldeirão dam

6. CONCLUSIONS

Ambient vibration tests have been successfully performed in a group of six concrete dams located in Portugal, with distinct characteristics and typologies, which during the tests were submitted to different operational and ambient excitations, showing the suitability of operational modal analysis to concrete dams. The studied group of structures included four arch dams with very different heights (Alto Lindoso dam, Santa Luzia dam, Bouçã dam and Caldeirão dam), an arch-gravity dam (Castelo do Bode dam) and a multiple arch dam (Aguieira dam). Two distinct acquisition systems were available to perform the tests and each of them was used depending on the characteristics and geometry of the structure.

Different vibration levels were measured, which depending on the operational conditions could go from few micro g to few milli g. Nevertheless, despite the very low vibration levels, satisfactory results were obtained in all the applications.

The modal identification developed in the three double-curvature arch dams with different heights was achieved through the application of the SSI-cov method. Seven to eight vibration modes were identified with the analysis of the two highest structures, while just two modes were identified in the third example. In all the three cases, the first mode identified is antisymmetric while the second mode is symmetric, however the first natural frequency may vary from around 3 Hz to around 12 Hz.

The results obtained are being used to numerically test the accuracy that would be achieved in the modal identification if lower cost accelerometers had been used during the tests instead.

ACKNOWLEDGEMENTS

This work was financially supported by: UID/ECI/04708/2019- CONSTRUCT - Instituto de I&D em Estruturas e Construções funded by national funds through the FCT/MCTES (PIDDAC); PTDC/ECM-EST/0805/2014|16761 – DAM_AGE - Advanced Online Dynamic Structural Health Monitoring of Concrete Dams, funded by FEDER funds through COMPETE2020 - Programa Operacional Competitividade e Internacionalização (POCI) – and by national funds through FCT - Fundação para a Ciência e a Tecnologia; FCT PhD Scholarship SFRH/BD/100587/2014 provided to the first author. The authors would like also to acknowledge all the collaboration and support provided by EDP Produção.

FCT
Fundação para a Ciência e a Tecnologia

REFERENCES

[1] Cunha, A., et al., *Recent perspectives in dynamic testing and monitoring of bridges.* Structural Control and Health Monitoring, 2013. **20**(6): p. 853-877.

[2] Gomes, J. and J.V. Lemos, *Characterization of the dynamic behavior of an arch dam by means of forced vibration tests*, in *1st Meeting of EWG Dams and Earthquakes*. 2016, Balkema: Saint Malo, France.

[3] Gauron, O., et al., *Forced-Vibration Tests and Numerical Modeling of the Daniel-Johnson Multiple-Arch Dam.* Journal of Performance of Constructed Facilities, 2018. **32**(2).

[4] Deinum, P.J., et al., *Vibration tests on emosson arch dam, Switzerland.* Earthquake Engineering & Structural Dynamics, 1982. **10**(3): p. 447-470.

[5] Proulx, J., et al., *An experimental investigation of water level effects on the dynamic behaviour of a large arch dam.* Earthquake Engineering and Structural Dynamics, 2001. **30**(8): p. 1147-1166.

[6] Darbre, G.R. and J. Proulx, *Continuos ambient-vibration monitoring of the arch dam of Mauvoisin.* Earthquake Engineering and Structural Dynamics, 2002. **31**(2): p. 475-480.

[7] Mendes, P., *Observação e Análise do Comportamento Dinâmico de Barragens de Betão*. 2010, Faculdade de Engenharia da Universidade do Porto.

[8] Pereira, S., et al., *Dynamic monitoring of a concrete arch dam during the first filling of the reservoir.* Engineering Structures, 2018. **174**: p. 548-560.

[9] EDP. *Energias de Portugal*. [cited 2018 21/09/2018]; Available from: http://www.a-nossa-energia.edp.pt/centros_produtores/.

IOMAC'19

8th International Operational Modal Analysis Conference

2019 May13-15 Copenhagen

MONITORING AND STRUCTURAL IDENTIFICATION OF A "STAR-SHAPED" REINFORCED CONCRETE BELL TOWER

M. Diaferio[1],D. Foti[2], N.I. Giannoccaro[3],S. Ivorra[4], G. Notarangelo and M. Vitti

[1]Polytechnic of Bari, Department of Civil Engineering and Architecture, Bari, *mariella.diaferio@poliba.it*.
[2]Polytechnic of Bari, Department of Civil Engineering and Architecture, Bari, *dora.foti@poliba.it*.
[3]University of Salento, Department of Innovation Engineering, Lecce, *ivan.giannoccaro@unisalento.it*.
[4]University of Alicante, Department of Civil Engineering, Alicante, *sivorra@ua.es*.

ABSTRACT

The object of present study is the bell tower of the church of Santa Maria Assunta of Lamadacqua in Noci (Bari, Italy) that has been subject to restoration together with the adjacent church. The bell tower has a rather peculiar shape with section septa varying from bottom to top. The structure is entirely in reinforced concrete (r.c.) and is in adherence with the church made of masonry. The structure has undergone degradation phenomena caused mainly by exogenous phenomena, such as wind and atmospheric phenomena. Therefore, a series of interventions for the recovery and the structural reinforcement have been designed and realized. In order to get more information on the effects of the structure's interventions the behaviour of the tower to environmental vibrations was monitored using special accelerometers positioned on the bell tower and on the spiers. The acquired data were used to dynamically identify the structure and calibrate the FE model of the bell tower.

Keywords: Operational modal Analysis (OMA), modal parameters identification, Reformed structure

1. INTRODUCTION

The present research deals with an experimental technique with special accelerometers aimed at identifying the modal parameters of a reinforced concrete (r.c.) bell tower through a Finite Element (FE) model calibrated on sampled environmental vibrations.

Generally, this kind of investigation is particularly suitable for structures with a predominant vertical development [1-4], such as towers, because through an in-situ sampling with accelerometers, it is possible to record very clearly the low intensity vibrations due to ambient loads, and then to identify the structure using the Operational Modal Analysis (OMA) technique [5-7]. Being a non-invasive method, it is easy to find its application in literature for masonry buildings and, in particular, for historical-cultural heritage such as civic towers and bell towers [8-15]. However, the technique is better used for r.c. buildings, which give a clearer response to environmental vibrations in presence of similar characteristics, such as slenderness and deformability [16-18]. Moaveni and Conte [19] investigate the performance of FE model updating and its accuracy for the damage identification for a modern r.c. slender structure.

The bell tower object of the present study is characterized by a "star-shaped" plan (Figure 1), for this reason, probably represents one of the few chances to study the behaviour of r.c. structure of modern heritage with an irregular system. Examples are shown in [20, 21] where a modal analysis of the structure, composed by a church and its r.c. bell tower, was carried out through finite element models to understand the overall dynamic behaviour and to analyse/propose a damped-interconnection retrofit as pounding mitigation technique.

The structure has undergone degradation phenomena caused mainly by exogenous phenomena, such as wind and atmospheric phenomena. Therefore, a series of interventions for the recovery and the structural reinforcement have been designed and realized.

The behaviour of the structure to environmental vibrations after the restoring interventions has been experimentally monitored in-situ using special accelerometers positioned on the bell tower and on the spiers. The acquired data were used to dynamically identify the structure and calibrate the FE model of the bell tower, taking into account that the geometry of the bell tower is non-conventional.

Figure 1. The Church of Santa Maria Assunta (on the right) and its bell tower (in r.c., on the left).

2. BRIEF DESCRIPTION OF THE TOWER GEOMETRY, EXPERIMENTAL TESTS AND PRELIMINARY ANALYSIS

The object of the present study is the bell tower of the Church of Santa Maria Assunta of Lamadacqua in Noci (Bari, Italy) that has been subject to restoration together with the adjacent church. The project was drafted by Plinio Marconi, architect and urban planner; the structures were completed in 1963 in their entirety.

The Church of Santa Maria Assunta has been realized with aload-bearing structure in soft stone ashlars (tufa) masonry with a thickness of 75 cm and with a single face. The roof is pitched and made in reinforced concrete (r.c.) with a double strut scheme. The bell tower to the left of the building, instead, is a structure entirely in r.c. with section septa varying from bottom to top. In the space between the church and the bell tower there is a small room in load-bearing masonry and a horizontal floor in r.c. simply leaning on the main structures (Figure 1).

The bell tower has a rather peculiar shape; it is about 14.00 meters tall, of which the first 5 meters in r.c. septa; from here three lateral spiers and the central spire rise. On the top of them there are some metal struts that support the three bells.

From a careful visual inspection, it was possible to outline the conservative state of the structure. The structure has undergone degradation phenomena mainly caused by exogenous phenomena, such as wind and atmospheric phenomena. The conformation of the spiers similar to a cantilever beam and the unobstructed area on which the structure stands means that the wind's kinetic action causes particularly critical bending moment stresses at the base, with tensile stresses too high for concrete. Degradation phenomena are noted, such as diffuse cracks in correspondence of the cover plates, total and partial expulsions of them, oxidation of the reinforcing rods. Therefore, a series of interventions for the recovery and the structural reinforcement have been designed.

From the point of view of structural modelling, the walls are of the bell tower, the sail and the veil positioned on the front entrance of the church are in reinforced concrete with mediocre mechanical characteristics.

The bell tower is affected by cracks and injuries partly caused by problems of capillary rising and, in part, by the scarce mechanical characteristics of the materials utilised. In this regard, the detailed survey of degradation and instability was able to confirm the important cracks patterns. In particular, the shape of the cracks on the three spiers of the bell tower is caused by a concomitance of actions and reactions to which the structure is subject (Figure 2). In particular, the exogenous degradation, that is the alteration of the characteristics of the materials constituting the structure, was caused by external agents such as wind. The area in which the structure rises, in fact, can be considered without obstacles and this causes an increase in the kinetic pressure that the wind exerts on the structures it meets. Moreover, in the case of a cantilever structure, the action of the wind causes particularly critical bending moment stresses at the base with tensile stresses to which the concrete is not able to resist. Among the three spiers at the top of the bell tower, the one adjacent to the remaining part of the structure is damaged to a lesser degree; this could be caused by the holding reaction that the remaining structure exerts on it, with a consequent reduction of the tensile stresses.

Figure 2. Detail of damages observed on the r.c. structures on the Church of Santa Maria Assunta bell tower.

The intervention provided a set of works designed to operate a structural reinforcement of the bell tower as localized reinforcement on an existing building in accordance with Chap. 8.4.3, DM 14.01.2008 [22]. Of course, the intervention on the existing construction must improve the constructive regularity, resistance and ductility, so that it intervenes more intensely, for example, on the more resistant structural elements or on the mechanisms of collapse in order to transform them from fragile to ductile.

3. DESCRIPTION OF THE EXPERIMENTAL TESTS CAMPAING

The tower was instrumented with seventeen 393B31 uniaxial piezo-accelerometers with a sensitivity of 10.000 mV/g, placed at three different levels on the tower (Figure 3). The accelerometers were connected to a centralized data acquisition system National Instruments DAQ model NI 9232 mounted on a NI cDAQ-9188 Chasis CompactDAQ. To guarantee the recordings in two perfectly orthogonal directions in each acquisition point, a cubic metallic device has been utilized.

Three ambient tests have been developed with a duration of 10 min. All tests have been developed with a sampling frequency of 1024 Hz and a decimation for the analysis between 0-51.2 Hz. A low pass filter was applied for a cut frequency of 25 Hz. Regarding the environmental tests, the aim was to perform a statistical analysis on the repeatability of the identified modal parameters.

The location of the sensors have been selected to detect accelerations in the North-South direction, similarly to those in the orthogonal direction (Figure 3). At each level they are applied in two opposite points of the structure and they provide together the oscillations in both directions; in this way they also allow to study the possible torsional motion of the structure. To analyze the structure's main modes and frequencies, three environmental noise recordings were carried out.

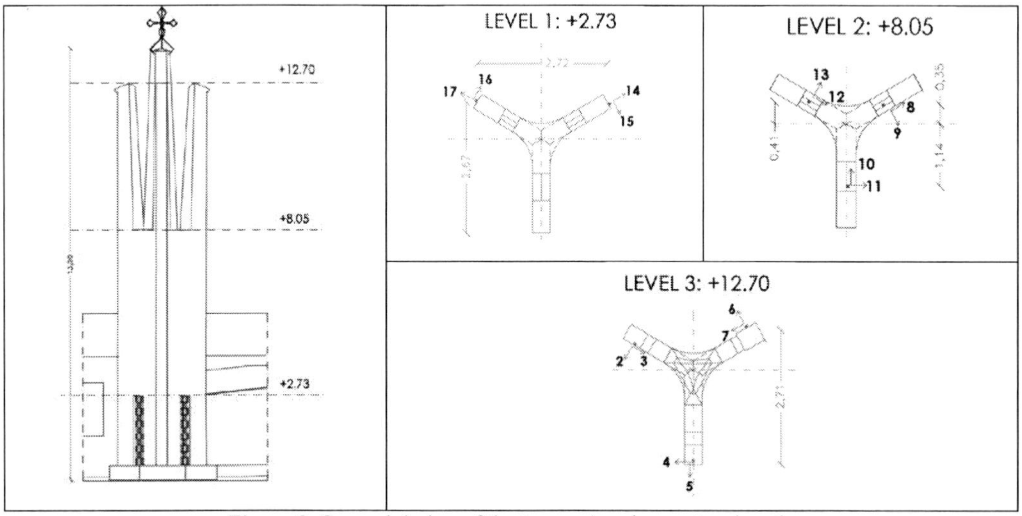

Figure 3. General design of the tower. Accelerometers location.

The frequencies of the bell tower were identified by mean of Operational Modal Analysis techniques using Artemis software [23]. For the OMA analysis, the structure geometry was simplified as showed in Figure 4a. In Figure 4b the location of each accelerometer and its direction is showed. Finally, in Figure 4c the slave nodes are presented.

In Table 1 the estimated frequencies are summarized. Main modes are local modes of the top of the tower. The two main are bending modes (5.665 Hz 5.883 Hz) and the third a torsional one (6.537 Hz).

After the retrofitting process, where cracks have been consolidated with new cement mortars and new frame elements and connections with the r.c. structure other experimental campaign have been developed to identify the new main frequencies and mode shapes. Table 1 shows these results under ambient vibrations.

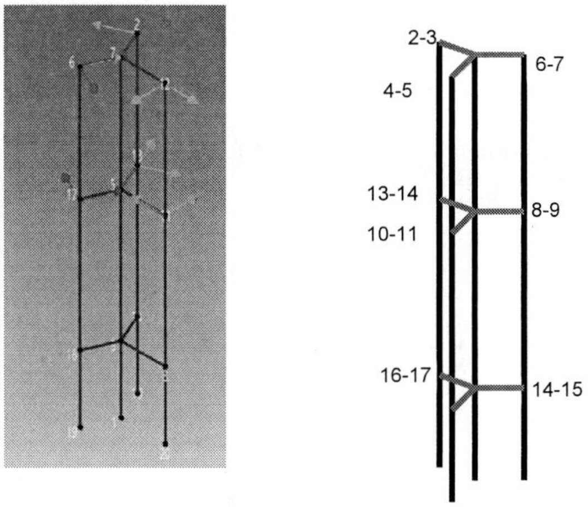

node(**1**,**1**)=node(**10**,**1**)=node(**20**,**1**)=**0**
node(**1**,**2**)=node(**10**,**2**)=node(**20**,**2**)=**0**
node(**1**,**3**)=node(**10**,**3**)=node(**20**,**3**)=**0**
node(**3**,**3**)=node(**5**,**3**)=node(**7**,**3**)=**0**
node(**3**,**1**)=**0**
node(**3**,**2**)=**0**
node(**7**,**2**)=node(**12**,**2**)
node(**5**,**2**)=node(**11**,**2**)

Figure 4. Simplified model of the tower. (a) Nodes. (b) Accelerometers. (c) Slave nodes

Table 1. Experimental frequency values .

Damaged structure			**Retrofitted Structure**		
Frequency [Hz]	Damping [%]	Complexity [%]	Frequency [Hz]	Damping [%]	Complexity [%]
5.665	1.901	2.34	6.44	2.08	2.814
5.883	1.063	1.123	6.696	3.853	15.512
6.537	1.739	0.749	6.792	2.024	0.587
7.14	2.16	3.857	7.461	1.912	2.92
8.609	1.533	9.7	9.26	1.174	1.942

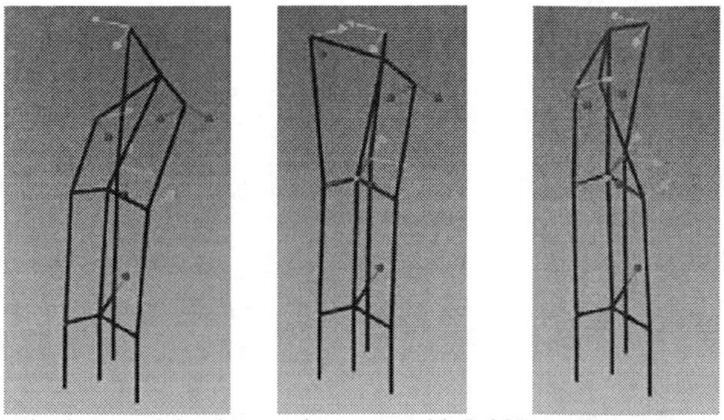

Figure 5. Mode shapes of the damaged structure (a) 5.665 Hz. (b) 5.883 Hz. (c) 6.537 Hz

4. NUMERICAL ANALYSIS

In order to verify the efficacy of the restoring interventions, a numerical model of the bell tower has been defined by means of Straus software [24], which operates in the framework of the finite element method.

The septa, which compose the bell tower have been modelled by 2853 QUAD4 elements, they are four-node shell elements, while the 120 UNP profiles, inserted to realise the three frames, which support the three bells, have been modelled by beam elements.

In Table 2 the mechanical properties of the structural materials adopted in the numerical model are shown.

Moreover, the presence of the three bells has been modelled by inserting three concentrated masses of 100 kg at the middle of the upper rods of the UNP frames.

Table 2. Mechanical properties of structural materials.

Material	Elastic modulus [MPa]	Density [kg/m^3]	Poisson's ratio
Concrete	23237	2500	0.2
Steel	206000	7860	0.2875

During the retrofitting interventions, in order to avoid the interaction between the bell tower and the church a foam was inserted between the masonry walls and the septa; thus, the finite element model assumes the bell tower as an isolated structure fixed at the base.

Figure 6 shows the numerical model; it has been defined assuming the septum which is not in contact with the church, oriented along the y axis, while the slope between the other two septa and the x axis is of about 30° in accordance with the geometrical survey.

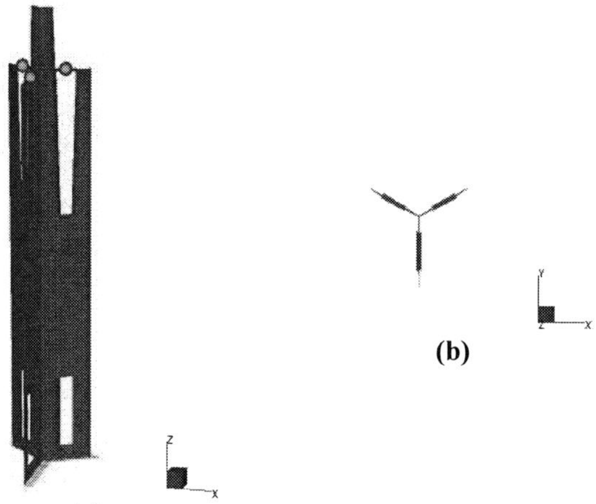

(b)

(a)

Figure 6. Finite element model of the bell tower of Santa Maria Assunta of Lamadacqua in Noci (Bari, Italy): a)3D view; b) plan view.

The frequency values and the mode shapes of the numerical model have been evaluated. In Table 3 the first three frequency values are reported.

Table 3. Frequency values of the FE model.

Damaged structure		Retrofitted structure	
Mode #	Frequency [Hz]	Mode #	Frequency [Hz]
1	5.47	1	5.59
2	6.17	2	6.33
3	6.21	3	8.16

In Figure 7 the shapes of the first three natural modes for the retrofitted structure are shown. The first mode shape is a bending mode along the direction orthogonal to the septum not in contact with the church. The second mode is a bending mode along the y axis, i.e. the direction of the septum not in contact with the church; while the third mode is a torsional mode.

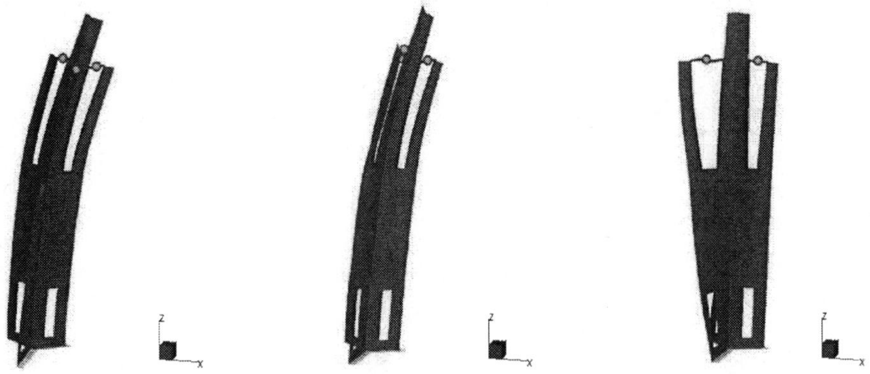

(a) (b) (c)

Figure 7. First three natural modes of the finite element model of the retrofitted bell tower of Santa Maria Assunta of Lamadacqua in Noci (Bari, Italy): a) first mode: bending mode along the x axis, b) second mode: bending mode along the y axis; c) third mode: torsional mode.

5. CONCLUSIONS

A reinforced concrete structures have been studied pre and post retrofitting. OMA analysis has performed to obtain main frequencies and mode shapes. Results of OMA analysis shows that the intervention has increased the stiffness of all vibration modes.

Similar results have been observed with the numerical simulation. The new steel frames on the top of the structure increases de main frequencies of all modes of vibration to higher values.

ACKNOWLEDGEMENTS

Authors acknowledge the Italian project PRIN 2015: "Mitigating the impacts of natural hazards on cultural heritage sites, structures and artefacts".

REFERENCES

[1] Diaferio, M., Foti, D., Giannoccaro, N.I., Ivorra, S. (2017). Model updating based on the dynamic identification of a baroque bell tower. International Journal of Safety and Security Engineering, 7(4), 519–531.

[2] Foti, D., Diaferio, M., Giannoccaro, NI, Ivorra, S. (2015). Structural identification and numerical models for slender historical structures. In: P. Asteris & V. Plevris (Eds.), Handbook of Research on Seismic Assessment and Rehabilitation of Historic Structures. Hershey, PA: Engineering Science Reference, Chapter 23, pp. 674-703.

[3] Diaferio, M., Foti, D., Giannoccaro, N.I., Ivorra, S. (2014). Optimal model through identified frequencies of a masonry building structure with wooden floors, International Journal of Mechanics, 8(1), 282-288.

[4] Foti, D. (2015). Non-destructive techniques and monitoring for the evolutive damage detection of an ancient masonry structure, Key Engineering Materials, 628,168-177.

[5] Ivorra, S., Brotóns, V., Foti, D., Diaferio, M. (2016). A preliminary approach of dynamic identification of slender buildings by neuronal networks. International Journal of Non-Linear Mechanics, 80, 183-189.

[6] Bru, D., Ivorra, S.,Baeza, F.J., Reynau, R., Foti, D. (2015). OMA dynamic identification of a masonry chimney with severe cracking condition. Proceedings of the 6th International Operational Modal Analysis Conference, IOMAC 2015.

[7] Gentile, C.,Saisi, A.,Cabboi, A. (2014).Structural Identification of a Masonry Tower Based on Operational Modal Analysis. International Journal of Architectural Heritage, 9(2), 98-110.

[8] Ivorra, S, Giannoccaro, N.I., Foti, D. (in press). Simple model for predicting the vibration transmission of a squat masonry tower by base forced vibrations. Structural Control and Health Monitoring.

[9] Diaferio, M., Foti, D., Giannoccaro, N.I., Ivorra, S. (2018). Measuring the modal parameters of a cultural heritage tower by using strong-motion signals. AKTA IMECO, October 2018, Vol. 7, n. 3, pp.86 – 94, ISSN: 2221-870X.

[10] Diaferio, M., Foti, D., Giannoccaro, N.I. (2015). Identification of the modal properties of a squat historic tower for the tuning of a FE model. Proceedings 6th International Operational Modal Analysis Conference, IOMAC 2015; Abba Hotel, Gijon; Spain; 12 - 14 May.

[11] Bartoli, G., Betti, M., Giordano, S. (2013). In situ static and dynamic investigations on the ' Torre Grossa' masonry tower. Engineering Structures, 52, 718-733.

[12] Diaferio, M., Foti, D., Gentile, C., Giannoccaro, N.I., Saisi, A. (2015). Dynamic testing of a historical slender building using accelerometers and radar. Proceedings of 6th International Operational Modal Analysis Conference, IOMAC 2015; Abba Hotel, Gijon; Spain; 12-14 May.

[13] Snoj, J., Österreicher, M., Dolšek, M. (2013). The importance of ambient and forced vibration measurements for the results of seismic performance assessment of buildings obtained by using a simplified non-linear procedure: Case study of an old masonry building. Bulletin of Earthquake Engineering, 11(6), 2105–2132.

[14] Tronci E.M., Pietrosanti D., Cordisco G., De Angelis M. (2017). Vibration analysis of the civic tower in Rieti. Procedia Engineering, 199, 2268-2273.

[15] Gupta, A., Zhao, W., Regan, C., Seiler, P., Kapania, R.K. (2018). Identification of Symmetrical Structures with Fabrication and Damage Induced Asymmetry. In: Conte, J., Astroza, R., Benzoni, G., Feltrin, G., Loh, K., Moaveni, B. (eds) Experimental Vibration Analysis for Civil Structures. EVACES 2017.

[16] Lepidi, M., Gattulli, V., & Foti, D. (2009). Swinging-bell resonances and their cancellation identified by dynamical testing in a modern bell tower. Engineering Structures, 31(7), 1486-1500.

[17] Ivorra, S., Pallarés, F. J., & Adam, J. M. (2009). Dynamic behaviour of a modern bell tower—A case study. Engineering Structures, 31(5), 1085-1092.

[18] Ivorra, S., Foti, D, Gallo, V., Vacca, V., Bru, D. (2019). Bell´s dynamic interaction on a singular concrete bell tower: A case of Study. Engineering Structures, 183, 965-975.

[19] Moaveni, B., Conte, J. P., & Hemez, F. M. (2009). Uncertainty and sensitivity analysis of damage identification results obtained using finite element model updating. *Computer Aided Civil and Infrastructure Engineering*, 24(5), 320-334.

[20] Pratesi, F., Sorace, S., &Terenzi, G. (2013). Non-linear FE modelling of seismic pounding and damped-mitigating interconnection between ar/c tower and a masonry church. XII International Conference on Computational Plasticity. Fundamentals and Applications COMPLAS XII

[21] Pratesi, F., Sorace, S., & Terenzi, G. (2014). Analysis and mitigation of seismic pounding of a slender R/C bell tower. Engineering Structures, *71*, 23-34.

[22] D.M. 14/1/2008, Nuove Norme Tecniche (*in Italian*).

[23] Artemis Modal Pro v5.3. Structural Vibrations Solutions. Aalborg, Denmark. 2016.

[24] Strauss 7 Finite element analysis system. Strand7 Pty Ltd. www.strauss7.com

IOMAC'19

8th International Operational Modal Analysis Conference

2019 May 13-15 Copenhagen

OMA APPLICATION FOR ESTIMATION OF TENSION FORCE IN A CABLE WITH A SMALL SAG

Wojciech Pakos[1], Jacek Grosel[2] and Wojciech Sawicki[3]

[1] PhD, Wrocław University of Science and Technology Wrocław, Poland, wojciech.pakos@pwr.edu.pl.
[2] PhD, Wrocław University of Science and Technology Wrocław, Poland, jacek.grosel@pwr.edu.pl.
[3] PhD, Wrocław University of Science and Technology Wrocław, Poland, wojciech.sawicki@pwr.edu.pl.

ABSTRACT

The paper presents the method for estimation the tension force in a cable with a small sag ($0 \leq d/L \leq 1/8$). In the case of a cable with negligible sag (string problem), the relation between the tension force and the eigenfrequency is relatively simple and could be easily applied to determine the tension strength on the basis of dynamic measurements. In case of cables with a small sag (i.e. large Irvine parameter), it is required to use modal analysis techniques. The article contains a description of the laboratory stand, test methodology, measurement results and their analysis, and discussion of results and conclusions.

Keywords: Operational, Modal, Analysis, Cable, Estimation, Force

Cables are structural elements very often used in construction. They are used e.g.: in roofs, as lashing cable at high constructions (e.g. masts), as hangers for hanging installation pipes, in bridge constructions and in other suspension constructions. It is very important to accurately estimate the forces in the cables during construction as well as during the subsequent use of the structure. To determine the forces in the cables, special force sensors are now often installed near the anchorages of the cables. Such sensors can be successfully used in newly built constructions in which both the appropriate technical parameters of the sensors and the method of their assembly can be predicted at the design stage. In the case of existing structures, in which the use of appropriate force sensors is impossible or at least difficult for technical or economic reasons, other techniques for determining forces in cables are sought. One of the basic, often used techniques of measuring forces in cables are vibration measurements. Nam and Nghia used this technique at work [1]. Nam and Nghia presented a way to estimate the value of forces in the cables of the cable stayed bridge based on the frequency measurement. Huang et al. in paper [2] presented the method of determining forces in vertical hangers in suspension bridges. They adopted the model of a cable taking into account bending stiffness. Yang et al. in paper [3] presented a regressive model of force identification in a cable with the use of measurement techniques.

The estimation of forces in cables based on vibration measurements is often used in practice, due to the numerous advantages of this approach, e.g. this technique can be used without interfering in the construction, in hard to reach places (e.g. vibration measurements with laser sensors). Although the basic principles of determining force in cables by measuring vibrations are easy to understand and use, they can often lead to significant errors in estimating the value of force. The basic error may be the adoption of equations for the tendon with negligibly small deflection (string problem), from which the force will be determined. In this paper, a linear model of the cable with a small sag ($0 \leq d/L \leq 1/8$), proposed by Irvine [4] was used to determine the force value. This model well describes the real work of many cable structures and is commonly used for the calculation of suspended bridges.

1. DESCRIPTION OF THE TEST STAND.

The research was carried out on the following geometric and material data of the cable: type 1x19, diameter ∅ = 5 mm, cross-sectional area A = 14.6 mm^2, mass m = 0.1212 kg/m, minimum breaking load H_{MBL} = 22.78 kN, Young's modulus E = 140 kN/mm^2, length of the cable L = 5.25 m. The length of the cable is understood as the horizontal projection of the distance between supports located at the same height. The scheme of the tested cable is shown in figure 2. The cable was fixed to one of the supports, by a manual tension regulator (see fig. 1 and fig. 2). The other side of the cable was mounted to the support by means of an eye holder forming a pin support.

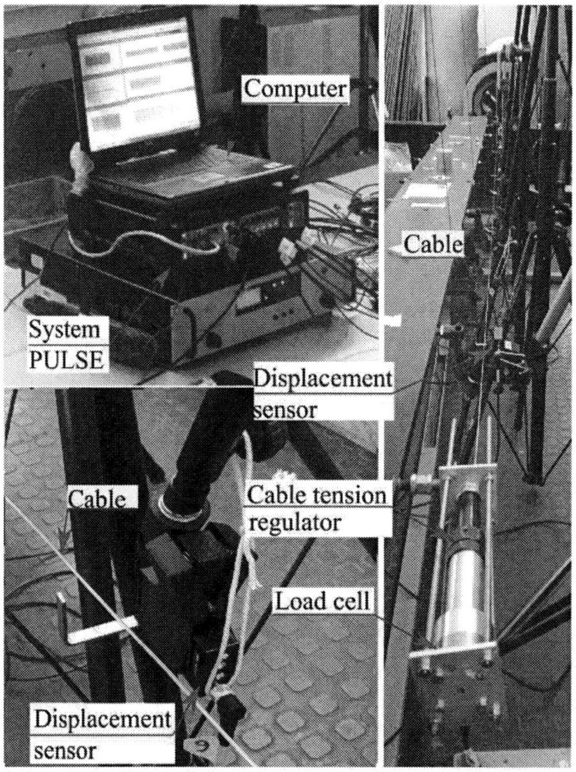

Figure 1. The experimental test stand and equipment used in the experiments.

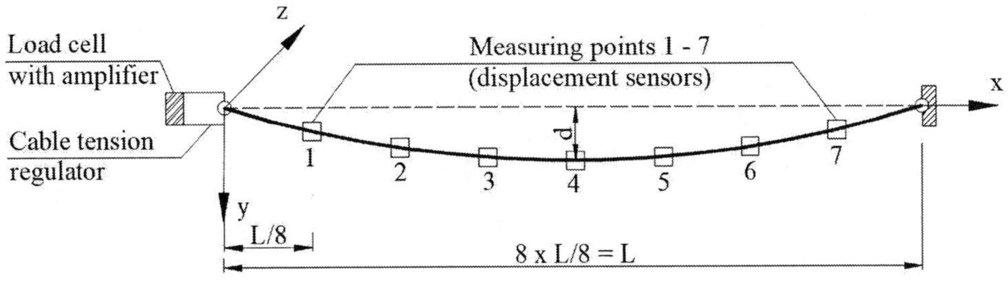

Figure 2. Model of a tested cable.

Non-contact vibration measurement was performed with seven displacement sensors type ZADM 034 made by Baumer company (see fig. 3), sensors were spaced at intervals $L/8$ between the supports (see fig.1 and fig. 2). The basic sensor data is:

- measuring field size – 24 mm,
- measuring distance (to object) – from 0 to 40 mm,
- resolution < 0,05 mm,
- smallest object recognizable – 1 mm.

Figure 3. The displacement sensor (ZADM 034 Baumer).

2. EQUATIONS AND MATHEMATICAL EXPRESSIONS

To determine the force in the tendon, generally known relationships for a model of a cable with a small sag ($0 \leq d/L \leq 1/8$) given by Irvine [4] were used. In the formulae given below the following symbols are assumed: L – length of the cable understood as the horizontal distance between supports located at the same height, m – mass per unit of cable length, A – cross-sectional area, H – force, E – Young's modulus, g – acceleration of gravity, d – deflection of the cable in the middle of the span.

Antisymmetric eigenforms in plane of the sag of a cable

Eigenform corresponding to i^{th} eigenfrequency (even eigenfrequencies)

$$Y_{2i}(x) = A_{2i} \cdot \sin\left(\frac{2i\pi x}{L}\right), \quad i = 1, 2, 3, \ldots \tag{1}$$

where A_{2i} is a mode amplitude.

i^{th} eigenfrequency

$$\omega_{2i} = \frac{2i\pi}{L}\sqrt{\frac{H}{m}}, \qquad i = 1, 2, 3, \ldots \tag{2}$$

Symmetric eigenforms in plane of the sag of a cable (odd eigenfrequencies)

Eigenform corresponding to each ith eigenfrequency describes the following relationship

$$Y_{2i-1}(x) = A_{2i-1}\cdot\left[1 - \tan\left(\frac{\overline{\omega}_i}{2}\right)\sin\left(\frac{\overline{\omega}_i x}{L}\right) - \cos\left(\frac{\overline{\omega}_i x}{L}\right)\right], \qquad i = 1, 2, 3, \ldots \tag{3}$$

where A_{2i-1} is the amplitude of mode, while $\overline{\omega}_i$ is an additional dimensionless frequency determined from formula

$$\tan\left(\frac{\overline{\omega}_i}{2}\right) = \frac{\overline{\omega}_i}{2} - \frac{4}{\lambda^2}\left(\frac{\overline{\omega}_i}{2}\right)^3 \tag{4}$$

and is related to the ith eigenfrequency corresponding to symmetric eigenforms in plane of the sag of a cable with the following relationship

$$\overline{\omega}_i = \frac{\omega_{2i-1}L}{\sqrt{\frac{H}{m}}}, \quad i = 1, 2, 3, \ldots \tag{5}$$

where Irvine parameter is given by relationship [4]

$$\lambda^2 = \left(\frac{mgL}{H}\right)^2\cdot\frac{E}{H/A} = \left(\frac{8d}{L}\right)^2\cdot\frac{EA}{H} \tag{6}$$

However, d is the value of y(x) at the point x = L/2 and, assuming a static small sag of the cable in the form of a parabola, can be expressed as

$$d = \frac{mgL^2}{8H} \tag{7}$$

Formula (4) describes eigenforms when a large Irvine parameter λ^2 appears. With a small parameter λ^2 analytical formulas in the case of eigenfrequencies and their corresponding symmetrical forms in plane of the sag take the form as in the formulas describing antisymmetric eigenforms in the plane of the sag [4]

$$Y_{2i-1}(x) = A_{2i-1}\cdot\sin\left(\frac{(2i-1)\pi x}{L}\right), \qquad i = 1, 2, 3, \ldots \tag{8}$$

$$\omega_{2i-1} = \frac{(2i-1)\pi}{L}\cdot\sqrt{H/m}, \qquad i = 1, 2, 3, \ldots \tag{9}$$

For the string problem, i.e. for the cable model with negligible small sag, eigenfrequencies and eigenforms are expressed in the following relations

$$Y_i(x) = A_i\cdot\sin\left(\frac{i\pi x}{L}\right), \qquad i = 1, 2, 3, \ldots \tag{10}$$

$$\omega_i = \frac{i\pi}{L}\cdot\sqrt{H/m}, \qquad i = 1, 2, 3, \ldots \tag{11}$$

3. DESCRIPTION OF THE METHOD OF DETERMINING THE FORCE IN THE CABLE.

The force in the cable was determined as follows:

- The cable tension regulator has been set to any (search) force in cable.
- Measurements of vibrations (displacements) were made using measuring devices.
- The recorded vibrations (displacements) were subjected to the operational modal analysis OMA, by means of which the eigenfrequencies and the corresponding eigenforms were determined.
- Eigenfrequencies and eigenforms obtained from measurements were compared with the eigenfrequencies and eigenforms determined by means of formulas (1) - (10).
- On the basis of the conformity of the measured and calculated first two eigenfrequencies and the eigenforms (first symmetrical and first antisymmetrical eigenform and eignefrequencies), the value of force in the cable was determined.

4. ESTIMATION OF CABLE TENSION

In figure 4 and in table 1, the first two natural eigenfrequencies obtained from experimental tests (OMA) and from numerical calculations are shown. Numerical calculations were made for the mathematical model of cable proposed by Irvine - formulas (2) and (4), and for the commonly known problem of string - formula (11). Figure 4 shows the first two eigenfrequencies, corresponding to the first symmetrical and first antisymmetric eigenforms according to the Irvine parameter. The eigenfrequencies are divided by the first eigenfrequency of the string (11), thanks to this, normalized frequencies values were obtained.

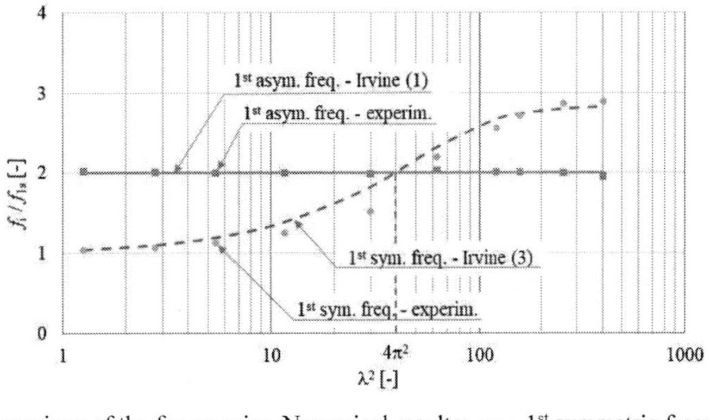

Figure 4. Comparison of the frequencies. Numerical results: – – 1st symmetric frequencies, — 1st antisymmetric frequencies. Experimental results: • 1st symmetric frequencies, ▪ 1st antisymmetric frequencies.

Figures 5-8 present the first symmetrical and first antisymmetric eigenforms for two selected tests: number 1 and number 7 (see table 1). The eigenforms in Figures 5 and 6 correspond to a small Irvine parameter $\lambda^2 = 1.3$, whereas the eigenforms in Figures 7 and 8 correspond to the large Irvine parameter $\lambda^2 = 121.3$. From both measurements and numerical calculations based on the considered cable model with small sag, a similar shape of eigenforms was obtained. It should be emphasized that for the large Irvine parameter the characteristic first symmetrical eigenform with three local extremes was obtained (see fig. 7a and fig. 7b). Depending on the value of coefficient λ^2, the first symmetrical eigenform has one extreme when $\lambda^2 < 4\pi^2$ and can have three extremes when $\lambda^2 > 4\pi^2$ [4]. In the latter case, the eigenfrequency corresponding to the first symmetrical eigenform is higher than the eigenfrequency corresponding to the first antisymmetric eigenform (see fig. 4). In the case of a cable for which λ^2 is close to or equal to $4\pi^2$, the eigenfrequencies corresponding to the symmetric and antisymmetric eigenforms converge to the same value. In this case, the sole measurement of the frequency needed to determine the value of forces is insufficient. Then, thanks to the use of OMA, it can be unequivocally determine eigenform and the corresponding eigenfrequency, it can be also determined which eigenfrequencies is smaller. This problem can be seen in the case of measurements done in test number 6. The experimentally determined eigenfrequencies differ from each other by approximately 8%. On the figure 9 and figure 10 the individual eigenforms corresponding to these eigenfrequencies are shown.

Table 1. Comparison between experimental and numerical results.

Test	Force [N]	λ^2 [-]	Mode	Frequency Experimental [Hz]	Irvine [1] [Hz]	String [2] [Hz]
1	398.1	1.3	1	5.67	5.73	5.46
			2	10.99	10.92	10.92
2	305.5	2.8	1	5.10	5.30	4.78
			2	9.57	9.56	9.56
3	244.5	5.4	1	4.80	5.14	4.28
			2	8.52	8.56	8.56
4	189.8	11.7	1	4.69	5.25	3.77
			2	7.53	7.54	7.54
5	138.3	30.1	1	4.88	5.88	3.22
			2	6.38	6.44	6.44
6	108.2	62.9	1	6.25	6.61	2.85
			2	5.77	5.69	5.69
7	86.9	121.3	1	6.50	6.81	2.55
			2	5.10	5.10	5.10
8	79.4	159.4	1	6.61	6.68	2.44
			2	4.87	4.87	4.87
9	67.6	257.9	1	6.43	6.30	2.25
			2	4.48	4.50	4.50
10	58.3	402.9	1	6.01	5.90	2.09
			2	4.06	4.18	4.18

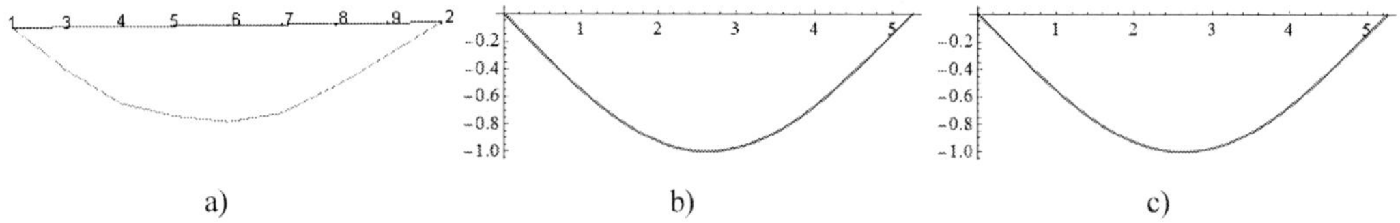

a) b) c)

Figure 5. The first symmetric eigenform corresponding to the first symmetric eigenfrequency for the force in cable H = 398.1 N, λ^2 = 1.3; (a) experimental results f_{e1} = 5.67 Hz, (b) Irvine formulas f_{I1} = 5.73 Hz, (c) String formulas f_{s1} = 5.46 Hz.

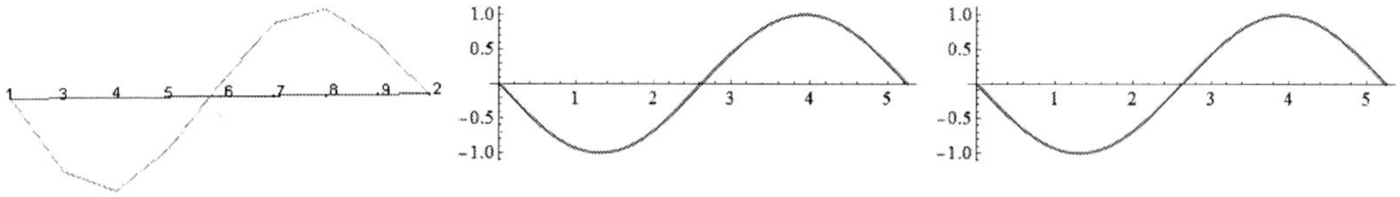

a) b) c)

Figure 6. The first antisymmetric eigenform corresponding to the first antisymmetric eigenfrequency for the force in cable H = 398.1 N, λ^2 = 1.3; (a) experimental results f_{e2} = 10.99 Hz (b) Irvine formulas f_{I2} = 10.92 Hz, (c) String formulas f_{I2} = 10.92 Hz.

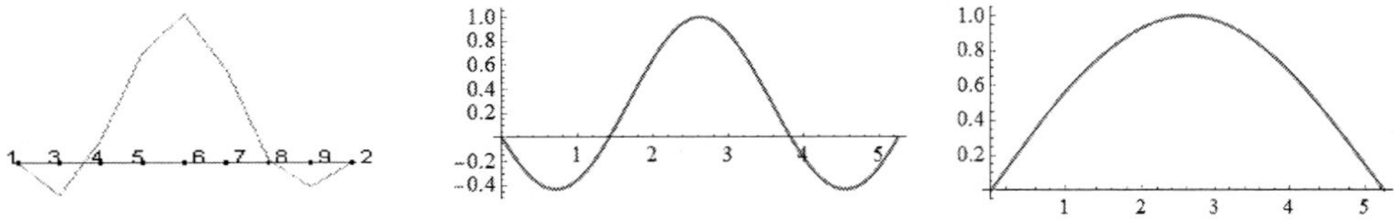

a) b) c)

Figure 7. The first symmetric eigenform corresponding to the first symmetric eigenfrequency for the force in cable $H = 86.9$ N, $\lambda^2 = 121.3$; (a) experimental results $f_{e1} = 6.607$ Hz, (b) Irvine formulas $f_{I1} = 6.68$ Hz, (c) String formulas $f_{s1} = 2.44$ Hz.

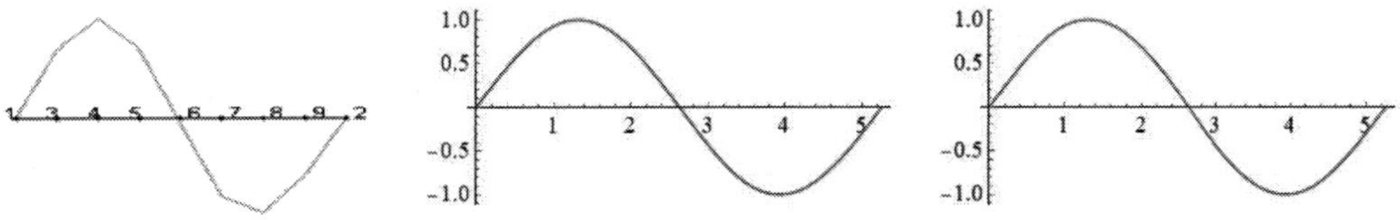

a) b) c)

Figure 8. The first antisymmetric eigenform corresponding to the first antisymmetric eigenfrequency for the force in cable $H = 86.9$ N, $\lambda^2 = 121.3$; (a) experimental results $f_{e2} = 4.87$ Hz (b) Irvine formulas $f_{I2} = 4.87$ Hz, (c) String formulas $f_{I2} = 4.87$ Hz.

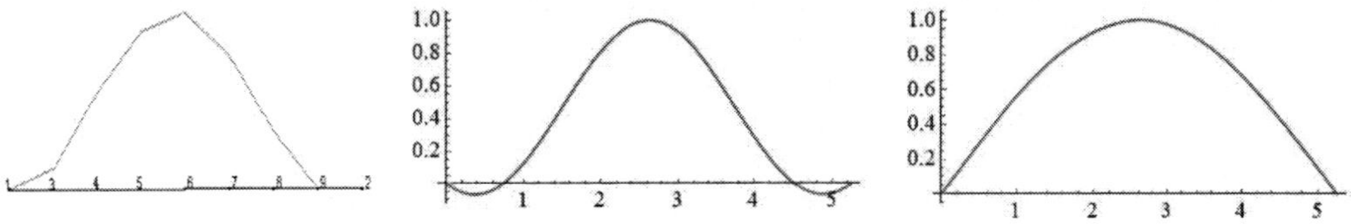

a) b) c)

Figure 9. The first symmetric eigenform corresponding to the first symmetric eigenfrequency for the force in cable $H = 108.2$ N, $\lambda^2 = 62.9$; (a) experimental results $f_{e1} = 6.25$ Hz, (b) Irvine formulas $f_{I1} = 6.61$ Hz, (c) String formulas $f_{s1} = 2.85$ Hz.

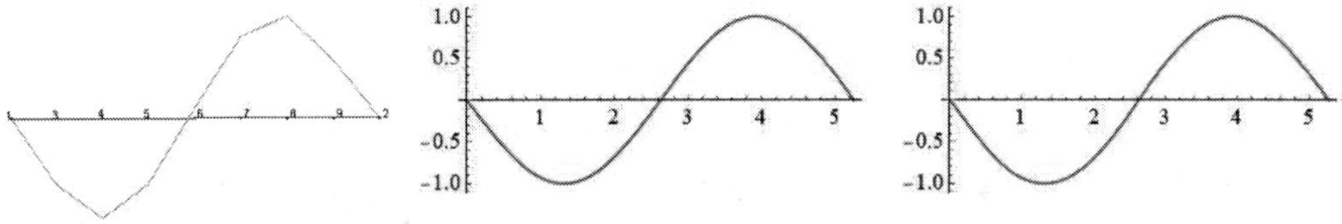

a) b) c)

Figure 10. The first antisymmetric eigenform corresponding to the first antisymmetric eigenfrequency for the force in cable $H = 108.2$ N, $\lambda^2 = 62.9$; (a) experimental results $f_{e2} = 5.77$ Hz (b) Irvine formulas $f_{I2} = 5{,}69$ Hz, (c) String formulas $f_{I2} = 5{,}69$ Hz.

By comparison the eigenfrequencies and eigenforms obtained from experimental studies with numerically calculated ones, it can be easily determine the force in a cable. Figure 9 shows the dependence of Irvine parameter λ^2 on the force in the cable. The value of the λ^2 parameter and the corresponding value of the force in the cable corresponding to this parameter are marked with a red dashed line. These are the values obtained for test 2 and 8 respectively.

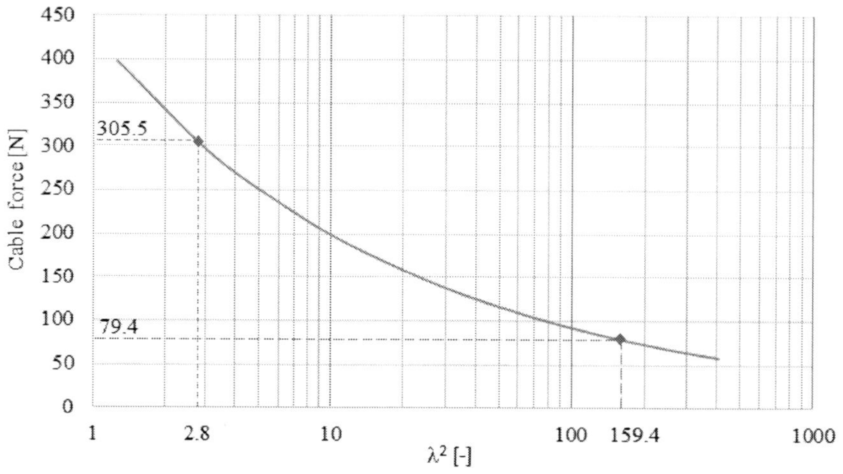

Figure 11. Dependence of Irvine parameter λ^2 on the force in the cable.

5. CONCLUSIONS

The article presents the method of determining force in a cable with a small sag ($0 \leq d/L \leq 1/8$). To determine the force in the cable, operational modal analysis (OMA) and the generally known and widely used mathematical model of the cable proposed by Irvine [1] were used. Chapter 4 gives the necessary formulas to determine the eigenforms and eigenfrequencies in plane of the sag of the cable. Chapter 2 describes the test stand, and chapter 3 describes of the method of determining the force in the cable. In the paper it is shown that with the help of measurements eigenfrequencies and eigenforms it is possible to correctly determine the forces in the cable with a relatively large sag, i.e. for a cable with a large Irvine parameter. It should be emphasized that for the large Irvine parameter the characteristic first symmetrical form with three local extremes was obtained (see fig. 7a and fig. 7b). This form does not appear when considering the cable of negligible small sag (the issue of the string). The comparability of results obtained from experimental and numerical calculations allows to confirm the effectiveness of using OMA to determine forces in a cable with a small sag. On the basis of the conducted research, it can be stated that the measurement of the first two eigenfrequencies and coresponding eigenforms (the first symmetric and the first antisymmetric) is necessary and at the same time sufficient to correctly determine the value of force in the cable with a small sag.

REFERENCES

[1] Nam. H., & Nghia. N. T. (2011). Estimation of cable tension using measured natural frequencies. *Procedia Engineering The Twelfth East Asia-Pacific Conference on Structural Engineering and* Construction. 14. 1510–1517.

[2] Huang. Y. H., Fu. J. Y., Wang. R. H., Gan. Q., Rao. R., Liu. A. R. (2014) Practical formula to calculate tension of vertical cable with hinged-fixed conditions based on vibration method. *JVE International Ltd. Journal of Vibroengineering*. 14(2). 997-1009.

[3] Yang. D.-W., Lu. D.-G. & Zhou. W.-S. (2018) Regression Model for Cable Tension Identification Based on Vibration Method Using Calibration Test: From Factory to Construction. In: *9th European Workshop on Structural Health Monitoring*. Manchester, UK.

[4] Irvine. H. M., Caughey T. K., (1974) The linear theory of free vibrations of a suspended cable, *Proceedings of the Royal Society Series*. 341(A).

IOMAC'19

8th International Operational Modal Analysis Conference

2019 May 13-15 Copenhagen

OMA AS A TOOL FOR NONLINEARITY DETECTION

Jacek Grosel[1], Wojciech Sawicki[2], Zbigniew Wojcicki[3], Jakub Marcinowski[4] and Volodymyr Sakharov[5]

[1] PhD, Wroclaw University of Science and Technology, Poland, jacek.grosel@pwr.edu.pl
[2] PhD, Wroclaw University of Science and Technology, Poland, wojciech.sawicki@pwr.edu.pl
[3] Prof, Wroclaw University of Science and Technology, Poland, zbigniew.wojcicki@pwr.edu.pl
[4] Prof, University of Zielona Gora, Poland, j.marcinowski @ib.uz.zgora.pl
[5] Prof, University of Zielona Gora, Poland, v.sakharov@ib.uz.zgora.pl

ABSTRACT

The study presents vibration measurements and the results of Operational Modal Analysis of the Monument of Christ the King, a structure that has been analysed by the authors repeatedly. The main purpose of the work is to determine the differences in modal parameters obtained during measurements and to try to find the reason for these differences: if they are caused by environmental influences (wind, temperature), by the non-linear characteristics of the object, or if they represent the errors of the method. The paper presents the results of one seven-day measurement run and shows the impact of the above mentioned factors on the values of eigenfrequencies obtained as a result of OMA.

Keywords: Nonlinearity, Vibrations, Measurements, Wind, Temperature, OMA

1. INTRODUCTION

1.1. General information

The basic assumption of OMA is that the structure under study is an LTI system (linear time-invariant structure) [1] . In the case of structures with nonlinear features, the level of recorded/measured vibrations may affect the obtained results of modal analysis. This has to be taken into account when performing modal analysis.

OMA is often used to monitor the condition of a structure (eg. [2]). In this, as well as in other applications (eg. FEM validation [3]), it is important to be sure that the change of modal parameters does not result from factors other than changes in the construction characteristics. If the change of modal characteristics is caused by environmental factors (temperature, humidity, wind) and this is not detected, the results will be misleading and incorrectly ascribed i.e. to structure deterioration.

This article is an analysis of the possible occurrence of phenomena that may influence modal analysis results.

2. MEASUREMENT DESCRIPTION

2.1. The Statue of Jesus Christ

The statue of Jesus Christ the King of the Universe (Fig.1a) now holds the title of Largest Statue of Jesus Christ. It is 3 m taller than the better known Rio de Janeiro statue of Christ the Redeemer. The statue in Świebodzin is 33 m high (plus a 2 m high crown) and weighs 260 tons. Built on an 12 m embankment of stones and rubble, the statue together with its mound are 48 m tall. The hands are 6 m long and the distance between the ends of the fingers is 26 m. The statue is topped by a 2 m high gilded crown with a diameter of 3.5 m.

The monument is not a typical construction, as the covering shell is composed of concrete and fibreglass mounted on a steel truss structure. This steel rod construction is the main load-bearing internal structure of the statue. It rests on a 1 m thick circular plate supported by six reinforced concrete columns, placed in a circle with a radius of 5.2 m. These columns are in turn founded on a square reinforced concrete plate placed 12 m beneath the mound peak.

Figure 1. View of the Statue.

The walls of the 2.4 m long lower segments of the statue are composed of three layers: the outer and inner layers of steel rebar with steel mesh enclose an inner 10 cm layer of hard rockwool. The segments are banded with steel ribbons and connected to the internal steel structure by additional steel rods welded to the steel ribbons. These segments were fabricated off-site, then affixed to the bearing structure on-site. The figure's arms and chest were fabricated on-site, next to the statue under construction. Following assembly, the walls of the statue were covered by 5-7 cm layers of shotcrete on both sides. Finally, a 4-6 mm layer of glass fiber reinforced polymer (GFRP) forms the external surface (skin) of the figure. It is attached to the steel bar mesh connected to the internal spatial truss.

2.2. The equipment for vibration measurement

The paper presents the results of measurements carried out between the 19th and the 27th of December 2018. The vibrations were measured continuously, recording the accelerations in batches. 303 measurement batches were registered, each of which lasted approximately 35 minutes. The accelerations were measured with seismic high sensitivity accelerometers DeltaTron 8340, Bruel&Kjaer (Fig 2a). Each accelerometer DeltaTron 8340 has a mass 775g and sensitivity 1mV/ms^{-2}. Measurement were performed at four measuring points:

channel 1 - at the statue's chest level in the horizontal direction, towards the front of the figure,

channel 2 - the highest measurement point was placed in the head of the statue that is at the height of about 32 m above the ground level, vibrations were recorded in the horizontal direction, towards the back of the figure,
channel 3 - in the right hand of the statue, at the wrist, in the vertical direction, downwards,
channel 4 - in the right hand of the statue, at the wrist, in the horizontal direction, towards the front of the figure.
Channels 1,3,4 were located on shoulder-height, about 27 m above the ground level.

The OMA package (Operational Modal Analysis Pro developed by: Structural Vibration Solutions A/S) and EFDD algorithm was applied by the authors for obtaining eigenfrequencies and eigenforms.

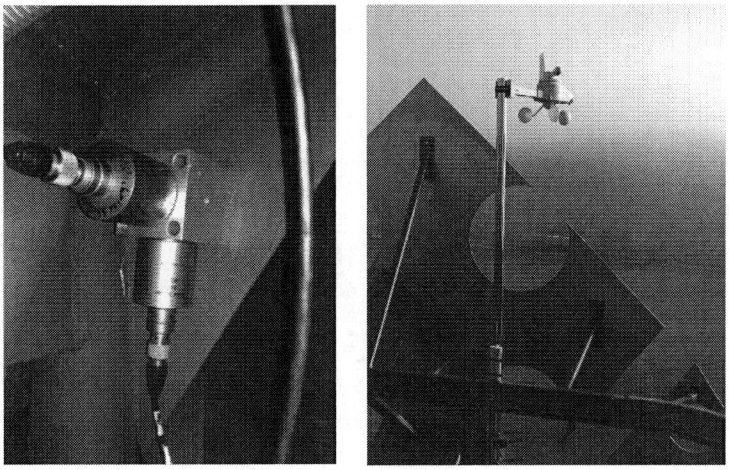

Figure 2. Accelerometers inside the Statue (channel 3 and 4) and a view of the weather station on the Statue's head.

2.3. The equipment for wind and temperature measurement

In addition to the acceleration measurements, meteorological parameters regarding wind and temperature were measured. The measurements took place in seven-minute cycles and after such a period the following measured values were recorded: average wind speed, maximum wind speed (gusts of wind), wind direction and air temperature. The weather station MA 10050, used for measurements, consists of a gateway with corresponding measuring sensors that measure weather data. The main part of the meteorological station is the wind sensor (MA10660), which can measure the wind speed and its direction. The wind speed is measured in the range of 0.3 – 50 m/s (1 –180 km/h) with an accuracy of 0.1 m/s (0.4 km/h), while the wind direction is determined as one of 16 positions, which gives angular resolution of 22.5°.The sensors transmit the readings wireless via radio to the gateway. The gateway collects weather data every 7 minutes and transmits them to a server. Finally, the data can be accessed via internet.

The wind sensor was placed at the top of the statue (Fig. 2b). Over 1500 records of wind conditions and temperature were registered during the measurement period (8 days)s. As over 90% of the registered data, including with maximum speeds and gusts of wind, were blowing in the northwest direction, the parameter of wind direction has been omitted in further analysis.

Results of wind and temperature measurement are shown in Fig. 3 and 4. The maximum wind speed was recorded at the beginning of the third day and reached a speed about 30 km/h (8.3 m/s). This day also showed maximum wind gusts up to 59.9 km/h (16.6 m/s). On this day (during periods of maximum gusts), there was also a maximum temperature of +9°C. During the measurement period, the temperature was mainly positive in the range of up to +9°C. The exception was on the first and sixth day when the temperature decreased up to -1°C.

3. MEASUREMENT RESULTS

On the basis of recorded 303 batches of measurements four eigenfrequencies were identified. For every eigenfrequency the minimum, maximum, mean value and variability is listed in Table 1. Also number of measurement batches with founded *i*-th eigenfrequency is given in Table 1. Besides the four listed eigenfrequencies few others eigenfrequencies were found but in lower number of measurement butches.

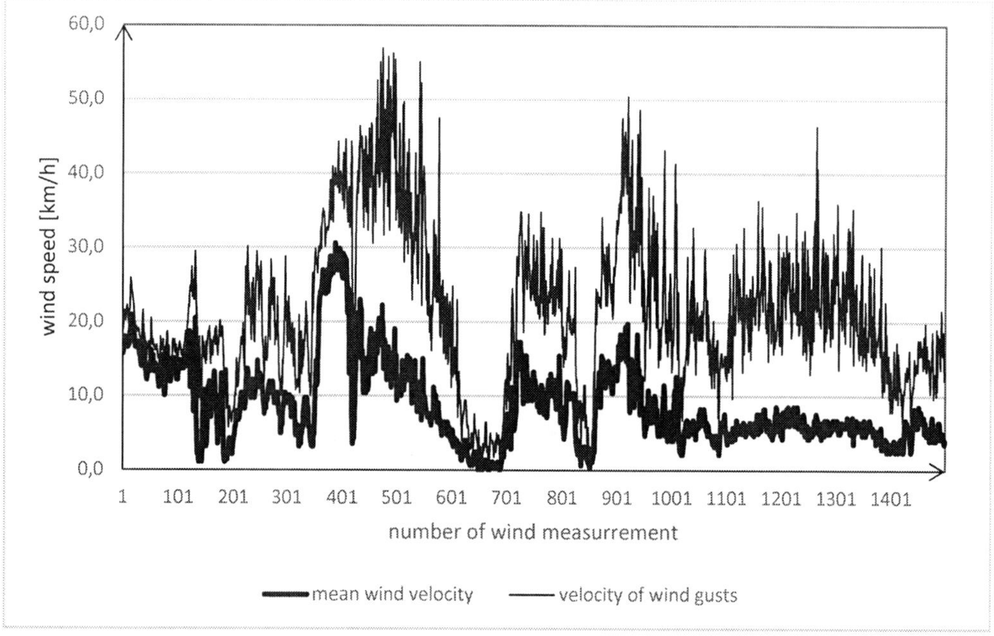

Figure 3. Wind velocity measured on the statue's head.

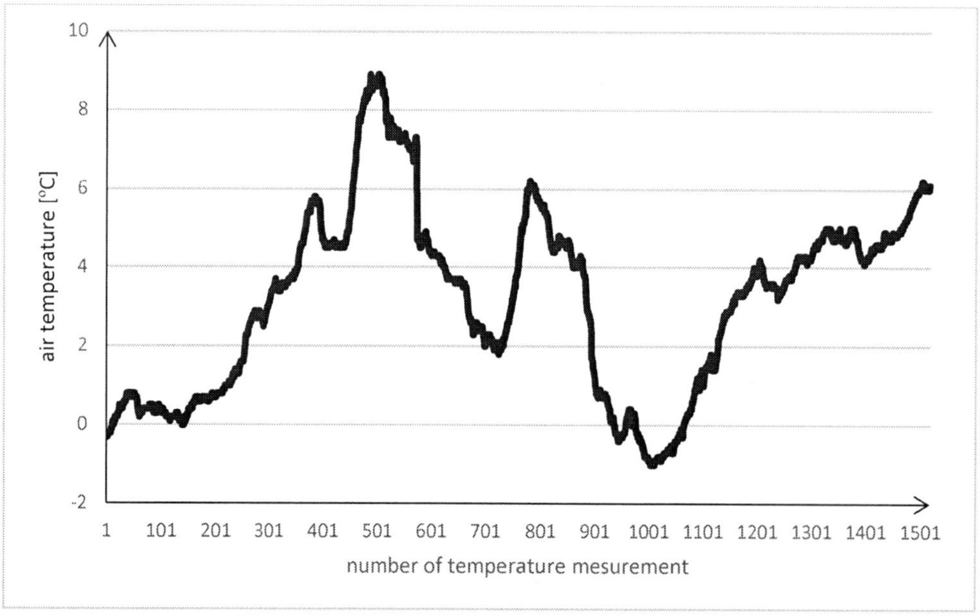

Figure 4. Air temperature measured on the statue's top.

For example frequency 6.45 Hz was found in 80 butches and frequency 4.81 Hz was found in 20 butches. These frequencies were not analysed.

Table 1. List of analysed eigenfrequencies.

Mode	Frequency				Number of batches with *i*-th eigenfrequency
	Lowest value [Hz]	Highest value [Hz]	Mean value [Hz]	Variability [%]	
1	*2*	*3*	*4*	*5=(3-2)/4*	*6*
1st - f_1	1.291	1.368	1.332	5.8	297
2nd - f_2	2.090	2.620	2,175	7.9	301
3rd - f_3	3.524	3.914	3.801	10.3	230
4th - f_4	8.449	8.694	8.535	2.9	276

Values of the four analysed eigenfrequencies are in good accordance with values obtained in the previous investigations [4,5,6]. Figures 5 and 6 show the values of f_2 and f_4 in subsequent measurements, respectively. One can observe some regularities in these dependencies. In order to verify these relationships charts showing dependency of eigenfrequency on the temperature or wind speed were prepared - Figures 7 and 8. It can be seen that the dependency is moderate, the highest value of the coefficient of determination (for a linear function) is about 0.5 when the lowest one is close to zero. The other situation is when eigenfrequency dependency on vibration level (RMS of acceleration measured in channel 1÷4) is considered. For the first and the second eigenfrequency coefficient of determination (for a logarithmic function) is bigger than 0.85. For the third eigenfrequency the coefficient is close to zero – 0.02 and for the fourth eigenfrequency is moderate and equals to 0.33. The representative draw is shown as Fig. 9.

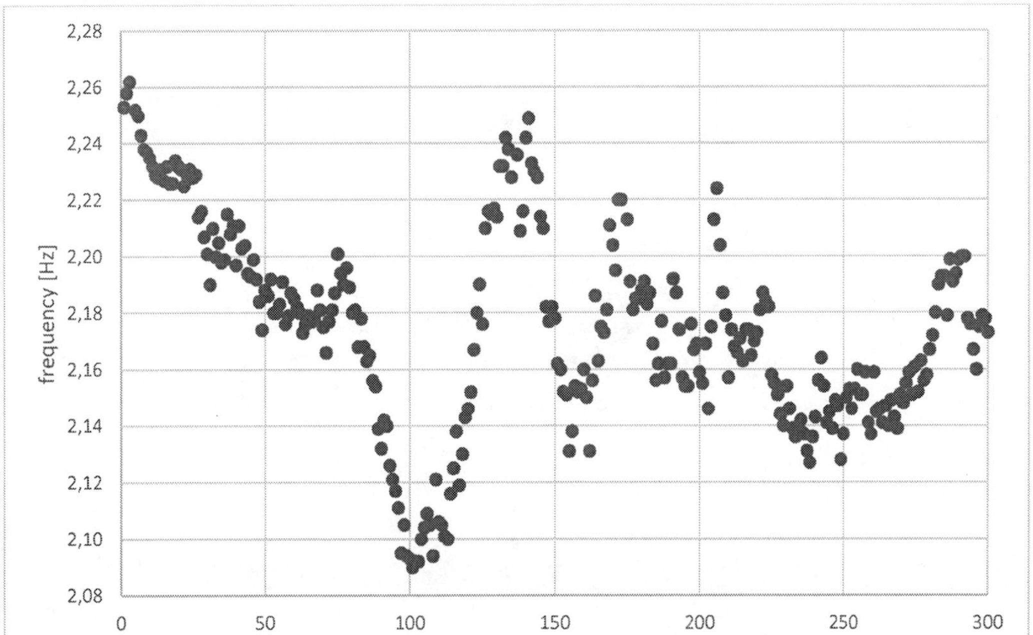

Figure 5. The second eigenfrequency f_2 in subsequent butches

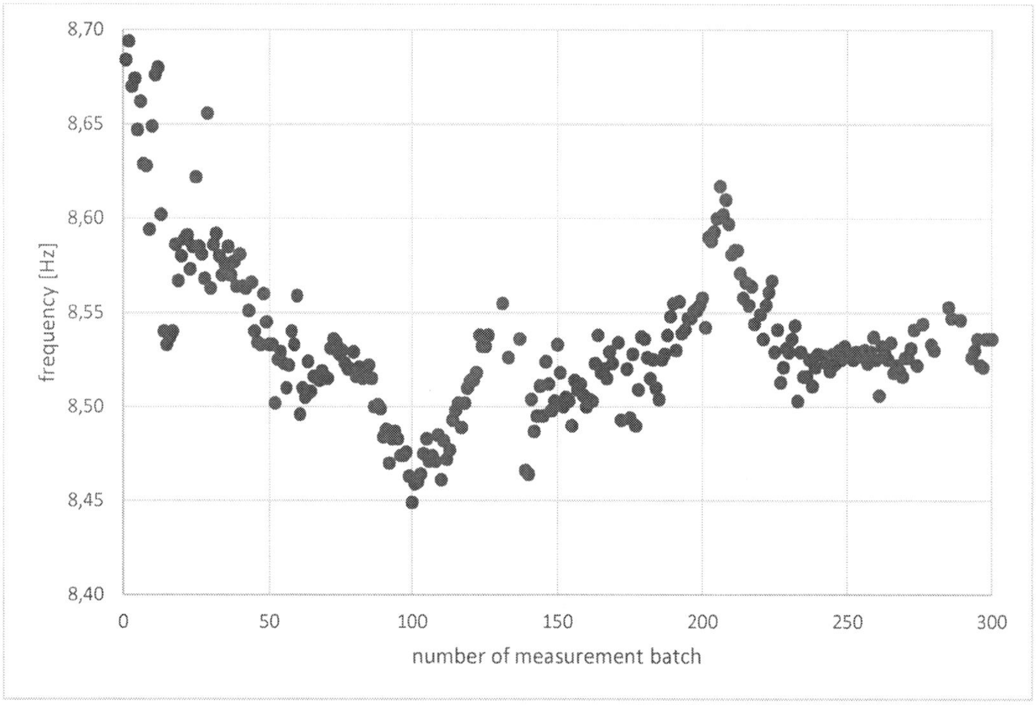

Figure 6. The fourth eigenfrequency f_4 in subsequent butches

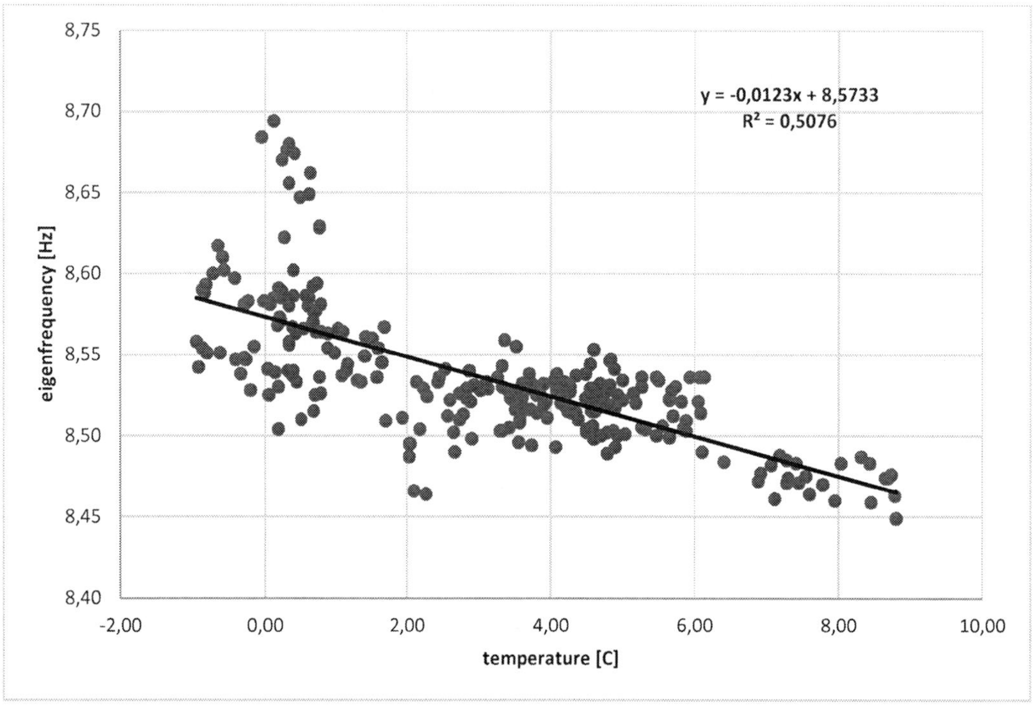

Figure 7. Dependency of the fourth eigenfrequency f_4 on the air temperature

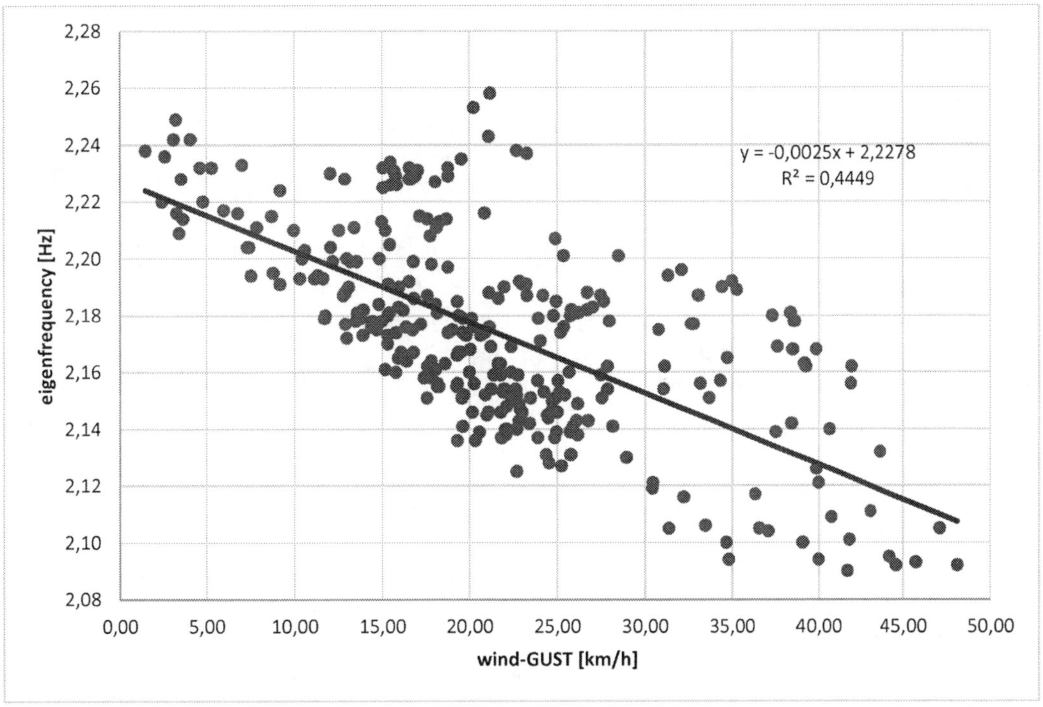

Figure 8. Dependency of the second eigenfrequency f_2 on the wind speed

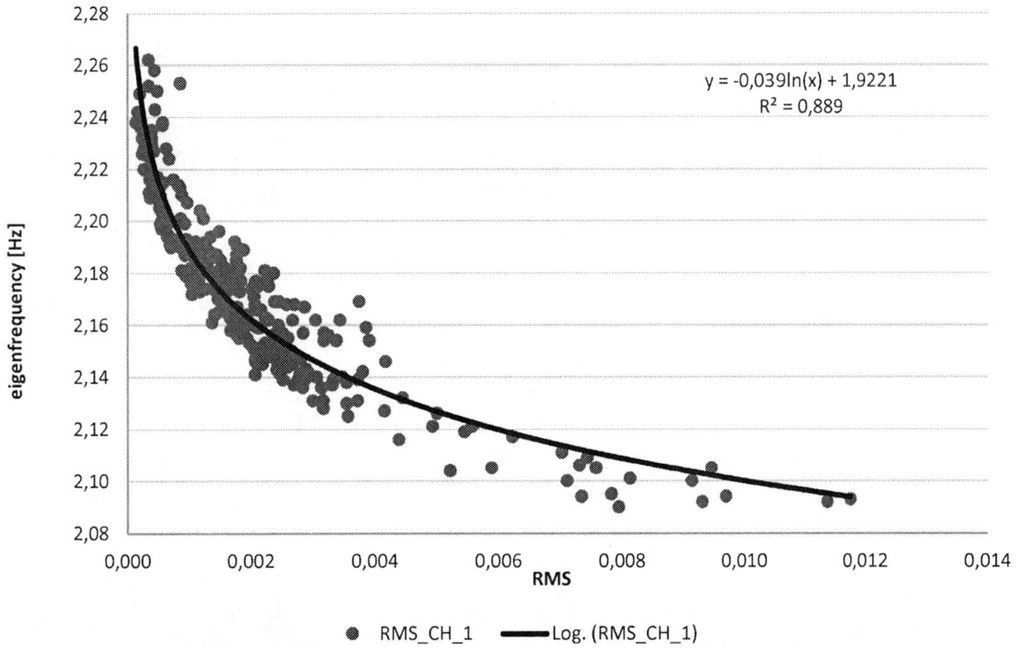

Figure 9. Dependency of the second eigenfrequency f_2 on the RMS of acceleration (channel 1)

4. CONCLUSIONS

The paper presents the results of modal analysis carried out on the basis of vibrations recorded under various external conditions. Based on the measurements taken and their analyses, it can be concluded that there is no significant correlation between wind speed (average or gusts) and eigenfrequencies. Similarly, there is no correlation in the relationship between environment temperature and eigenfrequencies. However, there is a significant correlation between the level of recorded vibrations and eigenfrequencies. As the level of vibrations increases, the frequency decreases, which means that with increasing displacement of the structure, its stiffness decreases. This indicates the non-linear nature of the structure's work.

Because there is a correlation between the level of vibration and the eigenfrequencies, an analysis of vibration levels should be carried out in parallel to modal analysis when applying OMA to monitor structure status. The two analysis results should then be compared to eliminate the influences of non-linearity in the process of monitoring the condition of the structure.

REFERENCES

[1] Brincker, R., Ventura, C. (2015). Introduction to operational modal analysis. Chichester, Wiley.

[2] Bru, D., Ivorra, S., Baeza, F., J., Reynau, R. Foti, D. (2015) OMA dynamic identification of a masonry chimney with severe cracking condition. In: *Proc. 6th Int. Operational Modal Analysis Conf.* Gijón, Spain

[3] Poprawa, G., Salamak, M., Pradelok, S., Łaziński, P. (2017) Operational modal analysis in model updating of a truss railway bridge In: *Proc. 7th Int. Operational Modal Analysis Conf.* Ingolstadt, Germany, 64-68

[4] Grosel, J., Sawicki, W., Marcinowski, J., Wojcicki, Z. (2017) OMA post-renovation study of the Christ the King monument preparation for windload analysis. In: *Proc. 7th Int. Operational Modal Analysis Conf.* Ingolstadt, Germany, 150-153

[5] Grosel, J., Sawicki, W., Marcinowski, J., Wojcicki, Z., (2015) Monument of Christ the King - OMA study. In: *Proc. 6th Int. Operational Modal Analysis Conf.* Gijón, Spain, 39-45

[6] Grosel, J., Sawicki, W., Marcinowski J, Wojcicki Z., (2018) Nonlinearity identification of Jesus Christ the King monument on the basis of modal parameters In: *Theoretical Foundation of Civil Engineering* (27RSP) (TFoCE 2018), Rostov-on-Don, Russia, 1-6

IOMAC'19

8th International Operational Modal Analysis Conference
2019 May13-15 Copenhagen

OPERATIONAL ANALYSIS OF TWO STRUT-FRAME BRIDGES IN THE SOUTHERN EAST OF FRANCE

PERRAULT Matthieu[1], *REGNIER Julie*[1], *MERCERAT Diego*[1], *DAVI Denis*[2], *LANGLAUDE Philippe*[1] *and PERNOUD Michel*[1]

[1] Cerema, Team MOUV-GS, France, 06309 Sophia-Antipolis, matthieu.perrault@cerema.fr.
[2] Cerema, DOA, France, 13290 Aix-en-Provence, denis.davi@cerema.fr.

ABSTRACT

Two strut-frame bridges were instrumented in the framework of an INTEREG project RISVAL. The overall scope of our action in RISVAL is to assess the optimal setup to instrument a bridge according to the objective of the instrumentation (health monitoring, model updating, damage detection…). The first bridge was instrumented with few 3D sensors while in the second one, the spatial distribution of the sensors was higher. The second instrumentation helps to identify the mode shapes, especially the first longitudinal one. With this observation we were able to propose a numerical model with modified boundary conditions that respect the observed modes order. The boundary conditions chosen suggest that the expansion joints between the road and the bridge are malfunctioning at least under ambient vibrations. Finally, we discussed the pertinence of ambient vibrations characterization especially for the boundary conditions to describe the dynamic behavior of the structure under seismic loading.

Keywords: strut-frame bridge, Operational, Modal, Analysis, expansion joint

1. INTRODUCTION

Operational Modal Analysis (OMA) based on ambient vibration measurements has gain on popularity since the mid 90's, these methods are used in several fields of the vibration mechanics (aerospace, rotation, machinery, on-road testing) and civil engineering structures such as buildings and bridges. A complete review of the application of OMA can be found in [1]–[3]. In civil engineering, an actual in-situ measurement will improve the quality of the models since their dynamic behavior is affected by the surrounding environment (soil and soil structure interaction). Contrary to the EMA (Experimental Modal Analysis or so-called input/output methods), the OMA is interesting because it does not required sources of excitations that can be huge considering the size of the structures involved.

The modal response of the structure can be affected by environmental conditions such as the temperature and operational conditions such as the traffic load or the state of the roadway expansion joints [4], [5]. Whatever the objectives of the ambient vibration instrumentation are: health monitoring, model updating or damage detections, the knowledge of the variability of the dynamic properties is needed. In the framework of an INTERREG project called RISVAL, we are currently instrumented more than 20 bridges on the A51 highway in France. We selected these structures such that various typologies of bridges and foundations are available and in the same time for one typology several bridges are instrumented. The scope of this project is to define the optimal configuration of sensors to describe the dynamic behavior of the structures depending on the objectives of the instrumentation (damage detection, health monitoring, model updating…).

In this article, we focus on strut-frame bridge configuration. We instrumented two bridges with this configuration and compare the results of the modal analysis (frequency domain decomposition as proposed by [6]) with a numerical model (2D).

2. INSTRUMENTATIONS AND MODAL ANALYSIS

2.1. Instrumentation configurations

The two bridges we instrumented (see Figure 1), thereafter called bridge A and bridge B, are 3-span strut-frame bridges. Bridge A is 66 m long (18 m-30 m-18 m) and bridge B is 48 m long (11 m-26 m-11 m).

Figure 1. Photos of the two instrumented strut-frame bridges: bridge A (left) and bridge B (right). From Google Street View.

We used a Cityshark II ambient vibrations station [7] that allows the simultaneous recording of 6 3-component sensors. The sensors are Guralp CMG-40T that are broadband seismometers with a flat response to velocity from 30 seconds to 50 Hz. The length of the recordings is 30 min at a 200 Hz sampling frequency.

We first instrumented bridge A, with a configuration of 6 sensors along the longitudinal direction on a sidewalk: one sensor at the level of the first abutment, one at the middle of the first span, two on the second span, one at the middle of the third span and one at the level of the second abutment.

Because the configuration is a single data set, all the mode shapes cannot be clearly identified (cf. part 2.2) especially those that involve torsion of the deck. We then instrumented bridge B with a higher spatial distribution (31 points, see Figure 2). The measurement was done using six data sets (A-B-C-D-E-F). Therefore, we define a reference sensor (REF on Figure 2), that was common to all the data sets. The reference was placed avoiding setting it at a node of a mode.

2.1. Modal Analysis

The modal analysis was done by Frequency Domain Decomposition (FDD,[6], [8], [9]). FDD is a non-parametric method, i.e. no a priori information of the bridge model is needed. It consists in computing the Fourier spectra of the cross-correlation matrix of simultaneous recordings done in a structure. [6] showed that the Power Spectra Density obtained can be decomposed into singular vectors (i.e. an estimate of the mode shapes) and scalar singular values (i.e. the resonance frequencies).

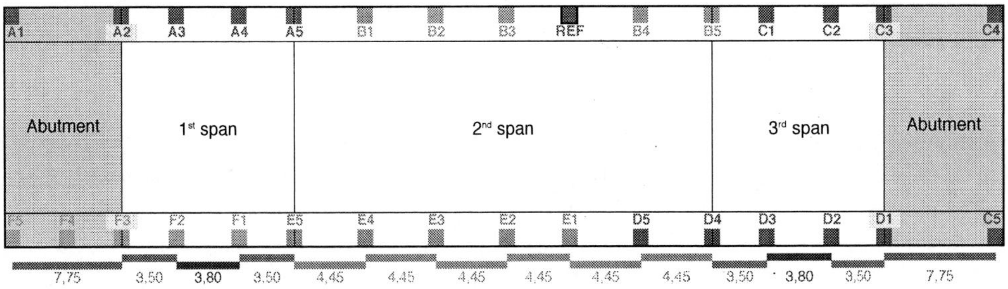

Figure 2. Instrumentation configuration of bridge B. Each square represents the location of a sensor. 6 different 6-sensor configurations were done (e.g. the first configuration: REF-A1-A2-A3-A4-A5). A reference sensor (REF) was always at the same place during the whole experiment.

Figures 3 and 4 show the results of the modal analysis for the bridge A and bridge B, respectively. Both figures show the two first singular values of the pseudo spectral density matrices and the mode shapes that we identified. Table 1 provides the value of the resonance frequencies that were identified. In the spectra figures, the colored peaks show the frequency range in which the Modal Assurance Criterion (MAC, [10]) is upper than 80% comparing the mode shape at a frequency with the mode shape at the main frequency of the mode. The mode shapes are represented in the XY system for the first mode (transversal) and in the XZ system for the other modes, where the X-axis corresponds to the longest horizontal direction of the bridge, Y-axis to the perpendicular horizontal direction and Z-axis to the vertical direction.

The modal analysis of bridge B, that was more detailed considering the high number of measurements, helped us to understand and identify the mode shapes obtained for bridge A. In particular, the first longitudinal mode of bridge A (in green in Figure 3) has been identified by comparison with the first longitudinal mode of bridge B. The main component of this mode is vertical, whereas it corresponds to a longitudinal behavior of the struts. Because there is only a very small longitudinal displacement of the two bridges at the abutments, it explains why this mode is mainly vertical: the deck of the spans has a vertical behavior in order to compensate for the displacement of the struts.

The order of the three first modes is not the same for the two bridges: transversal – vertical – longitudinal for bridge A, transversal – longitudinal – vertical for bridge B. It can be explained by a geometrical difference due to the dimensions of main carrying element, bridge A is a slab bridge and bridge B is T-beam bridge, so the bridge B may be more rigid in the vertical axis or/and boundary conditions (blocked or not).

The high density of measurement points performed on bridge B allows assessing seven modes for frequencies under 20 Hz. In particular, the synchronous measurements on both sidewalks allow identifying three torsional modes. Two peaks of bridge A (7.14 Hz and 9.67 Hz) are not well identified, we think they can be torsional modes. A second measurement on bridge A, with a higher density of sensors, could improve the modal identification.

In the following, we focus on the assessment of a numerical model for bridge A. The measurement on bridge B (that was easier to access) was performed retrospectively to clarify the identification of the mode shapes of bridge A. No numerical modelling has been yet performed on that bridge.

Table 1. Experimental resonance frequencies of bridge A and bridge B assessed by Frequency Domain Decomposition.

Mode	Bridge A	Bridge B
1	3.10 Hz (transversal mode)	3.99 Hz (transversal mode)
2	3.76 Hz (1st vertical mode)	5.15 Hz (longitudinal mode)
3	4.85 Hz (longitudinal mode)	7.78 Hz (1st vertical mode)
4	7.14 Hz (non identified)	8.87 Hz (torsional mode)
5	7.33 Hz (2nd vertical mode)	13.56 Hz (torsional mode)
6	9.67 Hz (non identified)	16.19 Hz (2nd vertical mode)
7	-	19.32 Hz (torsional mode)

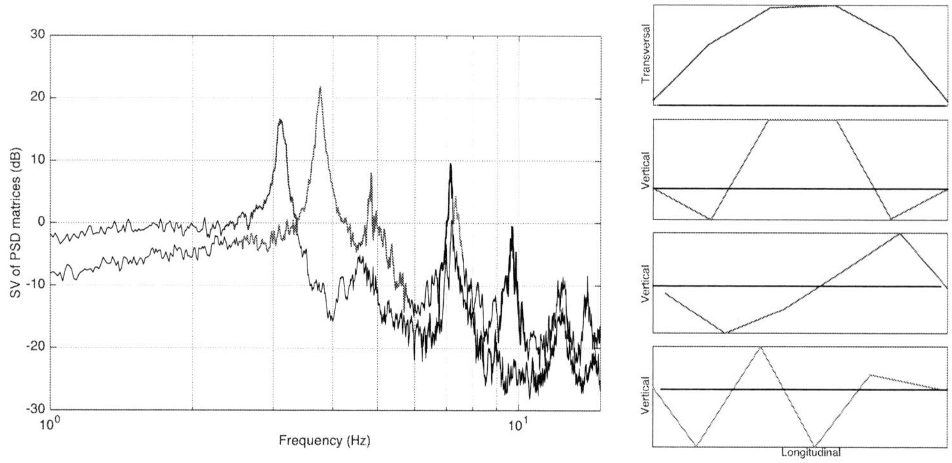

Figure 3. Modal analysis of bridge A. Four modes (in color) are identified until 10 Hz, and two other peaks (in black) could correspond to torsional modes. The blue mode (XY system) is a transversal mode, the red mode is the first vertical mode, the green one is a longitudinal mode and the orange one is the second vertical mode.

3. NUMERICAL MODELISATION

The bridge A was modelled using the software *ST1* [11], a linear elastic structural analysis program for frame elements developed by the Cerema. The geometry and properties of constitutive materials were assessed from the design documents of the engineered structure obtained from the operator of the highway (ESCOTA). On each abutment the deck is simply supported by elastomeric bearings with a dimension of 300 x 300 x 78 mm. The deck and the struts are rigidly connected and at the base of the struts are designed using reduced reinforced concrete sections (so called Freyssinet hinges). The accuracy of the model mass distribution was checked by comparison with the structure initial design documents, such that the axial dead load at the base of the strut (600 t) and the bending deformation at the middle of the deck (around 5mm during the loading test with four trucks of 20 to 23 t) satisfyingly match.

The tested models considered the material characteristics as listed in the Table 2. The first model properties were based also on the recommendations of the Eurocode 8-2: Concrete nominal resistance (f_{ck}) of 35 MPa, a Young modulus of the concrete of 40 000 MPa, a shear modulus of the elastomeric bearing of 1 MPa. The Freyssinet hinges are considered as perfect hinges with axes in the transverse direction. Finally, the footings and soil are considered as perfectly rigid.

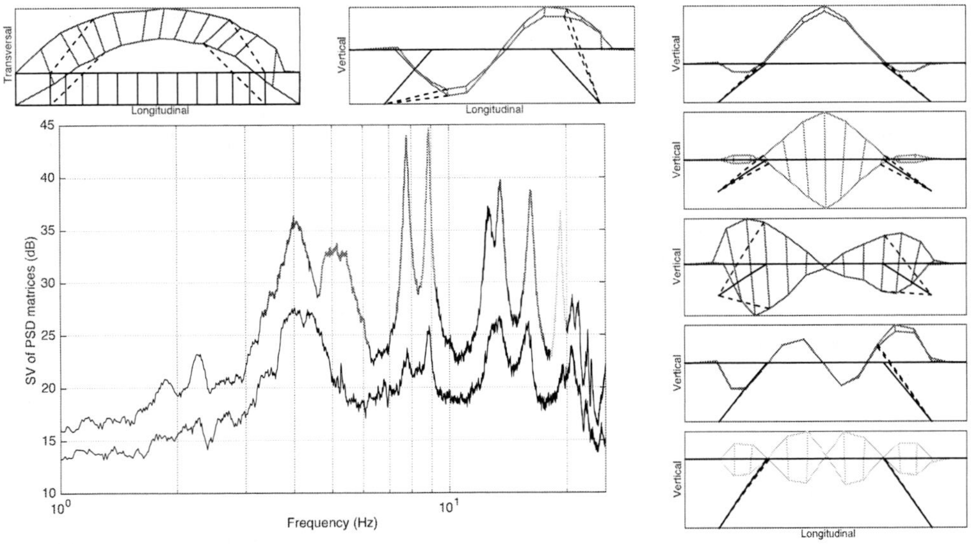

Figure 4. Modal analysis of bridge B. Seven modes (in color) are identified until 20 Hz: a transversal mode, a longitudinal mode, the first vertical mode, two torsional modes, the second vertical mode and another torsional mode.

The influence of those parameters has been tested in the models 2 to 5. Compared to the first model, the second one considers a refinement at the connection between the strut and the foundation, where instead of considering a perfect hinge we modelled the real mechanical properties (i.e. reduced section and inertia). In the third model, the Young modulus of the concrete was increased (according to on-site investigations made by the Cerema in 1983) with different values adopted for the deck and the strut (50 and 45 MPa respectively). In the fourth model, we tried a very high shear modulus for the elastomeric bearings (up to 50 MPa in order to match with recorded natural frequencies). Finally, in the last model we tested rigid boundary conditions in addition to the elastomeric bearings, in both longitudinal and transversal translational degrees of freedom at the abutments.

Table 2. Numerical models tested.

	Model 1	Model 2	Model 3	Model 4	Model 5
Freyssinet hinges	Perfect hinges	Reduced section	Reduced section	Reduced section	Reduced section
Concrete	F_{c28}=35Mpa	F_{c28}=35Mpa	F_{c28_strut}=45Mpa $F_{c28\ deck}$=50Mpa	F_{c28}=35Mpa	F_{c28_strut}=45Mpa $F_{c28\ deck}$=50Mpa
Elastomeric bearings	G=1MPa	G=1MPa	G=1MPa	G=50MPa	G=1MPa
Boundary condition at bridge edges (translational DOF)	2 DOF (longitudinal and transversal)	2 DOF (longitudinal and transversal)	2 DOF (longitudinal and transversal)	2 DOF (longitudinal and transversal)	0 DOF

3.1. Comparison between experimental and numerical results

The comparison of the resonance frequencies of the first fourth modes derived from the experimental modal analysis is synthetized in the Table 3. The first 4 numerical models do not provide the same modes order as found in the recordings. Only the last model with the modification of the boundary conditions succeeds to reproduce the recorded dynamic properties. Although, the differences between the frequencies are large and need to be adjusted.

In the first numerical models, the longitudinal mode is the fundamental resonance mode of the bridge. From model 1 to model 3, we tested various variations of the bridge properties, but we fail in reproducing the experimental results. In the third model, we tested a very high value of the shear modulus for the elastomeric bearings considering that under ambient vibration the rigidity of the bearing may be significantly increased. It improves the fitting of the resonance frequencies (the error between the experimental and the numerical first two modes are below 2%) but the order of the modes was still not reproduced. From model 4 to model 5, we considered different boundary conditions at the abutment that may reflect some disorders within the expansion joints. It can be related to the fact that the joints can be filled with gravels and dirt. This unexpected behaviour of the joints may lead the edges of the deck to be locked of the longitudinal and transversal translational degrees of freedom. Therefore, the fifth model considers no movement of the deck at the abutments. This model is the only one that respects the order of instrumented recorded modes.

Table 3. Comparison between experimental and numerical resonance frequencies.

		Experimental	Numerical									
			Model-1		Model-2		Model-3		Model-4		Model-5	
Mode		[Hz]	**[Hz]**	Error %	**[Hz]**	Error %	**[Hz]**	Error %	**[Hz]**	Error %	**[Hz]**	Error %
1	Transversal	3.10	**2.54**	18.1	**2.43**	21.6	**2.61**	15.8	**3.09**	0.3	**3.69**	19.0
2	1st Vertical	3.76	**3.49**	7.2	**3.52**	6.4	**3.83**	1.9	**3.83**	1.9	**3.83**	1.9
3	Longitudinal	4.85	**1.58**	67.4	**1.72**	64.5	**1.86**	61.6	**2.37**	51.1	**8.38**	72.8
4	2nd Vertical	7.33	**7.61**	3.8	**7.70**	5.0	**8.40**	14.6	**8.40**	14.6	**9.48**	29.3

4. DISCUSSION

In the comparison between the experimental data and the numerical model, our main observation concerns the expansion joints malfunction under ambient vibrations. The impact of boundary conditions on frequencies and mode shape has been highlighted in previous studies. [5] discusses the effect of operational and environmental conditions on structural health monitoring and he reported a study of [12] in which the expansion joints were closed preventing the structure from expanding with an alteration of the boundary conditions. In [4] the expansion of the bridge due to the temperature can alter the boundary conditions and consequently the resonances frequencies. A sensitivity study of the expansion joint rigidity on the resonance frequency, performed by [13]), indicates that the first 3 eigen modes are largely impacted (by more than 60 %) when the rigidity of the expansion joint is increased.

When using the ambient vibration data to characterize the dynamic behavior of the bridge, the main question concerns the validity of the characterization for stronger movements. All materials have a non-linear behavior. Although, the consideration of non-linear behavior implies more complexity. A large number of studies were performed to describe the non-linear behavior of materials and the way to implement it in the numerical codes. But what about the boundary conditions? During strong seismic loadings, we expect that the debris and the gravels are ejected from or crushed in the expansion joints, freeing the longitudinal and transversal movements at the abutments. In this case the boundary conditions will no longer be the same and the characterization from ambient vibrations will not correspond to the dynamic behavior under seismic loading. It could explain that model 4 represents well the behavior of the bridge, even if the longitudinal mode does not correspond to the experimental one. In order to fit the experimental longitudinal mode, an additional hypothesis on the boundary conditions (blocked) had to be done.

5. CONCLUSIONS

Ambient vibrations were measured on two strut-frame bridges in order to assess their real dynamic parameters (i.e. frequencies and mode shapes). The second bridge (that was easier to access) instrumentation is more detailed than the first instrumentation and it was performed to improve the modal identification of bridge A. Finally, four modes were identified for bridge A.

A 2D linear elastic numerical model is then proposed to represent the behavior of bridge A. Different hypothesis were made in order fit the experimental frequencies. From the first model based on the Eurocode 8-2 recommendations and on data from the engineering documentation of the bridge, two main modifications succeed in improving the fit of the experimental result. In the model 4, the increase of the shear modulus of the elastomeric bearings decreases the gap between the frequencies but the order of the resonance frequencies was not respected. The model 5 considers modified boundary conditions at the abutments with no longitudinal and transversal translational degrees of freedom. This model succeeds in reproducing the observation although the frequencies need to be adjusted. The boundary conditions suggest some disorder at the expansion joints. One explanation could be that the joints are filled with gravels and dirt.

An uncertainty remains concerning the states of the joints, and their behavior in case of stronger motions. Under ambient vibrations, they seem to be locked, whereas the movement under higher solicitations may free the translational degrees of freedom. Further investigations involving recordings under stronger solicitations could be performed to check the validity of the characterisation under ambient vibrations.

REFERENCES

[1] B. Peeters et G. De Roeck, « One-year monitoring of the Z 24-Bridge: environmental effects versus damage events », *Earthq. Eng. Struct. Dyn.*, vol. 30, n° 2, p. 149–171, 2001.

[2] E. Reynders, « System identification methods for (operational) modal analysis: review and comparison », *Arch. Comput. Methods Eng.*, vol. 19, n° 1, p. 51 124, 2012.

[3] R. Brincker et C. Ventura, *Introduction to operational modal analysis*. John Wiley & Sons, 2015.

[4] P. Cornwell, C. R. Farrar, S. W. Doebling, et H. Sohn, « Environmental variability of modal properties », *Exp. Tech.*, vol. 23, n° 6, p. 45–8, 1999.

[5] H. Sohn, « Effects of environmental and operational variability on structural health monitoring », *Philos. Trans. R. Soc. Math. Phys. Eng. Sci.*, vol. 365, n° 1851, p. 539 560, 2007.

[6] R. Brincker, L. Zhang, et P. Andersen, « Output-only modal analysis by frequency domain decomposition », in *The International Conference on Noise and Vibration Engineering*, 2001, p. 717–723.

[7] J.-L. Chatelain *et al.*, « CityShark: A user-friendly instrument dedicated to ambient noise (microtremor) recording for site and building response studies », *Seismol. Res. Lett.*, vol. 71, n° 6, p. 698 703, 2000.

[8] C. Michel, P. Guéguen, et P.-Y. Bard, « Dynamic parameters of structures extracted from ambient vibration measurements: An aid for the seismic vulnerability assessment of existing buildings in moderate seismic hazard regions », *Soil Dyn. Earthq. Eng.*, vol. 28, n° 8, p. 593 604, 2008.

[9] C. Michel, P. Guéguen, S. El Arem, J. Mazars, et P. Kotronis, « Full scale dynamic response of an RC building under weak seismic motions using earthquake recordings, ambient vibrations and modelling », *Earthq. Eng. Struct. Dyn.*, vol. 39, n° 4, p. 419 441, 2010.

[10] R. J. Allemang et D. L. Brown, « A correlation coefficient for modal vector analysis », in *Proceedings of the 1st international modal analysis conference*, 1982, vol. 1, p. 110 116.

[11] *ST1 Structural software*. Cerema, 2018.

[12] R. Rohrmann, « Structural causes of temperature affected modal data of civil structures obtained by long time monitoring », 2000.

[13] Z. Li, A. Li, et J. Zhang, « Effect of boundary conditions on modal parameters of the Run Yang Suspension Bridge », *Smart Struct Syst*, vol. 6, n° 8, p. 905 920, 2010.

IOMAC'19

8th International Operational Modal Analysis Conference
2019 May13-15 Copenhagen

OPERATIONAL MODAL ANALYSIS IN COMMISSIONING DYNAMIC TESTS OF DIFFERENT TYPES OF FOOTBRIDGES - EXPERIENCES AND CONCLUSIONS

Grzegorz Poprawa[1], Marek Salamak[2], Stefan Pradelok[3]

[1] Ph.D., Silesian University of Technology, grzegorz.poprawa@polsl.pl.
[2] Associate Professor, Silesian University of Technology, marek.salamak@polsl.pl.
[2] Ph.D., Silesian University of Technology, stefan.pradelok@polsl.pl.

ABSTRACT

Dynamic testing of newly constructed bridges is common practice in many European countries. Dynamic response is especially important in the case of footbridges; this is due to their low mass and stiffness compared to road and rail bridges and the specific load that these structures carry. The paper describes the use of Operational Modal Analysis (OMA) in commissioning dynamic tests of newly constructed footbridges in Poland. The subject of the described works were nine footbridges of various types and span length ranging from 30 to 60 m. As a result of conducted experiments, the method for implementing OMA in routine dynamic tests was developed. OMA has worked well in all described cases. In most of the described experiments, it was possible to identify all relevant modes with natural frequencies up to 5 Hz. The quality, unambiguity, and range of identification in each case exceeded what was possible to achieve using approach still common today – simple methods of signal processing and spectral analysis.

Key Words: footbridge, operational modal analysis, dynamic test, load test

1. INTRODUCTION

Pedestrian bridges constitute a group of structures particularly prone to excessive vibrations. Relatively small loads allow to construct lightweight and slender structures, so the dynamic response can be difficult to predict at the design stage. It is mainly because of difficulties in damping estimation. At the same time, the fundamental loads of footbridges are rhythmically moving pedestrians. If the rhythm of such excitation is close to the resonance zones of the footbridge, vibrations with significant amplitudes can be excited. Since the Millennium Footbridge case in London [1], the dynamic response problem of pedestrian footbridges has become not only well known but has also initiated many new research topics. One of them was the phenomenon of lock-in between transverse movements of crowd of pedestrians and transverse forms of natural vibrations. Since the beginning of this century, the problem of pedestrian traffic on a vibrating deck has been studied by many researchers [2], [3]. Footbridge prone to excessive vibrations that are rarely directly dangerous for the structure itself may fail to meet the serviceability limit conditions, significantly reduce the comfort of people using the structure and reduce bridge fatigue life [4].

Figure 1. Four examples of load tested footbridges: a) tied-arch footbridge; b) double span frame footbridge; c) fixed arch footbridge; d) suspension footbridge.

Dynamic tests of footbridges are a common form of assessment of their susceptibility to excessive vibrations associated with pedestrian traffic. There are many examples of such experiments in the literature, for example [5], [6]. Most of the dynamic tests focus on conducting experiments that are simulating possible operational scenarios. A group of people systematically recreates various possibilities of movement on the deck. Typical dynamic load patterns, in footbridge tests, consists of walking and running as well as jumps or squats of either one and more people. Trials are either free or synchronized to a certain frequency. In addition to simple methods of modal parameters extraction by analysis of signals generated during dynamic tests, more and more often in footbridge studies, advanced methods of modal analysis are used, namely EMA (input-output modal analysis) and OMA (output only modal analysis). Tests involving the usage of EMA method [7] tend to rely on using bulky, expensive vibration exciters and large labor expenditures for the preparation and implementation of tests. This makes it difficult to carry out such experiments on a mass scale, e.g., in the case of small, typical footbridges with a relatively simple static system. In turn usage of OMA fits well into the problem of identifying modal parameters of various objects with relatively small expenditure in the preparation of the experiment relying on often freely available alternative sources of vibrations [8]. The use of OMA in footbridge tests has recently been described, among others in [9]–[11]. The use of OMA extended with controlled excitations is described in [12].

In this paper, the author's approach to commissioning tests of newly constructed footbridges in Poland using OMA as modal identification method was described. The research group consists of nine independent superstructures with the longest span in range from 30 to 60 m (Figure 1). The work focuses, in addition to the presentation of basic results, on the discussion of the author's approach to routine dynamic tests of footbridges and benefits of OMA method in this type of experiments. Authors also described errors that they did not avoid when implementing OMA into their research practice of testing various footbridges.

2. COMMISSIONING TESTS OF NEWLY BUILT FOOTBRIDGES IN POLAND

Commissioning tests of newly built footbridges in Poland usually rely on static and dynamic load tests. The overriding goal of these tests is to verify the design assumptions and to assess whether the actual response of the structure corresponds to the design predictions. In dynamic tests, the damping properties and structural susceptibility to excessive vibrations caused by pedestrians are experimentally determined, and comfort criteria are checked.

- Static load test (Figure 2a). It involves inducing static load effects corresponding to a minimum 75% of a design characteristic crowd load. For this purpose, a structure is loaded with ballast, which may be pallets with building materials, concrete road plates or tanks filled with water. The number of ballast units and their spatial distribution on a footbridge deck results from static calculations. During the static load test, vertical displacements of a bridge at several preselected key locations are measured. This test gives an idea of real stiffens of a structure. Static tests of footbridges are similar to the load tests of road or railway bridges.
- Dynamic load test (Figure 2b). It consists of observing the dynamic response of the footbridge to an excitation like the one occurring during footbridge operation and on the experimental verification of the design assumptions regarding modal parameters of the structure. Typical dynamic load test, consists of multiple trials: walking, running as well as jumps or squats of one and many people, free and synchronized. Measured quantities are vertical displacements and accelerations at several preselected key locations on a superstructure.

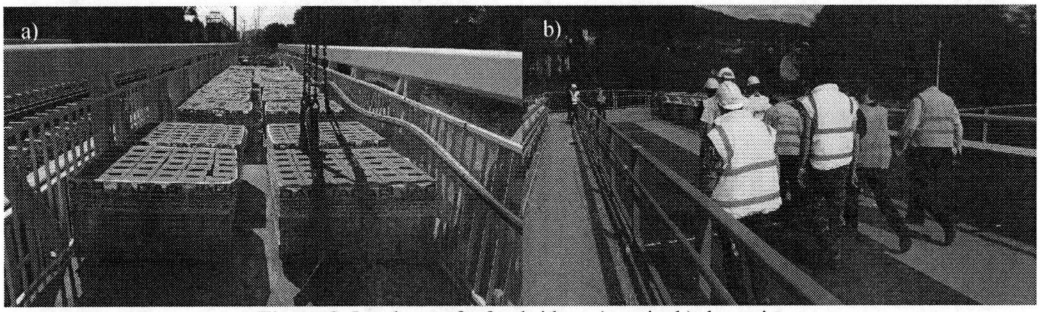

Figure 2. Load test of a footbridge: a) static; b) dynamic.

In the paper the discussion of the static load tests results was skipped. Only key results regarding dynamic tests were discussed. In all dynamic tests described in this paper the main goals were:

- identification of modal parameters (mode shape, natural frequency and modal damping) of the footbridge, global modes with a frequency below 5 Hz and thus verification of design assumptions,
- verification of serviceability criteria (maximal value of deck accelerations in few selected key locations) during tests simulating real exploitation scenarios,
- assessment of structural susceptibility to vandal excitations (synchronized jumps, squats).

3. GENERAL CHARACTERISTICS OF TESTED FOOTBRIDGES AND TEST PROCEDURES IN GENERAL

The experiments were carried out on nine footbridges, including seven different structural systems. All described dynamic tests were part of the commissioning tests that included a static load test and a dynamic load test. The basic characteristics of the examined footbridges are summarized in Table 1.

During tests, mainly vertical and transverse vibrations of the superstructure were observed. The experiments described in the article were carried out using two or four LVDT sensors and from 9 to 14 piezoelectric single axis accelerometers with a sensitivity of 1 V/g. Each experiment was based on a single setup of accelerometers. The locations of the measurement points are marked schematically on appropriate sketches in the next paragraph. Vibrations of support nodes were not observed. LMS SCADAS frontend with LMS Test.Xpress software was used to record signals. All signals were sampled with a sampling frequency of 256 Hz. All measurements were taken by the ISO 17025 accredited laboratory. Identification of modal parameters was carried out using time domain identification algorithm – SSI-COR BR [13]. The frequency range of interest covered the range 0 ÷ 5 Hz for vertical vibrations and 0 ÷ 2.5 Hz for horizontal vibrations. Usually, the experiments were planned to enable unambiguous identification of few additional modes with a higher natural frequency. The described limitations were related to the commercial nature of the work, in which the time and financial frames were strictly defined. All experiments took place during routine commissioning tests not special and extensive research experiment.

Due to the limitations of this text, the detail description of the damping estimation capabilities was omitted. In case of damping estimation OMA also worked well, giving in general results comparable with the damping estimated by the logarithmic decrement method.

Table 1. Comparison of fundamental characteristics of tested footbridges.

Mark	Structural system	Span lenght [m]	Number of spans	Structural material	Obstacle	Usable width [m]	Number of accelerom.
FB 1	continous beam	32.50	2	steel	expressway	4.7	11
FB 2	suspension bridge	58.50	1	steel/concrete	expressway	4.1	9
FB 3	fixed arch	43.44(62.15)	1	steel/concrete	expressway	3.0	14
FB 4	simply supported truss	31.50	1	steel/concrete	river	3.0	10
FB 5	tied-arch	50.00	1	steel	expressway	3.0	11
FB 6.1	double span frame	32.60	2	steel/concrete	expressway	3.9	12
FB 6.2	double span frame	32.60	2	steel/concrete	expressway	3.9	12
FB 7.1	simply supported truss	44.00	1	steel/concrete	city road	3.0	14
FB 7.2	simply supported truss	44.00	1	steel/concrete	city road	3.0	14

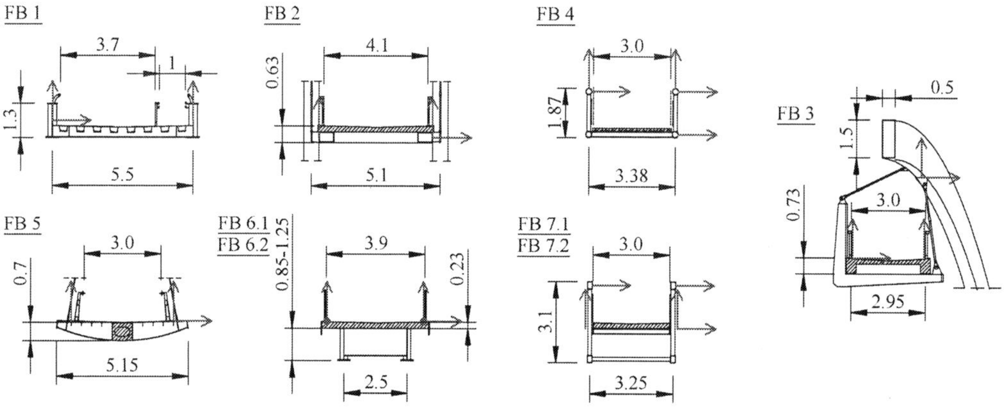

Figure 3. Cross sections of all tested footbridges.

In the descriptions of individual experiments, wherever possible, results (natural frequency and corresponding damping) were presented in the form of mean value and expanded uncertainty of the experimentally estimated value. In all cases, the identified natural frequency was referred to the one from the numerical modal analysis using the FE model that was prepared for the needs of the dynamic load test project. In the author's test practice, in most cases, load tests results are not leading to an updated FE model.

In Figure 3 the cross-sections of the seven structural systems described in section 4 are shown. On individual sketches, the approximate location and direction of the deck acceleration measurements are marked. In each of the described cases, slave nodes were used for the purpose of mode shape visualization and validation. All transducers were arranged using some basic engineering assumptions in a way to minimize duplication of information in recorded data.

4. EXPERIENCES FROM FIELD TESTS OF FOOTBRIDGES USING OMA

4.1. Continuous-beam through twin girder steel footbridge with orthotropic deck FB 1

It was the first footbridge tested by the authors using OMA approach. It is particularly interesting because it is completely made of steel and it is quite slender. The superstructure of this two-span continuous footbridge (Figure 4) consists of two slim steel plate girders connected by an orthotropic plate. As a result, the footbridge is characterized by high susceptibility to vibrations caused by pedestrian traffic. This footbridge is especially prone to vandal excitation. The location of the footbridge on the outskirts of the city and the expected low pedestrian traffic were key factors in deciding to accept a low level of comfort and allow the footbridge to be operated without installing tuned mass dampers. Vehicles passing under the footbridge were a good source of environmental excitations. The quality of the signal was good, and the distribution of accelerometers allowed clear identification of four basic forms of natural vibrations (Table 2). The higher density of measuring points within one of the spans served as a mean of improving the observability of the basic four mode shapes.

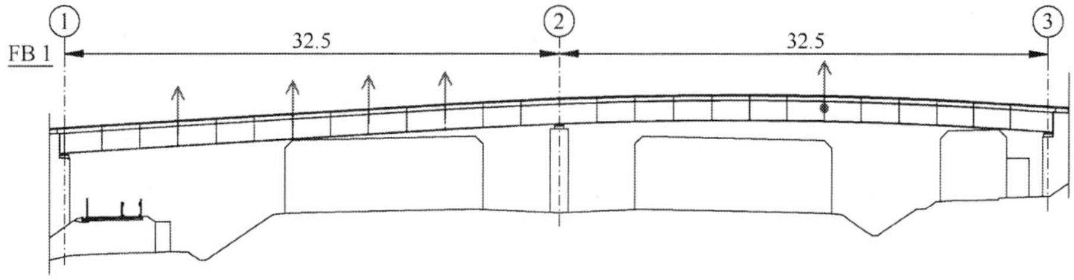

Figure 4. Continuous-beam through twin girder steel footbridge FB 1.

Table 2. Identification results - footbridge FB 1.

Mode no.	FE Model Freq. [Hz]	OMA Ave. Freq. [Hz]	Ave. Damp. [%]	Freq. 2*σ [Hz]	Damp. 2*σ [%]	Mode shape description
1	2.60	2.60	0.36	0.00	0.13	vertical bending I
2	2.74	3.32	1.87	0.00	0.14	torsion I
3	4.04	3.91	0.50	0.02	0.29	vertical bending II
4	4.25	5.42	1.34	0.01	0.54	torsion II

4.2. Single span suspension footbridge FB 2

The deck of this interesting footbridge is a steel grillage on which the reinforced concrete slab is laid. The deck is suspended to two steel pylons inclined inwards (Figure 5). A few mistakes were made in the planning and implementation phases of this experiment. The recorded signals were too short, and the observation of the dynamic response was limited to the half of the bridge and one lower pylon in axis no. 1 (Figure 1d). Lack of verification of signal quality and lack of preliminary estimation of modal parameters on site prevented a proper reaction to these deficiencies. Despite this, it was possible to identify most of the FEM predicted modes (Table 3). The test results showed a good agreement with the FE model prediction. Available signals did not allow for the estimation of experimental expanded uncertainty. No excessive vibrations due to the forced loading were observed.

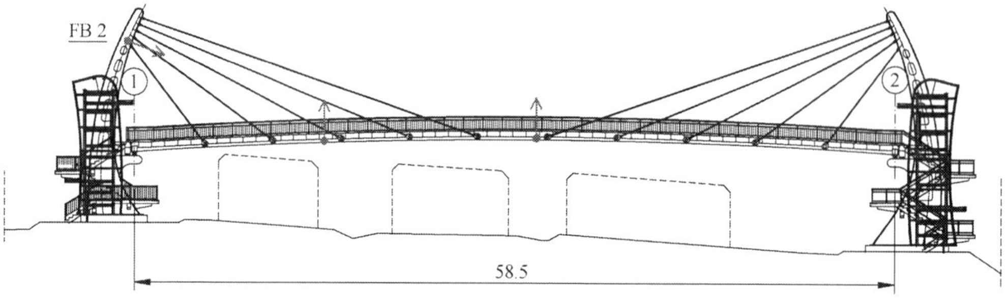

Figure 5. Single span suspension footbridge FB 2.

Table 3. Identification results - footbridge FB 2.

Mode no.	FE Model Freq. [Hz]	OMA Freq. [Hz]	Damp. [%]	Freq. 2*σ [Hz]	Damp. 2*σ [%]	Mode shape description
1	1.51	1.50	1.77	-	-	vertical bending I
2	1.68	1.77	1.32	-	-	lateral deck I
3	2.38	2.26	1.00	-	-	lateral pylon I
4	2.94	2.53	0.31	-	-	vertical bending II
5	3.34	undetected		-	-	lateral pylon
6	3.67	undetected		-	-	lateral pylon
7	3.93	4.03	1.38	-	-	torsional I
8	5.50	5.07	0.24	-	-	vertical bending III

4.3. Semi-through fixed steel arch footbridge FB 3

In case of this interesting footbridge the main structural element is a fixed steel arch with a box cross-section arranged diagonally over the footbridge deck (Figure 1c). The deck is constructed as a reinforced concrete slab suspended to the arch and additionally supported at both ends on reinforced concrete pillars (Figure 6). Despite the complicated structural system with numerous mods with quite low frequency (Table 4), this footbridge proved to be resistant to extensive vibrations caused by pedestrians.

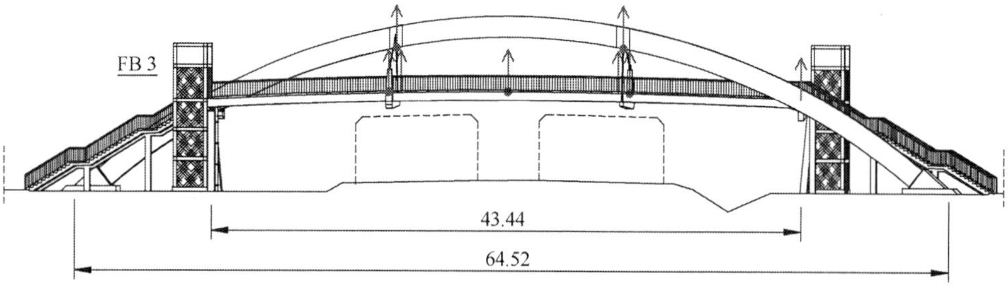

Figure 6. Semi-through fixed steel arch footbridge FB3.

This is the first case of footbridge where authors recorded dynamic response of superstructure during whole test process. Starting from the measurement of vibrations caused by the environmental excitations (mainly very busy road beneath) through vibrations during the static load test (with modified mass), until the end of all dynamic trials conducted as a last part of the test. Such approach allowed for the registration of very long data sets without significantly prolonging the duration of the entire load test. In Figure 7 a Short Time Fourier Transform (STFT) of signals from mid span are shown. It is easy to see the gradual change in the frequency of vibrations of certain modes during loading of the structure, followed by stabilization and then the change to the initial value during gradual unloading.

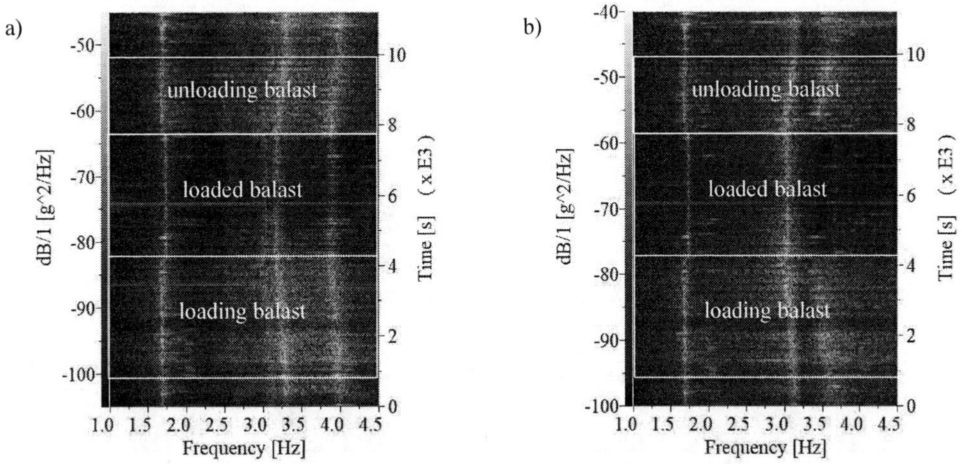

Figure 7. STFT of the accelerations in the middle of the footbridge (FB 3) deck during static load test: a) horizontal; b) vertical.

Table 4. Identification results - footbridge FB 3.

Mode no.	FE Model Freq. [Hz]	OMA Ave. Freq. [Hz]	Ave. Damp. [%]	Freq. 2*σ [Hz]	Damp. 2*σ [%]	Mode shape description
1	1.45	1.69	0.75	0.03	0.18	lateral arch I
2	2.75	3.13	0.88	0.01	0.32	lateral arch II
3	3.49	3.30	1.12	0.01	0.42	vertical bending II
4	3.79	3.62	1.63	0.01	0.26	vertical bending I
5	4.19	3.99	1.17	0.02	0.54	lateral deck I
6	4.79	undetected / observability		-	-	lateral arch III
7	5.25	5.69	0.64	0.00	0.40	vertical bending III

4.4. Single span through steel truss footbridge FB 4

This simply supported single-span beam footbridge with twin through truss girders (Figure 8) as the only one presented was built in a sheltered and quiet area, and it was crossing a small river. As a result, during the tests, no useful sources of environmental excitations were available. The lack of useful environmental excitations forced artificial improvement of signal quality. During the recording of the signals for OMA, two people were moving along the deck, trying to be as unforeseeable as possible. This approach gave satisfying results. Nevertheless, the process of identifying modal parameters was quite difficult. The greatest differences between the identified and calculated natural frequencies were observed in the case of this footbridge.

As in the previously described case (pt. 4.3), also here the entire OMA experiment was prepared before static tests. Example of mid span time data of displacements and accelerations is shown in Figure 9. The effects of mas modification during static load test is visible on displacements diagram. After static load test, dynamic load test followed. The footbridge proved to be susceptible to human-induced vibrations, especially running and vandal excitation. The largest recorded amplitudes of accelerations were obtained during a synchronized running test (3.0 Hz) of a group of people (the peak value of accelerations visible in Figure 9). Five accelerometers within a single cross-section of the truss (Figure 3) were necessary to distinguish local modes associated with lateral movements of the upper chord from the global modes. The asymmetrical, layout of transducers allowed for unambiguous identification of all sought-after basic forms of vibrations (Table 5) but was insufficient to clearly distinguish higher order modes.

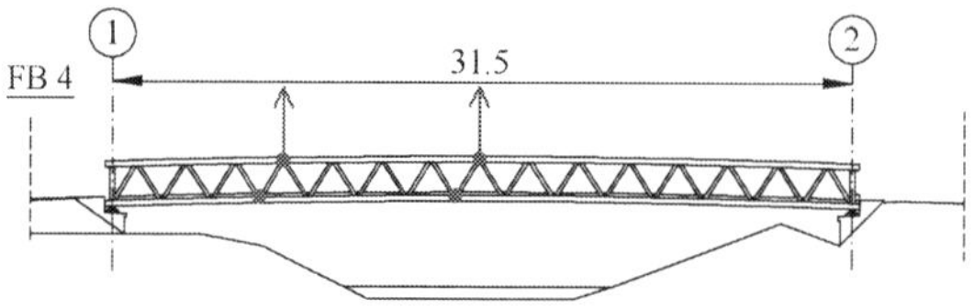

Figure 8. Single span through steel truss footbridge FB 4.

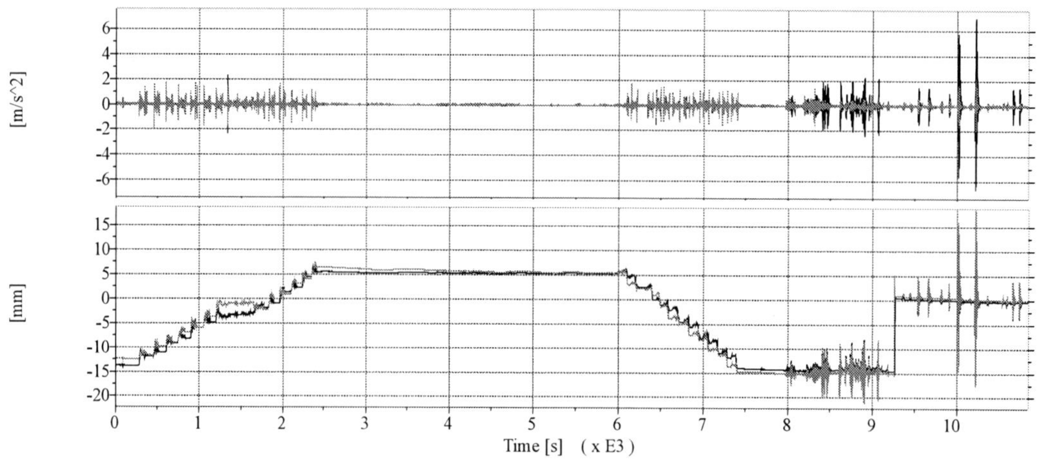

Figure 9. Acceleration and displacement time histories in the middle of the tested span (FB 4).

Table 5. Identification results - footbridge FB 4.

Mode no.	FE Model Freq. [Hz]	OMA Ave. Freq. [Hz]	OMA Ave. Damp. [%]	OMA Freq. 2*σ [Hz]	OMA Damp. 2*σ [%]	Mode shape description
1	2.37	3.08	0.64	0.00	0.06	vertical bending I
2	2.99	3.94	0.83	0.05	0.42	torsion rigid I
3	4.85	6.35	0.51	0.11	0.33	torsional flexible I

4.5. Tied-arch steel footbridge FB 5

This is another example of a structure with a quite complex structural system and good dynamic properties. Steel box girder deck partially filled with concrete is suspended to two inclined inwards arches (Figure 3). During the tests of this steel tied-arch footbridge (Figure 10) the expressway running under the deck was not yet put into use (Figure 1a). Fortunately, on the day of the test, a moderately strong monotonous wind blew, this created excellent conditions for OMA experiment. The employed layout of accelerometers allowed for the unambiguous identification of most of the basic global modes predicted by the FE model (Table 6). Lateral vibration mode associated with the deck was not detected.

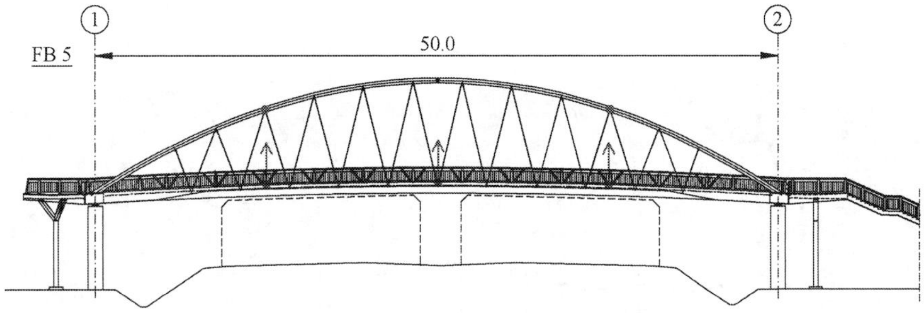

Figure 10. Tied-arch steel footbridge FB 5.

Table 6. Identification results - footbridge FB 5.

Mode no.	FE Model Freq. [Hz]	OMA Ave. Freq. [Hz]	Ave. Damp. [%]	Freq. 2*σ [Hz]	Damp. 2*σ [%]	Mode shape description
1	1.58	1.46	0.98	0.02	0.48	lateral arch I
2	2.73	2.58	0.63	0.02	0.33	lateral arch II
3	3.17	3.39	1.41	0.67	0.91	vertical bending II
4	4.31	4.09	0.12	0.00	0.11	lateral arch III
5	4.33	undetected		-	-	lateral deck I
6	4.67	4.49	0.29	0.02	0.14	vertical bending I
7	6.31	6.73	0.35	0.03	0.28	vertical bending III

4.6. Two identical double span composite frame footbridges FB 6.1 and FB 6.2

Next experiment regarded two identical two-span frame footbridges (Figure 11). Their superstructure consists of a composite beam connected rigidly to the reinforced concrete pillar. The tests were carried out before the final finishing works on the footbridges. The deck of one of them was still supported on temporary bearings (Figure 12a). The other structure (on its final bearings), was damaged during construction by an oversized vehicle. The damaged part of the steel beam has been cut out and replaced with a new steel element (Figure 12b). Additionally, as a result of the collision, a reinforced concrete pillar was cracked. In consequence, identification results obtained for an undamaged footbridge (Table 7) differ from those obtained for a damaged footbridge (Table 8). In Figure 13a MAC values are shown comparing the mode shapes of the five identified natural frequencies of both footbridges (FB 6.1 and FB 6.2). Significant difference in terms of the two first identified modes is clearly visible. Other three mode shapes are very similar. The fact that the final construction works were not finished makes it impossible to reliably assess the impact of damage on the observed differences in modal parameters. Observed dynamic response during dynamic load test of both footbridges indicates very good dynamic properties – both structures are unsusceptible to excessive vibrations. A busy road under one of the spans (Figure 1b) was an excellent source of random excitations.

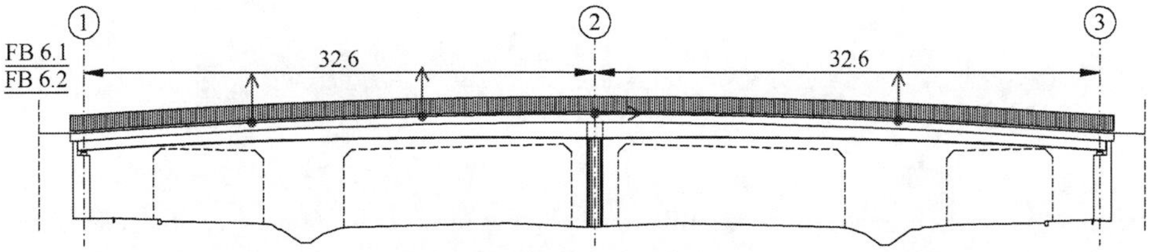

Figure 11. Double span composite frame footbridge FB 6.1 and FB 6.2.

Figure 12. Frame footbridge: a) temporary supports in undamaged footbridge FB 6.1; b) repaired section of steel element in damaged footbridge FB 6.2.

Table 7. Identification results – undamaged footbridge FB 6.1.

Mode no.	FE Model Freq. [Hz]	OMA Ave. Freq. [Hz]	OMA Ave. Damp. [%]	OMA Freq. 2*σ [Hz]	OMA Damp. 2*σ [%]	Mode shape description
1	1.97	undetected		-	-	vertical bending I pier +
2	2.92	2.80	0.92	0.01	0.15	lateral I
3	2.97	3.03	0.50	0.00	0.05	vertical bending I pier -
4	3.32	3.92	0.72	0.00	0.32	vertical bending II
5	4.74	4.98	0.79	0.01	0.48	torsional I
6	5.09	5.27	0.61	0.03	0.19	torsional II

Table 8. Identification results – damaged footbridge FB 6.2.

Mode no.	FE Model Freq. [Hz]	OMA Ave. Freq. [Hz]	OMA Ave. Damp. [%]	OMA Freq. 2*σ [Hz]	OMA Damp. 2*σ [%]	Mode shape description
1	1.97	undetected		-	-	vertical bending I pier +
2	2.92	3.08	0.65	0.02	0.01	lateral I
3	2.97	3.31	0.69	0.00	0.02	vertical bending I pier -
4	3.32	4.13	0.47	0.00	0.04	vertical bending II
5	4.74	4.97	0.53	0.00	0.22	torsional I
6	5.09	5.29	0.58	0.01	0.07	torsional II

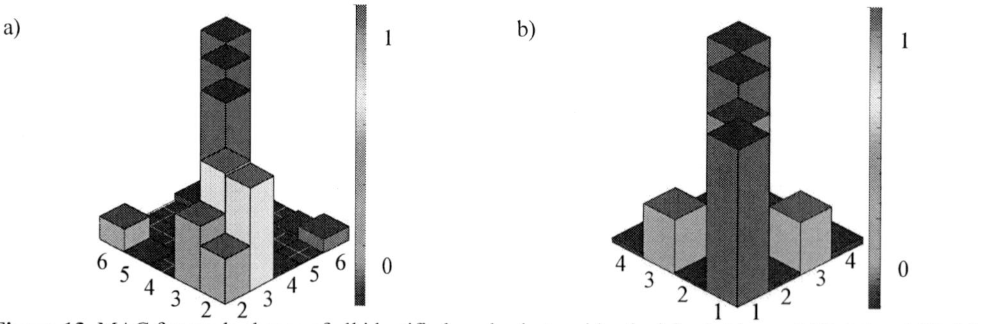

Figure 13. MAC for mode shapes of all identified modes in two identical footbridges: a) FB 6.1 and FB 6.2; b) FB 7.1 and FB 7.2.

4.7. Two identical single span semi-through steel truss footbridges FB 7.1 and FB 7.2

The last case described in the paper concerns another pair of two identical footbridges. These single-span steel twin truss girder footbridges have a semi-through concrete deck (Figure 14). The tests were carried out in two consecutive days. The FB 7.1 bridge was tested on a sunny and windless day and the FB 7.2 footbridge on a rainy day with full cloud cover. Based on the experiences from the tests of the previously described truss footbridge (pt. 4.4) three cross-sections spaced evenly over the length of the span were observed. Identification results obtained for both footbridges (Table 9, Table 10) are similar, and minor differences in regard to modal parameters were considered irrelevant. In both examples, the first two modes are closely spaced – the first vertical bending and the first lateral bending mode. This was not predicted by the model but effectively identified during the tests. In Figure 13b MAC values are shown comparing the mode shapes of the four identified modes of both footbridges (FB 7.1 and FB 7.2). Only second mode shape (first vertical bending) shows some minor differences mainly due to slight lateral movement in one of the footbridges. Both footbridges are prone to human-induced vertical vibrations in the form of the first vertical bending mode. This may be a problem in the operation of the structure, but no beat phenomenon was observed. The damping of the first vertical bending mode is the lowest of all cases described in the paper.

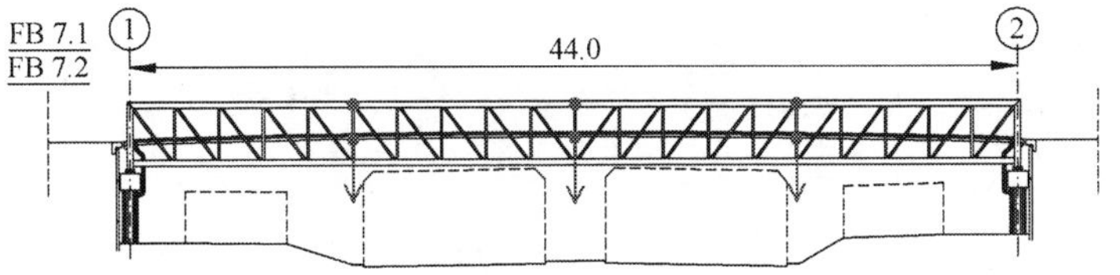

Figure 14. Single span semi-through steel truss footbridge FB 7.1 and FB 7.2.

Table 9. Identification results - footbridge FB 7.1

Mode no.	FE Model	OMA				Mode shape description
	Freq. [Hz]	Ave. Freq. [Hz]	Ave. Damp. [%]	Freq. 2*σ [Hz]	Damp. 2*σ [%]	
1	2.49	2.46	0.16	0.01	0.04	vertical bending I
2	3.12	2.42	0.64	0.02	0.24	lateral bending I
3	3.90	4.13	0.26	0.02	0.12	torsional I
4	7.13	6.08	0.97	0.13	0.25	lateral bending II

Table 10. Identification results - footbridge FB 7.2.

Mode no.	FE Model	OMA				Mode shape description
	Freq. [Hz]	Ave. Freq. [Hz]	Ave. Damp. [%]	Freq. 2*σ [Hz]	Damp. 2*σ [%]	
1	2.49	2.44	0.15	0.00	0.05	vertical bending I
2	3.12	2.39	0.38	0.01	0.13	lateral bending I
3	3.90	4.16	0.14	0.00	0.04	torsional I
4	7.13	6.10	0.84	0.02	0.14	lateral bending II

5. TEST PROCEDURE IN ROUTINE TESTS OF FOOTBRIDGES

Routine load tests of footbridges are subject to several restrictions:

- tests must be adapted to the schedule of works on the construction site,
- crane and ballast are needed to carry out static tests,

- a group of people is needed to carry out dynamic tests,
- static and dynamic test is usually carried out on the same day to mitigate additional costs,
- extended scope of the test program takes more time and generates additional costs.

Figure 15 depicts the diagram showing authors approach to the dynamic tests of footbridges in the situation when the acquired signals are to be used for OMA identification. The diagram was developed on the basis of experiences from tests described in the paper, and assuming that the experiment consists of two parts, static and dynamic, that are being carried out on the same day.

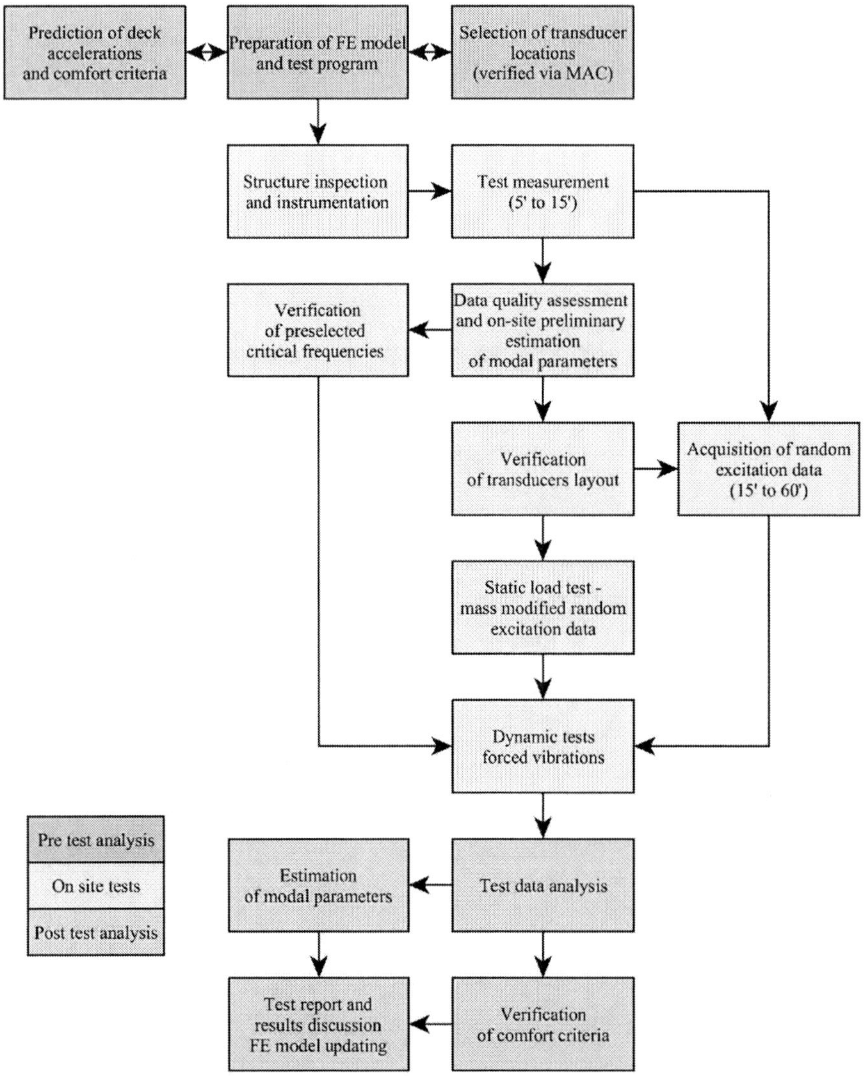

Figure 15. Diagram of the identification experiment.

In the author's opinion, when doing similar experiments, it is important to start signal acquisition before the static load test, and then continue it, until the end of the dynamic tests. In load testing there are moments that apparently nothing happens but at the same time useful data can be acquired. This allows us to take full advantage of the available time to obtain signals useful from the perspective of OMA without unnecessarily extending the entire process. Other important thing is on-site initial identification of modal parameters based on the relatively short test measurement. Initial identification allows for detection and removal of possible errors in the measurement system. It allows also to verify if planned synchronized forced excitation trials are going to take place using the correct forcing frequency.

6. CONCLUSIONS

The paper presents results from commissioning tests of nine newly constructed footbridges located in Poland. Commissioning trails are most often composed of a static and dynamic load test. This paper focuses only on dynamic trials. In all discussed cases OMA was used to identify modal parameters.

Presented tests results showed that the most susceptible to excessive vibrations are footbridges in the form of two-span steel structure (pt. 4.1) and single-span truss structure (pt. 4.4, pt. 4.7). This susceptibility concerns only vertical vibrations. None of the tested footbridges showed excessive transverse vibrations and possibility of occurring lock-in effect. Interestingly, more complicated structural systems (described in pt. 4.2, pt. 4.3, pt. 4.5 and pt. 4.6) are characterized by little or no susceptibility to excessive vibrations.

OMA has worked well in all described cases. Even when certain elements of the experiment have not been planned and implemented in the best possible way. The quality, unambiguity, and range of identification in each case exceeded what was possible to achieve using simple methods of signal processing and spectral analysis. This is even more important in the case of structures with a more complicated structural system. The use of OMA minimizes the risk of misinterpretation of the dynamic response of the footbridge, e.g., wrong mode identification, failure to detect a mode or failure to detect closely spaced modes. In the opinion of the authors, OMA fits very well in the routine commissioning tests of footbridges carried out in Poland. An effective identification experiment can shorten the time from identifying the problem with the dynamic response to its solution and opening the footbridge to the traffic. The use of OMA in the commissioning of new footbridges has several advantages:

- OMA doesn't require bulky vibration exciters,
- useful environmental excitations are often freely available,
- in case of medium span footbridges and properly planned experiment, OMA allows for identifying all or almost all basic modes in the frequency range from 0 to 5 Hz, with a single setup of accelerometers and a relatively small number of transducers,
- OMA gives possibility to detect closely spaced modes, repeated modes and work well in case of high modal density,
- The discussed cases are showing that the damping estimated using SSI algorithm (on basis of environmental excitations) does not deviate significantly from the damping estimated from forced vibration data (using the logarithmic decrement method and reasonable level of excitation).

OMA integrates well with the current load test process requiring only high sensitivity measurement chain and some additional work to prepare the structure for testing without significantly extending duration of the experiment itself. The most common difficulties encountered in the described experiments were related to lack of verification of registered signals in the field and fact that available environmental excitations were not always enough to sufficiently excite all modes of interest. In the described cases, the authors obtained a satisfactory scope of identification using a single setup of 9 to 14 single-axis accelerometers. Most of the described footbridges were located above busy roads generating useful random excitations. The most difficult case was the footbridge crossing the river, located far from potential sources of natural excitations (pt. 4.4). The experience gained in subsequent experiments allowed authors to develop a method of conducting routine dynamic tests of different footbridges using OMA (Figure 15).

The fact that the static load test is also an element of commissioning tests allows for registration of a dynamic response of a structure with a modified mass. This data can further lead to normalized mode shapes [14]. In this way, the significant drawback of OMA can probably be compensated. Further work in this area is needed.

ACKNOWLEDGEMENTS

We would like to thank the employees of Field Test Laboratory (ISO 17025 accredited) at the Faculty of Civil Engineering of the Silesian University of Technology in Poland for their help in conducting all described field tests.

REFERENCES

[1] P. A. Dallard *et al.*, "The London Millennium Footbridge," *Struct. Eng.*, vol. 79, no. 22, pp. 17–33, 2001.

[2] SETRA, *Footbridges - Assessment of vibrational behaviour of footbridges under pedestrian loading*. 2006.

[3] C. Maraveas, Z. C. Fasoulakis, and K. D. Tsavdaridis, "A Review of Human Induced Vibrations on Footbridges," *Am. J. Eng. Appl. Sci.*, vol. 8, no. 4, pp. 422–433, Apr. 2015.

[4] S. Pradelok, "The influence of higher modes vibrations on local cracks in node of lattice girders bridges," *Arch. Civ. Eng.*, vol. Vol. 58, nr 2, pp. 209–221, 2012.

[5] M. Salamak and P. Lazinski, "Experimental identification of the dynamic properties of three different footbridge structures," presented at the Footbridge 2008, Third International Conference, 2008.

[6] G. Poprawa, M. Salamak, and P. Klikowicz, "Dynamic identification of composite beam pedestrian bridges," in *Advance and trends in engineering sciences and technologie II. Proceedings of the 2nd International Conference on Engineering Sciences and Technologies, 29 June - 1 July 2016, High Tatras Mountains, Tatranské Matliare, Slovak Republic.*, 2016, pp. 231–236.

[7] A. Pavic, P. Reynolds, M. Willford, and J. Wright, "Key results of modal testing of the Millennium Bridge, London," presented at the Footbridge 2002, First International Conference, 2002.

[8] G. Poprawa, S. Pradelok, M. Salamak, and P. Łaziński, "Operational modal analysis in model updating of a truss railway bridge," in *Proceedings of 7th IOMAC*, Ingolstadt, 2017, pp. 64–67.

[9] R. Cantieni, A. Bajrić, and R. Brincker, "Damping Characteristics of a Footbridge: Mysteries and Truths," in *Dynamics of Coupled Structures, Volume 4*, M. Allen, R. L. Mayes, and D. Rixen, Eds. Cham: Springer International Publishing, 2016, pp. 283–292.

[10] J. Kortiš, Ľ. Daniel, M. Farbák, L. Maliar, and M. Škarupa, "Operational Modal Analysis of the Cablestayed Footbridge," *Civ. Environ. Eng.*, vol. 13, no. 2, pp. 92–98, Dec. 2017.

[11] Ł. Pyrzowski, M. Miśkiewicz, J. Chróścielewski, and K. Wilde, "Load Testing of GFRP Composite U-Shape Footbridge," *IOP Conf. Ser. Mater. Sci. Eng.*, vol. 245, Oct. 2017.

[12] E. Reynders, D. Degrauwe, G. De Roeck, F. Magalhães, and E. Caetano, "Combined Experimental-Operational Modal Testing of Footbridges," *J. Eng. Mech.*, vol. 136, no. 6, pp. 687–696, Jun. 2010.

[13] B. Peeters and G. De Roeck, "Reference-based stochastic subspace identification for output-only modal analysis," *Mech. Syst. Signal Process.*, vol. 13, no. 6, pp. 855–878, 1999.

[14] E. Parloo, B. Cauberghe, F. Benedettini, R. Alaggio, and P. Guillaume, "Sensitivity-based operational mode shape normalisation: Application to a bridge," *Mech. Syst. Signal Process.*, vol. 19, no. 1, pp. 43–55, Jan. 2005.

IOMAC'19

8th International Operational Modal Analysis Conference
2019 May 13-15 Copenhagen

OPERATIONAL MODAL ANALYSIS OF A DAMAGED BELL TOWER

Andrea Belleri[1], Simone Castelli[2], Alessandra Marini[3], Nicola Bettini[4], and Babak Moaveni[5]

[1] Assistant Professor, Department of Engineering and Applied Sciences, University of Bergamo, andrea.belleri@unibg.it
[2] Graduate Student, Department of Engineering and Applied Sciences, University of Bergamo, simone.castelli@unibg.it
[3] Associate Professor, Department of Engineering and Applied Sciences, University of Bergamo, alessandra.marini@unibg.it
[4] CEO, Di.Mo.Re srl, Via Oberdan 1/A, Brescia, Italy, nicola.bettini@dimore-strutture.com
[5] Associate Professor, Department of Civil and Environmental Engineering Tufts University, babak.moaveni@tufts.edu

ABSTRACT

This paper presents the operational modal analysis (OMA) and finite element (FE) modeling of the bell tower of the church of Castro located in Bergamo, Italy. This procedure was dictated by the need to identify the actual damage state of the structure detected by visual inspections. The 39m high reinforced concrete tower has a hollow section with a double concavity. Piezoelectric accelerometers were used to record ambient vibration in subsequent setups using the roving technique for high resolution system identification. After performing the system identification, two types of 3D structural models were considered compared, using shell and beam elements, respectively. Finally, the FE models were updated to identify the boundary conditions and the state of deterioration. The knowledge of the actual state of structural damage will be required to define the retrofit strategy.

Keywords: Bell tower, FDD, FE update, Damage state.

1. INTRODUZIONE

This paper presents the results related to the modal dynamic identification of the bell tower in Castro (BG) in Italy. The church of San Giacomo (Figure 1), with its adjoining bell tower, is in the municipality of Castro in the province of Bergamo in the upper area of Lake Iseo at an altitude of about 200 m. Located in the old part of the village, near to the lake, it was designed in 1966 by the architect Vittorio Sonzogni and built in 1969 to replace the pre-existing church. The reinforced concrete bell tower reaches the height of 37m and is characterized by a square section with an internal concavity on the four sides tapered at the top. There are also elongated openings alternating on the sides and horizontal joints with a regular pattern that hide the casting shots.
The bell tower is in an evident state of deterioration, with the presence of a high discontinuity at the third level, probably due to a number of factors: the concavity of the sections and elevations generates a clear washout of the concrete in the central area of each side, recognizable by the chromatic alteration of the surfaces; the areas of discontinuity of the surface such as the openings and the horizontal joints

collect a greater quantity of rainwater percolating from the top. In these areas, there is a greater presence of deterioration due to the corrosion of the reinforcing bars and the spalling of the concrete cover; the incorrect disposal of the conglomerate shows gravel nests on the surfaces.

Figure 1. View of the church with the adjacent bell tower.

For such reasons a dynamic identification was carried out with the roving technique to evaluate the damage extension and provide a reference finite element model for setting up the retrofit intervention. To record the environmental vibrations, 4 high sensitivity piezoeletric accelerometers (Wilcoxon 731A) were used. The sensors were placed at the various positions according to the scheme depicted in **Figure 2**: 2 sensors remained in the same position for all the acquisitions (reference) while the others were moved at each registration (rovering) and changed in directions according to the Type A and Type B positions (**Figure 2**). Configuration A allows the identification of the torsion at each level, while the configuration B allows the estimation of the modal forms in the orthogonal direction.

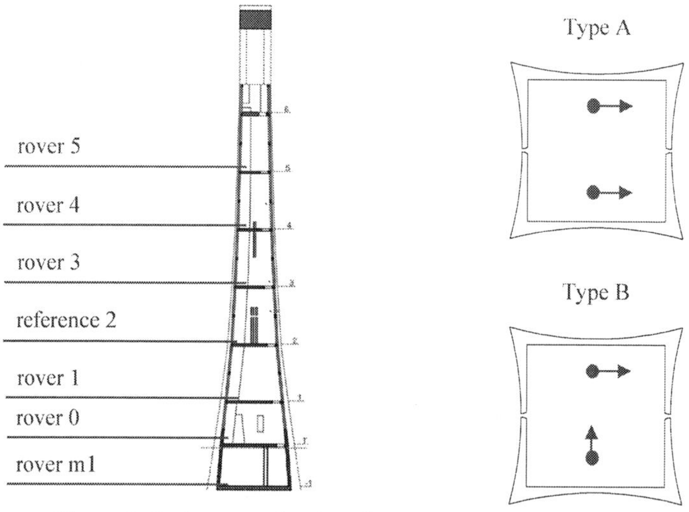

Figure 2. Environmental registration setup.

2. FREQUENCY DOMAIN DECOMPOSITION

For the dynamic modal identification, the FDD algorithm was selected [1, 2]. Frequency Domain approaches are based on the processing of a time-correlated signal through a Discrete Fourier Transform (DFT). Frequency Domain Decomposition methods operate a Singular Value Decomposition (SVD) at each line of the frequency spectrum. This procedure separates noisy data from disturbances of various sources and appears able to pick-up close modes with better accuracy. Typical underlying hypotheses of Frequency Domain Decomposition (FDD) methods are: white noise input, low structural modal damping ratios and geometrically-orthogonal mode shapes of close modes.

Figure 3 shows an example of the FDD results, the first peak was discarded because it corresponded to a local vibration mode. It is worth to note how the first two frequencies are very close to each other and it was possible to identify them only through a careful choice of the frequency resolution. The results of the identification are shown in Table 1 in terms of frequencies.

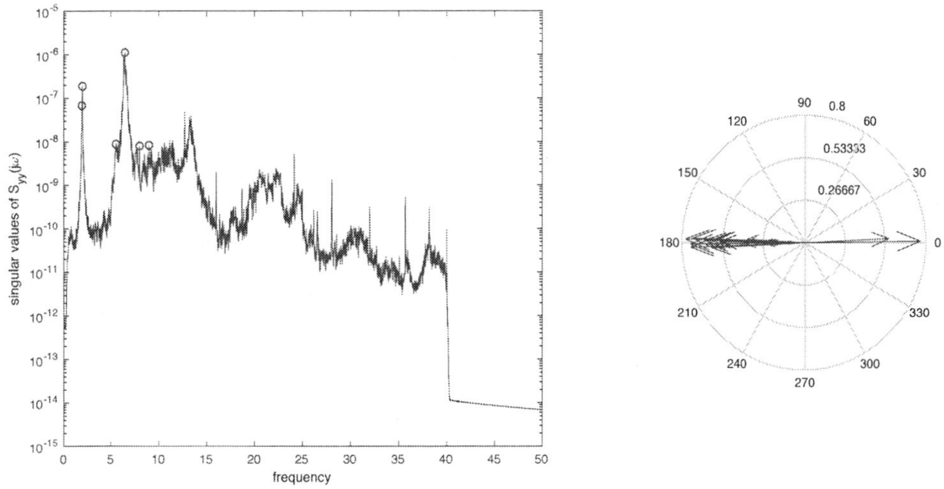

Figure 3. Singular Value Decomposition and Pick Peacking, Compass Plot.

Table 1. Estimated frequencies.

Mode	Frequency		
	Mean [Hz]	Median [Hz]	Standard deviation [Hz]
1	1.92	1.91	0.027
2	1.98	1.98	0.016
3	5.57	5.51	0.117
4	6.46	6.45	0.027
5	8.07	8.00	0.166
6	8.68	8.53	0.301

3. FEM UPDATE

A finite element model was built using the Midas Gen [3] software using four-node shell elements (**Figure 4**) fix-connected at the base. To capture the soil-structure interaction, the rotational degrees of freedom were released and two elastic springs were positioned to simulate rotational rigidity along the principal directions. The mechanical properties of the concrete were calibrated from compressive tests on the bell tower concrete. An additional model was built in Opensees [4] using beam elements in which scale factors were inserted to match the dynamic characteristics of the plate model, especially for the torsional part. **Table 2** highlights the lack of precision of the beam elements model particularly for the higher vibration modes. For such reason the shell elements model was considered in the following. **Figure 5** shows the comparison between the first two modal shapes of the identified and FE cases.

Figure 4. FEM model with shell elements.

Table 2. Comparison between estimated and calculated frequencies before update.

Mode	Frequency		
	OMA [Hz]	FEM Beam (OpenSees) [Hz]	FEM Plate (Midas) [Hz]
1	1.92	2.63	2.61
2	1.98	2.94	2.92
3	5.57	8.89	7.10
4	6.46	11.12	8.85
5	8.07	12.30	8.87
6	8.68	20.78	13.26

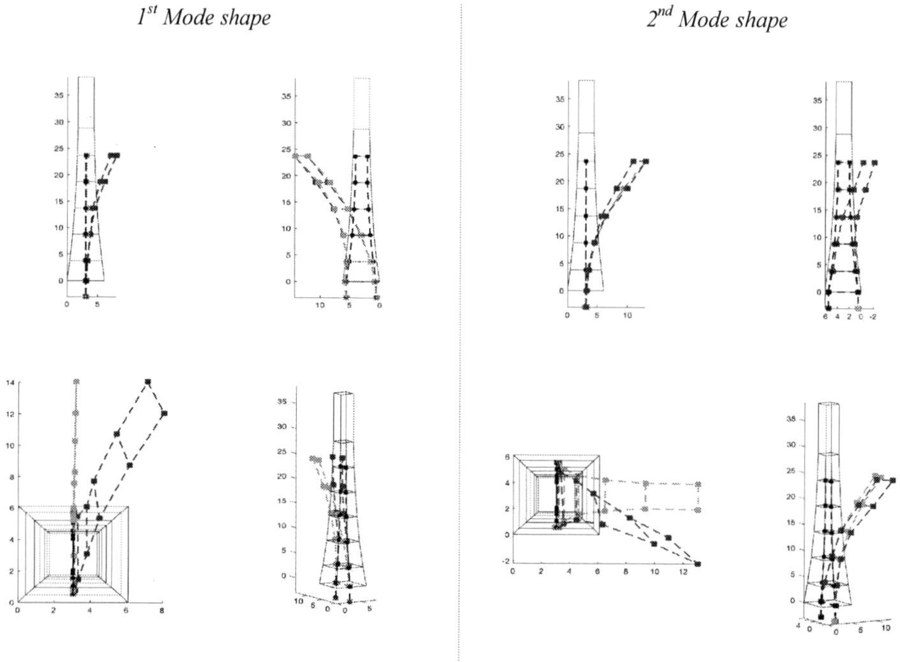

Figure 5. Comparison of first and second mode shapes before update: OMA (blue) and FEM (green).

A finite element model update was performed first by making a sensitivity analysis on the parameters governing the dynamic problem: that is, by varying the stiffness of the springs at the base, the percentage of damage in the crack and the Young's modulus of concrete for the FEM model. In this way, it was possible to define sensitivity surfaces for each modal frequency, fitting the results obtained. The sensitivity analyses on the amount of damage in the cracked region have shown that the latter does not lead to large variations in terms of modal frequencies but provides a plan rotation of the modal shapes. The stiffness of the rotational springs at the base of the model is fundamental for matching the modal curvature at the base while the scaling of the modulus of elasticity of the concrete significantly influences the modal frequencies. Therefore, by tuning each parameter at the time it was possible to obtain the results shown in **Figure 6** and **Figure** 7 which highlight a good performance of the tuning process. The MAC values of the first 4 mode shapes are 0.95, 0.96, 0.89, and 0.89 respectively.

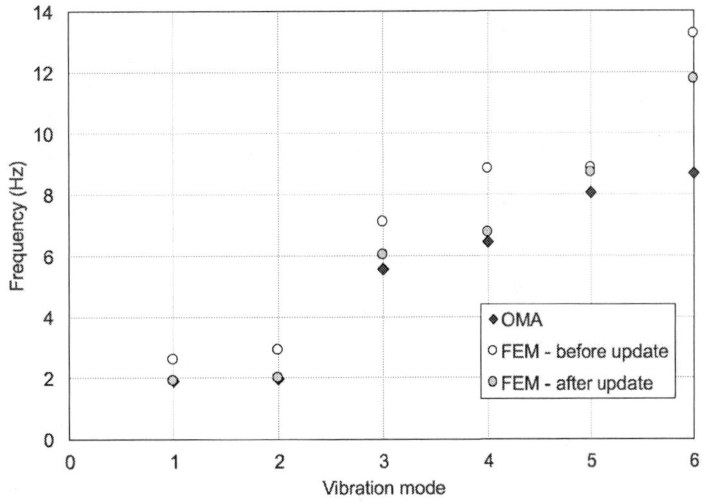

Figure 6. Comparison of modal frequencies.

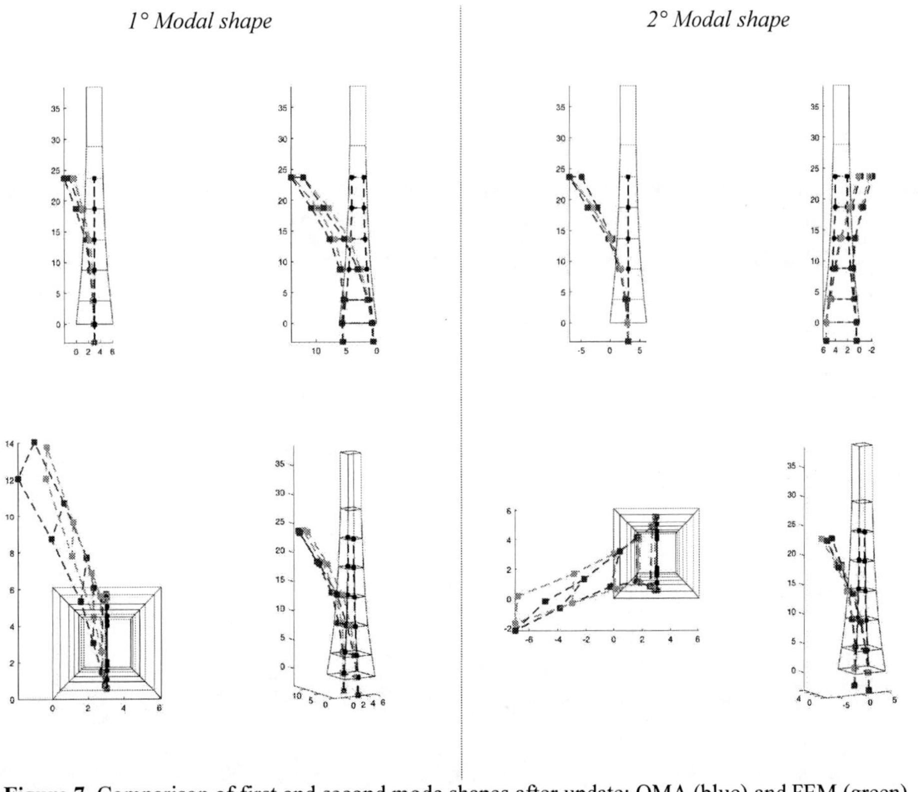

Figure 7. Comparison of first and second mode shapes after update: OMA (blue) and FEM (green).

4. CONCLUSIONS

The study had as objective the dynamic identification of a reinforced concrete bell tower of San Giacomo church in the municipality of Castro (Italy). Currently the tower is strongly degraded with an evident crack on the third level. A dynamic identification was performed using the roving technique. The FDD algorithm was applied on each record set and then combined to obtain the full model mode shapes. To accomplish a finite element update, two types of models were developed, namely a beam elements model and shell elements model. The former resulted in a less accurate model, particularly when referring to the torsional component therefore in the update the more accurate shell elements model was selected.

A sensitivity analysis was conducted to highlight the influence of the various parameters on the dynamic properties. In particular, it was found that: the amount of damage in the cracked region produced a plan rotation of the modal shapes compatible with the OMA results; the stiffness of the rotational springs at the base of the model can be selected to match the modal curvature at the base of the tower; the concrete modulus of elasticity significantly influences the modal frequencies. Therefore, after tuning each parameter at the time, it was possible to obtain a good match with the identified OMA dynamic properties and quantify the damage in the cracked region. The updated model will be used to define the retrofit strategy.

ACKNOWLEDGEMENTS

The authors express their gratitude to Eng. J. Zanni and Eng. G. Cottinelli for their help during the experimental campaign.

REFERENCES

[1] Brincker, R., Zhang, L., & Andersen, P. (2000). Modal identification of output-only systems using frequency domain decomposition. *Smart Materials and Structures*, 10(3), 441

[2] Brincker, R., & Andersen P. (2000). Ambient response analysis of the heritage court tower building structure. In: *Proc. of the XVIII IMAC* (pp 1081-1094). San Antonio, Texas, USA.

[3] MidasGEN 2017 (v2.1), MIDAS Information Technologies Co. Ltd.

[4] McKenna, F. (2011). OpenSees: A Framework for Earthquake Engineering Simulation. Computing in Science & Engineering, 13(4), 58-66.

DAMAGE DETECTION UNDER CHANGING OPERATIONAL CONDITIONS

IOMAC'19

8th International Operational Modal Analysis Conference

2019 May13-15 Copenhagen

A NUMERICAL BENCHMARK FOR SYSTEM IDENTIFICATION UNDER OPERATIONAL AND ENVIRONMENTAL VARIABILITY

Konstantinos Tatsis [1], *and Eleni Chatzi* [2]

[1] PhD, ETH Zürich, tatsis@ibk.baug.ethz.ch.

[2] Associate Professor, ETH Zürich, chatzi@ibk.baug.ehhz.ch.

ABSTRACT

Structural Health Monitoring (SHM) has been experiencing a very rapid growth during last decades, with a wide range of methods developed to support decisions for maintenance planning over a broad spectrum of operational and environmental conditions. Despite this progress, performance evaluation of various approaches is usually carried out on different case studies, rendering side-by-side comparison difficult. This contribution presents a numerical benchmark for system identification under changing environmental and operational conditions. The considered system is modelled with an open access Finite Element code, which is supplemented with a Graphical User Interface (GUI) and enables the extraction of modal properties and dynamic response data for a number of predefined damage patterns and operational as well as environmental scenarios. This benchmark, generated as part of COST Action TU1402 on Quantifying the Value of Information, is to serve as a reference case study for validation of decision-making tools relying on the Value of Information.

Keywords: Structural dynamics, Damage assessment, Data analysis, Value of information, Benchmark

1. INTRODUCTION

The very rapid growth of research in the field of SHM, renders benchmarking an important step for performance assessment. The existence of a baseline, which will enable the straightforward and quantitative evaluation of the large assortment of solution methods, will undoubtedly assist in consolidating the recent advances in the field. Among various identification methods, a number of contributions is focused on the identification of systems featuring environmental variability under different operational conditions. To this end, the present work aims at providing a simple numerical benchmark that can address such aspects.

Benchmarking is not a new idea in the context of SHM, since a number of standardized problems is already available for performance evaluation. The first study within that context is provided by Farrar et al. [1] on the dynamic testing of the I-40 bridge. Using the same structure as test-bed, Maeck and De Roeck [2] conducted a well-known benchmark by imposing a series of damage scenarios thereto, offering thus the material for testing and validation of detection, localization and quantification methods. Similarly, Molina et al. [3] established an experimental study using a composite steel-concrete two-story frame. A full-scale study on a bridge structure was set-up by the Center of Structural Monitoring and Control at Harbin Institute of Technology [4] in recent years, while Smith and Randall [5] established a benchmark based on the data from the Case Western Reserve University (CWRU) Bearing Data Centerand Joyce et al. [6] offered a test case for high-rate problems. Such contributions are not limited to experimental cases, since a number of noteworthy numerical studies is also available, with the IASC-ASCE SHM Task group offering one of the most influential benchmarks [7], which is essentially the numerical part of the companion experimental work by Dyke et al. [8]. Lastly, it should be underlined that benchmark studies are well extended to more complex and challenging systems featuring nonlinear behavior, like the work carried out by Tiso and Noël [9].

This paper introduces a simple numerical benchmark which is generated as part of COST Action TU1402 on Quantifying the Value of Information and is to serve as a reference case study for validation of decision-making tools relying on the Value of Information. The benchmark model is herein described along with the open source code for generation of simulated data. Although a default set-up of the benchmark is presented, the interested researchers are encouraged to extend and enhance the functionalities as desired. Within this context, the paper is organized as follows: the second section presents the numerical model used as benchmark along with the employed damaged patterns and the different operational loads. The third section describes the process followed for response simulation, while the fourth section serves as a manual for the Graphical User Interface (GUI), which is publicly available in GitHub.

2. BENCHMARK MODEL

The structure considered as benchmark model is a two-span beam as illustrated in Figure 1. The height of the beam is $h = 0.6$ units, the width is equal to $w = 0.1$ units and each span has a length of $L = 10$ units. The model is assigned a linear elastic material with Young's modulus $E = 2.1e11$, Poisson's ratio $\nu = 0.3$ and material density $\rho = 7800$ units. The structure is represented by a FE model which is constructed with isoparametric quadrilateral elements for plane-stress problems and a predefined discretization scheme with 200 and 6 elements in x and y directions, respectively, is used. To minimize the effect of locking, the implemented elements comprise 9 nodes and their stiffness and mass matrices are integrated with a Gauss scheme of 3×3 point rule.

Elastic boundaries are assumed for all three support points, in both x and y directions, with a support

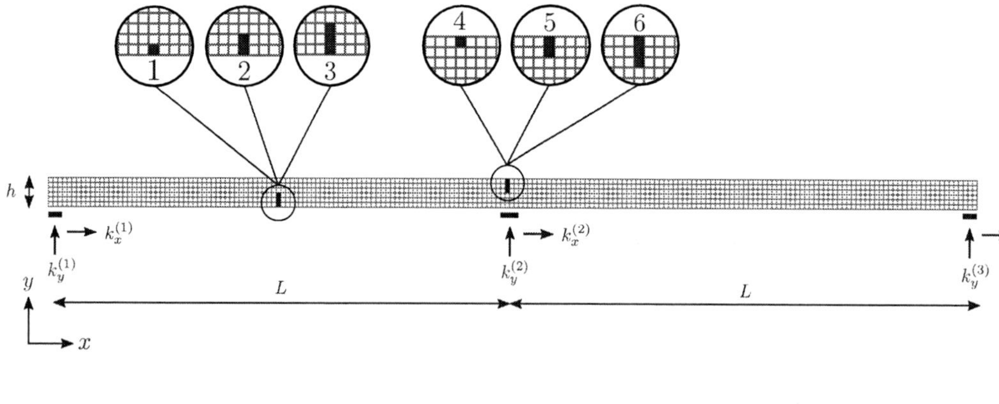

Figure 1: Finite element model of the benchmark structure.

width of 0.3 units for the two extremities and 0.4 units for the midpoint. It should be noted that all mentioned properties are merely proposed as default values for the reference state and the users are allowed to adjust them as deemed necessary. Except for the system dimensions, as will be presented in Section 4., a temperature-dependent model can be assigned to each variable, including boundary conditions, enabling thus the simulation under different environmental conditions.

2.1. Damage patterns

In addition to the reference structure described above, two groups of damaged cases, with a total of six scenarios as numbered in Figure 1, are studied, where each group is materialized with a stiffness reduction in the specified area. The first group assumes a damaged region in the mid of the first span, starting from the lower level of the cross section, while the second one comprises a damaged region above the mid-point support. Both groups advance from an area consisting of a single element up to a zone of three elements, as shown in Figure 1, with a width of 0.1 units and a height ranging from 0.1 to 0.3 units, with the latter being equal to half of the cross section height. It should be noted that these scenarios are not intended to represent the mechanisms and physics of actual damage but instead, provide the means for performance testing of various SHM methods in system changes. To this end, the amount of damage for each scenario is not *a priori* defined, but it can be specified through the percentage of stiffness reduction which ranges between 10 and 100%. To further enable the simulation of degradation effects, such as corrosion [11, 12], the thickness of the structure can be spatially reduced by specifying a thickness wastage pattern in the longitudinal direction.

2.2. Load cases

For each model case, three default sets of excitations can be used, as illustrated in Figure 2. These include (a) a mass of 100 units moving along the structure with a unit speed towards positive direction of x axis, and two fixed-point loads at the (b) left- and (c) right-hand side spans respectively. Although the excitation signal of the moving load is of deterministic nature, the signals of fixed-point loads are modeled as independent Gaussian white noise whose time series are stored in data files which can be modified accordingly.

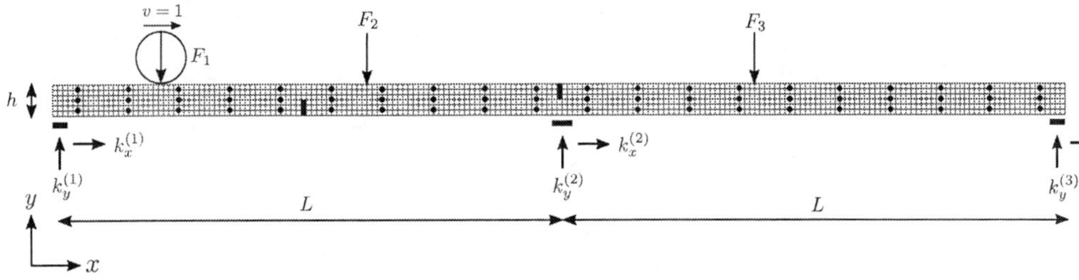

Figure 2: Load cases and measurement positions

3. RESPONSE SIMULATION

This section is focused on the numerical integration of the equations of motion, which is carried out to obtain the response induced by the different load cases. Given the initial order of the model, the equations are solved in the modal domain which is described by the generalized coordinates $\mathbf{q}$. These are related to the physical degrees of freedom by $\mathbf{u} = \mathbf{\Phi}\mathbf{q}$, where $\mathbf{\Phi}$ is the mode shape matrix and the equations of motion in modal coordinates are then given by

$$\hat{\mathbf{M}}\ddot{\mathbf{q}}(t) + \hat{\mathbf{C}}\dot{\mathbf{q}}(t) + \hat{\mathbf{K}}\mathbf{q}(t) = \mathbf{\Phi}^{\mathrm{T}}\mathbf{F}(t) \qquad (1)$$

where $\hat{\mathbf{M}}$, $\hat{\mathbf{C}}$ and $\hat{\mathbf{K}}$ are the modal mass, damping and stiffness matrices, respectively, while $\mathbf{F}$ is the vector of forces acting on the physical degrees of freedom. Although the mass and stiffness matrices are internally defined upon selection of a model case, the damping matrix is assumed to be proportional, obtained as follows

$$\mathbf{C} = \alpha\mathbf{M} + \beta\mathbf{K} \tag{2}$$

and the values of coefficients α and β are left for the user to specify, as will be described in the following section.

By default, the equations of motion are integrated using an implicit Newmark scheme [13], with parameters $\gamma = 1/2$ and $\beta = 1/6$. To render the analysis computationally affordable and enable the efficient execution of a series of jobs, the dynamics of the system are represented by the first ten vibration modes, which also constitutes a default setting and can be modified as deemed necessary. For each model scenario and load case, the acceleration and strain response from a number of structural points are exported as measured signals. The location of these points is depicted in Figure 2, for which the vertical component of acceleration and all three components, ϵ_{xx}, ϵ_{yy} and τ_{xy} of strains are measured.

4. DATA GENERATION

The modeling features described above, along with the response simulation scheme, are included into an open access Python code which is made available through GitHub. The code is wrapped with a Graphical User Interface (GUI) and offers the possibility of performing eigenvalue and time history analyses on the model under different operational and environmental conditions. Moreover, it provides the capability of extracting acceleration and strain measurements from a number of sensing points, which are arranged in a structured grid as shown in Figure 2. It should be noted here that both back-end and front-end of the benchmark model are publicly available in the form of an open source code and the readers are encouraged to contribute and freely extend the functionalities presented herein.

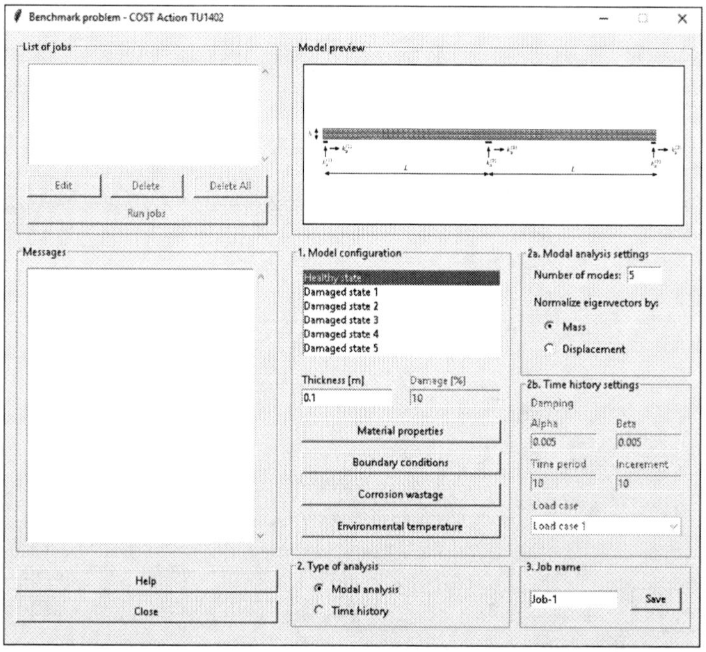

Figure 3: Graphical user interface for generation of simulated data.

A snapshot of the GUI for data generation is shown in Figure 3, where the user is given the capability of creating a list of different model scenarios, which are shown in the top-left frame named "List of jobs". Such a scenario may be created by following the numbered frames under model preview, starting

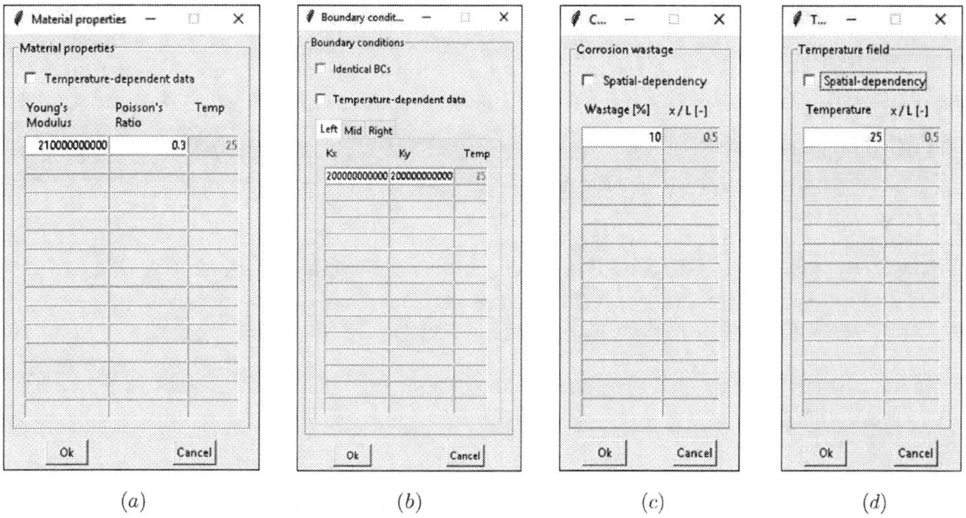

Figure 4: Graphical user interface for specifying (a) material properties, (b) boundary conditions, (c) corrosion wastage and (d) environmental temperature

from "1. Model configuration". This step includes the selection of a model state, choosing among the healthy and a number of damaged ones as described in Section 2., and the specification of a thickness and damage value. The latter is evidently relevant only for damaged models and defines the percentage of stiffness reduction applied on the damaged region of each model case. To finalize the model set-up, the user is called to specify the temperature-dependent material properties and elastic boundary conditions, as well as the spatially-distributed corrosion wastage and environmental temperature. A snapshot of the corresponding windows, which can be opened by the buttons under thickness and damage entries, is shown in Figure 4.

Upon definition of the model parameters, the user is asked to select the type of analysis, which can be either modal or time history. Depending on the choice, the corresponding settings should be then specified in either "2a. Modal settings" or "2b. Time history settings" frame, respectively. Once the scenario is fully defined, it can be added to the list of jobs by specifying the name and subsequently clicking on "Save" button in frame "5. Job name". The name of the job will be displayed then in the list of jobs and can be retrieved for editing upon selection and clicking on the "Edit" button. Similarly, any job, or all them, can be deleted by clicking on "Delete" or "Delete All" buttons, respectively. The available jobs can be submitted for analysis by hitting on "Run jobs" button and the progress of execution will be displayed in the "Messages" frame. The results of each job will be finally stored in a .dat file named in accordance with the job name.

5. CONCLUSIONS

This paper presented a benchmark study for system identification under environmental and operational variability. The considered structure is a simple two-span beam supported on elastic boundaries and modeled with plane stress elements. The system is supplemented with a number of predefined damage patterns and loading conditions, while it provide the possibility of defining temperature-dependent parameters. Along with the paper, an open source python code, which is wrapped with a GUI, is provided in order to enable the generation of dynamic response signals.

ACKNOWLEDGEMENTS

The authors would like to gratefully acknowledge the European Research Council via the ERC Starting Grant WINDMIL (ERC-2015-StG #679843) on the topic of Smart Monitoring, Inspection and Life-Cycle Assessment of Wind Turbines.

REFERENCES

[1] Farrar, C.R. and Baker, W.E. and Bell, T.M. and Cone, K.M. and Darling, T.W. and Duffey, T.A. and Eklund, A. and Migliori, A. Dynamic characterization and damage detection in the I-40 bridge over the Rio Grande. *Los Alamos National Lab*, NM(United States).

[2] Maeck, J. and De Roeck, G. (2003) Description of Z24 benchmark. *Mechanical Systems and Signal Processing*, 17(1), 127-131.

[3] Molina, F. and Pascual, R and Golinval, J. (2003) Description of the steelquake benchmark. *Mechanical Systems and Signal Processing*, 17(1), 77-82.

[4] Li, S. and Li, H. and Lan, C. and Zhou, W. and Ou, J. (2014) SMC structural health monitoring benchmark problem using monitored data from an actual cable-stayed bridge. *Structural Control and Health Monitoring*, 21, 156-172.

[5] Smith, W. and Randall, R. (2015) Rolling element bearing diagnostics using the Cave Western Reserve University data: A benchmark study. *Mechanical Systems and Signal Processing*, 64-65, 100-131.

[6] Joyce, B. and Dodson, J. and Laflamme, S. and Hong, J. (2018) An experimental test bed for developing high-rate structural health monitoring methods. *Shock and Vibration*, 2018.

[7] Johnson, E.A. and Lam,H.F. and Katafygiotis, L.S. and Beck, J.L. (2004) Phase I IASC-ASCE Structural Health Monitoring Benchmark Problem Using Simulated Data. *Journal of Engineering Mechanics*, 130(1), 3-15.

[8] Dyke, S. and Bernal, D. and Beck, J. and Ventura, C. (2003) Experimental phase of the structural health monitoring benchmark problem. *Proceedings of the 16th ASCE engineering mechanics conference.*

[9] Tiso, P. and Noël, J. (2017) A new, challenging benchmark for nonlinear system identification. *Mechanical Systems and Signal Processing*, 84, 185-193.

[10] Odgaard, P. and Stoustrup, M. and Kinnaert, M. (2009) Fault tolerant control of wind turbines - a benchmark model. *Proceedings of the 7th IFAC Symposium on Fault Detection, Supervision and Safety of Technical Processes.*

[11] Dunbar, T. and Pegg, N. and Taheri, F. and Jiang, L. (2004) A computational investigation of the effects of localized corrosion on plates and stiffened panels. *Marine Structures*, 17(4), 385-402.

[12] Sultana, S. and Wang, Y. and Sobey, A.J. and Wharton, J.A. and Shenoi, R.A. Influence of corrosion of the ultimate compressive strength of steel plates and stiffened panels. *Thin-Walled Structures*, 96, 95-104.

[13] Chopra, A. (2017) Dynamics of structures: theory and applications to earthquake engineering. *Prentice-Hall* Englewood Cliffs, NJ, USA.

IOMAC'19

8th International Operational Modal Analysis Conference

2019 May13-15 Copenhagen

A NONLINEAR ROBUST OUTLIER DETECTION APPROACH FOR SHM.

N. Dervilis[1], T. Zhang[1], L.Bull[1], E.J. Cross[1], T.J. Rogers[1], R. Fuentes[1], V. Dertimanis[2], I. Abdallah[2] E. Chatzi[2], K. Worden[1]

[1]Dynamics Research Group, Department of Mechanical Engineering, University of Sheffield, Mappin Street, Sheffield S1 3JD, UK

[2]Department of Civil, Environmental and Geomatic Engineering, ETH Zürich, Zürich, Switzerland

E-mail:n.dervilis@sheffield.ac.uk

ABSTRACT

The higher levels of structural health monitoring (SHM) - localisation, classification and severity assessment - are only accessible using supervised learning in the data-based approach. Unfortunately, one does not often have data from damaged structures; this forces a dependence on unsupervised learning i.e. novelty detection. This means that detection is sensitive to benign environmental and operational variations (EOVs) in or around the structure. The key novel element of this work is the combination of robust multivariate statistical methods into the structural health monitoring (SHM) field. In this paper, nonlinear robust outlier statistics are investigated, focussed mainly on a high level estimation of the "masking effect" of inclusive multiple outliers that may appear in the system by utilising nonlinear robust regression and offering no *a priori* division between the damaged and the undamaged condition, a holistic and robust inclusive outlier detection.

Keywords: robust regression, outlier analysis, SHM

1. INTRODUCTION

When SHM technology is adopted as a tool for monitoring a structure then the system has to run continuously and on-line. In turn, the effects of the environmental variations must be considered and identified before using a reliable feature for revealing any structural condition.

One of the most challenging issues in SHM methodologies is the influence of temperature on structural response. Especially for bridges, which is the concern of this study, temperature is generally considered to be an important environmental factor which affects the dynamic response of the structure, due to the influence on the stiffness of structural parameters and on the boundary conditions of a structure [3-9].

Various methods and algorithms have been proposed in order to counteract and remove the influence of external variations, such as principal component analysis, auto-associative neural networks or more recently cointegration and polynomial chaos expansion models [3,10]. Although these methods exhibit a series of advantages and disadvantages in terms of removing the influence of operational and environmental conditions, very little effort has been carried out in terms of characterising and distinguishing which of the outliers-leverage points indicated in data are "good" in terms of representing environmental/operational variations and which are "bad" in terms of representing damage or structural degradation. For more details regarding the different nature of outliers in multivariate statistics the reader can consult [11, 12].

A recent paper by Dervilis *et al.* [1-2] explores an approach of robust regression and robust multivariate statistics as a means of characterising and distinguishing the influence of environmental and operational conditions on the structural response.

This paper will discuss the performance of robust regression analysis for nonlinear systems. The layout of the paper is as follows. Section Two briefly covers the main features of the minimum covariance determinant and fast least-trimmed-squares estimator, while Sections Three and Four present and implement an idea for a generalised linear regression model. Section Five discusses how the previous approaches can be adopted to a real life experimental example. The paper finishes with some overall conclusion and future work.

2. MINIMUM COVARIANCE DETERMINANT AND FAST LEAST TRIMMED SQUARES ESTIMATOR.

The application of robust computation of location and covariance estimation of multivariate data is of significant interest in the investigation of inclusive outliers. The method introduced here is called the Minimum Covariance Determinant estimator (MCD). The computation of the MCD estimator is not a trivial procedure and requires an extensive calculation. In the current study, the FAST-MCD algorithm is implemented [11-14] using the code provided via a statistical Matlab library called, LIBRA [14]. A brief description of the algorithm is provided by explaining the basic steps of the FAST-MCD technique.

A multivariate data matrix $[X] = (\{x_1\}, ..., \{x_m\})^T$ is assumed of m points in an n-dimensional space ($n \times m$) where $\{x_i\} = (x_{i1}, ..., x_{in})^T$ is the observation. Robust estimates of the centre μ and the scatter matrix σ of X can be calculated by the MCD estimator. The MCD tool looks for the $h(>m)$ observations out of m whose classical covariance matrix has the lowest possible determinant. The raw MCD estimate of location (arithmetic mean) is then computed from the average of these h points and the raw MCD estimation of the scatter is the covariance matrix multiplied by a consistency factor.

As can be noted, the calculation of the lowest determinant is critical as one moves from one approximation of MCD to another one with lower determinant. This tool and the proof that follows it are not obvious and can be found in the appendix of [2,13].

Based on the raw MCD estimates, a reweighting step can be added in order to increase the finite sampling efficiency. The advantage is that MCD estimates can resist up to $(m - h)$ outliers and in turn, parameter h controls the robustness of the estimator. The highest resistance compared to contamination is achieved by calculating $h = (n+m+1)$. It is proposed that when a large proportion of contamination is assumed then $h = an$ with $a = 0.5$. Detecting outliers can be challenging when m/n is small because some data points can become coplanar. This is a general problem in the machine learning community called the "curse of dimensionality". It is recommended [14] that when $m > 5$, a should be 0.5. Generally, the MCD estimates of location and scatter are affine equivariant, which means that they are invariant under affine transformation behaviour. This is crucial as the underlying model is then immune to different variable scales and data rotations. Rousseeuw and Van Driessen (1999) [13] developed the FAST-MCD algorithm based on a Concentration step (C-step). C-steps select the h observations with the smallest distances and the scatter matrix with the lower determinant [13].

Many regression estimators break down in the presence of outliers. Generally, there are different kinds of outliers. Via this robust data mining methodology and with a simple re-arrangement one could uncover hidden patterns of the collected databases and in this current study this leads one to identify the difference between environmental and operational abnormalities and damage outliers.

The fast least-trimmed-squares (LTS) estimator as proposed by Rousseeuw et al. [9-17] is utilised here. Generally, in order to fit a linear regression model one assumes that,

$$y_i = \theta_i x_{i1} + ... + \theta_n x_{in} + \theta_0 \; for \; i = 1...m \quad (1)$$

where θ_i are the regression coefficients and $(\{x_i\}, y_i)$ are the data point coordinates. The basic objective of this algorithm is to minimise the function:

$$\sum_{i=1}^{h} (r^2)_{i:n} \; for \; i = 1...m \tag{2}$$

where r^2 is the squared residual which is the difference between the observed values and the predicted value $(y - \hat{y})$. The objective in this work is to find in a similar fashion with the MCD estimator, h-subsets with the smallest least squares function (1). The LTS regression line is the least square model of these h-points.

Rousseeuw *et al.* [9-17] state the major advantages of the algorithm against the classic least median squares (LMS) such as a smooth objective function, less sensitivity in the presence of local effects as well as statistical efficiency as the LTS estimator is asymptotically normal. As a major step further, the fast-LTS can deal with large data sets and is computationally inexpensive and much faster than least median squares (LMS). For more details on technical details and implementation of these methods for SHM purposes, readers are referred to [1,2]. The results that follow are presented in the form of a residual outlier map and it can be used in order to classify the observations according to the robust regression model. This visualisation plot displays the standardised LTS residuals (the residuals divided by a robust estimate of their scale) versus the robust distances calculated by applying the MCD estimator on the input variable (see Fig.1). An extensive analysis regarding this map can be found in [2,13].

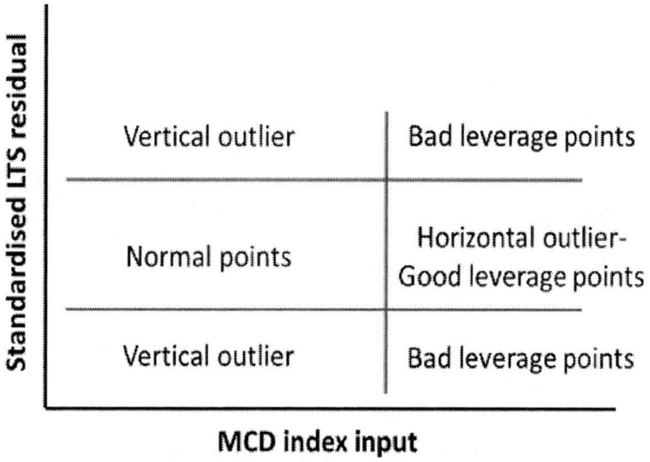

Figure 1: Residual outlier map.

3. TOWARDS AUTOMATIC NONLINEAR ROBUST REGRESSION ANALYSIS VIA A BAYESIAN CLASSIFICATION AND REGRESSION TREE (BCART)

As shown in the previous studies, the necessity of an nonlinear robust regression analysis is important after the identification and characterisation of the different outliers/leverage points in different families. This analysis is possible if one changes the basis functions of the LTS algorithm by introducing a generalised linear model, but this is non-automated and requires substantial input from the user (bilinear model or example). In turn, given the inevitable presence of uncertainties from the environment, stationary data acquisition is not guaranteed. To explore the potential relations behind the data while accommodating the issue of nonstationary and nonlinear behaviour, a Bayesian Classification and

Regression Tree (BCART) can be brought into utilisation [21-22]. BCART models have been shown to be successful in addressing nonstationary regression problems effectively, and have been adopted and applied across numerous research fields including SHM.

The BCART is essentially a semi-probabilistic model, as a matter of the fact that the splitting criterion is deterministically conveyed through a probabilistic optimisation process [21-22]. On behalf of the formation of the tree structure, the process is completely probabilistic, by assuming its form in a Markov Chain Monte Carlo (MCMC)-based random walk. In the current BCART model, the tree structure along with its splitting rule (basically this combination is referred to as the tree) will be represented as a state in a Markov chain.

Hence, the construction process of the treed model is, in a certain sense, tantamount to a random walk in the Markov space, and the chief objective for the random walk is to expediently discover the states satisfying the splitting criterion (in a global sense) best. Accordingly, the random walk will perform in a guided way which embodies in two aspects: 1. The alteration of the tree structure, which is equivalent to the pace of the walk in the Markov space. 2. The Metropolis-Hastings Algorithm [21-22]. The algorithms will be compared using experimental data from the well-known Z24 bridge SHM dataset.

4. A SIMPLE STRATEGY: THE Z24 BRIDGE EXAMPLE

The Z24 Bridge was a concrete highway structure in Switzerland connecting Koppigen and Utzenstorf, and in the late 1990s; before its demolishment procedure, it was used for SHM purposes under the "SIMCES" project [3,20]. During a whole year of monitoring of the bridge, a series of sensor systems captured modal parameter measurements, as well as a family of environmental measurements such as air temperature, soil temperature, humidity, wind speed etc. The critical point in this benchmark project was the introduction of different types of real progressive damage scenarios towards the end of the monitoring year. For the purposes of this study, the four natural frequencies that were extracted over a period of year, including the period of structural failure of the bridge are used Fig.2.

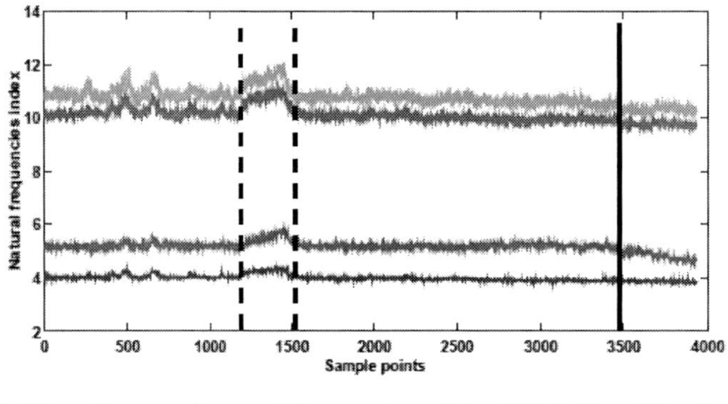

Figure 2: Time history of natural frequencies of the Z24 Bridge (The dotted lines represent the very cold temperature fluctuations and the black solid line the introduction of damage).

The Z24 bridge was extensively analysed using robust methods such as LTS and MCD techniques as means of exploring environmental variations for SHM purposes in previous and ongoing work [1, 2]. It was found that environmental variations due to sub-zero temperatures manifest themselves as vertical outliers (in comparison with damaged condition which appear as horizontal outliers or bad leverage points). This was a very vital information as it showed that the nature of outliers between operational/environmental variations and damage have totally different characteristics (see an example in Fig.3).

In this study a simple strategy is followed in order to allow the LTS technique to account for the complex behaviour of the bridge as in the Z24 bridge the environmental variations on the natural frequency are mainly caused due to low temperature values and the damage outliers can skew the regression output of the BCART model. As can be seen in Fig.4 after deriving the treed model with the multiple linear regression splits automatically, the LTS was applied in each region to correct as robustly as possible the BCART regression lines (blue solid line). The results of the robust linear regression correction (red line) are very promising as can be seen in Fig.4 as well as in Figs.5 and 6 the results flag the problematic skewness due the vertical outliers and bad leverage points due to very low temperatures and damage. The generalised BCART-LTS model performed very well in robustly characterising the measurements as normal/good leverage points. However, it can be noted that some few points are not precisely classified as normal points which means that more analysis in the treed model might be needed in order to have a fully correct model that describes the Z24 bridge (e.g. Treed Gaussian Processes). Also, in the region of split 6, 7 in Fig. 4 the LTS corrects a little the treed regression but because the outliers are so many compared to normal (almost equal clusters) the results are not perfect here. It has to be noted that all analysis here is inclusive which means that the data coming from outliers or damage in this case is included. This can be improved as it will be shown in future work. On the other hand, if one looks to the data under normal condition including the environmental fluctuations the strategy followed here is very successful (see for example split 2 and 5).

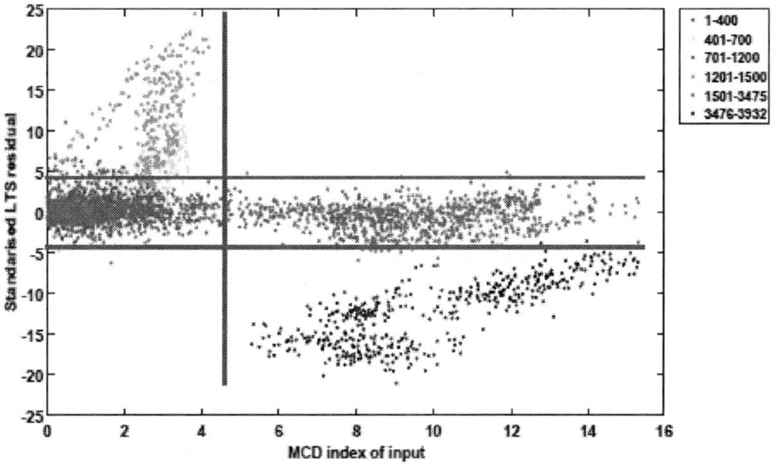

Figure 3: Plot of LTS residual versus MCD robust distance for regression between temperature and second natural frequency [2] (linear LTS regression).

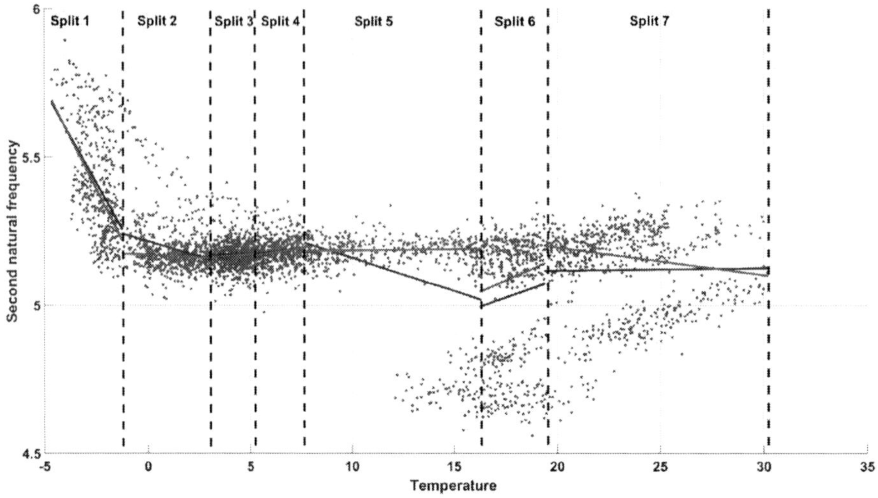

Figure 4: Plot of the regression output of the Treed Bayesian linear regression (blue solid line) and the robust linear regression correction (red line) on each leave of the tree (seven in this case).

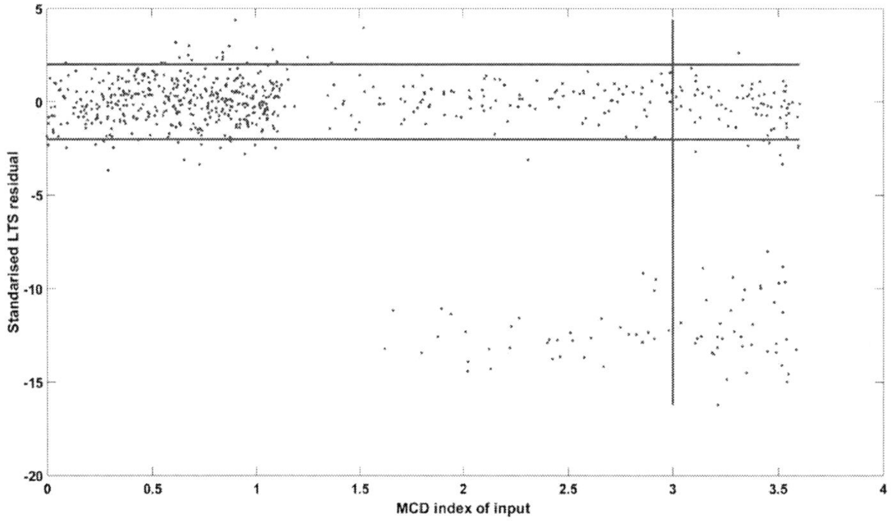

Figure 5: Plot of LTS residual versus MCD robust distance for regression between temperature and second natural frequency [2] (linear LTS regression) for split 5 of Fig.4.

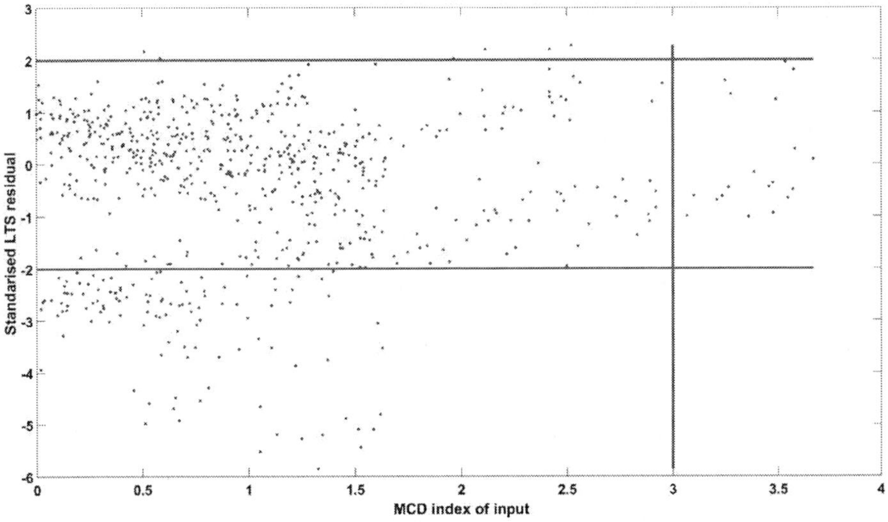

Figure 6: Plot of LTS residual versus MCD robust distance for regression between temperature and second natural frequency [2] (linear LTS regression) for split 7 of Fig.4.

5. CONCLUSIONS

The approach proposed in this paper is a first attempt to move LTS robust regression to a nonlinear perspective using the ideas of treed regression models. After it was pointed out in previous work [2-5] that environmental and operational variations can manifest themselves differently (vertical outliers) in physical appearance compared to damage measurements, an effort to classify these vertical outliers as normal operational points or good leverage points is proposed.

In a lot of real life cases, the data structure and the outlier generating mechanisms dictate which method will outperform the others and reveal the internal variability. This is the reason that this proposed method brings new ground in identifying, during monitoring operation, which of the suspicious data is sourced from damaged or undamaged condition and which of the abnormal behaviour is due to the influence of external factors.

In this paper, robust outlier statistics are used, focussed mainly on a high-level estimation of the "masking effect" of inclusive outliers, not only for determining the presence or absence of novelty something that is of fundamental interest but also to examine the normal condition set under the suspicion that it may already include multiple abnormalities. Further research is carried out in order to move from generalised linear BCART-LTS to pure nonlinear robust regression analysis.

ACKNOWLEDGEMENTS

The authors gratefully acknowledge the support of the UK Engineering and Physical Sciences Research Council (EPSRC) through Grant reference numbers EP/R003645/1, EP/R004900/1.

REFERENCES

[1] N. Dervilis, E.J. Cross, R.J. Barthorpe, K. Worden, Robust methods of inclusive outlier analysis for structural health monitoring, Journal of Sound and Vibration (2014) 333 (20) (2014) 5181 – 5195.

[2] N. Dervilis, K. Worden, E. J. Cross, On Robust Regression Analysis as a Means of Exploring Environ-mental and Operational conditions for SHM Data, Journal of Sound and Vibration (2014)(under review /submitted).
[3] E.J. Cross, On structural health monitoring in changing environmental and operational conditions, Ph.D. thesis (University of Sheffield, 2012).
[4] L.D. Avendaño-Valencia, E.N. Chatzi, K.Y. Koo, J.M. Brownjohn, 2017. Gaussian Process time-series models for structures under operational variability. Frontiers in Built Environment, 3, p.69.
[5] M.D. Spiridonakos, E.N. Chatzi, B. Sudret, 2016. Polynomial chaos expansion models for the monitoring of structures under operational variability. ASCE-ASME Journal of Risk and Uncertainty in Engineering Systems, Part A: Civil Engineering, 2(3), p.B4016003.
[6] E.J. Cross, K. Y. Koo, J. M. W. Brownjohn, K. Worden, Long-term monitoring and data analysis of the Tamar Bridge, Mechanical Systems and Signal Processing 35 (1) (2013) 16–34.
[7]B. Peeters, J. Maeck, G. De Roeck, Vibration-based damage detection in civil engineering: excitation sources and temperature effects, Smart materials and Structures 10 (3) (2001) 518.
[8]S. Alampalli, Effects of testing, analysis, damage, and environment on modal parameters, Mechanical Systems and Signal Processing 14 (1) (2000) 63–74.
[9] P. Cornwell, C. R. Farrar, S. W. Doebling, H. Sohn, Environmental variability of modal properties, Experimental Techniques 23 (6) (1999) 45–48.
[10] E J. Cross, K. Worden, Q. Chen, Cointegration: a novel approach for the removal of environmental trends in structural health monitoring data, Proceedings of the Royal Society A: Mathematical, Physical and Engineering Science 467 (2133) (2011) 2712–2732.
[11] A.M. Leroy, P. J. Rousseeuw, Robust regression and outlier detection, Wiley Series in Probability and Mathematical Statistics, New York: Wiley, 1987 1.
[12] P.J. Rousseeuw, B. C. Van Zomeren, Unmasking multivariate outliers and leverage points, Journal of the American Statistical Association 85 (411) (1990) 633–639.
[13] P.J. Rousseeuw, K. Van Driessen, A fast algorithm for the minimum covariance determinant estimator, Technometrics 41 (3) (1999) 212–223.
[14] S. Verboven, M. Hubert, LIBRA: a MATLAB library for robust analysis, Chemometrics and Intelligent Laboratory Systems 75 (2) (2005) 127–136.
[15] M. Hubert, P. J. Rousseeuw, S. Van Aelst, High-breakdown robust multivariate methods, journal of Statistical Science (2008) 92–119.
[16] D.A. Jackson, Y. Chen, Robust principal component analysis and outlier detection with ecological data, Environmetrics 15 (2) (2004) 129–139.
[17] P. Rousseeuw, M. Hubert, High-Breakdown Estimators of Multivariate Location and Scatter, in: Robust-ness and Complex Data Structures, Springer, 2013, pp. 49–66.
[18] P.J. Rousseeuw, K. Van Driessen, Computing LTS regression for large data sets, Data mining and knowledge discovery 12 (1) (2006) 29–45.
[19] P.J. Rousseeuw, Least median of squares regression, journal = Journal of the American statistical association 79 (388) (1984) 871–880.
[20] G.D. Roeck, The state-of-the-art of damage detection by vibration monitoring: the SIMCES experience, Journal of Structural Control 10 (2) (2003) 127–134.
[21] T. Zhang, On Treed Gaussian processes for modelling structural dynamic systems. Diss. University of Sheffield, 2018.
[22] H.A. Chipman, E. I. George and R. E. McCulloch. 1998, Bayesian CART model search, Journal of the American Statistical Association, 93(443):935–948.

IOMAC'19

8th International Operational Modal Analysis Conference
2019 May13-15 Copenhagen

COMPARISON OF TIME DOMAIN AND FEATURE DOMAIN DAMAGE DETECTION

Jyrki Kullaa

Dr., Metropolia University of Applied Sciences, jyrki.kullaa@metropolia.fi

ABSTRACT

In vibration-based structural health monitoring, data analysis for damage detection can be done in the time domain or in the feature domain. Both approaches have their advantages and disadvantages, which are discussed in this paper. Time domain data analysis is based on a sensor network, in which each sensor reading is estimated from the whole sensor network using Bayesian virtual sensing for noise reduction. In the feature domain analysis, damage-sensitive features are first identified from the response data. A numerical experiment is carried out to illustrate the main characteristics of the methods by simulating vibration measurements of a bridge deck with environmental influences and damage. The excitation or environmental variables are not measured. The feature-domain method was able to detect smaller damage but the number of false alarms was higher than that when using the time-domain algorithm.

Keywords: Structural health monitoring, Damage detection, Virtual sensing, Noise reduction, Environmental or operational effects, Time domain, Feature domain, System identification, Dimensionality

1. INTRODUCTION

Structural health monitoring (SHM), based on vibration measurements, is a global approach, meaning that damage can be detected remotely from the sensor. This is an advantage, because the location of damage is often unknown, and a limiting number of sensors is only available. Visual inspection of the measured time records is not sufficient for detection of minor damage, but a more sophisticated data analysis is necessary. The objective is to track changes in the vibration characteristics of the structure. Typically, this is done by extracting damage-sensitive features from the time histories. The most common features are the modal parameters: natural frequencies, mode shape vectors, and damping. They are extracted using system identification techniques particularly developed for output-only data. Another approach that is applied less frequently is data analysis directly in the time domain. Each sensor is estimated using the remaining sensors in the network. This approach requires that the number of sensors is larger than the number of active modes.

Because ambient excitation cannot be measured, the analysis must be based on the response data only. In addition, environmental or operational variability can change the dynamic characteristics of the structure, which should not be interpreted as damage. In this paper, the environmental or operational variables are not measured.

Time domain and feature domain approaches for damage detection are studied and compared in this paper. A unified statistical data analysis algorithm for damage detection is applied to both methods. The same measurement data are used in order to make the comparison possible. Comparison of different algorithms or features for damage detection is beyond the scope of this work.

The paper is organized as follows. Characteristics of time-domain and feature-domain approaches for damage detection are discussed and compared in Section 2. Bayesian virtual sensors for the time-domain analysis are derived in Section 3. Damage detection under varying environmental or operational conditions is outlined in Section 4. Detection and localization of an open crack in a bridge girder is studied in Section 5, in which a numerical finite element model is used to generate vibration measurements under different environmental and operational conditions. Concluding remarks are given in Section 6.

2. CHARACTERISTICS OF TIME-DOMAIN AND FEATURE-DOMAIN METHODS

In this section, the most relevant differences between the time-domain and the feature-domain approaches in SHM are discussed. Both methods require simultaneous sampling of all sensors in the network. The excitation remains unknown, and response data are only available. In both domains, the same technique is applied, in which the environmental or operational variables are not measured, but can be treated as latent variables. Training data under different environmental or operational conditions are required. The elimination of environmental or operational influences is discussed in Section 4. An example with a comparison is presented in Section 5.

In the present paper, damage detection in either domain is based on the data covariance matrix. In the time-domain, spatial correlation only is applied, which means that the correlation between sensors at the same time instant is only considered. For those time-domain algorithms that use spatiotemporal correlation, some of the characteristics below do not apply. These include Kalman filter (KF) approaches for damage detection [1]. In the feature-domain, system identification is applied, in which spatiotemporal correlation is utilized.

Several things can affect the time-domain and feature-domain damage detection. These include the excitation (frequency content, stationarity, amplitude), sensors, data management, computational effort, automation, outliers, non-linearities, and damage localization. They are not discussed further in this paper due to space limitations. Two important characteristics that are quite different in the two approaches, data dimensionality and feature extraction, are investigated in the following.

Data dimensionality clearly distinguishes the time-domain and the feature-domain methods. Let us assume that the number of uniaxial sensors in the sensor network is p, or more specifically, p signals are acquired. The number of data points, or samples, in a single measurement is N. The size of the data matrix is then $N \times p$. In the time-domain, the data dimensionality is p.

In the feature-domain, the number of data points is one. Let us assume that the number of identified modes is n. The modal parameters and the corresponding dimensionalities are: natural frequencies (n), damping (n), real mode shapes ($(p-1)\cdot n$), or complex mode shapes ($2(p-1)\cdot n$). Due to scaling, one sensor (DOF) must be removed from each mode shape vector. The dimensionality in the feature-domain may be significantly larger than that in the time-domain.

For a statistical data analysis, a large number of samples is advantageous. Therefore, the time-domain analysis might appear superior. There are, however, other criteria. The main criterion is obviously the detection performance, which is investigated in Section 5.

Feature-domain approach requires that some dynamic characteristics, or features, are extracted from the measured time histories. Often, special system identification algorithms are applied. Currently, there are no fully automatic system identification algorithms, but they include some parameters that have to be adjusted. For example, a stabilization diagram is often used to select the model order based on the stability of the identified modes and to separate the physical modes from the purely mathematical modes [2].

Another issue is mode pairing [3]. The number of identified modes can vary between measurements. Some modes are not identified or additional modes may appear. In cases of closely spaced modes, the modes may be in a different order. Mode pairing should also be automatic and reliable, which may be a challenge. In the case of missing modes, the corresponding measurements have to be discarded or the missing features have to be estimated using the other measurements.

In the time-domain, these challenges do not exist, if all sensors work normally. Sensor faults can be detected with similar methods as damage [4].

The main restriction of the time-domain method is that the number of sensors must be greater than the number of active modes. This may be a problem with large structures having several modes in the low frequency range. In those cases, a feature domain method may be the best choice.

3. BAYESIAN VIRTUAL SENSING

Virtual sensing (VS) gives an estimate of a quantity of interest using the available measurements. Empirical VS is a data-based approach, estimating a physical sensor using hardware redundancy. This study applies empirical virtual sensing to noisy measurements to estimate virtual sensors having a smaller measurement error and a higher SNR than the hardware.

Consider a sensor network measuring p simultaneously sampled variables $\mathbf{y} = \mathbf{y}(t)$ at time instant t. The measurement $\mathbf{y}$ includes a measurement error $\mathbf{w} = \mathbf{w}(t)$:

$$\mathbf{y} = \mathbf{x} + \mathbf{w} \tag{1}$$

where $\mathbf{x} = \mathbf{x}(t)$ are the true values of the measured degrees of freedom. The objective is to find a less noisy estimate for the true values $\mathbf{x}$ utilizing the noisy measurements $\mathbf{y}$ from the sensor network.

Equation (1) can be written in the following form at each time instant t [5].

$$\begin{Bmatrix} \mathbf{x} \\ \mathbf{y} \end{Bmatrix} = \begin{bmatrix} \mathbf{I} & \mathbf{0} \\ \mathbf{I} & \mathbf{I} \end{bmatrix} \begin{Bmatrix} \mathbf{x} \\ \mathbf{w} \end{Bmatrix} \tag{2}$$

For simplicity, assume zero-mean variables $\mathbf{x}$ and $\mathbf{y}$. The partitioned covariance matrix is

$$\begin{aligned} \begin{bmatrix} \boldsymbol{\Sigma}_{xx} & \boldsymbol{\Sigma}_{xy} \\ \boldsymbol{\Sigma}_{yx} & \boldsymbol{\Sigma}_{yy} \end{bmatrix} &= E(\begin{Bmatrix} \mathbf{x} \\ \mathbf{y} \end{Bmatrix} \begin{bmatrix} \mathbf{x}^T & \mathbf{y}^T \end{bmatrix}) = \begin{bmatrix} \mathbf{I} & \mathbf{0} \\ \mathbf{I} & \mathbf{I} \end{bmatrix} E(\begin{Bmatrix} \mathbf{x} \\ \mathbf{w} \end{Bmatrix} \begin{bmatrix} \mathbf{x}^T & \mathbf{w}^T \end{bmatrix}) \begin{bmatrix} \mathbf{I} & \mathbf{0} \\ \mathbf{I} & \mathbf{I} \end{bmatrix}^T \\ &= \begin{bmatrix} \mathbf{I} & \mathbf{0} \\ \mathbf{I} & \mathbf{I} \end{bmatrix} \begin{bmatrix} \boldsymbol{\Sigma}_{xx} & \mathbf{0} \\ \mathbf{0} & \boldsymbol{\Sigma}_{ww} \end{bmatrix} \begin{bmatrix} \mathbf{I} & \mathbf{I} \\ \mathbf{0} & \mathbf{I} \end{bmatrix} = \begin{bmatrix} \boldsymbol{\Sigma}_{xx} & \boldsymbol{\Sigma}_{xx} \\ \boldsymbol{\Sigma}_{xx} & \boldsymbol{\Sigma}_{xx} + \boldsymbol{\Sigma}_{ww} \end{bmatrix} \end{aligned} \tag{3}$$

where $E(\cdot)$ denotes the expectation operator and the measurement error $\mathbf{w}$ is assumed to be zero mean Gaussian, independent of $\mathbf{x}$, with a (known) covariance matrix $\boldsymbol{\Sigma}_{ww}$.

A linear minimum mean square error (MMSE) estimate for $\mathbf{x}\,|\,\mathbf{y}$ ($\mathbf{x}$ given $\mathbf{y}$) is obtained by minimizing the mean-square error (MSE) [5, 6]. The expected value, or the conditional mean, of the predicted variable is

$$\hat{\mathbf{x}} = E(\mathbf{x}\,|\,\mathbf{y}) = \boldsymbol{\Sigma}_{xx}(\boldsymbol{\Sigma}_{xx} + \boldsymbol{\Sigma}_{ww})^{-1}\mathbf{y} = \boldsymbol{\Sigma}_{xx}\boldsymbol{\Sigma}_{yy}^{-1}\mathbf{y} \tag{4}$$

and the estimation error is

$$\mathrm{cov}(\mathbf{x}\,|\,\mathbf{y}) = \boldsymbol{\Sigma}_{xx} - \boldsymbol{\Sigma}_{xx}(\boldsymbol{\Sigma}_{xx} + \boldsymbol{\Sigma}_{ww})^{-1}\boldsymbol{\Sigma}_{xx} = \boldsymbol{\Sigma}_{xx} - \boldsymbol{\Sigma}_{xx}\boldsymbol{\Sigma}_{yy}^{-1}\boldsymbol{\Sigma}_{xx} \tag{5}$$

The data covariance matrix $\boldsymbol{\Sigma}_{yy}$ can be estimated from the measurement data. If the noise covariance matrix can be approximated, then $\boldsymbol{\Sigma}_{xx}$ can be computed: $\boldsymbol{\Sigma}_{xx} = \boldsymbol{\Sigma}_{yy} - \boldsymbol{\Sigma}_{ww}$. In this study, the measurement errors are assumed uncorrelated between sensors resulting in a diagonal noise covariance matrix. It was shown that the Bayesian virtual sensors are more accurate than the physical hardware [7].

Bayesian virtual sensing is a noise reduction algorithm in the time domain applied to each measurement separately. Because of their higher accuracy, the virtual sensors replace the actual measurements in the subsequent time-domain data analysis ($\mathbf{y} \leftarrow \hat{\mathbf{x}}$) (4) as shown in the following section.

4. DAMAGE DETECTION UNDER DIFFERENT ENVIRONMENTAL OR OPERATIONAL CONDITIONS

The damage detection algorithm used in this paper is briefly outlined. Each variable in turn is estimated using the remaining variables using the MMSE estimation [8]. Each observation $\mathbf{y}$ is partitioned into observed variables $\mathbf{v}$ and estimated variables $\mathbf{u}$ (typically a single variable u):

$$\mathbf{y} = \begin{Bmatrix} \mathbf{y}_u \\ \mathbf{y}_v \end{Bmatrix} \tag{6}$$

Here $\mathbf{y}$ can represent the actual measurement, virtual sensors, or the feature vector. All cases are studied in Section 5.

For simplicity, assume zero-mean variables $\mathbf{y}$. The partitioned data covariance matrix $\boldsymbol{\Sigma}_y$ is

$$\boldsymbol{\Sigma}_y = E(\mathbf{y}\mathbf{y}^T) = \begin{bmatrix} \boldsymbol{\Sigma}_{y,uu} & \boldsymbol{\Sigma}_{y,uv} \\ \boldsymbol{\Sigma}_{y,vu} & \boldsymbol{\Sigma}_{y,vv} \end{bmatrix} \tag{7}$$

The precision matrix $\boldsymbol{\Gamma}_y$ is defined as the inverse of the covariance matrix $\boldsymbol{\Sigma}_y$ and is also written in a partitioned form:

$$\boldsymbol{\Gamma}_y = \boldsymbol{\Sigma}_y^{-1} = \begin{bmatrix} \boldsymbol{\Gamma}_{y,uu} & \boldsymbol{\Gamma}_{y,uv} \\ \boldsymbol{\Gamma}_{y,vu} & \boldsymbol{\Gamma}_{y,vv} \end{bmatrix} \tag{8}$$

A linear minimum mean square error (MMSE) estimate for $\mathbf{y}_u \mid \mathbf{y}_v$ is obtained by minimizing the mean-square error (MSE) and can be computed either using the covariance or precision matrix [6, 9]. If each sensor signal is estimated in turn, the formulas based on the precision matrix result in a more efficient algorithm [6]. The expected value of the estimated variable is

$$\hat{\mathbf{y}}_u = E(\mathbf{y}_u \,|\, \mathbf{y}_v) = -\boldsymbol{\Gamma}_{y,uu}^{-1}\boldsymbol{\Gamma}_{y,uv}\mathbf{y}_v \tag{9}$$

and the error covariance MSE is

$$\mathrm{cov}(\mathbf{y}_u \,|\, \mathbf{y}_v) = \boldsymbol{\Gamma}_{y,uu}^{-1} \tag{10}$$

The residuals for the variable u are then generated:

$$\varepsilon_u = \mathbf{y}_u - \hat{\mathbf{y}}_u \quad (11)$$

The training data consist of several measurements in order to take different environmental or operational conditions into account. Specifically, the data covariance matrix (7) is estimated using all training data. The environmental or operational influences can thus be eliminated [8]. Once damage occurs, the correlation structure does not fit the experimental data producing a larger residual, which will then trigger an alarm.

All residuals are standardized according to the training data. All samples, training and test data, are subjected to principal component analysis (PCA). The first principal component (PC) is retained in order to find the direction with the largest change in the data space, which is supposed to indicate damage. The first PC is plotted on a control chart with corresponding control limits [10]. Data points falling outside the control limits will trigger an alarm.

5. NUMERICAL EXAMPLE

Numerical simulations were performed using a finite element model of a stiffened bridge deck (Figure 1). The structure was 30 m long and 11 m wide. It had four longitudinal and three lateral stiffeners. The modelling was done using four-node discrete Kirchhoff quadrilateral shell elements with a diagonal mass matrix. The deck was made of concrete with a Young's modulus of E = 40 GPa (at temperature T = 0°C), Poisson ratio of ν = 0.15, density of ρ = 2500 kg/m^3, and thickness of 250 mm. The stiffeners were made of steel (E = 207 GPa, ν = 0.30, ρ = 7850 kg/m^3). The longitudinal stiffeners had a web with a thickness of t = 16 mm and a height of h = 1.4 m. The bottom flange had a thickness of t = 50 mm and a width of b = 700 mm. The lateral stiffeners were 1.4 m high and 30 mm thick plates.

The nodes of the bottom flanges were simply supported at both ends of the bridge. Longitudinal displacements were fixed only at one end of the bridge. The corners of the concrete deck were supported in the lateral and vertical directions.

The temperature had an effect on the concrete deck. It was assumed that the temperature along the width was constant, and along the length it was linearly varying including a zero-mean Gaussian noise with a standard deviation of σ_T = 0.2°C in each row of elements. The ends of the bridge were at random temperatures between –20°C and +40°C. The relationship between the temperature and the Young's modulus was stepwise linear as shown in Figure 2 left. There was thus an infinite number of possible distributions of the Young's modulus in the bridge deck. Different realizations of the distribution of the Young's modulus along the bridge are plotted in Figure 2 right. The Young's modulus of each element was constant, determined using the temperature at the midpoint. Notice that the temperature or the Young's modulus were not measured, but they were considered latent variables.

Two independent random loads in the vertical direction were applied to nodes shown with green squares in Figure 1. Because ambient excitation was assumed, the steady state response was measured. For the steady state analysis, periodic pseudorandom excitations in the frequency range between 0 and 8.33 Hz with random amplitudes and phases were generated [11] and the analysis was performed in the frequency domain [12]. The excitation was not measured.

The response was computed with a modal superposition algorithm using the first seven modes. The analysis period was 20.48 s with a sampling frequency of 50 Hz. One measurement period then included 1024 samples from each sensor.

Vertical accelerations were measured at 28 points shown in Figure 1. An equal amount of noise was added to the signals, so that the average signal-to-noise ratio was approximately SNR = 18, 21, 24, 27, 30, 33, 36, 39, 42, 45, 48, 51, 54, 57, or 60 dB. The effect of the noise level was investigated.

700 measurements were acquired from the undamaged structure under random environmental conditions. Damage was a crack in a steel girder, which was simulated by removing the contact between elements at selected nodes. The damage location is plotted in red in Figure 1. Six different crack configurations were modelled with an increasing severity by removing the contact at 1–6 nodes, respectively. The nodes are shown in the detailed plot in Figure 1 showing the order in which the nodes were separated. Each damage scenario was monitored with ten measurements under random environmental and operational conditions. As a result, the last 60 measurements were from a damaged structure.

Figure 3 left shows the first seven natural frequencies in all 760 measurements. The variability due to environmental variation is clearly seen. Visually, there are no clear changes in natural frequencies due to damage. Figure 3 right shows the first two natural frequencies in all 760 measurements.

The training data were the first 365 measurements. They were also used to design the control charts. The test data were the last 395 measurements, from which the last 60 were from the damaged structure.

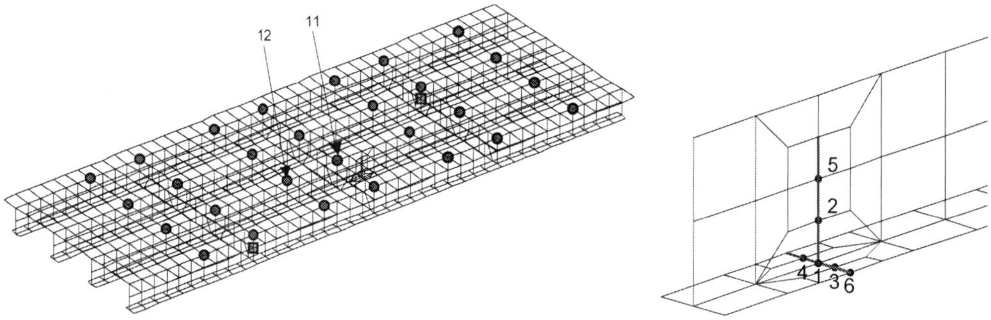

Figure 1. Left: Finite element model representing the actual structure. The 28 sensor positions are shown as red circles and the two excitation points as green squares. Damage is shown with red lines. Sensor 11 is located nearest to the crack. Right: A detail of the steel girder with damage. The crack is shown with red lines and the numbers indicate the order in which the connecting nodes separated resulting in an increasing crack size.

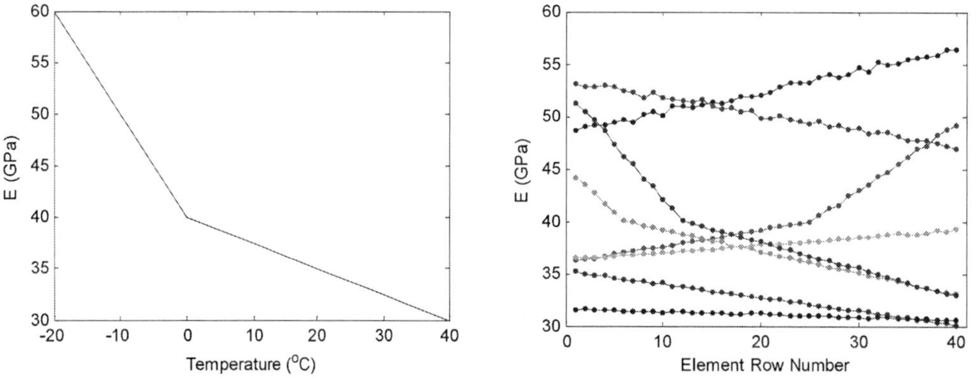

Figure 2. Left: The effect of temperature on the Young's modulus of the concrete. Right: Eight realizations of the longitudinal distributions of the Young's modulus of the concrete.

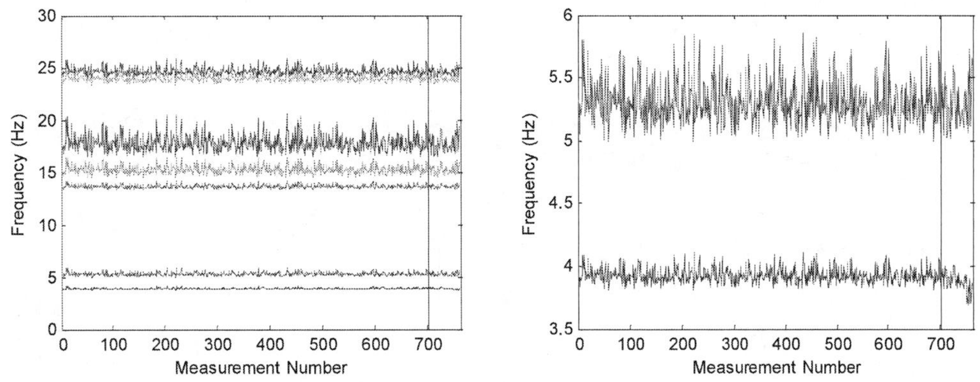

Figure 3. Left: The first seven natural frequencies indicating the influences of the environmental variables and damage. Right: The first two natural frequencies. The data before the vertical line are from the undamaged structure.

5.1. Time-domain analysis

The standard deviation of the noise was assumed to be known. The empirical Bayesian virtual sensors were estimated using the physically measured 28 accelerations. It was seen that the Bayesian virtual sensors were more accurate than the actual measurement. The standard deviation of the noise was reduced to less than one third on average. This noise reduction property was utilized in damage detection as shown next.

The residuals were computed as discussed in Section 4. Because the distribution of the first PC scores of the residuals was unknown, a generalized extreme value distribution was identified [13]. The PC scores were divided into subgroups (of size n = 1024) and the subgroup minima and maxima were recorded. Extreme value distributions were identified for both the subgroup minima and maxima of the in-control samples (training data). The control limits were computed from these distributions by choosing the probability of exceedance (here 0.001). The extreme values were plotted on a control chart to see if the test data exceeded the control limits thus indicating damage. Because the subgroup size was 1024, each measurement was represented by one data point.

The EVS control charts for damage detection for two different SNRs are shown in Figures 4 and 5. The left charts were plotted using the actual measurements, whereas the charts in the right were plotted using the virtual sensors. With an average SNR equal to 36 dB, damage level 6 was only detected, while levels 4–6 were detected using the virtual sensors (Figure 4). Similarly, with an average SNR equal to 60 dB, damage levels 3–6 were detected using the actual measurements, whereas all levels 1–6 were detected using the virtual sensors (Figure 5). It is noticeable that no false indications of damage occurred.

Damage was assumed to locate in the vicinity of the sensor u with the largest Mahalanobis distance [9] of the residuals (11). The Mahalanobis distances of the residuals for each sensor are plotted in Figure 6 with two different SNRs. For virtual sensors with all SNRs, damage was correctly localized to sensor 11 that was the nearest sensor from the crack (Figure 1). The only case in which the localization failed, was when analysing the actual measurements with SNR = 18 dB.

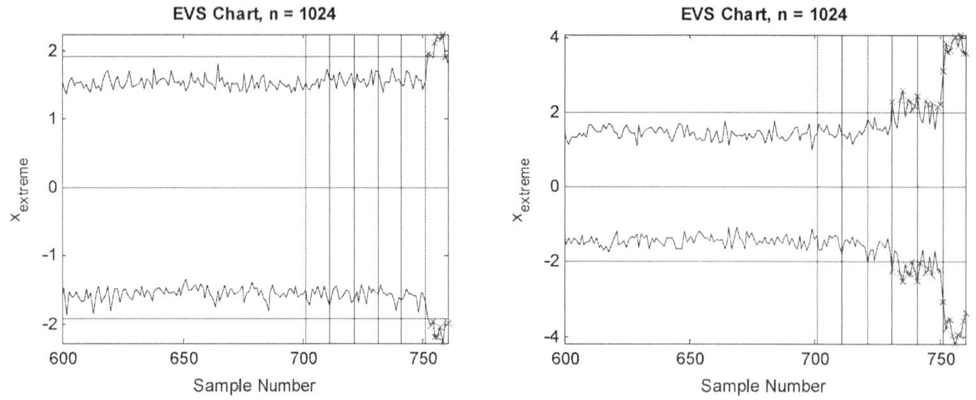

Figure 4. EVS control charts using the actual measurements (left) with an average SNR = 36 dB and the Bayesian virtual sensors (right). The vertical lines indicate the six damage levels with an increasing severity.

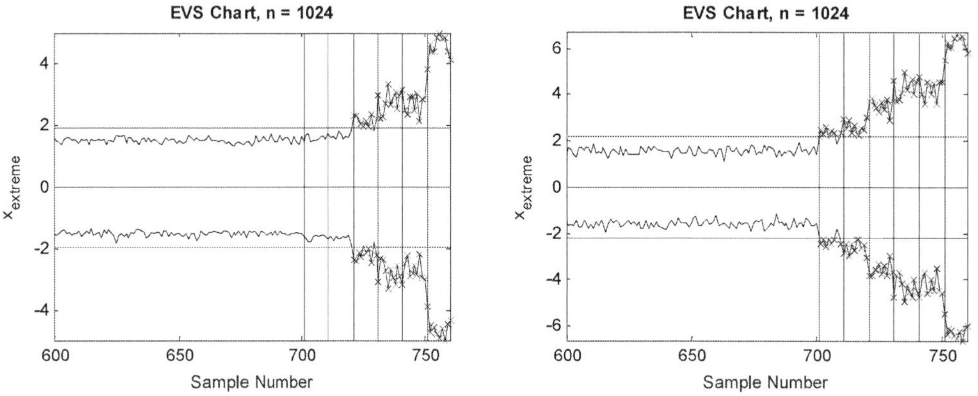

Figure 5. EVS control charts using the actual measurements (left) with an average SNR = 60 dB and the Bayesian virtual sensors (right). The vertical lines indicate the six damage levels with an increasing severity.

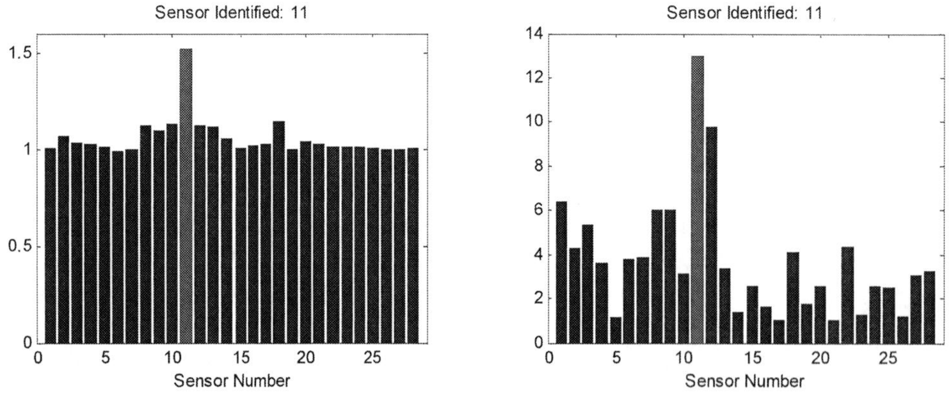

Figure 6. Damage localization using virtual sensors. Left: SNR = 36 dB. Right: SNR = 60 dB.

5.2. Feature-domain analysis

The feature-domain analysis started by identifying the lowest natural frequencies and mode shapes from the 28 sensor measurements using a covariance-based stochastic subspace identification (cov-SSI) [2]. The same data were used as in the time-domain analysis. Because the frequency band of the excitation was 0...8.33 Hz, only the two lowest modes could be identified. Stabilisation diagram with an automatic selection of the model order was used.

The first two natural frequencies and the corresponding mode shape magnitudes were used as damage-sensitive features. The data dimensionality was p = 2+2(28–1) = 56. The number of data points in the training data was only 365, which was statistically insufficient.

The first principal component scores of the residuals (11) were plotted on the Shewhart, or xbar, control chart [10]. Control charts for two different noise levels are shown in Figure 7 with a subgroup size of 10. Hence, each damage level is plotted with a single data point.

With SNR = 24 dB, damage levels 3–6 were detected. For a SNR higher or equal to 36 dB, all damage levels were detected. The probability of detection of the feature-domain analysis was therefore higher than that of the time-domain analysis. However, the proportion of false alarms was higher in the feature-domain than in the time-domain analysis.

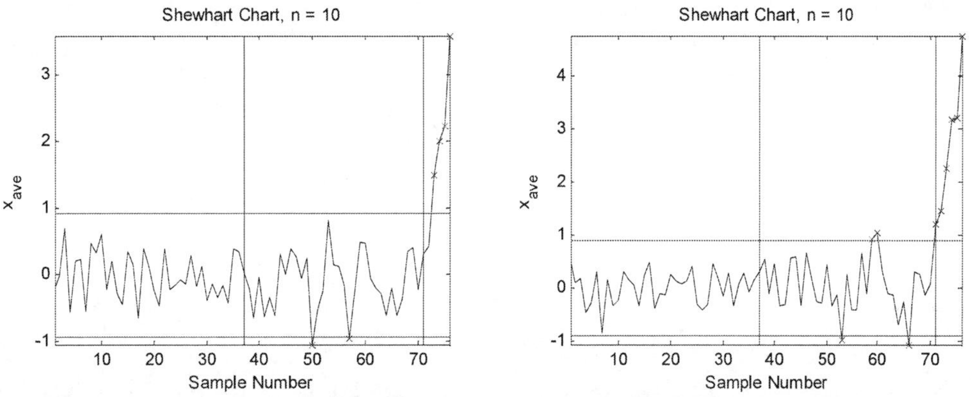

Figure 7. Shewhart control charts of the first two natural frequencies and the corresponding mode shape amplitudes (p = 56) with SNR = 24 dB (left) and SNR = 36 dB (right). The data before the leftmost vertical line were used as the training data, and the other vertical line indicates the first damage level. The subgroup size is 10. Therefore, each damage level is presented by one data point in the charts. Logarithmic scaling was applied to the vertical axis for clarity.

5.3. Comparison of time-domain and feature-domain analyses

In this section, the results of the data analyses in the time-domain and in the frequency-domain are compared. As mentioned in Section 2, the detection performance is probably the most important criterion. The probability of detection (POD) is depicted in Figure 8 for the time-domain and feature-domain algorithms. The probability of detection of different crack sizes is plotted as a function of the average SNR of the measurement data.

First, it can be seen that in the time-domain the virtual sensors resulted in a better detection performance than the actual measurements. This is due to the fact that virtual sensors had a higher SNR than the corresponding hardware. Second, the feature-domain data analysis was more sensitive to damage or less sensitive to noise. A smaller crack size could be detected in the feature-domain than in the time-domain with the same SNR. However, the number of false alarms was larger in the feature-domain. In the-time domain, no false alarms occurred.

As an example, when the SNR was equal to 30 dB, the time-domain analysis was not able to detect any crack sizes using the actual measurements. Using the virtual sensors, the largest crack size (damage level 6) was detected with POD = 1, and damage levels 4 and 5 were detected with a low POD, 0.1 and 0.2, respectively. The proportion of false alarms was 0. In the feature-domain, damage levels 2–6 were detected with POD = 1, but damage level 1 was not detected. The proportion of false alarms was 0.06.

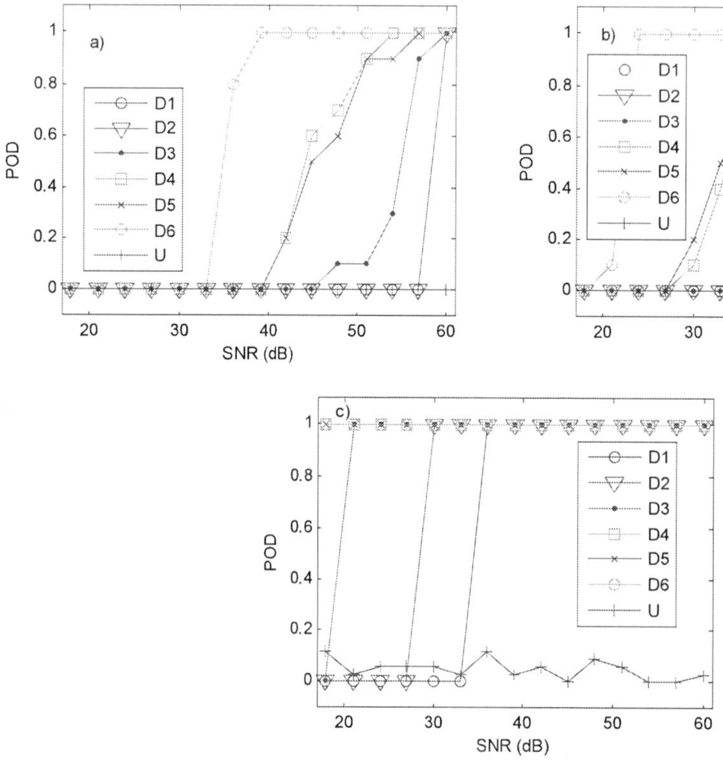

Figure 8. Detection ratio, or probability of detection (POD), of each damage level 1–6 with different SNRs. a) Time-domain analysis using actual measurements; b) Time-domain analysis using virtual sensors; and c) Feature-domain analysis with $p = 56$. D = damage, U = undamaged.

6. CONCLUSIONS

Time-domain and feature-domain approaches for damage detection were studied and compared. A unified data-driven algorithm that takes into account environmental or operational influences was proposed. Spatial correlation was only utilized in the time-domain. The lowest identified natural frequencies and the corresponding mode shape magnitudes were used as damage-sensitive features in the feature-domain.

Because a comparison of numerous different features and damage detection algorithms was beyond the scope of this paper, the conclusion is made based on the observations made using the selected modal parameters and the proposed algorithms. It should be noted, however, that different features and algorithms might result in a different conclusion.

Averaging is advantageous in detection [14]. It decreases the variance and increases the SNR, resulting in an increasing probability of detection (POD). In system identification, a lot of averaging is made, which makes the features accurate resulting in a single data point per measurement. In the time-domain, averaging is more difficult, because the excitation is different in all measurements. Averaging between sensors in the same instant is, however, possible, which was shown in Section 3, resulting in virtual sensors that are more accurate than the corresponding measurement.

In the time-domain, Bayesian virtual sensors outperformed the actual measurements. The feature-domain analysis resulted in a higher POD, but also an increased number of false alarms. The feature-domain damage detection analysis requires less memory than the time-domain analysis, because the number of data points is smaller. The time-domain data analysis is automatic, but in the feature-domain method, system identification may require some user interaction. In the time-domain, damage localization was straightforward and resulted in a correct localization.

The dimensionality may become too large in the feature-domain, and a large amount of training data must be acquired. In the time-domain, the main restriction is that the number of sensors must be larger than the number of active modes. If this is not the case, the feature-domain approach is suggested.

It is important to further develop both approaches for a higher detection performance. In addition, as was seen in this paper, if time-domain analysis is adopted, the measurement error should be kept minimum. Experimental verification is essential, because it may reveal further challenges that were not present when using the simulated data.

ACKNOWLEDGEMENTS

This research has been supported by Metropolia University of Applied Sciences.

REFERENCES

[1] Bernal, D. (2013). Kalman filter damage detection in the presence of changing process and measurement noise. *Mechanical Systems and Signal Processing*, 39(2013), 361–371.

[2] Peeters, B. (2000). *System identification and damage detection in civil engineering*. Ph.D. thesis. KU Leuven, Department of Civil Engineering, 238 p.

[3] Kullaa, J. (2003). Damage detection of the Z24 Bridge using control charts. *Mechanical Systems and Signal Processing*, 17(1), 163–170.

[4] Kullaa, J. (2011). Distinguishing between sensor fault, structural damage, and environmental or operational effects in structural health monitoring. *Mechanical Systems and Signal Processing* 25(8), 2976–2989.

[5] Scharf, L.L. (1991). *Statistical signal processing: detection, estimation, and time series analysis*. Reading, MA, Addison-Wesley.

[6] Kullaa, J. (2010). Sensor validation using minimum mean square error estimation. *Mechanical Systems and Signal Processing*, 24(2010), 1444–1457.

[7] Kullaa, J. (2018). Bayesian virtual sensing in structural dynamics. *Mechanical Systems and Signal Processing*, 115(2019), 497–513.

[8] Kullaa, J. (2009). Eliminating environmental or operational influences in structural health monitoring using the missing data analysis. *Journal of Intelligent Material Systems and Structures*, 20(11), 1381–1390.

[9] Bishop, C.M. (2006). *Pattern recognition and machine learning*. New York, Springer.

[10] Montgomery, D.C. (1997). *Introduction to statistical quality control*, 3rd edition, New York, Wiley.

[11] Brandt, A. (2011). *Noise and vibration analysis: signal analysis and experimental procedures*, Chichester; Hoboken, N.J., Wiley.

[12] Clough, R.W. & Penzien, J. (1993). *Dynamics of structures.* 2nd edition, New York, McGraw-Hill.

[13] Worden, K., Allen, D., Sohn, H. & Farrar, C.R. (2002). Damage detection in mechanical structures using extreme value statistics, In: *SPIE Proceedings, Vol. 4693, 9th Annual International Symposium on Smart Structures and Materials* (pp. 289–299). San Diego, CA.

[14] Kay, S.M. (1998). *Fundamentals of statistical signal processing. Detection theory*, Upper Saddle River, NJ, Prentice-Hall.

IOMAC'19

8th International Operational Modal Analysis Conference

2019 May13-15 Copenhagen

CONTINUOUS OMA FOR DAMAGE DETECTION AND LOCALIZATION IN THE SCIRI TOWER IN PERUGIA, ITALY

Ilaria Venanzi [1], *Alban Kita* [2], *Nicola Cavalagli* [3], *Laura Ierimonti* [4] *and Filippo Ubertini* [5]

[1] Assistant Professor, University of Perugia, ilaria.venanzi@unipg.it.

[2] Ph.D. Student, University of Perugia, alban.kita@unipg.it.

[3] Assistant Professor, University of Perugia, nicola.cavalagli@unipg.it.

[4] Post-doctoral Fellow, University of Perugia, laura.ierimonti@unipg.it.

[5] Full Professor, University of Perugia, filippo.ubertini@unipg.it.

ABSTRACT

This paper presents a methodology for earthquake-induced damage detection and localization in masonry towers using long-term vibration monitoring data. An inverse calibration problem is solved to evaluate the evolution in time of the damage-dependent structural parameters, by using a surrogate quadratic model of natural frequencies and modal shapes. An historic civic tower, named Sciri Tower and located in Perugia, Italy, continuously monitored since December 2016, is selected as the case study. The validation of the procedure is carried out through nonlinear dynamic analyses exploiting a finite element model of the tower and of the surrounding building aggregate calibrated on the basis of data from ambient vibration tests. Accelerograms measured during real earthquakes, occurred during the monitoring period, are adopted for the simulations. The results demonstrate that the proposed procedure is capable of correctly detecting and localizing earthquake-induced damages, even in the case of small-intensity earthquakes where no significant changes in structural conditions are detected from visual inspections.

Keywords: Conference, Operational, Modal, Analysis

1. INTRODUCTION

Vibration-based Structural Health Monitoring (SHM) using modal parameters as damage-sensitive features is widely recognized as a valid tool for the historic buildings' preventive conservation [1, 2, 3, 4]. The application of long-term SHM systems allows to highlight if an historical structure has undergone permanent damage after an earthquake or if it is accumulating damage during a seismic sequence [5, 6] and also allows to prioritize the inspection activities and the restoration interventions.

In order to localize the damage, it is useful to construct and calibrate a FE model of the structure, with particular attention on the effects of surrounding aggregate buidings [7]. Continuous vibration data can be used for online FE model calibration in order to relate the modification of modal parameters to the local variation of mechanical quantities [8].

This paper presents an improved version of the method proposed in [8] for quick automated damage detection and localization in historic masonry towers and its validation based on field data. A civic tower, named Sciri Tower and located in Perugia, Italy, continuously monitored for 10 months, has been selected as the case study. A FE model is calibrated using data from Ambient Vibration Tests (AVT). The structure is ideally subdivided into four macrostructural elements in order to discriminate the damage-dependent structural parameters belonging to different zones. The online minimization of the relative differences between experimental and numerical modal parameters allows the continuous identification of damage-dependent parameters. A quadratic surrogate model relating natural frequencies and mode shapes to elastic parameters is adopted, in order to reduce the computational effort required by the online optimization procedure.

2. EARTHQUAKE-INDUCED DAMAGE ASSESSMENT AND LOCALIZATION

The proposed methodology for earthquake-induced damage assessment and localization is based on the following steps. Firstly, a reliable numerical FE model, tuned on the basis of AVT, is constructed and a surrogate model linking natural frequencies and eigenvector components to elastic parameters of macrostructural elements is built. Operational Modal Analysis is continuusly performed at time intervals δt_{id}, using monitoring data, by means of a fully automated SSI data-driven technique developed in a previous study [9]. The effects of environmental conditions are removed from identified natural frequencies, using Multi Linear Regressive (MLR) filters [10]. The evolution with time of the identified frequencies variations $\delta f^{\exp}$ is computed and a continuous model updating is carried out. A set of damage-dependent parameters of the Finite Element Model is optimized, collected in the design variables vector $\mathbf{U} = (U_1, ..., U_n, U_{n+1}, ..., U_{2n}, U_{2n+1}, ..., U_{n \cdot m})$, where n is the number of uncertain parameters (e.g. typically the elastic modulus and the shear modulus of macroelements) and m is the number of different zones in which the tower can be ideally divided (e.g. at heights 1,...,m). A functional J is continuously minimized in order to compute the damage-dependent parameters corresponding to the observed frequency decays and natural mode shapes:

$$J(\mathbf{U}) = \sum_{i=1}^{l} (\alpha_i \epsilon_i(\mathbf{U}) + \beta_i \delta_i(\mathbf{U})) \tag{1}$$

where

$$\epsilon_i = \left| \frac{\Delta f_i^{\exp}}{f_i^{\exp}} - \frac{\Delta f_i^{\mathrm{FEM}}(\mathbf{U})}{f_i^{\mathrm{FEM}}(\mathbf{U})} \right| \qquad \delta_i = 1 - MAC_{ii}(\mathbf{U}) \tag{2}$$

In which MAC represents the Modal Assurance Criterion between the identified mode shapes and those obtained from the model, α_i and β_i are weighting coefficients and l is the number of identified modes.

In order to reduce the computational time required by the minimization analyses, a surrogate quadratic model can be adopted:

$$f_i^{\mathrm{FEM}}(\mathbf{U}) = \sum_{j=1}^{n} A_{i,j} U_j^2 + \sum_{j=1}^{n} B_{i,j} U_j + C_i \quad \Phi_i^{\mathrm{FEM}}(\mathbf{U}) = \sum_{j=1}^{n} D_{i,j} U_j^2 + \sum_{j=1}^{n} E_{i,j} U_j + F_i \tag{3}$$

where $A_{i,j}$, $B_{i,j}$, C_i, $D_{i,j}$, $E_{i,j}$ and F_i, are coefficients relating the ith identified modal properties to the jth uncertain parameter ($j = 1, .., n$) and are calibrated through first order series approximation around the nominal values. The optimization problem is solved continuously for each set of natural frequencies and mode shapes by using the genetic algorithm [11].

3. THE THE LONG-TERM SHM OF THE SCIRI TOWER

3.1. The Sciri tower

The Sciri tower is the 41 m high civic tower located in *Via dei Priori* in the historical center of Perugia, Italy (Fig. 1). It was built in the 13th century and it is surrounded by neighboring masonry buildings up to the first 17 m on three sides, while the fourth side is free and facing *Via dei Priori* towards North. The masonry is homogeneous and regular and it is made of squared white limestone blocks. The tower has a quadrangular cross-section (7,15 x 7,35 m) and it can be ideally divided in two structural portions (Fig. 2): the lower and the upper parts. The lower part, up to a height of 8.4 m, is characterized by about 2.1 m thick walls with some small openings and a stone masonry vaulted slab which stands above the rooms of an old chapel. The upper part, rising up to 41 m, has slender continuous walls (thickness from 1.6 to 1.4 m) with four 1.5 m wide brick masonry vaulted slabs at different heights. Moreover, a brick masonry ceiling vault completes the tower on the top.

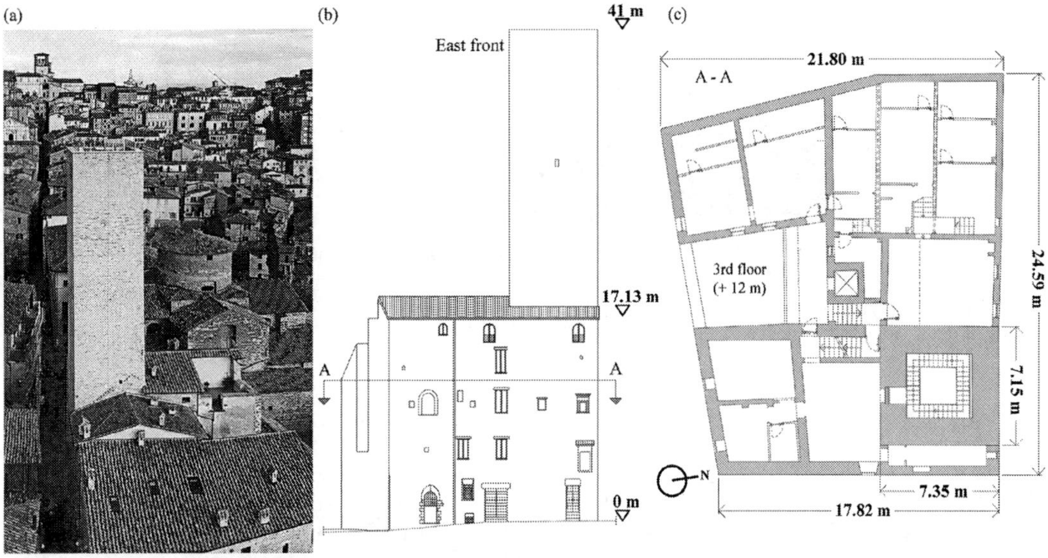

Figure 1: The Sciri Tower: picture of the tower (a), East front (b) and plan view at 12 m height (c).

Ambient Vibration test were carried out on May 22nd, 2017 in order to identify the modal parameters of the tower. A set of 12 high sensitivity (10 V/g) uniaxial accelerometers have been used to measure ambient micro vibrations in operational conditions. Data have been acquired in 30 minutes-long files with a sampling frequency of 1652 Hz. The layout of the accelerometers (denoted as A1, A2,... A12) is depicted in Fig. 2. Sensors have been installed on levels 1, 3, 4 and 5 of the tower, while the DAQ system has been positioned on level 2. Seven vibration modes have been identified within the range from 0 to 11 Hz: two flexural modes in NW direction (x direction as depicted in Fig. 2, denoted as Fx1 and Fx2, respectively), two flexural modes in SW direction (y direction, denoted as Fy1 and Fy2, respectively), one torsional mode, namely Tz1 and finally, two higher order flexural modes, Fx3 and Fy3. The natural frequencies (f_i) and damping ratios (ξ_i) of the seven identified modes from AVT are reported in Table 1 toghether with the natural frequencies obtained by means of MLR model at the reference temperature of 20°C (mean annual value for the city of Perugia).

3.2. The continuous monitoring system

The Sciri tower has been continuously monitored since December 13th, 2017. The continuous permanent dynamic monitoring system comprises three accelerometers and two thermocouples, as schematically indicated in Fig. 2. Accelerometers Ap1, Ap2 and Ap3 are installed at height of 36.7 m. The thermo-

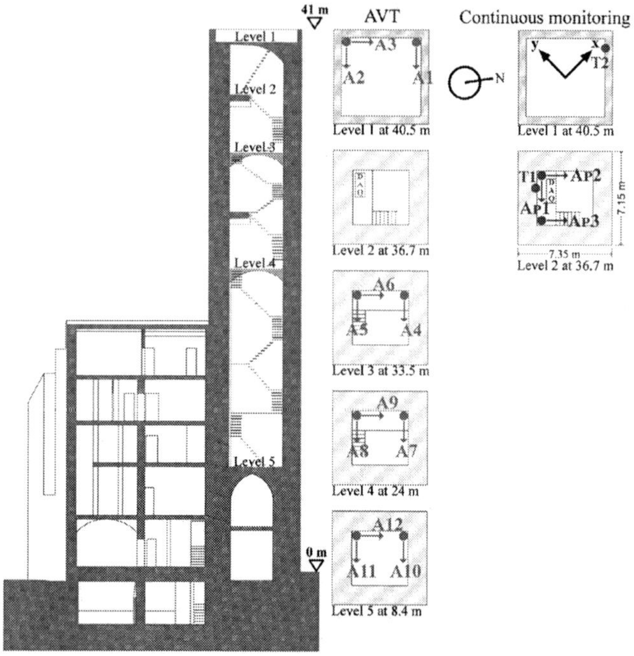

Figure 2: Sensors layout for AVT (left) and continuous monitoring (right).

Table 1: Experimental identified natural frequencies and damping ratios from AVT and frequencies estimated through MLR at 20° C.

Mode no.	Mode type	f_i [Hz]	ξ_i [%]	$f_{i,20°C}^{MLR}$ [Hz]
1	Fx1	1.709	0.740	1.722
2	Fy1	1.914	0.932	1.925
3	Fx2	5.615	0.581	5.615
4	Fy2	5.986	1.054	6.006
5	Tz1	8.428	2.081	8.399
6	Fx3	9.902	1.638	9.896
7	Fy3	10.970	1.740	10.928

couples are installed at levels 2 (indoor) and 1 (outdoor), respectively, measuring the surface temperature of the wall. Data are consecutively stored in separate files containing 30 minute acceleration time series with a sampling frequency of 100 Hz, while temperature data are recorded with a sampling frequency of 0.1 Hz. A wi-fi data connection allows to transfer the data from the tower to the Laboratory of Structural Dynamics of University of Perugia, located at a distance of about 2.5 km, where they are stored and processed. Multiple linear regressive filters are adopted to take into account and remove the effects of changes in environmental conditions.

From January 16th to January 23th 2017 the tower has been preliminary monitored for one week, using accelerometers A4, A5 and A6 (see Fig. 2). On January 18th 2017, a seismic sequence occurred with epicenters close to L'Aquila, in central Italy, at about 100 km distance from the Sciri tower. Four main shocks with moment magnitude greater than 5 have been recorded from 09:25 to 13:33 UTC (Montereale: at 9:25 a.m., Mw 5.3; Capitignano: 10:14 a.m., Mw 5.4; Capitignano: 10:25 a.m., Mw 5.3; Cagnano Amiterno: 13:33 a.m., Mw 5.1). The seismic events led to non negligible variations of the natural frequencies of the tower. Figs. 3a)-b) show the time histories of the natural frequencies of vibration of six modes of the tower continuously identified and tracked during the preliminary monitoring period (modes Fx1, Fy1, Fx2, Fy2, Tz1 and Fy3) from January 16th to January 23th 2017. As it is visible

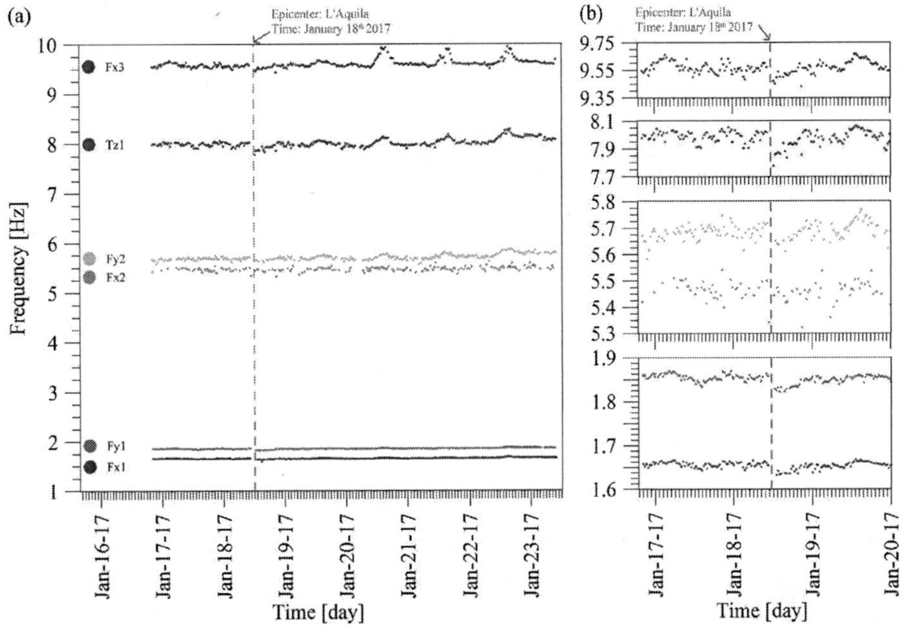

Figure 3: Frequency tracking from January 16th to January 23rd, 2017.

Table 2: Frequency decays during seismic sequence of January 18th 2017.

Mode no.	1	2	3	4	5	6
$(\Delta f_i/f_i)^{\text{exp}}$ [%]	1.27	1.48	0.71	1.01	1.14	1.10

from the figures, the seismic events clearly led to small frequency decays. Table 2 reports the relative frequency decays after the first two seismic events.

4. FINITE ELEMENT MODEL AND SURROGATE MODEL

A 3D Finite Element Model of the Sciri tower and of the surrounding aggregate has been built by using the ABAQUS 6.10 platform [12] (Fig. 4). A free meshing of solid tetrahedral elements, with mean elements' dimension of about 50 cm, has been adopted. Floors and walls of the tower and of the surrounding buildings have been included in the model and the whole structure has been assumed fixed to the ground, considering soil-structure interaction as negligible [13]. For FEM tuning, the model has been partitioned into several regions to allow discrimination of the materials of the walls and floors and an accurate calibration, through sensitivity analysis, has been carried out. The initial mechanical parameters of the material, assumed with isotropic constitutive behavior, are computed for square stone masonry according to the Italian technical standard code [14], as explained in [15]. Table 3 summarizes the initial and the updated values of the uncertain parameters before and after calibration. Table 4 summarizes the comparison between the target frequencies (denoted as $f_{i,20°C}^{\text{MLR}}$) and those numerically predicted from the tuned FE model (f_i^{FEM}).

In order to construct the surrogate model, the FE model (tower and building aggregate) has been subdivided in four macroelements, as illustrated in Fig. (4c): i) Macroelement 1 (M1): the building aggregate and a portion of the tower up to the top height of the roof of the same aggregate (0-18.9 m); ii) Macroelement 2 (M2): the portion of the tower between the height of 18.9 and 26.8 m; iii) Macroelement 3 (M3): the portion of the tower between the height of 26.8 and 33.8 m; iv) Macroelement 4 (M4): the portion of the tower between the height of 33.8 and 41.0 m. The damage-dependent parameters to be identified are

Table 3: Mechanical parameters of the FE model before and after tuning.

	Young's modulus E $[kN/m^2]$	Shear modulus G $[kN/m^2]$	Poisson's ratio ν []	Mass density w $[t/m^3]$
before tuning	4.032e+06	1.612e+06	0.25	2.20
after tuning	5.77e+06	2.308e+06	0.25	2.20

Table 4: Comparison between experimental and numerical modal parameters after tuning.

Mode	$f_{i,20°C}^{MLR}$ [Hz]	f_i^{FEM} [Hz]	$\Delta f_i/f_i$ [%]	MAC []
Fx1	1.722	1.754	1.870	0.970
Fy1	1.925	1.967	2.140	0.973
Fx2	5.615	5.770	2.757	0.972
Fy2	6.006	6.195	3.152	0.651
Tz1	8.399	8.005	-4.686	0.747
Fx3	9.896	9.894	-0.022	0.965
Fy3	10.928	10.858	-0.641	0.840
			$(\Delta f/f)_{mean} = 2.181\%$	MAC_{mean}=0.874

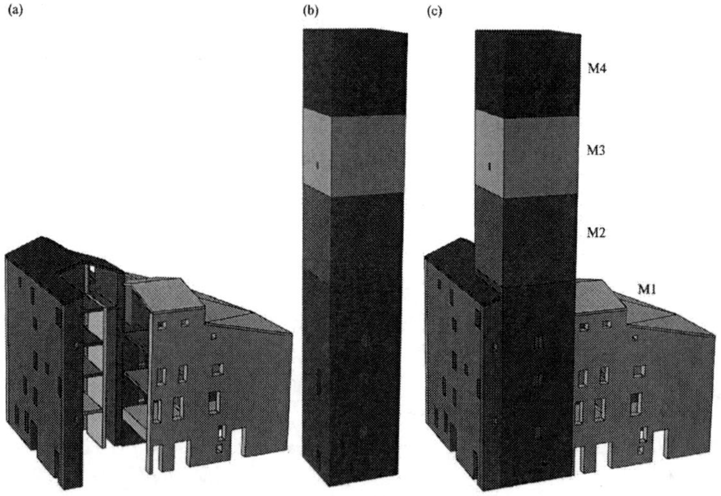

Figure 4: Finite element model of the aggregate (a), the Sciri tower (b) and the whole building (c).

Table 5: Results of the damage localization procedure.

An.	α	β	J_{opt}	Δk [%]	ΔE_2 [%]	ΔE_3 [%]	ΔE_4 [%]	f_i^{FEM} [Hz]	MAC []
1	1	0	0.01	-0.80	-0.02	0.00	0.00	1.751;1.963;5.758;6.185;7.994;9.863	0.970;0.973;0.972;0.652;0.745;0.964
2	1	1	0.74	-0.80	-0.02	-0.01	0.00	1.751;1.963;5.758;6.185;7.994;9.863	0.970;0.973;0.972;0.652;0.745;0.964
3	1	5	3.60	19.10	-0.03	-0.02	-0.01	1.812;2.028;5.957;6.388;8.208;9.808	0.973;0.976;0.969;0.657;0.758;0.982
4	1	10	7.01	21.90	-0.03	-0.02	-0.01	1.817;2.034;5.971;6.409;8.228;9.661	0.974;0.978;0.968;0.662;0.754;0.984
5	0	1	0.68	23.70	-0.03	-0.02	-0.01	1.820;2.037;5.978;6.422;8.241;9.549	0.975;0.979;0.966;0.666;0.750;0.984
6	5	1	0.80	-0.80	-0.03	0.00	0.00	1.751;1.963;5.758;6.185;7.994;9.863	0.970;0.973;0.972;0.652;0.745;0.964
7	10	1	0.88	-0.80	-0.03	-0.01	0.00	1.751;1.963;5.758;6.185;7.994;9.863	0.970;0.973;0.972;0.652;0.745;0.964

collected in the vector of the design variables of the optimization problem $\mathbf{U}$, as follows:

$$\mathbf{U} = (k, E_2, E_3, E_4) \tag{4}$$

where k is a coefficient that multiplies the elastic moduli of all the walls belonging to M1 of the FE model and E_i (i=2,3,4) are the elastic moduli of masonry of M2, M3 and M4, respectively. The variation of the components of vector $\mathbf{U}$ with respect to initial values, identified by the damage localization procedure, is related to the occurrence of damage in the structure. The coefficients of the quadratic model (Eqs. (3)), $A_{i,j}$, $B_{i,j}$, C_i, $D_{i,j}$, $E_{i,j}$, F_i, with $i = 1, ..., l$, (l the number of identified modes) and $i = 1, ..., n$, (n the total number of uncertain parameters) are computed through finite difference analysis. Each component of $\mathbf{U}$ is varied by $\pm 5\%$ and the corresponding natural frequencies are computed from the FE model. The coefficients of the quadratic model are computed by imposing equivalence between the first and second derivative of $f_i^{\mathbf{FEM}}$ and $\Phi_i^{\mathbf{FEM}}$, expressed in terms of the unknown coefficients, with the first and second order finite differences obtained from the analysis. The assumption of quadratic equations to describe the relationship between the design variables and the modal parameters is verified through a preliminary parametric analysis.

5. RESULTS OF DAMAGE DETECTION AND LOCALIZATION

The proposed methodology for damage detection and localization has been applied in order to assess the damage occurred as a consequence of the seismic sequence of January 18th. An optimization procedure has been carried out to minimize the objective function (Eqs. 1 and 2). In Eq. (2), the experimental frequency decays, $\Delta f_i / f_i^{exp}$ are those reported in Table 2, the experimental natural frequencies can be found in Table 4, while the MAC are computed using the experimental modal shapes and those computed with the surrogate equations. The selected optimization algorithm is the genetic algorithm that allows to find a global minimum for the objective function. The optimization has been repeated by adopting different values of the coefficients α and β, in order to weight differently the two terms of Eq. (1). Table 5 reports the results of the damage localization procedure. The obtained relative variation of k (-0.80%) is much higher than those of E_2, E_2, and E_3, thus indicating that the slight damage is mainly localized in Macroelement 1, in the lower part of the structure (Fig. 4c)). This is probably due to the fact that, during the seismic event, the different deformations of the tower and the surrounding building aggregate led to slight deterioration of the connection between the two parts of the structure. Conversely, the damage to the Macroelement 4, at the top of the structure, is almost negligible.

6. RESULTS VALIDATION THROUGH NONLINEAR DYNAMIC ANALYSIS AND IN-SITU VISUAL INSPECTIONS

In order to validate the proposed improved methodology for earthquake-induced damage detection and localization, a non-linear dynamic FE analysis has been carried out. In order to reproduce the non-linear mechanical behavior of the masonry, the classic concrete damage plasticity (CDP) model [16] for cyclic loading and damage implementation, with tension and compression damage, has been used [17]. The behavior of the masonry has been reproduced up to the ultimate limit state, considering damage in tension. Given the lack of results of specific tests carried out on site, the mechanical properties assigned to

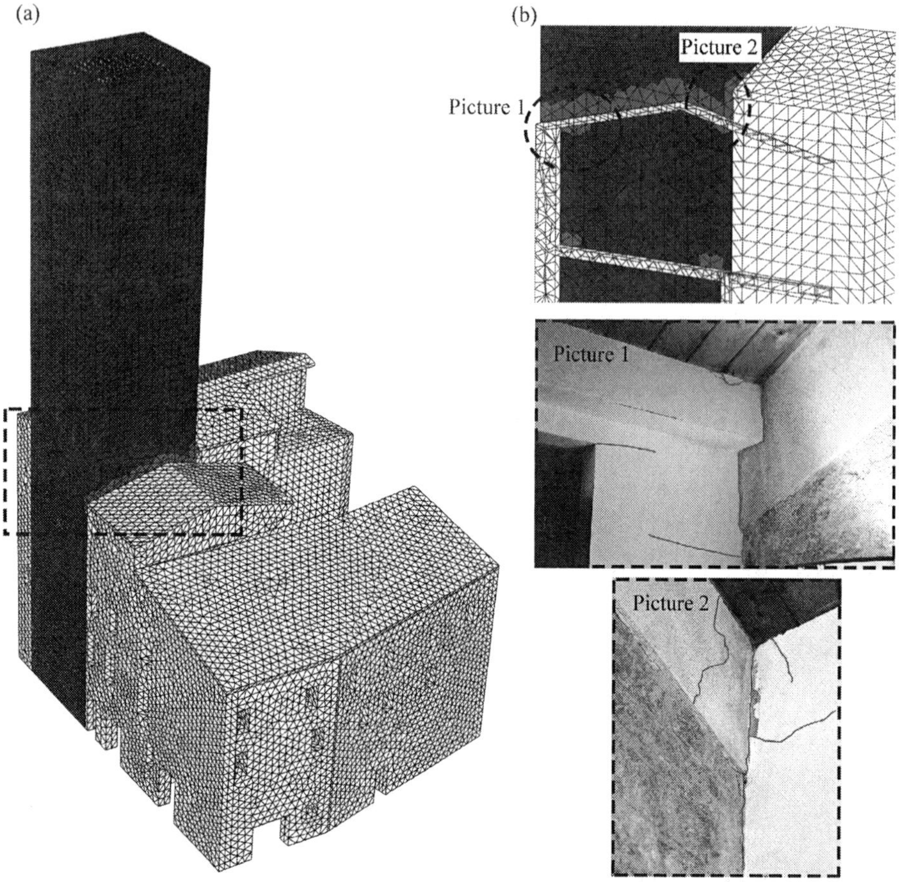

Figure 5: Results of nonlinear dynamic analysis obtained from the sequential application of the two main shocks of January 18th 2017: general overview of the damaged FE model (a), zoom of damage in the West façade in correspondence to the roof with some picture evidence (b).

the materials in different portions of the structure have been estimated from the literature.
The accelerograms of the two main shocks of January 18th 2017 seismic sequence recorded by the seismic station closest to the Sciri tower, i.e. Castelnuovo-Assisi, have been used as inputs for the analysis. Such ground motion waveforms have been scaled in order to reproduce the experimental Peak Response Accelerations measured on top of the tower.
Non-linear dynamic analyses have been carried out to localize earthquake-induced damage by considering the two main scaled waveforms concatenated. Fig. 5 shows the map of the tension damage of the FE numerical model, obtained by the numerical analysis. Some small damage is localized at the contact between the tower and the building aggregate, at the outer corners of the tower (internally to the aggregate) and in correspondence to the horizontal elements and structural walls). Visual inspections, carried out by the authors, revealed a limited, but clearly visible, damage state in the aforementioned contact points between the tower and the aggregate, that has been reported by building occupants as occurred after the 2016-2017 Central Italy seismic sequence (Fig. 5b)). Therefore, the results of the non-linear dynamic analysis confirm those obtained from the localization procedure and evidence provided by in-situ visual inspections.

7. CONCLUSIONS

The paper presents a methodology for earthquake-induced damage detection and localization in masonry towers using long-term vibration monitoring data and numerical modeling. The methodology has been applied to the case study of the *Sciri Tower*, an historic civic masonry tower located in Perugia, Italy, continuously monitored for 10 months. Data have been used to perform online identification in order to track the evolution of modal parameters with time. A Multiple Linear Regressive model has been used to remove the effects of changing environmental conditions on natural frequencies. The damage localization task has been performed by solving an inverse FE model calibration problem, where equivalent elastic properties of macrostructual elements have been identified by minimizing an objective function of experimentally identified and numerically predicted damage-induced decays in natural frequencies and changes in eigenvector components. To minimize the computational effort of this calibration procedure, a quadratic surrogate model has been constructed using a tuned numerical FE model of the structure. Frequency decays observed after the far-field earthquake have been used to localize possible earthquake-induced damage. The results have been validated by using a non-linear dynamic analysis and visual inspections. It is demonstrated that the proposed procedure is capable of correctly localizing earthquake-induced damage at the connection between the tower and the aggregate, that was also confirmed by visual inspections.

ACKNOWLEDGEMENTS

This project has received funding from the European Union's Framework Programme for Research and Innovation HORIZON 2020 under grant agreement No 700395.

REFERENCES

[1] Alvandi, A. and Cremona, C. (2006) Assessment of vibration-based damage identification techniques. *Journal of Sound and Vibration*, 292(1-2), 179-202.

[2] Ramos, L.F. and Marques, L. and Lourenço, P.B. and De Roeck, G. and Campos-Costa, A. and Roque, J. (2010) Monitoring historical masonry structures with operational modal analysis: Two case studies. *Mechanical Systems and Signal Processing*, 24(5), 1291-1305.

[3] Masciotta, M.G. and Ramos, L.F. and Lourenço, P.B. (2017) The importance of structural monitoring as a diagnosis and control tool in the restoration process of heritage structures: A case study in Portugal. *Journal of Cultural Heritage*, 27, 36-47.

[4] Ubertini, F. and Cavalagli, N. and Kita, A. and Comanducci, G. (2018) Assessment of a monumental masonry bell-tower after 2016 Central Italy seismic sequence by long-term SHM. *Bulletin of Earthquake Engineering*, 16, 775-801.

[5] Saisi, A. and Gentile, C. and Guidobaldi, A. (2015) Post-earthquake continuous dynamic monitoring of the Gabbia Tower in Mantua, Italy. *Construction and Building Materials*, 81, 101-112.

[6] Ditommaso, R. and Mucciarelli, M. and Parolai, S. and Picozzi, M. (2012) Monitoring the structural dynamic response of a masonry tower: comparing classical and time-frequency analyses. *Bulletin of Earthquake Engineering*, 10(4), 1221-1235.

[7] Formisano, A. (2017) Theoretical and Numerical Seismic Analysis of Masonry Building Aggregates: Case Studies in San Pio Delle Camere (L'Aquila, Italy). *Journal of Earthquake Engineering*, 21(2), 227-245.

[8] Cabboi, A. and Gentile, C. and Saisi, A. (2017) From continuous vibration monitoring to FEM-based damage assessment: Application on a stone-masonry tower. *Construction and Building Materials*, 156, 252-265.

[9] Ubertini, F. and Carmelo, G. and Materazzi, A.L. (2013) Automated modal identification in operational conditions and its application to bridges. *Engineering Structures*, 46, 264-278.

[10] Ubertini, F. and Comanducci, G. and Cavalagli, N. and Pisello, A.L. and Materazzi, A.L. and Cotana, F. (2017) Environmental effects on natural frequencies of the San Pietro bell tower in Perugia, Italy, and their removal for structural performance assessment. *Mechanical Systems and Signal Processing*, 82, 307-322.

[11] Venanzi, I. and Materazzi, A.L. and Ierimonti, L. (2015) Robust and reliable optimization of wind excited cable-stayed masts. *Journal of Wind Engineering and Industrial Aerodynamics*, 147, 368-379.

[12] , Simulia, corp. (2010) *Abaqus Analysis User's Manual. Volume III: Materials*. Dessault Systèmes, USA.

[13] Venanzi, I. and Salciarini, D. and Tamagnini, C. (2014) The effect of soil-foundation-structure interaction on the wind-induced response of tall buildings. *Engineering Structures*, 79, 117-130.

[14] , Ministero delle Infrastrutture e dei Trasporti, (2018) *Nuove norme tecniche per le costruzioni. Decreto 14 gennaio 2008*. Supplemento ordinario alla Gazzetta Ufficiale.

[15] Cavalagli, N. and Comanducci, G. and Ubertini, F. (2018) Earthquake-Induced Damage Detection in a Monumental Masonry Bell-Tower Using Long-Term Dynamic Monitoring Data. *Journal of Earthquake Engineering*, 22(suppl), 96-119.

[16] Lubliner, J. and Olive, J. and Oller, S. and Onate E. (1989) A Plastic-Damage Model for Concrete. *International Journal of Solids and Structures*, 25(3), 229-326.

[17] Valente, M. and Milani, G. (2016) Seismic assessment of historical masonry towers by means of simplified approaches and standard (FEM). *Construction and Building Materials*, 108, 74-104.

IOMAC'19

8th International Operational Modal Analysis Conference

2019 May13-15 Copenhagen

DAMAGE DETECTION UNDER PROGRESSIVE OPERATIONAL DEGRADATION OF STRUCTURES IN REAL TIME

Basuraj Bhowmik[1], Tapas Tripura[2], Budhaditya Hazra[3] and Vikram Pakrashi[4]

[1]PhD, Department of Civil Engineering, Indian Institute of Technology, Guwahati, Assam, India; basurajbhowmik@gmail.com.
[2]Masters student, Department of Civil Engineering, Indian Institute of Technology, Guwahati, Assam, India; tripuratapas@gmail.com.
[3]Assistant Professor, Department of Civil Engineering, Indian Institute of Technology, Guwahati, Assam, India; budhaditya.hazra@iitg.ac.in.
[4]Assistant Professor, School of Mechanical and Materials Engineering, University College Dublin, Ireland; vikram.pakrashi@ucd.ie.

ABSTRACT

The importance of real time structural health monitoring (SHM) can be envisaged from recent infrastructural mishaps that left disasters in its wake and incurred socio-economic losses worldwide. Sudden collapse of bridges due to excess operational design load and steady degradation of buildings due to excitations are real time events that require online algorithms to assess their detrimental effects. The paper demonstrates the applicability of real time algorithms universally formulated under the broad spectrum of first order eigen perturbation (FOEP) methods. The effect of nonlinearity change due to progressive degradation of a numerically simulated base-isolated system is considered. Using time series models in conjunction with FOEP algorithms, the paper proposes to effectively capture the progressive deterioration incurred due to steady loss in stiffness, accumulation of fatigue and/or creep, leading to crack propagation. The applicability of FOEP techniques in assessing progressive damage renders their utility as ideal candidates for real time SHM.

Keywords: Structural degradation, deterioration, real time, first order eigen perturbation, recursive canonical correlation analysis

1. INTRODUCTION

Degradation of a system is an inherent process that is influenced by internal resistance and external factors including environmental, operational conditions with varying levels of excitation [1-3]. Degradation, such as damage accumulation over time, results in an irreversible process that decreases the system ability to withstand sustained loading. Repeated cycles of loading over time leads to failure when the accumulated damage exceeds the bearing threshold level for the system, thereby compromising its reliability [4]. Therefore, it becomes imperative to understand and model the degradation patterns of the system to prevent potential performance failures and avoid subsequent socio-economic losses. In order to carry out a continuous monitoring process for systems subjected to varying levels of excitation, techniques that provide in-situ estimation of system's health needs to be employed. As most of the existing monitoring processes are *offline* in nature, the need for developing *real time* algorithms is of paramount importance [5-7]. In this paper, monitoring of systems based on real time methodologies centred around *first order eigen perturbation* (FOEP) techniques is provided.

Dynamic excitation of engineering systems causes irreversible changes to the material behaviour that decreases the system's capability to carry the intended loading. As damage manifests itself primarily in deteriorating levels of stiffness, a simultaneous fatigue process is triggered due to cyclic patterns of loading, often leading to creep and other detrimental effects [1]. It becomes clear that an adequate approach should account for the joint treatment of both the system dynamics and its corresponding deterioration process. Monitoring techniques involving scrutinizing crack propagation paths, changes in operational temperature conditions and excess of vibration in rotating components, provide data patterns to identify the condition of a system [2]. In comparison with failure data, operational degradation data provide crucial information on the failure behaviour of a system that can expedite reliability assessment and logistic decision regarding the state of the structure. Therefore, it becomes necessary that the vibrating systems are continuously monitored to identify the minute changes in its operational condition. Towards this, real time approaches that provide on-site estimation of the system health are developed in this paper using the principles of *recursive canonical correlation analysis* (RCCA).

A survey of literature reveals that the existing monitoring schemes are primarily offline in nature that requires the data to be gathered in the first step and processed in the next [1-4]. To provide early warning and ascertain the safety of the individuals near the monitored system, early detection approaches based on real life data should be developed. In this paper, an attempt has been made to identify the degrading patterns of damage of vibrating systems using RCCA, which is pivoted around the concepts of FOEP approaches [5-7]. The method utilizes the output responses obtained from an array of sensors in real time and provides transformed responses at each time stamp. In the process of updating the eigenspace characteristics of the covariance estimate, recursive damage sensitive features (RDSFs) track its evolution that effectively aids in detecting damage in real time [6]. The objective of the present work is to expound the applicability of real time approaches such as RCCA to monitor a vibrating system undergoing a state of degradation and eventually, a collapse. Numerical simulations contemplating the aforesaid scenario, backed by sufficient experimental evidence on a 2-storey model, demonstrate the efficacy of the proposed RCCA based scheme in detecting degradation patterns in real time.

2. RECURSIVE CANONICAL CORRELATION ANALYSIS (RCCA)

Canonical correlation analysis (CCA) is an exploratory tool widely used in statistical signal processing [8]. Blind source separation (BSS) based formulation of CCA has found widespread application in detecting damage in dynamic systems and identifying structural modal parameters [9]. As the application of these methods utilize gathered data to identify the dynamic parameters of a system, implementation towards continuous monitoring of structures subjected to continuous degradation, is hindered. To tailor traditional CCA towards a recursive implementation, techniques based on FOEP that provide recursive eigenspace estimates at each sample point, is discussed. The RCCA based approach updates the eigenspace at each instant of time which subsequently provides information regarding the state of the monitored infrastructure [7]. An important aspect to be considered here is that the FOEP based RCCA method updates the *eigenspace characteristics* at each time instant, instead of updating the block covariance matrices $\begin{bmatrix} 0 & \mathbf{C_{xy}} \\ \mathbf{C_{xy}} & 0 \end{bmatrix}$ and $\begin{bmatrix} \mathbf{C}_{xx} & 0 \\ 0 & \mathbf{C}_{yy} \end{bmatrix}$ for a general vector valued multivariate data $\boldsymbol{X}$ and $\mathbf{Y}$ thereby reducing the time complexity of the recursive implementation [5-7].

2.1. RCCA: Derivation

The theoretical treatment of RCCA is derived from estimating the eigenspace updates using the FOEP approach. Towards this are recursive implementation of RCCA the matrices $\mathbf{C_{xx}}$ and $\mathbf{C_{xy}}$ are expressed for $(k+1)^{th}$ instant in terms of their estimates at k^{th} instant using the following equation

$$\mathbf{C}_{\mathrm{xx}}(k+1) = \frac{k}{k+1}\mathbf{C}_{\mathrm{xx}}(k) + \frac{1}{k+1}\mathbf{X}_{\mathrm{k+1}}\mathbf{X}_{\mathrm{k+1}}^{\mathrm{T}}$$

$$\mathbf{C}_{\mathrm{xy}}(k+1) = \frac{k}{k+1}\mathbf{C}_{\mathrm{xy}}(k) + \frac{1}{k+1}\mathbf{X}_{\mathrm{k+1}}\mathbf{Y}_{\mathrm{k+1}}^{\mathrm{T}} \tag{1}$$

It should be noted that the FOEP based formulation does not take into consideration the nature of the involved dataset and can effectively provide recursive estimates for both stationary and non-stationary processes [7]. The approach being purely data-driven in nature, it can effectively account for the indeterministic patterns of deterioration for a system. As CCA accommodates block covariance estimates, it can be inferred that its recursive variant can effectively provide detection results for multi-directional dependencies as well. Considering the evolution of data from zero mean process, the eigen decomposition of the covariance estimate at the $(k+1)^{th}$ instant ($\mathbf{C}_{\mathrm{xx}}(k+1)$) can be obtained as:

$$\boldsymbol{\Phi}_{k+1}\boldsymbol{E}_{k+1}\boldsymbol{\Phi}_{k+1}^{T} = \frac{1}{k+1}\boldsymbol{\Phi}_{k}\left[(k)\boldsymbol{E}_{k} + \boldsymbol{v}_{k+1}\boldsymbol{v}_{k+1}^{T}\right]\boldsymbol{\Phi}_{k}^{T} \tag{2}$$

where, the POC vector at the $k+1^{th}$ time stamp is given by: $\boldsymbol{v}_{k+1} = \boldsymbol{\Phi}_{k}^{T}\boldsymbol{X}_{k+1}$.

On examining the term $(k)\boldsymbol{E}_{k} + \boldsymbol{v}_{k+1}\boldsymbol{v}_{k+1}^{T}$, one can easily observe that it bears a diagonally dominant structure. This can be validated by the fact that the eigenvalues of the term are close to the diagonal portion and the eigenvectors can be approximated to unity. This ensures the use of Gershgorin's theorem to evaluate the EVD of this term (of the form $\boldsymbol{\Sigma}_{k+1}\boldsymbol{\Lambda}_{k+1}\boldsymbol{\Sigma}_{k+1}^{T}$) for low to moderate values of damping and for finite sample size of the response, obtained as [5]:

$$\boldsymbol{\Phi}_{k+1}\boldsymbol{E}_{k+1}\boldsymbol{\Phi}_{k+1}^{T} = \frac{1}{k+1}[\boldsymbol{\Phi}_{k}\boldsymbol{\Sigma}_{k+1}][\boldsymbol{\Lambda}_{k+1}][\boldsymbol{\Phi}_{k}\boldsymbol{\Sigma}_{k+1}]^{T} \tag{3}$$

Thereby yielding the following set of recursively updated eigenspace at each time stamp:

$$\left.\begin{aligned}\boldsymbol{\Phi}_{k+1} &= \boldsymbol{\Phi}_{k}\boldsymbol{\Sigma}_{k+1}\\ \boldsymbol{E}_{k+1} &= \frac{\boldsymbol{\Lambda}_{k+1}}{k+1}\end{aligned}\right\} \tag{4}$$

The above derivation for RCCA is based on the premise that the excitation on the dynamical system is uniaxial. However, as CCA deals with block covariance matrices, it can be inferred that its recursive variation will be able to accommodate the eigenspace estimates for multi-directional dependencies as well [9]. In order to understand the structure of the matrices for multiple excitation sources, consider the basic CCA equation for k^{th} sample point as:

$$\boldsymbol{R}(k)\boldsymbol{z}(k) = \boldsymbol{\gamma}(k)\boldsymbol{S}(k)\boldsymbol{z}(k) \tag{5}$$

Where, $\boldsymbol{R}$ and $\mathbf{S}$ are block covariance matrices that can be expressed as: $\mathbf{R} = \begin{bmatrix} 0 & \mathbf{C_{xy}} \\ \mathbf{C_{xy}} & 0 \end{bmatrix}$ and $\mathbf{S} = \begin{bmatrix} \mathbf{C}_{xx} & 0 \\ 0 & \mathbf{C}_{yy} \end{bmatrix}$. The rank one update using FOEP provides recursive eigenspace at every time instant. Conforming to this notion, the perturbed eigen decomposition can be obtained as:

$$(\boldsymbol{R} + \boldsymbol{\Delta R})(\boldsymbol{z} + \boldsymbol{\Delta z}) = (\boldsymbol{\gamma} + \boldsymbol{\Delta\gamma})(\boldsymbol{S} + \boldsymbol{\Delta S})(\boldsymbol{z} + \boldsymbol{\Delta z}) \tag{6}$$

Recognizing the negligible magnitude of the perturbed matrices, each of the perturbations correspond to obtaining the matrices at the $k+1^{th}$ time instant that underlies the key essence of the FOEP approach. The corresponding eigen decomposition therefore, aligns with the case of a generalized EVD, and can be expressed as:

$$\boldsymbol{z}(k+1) = \boldsymbol{\gamma}(k+1)\boldsymbol{R}(k+1)^{-\mathbf{1}}\boldsymbol{S}(k+1)\boldsymbol{z}(k+1) \tag{7}$$

The above structure forms the basis of the multi-directional capabilities that RCCA can accommodate. Using Woodbury's identity, the solution to generalized EVD can be obtained. This matrix structure provides evidence to the ability of RCCA to accommodate cases involving multi-directional dependencies.

3. RECURSIVE DAMAGE SENSITIVE FEATURES

The proposed RCCA method provides eigenspace updates recursively, at each time stamp. As the eigenspace by itself is not enough to capture the degradation events, RDSFs are employed that tracks the behaviour of damage patterns. In this work, the primary RDSF considered is the evolution of time varying auto regressive (TVAR) coefficients that are modelled on the transformed responses.

3.1. TVAR coefficients

The use of TVAR coefficients as an effective RDSF has been well cited in the literature [5,7]. The proposed RCCA based approach generates the transformed responses online on to which time series models are fit. As the damage occurring to a dynamic system is a real time event, the use of TVAR models to capture an online event is therefore, justified. The plots of TVAR coefficients undergo a change in the mean level at the onset of a damage. The near mono-component nature of the transformed response ensures that low model order is sufficient to capture its dynamics; therefore, in the proposed framework, a model order of 2 (two) is pre-selected for all the cases. The basic time series fit for a TVAR model can be expressed as [5,7]:

$$\boldsymbol{\mu}(k+2) = \boldsymbol{a}_1(k+2)\boldsymbol{\mu}(k+1) + \boldsymbol{a}_2(k+2)\boldsymbol{\mu}(k) + \boldsymbol{\varepsilon}(k+2) \tag{8}$$

Here, $\boldsymbol{a}_1(k+2)$ and $\boldsymbol{a}_2(k+2)$ are the associated TVAR coefficients and the error arising due to modelling is represented by $\boldsymbol{\varepsilon}(k+2)$ which is inconsequential, considering its negligible magnitude. As these coefficients are expected to show alterations in their values at the instant of damage, tracking them in real time serves as a RDSF.

4. PROPOSED ALGORITHM

The proposed RCCA approach detects gradually degrading behaviour of systems subjected to repeated excitation. The algorithm provides a set of transformed response at the onset of each streaming data. The eigenspace spanned by the block covariance estimate gets updated online. The RDSFs monitor the characteristic of the eigenspace and manifest as undulations when visually examined. The instant of damage along with the location of its possible occurrence can be eventually justified using the RDSF plots.

The basic steps of the proposed method are enumerated below for reference:

(i) First, traditional CCA is employed on some initial data points (around 100 in number) to estimate the initial eigenspace. The number of data points chosen are pre-selected, only used for initial stabilizing and subsequent calculations for the recursive approach.

(ii) The RCCA algorithm operates on the real time streaming of the input data which generates a set of transformed response at each time stamp.

(iii) The set of transformed responses are fit with suitable time series models from which TVAR plots are obtained. This acts as RDSF plot for determining the degrading state of the system.

(iv) Once the RDSF identifies the onset of degradation, it proceeds by fitting time series models on to the neighbouring degrees of freedom (DOF). The cumulative event of the possible degradation of the floors is then examined in a recursive framework to justify the extent of deterioration the system has undergone.

5. NUMERICAL CASE STUDY

To illustrate the application of the proposed RCCA based damage identification method, a numerical simulation is performed on a 5-DOF system modelled with a Buoc-Wen (B-W) oscillator at its base. Temporal damage to the system is considered by altering the nonlinear force term at the base of the model. The governing differential equation of the oscillator can be expressed by:

$$\boldsymbol{M}\ddot{\boldsymbol{X}} + \boldsymbol{C}\dot{\boldsymbol{X}} + \boldsymbol{K}\boldsymbol{X} = \boldsymbol{\Gamma F} - \boldsymbol{M I}\ddot{\boldsymbol{X}}_g \tag{9}$$

The numerical values for the assembled mass (**M**), damping (**C**), and stiffness (**K**) matrices respectively, can be found in Bhowmik et al. [7]. In Eq. (9), Γ represents the location of the base at the point of application of the nonlinear force (f) due to the LRB base isolator, given by:

$$f = \kappa \boldsymbol{Z Q}_{pb} - k_b \boldsymbol{X}_b - c_b \dot{\boldsymbol{X}}_b \tag{10}$$

The quantities $k_b and\ c_b$ represent the base shear stiffness and the damping, respectively, while the parameter $\boldsymbol{Q}_{pb} = \left(1 - \frac{k_{yield}}{k_{initial}}\right) \boldsymbol{Q}_y$, with $\boldsymbol{Q}_y$ as the yield force. The term κ controls the level of nonlinearity associated with the system. A change in the level of the nonlinear force parameter induces a global damage to the system which is permanent in nature and does not wear off as time progresses. The relations for the evolutionary variable can be found in [7] and is not reported here for brevity.

5.1. Spatial damage detection results

The numerically simulated B-W system is inflicted with a discreet local damage that progresses over the passage of time. This corresponds to a degradation event where the top floor of a building supposedly collapses at the onset of an earthquake of a strong magnitude. As the deterioration of the system is not arrested spontaneously, the effect of the collapse is reflected onto the next DOF which might suffer a lower percentage of damage. The same phenomena continue until the remainder of the excitation or the collapse event terminates due to resistive stiffness of the members. In order to understand the applicability of the proposed method towards detecting such events in real time, consider the B-W model to undergo a reduction in the top floor by 70% at 10s into the excitation phase. The collapse event is simulated to continue to the fourth floor where the storey suffers a 50% damage at 20s. The progression of events cumulates onto the third floor at 30s and the second floor at 35s, where the respective levels of degradation attenuate at 30% and 10%, respectively.

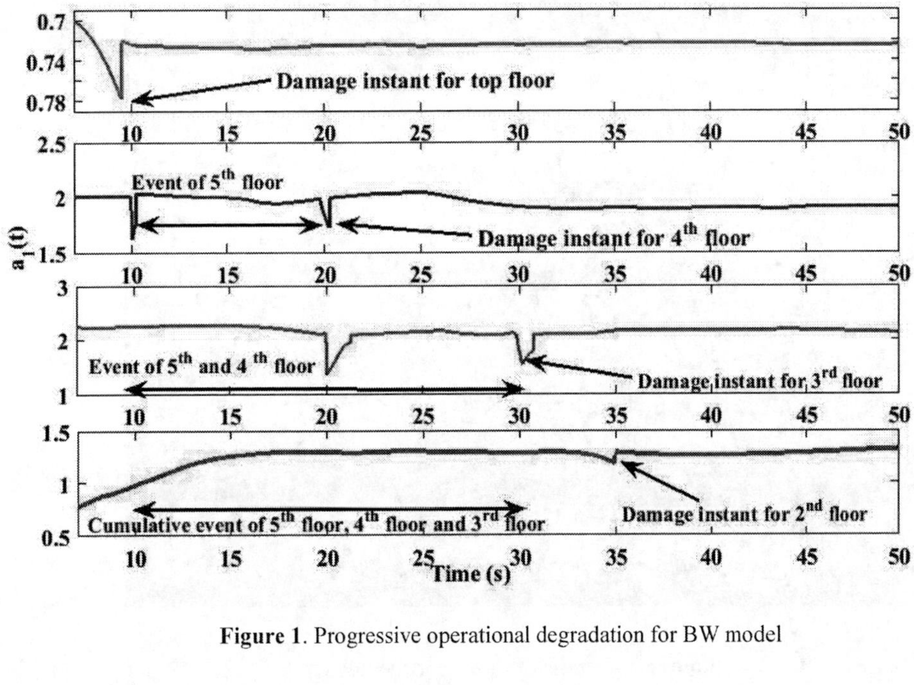

Figure 1. Progressive operational degradation for BW model

The application of the proposed RCCA method provides transformed responses corresponding to each floor level. From the plot of the TVAR coefficient shown in Figure 1, the absence of any activity before the 10s mark indicates that no damage has occurred prior to that instant. A sudden spike in the mean level of the plot at 10s confirms the onset of degradation. The succeeding plot shows a clear peak at 20s, which indicates the intrusion of damage onto the structural members at that instant but the resulting activities prior to the time stamp indicate the cumulative event that both the floors have suffered. The same notion can be applied when the TVAR plot for the third floor indicates a cumulative event of all the floors combined and demarcates the individual event of a 30% damage at the 30s mark. Proceeding to the second floor, the wavy undulations of the TVAR plot indicates the cumulative event of the damage event of all the floors. It should, however, be noted that identification of a low level of damage of the order of 10% in real time is a difficult feat, especially when attempted in a real time framework. Based on the above findings, it becomes clear that the proposed RCCA method can detect operational degradation for a broad spectrum of damage levels in real time.

6. EXPERIMENTAL VERIFICATIONS

To substantiate the robustness of the proposed approach, an experimental setup is devised consisting of a two-storey aluminium shear building prototype placed with a water dispenser at its top floor. The model is bolted on top of a shake table, 1.5m high, with inter-storey distance of 0.74m fixed on a base plate. The water dispenser of height 0.26m is firmly affixed to the roof plate using commercially available epoxy resin, as shown in Figure 2. The experimental setup is excited using Gaussian broadband noise and the streaming acceleration data are collected using *QuantumX MX410 HBM* Data Acquisition (DAQ) system at a sampling frequency of $400Hz$. The shear building model is instrumented at the floor levels in orthogonal directions using PCB Piezotronics triaxial accelerometers of sensitivity $100mV/g$, bearing a frequency range of $0.5 - 10000Hz$. The sloshing of the water in the dispenser during the vibratory motion of the setup provides nonlinearity. The flow of the water is controlled at 2L/min which can be considered as a steady degradation event, considering a dynamic mass loss in real time [10].

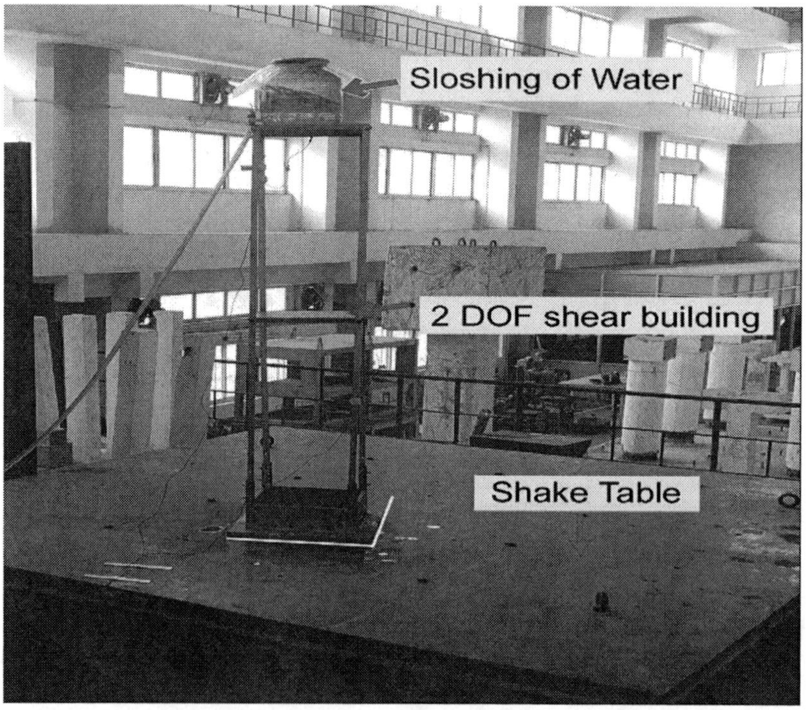

Figure 2. Details of the experimental setup

The main objective of this experimental trial is to assess the efficacy of the proposed algorithm for a multi-directional case, closely emulating a practical scenario, where the ground motions might excite a structure from a non-orthogonal alignment. The experimental trials were conducted with the model positioned at a non-orthogonal direction with respect to the global cartesian coordinates. The trials proceed by allowing the water to drain out at 0s from the start of the excitation. The response observed at the instrument end was provided as input to the proposed RCCA method to identify the degradation event, online. TVAR models on the transformed responses indicate the steady mass loss event through a consistent change in the mean level of the plot, as evident from Figures 3 and 4. In line with the experimental trials, the steady change in the mean level commences at 0s that continues for the remainder of the excitation, indicating that the water has completely drained out of the dispenser.

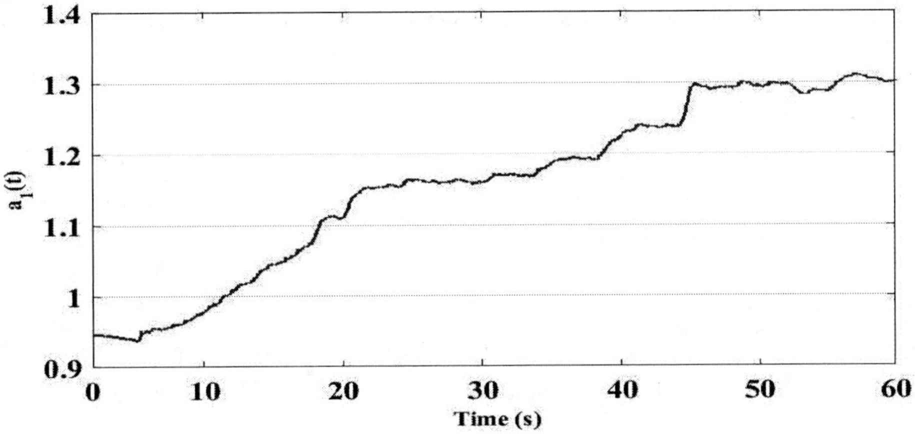

Figure 3. Plot of 1st TVAR coefficient for experimental trial.

It should be noted that the proposed method evidently accommodates multi-directional dependencies as observed through the trials. The experimental findings hold promise that RCCA algorithm can be applied for real life scenario involving studies on buildings subjected to excitation from randomly aligned orientations. Conforming to these findings, the robustness of the proposed method is eventually justified.

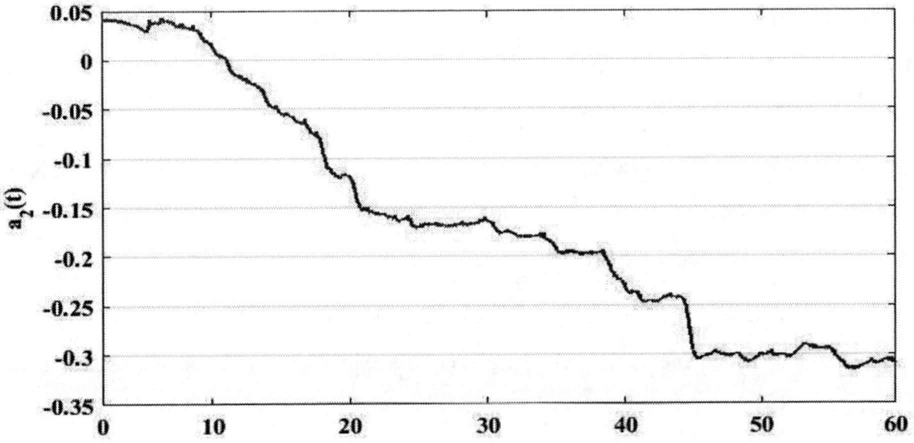

Figure 4. Plot of 2nd TVAR coefficient for experimental trial.

7. CONCLUSIONS

A real time approach using the principles of RCCA to capture the events of operational degradation is presented. The recursive eigenspace characteristics of the covariance matrix provide information regarding the state of the system, if inflicted with damage. Damage being a progressive event, requires algorithms to function in real time to efficiently capture the phenomenon. The authors have attempted to identify degradation patterns based on the principles of RCCA by extracting information from the recursive eigenspace updates that reflect the present health of a monitored system. The use of RDSFs such as TVAR coefficients provide real time updates of the state of the vibrating system. As previously mentioned, the sudden change in the mean level over time indicates the onset of damage to the system. The proposed method identifies progressive damage to a numerically simulated B-W model having a wide range of damage spectrum. Real time deterioration of the order of about 10% was successfully reported, which is difficult to attain in a recursive framework. Experimental case studies reveal that the method successfully accommodates multi-directional dependencies and yields accurate detection results for dynamically altering systems. Through the aid of RDSFs such as TVAR coefficients, the phenomenon of mass loss occurring to the experimental setup was accurately captured. Detection results for case studies with multi-directional dependencies provide substantial evidence that the FOEP based RCCA approach is capable to monitor real life engineering structures of larger magnitude. The applicability of the proposed method towards real life examples, case studies and benchmark data remain a future work to be addressed along these lines.

REFERENCES

[1] Sobczyk, K., & Spencer Jr, B. F. (2012). *Random fatigue: from data to theory*. Academic Press..

[2] Sobczyk, K. (2006). Stochastic dynamics and reliability of degrading systems. *TECHNICAL SCIENCES, 54*(1).

[3] Du, D. B., Zhang, J. X., Zhou, Z. J., Si, X. S., & Hu, C. H. (2018). Estimating Remaining Useful Life for Degrading Systems with Large Fluctuations. *Journal of Control Science and Engineering, 2018*.

[4] Shahraki, A. F., Yadav, O. P., & Liao, H. (2017). A review on degradation modelling and its engineering applications. *International Journal of Performability Engineering, 13*(3), 299.

[5] Krishnan, M., Bhowmik, B., Hazra, B., and Pakrashi, P, (2018). 'Real time damage detection using recursive principal components and time varying auto-regressive modeling', *Mechanical Systems and Signal Processing*, Volume 101, Elsevier, pp. 549 – 574.

[6] Krishnan, M., Bhowmik, B., Tiwari, AK., and Hazra, B. (2017). 'Online damage detection using recursive principal component analysis and recursive condition indicators,' *Smart Materials and Structures*, IOP Publishing. 26(8), 085017.

[7] Bhowmik, B., Krishnan, M., Hazra, B.,and Pakrashi, V. (2018) . 'Real time unified single and multi-channel structural damage detection using recursive singular spectrum analysis', *Structural Health Monitoring*, SAGE Publications. pp. 475921718760483, doi=10.1177/1475921718760483.

[8] Borga, M. (2001). Canonical correlation: a tutorial. On line tutorial *http://people. imt. liu. se/magnus/cca*. 4(5).

[9] Hazra B, Sadhu A, Roffel AJ and Narasimhan S. (2012) Hybrid Time-Frequency Blind Source Separation Towards Ambient System Identification of Structures, *Computer-Aided Civil and Infrastructure Engineering*, 27(5), pp. 314–332.

[10] Pakrashi, V., Fitzgerald, P., O'Leary, M., et al. "Assessment of structural nonlinearities employing extremes of dynamic responses". (2016) *Journal of Vibration and Control*; 24: 137–152.

IOMAC'19

8th International Operational Modal Analysis Conference
2019 May13-15 Copenhagen

HANKEL MATRIX NORMALIZATION FOR ROBUST DAMAGE DETECTION

Szymon Gres[1], Michael Döhler [2], Palle Andersen[3], Lars Damkilde[1], Laurent Mevel[2]

[1] Aalborg University, Department of Civil and Structural Engineering,
Thomas Manns Vej 23, 9000 Aalborg, Denmark

[2] Inria, Ifsttar, Univ. Rennes,
Campus de Beaulieu, 35042 Rennes, France

[3] Structural Vibration Solutions A/S,
NOVI Science Park, 9220 Aalborg, Denmark

ABSTRACT

In the context of detecting changes in structural systems, multiple vibration-based damage detection methods have been proposed and successfully applied to both mechanical and civil structures over the past years. One of the popular schemes is based on a robust subspace-based residual and enjoys favorable statistical and computational properties, like invariance to changes in the excitation covariance and numerical stability. This paper presents an alternative Gaussian residual that is based on the difference of normalized Hankel matrices between reference and damaged states, which can be easily computed. The statistical properties of the residual are reported and used for efficient hypothesis testing. Its robustness to excitation changes is shown. The proposed scheme is evaluated in numerical simulations, validating its robustness, and tested on real data sets from a full scale bridge.

Keywords: damage detection, hypothesis testing, robust residual, Hankel matrix normalization

1. INTRODUCTION

Monitoring of the structural integrity based on measurements refers to detecting changes with some damage-sensitive features derived from the data. In that context, many works employ modal parameter estimates e.g. natural frequencies [14], which can be evaluated for damages using control charts [10]. The evaluation of data-based residuals in context of SHM often relies on an outlier analysis [16], cointegration [4] and many other techniques from the statistical signal processing field.

The performance of modal parameter-based methods depends on several factors e.g. the quality of parameter estimation from the data and the ability to track the selected estimates after identifying them in the healthy state of the system. This, and the subsequent necessary automation, has been shown to be a complex task. Hence it is desirable to compute relevant features directly on the data without any need of modal parameter estimation. Together with a statistical evaluation of such features, it can yield automated damage detection. In addition to the statistical variability due to limited data length, those data-based damage features are inherently dependent on the natural changes in the ambient excitation conditions. That poses a major challenge in the evaluation of such indicators, since excitation conditions are in principle unknown and unmeasured, hence any related change may be incorrectly classified as damage. A solution to this problem lies in the design of a damage detection residual, whose mean value is independent of changes in excitation conditions.

Subspace-based damage detection methods [2, 7] are a well-known group of methods that have been successfully applied to vibration-based SHM of engineering structures, e.g. in [5]. In its classical form the subspace-based residual is linked to changes in the subspace spanned by the Hankel matrix built from the output covariance sequences of the tested data by confronting it with its left null space from the reference, undamaged, state. It is well-known that the Hankel matrices of the output covariance sequences contain information about the system matrices, which define the dynamic behavior of a structural system. However, they are dependent on the excitation conditions, which can rapidly change based on the environment. A damage detection scheme based on Hankel matrices should hence be designed to monitor the changes only in the structural system, which requires appreciation of this environmental variation.

In this context, a new residual is proposed using the difference between the Hankel matrix in the reference state and the excitation normalized Hankel matrix in the tested, potentially damaged, state. As such, the aforementioned residual is evaluated in the local asymptotic approach framework for Gaussian residuals [3]. To decide about the health of the system, the value of the resulting hypothesis test is compared to a threshold. The robustness of the new approach is achieved via a normalization scheme that is adapted from the multi-setup subspace-based system identification [6]. Subsequently, the proposed approach is tested on numerical simulations and experimental data from a full scale bridge.

2. BACKGROUND AND PROBLEM STATEMENT

In this section some background on the computation of Hankel matrices of output covariance sequences from the data are recalled. Next some numerical experiment is set up to illustrate the effect of a changing excitation properties on the empirical damage detection metric employing Hankel matrices. It is illustrated that the empirical methods do not work satisfactory when the covariance of the excitation is varying, thus this simple example should be an illustration of the new scheme proposed in the next section.

Let $R_i = \mathrm{E}(y_k y_{k-i}^{\mathrm{pc}T})$ be the theoretical covariance of the discrete measurements y_k at time lag i, also called *output covariances*, where superscript 'pc' denotes r_0 selected channels, also called projection channels. The collection of R_i can be stacked to form a block Hankel matrix $\mathcal{H} \in \mathbb{R}^{(p+1)r \times qr_0}$

$$\mathcal{H} = \begin{bmatrix} R_1 & R_2 & \vdots & R_q \\ R_2 & R_3 & \vdots & R_{q+1} \\ \vdots & \vdots & \vdots & \vdots \\ R_{p+1} & R_{p+2} & \vdots & R_{p+q} \end{bmatrix} \tag{1}$$

where p, q are parameters with usually $p = q+1$, r labels the total number of channels and r_0 denotes the number of reference channels. The estimates $\hat{R}_i$ and consequently $\hat{\mathcal{H}}$ can be computed from the sample covariance from past $\mathcal{Y}^+$ and future $\mathcal{Y}^-$ data horizons such that $\hat{\mathcal{H}} = \mathcal{Y}^+\mathcal{Y}^{-T}$ and

$$\mathcal{Y}^+ = \frac{1}{\sqrt{N}} \begin{bmatrix} y_{q+1} & y_{q+2} & \vdots & y_{N+q} \\ y_{q+2} & y_{q+3} & \vdots & y_{N+q+1} \\ \vdots & \vdots & \vdots & \vdots \\ y_{p+q+1} & y_{p+q+2} & \vdots & y_{p+q+N} \end{bmatrix}, \quad \mathcal{Y}^- = \frac{1}{\sqrt{N}} \begin{bmatrix} y_q^{\text{pc}} & y_{q+1}^{\text{pc}} & \vdots & y_{N+q-1}^{\text{pc}} \\ y_{q-1}^{\text{pc}} & y_q^{\text{pc}} & \vdots & y_{N+q-2}^{\text{pc}} \\ \vdots & \vdots & \vdots & \vdots \\ y_1^{\text{pc}} & y_2^{\text{pc}} & \vdots & y_N^{\text{pc}} \end{bmatrix},$$

where $N + p + q$ is total a number of samples.

The numerical example is a theoretical 6 DOF chain-like system that, for any consistent set of units, is modeled with a proportional damping matrix, spring stiffness $k_1 = k_3 = k_5 = 100$ and $k_2 = k_4 = k_6 = 200$ and mass $m_i = 1/20$. The system is subjected to noise with a changing excitation covariance Q acting at all DOFs. Responses are measured at 1, 3 and 6 DOF. The simulation campaign consists of the reference built with $N_0 = 2 \cdot 10^6$ data points and the tested states, each simulated with $N = 10^5$ data points. Different excitation covariance scenarios are considered, namely

- first, the most simple theoretical case, when Q is the identity matrix $\mathcal{I}_6$,
- second, where every excitation amplitude is scaled with a random scalar constant a such that $Q = a \cdot \mathcal{I}_6$,
- third, the most general case, where $Q = a \cdot bb^T$ where $b \in \mathbb{R}^{6\times 6}$ is a randomly generated matrix whose entries follow a standard Gaussian distribution.

Each data set simulated beside the reference one corresponds to a different damage level occurring during the respective excitation scenario. The damage is modeled as a gradual stiffness reduction of the second (unmeasured) spring. Gaussian white noise with standard deviation equal to 5% of the standard deviation of the output is added to the response at each measurement channel.

An empirical way to counter non-complex changes in the excitation covariance is to normalize the data with e.g. the standard deviations related to the output covariance R_0, as proposed in [9]. As such, a residual for damage detection that incorporates such normalization can be developed based on the Mahalanobis distance [12] computed on estimates of the Hankel matrices from respectively reference ($\hat{\mathcal{H}}_{ref}$) and tested states ($\hat{\mathcal{H}}_{test}$). Such distance metric d writes as

$$d(\hat{\mathcal{H}}_{ref}, \hat{\mathcal{H}}_{est}) = \sqrt{\text{vec}(\hat{\mathcal{H}}_{ref}^W - \hat{\mathcal{H}}_{test}^W)^T \Sigma_{\hat{\mathcal{H}}_{ref}^W}^{-1} \text{vec}(\hat{\mathcal{H}}_{ref}^W - \hat{\mathcal{H}}_{test}^W)}\,, \quad (2)$$

where $\hat{\mathcal{H}}^W = W^{-1}\hat{\mathcal{H}}W_{\text{pc}}^{-1}$ and $\Sigma_{\hat{\mathcal{H}}_{ref}^W}$ is the covariance of the normalized Hankel matrix in the reference state, computed using the sample mean scheme e.g. after [7]. The normalization factors W and W_{pc} write as

$$W = \mathcal{I}_{(p+1)r} \otimes W_r, \; W_r = \left(\text{E}(y_k y_k^T)\right)^{1/2}$$

and

$$W_{\text{pc}} = \mathcal{I}_{(p+1)r} \otimes W_{r,\text{pc}}, \; W_{r,\text{pc}} = \left(\text{E}(y_k^{\text{pc}} y_k^{\text{pc}T})\right)^{1/2},$$

where $(\cdot)^{1/2}$ denotes the matrix square root. The results from that scheme are depicted in Figure 1.

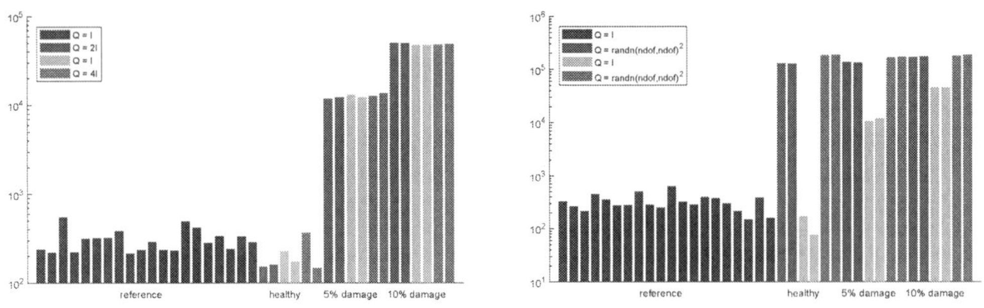

Figure 1: Damage detection with metric d (2).

When normalizing in this way, a different scaling of the noise covariance can be handled as illustrated in Figure 1 (left), whereas more complex Q matrices yield to false alarms and bad performance for the detection in Figure 1 (right). To mitigate these issues, a more robust normalization needs to be considered.

3. DAMAGE DETECTION RESIDUAL BASED ON ROBUST NORMALIZATION

In this section a new damage detection residual is introduced based on a robust normalization of the Hankel matrices. The newly developed metric fits in a well-known framework, namely the local asymptotic approach for change detection [3, 7]. Decision about the damage is taken with a statistical test which follows a χ^2 distribution, and whose mean is robust to changes in the excitation covariance under the null hypothesis. The proposed scheme is validated with a numerical simulation and tested on a full scale bridge example.

3.1. Normalization scheme

Let $\mathcal{H}_{ref}$ and $\mathcal{H}_{test}$ be the exact Hankel matrices of rank n, computed for a system subjected to excitation with different covariances Q_{ref} and Q_{test}. The SVD of the juxtaposed $\mathcal{H}_{ref}$ and $\mathcal{H}_{test}$ writes

$$\begin{bmatrix}\mathcal{H}_{ref} & \mathcal{H}_{test}\end{bmatrix} = \begin{bmatrix}U_s & U_{ker}\end{bmatrix}\begin{bmatrix}D_s & 0\\ 0 & 0\end{bmatrix}\begin{bmatrix}V_{s,ref}^T & V_{s,test}^T\\ V_{ker,ref}^T & V_{ker,test}^T\end{bmatrix}, \tag{3}$$

where $\mathrm{rank}(\begin{bmatrix}\mathcal{H}_{ref} & \mathcal{H}_{test}\end{bmatrix}) = n$, $U_s \in \mathbb{R}^{(p+1)r\times n}$ are the left singular vectors, $D_s \in \mathbb{R}^{n\times n}$ are the non-zero singular values and $V_s^T = \begin{bmatrix}V_{s,ref}^T & V_{s,test}^T\end{bmatrix} \in \mathbb{R}^{n\times 2qr_0}$ are the right singular vectors corresponding to $\mathcal{H}_{ref}$ and $\mathcal{H}_{test}$ respectively. Now define $\mathcal{Z}_{ref} = D_s V_{s,ref}^T$ and $\mathcal{Z}_{test} = D_s V_{s,test}^T$, where both $\mathcal{Z}_{ref}$ and $\mathcal{Z}_{test}$ are full row rank. Since the converged Hankel matrices share the same observability matrix in the reference state (independently of the excitation), it holds

$$\begin{bmatrix}\mathcal{H}_{ref} & \mathcal{H}_{test}\end{bmatrix} = U_s\begin{bmatrix}\mathcal{Z}_{ref} & \mathcal{Z}_{test}\end{bmatrix}. \tag{4}$$

To compare $\mathcal{H}_{ref}$ with $\mathcal{H}_{test}$ a proper normalization of the latter matrix must be deployed, to take into account a possible change in the excitation. In order to do so, a normalization scheme is proposed that is based on the multi-setup normalization strategy from [6]. The scheme writes

$$\overline{\mathcal{H}}_{test} = \mathcal{H}_{test}\mathcal{Z}_{test}^{\dagger}\mathcal{Z}_{ref}, \tag{5}$$

where $\overline{\mathcal{H}}_{test}$ is a Hankel matrix sharing the same stochastic controlability matrix as $\mathcal{H}_{ref}$. Based on the latter expression a residual for damage detection robust to changes in the excitation covariance can be defined.

3.2. Residual definition and its asymptotic properties

The damage detection problem can be focused on a subset of parameters that are functions of the structural properties of the considered system. Typical parameters in engineering applications are the estimates of modal parameters or stiffness/mass properties of the system [1]. For that, let $\theta \in \Theta$ denote a general parameterization of the structural properties of the considered problem in a parameter space Θ. Also, let $\theta^* \in \Theta$ denote those properties under the reference state of the structure. The theoretical residual is defined as

$$\zeta(\theta) = \text{vec}\left(\mathcal{H}_{test}(\theta)\mathcal{Z}_{test}^{\dagger}\mathcal{Z}_{ref} - \mathcal{H}_{ref}(\theta_*)\right), \tag{6}$$

where $\mathcal{Z}_{ref}$ and $\mathcal{Z}_{test}$ are obtained from the SVD in (3) by truncating it at model order n. An estimate of the residual $\hat{\zeta}^{\theta}$ can be obtained from the estimates of the Hankel matrices $\hat{\mathcal{H}}_{ref}^{\theta^*}$ and $\hat{\mathcal{H}}_{test}^{\theta}$ computed from the measurement data. Here, we assume that Hankel matrices for both reference and tested states are computed on data sets with equal length N. Consequently, the system residual writes as

$$\hat{\zeta}^{\theta} = \sqrt{N}\text{vec}\left(\hat{\mathcal{H}}_{test}^{\theta}\hat{\mathcal{Z}}_{test}^{\dagger}\hat{\mathcal{Z}}_{ref} - \hat{\mathcal{H}}_{ref}^{\theta^*}\right), \tag{7}$$

where $\hat{\mathcal{Z}}_{ref}$ and $\hat{\mathcal{Z}}_{test}$ are derived from the relation

$$\left[\hat{\mathcal{H}}_{ref}^{\theta_*} \quad \hat{\mathcal{H}}_{test}^{\theta}\right] \approx \hat{U}_s\left[\hat{\mathcal{Z}}_{ref} \quad \hat{\mathcal{Z}}_{test}\right], \tag{8}$$

truncating the SVD analogous to (3) at order n. The asymptotic properties of the residual in (7) are functions of the statistical properties of the computed Hankel matrices. To recall

$$\begin{aligned} &\text{under } \mathrm{H}_0 : \sqrt{N}\text{vec}\left(\hat{\mathcal{H}}_{ref}^{\theta_*} - \mathcal{H}_{ref}(\theta_*)\right) \xrightarrow{\mathcal{L}} \mathcal{N}(0, \Sigma_{\mathcal{H}_{ref}(\theta_*)}), \\ &\text{under } \mathrm{H}_1 : \sqrt{N}\text{vec}\left(\hat{\mathcal{H}}_{test}^{\theta} - \mathcal{H}_{test}(\theta_*)\right) \xrightarrow{\mathcal{L}} \mathcal{N}(\delta_{\mathcal{H}}, \Sigma_{\mathcal{H}_{test}(\theta_*)}), \end{aligned} \tag{9}$$

where $\Sigma_{\mathcal{H}_{ref}(\theta_*)}$ and $\Sigma_{\mathcal{H}_{test}(\theta_*)}$ are the respective asymptotic covariances of $\hat{\mathcal{H}}_{ref}^{\theta^*}$ and $\hat{\mathcal{H}}_{test}^{\theta}$, and $\delta_{\mathcal{H}}$ is the mean value of the vectorized Hankel matrix in the possibly damaged state.

Lemma 1 *The residual in (7) is asymptotically Gaussian with the following properties*

$$\text{under } \mathrm{H}_0 : \hat{\zeta}^{\theta_*} \xrightarrow{\mathcal{L}} \mathcal{N}(0, \Sigma_{\zeta}), \tag{10}$$

$$\text{under } \mathrm{H}_1 : \hat{\zeta}^{\theta} \xrightarrow{\mathcal{L}} \mathcal{N}(\delta, \Sigma_{\zeta}), \tag{11}$$

where δ is the mean value of the residual under under H_1 and Σ_{ζ} is its asymptotic covariance, which depends on the variance of both $\hat{\mathcal{H}}_{test}^{\theta}$ and $\hat{\mathcal{H}}_{ref}^{\theta^*}$.

The derivation of the expressions for Σ_{ζ} is excluded from this paper due to space limitations.

3.3. Hypothesis testing

Based on the local approach, the residual in (10) is asymptotically Gaussian under both hypotheses. The decision about the damage can be achieved by applying the Generalized Likelihood ratio (GLR) test [2], which is asymptotically χ^2 distributed [8]. It writes in its simplest form as

$$t_{\text{global}}^{\text{np}} = (\hat{\zeta}^{\theta})^T \,\hat{\Sigma}^{-1}\, \hat{\zeta}^{\theta}, \tag{12}$$

where $\hat{\Sigma}$ is a consistent estimate of Σ_{ζ}. The performance of the proposed test is investigated on the numerical example from Section 2..

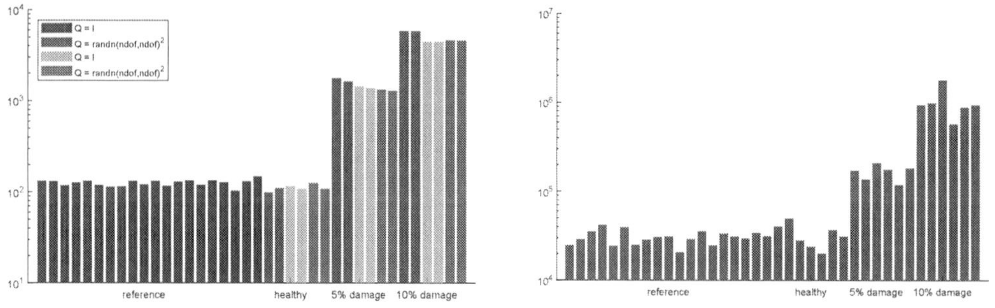

Figure 2: Damage detection based on the robust normalization. Three randomly chosen excitation levels in the tested data sets (left). Random excitation in every data set (right).

It can be observed that the test is able to separate the different damages despite being computed for different values of the excitation. Figure 2 (right) displays the same type of information for Q changing all the time for each data set. This shows that the damage can be detected without any prior knowledge of the excitation properties.

4. APPLICATION

The Z24 bridge is a benchmark for many studies involving e.g. damage detection [15] or removal of the environmental characteristics from the parameters estimated from the data [13]. Before its demolition in 1998, a progressive damage campaign was carried out and consisted of a series of ambient and forced vibration tests conducted while inducing different kinds of damage on the bridge. A complete description of this experimental campaign can be found in [11]. The progressive damage tests took place between August and September where some significant changes in the temperature conditions were experienced during its execution. The approach proposed in this paper doesn't account for the temperature variation. Therefore, only several data sets from the beginning of the experimental campaign are analyzed and assumed not to be significantly perturbed by these temperature changes.

The analyzed measurement corresponds to the mix of forced excitation from two shakers and ambient excitation from wind and traffic under the bridge. The vibration tests were conducted with 28 moving and 5 fixed sensors measuring vertical, transverse and lateral accelerations of the bridge. For the purpose of this study only the measurements from 5 fixed sensors are analyzed. The data was sampled with a frequency of 100 Hz and each measurement lasted for 655.36 seconds. A total number of 54 data sets were analyzed, from which the first 18 measurements are under healthy conditions. The first 6 data sets are selected for the reference state computation. Data sets between numbers 19 and 36 correspond to damage state 1, namely lowering one of the bridge piers by 20mm, and data sets from 37 to 54 correspond to the damage state 2, lowering the same pier by another 20mm. The view on the bridge with positions and directions of the sensors used for this study is shown on Figure 3.

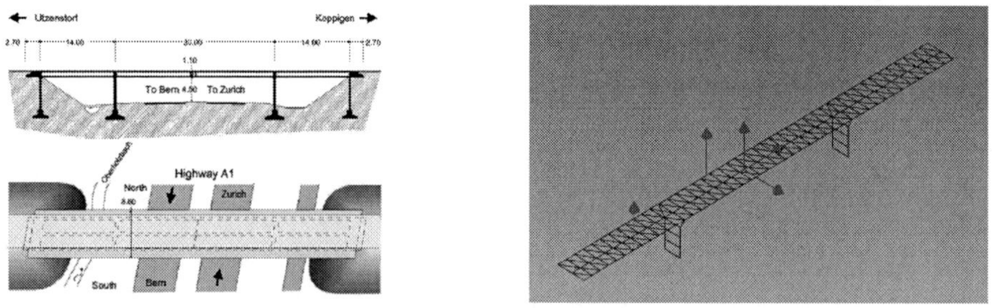

Figure 3: Front view and top views of the Z24 bridge (left). Geometry and analyzed sensors of the Z24 bridge ARTEMIS MODAL PRO 6.0 (right).

The test from (12) is computed with 10 time lags to create a Hankel matrix of model order of 6. The reference state is computed from the first 6 measurements in the healthy state. The number of blocks for the covariance of the reference and the tested Hankel matrices is selected to 400. The results are depicted in Figure 4.

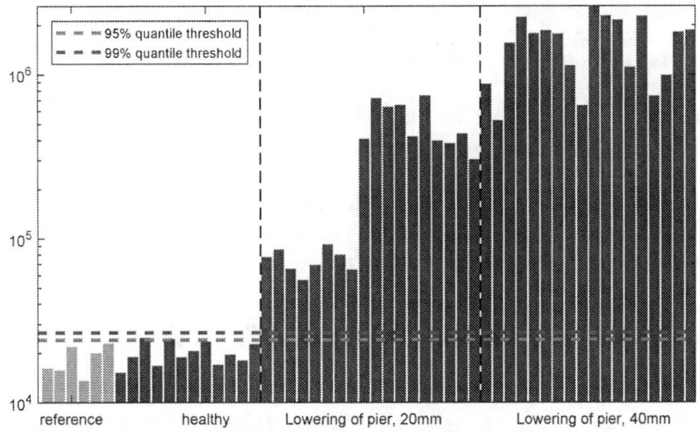

Figure 4: Damage detection in the Z24 bridge. Damage detection test after (12) .

As expected, the results exhibit no false alarms in the healthy state of the structure. Moreover, two damage levels inflicted on the bridge are clearly detected. The plotted detection thresholds correspond to two quantiles, 95% and 99%, of the empirical distribution of the test values in the reference state. Two different levels of the χ^2 test for the damage state 1 might indicate the lowering of the bridge pier in two steps by 10mm.

5. CONCLUSIONS

In this paper we proposed a new damage detection residual based on the difference of Hankel matrices in different states of the structure. The robustness of the new approach is achieved via a robust normalization scheme. It is empirically shown that the mean value of the proposed test under healthy conditions of the system does not depend on the variances of the excitation. The new method has been evaluated on numerical simulations of a simple system and on full scale experimental data from the Z24 bridge. Both cases represent case studies under complex excitation conditions. The experimental results exhibit no outliers in the healthy state, which helps to avoid false alarms and to define an accurate detection threshold.

REFERENCES

[1] E. Balmès, M. Basseville, L. Mevel, H. Nasser, and W. Zhou. Statistical model-based damage localization: A combined subspace-based and substructuring approach. *Structural Control and Health Monitoring*, 15(6):857–875, 2008.

[2] M. Basseville, M. Abdelghani, and A. Benveniste. Subspace-based fault detection algorithms for vibration monitoring. *Automatica*, 36(1):101 – 109, 2000.

[3] A. Benveniste, M. Basseville, and G. Moustakides. The asymptotic local approach to change detection and model validation. *IEEE Transactions on Automatic Control*, 32(7):583–592, Jul 1987.

[4] E. J. Cross, K. Worden, and Q. Chen. Cointegration: a novel approach for the removal of environ-

mental trends in structural health monitoring data. *Proceedings of the Royal Society A: Mathematical, Physical and Engineering Sciences*, 467(2133):2712–2732, 2011.

[5] M. Döhler, F. Hille, L. Mevel, and W. Rücker. Structural health monitoring with statistical methods during progressive damage test of s101 bridge. *Engineering Structures*, 69:183 – 193, 06 2014.

[6] M. Döhler and L. Mevel. Modular subspace-based system identification from multi-setup measurements. *IEEE Transactions on Automatic Control*, 57(11):2951–2956, 2012.

[7] M. Döhler, L. Mevel, and F. Hille. Subspace-based damage detection under changes in the ambient excitation statistics. *Mechanical Systems and Signal Processing*, 45(1):207 – 224, 2014.

[8] M. Döhler, L. Mevel, and Q. Zhang. Fault detection, isolation and quantification from gaussian residuals with application to structural damage diagnosis. *Annual Reviews in Control*, 42:244–256, 2016.

[9] S. Gres, M. D. Ulriksen, M. Döhler, R. J. Johansen, P. Andersen, L. Damkilde, and S. A. Nielsen. Statistical methods for damage detection applied to civil structures. *Procedia Engineering*, 199:1919 – 1924, 2017. X International Conference on Structural Dynamics, EURODYN 2017.

[10] J. Kullaa. Damage detection of the Z24 bridge using control charts. *Mechanical Systems and Signal Processing*, 17(1):163 – 170, 2003.

[11] J. Maeck and G. D. Roeck. Description of Z24 benchmark. *Mechanical Systems and Signal Processing*, 17(1):127 – 131, 2003.

[12] P. C. Mahalanobis. On the generalised distance in statistics. In *Proceedings National Institute of Science, India*, volume 2, pages 49–55, Apr. 1936.

[13] E. Reynders, G. Wursten, and G. D. Roeck. Output-only structural health monitoring in changing environmental conditions by means of nonlinear system identification. *Structural Health Monitoring*, 13(1):82–93, 2014.

[14] O. Salawu. Detection of structural damage through changes in frequency: a review. *Engineering Structures*, 19(9):718 – 723, 1997.

[15] A. Teughels and G. D. Roeck. Structural damage identification of the highway bridge z24 by fe model updating. *Journal of Sound and Vibration*, 278(3):589 – 610, 2004.

[16] K. Worden, G. Manson, and N. Fieller. Damage detection using outlier analysis. *Journal of Sound and Vibration*, 229(3):647 – 667, 2000.

IOMAC'19

8th International Operational Modal Analysis Conference
2019 May13-15 Copenhagen

LOAD VECTOR BASED DAMAGE LOCALIZATION WITH REJECTION OF THE TEMPERATURE EFFECT

Md Delwar Hossain Bhuyan[1], *Nicolas Le Touz*[2,3], *Guillaume Gautier*[3,2], *Michael Döhler*[3,2], *Falk Hille*[1], *Jean Dumoulin*[2,3], *Laurent Mevel*[3,2]

[1] BAM Federal Institute of Materials Research and Testing, Berlin, Germany, {md-delwar-hossain.bhuyan, falk.hille}@bam.de
[2] Ifsttar, COSYS/SII, Bouguenais, France, {nicolas.le-touz, jean.dumoulin}@ifsttar.fr
[3] Univ. Rennes, Inria, Rennes, France, {guillaume.gautier, michael.doehler, laurent.mevel}@inria.fr

ABSTRACT

The Stochastic Dynamic Damage Locating Vector (SDDLV) approach is a vibration-based damage localization method based on both a finite element model of a structure and modal parameters estimated from output-only measurements in the damage and reference states. A statistical version of the approach takes into account the inherent uncertainty due to noisy measurement data. In this paper, the effect of temperature fluctuations on the performance of the method is analyzed in a model-based approach using a finite element model with temperature dependent parameters. Robust damage localization is carried out by rejecting the temperature influence on the identified modal parameters in the damaged state. The algorithm is illustrated on a simulated structure.

Keywords: damage localization, SDDLV, load vector, temperature rejection, statistical evaluation

1. INTRODUCTION

Vibration-based structural health monitoring (SHM) techniques have been actively developed in the last decades [1–3], for example for the monitoring of bridges, buildings or offshore structures. Monitoring-based structural damage assessment is usually divided into subtasks of increasing difficulty [4]: damage detection (level 1) has been of great effort in the last decade, whereas damage localization (level 2) is more a focus of current research [5–7].

Physical changes in the structure due to damage induce changes in the dynamic properties of the structure, which can be monitored through output-only vibration measurements. Nonetheless, the dynamics of structure can also be affected by some environmental variability e.g. changes in temperature, loads, boundary conditions, winds etc. [8–10].

The Stochastic Dynamic Damage Locating Vector (SDDLV) approach [11] is a vibration-based damage localization method based on both a finite element model of a structure and modal parameters estimated from output-only measurements in the damage and reference states. A vector is obtained in the null space of the changes in the transfer matrix between both states and then applied as a load vector to the model. The damage localization is related to the resulting stress where it is close to zero. In previous work [7, 12, 13], the statistical SDDLV approach has been proposed, taking into account the uncertainties in the measurement data. So far, environmental variability has not been considered, in particular the effect of temperature changes. Since the damage localization approach operates based on the modal parameter estimates, it is proposed to reject the temperature variations by correcting these estimates in a preprocessing step. The objective of this paper is to show that the robustness of the damage localization method is improved significantly with the proposed temperature rejection strategy.

This paper is presented as follows. In Section 2, the SDDLV method and the rejection of the temperature effect are presented, and the modeling issues are derived in Section 3. The proposed approach is applied on a numerical simulation in Section 4.

2. DAMAGE LOCALIZATION WITH S-SDDLV ROBUST TO TEMPERATURE CHANGES

In this section, the dynamic modeling of a structure, modal parameters estimates and the temperature rejection approach on the modal parameters estimates are presented in Sections 2.1., 2.2. and 2.3., respectively. Finally, the deterministic computation of the damage indicator and its statistical evaluation is shown in Section 2.4..

2.1. Dynamic modeling of structure

The behavior of a mechanical structure can be described by a linear time-invariant (LTI) dynamic system

$$M\ddot{\mathcal{X}}(t) + C\dot{\mathcal{X}}(t) + K\mathcal{X}(t) = f(t) \tag{1}$$

where M, C, $K \in \mathbb{R}^{d\times d}$ are the mass, damping and stiffness matrices, respectively, t indicates continuous time and $\mathcal{X} \in \mathbb{R}^d$ denotes the displacements at the d degrees of freedom (DOF) of the structure. The external force $f(t)$ is not measurable and modeled as white noise. The external force $f(t)$ is not measurable. Observing system (1) at r sensor coordinates, it can be transformed to the corresponding continuous-time state-space model

$$\begin{cases} \dot{x}(t) = A_c x(t) + B_c e(t) \\ y(t) = C_c x(t) + D_c e(t) \end{cases} \tag{2}$$

with state vector $x \in \mathbb{R}^n$, output vector $y \in \mathbb{R}^r$, the state transition matrix $A_c \in \mathbb{R}^{n\times n}$ and output matrix $C_c \in \mathbb{R}^{r\times n}$, where $n = 2d$ is the system order and r is the number of outputs [11]. The input influence and direct transmission matrices are of size $B_c \in \mathbb{R}^{n\times r}$ and $D_c \in \mathbb{R}^{r\times r}$ respectively. Matrices A_c and C_c contain information on the modal parameters of the structure and can be identified from measurements.

2.2. Modal parameters extraction

From Stochastic Subspace Identification (SSI) [14], modal parameter estimates and subsequently, the estimates of system matrices $\widehat{A}_c$ and $\widehat{C}_c$ can be obtained from output only measurements.

The environmental variability, e.g. due to temperature changes may affect the structural properties or boundary conditions and thus the modal parameter estimates [8]. These effects should be taken into account in the presented models. In the following, the rejection of temperature effect is derived from the modal parameter estimates in the damaged state.

2.3. Temperature rejection

The analysis of temperature variation on the modal parameters of the structure is a subject of increasing interest in the last couple of years [8–10]. Since the considered SDDLV approach operates on the modal parameter estimates, the temperature effect can be rejected from these estimates by a sensitivity analysis.

Assume that $T \in \mathbb{R}^p$ be a temperature parameter vector that describes the monitored system in the current state at p different positions of the structure, and let $T_0 \in \mathbb{R}^p$ be its value in the reference system. To obtain the required sensitivity matrix, the derivative of the modal parameters $(\lambda_{(c,l)}, \varphi_l)$ with respect to the temperature change is computed for each mode l for the eigenvalues $\lambda_{c,l}$ and mode shapes φ_l, $l = 1, \ldots, m$. Denote $\lambda_c = [\lambda_{c,1} \ldots \lambda_{c,m}]^T$ and $\varphi = [\varphi_1 \ldots \varphi_m]$ the collection of eigenvalues and mode shapes, respectively, and let

$$\theta = \begin{bmatrix} \lambda_c \\ \text{vec}(\varphi) \end{bmatrix}$$

be the full modal parameter vector of the system. These parameters are temperature dependent, $\theta = \theta(T)$. The Taylor expansion of the parameter vector writes as

$$\theta(T) \approx \theta(T_0) + \mathcal{J}_{\theta,T}(T - T_0), \tag{3}$$

where $\mathcal{J}_{\theta,T} = \frac{\partial \text{vec}(\theta)}{\partial \text{vec}(T)}$ is the sensitivity matrix. Now, the rejection of temperature variation from the considered parameter vector θ in the damaged state can be obtained from (3)

$$\theta(T_0) \approx \theta(T) - \mathcal{J}_{\theta,T}(T - T_0). \tag{4}$$

The derivative $\mathcal{J}_{\theta,T}$ of the modal parameters with respect to the temperature vector is obtained by first deriving the modal parameters with respect to the stiffness parameters of the system as described in detail in [15] at the reference temperature. Then, the relation between the temperature vector and the material properties is used to obtain the derivative of the stiffness parameters with respect to the temperature vector in the second step, e.g. using a finite difference approach.

2.4. Computation of the damage indicator

The SDDLV is an output-only damage localization method based on interrogating changes $\delta G(s) = \tilde{G}(s) - G(s)$ in the transfer matrix $G(s) \in \mathbb{C}^{r \times r}$ of a system at the sensor coordinates in both damaged (with tilde) and reference states [11], where

$$G(s) = R(s)D_c \quad \text{where} \quad R(s) = C_c(sI - A_c)^{-1} \begin{bmatrix} C_c A_c \\ C_c \end{bmatrix}^{\dagger} \begin{bmatrix} I \\ 0 \end{bmatrix} \tag{5}$$

and s is a Laplace variable in the complex plane. Note that $G(s)$ in the reference state is obtained at the reference temperature T_0, and $\tilde{G}(s)$ in the damaged state is obtained with the temperature rejection approach where the temperature effect is removed from the estimates of modal parameters (4) and subsequently the system matrices.

The changes $\delta G(s)$ are linked to physical properties of the structure. The structural damage is indicated by losses of stiffness that are confined to some part or a region of the structure, affecting the flexibility of the system, which is linked to $\delta G(s)$. A load vector $v(s) \in \mathbb{C}^r$ in the null space of $\delta G(s)$ is obtained from the null space of $\delta R(s)^T$ using a singular value decomposition (SVD). Then this load vector is applied to the Finite Element (FE) model of the healthy structure at the reference temperature for the computation of a stress field over the structure. This stress is stacked in vector $S(s)$, which yields a linear relationship to the load, and which can be expressed by a matrix $L_{model}(s) \in \mathbb{C}^{l \times r}$ based on the FE model of the structure satisfying

$$S(s) = L_{model}(s)v(s). \tag{6}$$

The stress vector $S(s)$ indicates potential damage for elements with corresponding entries in $S(s)$ that are close to zero. When estimated, these stresses are not exactly zero but small in practice because of modal truncation, model errors and variance errors from measurements.

To decide if the estimated stress components are zero, the covariance of the stress vector Σ_S has been estimated in [7, 12, 13], since its identification is subject to uncertainty because of unknown excitation, measurement noise and limited data length. The uncertainties in the estimates are penalizing the quality and precision of the damage localization results. For making decisions about damaged elements of the structure, these uncertainties need to be taken into account to decide whether stress of an element is significantly close to zero or not. Then, an appropriate hypothesis test is performed on each structural element t by selecting the respective stress components S_t in $S(s)$ as well as the respective covariance submatrix Σ_t of Σ_S, and computing the test statistic for each structural element t

$$\chi_t^2 = S_t^T \Sigma_t^{-1} S_t \tag{7}$$

tested for damage. Since stress over damaged elements is zero in theory, potential damage is located in some of the elements t corresponding to the lowest value of χ_t^2 among all elements.

Notice that the correction of the modal parameters with respect to the effect of temperature variation is a deterministic step. In that sense, the variances of the modal parameters after correction should not be affected and corrected. Still, the variances of the transfer functions, the load vector and then the stress are affected by the temperature rejection strategy by virtue of the perturbation approach that is used here to derive those covariances and then they should be adjusted accordingly.

2.5. Summary of the algorithm

The proposed algorithm of the damage localization approach runs as follows with the proposed temperature rejection strategy.

1. The FE model of the structure is obtained at reference temperature vector T_0, and matrix $L_{model}(s)$ is extracted from it for the stress computation (Equation (6)).

2. Vibration measurements are recorded in the undamaged state at reference temperature T_0. The modal parameters are identified from these measurements and used for estimation of the system matrices $\widehat{A}_c$ and $\widehat{C}_c$ in the reference state, as well as their covariance is obtained (see [13]).

3. Based on the FE model and a relation between the temperature vector T and the material properties of the structure, the sensitivity $\mathcal{J}_{\theta,T}$ of the modal parameters with respect to temperature changes is obtained (see Equation (3)).

4. Vibration measurements are recorded in the damaged state at an arbitrary temperature vector T. The estimates of the modal parameters are obtained and corrected using the temperature rejection strategy (4) and subsequently, the $\widehat{A}_c$ and $\widehat{C}_c$ are computed in the damaged state rejecting the temperature variation by the sensitivity analysis.

5. In order to compute the stress field $S(s)$ (6) for damage localization, the load vector $v(s)$ in the null space of the transfer matrix difference $\delta G(s)$ between the healthy and damaged systems is applied to the FE model of the structure in the reference state at the reference temperature.

6. Finally, based on this temperature rejection strategy, the robust damage localization framework can be finalized by the computation of stress $S(s)$ (6) and the statistical evaluation by χ_t^2-test (7).

3. NUMERICAL APPLICATION

The damage localization method has been applied on a 3D rectangular beam model in order to investigate the temperature effect on the dynamic properties of the structure in the computation of stress for damage localization.

In this application, the outcome of the localization results with temperature rejection is compared to not using any temperature rejection. To get these results from simulated datasets, the modes of the system are estimated using a stabilization diagram procedure with SSI [14] in both reference and damaged states. Since the modal parameters of the structure are varying due to the temperature variations, these modal parameters are corrected in the damaged state by sensitivity analysis (4). Then, the system matrices are assembled from the modes [13]. Finally, the estimated stress is computed by considering temperature rejection and its statistical χ_t^2 -test is evaluated for each structural element for damage localization.

3.1. Beam model

In this study, a 3D Beam model, matching a designed and realized mock-up by I4S Team [16], has been considered for damage localization under temperature effect. The structure is modeled with 4 main beam elements of length 1 m. The elements are modeled as rectangular hollow structural sections (HSS) with internal 0.142 m × 0.042 m and external 0.15 m × 0.05 m sections, as depicted in Figure 1. The mass density, Young modulus (E) and Poisson ratio are 7800 kg.m^{-3}, 70 GPa (at 20°C) and 0.33, respectively. Each section is enclosed by two plates of length 0.1 m with external 0.18 m × 0.08 m and internal 0.142 m × 0.042 m sections, respectively. Finally, at the beam ends, two plates of length 0.2m and section 0.3 m × 0.08 m are mounted. All beam sections have the same physical properties as the main beam elements.

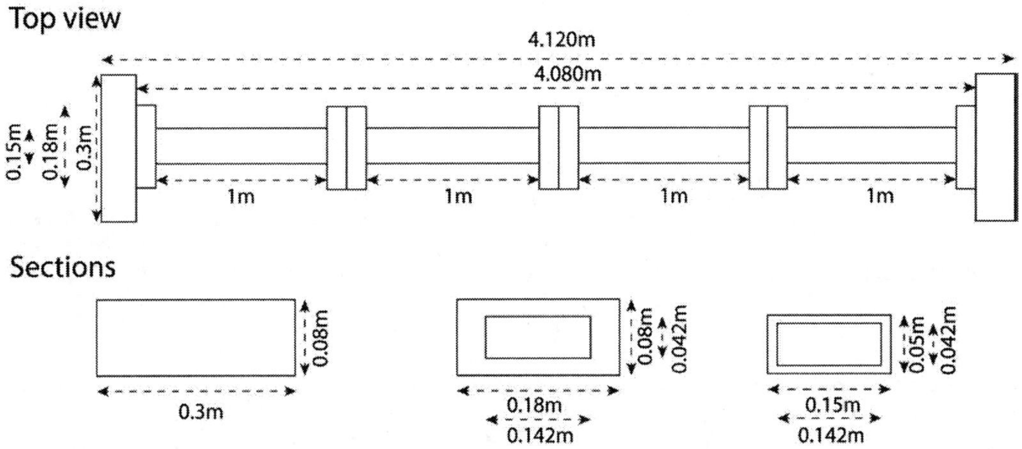

Figure 1: 3D Model with 30 beam elements (180 DOFs)

Each main beam element is discretized into 5 small elements and hence, the total number of elements is 30, and the number of degrees of freedom of the structure is 180. Damping is defined such that the damping ratio of all modes is 0.2%. Note that the damaged position is modeled at elements 12-14 (1.45 m from left end) by 30% stiffness loss. For the damaged and undamaged states, the acceleration data length for each simulated set is N = 100,000, generated from collocated white noise excitation using four sensors in the Y-direction at 0.43 m, 1.49 m, 2.49 m, and 3.47 m from the left support end with a sampling frequency of 2000 Hz, and 5% white noise was added to the output data.

3.2. Temperature model and measurements

A numerical temperature model is used for the computation of a temperature field in the structure from the knowledge of the environmental conditions. It is supposed that the structure is submitted to natural convective exchange with the air, radiative exchange with the environment and outside energy contributions such as solar radiation. Applying a heat source at element 17, the temperature field is computed at the elements of the finite element model. Their stiffness is then computed from the obtained temperatures and used for the data simulation for different magnitudes of the heat flux.

For damage localization, the temperatures at all elements are supposed to be measured, e.g. by an infrared camera in practice, but here computed from the model. In the damaged state, these temperatures are taken into account for the temperature rejection.

3.3. Modal analysis

In the SDDLV approach, the number of considered modes cannot be higher than the number of sensors. The first four modes of the structure are identified (see Table I) from the simulated measurements using stochastic subspace identification (SSI). The identified mode shapes of the first four modes are illustrated in Figure 2 for the respective healthy state together with the mode shapes obtained from the FE model in the healthy state. Moreover, Figure 3(a)-(b) shows that how the first and second modal frequencies are varying in terms of increasing heat flux for both healthy and damaged conditions.

Table I: Frequency (f [Hz]) from healthy state (ref. temperature 293 K) and damaged states (heat flux 40 W.m^{-2}).

Mode	Healthy state	Damaged state
1	22.14	21.03
2	61.10	59.00
3	118.6	113.3
4	204.5	194.2

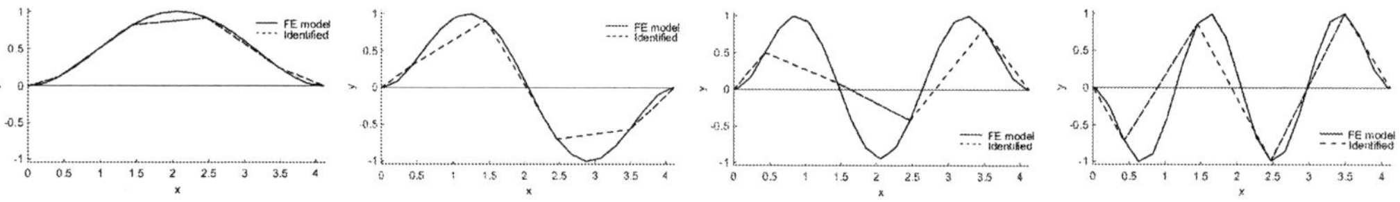

(a) First mode (b) Second mode (c) Third mode (d) Fourth mode

Figure 2: Mode shapes of the first four vertical modes in the healthy state from data and FE model.

In the following, localization results at all structural elements are presented under temperature influence using one dataset and one Laplace variable s.

3.4. Localization results in all elements

To analyze the impact of temperature variation on both the stress computation and its statistical evaluation for damage localization, results for each element are illustrated in Figures 4 and 5 taking into account the temperature rejection approach or not (with/without). The value for the Laplace variable s is chosen as $s_1 = -1 + 700i$ in the vicinity of the identified poles. To compare the ratios between test results for the healthy and damaged elements, the computed test values are normalized in the figures such that the smallest of the 30 values – indicating damage – is 1.

In Figures 4(a)-4(c), the values of the theoretical, estimated stress and its statistical evaluation are displayed when temperature is simulated as varying between healthy and damage states, and similarly, the test values (theoretical, estimated stress and its statistical evaluation) are illustrated in Figures 5(a)-5(c) when temperature rejection is applied. It can be seen that it is difficult to localize the damaged elements

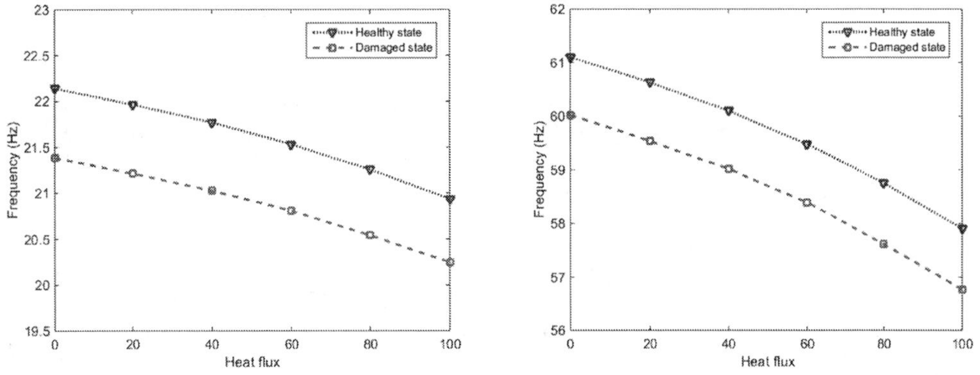

(a) First frequency **(b)** Second frequency

Figure 3: Temperature effect on the first (a) and second (b) frequencies in the healthy and damaged states.

correctly at positions 12, 13 and 14 in Figure 4, while it is easier to discriminate between the damaged and undamaged elements in Figure 5. In addition, it can also be noticed that the contrast ratio between the test values for the damaged and undamaged elements leads to a higher value for the ratio of the statistical evaluation in Figure 5 than in Figure 4, while rejecting the temperature variations.

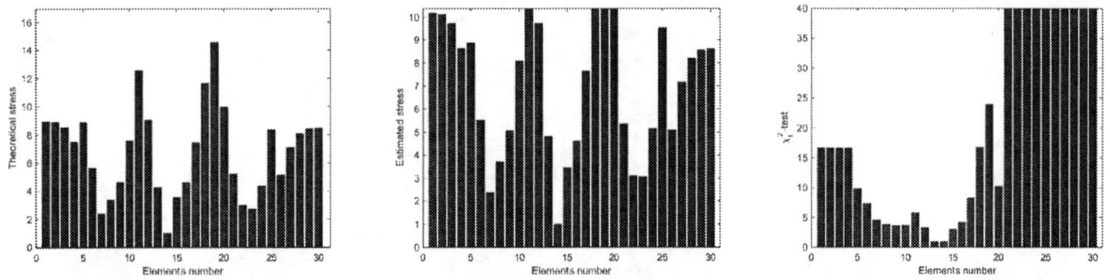

(a) Theoretical stress **(b)** Estimated stress **(c)** Statistical test

Figure 4: Without temperature rejection – Localization results at all elements for stress computation and its statistical evaluation. Damaged elements are 12, 13 and 14.

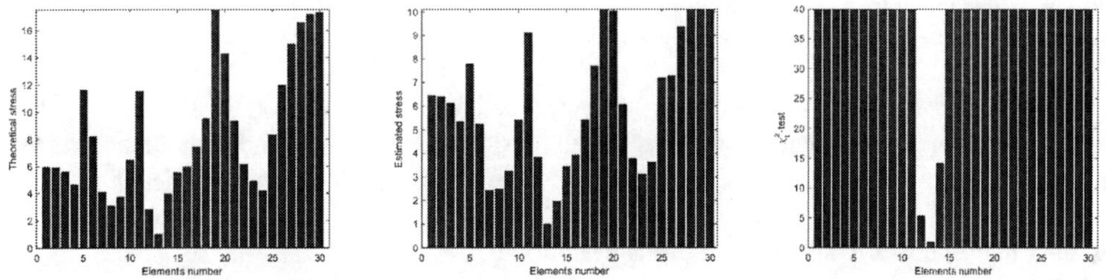

(a) Theoretical stress **(b)** Estimated stress **(c)** Statistical test

Figure 5: With temperature rejection – Localization results at all elements for stress computation and its statistical evaluation. Damaged elements are 12, 13 and 14.

3.5. Performance evaluation of damage localization with and without temperature rejection

To investigate the performance of the damage localization method under temperature variation, the success rate (or probability) of damage localization is evaluated for 100 sets of simulated measurement data in a Monte Carlo experiment. In order to indicate if an element is potentially damaged or not, the χ_t^2 value is computed for each structural element. For each Monte Carlo realization, damage localization is seen as successful when the lowest χ_t^2 value among all elements is indeed at the damaged element, and the success rate is the percentage of realizations for which the χ_t^2 value at the damaged element is the smallest χ_t^2 value. The success rate depends on the chosen value for Laplace variable s and serves as the performance indicator for the method. Notice that the generation of several datasets allows the evaluation of the success rate, while in reality usually only one dataset is available.

In order to evaluate the influence of the Laplace variable s on the success rate of the damage localization procedure, each dataset in the Monte-Carlo simulations is evaluated for a set of values of s with different real and imaginary parts in order to obtain the success rate in dependence of s. The range of for the Laplace variable s has been chosen in the vicinity of the identified poles to reduce the effects of modal truncation in the transfer matrix estimates [11].

Considering using temperature rejection or not, the success rates of damage localization are shown in Figure 6 in dependence of the imaginary part of parameter s for a fixed real part $\mathrm{Re}(s) = -1$ (since the choice of the real part of the Laplace variable has little impact on the results), at a heat flux of 80 Wb/m^2. It can be clearly seen that the temperature rejection approach significantly improves the damage localization performance for nearly all values of s in comparison to not using it.

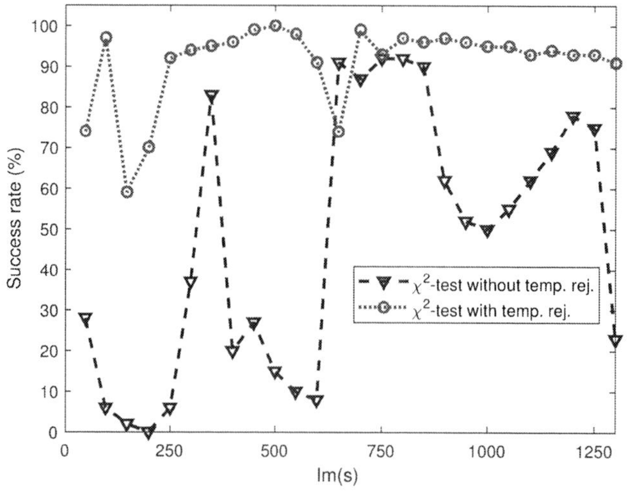

Figure 6: With/without temperature rejection: Success rates of damage localization for different values of s at a heat flux of 80 Wb/m^2. Damaged elements are 12, 13 and 14.

In Figure 7, the mean of the success rates of damage localization for values of s with $\mathrm{Im}(s)$ =100, 150, ..., 1300 are shown in dependence of the heat flux in the damaged state with and without the temperature rejection approach. Without using the rejection, the success rate decreases when the heat flux increases, since no heat flux is present in the healthy state. With the rejection, the localization success rate is constantly high and nearly independent of the heat flux.

4. CONCLUSIONS

In this paper, a temperature rejection strategy has been presented, correcting the modal parameter estimates through a sensitivity analysis before applying a subsequent damage localization approach previously developed. The result shows that temperature rejection on the modal parameters is a useful preprocessing step to improve the performance of the damage localization results. It can be concluded that the risk of poor performance of the damage localization method due to the effect of temperature variation can be reduced using this temperature rejection strategy.

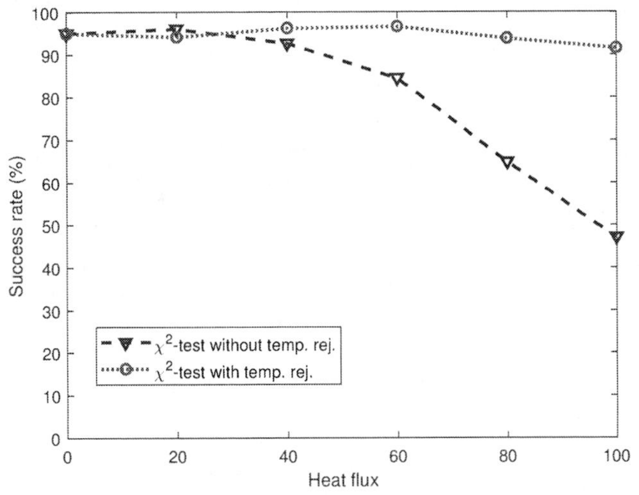

Figure 7: With/without temperature rejection: Success rates of damage localization for different heat flux. Damaged elements are 12, 13 and 14.

ACKNOWLEDGEMENTS

The support from DAAD/German Federal Ministry of Education and Research and the French Ministries of Foreign Affairs (MAEDI) and Education (MENESR) in the PROCOPE program is gratefully acknowledged.

REFERENCES

[1] C.R. Farrar, S.W. Doebling, and D.A. Nix. Vibration-based structural damage identification. *Philosophical Transactions of the Royal Society A: Mathematical, Physical and Engineering Science*, 359(1778):131–149, 2001.

[2] E.P. Carden and P. Fanning. Vibration based condition monitoring: a review. *Structural Health Monitoring*, 3(4):355–377, 2004.

[3] W. Fan and P. Qiao. Vibration-based damage identification methods: a review and comparative study. *Structural Health Monitoring*, 10(1):83–111, 2011.

[4] C.R. Farrar and K. Worden. An introduction to structural health monitoring. *Philosophical Transactions of the Royal Society A: Mathematical, Physical and Engineering Sciences*, 365(1851):303–315, 2007.

[5] S. Allahdadian, M. Döhler, C. Ventura, and L. Mevel. Damage localization of a real structure using the statistical subspace damage localization method. In *Proc. 11th International Workshop on Structural Health Monitoring (IWSHM)*, Stanford, CA, USA, 2017.

[6] M.D.H. Bhuyan, G. Gautier, M. Döhler, L. Mevel, Y. Lecieux, and F. Schoefs. Statistical damage localization in mechanical systems based on load vectors. In *International Federation of Automatic Control (IFAC), World Congress*, 9-14 July, 2017, Toulouse, France.

[7] M.D.H. Bhuyan, M. Döhler, Y. Lecieux, L. Mevel, and F. Schoefs. Statistical damage localization with stochastic load vectors using multiple mode sets. *Structural Health Monitoring*, 16(5):518–535, 2017.

[8] H. Sohn. Effects of environmental and operational variability on structural health monitoring. *Philosophical Transactions of the Royal Society A: Mathematical, Physical and Engineering Sciences*, 365(1851):539–560, 2007.

[9] M. Basseville, F. Bourquin, L. Mevel, H. Nasser, and F. Treyssède. Handling the temperature effect in vibration monitoring: two subspace-based analytical approaches. *Journal of Engineering Mechanics*, 136(3):367–378, 2010.

[10] K. V. Buren, J. Reilly, K. Neal, H. Edwards, and F. Hemez. Guaranteeing robustness of structural condition monitoring to environmental variability. *Journal of Sound and Vibration*, 386:134–148, 2017.

[11] D. Bernal. Load vectors for damage location in systems identified from operational loads. *Journal of Engineering Mechanics*, 136(1):31–39, 2010.

[12] M. Döhler, L. Marin, D. Bernal, and L. Mevel. Statistical decision making for damage localization with stochastic load vectors. *Mechanical Systems and Signal Processing*, 39(1-2):426–440, 2013.

[13] L. Marin, M. Döhler, D. Bernal, and L. Mevel. Robust statistical damage localization with stochastic load vectors. *Structural Control and Health Monitoring*, 22:557–573, 2015.

[14] M. Döhler and L. Mevel. Fast multi-order computation of system matrices in subspace-based system identification. *Control Engineering Practice*, 20(9):882–894, 2012.

[15] W. Heylen, S. Lammens, and P. Sas. *Modal Analysis Theory and Testing*. Katholieke Universiteit Leuven, Belgium, 1998.

[16] G. Gautier, L. Mevel, J. Dumoulin, M. Döhler, M. Le Pen, D. Siegert, and E. Merliot. An experimental setup for subspace based damage identification methods. In *European Geosciences Union, General Assembly*, 09-13 April, 2018, Vienna, Austria.

IOMAC'19

8th International Operational Modal Analysis Conference
2019 May13-15 Copenhagen

MINIMUM DETECTABLE DAMAGE FOR STOCHASTIC SUBSPACE-BASED METHODS

A. Mendler[1], *S. Allahdadian*[2], *M. Döhler*[3] , *L. Mevel*[4], *C.E. Ventura*[5]

[1] Ph.D. Candidate, University of British Columbia, Department of Civil Engineering, Canada, alexander.mendler@ubc.ca.

[2] Researcher, University of British Columbia, Department of Civil Engineering, Canada, saeid@civil.ubc.ca.

[3] Researcher, Inria, Ifsttar, I4S, Rennes, France, michael.doehler@inria.fr.

[4] Senior researcher, Inria, Ifsttar, I4S, Rennes, France, laurent.mevel@inria.fr

[5] Professor, University of British Columbia, Department of Civil Engineering, Canada, ventura@civil.ubc.ca.

ABSTRACT

Detecting small and local damages on structures based on ambient vibrations is a major challenge in structural health monitoring. However, being able to identify the minimum damage is essential for quantifying the effectiveness of the instrumentation and for defining the limitations of low-frequency vibration monitoring in general. This paper shows how subspace-based methods could be used by engineers to predict the minimum damage that can be detected. The method employs a Gaussian subspace-based residual vector as a damage-sensitive criterion and evaluates its deviation from zero mean through two different statistical hypothesis tests, a parametric version and a non-parametric one. A sensitivity analysis is carried out to parametrize the deviation from the nominal state, and link it to physical parameters in a finite element model through the Fisher information matrix. This link can also be used to predict the minimum detectable damage, *e.g.* by prescribing a minimum probability of detection based on code-based reliability concepts. Ultimately, the developed theory is verified by means of a numerical example.

Keywords: Ambient vibrations, statistical hypothesis test, Fisher information, finite element model

1. INTRODUCTION

In the literature, many techniques have been proposed to monitor the health state of structures based on ambient vibrations [1]. Moreover, there seems to be a general consent that output-only methods based on ambient vibrations may not be sensitive enough to diagnose small and local damages, due to the low damage-related information content of low-level or low-frequency vibrations. Therefore, it has become a key issue to quantify the minimum detectable damage that vibration-based methods can sense based on the global system response (for instance in percent of a stiffness parameter), because it allows to explicitly assess the efficiency of a monitoring system, and helps to transition state-of-the-art technology into engineering practice [2].

Stochastic subspace-based methods offer means to quantify the minimum detectable damage, because the healthy and the damaged state can be linked through a statistical framework using the Fisher information matrix. The foundations were laid in 1987 by introducing the underlying statistical expressions, also called the asymptotic local approach [3]. In 2000, the first attempt to use subspace-based methods for damage detection was documented [4]. In essence, a subspace-based residual is computed with zero mean in the reference state and non-zero mean in the damaged state. To give physical meaning to the statistical criterion, it was linked to mechanical parameters in a finite element (FE) model that would experience changes due to damage in the real structure. This was, for example, done by means of a sensitivity analysis of the residual toward the affected parameters [5]. An improved residual was published in 2014 that was more robust toward variations in the ambient excitation characteristics [6]. In this paper, a predictive formula is developed that takes as input the vibration data of a healthy structure and the parameters of a corresponding FE model, and predicts the minimum damage by requiring a minimum damage resolution for decision making. The derivation is shown for two damage diagnosis tests, the parametric and non-parametric detection test, and validated by means of a numerical example.

2. BACKGROUND

2.1. Stochastic Subspace

This first section recaps how the stochastic subspace can be estimated from ambient vibrations. The starting point is a discrete state space model used to describe a linear and time-invariant mechanical system with m degrees of freedom (DOF) under random excitation:

$$\begin{cases} \mathbf{x}_{k+1} & = \mathbf{A}\mathbf{x}_k + \mathbf{w}_k \\ \mathbf{y}_k & = \mathbf{C}\mathbf{x}_k + \mathbf{v}_k, \end{cases} \tag{1}$$

where $\mathbf{A} \in \mathbb{R}^{n \times n}$ and $\mathbf{C} \in \mathbb{R}^{r \times n}$ are the state transition and the output matrix and $n = 2m$. The vectors $\mathbf{x}_k \in \mathbb{R}^{n \times 1}$ and $\mathbf{y}_k \in \mathbb{R}^{r \times 1}$ are the state vector and the measurement vector at time instant k, and $\mathbf{w}_k \in \mathbb{R}^{n \times 1}$ and $\mathbf{v}_k \in \mathbb{R}^{r \times 1}$ are noise terms modeled as white noise. First, the output covariances $\mathbf{R}_i = \mathbf{E}(\mathbf{y}_{k+i}\mathbf{y}_k)$ are estimated and assembled in the block Hankel matrix

$$\mathcal{H}_{p+1,q} = \begin{bmatrix} \mathbf{R}_1 & \mathbf{R}_2 & \dots & \mathbf{R}_q \\ \mathbf{R}_2 & \mathbf{R}_3 & \dots & \mathbf{R}_{q+1} \\ \vdots & \vdots & \ddots & \vdots \\ \mathbf{R}_{p+1} & \mathbf{R}_{p+2} & \dots & \mathbf{R}_{p+q} \end{bmatrix}; \qquad \mathbf{R}_i = \mathbf{R}_{yy,i} = \frac{1}{N-i}\sum_{k=1}^{N-i} \mathbf{y}_{k+i}\mathbf{y}_k^T. \tag{2}$$

The time lags $i = 1, \dots, p+q$ are used to evaluate the similarity of the time-shifted wave patterns at different sensor locations, where p and q should be chosen sufficiently large with $\min(pr, qr) \geq n$ and often $p + 1 = q$. Secondly, the matrix is decomposed into its subspaces by means of a singular value decomposition separating the orthonormal singular vectors related to structural information $\mathbf{U}_1$ from those related to noise processes $\mathbf{U}_0$, also referred to as the left null-space.

$$\mathcal{H}_{p+1,q} = \begin{bmatrix} \mathbf{U}_1 & \mathbf{U}_0 \end{bmatrix} \begin{bmatrix} \mathbf{D}_1 & \mathbf{0} \\ \mathbf{0} & \mathbf{D}_0 \end{bmatrix} \begin{bmatrix} \mathbf{V}_1^T \\ \mathbf{V}_0^T \end{bmatrix} \tag{3}$$

2.2. Damage Diagnosis

A damage-sensitive criterion is formed by multiplying the left null-space from the training phase with the block Hankel matrix estimated from test data. When vectorized by means of the column stacking operator $vec(\cdot)$ and scaled by the square root of the sample size, it is also called the Gaussian residual.

$$\zeta = \sqrt{N} vec(\mathbf{U}_0^T \mathcal{H}_{p+1,q}) \sim \begin{cases} \mathcal{N}(\mathbf{0}, \boldsymbol{\Sigma}) & healthy \\ \mathcal{N}(\boldsymbol{\mathcal{J}}\boldsymbol{\delta}, \boldsymbol{\Sigma}) & damaged, \end{cases} \tag{4}$$

where the covariance $\boldsymbol{\Sigma}$ is estimated as the sample covariance from realizations ζ_k of the residual computed on blocks of the available data [6] with

$$\boldsymbol{\Sigma} = \frac{1}{n_b - 1} \sum_{k=1}^{n_b} \zeta_k \zeta_k^T . \tag{5}$$

If no damage is present, the residual follows a normal distribution with zero mean and covariance $\boldsymbol{\Sigma}$. Any abnormality in the test data causes a deviation from zero mean that can be parametrized as $\boldsymbol{\mathcal{J}\delta}$, that is, the sensitivity of the Gaussian residual toward changes in any structural parameters $\boldsymbol{\mathcal{J}} = \partial \mathbf{E}(\frac{1}{\sqrt{N}}\zeta)/\partial \boldsymbol{\theta}$ multiplied by the parameter change vector $\boldsymbol{\delta} = \sqrt{N}(\boldsymbol{\theta} - \boldsymbol{\theta}_0)$. To assess the significance of the deviation, the general likelihood ratio can be employed. It quantifies the likelihood that the residual is drawn from the probability distribution corresponding to the damaged structure rather than the healthy one. Using the matrices from above, the likelihood ratio can be expressed as [6]

$$t = \zeta^T \boldsymbol{\Sigma}^{-1} \boldsymbol{\mathcal{J}} \left(\boldsymbol{\mathcal{J}}^T \boldsymbol{\Sigma}^{-1} \boldsymbol{\mathcal{J}} \right)^{-1} \boldsymbol{\mathcal{J}}^T \boldsymbol{\Sigma}^{-1} \zeta \sim \begin{cases} \chi^2(k, 0) & healthy \\ \chi^2(k, \lambda) & damaged \end{cases} . \tag{6}$$

The test statistic t is scattered due to the stochastic nature of the method. As shown in [7], it follows a chi-squared distribution with k degrees of freedom and a non-centrality of zero $\lambda = 0$ in the healthy state. In the damaged state, the non-centrality is $\lambda = \boldsymbol{\delta}^T(\boldsymbol{\mathcal{J}}^T \boldsymbol{\Sigma}^{-1} \boldsymbol{\mathcal{J}})\boldsymbol{\delta}$, and serves as a measure for the severity of damage, see Fig. 1. If no parametrization is available, the sensitivity of the parametrization toward the residual vector defaults to unity $\boldsymbol{\mathcal{J}} = \mathbf{I}$, and the general likelihood ratio from Eq. (6) collapses into

$$t = \zeta^T \boldsymbol{\Sigma}^{-1} \zeta \sim \begin{cases} \chi^2(k, 0) & healthy \\ \chi^2(k, \lambda) & damaged \end{cases} . \tag{7}$$

To decide whether the structure is damaged or not, the test statistic from Eq. (6) or (7) is compared against a threshold t_{crit}, and an alarm is sound if $t > t_{crit}$.

2.3. Parametrization

Damage can be parametrized, meaning the deviation in the mean residual from Eq. (4) can be linked to the structural parameter that caused it. To do that, two *modal* parameter vectors have to be established, storing all poles and mode shapes that characterize the vibration behaviour in discrete-time and continuous-time. Moreover, a *physical* parameter vector $\boldsymbol{\theta}$ is defined, which holds structural parameters that may experience changes. For a mass-and-spring system with one DOF, a full parametrization writes

$$\boldsymbol{\theta}_d = \begin{bmatrix} Re(\lambda) \\ Im(\lambda) \\ vec(Re(\phi)) \\ vec(Im(\phi)) \end{bmatrix}, \boldsymbol{\theta}_c = \begin{bmatrix} Re(\mu) \\ Im(\mu) \\ vec(Re(\phi)) \\ vec(Im(\phi)) \end{bmatrix}, \boldsymbol{\theta} = \begin{bmatrix} m \\ c \\ k \end{bmatrix} . \tag{8}$$

Linking the mean residual to a change in the parameter vector $\boldsymbol{\theta}$ is done by means of three consecutively performed first-order sensitivity analyses [8]. The first Jacobian matrix holds the sensitivity of the mean residual toward the discrete poles and mode shapes evaluated based on operational modal analysis concepts [4, 6, 9]. The second Jacobian matrix links the modal parameters to the ones of the analytical model, which are in continuous-time [9]. The third Jacobian matrix links the analytical modal parameters to the structural parameters [5], *e.g.* by means of the direct sensitivity approach [10].

$$\boldsymbol{\mathcal{J}} = \frac{\partial}{\partial \boldsymbol{\theta}} \mathbf{E}(\tfrac{1}{\sqrt{N}}\zeta) = \boldsymbol{\mathcal{J}}^{\zeta}_{\boldsymbol{\theta}_d} \boldsymbol{\mathcal{J}}^{\boldsymbol{\theta}_d}_{\boldsymbol{\theta}_c} \boldsymbol{\mathcal{J}}^{\boldsymbol{\theta}_c}_{\boldsymbol{\theta}} \tag{9}$$

If the modal parameter vectors are incomplete, modal truncation occurs and biases the damage diagnosis. However, the physical parameter vector can be defined by the user, meaning a reduced set of monitoring parameter can be chosen, and no bias is introduced if damage only affects the selected parameters.

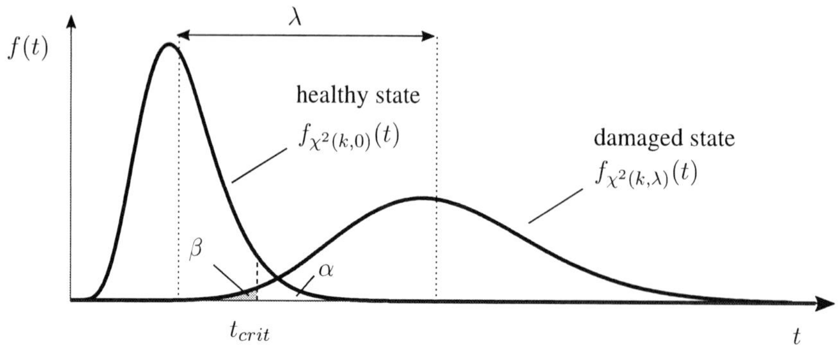

Figure 1: Statistical distribution of the test statistic for damage detection.

3. LINKING HEALTHY AND DAMAGED STATE

3.1. Parametric Detection Test

As mentioned above, different structural health states can be linked through the non-centrality parameter, which changes from $\lambda = 0$ in the healthy state to $\lambda = \boldsymbol{\delta}^T(\boldsymbol{\mathcal{J}}^T\boldsymbol{\Sigma}^{-1}\boldsymbol{\mathcal{J}})\boldsymbol{\delta}$ in the damaged one. On close inspection, it becomes clear that the bracket term can be calculated based on healthy vibration data, so all information on the future shift in the test statistic due to damage is already available. It corresponds to the information matrix or the Fisher information matrix of the parameter $\boldsymbol{\theta}$ contained in the residual $\boldsymbol{\zeta}$.

$$\mathbf{F} = \boldsymbol{\mathcal{J}}^T\boldsymbol{\Sigma}^{-1}\boldsymbol{\mathcal{J}} \tag{10}$$

As explained in Section 2.3., all physical parameters to be monitored are user-defined, and the only requirement is that structural changes only occur in the physical parameters that are stored in $\boldsymbol{\theta}$. In the special case, where damage is limited to a single parameter θ_i in $\boldsymbol{\theta}$, the shift of the mean value from zero is only due to the damage in that very parameter $\boldsymbol{\mathcal{J}}\boldsymbol{\delta} = \boldsymbol{\mathcal{J}}_i\delta_i$, where $\boldsymbol{\mathcal{J}}_i$ is the ith column of the sensitivity matrix. For this case, the Fisher information reduces to a scalar value, and the relation between the healthy and damaged state writes

$$\lambda = F_{ii}\delta_i^2. \tag{11}$$

That means that the non-centrality parameter λ from the statistical test can be linked to a physical parameter change of a single structural parameter δ_i in an analytical computer model through the main diagonal value of the Fisher information, making F_{ii} a measure for the detectability of damage [11].

3.2. Non-parametric Detection Test

In the non-parametric test from Eq. (7), the test statistic t is evaluated without taking into account the sensitivity matrix $\boldsymbol{\mathcal{J}}$, but this section explains why the healthy and damaged state can still be linked through the Fisher information according to Eq. (10) and (11). For this purpose, a new vector $\mathbf{z}$ with unit variance is defined by pre-multiplying $\boldsymbol{\Sigma}^{-1/2}$ to the residual of the damaged state from Eq. (4).

$$\mathbf{z} = \boldsymbol{\Sigma}^{-1/2}\boldsymbol{\zeta} \sim \mathcal{N}(\boldsymbol{\Sigma}^{-1/2} \cdot \boldsymbol{\mathcal{J}}\boldsymbol{\delta}, \mathbf{I})$$

Squaring up this vector yields the non-parametric test statistic

$$t = \mathbf{z}^T\mathbf{z} = \boldsymbol{\zeta}^T\boldsymbol{\Sigma}^{-1}\boldsymbol{\zeta} \sim \chi^2(k, \lambda), \tag{12}$$

with the non-centrality parameter

$$\lambda = \boldsymbol{\mu}^T\boldsymbol{\mu} = (\boldsymbol{\Sigma}^{-1/2}\boldsymbol{\mathcal{J}}\boldsymbol{\delta})^T(\boldsymbol{\Sigma}^{-1/2}\boldsymbol{\mathcal{J}}\boldsymbol{\delta}) = \boldsymbol{\delta}^T(\boldsymbol{\mathcal{J}}^T\boldsymbol{\Sigma}^{-1}\boldsymbol{\mathcal{J}})\boldsymbol{\delta}. \tag{13}$$

3.3. Practical Considerations

This section presents an approach to interpret the non-centrality λ from an engineering perspective. Obviously, λ quantifies the degree of separation between the distributions related to the healthy and damaged state (see Fig. 1), so it can be interpreted as some kind of reliability index. The larger the non-centrality, the lower the probability that the structure is mistakenly diagnosed as healthy although it is not, and vice versa. However, there will always be an overlap between the two states. The following paragraphs give guidance on how to choose an appropriate λ for a specific monitoring application by tying it back to code-based reliability concepts.

3.3.1. Reliability Concept

The first question one should ask oneself is "how often do I want the test to diagnose the structure as damaged although it is not"? Based on the accepted false-negative rate (type I error α), a safety threshold value can be defined for the test statistic, see t_{crit} in Fig. 1. For civil engineering structures, a typical type I error could be in the range of $\alpha = [0.3\%, 5\%]$ or lower, meaning one out of 20 - 300 tests diagnoses a healthy structure as damaged.

The second question is "how often do I want the test to diagnose the structure as undamaged although damage is present"? The false-positive rate (type II error β) is critical and depends on the allowable damage consequences. For load-bearing components, for example, it is recommended to choose the type II error according to the national reliability concept. In Canada and the U.S.A., the reliability index for assessment is defined as 3.25 and 2.5, which is equivalent to a false-negative rate of $\beta = 0.06\%$ and $\beta = 0.6\%$, respectively. The Eurocode does not define a reliability index for assessment, but the ISO norm requires a reliability index of 4.7, so $\beta = 10^{-6}$ [12].

3.3.2. Corresponding Non-centrality

Once the type I and II errors are defined, the non-centrality parameter λ can be solved for as the distance between the mean values of the healthy and damaged state PDF. There is still one unknown, that is the number of degrees of freedom k, but since this value depends on the kind of damage diagnosis test that is performed (*e.g.* parametric, or non-parametric detection test, or others), it is treated as a known constant here and referred to Section 3.3.3. below. Graphically, the defined type I error α describes the area under the healthy state PDF to the right of the safety threshold t_{crit}, see Fig. 1. When setting up the corresponding equation, the only unknown is t_{crit}, which can be solved for, *e.g.* by means of the cumulative distribution function (CDF) for the healthy state $F_{\chi^2(k,0)}(t_{crit})$ and numerical iteration.

$$\alpha = 1 - \int_0^{t_{crit}} f_{\chi^2(k,0)}(t)dt = 1 - F_{\chi^2(k,0)}(t_{crit}) \tag{14}$$

The type II error β corresponds to the area below the damaged state PDF to the left of the safety threshold. The only unknown in the following equation is the desired non-centrality λ, which can be solved for in the same manner as for the safety threshold using the CDF of the damaged state $F_{\chi^2(k,\lambda)}(t_{crit})$.

$$\beta = \int_0^{t_{crit}} f_{\chi^2(k,\lambda)}(t)dt = F_{\chi^2(k,\lambda)}(t_{crit}) \tag{15}$$

3.3.3. Number of Degrees of Freedom

The number of degrees of freedom k of the chi-squared distribution can be interpreted as a measure for the dimensionality of the damage detection problem, so it depends on the specific monitoring application. Mathematically, k corresponds to the number of statistical processes that influence the dynamic behaviour of the structure. In some special cases, k coincides with the number of parameters to be monitored. Suppose, all contributing factors are collected in a parameter vector $\boldsymbol{\theta}$ in Eq. (8). Further suppose that the individual parameters θ_i do not influence each other and their effect on the residual can be clearly distinguished; then, the sensitivity matrix $\mathcal{J}$ has full rank, and k corresponds to the number of columns in the sensitivity matrix, which is equal to the number of parameters in $\boldsymbol{\theta}$. For the non-parametric test, k is equal to the rank of the (converged) covariance matrix. However, this theoretical criterion is not very meaningful for practical applications, because the singular values of the covariance estimate decrease continuously without showing a distinct jump.

Alternatively, auxiliary empirical tools can be used to estimate k. For example, the statistical distribution from Eq. (6) and (7) for the healthy state could be evaluated in a Monte Carlo simulation. Then, it could be subdivided into bins, and a least-square fit could be performed with k being the only variable in the target function of a central chi-square distribution ($\lambda = 0$).

$$f_{\chi^2(k,0)}(t) = \frac{1}{2^{k/2}\Gamma(k/2)} t^{k/2-1} e^{-t/2}. \tag{16}$$

3.4. Predictive Formula

By bringing together the considerations from previous sections, a predictive formula can be developed for the minimum detectable damage. The starting point is a fundamental statistical equation, the asymptotic local approach. It describes the relation between the parameter change vector $\boldsymbol{\delta}$ and the chosen parametrization and includes a scaling factor for the measurement duration, which guarantees that the residual follows a normal distribution and that the log-likelihood of the general likelihood test is well-defined. [3]

$$(\boldsymbol{\theta} - \boldsymbol{\theta}_0) = \boldsymbol{\delta}/\sqrt{N}$$

A predictive formula for the minimum detectable damage in each individual parameter i is obtained by substituting $N = Tf_s$ as well as the relation $\lambda = \delta_i^2 F_{ii}$ from Eq. (11). When normalized by the reference parameter vector, the parameter change is given in percent and can be associated with a measure for the damage severity $\Delta_i = (\theta_i - \theta_{0,i})/\theta_{0,i}$.

$$\Delta_i = \frac{1}{\theta_{0,i}} \sqrt{\frac{\lambda}{Tf_s \cdot F_{ii}}} [\%] \tag{17}$$

This formula for the minimum detectable damage Δ_i includes three variables, namely the measurement duration and sampling frequency, T and f_s, and the non-centrality parameter λ, which is a function of the accepted type I and II errors α and β and the number of degrees of freedom k. The relative magnitude of the monitoring parameter $\theta_{0,i}$, on the other hand, depends on the structural system, and the Fisher information F_{ii} depends on the sensor configuration as well as T, f_s and $\theta_{0,i}$.

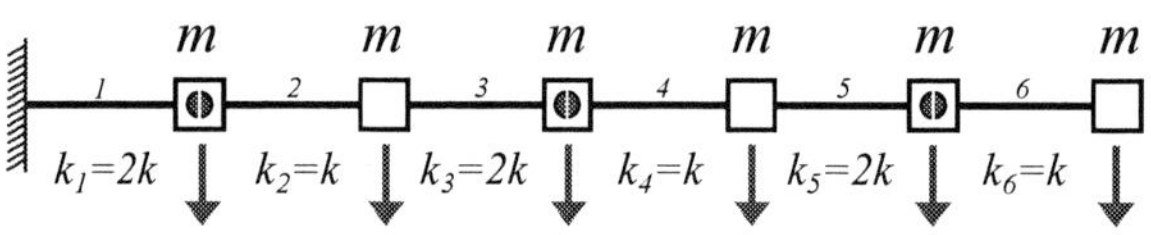

Figure 2: 6-DOF mass-and-spring system instrumented with three sensors (round symbols).

4. APPLICATION

For validation, the methodology was applied to a 6-DOF mass-and-spring system with a fundamental frequency of 2.03 Hz (T = 0.49 s). Lumped masses of 1.0 t were connected through beams with alternating stiffness values, where k = 2000 MN/m (see Fig. 2). Rotational DOFs were fixed and gravity effects were neglected. Every mode of vibration was assumed to be lightly damped with a modal damping ratio of 2% critical damping. A white noise excitation was generated and applied along all DOFs. Three sensors were placed at the masses 1, 3, 5 sampling the signal at 128 Hz. The type I and II errors were set to $\alpha = \beta = 2\%$ for demonstration purposes. For clarity, the following sections are organized in the three main states of the damage diagnosis: the reference state, the training state and the test state.

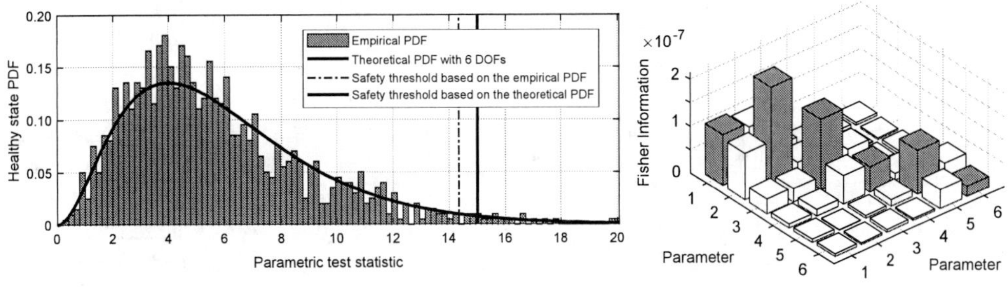

Figure 3: Healthy state PDF of the parametric test (left), and Fisher information matrix (right).

4.1. Reference State

In the reference state, all matrices were determined for the damage diagnosis test and for the prediction of the minimum detectable damage. Firstly, the parametrization was defined, and to avoid modal truncation, all six modes of vibration were considered. A common engineering assumption is to only consider a stiffness decrease due to damage, so the parameter vector from Eq. (8) reduced to

$$\boldsymbol{\theta}_0 = [k_1, k_2, k_3, k_4.k_5, k_6]^T. \tag{18}$$

Secondly, the residual vector from Eq. (4) was evaluated based on vibration data of the healthy structure, and both its covariance $\Sigma(\zeta)$ and sensitivity toward the parameter vector from Eq. (18) were calculated according to Eq. (5) and (9). Moreover, the Fisher information matrix was computed based on Eq. (10) and visualized as shown in Fig 3. In this example, the measurement duration was set to a large value of $T_0 = 300$ min to reduce the uncertainties in the Gaussian residual and all matrices derived from it.

4.2. Training State

In the training state, the healthy state PDF from Fig. 1 was determined with the only unknown being the number of degrees of freedom k. For the non-parametric test, no theoretical value was available for k, so it had to be determined empirically. To do so, 1,000 ambient vibration records with a measurement duration of $T = 1$ min were created in a Monte Carlo experiment while applying the damage diagnosis test from Eq. (7) to each record. Then, the empirical distribution was plotted in a histogram and the curve from Eq. (16) was fitted. A minimum error was achieved for $k = 82$, a value that was higher than the number of parameters to be monitored but lower than the number of rows/columns in the covariance matrix (160). That means the covariance matrix was not of full rank.
For the parametric test, the number of degrees of freedom was set to the theoretical value of $k = 6$, as six parameters were to be monitored, see Eq. (18), but its distribution was evaluated as well for comparison, see Fig. 3. The empirical distribution (in bright blue) appeared to follow the theoretical one (solid black line), so the assumption of a full rank sensitivity matrix was justified. Moreover, the curve fitting approach could be validated, as it resulted in the same value for the number of degrees of freedom.

The healthy state was now fully defined, because the non-centrality parameter was assumed to be zero $\lambda = 0$, and the safety threshold t_{crit} could be determined as the quantile value of the chi-square distribution corresponding to the predefined type I error $Q[f_{\chi^2(k,0)}(t)] = \alpha$. This approach was convenient and efficient because an empirical evaluation in the training state is circumvented for the parametric test.

4.3. Predicting the Minimum Damage

Having completed the training phase, the minimum detectable damage could be predicted according to Eq. (17) with the only remaining unknown being the (minimum) non-centrality parameter λ. It could be determined as the distance between the mean values of the healthy and damaged state, see Fig. 1, taking as input the accepted type I and II error, α and β, as well as the number of degrees of freedom k of the healthy state PDF, see Eq. (14) and (15).

4.4. Test State

In the test phase, different damage scenarios were simulated by decreasing the beam stiffness by the minimum damage $k_{dam,i} = k_i(1 - \Delta_i)$, one at the time, and it was observed whether the test statistic reacted in the predicted manner. Therefore, the damaged state PDF was evaluated empirically in another Monte Carlo experiment with 100 data sets and $T = 1$ min. A correct prediction was characterized by an empirical damaged state PDF identical to the theoretical one or by a measured type II error β_{emp} identical to the theoretical one used for the prediction. In this paper, the power of the test was used to verify the predictions, *i.e.* the probability that a damaged structure is correctly classified as damaged.

$$Power = 1 - \beta_{emp} \stackrel{!}{=} 1 - \beta = 98\% \quad (19)$$

For visualization, representative results of the experiments were plotted in Fig. 4 and 5, where the empirical distributions of the test statistic were plotted in a blue histogram, together with the predicted damage state PDF (solid black line) and vertical dotted lines indicating the theoretical safety threshold. Please note that the figures only show the results from one single run, which are subject to uncertainties in both the reference and the test state. To quantify these uncertainties, the experiment was repeated 21 times, and the mean results are given in Table 1 and 2 including the standard deviations.

4.4.1. *Parametric Damage Detection Test*

The accuracy of the predictions could be validated visually in Fig. 5, as the empirical distributions in the damaged states followed the predicted ones. The similarity was confirmed by the values for the power of the test in Table 1, which ranged between 93.3% and 97.5% for Beam 1 - 6, so the maximum deviation from the target value of 98% was 4.7%. The mean power of the test averaged over all damage scenarios was 95.9%, and thus 2.1% below the target value. The inaccuracies could be tied back to a slight bias in the healthy state PDF, meaning the theoretical safety threshold value marginally overestimated the empirical 2% quantile of the empirical distribution. Nonetheless, it was deemed beneficial to use the theoretical safety threshold because it allowed for the time-consuming part of the training state (the empirical evaluation) to be skipped. In other words, there appeared to be a trade-off between increasing the accuracy of the predictions and maximizing the numerical efficiency of the estimation procedure.

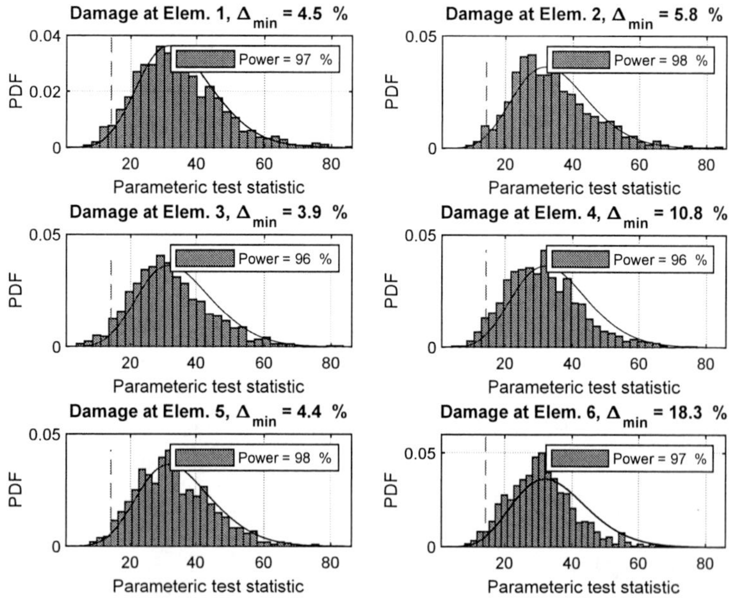

Figure 4: Validating the minimum detectable damage for the parametric test.

Table 1: Empirical power of the test for both damage detection tests, averaged over 21 runs.

No.	Detection test	Power of the test μ/σ [%]						
		Beam 1	Beam 2	Beam 3	Beam 4	Beam 5	Beam 6	Averaged
1	Parametric	96.7/1.8	97.5/1.6	96.4/1.8	95.2/2.6	96.3/2.3	93.3/4.4	95.9/2.4
2	Non-parametric	95.7/2.4	96.9/2.4	93.4 /3.5	92.5/3.1	93.5/2.7	96.4/3.0	94.7/2.8

The minimum detectable damage ranged between 4.0% and 18%, which was very low considering the short measurement duration of 1 min. Interestingly, a large Fisher information did not inevitably correspond to a high damage sensitivity, because the predictive formula also takes into account the parameter's magnitude $\theta_{0,i}$. For example, the main diagonal value of the Fisher information of Parameter 2 was greater than for Parameter 1, see Fig. 3. However, the beam stiffness of Beam 1 was twice as high reducing the minimum damage in Beam 1 to 4.55%, and thus, below 5.83% in Beam 2.

4.4.2. Non-Parametric Damage Detection Test

The accuracy of the predictions could be validated for the non-parametric test as well, see Figure 5, and the values for the power of the test ranges between 92.5% and 96.9%, with a maximum deviation of 5.5% and an averaged deviation of 2.3% from the target value of 98%, see Table 1.

The inaccuracies in the prediction, in particular in comparison to the parametric detection test, were most likely due to the additional bias that is introduced through the empirical curve-fitting. Notwithstanding, the results showcased that the empirical curve-fitting was a suitable approach to roughly estimate the number of degrees of freedom k of the chi-square distribution, so it was a helpful empirical means to fill the theoretical gap. Another contribution was the verification that the Fisher information from the parametric test could indeed be used for the non-parametric test. Since the number of DOFs of the healthy state PDF was greater for the non-parametric test, the distribution was wider, and a greater non-centrality was necessary (greater damage), so the damaged distribution could be discriminated from the healthy one. In other words, the non-parametric test was less sensitive to small damages than the parametric detection test. A great advantage of the non-parametric test was, however, that no parametrization was required for the damage diagnosis, so it could be appropriate for monitoring applications where no accurate finite element model is available.

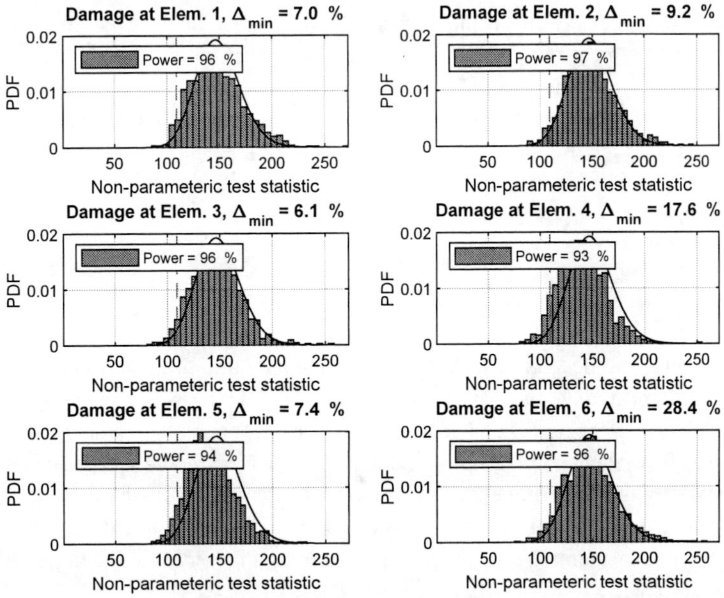

Figure 5: Validating the minimum detectable damage for the non-parametric test.

Table 2: Minimum detectable damage for both damage detectiont tests, averaged over 21 runs.

No.	Detection test	Minimum detectable damage μ/σ (%)					
		Beam 1	Beam 2	Beam 3	Beam 4	Beam 5	Beam 6
1	Parametric	4.55/0.12	5.83/0.15	4.02/0.1	11.03/0.45	4.49/0.20	17.94/0.84
2	Non-parametric	7.13/0.73	9.07/0.26	6.23/0.19	17.02/0.42	6.98/0.24	27.79/0.78

4.5. Discussion

The presented example, although simple, showcased the accuracy of the predictive formula for both the parametric and non-parametric damage detection test. One of the basic assumptions was a full rank sensitivity matrix, an assumption that is fulfilled for a 6-DOF mass-and-spring system. Before closing this paper, the findings for the monitoring problem at hand are generalized for varying design parameters. The following list of remarks also aids in understanding the physical meaning of the predictive formula in Eq. (17) from a theoretical standpoint.

- *Remark 1*: The larger the sample size N, the higher the damage sensitivity of the subspace-based damage detection tests, in an asymptotic manner. The sample size could be increased by extending the measurement duration T or tuning the sampling frequency f_s.
- *Remark 2*: In the presented example, it appeared that increasing the magnitude of the reference parameter $\theta_{0,i}$ leads to a decreasing (relative) minimum detectable damage Δ_i, despite the fact that $\theta_{0,i}$ also influences the Fisher information. That means, for example, that smaller damage percentages can be detected in stiff elements.
- *Remark 3*: The stricter the requirements regarding the reliability of the test, defined through the non-centrality parameter λ, the smaller the sensitivity of the damage diagnosis toward small damages.
- *Remark 4*: The parameters to be monitored remain user-defined, and it is possible to monitor changes in the mass, stiffness and/or damping properties.

The central element of this paper was the Fisher information matrix. It was used as a measure for the detectability of damage and linked the non-centrality in the statistical test to structural changes in a corresponding finite element model. However, it appeared that the minimum detectable damage also depended on the magnitude of the structural parameter to be monitored, see $\theta_{0,i}$ in Eq. (17). In this sense, a more suitable measure for the detectability of damage could be obtained by rearranging the predictive formula, for example, for the minimum measurement duration.

$$T = \frac{\lambda}{f_s \Delta_i^2} \left(\frac{1}{\theta_{0,i}^2 \cdot F_{ii}} \right) [s] \tag{20}$$

5. CONCLUSIONS

In this paper, a formula was developed that allows for the prediction of the minimum detectable damage for subspace-based damage diagnosis. By applying it to a simple mass-and-spring system, it was possible to illustrate both the effectiveness and accuracy of the predictions. A notable theoretical contribution was the extension of the theory to the non-parametric test, where theoretical concepts are mixed with auxiliary empirical means to determine the healthy state. Moreover, a code-based reliability concept was introduced that can be used to fix the non-centrality parameter based on user-defined requirements. Ultimately, the minimum measurement duration was proposed as a measure for the detectability of damage.

A major limitation is that the predictive formula only holds true for full rank sensitivitiy matrices, a condition that may be violated for any structure where different structural parameters cause a similar deviation in the Gaussian residual. This matter will be the subject of future studies.

ACKNOWLEDGMENTS

The financial support from the German Academic Exchange Service (DAAD) and the Natural Sciences and Engineering Research Council of Canada (NSERC) is gratefully acknowledged.

REFERENCES

[1] Farrar, C., & Worden, K. (2012). *Structural health monitoring: A machine learning perspective*. Oxford, U.K.: Wiley.

[2] Schnellenbach-Held, M., Karczewski, B., & Kühn, O. (2014). *Intelligente Brücke - Machbarkeitsstudie für ein System zur Informationsbereitstellung und ganzheitlichen Bewertung in Echtzeit für Brückenbauwerke*. Berichte der Bundesanstalt für Strassenwesen Brücken- und Ingenieurbau. Bremen, Germany: Fachverlag NW.

[3] Benveniste, A., Basseville, M., & Moustakides, G. (1987). The asymptotic local approach to change detection and model validation. *IEEE Transactions on Automatic Control, 32*(7), 583–592.

[4] Basseville, M., Abdelghani, M., & Benveniste, A. (2000). Subspace-based fault detection algorithms for vibration monitoring. *Automatica, 36*(1), 101–109.

[5] Balmès, É., Basseville, M., Mevel, L., Nasser, H., & Zhou, W. (2008). Statistical model-based damage localization: a combined subspace-based and substructuring approach. *Structural Control and Health Monitoring, 15*(6), 857–875.

[6] Döhler, M., Mevel, L., & Hille, F. (2014). Subspace-based damage detection under changes in the ambient excitation statistics. *Mechanical Systems and Signal Processing, 45*(1), 207–224.

[7] Döhler, M., Mevel, L., & Zhang, Q. (2016). Fault detection, isolation and quantification from Gaussian residuals with application to structural damage diagnosis. *Annual Reviews in Control, 42*, 244–256.

[8] Döhler, M., Kwan, K., & Bernal, D. (2013). Optimal sensor placement with a statistical criterion for subspace-based damage detection. In *Proceedings of the IMAC - 31st International Modal Analysis Conference* (Vol. 4, pp. 219–229). New York: Springer.

[9] Basseville, M., Mevel, L., & Goursat, M. (2004). Statistical model-based damage detection and localization: subspace-based residuals and damage-to-noise sensitivity ratios. *Journal of Sound and Vibration, 275*(3-5), 769–794.

[10] Heylen, W., & Sas, P. (1997). *Modal analysis theory and testing*. Belgium: K. U. Leuven.

[11] Allahdadian, S. (2017). *Robust statistical subspace-based damage assessment* (Doctoral dissertation, University of British Columbia, Vancouver).

[12] Wenzel, H. (2009). *Health monitoring of bridges*. Chichester U.K.: Wiley.

IOMAC'19

8th International Operational Modal Analysis Conference
2019 May13-15 Copenhagen

MODAL STRAIN-BASED DAMAGE DETECTION ON A PRE-STRESSED CONCRETE BEAM UNDER CHANGING TEMPERATURE

Dimitrios Anastasopoulos [1], *Edwin P.B. Reynders* [2], *and Guido De Roeck* [3]

[1] PhD candidate, Dept. of Civil Engineering, KU Leuven, Leuven, Belgium, dimitrios.anastasopoulos@kuleuven.be
[2] Professor, Dept. of Civil Engineering, KU Leuven, Leuven, Belgium, edwin.reynders@kuleuven.be
[3] Emeritus Professor, Dept. of Civil Engineering, KU Leuven, Leuven, Belgium, guido.deroeck@kuleuven.be

ABSTRACT
Vibration-based SHM constitutes a non-destructive condition assessment method that is used for monitoring civil infrastructure. However, the commonly employed dynamic characteristics, natural frequencies and mode shapes, are relatively insensitive to local damage of moderate severity while the sensitivity of natural frequencies to temperature fluctuations may be sufficiently high to mask the effect of damage. Modal strains are more sensitive to local damage but the influence of temperature on modal strains is not well-known. In this context, a prestressed concrete beam is monitored under changing temperature conditions in the framework of a progressive damage test to investigate the influence of temperature versus damage on modal strains. The modal strains are identified from a strain-based modal analysis where dynamic strains measured with multiplexed FBG strain sensors are used. The level of damage that can be identified from the modal strains with/without accounting the influence of temperature is quantified.

Keywords: structural health monitoring, fiber optic sensors, modal strains, system identification, experimental modal analysis

1. INTRODUCTION

Vibration-Based Structural Health Monitoring (VBSHM), can be a successful non-destructive approach for damage identification and structural condition assessment of civil structures [1, 2]. The idea behind VBSHM is to identify changes in the modal characteristics of a structure that are directly related to damage [1, 2, 3]. The main challenge for VBSHM is to identify modal characteristics that are as sensitive as possible to structural damage and at the same time as insensitive as possible to measurement noise, loading, and environmental factors such as temperature [3, 4]. Natural frequencies are probably the most commonly used modal characteristics for damage identification [5, 6]. However, natural frequencies are influenced by environmental factors, such as temperature, and that influence can be high enough to completely mask the presence of even severe damage, necessitating data normalization [2, 7, 8]. A promising alternative can be the monitoring of modal characteristics obtained from dynamic strain measurements, such as modal strains and curvatures which are more sensitive to local damage than modal displacements, offering in this way a higher accuracy in damage detection and localization [9, 10, 11].

The introduction of fiber-optic sensors (FOS) that can accurately measure dynamic strains and offer ease of installation, resistance in harsh environment and long-term stability, contributed to an increased interest in adopting these sensors for VBSHM applications [12]. Fiber Bragg grating (FBG) sensors [13] share the important advantages of other FOS, but additionally they are easy to multiplex (i.e. many different sensors can be inscribed into the same glass fiber) and they have a relatively low cost. FBGs are being used for real-time monitoring of a wide range of structures, including bridges [14].

Measuring the very small dynamic strains that occur in civil structures during ambient or operational excitation with high accuracy and precision and in a dense grid has become possible thanks to the recent development of two approaches [11, 15]. The second approach is implemented in this article for SHM purposes by repetitively identifying modal strains and monitoring their changes over time. The modal-strain based damage identification has been proved to be a successful approach for early stage, local damage identification [11] of beam structures. In the present paper, the influence that temperature has on modal strains and how this influence is compared with the influence of damage is investigated. The method is presented through application on a prestressed concrete beam, which is subjected to a progressive damage test (PDT). Modal tests are performed at the end of each loading cycle for a period of time between 72 h and 90 h under different temperature conditions. The beam is monitored with four chains of multiplexed FBG sensors and is excited with an electrodynamic shaker. The data are used in a strain-based modal analysis. The obtained modal characteristics of the various damage stages are then compared and shifts in their values are related to the presence and location of structural damage.

2. EXPERIMENTAL SETUP

2.1. Test structure

A prestressed concrete beam serves as the test structure. The length of the beam is 5.0 m and it has a rectangular cross-section of 24x20 cm with chamfered edges (Figure 1). High-strength concrete (HSC) of the category C70/85 was used. The longitudinal reinforcement of the beam consists of 5 prestressed low relaxation strands with a nominal diameter of 12.5 mm and characteristic tensile strength σ_{pk} = 1860 MPa. Three strands are positioned at the bottom of the beam and two at the top (Figure 1). The strands are given an initial stress of σ_{p0} = 744 MPa (50% of $\sigma_{p0,max}$), where $\sigma_{p0,max} = 0.8\sigma_{pk}$ = 1488 MPa. Closed-loop stirrups, with a nominal diameter of 6 mm and a centre-to-centre distance of 150 mm are provided to withstand the shear forces (Figure 1).

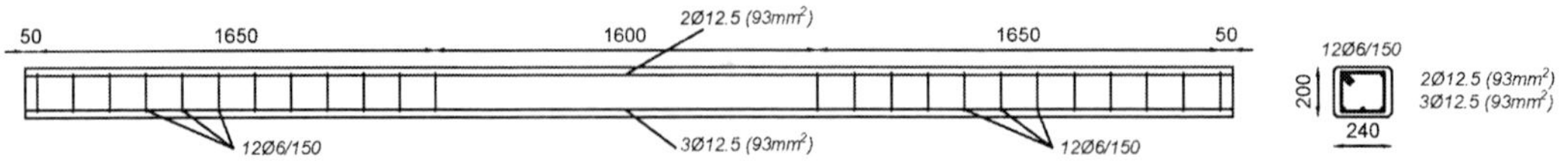

Figure 1: The reinforcement of the prestressed beam (dimensions in mm).

2.2. Quasi-static progressive damage test

The beam is subjected to a 4-point progressive damage test (PDT). The static boundary conditions approximate these of a simply supported beam. The static steel roller supports are at 50 cm from the ends of the beam. The quasi-static load is applied through two hydraulic jacks, controlled with a hydraulic pump which is operated manually, at two points located 1.0 m respectively from the center of the beam, as shown in Figure 2. Therefore, a zone of constant bending moment is created in between the two hydraulic jacks, where most of the bending cracks are expected during the PDT. An overview of the complete setup of the PDT is displayed in Figure 3.

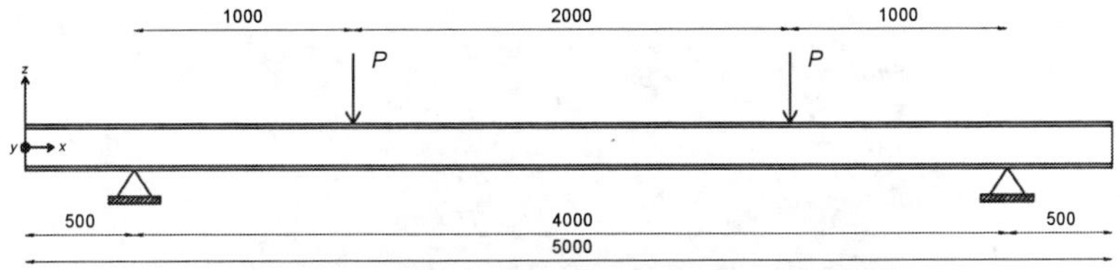

Figure 2: Schematic representation of the PDT - front view (dimensions in mm).

Figure 3: The PDT setup, showing the deflection of the beam under static loading by the hydraulic jacks.

A progressive damage loading scheme is followed, consisting of 9 loading cycles of increasing load, where the load step is 30 kN for the first 2 cycles and 10 kN from the third cycle on. The beam failed during the 9th loading cycle for a load of 2P $\approx$ 160 kN. The type of the failure was crushing of the concrete in the middle of the beam. The beam exceeded its cracking load after the second loading cycle (loading cycle amplitude of 60 kN) for a total load of 2P $\approx$ 55 kN (Figure 2). The crack pattern, up to the failure of the beam, is shown in Figure 4.

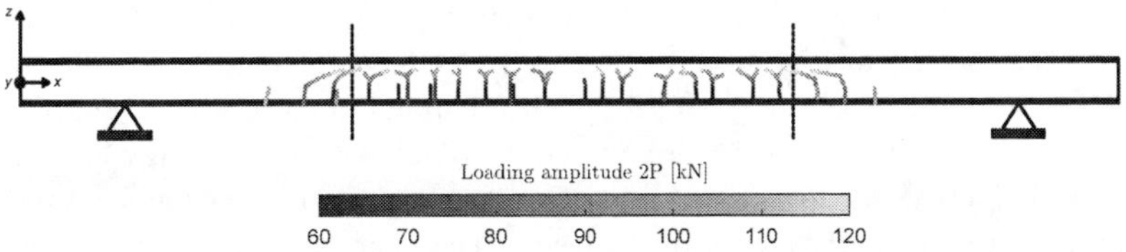

Figure 4: The crack pattern of the beam. The dashed lines indicate the locations that the quasi-static load is applied during the PDT.

2.3. Modal test setup

The beam is repeatedly subjected to vibration tests to identify its modal characteristics, i.e. natural frequencies and strain mode shapes. The vibration tests are performed before and after each PDT loading cycle, and for a range of temperatures. The dynamic boundary conditions approximate these of a free-free vibrating beam. This is achieved by using inflated tires (Figure 5). The tires are placed below the beam at both ends and when they are inflated the beam is detached from its static supports and rests solely on the fexible tires. Hence, it is considered to be in dynamically decoupled (free-free) boundary conditions. The assumption of free-free boundary conditions is confirmed when the identified natural frequency of the highest rigid-body mode of the beam ($\approx$ 16 Hz) is compared with the identified natural frequency of the lowest vibration mode of the beam ($\approx$ 36 Hz). The difference is sufficient to consider the beam decoupled by its supports.

Figure 5: One of the inflated tires used to approximate dynamic free-free boundary conditions.

The beam is excited by a Gaussian white noise force signal in the frequency bandwidth (0-400) Hz. The signal is applied in the vertical direction of the beam through an electrodynamic shaker that is connected with the beam at a single location, at 3.5 m from its left end (Figure 6)). The duration of every modal test is 70 s. The amount of modal tests and the temperature range that is achieved for each damaged state are summarized in Table 1.

Table 1: Amount of modal tests and temperature range for each state.

State	Amount of tests	Temperature range (T_{min}-T_{max}) [°C]	T_{max}-T_{min} [°C]
Undamaged	161	22.0-32.6	10.6
After 30 kN	144	21.6-34.5	12.9
After 60 kN	166	18.3-34.3	16.0
After 70 kN	126	19.4-34.3	14.9
After 80 kN	107	22.3-34.5	12.2
After 90 kN	115	23.6-34.6	11.0
After 100 kN	109	23.3-34.5	11.2
After 110 kN	139	22.9-34.3	11.4
After 120 kN	112	22.0-34.6	12.6

The dynamic strains of the beam are measured with four chains of multiplexed FBG strain sensors from FBGS attached to the four edges of the beam (Figure 6). Each chain contains 20 FBG sensors and is attached to the side beam along its longitudinal direction through a custom clamping system [11], to measure axial dynamic strains. The distance between two consecutive clamping blocks is 25 cm and one FBG sensor exists between them, measuring the average strain or macrostrain between both blocks in a quasi-distributed way along the length of the beam. The fibers are prestressed to ensure that they would remain in tension while they are also covered with thermal insulation, to ensure that temperature fluctuations in the laboratory would not affect the measurements.

When dynamic strains are measured, the ability to determine the Bragg wavelength shift with adequate accuracy and precision is essential. Therefore, the strain acquisition system is an interrogator of relatively high wavelength accuracy ($\pm$1 pm) and precision (<0.1 pm), the FAZ Technologies FAZT-I4. When the measured wavelength shifts are lower than the resolution of the acquisition system, the implementation of a method that will interpolate the wavelength spectrum down to the desired resolution level is mandatory [15]. However, the resolution of the I4 is adequate for the presented work and therefore, no method needs to be implemented. The position-averaged root mean square (RMS) strain value of the dynamic strain measurements is 0.04 $\mu\epsilon$, similar to the strain levels that stiff civil structures, like stiff bridges, exhibit during ambient or operational excitation. The FAZT-I4 sampling frequency is f_s = 1000 Hz.

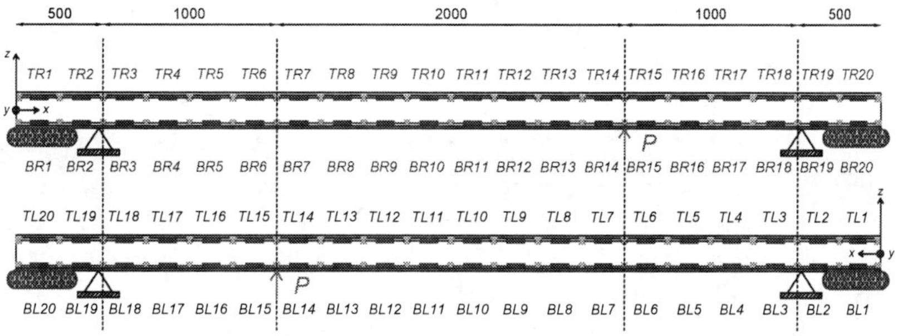

Figure 6: The setup of the FBGs. Left-right and right-left front view. The yellow rectangles represent the clamping blocks. The blue rectangles represent the FBG senors in between the clamping blocks. TR stands for top tight, BR for bottom right, TL for top left and BL for bottom left side of the beam. P indicates the location that the white noise force signal is applied (dimensions in mm).

2.4. Temperature influence setup

The influence of temperature changes on the modal characteristics of the beam is investigated. A temperature range of at least 10°C is aimed at. To this end, the beam is covered with a tent structure, as shown in Figure 7(a). Six portable 2 kW floor fan heaters are used to increase the temperature in the tent. The fans heaters are uniformly distributed in the tent to create uniform temperature conditions.

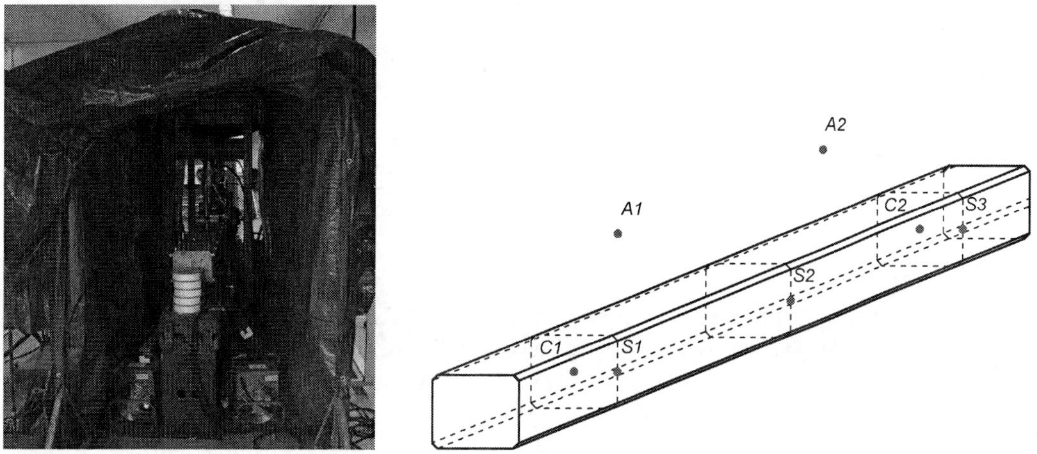

(a) (b)

Figure 7: (a) The temperature influence setup. Two of the fan heaters can be seen next to the beam. (b) The setup of the thermocouples. S1-S3 are the surface sensors, C1, C2 are the core sensors and A1, A2 are the air sensors.

The temperature is measured with thermocouples at seven locations. Two sensors are measuring the temperature inside the core of the beam, three on its surface and two are measuring the air temperature inside the tent. The layout of the sensors is shown in Figure 7(b). The concrete core temperature is measured at the locations where the static supports are applied during the PDT. In this way, the holes that have been made to reach the core with the thermocouples do not influence the crack formation during the PDT.

The highest temperature that can be achieved is $\approx$ 35°C. The temperature influence test consists of two phases: a heating up phase during which the fan heaters are switched on, and a cooling down phase during which they are switched off. The heating up phase, from room temperature to 35°C, lasts for $\approx$ 24 h. The cooling down phase from 35°C to room temperature lasts between 48 h and 90 h, depending on the room temperature outside the tent. Every half an hour, a modal test is performed (Section 2.3.). The temperature of the beam is defined as the average measured temperature of the two thermocouples that are measuring the core temperature and the three thermocouples that are measuring the surface temperature, when the absolute temperature difference among all of them is $< 1°C$. Then, the temperature of the beam is considered uniform. The air temperature is changing much faster than this of the beam and the two are in agreement only in steady-state room temperature. Thus, the air temperature is discarded.

A typical heating up/cooling down temperature time history, as recorded from the seven thermocouples is shown in Figure 8. The fluctuations of the air temperature between 35°C and 39°C are due to the safety thermostats of the fan heaters. After they reach the maximum temperature defined by their thermostats, the heaters are automatically switching off. They are switching on again when the temperature drops below 35°C. The cooling down lasts for 90 hours, as the lowest possible temperature is desired. To facilitate the process, the laboratory is ventilated during a cool day, at the end of the measurements. The lowest temperature of 18.3°C is achieved during this day.

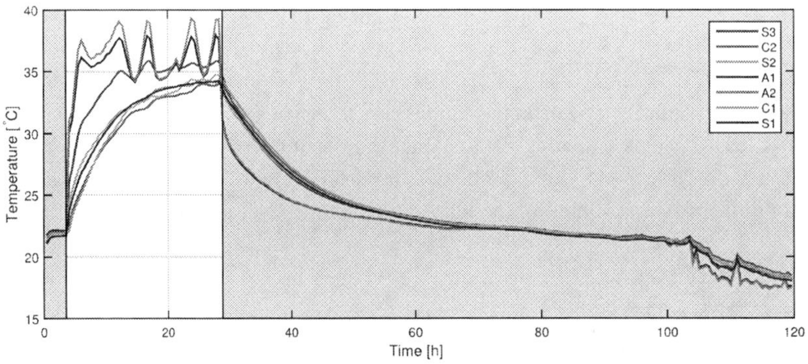

Figure 8: Typical heating up/cooling down temperature time history. The shaded parts of the graph indicate the time ranges that the temperature of the beam is considered to be uniform.

3. EXPERIMENTAL RESULTS

Dynamic strain data obtained from the FBG sensors are used for identifying the modal characteristics of the beam. In order to simulate in-situ conditions, only the measured dynamic strains are used in the system identification, resulting in an output-only modal analysis. The system identification is conducted with MACEC, a MATLAB toolbox for experimental and operational modal analysis [16]. The data-driven stochastic subspace identification SSI-data technique [17, 18] is applied, which is an output-only identification technique. The model order is chosen in steps of 2 and the maximum order is 100. The half number of Hankel block rows i is 40. The static or DC offset is removed first from all measured signals. Furthermore, a fourth-order Butterworth filter with a high-pass frequency of 4 Hz is applied to all channels to remove the influence of the small temperature fluctuations on the strain measurements during the modal tests. Four vertical bending modes are identified in the bandwidth (0-400) Hz and are manually selected from stabilization diagrams [19]. The lateral bending modes are not identified as the shaker excitation is in the vertical direction of the beam. Therefore, the lateral modes are not excited.

3.1. Influence of damage versus temperature on natural frequencies

The evolution of the natural frequencies, throughout the PDT, for the first two modes (B1 and B2) is shown in Figure 9. The presented values are the ones measured for a uniform beam temperature of 24°C. A gradual reduction of the natural frequency values is observed, which is correlated with the increased level of damage of the beam. The trend is similar for the other modes and thus their reduction is not graphically presented. The percentile reduction of the natural frequency values is about 3.5% for modes B1 and B2, when the undamaged beam natural frequencies are compared with the natural frequencies after the 8th loading cycle (loading cycle amplitude of 120 kN).

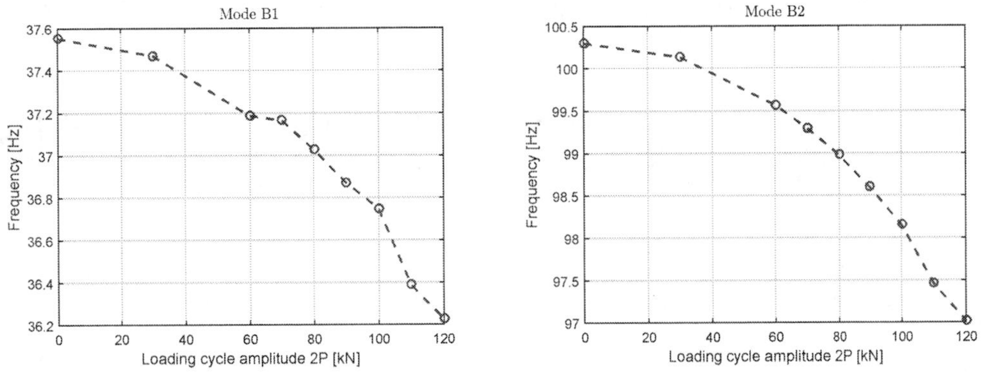

Figure 9: Evolution of the natural frequencies (strain-based modal analysis) for modes B1 and B2 at a uniform beam temperature of 24°C. The 0 kN loading cycle amplitude corresponds to the undamaged beam.

Moreover, the influence that the damage and the temperature have on the natural frequencies of the vertical bending modes of the beam is investigated. The identified natural frequencies versus the corresponding temperature are presented in Figure 10, for all loading cycles and for modes B1 and B2. The trend is similar for the other modes and thus their evolution is not graphically presented here. For each loading cycle, a straight line is fitted between the natural frequency values and the temperature at which they have been identified, to describe the relationship between the natural frequencies and the temperature for the specific damaged state of the beam. The temperature range is between 10°C and 15°C among the loading steps, allowing for a clear trend between natural frequency and temperature to be established.

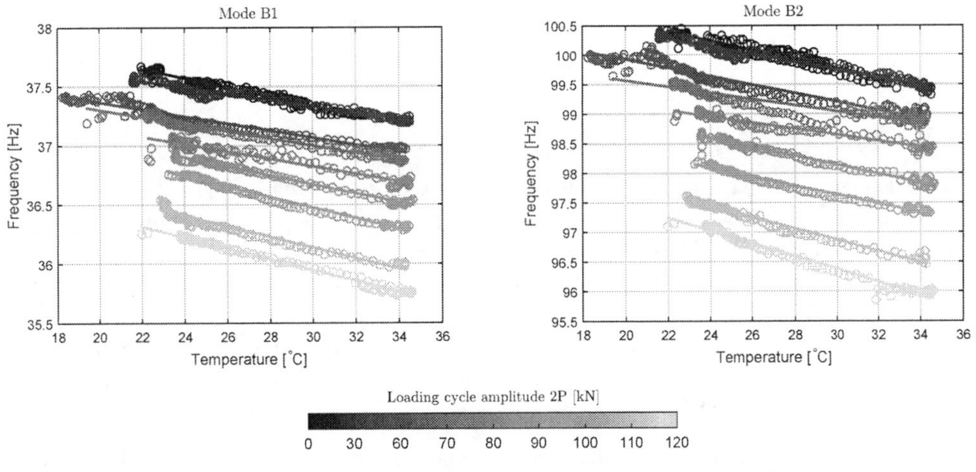

Figure 10: Evolution of the natural frequency for the vertical bending modes B1 and B2 for the first 8 loading cycles. The 0 kN loading cycle amplitude corresponds to the undamaged beam.

As it can be seen in Figure 10, there is a clear linear reduction of the natural frequencies of the beam when its temperature is increasing. An increase of $\Delta T = 10°C$ in temperature results in a decrease of about $\Delta f = 0.8\%$ for the natural frequencies, which translates to a change of about $\Delta E = 0.8$ GPa for the dynamic Young's modulus. The nominal value of the dynamic Young's modulus is E(24°C) = 46 GPa. The relationship appears to be relatively consistent among the different modes and among the different damaged states. The influence of temperature on the natural frequencies of the beam is quite large when compared to this of damage, given that a change of temperature by 40°C can create a change in the natural frequency values of 3.5%, the same as the one due to damage.

3.2. Influence of damage versus temperature on strain mode shapes

The strain mode shapes ϕ_t of a test t are normalized to unit modal strain [17]. A normalization scheme [20] is applied here that allows for a consistent re-scaling of the strain mode shapes so they can be directly compared within the different loading cycles and temperatures. It consists of two normalization steps: first rotating ϕ_t such that one of its components $\phi_{t,l}$ has zero imaginary part and second re-scaling ϕ_t such that its Euclidean norm has unit length. Application of the first step yields:

$$\phi_{1t} = \phi_t e^{-i\alpha_{t,l}} \tag{1}$$

where $\alpha_{t,l}$ is the phase angle of $\phi_{t,l}$. Application of the second step results in:

$$\phi_{2t} = \frac{\phi_{1t}}{||\phi_{1t}||} \tag{2}$$

The influence of the temperature fluctuations throughout the PDT on the strain mode shapes is investigated. First, for each damage state (or PDT step), the strain mode shapes are grouped in temperature groups that have a range of 2°C per group. Then, the sample mean strain mode shape $E[\phi_2^j]$, the sample standard deviation of the strain mode shapes $\sigma[\phi_2^j]$ and the 95% confidence interval of the sample mean strain mode shape $CI[\phi_2^j]$ are obtained for each temperature group j from Equations 3 - 5 respectively:

$$E[\phi_2^j] = \frac{1}{n_s}\sum_{s=1}^{n_s} \phi_{2,s}^j \tag{3}$$

$$\sigma[\phi_2^j] = \frac{1}{n_s}\sqrt{\sum_{s=1}^{n_s}(\phi_{2,s}^j - E[\phi_2^j])^2} \tag{4}$$

$$CI[\phi_2^j] = [-2\sigma[\phi_2^j], 2\sigma[\phi_2^j]] \tag{5}$$

where n_s denotes the number of tests within the temperature group j and $\phi_{2,s}^j$ is the strain mode shape of a mode of test s. Combined graphs are given, where the mean strain mode shapes with their 95% confidence interval, $E[\phi_2^j] \pm CI[\phi_2^j]$ and for the different temperature groups within the same damaged state are plotted on the same graph, versus the median temperature of the temperature group for which they are obtained. The mean strain mode shapes of the different temperature groups of modes B1, B2 and B3 are displayed in Figures 11(a)-(c), for the 2nd loading cycle (loading amplitude of 60 kN), where the largest temperature range is recorded (Table 1). In Figure 11(d) the zone between the points where the load is applied (1500-3500 mm) for mode B1 is displayed in detail.

The confidence intervals $CI[\phi_2^j]$ of the mean strain mode shapes that are obtained at different temperatures are all completely overlapping, as shown with more detail in Figure 11(d). The same observation applies for all modes. Thus, it can be concluded that there is no clear influence of the temperature on the strain mode shapes, for the given temperature range of 16°C, as all mean strain mode shapes lie within the same narrow bounds of uncertainty.

Furthermore, the influence of the damage on the strain mode shapes of the beam is investigated. Since no influence of the temperature on the strain mode shapes is identified, the mean strain mode shapes $E[\phi_2]$ over all tests (sample) within a loading cycle are considered as representative of this damaged state. The sample mean strain mode shapes $E[\phi_2]$ of the different damaged states are plotted on the same graph in Figures 12(a)-(c) including the 95% confidence interval of the sample ($CI[\phi_2] = [-2\sigma[\phi_2], 2\sigma[\phi_2]]$), $E[\phi_2] \pm CI[\phi_2]$.

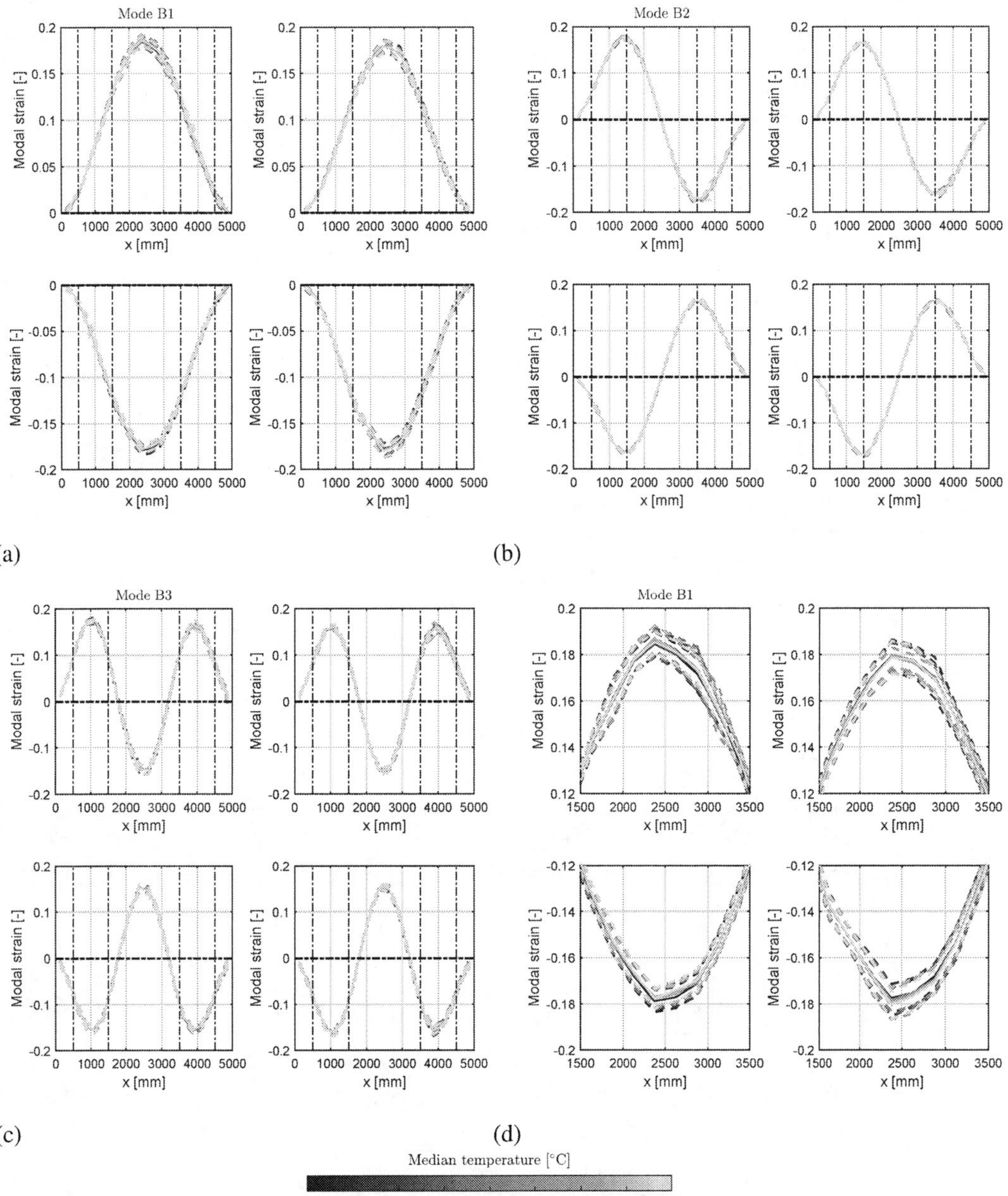

Figure 11: (a), (b) and (c), mean strain mode shapes $E[\phi_2^j]$ for modes B1-B3, after the 2nd loading cycle (60 kN), for the different temperature groups j, (d), detail of the zone 1500-3500 mm for mode B1. The dashed lines correspond to the $CI[\phi_2^j]$. The top subplots correspond to the top fibers and the bottom to the bottom fibers. The left subplots correspond to the side of the beam with positive y-coordinates while the right subplots to the side of the beam with negative y-coordinates.

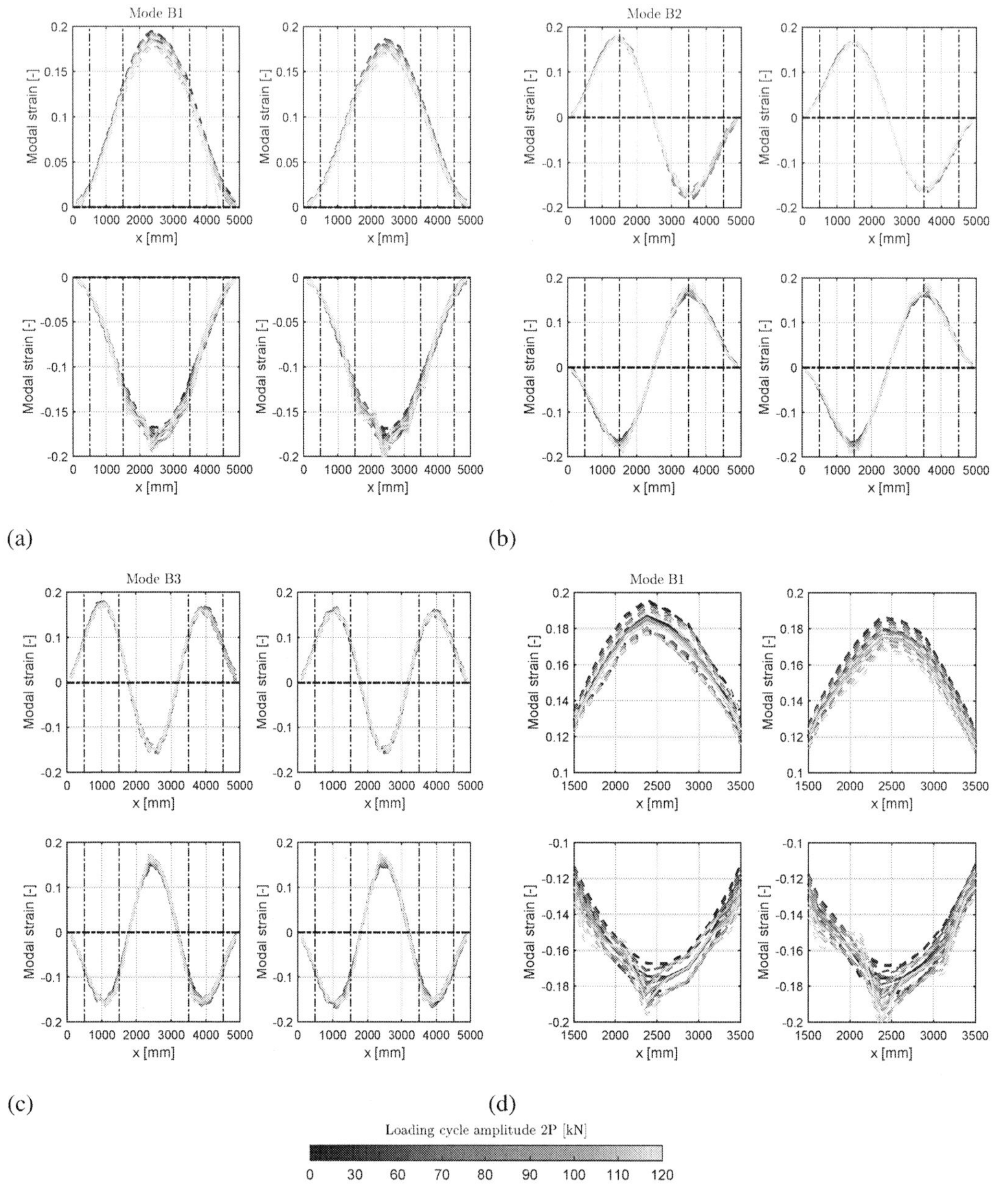

Figure 12: (a), (b) and (c), evolution of mean strain mode shapes $E[\phi_2]$ for modes B1-B3, for the first 8 loading cycles, (d), detail of the zone 1500-3500 mm for mode B1. The 0 kN loading cycle amplitude corresponds to the undamaged beam. The dashed lines correspond to the $CI[\phi_2]$. The top subplots correspond to the top fibers and the bottom to the bottom fibers. The left subplots correspond to the side of the beam with positive y-coordinates while the right subplots to the side of the beam with negative y-coordinates.

Moreover, the variance of the sample mean values of the strain mode shapes $\sigma[E[\phi_2]]$ of a single loading cycle is calculated:

$$\sigma[E[\phi_2]] = \frac{\sigma[\phi_2]}{\sqrt{N_s}} \tag{6}$$

where N_s is the total number of tests that are conducted within a loading cycle. The mean strain mode shape $E[\phi_2]$ of mode B1 at each loading cycle, including the 95% confidence interval, $CI[E[\phi_2]] = [-2\sigma[E[\phi_2]], 2\sigma[E[\phi_2]]]$, which is obtained from the variance of the mean of the strain mode shape, is shown in Figure 13(a), $E[\phi_2] \pm CI[E[\phi_2]]$. In Figure 13(b) the zone between the points at which the load is applied (1500-3500 mm) for mode B1 is presented in detail. Similar accuracy is obtained for mode B2 and B3 and thus the modes are not presented.

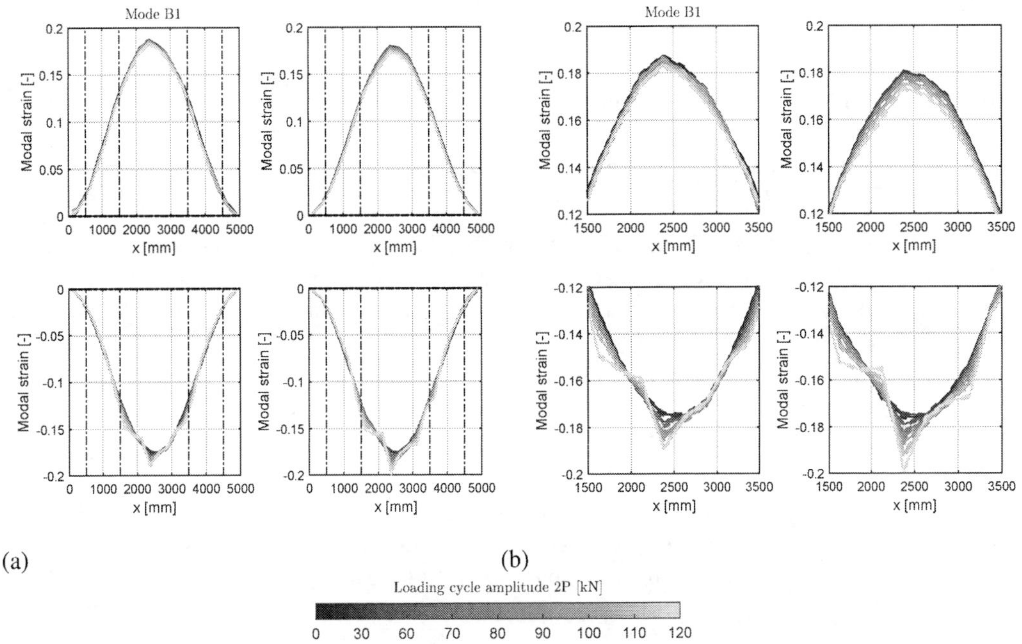

Figure 13: (a) evolution of the mean strain mode shape $E[\phi_2]$ of mode B1, for the first 8 loading cycles and (b), detail of the zone 1500-3500 mm for mode B1. The 0 kN loading cycle amplitude corresponds to the undamaged beam. The dashed lines correspond to the $CI[E[\phi_2]]$. The top subplots correspond to the top fibers and the bottom to the bottom fibers. The left subplots correspond to the side of the beam with positive y-coordinates while the right subplots to the side of the beam with negative y-coordinates.

The evolution of the strain mode shapes during the different loading cycles is prominent and follows the evolution of the cracks, even though the cracks are nearly closed after the static unloading of the beam due to the prestressing force. Strain amplitude changes are observed in the vicinity of the damaged area (between the points of the load application) for all modes, as can be seen from the strain mode shapes in Figures 12 and 13. The largest changes of the modal strain amplitude correspond to the damaged state after the end of the 8th loading cycle at 120 kN (70% of the failure load at 160 kN), when the FBG chains were detached to avoid damaging them during a PDT loading cycle. More specifically, the amplitude of the bottom strain mode shapes is increasing with the increasing level of damage at the vicinity of the damaged zone (e.g. Figures 12(d) and 13(b)-bottom subplots) and the changes are more prominent at the locations of the cracks (Figure 4). On the contrary, the amplitude of the top strain mode shapes is decreasing in a uniform pattern at the vicinity of the damaged zone (e.g. Figure 12(d) and 13(b)-top subplots). This increase/decrease of the strain amplitude for the bottom/top strain mode shapes is related to the shift of the neutral axis of the beam due to the increasing level of damage. Changes in the amplitude of the strain mode shapes are already identified after the end of the 2nd loading cycle with force amplitude of 60 kN, when the beam reached its crack load, indicating early crack identification. The $CI[E[\phi_2]]$ as obtained from the variance of the mean values of the strain mode shapes is narrow for all modes throughout the PDT indicating high identification accuracy and most important that the changes that are observed on the strain mode shapes are due to the increasing level of damage, as they exceed the statistical identification uncertainty (Figure 13).

4. CONCLUDING REMARKS

In this article, a new method was presented for VBSHM by means of quasi-distributed longitudinal macrostrain FBG sensing. The method was demonstrated and validated by progressive damage testing of a prestressed concrete beam, subjected to changing temperature conditions. The high prestressing force that is not combined with the influence of a high self-weight of the beam is a very challenging case for VBSHM, as the prestressing force results in almost closed cracks after the unloading of the beam. Thus, the changes in the dynamic stiffness are very small when the beam is unloaded, even when the cracks are clearly visible when the beam is loaded. This is a case that seldom occurs on real structures, such as bridges, where the high self-weight of the deck of a bridge would probably keep cracks at least partially open, even when there is no traffic on top. This would facilitate the identification of the damage through VBSHM means.

The identified natural frequencies of the beam were found to be influenced both by damage and temperature changes. The influence of temperature was large enough to super-pass the influence of damage and potentially mask its presence. This confirms the necessity of data normalization when natural frequencies are implemented for SHM purposes.

The strain mode shapes were found to be insensitive to temperature changes, regardless of the level of damage in the beam. This is an important conclusion, since a temperature-insensitive modal characteristic can be directly used for damage detection, without requiring data normalization. However, this needs to be further confirmed in-situ on a full size civil structure where more complex boundary conditions apply and the temperature is not uniform along the structure. Moreover, the strain mode shapes exhibit high sensitivity to local damage, which is pronounced already from an early damaged state, as it has been confirmed in previous research for more complex beam structures[11].

ACKNOWLEDGEMENTS

The research presented in this paper has been performed within the framework of the project G099014N "Robust vibration-based damage identification with a novel high-accuracy strain measurement system", funded by the Research Foundation Flanders (FWO), Belgium. Their financial support is gratefully acknowledged. The authors wish to express their gratitude to Ergon NV for supplying the concrete beam that served as a test object in this study.

REFERENCES

[1] S. W. Doebling, C. R. Farrar, and M. B. Prime. A summary review of vibration-based damage identification methods. *The Shock and Vibration Digest*, 30(2):91–105, 1998.

[2] J. M. W. Brownjohn, A. De Stefano, Y. L. Xu, H. Wenzel, and A. E. Aktan. Vibration-based monitoring of civil infrastructure: challenges and successes. *Civl Structural Health Monitoring*, 1(3–4):79–95, 2011.

[3] W. Fan and P. Qiao. Vibration-based damage identification methods: a review and comparative study. *Structural Health Monitoring*, 10(1):83–111, 2010.

[4] A. Deraemaeker, E. Reynders, G. De Roeck, and J. Kullaa. Vibration based Structural Health Monitoring using output-only measurements under changing environment. *Mechanical Systems and Signal Processing*, 22(1):34–56, 2008.

[5] B. Peeters and G. De Roeck. One-year monitoring of the Z24-bridge: environmental effects versus damage events. *Earthquake Engineering and Structural Dynamics*, 30(2):149–171, 2001.

[6] E. J. Cross, K. Y. Koo, J. M. W. Brownjohn, and K. Worden. Long-term monitoring and data analysis of the Tamar Bridge. *Mechanical Systems and Signal Processing*, 35(1–2):16–34, 2013.

[7] E. Reynders, G. Wursten, and G. De Roeck. Output-only structural health monitoring in changing environmental conditions by means of nonlinear system identification. *Structural Health Monitoring*, 13(1):82–93, 2014.

[8] K. Worden and E. J. Cross. On switching response surface models, with applications to the structural health monitoring of bridges. *Mechanical Systems and Signal Processing*, 98:139–156, 2018.

[9] J.F. Unger, A. Teughels, and G. De Roeck. Damage detection of a prestressed concrete beam using modal strains. *Structural Engineering*, 131(9):1456–1463, 2005.

[10] E. Reynders, G. De Roeck, P.G. Bakir, and C. Sauvage. Damage identification on the Tilff bridge by vibration monitoring using optical fibre strain sensors. *ASCE J. of Engineering Mechanics*, 133(2):185–193, 2007.

[11] D. Anastasopoulos, M. De Smedt, L. Vandewalle, G. De Roeck, and E. Reynders. Damage identification using modal strains identified from operational fiber-optic Bragg grating data. *Structural Health Monitoring*, 17(6):1441–1459, 2018.

[12] B. Glisic and D. Inaudi. *Fibre Optic Methods for Structural Health Monitoring*. John Willey & Sons, West Sussex, U.K., 2007.

[13] G. Meltz, W. W. Morey, and W. H. Glenn. Formation of bragg gratings in optical fibers by a transverse holographic method. *Optics Letters*, 14(15):823–825, Aug 1989.

[14] T. H. T. Chan, L. Yu, H. Y. Tam, Y. Q. Ni, S. Y. Liu, W. H. Chung, and L. K. Cheng. Fiber Bragg grating sensors for structural health monitoring of Tsing Ma bridge: background and experimental observation. *Engineering Structures*, 28(5):648–659, 2006.

[15] D. Anastasopoulos, P. Moretti, T. Geernaert, B. De Pauw, U. Nawrot, G. De Roeck, F. Berghmans, and E. Reynders. Identification of modal strains using sub-microstrain FBG data and a novel wavelength-shift detection algorithm. *Mechanical Systems and Signal Processing*, 86A:58–74, 2017.

[16] E. Reynders, M. Schevenels, and G. De Roeck. MACEC 3.3: a Matlab toolbox for experimental and operational modal analysis. Report BWM-2014-06, July 2014.

[17] B. Peeters and G. De Roeck. Reference-based stochastic subspace identification for output-only modal analysis. *Mechanical Systems and Signal Processing*, 13(6):855–878, 1999.

[18] E. Reynders, R. Pintelon, and G. De Roeck. Uncertainty bounds on modal parameters obtained from Stochastic Subspace Identification. *Mechanical Systems and Signal Processing*, 22(4):948–969, 2008.

[19] E. Reynders, J. Houbrechts, and G. De Roeck. Fully automated (operational) modal analysis. *Mechanical Systems and Signal Processing*, 29:228–250, 2012.

[20] E. Reynders, K. Maes, G. Lombaert, and G. De Roeck. Uncertainty quantification in operational modal analysis with stochastic subspace identification: validation and applications. *Mechanical Systems and Signal Processing*, 66–67:13–30, 2016.

IOMAC'19

8th International Operational Modal Analysis Conference

2019 May13-15 Copenhagen

MODAL TRACKING OF TWO WHARF STRUCTURES UNDER ENVIRONMENTAL, OPERATIONAL AND EARTHQUAKE LOADS

R. Boroschek[1], *E. Peña*[2], *P. Villalpando*[2], *N. Novoa*[3]

[1] Univ. Chile and RBA, rborosch@ing.uchile.cl, ruben.boroschek@rba-global.com

[2] RBA Emilio.pena@rba-global.com, pastor.villalpando@rba-global.com

[3] PRDW Aldunate Vásquez Ingenieros Ltda., nnovoa@prdw.com

ABSTRACT

A motion monitoring system was installed in two wharves in Chile for response and damage detection under operational, sea wave and earthquake demand. Each of the systems consists of at least 18 acceleration channels and a recording system adapted to harsh environments. During a year of monitoring 10 earthquakes have been recorded, one of them with Magnitude Mw 6.2, and also more than 400 impacts produced by the ships berthing. An online near real-time analysis of the state of health is performed and communicated to stakeholders. This article presents the process to obtain modal properties together with a tracking technique for damage detection that takes into consideration the environmental variables. In these projects the platform is not only responsible for analyzing the signal and calculating the properties, it must also generate a report for each event automatically, informing the change in state that has occurred.

Keywords: wharf, damping, system identification

1. INTRODUCTION

This extended abstract highlights the monitoring of two wharves located in two different regions of Chile, subjected to weather actions such as waves, earthquakes and impacts caused by ship berths and heavy equipment assemblies on top. A vibration measurement system composed of accelerometers is implemented, permanently measuring vibrations, to detect changes in the health status of the structure based on methods of identification and monitoring over time. For this the system analyzes all types of vibrations, which are classified into two types: the first category corresponds to operational and environmental vibrations which are continuous; the second category corresponds to events, which have durations bounded in time, and the occurrence of extreme accelerations. For both types of vibrations, the frequencies, damping and modal forms are evaluated automatically by means of the "Stochastic Subspace Identification" [1] and a tracking algorithm.

1.1. The Structures and its monitoring system

The first pier is located in Caleta Hornos, Coquimbo Region, 37 km north of La Serena, with an area of 34x18 m2 (Fig. 1). The second is Caleta Maullín, Los Lagos Region, 74 km west of Puerto Montt, with an area of 47.2x24.5 m2 (Fig. 2). Both are located in Chile. Each monitoring system consists of at least 18 channels of acceleration in 6 positions, strategically located to properly defined modal properties in the longitudinal, transverse, torsional and vertical directions

Figure. 1 –Caleta Hornos

Figure. 2 –Caleta Maullín

2. RESULTS

Both wharves are constantly evaluated for their state of health, which is inform to the project owners. System identification is performed online. Figures 3 show the identified and tracked frequency for Hornos wharf for a period of 7 month. Figure 4 show a zoom of the signal together with externa environmental temperature measurements. The variation of properties due to sea level, temperature and added masses can be seen in the figures.

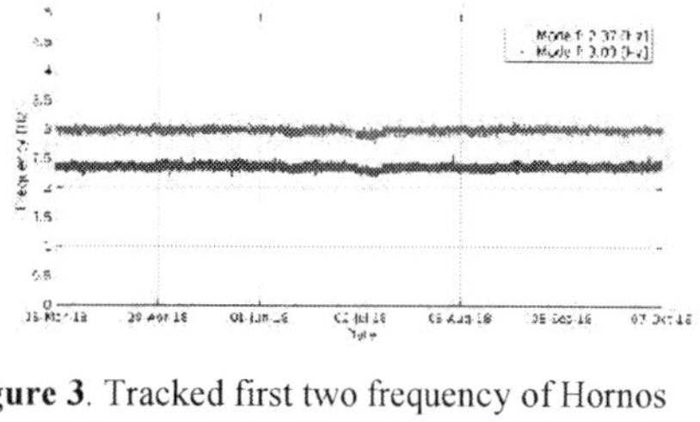

Figure 3. Tracked first two frequency of Hornos

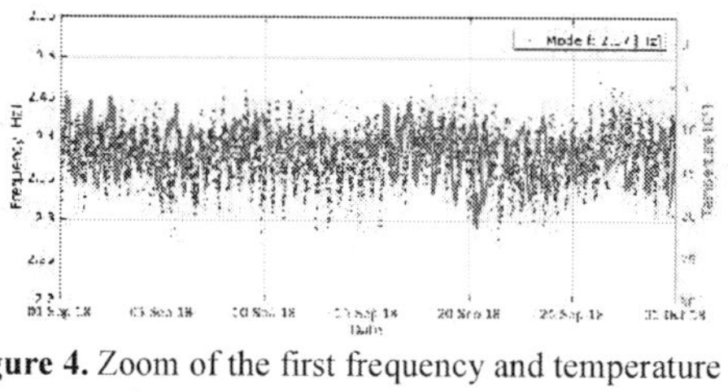

Figure 4. Zoom of the first frequency and temperature measurements.

3. CONCLUSIONS

The results of the monitoring show a high level of variation of the identified frequency and damping, modal shape show small changes. These variations present a cyclic behavior mainly contained in periods of one day (for example the predominant frequency change is around 0.12 [Hz] in Hornos and 0.29 [Hz] Maullín) or weekly (around 0.15 [Hz] in Hornos and 0.25 [Hz] Maullín, for the first mode). Damping values present average values between 2.4 [%] and 2.7 [%] for the first mode, with a dispersion of 1.1 [%], and between 1.2 and 2.1 [%] for higher modes, with a maximum dispersion of 1.1 [%], under environmental actions. For earthquake loading (0.2 g deck acceleration) the damping increases to 4-5%. These variations are attributable to changes in temperature (Day-Night), rise or fall of tides, the level of loading on top of the structure and the amplitude of the response.

ACKNOWLEDGEMENTS

The Port Works Directorate of the Ministry of Public Works of Chile is thanked for their support and funding of this project.

REFERENCES

[1] B. Peeters and G. de Roeck. (1999). Reference-based stochastic subspace identification for output-only modal analysis, *Mecanical systemes and signal processing*, vol. 6, n° 13, pp. 855-878.

IOMAC'19

8th International Operational Modal Analysis Conference
2019 May13-15 Copenhagen

OMA-BASED STRUCTURAL HEALTH MONITORING OF A WOODEN MAST STRUCTURE EXPOSED TO AMBIENT VIBRATIONS

Pernille Lysgaard Andersen[1], *Silja Tea Nielsen*[2], *Sandro D. R. Amador*[3], *Evangelos Katsanos*[4] *and Rune Brincker*[5]

[1] Student, Technical University of Denmark (DTU), Department of Civil Engineering, pernille@lysgaard-andersen.dk.
[2] Student, Technical University of Denmark (DTU), Department of Civil Engineering, siljatea@gmail.com.
[3] Assistant Professor, Technical University of Denmark (DTU), Department of Civil Engineering, sdio@byg.dtu.dk.
[4] Assistant Professor, Technical University of Denmark (DTU), Department of Civil Engineering, vakat@byg.dtu.dk.
[5] Professor, Technical University of Denmark (DTU), Department of Civil Engineering, runeb@byg.dtu.dk.

ABSTRACT
OMA-based Structural Health Monitoring (SHM) relies on the modal parameters in order to identify the health condition of a structure. These parameters are affected both by structural changes and the varying environmental/operational conditions. In order to robustly detect structural modifications in the monitored structures, an OMA-based SHM approach must distinguish between the different sources of change. Along these lines, this study aims at detecting structural changes in a structure subjected to varying environmental conditions. The investigated structure consists of a wooden mast and a steel frame top site, and is monitored by a modern vibration-based acquisition system while a weather station captures the environmental conditions. The measurements provided are used to: establish an environmental model for the mast structure; remove the effect of the environmental conditions from the estimated modal parameters and finally detect structural changes such as induced damages, hereby assessing the efficiency of the deployed OMA-based SHM approach.

Keywords: Operational Modal Analysis, Structural Health Monitoring, Changing environmental/operational conditions, Damage detection

1. INTRODUCTION

Critical infrastructures including road networks, bridges, energy plants, and power grids as well as ports, marine, and offshore facilities are structural systems of increased importance for the welfare and sustainable development of modern societies. Therefore, securing the safe operation and structural integrity of those structural systems should be highly prioritised. This is often pursued by surveying the structural systems with human-driven inspections and rather ad hoc monitoring campaigns. These methods can be associated with significant time and monetary burden while the reliability can be adversely affected by human errors. Demanding challenges need also to be met in case of monitoring hardly accessible structures. Therefore, robust techniques should be adopted to perform structural health monitoring (SHM) on a continuous, systematic and reliable basis.

Numerous SHM methods have been already proposed in the literature. Measuring structural vibrations and consequently identifying the modal properties in form of the natural frequencies, damping ratios and mode shapes of a structure constitute a widely used framework to assess the health of a monitored structure [1, 2]. Within this framework, operational modal analysis (OMA) can accommodate the purposes of monitoring a structure while in operation [3, 4]. The choice of an identification technique, which enables a reliable and stable estimation of the modal properties, is of high relevance for SHM campaigns. Moreover, continuity of the vibration-based monitoring requires automation of OMA and the pertinent modal identification. This can be problematic, especially in cases where noise-related modes interfere extensively with the physical ones [5]. Reliable application of the OMA-based SHM methods also relies on identifying and then, eliminating the influence of the environmental and operational (e.g., temperature, moisture and wind speed) variability (EOV) on the modal properties [2, 5, 6]. Various methods have been already used to lessen the EOV effects on the modal properties including models that follow the principal component analysis [2, 7], multivariate linear regression [8], and auto regressive models [9, 10]. One full year is commonly considered as a reasonable time frame to estimate reliable EOV models; however, time restrictions have led researchers to perform the essential EOV-based correction of the identified modal properties by using data obtained after a few months of monitoring [1, 9]. The meticulous design and installation of the measurement system as well as the establishment of quality assurance criteria for the monitoring data can further increase reliability of any SHM campaign [11]. Ultimately, all of these refinements allow SHM to be applied for damage detection [7, 9, 12, 13].

As can be seen from the above many advancements have been already made in SHM, however for the present study it is chosen to deliberately avoid a highly complex SHM scheme. This allows for a transparent investigation of how the different parts of the SHM scheme affects the final outcome. Along these lines, the present experimental study focuses on utilizing a state-of-the-art OMA technique on an automated basis in order to monitor the health of a medium-sized wooden mast with a top mass subjected to wind-induced load. The experimental model is placed in an outdoor environment and thus, it is necessary to develop an EOV model in order to eliminate the influence of EOV on the modal properties. The measuring system is designed with contemporary sensors and the quality of the measurements as well as the performance of the identification technique are continuously evaluated during the 32 day long monitoring campaign. Moreover, damages are induced to the wooden mast to investigate whether the detection of those structural changes is feasible by the designed SHM system. The objectives of this study are briefly described below:

- experimental identification of natural frequencies of the wooden mast in order to detect deliberately induced damages
- evaluation of the quality and reliability of the monitoring data used for the modal identification
- application of an environmental model to eliminate the effects of EOV on the identified natural frequencies

2. METHODOLOGY

The theoretical background and methodology applied for the SHM scheme are described in this section. This includes description of the time domain poly reference (TDPR) identification technique, the environmental model used to correct the identified natural frequencies, and the damage detection procedure.

2.1. Identification by Time Domain Poly Reference

The TDPR is an autoregression (AR) based identification technique where an AR model is fitted to the correlation functions (CFs) of the structural response, as these can be interpreted as free decays. The AR model is described at the discrete time instant n by the difference equation

$$\mathbf{y}(n) - \mathbf{A}_1\mathbf{y}(n-1) - \mathbf{A}_2\mathbf{y}(n-2) - ... - \mathbf{A}_{na}\mathbf{y}(n-na) = \mathbf{0} \tag{1}$$

where $\mathbf{y}(n)$ holds nc free decays with np number of samples and na is the number of previous time instances to include in the consideration. $\mathbf{A}_k$ is the AR matrices to be estimated, which is accomplished by setting up an overdetermined system with $np - na$ set of equations and performing least square regression defined by

$$\mathbf{A}\mathbf{H}_1 = \mathbf{H}_2 \qquad \Leftrightarrow \qquad \hat{\mathbf{A}} = \mathbf{H}_2\mathbf{H}_1^+ \tag{2}$$

where $[\cdot]^+$ denotes the pseudo-inverse and $\mathbf{A}$ holds the AR matrices $\mathbf{A} = [\mathbf{A}_{na},\ \mathbf{A}_{na-1},\ \dots,\ \mathbf{A}_1]$. $\mathbf{H}_1$ and $\mathbf{H}_2$ are Hankel block matrices, set up as

$$\mathbf{H}_1 = \begin{bmatrix} \mathbf{y}(1) & \mathbf{y}(2) & \dots & \mathbf{y}(np-na) \\ \mathbf{y}(2) & \mathbf{y}(3) & \dots & \mathbf{y}(np-(na-1)) \\ \vdots & \vdots & \ddots & \vdots \\ \mathbf{y}(na) & \mathbf{y}(na+1) & \dots & \mathbf{y}(np-1) \end{bmatrix}, \ \mathbf{H}_2 = \begin{bmatrix} \mathbf{y}(na+1) & \mathbf{y}(na+2) & \dots & \mathbf{y}(np) \end{bmatrix} \tag{3}$$

The difference equation given in Equation (1) is reformulated to a state space formulation containing the companion matrix, and the modal parameters are then determined by eigenvalue decomposition of this companion matrix. A more detailed description of the applied TDPR technique is provided by [14].

The CFs are found by first determining the spectral densities (SDs) with the use of the Welch averaging technique with 50% overlap and by convolution. A band-pass frequency domain window is applied to the SDs to keep a narrow band of frequencies only containing modes of the structure close to each other. The identification procedure is thus split up in several narrow band analyses of grouped modes, as this minimises disturbance from noise modes. The CFs are then estimated by taking the SDs back to the time domain through inverse fast fourier transform. To avoid bias from noise in the beginning of the CFs and the noise tail, only the intermediate part of the CFs are applied for identification. Optimized condensation of the CFs are implemented to pick out the physical modes from the noise modes. This is accomplish by following the procedure presented in [15]. By applying condensation it is necessary to request and therefore know the number of physical modes in each frequency band. nr number of CFs are gathered in $\mathbf{Y} = [\mathbf{y}_1(n),\ \mathbf{y}_2(n), \dots,\ \mathbf{y}_{nr}(n)]$ and used as the input in the Hankel block matrices given in (3) with $na = 2$ block rows. The size of $\mathbf{Y}$ is $nc \times nr = 6 \times 6$ and the number of samples is different in each analysis of grouped modes but is at least $np = 256$ why the system is well overdetermined to obtain a satisfactory estimate of the AR matrices, $\hat{\mathbf{A}}$.

2.2. Environmental Model

In order to describe the effect from the EOV on the natural frequencies, an environmental model is established by fitting a set of predictors, p_j, to the identified natural frequency of each mode, n. This is accomplished by performing multivariate linear least squares regression. The linear regression model to predict the natural frequencies, $\hat{f}_n$, is described as

$$\hat{f}_n(p_j(t)) = \beta_{0,n} + \sum_{j=1}^{J} \beta_{j,n} p_j(t) \tag{4}$$

where β are the regression coefficients, estimated by setting up a matrix equation and performing least square regression as

$$\mathbf{f}_n = \mathbf{P}\boldsymbol{\beta}_n \qquad \Leftrightarrow \qquad \hat{\boldsymbol{\beta}}_n = \mathbf{P}^{+}\mathbf{f}_n \tag{5}$$

where $\boldsymbol{\beta}_n$ holds the regression coefficients, $\mathbf{P}$ contain the predictors for all time instances, i, and the identified natural frequency at each instance, i, are located in $\mathbf{f}_n$. The environmental model can account for several parameters, herein air temperature, relative humidity, wind speed, and wind direction are investigated. The environmental parameters are averaged over the measurement duration in order to be applied as predictors. Cross terms of these predictors are applied as well. To determine the optimal model and set of predictors, a 80/20 percent split of data from the healthy structure is applied to obtain a training and a test set respectively. The optimal model is chosen based on a balance between its predicting abilities in the test set and simplicity. The predicting ability is evaluated through the root mean square (rms) error.

2.3. Damage Detection

In this study, damage detection is based on the natural frequencies estimated at each time instance, i, and corrected in order to minimize the influence from the environmental conditions. The corrected natural frequencies, f_n^c, are determined as

$$f_{i,n}^c = \mathrm{M}[f_n] + \varepsilon_{i,n} \qquad \text{where} \qquad \varepsilon_i = f_{i,n} - \hat{f}_{i,n} \tag{6}$$

where $\mathrm{M}[\cdot]$ is the median operator applied on the identified natural frequencies from the healthy test data set. The mean value of the corrected frequencies are expected to be constant as long as the structure is healthy while changes from the mean indicate damage. The definition of damage detection applied here is therefore based on statistical process control, where a value outside a band around the mean value is defined as an outlier. Previous studies apply different control limits, for example, in [10, 13] the boundaries of a 95% confidence interval are used, which corresponds to a deviation of two times the standard deviation from the mean value. A factor of three times the standard deviation corresponds to a 99.7% confidence level. Instead of creating the limits based on standard deviation and the mean value, it is chosen to construct them from median absolute deviation (MAD) value, due to a limited amount of data [16]. The control limits of each mode, L_n, are defined by

$$L_n = \mathrm{M}[f_n] \pm 3 \cdot \mathrm{MAD}_n \qquad \text{where} \qquad \mathrm{MAD}_n = 1.4826 \cdot \mathrm{M}[f_n^c - \mathrm{M}[f_n^c]] \tag{7}$$

Chosing a factor of three on the deviation measure is considered conservative [16], meaning that it leads to a seldom but expected occurrence of outliers (values outside of these limits). Therefore, the final decision taken herein for defining the damage detection criterion is the following: the indication of a damage-related change in the median value of the natural frequencies corresponds to a continuity of outliers.

3. TEST SET-UP

The monitored experimental model is a medium sized monopile-like structure consisting of a 3.6 m high wooden mast with a square cross section of 0.1 m × 0.1 m, see Figure 1. A steel girder is placed at the top of the mast and it is founded rigidly on a concrete block. The connections at the base and the top are both carried out as bolted steel connections while they are deliberately designed to host realistic imperfections. The model is placed outside lab facilities, thus it is exposed to natural loads mainly related to wind-induced lateral loads. The sensors used for measuring the structural response are triaxial geophones, chosen for their high sensitivity and low noise floor. Three of these sensors are placed on the corners of the top site as presented in Figure 1 (top right). The measured corner displacements (x_j, y_j, z_j) are converted into the three translational (x_c, y_c, z_c) and three rotational $(\theta_{x,c}, \theta_{y,c}, \theta_{z,c})$ degrees of freedom

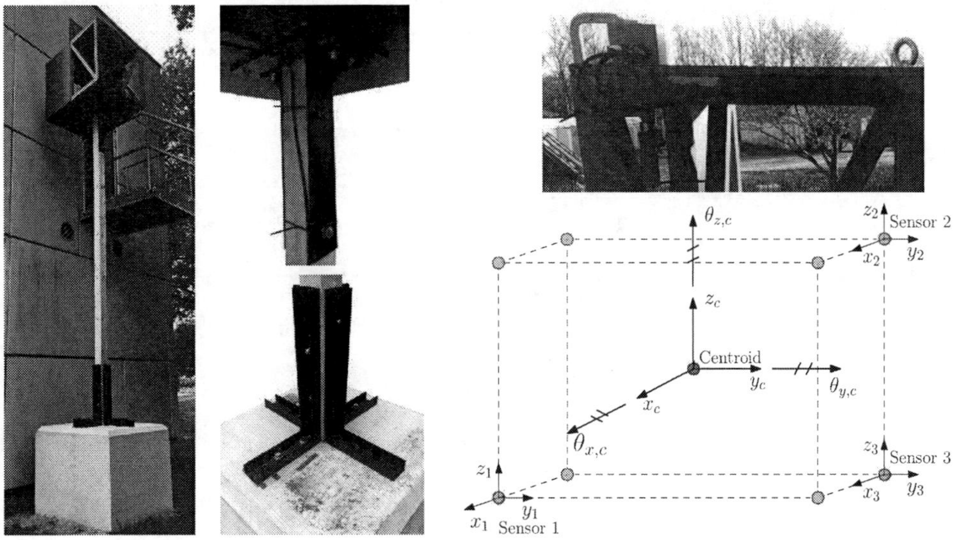

Figure 1: Left: Photo of the experimental model. Middle: Photos of connections. Top right: Sensor mounting with clamp, strips and tape. Bottom right: Diagram of top site with the sensor placements shown with orange dots. The nine corner directions and six centroid DOFs are shown with arrows.

(DOFs) at the centroid of the top site illustrated in Figure 1 (bottom right). This transformation is achieved by considering rigid body movements of the top site.

The monitoring campaign is initiated at 2018/10/03 and finalised at 2018/11/05 while measurements are performed on an hourly basis with a sampling frequency of $f_s = 100$Hz and a duration of $T = 1200$s. The damage is initially induced at 2018/10/30. Three different filters are applied to the measurments in the frequency domain, one for integration (i.e., from velocity to displacement time series), one for correction of the dynamic system of the geophone per se, and one for filtering out frequencies below 0.5Hz and above 25Hz. Additional information on the test set-up and signal processing can be found in [17].

4. QUALITY ASSESSMENT OF MEASUREMENTS

A representative example of the measured signals is presented in Figure 2 (left) as the singular value plot of the SD matrix. To approach robust and reliable monitoring campaign, the quality of each measurement is assessed prior to its use for identification purposes. The quality is assessed based on two parameters: A residual measure accounting for the transformation from the corner signals to the centroid DOFs and the signal to noise ratio (SNR) of the measurement. As it concerns the first parameter, the residual value indicates errors in the recorded signal as it detects discrepancy between the recorded and estimated signals. Furthermore, the SNR must be high to ensure that the physics are clearly represented in the measurement. By applying appropriate thresholds, measurements with signal errors and low SNR are discarded. More details about the applied thresholds can be found in [17]. The evaluation of all measurements is presented in Figure 2 (right), where it can be seen that a total of five measurements are discarded. However, an additional measurement was removed due to manual detection of a signal error, thus the presented quality assessment is incomplete. In total 99.1% of measurements are of sufficient quality to be used for identification.

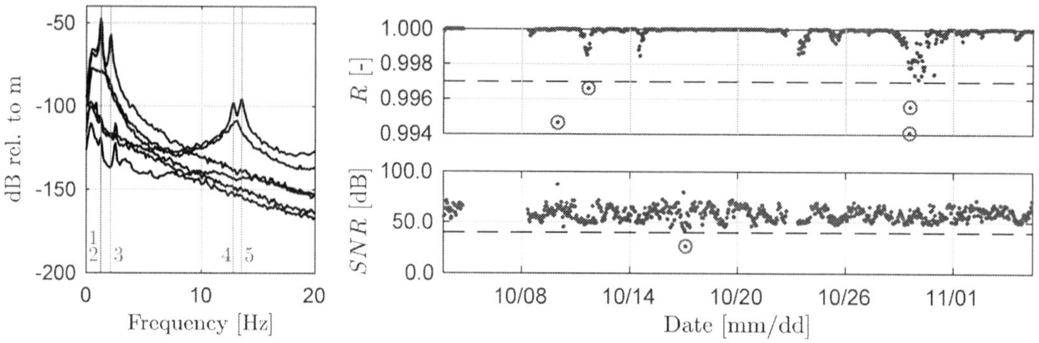

Figure 2: Left: Singular value plot of the spectral density of the signal after signal processing with indication of the first five modes (|). Right: Quality assessment values shown for all measurements (•), shown with the chosen threshold (– –) and indication of discarded measurements (○)

5. RESULTS

The SHM scheme adopted herein and the assosiated results follow the methodology presented in section 2. Therefore, results concerning the system identification, the environmental model, and the final damage detection are described in the following sections. `Matlab` [18] is utilised to perform relevant calculations.

5.1. Identified Modal Parameters

The signals used for modal identification is presented by an example in Figure 2 (left). It can be seen that the three first modes (i.e., the first two bending modes and the first torsional one) are adjacent ones (i.e., 1.26Hz to 2.13Hz) while such a modal proximity can also be detected for the second couple of bending modes (i.e., 12.7Hz to 13.4Hz). The latter allows for creating two modal groups for identification, containing modes 1-3 and 4-5 respectively. The identified natural frequencies, damping ratios, and pertinent mode shapes are presented in Figure 3 to exemplify the monitoring results. As the identified mode shapes tend to mix with other mode shapes in their proximity, these are separated by projecting the direction of a mode onto a subspace of identified modes. This is done according to [14] by

$$\mathbf{a}_{p,n} = \mathbf{A}\hat{\mathbf{t}} \qquad \text{where} \qquad \hat{\mathbf{t}} = \mathbf{A}^{+}\mathbf{b}_n \tag{8}$$

where $\mathbf{a}_{p,n}$ is the projected mode shape vector, $\mathbf{A}$ is a subspace of mixing modes shapes and $\mathbf{b}_n$ is the direction vector for the nth mode. The direction vectors are applied as rough estimates with values of unity placed at the DOFs in $\mathbf{b}_n$ that are expected to be activated for each mode. In [17] it is shown that the projected mode shape, $\mathbf{a}_{p,n}$, is not affected by the rough estimate of $\mathbf{b}_n$ as long as $\mathbf{b}_n$ contains values in the correct translational or rotational DOFs.

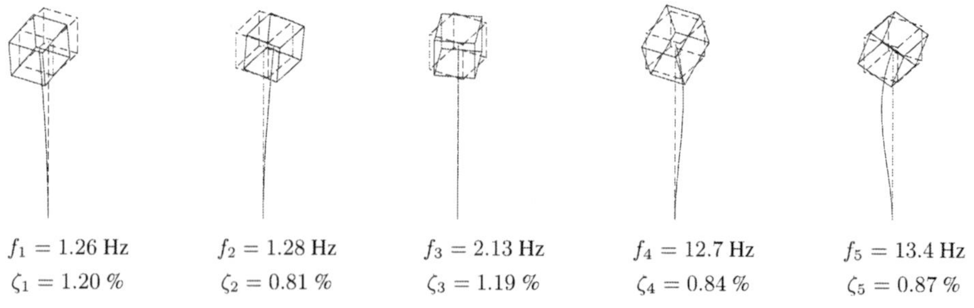

Figure 3: Example of identified modal parameters from the measurement at 2018/10/15 16:00:07. The mode shapes, $\mathbf{a}_{p,n}$, are separated by projection and visualised by expansion to the wooden pile and the top site.

For illustrative purposes, the mode shapes presented in Figure 3 are expanded to include the geometry of the top site and wooden pile in addition to the top site centroid DOFs. This is accomplished by considering rigid body movements of the top site and polynomial formulation for the wooden mast deflections from foundation level $z = 0$ to the centroid of top site $z = L$ given as

$$\begin{bmatrix} x(z) \\ y(z) \end{bmatrix} = \begin{bmatrix} (L \cdot \theta_{y,c} - 2 \cdot x_c) \cdot z^3/L^3 - (L \cdot \theta_{y,c} - 3 \cdot x_c) \cdot z^2/L^2 \\ (L \cdot \theta_{x,c} - 2 \cdot y_c) \cdot z^3/L^3 - (L \cdot \theta_{x,c} - 3 \cdot y_c) \cdot z^2/L^2 \end{bmatrix} \tag{9}$$

where $L = 3.6 + 0.4$ m and x_c, y_c, $\theta_{x,c}$ and $\theta_{y,c}$ correspond to the centroid DOFs in the projected mode shapes $\mathbf{a}_{p,n}$.

The performance of the TDPR identification on a fully automated basis is considered successful as the first five modes of the experimental model are identified for all measurements available from the monitoring campaign after quality assessment. Based on this, the identification procedure is considered stable. The identified frequencies of the first mode prior to the EOV based correction can be seen in Figure 4 (top) considering all measurements taken from the healthy structure (prior to the deliberately induced damages). Daily patterns in the identified natural frequencies can be observed. Besides this variation no sudden outliers are found, thus the procedure can also be considered to be consistent.

5.2. Environmental Model

Preliminary analyses undertaken by the authors showed that the identified natural frequencies are strongly correlated with air temperature while less correlated with the additional environmental factors investigated; relative humidity of the air, wind speed, and wind direction. Figure 4 illustrates the changes of the first frequency in relation to the air temperature. As expected the natural frequencies decrease with increasing temperature. When correcting the frequencies based on the air temperature solely, the MAD value of the first-mode natural frequency in test data set decreases from 6.34mHz to 3.42mHz. When the additional environmental factors are considered, the corresponding MAD values are further reduced to 3.32mHz. However, such a minor change (from 3.42mHz to 3.32mHz) is found dispensable over the simplicity of developing the environmental model for the current SHM scheme based on air temperature only. Similar tendencies are observed for the remaining four modes thus the decision applies to all modes. The corrected frequencies of the first mode after application of the environmental model can be seen in Figure 4 (bottom). It should be mentioned that correction does not completely remove the daily, environmental-related pattern. Therefore, refinement of the environmental model should be pursued by using, e.g., a larger data set with measurements from a longer period of time or a dynamic modelling approach.

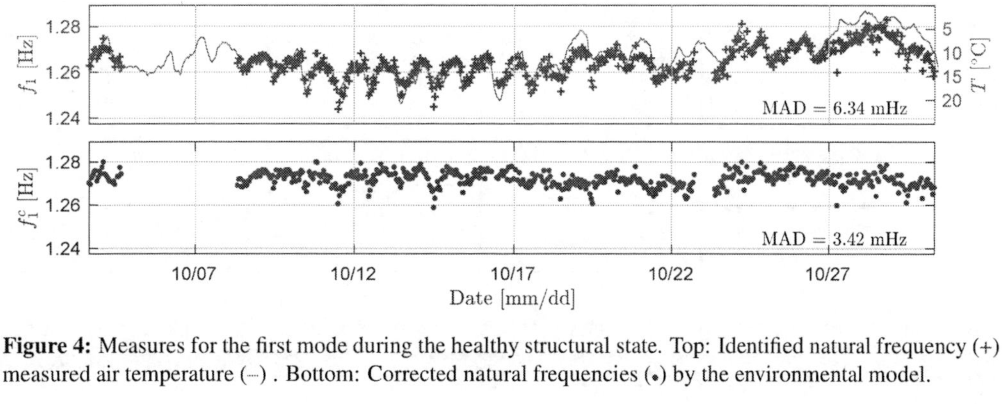

Figure 4: Measures for the first mode during the healthy structural state. Top: Identified natural frequency (+) and measured air temperature (–) . Bottom: Corrected natural frequencies (•) by the environmental model.

5.3. Damage Detection

Damage is induced to the wooden pile as eleven cuts near the foundation in six steps, as presented in Figure 5 and Table 1. The identified and environmentally corrected natural frequencies based on measurements taken during the damage induction period are presented in Figure 6. It is seen that damage is indicated by continuous outliers already at the first damage step. The latter is more profound for the second mode while more convincing damage detection can be seen both for the first and second mode after the induction of the second damage step. On the other hand, the third mode is seen to be less sensi-

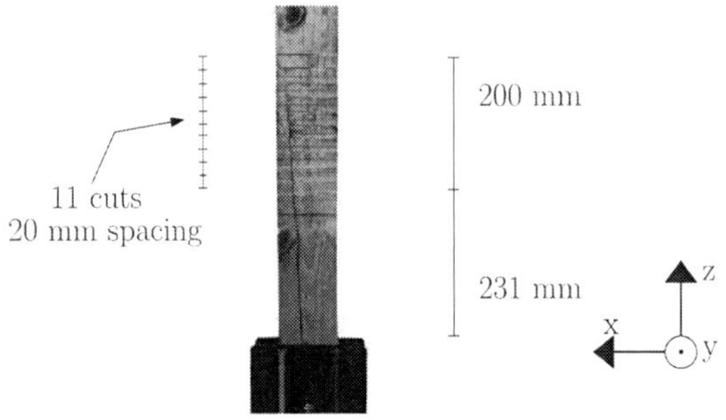

Figure 5: Illustration of the induced damages.

Table 1: Reduction of cross section for each damage step

Damage step	Reduction [%]
1	1.1
2	4.5
3	6.9
4	8.2
5	9.7
6	21.8

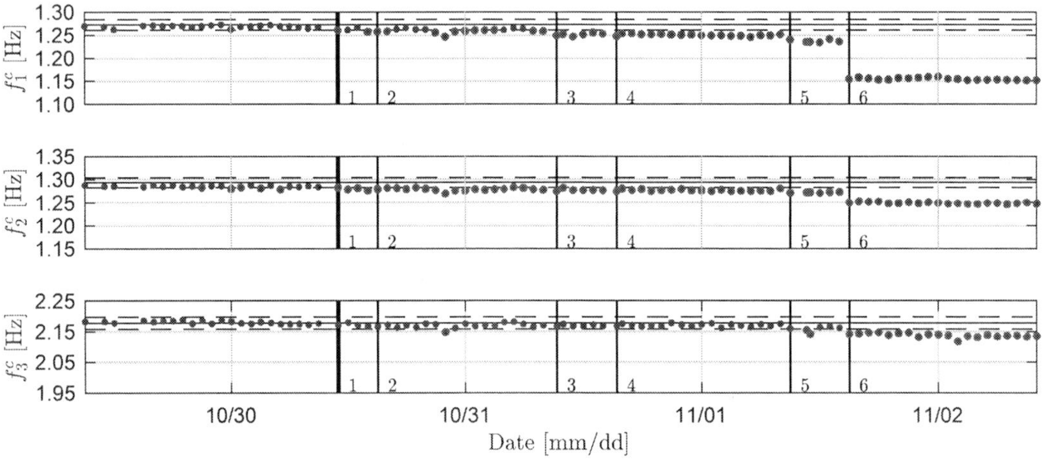

Figure 6: Corrected natural frequencies (•) at damaged structural state of the monitoring campaign. (○) indicates an outlier, (- -) is the control limits, (–) is the median and (|) indicates the damage step.

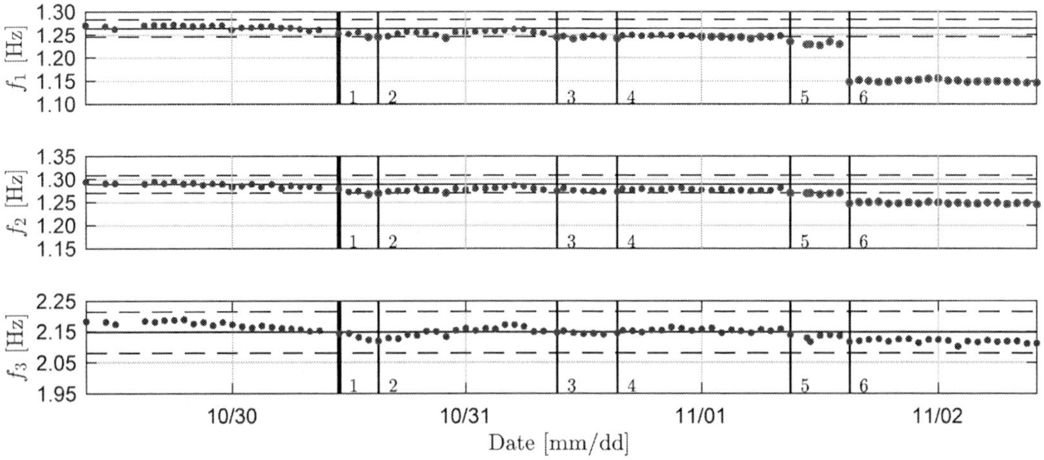

Figure 7: Natural frequencies (•) at damaged structural state of the monitoring campaign. (○) indicates an outlier, (- -) is the control limits, (–) is the median and (|) indicates the damage step.

tive to damage as only the last damage step (21.8% cross sectional reduction) can be identified. The high sensitivity of the first two modes is expected as the vibration profiles corresponding to these modes result in large bending moments close to the foundation, thus the location of the damage is critical for these modes. The rather noticeable decrease in the identified first-mode natural frequency after the last damage step can be explained by the fact that the induced damage reduces mostly the moment of inertia in the direction of the first mode.

Damage detection based on uncorrected frequencies is possible as well, as it can be seen from Figure 7. This indicates that the success of damage detection is not only a result of the temperature correction but also caused by reliability of the SHM and identification followed herein. However, the uncorrected frequencies are less sensitive to damage compared to the temperature corrected frequencies, as continuous outliers for the first and second-mode natural frequencies are first seen at the fourth and fifth damage step, respectively.

6. CONCLUSIONS

This study concerns a fully experimental application of SHM, in which detection of gradually induced damage close to the base of the wooden mast is attempted through identification of the first three natural frequencies. The results of the study show that

- deliberately induced damage is detected through pertinent changes in the natural frequencies
- when accounting for the effect of air temperature variability on the identified natural frequencies through a linear regression model, the natural frequencies show to be more sensitive to damage.
- 99.1% of measurements are found to be of satisfactory quality, while the TDPR identification technique succeeded for 100% of the measurements. Furthermore, the environmental model based on air temperature solely reduced the variability of the identified natural frequencies by 46%.

It is notable that the temperature correction applied in the present study is only based on 27 days of measurements. However, data describing the healthy structure over a longer time frame (i.e., a full year) are commonly considered to be necessary for developing a reliable environmental model. Therefore, the established environmental model may not facilitate long term forecasts despite the rather satisfactory performance that this model was found to have regarding correction of the identified natural frequencies. The latter can be considered beneficial when applying continuous updating of the environmental model in order to obtain reliable results within a short time frame. The quality assessment of the measurements showed to influence the success of identification, however refinement of the relevant criteria should be pursued while their automated performance may further increase the robustness of any SHM scheme.

ACKNOWLEDGEMENTS

The authors acknowledge the funding received from Centre for Oil and Gas - DTU/Danish Hydrocarbon Research and Technology Centre (DHRTC).

REFERENCES

[1] Rainieri, C., Gargaro, D. and Fabbrocino, G. (2015) Statistical tools for the characterization of environmental and operational factors in vibration-based SHM. In: *Structural Health Monitoring and Damage Detection*, 7, (pp. 175-184). Springer.

[2] Magalhães, F., Cunha, A. and Caetano, E. (2012) Vibration based structural health monitoring of an arch bridge: from automated OMA to damage detection. In: *Mechanical Systems and Signal Processing*, 28, (pp. 212-228). Elsevier.

[3] Weijtjens, W., Verbelen, T., Capello, E. and Devriendt, C. (2017) Vibration based structural health monitoring of the substructures of five offshore wind turbines. In: *Procedia engineering*, 199, (pp. 2294-2299). Elsevier.

[4] Peeters, B., Couvreur, G., Razinkov, O., Kündig, C., Van der Auweraer, H. and De Roeck, G. (2009) Continuous monitoring of the Øresund Bridge: system and data analysis. In: *Structures and Infrastructure Engineering*, 5(5), (pp. 392-405). Taylor & Francis.

[5] Carden, P.E. and Brownjohn, J. (2008) Fuzzy clustering of stability diagrams for vibration-based structural health monitoring. In: *Computer-Aided Civil and Infrastructure Engineering*, 23(5) (pp. 360-372). Wiley Online Library.

[6] Cross, E.J., Koo, K.Y., Brownjohn, J. and Worden, K. (2013) Long-term monitoring and data analysis of the Tamar Bridge. In: *Mechanical Systems and Signal Processing*, 35(1-2) (pp. 16-34). Elsevier.

[7] Diord, S., Magalhães, F., Cunha, A., Caetano, E. and Martins, N. (2017) Automated modal tracking in a football stadium suspension roof for detection of structural changes. In: *Structural Control and Health Monitoring*, 24(11) (pp. e2006). Wiley Online Library.

[8] Laory, I., Trinh, T.N., Smith, I.F.C and Brownjohn, J. (2014) Methodologies for predicting natural frequency variation of a suspension bridge. In: *Engineering Structures*, 80, (pp. 211-221). Elsevier.

[9] Peeters, B. and De Roeck, G. (2001) One-year monitoring of the Z24-Bridge: environmental effects versus damage events. In: *Earthquake engineering & structural dynamics*, 30(2) (pp. 149-171). Wiley Online Library.

[10] Ramos, L., Mevel, L., Lourenço, P.B. and De Roeck, G. (2008) Dynamic monitoring of historical masonry structures for damage identification. In: *Proc. 26th International Modal Analysis Conference*, Orlando, Florida, USA

[11] Vardanega, P.J., Webb, G.T., Fidler, P.R.A. and Middleton, C.R. (2016) Bridge monitoring. In: *Innovative Bridge Design Handbook*, (pp. 759-775). Elsevier.

[12] Brincker, R., Andersen, P. and Cantieni, R. (2001) Identification and level I damage detection of the Z24 highway bridge. In: *Experimental techniques*, 25(6) (pp. 51-57). Springer.

[13] Andersen, P. (1997) Identification of civil engineering structures using vector ARMA models. *Doctoral dissertation*, Department of Building Technology and Structural Engineering, Aalborg University, Denmark.

[14] Brincker, R. and Ventura, C. (2015) Introduction to operational modal analysis John Wiley & Sons

[15] Olsen, P., Juul, M. and Brincker, R.(2019) Condensation of the correlation functions in modal testing. In: *Mechanical Systems and Signal Processing*, 118, (pp. 377-387), Elsevier.

[16] Leys, C., Ley, C., Klein, O., Bernard, P and Licata, L (2013) Detecting outliers: Do not use standard deviation around the mean, use absolute deviation around the median. In: *Journal of Experimental Social Psychology*, 49(4) (pp. 764-766). Elsevier.

[17] Andersen, P.L. and Nielsen, S.T. (2019) OMA Based Monitoring of a Wind Loaded Structure, Appendix C.3 *Master Thesis*, Civil Engineering, Technical University of Denmark.

[18] MathWorks. Matlab 2017b. https://se.mathworks.com/products/simulink.html

IOMAC'19

8th International Operational Modal Analysis Conference

2019 May13-15 Copenhagen

OMA IDENTIFICATION ON A SCALED MASONRY BUILDING PRE AND POST REINFORCED WITH TRM

D. Bru[1], S. Ivorra[2], M. Buitrago[3], E.Bertolessi[4]

1 Department of Civil Engineering, University of Alicante. San Vicente Del Raspeig, Apartado 99, 03080, Spain, david.bru@ua.es.

2 Department of Civil Engineering, University of Alicante. San Vicente Del Raspeig, Apartado 99, 03080, Spain, sivorra@ua.es.

3 ICITECH, Universitat Politècnica de València, Camino de Vera, s/n, 46022 Valencia, Spain, mabuimol@upv.es.

4 ICITECH, Universitat Politècnica de València, Camino de Vera, s/n, 46022 Valencia, Spain, elber4@upv.es.

ABSTRACT

This document shows the dynamic identification developed on a scaled masonry building (3.11x4.11x2.15 m) at the ICITECH of the Universitat Politècnica de València. Eight seismic accelerometers have been placed to identify bending and torsional modes. The identification analysis was performed on the original structure. The structure was then subjected to dynamic tests until reaching some important failures and several cracks. At that moment another identification analysis was performed. Later, the scaled model was reinforced with Textile Reinforced Mortars (TRM) applied on the outer surface of the walls. The reinforced building was again analysed with dynamic identification. Finally the structure was tested by the same previously applied procedure until reaching the failure. Again, a final dynamic identification analysis was carried out. ARTEMIS software was adopted to develop all the OMA analyses.

Keywords: Masonry, OMA, damping, TRM.

1. INTRODUCTION

Masonry walls are a traditional structural system used in many buildings, and it can be found today as the constructive solution for new buildings. However, these elements show a brittle behavior for in plane and out plane loads, especially for seismic or dynamic loads [1]. In particular, the more usual failure modes for in plane loads are toe crushing, rocking, diagonal cracking or sliding [2]. In case of out of plane loads, these elements shows a very slow bending strength. Different reinforcement techniques can be used to improve the in plane and out plane behavior of the masonry walls. Fiber reinforced polymers (FRP) has been used for different authors such as [3]. However, these solutions show problems related with the contact between them and the masonry. Other solution is the textile reinforced mortar (TRM) [4]. These materials show a better compatibility with masonry and avoid problems related to debonding or permeability issues.

The main objective of this research is the evaluation of the TRM reinforcement for dynamic loads. In particular, changes in the vibration frequencies, modal shapes, and damping factor [5] have been evaluated by means of OMA (Operational modal analysis), before and after the reinforcement process.Length of the documents

2. MASONRY BUILDING AND REINFORCEMENT MATERIAL

A scaled masonry building, with 3 walls as the main vertical structure and joists – hollow concrete bricks as the roof, was built at ICITECH of Universitat Politècnica de València (Valencia, Spain) with the aim of assessing the general structural behavior for dynamic loads. In particular, the cracking pattern and the changes in modal parameters as damping, frequencies and modal shapes has been evaluated. Figure 1 shows the general view of the building.

The masonry walls were constructed using clay bricks laid by means of 10 mm thick lime mortar joints adopting an english bond disposition. Wood beams were used on top of the door and the window. Table 1 shows the dimensions and compression strength of bricks and the mean compression strength of lime mortar at 28 days and 94 days (days in which tests, described later, were performed).

Table 1. Geometric characteristics and compression strength of bricks and lime mortar.

Bricks		Lime mortar	
Dimensions [mm]	230 x 110 x 50	Compression strength at 28 days [MPa]	4.25
Compression strength [MPa]	13.99	Compression strength at 94 days [MPa]	5.98

Foundations were prepared for constrain displacements with the use of steel plates and anchors to the main concrete slab of the laboratory, Figure 1. In addition, the building might have connected at the top of the lateral walls to a servo-hydraulic jack by means of a steel beam supported by props. Dimensions of the walls and its disposition are shown in Figure 1.

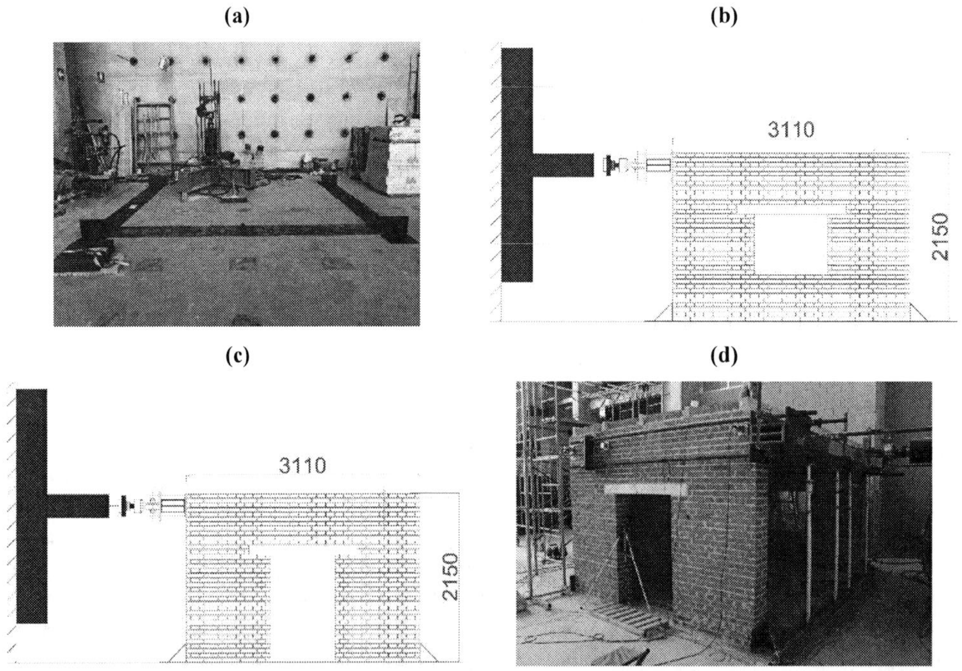

Figure 1. (a) System used for the foundation; (b) dimensions of the windowed wall; (c) dimensions of the door wall; and (d) a 3D view of the actual building.

Later, the building was reinforced with Textile Reinforced Mortar (TRM) materials with the aim of evaluating the efficacy of cementitious-based strengthening to: (i) improve the seismic behavior of masonry structures, and (ii) avoid a seismic-induced premature failure of poor-quality masonries. The adopted TRM retrofitting technique comprised a 25x25 mm glass textile grid embedded into a 10 mm thick cementitious layer applied along the outer face of the overall building. Table 2 shows the mechanical properties of the reinforced material used in this research.

Table 2. Mechanical properties or reinforced materials.

Mortar		Textile mesh	
Compression strength at 28 days [MPa]	15	Tensile strength [kN/m]	45
Elastic modulus [MPa]	8000	Elastic modulus [MPa]	72000

When this kind of reinforcement is applied on damaged structures, it comprises different steps. Indeed, the masonry support was preliminarily treated injecting the wider cracks to restore the original load bearing capacity of the damaged masonries. Then, a 5 mm thick cementitious layer was applied on the outer face of the walls. This layer is necessary to allow the bond between the masonry support and the glass textile grid. It is worth mentioning that, conversely to FRP composites, TRM materials allow to comply with the current requirements of compatibility and reversibility of the retrofitting with respect to brittle supports due to the presence of a mortar matrix instead of an epoxy one [6]. Finally, the glass grid was covered with a second 5 mm thick layer of the cementitious binder. The layers composing the TRM composite adopted in the present investigation are showed in Figure 2.

(a) **(b)**

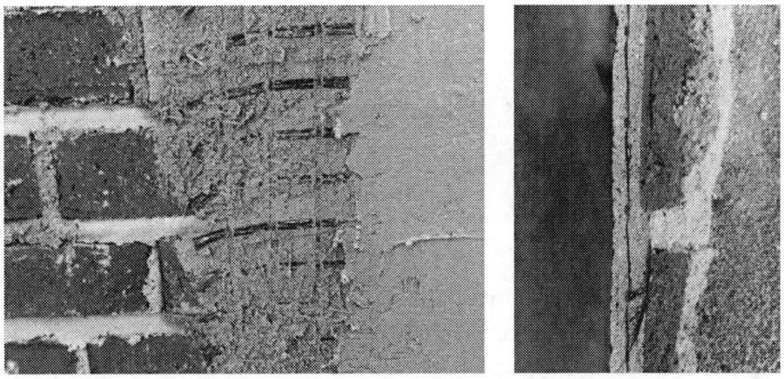

Figure 2. Different layers of the adopted Textile Reinforced Mortar (TRM) material: (a) front view; and (b)

3. MONITORING AND DESCRIPTION OF THE MODAL ANALYSIS

The methodology for dynamic identification has been divided in four phases: (i) Unreinforced pre-damage; (ii) Unreinforced post-damage; (iii) Reinforced pre-damage; (iv) Reinforced post-damaged. Ambient vibrations has been registered during all phases with a sampling frequency of 1000 Hz. Two records of 5' have been done in each phase, and the mean values have been used. For data acquisition, 8 piezoelectric accelerometers of sensitivity equal to 10 V/g have been employed. They were located according to Figure 3. Signals have been registered using a data acquisition device model Kyowa PCD-320 and signal conditioner model PCB 482A22.

With the aim to introduce a general damage distribution, similar to the seismic loads, a series of cyclic loads with increasing amplitude of the displacement from 0.2mm to 12mm and increasing frequency range from 0.3Hz to 10 Hz have been used. The horizontal load has been applied by means of a hydraulic jack with a displacement load control. In this paper the results showed are related with the initial phases previously to the damage and the final phases after the full damage procedure. It is important to note that the reinforced building is the unreinforced building repaired after all the damage phases.

Finally, Operational Modal Analysis (OMA) was used to analyze the vibration frequencies and the damping factor. The technique used is the Enhanced Frequency Domain Decomposition (EFDD), according to the Artemis software.

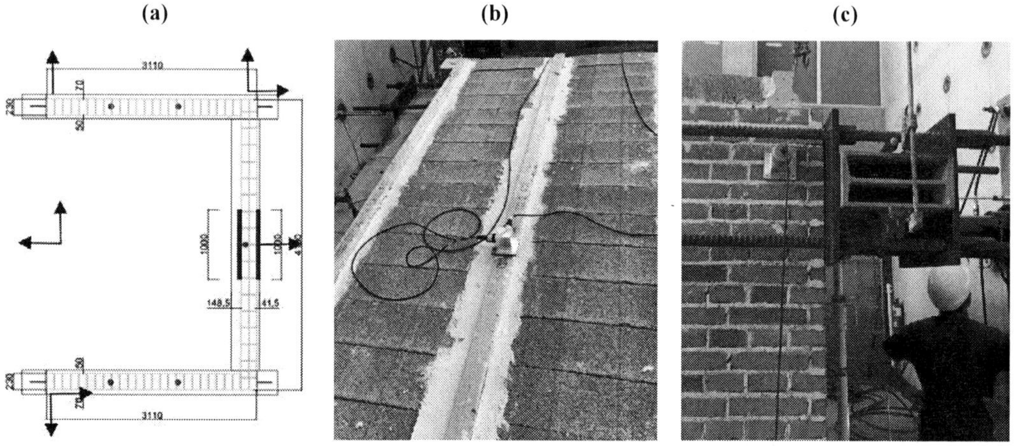

Figure 3. (a) General view of sensors location; (b) roof sensors; (c): wall sensors.

4. RESULTS

In case of unreinforced masonry building, Figure 4 shows the crack pattern distribution after the damage process and the inner masonry wall before the cracks appear. Transversal walls resulted to be the most damaged walls, while the perpendicular massive panel did not suffer any damage. Classical diagonal cracks of 45° were in the windows corner due to the shear stress for a maximum horizontal displacement of 12mm. No cracks in the wall without openings, and no problems due to out of the plane bending, was detected. As expected, stepped cracks opened and widened mainly along both bed and head mortar joints connecting the corners of the openings to the corners of the transversal walls, Figure 6.

Regarding modal analysis, Figure 4 shows the singular values for the Enhanced Frequency Domain Decomposition technique. In particular a value range from 0 to 500 Hz have been evaluated. Figure 5 and Table 3, resume the modal shapes, vibration frequencies and damping factor for the first four vibration modes. As expected, there is a general tendency to decrease the vibration frequency with increasing damage. In particular a reduction equal to 24.4%, 26.8%, 33.4% and 30.2% for the first, second, third, and fourth vibration mode has been evaluated. Damping factor shows an inverse behavior with increases of 76.8%, 126.1%, 195.9% and 72% from the fist to the fourth vibration mode. This means that cracking increases the energy dissipation due to the material friction in the joints. Finally, the Modal Assurance Criterion (MAC) has been used with the aim to evaluate the changes in the modal shapes due to the damage process. Table 4 shows few differences for the first two modes, however, for the third and fourth mode the differences are more important. This means that the cracking process affects more directly the higher vibrations modes.

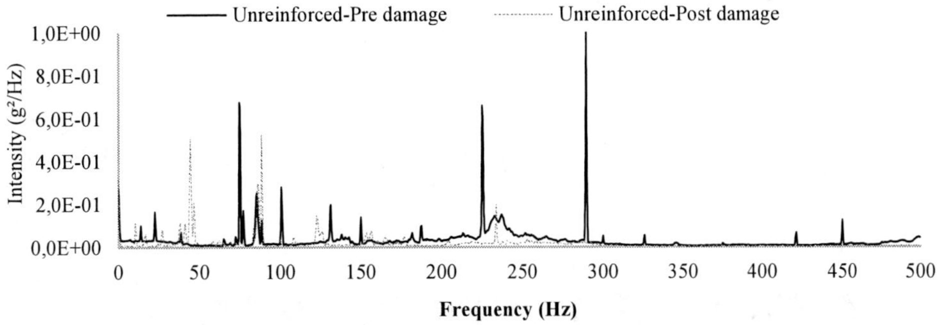

Figure 4. Spectral density for unreinforced building pre and post damaged.

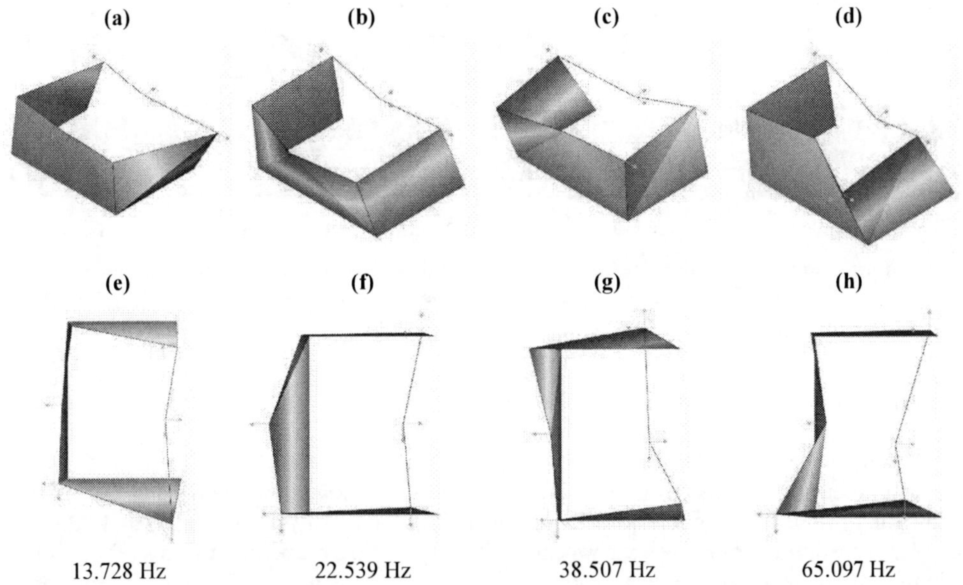

Figure 5. Frequencies and modal shapes for unreinforced and pre-damage building. General view: (a), (b), (c), (d). Plan view: (e), (f), (g), (h).

Table 3. Frequencies and damping factor for unreinforced pre/post damage masonry building.

Pre-damage		Post-damage	
Frequency (Hz)	Damping (%)	Frequency (Hz)	Damping (%)
13.728	2.41	10.375	4.26
22.539	1.53	16.507	3.46
38.507	0.74	25.636	2.19
65.097	0.50	45.445	0.86

Table 4. MAC values between unreinforced pre and post damage masonry building.

Hz	13.73	22.54	38.50	65.09
10.37	0.914	0.018	0.181	0.009
16.50	0.03	0.808	0.105	0.424
25.63	0.028	0.036	0.281	0.432
45.44	0.007	0.198	0.027	0.214

(a) (b)

Figure 6. Windowed wall undamaged (a) and crack pattern produced at the end of the investigation (b).

In case of reinforced masonry building, Figure 8 shows the crack pattern distribution after the second dynamic test. The building shows a damage configuration very similar to the non-reinforced one. However, the cracks near the window opening are less important than in case of the non-reinforced masonry structure.

Regarding the parameters evaluated during the operational modal analysis, Figure 7 shows the bending and torsional frequencies. Moreover, Figure 8 and Table 4, resume the damping factor, modal shapes, and vibration frequencies for the main vibration modes. It is important to highlight that after the reinforcement process the stiffness of the building was improved regarding the original values (non-damage building). In case of the four principal frequencies, the improvement factor was 1.05, 1.087, 1.263 and 1.05 respectively. However, after the masonry lateral walls crack, the stiffness of the building shows similar values that the un-reinforced building with cracks. Regarding the damping factor, a lower value has been evaluated both before and after the reinforcement process. This effect is due to the elastic behavior of the reinforcement material, and the reduction of the friction in the joints. Finally, no important changes have been detected in the modal shapes after the second dynamic test, Table 6.

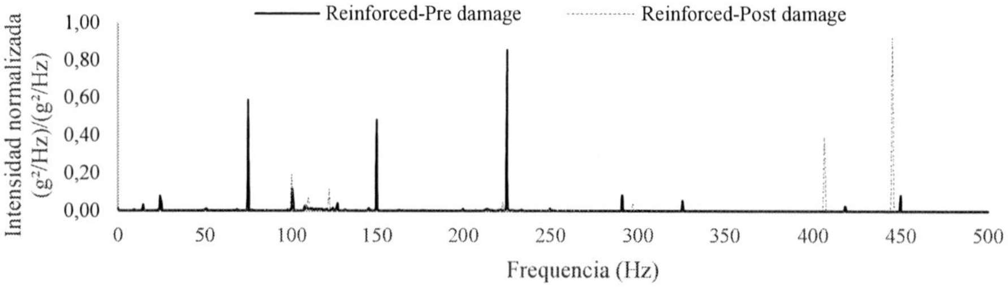

Figure 7. Spectral density values for reinforced building pre and post damaged.

Table 5. Frequencies and damping factor for reinforced pre/post damage masonry building.

Pre-damage		Post-damage	
Frequency (Hz)	Damping (%)	Frequency (Hz)	Damping (%)
14.461	1.23	9.613	3.32
24.517	1.51	15.854	2.35
48.647	0.35	25.429	1.39
68.517	0.69	35.210	1.16

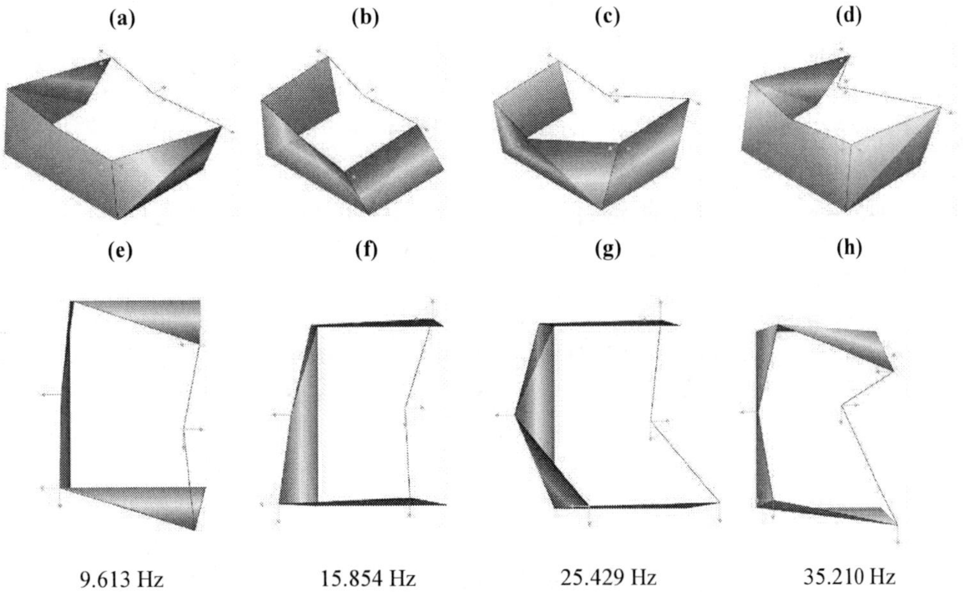

Figure 8. Frequencies and modal shapes for reinforced and post-damage building. General view: (a), (b), (c), (d). Plan view: (e), (f), (g), (h).

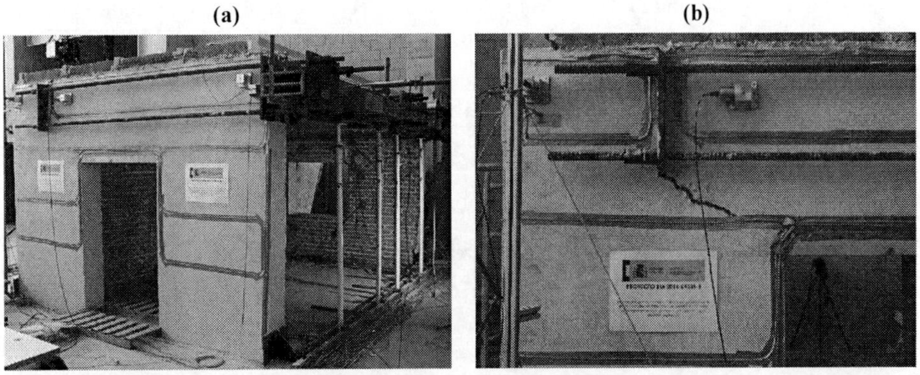

Figure 9. Reinforced structure before (a) and after (b) the damage

Table 6. MAC values between reinforced pre and post damage masonry building.

Hz	14.46	24.52	48.65	68.65
9.61	0.983	0.006	0.023	0.041
15.85	0.003	0.837	0.029	0.023
25.43	0.018	0.2	0.135	0.224
35.210	0.647	0.045	0.098	0.118

5. CONCLUSIONS

The dynamic behavior of masonry building before and after reinforcing with TRM was assessed. After the cyclic loads, the damping factor, the modal shapes and the vibration frequency have been evaluated. The following conclusions may be drawn for unreinforced and reinforced masonry building due to the cracking process: Reduction of vibration frequencies by 20-30%, increase of the damping factor by more than 100%. However no significant changes in the modal shapes have been evaluated for the first vibration modes. Regarding the effect of the TRM, the most important conclusions are related with the possibility of recovering the pre-damage stiffness of the building, and the negative effect in the damping factor due to the elastic behavior of these materials.

ACKNOWLEDGEMENTS

The authors want to acknowledge Spanish Ministry of Economy, Industry and Competitiveness for the funding provided through Projects BIA2015-69952-R and BIA 2014-59036-R, and also the Grupo Mapei and the Grupo Puma for their invaluable assistance.

REFERENCES

[1] Magenes, G., Calvi, G.M. In-plane seismic response of brick masonry walls, *Earthq. Eng. Struct. Dyn.* 26 (1996) 1091–1112.

[2] Bhattacharya, S., Nayak, S., Dutta, S.C. A critical review of retrofitting methods for unreinforced masonry structures, *Int. J. Disaster Risk Reduct.* 7 (2014) 51–67. doi:10.1016/j.ijdrr.2013.12.004.

[3] Triantafillou, T.C., Strengthening of masonry structures using epoxy-bonded FRP laminates, J. Compos. Constr. 2 (1998) 96–104. doi:10.1061/(ASCE)1090-0268(1998)2:2(96).

[4] Bilotta, A., Ceroni, F., Lignola, G.P., Prota, A., Use of DIC technique for investigating the behavior of FRCM materials for strengthening masonry elements, Compos. Part B Eng. 129 (2017) 251–270. doi:10.1016/j.compositesb.2017.05.075.

[5] Bru, D., Baeza, F. J., Varona, B., Garcia-Barba, J., Ivorra, S., Static and dynamic properties of retrofitted timber beams using glass fiber reinforced polymers, *Materials and Structures* 49(1-2) 181-191. doi: 10.1617/s11527-014-0487-0.

[6] Kouris L.A.S., Triantafillou T.C. (2018). State-of-the-art on strengthening of masonry structures with textile reinforced mortar (TRM). *Construction and Building Materials* 188:1221-1233. doi: 10.1016/j.conbuildmat.2018.08.039.

IOMAC'19
8th International Operational Modal Analysis Conference
2019 May13-15 Copenhagen

REAL TIME STRUCTURAL DAMAGE DETECTION IN THE PRESENCE OF DETERMINISTIC OPERATIONAL POWER LINE NOISE

Basuraj Bhowmik[1], *and Budhaditya Hazra*[2]

[1]PhD, Department of Civil Engineering, Indian Institute of Technology, Guwahati, Assam, India; basurajbhowmik@gmail.com.
[2] Assistant Professor, Department of Civil Engineering, Indian Institute of Technology, Guwahati, Assam, India; budhaditya.hazra@iitg.ac.in.

ABSTRACT

The application of real time structural damage detection schemes towards continuous monitoring of system health is an emerging topic of interest. This paper presents the use of real time algorithms belonging to the family of first order eigen perturbation (FOEP) techniques to detect damage, online. Integration of such algorithms towards numerical simulations and experimental validations shows promise in the field of structural health monitoring (SHM). However, the presence of operational noise arising during faults in experimentation, behaviour induced habits and AC voltage sources impedes the possibility of identifying the actual damage patterns. Towards this, the paper uses real time FOEP algorithms that essentially segregates the noise and the harmonic components from the mixed signal, thereby eliciting the vibrating components of the pure signal. Applications to both numerical simulations backed by experimental case studies demonstrate the utility of FOEP family of algorithms as ideal candidates for baseline free SHM.

Keywords: Operational noise, noise separation, real time, time series analysis, online damage detection

1. INTRODUCTION

The presence of noise during physical processes as random variations of one or more characteristics of entities such as voltage, current or data of any random signal, is inevitable. In most applications, it becomes essential that the noise is first removed or reduced to an extent such that the actual quality of data is not compromised [1]. Resorting to spectral approaches to minimize the signal bandwidth, nonlinear filtering techniques and compressing the spectrum of the noise content of a signal are some of the prevalent approaches towards noise removal strategies [1,2]. Recent advancements in signal processing has witnessed a growing inclination towards advanced digital filtering techniques involving bandpass filtering, windowed filtering approaches, to name a few [3]. However, these techniques call for extensive computational prowess that are at times unavailable on site during experimentation facilities. This results in incorrect data acquisition, unexpected outliers in the data set and unwanted clustering at the receiver due to reduction in the bandwidth limit of the maximum speed of the streaming data [1]. In this context, this paper focusses on delivering strategies that apply *real time operational noise separation techniques* for numerically simulated dynamic systems in conjunction with experimental observations.

Noise can be defined as any disturbance that interferes with the actual operation of a device or system. It originates mainly due to human-induced faults during experimentation, changes in environmental and operational conditions and external interference from instruments in the vicinity. Separation of deterministic signal components such as noise from information-rich signals needs to be carried out in unison with data acquisition [4]. As most of the signal decontamination approaches are *offline* in nature, stochastic signal interference with the acquired datasets deteriorates the signal quality, thereby affecting the post-processing techniques, which often leads to erroneous results. Again, removal of certain noise components cause distortion in the dataset as some of the suppressed frequency components constitute a crucial aspect of the dynamics of the system. Therefore, it becomes imperative that the noise separation techniques are tailored to a *real time framework* where the decontamination can function simultaneously with the onset of streaming data, without eliminating the vital components of the signal. This can be achieved using *first order eigen perturbation* (FOEP) techniques that aid in recursively delineating the noise components of the signal [5-7].

A survey of literature reveals that the existing noise-reduction schemes are primarily offline in nature that requires the data to be gathered in the first step and processed in the next [1-4]. Due to obvious reasons, the data sometimes get contaminated to an extent that it becomes practically impossible to carry out analysis and calls for repeated experimental trials. The key motivation driving the present work lies in the essential requirement of recursive approaches that *eliminates operational noise online* in tandem with data acquisition. In this context, a new class of algorithm, viz., recursive canonical correlation analysis (RCCA), is developed that utilizes the eigenspace characteristics of the covariance estimate obtained from a set of physical response. The set of transformed response corresponding to each sample point reveals the nature of the associated signal, which can be further utilized for noise truncation from the actual dataset. Towards this, the present work focuses on providing solution for segregating the noise components from the response signal in real time. This subsequently aids in identifying accurate damage patterns for a vibrating system at the possible onset of an event [8]. However, identifying the predominant noise component of a signal in real time provides a formidable challenge that is addressed by the authors in the current study. The working methodology along with applications towards numerically simulated dynamical systems backed by case studies from experimental test beds is provided in detail in the subsequent sections.

2. RECURSIVE CANONICAL CORRELATION ANALYSIS (RCCA)

Canonical correlation analysis (CCA) is a standard statistical tool that has been extensively used in econometrics, meteorology and medical studies. Its recent exploration in signal processing has opened avenues towards utility in detecting damage in dynamic systems [9,10]. The algorithm proceeds by finding two basis vectors in which the correlation matrix between the variables is diagonal and mutually maximized by projecting the original set of variables onto an optimum subspace [9]. While the technique has shown promise in detecting structural damage, the inherent formulation of CCA makes it an *offline* method. To tailor it towards an online implementation, FOEP formulations are carried out that provides eigenspace estimates, in real time. An important aspect to be considered here is that the FOEP based RCCA method updates the eigenspace characteristics at each time instant, instead of updating the block covariance matrices $\begin{bmatrix} 0 & \mathbf{C_{xz}} \\ \mathbf{C_{xz}} & 0 \end{bmatrix}$ and $\begin{bmatrix} \mathbf{C}_{xx} & 0 \\ 0 & \mathbf{C}_{zz} \end{bmatrix}$ for a general vector valued multivariate data $\mathbf{x}$ and $\mathbf{z}$ thereby reducing the time complexity of the recursive implementation [5-7].

2.1. RCCA: Derivation

The theoretical treatment of RCCA is derived from estimating the eigenspace updates using the FOEP approach. Towards are recursive implementation of RCCA the matrices $\mathbf{C_{xx}}$ and $\mathbf{C_{xz}}$ are expressed for k^{th} instant in terms of their estimates at $(k-1)^{th}$ instant using the following equation

$$\mathbf{C}_{\mathrm{xx}}(k) = \frac{k-1}{k}\mathbf{C}_{\mathrm{xx}}(k-1) + \frac{1}{k}\mathbf{X}_{\mathrm{k}}\mathbf{X}_{\mathrm{k}}^{\mathrm{T}}$$

$$\mathbf{C}_{\mathrm{xz}}(k) = \frac{k-1}{k}\mathbf{C}_{\mathrm{xz}}(k-1) + \frac{1}{k}\mathbf{X}_{\mathrm{k}}\mathbf{Z}_{\mathrm{k}}^{\mathrm{T}} \tag{1}$$

It should be noted that the FOEP based formulation does not take into consideration the nature of the involved dataset and can effectively provide recursive estimates for both stationary and non-stationary processes [7]. As the dynamics of structural systems generally evolve from zero mean processes, the eigen decomposition of the covariance estimate for ($\mathbf{C}_{\mathrm{xx}}(k)$) can be obtained as:

$$\boldsymbol{V}_k\boldsymbol{\epsilon}_k\boldsymbol{V}_k^T = \frac{1}{k}\boldsymbol{V}_{k-1}\left[(k-1)\boldsymbol{\epsilon}_{k-1} + \boldsymbol{\mu}_k\boldsymbol{\mu}_k^T\right]\boldsymbol{V}_{k-1}^T \tag{2}$$

where, the POC vector at the kth time stamp is given by: $\boldsymbol{\mu}_k = \boldsymbol{V}_{k-1}^T\boldsymbol{X}_k$.

It now becomes essential that the term $(k-1)\boldsymbol{\epsilon}_{k-1} + \boldsymbol{\mu}_k\boldsymbol{\mu}_k^T$ has a diagonally dominant structure for the application of Gershgorin's theorem. This can be validated by the fact that the eigenvalues of the term are close to the diagonal portion and the eigenvectors can be approximated to unity. This ensures the use of Gershgorin's theorem to evaluate the EVD of this term (of the form $\boldsymbol{P}_k\boldsymbol{\Psi}_k\boldsymbol{P}_k^T$) for low to moderate values of damping and for finite sample size of the response, obtained as [5]:

$$\boldsymbol{V}_k\boldsymbol{\epsilon}_k\boldsymbol{V}_k^T = \frac{1}{k}[\boldsymbol{V}_{k-1}\boldsymbol{P}_k][\boldsymbol{\Psi}_k][\boldsymbol{V}_{k-1}\boldsymbol{P}_k]^T \tag{3}$$

which yields the following set of recursively updated eigenspace at each time stamp:

$$\left.\begin{aligned} \boldsymbol{V}_k &= \boldsymbol{V}_{k-1}\boldsymbol{P}_k \\ \boldsymbol{\epsilon}_k &= \frac{\boldsymbol{\Psi}_k}{k} \end{aligned}\right\} \tag{4}$$

The above derivation for RCCA is based on the premise that the excitation on the dynamical system is uniaxial. However, as CCA deals with block covariance matrices, it can be inferred that its recursive variation will be able to accommodate the eigenspace estimates for multi-directional dependencies as well [9]. In order to understand the structure of the matrices for multiple excitation sources, consider the basic CCA equation for k^{th} sample point as:

$$\boldsymbol{M}(k)\boldsymbol{y}(k) = \boldsymbol{\gamma}(k)\boldsymbol{N}(k)\boldsymbol{y}(k) \tag{5}$$

Where, $\mathbf{M}$ and $\mathbf{N}$ are block covariance matrices that can be expressed as: $\mathbf{M} = \begin{bmatrix} 0 & \mathbf{C_{xz}} \\ \mathbf{C_{xz}} & 0 \end{bmatrix}$ and $\mathbf{N} = \begin{bmatrix} \mathbf{C}_{xx} & 0 \\ 0 & \mathbf{C}_{zz} \end{bmatrix}$. The rank one update using FOEP provides recursive eigenspace at every time instant. Conforming to this notion, the perturbed eigen decomposition can be obtained as:

$$(\boldsymbol{M} + \boldsymbol{\Delta M})(\boldsymbol{y} + \boldsymbol{\Delta y}) = (\boldsymbol{\gamma} + \boldsymbol{\Delta\gamma})(\boldsymbol{N} + \boldsymbol{\Delta N})(\boldsymbol{y} + \boldsymbol{\Delta y}) \tag{6}$$

Recognizing the negligible magnitude of the perturbed matrices, each of the perturbations correspond to obtaining the matrices at the $k + 1^{th}$ time instant that underlies the key essence of the FOEP approach. The corresponding eigen decomposition therefore, aligns with the case of a generalized EVD, and can be expressed as:

$$\boldsymbol{y}(k+1) = \boldsymbol{\gamma}(k+1)\boldsymbol{M}(k+1)^{-1}\boldsymbol{N}(k+1)\boldsymbol{y}(k+1) \tag{7}$$

The above structure forms the basis of the multi-directional capabilities that RCCA can accommodate. In practical cases, the algorithm promises to potentially analyse systems that are subjected to biaxial excitations, an instance of which is reported in this paper.

3. RECURSIVE DAMAGE SENSITIVE FEATURES

Based on the above discussions, it becomes easy to realize that the proposed RCCA method provides eigenspace updates at each time stamp. However, the eigenspace by itself is not enough to indicate the underlying damage patterns that arises due to the damage inflicted on the system [6,7]. To effectively distinguish between damaged and pristine state of the system and to identify the exact instant of damage in real time, recursive damage sensitive features (RDSFs) are employed that tracks the behaviour of damage patterns. In this work, the primary RDSF considered is the evolution of time varying auto regressive (TVAR) coefficients that are modelled on the transformed responses. Additionally, the use of recursive kurtosis helps in identifying the nature of the transformed responses from which the deterministic noise can be segregated [6].

3.1. TVAR coefficients

The use of TVAR coefficients as an effective RDSF has been well cited in the literature [6,7]. The proposed RCCA based approach generates the transformed responses online on to which time series models are fit. As the damage occurring to a dynamic system is a real time event, the use of TVAR models to capture an online event is therefore, justified. The plots of TVAR coefficients undergo a change in the mean level at the onset of a damage. The near mono-component nature of the transformed response ensures that low model order is sufficient to capture its dynamics; therefore, in the proposed framework, a model order of 2 (two) is pre-selected for all the cases. The basic time series fit for a TVAR model can be expressed as [5,7]:

$$\mu(k) = a_1(k)\mu(k-1) + a_2(k)\mu(k-2) + \varepsilon(k) \tag{8}$$

Here, $a_1(k)$ and $a_2(k)$ are the associated TVAR coefficients and the error arising due to modelling is represented by $\varepsilon(k)$ which is inconsequential, considering its negligible magnitude. As these coefficients are expected to show alterations in their values at the instant of damage, tracking them in real time serves as a RDSF.

3.2. Recursive kurtosis

The set of transformed responses obtained at each time instant using the proposed method comprises of a noise component that needs to be eliminated for subsequent damage detection. In order to effectively determine the operational noise, recursive kurtosis on each of the transformed responses is carried out in unison with TVAR modelling [5]. Using concepts of statistics, it is a well-known fact that kurtosis of noise components should provide a constant value throughout an ensemble average. Conforming to this, the recursive variation of kurtosis spanned over the entire sample can be expressed as:

$$\chi_{a_i}(k) = \left. \left(\frac{(k-1)\chi_{a_i}(k-1)}{k} + \frac{a_i(k)a_i(k)a_i(k)a_i(k)}{k} \right) \middle/ \left(\frac{(k-1)\sigma_{a_i}^2(k-1)}{k} + \frac{a_i(k)a_i(k)a_i(k)_i(k)}{k} \right)^4 \right. \tag{9}$$

4. PROPOSED ALGORITHM

The proposed RCCA approach deals with detecting global or temporal damage in real time. The algorithm provides a set of transformed response at the onset of each streaming data. The eigenspace spanned by the block covariance estimate gets updated online. At a possible damage instant, the distortions in the eigenspace are tracked using the proposed RDSFs that are tracked in real time [5-7]. Once the transformed responses are obtained, recursive kurtosis on each component helps in identifying the nature of the signal. The noise component is then eliminated and the damage detection module proceeds using a *subset of the transformed responses*, which forms the basis of the present identification work.

The basic steps of the proposed method are enumerated below for reference:

(i) First, traditional CCA is employed on some initial data points (around 100 in number) to estimate the initial eigenspace. The number of data points chosen are pre-selected, only used for initial stabilizing and subsequent calculations for the recursive approach.

(ii) The RCCA algorithm operates on the real time streaming of the input data which generates a set of transformed response at each time stamp.

(iii) Recursive kurtosis employed on each transformed response reveals the nature of the signal associated with the dataset. For instance, if the excitation contains a harmonic component of greater magnitude compared to the random noise component, the recursive kurtosis tracked over the ensemble will approximate to a value of 1.5 and slowly attenuate with the progression of samples.

(iv) Once the RDSF identifies the noise component, a subset of transformed response is then considered for identifying the instant of damage to the system. TVAR models are subsequently fit to the resulting subset and tracked over time to accurately detect damage. A change in the mean level of the plots indicate the exact instant of damage.

5. NUMERICAL CASE STUDY

To illustrate the application of the proposed RCCA based damage identification method, a numerical simulation is performed on a 5-DOF system modelled with a Buoc-Wen (B-W) oscillator at its base. Temporal damage to the system is considered by altering the nonlinear force term at the base of the model. The governing differential equation of the oscillator can be expressed by:

$$\boldsymbol{M\ddot{X}} + \boldsymbol{C\dot{X}} + \boldsymbol{KX} = \boldsymbol{\Gamma F} - \boldsymbol{MI\ddot{X}_g} \tag{10}$$

The numerical values for the assembled mass (**M**), damping (**C**), and stiffness (**K**) matrices respectively, can be found in Bhowmik et al. [7]. In Eq. (10), Γ represents the location of the base at the point of application of the nonlinear force (f) due to the LRB base isolator, given by:

$$\boldsymbol{f} = \kappa \boldsymbol{Z} \boldsymbol{Q}_{pb} - k_b \boldsymbol{X}_b - c_b \dot{\boldsymbol{X}}_b \tag{11}$$

The quantities k_b *and* c_b represent the base shear stiffness and the damping, respectively, while the parameter $\boldsymbol{Q}_{pb} = \left(1 - \frac{k_{yield}}{k_{initial}}\right) \boldsymbol{Q}_y$, with $\boldsymbol{Q}_y$ as the yield force. The term κ controls the level of nonlinearity associated with the system. A change in the level of the nonlinear force parameter induces a global damage to the system which is permanent in nature and does not wear off as time progresses. The relations for the evolutionary variable can be found in [7] and is not reported here for brevity.

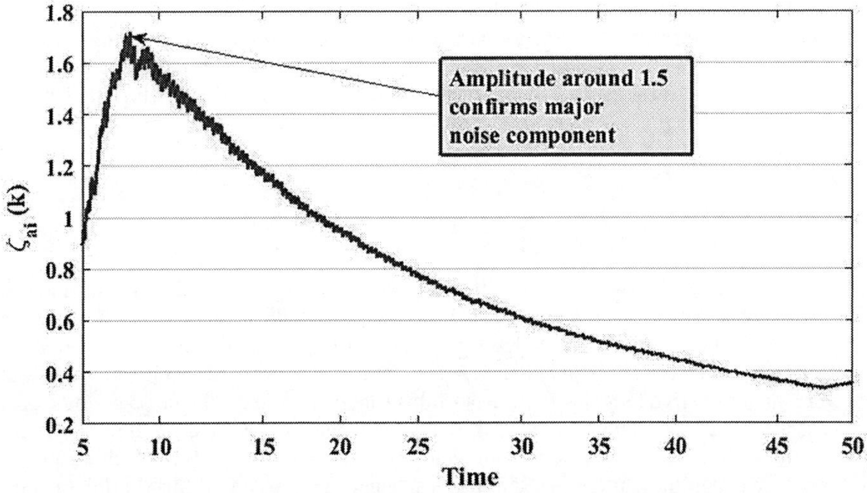

Figure 1. Indicating the presence of noise out of the first transformed response

5.1. Temporal damage detection results

The essence of damage to the B-W system is captured by changing the value of the nonlinear term in the equation of motion of the system. A numerically simulated study is considered with a 15% change in the value of κ at 31s from the start of the excitation. The proposed RCCA method provides transformed responses corresponding to a predominantly harmonic excitation with significant noise levels. As the major component of the excitation is harmonic, recursive kurtosis on the transformed responses yields a single set of response that shows a peak around the 1.5 amplitude mark. As illustrated in Figure 1, this identifies the major noise component associated with the signal, the magnitude of which reduces with the progression of samples. The algorithm proceeds by removing the operational noise and uses a subset of transformed response to eventually identify the instant of damage. As observed from Figure 2, the appearance of a sudden spike associated with the change in the mean level of the TVAR plots indicate the damage to the system at 31s from the start of the excitation.

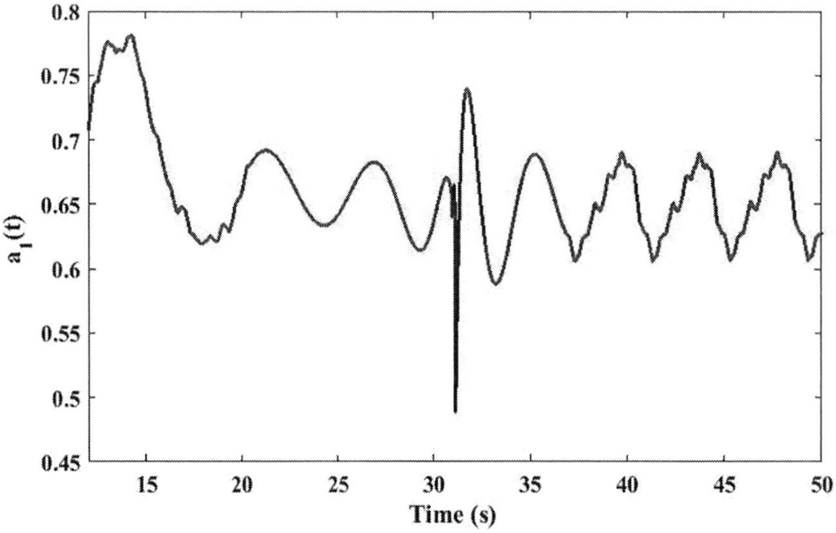

Figure 2. Temporal damage detection for the B-W system

It can be inferred from the above figure that the modulatory nature of the transformed response arises due to the nature of the input excitation which is predominantly harmonic. It can therefore, be easily understood that the proposed method is useful in segregating the deterministic noise component from the streaming dataset. The utility of the method in determining noise from a set of mixed transformed responses reflects its efficacy. The subsequent removal of operational unwanted characteristics of the response in *real time,* holds promise that the proposed approach should fare well when implemented in real life scenarios, which is presented next in detail.

6. EXPERIMENTAL VERIFICATION

The present study explores the applicability of the proposed noise removal scheme towards numerical simulations that are extensively backed by experimental case studies. In order to substantiate the robustness of the method, an experimental setup consisting of an aluminium beam of dimensions $120\ cmx3.5\ cmx3.5\ cm$ fixed on top of a shake table, is devised. For detailed specification of the setup, the readers are kindly referred to [5-7]. The intent of this trial was to assess the noise removal prowess of the proposed technique for practical case studies where human induced errors and interference with appliances in the vicinity is sometimes predominant. The experimental setup has a thin rubber strip attached to the free end of the cantilever beam that is snapped at an instant of time in order to emulate a damage condition. The experimental trial commences by subjecting the setup to earthquake excitation of scaled magnitude for a period of about 80s. The aluminium beam model is instrumented using Honeywell accelerometers at $1, 30, 47$ *and* $81cm$ from the free end. As the trial commences, a QuantumX MX410 HBM Data Acquisition System (DAQ) sampled at 75 Hz acquires the streaming acceleration response in real time. It is obvious to understand that the sampled data would contain traces of noise arising due to interference with electrical appliances in the vicinity of the setup [8]. The rubber strip serves the purpose of providing a stiffening type of nonlinearity, the snapping of which can be construed as damage.

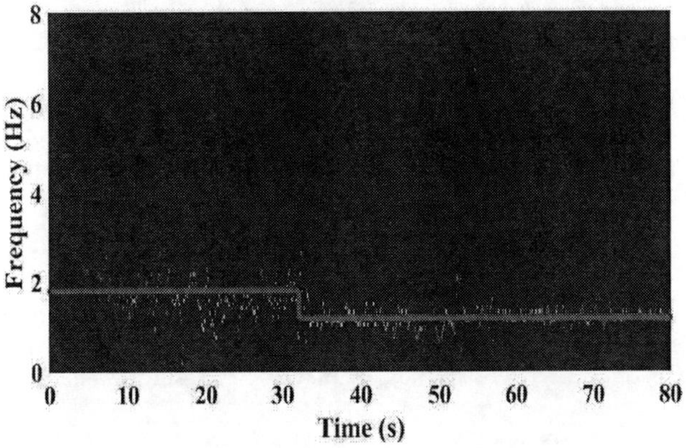

Figure 3. Use of HHS as a preliminary representation of a possible damage event.

In order to simulate a real-time damage scenario, the rubber strip attached to the free end of the cantilever beam is snapped accurately at a fixed time instant, during the vibration of the beam [11]. The uncertainties during experimentation arising due to faulty instrumentation and nearby interference are considered while acquiring the response from the DAQ. A real time damage in the present context is emulated by snapping the rubber strip at 33s from the start of the excitation. The snapping action of the rubber closely emulates a real life scenario where the stiffness of a structural element suddenly degrades due to the event of earthquake, fire or any other natural or human-induced mishap. A preliminary first-hand representation of the damage event can be obtained by plotting a Hilbert Huang spectrum (HHS) that identifies the changes in frequency with respect to time [12]. As clearly evident from Figure 3 the shift in the mean level of the plot indicates a possible event. However, the shift in the mean plot of the HHS should not be straightaway adjudged as a damage event as the presence of noisy background compromises the reliability of such a visual indicator. Hence, an accurate estimation of the same can be done using the proposed RCCA based noise removal approach.

The set of transformed responses obtained at each time stamp is considered for identifying the damage event online. Traditional noise removal schemes utilize the response data to bandpass a fixed spectrum of noise component and proceed with subsequent analysis. However, in the proposed approach, the actual set of response is taken into consideration and the RCCA method is utilized to yield transformed responses in real time. As previously discussed, the recursive kurtosis of the predominant noise component yields almost a constant value throughout the duration of the excitation. This helps in identifying the operational noise that arises due to interference with nearby machinery. A subset of the transformed responses is then chosen which eliminates the affect of noise in the dataset for identifying damage patterns in real time. It should be noted that the removal of noise from the ensuing dataset does not compromise the quality of the signal and renders the damage identification process, efficient. As observed from Figure 4, the plot of the TVAR coefficient indicates a change in the mean level at 33s from the start of the excitation, which identifies the instant of damage to the system. However, the appearance of certain activity in the later stages of the excitation is due to the non-stationary nature of the input excitation taken into consideration. The wavy patterns at the far end of the excitation are inconsequential, and can therefore, be safely ignored. Hence, the applicability of the proposed real time noise removal approach towards practical case studies is eventually justified.

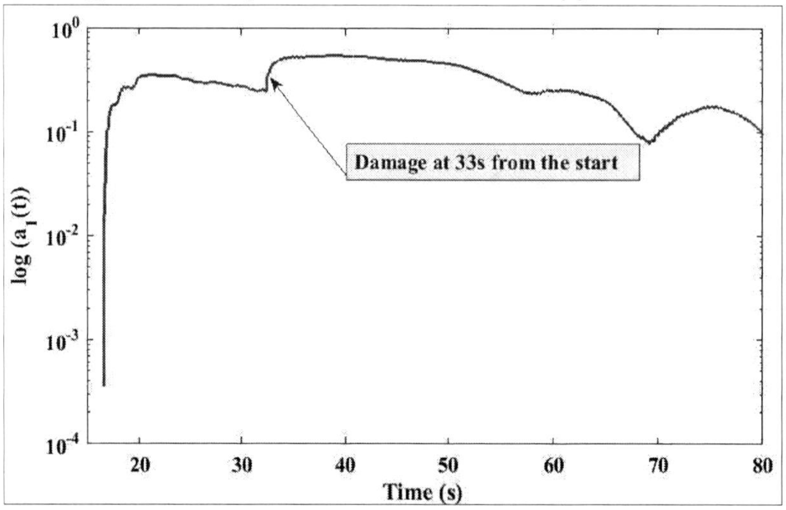

Figure 4. RDSF plot for the experimental trial

7. CONCLUSIONS

A real time noise removal approach using the principles of RCCA is presented. The method provides a set of transformed responses which are examined using higher order moments such as recursive kurtosis, to identify the noise component of the signal. Further, the recursive eigenspace characteristics of the covariance matrix provide information regarding the state of the system, if inflicted with damage. Once the operational noise component is eliminated, the algorithm proceeds with a subset of the transformed responses to accurately identify the damage instant. The use of RDSFs such as TVAR coefficients provide real time updates of the state of the vibrating system. As previously mentioned, the sudden change in the mean level over time indicates the onset of damage to the system. The proposed method identifies damage in real time of the order of 15% for temporal damage, using a subset of responses. Numerically simulated case studies reveal that the proposed RCCA based noise reduction technique is particularly helpful in segregating the deterministic noise component from the signal. Even with a subset of transformed responses, the method has shown to accurately depict the instant of damage in real time, which is a novel feat, that has not been attempted so far. Presented experimental verification shows that the noise reduction scheme is equally efficient in removing the outliers for a practical scenario considering the inevitable interference arising during experimentation. The findings from the experimental studies are of immense significance as the method hold promise in detecting damage events for real life case studies involving actual structures that are subjected to continuous excitation levels. Application of the method towards varied nonlinear systems and extensive practical studies is kept as a possible extension of the current work to be dealt with in the future.

REFERENCES

[1] Brocker, J., Parlitz, U., & Ogorzalek, M. (2002). Nonlinear noise reduction. *Proceedings of the IEEE*, 90(5), 898-918.

[2] Schreiber, T. (1993). Extremely simple nonlinear noise-reduction method. *Physical Review E*, 47(4), 2401.

[3] Kantz, H., Schreiber, T., Hoffmann, I., Buzug, T., Pfister, G., Flepp, L. G., & Brun, E. (1993). Nonlinear noise reduction: A case study on experimental data. *Physical Review E*, 48(2), 1529.

[4] Just, W., Kantz, H., Rödenbeck, C., & Helm, M. (2001). Stochastic modelling: replacing fast degrees of freedom by noise. *Journal of Physics A: Mathematical and General*, 34(15), 3199.

[5] Krishnan, M., Bhowmik, B., Hazra, B., and Pakrashi, P, (2018). 'Real time damage detection using recursive principal components and time varying auto-regressive modeling', *Mechanical Systems and Signal Processing*, Volume 101, Elsevier, pp. 549 – 574.

[6] Krishnan, M., Bhowmik, B., Tiwari, AK., and Hazra, B. (2017). 'Online damage detection using recursive principal component analysis and recursive condition indicators,' *Smart Materials and Structures*, IOP Publishing. 26(8), 085017.

[7] Bhowmik, B., Krishnan, M., Hazra, B.,and Pakrashi, V. (2018) . 'Real time unified single and multi-channel structural damage detection using recursive singular spectrum analysis', *Structural Health Monitoring*, SAGE Publications. pp. 475921718760483, doi=10.1177/1475921718760483.

[8] Cahill, P., Hazra, B., Karoumi, R., Mathewson, A., & Pakrashi, V. (2018). Vibration energy harvesting based monitoring of an operational bridge undergoing forced vibration and train passage. *Mechanical Systems and Signal Processing*, 106, 265-283.

[9] Borga, M. (2001). Canonical correlation: a tutorial. On line tutorial *http://people. imt. liu. se/magnus/cca*. 4(5).

[10] Thorndike, RM., (2000). Canonical correlation analysis. *Handbook of applied multi- variate statistics and mathematical modeling*. Elsevier, pp. 237–263.

[11] Pakrashi, V., Fitzgerald, P., O'Leary, M., et al. "Assessment of structural nonlinearities employing extremes of dynamic responses". (2016) *Journal of Vibration and Control*; 24: 137–152.

[12] Huang NE, Shen Z, Long SR, et al. (1998) "The empirical mode decomposition and the Hilbert spectrum for nonlinear and non-stationary time series analysis". *Proceedings of the Royal Society London A*; 454(1971): 903–995.

IOMAC'19

8th International Operational Modal Analysis Conference

2019 May13-15 Copenhagen

STRUCTURAL ANOMALY DETECTION BASED ON PROBABILISTIC METRIC DISTANCE OF TRANSMISSIBILITY FUNCTIONS

Wang-Ji Yan[1], *Dimitrios Chronopoulos*[2]

Marie Skłodowska-Curie Fellow,Institute for Aerospace Technology & The Composites Group, The University of Nottingham, United Kingdom, civilyanwj@gmail.com

Associate Professor, Institute for Aerospace Technology & The Composites Group, The University of Nottingham, United Kingdom, ezzdc1@exmail.nottingham.ac.uk

ABSTRACT

Transmissibility function (TF) has been extensively used as damage-sensitive features in structural condition assessment. Based on the theoretical findings of circularly-symmetric complex Gaussian ratio distribution for transmissibility, the study proposes a new data-driven damage detection algorithm by accommodating multiple uncertainties of frequency responses. Based on the analytical probability density function of TFs of the healthy and of different possibly damage scenarios, a probabilistic metric is calculated as a damage index to identify the dissimilarity between the probability distributions of TFs under different states, which allows the automatic identification of structural anomaly. Numerical studies are carried out to verify the effectiveness and accuracy of the proposed methodology.

Keywords: Transmissibility function, Uncertainty quantification, Damage detection, Probabilistic metric, Operational variation

1. INTRODUCTION

The anticipated service life of engineering structures decreases due to hostile-loading environments and lack of timely maintenance. Assessing the structural condition of engineering structures have attracted widespread attention [1,2]. Output-only vibration testing without resorting to expensive excitation setups are particularly attractive as it can realize real-time safety monitoring for the structures without interrupting their normal operations. Therefore, considerable efforts have been spent in extracting damage features from ambient vibration measurements [3].

Over the past few years, transmissibility function (TF) as a mathematical representation of the output-to-output relationship has proven to be an attractive tool in SHM due to its unique properties [4]. Without measuring the input or assuming a specific input model, TF-based damage detection has aroused considerable interest due to its advantages [5]. For example, there is no need to undertake a modal identification, while it is not necessary to have any analytic or numerical model of the structure [6].

Motivated by the fact that structural damage will cause dissimilarity of the probability distributions of frequency responses, and Symmetric Kullback-Leibler (SKL) Divergence is able to measure the degree of difference between two probability distributions [7], the study proposes a new statistical data-driven damage detection algorithm by accommodating multiple uncertainties of transmissibility measurements. It has been strictly proved that TFs follow circularly-symmetric complex Gaussian ratio distribution [8,9]. As a result, SKL divergence-based damage index is calculated to detect the dissimilarity between two probability distributions of TFs corresponding to different states, which allows the automatic identification of anomaly. Numerical studies are carried out to verify the effectiveness of the proposed methodology.

2. THEORETICAL BACKGROUND

2.1. Analytical probabilistic model of transmissibility functions

For a linear system subjected to a stationary excitation, discrete measurements $\boldsymbol{y}(t) = \{y_1(t), y_2(t), \cdots, y_{n_o}(t)\}$ are available for n_o measured dofs, and its corresponding FFT coefficients are denoted by $\boldsymbol{Y}(\omega_k) = \{Y_1(\omega_k), Y_2(\omega_k), \cdots, Y_{n_o}(\omega_k)\}$. The sampling frequency is assumed to be $\frac{1}{\Delta t}$. A TF $T_{i,o}^{(k)}$ is defined as the ratio of FFT of an arbitrary response $Y_i(\omega_k)$ to a reference response $Y_o(\omega_k)$:

$$T_{i,o}^{(k)} = \frac{Y_i(\omega_k)}{Y_o(\omega_k)} \tag{1}$$

Using the new theorem on multivariate circularly-symmetric complex Gaussian ratio distribution [8], the probability density function (PDF) of multiple TFs are given by [9]:

$$p_{T_k}(\boldsymbol{\tau}_k) = \frac{(n_o - 1)!}{\pi^{(n_o-1)}|det\,\boldsymbol{\Lambda}_k|(\zeta_k^* \boldsymbol{\Lambda}_k^{-1} \zeta_k)^{n_o}} \tag{2}$$

where $\zeta_k = \left[1, \boldsymbol{\tau}_k^T\right]^T = \left[1, \tau_{1,o}^{(k)}, \tau_{2,o}^{(k)}, \cdots, \tau_{(n_o-1),o}^{(k)}\right]^T$ denotes the value of random vector $\{1, T_k\} = \{1, T_{1,o}^{(k)}, T_{2,o}^{(k)}, \cdots, T_{i,o}^{(k)}, \cdots, T_{(n_o-1),o}^{(k)}\}$; $\tau_{i,o}^{(k)}$ denotes the value of the random variable $T_{i,o}^{(k)}$; $\boldsymbol{\Lambda}_k$ denotes the covariance matrix of FFT coefficients vector $\boldsymbol{Y}(\omega_k)$. It is worth mentioning here that, in this work, all 'k' shown in the bracket, in the subscript or in the superscript denote frequency f_k.

2.2. Symmetric KL divergence

KL divergence is a measure of how one probability distribution is different from the reference probability distribution. In probability theory, KL divergence is also known as information divergence, information gain, or relative entropy. Applications include characterizing the relative (Shannon) entropy in information systems, randomness in continuous time-series, and information gain when comparing statistical models of inference. For two continuous PDFs $p_1(x)$ and $p_2(x)$, KL divergence is defined to be the integral given by [7]

$$D_{KL}(p_1(x)\|p_2(x)) = \int_X p_1(x)\, log \frac{p_1(x)}{p_2(x)} dx \tag{3}$$

The KL divergence from $p_1(x)$ to $p_2(x)$ is generally not the same as that from $p_2(x)$ to $p_1(x)$. It is not a true "distance" measure between the two distributions since it is not symmetric, i.e. $D_{KL}(p_1(x)\|p_2(x)) \neq D_{KL}(p_2(x)\|p_1(x))$, and does not satisfy the triangle inequality. Therefore, the symmetric KL (SKL) divergence between $p_1(x)$ and $p_2(x)$ will be employed in this study to formulate damage index to make sure it satisfy the definition of 'distance'. SKL divergence is defined as [7]

$$SKL(p_2(x); p_1(x)) = \int_X [p_1(x) - p_2(x)] \, log \frac{p_1(x)}{p_2(x)} dx \tag{4}$$

The above equation represents a non-negative measure between two PDFs.

2.3. Damage index based on SKL divergence

The TF between $i - th$ and $j - th$ DOFs for the healthy state and damaged state are denoted by $T_{ij}^h(\omega_k)$ and $T_{ij}^d(\omega_k)$, while their PDFs are denote by $p_{ij}^h(x)$ and $p_{ij}^d(x)$, respectively. The divergence of $p_{ij}^h(x)$ from $p_{ij}^d(x)$ relate to the idea that the distribution of damaged state will deviate the distribution of healthy state. Therefore, one can achieve a SKL divergence $SKL_{ij}(\omega_k)$ at frequency ω_k between the possibly damaged state $T_{ij}^d(\omega_k)$ and the healthy state $T_{ij}^h(\omega_k)$:

$$SKL_{ij}(\omega_k) = \int_X \left[p_{ij}^h(x) - p_{ij}^d(x)\right] log \frac{p_{ij}^h(x)}{p_{ij}^d(x)} dx \tag{5}$$

As a result, the damageindicator DI can be obtained by incorporating $SKL_{ij}(\omega_k)$ corresponding to different measurements at different frequency points:

$$DI = \sum_{k=1}^{N_\omega} \sum_{\substack{j=1 \\ j \neq i}}^{n_o} \sum_{i=1}^{n_o} SKL_{ij}(\omega_k) \tag{6}$$

where n_ω denotes the number of frequency ordinates; where n_o denotes the number of measurements.

3. CASE STUDY

The theory proposed in the above will be verified by a numerical example. This section details the processing of synthesis data based on simulated response of a 10-storey shear building that forms the cornerstone of the work. The stiffness at each floor is assumed to be $1.50 \times 10^6 N/m$, while mass at each floor is assumed to be $1000kg$. Classical Rayleigh damping is assumed. To simulate the responses of the structure, the structure is excited by ambient input modeled as Gaussian white noise at the 5-th dof, while the prediction error is also assumed to be Gaussian white noise.

Table 1. damage scenarios

Scenarios	Damage Element	Damage extent
1	5	10%
2	5	30%
3	5	30%
	10	20%
	4	20%
4	5	30%
	10	20%

Table 2. DI values for different damage scenarios

Scenarios		DI values
Undamaged	0	151.499
Damaged	1	201.883
	2	598.411
	3	852.798
	4	1114.588

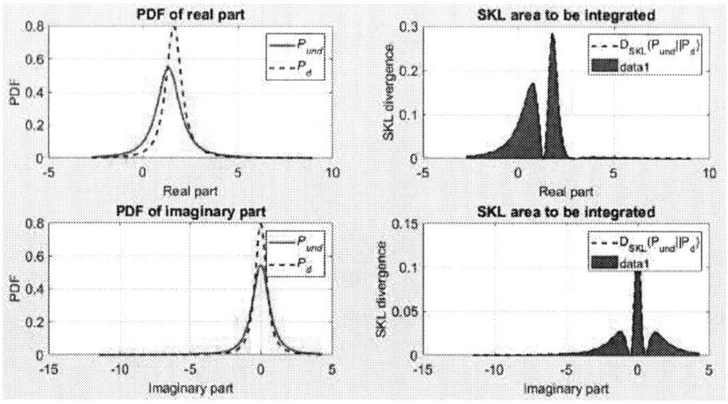

Figure 1. PDF and SKL of $T_{1,2}^{(k)}$ at $\omega_k = 27.72\pi\ rad/s$ corresponding to healthy and damaged states

In addition to the undamaged structure, four damage patterns are studied as a part of the problem. The damage patterns are defined in **Table** 1. 500 samples are generated for the healthy state, which serves as the baseline of calculating SKL divergence. The TF of the first sensor and the second sensor $T_{1,2}^{(k)}$ at $\omega_k = 27.72\pi$ rad/s is observed in detail. The PDF of $T_{1,2}^{(k)}$ corresponding to the healthy state and the second damage state are shown in **Figure** 1. The damage indicator of the TFs acquired from the data sets corresponding to measurements of different states are computed using Eq.(6). The DI incorporating SKL of different transmissibility functions at diffenent frequencies are shown in **Table** 2. As is seen from **Table** 2, the DI values are proportional to the damage level, indicating that the disimilarity of TFs different states increases with the level of damage. Therefore, the proposed damage index can reflect the damage extent, and SKL can be employed as a reasonable damage index for structural anomaly detection.

4. CONCLUSIONS

Condition assessment for infrastructure protection and health monitoring of structures has been a subject of strong research within the engineering community. The difficulty of achieving controlled input has led to the development of new output-only SHM approaches. TF has been extensively used as damage-sensitive features in structural condition assessment. Based on the theoretical findings of circularly-symmetric complex normal ratio distribution for scalar TFs, the study proposes a new statistical data-driven damage detection algorithm by accommodating multiple uncertainties of frequency responses, which has rarely been considered in the literature available. Based on the PDF of TFs of the healthy and of different possibly damage scenarios, symmetric KL divergence is calculated as an index to quantify the dissimilarity between PDFs of TFs under different damage conditions, which can reflect the structural anomaly properly. A numerical case study is employed to prove that the proposed method is able to diagnose the existence of damage and assess the overall health condition of a structure using ambient vibration testing.

ACKNOWLEDGEMENTS

The research described in this paper was financially supported by the European Union's Horizon 2020 research and innovation program under the Marie Skłodowska-Curie grant agreement No 741284.

REFERENCES

[1] Worden, K., Farrar, C.R., Manson, G., & Park, G. (2007). The fundamental axioms of structural health monitoring. Proc. R. Soc. A, 463, 1639-64.

[2] Chronopoulos, D., Droz, C., Apalowo, R., Ichchou, M., & Yan, W. J. (2017). Accurate structural identification for layered composite structures, through a wave and finite element scheme. Composite Structures, 182, 566-578.

[3] Brownjohn, J. M. (2007). Structural health monitoring of civil infrastructure. Philosophical Transactions of the Royal Society of London A: Mathematical, Physical and Engineering Sciences, 365 (1851), 589-622.

[4] Yan, W. J., Zhao, M. Y., Sun, Q., & Ren, W. X. (2019). Transmissibility-based system identification for structural health Monitoring: Fundamentals, approaches, and applications. Mechanical Systems and Signal Processing, 117, 453-482.

[5] Simon, C., & Arnaud, D. (2013). Damage localization using transmissibility functions: A critical review. Mechanical Systems and Signal Processing, 38 (2), 569-584.

[6] Maia, N.M.M., Almeida, R., Urgueira, A.P.V., & Sampaio, R.P.C. (2011). Damage detection and quantification using transmissibility. Mechanical Systems and Signal Processing, 25 (7), 2475-2483.

[7] Goldberger, J., Gordon, S., & Greenspan, H. (2003, October). An efficient image similarity measure based on approximations of KL-divergence between two Gaussian mixtures. [C]//null. IEEE, 2003: 487

[8] Yan, W.J., & Ren, W.X. (2016). Circularly-symmetric complex normal ratio distribution for scalar transmissibility function. Part I: theory. Mechanical Systems and Signal Processing, 80, 58-77.

[9] Yan, W.J., & Ren, W.X. (2016). Circularly-symmetric complex Normal ratio distribution for scalar transmissibility functions. Part II: application. Mechanical Systems and Signal Processing, 80, 78-98.

IOMAC'19

8th International Operational Modal Analysis Conference
2019 May13-15 Copenhagen

SUBSPACE-BASED DAMAGE DETECTION WITH REJECTION OF THE TEMPERATURE EFFECT AND UNCERTAINTY IN THE REFERENCE

Eva Viefhues [1], *Michael Döhler* [2], *Qinghua Zhang* [2], *Falk Hille* [1], *and Laurent Mevel* [2]

[1] BAM Federal Insitute for Materials Research and Testing, Berlin, Germany, (eva.viefhues, falk.hille)@bam.de

[2] Inria, Ifsttar, Univ. Rennes, Rennes, France, (michael.doehler, qinghua.zhang, laurent.mevel)@inria.fr

ABSTRACT

Temperature variation can be a nuisance that perturbs vibration based structural health monitoring (SHM) approaches for civil engineering structures. In this paper, temperature affected vibration data is evaluated within a stochastic damage detection framework, which relies on a null space based residual. Besides two existing temperature rejection approaches – building a reference state from an averaging method or a piecewise method – a new approach is proposed, using model interpolation. In this approach, a general reference model is obtained from data in the reference state at several known reference temperatures. Then, for a particular tested temperature, a local reference model is derived from the general reference model. Thus, a well fitting reference null space for the formulation of a residual is available when new data is tested for damage detection at an arbitrary temperature. Particular attention is paid to the computation of the residual covariance, taking into account the uncertainty related to the null space matrix estimate. This improves the test performance, contrary to prior methods, for local and global damages, resulting in a higher probability of detection (PoD) for the new interpolation approach compared to previous approaches.

Keywords: statistical method, subspace-based method, temperature rejection, model interpolation, uncertainty

1. INTRODUCTION

In structural health monitoring of civil engineering structures, the effects of environmental variability often limit the possible application of existing damage diagnosis approaches. Methods that are sensitive to changes due to damages mostly are prone to false alarms, when temperature affects the dynamical behavior of the structure in a more significant way than small, local damages would. Thus, the environmental variability is an crucial issue for the practicability of vibration based SHM. In [1] examples of

SHM projects are listed, which gave evidence of the importance of considering temperature effects.

Several approaches are proposed within the literature for temperature rejection methods in vibration based damage diagnosis tools. Some of them consider data features, which are blind to environmental variations. In [2], a regression analysis of the natural frequencies was performed, requiring the estimation of those quantities. Other approaches [3, 4] adopt a novelty detection point of view, with the definition of the system under normal reference conditions.

In this paper the stochastic subspace-based methods will be used for damage diagnosis robust to temperature variations. These statistical approaches have been shown to be able to handle noises and uncertainties in the reference null space. The stochastic subspace-based method has already been basis for some work on temperature rejection too. In [8], a damage diagnosis test is proposed, where the system parameter matrix estimates are averaged with respect to temperature. This temperature depending average is used for the determination of a reference and therefore for the statistical tests. In [6] the generic stochastic subspace-based method was modified for temperature compensation, by considering the reference measurements piecewise. The temperature parameter is then used to find the best fitting reference null space.

The now proposed temperature rejection approach relies on the model interpolation approach from [7]. Assume that the dynamic behavior of a system depends on a parameter p, for example, the temperature of a monitored structure. Given some data sets, each being collected on the system when p stays around a specific value, then each of these data sets can be used to build a model, which is valid locally in the range of p. Naturally, when p varies within the same range, new models can be obtained by interpolating the available local models. However, with the stochastic subspace method, the available local models are in state-space form, and each of them are represented in an arbitrary state basis, independent from each other. This lack of coherence between the state bases of the local models makes the interpolation of local models non trivial. The method proposed in [7] has the advantage of being insensitive to this lack of coherence. In the context of the current paper and the temperature rejection, the considered varying physical parameter is assumed to be the temperature.

In the following, the basics of subspace-based damage diagnosis are introduced shortly. In Section 3. two existing temperature rejection approaches for the stochastic subspace-base damage diagnosis are described, and the new approach using model interpolation is derived. After considering the issue of uncertainty considerations, the three temperature rejection approaches are compared regarding their probability of detection in Section 4..

2. SUBSPACE-BASED DAMAGE DIAGNOSIS

Assume the structure of interest to be modeled by a linear mechanical model, which is influenced by the temperature T. At some temperature $T = T_j$, the corresponding stochastic discrete time state-space model writes as

$$\begin{aligned} x_{k+1,j} &= A_j x_{k,j} + w_{k,j} \\ y_{k,j} &= C_j x_{k,j} + v_{k,j}, \end{aligned} \quad (1)$$

where $x \in \mathbb{R}^n$ denotes the state, k the index of the sample within each experiment, N the total number of samples for each experiment, $y \in \mathbb{R}^r$ is the measured output. The system matrices $A_j = A(T_j)$ and $C_j = C(T_j)$ are the state transition matrix with dimension $n \times n$ and the observation matrix with dimension $r \times n$, respectively. White noise is assumed for the state noise w and output noise v. Denote the cross-covariances between the signal $y_{k,j}$ and its time-shifted version $y_{k-i,j}$ as the *output covariances*

$R_{i,j} = \mathbf{E}(y_{k,j} y_{k-i,j}^T) = C_j A_j^{i-1} G_j$, where $G_j = \mathbf{E}(x_{k+1,j} y_{k,j}^T)$. Then a block Hankel matrix is built:

$$\mathcal{H}_j \stackrel{\text{def}}{=} \begin{bmatrix} R_{1,j} & R_{2,j} & \dots & R_{q,j} \\ R_{2,j} & R_{3,j} & \dots & R_{q+1,j} \\ \vdots & \vdots & \ddots & \vdots \\ R_{p+1,j} & R_{p+2,j} & \dots & R_{q+p,j} \end{bmatrix}. \tag{2}$$

By definition $\mathcal{H}_j$ depends on the system matrices and therefore will change if the dynamical system changes due to damages. For damage diagnosis, the left null space matrix of $\mathcal{H}_j$ in the reference state is considered. For the so called *reference null space* S it holds $S^T \mathcal{H}_j = 0$ for some j. A data-based residual vector ζ can be defined as

$$\zeta = \sqrt{N} \text{vec}(S^T \hat{\mathcal{H}}), \tag{3}$$

with vec$(\cdot)$ as the column stacking vectorization operator and $\hat{\mathcal{H}}$ as the estimate of the Hankel matrix from data in the monitoring state at an arbitrary temperature T. Notice that for every $\mathcal{H}_j$, there exists a different null space S_j. This makes the choice of a unique null space impossible as temperature varies.

If the system deviates from the reference state, S is no longer the null space of the monitored data Hankel matrix and the mean value of ζ deviates from 0. The evaluation of the residual ζ is done by means of some hypothesis tests, as proposed e.g. in [8, 9]. The test writes as

$$t = \zeta^T \Sigma_\zeta^{-1} \zeta, \tag{4}$$

where Σ_ζ is the asymptotic residual covariance. The test statistic t is asymptotically χ^2 distributed and compared to a threshold, which has to be computed in a training phase in the reference state for a given type I error. Note that besides changes due to damage, changes due to temperature will also lead to a deviation of the residual mean from 0 when the temperature for the computation of S does not correspond to the temperature of $\hat{\mathcal{H}}$.

Conventionally, the asymptotic covariance $\Sigma_\mathcal{H} = \lim \text{cov}(\sqrt{N} \text{vec}(\hat{\mathcal{H}}))$ corresponding to the computed matrix $\hat{\mathcal{H}}$ is considered in the computation of Σ_ζ as

$$\Sigma_\zeta = \mathcal{J}_{\zeta,\mathcal{H}} \Sigma_\mathcal{H} \mathcal{J}_{\zeta,\mathcal{H}}^T \tag{5}$$

where $\mathcal{J}_{\zeta,\mathcal{H}} = I \otimes S^T$. An estimate $\hat{\Sigma}_\mathcal{H}$ of the covariance $\Sigma_\mathcal{H}$ is obtained from a sample covariance [9]: A data sample y_k, $k = 1, ..., N$, is separated into n_b blocks, each of the length N_b, with $n_b \cdot N_b = N$. With the output covariance estimates computed for each data block h, the Hankel matrix $\hat{\mathcal{H}}^{(h)}$ can be computed and the sample covariance yields

$$\hat{\Sigma}_\mathcal{H} = \frac{N_b}{n_b - 1} \sum_{h=1}^{n_b} \text{vec}\left(\hat{\mathcal{H}}^{(h)} - \hat{\mathcal{H}}\right) \text{vec}\left(\hat{\mathcal{H}}^{(h)} - \hat{\mathcal{H}}\right)^T. \tag{6}$$

3. TEMPERATURE REJECTION WITHIN SUBSPACE-BASED DAMAGE DETECTION

The stochastic subspace-based method is promising when it comes to damage detection of structures, which are exposed to temperature variations. By choosing an adequate reference null space for the residual and a proper residual covariance for the hypothesis testing, the damage detection tests can be made robust to temperature variation.

In the following two existing temperature rejection approaches – an averaging and a piecewise approach – will be recalled shortly. Finally a new method is introduced, where an interpolated reference null space is considered.

3.1. Averaging and piecewise approaches for temperature rejection

A simple temperature rejection approach [8] uses the reference null space of *averaged* Hankel matrices in the reference state and an averaged residual covariance. Measurements $\mathcal{Y}_j = [y_{1,j} \ y_{2,j} \ \dots \ y_{N,j}]$ at $j = 1, \dots, m$ different reference temperatures T_j are merged to one big data set $\bar{\mathcal{Y}} = \begin{bmatrix} \mathcal{Y}_1 & \mathcal{Y}_2 & \dots & \mathcal{Y}_m \end{bmatrix}$. The null space $\bar{S}$ of the *averaged* system and the corresponding data covariance $\bar{\Sigma}_{\mathcal{H}}$ follow from Equations (2) and (6), computed on the merged data set $\bar{\mathcal{Y}}$. Note that for this method no information about the reference temperatures is used.

Taking into account the temperature measurement information into the temperature rejection method can improve the test performance, as the reference null space can be determined more accurately for a specific temperature range. In [6] an approach was proposed, where reference null space matrices S_j and corresponding covariances $\Sigma_{\mathcal{H}_j}$ are estimated "piecewise" on reference data $\mathcal{Y}_j$ at each available reference temperature T_j, $j = 1, \dots, m$. In the tested state, the current temperature T is recorded and the *nearest* reference null space with respect to this temperature is used to compute the residual and the hypothesis test.

3.2. Model interpolation for temperature rejection

The basic idea of the new temperature rejection method is to provide an adequate reference null space for each tested temperature T. This approach is based on a linear parameter varying (LPV) system model interpolation with model reduction method proposed in [7]. In this model interpolation method, the local state-space models (1), obtained at $j = 1, \dots, m$ reference temperatures T_j, are combined to build a large global state-space model. Because each local state-space model (1) has been estimated with an arbitrary state basis, it is not possible to directly interpolate the matrices involved in (1) before making the local models coherent. The method proposed in [7] has the advantage of not requiring the formulation of coherent local models. From this LPV model a local model for the required tested temperature T can be interpolated in the testing step. Then, this local model corresponds well to a reference system at temperature T, and can be used to obtain the null space and covariance matrices for damage detection. Following [7], the local models (1) are combined into a large state-space model as

$$\begin{aligned} \underline{x}_{k+1} &= \underline{A}\,\underline{x}_k + \underline{w}_k \\ y_k &= \underline{C}(T)\,\underline{x}_k + \underline{v}_k, \end{aligned} \tag{7}$$

where

$$\underline{x}_k = \begin{bmatrix} x_{k,1}^T & \dots & x_{k,m}^T \end{bmatrix}^T, \ \underline{w}_k = \begin{bmatrix} w_{k,1}^T & \dots & w_{k,m}^T \end{bmatrix}^T$$

$$\underline{C}(T) = \begin{bmatrix} \rho_1(T)C_1 & \cdots & \rho_m(T)C_m \end{bmatrix}, \ \underline{v}_k = \sum_{j=1}^{m} \rho_j(T)\, v_{k,j}(t)$$

$$\underline{A} = \begin{bmatrix} A_1 & & \\ & \ddots & \\ & & A_m \end{bmatrix}, \quad \underline{G} = \begin{bmatrix} \rho_1(T)G_1 \\ \vdots \\ \rho_m(T)G_m \end{bmatrix}.$$

The weighting functions $\rho(T)$ are typically bell-shaped functions, centered at T, such that

$$\sum_{j=1}^{m} \rho_j(T) = 1 \quad \text{for all} \quad T \in \mathbb{T} \quad \text{and} \quad \rho_j(T) : \mathbb{T} \Rightarrow [0, 1]. \tag{8}$$

This large global model of order mn is then reduced. Using the well-known balanced reduction method, due to its reliable numerical behavior, the state vector $\underline{x}_k$ is transformed linearly, removing the smallest Hankel singular values. Then only the n largest Hankel singular values are kept, and the resulting state space model is of order n, like any of the local models. This method was developed based on the availability of system matrix estimates at different temperatures.

However, the damage detection test (4) is not directly formulated with the matrices involved in state-space models like those of (1) or those of the interpolated local model. Instead, it is based on the Hankel matrix of the output covariances and its null space in the reference state of the system. Direct interpolation of the temperature-dependent null space is a non trivial task, because each corresponding local model is related to an arbitrary state basis. In this paper, this interpolation will be made through the interpolation of the Hankel matrices corresponding to different reference temperatures T_j and the production of a global, interpolated Hankel matrix $\underline{\mathcal{H}}(T)$ corresponding to the reference state at temperature T. Considering the definition of the output covariances R_i, the output covariances of system (7) can be written as

$$\underline{R}_i(T) = \underline{C}(T)\underline{A}^{i-1}\underline{G} = \sum_{j=1}^{m} \rho_j^2(T) C_j A_j^{i-1} G_j = \sum_{j=1}^{m} \rho_j^2(T) R_{i,j}. \tag{9}$$

This leads to the interpolated Hankel matrix

$$\underline{\mathcal{H}}(T) = \sum_{j=1}^{m} \rho_j^2(T) \mathcal{H}_j \tag{10}$$

and thus to the null space matrix $\underline{S}(T)$ of the interpolated Hankel matrix, i.e. the left null space of (10). The covariance $\underline{\Sigma}_{\mathcal{H}}(T)$ of the interpolated Hankel matrix follows as

$$\underline{\Sigma}_{\mathcal{H}}(T) = \sum_{j=1}^{m} \rho_j^4(T) \Sigma_{\mathcal{H}_j}. \tag{11}$$

3.3. Behavior of the temperature rejection approaches

For the evaluation of the temperature rejection approaches, hypothesis tests on an 8-mass-spring damper are performed at different tested temperatures between 0°C and 20°C. The temperature effect is modeled as a decrease or an increase of stiffness at all elements of maximum 8%. In the reference state, data is simulated at $m = 5$ reference temperatures, namely at 0, 5, 10, 15, and 20 °C. Two different data lengths are used (40,000 and 80,000 data samples, respectively) at each considered reference temperature when setting up the reference state, i.e. for the computation of the null space and the covariance matrix.

For the damage detection tests, datasets of length N=200,000 are generated in the reference and damaged states in the whole temperature range between 0°C and 20°C for the computation of $\hat{\mathcal{H}}$.

The test values in the reference state are plotted in Figure 1 with the different temperature rejection methods. The red lines show the results when 10°C is taken as the reference temperature and no further temperature rejection is considered. It can be observed that for other tested temperatures than the chosen reference temperature, the test values differ significantly from those computed at the reference temperature. This is most likely due to the fact that the considered reference null space does not fit properly to the data, if the temperature in the tested state is different from the one at the reference state, to the point that a change in the system is incorrectly detected. Then, it will not be possible to define a threshold for damage detection. A well defined threshold is mandatory for a good test performance with few false alarms. Notice that the observed effect is independent from the length of the dataset used for the computation of the reference null space.

The test values of the averaging method (blue lines) follow a flat curve, and the impact of data length is not obvious. Stability of the test values for different tested temperatures is a first requirement to ensure, so that a reliable threshold avoiding too many false alarms can be found.

For the piecewise approach, the $m = 5$ reference temperatures 0, 5, 10, 15, and 20 °C can be clearly identified as the minima of the green curves. It can be seen that using more data at each temperature state gives more stable test values. However, if the tested temperature differs from the reference temperature used for the null space computation, the test values are rising, as a change is detected.

The new temperature rejection method aims at providing an adequate reference for each tested temperature (pink lines). With the reference temperatures 0, 5, 10, 15, and 20 °C, the test values in the reference state vary in a certain range. They do not show a specific increase or decrease according to the reference temperatures. The values become more stable when the data length increases.

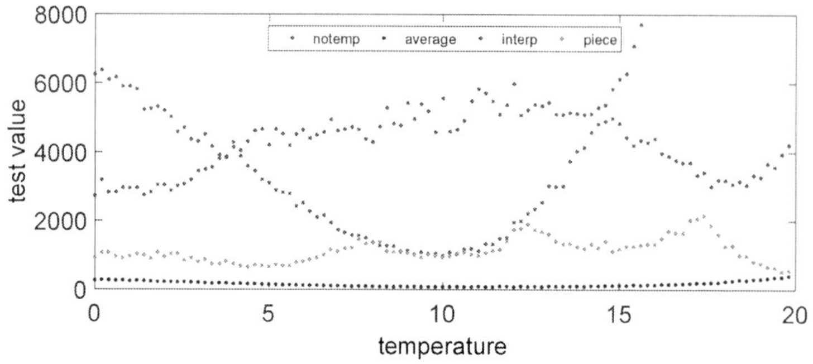

(a) 40,000 data points at each reference temperature

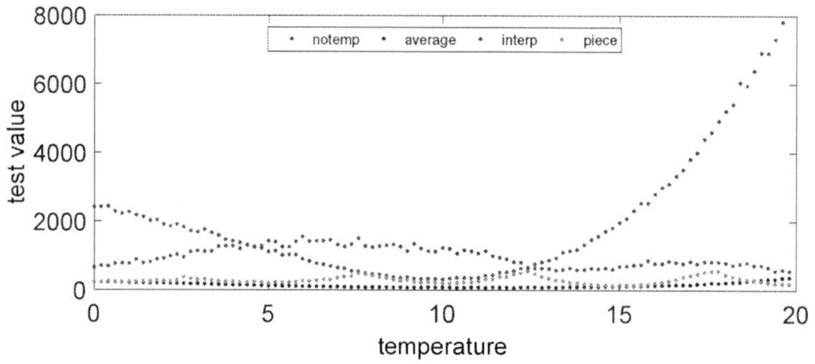

(b) 80,000 data points at each reference temperature

Figure 1: Test values in reference case for short and long data sets in the reference state

To consider the performance of the hypothesis test when damage occurs, the shift of the test values in the damaged state from those in the reference state is the relevant criterion. In Figure 2 test values in the reference and in the damaged state are presented, where the long data set in the reference state was considered. The damage is defined as a global damage with 2% loss of stiffness at all elements. To detect global damages, such as the loss of external pre-stressing or extensive cracking, is challenging compared to detecting local ones, because the effect of the damage on the dynamical behavior is similar to the temperature effect.

When using the averaging method, the shift of the test values in the damaged case is sometimes positive and sometimes negative, depending on the temperature in the tested state. This can be explained as follows: The reference null space is computed from merged data with mean temperature at 10°C. For tested temperatures under 10°C, temperature and damage affect the stiffness in a similar way but in different directions. The effects of temperature and damage cancel out each other. When they act in the same direction, as it is the case for temperatures above the reference temperature, the shift between reference and damaged test values is very high. However, reducing the number of false alarms in the reference state will require a relatively high threshold for the damage test value, and lots of damages that come along with higher test temperatures will not be detected. Basically, this phenomenon of crossing test value curves is most likely a problem of a badly chosen reference for the computation of the residual.

While the results of the piecewise computation show the same problem of badly fitting reference at each temperature state, the interpolated reference null space overcomes this problem. The test values in the damaged case are clearly shifted positively from those of the reference state for every tested temperature. Even if the effects of damage and temperature do not have the same direction, they do not cancel out each other. This allows for the definition of an adequate global threshold with few false alarms.

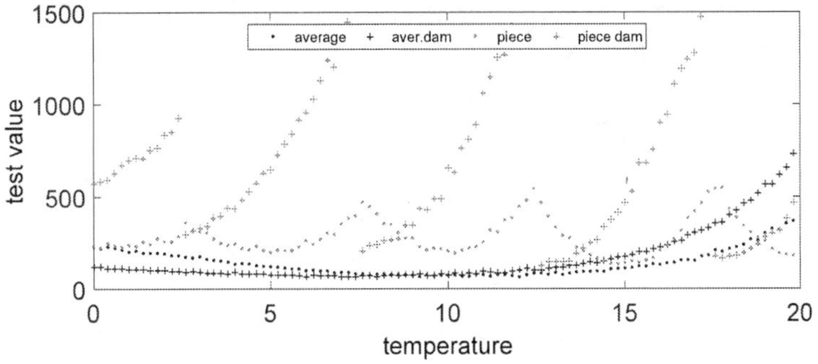

(a) Averaging and piecewise method

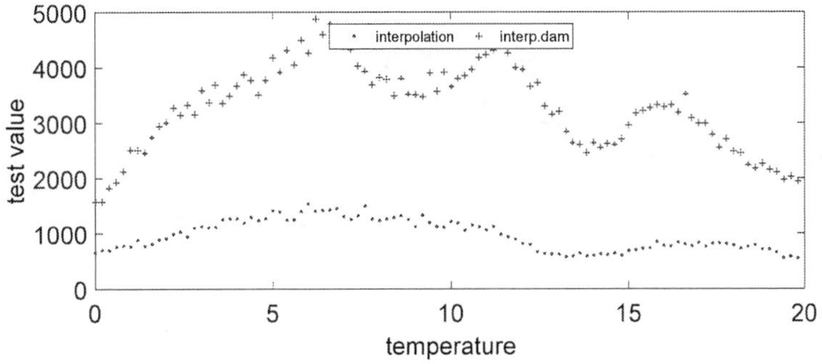

(b) Interpolation method

Figure 2: Test values in reference and damaged case for global damage

4. UNCERTAINTY CONSIDERATIONS FOR SUBSPACE-BASED DAMAGE DETECTION WITH TEMPERATURE EFFECTS

4.1. Covariance computation with uncertainties in the reference null space

In the subspace-based damage detection the accuracy of the residual covariance estimate is very important for the performance of the hypothesis testing. The conventional computation of the estimate of the residual covariance described in (5) only considers the uncertainties of the data itself. However, the null space matrix S taken as reference is usually estimated, computed from measurements and thus afflicted with uncertainties. In [10] it is described how those uncertainties can be taken into account. The residual covariance estimate can be formulated as

$$\hat{\Sigma}_{\zeta} = \mathcal{A} \begin{bmatrix} N/M\hat{\Sigma}_{\mathcal{H}} & 0 \\ 0 & \hat{\Sigma}_{\mathcal{H}} \end{bmatrix} \mathcal{A}^T, \text{ with } \mathcal{A} = \begin{bmatrix} \mathcal{J}_{\zeta,S}\,\mathcal{J}_{S,\mathcal{H}} & \mathcal{J}_{\zeta,\mathcal{H}} \end{bmatrix}, \qquad (12)$$

where the estimate of the Hankel matrix covariance $\Sigma_{\mathcal{H}}$ is used. N and M are the length of the data sets used in the computation of $\hat{\mathcal{H}}$ in the testing state and S, respectively. A detailed definition of the sensitivities $\mathcal{J}$ can be found in [10]. This extended covariance computation can increase the performance of the damage detection test significantly. Studies in [11] demonstrated, that if the estimation of the reference null space S is significantly afflicted with uncertainties, because no long data sets in the reference state are available, these uncertainties should not be neglected.

The test values in the undamaged and damaged state considering the uncertainty in the reference are presented in Figure 3 for the piecewise (a) and the interpolation (b) method. Both approaches show high dependency on the data length when the uncertainty of the reference is neglected (see Figure 1). By taking this uncertainty into account, stable results in the undamaged case can be obtained, even for short data lengths. However, the shift of the test values in the damaged case increases when more data is used. This will result in better test performances.

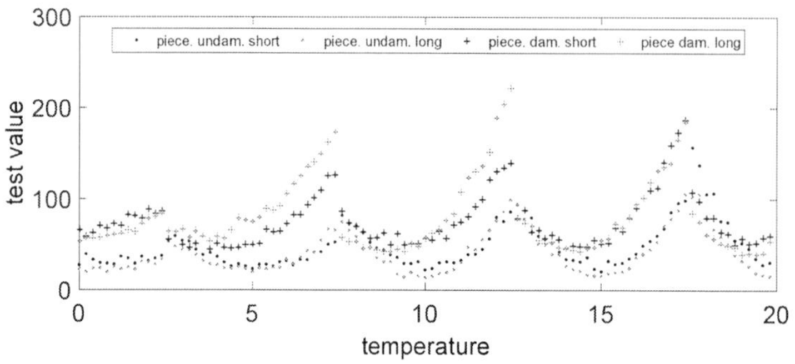

(a) Piecewise approach

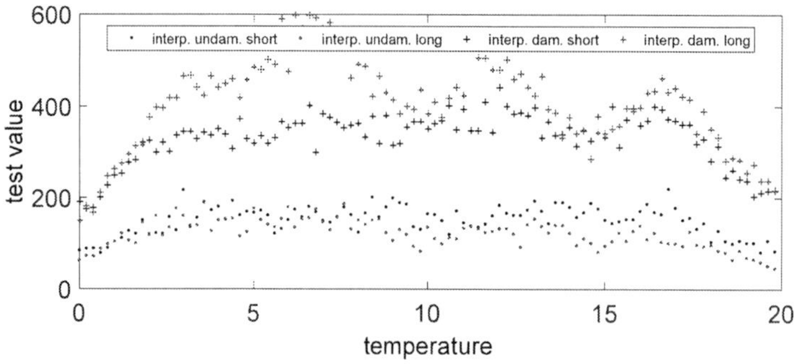

(b) Interpolation approach

Figure 3: Test values (undamaged and damaged) with consideration of uncertainty in the reference for short (40,000) and long (80,000) data sets

In Figure 4 the probability of detection (PoD) of the 8-mass-spring damper with a local damage at element 3 is plotted with respect to the damage size considering the impact of the uncertainty of S in the covariance computation. 5 temperatures are taken into account in the reference state for computation of the temperature rejection methods. The considered temperatures in the reference training state and in the testing state are between 0°C and 20°C. The threshold to detect damages is defined such that the false alarm rate is beneath 1% in the reference training state. Note that in the piecewise approach, a threshold is computed individually for each reference temperature state.

It can be seen that for the averaging and the piecewise approach the effect of different uncertainty computations to the PoD of the damage detection test is negligible. In these approaches the main reason for bad test performance is the bad fitting reference null space in the considered tested temperature state.

For the interpolation approach (Figure 2) it has already been shown that a better fitting reference null space is provided. The only issue for the test performance is the uncertainty of the estimated reference null space based on the interpolation. Figure 4 shows that the PoD is improved significantly when taking into account the uncertainty of the estimation of S in the residual covariance computation. This effect will fade when very long data sets in the reference state are available.

Instead of interpolating the covariance of the Hankel matrix as in (11), it can also be calculated again as

$\Sigma_{\mathcal{H}_T}$ on the data for each tested temperature state using the test data (dashed line) and then used in the residual covariance. This yields a similar performance for the PoD, meaning that the computation of a correct S is the crucial part of the method.

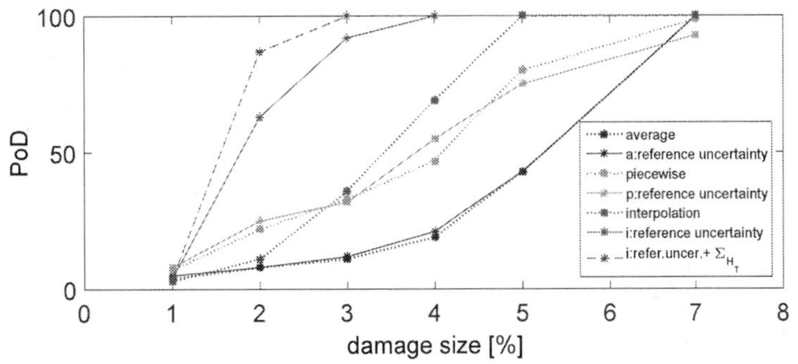

Figure 4: Probability of detection wrt. damage size and the uncertainty on the null space computation

4.2. Test performance with temperature rejection approaches

In this section the test performance of the three temperature rejection approaches is evaluated. The performance for different damage types and with respect to the amount of data in the reference state is examined. The covariance in the tests is computed taking into account the uncertainty on the null space as in equation (12). The temperature setup and threshold computation are defined as described in Section 4.1..

In Figure 5a the PoD of a local damage for different damage sizes is shown. Damage is simulated as loss of stiffness in [%] at element 3. Among all presented approaches, temperature rejection leads to better test performance. While the interpolation approach already detects damages of very small damage size, the averaging approach only works properly if the damage is big enough.

It has to be noted that the test performance of the interpolation method relies on the chosen weighting function. The circle and the diamond in Figure 5a denote the PoD of 3% damage, when a very narrow or a very wide bell shaped weighting function is used. It can be seen that the test performance decreases significantly in this case. If the weighting function is very wide and flat, the resulting reference null space will take into account every measured reference temperature point with nearly the same weight – similar to the averaging method. If the weighting function is very narrow, this may lead to a more or less piecewise method. Thus, finding an accurate weighting function is an important issue that should be addressed during the computation of the reference null space. The method here provides the possibility to introduce knowledge of the temperature dependent behavior of the structure into the reference state without requiring explicit knowledge of the temperature modeling. If the temperature effect is mostly linear, good results may be achieved with linear interpolation of the two nearest local models. If sudden temperature effects at specific temperatures are expected, this may also be taken into account by choosing discrete weighting functions.

Global damage (Figure 5b) may be considered as a loss of stiffness at all elements. The resulting effect on the dynamical behavior is very similar to that induced by temperature variations. The averaging method is not able to distinguish between the causes, and thus does not perform better as if no temperature changes would have taken into account. However, the piecewise and the interpolation approach both refer to a reference temperature point for the computation of the reference null space. They test if the system behavior has changed with respect to a particular reference null space and show good test performance. The interpolation method is more sensitive to damages than the piecewise method, due to the well fitting reference null space.

For SHM of civil structures, the availability of data from the reference state always is an issue – for

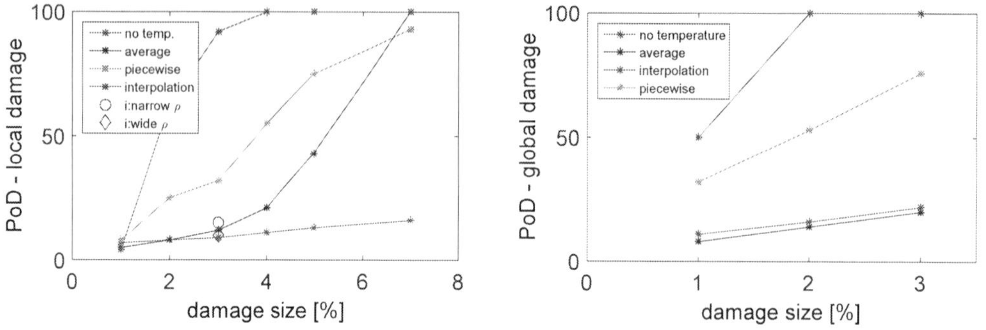

(a) Damage with local effects

(b) Damage with global effects

Figure 5: Probability of detection wrt. the damage size for different damage types.

example the temperature in the measured reference states cannot be influenced and data have to be shortened to ensure temperature stability within one given dataset. In Figure 6a the PoD for different numbers of temperatures in the reference state is presented. The PoD of the piecewise approach increases with more reference temperatures. If there are measurements for a dense grid of temperature points, one can choose a quite correct reference null space from measurements and thus good results can be obtained. However, it can be seen, that the performance of the interpolation method depends on an optimization of the weighting function that should be chosen in accordance with the reference temperatures. Here the same weighting function is used for each setup. Since this weighting function was chosen for 5 reference temperatures, it leads to bad test performance for a different number of reference temperatures.

Figure 6b shows that the sample length in the reference state affects the interpolation and the piecewise approach only slightly. Long datasets usually lead to better estimates of the reference null spaces. However, by dealing with the uncertainty of S in the covariance residual computation as in (12), those uncertainties are already handled.

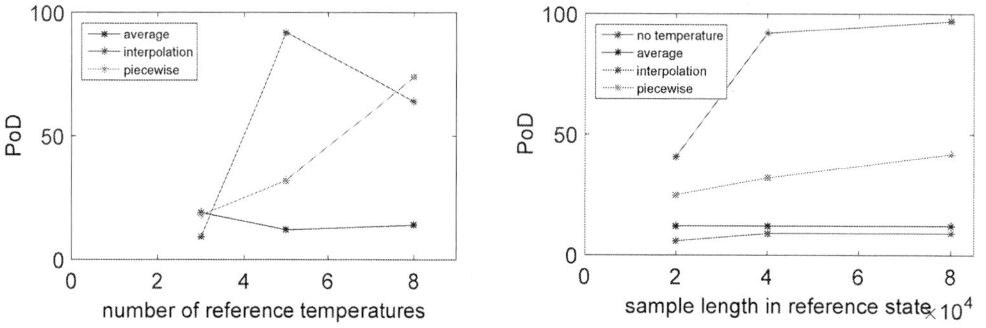

(a) Different number of reference temperatures

(b) Different data length in reference state

Figure 6: Probability of detection wrt. reference null space computation

5. CONCLUSIONS

In this paper a new temperature rejection method for subspace-based damage detection has been proposed and experimentally compared with two existing methods. Based on the interpolation of models, it could be shown that the new interpolation approach gives good results for both global and local damages. The local reference null space computed from an interpolated reference Hankel matrix at each tested temperature fits better to the test data, than the averaging or the piecewise approaches. Moreover, taking into account the uncertainty in the computation of the reference null space improves significantly the performance of damage detection.

The choice of the weighting function in the interpolation method provides the possibility to introduce specific monitoring rules into the data driven method, without requiring explicit knowledge of the temperature model.

ACKNOWLEDGEMENTS

The financial support from DAAD/German Federal Ministry of Education and Research and and the French Ministries of Foreign Affairs (MAEDI) and Education (MENESR) in the PROCOPE program is gratefully acknowledged.

REFERENCES

[1] Sohn, H. (2007) Effects of environmental and operational variability on structural health monitoring. *Philosophical transactions. Series A, Mathematical, physical, and engineering sciences*, 365(1851), 539-560.

[2] Peeters, B., De Roeck, G. (2000) One year monitoring of the Z24 bridge: environmental influences versus damage effects. *Proc. IMAC-XVIII* (pp.1570-1576). San Antonio, TX, USA.

[3] Worden, K. (2002) Inferential parameterisation using principal curves. *Proc. 3rd International Conference of Identification in Engineering Systems*. Swansea, Wales, UK.

[4] Manson, G. (2002) Identifying damage sensitive, environmental insensitive features for damage detection. *Proc. 3rd International Conference of Identification in Engineering Systems*. Swansea, Wales, UK.

[5] Basseville, M., Bourquin, F., Mevel, L., Nasser, H., Treyssede, F. (2010) Handling the temperature effect in vibration monitoring: two subspace-based analytical approaches. *Journal of Engineering Mechanics*, 136(3), 367-378.

[6] Fritzen, C. P., Mengelkamp, G., Güemes, A. (2003) Elimination of temperature effects on damage detection within a smart structure concept. *Proc. 4th International Workshop on Structural Health Monitoring* (pp. 15301538). Stanford, CA, USA.

[7] Zhang, Q. (2018) LPV system local model interpolation based on combined model reduction. *Proc. 18th IFAC Symposium on System Identification* (pp. 1104-1109). Stockholm, Sweden.

[8] Balmes, E., Basseville, M., Bourquin, F., Mevel, L., Nasser, H., Treyssede, F. (2008) Merging sensor data from multiple temperature scenarios for vibration monitoring of civil structures. *Structural Health Monitoring*, 7(2), 129-142.

[9] Döhler, M., Mevel, L., Hille, F. (2014) Subspace-based damage detection under changes in the ambient excitation statistics. *Mechanical Systems and Signal Processing*, 45(1), 207-224.

[10] Viefhues, E., Döhler, M., Hille, F., Mevel, L. (2018) Asymptotic analysis of subspace-based data-diven residual for fault detection with uncertain reference. *Proc. 10th IFAC Symposium on Fault Detection, Supervision and Safety for Technical Processes* (pp. 414-419). Warsaw, Poland.

[11] Viefhues, E., Döhler, M., Hille, F., Mevel, L. (2017) Stochastic subspace-based damage detection with uncertainty in the reference null space. *Proc. 11th International Workshop on Structural Health Monitoring* (pp. 1007-1014). Stanford, CA, USA.

IOMAC'19

8th International Operational Modal Analysis Conference
2019 May13-15 Copenhagen

VIBRATION-BASED CONTINUOUS MONITORING OF A BASE ISOLATED BUILDING

Laura Ierimonti [1] *Ilaria Venanzi* [2], *Nicola Cavalagli* [3], *Marco Mezzi* [4], *Filippo Ubertini* [5]

[1] Ph.D, University of Perugia, Department of Civil and Environmental Engineering, laura.ierimonti@unipg.it.
[2] Assistant Professor, University of Perugia, Department of Civil and Environmental Engineering, ilaria.venanzi@unipg.it.
[3] Assistant Professor, University of Perugia, Department of Civil and Environmental Engineering, nicola.cavalagli@unipg.it.
[4] Associate Professor, University of Perugia, Department of Civil and Environmental Engineering, marco.mezzi@unipg.it.
[5] Full Professor, University of Perugia, Department of Civil and Environmental Engineering, filippo.ubertini@unipg.it.

ABSTRACT

The paper presents the results of a research project aimed at assesing the aging of base isolators, installed on a reinforced concrete building located in a seismic area. The main scope is to optimally plan maintenance activities of the isolators in long term by using continuous monitoring data. The Bayesian model updating is sequentially performed by using the continuous recorded data in order to online calibrate isolators' parameters and track their evolution in time in a probabilistic perspective. The case study is a school building located in Bojano, near Campobasso (Italy) which is a three storey reinforced concrete building, with an irregular floor plan and equipped with a base isolation system. Data obtained from Ambient Vibration Tests (AVT) are used to preliminary calibrate a FEM of the structure and to assess the initial dynamic characteristics. Then, the continuous monitoring data, used in conjunction with the Bayesian model updating, allow the tracking of isolators' stiffness evolution.

Keywords: Base isolated building, Structural Health Monitoring, Bayesian Model Updating, Isolators' aging

1. INTRODUCTION

Structural health monitoring (SHM) of structures is a powerful tool to track any changes in time of the structural modal parameters, which are commonly considered related to the material's damage and deterioration [5, 11]. In the case of a base-isolated building the base-isolation system may deteriorate with time or get damaged due to an earthquake [6, 16]. Hence, it is advisable to install a continuous monitoring system capable of measuring in real time the variation of the dynamic response of the structure and, consequently, allowing the on-line damage detection. The main goal is to reach an accurate response prediction of the real structure by using an updated FEM. Considering all the uncertainties in-

volved in the process of numerical modeling and data measurement [17, 19], over the last decade the probabilistic-based model updating techniques have become widely used in civil engineering. In particular the Bayesian statistical framework is able to handle the inherent ill-conditioning and possible nonuniqueness in model updating applications [1, 20]. Several research works have been carried out on the application of Bayesian Model Updating to different structural problems[10, 12, 13]. Despite the potential of these tecniques, only a few recent contributions deal with Bayesian model updating and SHM [2, 3, 18].
The present paper presents the results of a research project aimed at evaluating the deterioration in time of base isolators, installed on reinforced concrete buildings exposed to seismic events, in order to optimally plan maintenance activities and possible replacement of the isolators. A sequential Bayesian approach is proposed and used for model updating. The posterior distribution of the uncertain parameters is computed by expliting the Markov-Chain Monte Carlo method with the Metropolis Algorithm [7, 9, 14]. The results show the advantage of using long-term monitoring data in conjunction with a sequential Bayesian model updating approach, for the correct estimation of the uncertain parameters' distribution.

2. THE METHODOLOGY

The proposed methodology consists in a continuous Bayesian model updating based on the well known Bayes' theorem. It is aimed at the evaluation of the posterior probability distribution $p(\Theta|\mathbf{d}, M, t)$ of the uncertain parameter Θ in a predefined time interval t, conditional on a set of measured data $\boldsymbol{d}$ of the system and on the assumed mathematical model M:

$$p(\Theta|\boldsymbol{d}, M, t) = c_0 p(\boldsymbol{d}|\Theta, M, t)p(\Theta|M, t) \tag{1}$$

In the previous equation c_0 is a normalizing constant to ensure that the posterior distribution integrates to one; Θ is the vector collecting the jth updating parameter with $J = 1, .., N$; the index N represents the total number of the uncertain parameters selected as the most sensitive to the dynamic modification of the structure; $p(\boldsymbol{d}|\Theta, M, t)$ is the likelihood function which represents the probability of obtaining the measured data $\boldsymbol{d}$ conditional on the uncertain parameters Θ and on the model M; $p(\Theta|M, \boldsymbol{t})$ is the prior distribution of the uncertain parameters Θ; $t = 1, .., T$ is the index of the time intervals; T is the current time interval. Since only one FEM is used in the following analyses, the reference mathematical model M is dropped hereafter.
Differently from the classical approach, the proposed methodology includes the time interval t which represents the time frame at which the Bayesian model updating is performed. Hence, it is possible to check continuously any modification in the dynamic behavior of the structure and consequently, in the isolators' characteristics due to aging or due to a strong seismic event. The likelihood function $p(\boldsymbol{d}|\Theta, t)$, is central to the process of estimating the unknown parameters and it is modeled as a Gaussian distribution with zero mean and an unknown variance and it quantifies the discrepancy between the experimental data and the FEM results [3, 4, 7, 8, 10, 15].

The proposed methodology, presented in Fig.1, consists in the following steps:

1. Preliminary execution of AVTs on the structure and subsequent identification of the modal properties by using modal identification techniques. For the present application a Stochastic Subspace Identification (SSI) methodology is adopted [5]. At this stage it is appropriate to establish the standard deviation $\sigma_{f_{i,t}}^{\text{exp}}$ and the mean values $\mu_{f_{i,t}}^{\text{exp}}$ of the ith experimental frequency, f_i, where index $i = 1, .., m$ refers to the ith vibration mode;
2. Preliminary calibration of the FEM by varying the updating parameters θ_j as a function of $\mu_{f_{i,t}}^{\text{exp}}$ in order to optimally fit the experimental data (AVT) and the FEM results.

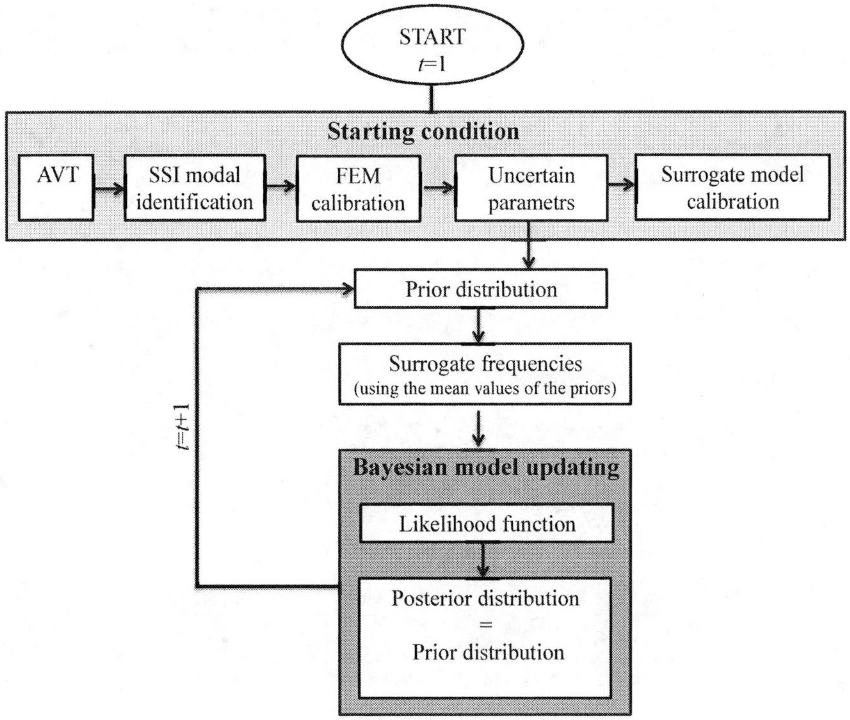

Figure 1: The continuous Bayesian model updating methodology.

3. Calibration of the surrogate model in order to considerably reduce the computational effort in the continuous Bayesian approach. Given the assumption of a linear behavior of the structure with respect to small changes of the uncertain parameters, this step will be dropped for $t > 1$.

4. Definition of the prior distribution:

$$p(\boldsymbol{\Theta} | \boldsymbol{\mu}_{\Theta}, \boldsymbol{\Sigma}_{\Theta}, t) \tag{2}$$

where $\boldsymbol{\mu}_{\Theta}$ contains the jth mean value of θ_j ; $\boldsymbol{\Sigma}_{\Theta}$ is the diagonal co-variance matrix. Values of μ_{θ_j} and $\sigma^2_{\theta_j}$ are preliminary defined (step 1) for $t = 1$ and then adjusted according to step 8.

5. Evaluation of the surrogate natural frequencies $f^{\text{surr}}_{i,t}$ by using the selected mean value μ_{θ_j} of the uncertain parameter θ_j.

6. Evaluation of the likelihood as following:

$$p(\boldsymbol{d} | \Theta, t) = \frac{1}{\left[2\pi \prod_{i=1}^{m} (\sigma^{\text{exp}}_{f_{i,t}})^2\right]^{(mD(t))/2}} exp\left(-\frac{1}{2(\sigma^{\text{exp}}_{f_{i,t}})^2} \sum_{t=1}^{T} \sum_{i=1}^{m} (\mu^{\text{exp}}_{f_{i,t}} - f^{\text{surr}}_{i,t})^2\right) \tag{3}$$

where $D(t)$ is the total number of data associated to the ith frequency at time step t.

7. Evaluation of the posterior distribution of the parameters $\boldsymbol{\Theta}$ according to Eq. (1). For the purposes of the present work the Markov chain Monte Carlo samples (MCMC) is used.

8. Definition of the new prior for the step $t + 1$ as the posterior distribution evaluated at the previous step.

Figure 2: The School building in Bojano.

9. Repeat steps 1-8 until the current data set T is reached.

The main advantage of the proposed methodology is the possibility to evaluate in a timely and continuous manner any variation in the structure, since the dynamic characteristics are commonly considered as a sign of possible damages. Indeed, in the standard Bayesian model updating, as the number of data set increases, the estimation accuracy decreases and the posterior distribution tends to converge. On the contrary the use of a continuous Bayesian model updating allows to capture variations over time and to optimally schedule maintenance operations.

3. THE CASE STUDY

3.1. The Bojano school building

The case study is a school building located in Bojano, near Campobasso, in Italy (Fig. 2). The structure is a three-storeys reinforced concrete building which is non-homogeneous for volumes and materials and structurally irregular, both in plan and in elevation.
The school building is equipped with a base isolation system for the mitigation of the seismic-induced demand force and deformations. The isolation system is composed by 54 isolators installed between the foundation beams and the ground floor which can be divided into two main typologies: Lead Rubber Bearings (LRB) and sliding devices (SD). The main characteristics of the devices are summarized in Table 1 where the acronym SD-HC stands for sliding device with high capacity in terms of vertical load carried, and SD-LC stands for low-capacity device.

3.2. Ambient Vibration Tests and modal identification

In order to identify the structural dynamic proprieties of the school building in Bojano, an Ambient Vibration Test (AVT) was carried out on September 3rd, 2018 with a duration of about 12 hours in order to extract several significant data sets. A total of 9 high sensitivity (10 V/g) uni-axial accelerometers,

Table 1: Isolator characteristics.

Characteristic	LRB type A	LRB type B	SD-HC	SD-LC
Diameter [mm]	700	600	-	-
Lead core diameter [mm]	110	80	-	-
Tangential elastic modulus [Mpa]	0.6	0.4	-	-
Horizontal stiffness [kN/m]	1227	611	-	-
Damping	0.2	0.2	-	-
Vertical load [kN]	-	-	2200	600
Number	25	16	8	5

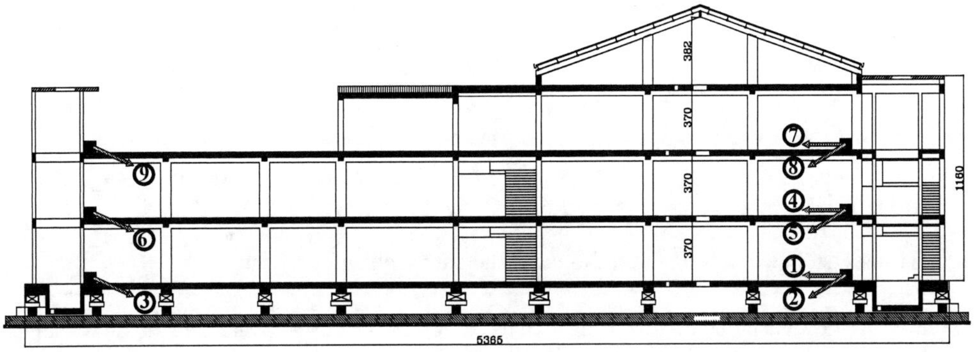

Figure 3: AVT set-up configuration with the position of the 9 accelerometers (dimensions in mm).

model PCB393B12, were installed on each floor (three per floor) in order to measure micro tremors induced by ambient vibrations like traffic, wind and daily activities. Data were acquired with the DAQ (data acquisition) system, a real-time operating system with a chassis, model cDAQ9184, connected to the PC via Ethernet to the 9 modules that provide direct connectivity to the sensors. The data were recorded for a duration of 30 minutes with a sampling frequency of 1652 Hz, which is the default rate, and then down-sampled to 100 Hz. The structural configuration and the level of excitation allowed to consistently identify in the observation period two global modes within the range from 0 to 12 Hz by the SSI identification technique, one torsional and one translational. The natural frequencies of the identified modes are reported in Table 2.

Table 2: Natural frequencies of the identified vibration modes

Mode no.	Frequency [Hz]
1	7.12
2	10.86

3.3. The long-term monitoring system and modal identification

The permanent monitoring system (Fig. 4) was installed by the Department of Civil and Environmental Engineering of University of Perugia in March 2017 within the framework of the ReLuis project. it is characterized by:

- a data acquisition system;
- n. 3 unidirectional accelerometers (1,2,3), model PCB393B12 installed on the beams at the third level;

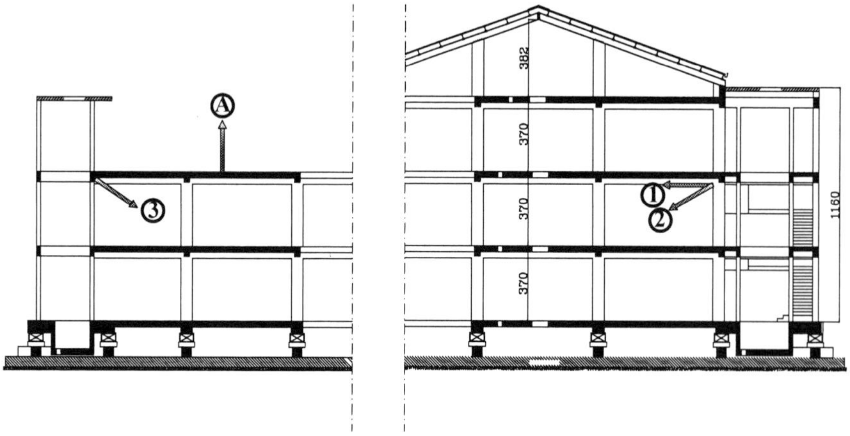

Figure 4: Continuous monitoring configuration.

- n. 1 anemometer (A) for the recording of the mean-wind velocity and direction, model ANS-VV1-B, installed on the walkable terrace at the third level;
- a wiring system connecting the sensors and the data acquisition system;

The monitoring system started the real-time activity on March 17th 2017. Data are stored with an hourly basis with a sampling frequency of 100 Hz. For the purposes of the current paper only the monitoring data recorded after the AVT (September 2018) are analyzed for the numerical application, since the AVT information are used for the model updting.

3.4. The calibration of the FEM and of the surrogate model

The FEM consists in a frame of unidimensional beam element with different cross sections. The slabs are modeled with shell elements with rigid in-plane behavior. Nonstructural partition walls are included in the model and schematized as shell elements with the aim of reproducing the real stiffness of the structure for low vibration levels (daily activities).
The isolation system is modeled by 54 nodes bounded at the base with *N-links* elements. The calibrated values of the isolators' stiffness are summarized in Table 3. It is worth noticing that the values of the sliders' stiffness can be related to the sliding friction until the front detachment.

Table 3: Isolators' stiffness after FEM calibration.

Isolator	Stiffness [10^7 kN/m]
LRB type A	7.118
LRB type B	0.8326
SD-HC	400.7
SD-LC	133.1

In order to reduce the computational effort of the continuous Bayesian model updating, a quadratic polynomial surrogate model, is reconstructed:

$$\mathbf{f} = \mathbf{A}\mathbf{\Theta}^2 + \mathbf{B}\mathbf{\Theta} + \mathbf{C} \tag{4}$$

where $\mathbf{A}$ is coefficients matrix of the second order terms, $\mathbf{B}$ is coefficients matrix of the first order terms, $\mathbf{C}$ is the vector collecting the known terms. The quadratic model is chosen for the present application since it turned out to be sufficiently accurate with a percentage error less than 1.8% for the selected range of the uncertain parameters $\mathbf{\Theta}$ (equal to 10%). It is worth noticing that the surrogate model is calibrated by using the only frequencies (the mode shapes are neglected) since the number of sensors available is not sufficient to reconstruct them with a good accuracy.

3.5. The continuous Bayesian model updating

With the main objective of exploiting the potentiality of the continuous Bayesian model updating, the isolators's stiffness are chosen as the main uncertain parameters. Consequently the vector of the uncertain parameters can be defined as $\Theta = (k_1, k_2, k_3, k_4)$. The Θ parameters are assumed as statistically independent and, consequently, the prior distribution can be stated as:

$$p(\Theta|\mu_\Theta, \Sigma_\Theta, t) = p(k_1|\mu_{k_1}, \sigma_{k_1}, t)p(k_2|\mu_{k_2}, \sigma_{k_2}, t)p(k_3|\mu_{k_3}, \sigma_{k_3}, t)p(k_4|\mu_{k_4}, \sigma_{k_4}, t) \quad (5)$$

The frame time t is defined as 1 month of measurements and, for the purposes of the current paper, two months of data are analyzed (September/October, 2018). The prior knowledge about k_1, k_2, k_3, k_4 is expressed as a Gaussian distribution. At time $t = 1$, in absence of any information, the mean values are chosen as the nominal values (Table 3) and, since the prior acts as regulator in the Bayesian process, high level of uncertainty is preliminary assigned. Hence, coefficients of variation are assumed as 30 percent. At time $t > 1$ this parameters are continuously updated according to Section 2.
The available monitoring data between March 2017 and September 2018 are used to define the prior knowledge on the frequencies standard deviation $\sigma^{\text{exp}}_{f_{i,t}}$, which are set to 0.5 percent.

4. NUMERICAL RESULTS

In this Section some preliminary numerical results are presented. Fig. 5 shows the Bayesian model updating at $t = 1$, that is in correspondence of the first time step (September 2018). From the Figure it can be observed a small variation in terms of mean values and a substantial modification of σ_{k_1} and σ_{k_3}. Fig. 6 shows the Bayesian model updating at the second time step $t + 1$, corresponding to October 2018. In this step the parameters of the prior distribution are sequentially assumed as those calculated from the posterior distribution in the previous step. Results show a more pronounced variation of the mean values with respect to the previous time step as conformed in Table 4 and also a variation in terms of standard deviation, due to the increasing number of the available data. This trend is consistent with

Table 4: Mean values of the Θ posterior distributions evaluated on September and October 2018.

Reference period	k_1 [10^7]	k_2 [10^7]	k_3 [10^7]	k_4 [10^7]
Prior ($t = 1$)	7.118	0.8326	401	133
September	6.980	0.810	398	131
October	7.246	0.884	421	129

Table 5 which reports the frequencies mean values identified during the analyzed time steps. Hence, as the frequencies tend to increase (from September to October), the updated k parameters increase consequently. This effect can be probably associated to environmental effects, i.e., temperature and humidity, and is consistent with the expected increase in rubber stiffness with decreasing temperature.

Table 5: Mean values of the main frequencies identified by the monitoring system on September and October 2018.

Reference period	f_1 [Hz]	f_2 [Hz]
September	7.09	10.82
October	7.15	10.94

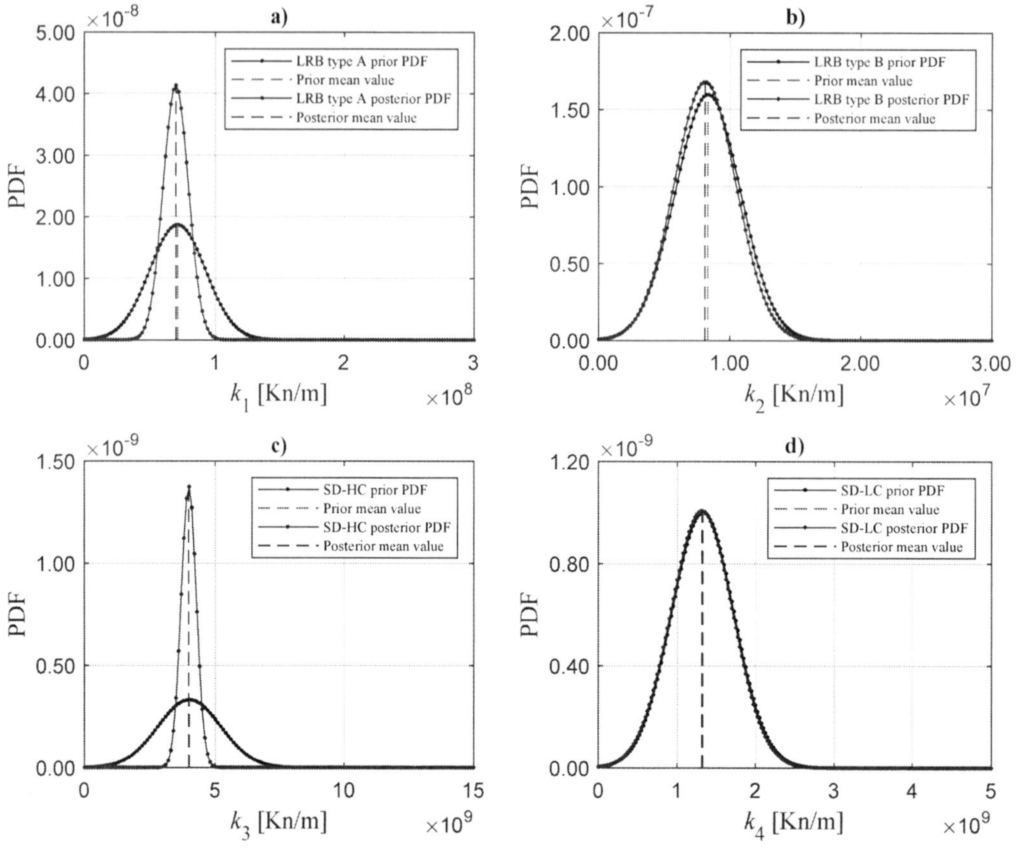

Figure 5: Bayesian model updating with data at $t = 1$ (September 2018).

5. CONCLUSIONS

The present paper shows preliminary results on the potential of the Bayesian model updating technique for evaluating the deterioration in time of a base isolation system, installed on a reinforced concrete building located in a seismic area. The measured data are divided in time steps on which the complete FEM Bayesian updating is performed. The use of long term monitoring data allow to optimally check variation in the structural dynamic proprieties and eventually plan maintenance activities and possible replacement of the isolators. As confirmed by the numerical results, the proposed approach is able to check any variation of the structural global condition which can be associated to environmental effects (small and temporary variations due to temperature or humidity). Consistently, it is possible to check irreversible damages which can occur during the lifetime of the structure.

REFERENCES

[1] J.L. Beck and L.S. Katafygiotis. Updating models and their uncertainties. i: Bayesian statistical framework. *Journal of Engineering Mechanics*, 124(4):455–461, 1998.

[2] I. Behmanesh and B. Moaveni. Accounting for environmental variability, modeling errors, and parameter estimation uncertainties in structural identification. *Journal of Sound and Vibration*, 374:92–110, 2016.

[3] I. Behmanesh, B. Moaveni, G. Lombaert, and C. Papadimitriou. Hierarchical bayesian model updating for structural identification. *Mechanical Systems and Signal Processing*, 64–65:360–376,

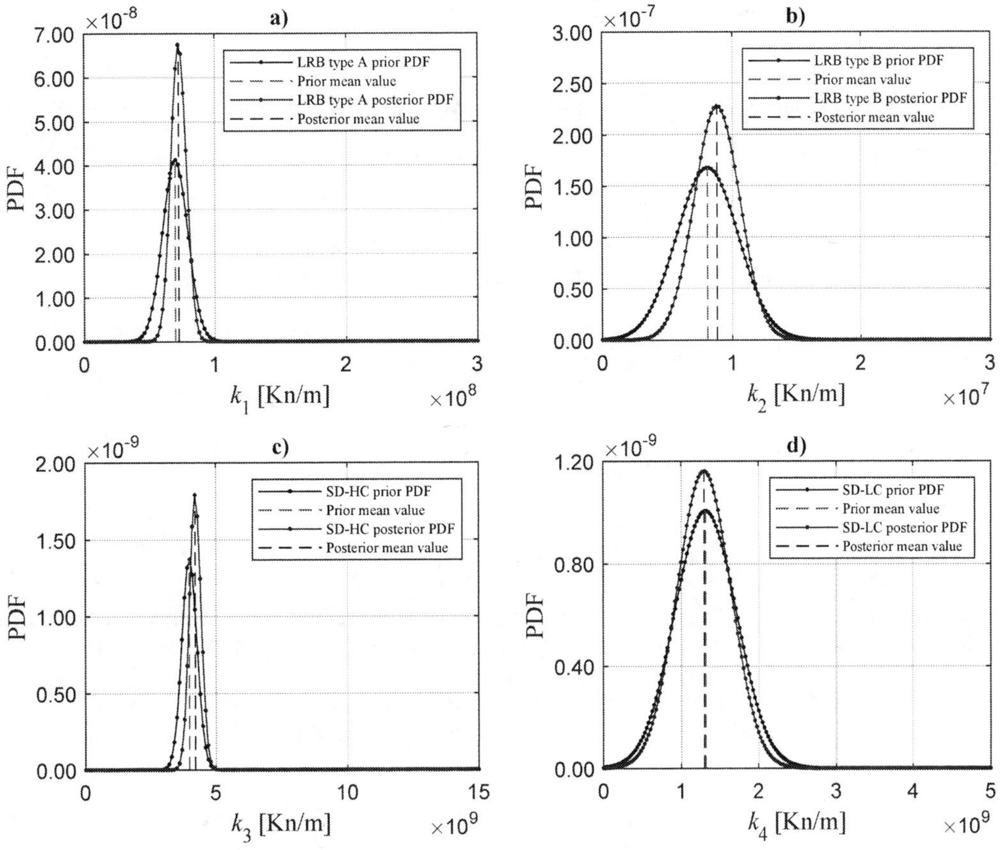

Figure 6: Bayesian model updating with data at $t + 1$ (October 2018).

2015.

[4] I. Behmanesh, B. Moaveni, and C. Papadimitriou. Probabilistic damage identification of a designed 9-story building using modal data in the presence of modeling errors. *Engineering Structures*, 131:542–552, 2017.

[5] N. Cavalagli, G. Comanducci, and F. Ubertini. Earthquake-induced damage detection in a monumental masonry bell-tower using long-term dynamic monitoring data. *Journal of Earthquake Engineering*, 22(supl):96–119, 2018.

[6] M.H. Gheryani, H.A. Razak, and M. Jamel. Dynamic response changes of seismic isolated building due to material degradation of hdrb. *Arabian Journal for Science and Engineering*, 40(12):3429–3442, 2015.

[7] W.R. Gilks, S. Richardson, and D.J. Spiegelhalter. *Markov Chain Monte Carlo in Practice*. Chapman & Hall, Boca Raton, FL, 1998.

[8] B. Goller and G.I. Schuller. Investigation of model uncertainties in bayesian structural model updating. *Journal of Sound and Vibration*, 330(25):6122–6136, 2011.

[9] W. K. Hastings. Monte carlo sampling methods using markov chains and their applications. *Biometrika*, 57(1):97–109, 1970.

[10] J. Jang and A. Smyth. Bayesian model updating of a full-scale finite element model with sensitivity-based clustering. *Structural Control and Health Monitoring*, 24(11), 2017.

[11] Yavuz Kaya and Erdal Safak. Real-time analysis and interpretation of continuous data from structural health monitoring (shm) systems. *Bulletin of Earthquake Engineering*, 13(3):917–934, 2015.

[12] H.-F. Lam, J. Hu, and J.-H. Yang. Bayesian operational modal analysis and markov chain monte carlo-based model updating of a factory building. *Engineering Structures*, 132:314–336, 2017.

[13] H.-F. Lam, F.-L. Zhang, Y.-C. Ni, and J. Hu. Operational modal identification of a boat-shaped building by a bayesian approach. *Engineering Structures*, 138:381–393, 2017.

[14] N. Metropolis, A.W. Rosenbluth, M.N. Rosenbluth, A.H. Teller, and E. Teller. Equation of state calculations by fast computing machines. *The Journal of Chemical Physics*, 21(6):1087–1092, 1953.

[15] R. Rocchetta, M. Broggi, Q. Huchet, and E. Patelli. On-line bayesian model updating for structural health monitoring. *Mechanical Systems and Signal Processing*, 103:174–195, 2018.

[16] G. Russo and M. Pauletta. Sliding instability of fiber-reinforced elastomeric isolators in unbonded applications. *Engineering Structures*, 48:70–80, 2013.

[17] E. Simoen, G. De Roeck, and G. Lombaert. Dealing with uncertainty in model updating for damage assessment: A review. *Mechanical Systems and Signal Processing*, 56-57:123–149, 2015.

[18] H. Sun, A. Mordret, G.A. Prieto, M.N. Toksz, and O. Bykztrk. Bayesian characterization of buildings using seismic interferometry on ambient vibrations. *Mechanical Systems and Signal Processing*, 85:468–486, 2017.

[19] I. Venanzi, A.L. Materazzi, and L. Ierimonti. Robust and reliable optimization of wind-excited cable-stayed masts. *Journal of Wind Engineering and Industrial Aerodynamics*, 147:368–379, 2015.

[20] K.V. Yuen. *Bayesian Methods for Structural Dynamics and Civil Engineering*. John Wiley & Sons (Asia) Pte Ltd, 2 Clementi Loop, # 02-01, Singapore 129809, 2010.

FEM UPDATING USING OPERATING RESPONSES

IOMAC'19

8th International Operational Modal Analysis Conference
2019 May 13-15 Copenhagen

ACCURATE MODEL UPDATING OF A HISTORIC TOWER BY MEANS OF DYNAMICAL EXPERIMENTAL DATA

M. Diaferio[1], *D. Foti*[2], *N.I. Giannoccaro*[3] *and S. Ivorra*[4]

[1] Polytechnic of Bari, Department of Civil Engineering and Architecture, Bari, mariella.diaferio@poliba.it.
[2] Polytechnic of Bari, Department of Civil Engineering and Architecture, Bari, dora.foti@poliba.it.
[3] University of Salento, Department of Innovation Engineering, Lecce, ivan.giannoccaro@unisalento.it.
[4] University of Alicante, Department of Civil Engineering, Alicante, sivorra@ua.es.

ABSTRACT

The paper deals with the analysis of a historical masonry tower characterized by a squat profile and a square cross section. Due to the absence of asymmetry, a classical FE model of the tower gives as a result of the Modal Analysis the first two bending modes very close to each other. Only a detailed experimental study based on the application of Operational Modal Analysis (OMA) to environmental vibrations and the use of filtering processes allowed to update the model taking into account the effects of the surrounding conditions. The details of the aforementioned analyses and of the subsequent model updating are presented.

Keywords: Operational modal Analysis (OMA), digital filtering, post processing, modal parameters identification, Finite Element (FE) model updating

1. INTRODUCTION

This work presents detailed considerations about an extensive experimental analysis aimed at identifying the modal parameters of a historical tower through a comparison with the results of a Finite Element (FE) model. The tower is equipped with a clock and is characterized by a square layout (Figure 1). It is located on the eastern façade of the Swabian Castle of Trani (South-East of Italy), on its main entrance. The clock tower had been experimentally tested [1-4]; the data were recorded by means of a series of accelerometers installed at specific points of the structure [5, 6].

Slender structures such as towers are particularly suitable for this type of investigation [7-10] because even if they are subjected to actions of low intensity, as the ones due to ambient loads, they show vibrations which can be clearly recorded by means of the usually adopted accelerometers and may be analysed by techniques of Operational Modal Analysis [11-13].

On the other side, in case of squat buildings like the clock tower here considered, the amplitude of the vibrations induced by the environmental actions may be too low to guarantee a good ratio between the signal and the noise, and consequently it may be necessary to use a forced excitation (examples of squat structures or forced excitation are reported in [14-18]) in order to obtain enough dynamic information for the subsequent analyses.

In this paper the analysis of the environmental data obtained during the tests on the clock tower focuses on the evaluation of the dynamic behaviour of the structure through a comparison with a FE model.

The performed analysis may be considered very particular and innovative in this field of research for the use of a specific post processing elaboration, which may underline the relevant characteristics of the dynamic structural behaviour.

2. BRIEF DESCRIPTION OF THE TOWER GEMETRY, EXPERIMENTAL TESTS AND PRELIMINARY ANALYSIS

A brief description of the analysed tower and the modalities of the test is reported in this section with the aim of a complete comprehension of the following study and analysis; a detailed description is reported in refs [1, 2].

The clock tower is part of the Swabian Castle of Trani (South-East of Italy) and it is located on the eastern façade, on the main entrance of the castle. The tower has an overall height equal to 7.20 m from its main door; it has a square cross section, with the inner side of about 2.05 m, constant along the total height, while the outer side is variable along the height because of the presence of a Trani stone covering. In fact, the outer side is 4.25 m at the base and 3.55 m at the intermediate height of 4.00 m and, from this level up to the top, it keeps constant. At the intermediate height of 4.60 m there is also a toroidal stringcourse. The tower façades are characterized by openings arranged on two different levels: (i) At the lower level, there is the doorway on the West side, while on the other sides, there are archivolted windows with a width of about 1.40 m and an average height of 60 cm (Figure 1b). (ii) At the upper level, there are archivolted windows smaller than the previous ones, with a width of 85 cm and a height of 55 cm, arranged on all sides with the exception of the East one, which is blind to host the large central clock. (Figure 1a). On the eastern facade, differently from the other ones, the total height of the wall is about 2.25 m. The top presents a gabled portal with an arched opening in the middle where a bell is located.

(a) *(b)* *(c)*

Figure 1. Clock tower of Trani's Swabian Castle: a) East, b) West; c) South

To evaluate the tower main frequencies and its mode shapes, the tower has been instrumented with 23 high sensitivity seismic accelerometers ICP PCB 393B31 with a sensitivity of 10 V/g. All the accelerometers were connected by flexible wired cables to a data acquisition system, the latter connected to a laptop with a specific acquisition software. The accelerometers were placed on four different levels on the four lateral sides of the tower: eight accelerometers at the four corners of the floor over the clock, six accelerometers at three corners at the intermediate level, six at the three corners at the lower level, one accelerometer at the base of the castle entrance as a reference sensor and, finally, two accelerometers on the upper arch (Figure 2a). Appropriate rectangular blocks, where the accelerometers were inserted with screws, were used for ensuring the orthogonality of each couple of accelerometers applied in the same point. Preliminary considerations [2] permitted to exclude 3 of the

23 accelerometers used because not properly running; for the following processing the 20 accelerometers schematically represented in Fig. 2 c) have been considered. Four consecutive acquisitions of environmental vibrations (called Test 1, Test 2, Test 3 and Test 4) were carried out by recordings of 15 minutes each with a sampling frequency of 1024 Hz.

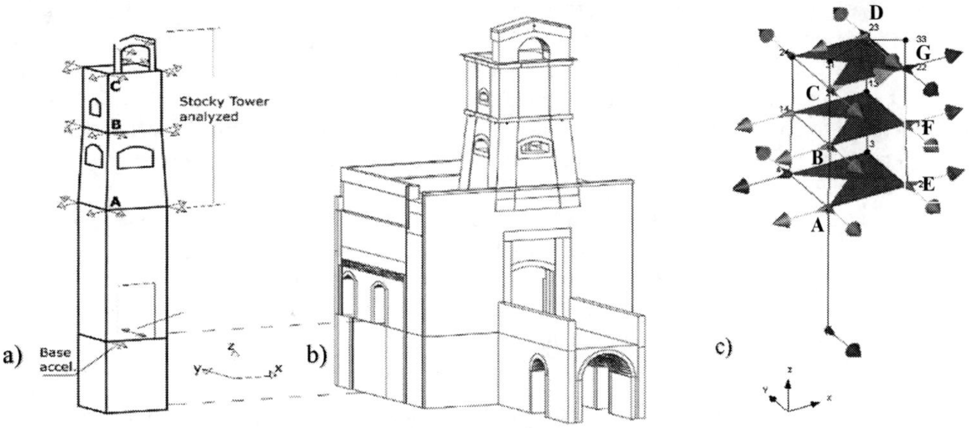

Figure 2. Experimental setup: a) Positions and directions of the 23 accelerometers; b) 3D view of the tower; c) Schematic representation of the positions and directions of the 20 considered accelerometers.

2.1. Preliminary modal parameter extraction

The specific software ARTeMIS [19] was used for the preliminary extraction of the modal parameters. Two different OMA methods were used for each analysis: the Enhanced Frequency Domain Decomposition (EFDD), which operates in the frequency domain, and the Stochastic Subspace Identification (SSI) using Unweighted Principal Components (UPC), which operates in the time domain. The identified frequencies for the four environmental tests is summarized in Table 1 [2] which have been obtained by considering the highest sampling frequency (equal to 1024 Hz) in order to improve the accuracy of the identification methods avoiding the undersampling. It is evident the good repeatability of the identified frequencies for all the environmental tests; moreover, similar results were obtained also adopting the EFDD technique.

Table 1. Identified frequencies for the four environmental tests using the SSI technique.

	Frequency			
Mode	Test1 [Hz]	Test2 [Hz]	Test3 [Hz]	Test4 [Hz]
1	7.52	7.5	7.48	7.53
2	10.32	10.36	10.34	10.31
3	13.28	13.33	13.35	13.51
4	21.85	21.83	21.83	22.08

So, nevertheless the squat profile of the analysed tower, the power of the recent OMA techniques, a very high number of samples (1024 samples per seconds) and the sensitivity of the available sensors seem to allow the identification of the frequencies. About the corresponding mode shapes, the information available for reconstructing their behaviour are only related to the points where the accelerometers are located, thus only a fitting procedure, defined by introducing some hypothesis, allows their estimation also for the not monitored points. As shown in [2] the mode shapes corresponding to the identified frequencies seem to be related to bending modes (exactly oriented along y and x axes, respectively) for the first two frequencies; the third frequency seems to be related to a torsional mode, the fourth frequency to a bending-torsional mode. Anyway, it must be considered that the mode shapes are not completely defined, depending on the aforementioned interpolation procedure, therefore, a strict comparison with a FE model is necessary to confirm the results. In this perspective, the following accurate post-processing, shown in sect. 3, becomes decisive to update the FE model of the tower.

2.2. Comparison with a preliminary FE model

The main aim of the study is the evaluation of the vulnerability of the examined structure. Thus, a reliable numerical model is needed; here such model has been defined by means of Straus software [20], which operates in the framework of the finite element method. The model has been defined on the basis of a visual inspection of the structure, a geometrical survey and an analysis of the available documents. Moreover, an experimental campaign has been performed on the structure by means of ground penetrating radar tests with the aim of evaluating the typesetting of the masonry walls. Based on the aforementioned analysis a finite element model has been defined, all the walls and the vault have been modelled by means of a total of 9114 shell elements. In detail, 8-nodes quadrilateral elements have been used for all the plate elements, except for the ones located at the connection between the vault and the walls where 6-node triangular elements have been adopted in order to better describe this connection. All the openings have been inserted into the model, and in order to consider the presence of a rigid floor at the top of the tower an internal restraint has been introduced at this level, which imposes that the in-plane deformations will be null during the motion.

Considering that the castle is more rigid than the clock tower, the tower has been assumed pinned at the base. In order to better describe the real geometry of the tower, which for the first 4,00 m has a variable wall thickness, this part of the tower has been divided into five parts of constant thickness, which have been aligned along the inner side. Thus, fourteen plate sections have been defined whose thicknesses have been chosen in accordance with the geometrical survey and whose elastic modulus and density have been evaluated by weighted average. In detail, the tower walls are composed by external blocks made in Trani's stone and tufa internal blocks whose thicknesses have been evaluated by means of the ground penetrating radar tests. Thus, the elastic modulus and the density of the sections have been evaluated by weighted average where the weighting factors are the thickness of the different materials, which composed the walls. In such weighted average it has been assumed for the Trani stone an elastic modulus of 2400 MPa and a density of 2200 Kg/m^3, while for the tufa blocks an elastic modulus of 1000 MPa and a density of 1600Kg/m^3.

In Fig. 3 a view of the model is reported where the different colours are representative of the different plate sections.

In Table 2 the first four natural frequencies of the model and the modal participation factors are shown.

Table 2. First four frequencies and modal participation factors for the preliminary finite element model.

Mode	Frequency [Hz]	Modal participation factors [%]					
		X	Y	Z	RX	RY	RZ
1	6.548	66.889	0	0	0	89.266	21.773
2	6.6027	0	56.601	0	85.089	0	15.330
3	12.238	0	11.106	0	4.208	0	3.007
4	1.4169	3.199	0	0	0	0	15.000

It can be seen that the first couple of bending modes are very close each other, and even if uncertainties still exist on the values adopted for the mechanical characteristics of the materials, these uncertainties may be responsible of a variation of the frequency values but do not justify a significant variation of the ratio between the first couple of frequencies.

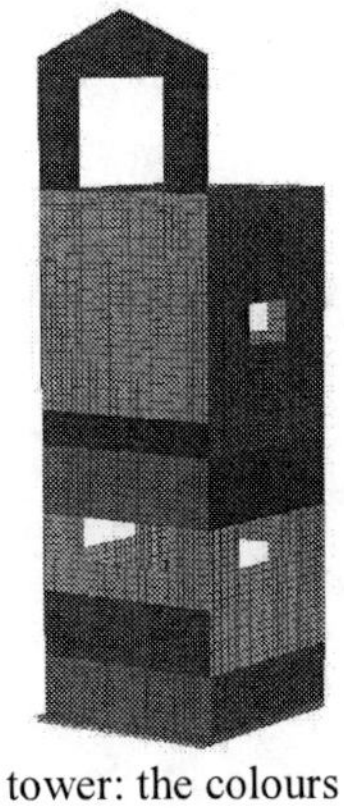

Figure 3. Finite element model of the clock tower: the colours are representative of different plate sections.

3. DETAILED ANALYSIS FOCUSED ON THE ENVIRONMENTAL DATA AND ON MODEL MODIFICATION

Due to the relevant difference between the FE model behaviour and the experimental identification especially regarding the first two flexional modes the authors got the necessity of improving the analysis of the environmental data in order to understand if the first couple of very close frequencies detected by the model are simply numerically too close for being estimated with the traditional OMA methods or if the model symmetry has been really corrupted by other effects. At this aim, in the following sections, a detailed analysis on the experimental data will be presented with the aim of refining the results of the classical OMA.

3.1. Direct analysis of the single acquisition channels

The first step has been to carry out a direct analysis of the single channel data for searching the frequency components with respect to the measured directions. Naming $a_j(t_i)$ the time series of the jth acquisition channel (j varying from 1 to 20 considered accelerometers) the single sided amplitude spectrum $P_j(f_k)$ has been calculated by (2), considering the Fast Fourier Trasform (FFT) algorithm [21] applied to the signal $ae_j(t_i)$ depurated by its static effect through (1), m_j is the average value of $a_j(t_i)$ over all the t_i of the acquisition and f_k defines the succession of frequencies, multiples of the invers of the sampling frequency (1024 Hz).

$$ae_j(t_i) = a_j(t_i) - m_j \quad (1)$$

$$P_j(f_k) = 2 * |fft(ae_j(t_i)| \quad (2)$$

As a first step, the single sided amplitude spectrum for the accelerometers placed in different positions but with the same acquisition direction, have been compared in a frequency range, which includes the first two identified frequencies. In Figures 4 and 5 the single-sided amplitude spectrum in the range [5-11] Hz for the accelerometers placed in the points A, B, C, E, F, G indicated in Fig. 2c) measuring acceleration in y direction (Fig.4) and in x direction (Fig.5) are shown.

It is evident from Figure 4 (and also from the data of other accelerometers and other tests) that something relevant happens around 7.5 Hz for the accelerometers directed along y axis and something relevant is happening around 10.3 Hz for the accelerometers oriented along x axis. Anyway, it is not possible to establish if these phenomena are related or not to the first flexional modes of the structure and, moreover, a small effect could be also recognized around 7.5 Hz for the accelerometers oriented along x axis.

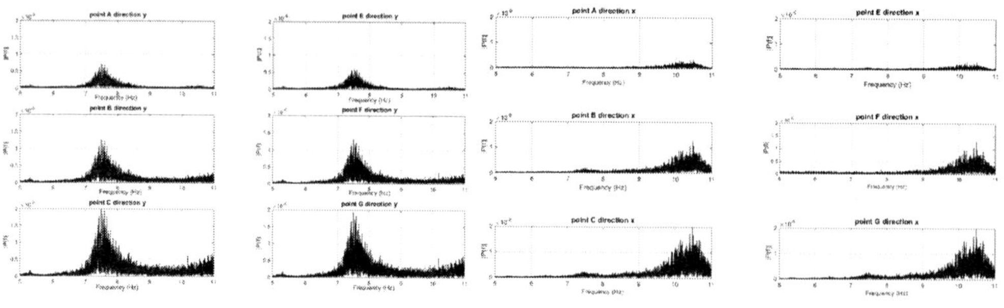

Figure 4. Amplitude spectrum along y direction (left) and x direction (right) points A, B, C, E, F, G, Test1.

3.2. Application of the OMA only on predefined direction data

A further methodology improved to complete the analysis of the dynamic behaviour of this highly symmetrical structure was the application of the previously indicated OMA techniques to two different data sets obtained by collecting the accelerometers data with respect to the acquisition directions, x and y, that are the directions of the first two modal shapes. In Fig. 5a the positions and directions of the accelerometers oriented along the x axis are shown, while in Fig. 5b the positions and directions of the accelerometers oriented along the y axis are shown. In Fig 6 the results of the SSI technique applied to the first test obtained considering the two configurations in Fig. 5 are reported. The results for all the performed tests are summarized in Table 3 and Table 4.

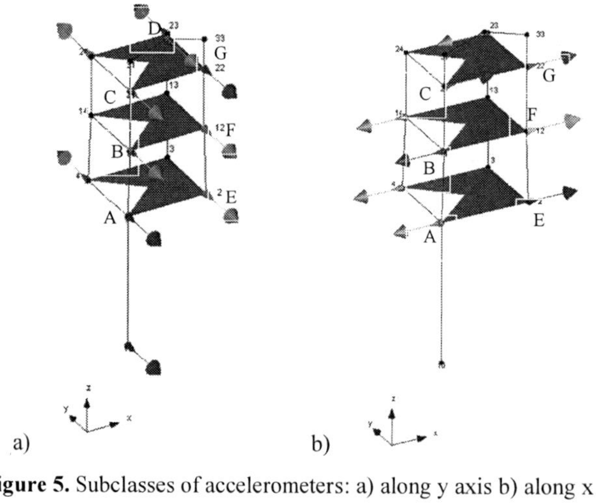

Figure 5. Subclasses of accelerometers: a) along y axis b) along x axis

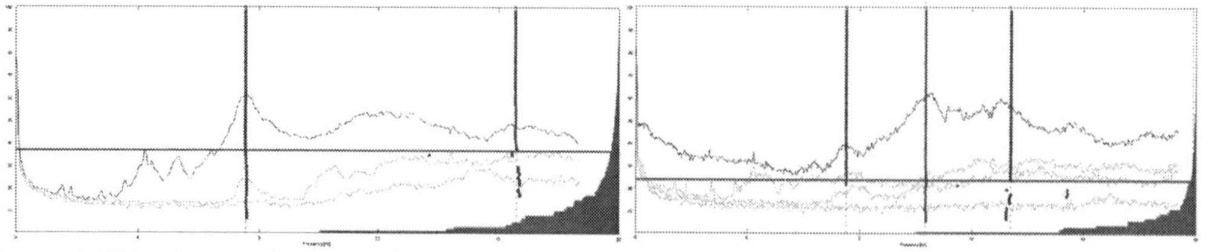

Figure 6. SSI estimation for the accelerometers data in Fig. 5a (left) and Fig. 5b (right), Test1, range [0-20] Hz

An accurate analysis of the data shown in Tables 3 and 4 in conjunction with a visual deep inspection of the fitting of the mode shapes for all the analyses, and a comparison with the useful information of the FE model, permits to extract the following considerations:

- The first two bending modes are effectively very close, with the value of 7.51 Hz along y axis, about 7.52 Hz along x axis;

- Other modes related to local and torsional effects appear at 10.33 and 13.52 Hz (related to x direction), and 16.49 and 26.64 Hz (related to y direction) ;
- The modes at about 22.3 Hz and 31.4 Hz are pure torsional modes, clearly extracted in all the cases (all accelerometers and the two considered subsets).

The considerations have been used for tuning the FE model, in such a way that could be close to the experimental behaviour.

Table 3. Identified frequencies for the four environmental tests using the SSI technique with only accelerometers along y axis.

Mode	Frequency					Notation
	Test1 [Hz]	Test2 [Hz]	Test3 [Hz]	Test4 [Hz]	Average	
1	7.54	7.54	7.53	7.57	7.54	Flexional
2	16.57	16.27	16.75	16.38	16.49	Flexional
3	22.33	22.24	22.09	22.39	22.26	Torsional
4	26.42	26.65	26.66	26.83	26.64	Flexional
5	31.22	31.27	31.60	31.47	31.39	Torsional

Table 4. Identified frequencies for the four environmental tests using the SSI technique with only accelerometers along x axis.

Mode	Frequency					Notation
	Test1 [Hz]	Test2 [Hz]	Test3 [Hz]	Test4 [Hz]	Average [Hz]	
1	7.52	7.56	7.51	7.47	7.51	Flexional
2	10.35	10.35	10.33	10.3	10.33	Flexional
3	13.39	13.49	13.51	13.72	13.52	Flexional
4	22.29	22.26	23.06	22.33	22.48	Torsional
5	31.13	31.12	31.5	31.72	31.37	Torsional

4. ACCURATE MODEL UPDATING AND FINAL RESULTS

The update of the FE model has been performed by varying the elastic modulus of the tufa and Trani's blocks in order to match the experimental results. Finally it was adopted for the Trani stone an elastic modulus of 3200 MPa and for the tufa blocks an elastic modulus of 1260 MPa, and then applied the same procedure of weighted average previously described. Table 4 shows the comparison between the experimental and the numerical results.

Regarding mode n.4 in Table 5, it must be underlined that this mode refers to a local mode of the arch that was equipped with only a single accelerometer (named with the letter D in Fig 2c). Calculating and plotting (Fig.7) the single-sided amplitude spectrum $P(f)$ of the accelerometer placed on the top of the arch (point D), it is possible to recognize (around 13-14 Hz highlighted by an arrow) a phenomenon that may be related to the presence of the local mode evaluated by the model.

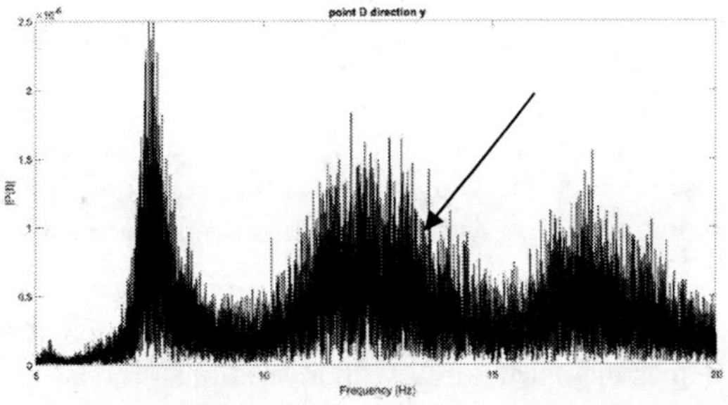

Figure 7. Amplitude spectrum along y direction, point D Test1.

Table 5. Comparison between the numerical and experimental results.

Mode	Experimental frequency [Hz]	Numerical frequency [Hz]	Difference [%]
1	7.51	7.50	0.13
2	7.54	7.58	0.53
3	10.33		-
4		14.24	-
5	13.52		-
6	16.49	16.25	1.45
7	22.26	21.94	1.43
8	26.64		-
9	31.39	29.37	6.43

5. CONCLUSIONS

In this paper the authors tackled the problem of the identification of the modal parameters of squat and highly symmetrical structures, like the tower analysed. Several tools have been used for achieving a good confidence on the identification: analysis of each channel spectrum, application of OMA techniques to all the accelerometers and to specific subsets, continuous comparison with an accurate FE model, based on precise geometrical information of the structure. It must be underlined that only the application of all the shown steps has permitted to achieve the final accuracy on the model updating and has permitted to establish the presence of two very close frequencies not detectable with a direct analysis.

ACKNOWLEDGEMENTS

Authors acknowledge the Italian project PRIN 2015: "Mitigating the impacts of natural hazards on cultural heritage sites, structures and artefacts".

REFERENCES

[1] Ivorra, S, Giannoccaro, N.I., Foti, D. (in press). Simple model for predicting the vibration transmission of a squat masonry tower by base forced vibrations. Structural Control and Health Monitoring.

[2] Diaferio, M., Foti, D., Giannoccaro, N.I., Ivorra, S. (2018). Measuring the modal parameters of a cultural heritage tower by using strong-motion signals. AKTA IMECO, October 2018, Vol. 7, n. 3, pp.86 – 94, ISSN: 2221-870X.

[3] Diaferio, M., Foti, D., Giannoccaro, N.I. (2015). Identification of the modal properties of a squat historic tower for the tuning of a FE model. Proceedings 6th International Operational Modal Analysis Conference, IOMAC 2015; Abba Hotel, Gijon; Spain; 12 - 14 May.

[4] Prete, F. (2014). I centri storici tra cultura, arte e tecniche. Il caso studio di Trani/Historical centres among culture, art and techniques. The case study of Trani. Bari: Adriatica Editrice (in Italian/English).

[5] Giannoccaro, N.I., Spedicato, L., Foti, D. (2016). A digital analysis for the experimental accelerometers data used for building dynamical identification. Proceedings of the 2016 IEEE Workshop on Environmental, Energy and Structural Monitoring Systems, Bari, June 2016, 141-146, ISBN: 978-5090-2369-1.

[6] Ramos, L.F., Marques, L., Lourenco, P.B., De Roeck, G., Campos-Costa, A., Roque, J. (2010). Monitoring historical masonry structures with operational modal analysis: Two case studies. Mechanical Systems and Signal Processing, 24, 1291-1305.

[7] Diaferio, M., Foti, D., Giannoccaro, N.I., Ivorra, S. (2017). Model updating based on the dynamic identification of a baroque bell tower. International Journal of Safety and Security Engineering, 7(4), 519–531.

[8] Foti, D., Diaferio, M., Giannoccaro, NI, Ivorra, S. (2015). Structural identification and numerical models for slender historical structures. In: P. Asteris & V. Plevris (Eds.), Handbook of Research on Seismic Assessment and Rehabilitation of Historic Structures. Hershey, PA: Engineering Science Reference, Chapter 23, pp. 674-703.

[9] Diaferio, M., Foti, D., Gentile, C., Giannoccaro, N.I., Saisi, A. (2015). Dynamic testing of a historical slender building using accelerometers and radar. Proceedings of 6th International Operational Modal Analysis Conference, IOMAC 2015; Abba Hotel, Gijon; Spain; 12-14 May.

[10] Foti, D. (2015). Non-destructive techniques and monitoring for the evolutive damage detection of an ancient masonry structure, Key Engineering Materials, 628,168-177.

[11] Ivorra, S., Brotóns, V., Foti, D., Diaferio, M. (2016). A preliminary approach of dynamic identification of slender buildings by neuronal networks. International Journal of Non-Linear Mechanics, 80, 183-189.

[12] Bru, D., Ivorra, S., Baeza, F.J., Reynau, R., Foti, D. (2015). OMA dynamic identification of a masonry chimney with severe cracking condition. Proceedings of the 6th International Operational Modal Analysis Conference, IOMAC 2015.

[13] Gentile, C., Saisi, A., Cabboi, A. (2014). Structural Identification of a Masonry Tower Based on Operational Modal Analysis. International Journal of Architectural Heritage, 9(2), 98-110.

[14] Bartoli, G., Betti, M., Giordano, S. (2013). In situ static and dynamic investigations on the ' Torre Grossa' masonry tower. Engineering Structures, 52, 718-733.

[15] De Sortis, A., Antonacci, E., Vestroni, F. (2005). Dynamic identification of a masonry building using forced vibration tests. Engineering Structures, 27(2), 155–165.

[16] Snoj, J., Österreicher, M., Dolšek, M. (2013). The importance of ambient and forced vibration measurements for the results of seismic performance assessment of buildings obtained by using a simplified non-linear procedure: Case study of an old masonry building. Bulletin of Earthquake Engineering, 11(6), 2105–2132.

[17] Tronci E.M., Pietrosanti D., Cordisco G., De Angelis M. (2017). Vibration analysis of the civic tower in Rieti. Procedia Engineering, 199, 2268-2273.

[18] Gupta, A., Zhao, W., Regan, C., Seiler, P., Kapania, R.K. (2018). Identification of Symmetrical Structures with Fabrication and Damage Induced Asymmetry. In: Conte, J., Astroza, R., Benzoni, G., Feltrin, G., Loh, K., Moaveni, B. (eds) Experimental Vibration Analysis for Civil Structures. EVACES 2017.

[19] Artemis Modal Pro v4.5. Structural Vibrations Solutions. Aalborg, Denmark. 2016.

[20] Strauss 7 Finite element analysis system. Strand7 Pty Ltd. www.strauss7.com

[21] The Mathworks, "MATLAB." Natick, MA, 2015.

IOMAC'19

8th International Operational Modal Analysis Conference
2019 May13-15 Copenhagen

DETECTING STRUCTURAL CHANGES WITH THE ONE-STEP FE MODEL UPDATING TECHNIQUE

A. L. Caballero [1], *S. D. R. Amador* [2], *S. Andersen* [3], *S. P. N. Poulsen* [4] *and R. Brincker* [5]

[1] Research Assistant, Technical University of Denmark, alcar@byg.dtu.dk
[2] PostDoc, Technical University of Denmark, sdio@byg.dtu.dk
[3] PostDoc, Technical University of Denmark, seba@byg.dtu.dk
[4] Associate Professor, Technical University of Denmark, pnp@byg.dtu.dk
[5] Professor, Technical University of Denmark, runeb@byg.dtu.dk

ABSTRACT

Differently from the sensitivity based finite element (FE) model updating technique in which the discrepancies between the FE and experimental modal properties are reduced iteratively by modifying the FE modelling assumptions, the one-step FE model updating technique based on modal orthogonality and the local correspondence (LC) principle updates the FE model in a single step. When updating an FE model with the one-step updating approach, it is assumed that the discrepancies between a FE model and the (physical) modelled structure are small and distributed over the model's degrees of freedom. If this assumption is fulfilled, it is verified that the one-step method efficiently updates the FE model, so that its modal properties match very well the ones obtained from experimental vibration tests. In this paper, the performance of the one-step updating technique in detecting localized changes is investigated by means of a practical application example in which the experimental modal properties of a t-shaped steel structure are used to update the corresponding FE model.

Keywords: FEM updating, one-step FEM updating, operational modal analysis; local correspondence principle; sensitivity method; matrix mixing technique, modal orthogonality

1. INTRODUCTION

One of the main objectives of finite element (FE) model updating is to improve the precision of the model being updated, so that it can predict, in a more accurate way, the structural behaviour of the modelled physical structure. Traditionally, basically two main FE updating approaches based on experimental modal properties are widely used to improve the accuracy of the FE models: the sensitivity [1] and the one-step based methods [2]. The sensitivity methods basically consists of iteratively updating a selected number of FE model parameters in order to optimize a cost function that measures the differences between the modal properties estimated with the FE model and those experimentally determined from vibration tests. It turns out that sensitivity based updating techniques can be time consuming, particularly when a complex FE model containing a very high number of Degrees of Freedoms (DoFs) is iteratively updated.

Furthermore, depending on the complexity of the FE model and the number of modelling parameters being optimized, issues such as cost function converging to local minima or convergence not being reached might as well occur. The one-step updating techniques, on the other hand, updates the FE modes in a single step by making use of the orthogonality equations of the mass and stiffness matrices [3, 4]. These techniques are regarded as perturbation-based updating approaches, meaning that the errors, i.e. the discrepancies between FE model and the modelled physical structure, are assumed to be small and distributed over the DoFs of the FE model. In [3, 4], it is shown that if these assumptions are fulfilled, the one-step updating based on mode shape orthogonality, matrix mixing [2] and local correspondence [5] can update the FE model so that the FE modal properties match very well the ones experimentally obtained from operational modal analysis (OMA).

In this paper, it is investigated how the one-step updating approach performs in terms of localization of structural changes when dealing with localized discrepancies between model and physical structure. To this end, the paper aim at assessing the capacity of the one-step method introduced in [3, 4] to provide information about localized mass changes in a structure. In order to assess its performance from a practical perspective, the aforementioned one-step approach is applied to detect localized mass changes in a FE model of a t-shaped steel structure in the final part of the paper.

2. FE MODEL UPDATING BASED ON THE LINEAR CORRESPONDENCE PRINCIPLE

The one-step updating equations establish a clear correspondence between the physical properties of the FE model, mass and stiffness matrices, to the FE modes. This allows the introduction of the experimental identified modal properties in substitution of the corresponding FE modal properties [3] [4]. Moreover, the number of DoFs measured in experimental vibration tests is much lower than the number of DoFs defined in FE models, thus an expansion of the experimental mode shapes is required. To carry out this task, an algorithm based on the local correspondence (LC) principle [5] is used to express the experimental mode shapes as linear combinations of FE modes.

2.1. One-step method

The one-step updating procedure is based on the orthogonality of the FE modes with respect to the stiffness and mass matrices (see e.g. [7]). In case of mass normalized modes, this orthogonality condition can be expressed as:

$$\mathbf{B}^T\mathbf{M}\mathbf{B} = \mathbf{I} \tag{1}$$

$$\mathbf{B}^T\mathbf{K}\mathbf{B} = \lceil \omega_n^2 \rfloor \tag{2}$$

where $\mathbf{B} = \begin{bmatrix}\mathbf{b}_1 & \mathbf{b}_2 & \cdots \mathbf{b}_N\end{bmatrix}$ is a $N \times N$ matrix gathering all the FE mode shape vectors, $\mathbf{b}_n$ $\left(\forall n \in \{1, 2, \ldots, N\}\right)$, and $\lceil \omega_n^2 \rfloor$ is a diagonal matrix containing the squared angular frequencies of the FE modes, with N denoting the number of DoFs in the FE model. Then, the inverse of the mass matrix can be expressed as:

$$\mathbf{M}^{-1} = \mathbf{B}\mathbf{B}^T = \sum_{i=1}^{N} \mathbf{b}_i\mathbf{b}_i^T \tag{3}$$

The sum of the outer products can be divided in two sets. For this method, the first set contains the modes to be updated (m) and the second comprises the rest of the FE modes that remains unchanged:

$$\mathbf{M}^{-1} = \sum_{i=1}^{m} \mathbf{b}_i\mathbf{b}_i^T + \sum_{i=m+1}^{N} \mathbf{b}_i\mathbf{b}_i^T \tag{4}$$

The updating will basically consist in the replacement of the first set by the outer products of the expanded experimental modes, $\mathbf{a}_n$:

$$\mathbf{M_u}^{-1} = \sum_{i=1}^{m} \mathbf{a}_i\mathbf{a}_i^T + \sum_{i=m+1}^{N} \mathbf{b}_i\mathbf{b}_i^T \tag{5}$$

The set containing the outer products of the non-updated modes is expressed as:

$$\sum_{i=m+1}^{N} \mathbf{b}_i\mathbf{b}_i^T = \mathbf{M}^{-1} - \sum_{i=1}^{m} \mathbf{b}_i\mathbf{b}_i^T \tag{6}$$

Finally, introducing equation (6) into equation (5) yields the one-step updating equation for the mass matrix:

$$\mathbf{M_u}^{-1} = \mathbf{M}^{-1} - \sum_{i=1}^{m} \mathbf{b}_i\mathbf{b}_i^T + \sum_{i=1}^{m} \mathbf{a}_i\mathbf{a}_i^T \tag{7}$$

With the same procedure, the updated stiffness matrix is obtained:

$$\mathbf{K_u}^{-1} = \mathbf{K}^{-1} - \sum_{i=1}^{m} \omega_{\mathrm{b}\,i}^{-2}\mathbf{b}_i\mathbf{b}_i^T + \sum_{i=1}^{m} \omega_{\mathrm{a}\,i}^{-2}\mathbf{a}_i\mathbf{a}_i^T \tag{8}$$

2.2. LC principle

As previously mentioned, the experimental mode shapes need to be expanded. For this task, an algorithm based on the LC principle [5] is used to express the experimental mode shapes as linear combinations of FE modes. The LC principle is based on the expansion theorem that states that any deformation of a mechanical system can be expressed as a linear combination of mode shape vectors. For each experimental mode shape, a chosen number of FE mode shapes are reduced to the experimental DoFs and then, the LC principle selects which of these FE mode shapes to include in an optimal FE mode shape cluster. Then a transformation matrix that relates the experimental mode shape vector and the optimal cluster of FE modes is estimated in a linear least squares sense. Finally, the experimental modal vector can be expanded to all DoFs of the FE model by means of the estimated transformation matrix. A more detailed description of the LC expansion itself as well as the optimization of the cluster of modes used in the expansion of the experimental mode shape vectors can be found, for instance, in [5, 3]. A brief description of the LC expansion is herein presented in the following paragraphs for completeness. Letting $\mathbf{B}_{\mathrm{r}n}$ be the optimal mode shape cluster at experimental DoFs, the nth experimental mode shape vector at the experimental DoFs, $\mathbf{a}_{\mathrm{r}n}$, can be expressed as:

$$\mathbf{a}_{\mathrm{r}n} = \mathbf{B}_{\mathrm{r}n}\mathbf{t}_n \tag{9}$$

with $\mathbf{t}_n$ standing for the transformation matrix. An estimate for this matrix is obtained in linear least squares sense from

$$\hat{\mathbf{t}}_n = \mathbf{B}_{\mathrm{r}n}{}^{+}\mathbf{a}_{\mathrm{r}n} \tag{10}$$

where $(\bullet)^{+}$ denotes the pseudo-inverse of a matrix. Once the transformation matrix estimate, $\hat{\mathbf{t}}_n$, is obtained, the experimental mode shape vector at the experimental DoFs is expanded by simply replacing $\mathbf{B}_{\mathrm{r}n}$ by the optimal mode shape cluster at all the FE DoFs, $\mathbf{B}_n$, in equation (9):

$$\hat{\mathbf{a}}_n = \mathbf{B}_n\hat{\mathbf{t}}_n \tag{11}$$

Finally, the expanded experimental mode shape vector is mass normalized to be used in equations (7) and (8):

$$\mathbf{a}_n = \frac{\hat{\mathbf{a}}_n}{\sqrt{\hat{\mathbf{a}}_n^T\mathbf{M}\hat{\mathbf{a}}_n}} \tag{12}$$

3. CASE STUDY

In this section, a brief description of the experimental and modelling setups is presented and the ad-hoc updating steps for this particular case are explained.

3.1. Experimental tests

In order to assess the efficiency of the previously explained updating technique in cases of localized mass changes, experimental data from the t-structure depicted in Figure 1a was used. The experimental tests and the data processing were carried out in [6]. Using OMA techniques [7], the experimental natural frequencies for the first 8 modes and the corresponding mode shape vectors for the experimental DoFs (see Figure 1b) were obtained. The mass perturbations were placed at two different locations (see Figure 1c), the coordinates of the locations are gathered in Table 1.

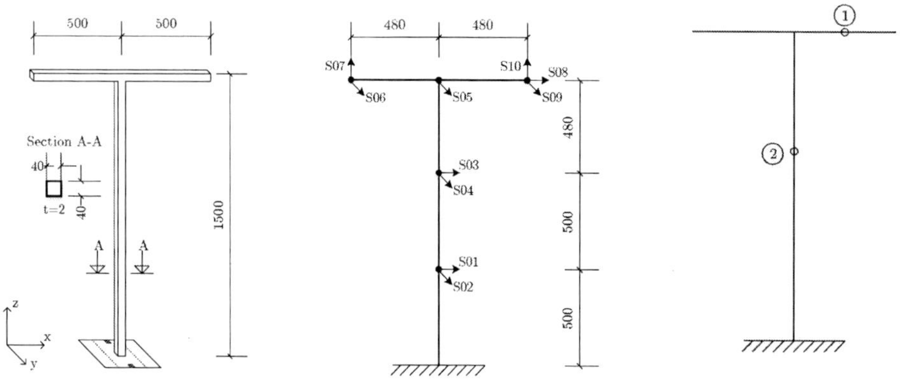

(a) Geometry and global coordinates **(b)** Experimental DoFs **(c)** Locations of the mass perturbations

Figure 1: Illustration of the tested t-structure

Table 1: Coordinates of the localized mass perturbations

Location	x coord [m]	y coord [m]	z coord [m]
1	0.25	0	1.48
2	0	0	0.92

3.2. FE Model

The FE model was built using an FE modelling Matlab toolbox developed in the civil engineering department of the Technical University of Denmark (DTU). It was decided to compute the global mass matrix using particle-lumped mass matrix for the beam elements [8]. The particle lumping technique allows for a more intuitive analysis of the updated mass matrix, since it only has values in the diagonal. The discretization of the structure was fine enough to obtain reasonable values for the natural frequencies compared to the natural frequencies of a model using a consistent mass matrix.

3.3. Updating procedure

For this structure, the first stage is to update the FE model using the experimental mode shape vectors and natural frequencies of the structure without any mass change. This updated FE model is hereinafter referred as the reference FE model, since it will be used as reference for detecting mass changes with the one-step updating technique. In the second step, the reference mass matrix is updated with the modal information obtained from tests in which localized masses are added to the physical structure. The updated mass matrix obtained from the second step are hereinafter denoted as updated matrices. Usually, in FE model updating with one-step approach, the experimental mode shapes are mass scaled. However, since only localized mass changes are addressed in context of this paper, it is obvious to assume that the stiffness matrix remains unchanged when the model is updated. Under this circumstance, the experimental mode shapes can be stiffness scaled. In order to perform the stiffness scaling, it is assumed that the same modal stiffness for the reference and updated modes:

$$k_{u\,i} = k_i \rightarrow m_{u\,i} = \left(\frac{\omega_i}{\omega_{u\,i}}\right)^2 m_i \tag{13}$$

where m_i and k_i are the reference modal mass and stiffness of mode i; $m_{u\,i}$ and $k_{u\,i}$ are the modal mass and stiffness of mode i of the updated FE model.

The differences between the updated mass matrix and the reference mass matrix are the basis for the mass detection analysis. Lumped mass matrices only have terms in their diagonal in the positions corresponding to nodal translational DoFs (and zeros for the rotational DoFs). For a given node, the subtraction of each translational DoF (x, y and z) in the reference mass matrix from the corresponding translational DoF in the updated mass matrix yields the mass added to the physical model. The difference between reference and updated nodal masses are then evaluated in order to assess the performance of the one-step updating approach in detecting the localized mass changes.

4. RESULTS OF THE CASE STUDY

The results from the two mass perturbation cases are now presented, processed and analysed. In both cases, the results presented belong to the maximum perturbation tested.

4.1. Location 1: mass perturbation- 304 gr

The largest localized perturbation tested in Location 1 (see Figure 1c) was 304 gr, which corresponds to a 4.05% of the total mass of the structure (7.5 kg). Figure 2 shows the nodal mass increments along the t-structure (the illustrations of the t-structure are none dimensional) detected for each global direction x, y and z (see Figure 1a). The mass detection in the x direction is constant alongside the horizontal beam and lower than the other two cases. Most of the mass change detected in the y and z directions is in the beam side of the localized mass, but the maximum mass change is close to the edge. Moreover, the sum of the nodal mass increments for the three cases is a much lower value than the actual perturbation of 304 gr. It was expected that this updating technique was going to express the mass perturbation as a distributed mass change along the structure, yet the results presented so far provide very vague information about the possible location of the mass perturbation.

Since the mass matrix is a diagonal matrix, the inverse mass matrix is also diagonal. Observing equation (4), each diagonal term of the inverse mass matrix is formed by the contribution of the outer products of the updated mode shapes and the outer products of the rest of mode shapes. One of the reasons behind the underestimation of the mass is the low contribution of the outer products of the updated mode shapes to the inverse mass matrix terms. Thus, the nodal increments at each DoF were normalized according to the contribution of the outer products of the updated mode shapes to the term of the inverse mass matrix corresponding to that DoF. As an example, the nodal mass for node 10 in the x direction is placed at the diagonal term (55,55) of the mass matrix. The mass increment detected at the latter position is 0.194%. The value for the term (55,55) in the inverse mass matrix is 7.5911 and the value in the matrix composed by the outer products of the $m = 8$ updated mode shapes is 0.4872 (see expression (14)). Then, the detected mass increment 0.194% is multiplied by 7.5911/0.4872. Following this procedure for all the

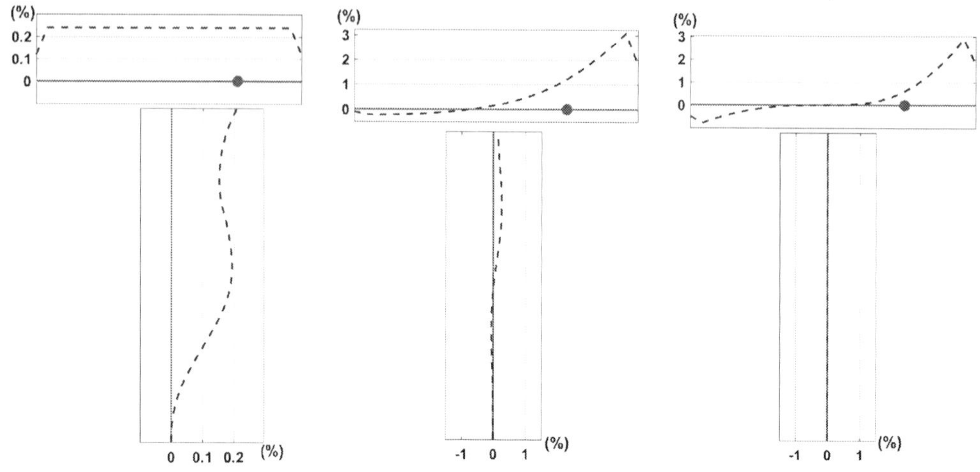

(a) x direction **(b)** y direction **(c)** z direction

Figure 2: Location 1- nodal mass increments detected in global directions x, y and z

DoFs, the new normalized increments are shown in Figure 3 for the global directions x, y and z.

$$\underbrace{\frac{1}{\mathbf{M}(55,55)}}_{7.59} = \underbrace{\sum_{i=1}^{m} \mathbf{b}_i(55)\mathbf{b}_i^T(55)}_{0.49} + \underbrace{\sum_{i=m+1}^{N} \mathbf{b}_i(55)\mathbf{b}_i^T(55)}_{7.1} \tag{14}$$

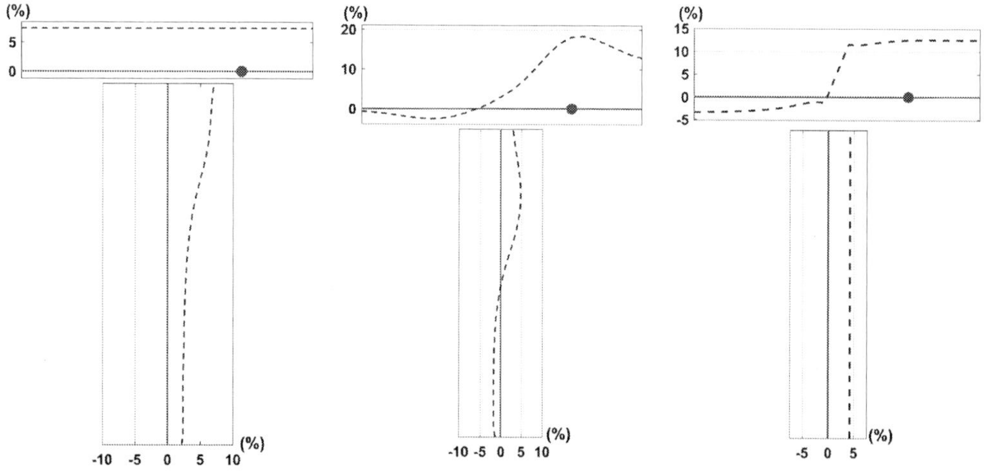

(a) x direction **(b)** y direction **(c)** z direction

Figure 3: Location 1- normalized nodal mass increments detected in global directions x, y and z

Most of the normalized mass increment detected in the x direction (Figure 3a) is in the horizontal beam and it is constant. This might just be because there is only one experimental DoF in the x direction measured on the horizontal beam (see Figure 1b). The largest part of the normalized mass increment detected in z direction (Figure 3c) is in the side of the horizontal beam where the localized mass was placed and it is almost constant. The reason for this might be the fact that there are two experimental

DoFs measured in the z direction, one at each edge of the horizontal beam. The most interesting result is provided by the normalized mass increment detected in the y direction (Figure 3b). Most of the mass increment is detected again in the beam side of the localized mass but in this case, the largest mass increment coincides with the placement of the localized mass. Three experimental DoFs in the y direction were measured (two in the edges and one in the center).

Furthermore, the total normalized mass increments for the different directions were calculated. The results are shown in Table 2 and have the same order of magnitude than the actual localized mass perturbation, which imply that the normalization approach has some physical significance.

Table 2: Location 1- Total normalized mass increments

Localized mass [gr]	mass in x [gr]	mass in y [gr]	mass in z [gr]
304	416	246	354

4.2. Location 2: mass perturbation- 152 gr

The largest localized perturbation tested in Location 2 (see Figure 1c) was 152 gr, which corresponds to a 2.03% of the total mass of the structure (7.5 kg). In this case, there is no mass detection in the z direction since the mass in Location 2 is not activated by the first 8 modes in this direction (see modes in Figure 6 in Appendix). Figures 4a and 4b show the nodal mass increments in the x and y direction, respectively. The nodal mass increment is maximum very close to the placement of the punctual mass for direction y. For the x direction, the maximum mass change is detected lower than the punctual mass location.

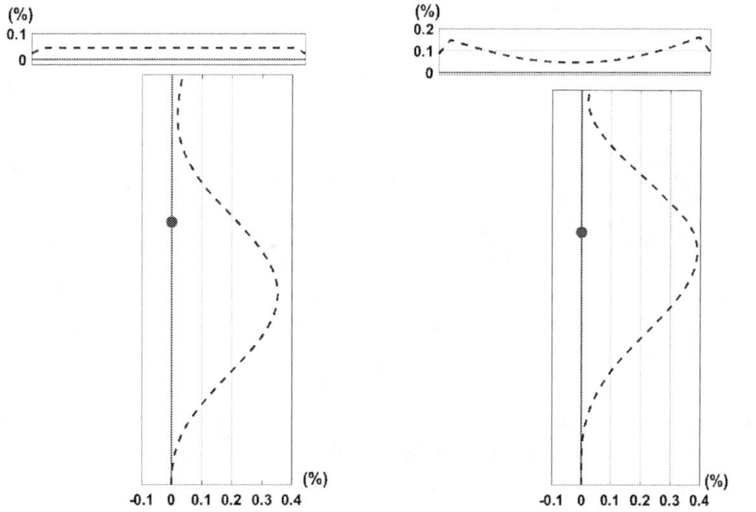

(a) x direction **(b)** y direction

Figure 4: Location 2- nodal mass increments detected in global directions x and y

As for location 1, the nodal mass increments were normalized with the same procedure. Figure 5a and Figure 5b show the normalized nodal increments detected in the x direction and y, respectively. For the y direction, the normalized mass increments are distributed similarly as the originally detected increments. However, for the x direction, the normalized mass increments are approximately constant and at maximum from the base of the structure until the proximity of the punctual mass placement, where the mass increments decrease abruptly.

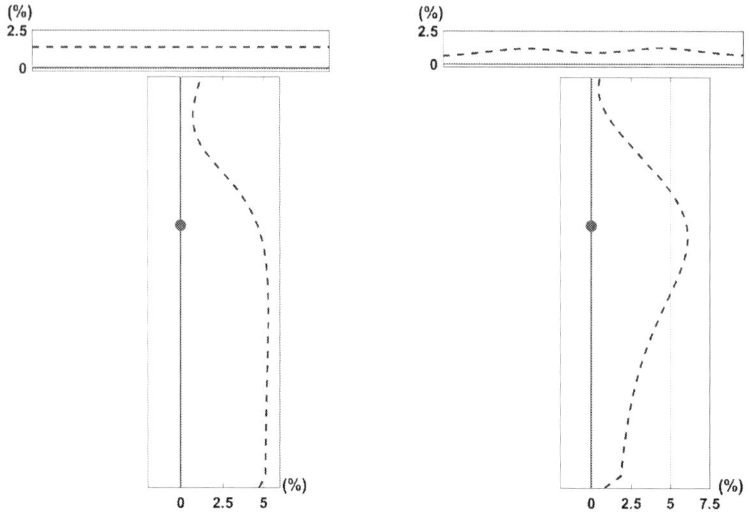

(a) x direction

(b) y direction

Figure 5: Location 2- normalized nodal mass increments detected in global directions x and y

The summation of normalized mass increments for the two directions is presented in Table 3. Again, the estimations of the mass perturbation are in the same order of magnitude as the actual punctual mass.

Table 3: Location 2- Total normalized mass increments

Localized mass [gr]	mass in x [gr]	mass in y [gr]
152	234	187

5. CONCLUSIONS

This paper aimed at assessing the performance of the one-step updating method based on the LC principle and modal orthogonality when dealing with localized mass changes. The scaling method for the detected nodal mass increments based on the contribution of the outer products of the updated modes to the terms of the inverse mass matrix, described in the previous chapter, provided hints about the placement of the localized masses and estimations for the mass change in the same order of magnitude as the actual mass perturbation. As expected, the mass increments detected by the proposed updating procedure were distributed along the structure and varied for the different global directions. Nonetheless, it is clear that the distribution of the nodal mass increments can shed light on the position of a localized mass.

It can be concluded that the two most crucial factors for this updating technique in the detection of localized masses are the deformation outline of the mode shapes to be updated and the placement of the experimental DoFs. Since the mode shapes detected with OMA techniques are the low frequency modes, the outer products of these mode shapes have a low contribution to the inverse mass matrix. This fact seemed to have an underestimating effect in the updating of the mass matrix. In contrast, the contribution of low frequency mode shapes to the the inverse stiffness matrix is higher because the outer products of the mode shapes are divided by the their squared angular frequency to define the inverse stiffness matrix.

ACKNOWLEDGEMENTS

The authors acknowledge the funding received from the Centre for Oil and Gas - DTU/Danish Hydrocarbon Research and Technology Centre (DHRTC).

REFERENCES

[1] Friswell, M.I., Mottershead, J.E. and Link, M. (2011) The sensitivity method in finite element updating: A tutorial. *Journal of Mechanical Systems and Signal Processing*, 25, 2275-2296.

[2] Friswell, M.I. and Mottershead, J.E. (1993) Model updating in structural dynamics: a survey. *Journal of Sound and Vibration* , 167(2), 347-375.

[3] Amador, S., Juul, M., Friis, T. and Brincker, R. (2017) Finite element model updating using the local correspondence principle. *International Modal Analysis Conference*

[4] Juul, M., Amador, S., Skafte, A., Hansen, J., Lopez Aenlle, M. and Brincker, R. (2017) One-step FE model updating using local correspondence and mode shape orthogonality. *Journal of Shock and Vibration*

[5] Brincker, R., Skafte, A., Lopez Aenlle, M., Sestieri, A., D'Ambrogio, W. and Canteli, A. (2014) A local correspondence principle for mode shapes in structural dynamics. *Journal of Mechanical Systems and Signal Processing*, 45, 91–104.

[6] Glavind, S.T. (2016) Vibration-based identification of mass changes using statistical learning theory. M.Sc. thesis. Department of Engineering, AArhus University, Denmark.

[7] Brincker, R. and Ventura, C. (2015) *Introduction to operational modal analysis.* New York, Wiley.

[8] Pavlou, D. (2015) *Essentials of the finite element method.* London, Academic Press.

APPENDIX - MODAL SHAPES OF THE T-SHAPED STRUCTURE AFTER FE UPDATING WITH ONE-STEP APPROACH

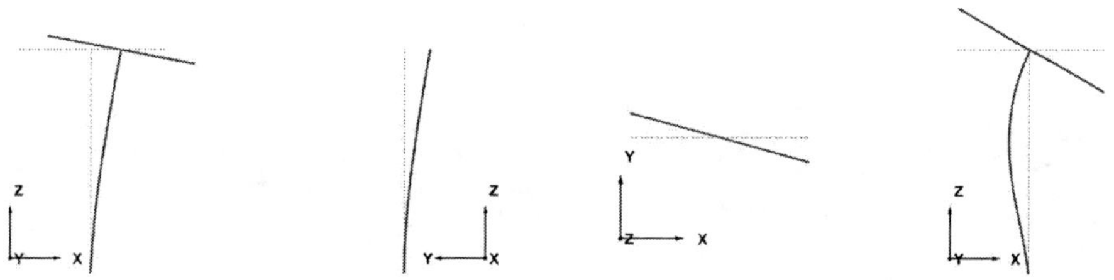

(a) Mode 1 **(b)** Mode 2 **(c)** Mode 3 **(d)** Mode 4

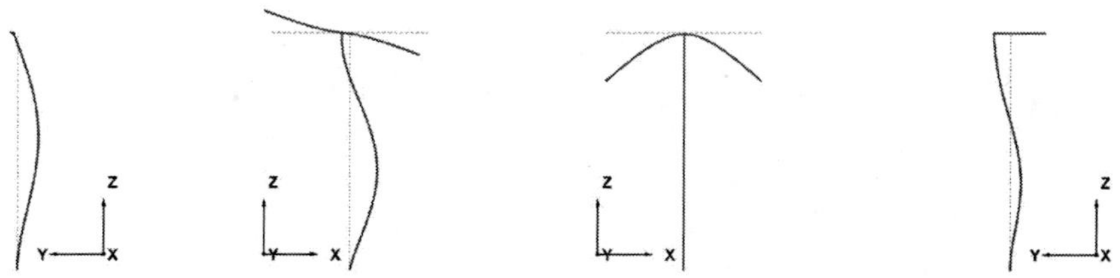

(e) Mode 5 **(f)** Mode 6 **(g)** Mode 7 **(h)** Mode 8

Figure 6: Mode shapes of the t-shaped steel structure obtained with the updated FE model

IOMAC'19

8th International Operational Modal Analysis Conference
2019 May13-15 Copenhagen

ESTIMATION OF ELASTIC PROPERTIES OF AN URM WALL BY APPLYING VIBRATION BASED AND GLOBAL SENSITIVITY TECHNIQUES

Alexander Opazo-Vega, MSc[1,2] *and Claudio Oyarzo-Vera, PhD*[3]

[1]Senior Lecturer, MSc, Universidad del Bío-Bío, aopazove@ubiobio.cl.
[2] PhD Student, Universidad Católica de la Santísima Concepción, aopazo@doctorado.ucsc.cl
[3] Senior Lecturer, Universidad Católica de la Santísima Concepción, coyarzov@ucsc.cl

ABSTRACT

Unreinforced masonry walls (URM) are structural elements usually observed in heritage buildings in Chile. The assessment of the elastic properties of this kind of structures is generally a challenging task, because of its orthotropic behaviour and the difficulties to extract and to handle in situ samples for destructive experimental tests. The study presented here aims to estimate the elastic mechanical properties of URM walls by applying vibration based non-destructive techniques. A representative segment of URM wall was built in the laboratory and subjected to a series modal tests using low energy impacts as excitation source. Modal properties of the wall were estimated through Enhanced Frequency Domain Decomposition (EFDD) and Stochastic Subspace Identification (SSI) methods. An orthotropic finite element model of the wall was successively updating through global sensitivity analysis techniques until the differences between experimental and numerically simulated modal properties were minimal. The results suggest that this approach can be extended to more complicated structural configurations.

Keywords: Unreinforced masonry, Impact test, Global sensitivity

1. INTRODUCTION

Masonry is one of the oldest building materials, so it has a significant presence in heritage buildings. Despite the above, the knowledge on the structural behaviour of this type of buildings is still limited due to the variability of its components [1]. Unreinforced masonry (URM) walls are usually constructed from hand-made units of natural or manufactured material, that are stacked following different arranges and glued together by mortar [2].

The mechanical behaviour of the walls depends on the origin of the raw materials, the bricks and mortar manufacture process and construction practice. In heritage buildings the standardization of these processes is scarce, so the mechanical properties must be estimated by applying experimental tests. The design codes generally recommend performing compression tests on masonry prisms to extract the characteristic compression strength of the combined material and the other mechanical properties are estimated from this parameter [3]. Previous work has revealed that mechanical properties of masonry estimated from prism compression test are not representative of the actual material performance in existing structures [4]. This problem arises because the prism specimens are altered during the processes of extraction, transport, and preparation of the test. Besides, the number of prism specimens that can be extracted from buildings is limited and the results obtained from this studies might be statistically questionable.

Based on the preceding, a series of non-destructive vibration-based assessment techniques for masonry heritage structures have emerged as an attractive alternative for field investigations [5-9]. Combining these techniques with finite element model updating make it possible to estimate the elastic properties of this kind of structures. However, due to the inherent high heterogeneity of URM structures (material variability, accumulated damage and interactions between components), it is necessary to perform complementary model updating analysis.

Global sensitivity analysis (GSA) [10] is a technique suitable for updating model variables even in the case of high uncertainty about the material characteristics. In general terms, GSA investigates how the variability in input factors affects the results of numerical models. GSA techniques considers the entire variability space of input factors. Hence, GSA model updating methods are less dependent initial conditions chosen for the input factors.

This paper describes a new approach to estimate the elastic properties of URM walls based on the combination of operational modal analysis, model updating, and two methods of global sensitivity analysis. This new approach was applied to a URM wall prototype with the purpose of identifying some relevant orthotropic elastic properties that minimize the differences between numerical estimations and its experimental response.

2. MATERIALS AND METHODS

2.1. URM wall prototype description and instrumentation

The tested specimen consisted of an unreinforced masonry wall, constructed with solid brick units with dimensions of 290 mm in length, 140 mm in width and 45 mm in thickness, connected through a pre-dosed cement mortar. The configuration of the bricks had a typical British buildings bricks arrangement. The final dimensions of the wall were 1160 mm long, 1200 mm high and 290 mm thick [11].

This study aimed to analyse the out-of-plane behaviour of the wall. Therefore, twenty low energy impacts were applied perpendicular to the plane of the wall and eight uniaxial accelerometers were installed in the same direction. The objective of this setup was to identify the first three out-of-plane modes of the specimen. The masonry wall and its instrumentation are presented in Figure 1.

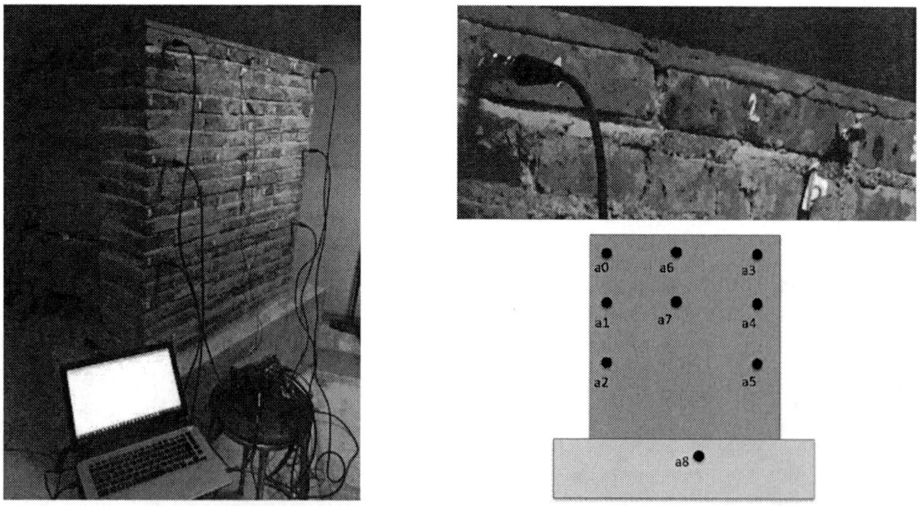

Figure 1. URM wall instrumentation for operational modal testing.

2.2. Operational modal analysis and model updating techniques

Enhanced Frequency Domain Decomposition (EFDD) [12] and Stochastic Subspace Identification (SSI-UPC) [13] were used to estimate the modal properties of the wall. These methods were chosen to extract the modal properties from two different sources, i.e., applying frequency and time domain techniques, and compare those results. For this purpose, the software package ARTeMIS Modal Pro [14] was used to determine modal frequencies, damping and shapes.

A finite element model was implemented in ANSYS® software [15] to represent the dynamic behaviour of the wall specimen. Tetrahedral 10-node elements were used to represent the wall, considering linear-elastic and homogeneous orthotropic properties for the masonry. Figure 2 shows the finite element mesh used for the model.

Figure 2. Analytical model for the URM wall (Images used courtesy of ANSYS, Inc.).

The finite element model of the wall specimen was updated by minimizing the differences between the experimental and numerical modal data. This minimization is performed by adjusting several uncertain model properties within a range of plausible values [16]. For this aim, an objective function is defined as a nonlinear least squares problem, as it is shown in Eq. (1).

$$Y = \min_{\boldsymbol{p}} F(\boldsymbol{p}) = \frac{1}{2} \|\boldsymbol{r}(\boldsymbol{p})\|^2 = \frac{1}{2} \left\| \begin{matrix} \boldsymbol{r}_f(\boldsymbol{p}) \\ \boldsymbol{r}_s(\boldsymbol{p}) \end{matrix} \right\|^2 \quad (1)$$

Where $\boldsymbol{r}$ is the residual vector that contains the frequency residuals $\boldsymbol{r}_f$ and mode shape residuals $\boldsymbol{r}_s$. The vector $\boldsymbol{p}$ represents the set of design variables. The expressions of the residuals $\boldsymbol{r}_f$ y $\boldsymbol{r}_s$ are shown in Eq. (2) and Eq. (3).

$$r_f(\boldsymbol{p}) = \frac{\lambda_j(\boldsymbol{p}) - \tilde{\lambda}_j}{\tilde{\lambda}_j} \qquad \text{with} \qquad \lambda_j = (2\pi f_j)^2 \quad (2)$$

$$r_s(\boldsymbol{p}) = \frac{\phi_j^l(\boldsymbol{p})}{\phi_j^r(\boldsymbol{p})} - \frac{\tilde{\phi}_j^l}{\tilde{\phi}_j^r} \quad (3)$$

In Eq. (2) $\lambda_j(\boldsymbol{p})$ and $\tilde{\lambda}_j$ are the jth analytical and experimental squared circular frequencies, respectively. While, in Eq. (3) $\phi_j(\boldsymbol{p})$ and $\tilde{\phi}_j$ are the jth analytical and experimental mode shapes. The superindexes $\boldsymbol{l}$ and $\boldsymbol{r}$ denote an arbitrary and a reference degree of freedom of mode shape ϕ_j (or $\tilde{\phi}_j$), respectively. In this model, the vector $\boldsymbol{p}$ had nine orthotropic elastic components that correspond to three Young's moduli (E_x, E_y, E_z), three Poisson coefficients (v_{xy}, v_{yz}, v_{xz}) and three shear moduli (G_{xy}, G_{yz}, G_{xz}).

Two methods of global sensitivity analysis were used to estimate adjusted values for the nine orthotropic elastic properties of the wall.

In a first stage, a method known as Element Effects Test (EET) [17] was used to analyse which elastic constants did not affect the Y function. Subsequently, a Regional Sensitivity Analysis (RSA) [18] was applied to determine the optimal ranges of values for the elastic constants that influenced the Y function.

EET corresponds to a technique that performs sampling of combinations of input variables by modifying one variable at a time. Its sensitivity indicator is the average of the "Elemental Effects (EE)". The EE represents the influence of the variation of an input parameter on the model's output function [17]. For a particular input parameter, its EE is calculated as follows: (i) the output function (Y_i) is evaluated for a set of initial input parameters, (ii) the output function (Y_{i+1}) is evaluated for another set of parameters that only differs in the parameter of interest increased by a value Δ, (iii) the difference between the two previous output function is calculated and divided by the value Δ. An example of EE evaluation is shown in Eq. (4), for the input parameter E_z.

$$EE_{E_z} = \frac{Y_{i+1}\left(E_x, E_y, (E_z + \Delta), v_{xy}, \ldots, G_{xz}\right) - Y_i\left(E_x, E_y, E_z, v_{xy} \ldots, G_{xz}\right)}{\Delta} \quad (4)$$

To calculate the sensitivity indicator of this method it is necessary to carry out multiple EE evaluations. These evaluations should consider different sets of parameters to represent the entire range of interest variables. In the study presented here, 1000 model evaluations were carried out to discriminate between influential and non-influential input factors.

On the other hand, the RSA method performs the sampling of input variables, modifying all variables at a time. RSA is a particularly suitable method to identify regions in the inputs space corresponding to high or low values of the output. In RSA the input samples are divided into two binary sets, "behavioural (B)" and "non-behavioural (NB)", depending on whether the associated output is above or below a prescribed threshold. A useful sensitivity indicator for this method is the maximum vertical difference between the empirical cumulative probability distribution functions (CDF) of B and NB models [18]. In Eq. (5) the mathematical expression of this indicator is shown, for an input parameter E_z.

$$S_{E_z} = \max_{E_z}\left|F_{E_z|Y_B}(E_z|Y \in Y_B) - F_{E_z|Y_{NB}}(E_z|Y \in Y_{NB})\right| \quad (4)$$

where $F_{E_z|Y_B}$ and $F_{E_z|Y_{NB}}$ are the empirical cumulative distributions functions of E_z when considering input samples associated with behavioural outputs (Y_B) and non-behavioural outputs (Y_{NB}), respectively.

The ranges of variables that have more significant influence in the B and NB models are obtained through the comparison between the slopes of the CDFs. For example, B models will concentrate more strongly on those ranges of values where the slope of their CDF is greater than the slope of the NB models. To define the B models, a threshold value $Y < 0.4$ was used. According to the recommendations of previous research [19], the sample size for the simulations should be between 100 and 1000 times the number of input parameters.

The SAFE Matlab toolbox was used to perform global sensitivity analyses [20]. The Latin hypercube sampling technique [21] was used to select the input variables since it shows better results with fewer simulations than a traditional random sample. The ranges considered for the input variables where experimentally estimated in previous investigations [11] and are shown in Table 1.

Table 1. Proposal of input parameters ranges for global sensitivity analysis.

	Orthotropic elastic properties		
	E_x, E_y E_z [MPa]	v_{xy}, v_{yz}, v_{xz}	G_{xy}, G_{yz}, G_{xz} [MPa]
min	100	0.05	100
max	800	0.25	800

3. RESULTS AND DISCUSSION

3.1. Experimental modal properties of the URM wall

Table 2 summarizes the frequencies identified by the EFDD and SSI-UPC methods. Figure 3 shows the vibration modes associated with each frequency. Examples of the frequency estimations using the two above mentioned methods are shown in Figures 4 and 5. In Table 2, "N" is the number of times the frequency was detected in the entire set of 20 performed tests.

Table 2. Frequencies identified through OMA methods.

Statistics	EFDD			SSI-UPC		
	f_1 [hz]	f_2 [hz]	f_3 [hz]	f_1 [hz]	f_2 [hz]	f_3 [hz]
Mean	13.20	57.37	68.28	13.11	58.49	68.20
CoV (%)	0.80	4.89	0.19	0.66	0.73	0.22
N	20	5	17	20	19	20

(a) (b) (c)

Figure 3. Typical modes shapes identified by SSI-UPC method.
(a) mode 1, (b) mode 2, and (c) mode 3.

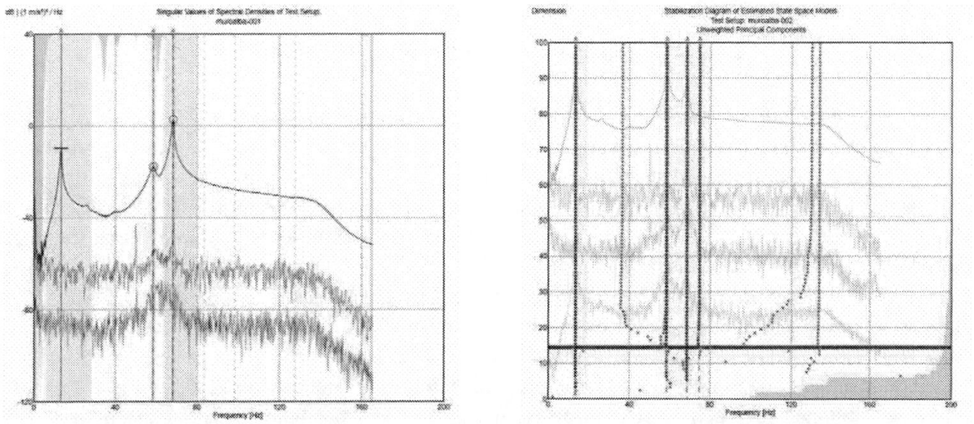

(a) (b)

Figure 4. Examples of the system identification results in ARTeMIS Modal Pro [ref].
(a) Singular values of spectral densities of test setup 1 (EFDD method), and (b) Stabilization diagram of estimated state space models for test setup 2 (SSI-UPC).

It can be seen from Table 2 that both EFDD and SSI methods identified similar frequency values. The coefficients of variation (CoV) were low, which demonstrates the accuracy of the tests. However, the second mode shape was more easily identifiable with SSI method (N=19) than the EFDD method (N=5). From Figure 3, we can see that the first and second modes have a noticeable flexural component, while the third frequency was torsional.

3.2. Model updating of the URM wall

3.2.1. Ranking of the contribution of input elastic properties in the output model variability

To assess the relative contribution of elastic properties to the Y function, EET global sensitivity analysis was used. The results of 1000 model simulations with different combinations of elastic properties values are presented in Figure 5.

We observed in Figure 5 that the Young´s modulus in the vertical direction (E_y) had the most significant influence (57.5%) on the Y function. On the other hand, four elastic properties (G_{xz}, v_{yz}, E_z, v_{xz}) had non-significant influence (>1%) on the Y function. Therefore, to minimize the computational cost, these four variables were not considered in the subsequent analyses.

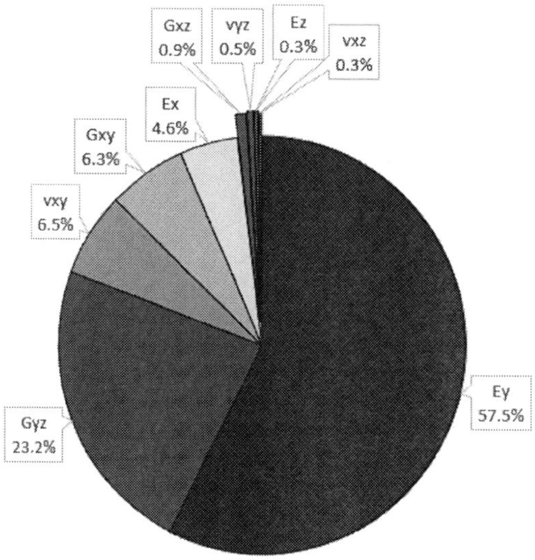

Figure 5. Ranking of elastic properties in the Y function.

3.2.2. Proposed ranges of values for the elastic properties of the URM wall

Regional Sensitivity Analysis (RSA) was used to propose ranges of values for the elastic properties of the wall. In total, 2500 numerical simulations were performed with different combinations of values for the properties E_y, G_{yz}, v_{xy}, G_{xy} and E_x. The models were defined as "behavioural" (B models) when the value of the Y function was less than 0.4. This definition of the B models guarantees that the average differences between the numerical and experimental frequencies do not exceed ±20%. Figure 6 presents scatter plots of Y function against the different input elastic properties considered in this study. In this Figure, the green points represent B models which is only a small proportion of the total simulations (11% of the total). Also, it is observed that only E_y and G_{xy} (Figure 6a and 6d) have sub-ranges of values that generate higher concentrations of B models. This situation is better illustrated in Figure 7 with the CDF curves obtained for each elastic property. It can be seen that when E_y is in the interval 130·to 260·MPa the slope of curve B is higher than that of curve NB. The same trend can be observed when G_{xy} is in the interval 560·to 800 MPa. Therefore, these two variables within the abovementioned ranges are recommended as updating variables for the URM wall model. For the other mechanical properties, a standard fixed value (for example, obtained from literature) can be proposed, since they did not have significant influence in minimizing the differences between the experimental and numerical model (function Y).

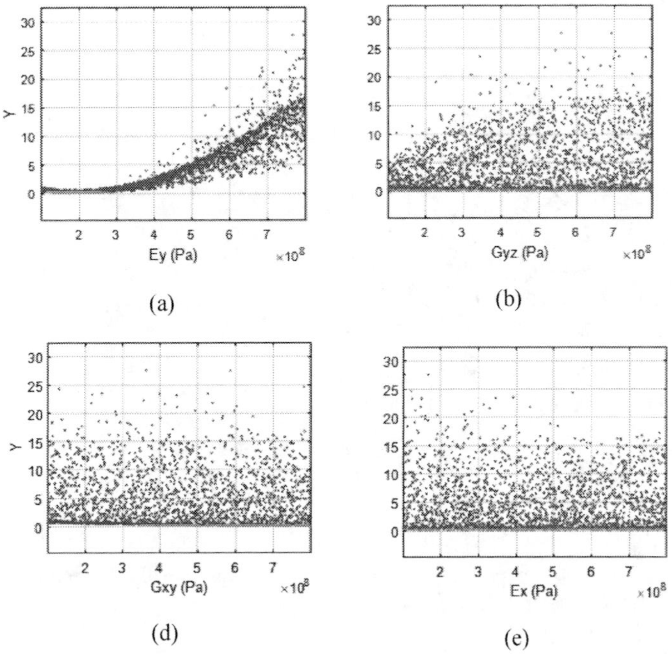

Figure 6. Scatter plots of Y function against elastic properties samples (B models: green dots).

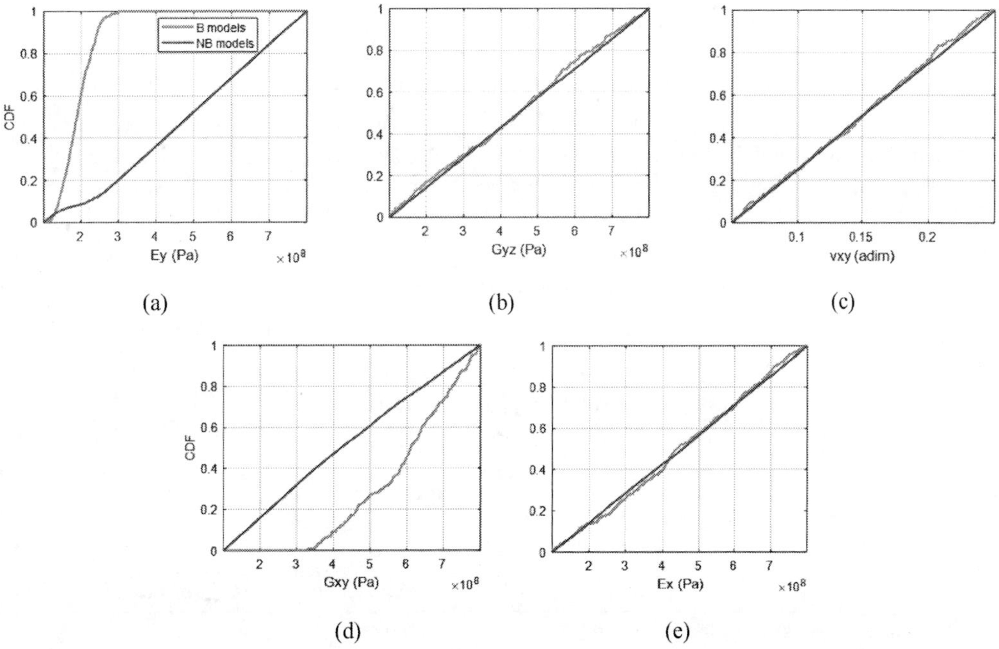

Figure 7. CDF curves for B and NB models for elastic properties.

Although our results differ from those proposed in Chilean masonry design codes [22-23], they are consistent with what was observed in the tested URM wall. The low values of E_y could be explained by the presence of cracks and partial loss of bonding in mortar-brick interface. On the other hand, the high values of G_{xy} could be justified by the transversal and longitudinal brick interlocking in the wall. The aforementioned situations are shown in Figure 8.

(a) (b)

Figure 8. (a) Cracking and bonding problems in observed URM specimen, and (b) Transversal and longitudinal interlocking of bricks in the wall.

To further limiting the mechanical properties range of values and assessing the effectiveness of the model updating process, we examined the 5% of the best and worst results, as shown in Table 3 and Table 4.

It is observed in Table 3 that 5% of the best models have excellent results. It is observed that the second and third frequencies overestimate the experimental values by only 7% on average, while the first frequency underestimates the measured values by 16%. Regarding to the mode shapes, the modal assurance criterion (MAC) was good for the first and third modes (>96%) but deficient for the second mode (74%). The mechanical properties of these models are within the ranges predicted by the RSA method.

The 5% of the worst models shown in Table 4 have significant errors in the estimation of frequencies, especially for the first and second mode (>80%). However, the MAC values were similar to those of 5% of the best models, suggesting that the elastic properties are better correlated with the frequencies than with the modes of vibration.

Table 3. Results of 5% best models

		Elastic properties		Model updating performance					
Statistics	Y function	E_y [MPa]	G_{xy} [MPa]	f_1 error [%]	f_2 error [%]	f_3 error [%]	MAC_1	MAC_2	MAC_3
Mean	0.13	183	740	-15.36	7.83	6.53	0.97	0.74	0.99
CoV (%)	8.55	7.03	6.71	18.88	49.38	-46.87	0.03	0.55	0.05

Table 4. Results of 5% worst models

		Elastic properties		Model updating performance					
Statistics	Y function	E_y [MPa]	G_{xy} [MPa]	f_1 error [%]	f_2 error [%]	f_3 error [%]	MAC_1	MAC_2	MAC_3
Mean	21.95	756	430	81.02	124.94	-16.66	0.97	0.58	0.99
CoV (%)	11.12	4.87	39.19	8.43	4.68	-71.76	0.09	23.50	0.37

4. CONCLUSIONS

In this paper, we have described a new approach to estimate the elastic properties of URM walls based on OMA techniques, FEM updating, and global sensitivity analysis. We have obtained satisfactory results showing that this methodology can be extended to more complicated structural configurations.

Global sensitivity analysis provides a powerful tool for estimating the elastic properties of URM walls that present high heterogeneity due to inherent material anisotropy, damage and brick-mortar interaction. In the first stage, it is recommended to use the EET method to detect the elastic properties that have little influence on the dynamic behaviour of the wall, to exclude them from the subsequent analysis to decrease the computational cost. Then the RSA method can be used to find the ranges of values of the relevant elastic properties that minimize the differences between the experimental and numerical modal properties.

For the studied URM wall, the SSI-UPC method was more effective than the EFDD in detecting the first three out-of-plane mode shapes. The most significant differences were seen in the second mode shape where the EFDD and SSI-UPC methods had 25% and 95% effectiveness, respectively. These results demonstrate the advantages of the SSI-UPC method for detecting modes with close frequencies.

The proposed elastic properties minimized the differences between the numerical and experimental frequencies to less than 20% in the first three modes, which is satisfactory for this type of applications. Further work needs to be done to establish whether the low MAC value of the second mode is related to local damage in the URM wall.

ACKNOWLEDGEMENTS

This work was carried out within the framework of the Civil Engineering Doctoral Program at Universidad Católica de la Santísima Concepcion (UCSC). Support was given by the UCSC Research Direction that funded the initial stage of this study (Proyecto DIN 06/2013).

REFERENCES

[1] Lourenço, P. B. (2004). Current experimental and numerical issues in masonry research. In: Sismica 2004-6° Congresso de Sismologia e Engenharia Sismica. Universidade do Minho. Guimaraes. 119-136.

[2] Wijanto, L. S. (2007). Seismic Assessment of Unreinforced Masonry Walls. Ph.D. Dissertation, University of Canterbury, Christchurch, New Zealand

[3] Paulay, T., & Priestley, M. N. (1992). Seismic design of reinforced concrete and masonry buildings. Wiley, New York, USA.

[4] Lumantarna, R., Biggs, D. T., & Ingham, J. M. (2012). Uniaxial compressive strength and stiffness of field-extracted and laboratory-constructed masonry prisms. Journal of Materials in Civil Engineering, 26(4), 567-575.

[5] Casciati, S., & Al-Saleh, R. (2010). Dynamic behavior of a masonry civic belfry under operational conditions. Acta mechanica, 215(1-4), 211-224.

[6] Chiorino, M. A., Ceravolo, R., Spadafor, A., Zanotti Fragonara, L., & Abbiati, G. (2011). Dynamic characterization of complex masonry structures: the Sanctuary of Vicoforte. International Journal of Architectural Heritage, 5(3), 296-314.

[7] Boscato, G., Russo, S., & Sciarretta, F. (2011). Mechanical performance of very old masonry walls after earthquake assessed by ND testing: the case of L'Aquila. In 9th Australasian Masonry Conference, Queenstown, New Zealand, 15th-18th February.

[8] Rainieri, C., & Fabbrocino, G. (2012). Estimating the elastic period of Masonry towers. In Topics in Modal Analysis I, Volume 5 (pp. 243-248). Springer, New York, NY.

[9] Fabbrocino, F. (2016). Estimation of the natural periods of existing masonry towers through empirical procedure. International Journal of Sustainable Materials and Structural Systems, 2(3-4), 250-261.

[10] Boscato, G., Russo, S., Ceravolo, R., & Fragonara, L. Z. (2015). Global sensitivity-based model updating for heritage structures. Computer-Aided Civil and Infrastructure Engineering, 30(8), 620-635.

[11] Chávez, M., Behrens, E., Oyarzo, C. (2015) Caracterización de las propiedades mecánicas de la albañilería basada en ensayos vibratorios no destructivos. In: XI Congreso Chileno de Sismología e Ingeniería Sísmica. Santiago, Chile.

[12] Brincker, R., Zhang, L., & Andersen, P. (2001). Modal identification of output-only systems using frequency domain decomposition. Smart materials and structures, 10(3), 441.

[13] Van Overschee, P., & De Moor, B. (1996). Subspace Identification for Linear Systems: Theory, Implementation, Applications. Kluwer Academics Publishers.

[14] ARTeMIS Modal Pro, Version 5.3, Structural Vibration Solutions A/S, Aalborg Denmark, Copyright 1999–2013.

[15] ANSYS® Academic Research Mechanical, Release 19.2

[16] Teughels, A., & De Roeck, G. (2004). Structural damage identification of the highway bridge Z24 by FE model updating. Journal of Sound and Vibration, 278(3), 589-610.

[17] Campolongo, F., Saltelli, A., & Cariboni, J. (2011). From screening to quantitative sensitivity analysis. A unified approach. Computer Physics Communications, 182(4), 978-988.

[18] Saltelli, A., Ratto, M., Andres, T., Campolongo, F., Cariboni, J., Gatelli, D., Saisana, M. & Tarantola, S. (2008). Global sensitivity analysis: the primer. John Wiley & Sons.

[19] Pianosi, F., Beven, K., Freer, J., Hall, J. W., Rougier, J., Stephenson, D. B., & Wagener, T. (2016). Sensitivity analysis of environmental models: A systematic review with practical workflow. Environmental Modelling & Software, 79, 214-232.

[20] Pianosi, F., Sarrazin, F., & Wagener, T. (2015). A Matlab toolbox for global sensitivity analysis. Environmental Modelling & Software, 70, 80-85.

[21] Forrester, A., Sobester, A., & Keane, A. (2008). Engineering design via surrogate modelling: a practical guide. John Wiley & Sons.

[22] Instituto Nacional de Normalización. (2009) Albañilería armada-requisitos para el diseño y cálculo, NCh1928.

[23] Instituto Nacional de Normalización. (2003) Albañilería confinada-requisitos para el diseño y cálculo, NCh2123.

IOMAC'19

8th International Operational Modal Analysis Conference
2019 May13-15 Copenhagen

EXPERIMENTAL AND OPERATIONAL MODAL ANALYSIS IN SUPPORT OF MODAL MODEL UPDATING – A TEST CASE.

Jacopo Valentino Covioli[1], *Giuliano Coppotelli*[2]

[1] PhD Student, Sapienza University of Rome, covioli.1804032@studenti.uniroma1.it.
[2] Professor, Sapienza University of Rome, giuliano.coppotelli@uniroma1.it.

ABSTRACT

The introduction of new equipment on board an aircraft requires fatigue evaluations for reliability prediction purposes. To do so, the model must be updated with experimental modal data. The purpose of this paper is to compare Experimental Modal Analysis (EMA) and Operational Modal Analysis (OMA) methods in determining modal parameters for a test case, consisting in a new equipment installed on board an in-service helicopter, in support of model updating for fatigue predictions. EMA data are obtained executing a Ground Vibration Test (GVT), during which the test item is excited by localized white noise input generated by a shaker. OMA data are collected in different flight conditions by a set of accelerometers located at the same positions of the EMA test setup. The OMA method is recursively applied for different flight conditions and flight phases. Following EMA and OMA method application, related modal parameters are quantitatively compared to detect deviations in the modal characterization of the test item.

Keywords: modal model updating, experimental modal analysis, operational modal analysis, helicopter, flight, frequency domain, harmonic.

1. INTRODUCTION

The introduction of new equipment on board an aircraft requires fatigue evaluations for reliability prediction purposes. This is particularly true when complex assemblies are required to be installed in areas exposed to combined stresses, most commonly vibrational, either random or harmonic. Beside a thorough characterization of the stress environment, an accurate equipment modal model is the basis to quantitatively determine whether the fatigue safe-life goal is met. Several techniques are available to estimate the modal parameters. Besides those techniques based on the measurements of both the input excitation and the corresponding output response, also known as Experimental Modal Analysis (EMA) techniques, the and Operational Modal Analysis (OMA) methods are gaining greater and greater interest in the scientific community because only the mesurement of the output response is required, provided that a random, in space and in the time domain, loading is characterizing the operating environment [1-3]. Albeit these assumptions are quite stringent, when compared to EMA methods, OMA techniques provide modal parameters for all the modes excited under real stress and constraint conditions, which might not be the case for EMA. The focus of the paper is the dynamic characterization of a new equipment installed on board an in-service helicopter, in support of model updating for fatigue predictions. The effects of such structural modifications to the fatigue properties were the ultimate goal of the activity. Experimental modal parameters were estimated with the EMA approach during a Ground Vibration Test. Keeping the measurement chain (accelerometers and acquisition system), sensors position and Degrees Of Freedom (DOFs) unaltered from the GVT, flight data were collected at 5 straight, level unaccelerated flight conditions. The Hilbert Transform Method (HTM), in its enhanced version, provided a direct estimation of the Frequency Response Functions (FRFs) for modal parameters fitting. Harmonic components in the FRF were removed by signal Kurtosis minima identification within the harmonic excitation band. Flight test OMA – HTM results were compared to EMA-GVT to determine whether any correlation was present.

2. THEORETICAL BACKGROUND

2.1. The Hilbert Transform Method

The Hilbert Transform Method takes advantage of analytic signals properties. The real and imaginary parts of an analytic signal are real functions, which could be mutually expressed by the Hilbert Transform [4]. Given a signal Power Spectral Density (PSD) $G_{y_i y_i}$ at the *i-th* driving point, it is possible to demonstrate [3] that, in case of purely random gaussian input

$$\overline{H_{ii}}(\omega) = \sqrt{G_{y_i y_i}(\omega)e^{j\phi_{ii}(\omega)}}$$

$$\phi_{ii}(\omega) = -\frac{1}{2}\mathrm{H}\left[\ln\left(G_{y_i y_i}(\omega)\right)\right]$$

where $\overline{H_{ii}}(\omega)$, $\phi_{ii}(\omega)$ are the bias FRF absolute value and phase at frequency ω respectively, H is the Hilbert transform Operator. For the FRF off diagonal terms, it is also possible to show that

$$\overline{H_{ij}}(\omega) = \frac{G_{y_i y_j}(\omega)}{\overline{H_{ii}}(\omega)}$$

Thus, starting from the auto and cross PSD of a signals set, it is possible to determine the FRF matrix

2.2. Harmonic identification

OMA methods, including the HTM, requires a white noise input to be present with no harmonic signal components acting in the band of interest. Thus, OMA application on helicopter structures shall be carried out with a clear understanding of rotor harmonics effects over the frequency band of interest. Harmonic signals identification is currently treated with several approaches, based on Singular Value Decomposition (SVD), Modal Assurance Criterion (MAC), Short Time Fast Fourier Transform (STFFT) and signal statistical properties [6,7]. For this research, a statistical approach was considered using the kurtosis index γ, expressed as

$$\gamma(y|\mu,\sigma) = \frac{E[(y-\mu)^4]}{\sigma^4} - 3$$

Where y represents the output signal, μ and σ are the signal average and standard deviation respectively, and E denotes the expectation value. With the formulation above, γ values range from positive (leptokurtic) to -1.5 (platykurtic), the latter indicating a pure harmonic component is present. A value of 0 indicates the signal as perfect random gaussian (mesokurtic).

3. TEST ITEM AND INSTRUMENTATION

The test item consisted on a 2 meters aluminium beam protruding starboard of a helicopter. The beam was interfaced with the helicopter through a truss structure secured on the helicopter main cabin floor. The aluminium beam extended for 1 meter from the helicopter fuselage shell. A 6kg payload was attached to the external beam tip. To ensure an adequate bending stiffness, two additional steel rods connected the beam tip and the supporting truss structure. Four triaxial accelerometers were installed along the beam, located at 30, 50, 70 and 90 centimetres from the truss structure side edge. The complete setup is illustrated in Figure 1.

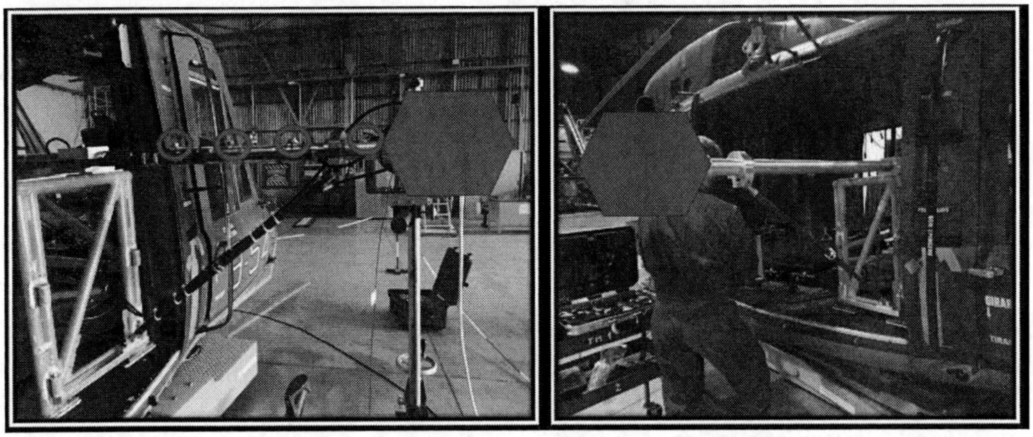

Figure 1. Test setup (blue hexagon: payload, red circles: accelerometers).

4. TEST RESULTS

4.1. Ground Vibration Test Results

To avoid skid modes, the GVT was conducted with the helicopter belly-supported with an electro-hydraulic towing cart. This resulted in a no contact condition between the skids and the ground, which was desired. The main beam was excited at the tip along the Z an X directions with a shaker. A random signal was fed in input, measured with a force cell located between the beam and the shaker sting. A total of two runs (one for each excitation direction) were conducted at a sampling frequency of 256Hz, with 30 averages. The resulting spectral resolution was 0.0625Hz. For each run, accelerometers responses along the helicopter X and Z axes were recorded. A total of 2 FRFs matrices were directly computed, with 8 DOFs. Coherence values were acceptable (minimum value 0.9) at frequencies higher than 5 Hz. Stable poles and modes shapes were calculated with Least Squares Complex Exponential Algorithm (LSCE)[4] up to a maximum fit order of 50. Poles stability criteria was set to 1% for the natural frequency and 5% for the damping ratio. Modes at frequencies lower than 6 Hz were excluded and observation of the stabilization diagram conducted to a further refinement, as shown in Figure 2. A set of 17 mode shapes was selected as result of the analysis process. Natural frequencies and damping ratios are reported in Table 1. It is important to note that, considering a rotor speed of 324 RPM with two blades, the Blade Passage Frequency (BPF) was 10.8 Hz. Thus, only the 7th and the 8th modes were potentially coupling within $\pm 5\%$ of the 6th and the 8th harmonic.

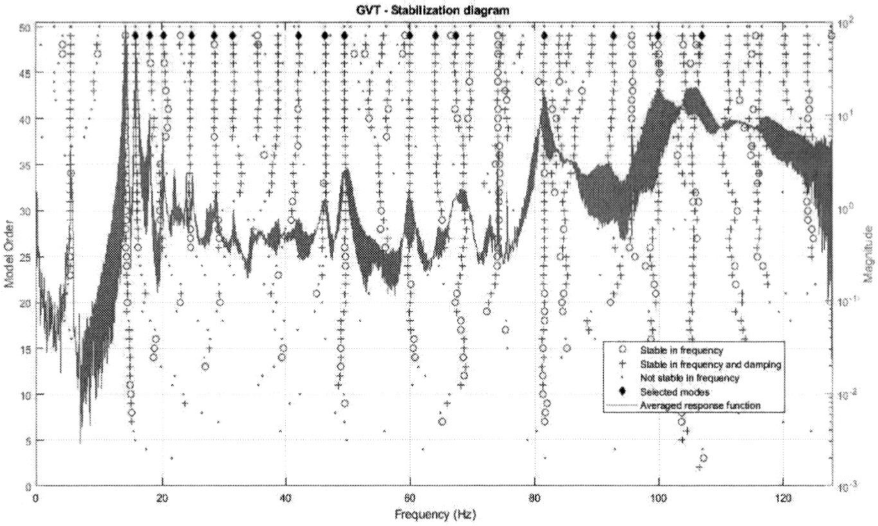

Figure 2. Stabilizatrion diagram from HTM.

Table 1. EMA modal parameters.

	Natural Frequency f_n [Hz]	Damping Ratio ξ [%]	Potential rotor coupling
1	14.29	0,58	-
2	15.87	0,92	-
3	18.07	1,75	-
4	20.31	1,97	-
5	25.08	1,28	-
6	28.89	1,16	-
7	31.86	1,77	6*BPF
8	42.29	2,09	8*BPF
9	46.54	1,60	-
10	49.62	1,57	-
11	59.88	1,96	-
12	64.26	1,46	-
13	67.24	2,27	-
14	81.55	1,20	-
15	92.79	1,86	-
16	99.93	0,78	-
17	106.98	1,47	-

4.2. OMA Flight Test Results

Flight test data were collected at 5 airspeeds from 40 to 110 knots Indicated Airspeed (IAS). Each test point consisted in a 30s stabilization in straight, level, unaccelerated flight. The flight test instrumentation layout was the same as for the GVT. The first analysis step consisted in identifying the harmonic response bands. For this purpose, the kurtosis was determined for each channel at each test point. An example is given in Figure 3. Spectral kurtosis minima lie at expected BPF minima. It is also important to note that the rotor transmission contribution (0.5*BPF) and its harmonics have a quite significant effect. At each airspeed, the frequency bands affected by harmonic excitation were identified imposing a spectral kurtosis threshold of -0.88. This value was determined by observation of all the test points.

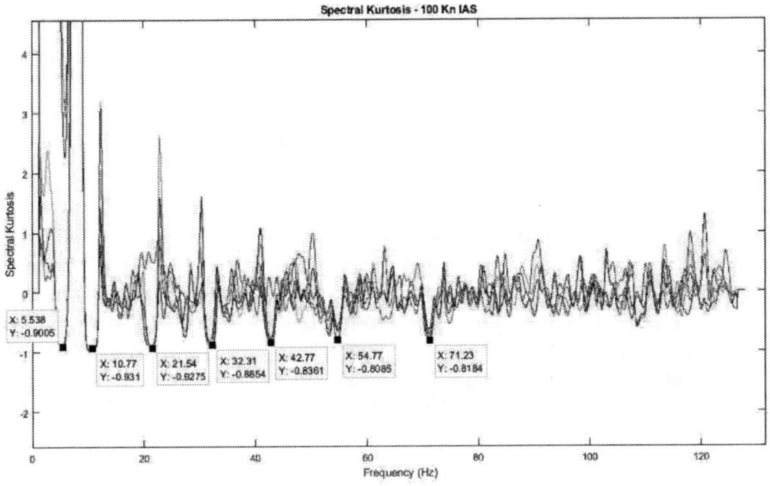

Figure 3. Spectral kurtosis.

The second step in data analysis was to estimate the biased FRFs using the HTM method. Then, modal parameters were estimated with the LSCE method, with the same stability criteria imposed for the EMA case. Poles and related mode shapes whose natural frequencies were inside a harmonic band were excluded as shown in Figure 4.

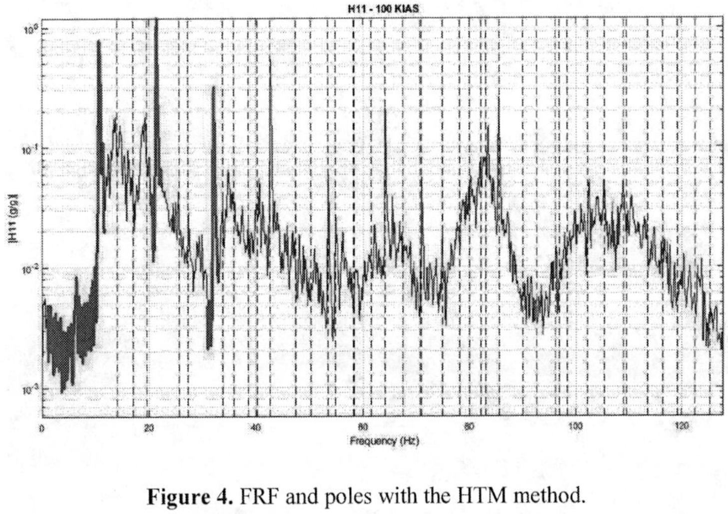

Figure 4. FRF and poles with the HTM method.

4.3. EMA and OMA test results comparison

An assessment on EMA and OMA parameters estimation results is quantitatively and qualitatively carried out. The Modal Assurance Criterion (MAC) was computed in its classical, complex (MACX) and complex-pole weighted (MACXP) form [8,9] between the EMA and OMA modes, at each airspeed. Maximum values observed over airspeeds are reported in Table 2.

Table 2. Maximum MAC values between EMA and OMA.

Airspeed	MAC		MACX		MACXP	
(KIAS)	Maximum value	EMA/OMA f_n (Hz)	Maximum value	EMA/OMA f_n (Hz)	Maximum value	EMA/OMA f_n (Hz)
40	0.6624	25.08/53.27	0.6854	25.08/53.27	0.1669	25.08/24.95
60	0.7929	25.08/98.67	0.9111	25.08/98.67	0.8193	25.08/25.73
80	0.7821	25.08/117.96	0.8410	28.89/109.4	0.0945	99.93/100.5
100	0.5427	25.08/70.99	0.6841	81.55/70.99	0.1148	67.24/67.51
110	0.6624	25.08/53.27	0.6854	25.08/53.27	0.1669	25.08/25.80

Overall, looking at MAC and MACX, there is a poor correlation between EMA and OMA modes that shall be investigated. Even if the 60 KIAS test point suggests a sort of correlation is present between EMA and OMA mode shapes, natural frequencies are very different. It is interesting to note that MACXP maximum values, although very low when compared to the common 0.9 threshold, are obtained in correspondence of approximately the same natural frequency. These results suggest some spatial aliasing is affecting the test set that the MACXP is optimized to compensate for [5]. Looking at the MACXP pattern of Figure 5, it is possible to infer that similar results might be obtained at MACXP maxima for each mode. Table 3 confirms the deduction in that EMA and OMA natural frequencies and associated damping ratios are similar, despite mode shapes are dissimilar, as evidenced in Figure 6 and 7. Regarding the spatial aliasing, the Auto MACX pattern of Figure 8 clearly shows large correlation in off diagonal positions between EMA modes, confirming the aliased condition.

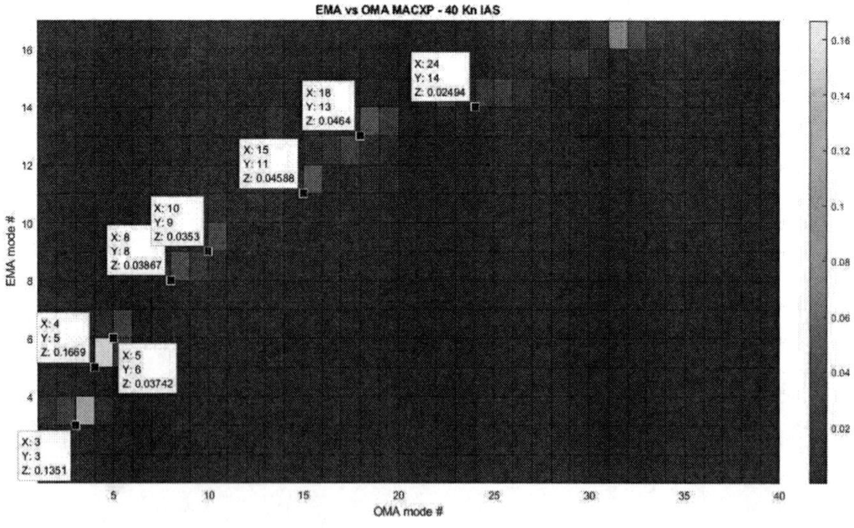

Figure 5. MACXP map – 40 KIAS

Table 3. Natural frequency and damping ratio comparison between MACXP correlated modes.

EMA/OMA – 40 KIAS				
EMA mode #	OMA mode #	MACXP	EMA/OMA f_n [Hz]	EMA/OMA ξ [%]
3	3	0.1315	18.07/19.10	1.75/8.62
5	4	0.1669	25.08/24.95	1.28/5.88
6	5	0.0374	28.89/27.26	1.16/1.26
8	8	0.0387	42.29/40.66	2.09/2.92
9	10	0.0353	46.54/46.61	1.60/2.51
11	15	0.0459	59.88/58.29	1.96/1.22
13	18	0.0464	67.24/67.22	2.27/2.06
14	24	0.02494	81.59/83.31	1.20/1.27

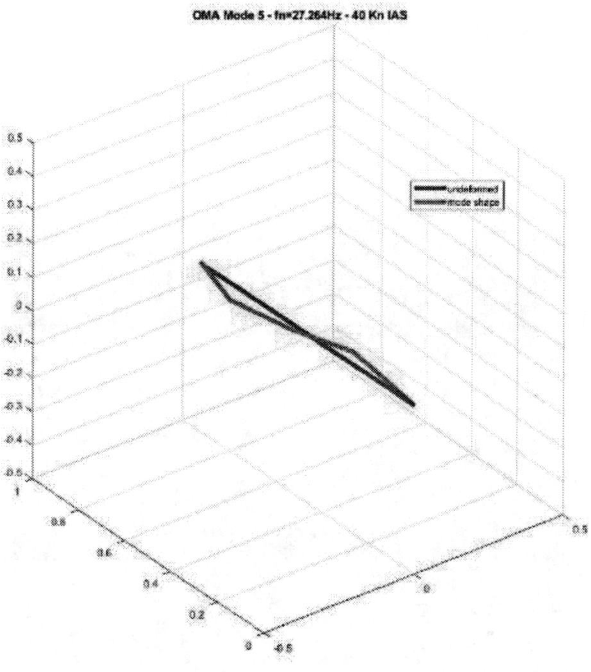

Figure 6. OMA mode shape #5

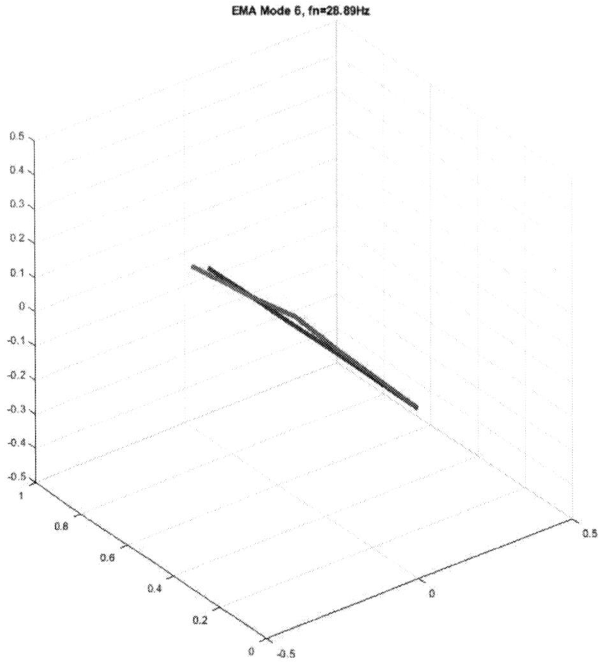

Figure 6. EMA mode shape #6

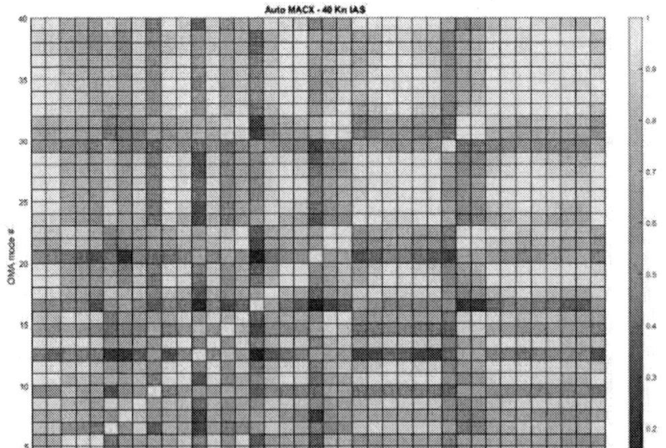

Figure 7. OMA Auto MACX map – 40 KIAS

5. MODEL UPDATING – PRELIMINARY RESULTS

Since the modal parameters estimated using the GVT and the OMAapproaches provided similar results, as highlighted by the MAXP correlation index, the modal basis used for updating the structureal model is not referring to any estimating method for the next part of the paper. A preliminary finite element model has been developed to assess the overall procedure. The test structure of Fig. 1 has been represented by a truss-like model, using beam and bar elements. Such a preliminary model does not take into account the supporting structure, located inside the helicopter cabin. Thus instead of a clamped beam end, two rotational springs (along the two bending axes) have been introduced to model the junction between the test article and the supporting structure. Additional model data are reported in Table 4.

Table 4. Model data

MATERIEL DATA					
	Element type	Material	Young Modulus	Density	Cross sectional area
			GPa	Kg/m^3	m^2
Main beam	Beam	Alluminum	73.1	2780	1.96 x 10^{-3}
Supporing beam	Rod	Steel	200	8000	1.52 x 10^{-4}

The resulting number of degrees of freedom is 150. The payload is simulated with a tip lumped mass of 6Kg. A representation of the model is depicted in Figure 9.

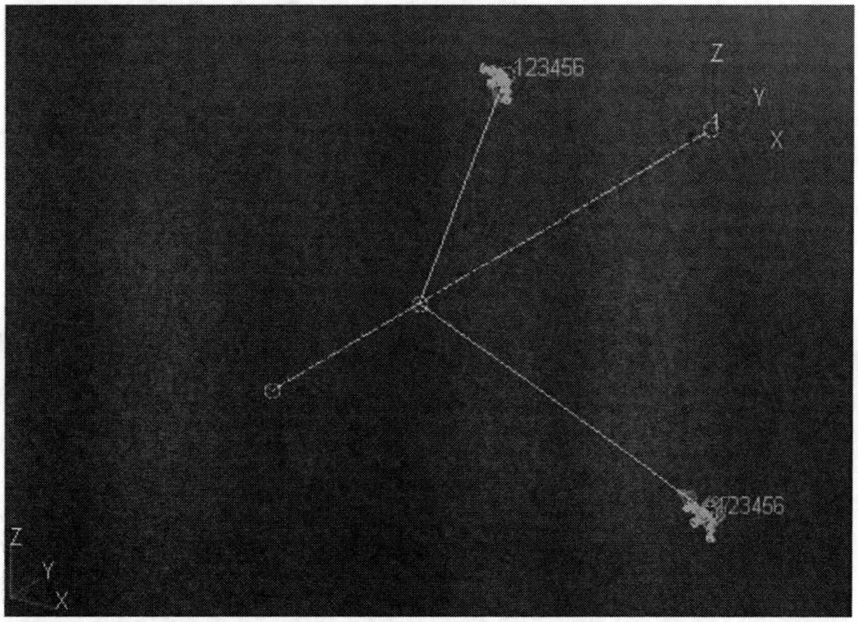

Figure 9. Test structure model

Starting from the nominal values of the structural parameters (such as Young modula, mass densities and the lumped spring torsional stiffness) the initial set of modal paramaters has been identified as the starting point for model validation. The lower frequency properties drove such numerical tuning with the experimental findings. The Finite Element Analysis (FEA) modes, indentified in the 13 - 17 Hz frequency range, has been paired the experimental counterparts following the highest MAC criteria. Results are presented in Table 5. From such a table it is evident that the numerical model is not accurate enough to catch the experimental dynamic behavior and therefore major improvements are required. However, instead of refining the F.E. model it has been chosen to update the actual numerical model by considering the third mode only. Indeed, this mode 3 is characterized by the higher mode correlation and the lower natural frequency shift with respect to the other twos. The following model tuning was accomplished with iterative methods [6], perturbing the spring stiffness values at the beam root as parameter, MAC and the natural frequency as the responses. The final result is presented in Table 6 and Figure 10.

Table 5. Experimental and numerical mode shapes pairing before updating

MODE SHAPE PAIRING BEFORE UPDATE				
FEA Mode		Experimental Mode		MAC
#	[Hz]	#	[Hz]	%
1	8.08	15	92.79	61.9
2	13. 73	9	46.54	24.3
3	15.31	1	14.29	89.5

The updated model was obtained after 10 iterations with a 16% total variation on the perturbed parameter (rotational spring stiffness along Z axis of Figure 9) from the initial condition at 3000 Nm^4. Considering an equivalent alluminum circular beam cross section, its area should be excessively small (4.1 x 10^{-2} mm^2). Thus, the resulting model is not representative of the physical propeties of the actual structure but dynamically equivalent.

Table 6. Experimental and model mode shapes pairing before updating

MODEL UPDATING RESULTS				
Updated mode		Experimental mode		MAC
#	[Hz]	#	[Hz]	%
3	14.21	1	14.29	96.4

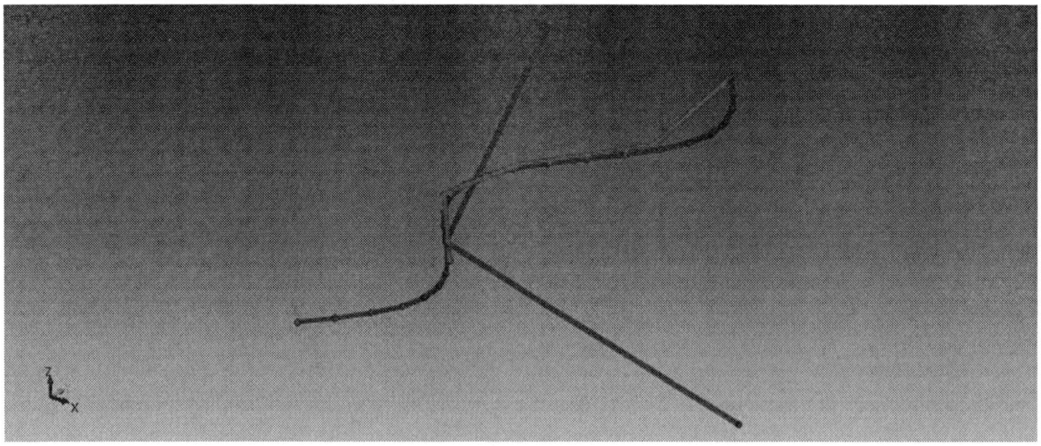

Figure 10. Updated modes compared to experimental

6. CONCLUDING REMARKS

In this paper, a comparison between EMA and OMA methods for the modal characterization of a helicopter structural modification was carried out. Identical sensors position, measurements chain and modal extraction methods helped to reach the highest possible level of comparability between the two methods. Ground and flight test data were processed with classical EMA and recent OMA methods respectively to fit modal parameters. Modal fit results pointed out that spatial aliasing prevented a straightforward correlation between EMA and OMA mode shapes. Nevertheless, natural frequencies and damping ratios were extracted from OMA data and associated to the corresponding EMA dataset, taking advantage of a pole-weighted MAC. Overall, EMA and OMA methods provided similar results when dealing with natural frequencies and damping. The model updating process, although accurate, was limited to only one mode. Considering the close correlation between EMA and OMA in terms of poles, it is possible to say that the modelling accuracy shall be refined to improve the agreement between the test and the model before updating, eventually including additional GVT runs to improve mode shapes characterisation over the entire structure.Further studies will focus on three research paths. First, the process will be repeated applying different OMA techniques and changing analysis parameters to eventually improve modal estimates. Second, a finite element model of the structure under test will be validated both with EMA and OMA data. Lastly, the MACXP maxima pattern for natural frequency and damping identification will be consolidated to be used in modal parameters identification.

ACKNOWLEDGEMENTS

The authors would like to thank the Italian Air Force for providing their valuable support in this research.

This research has been supported by "F.E. model updating of remotely piloted aircraft (RPA) using flight test data", 2015, University of Rome *"La Sapienza"*.

REFERENCES

[1] L. Hermans, H. Van der Auweraer, Industrial Applicability of Modal Analysis on Op- erating Data", Proc. NATO Advance Study Institute on Modal Analysis and Testing, Seimbra (P), (1998).

[2] R. Brincker, L. Zhang, P. Andersen, Modal Identification from Ambient Responses Using Frequency Domain Decomposition, XVIII IMAC, S. Antonio, TX, (USA), (2000).

[3] A. Agneni, L. Balis Crema, G. Coppotelli, (2010) Output-Only Analysis of Structures with Closely Spaced Modes, Mechanical System and Signal Processing. Special Issue: Operational Modal Analysis, Vol 24, N. 5, July, pp. 1240-1249, ISSN: 0888-3270, doi: 10.1016/j.ymssp.2009.10.013.

[4] Mertins, A.(1999) *Signal Analysis*. Chichester, John Wiley Sons Ltd.

[5] Jacobsen, N-J., Andersen, P., & Brincker, R. (2007). Eliminating the Influence of Harmonic Components in Operational Modal Analysis. In Conference Proceedings: IMAC-XXIV : A Conference & Exposition on Structural Dynamics Society for Experimental Mechanics

[6] Brown, D., Allemang, R., Zimmerman, R., and Mergeay, M.(1979). Parameter Estimation Techniques for Modal Analysis. SAE Technical Paper 790221.

[7] Agneni A, Coppotelli G., Grappasonni C (2012). A Method for the Harmonic Removal in Operational Modal Analysis of Rotating Blades. MECHANICAL SYSTEMS AND SIGNAL PROCESSING, vol. 27, p. 604-618, ISSN: 0888-3270, doi: 10.1016/j.ymssp.2011.09.013

[8] P. Vacher, B. Jacquier, A. Bucharles, "Extensions of the MAC criterion to complex modes. In: *Proceedings of ISMA 2010 including USD2010* (pp. 2713-2726).

[9] Covioli J. V., Coppotelli G., De Paolis P., D' Argenio A., and Mariani S.. "Study on a modified mode tracking technique in support of aeroelastic stability verification by flight testing", AIAA Scitech 2019 Forum, AIAA SciTech Forum, (AIAA 2019-1536), https://doi.org/10.2514/6.2019-1536

IOMAC'19
8th International Operational Modal Analysis Conference
2019 May13-15 Copenhagen

FE MODELLING FOR SEISMIC ASSESSMENT OF AN ANCIENT TOWER FROM AMBIENT VIBRATION SURVEY

C. Gentile[1], *A. Saisi*[2], *P. Borlenghi*[3]

[1] Professor, Department of Architecture, Built environment and Construction engineering (DABC), Politecnico di Milano, e-mail address: carmelo.gentile@polimi.it
[2] Assistant Professor, Department of Architecture, Built environment and Construction engineering (DABC), Politecnico di Milano, e-mail address: antonella.saisi@polimi.it
[3] Ph.D. Candidate, Department of Architecture, Built environment and Construction engineering (DABC), Politecnico di Milano, e-mail address: paolo.borlenghi@polimi.it

ABSTRACT

The paper exemplifies the application of the methodology involving historical and architectural research complemented by ambient vibration survey in the structural assessment of the so-called Zuccaro's tower in Mantua, Italy. The tower is about 43.0 m high and built in solid brick masonry. The good knowledge of the structural geometry and the large number of identified vibration modes allowed to establish a 3D numerical model of the tower for the quantitative assessment of its seismic vulnerability. It is worth underlining that: (a) the elastic parameters of the model, which were identified by minimizing the difference between numerical and experimental resonant frequencies, exhibited an excellent agreement with the available characterization of the masonry material (which was found in the archives and dates back to the '90s); (b) the proposed methodology involves only non-destructive tests and might allow relatively quick seismic assessment of ancient towers at the territorial level.

Keywords: Non-destructive testing, Masonry towers, Ambient vibration test, Model updating

1. INTRODUCTION

The assessment of ancient masonry towers is a challenging multidisciplinary activity, involving different tasks. Once the geometry of the building has been retrieved through the topographic survey, qualitative information results from historical research and direct inspections so that important data are made available on the geometric arrangement, the construction techniques and the mapping of discontinuities and damages. Operational modal testing and analysis (even carried out using a reduced number of sensors) could supplement the previous investigation steps, contributing to the diagnosis of historic towers with quantitative parameters, which are representative of the structural condition.

The paper exemplifies the application of the methodology involving historical and architectural research, complemented by the dynamic survey, for the structural assessment of the Zuccaro's tower in Mantua, Italy (Fig. 1). The tower is approximately 43 m high, built in solid brick masonry with eight timber floors and a masonry cross-vault covering the ground level. The relatively good knowledge of the structural geometry, along with the complete inspection carried out and the large number of identified vibration modes allowed to establish a 3D numerical model of the tower. It is worth underlining that:

(a) the developed model reproduces with good accuracy the geometry and out-of-plumb of the tower, the connection with the neighboring buildings, the stiffening of timber floors and the observed characteristics of the lower 7 vibration modes;
(b) the elastic parameters of the model, which were identified by minimizing the difference between numerical and experimental resonant frequencies, exhibited an excellent agreement with the available characterization of the masonry material (which was found in the archives and dated back to the '90s). Furthermore, the proposed methodology involves only non-destructive tests and might allow relatively quick seismic assessment of ancient towers at the territorial level.

2. THE ZUCCARO'S TOWER IN MANTUA, ITALY

The Zuccaro's Tower (Fig. 1) is an ancient defensive structure built in Mantua during the Middle Ages. It is about 43 m high and has an approximately square plan with a side of 8.5 m. The masonry walls are built in solid bricks and lime mortar with a thickness ranging from 1.1m, at the base, to 0.8m at the top. The tower includes eight timber floors and a masonry cross vault at the first level. Furthermore, it is surrounded by buildings on three sides up to the height of 10 m, and the only entrance is from the S-W side, toward *don Tazzoli* Street.

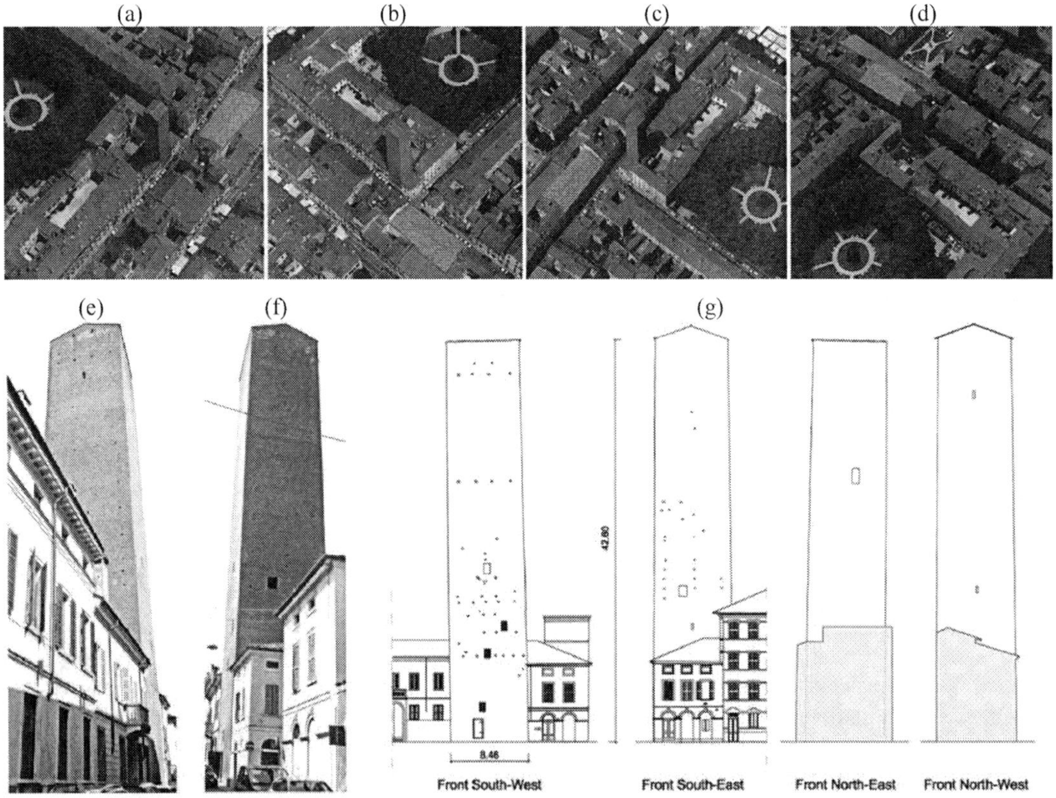

Figure 1. The investigated tower: 3D views from Google Earth of the west (a), south (b), east (c) and north corners (d); pictures from the ground level from the west (e) and south corners (f); and geometric survey of the external façades (g).

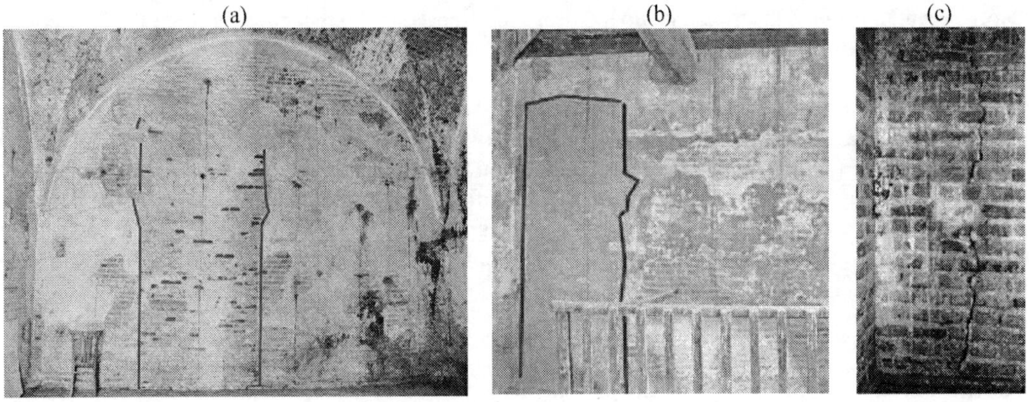

Figure 2. Details of masonry cracks and discontinuities: (a) ground floor, N-E front, (b) 1st floor, S-E front and (c) 3rd floor, S-W front.

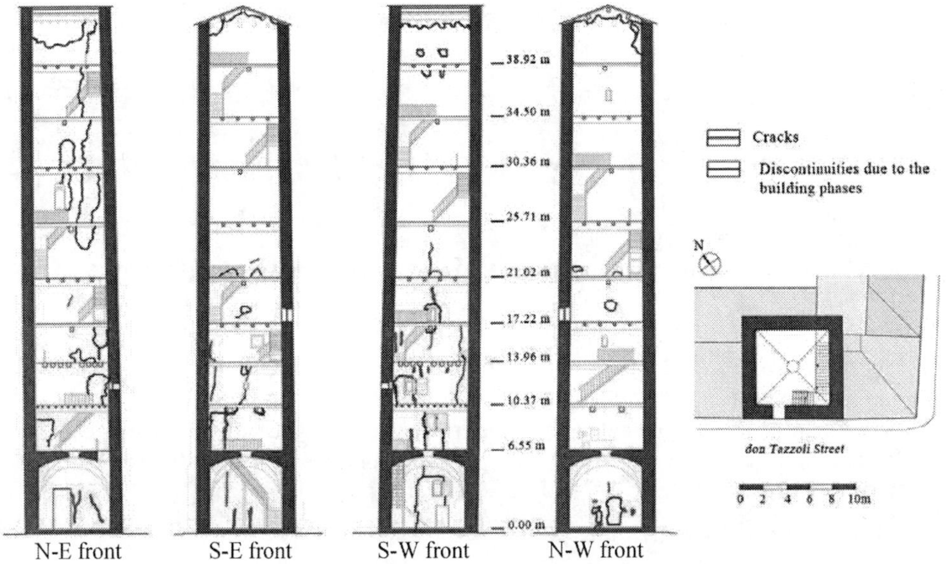

Figure 3. Damage survey and crack patterns of the inner fronts.

2.1. Historical and documentary research

The original defensive role of the structure is demonstrated by its morphology and position: the openings are very few and small, and the location was at the limits of the Middle Ages fortifications. As reported by Saisi et al. [1], the first historical record regarding the existence of the tower dates back to 1143, but the lack of information regarding several transformations makes difficult to reconstruct the evolution phases of the structure completely. In 1533 the building was subjected to some not well-documented repairing interventions after the damages caused by lightning, while in 1717 a new access from *don Tazzoli* Street was opened and the roof rebuilt. Other information regarding the relationship with the neighboring constructions is obtained from the historical cartography [1]. During the XVI and XVII centuries, the tower was represented in a building aggregate, surrounded by low-rise buildings on two sides, with an entrance from the N-E front. Nowadays, the only entrance is on the opposite side, the former one was closed (Fig. 2a), and another construction is present on N-E side. Another map from the first half of the XIX century reveals the presence of an external staircase, which probably connected *don Tazzoli* Street with an upper entrance, as confirmed by the presence of infilled openings on that front (Fig. 2b).

More recently, in the 60s, some documents from the Local Superintendence reported the concerning about the bad state of preservation of the tower, requesting necessary inspections and interventions. Subsequently, a fire occurred in 1979, and several interventions were carried out in 1982, from the substitution of timber floors, roof and internal staircase to local masonry rebuilding, and the opening of new windows. Between 1994 and 1997 an extensive experimental campaign was carried out by ISMES [2], including the installation of a static monitoring system and the characterization of masonry materials: the average elastic modulus identified from the double flat jack tests (DFJT) at the base level was equal to 3.18 GPa. After the campaign, a strengthening intervention was carried out involving the substitution of the roof and timber floors, and the injection of expanding mortars in the main cracks.

2.2. Recent on-site investigations

An extensive campaign devoted to geometry and crack surveying was recently carried out by Saisi et al. [1]. Through visual inspection, it was possible to identify some sharp discontinuities and deep cracks around the corner between the S-W and S-E inner fronts (Fig. 2c) starting from the base up to 17.22 m. Furthermore, it was possible identifying some deep and thick cracks on the cross vault at the first level and extended dark areas on the inner walls' surfaces probably caused by the fire occurred in 1979. Furthermore, it is worth considering the presence of large areas with fragmentary and non-homogeneous brick masonry, especially in the N-E inner front, starting around 21.0 m (Fig. 3).

3. AMBIENT VIBRATION TESTS AND OPERATIONAL MODAL ANALYSIS

3.1. Testing procedure

Two ambient vibration tests were carried out to study the dynamic behavior of the tower. The first test was performed on 23-24 October 2016 with few sensors (i.e., four seismometers) placed at the top floor (Fig. 4a). A second test was carried out on 11-12 December 2017 with a larger number of measuring points (Fig. 4b-c) to evaluate the mode shapes of the building.

During the test of October 2016, two opposite corners at the 9th floor were instrumented employing four seismometers (electro-dynamic velocity transducers, SARA SS45, Fig. 4d). The structural response induced by ambient vibrations was recorded for twelve hours, during the night, with temperatures ranging between 10.3°C and 12.6°C, and a sampling rate of 200 Hz. The data were stored in 12 sets of 3600 s.

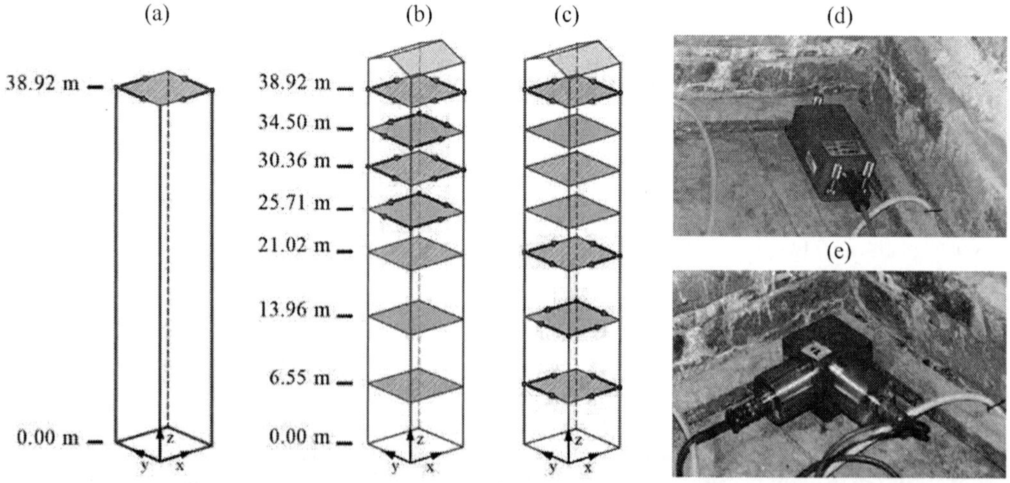

Figure 4. Sensors layout in the AVTs of the 23-24 October 2016 (a) and 11-12 December 2017 (b)-(c), and sensors employed in the first (d) and second (e) test.

(a) (b)

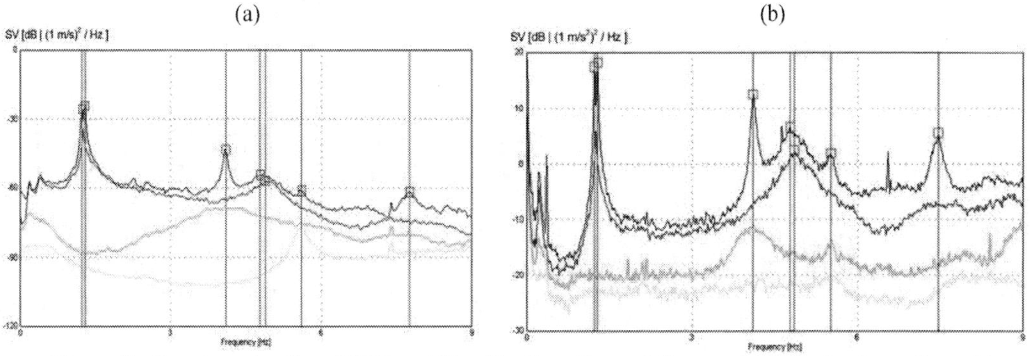

Figure 5. Singular value lines (FDD) and identification of natural frequencies from the data collected in October 2016 (a) and December 2017 (b).

The test of December 2017 was conducted with 14 points instrumented along the height of the tower, employing 28 WR 731A accelerometers (10 V/g sensitivity and ± 0.50 g peak acceleration, Fig. 4e) and a multi-channel acquisition system with NI 9234 data acquisition modules (24-bit resolution, 102 dB dynamic range and anti-aliasing filters). During the test of December 2017, the temperature ranged between −0.1°C and +2.0°C and the sampling frequency was set equal to 200 Hz.

3.2. Operational modal analysis (OMA) and results

As previously pointed out, the modal identification was performed by considering the accelerations induced by micro-tremors and wind. Time series of 3000 s were considered, and different output-only identification algorithms were employed to obtain an estimate of natural frequencies and mode shapes. The Frequency Domain Decomposition (FDD) [3] and the data-driven Stochastic Subspace Identification (SSI-data) [4], both available in the commercial software ARTeMIS [5], were applied to the recorded data.

The local maxima of the first singular value (SV) line, obtained from the processing of the recorded data, represent the vibration modes of the structure. Fig 5 shows the first four SV lines obtained from both tests where 7 modes were identified in the frequency range of 0-9 Hz. The estimates of the mode shapes are shown in Figs. 6 and 7 for the tests of October 2016 and December 2017 respectively. The sequence of the first five modes is consistent with past experimental studies on similar towers [6, 7, 8], while the last two modes seem to be very peculiar of this structure. In more detail, the first two modes are closely spaced well-defined bending modes in opposite directions (B_{y1} and B_{x1}), followed by a torsion mode (T_1) and another couple of higher-order bending modes (B_{y2} and B_{x2}). The peculiar shape of the last two modes is known as warping (W_1 and W_2) [1], which represent a distortion of the structure's cross-section (Figs. 7f-g). In the case of the investigated tower, the warping distortion is conceivably related to the length of the structure's side and the absence of rigid floors.

Regardless the differences in the external temperatures between the two tests, the excellent correspondence of the first five frequencies (Tab. 1) demonstrates that the global dynamic behavior of the tower can be evaluated by sensing just the upper level, confirming the possibility of permanently installing in the structure a cost-effective monitoring system employing 3-4 accelerometers or seismometers. It is further noticed that the higher modes (W_1 and W_2) seem to exhibit a stronger sensitivity to the variations of temperatures.

4. FINITE ELEMENT MODELLING AND MODEL UPDATING

4.1. The Abaqus model

The numerical simulations were carried out with the FE code ABAQUS [9] by means of a detailed 3D model using eighth-node brick elements (C3D8). To obtain a regular distribution of masses and a good representation of the opening distribution and thickness variations, a relatively large number of

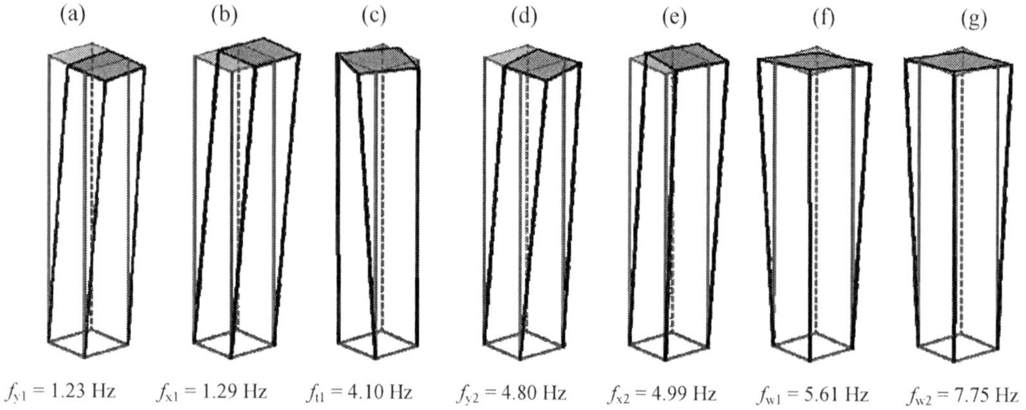

Figure 6. Vibration modes identified employing few seismometers (October 2016).

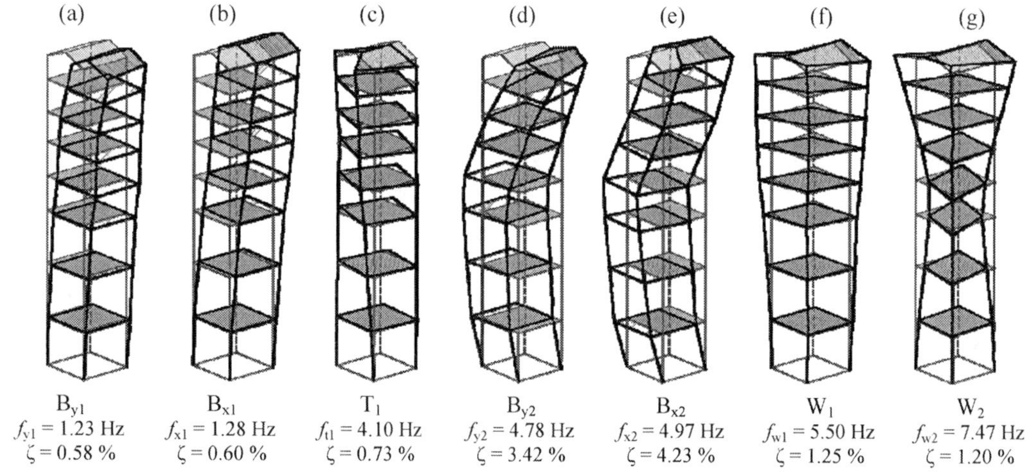

Figure 7. Vibration modes identified employing a large number of accelerometers (December 2017).

Table 1. Comparison between the natural frequencies identified in October 2016 and December 2017.

Mode no.	Mode type	$f_{oct-2016}$ (Hz)	$f_{dec-2017}$ (Hz)	Error (%)
B_{y1}	Bending mode in N-E/S-W direction	1.23	1.23	0.00
B_{x1}	Bending mode in N-W/S-E direction	1.29	1.28	0.78
T_1	Torsion mode	4.10	4.09	0.24
B_{y2}	Bending mode in N-E/S-W direction	4.80	4.78	0.42
B_{x2}	Bending mode in N-W/S-E direction	4.99	4.97	0.40
W_1	Warping distortion mode	5.61	5.50	1.96
W_2	Warping distortion mode	7.75	7.47	3.61

elements have been used: the average element size is approximately equal to 0.5m. In addition, the mesh size is sufficiently refined to provide a negligible effect on modal parameters. Overall, the FE model consists of 10582 brick elements with 48438 active degrees of freedom (Fig. 8).

The vibration-based FE model updating (FEMU) of historic towers is mainly connected with the calibration of masonry elastic properties (*E* and *G*) and boundary conditions as reported by different scholars [6, 10]. Consequently, to reduce the number of updating parameters and consider just the ones affected by major uncertainties, some assumptions were introduced: (a) the effect of soil-structure interaction was neglected, and the tower was considered fixed at the base; (b) regarding the modelling of brick masonry, a linear elastic orthotropic material was adopted; (c) the relationship between Young's modulus and the shear modulus was considered equal to $G = \alpha \cdot E$; (d) a homogeneous distribution of weight per unit volume was assumed equal to 17 kN/m^3; and (d) a Poisson's ratio of 0.15 was held constant.

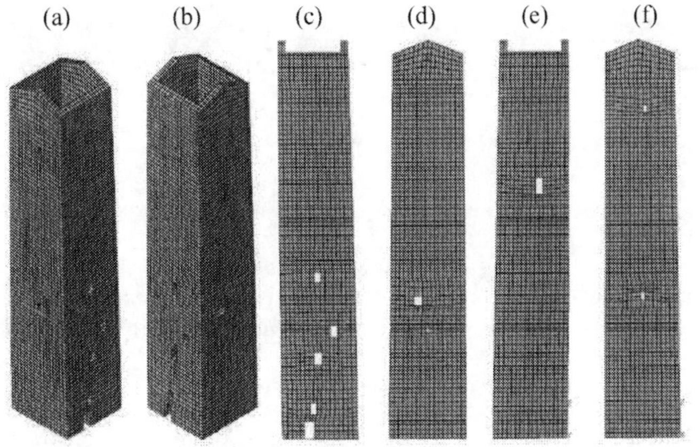

Figure 8. FE model of the Zuccaro's Tower, axonometric views of the West (a) and South corner (b), and parallel projections of the S-W (c), S-E (d), N-E (e), and N-W (f) façades.

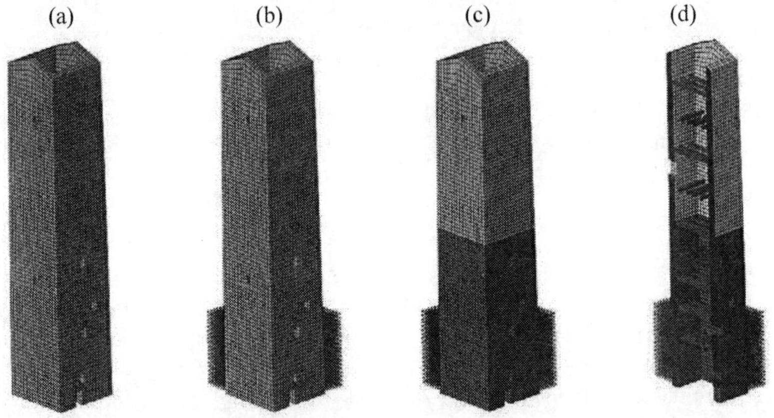

Figure 9. Developed models: (a) Model 0, (b) Model 1, (c) Model 2, and (d) Model 3 (optimised model).

To demonstrate the need for FEMU procedures, an initial model (Model 0, Fig. 9a) was developed just considering the results of the flat jack tests from the experimental campaign of ISMES [2] and the recommendations of the Italian Technical Code, without taking into consideration the effect of the nearby constructions. Thus, a FEMU technique based on the Douglas and Reid method [11] and the Particle Swarm Optimisation (PSO) algorithm [12] was applied to improve the correlation with experimental results. The response features chosen for the updating procedure were the natural frequencies. Despite the accurate geometry of the model and the quality of the structural identification procedures, some further considerations were needed to accurately represent all identified modes:

(1) the effect of surrounding buildings was simulated with a uniform distribution of 342 linear elastic translational springs on the S-E side and N-E side, with constants k_x and k_y respectively (Model 1, Fig. 9b);
(2) the presence of discontinuities and fragmentary masonry areas was simulated adopting a non-homogeneous distribution of Young's modulus E, namely, dividing the structure into two parts with constant elastic properties (Model 2, Fig. 9c);
(3) at last, the stiffening effect of the timber floors was simulated through a series of rigid beam elements connected with the vertical walls, thorough linear rotational springs with constant k_{RS} (Model 3, Fig. 9d).

Table 2. Summary of the developed FE models and corresponding average frequency discrepancy (DF_{ave}).

	Model 0	Model 1	Model 2	Model 3
Parameters optimization		×	×	×
Surrounding buildings effect		×	×	×
Effect of non-homogeneous masonry			×	×
Effect of timber floors				×
Number of vibration modes with $DF < 1$ %	0	3	5	7
DF_{ave} [%]	9.96	5.34	2.60	0.07
DF_{max} [%]	21.5	15.6	10.1	0.2

Hence, applying the sequence of the above steps (involving different assumptions on the modes' uncertainties), it was possible to obtain an excellent correlation with all identified natural frequencies.

4.2. Comparison between analytical and experimental results

The initial model (Model 0, Fig. 9a) was developed considering just the results of the material characterization campaign – average Young's modulus identified equal to 3.2 GPa – and the recommendations of the Italian Technical Code – $G = E/3$ –, without considering the effect of the nearby constructions. The correlation between the numerical and experimental response is measured through the frequency discrepancy, defined as follow:

$$DF_i = (f_i^{EXP} - f_i^{FEM}) / f_i^{EXP}\, 100 \quad [\%] \tag{1}$$

and particularly with its average DF_{ave} and the maximum DF_{max} index. Therefore, the initial model (Model 0, Fig. 9a) exhibits a poor correlation with the OMA results, showing a much stiffer response with all the natural frequencies exceeding the experimental ones, and a DF_{ave} and DF_{max} equal to 10% and 22% respectively (Tab. 2). Furthermore, it is worth to mention that Model 0 would have been conceivably very similar to a standard model developed according to the Italian Code, without the information collected with AVTs.

To improve the correlation with experimental results, Model 1 (Fig. 9b) considers the effect of the building aggregate where the tower is enclosed through a series of linear elastic springs. Based on the sensitivity analysis, the parameters selected for the model updating procedure were the average masonry elastic modulus E, the ratio $\alpha = G/E$, and the resulting spring stiffness in the two main directions $\sum k_x$ and $\sum k_y$. Hence, the optimal parameters provided by the model updating algorithm are reported in Table 3. As expected, there is a global reduction of the masonry elastic properties: the response of Model 0 was indeed much stiffer than the (real) structural response. Furthermore, the springs simulating the interaction with the neighboring buildings in the two directions have very different stiffness, presumably for the different morphology of surrounding constructions. In y-direction, the constraint effect is given by an entire building aggregate while in x-direction just an isolated block is present (Fig. 1a). Although the overall correlation was improved, and the first three resonant frequencies (B_{y1}, B_{x1}, and T_1) were well reproduced (Table 4), the numerical model is still stiffer than the real structure with four modes out of seven exceeding the experimental ones, apparently due to the presence of discontinuities in the masonry walls.

Model 2 (Fig. 9c) was implemented assuming two regions with constant elastic properties: E_L for the lower part (height ≤ 21.02 m) and E_U for the upper part (height > 21.02 m). The division of the areas at the height of 21 m (the 5th floor) is consistent with the starting point of non-homogeneities in the masonry of the N-E front, reported by the direct survey. As expected, the parameters resulting from the calibration show a remarkable reduction of the elastic properties of the upper part (E_U) while in lower part just a slight increase is reported (Table 3). Model 2 is capable of reproducing with high accuracy the lower 5 modes of the real structure (with the maximum frequency discrepancy being 0.4%), whereas it turns out to be too flexible to correctly reproduce the warping modes; this relative lack of stiffness is most likely due to the neglected effect of timber floors.

Finally, to improve the model calibration and the identification of the warping modes, it was necessary to consider the effect of the timber floors (Model 3, Fig. 9d). It is worth noting that these floors were substituted in the '90s, and the quality of the connections between the timber elements and the masonry walls is reasonably not negligible. Subsequently, rigid elements were placed at each floor, parallel to the rigid direction of the timber floors, to simulate the connections between the opposed masonry walls. Each connection between a rigid element and a brick element was modeled with a linear elastic rotation spring of constant k_{RS}. The model updating procedure led to the identification of the structural parameters reported in Table 3. The stiffening effect related to the introduction of rigid elements is clearly reflected in a slight decrease of both Young's moduli and compensated by an increase of ratio α, in a way that leaves the shear moduli approximately constant. Interestingly, the constants of both springs increase, demonstrating the difficulty of a clear identification most likely connected with the low sensitivity of these parameters. On the other hand, the numerical frequencies obtained with the above set of parameters are basically equivalent to the one estimated from the AVT of December 2017 with a DF_{max} much less than 1% (Fig. 10).

Table 3. Summary of the identified structural parameters.

Structural parameters	Model 0	Model 1	Model 2	Model 3
E (GPa) whole structure	3.20	2.97	-	-
E_L (GPa) height ≤ 21.02m	-	-	3.14	3.07
E_U (GPa) height > 21.02m	-	-	1.71	1.56
A	0.333	0.298	0.333	0.342
G (GPa) whole structure	1.067	0.885	-	-
G_L (GPa) height ≤ 21.02m	-	-	1.046	1.052
G_U (GPa) height > 21.02m	-	-	0.570	0.535
Σk_x (kN/m $\cdot 10^5$)	-	11.80	15.05	22.33
Σk_y (kN/m $\cdot 10^5$)	-	0.20	0.20	3.50
k_{RS} (kN/m $\cdot 10^5$)	-	-	-	0.169

Table 4. Comparison between experimental and numerical modal frequencies.

	f (Hz)				
Mode no.	FDD (2017)	Model 0	Model 1	Model 2	Model 3
B_{y1}	1.23	1.285	1.230	1.230	1.228
B_{x1}	1.28	1.295	1.281	1.281	1.280
T_1	4.10	4.433	4.096	4.100	4.100
B_{y2}	4.78	5.502	5.18	4.800	4.779
B_{x2}	4.97	5.436	5.37	4.974	4.969
W_1	5.50	6.680	6.36	4.94	5.499
W_2	7.47	8.224	7.87	6.91	7.486

5. CONCLUSIONS

The paper focuses on the structural identification of the Zuccaro's Tower in Mantua. After the seismic events of May 2012, a preliminary structural assessment of the state of preservation of the tower was performed [1]. During these investigations, the presence of non-homogeneous and fragmentary masonry areas was documented and confirmed by ambient vibration tests reporting anomalous distortions of the tower's cross-sections. To better understand the effects of these non-homogeneities and anomalies, deeper analyses were suggested. Therefore, the current research programme involved two main steps: (a) the development of an FE model that represents accurately the information collected on-site, involving structure's geometry, masonry quality and boundary conditions; and (b) the identification of uncertain model parameters by means of a FEMU technique based on the Douglas-Reid method and the PSO algorithm.

Based on the experimental data collected during an ambient vibration test, the FE model is iteratively calibrated. The results of the entire process summarised in Tables 2-4, suggest the following conclusions:

(1) Notwithstanding the very low level of excitation during the AVTs, seven vibration modes were identified in the frequency range of 0-9 Hz;

(2) Besides the initial model (Model 0) represented accurately the geometry surveyed and the material properties identified with the material characterization campaign, a very poor correlation with the actual structural response was obtained (DF_{ave} = 10%);

(3) On the contrary, applying the developed FE model updating procedure and considering the effects of local masonry non-homogeneities and timber floors, an excellent correlation with the experimental results was obtained (DF_{ave} = 0.05%).

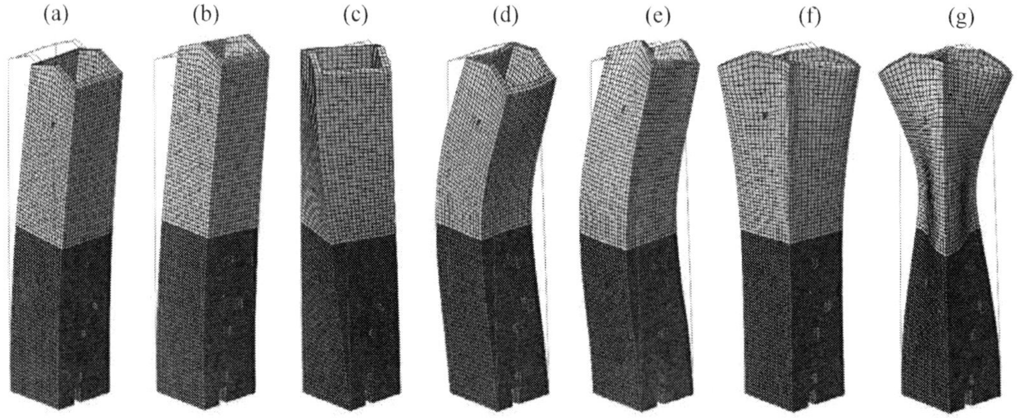

B_{y1}	B_{x1}	T_1	B_{y2}	B_{x2}	W_1	W_2
f_{EXP} = 1.23 Hz	f_{EXP} = 1.28 Hz	f_{EXP} = 4.10 Hz	f_{EXP} = 4.78 Hz	f_{EXP} = 4.97 Hz	f_{EXP} = 5.50 Hz	f_{EXP} = 7.47 Hz
f_{FEM} = 1.228 Hz	f_{FEM} = 1.280 Hz	f_{FEM} = 4.010 Hz	f_{FEM} = 4.779 Hz	f_{FEM} = 4.969 Hz	f_{FEM} = 5.499 Hz	f_{FEM} = 7.486 Hz
DF_{y1} = 0.17 %	DF_{x1} = 0.02 %	DF_{T1} = 0.00 %	DF_{y2} = 0.01 %	DF_{x2} = 0.02 %	DF_{W1} = 0.03 %	DF_{W2} = -0.21 %

Figure 10. Vibration modes of the updated Model 3 and comparison with the experimental results.

ACKNOWLEDGEMENTS

Sincere thanks are due to M. Cucchi (LPMSC, Testing Lab for Materials, Buildings and Civil Structures, Politecnico di Milano) and A. Ruccolo (Ph.D. candidate, Politecnico di Milano) who assisted the authors in conducting the field tests.

REFERENCES

[1] Saisi, A., Terenzoni, S., Ruccolo, A., & Gentile, C. (2019). Safety of the Architectural Heritage: Structural Assessment of the Zuccaro's Tower in Mantua. In: *Aguilar R., Torrealva D., Moreira S., Pando M.A., Ramos L.F. (eds) Structural Analysis of Historical Constructions* (pp 2422-2430). RILEM Bookseries, vol 18. Springer, Cham

[2] ISMES. (1990). Indagine Conoscitiva e Monitoraggio delle Strutture Murarie e del Terreno di Fondazione della Torre degli Zuccaro (MN) (In Italian).

[3] Brincker, R., Zhang, L., & Andersen, P. (2001). Modal identification of output-only systems using frequency domain decomposition. *Smart Materials and Structures* 10(3), 441-445.

[4] van Overschee, P., & De Moor, B. (1996). *Subspace identification for linear systems: Theory, implementation, applications.* New York, NY: Kluwer Academic Publishers.

[5] Structural Vibration Solutions (SVS). (2010). ARTeMIS Extractor 2010. Copenhagen, Denmark: Aalborg University.

[6] Gentile, C., Saisi, A., & Cabboi, A. (2015). Structural identification of a masonry tower based on operational modal analysis. *International Journal of Architectural Heritage* 9(2), 98–110.

[7] Foti, D., Diaferio, M., Giannoccaro, N. I., & Mongelli, M. (2012). Ambient vibration testing, dynamic identification and model updating of a historic tower. *NDT & E International* 47, 88-95.

[8] Ubertini, F., Comanducci, G., & Cavalagli, N. (2016). Vibration-based structural health monitoring of a historic bell-tower using output-only measurements and multivariate statistical analysis. *Structural Health Monitoring* 15(4), 438-457.

[9] Dassault Systemès. (2017). Abaqus CAE/2018.

[10] Ramos, L. F., Marques, L., Lourenço, P. B., De Roeck, G., Campos-Costa, A., & Roque, J. (2010). Monitoring historical masonry structures with operational modal analysis: Two case studies. *Mechanical Systems and Signal Processing* 24(5), 1291-1305.

[11] Douglas, B. M., & Reid, W. H. (1982). Dynamic tests and system identification of bridges. *ASCE Journal of Structural Engineering* 108(10), 2295-312.

[12] Kennedy, J., & Eberhart, R. (1995). Particle Swarm Optimization. In: *Proceedings of IEEE International Conference on Neural Networks* (pp. 1942-1948). Perth, WA, Australia.

IOMAC'19
8th International Operational Modal Analysis Conference
2019 May13-15 Copenhagen

FINITE ELEMENT MODEL UPDATING OF PIEZOELECTRIC TRANSDUCERS

Sau-Lon James Hu [1], *Liang Su* [2], *Shuai Cong*[3] *and Hua-Jun Li*[4]

[1] Professor, Department of Ocean Engineering, University of Rhode Island, Narragansett, RI 02882-1197,USA. E-mail:jameshu@uri.edu.
[2] Senior Engineer, Pilot National Laboratory for Marine Science and Technology, Qingdao 266100, PR China. Email:suliang.leo@gmail.com.
[3] Ph.D Candidate, College of Engineering, Ocean University of China, Qingdao 266100 , PR China. Email:congshuaiouc@outlook.com.
[4] Professor, Shandong Provincial Key Lab of Ocean Engineering, Ocean University of China, Qingdao 266100 , PR China. E-mail:huajun@ouc.edu.cn.

ABSTRACT
Building an accurate finite-element model for a piezoelectric transducer depends on the accuracy of the input material properties, including the elastic, dielectric and piezoelectric parameters, of the piezoelectric materials. But the values provided in the manufacturer's specification sheets for piezoelectric materials are often incomplete or inaccurate. Thus, it is highly desired to have a quick and accurate method of correcting the finite element models for piezoelectric transducers. This study develops and tests a finite element model updating method for piezoelectric tube transducers based on an extended cross-model cross-mode (CMCM) method. This proposed method updates the elastic material properties using a short-circuit model in the first step, and the dielectric and piezoelectric parameters using an open-circuit model in the second step. The only information required is the impedance function—which could be easily obtained from simple experiments —of the transducer. The high performance of the proposed two-step approach will be demonstrated through computer simulations.

Keywords: Impedance function, Piezoelectric transducer, Finite element model, Model updating

1. INTRODUCTION

The accuracy of the finite element (FE) model of a piezoelectric transducer depends on the accuracy of the material's constitutive properties, but the values provided in the manufacturer's specification sheets for piezoelectric materials are often incomplete or inaccurate. Because of the polycrystalline nature of piezoceramics and the statistical variations in their composition and production-related influences, the standard tolerance range of piezoelectric material is $\pm 20\%$. As a result, the properties of different transducers made with the same piezoelectric material may vary.

It is highly desired to have a quick and accurate model updating method for FE transducer models. Traditional methods of model updating for mechanical systems have been classified into two major types: direct matrix methods and indirect physical property adjustment methods [1]. The first of these two groups generally involves non-iterative methods, all of which are based on computing changes that are made directly to the mass and stiffness matrices. Such changes may have succeeded in generating modified models, but cannot be interpreted in a physical way. The second group comprises iterative methods that seek to find correction factors for each individual FE or for each design parameter related to each FE. These methods are in many ways more acceptable in that their parameters are much closer to physically realizable quantities. There are only a few published articles on the model-updating for piezoelectric transducers [2, 3, 4], and those articles have adopted methods which belong to the indirect physical property adjustment methods. In this study, the cross-model cross-mode (CMCM) method [5] —a direct, physical property adjustment model updating method— is extended to update a piezoceramic tube transducer. When the impedance function of this tube transducer is the only measured data, an iterative CMCM approach is developed to deal with the incompleteness of modal information as only a few measured resonant and anti-resonant frequencies are available. Sequentially, the elastic and dielectric-piezoelectric properties are updated in the short-circuit and open-circuit models, respectively.

2. CONSTITUTIVE EQUATIONS ASSOCIATED WITH PIEZOELECTRIC TUBE TRANSDUCER

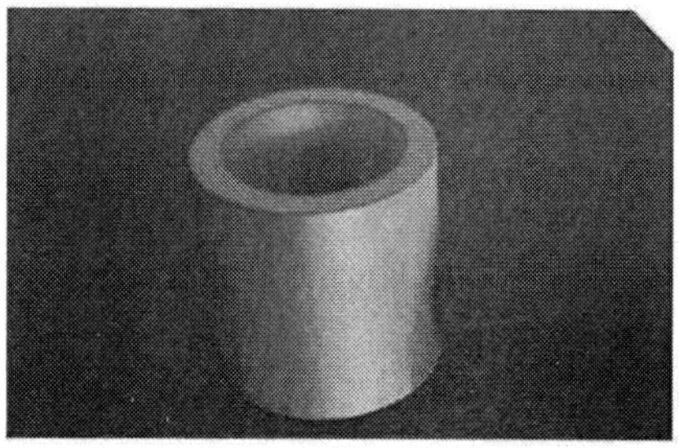

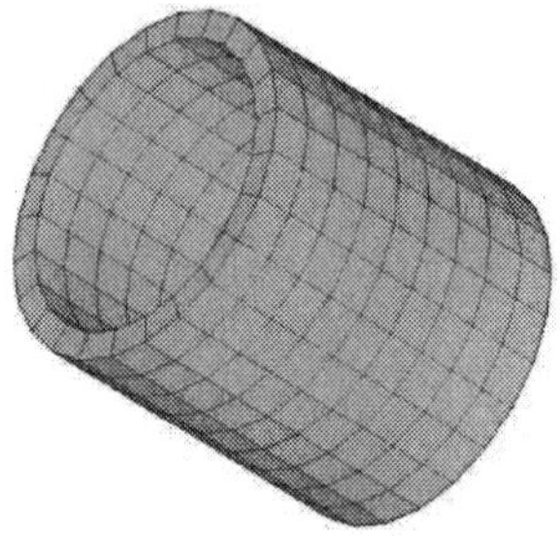

Figure 1: Tube transducer (Left), Finite element model of the transducer (Right)

Fig. 1 shows a piezoelectric tube transducer and its FE model. When the constitutive equations of the piezoelectric material are expressed in the so-called e-form, one has:

$$\mathbf{T} = \mathbf{c}^E\mathbf{S} - \mathbf{e}^t\mathbf{E} \quad (1)$$

$$\mathbf{D} = \mathbf{e}\mathbf{S} + \boldsymbol{\varepsilon}^S\mathbf{E} \quad (2)$$

where $\mathbf{T} \in \mathbb{R}^{6\times1}$ is stress vector, $\mathbf{S} \in \mathbb{R}^{6\times1}$ strain vector, $\mathbf{E} \in \mathbb{R}^{3\times1}$ electric field vector, $\mathbf{D} \in \mathbb{R}^{3\times1}$ electric displacement vector, $\mathbf{c}^E \in \mathbb{R}^{6\times6}$ elastic stiffness matrix with $\mathbf{E}$ being held constant, $\mathbf{e} \in \mathbb{R}^{3\times6}$ piezoelectric stress matrix (superscript t stands for the transpose) and $\boldsymbol{\varepsilon}^S \in \mathbb{R}^{3\times3}$ permittivity matrix with $\mathbf{S}$ being held constant [6, 7]. A widely used alternative and equivalent representation is writing the constitutive equations in the so-called d-from:

$$\mathbf{S} = \mathbf{s}^E\,\mathbf{T} + \mathbf{d}^t\,\mathbf{E} \quad (3)$$

$$\mathbf{D} = \mathbf{d}\,\mathbf{T} + \boldsymbol{\varepsilon}^T\,\mathbf{E} \quad (4)$$

where $\mathbf{s}^E \in \mathbb{R}^{6\times6}$ is elastic compliance matrix, $\mathbf{d} \in \mathbb{R}^{3\times6}$ piezoelectric strain matrix and $\boldsymbol{\varepsilon}^T \in \mathbb{R}^{3\times3}$ permittivity matrix at constant stress. From the constitutive equations of d-form and e-form, it is straightforward to obtain the following relationships between their parameters:

$$\mathbf{c}^E = \left(\mathbf{s}^E\right)^{-1} \tag{5}$$

$$\mathbf{e} = \mathbf{d}\left(\mathbf{s}^E\right)^{-1} \tag{6}$$

$$\boldsymbol{\varepsilon}^S = \boldsymbol{\varepsilon}^T - \mathbf{e}\mathbf{d}^t \tag{7}$$

For polarized piezoelectric material (such as PZT) which belongs to the 4 mm (C4V) crystal class, Eqs. 3 and 4 can be explicitly expressed as [8]:

$$\begin{Bmatrix} S_1 \\ S_2 \\ S_3 \\ S_4 \\ S_5 \\ S_6 \\ D_1 \\ D_2 \\ D_3 \end{Bmatrix} = \begin{bmatrix} s_{11}^E & s_{12}^E & s_{13}^E & 0 & 0 & 0 & 0 & 0 & d_{31} \\ s_{12}^E & s_{11}^E & s_{13}^E & 0 & 0 & 0 & 0 & 0 & d_{31} \\ s_{13}^E & s_{13}^E & s_{33}^E & 0 & 0 & 0 & 0 & 0 & d_{33} \\ 0 & 0 & 0 & s_{44}^E & 0 & 0 & 0 & d_{15} & 0 \\ 0 & 0 & 0 & 0 & s_{44}^E & 0 & d_{15} & 0 & 0 \\ 0 & 0 & 0 & 0 & 0 & s_{66}^E & 0 & 0 & 0 \\ 0 & 0 & 0 & 0 & d_{15} & 0 & \varepsilon_{11}^T & 0 & 0 \\ 0 & 0 & 0 & d_{15} & 0 & 0 & 0 & \varepsilon_{11}^T & 0 \\ d_{31} & d_{31} & d_{33} & 0 & 0 & 0 & 0 & 0 & \varepsilon_{33}^T \end{bmatrix} \begin{Bmatrix} T_1 \\ T_2 \\ T_3 \\ T_4 \\ T_5 \\ T_6 \\ E_1 \\ E_2 \\ E_3 \end{Bmatrix} \tag{8}$$

where $s_{66}^E = 2(s_{11}^E - s_{12}^E)$. As a thin tube transducer polarized in the thickness direction (Fig.1), the normal stress in the polarized (radial) direction and the respective transverse shear stress components are negligible [9]:

$$T_3 = T_4 = T_5 = 0 \tag{9}$$

If the electric field is only applied in polarized direction,

$$E_1 = E_2 = 0 \tag{10}$$

then Eq.8 becomes

$$\begin{Bmatrix} S_1 \\ S_2 \\ S_6 \\ D_3 \end{Bmatrix} = \begin{bmatrix} s_{11}^E & s_{12}^E & 0 & d_{31} \\ s_{12}^E & s_{11}^E & 0 & d_{31} \\ 0 & 0 & s_{66}^E & 0 \\ d_{31} & d_{31} & 0 & \varepsilon_{33}^T \end{bmatrix} \begin{Bmatrix} T_1 \\ T_2 \\ T_6 \\ E_3 \end{Bmatrix} \tag{11}$$

which are identical to the reduced constitutive equations in the d-form [9]. Notice that the reduced d-form parameters are also identical to those of the original constitutive equations.

Similarly, the e-form of the reduced constitutive equations yields

$$\begin{Bmatrix} T_1 \\ T_2 \\ T_6 \\ D_3 \end{Bmatrix} = \begin{bmatrix} \bar{c}_{11}^E & \bar{c}_{12}^E & 0 & -\bar{e}_{31} \\ \bar{c}_{12}^E & \bar{c}_{11}^E & 0 & -\bar{e}_{31} \\ 0 & 0 & \bar{c}_{66}^E & 0 \\ \bar{e}_{31} & \bar{e}_{31} & 0 & \bar{\varepsilon}_{33}^S \end{bmatrix} \begin{Bmatrix} S_1 \\ S_2 \\ S_6 \\ E_3 \end{Bmatrix} \tag{12}$$

From Eqs. 11 and 12, one shows

$$\begin{bmatrix} \bar{c}_{11}^E & \bar{c}_{12}^E & 0 & -\bar{e}_{31} \\ \bar{c}_{12}^E & \bar{c}_{11}^E & 0 & -\bar{e}_{31} \\ 0 & 0 & \bar{c}_{66}^E & 0 \\ \bar{e}_{31} & \bar{e}_{31} & 0 & \bar{\varepsilon}_{33}^S \end{bmatrix} = \begin{bmatrix} s_{11}^E & s_{12}^E & 0 & 0 \\ s_{12}^E & s_{11}^E & 0 & 0 \\ 0 & 0 & s_{66}^E & 0 \\ -d_{31} & -d_{31} & 0 & 1 \end{bmatrix}^{-1} \begin{bmatrix} 1 & 0 & 0 & -d_{31} \\ 0 & 1 & 0 & -d_{31} \\ 0 & 0 & 1 & 0 \\ 0 & 0 & 0 & \varepsilon_{33}^T \end{bmatrix} \tag{13}$$

It is realized the reduced e-form parameters are different to those of the original constitutive equations. Therefore, it would be better to update the d-form parameters than the e-form parameters for the tube transducers. Note that there are only four independent material parameters required to be updated: s_{11}^E, s_{12}^E, ε_{33}^T and d_{31}, where s_{11}^E and s_{12}^E can be replaced by engineering parameters: Young's modulus $Y_{11}^E = 1/s_{11}^E$ and Passion ratio $\nu_{12} = -s_{12}^E/s_{11}^E$.

3. DYNAMIC EQUATIONS OF PIEZOELECTRIC STRUCTURES

The system equations for a piezoelectric structure can be written:

$$\begin{bmatrix} \mathbf{M} & 0 \\ 0 & 0 \end{bmatrix} \begin{Bmatrix} \ddot{\mathbf{U}} \\ \ddot{\mathbf{\Phi}} \end{Bmatrix} + \begin{bmatrix} \mathbf{K}_{UU} & \mathbf{K}_{U\Phi} \\ \mathbf{K}_{\Phi U} & \mathbf{K}_{\Phi\Phi} \end{bmatrix} \begin{Bmatrix} \mathbf{U} \\ \mathbf{\Phi} \end{Bmatrix} = \begin{Bmatrix} \mathbf{F} \\ \mathbf{G} \end{Bmatrix} \tag{14}$$

where $\mathbf{U}$ = displacement vector, $\mathbf{\Phi}$ = electric potential vector, $\mathbf{M}$ = mass matrix, $\mathbf{K}_{UU}$ = displacement stiffness matrix, $\mathbf{K}_{U\Phi}$ = piezoelectric coupling matrix, $\mathbf{K}_{\Phi\Phi}$ = dielectric "stiffness" matrix, $\mathbf{F}$ = external force vector, and $\mathbf{G}$ = charge vector. When the electric potential $\mathbf{\Phi}$ is controlled, from Eq. 14, one writes

$$\mathbf{M}\ddot{\mathbf{U}} + \mathbf{K}_{UU}\mathbf{U} = \mathbf{F} - \mathbf{K}_{U\Phi}\mathbf{\Phi} \tag{15}$$

where the term $-\mathbf{K}_{U\Phi}\mathbf{\Phi}$ represents the piezoelectric load. From Eq. 15, the eigenvalue problem of the short circuit model, namely $\mathbf{\Phi} = \mathbf{0}$, is

$$(\mathbf{K}_{UU} - \omega^2\mathbf{M})\mathbf{U} = \mathbf{0} \tag{16}$$

Notice that the modal frequencies, ω, and mode shapes of the short-circuit model are the same as those when there was no piezoelectric electromechanical coupling.

In physics, an open circuit model corresponds to the charge condition $\mathbf{G} = \mathbf{0}$; from Eq.14, one writes

$$\mathbf{\Phi} = -(\mathbf{K}_{\Phi\Phi}^{-1}\mathbf{K}_{\Phi U})\mathbf{U} \tag{17}$$

Upon substituting Eq. 17 into Eq. 15, it yields

$$\mathbf{M}\ddot{\mathbf{U}} + (\mathbf{K}_{UU} - \mathbf{K}_{U\Phi}\mathbf{K}_{\Phi\Phi}^{-1}\mathbf{K}_{\Phi U})\mathbf{U} = \mathbf{F} \tag{18}$$

It results in the eigenvalue problem of an open circuit model:

$$(\tilde{\mathbf{K}}_{UU} - \omega_a^2\mathbf{M})\mathbf{U} = \mathbf{0} \tag{19}$$

where

$$\tilde{\mathbf{K}}_{UU} = \mathbf{K}_{UU} - \mathbf{K}_{U\Phi}\mathbf{K}_{\Phi\Phi}^{-1}\mathbf{K}_{\Phi U} \tag{20}$$

and ω_a denotes the modal frequencies of the open-circuit model. Note that $\tilde{\mathbf{K}}_{UU}$ is the condensed electro-elastic stiffness matrix which amounts to performing a static condensation to eliminate the degrees of freedom associated with $\mathbf{\Phi}$ [7, 10].

The modal frequencies of the short and open circuit models, ω and ω_a, are known to be the resonance and anti-resonance frequencies of the transducer, respectively. They are also the frequencies corresponding to the local minima and local maxima of the impedance function of a transducer [11]. As the impedance function of a transducer is easily measured, so are the modal frequencies of the short and open circuit models of the transducer.

4. EXTENDED CROSS-MODEL CROSS-MODE (CMCM) METHOD

Originally developed for mechanical systems, the CMCM model updating method [5] solves a set of linear simultaneous equations for physically meaningful correction factors from the measured modal data, together with modal data of the finite element model. The CMCM method is an accurate and efficiency method which has the advantages of both direct and iterative methods. While it is very cost-effective in computational time and needs only the first few measured modes, it also preserves the initial model configuration and physical connectivity of the updated model [5]. When only measured modal frequencies are available, the original CMCM method must be extended to involve an iterative procedure (see the flowchart in Fig. 2) [12]. It involves repeatedly applying the following two steps:

1. As no measured mode shapes are available, a plausible approximation for a measured mode shape is the corresponding analytical mode shape form the FE model.

2. Using the measured modal frequencies and the corresponding approximated measured mode shapes (from Step 1), one can proceed the original CMCM method to compute correction coefficients, and rebuild the updated FE model.

The iteration will continue until a converged solution with a preset tolerance is achieved.

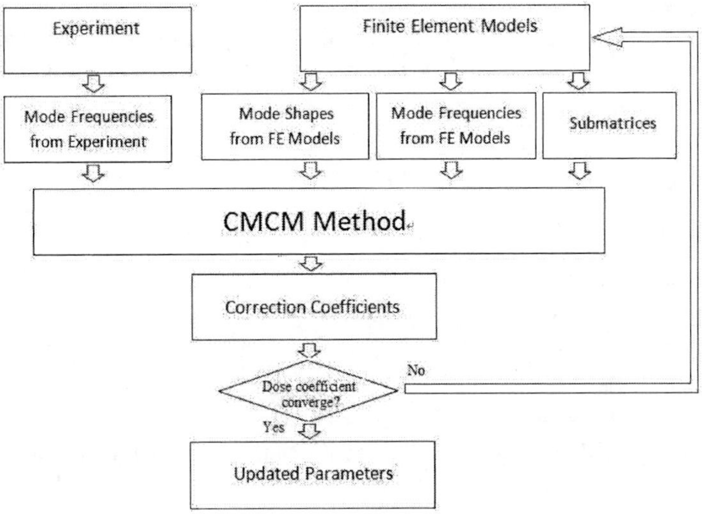

Figure 2: Flowchart of the iterative extended CMCM method with measured modal frequencies only

5. MODEL UPDATING OF PIEZOELECTRIC TUBE BY THE CMCM METHOD

It is assumed that the mass density and geometry of a piezoceramic tube transducer are measured accurately. To be updated are three groups of piezoelectric material parameters: elastic parameters, dielectric parameters and piezoelectric parameters. Referring to a measured impedance function, elastic parameters would solely decide the resonance frequencies which are the modal frequencies of the transducer in short circuit situation; dielectric parameters (permittivity) determine the unclamped capacitance; and all three groups of parameters affect the anti-resonance frequencies which are the modal frequencies of the transducer in open circuit condition. Therefore, one can proceed the piezoelectric tube transducer parameter updating as follows:

1. From the resonant frequencies of the measured impedance function, update the elastic parameters based on a short-circuit FE model.

2. From the measured impedance value at the very low frequency region, update the dielectric parameters (permittivity) in the poling direction.

3. From the anti-resonant frequencies of the measured impedance function, update the piezoelectric parameters based on an open-circuit FE model.

6. NUMERICAL EXAMPLE

Chosen for the numerical demonstration is a simulated transducer. Because the target values of parameters are known for the simulated transducer and can be compared with the updated values, the simulated transducer is employed to test the accuracy of the proposed method. This study focuses on using the 3D constitutive equations for the model updating of the tube transducer. Both the original analytical model and the target model are generated from using the same FE model built by ANSYS with the inner diameter $D_i = 16 \times 10^{-3}$ m, outer diameter $D_o = 19 \times 10^{-3}$ m and length $\ell = 20 \times 10^{-3}$ m (see Fig. 1b), but different sets of material coefficients. It is assumed that the analytical model is with a set of "wrong" coefficients. The goal is to correct those wrong coefficients from the measured modal information which is simulated from the same FE model with "right" coefficients. Because engineering parameters are more commonly provided in manufacture specification sheets, they are utilized as the intended updating quantities for the elastic material properties. The original and target values of these four sensitive parameters are listed in Table 1. The relative error provided in Table 1 is defined as the difference between the original value and the target value, and it is then normalized by the target value.

Table 1: Material properties of the original and target models

Parameter	Unit	Original Value	Target Value	Relative Error
Y_{11}^E	$10^{10}\,(N/m^2)$	6.3	6.66	5.4054%
ν_{12}	—	0.31	0.3333	6.9907%
d_{31}	$10^{-12}\,(C/N)$	−175	−210	16.6667%
$\varepsilon_{33}^T/\varepsilon_0$	—	1576	2294	31.2990%

Fig. 3 shows a comparison of the impedance function of the original model and that of the target model. There are three modes that significantly contributing to the impedance functions. For the impedance function of the target model, the three major resonant frequencies are 51.4, 55, and 82.6 KHz, and the three anti-resonant frequencies are 52.4, 55.8, and 101.6 KHz.

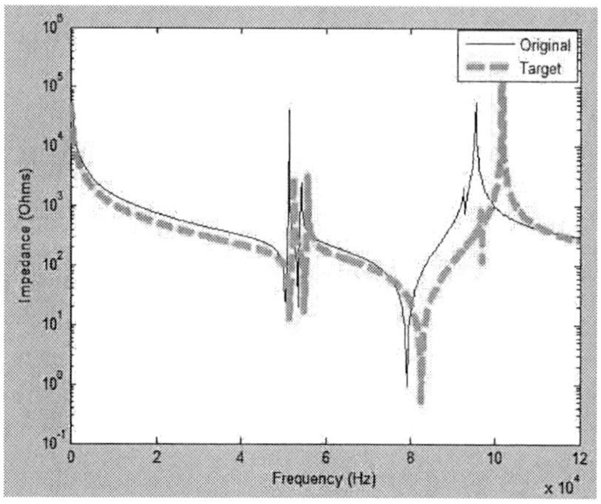

Figure 3: The comparison of the impedance function between the original and target models

Given the three modal frequencies of the target short-circuit model: 51.4, 55 and 82.6 KHz, and those of the target open-circuit model: 52.4, 55.8 and 101.6 KHz, the task is to apply the extended CMCM method to perform the model updating for the analytical piezoceramic tube transducer model.

The first step is to update the elastic parameters of the analytical piezoceramic tube transducer model, using the short circuit model (or pure mechanical model). Given the three modal frequencies of the target short circuit model, the extended CMCM method is applied to estimate α_1 and α_2 which are the correction coefficients of c_{11}^E and c_{12}^E, respectively. Fig. 4 shows the convergence of α_1 and α_2. After 14 iteration steps, these values converge to 0.1455 and 0.2755, respectively, and match the target values accurately. Because the mechanical boundary condition is free-free, the related permittivity of this unclamped transducer is the permittivity at constant stress. Accordingly, ε_{33}^T can be corrected easily from the value at very low frequency of the measured impedance function.

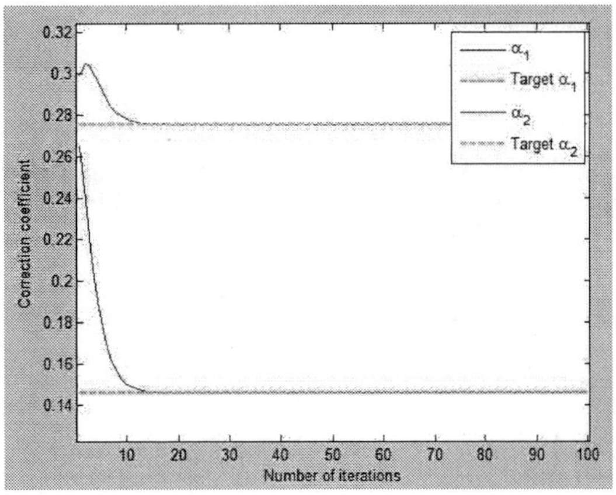

Figure 4: Iteration procedure of α_1 and α_2 on simulation model

After updating the elastic parameters and permittivity, the open-circuited FE model, together with the anti-resonant frequencies of the target model, can be employed to update the piezoelectric parameter d_{31} (or e_{31}). Given the three modal frequencies of the target open-circuit model: 52.4, 55.8, and 101.6 KHz, the extended CMCM method is applied to estimate α_3 which is the correction coefficient of $(e_{31})^2/\varepsilon_{33}^S$. Fig. 5 shows the convergence of the correction coefficient of α_3.

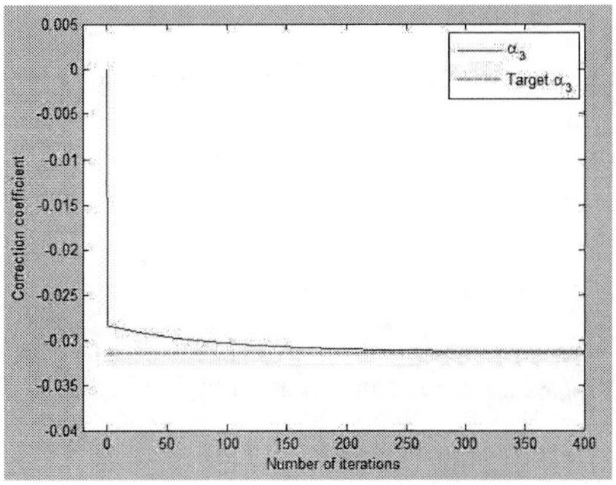

Figure 5: Iteration procedure of α_3 on simulation model

To summarize, the comparison among the original values, target values, and updated values is presented in Table 2. It is found that the updated parameters from the proposed method match perfectly with the corresponding target values.

Table 2: The comparison of properties between original, target and updated simulation models

Parameters	Unit	Original	Target	Updated	Relative error
Y_{11}^E	$(10^{10}N/m^2)$	6.3	6.66	6.66	0%
ν_{12}	—	0.31	0.3333	0.3333	0%
d_{31}	$(10^{-12}C/N)$	−175	−209.96	−210	0.019%
$\varepsilon_{33}^T/\varepsilon_0$	—	1576	2293.3	2294	0.0305%

7. CONCLUDING REMARKS

This study developed and tested a finite element model updating method for piezoelectric tube transducers where the only information required was the impedance function of the transducer which could be easily obtained from experiments. This proposed method updated the elastic material properties using a short circuit model in the first step by using the extended CMCM method, and updated the dielectric and piezoelectric parameters using an open-circuit model in the second step by applying the extended CMCM method again. The excellent performance of the proposed approach was demonstrated through a computer simulated piezoelectric tube transducers.

ACKNOWLEDGEMENTS

The research was financially supported by the National Natural Science Foundation of China (Grant No.51879250).

REFERENCES

[1] M. Friswell, J. E. Mottershead, Finite element model updating in structural dynamics, Vol. 38, Springer Science & Business Media, 1995.

[2] B. Piranda, S. Ballandras, W. Steichen, B. Hecart, A model-updating procedure to simulate piezoelectric transducers accurately, Ultrasonics, Ferroelectrics, and Frequency Control, IEEE Transactions on 48 (5) (2001) 1321–1331.

[3] M. Montemurro, H. Nasser, Y. Koutsawa, S. Belouettar, A. Vincenti, P. Vannucci, Identification of electromechanical properties of piezoelectric structures through evolutionary optimisation techniques, International Journal of Solids and Structures 49 (13) (2012) 1884–1892.

[4] M. Hamdi, A. Benjeddou, Robust multi-objective evolutionary optimization-based inverse identification of three-dimensional elastic behaviour of multilayer unidirectional fibre composites, in: Smart Structures and Materials, Springer, 2017, pp. 267–293.

[5] S.-L. J. Hu, H. Li, S. Wang, Cross-model cross-mode method for model updating, Mechanical Systems and Signal Processing 21 (4) (2007) 1690–1703.

[6] C. H. Sherman, J. L. Butler, Transducers and arrays for underwater sound, Springer, 2007.

[7] V. Piefort, Finite element modelling of piezoelectric active structures, Ph.D. thesis, Université Libre de Bruxelles (2001).

[8] American National Standards Institute, IEEE Standard on Piezoelectricity (1987).

[9] A. Erturk, D. J. Inman, Piezoelectric energy harvesting, John Wiley & Sons, 2011.

[10] W. P. Mason, Physical acoustics, Elsevier Science, 2013.

[11] A. Ballato, Equivalent circuits for resonators and transducers driven piezoelectrically, Tech. rep., DTIC Document (1990).

[12] H. Li, J. Wang, S.-L. J. Hu, Using incomplete modal data for damage detection in offshore jacket structures, Ocean Engineering 35 (17) (2008) 1793–1799.

IOMAC'19

8th International Operational Modal Analysis Conference

2019 May13-15 Copenhagen

IDENTIFICATION OF INFILL MASONRY WALLS STIFFENING CONTRIBUTION ON THE DYNAMIC BEHAVIOUR OF STEEL FRAMES

Vanni Nicoletti[1], Marco Regni[2], Elisa Speranza[3], Davide Arezzo[4], Sandro Carbonari[5] and Fabrizio Gara[6]

[1] Post doc, Dept. ICEA, Università Politecnica delle Marche, Ancona - Italy, v.nicoletti@univpm.it.
[2] PhD candidate, Dept. ICEA, Università Politecnica delle Marche, Ancona - Italy, m.regni@pm.univpm.it.
[3] PhD student, Dept. ICEA, Università Politecnica delle Marche, Ancona - Italy, e.speranza@pm.univpm.it.
[4] PhD student, Dept. ICEA, Università Politecnica delle Marche, Ancona - Italy, d.arezzo@pm.univpm.it.
[5] Assistant professor, Dept. ICEA, Università Politecnica delle Marche, Ancona - Italy, s.carbonari@univpm.it.
[6] Associate professor, Dept. ICEA, Università Politecnica delle Marche, Ancona - Italy, f.gara@univpm.it.

ABSTRACT

The paper deals with the influence of infill masonry walls on the dynamic behaviour of steel structures. The research is based on the experimental and numerical results obtained for a real scale laboratory mock-up, consisting of a one-storey two-bays steel-concrete composite frame. Ambient vibration tests followed by impact load tests were performed after the construction of the IMWs to estimate the dynamic properties of the entire structure and to investigate changes of modal parameters (natural frequencies and mode shapes) due to the contribution of the non-structural components. Furthermore, impact load tests were performed on some IMWs to identify their out-of-plane modal parameters; finally, a methodology to estimate parameters for a 2D modelling of the IMWs is proposed and validated. The numerical results show a very good agreement with the experimental ones, proving the reliability of the estimated IMWs stiffnesses through the proposed procedure.

Keywords: infill masonry walls, steel-concrete composite frames, ambient vibration tests, impact load tests, in-plane/out-of-plane infill dynamic behaviour.

1. INTRODUCTION

Infill Masonry Walls (IMWs) are the most common non-structural elements adopted all over the world in steel and reinforced concrete structures for architectural purposes. The interaction between infills and the surrounding frame under seismic loads have been in depth investigated for more than five decades and many theoretical models and predictive techniques have been developed to account for the influence of IMWs on the overall response of framed structural systems. These models, ranging from the simple replacement of an IMW by one or more equivalent struts [1-5] to detailed linear and non-linear finite element (f.e.) formulations [6-7], require the mechanical material properties of the masonry panels to be known. Anyway, in most cases, a force-displacement relationship is proposed to describe the IMW in-plane behaviour. For the latter purpose, many researchers performed static and cyclic lateral load tests considering several masonry typologies [8-10] to characterize their in-plane and, sometimes, out-of-plane behaviour and to investigate their material properties. It is generally found that each masonry typology presents different characteristics, depending on the type and quality of materials and the construction techniques, so that a standardization of parameters is rather difficult.

In this paper, the influence of IMWs on the dynamic behaviour of a steel-concrete composite structure is investigated. In details, a procedure to develop an accurate f.e. model which takes into account the mass and stiffness contributions of the IMWs is presented with reference to a real-scale mock-up located at the Materials and Structures Testing Laboratory of the Università Politecnica delle Marche. Impact load tests are performed on the IMWs to identify the experimental out-of-plane modal parameters (frequency and mode shapes) and to estimate the mechanical properties of the masonry walls through comparisons between experimental and numerical modal parameters. Afterwards, the infill walls, with their estimated properties, are included in the f.e. structural model. Finally, the modal parameters of the global f.e. model are compared with the experimental ones obtained from an in-situ ambient vibration measurement and the Operational Modal Analysis (OMA) of the global structure. Results are presented and discussed in terms of resonance frequencies and relevant mode shapes.

2. THE MOCK-UP

2.1. Structural description

The investigated mock-up is a steel-concrete composite structure (Figure 1) consisting of a pair of one-storey two-bay moment-resisting frames with a height of 3.00 m and spans of 4.20 m. The columns consist of HE160A hot rolled grade S355 steel profiles. The composite beams are also obtained with HE160A grade S355 steel profiles and a 120 mm thick slab realized with a C30/37 concrete cast on a collaborating EGB210 steel sheet. A ϕ6/200 wire fabric is also placed into the slab, which is connected to the beams by Nelson studs in order to ensure full shear connection. The beam-to-column connections are obtained by means of a beam end-plate bolted to a column flange. Nine concrete blocks are placed over the slab to simulate the presence of additional masses due to super-dead and live loads. Two IMWs (called W1 and W2) are built filling only one of the longitudinal bays. The latter are built with 250 x 250 x 60 mm hollow clay bricks with head and bed 10 mm thick mortar joints.

2.2. Mock-up dynamic characterization

Ambient vibration measurements and the OMA are carried out with the aim of identifying the modal parameters of the whole composite structure, namely the natural frequencies and mode shapes of the infilled structure. The dynamic test is performed exploiting six low-noise uniaxial piezoelectric accelerometers with sensitivity of 10 V/g, frequency range of 0.07 – 300 Hz and resolution of 1 μg, a 24-bit data acquisition system, coaxial cables and a laptop equipped with a LabView software. During the test, 2000 s long records sampled at a rate of 2048 Hz are acquired, in order to have enough data to obtain modal parameters with a good accuracy [11]. The accelerometers are placed over the floor slab: three measuring in longitudinal direction (1L, 2L and 3L) and the other three in the transverse direction (1T, 2T and 3T), as shown in Figure 2. The recorded data are processed with standard signal processing techniques before performing modal analyses. First, data are examined to cut those parts that show anomalous behaviours (signal clipping, intermittent noise, spikes and so on) due to sensor or measurement chain malfunctioning or due to signal saturation. Then, the contribution of spurious trends is eliminated by subtracting the contribution obtained by fitting the signals with a polynomial function and the high frequency contribution is eliminated by filtering with a Butterworth low pass filter characterized by order four and cut-off frequency of 20 Hz. Finally, signals are down-sampled to decrease the number of data and make faster the subsequent analyses. The Covariance-driven Stochastic Subspace Identification (SSI-COV) method is used to identify the modal parameters of the structure [12]. As results, the first three natural frequency (Table 1) and the relevant mode shapes (Figure 3) of the infilled steel-concrete composite frame are obtained.

3. PROPOSED METODHOLOGY FOR THE IMWS STIFFNESS ESTIMATION

3.1. IMWs impact load tests

The proposed procedure for the stiffness estimation of IMWs stems from the dynamic dentification of the out-of-plane behaviour through experimental tests. Impact load tests and the Experimental Modal Analysis (EMA) are performed with the aim to investigate the out-of-plane dynamic behaviour of the IMWs. Impact tests are performed on both the IMWs adopting one instrumented hammer equipped with a medium tip having sensitivity of 0.23 mV/N, measurement range ± 22240 N and frequency range of 0 – 650 Hz, two uniaxial shear piezoelectric accelerometers with sensitivity of 0.3 V/g and frequency range of 1 – 2000 Hz, a 24-bit data acquisition system, coaxial cables and a laptop equipped with a basic LabView software. Each IMWs is divided into twenty-five grid points (five columns and five rows) and the two accelerometers are fixed in two of them (B2 and C3) in order to identify as much vibration modes as possible. The impulse forces, instead, are applied in each grid points; in details, four or more strokes are applied in each point to obtain a reliable data set. A commercial software [13] is used to identify the modal parameters of the tested IMWs. Six and nine out-of-plane vibration modes are identified for walls W1 and W2, respectively. The experimental natural frequencies are listed in Table 2, while the relevant experimental mode shapes are shown in Figure 4.

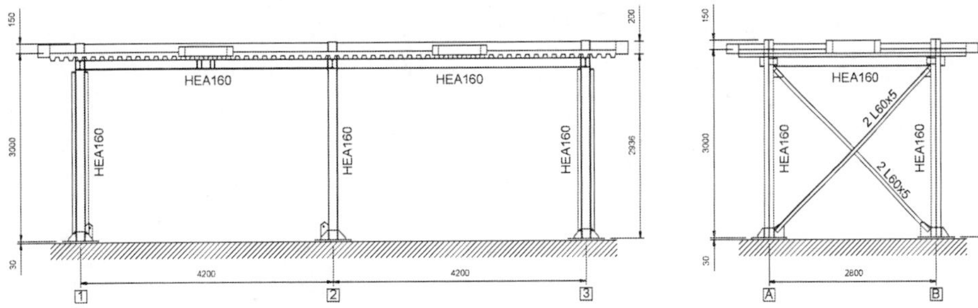

Figure 1. Steel-concrete composite mock-up.

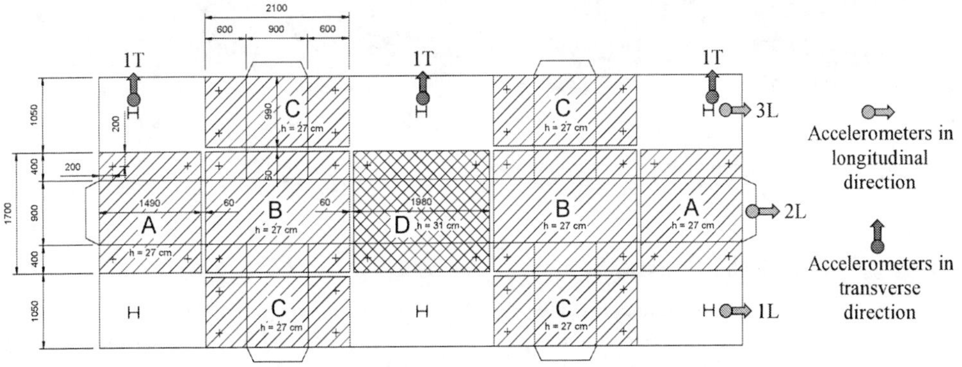

Figure 2. Accelerometers arrangement over the floor slab.

Table 1. Experimental natural frequencies of the infilled mock-up.

Mode	Mode typology	Frequency [Hz]
1	Transversal	8.40
2	Rotational/Longitudinal	14.66
3	Rotational	15.20

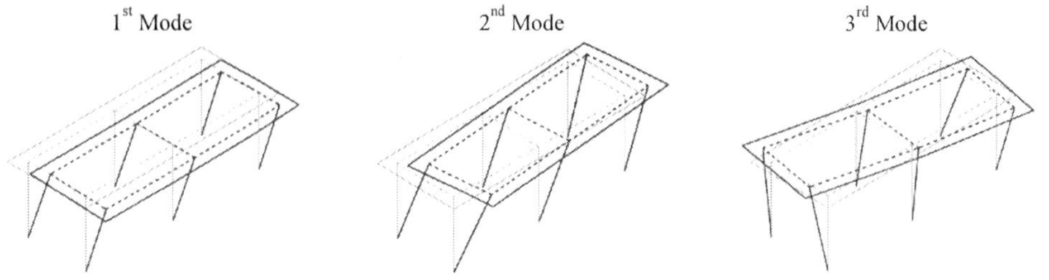

Figure 3. Experimental mode shapes of the infilled mock-up.

Table 2. Experimental natural frequencies for the tested IMWs.

Mode	Mode name	Frequency [Hz]	
		W1	W2
1	I	16.28	18.43
2	II vertical	27.82	28.41
3	II horizontal	/	43.39
4	III vertical	46.56	46.85
5	IV	56.37	57.39
6	IV vertical	/	64.50
7	VI horizontal	/	74.95

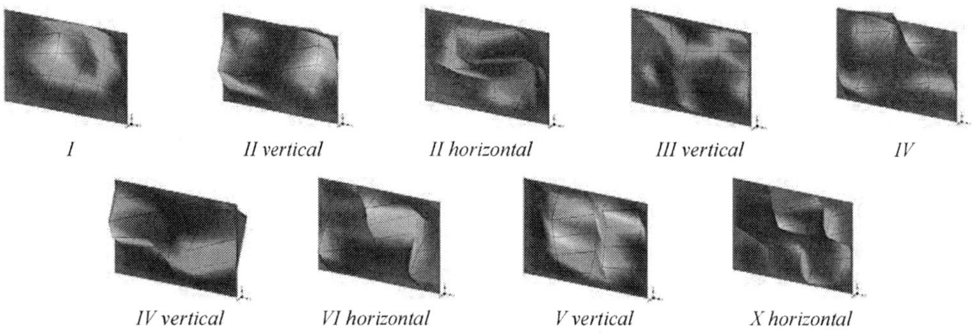

Figure 4. Experimental mode shapes of the tested IMWs.

3.2. Numerical estimation of IMWs stiffness

Numerical f.e. models of the investigated IMWs are developed by means of SAP2000 code. Each IMW is assumed to be clamped and modelled with bi-dimensional thin shell elements consistently with the geometric dimensions of the real panels (height, length and thickness). For the sake of simplicity, the material is considered homogeneous, elastic and isotropic. In this case, the governing differential equation for the free vibration of a plate is given by

$$D\nabla^4 w - \rho h \omega^2 w = 0 \tag{1}$$

where

$$D = Eh^3/12(1 - \nu^2) \tag{2}$$

In Eq. (1), w is the flexural displacement, ω is the angular frequency and ρ and h are the mass density and the thickness of the plate, respectively. Furthermore, in Eq. (2), D is the flexural rigidity of the plate and ν is the Poisson's ratio of the material, which is assumed to be 0.2 since it is assumed not to sensibly affect the out-of-plane vibrations of the plate. Finally, E is the elastic modulus of the material, which is considered to be the only unknown parameter. The latter is estimated by means of an iterative procedure that ends once the numerical out-of-plane modal parameters of the panel fit well the experimental ones previously identified. The Young moduli estimated through the above mentioned methodology are reported in Table 3.

4. IMWS STIFFNESS VALIDATION AND USES

To assess the reliability of the proposed methodology for the estimation of the stiffness contribution of the IMWs, a refined global f.e. model of the steel-concrete composite mock-up is used. In detail, a numerical model already available from a previous research and calibrated to simulate the behaviour of the frame without the IMWs is adopted. The latter is modified to include the IMWs, which are modelled through thin shell elements having geometric parameters consistent with the real dimensions of the panels. Concerning the mechanical properties of the IMWs material, the elastic moduli estimated through the proposed methodology are adopted, assuming that the material properties governing the out-of-plane response are the same of those governing the in-plane behaviour. The latter assumption stems from two basic considerations: (*i*) the proposed procedure ought to be simple and (*ii*) the behaviour of the wall can be considered to be similar to that of a homogenous isotropic plate for very low strains (such those experienced as a consequence of the ambient vibrations), disregarding its overall non-homogeneity. A classical modal analysis is performed on the developed model to obtain the numerical natural frequencies and the relevant mode shapes. Table 4 compares the experimental and numerical natural frequencies. It is worth noting that the resonance frequencies obtained from the f.e. model are in good agreement with the experimental ones. In Figure 5 the numerical and experimental mode shapes are compared; the model is able to capture very well the experimental mode shapes.

Table 3. Estimated elastic moduli E for the tested IMWs.

Wall name	Elastic modulus [MPa]
W1	2850
W2	3650

Table 4. Comparison between experimental and numerical natural frequencies for the infilled mock-up.

Mode	Frequency [Hz]	
	Experimental	Numerical
Transversal	8.40	8.43
Rotational/Longitudinal	14.66	14.20
Rotational	15.20	15.13

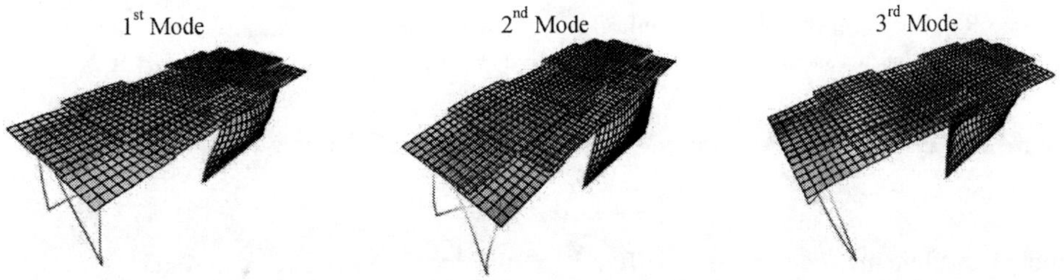

Figure 5. Numerical mode shapes of the infilled mock-up.

5. CONCLUSIONS

In this paper, the influence of IMWs on the dynamic behaviour of a steel-concrete composite structures has been investigated and a procedure to develop an accurate f.e. model which considers both the mass and stiffness contributions of the infills has been presented, with reference to a real-scale mock-up located at the Materials and Structures Testing Laboratory of the Università Politecnica delle Marche. Firstly, the IMWs built within the composite structure have been tested dynamically to identify their out-of-plane dynamic properties, which have been used as a benchmark to calibrate the stiffness of the tested IMWs adopting an iterative procedure based on the comparison between experimental and numerical modal parameters of the walls. Then, the IMWs have been modelled within a global f.e. model of the composite frame as thin, isotropic and homogeneous shell elements, considering the mechanical properties previously estimated. The modal parameters of the whole structure obtained from the numerical model have been compared with the experimental ones achieved by means of the OMA, based on ambient vibration measurements performed after the construction of the IMWs. Results (in terms of resonance frequencies and mode shapes) show a very good agreement, proving the reliability of the walls stiffness estimated through the proposed methodology.

REFERENCES

[1] Stafford-Smith, B., & Carter, C. (1969). A method for analysis for infilled frames. In: *Proc. Inst. Civ. Eng.* (pp. 31-48).

[2] Mainstone, R.J. (1974). Supplementary note on the stiffness and strength of infilled frames. *Building Research Station*, Watford, U.K.

[3] Crisafulli, F.J., & Carr A.J. (2007). Proposed macro-model for the analysis of infilled frame structures. *Bull. N.Z. Soc. Earthquake Eng.*, 40(2), 69-77.

[4] Vicente, R., Rodrigues, H., Arede, A., & Varum, H. (2016). Simplified macro-model for infill masonry walls considering the out-of-plane behaviour. *Earthquake Eng. Struct. Dyn.*, 45(4), 507-524.

[5] Di Trapani, F., Shing, P.B., & Cavaleri L. (2018). Macroelement model for in-plane and out-of-plane responses of masonry infills in frame structures. *Journal Struct. Eng.*, 144(2), 1-13.

[6] Koutromanos, I., Stavridis, A., Shing, P.B., & William, K. (2011). Numerical modelling of masonry infilled RC frames subjected to seismic loads. *Comp. Struct.*, 89(11-12), 1026-1037.

[7] Mazza, F. (2018). In-plane-out-of-plane non-linear model of masonry infills in the seismic analysis of r.c. framed buildings. *Earthquake Eng. Struct. Dyn.*, 1-22.

[8] Bosilikov, V., Page, A., Bokan-Bosilikov, V., & Zarnic R. (2003). Performance based studies of in-plane loaded unreinforced masonry walls. *Masonry Int.*, 16(2), 39-50.

[9] Frumento, S., Magenes, G., Morandi, P., & Calvi, G.M. (2009). Interpretation of experimental shear tests on clay brick masonry walls and evaluation of q-factors for seismic design. *Research report EUCENTRE 2009/02*, Pavia, IUSS Press.

[10] Petry, S., & Beyer, K. (2015). Cyclic test data of six unreinforced masonry walls with different boundary conditions. *Earthquake Spectra*, 31(4), 2459-2484.

[11] Canteni, R. (2005). Experimental methods used in system identification of civil engineering structures. In: *Proc. 1st Int. Conf. on Operational Modal Analysis* (pp. 249-260). Copenhagen, Denmark.

[12] Juang, J.N. (1994). *Applied system identification.* Prentice-Hall Englewood Cliffs, New Jersey, USA

[13] National Instruments. (2013). ModalVIEW: Application for Modal Testing and Analysis, AB Signal Inc.

iomac
International Operational Modal Analysis Conference

IOMAC'19

8th International Operational Modal Analysis Conference
2019 May13-15 Copenhagen

ON THE STRUCTURAL UPDATING USING OPERATIONAL RESPONSES OF A REALISTIC WING MODEL: THE RIBES TEST ARTICLE

Giuliano Coppotelli[1], *Federico Di Giandomenico*[2], *Corrado Groth*[4], *Stefano Porziani*[5], *Andrea Chiappa*[6] *and Marco Evangelos Biancolini*[7]

[1] Associate Professor, University of Rome "La Sapienza", giuliano.coppotelli@uniroma1.it
[2] Engineer, University of Rome "La Sapienza", fede.digiando@gmail.com
[3] Research Fellow, University of Rome "Tor Vergata", corrado.groth@uniroma2.it
[4] Research Fellow, University of Rome "Tor Vergata", stefano.porziani@uniroma2.it
[5] Research Fellow, University of Rome "Tor Vergata", andrea.chiappa@uniroma2.it
[6] Associate Professor, University of Rome "Tor Vergata", biancolini@ing.uniroma2.it

ABSTRACT

The assessing of the numerical model of a structure to improve its design is of great importance. When referring to the aircraft dynamic properties, a high accuracy numerical model could be achieved if the modal parameters are compared with those characterizing the flying vehicle. In this paper, the updating of the finite element model of a realistic wing model is carried out using the dynamic properties estimated from the analysis of the structure output responses. The experimental modal parameters are used as target characteristics in the structural updating process. The finite element dynamic representation of the wing model, designed and manufactured in order to replicate a typical metallic wing box structure, has been improved by tuning the most sensitive structural parameters.

Keywords: Operational Modal Analysis, F.E. Model, Experimental/Numerical Correlation, and Structural Updating

1. INTRODUCTION

For the Aeronautical Industry the assessing of the numerical model of a structure to improve its design is of great importance. When referring to the evaluation of the aircraft dynamic properties, a high accuracy numerical model could be achieved if the modal parameters are compared with those characterizing the flying vehicle. Operational Modal Analysis (OMA) techniques were developed in the recent years, allowing the estimate of the dynamic properties of a structure (natural frequencies, damping ratios and mode shapes) without measuring the input forces, Refs. [1, 2, 3, 4]. These techniques are not only sought for the reduction of the time-to-market of new designs, but also for the characterization of the actual boundary conditions of the structures, Ref. [5]. The main hypothesis on which all the OMA methods rely is the requirement that the input excitation is a stochastic broad-band loading. Several OMA procedures, both in the time and frequency domain, were developed in order to identify the modal parameters of an aeronautical structure in operative condition. The time-domain-based methodologies estimate the modal model from the state-space representation of the system obtained from the time domain data, Ref. [3]. In contrast, the frequency-domain-based approaches are focused on the identification of the spectral properties of the system from the power spectral density functions of the output responses, Ref. [6], or, from the (biased) frequency response functions obtained by exploiting the properties of the Hilbert transform, Ref. [2]. Current days numerical and and experimental structural characterizations could be considered of high accuracy. Since numerical techniques simulate reality, experimental modal analysis is essential to verify accuracy of the numerical model and correct it if considerable discrepancies are present. However, limits of both numerical and experimental analysis arise if correlation between them is considered, Refs. [7, 8, 9]. To better understand the mechanical component, requesting an higher and higher level of correlation between models, is a relevant issue for industrials. The main limiting issues for a common use of updating the techniques relate to the techniques themselves that fail to give useful updating information and require an high level of experience of the structural analyst. Generally, the finite element representation and the number of experimental information are actually the weak elements in any updating procedures. Numerical models still need to be improved to detect and take into account possible deviations from the linear elastic behavior, for example non-linear elasto-dynamic properties, the experimental data gives a picture of the real structural component only with a limited set of data. Thus, following the correlation between the two models through specific coefficients, structural updating techniques are introduced in order to modify the initial numerical model and approach numerical modal parameters and experimental ones. Yet, the selection of the structural parameters to be updated still represent a crucial choice that the analyst must face with. In this paper, the structural updating of the finite element model of a realistic wing model is carried out using as reference experimental dynamic properties those from the analysis of the wing output responses subjected to random excitation. The experimental modal parameters, achieved by several operational modal analysis methods, Refs. [1, 2, 3], are used as target characteristics in the structural updating process.

The structure behavior investigated in this paper is the one used in the "Radial basis functions at fluid Interface Boundaries to Envelope flow results for advanced Structural analysis" (RIBES) project. Such a project, led by the University of Rome *"Tor Vergata,"* was funded within the 7th European Union's Research and Innovation funding program, under the Clean Sky framework, and had a duration of two years. The aim of the RIBES project was on developing an innovative approach for loads mapping based on Radial Basis Functions (RBF) theory, Ref. [10], and a suite of tools devoted to the improvement of accuracy in coupled fluid-structure interaction (FSI) analyses. The research covered three main topics. The first one was the development of a load mapping procedure; then the development of a structural optimization procedure; finally, the setting up an experimental campaign. Outcomes from all the topics have been disseminated in literature, Refs. [11, 12, 13, 14], in this paper the latter will be expanded with response and operational analyses.

In the next sections, first the topology and geometry of the RIBES wing will be explained, highlighting the manufacturing methodologies employed, then the RIBES wing will be detailed, including the structural aspects of its design, testing and validation. The resulting F.E model has been improved taking advantages by properly tuning the most sensitive structural parameters, Refs. [15, 16, 17, 18, 19, 20].

2. THEORETICAL BACKGROUND

In this section some background on two operational modal analysis methods used to estimate the modal parameters, as well as the updating technique used to improve the correlation of the RIBES wing section model will be outlined. Both frequency and time domain methods are available in the numerical procedure called *NIMA* (Natural Input Modal Analysis) developed at the Department of Mechanical and Aerospace Engineering of the University of Rome *"La Sapienza"*.

2.1. Recalls on Operational Modal Analysis

2.1.1. Hilbert Transform Method, HTM

From the measurements of the output responses y_i, $i = 1, 2, \cdots, N_o$, (being N_o the number of measurement points) over N_t time samples, it is possible to build the so called output spectral density function matrix, $\mathbf{G}_{yy}(\omega_k) \in \mathcal{C}^{N_o \times N_o}$, $k = 1, \cdots, N_t/2$ composed by spectral density functions, $G_{y_i y_j}(\omega_k)$, defined between the i-th and j-th output responses, at the k-th spectral line

$$\mathbf{G}_{yy}(\omega_k) = \begin{pmatrix} G_{y_1 y_1}(\omega_k) & \cdots & G_{y_1 y_{N_o}}(\omega_k) \\ \vdots & \ddots & \vdots \\ G_{y_{N_o} y_1}(\omega_k) & \cdots & G_{y_{N_o} y_{N_o}}(\omega_k) \end{pmatrix} \tag{1}$$

By using the Hilbert transform the imaginary part of a causal function can be estimated starting from its real part, Ref. [21]. The polar representation of a driving point FRF ($H_{ii}(\omega)$) is given by introducing the amplitude ($|H_{ii}(\omega)|$) and the phase ($\phi_{ii}(\omega)$) functions as:

$$H_{ii}(\omega) = |H_{ii}(\omega)| e^{-j\phi_{ii}(\omega)} \tag{2}$$

or, by introducing the natural logarithm, could be expressed as

$$ln\,[H_{ii}(\omega)] = G_{ii}(\omega) - j\phi_{ii}(\omega) \tag{3}$$

in which $G_{ii}(\omega) = ln|H_{ii}(\omega)|$ is the gain function. Considering that the real part of the FRF is an even function and the imaginary part is an odd function, therefore the gain and the phase are even and odd, respectively. As a result the left-hand side of the Eq.(3) could be expressed as the sum of a pair of Hilbert transform functions such that

$$\phi_{ii}(\omega) \quad = \quad -\hat{G}_{ii}(\omega) \tag{4}$$

The gain function is related to the spectral density function as:

$$\mathbf{G}_{yy}(\omega_k) = \mathbf{H}(\omega_k)\mathbf{G}_{ff}(\omega_k)\mathbf{H}^H(\omega_k) \tag{5}$$

where the input spectral density matrix, defined between the N_i inputs, *i.e.*, $\mathbf{G}_{ff}(\omega_k) \in \mathcal{C}^{N_i \times N_i}$, is assumed to be derived from a white noise excitation. This implies that $\mathbf{G}_{ff}(\omega_k)$ is frequency independent, that is $\mathbf{G}_{ff}(\omega_k) = \mathbf{G}_{ff}$, and is a diagonal matrix when the input excitation is uncorrelated in the space domain. By applying the natural logarithm and performing the Hilbert transform, Eq.(5) becomes:

$$\mathcal{H}\left[\ln(G_{y_i y_i}(\omega))\right] = 2\mathcal{H}\left[\ln|H_{ii}(\omega)|\right] \tag{6}$$

in which the input spectral density contribution, $G_{f_i f_i}$, is null, as the Hilbert transform of a constant is zero. Combining the previous Eqs.(4) and (6) it is possible to write

$$\phi_{ii}(\omega) = -\frac{1}{2}\mathcal{H}\left[\ln(G_{y_i y_i}(\omega))\right] \tag{7}$$

Therefore, the FRF in the i-th driving point is available. It is possible to demonstrate that the off-diagonal terms of the FRF are derivable from the comparison between the commonly used H_1 and H_2 estimators, Refs. [2, 22]:

$$H_{ij}(\omega) = \frac{G_{y_i y_j}(\omega)}{\sqrt{G_{f_i f_i} H_{ii}^*(\omega)}} \tag{8}$$

Obviously the estimated functions are unbiased depending on the unknown input forces. The modal parameters are evaluated with a least square approximation, considering the expression of FRF in pole-residue terms. In the frequency range of definition of the FRF, the number of modes, N_m, is not known, therefore a stabilization diagram is introduced to estimate it by means of an iterative procedure. It is worth remarking that the structural properties are independent from the order used to describe the system, thus stable poles are representative of natural frequencies, Ref. [23].

2.1.2. Frequency Domain Decomposition, FDD

From the measurements of the output responses y_i, $i = 1, 2, \cdots, N_o$, (being N_o the number of measurement points) over N_t time samples, it is possible to build the so called output spectral density function matrix, $\mathbf{G}_{yy}(\omega_k) \in \mathcal{C}^{N_o \times N_o}$, $k = 1, \cdots, N_t/2$ from the evaluation of the spectral density functions, $G_{y_i y_j}(\omega_k)$, defined between the i-th and j-th output responses, at the k-th spectral line, as:

$$\mathbf{G}_{yy}(\omega_k) = \begin{pmatrix} G_{y_1 y_1}(\omega_k) & \dots & G_{y_1 y_{N_o}}(\omega_k) \\ \vdots & \ddots & \vdots \\ G_{y_{N_o} y_1}(\omega_k) & \dots & G_{y_{N_o} y_{N_o}}(\omega_k) \end{pmatrix} \tag{9}$$

Because such response spectral matrix is Hermitian, $\mathbf{G}^H_{y_i y_j}(\omega_k) = \mathbf{G}_{y_j y_i}(\omega_k)$, with real positive diagonal elements, the singular value decomposition of the output spectral density matrix, for each of the k-th available spectral lines could be written as, Ref. [1]:

$$\mathbf{G}_{yy}(\omega_k) = \mathbf{U}_k(\omega_k)\mathbf{\Sigma}_k(\omega_k)\mathbf{U}_k^H(\omega_k) \tag{10}$$

in which $\mathbf{U}_k(\omega_k) \in \mathcal{C}^{N_o \times N_o}$ is the matrix of left singular vectors and $\mathbf{\Sigma}_k(\omega_k) \in \mathcal{R}^{+(N_o \times N_o)}$ is the diagonal matrix of singular values. Under the hypothesis that the structure behaves as a single degree of freedom system around the peak of resonance, ω_n, the rank of $\mathbf{G}_{yy}(\omega_k)$ tends to one as the current frequency ω_k approaches one of the natural frequency of the structure, ω_n. The output spectral density matrix could be expressed in terms of the modal components as:

$$\mathbf{G}_{yy}(\omega_k) = \sum_{i=1}^{N_m} \left(\frac{\boldsymbol{\psi}^{(i)} \bar{\boldsymbol{\varphi}}^{(i)T}}{j\omega_k - \lambda_i} + \frac{\boldsymbol{\psi}^{(i)*} \bar{\boldsymbol{\varphi}}^{(i)H}}{j\omega_k - \lambda_i^*} + \frac{\bar{\boldsymbol{\varphi}}^{(i)} \boldsymbol{\psi}^{(i)T}}{-j\omega_k - \lambda_i} + \frac{\bar{\boldsymbol{\varphi}}^{(i)*} \boldsymbol{\psi}^{(i)H}}{-j\omega_k - \lambda_i^*} \right) \tag{11}$$

in which $\bar{\boldsymbol{\varphi}}^{(i)}$ takes into account the contribution of the input excitation to the i-th participation factor. By comparing Eq. (11) and Eq. (10) when $\omega_k = \omega_n$, a good estimate of the mode shape could be achieved from the singular vector corresponding to the only non-zero singular value. Moreover, from Eq.(11), the correlation matrix could be written in terms of the modal parameters as:

$$\mathbf{R}(\tau) = \sum_{i=1}^{N_m} \left(\boldsymbol{\psi}^{(i)} \bar{\boldsymbol{\varphi}}^{(i)} e^{\lambda_i \tau} + \boldsymbol{\psi}^{(i)*} \bar{\boldsymbol{\varphi}}^{(i)H} e^{\lambda_i^* \tau} \right) \tag{12}$$

If such correlation functions are evaluated by an inverse Fourier transform of the power spectral density matrix in the neighborhood of the identified natural frequency, and the mode shapes are well separated, then they correspond to the free decay of an equivalent SDOF system. Therefore, the logarithmic decrement technique could be applied to estimate the damping ratio, Ref. [6, 24].

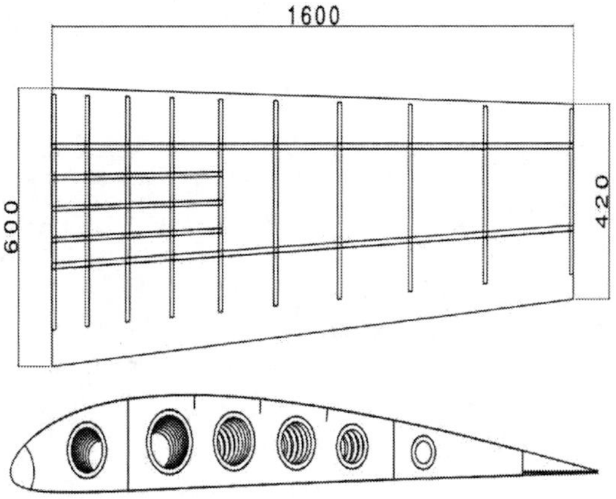

Figure 1: RIBES wing section topology.

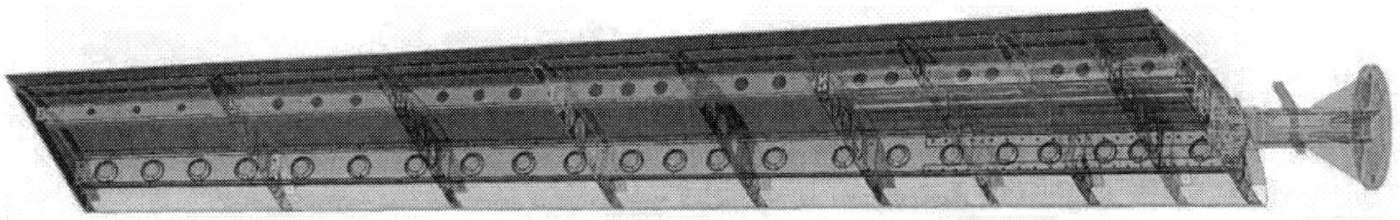

Figure 2: RIBES wing section drawing.

3. DESCRIPTION OF THE RIBES WING SECTION

As briefly mentioned before in the Introduction, the RIBES test article was conceived with two main requirements: to replicate a typical aeronautical design , to reproduce a realistic wing load distribution recurring to a low-speed wind tunnel. The restriction of respecting the typical assembly of a metallic aeronautical structure (composed by elements such as spars, ribs and stringers) and the necessity to build a model scaled to a wingspan of 1.6 m go in the direction of an excessively stiff structure, unsuitable to undergo significant deformations in a low-speed wind tunnel. A direct scaling of an existing wing was unfeasible for manufacturing reasons, since the reduction of skin thicknesses and rivets would have led to unmanageable dimensions. For this reason, extra care was given to the design phase, targeted to produce a model flexible enough, still respecting the project requirements. The final wing layout derived from a design phase that included coupled structural and fluid-dynamic studies, as well as manufacturing and maintenance considerations. The wing profile was devised in order to fulfill load shape requirements on the wing, and was obtained scaling the *"Götingen"* 398 airfoil so to obtain a thickness to chord ratio of $t/c = 11$, further modifying its leading edge to reduce and delay stall, Ref. [25]. Root and tip chords were chosen to be 0.6m and 0.42m respectively, with a taper ratio of 0.7. Wing topology consists in ten ribs and two C-shaped spars, located at 20% and 60% of the root chord. Fig. 1 shows the adopted arrangement for the wing, in which the three stringers covering the first four bays were added to increase upper skin stiffness, which resulted sensitive to buckling problems during wind tunnel loading. Model dimensioning took into account the operative wind tunnel conditions, namely 40 m/s for the flow velocity and 60 Kg of lift force. A 0.6 mm thickness was chosen for all the 2024-T3 Aluminum sheet panels composing the wing, with the exception of the 1 mm thick spars that were further reinforced in the most loaded root region. The final CAD geometry is visible in Fig. 2. External panels were fastened to the structure recurring to flush head CherryMAX rivets and treated with Alodine and primer for the paint. Measurements took place employing 25 strain gauges and 81 pressure taps distributed over the wing surface. Results from the experimental testing campaign were published on the RIBES website (http://ribes-project.eu/) along with the FEM and CFD models produced and used for the project activities. Further experimental testing, aimed to assess wing stiffness, proceeded via static loading, Ref. [26] and highlighted differences in the value of displacements between the FEM model and the test article. To better match the stiffness captured experimentally, a new and more refined model was developed with a higher level of detail, especially as concerns the riveted junctions. In the latter model, spring elements played the role of rivets, whilst in the former one attached panels were considered glued and modeled with boundary nodes coincident. A FEM modal analysis of the model published online (the first of the above mentioned) used Nastran as solver and showed the results summarized in Tab. 1, which reports the list of the first 8 vibrational frequencies.

Table 1: Natural frequencies for the RIBES model, published online.

Mode #	1	2	3	4	5	6	7	8
Natural frequency [Hz]	104.463	112.173	112.809	118.489	123.725	127.103	129.588	131.177

4. EXPERIMENTAL INVESTIGATION

As illustrated in Fig. 3 the RIBES wing section was suspended by means of bungee cords from the laboratory ceiling in order to perform operational modal analysis. This experimental configuration could be considered good enough to mimic free-free boundary conditions since the rigid body motion natural frequencies were estimated to be lower than 11.5 Hz, that is about an order of magnitude lower than the first elastic mode natural frequency.

Figure 3: Experimental setup of the RIBES wing section.

The dynamic characteristic of the structure has been estimated from the acceleration responses recorded during finger tapping excitation. This kind of excitation is proved to be random both in space and time. The measured out-of-plane degrees of freedom were 8, evenly distributed on the wing section. The acquisition parameters are reported in Tab. 2

Table 2: Acquisition parameters.

Sampling frequency, f_s (Hz)	1024
Number of Samples, T (s)	2^{16}
Cutoff High Pass Filter, f_{filt} (Hz)	0.6

The sample rate was chosen high enough in order to obtain the necessary bandwidth to estimate at least the first six modes, whereas the high number of sampling points improved the accuracy of the estimate. Besides, a high pass filter was employed to de-trend the signals to zero mean. Indeed, the DC offsets was eliminated because of the excessive noise in the low frequency region typical of the sensors. Because both the OMA methods, presented in the previous Section 2.1., operate in the frquency domain, the PSD matrix was the first evaluated. To this end, 64 data blocks, with an overlap of 90%, and a Hanning window were used to reduce noise variance and leakage related issues. No remarkable differences between the modal parameters estimated using the considered OMA methods have been observed. Only the damping ratios exhibited a larger deviation, compared to the other modal properties, that could be, however, considered acceptable. Therefore, the first six estimated natural frequencies, f_n, and damping ratios, ζ_n, reported in Tab. 3, are representative of both the OMA methods, although the damping ratios are the average between the methods. Finally, in Figs. 10, 11, 12, 13, 14 and 15, left, the first six estimated mode shapes are depicted regardless the estimated method.

Table 3: Estimated natural frequencies and damping ratios.

Mode #	Natural frequency, f_n (Hz)	Damping ratio, ζ_n (%)
1	90.057	1.15
2	110.682	0.01
3	122.722	0.02
4	145.830	0.41
5	182.480	0.54
6	202.086	0.49

5. CORRELATION AND UPDATING OF THE RIBES F.E. MODEL

The experimental vibrational test made use of eight accelerometers arranged over the wing model. In order to achieve a consistent comparison between empirical and numerical results, eigenvectors related to the frequencies of Tab. 4 were extracted at the same points at which the accelerometers were positioned in the experimental setup.

Table 4: Comparison between experimental and numerical results.

Model	Frequency			
	Experimental [Hz]	Numerical [Hz]	Error %	MAC %
1	90.057	87.72	2.6	99
2	110.682	113.08	2.2	95
3	122.722	117.30	4.4	91
4	145.830	147.17	0.9	96
5	182.480	189.67	3.9	43
6	202.086	210.64	4.2	62

Fig. 4 shows the numerical model of the wing, in which the sites of experimental and numerical data acquisition are connected by 3 Nastran "plot-only-elements" (in transparency). Fig. 5 reports the original RIBES FEM model (composed by 97130 linear plate elements), as available online. In the picture, the upper skin panel is not visible to give an insight of the inner structure. Several discrepancies arose

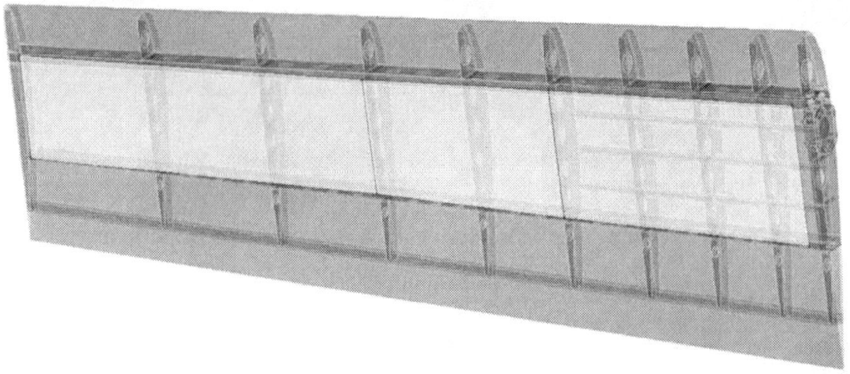

Figure 4: Pairing of the numerical-experimental degrees of freedom.

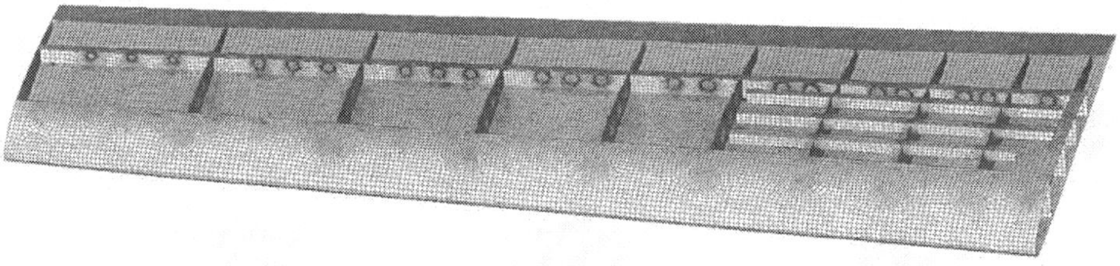

Figure 5: Original FEM model of RIBES wing section, from the RIBES website.

between experimental data and numerical results from the analysis conducted on the cited model. Fig. 6 shows the Modal Assurance Criterion (MAC) table, it gives a visual representation through a color scale of the matching between the experimental modes and numerical results from the original RIBES model. In this study, the MAC parameter compares available experimental eigenvectors with evaluated numerical eigenvectors. Its value can vary in the range $[0 - 1]$, which represent the case of orthogonality and the case of parallelism, respectively. From the picture, it is observable a poor matching between similar frequencies, while the highest values of the MAC are far from the diagonal, due to the shortcoming of the number of points to represent modal shapes, introducing aliasing phenomena in the space representation. Discrepancies can be attributed to the simplified assumption of modeling all the riveted junctions as perfectly glued, thus increasing the numerical model stiffness compared to the measured one, especially

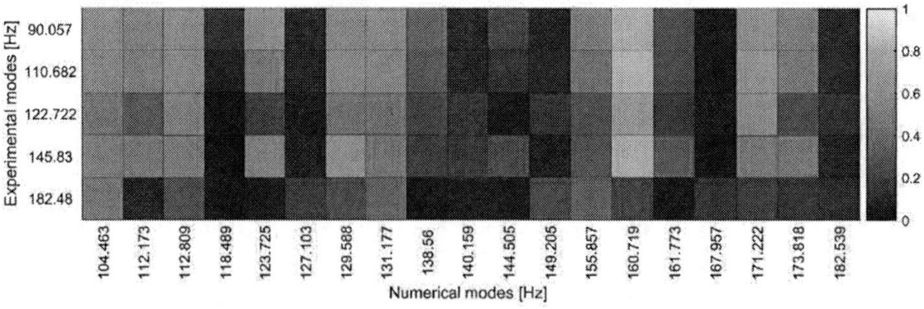

Figure 6: MAC table comparing numerical end experimental modes for the original RIBES FEM model.

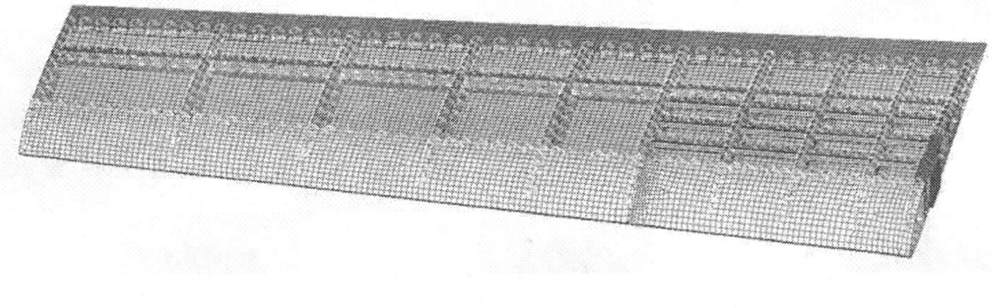

Figure 7: Stiffness-tuned FEM model of RIBES wing section.

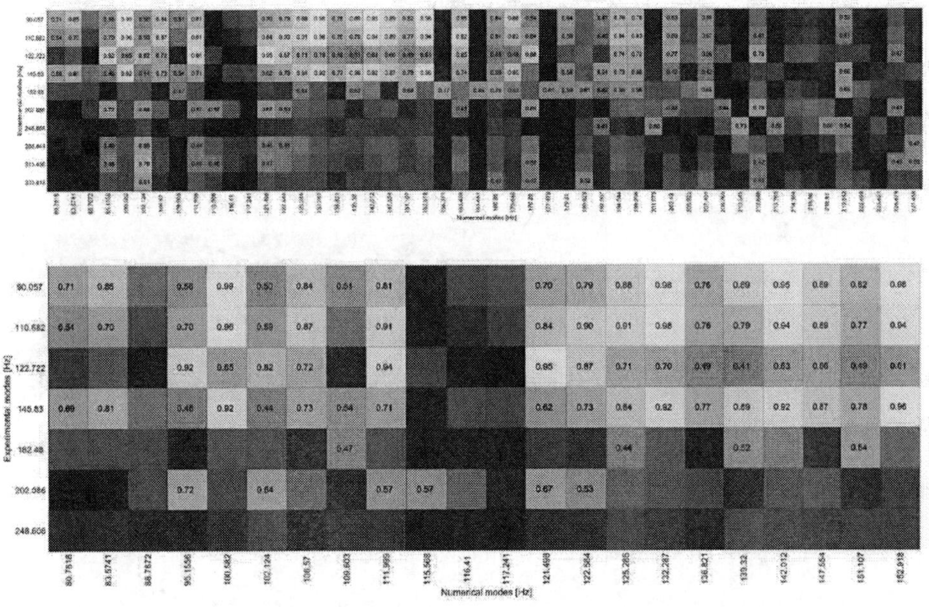

Figure 8: MAC table comparing numerical end experimental modes for the RIBES FEM model in Ref. [26].

in the root region where fastening occurs to a greater extent.

The improved model developed in Ref. [26], shown in Fig. 7 without the upper skin panel, was already modified adding a more detailed description of the riveted junctions and tuned in order to match the experimental static tests described in Ref. [26]. This improved numerical model was then analyzed and results compared to the experimental ones. In Fig. 7 are also visible the rivets, which were modeled using 1032 Nastran "CBUSH" elements and the Huth-Schwarmann formula, Ref. [27], to compute their stiffness. An additional improvement with respect to the previous model is the machined root rib, deploying solid parabolic tetrahedral elements. Numerical eigenvectors were compared to experimental modes by means of the MAC table shown in Fig. 8. Higher correlation numbers are obtained for similar numerical and measured frequencies, while modal shapes characterized by local plate vibrations have lower values. The first numerical mode matching experimental measurements with a correlation of 99% is found at 100.58 Hz while the empirical one is at 90 Hz. It is worth to notice that the weight of rivets, not taken into account so far, indeed play a significant role and it was introduced successively in the present model as concentrated masses in correspondence of spring elements (CBUSH). A total of 810 mass elements was added to the model for a total mass increase of 1.5 Kg. Updating the model with the weight of the rivets improved drastically the results, shifting the first matching mode down to

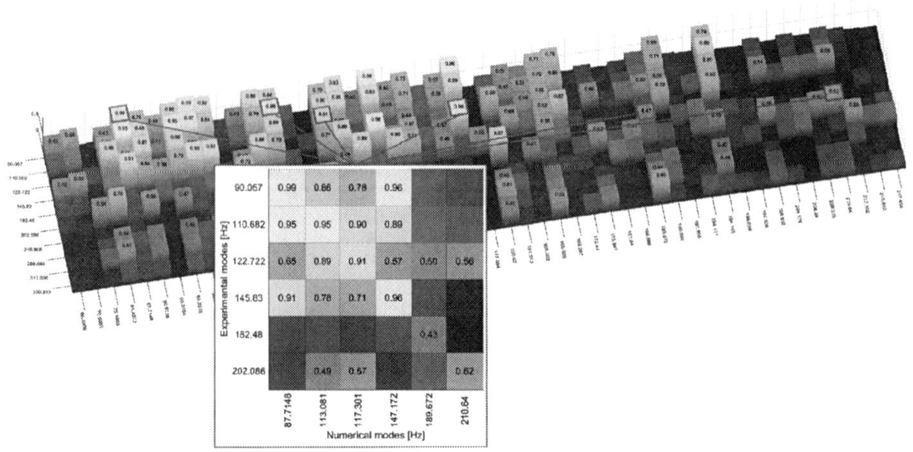

Figure 9: MAC table comparing numerical end experimental modes for the RIBES FEM model updated with rivets mass.

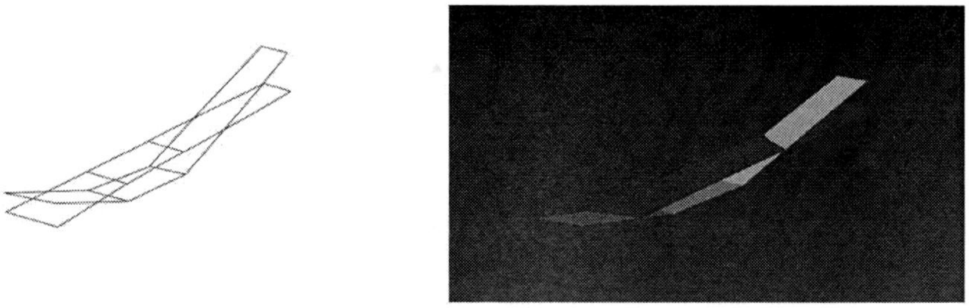

Figure 10: Comparison of the experimental/numerical mode shapes - Mode #1.

87.7 Hz. The resulting MAC table is shown in Fig. 9, with matching modes highlighted in red. Their values are closer to unity with respect to the previous case, proving that a more reliable representation of the measured dynamical behavior was achieved. A stricter agreement occurs also for the values of the frequency, up to the sixth mode. In Tab. 4 the comparison of the first 6 frequencies with the relative error is summarized. From Fig. 10 to Fig. 15, the first 6 mode shapes experimentally estimated are compared to those extracted by means of FEM. The deformed backbones of the test case (on the left) and of the numerical model (on the right) appear as the three-quadrilateral structures built across the measurement points, superimposed with their undeformed shapes. The visual examination of the reported cases shows that measured and simulated fields seem to refer to the same vibration modes. A doubt arises for the fifth matching, where the experimental shape appears excessively rotated with respect to the numerical result, yielding to the lowest value found for the MAC parameter (MAC=0.43).

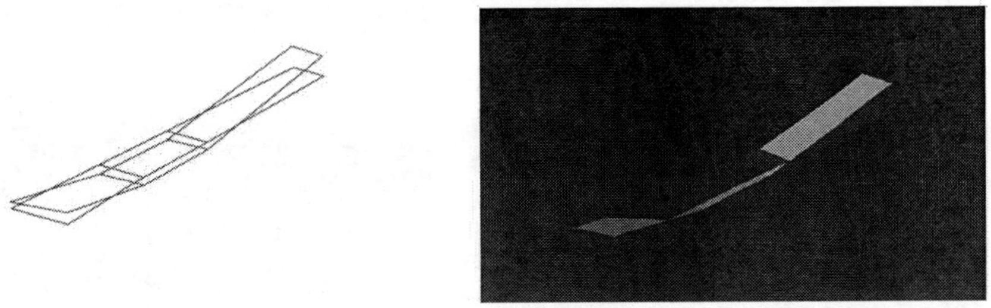

Figure 11: Comparison of the experimental/numerical mode shapes - Mode #2.

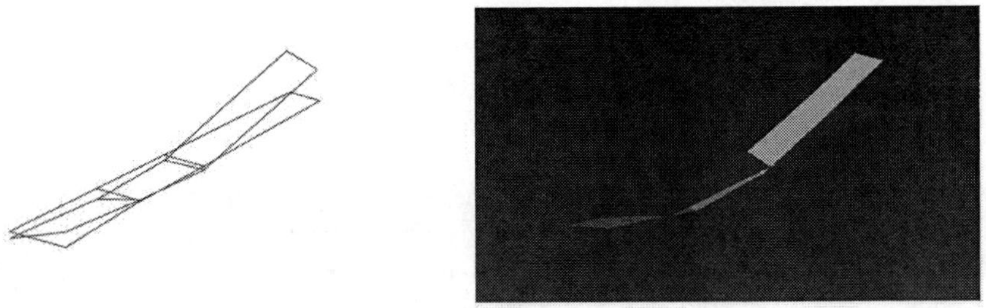

Figure 12: Comparison of the experimental/numerical mode shapes - Mode #3.

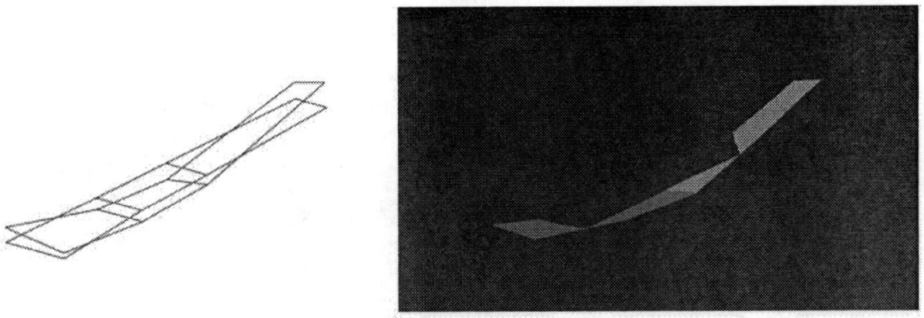

Figure 13: Comparison of the experimental/numerical mode shapes - Mode #4.

Figure 14: Comparison of the experimental/numerical mode shapes - Mode #5.

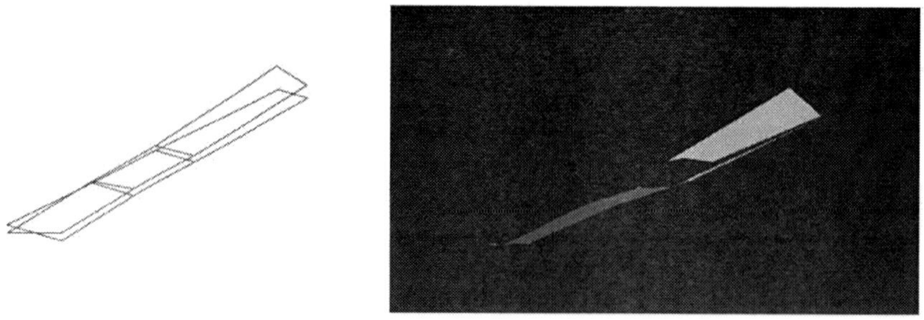

Figure 15: Comparison of the experimental/numerical mode shapes - Mode #6.

6. CONCLUDING REMARKS

In this paper the dynamic finite element model of a realistic wing model, developed within the "Radial basis functions at fluid Interface Boundaries to Envelope flow results for advanced Structural analysis" (RIBES) project, has been carried out using modal parameters estimated in the framework of Operational Modal Analysis (OMA). The chosen OMA methods for the estimate of the modal parameters identified practically the same dynamic properties. Higher uncertainties were associated to the estimate of the damping ratios. The F.E. model was preliminary updated by tuning both the stiffness and mass distribution. However, greater improvement was achieved after re-modeling all the riveted junctions. Indeed, it was found out that the simplified assumption regarding the rivet model, assumed to be perfectly glued, introduced an overall higher stiffness, especially in the root region where fastening occurs to a greater extent. By properly introducing the junction stiffness properties, using the "CBUSH" finite element in the NASTRAN code, it was possible to tune the dynamic model to the experimental findings. Finally, an additional improvement with respect to the previous model was gained by deploying solid parabolic tetrahedral elements when representing the machined root rib.

ACKNOWLEDGEMENTS

This research has been supported by *"F.E. model updating of remotely piloted aircraft (RPA) using flight-test data"*, 2015, University of Rome "La Sapienza".

REFERENCES

[1] R. Brincker, L. Zhang, P. Andersen, Modal Identification from Ambient Responses Using Frequency Domain Decomposition, XVIII IMAC, S. Antonio, TX, (USA), (2000).

[2] A. Agneni, L. Balis Crema, G. Coppotelli, (2010) Output-Only Analysis of Structures with Closely Spaced Modes, Mechanical System and Signal Processing. Special Issue: Operational Modal Analysis, Vol 24, N. 5, July, pp. 1240-1249, ISSN: 0888-3270, doi: 10.1016/j.ymssp.2009.10.013.

[3] P. Van Overschee, B. De Moor, Subspace Identification for Linear Systems, Kluver Academic Publisher, (1996).

[4] F. Poncelet, G. Kerschen, J.-C. Golinval, and D. Verhelst, Output-only modal analysis using blind source separation techniques, Mechanical Systems and Signal Processing, 2007, vol. 21, No. 6, pp. 2335-2358, doi: 10.1016/j.ymssp.2006.12.005.

[5] L. Hermans, H. Van der Auweraer, Industrial Applicability of Modal Analysis on Op- erating Data", Proc. NATO Advance Study Institute on Modal Analysis and Testing, Seimbra (P), (1998).

[6] R. Brincker, C. E. Ventura, P. Andersen, Damping Estimation by Frequency Domain Decomposition, XIX IMAC, Kissimee, FL, (USA), (2001).

[7] Heylen, W., and Avitabile, P., Correlations Considerations - Part 5 (degree of freedom correlation technique) 16th IMAC 1998, Santa Barbara, USA

[8] Imregun, M., and Visser, W.,J., A Review of Model Updating Techniques, The Shock and Vibration Digest, 23(1), 9 20, Jan. 1991

[9] Link, M., Identifiction of Physical Sistem Matrices Using Incomplete Vibration Test Data, 4th IMAC 1986, los Angeles, USA

[10] Biancolini, M.E., 2012. Mesh Morphing and Smoothing by Means of Radial Basis Functions (RBF). Handbook of Research on Computational Science and Engineering I, 347-380. doi:10.4018/978-1-61350-116-0.ch015.

[11] Biancolini, M., Chiappa, A., Giorgetti, F., Groth, C., Cella, U., Salvini, P., 2018. A balanced load mapping method based on radial basis functions and fuzzy sets. International Journal for Numerical Methods in Engineering 115, 1411-1429. URL: https://onlinelibrary.wiley.com/ doi/abs/10.1002/nme.5850, doi:10.1002/nme.5850, arXiv:https://onlinelibrary.wiley.com/doi/pdf/10.1002/nme.5850

[12] Beltramme, D., 2015. Advanced Optimization of the WT Model of the RIBES Project. Master's thesis. University of Rome "Tor Vergata". Rome, Italy.

[13] Cella, U., Biancolini, M.E., Groth, C., Chiappa, A., Beltramme, D., 2015. Development and validation of numerical tools for fsi analysis and structural optimization: the eu ribes project status, in: AIAS 44th National Congress, 2 / 5 September 2015, Messina, Italy.

[14] Groth, C., Porziani, S., Chiappa, A., Giorgetti, F., Cella, U., Nicolosi, F., Della Vecchia P., Mastroddi F., Coppotelli G. Biancolini, M. E. (2018). Structural validation of a realistic wing structure: the RIBES test article. Procedia Structural Integrity, 12, 448-456.

[15] Friswell, M.I., Mottershead, J.E., Finite Element Model updating in structural dynamics, Kluwer Academic Publishers, 1995

[16] Imregun, M., Visser, W.J. and Ewins, D.J., Finite element model updating using frequency response function data - I. Theory and initial investigations, Mechanical Systems and Signal Processing, (1995), 9(2), 187-202

[17] Ziaei Rad,S., Methods for updating numerical models in structural dynamics, PhD Thesis - Dept. of Mechanical Engineering, Imperial College of Science, Technology and Medicine, June 1997, London

[18] Coppotelli G., Balis Crema L. (2002). Effect of Limited DOFs and Noise in Structural Updating. In: International Modal Analysis Conference. p. 1091-1097, Los Angeles, California USA, 4-7 Feb.

[19] FEMtools^{TM} Model Updating Theoretical Manual, Version 3.5, Dynamic Design Solutions

[20] L. Balis Crema, G. Coppotelli, *Output-Only Approach for Finite Element Model Updating of AB-204 Helicopter Blade,* in Proc. of 46th AIAA/ASME/ASCE/AHS/ASC Structures, Structural Dynamics, and Material Conference, Austin, TX, USA, paper n. AIAA-2005-2249, (2005).

[21] E.A. Robinson, M.T. Silva, *Digital Signal Processing and Time Series Analysis*, San Francisco, CA, (USA), (1978).

[22] A. Agneni, L. Balis Crema, G. Coppotelli, *Time and Frequency Domain Model Parameter Estimation by Output Only Functions*, in *Proceedings of International Forum on Aeroelasticity and Structural Dynamics*, Amsterdam, NL, 2003.

[23] W. Heylen, S. Lammens, P. Sas, *Modal Analysis Theory and Testing*, Leuven, (1994).

[24] D.J. Ewins, Modal Testing: Theory and Practice, Research Studies Press Ltd., Tau- ton, Somerset, (England), (1995).

[25] Cella, U., 2015. Setup and Validation of High Fidelity Aeroelastic Analysis Methods Based on RBF Mesh Morphing. Ph.d thesis. University of Rome Tor Vergata.

[26] Groth, C, et Al., 2018. Structural validation of a realistic wing structure: the RIBES test article. Procedia Structural Integrity, 12, 448-456.

[27] Tate, M., Rosenfeld, S., 1946. Preliminary investigation of the loads carried by individual bolts in bolted joints. National Advisory Committee for Aeronautics. Technical Report. Technical Note.

[28] Zimmerman, D.C., and Kaouk, *Evaluation of the Minimum Rank Update in Damage Detection: an Experimental Study, IMAC 1993*, pp. 1061-1068

[29] Zimmerman, D.C., and Kaouk, *Structural Damage Detection Using a Subspace Rotation Algorithm, AIAA Journal*, Apr. 1992, pp. 2341-2350

[30] Zimmerman, D.C., and Kaouk, *Structural Damage Assessment Using a Generalized Minimum Rank Perturbation Theory, AIAA Journal, vol. 32, N. 4*, Apr. 1994, pp. 836-842

[31] Stubbs, N., *Global Non–Destructive Damage Detection in Solids – Experimental Verification, Int'l Journal of Analytical and Experimental Modal Analisys, 5(2)*,Apr. 1990, pp. 81-97

[32] Kowalski, A. and Dziewulak, B. (2006) A method for reinforcement of steel beams. *Journal of Structures*, 36(2), 115-127.

[33] Borzemski, S. (1990) An algorithm for a certain reliability problem. In: *Proc. 7th Int. Conf. on Systems Engineering* (pp. 242-250). Las Vegas, University of Nevada.

[34] Nowacki, W. (1970) *Theory of elasticity*. Warszawa, PWN.

IOMAC'19
8th International Operational Modal Analysis Conference
2019 May13-15 Copenhagen

OUTPUT-ONLY MODAL TESTING AND MODEL VALIDATION OF UNREINFORCED MASONRY INFILL WALLS IN REINFORCED CONCRETE FRAMES

Carlo Rainieri[1], Mariano Di Domenico[2], Maria Teresa De Risi[3] and Paolo Ricci[4]

[1] Assistant Professor, University of Molise, carlo.rainieri@unimol.it.
[2] PhD Candidate, University of Naples Federico II, mariano.didomenico@unina.it.
[3] Research Fellow, beneficiary of an AXA Research Fund postdoctoral grant, University of Naples Federico II, mariateresa.derisi@unina.it.
[4] Assistant Professor, University of Naples Federico II, paolo.ricci@unina.it.

ABSTRACT

Unreinforced masonry (URM) infill walls in reinforced concrete (r.c.) buildings are prone to seismic damage due to combined in-plane (IP) and out-of-plane (OOP) loadings. In particular, damage due to IP displacement demands promotes OOP collapse of URM infills (IP-OOP interaction). Thus, an experimental campaign based on static, cyclic and dynamic tests has been initiated to assess the influence of IP damage on the OOP response of masonry infills in r.c. frames. The present paper investigates the OOP dynamic response of 2D frames with URM infills in healthy state, when no cracking is present in the masonry panel as a result of IP static or cyclic tests. A finite element model of the frames is developed and validated against the results of output-only modal tests. Finally, sensitivity analyses are carried out to assess the relative influence of boundary r.c. elements on the OOP dynamic response of the panel.

Keywords: Infill walls, masonry, out-of-plane, model validation.

1. INTRODUCTION

Accurate predictive models for the response of masonry infills in reinforced concrete (r.c.) frames under earthquake loading still need to be developed. This mainly applies to the out-of-plane response. Different studies have pointed out the importance of gaining knowledge about the out-of-plane behavior of infills to prevent this type of failure mode. In fact, the currently available models often underestimate the out-of-plane strength of masonry infill panel [1, 2] and do not adequately take into account the influence of damage due to in-plane loading on the out-of-plane response [3, 4].

The infill inside an r.c. frame can be modeled as a plate, as shown by several experimental studies. However, the results are often very scattered or even in contrast with each other. This can be probably addressed to differences in the experimental setups [2]. Most of the studies available in the literature about the out-of-plane response of masonry infill panels are based on static or cyclic tests, while modal testing has been rarely used to gain knowledge about the out-of-plane response of masonry infills. Among the available studies it is worth mentioning an extensive experimental campaign aimed at assessing the influence of different variables (geometry, slenderness, constraints, and openings) on the fundamental out-of-plane frequency of infill masonry panels [5]. To this aim ambient vibration tests were carried out on the infill panels of three different r.c. structures in Portugal. Some dynamic tests in the laboratory have been also conducted by some Authors [5, 6], but limited results have been obtained in terms of knowledge enhancement about the out-of-plane response of masonry infills. Moreover, the adopted sensor layouts were not effective in terms of observability of those modes involving the panel as well as the surrounding r.c. frame, so that the behavior of the composite (r.c. frame + masonry infill) system was not exhaustively analyzed.

The calibration of the numerical model from the results of Operational Modal Analysis (OMA) tests to analyze the dynamic and seismic response of an infill masonry wall is described in a recent paper [7]. The results have pointed out the importance of including the surrounding r.c. frame in the test and the relevant role played by the constraints applied by the r.c. elements to the masonry panel. Nevertheless, a thorough understanding about the interaction between infill and surrounding r.c. frame and its influence on the out-of-plane response of the panel has not been achieved.

The present paper reports the first results of an experimental campaign based on out-of-plane OMA tests on unreinforced masonry infills within r.c. frames. In particular, two undamaged square masonry panels surrounded by an r.c. frame have been investigated. The results of modal tests are first compared with those provided by basic predictive formulations for the fundamental frequency of the panel. A simple Finite Element (FE) model of the specimens is validated afterwards with reference to the experimental results. The comparison of analytical, numerical and experimental results makes possible the quantitative assessment of the predictive capacity of basic formulations available in the literature to predict the fundamental OOP frequency of URM infills in r.c. frames. As a result, their suitability for use in code-based safety assessment of infill walls against seismic OOP actions is evaluated.

2. EXPERIMENTAL TESTS

2.1. Tested specimens and sensor layout

Two OMA tests have been carried out on two 2/3 scale infilled r.c. frames with the same geometry and designed according to the D.M. 14/01/2008 Italian seismic design code [8]. It is worth noting that the 2/3 scaling factor has been applied to lengths only, while the mechanical properties of materials (density, strength and elastic modulus) were not scaled in agreement with previous studies considering similar scaling [9, 10]. The mechanical properties of the materials are reported in Table 1.

Table 1. Construction materials' mechanical properties.

Mechanical property	symbol	Number of specimens	Average value [N/mm^2]
concrete compressive strength	f_{cm}	6	42.9 N/mm^2
masonry compressive strength (parallel to holes)	f_{mh}	3	4.63 N/mm^2
masonry compressive strength (perpendicular to holes)	f_{mv}	3	2.37 N/mm^2
masonry elastic modulus (parallel to holes)	E_{mh}	3	3452 N/mm^2
masonry elastic modulus (perpendicular to holes)	E_{mv}	3	1891 N/mm^2

C32/40 concrete and steel reinforcement bars with nominal characteristic yielding stress of 450 N/mm^2 were used to build the r.c. frames. Figure 1a shows the construction drawings of the r.c. frames, including geometric and reinforcement details.

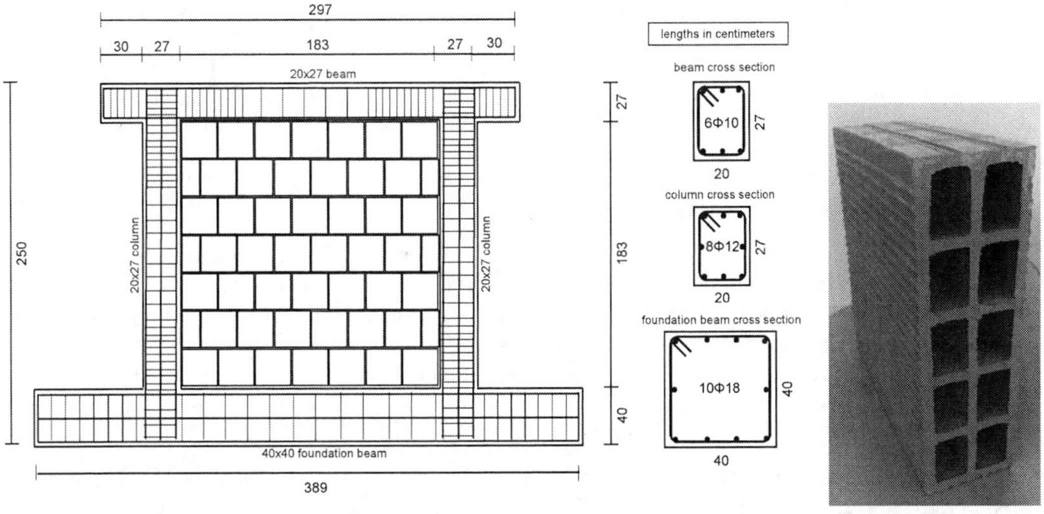

(a) (b)

Figure 1. Construction drawings of the tested specimens (a), hollow clay brick used to build the infill panel (b).

The infills of the r.c. frames consisted of 8 cm thick masonry panels with equal height and width (183 cm). The slenderness (height-to-thickness ratio) of the panels was approximately equal to 23. The panel was built by 25x25x8 cm^3 clay hollow bricks (Figure 1b) with horizontally oriented holes. The joints between the bricks and between the masonry panel and the surrounding r.c. frame were made of 1 cm thick horizontal and vertical joints of M5 class mortar.

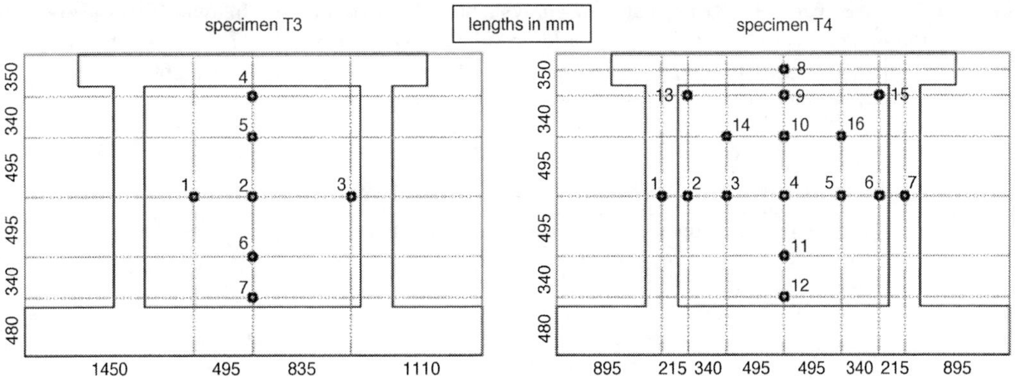

Figure 2. Sensor layout: first specimen T3 (left) and second specimen T4 (right).

The ambient vibration OOP response of the infilled frame has been measured by IEPE accelerometers with the following characteristics: 10 V/g sensitivity, ± 0.5 g measurement range, 0.000008 g rms broadband resolution, frequency range from 0.15 to 1000 Hz. A 24 bit digitizer was used to acquire the acceleration data. Since the main goal of the tests was the characterization of the fundamental OOP frequency of the panel, the ambient vibration OOP response of the first specimen has been measured only at seven points (Figure 2). No sensors have been placed on the r.c. members. In the second test, taking into account the relevant influence of the interaction with the surrounding r.c. frame and the need for additional sensors to more accurately observe and distinguish the different modes, the number of sensors has been increased up to sixteen and they have been installed on the masonry panel as well as the r.c. members (Figure 2).

While in all tests the foundation beam was always clamped to the floor at both ends, two different constraint conditions have been considered for the upper beam: free (i.e., allowing OOP drifts of the r.c. frame) and constrained at two inners sections (i.e., not allowing OOP drifts of the r.c. frame). In the following, only the results of the tests with free upper beam are discussed and used for model validation.

2.2. Modal identification results

The ambient vibration response of the specimens was acquired for 1800 s at a sampling frequency of 200 Hz. Before extracting the modal properties, the time series have been accurately inspected and validated [11]. Offsets have been also removed before modal parameter estimation. The modal parameters have been extracted by applying parametric as well non-parametric OMA procedures. In fact, powerful and well-established OMA techniques, such as the Frequency Domain Decomposition (FDD) [12] and the Covariance Driven Stochastic Subspace Identification (Cov-SSI) [13] have been applied.

FDD is a frequency domain, non-parametric, output-only modal identification technique based on the Singular Value Decomposition (SVD) of the output Power Spectral Density (PSD) matrix. Structural resonances are identified from the singular value plots through peak picking; the corresponding singular vectors are good estimates of the corresponding mode shapes.

The Cov-SSI method is a time domain, parametric, modal identification procedure based on a state-space description of the dynamic problem. The modal parameters are extracted from realizations of the state matrix and output matrix of the system obtained from measurements of its response to ambient vibrations through algebraic manipulations. In particular, the extraction of the modal properties by the Cov-SSI method is based on the decomposition of the Toeplitz matrix of covariances.

When FDD was applied, the PSDs have been estimated by applying the Hanning window and considering a 66% overlap. When Cov-SSI was applied, the number of block rows and the maximum model order have been set after a sensitivity analysis aimed at maximizing the quality of the resulting stabilization diagrams [14]. Modal identification results are summarized in Table 2, while a graphical representation of the experimental mode shapes is shown in Figure 3. The identified modes are normal, as confirmed by the complexity plots.

Table 2. Modal identification results.

Specimen	Mode #	Natural frequency [Hz]
	I	10.0
T3	II	19.2
	III	58.5
	I	9.3
T4	II	18.4
	III	53.9

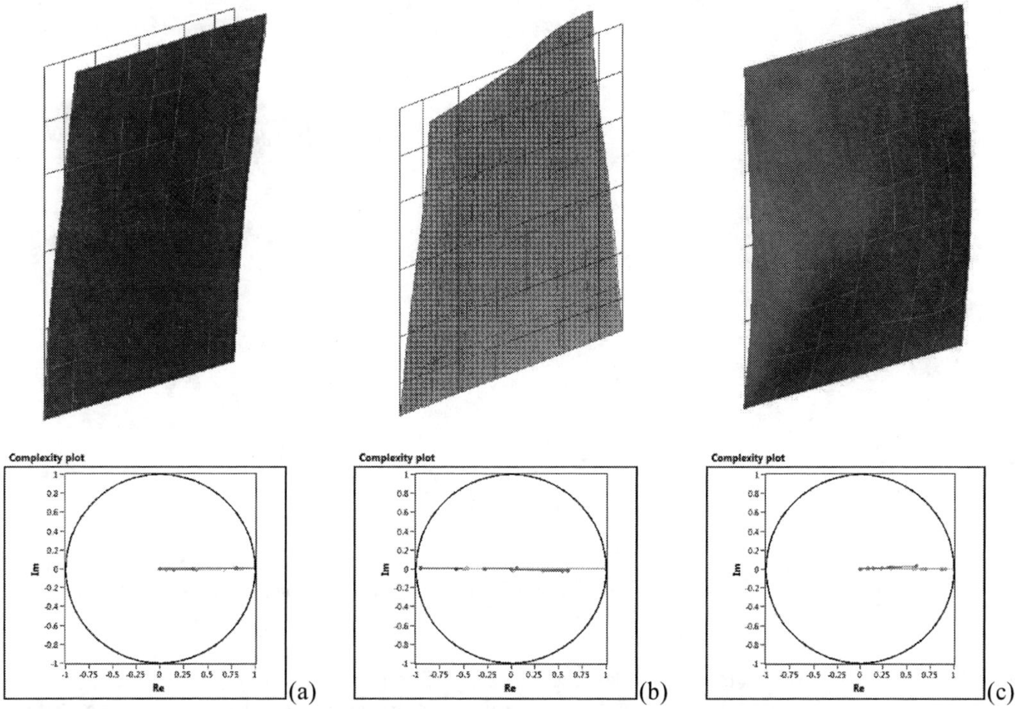

Figure 3. Experimental mode shapes and corresponding complexity plot: mode I (a), II (b) and III (c).

3. COMPARISONS WITH ANALYTICAL AND NUMERICAL MODELS

In this section, the experimental results are compared with the predictions of literature formulations and 2D and 3D FE models. The OOP vibration mode of the infill walls is considered first, while the overall modal response of the infill panel and the surrounding r.c. frame is analyzed afterwards.

Closed-form relationships for the prediction of the transverse vibration frequencies of elastic isotropic plates with different boundary conditions at the edges are available in the literature [15]. For instance, the first transverse frequency of a simply supported along all edges, elastic, and isotropic plate can be calculated according to Eq. (1):

$$f_1 = \frac{\pi(1+(w/h)^2)}{2w^2}\sqrt{\frac{Et^2}{12\rho(1-\nu^2)}} \tag{1}$$

where w is the plate width expressed in m, h is the plate height expressed in m, E is the material elastic modulus in N/mm^2, t is the plate thickness in mm, ρ is the material density expressed in kg/m^3, ν is Poisson coefficient.

Assuming w, h and t equal to 1.83 m, 1.83 m and 80 mm, respectively, and setting E equal to E_{mh} (Table 1), ρ equal to 800 kg/m^3 and ν equal to 0.25 (in agreement with code provisions [8]), a fundamental OOP frequency of 46.5 Hz is obtained.

Adopting the same mechanical and geometric properties as above, a 2D elastic and isotropic FE model of the infill wall has been set. SAP2000 [16] was used to develop the numerical model (Figure 4).

The infill wall has been modeled by 400 square shell elements. A sensitivity analysis has, in fact, demonstrated that further mesh refinements significantly increase the analysis duration without significant variations in the modal analysis results. The 2D FE model provided a value of the fundamental OOP frequency of 46.8 Hz, which is consistent with the prediction by Eq. (1).

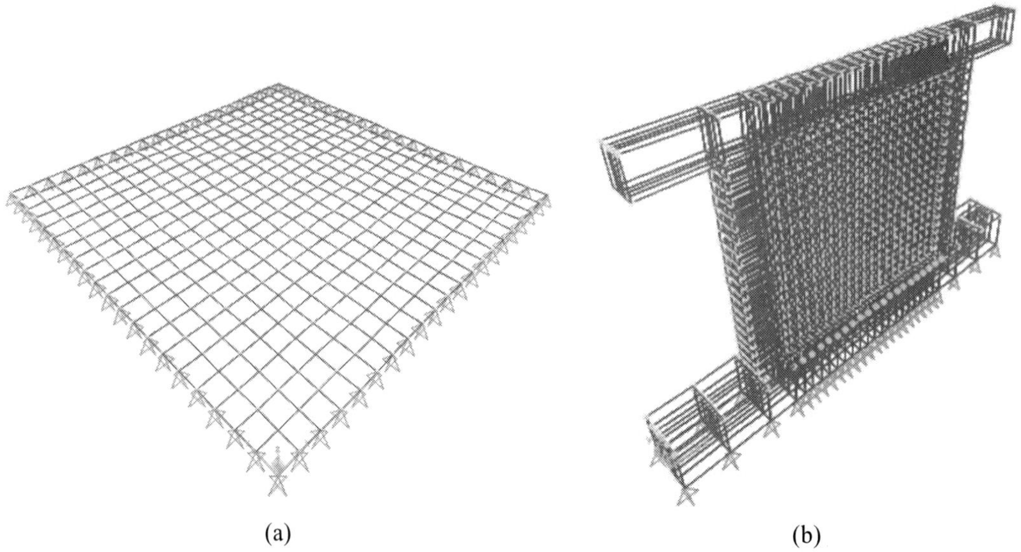

(a) (b)

Figure 4. 2D FE model of the infill walls (a) and 3D FE model of whole specimens (b).

This basic FE model of the infill wall has been further refined by taking into account the orthotropic nature of masonry and different combination of restraints at the edges. In particular, two different elastic moduli equal to E_{mh} and E_{mv} (Table 1) respectively, have been assigned to the shell elements, and the modal analysis results for the fundamental transverse frequency corresponding to different boundary conditions applied to the elastic orthotropic plate are reported in Figure 5a. The frequencies obtained from the refined 2D FE model are also shown in comparison with the experimental ones (Figure 5b).

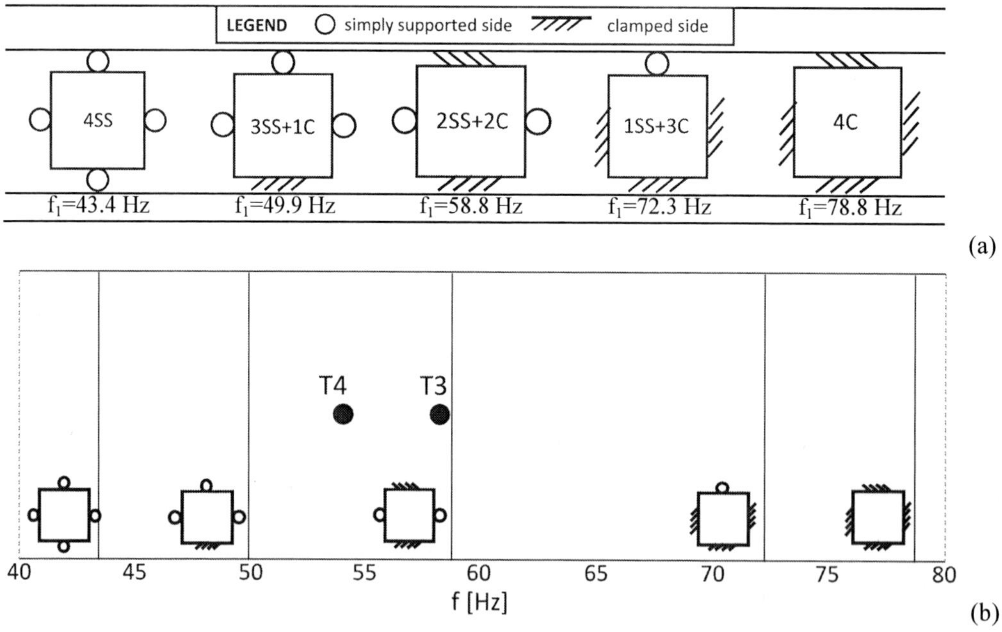

Figure 5. OOP frequencies from the 2D FE models (a) and comparisons with the experimental estimates (b).

The experimental estimates of the fundamental OOP frequency obtained from specimens T3 and T4 (53.9 Hz and 58.5 Hz, respectively) are significantly higher than the value predicted by modeling the masonry panel as a simply supported plate along the edges, even when the foundation beam is considered fully clamped. On the contrary, the best predictions are obtained when the constraint exerted by the upped beam on the masonry panel is modeled by a fully clamped edge. Moreover, comparing numerical and experimental results seems to confirm that vertical edges can be likely modeled as simply supported.

Interpreting the above outcomes may be not straightforward. Thus, a 3D FE model of the whole specimens has been also set (Figure 4b). In this case, r.c. elements have been modeled by solid elements with elastic and isotropic properties (namely, elastic modulus equal to E_{cm}, as reported in Table 1, and material density equal to 2500 kg/m^3), while the infill wall has been modeled by of solid elements with elastic and orthotropic properties as previously discussed for shell elements in the 2D model.

The 3D FE model has been used to predict the natural frequencies not only of the masonry infill but also of the whole system made by the panel and the surrounding r.c. frame. According to the 3D FE model, the first mode at the frequency of 13.5 Hz can be described as a cantilever deflection in the transverse direction of the entire r.c. frame + infill system, as shown in Figure 6a. The second mode is instead a torsional twist of the entire r.c. frame + infill system (Figure 6b) at the frequency of 25.4 Hz. The third mode of the system is basically associated to the out-of-plane deformation of the infill wall but it also involves the upper beam (Figure 6c).

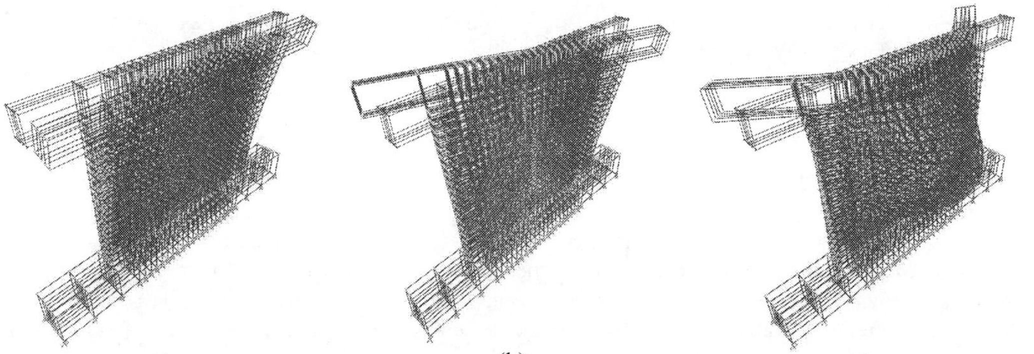

(a) (b) (c)

Figure 6. 3D FE model of the specimen: first (a), second (b) and third (c) mode shape.

Table 3. Comparisons between experimental (T4 specimen) and numerical (3D FE model) results.

Mode #	f_{exp} [Hz]	f_{FEM} [Hz]	MAC [%]
I	9.3	13.5	99.1%
II	18.4	25.8	98.3%
III	53.9	62.0	79.7%

Table 3 shows the comparison between the results of the 3D FE model and the experimental results with reference to the T4 specimen. The latter has been assumed as the reference for the experimental results because of the better spatial resolution of measurements. Moreover, the sensor layout for the T3 specimen has five over seven sensors placed in nodal points of the second mode shapes. As a consequence, the comparisons with the model in terms of mode shapes are more meaningful when the T4 specimen is considered. Table 3 points out that:

- the numerical 3D FE model reproduces quite well the first and the second mode shape while the third mode shape is caught only to a certain extent;
- the natural frequencies of the model are sufficiently close to the experimental values but these are systematically overestimated.

In other words, the numerical 3D FE model is able to catch the overall behavior of the structure but it is stiffer than the real r.c. frame + infill wall system. Thus, even if the comparisons confirm the validity of the numerical model, further refinements are needed. A sensitivity analysis of the modal parameters with respect to the mechanical properties of materials, for instance, might be helpful to identify the possible source of the bias. This activity is out of the scope of the present paper and it will be discussed in a future publication. However, at the current stage of analysis the following conclusions can be drawn from the joint analysis of the results of experimental and numerical modal analyses:

- The foundation beam acts as a clamp with respect to the infill lower edge (i.e., the infill lower edge does not rotate);
- The upper r.c. beam acts as a clamp with respect to the infill upper edge (i.e., the infill upper edge does not rotate);
- The columns acts as a simple support with respect to the infill vertical edges (i.e., the infill vertical edges rotate for consistency with the column twisting).

assuming a continuous connection between the infill wall and the r.c. frame and no defects. These are also the reasons why the experimental out-of-plane frequencies of the infill walls T3 and T4 are similar to those predicted by means of the 2D FE model with the horizontal edges clamped and with the vertical edges simply supported (Figure 5b).

4. CONCLUSIONS

The assessment of the out-of-plane vibration frequency of infill walls is fundamental to compute the out-of-plane seismic demand acting on them. This study reports a preliminary experimental and numerical assessment of the significant variables affecting the OOP dynamics of infill panels. The obtained results seem to confirm the effectiveness of basic 2D FE models in predicting the OOP frequency provided that the orthotropic nature of masonry is considered, the boundary conditions at the edges of the infill walls are correctly reproduced, and the mechanical properties of masonry are selected in an appropriate and potentially conservative manner. However, further work is needed to obtain refined numerical models that are fully representative of the actual dynamic behavior of the infill + r.c. frame system and to draw definite conclusions.

ACKNOWLEDGEMENTS

This work was developed under the support of AXA Research Fund Post-Doctoral Grant "*Advanced nonlinear modelling and performance assessment of masonry infills in RC buildings under seismic loads: the way forward to design or retrofitting strategies and reduction of losses*", and ReLUIS-DPC 2014-2018 *Linea CA -WP6 Tamponature* funded by the Italian Department of Civil Protection (DPC). These supports are gratefully acknowledged.

REFERENCES

[1] Abrams, D.P., Angel, R., & Uzarski, J. (1996). Out-of-plane strength of unreinforced masonry infill panels. *Earthquake Spectra*, 12(4), 825-844.

[2] Asteris, P.G., Cavaleri, L., Di Trapani, F., & Tsaris, A.K. (2017). Numerical modelling of out-of-plane response of infilled frames: State of the art and future challenges for the equivalent strut macromodels. *Engineering Structures*, 132, 110-122.

[3] Ricci, P., Di Domenico, M., & Verderame, G.M. (2018). Experimental assessment of the in-plane/out-of-plane interaction in unreinforced masonry infill walls. *Engineering Structures*, 173, 960-978.

[4] Ricci, P., Di Domenico, M., & Verderame, G.M. (2018). Experimental investigation of the influence of slenderness ratio and of the in-plane/out-of-plane interaction on the out-of-plane strength of URM infill walls. *Construction and Building Materials*, 191, 505-522.

[5] Furtado, A., Rodrigues, H., Arede, A., & Varum, H. (2017). Modal identification of infill masonry walls with different characteristics. *Engineering Structures*, 145, 118-134.

[6] Furtado, A., Rodrigues, H., Arede, A., & Varum, H. (2016). Experimental evaluation of out-of-plane capacity of masonry infill walls. *Engineering Structures*, 111, 48-63.

[7] De Angelis, A., & Pecce, M.R. (2018). Out-of-plane structural identification of a masonry infill wall inside beam-column RC frames. *Engineering Structures*, 173, 546-558.

[8] Consiglio Superiore dei Lavori Pubblici. *Decreto ministeriale 14 gennaio 2008 - Norme Tecniche per le Costruzioni NTC2008*. Supplemento ordinario n. 30 Gazzetta Ufficiale 4 febbraio 2008, n 29. (in Italian).

[9] Benedetti, D., Carydis, P., & Pezzoli, P. (1998). Shaking table tests on 24 simple masonry buildings. *Earthquake Engineering and Structural Dynamics*, 27, 67-90.

[10] Hashemi, A., & Mosalam, K.M. (2006). Shake table experiment on reinforced concrete structure containing masonry infill wall. *Earthquake Engineering and Structural Dynamics*, 35, 1827-1852.

[11] Bendat, J.S., & Piersol, A.G. (2000). *Random data: analysis and measurement procedures*, 3rd edn., John Wiley & Sons, New York, USA.

[12] Brincker, R., Zhang, L., & Andersen, P. (2001). Modal identification of output-only systems using frequency domain decomposition, *Smart Materials and Structures*, 10, 441-445.

[13] Peeters, B. (2000). *System Identification and Damage Detection in Civil Engineering*, Ph.D. Thesis, Katholieke Universiteit Leuven, Leuven, Belgium.

[14] Rainieri, C., Fabbrocino, G., & Cosenza, E. (2010). Some remarks on experimental estimation of damping for seismic design of civil constructions. *Shock and Vibration*, 17, 383-395.

[15] Blevins, R.D., & Plunkett, R. (1980). *Formulas for natural frequency and mode shape*. Van Nostrand Reinhold, New York, USA.

[16] Computers and Structures (2013). *SAP2000 version 16*, Walnut Creek, CA, USA.

IOMAC'19
8th International Operational Modal Analysis Conference
2019 May 13-15 Copenhagen

STRUCTURAL IDENTIFICATION OF AN HISTORICAL BUILDING IN A MASONRY AGGREGATE.

Valeria Pepe[1], *Alessandra De Angelis*[2], *and Maria Rosaria Pecce*[3]

[1] Ph.D. Student, University of Sannio, Benevento, Italy, vpepe@unisannio.it
[2] Ph.D., University of Sannio, Benevento, Italy, adeangelis@unisannio.it
[3] Full Professor, University of Sannio, Benevento, Italy, pecce@unisannio.it

ABSTRACT

The historical masonry buildings are usually complex structures with strong peculiarity that in many cases have been also rehashed with local demolitions, enlargement, strengthening interventions. Among the various uncertainties that afflict the historical buildings there is the constraint influence of adjacent constructions weekly connected. Typical examples are bell towers connected to churches, a single cell housing in a masonry aggregate, the parts of a building connected only in few points. In these cases the structural identification through a dynamic test and model updating could be a promising procedure to define a reliable structural model. In this paper the efficiency of ambient vibration tests in situ in evaluating the degree of interactions between two parts of an historical building is verified; in particular a part of a masonry building has been tested and modelled calibrating the restraints on one side to take into account the part of the building not tested.

Keywords: Masonry buildings aggregate, Structural identification, Operational modal analysis, Model updating.

1. INTRODUCTION

Historical masonry buildings are complex structures characterized by a wide range of uncertainties mainly due to irregularity in the internal masonry texture, imperfections related to out-of-plane rotations of vertical walls, local variability of material strength and stiffness, distribution of cracks, depth, geometry and material properties of the foundations [1]. A peculiarity of most of Italian historical masonry buildings is the fact that they should have been altered repeatedly over time with local demolitions and enlargements, so that one building could belong to a masonry aggregate. All the connections with the structures of adjacent buildings can have strong influence on the seismic behaviour of the investigated structure [2], therefore in order to avoid the analysis of the whole aggregate it is necessary to evaluate the effect of the constraints influence of the constructions connected to the part of interest. In this cases the structural identification by means of dynamic test can be an efficient tool that is currently a promising technique to collect information on the structural characteristics of architectural heritage [1,3,4]. In particular dynamic tests are able to provide information about flexibility of floors, constraints and global response of flexible structures like towers, vaults and domes, whereas modal analysis on massive or stiff masonry bodies can be affected by the crowd of local and global modes in narrow frequency ranges and by the spurious multiple harmonic components due to nonlinear behaviour of masonry [5] or to non-stationary input [6].

In this paper an ambient vibration tests in situ was performed on a case study structure to verify its efficiency in evaluating the degree of interactions between two parts of an historical building. Furthermore a numerical model was implemented in order to evaluate the constraint exerted by the part of building not tested.

2. DESCRIPTION OF THE CASE STUDY

The historical masonry building under investigation is De Simone Palace in figure 1, located in Benevento (Campania, Southern Italy). It belongs to a masonry aggregate and has a L-plant. The current building is the result of changes occurred along the time. It has been taking its name from the De Simone family who came from the County of Angiò in Provence and transformed this building into a location worthy of an important family as they were. This building was demolished and rebuilt after the earthquakes occurred in 1688 and 1705 and enlarged with a family chapel.

Figure 1. Historical photo of De Simone Palace.

In the XX century it was refurbished to host a boarding school; the old family chapel was demolished and a new elegant chapel was built. The present structure accommodates three types of activities: the public theatre (in yellow), the Department of Economics of University of Sannio (in red) and the Conservatory of Music "Nicola Sala" (in blue) in figure 2.

Figure 2. Overall view of Palazzo De Simone with the identification of the different activities.

The structural unit that has to be studied is the yellow building and it is composed of three parts (figure 3): A, B and C.

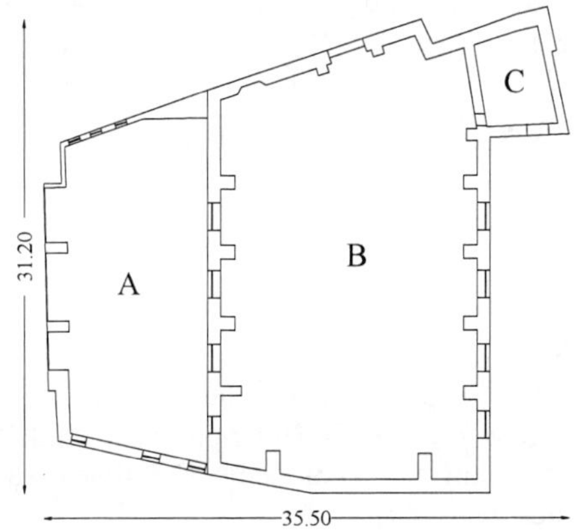

Figure 3. Plant of the part of the building under study.

The part A of the building has one floor, whereas parts B and C develop on two levels which are the ground and the first floor with a perimeter walkway as an intermediate level. On the first floor of the part B there is an accessible attic covered by a wood hipped roof.

At the first level of the yellow structure in figure 2, the new chapel built in the XX century is located in the part B. In figure 4 the plant of the chapel and the roof plant of the part B are depicted. The main in-plan dimensions are approximately Lx=32.20m and Ly=35.50m, the height is 21.65m.

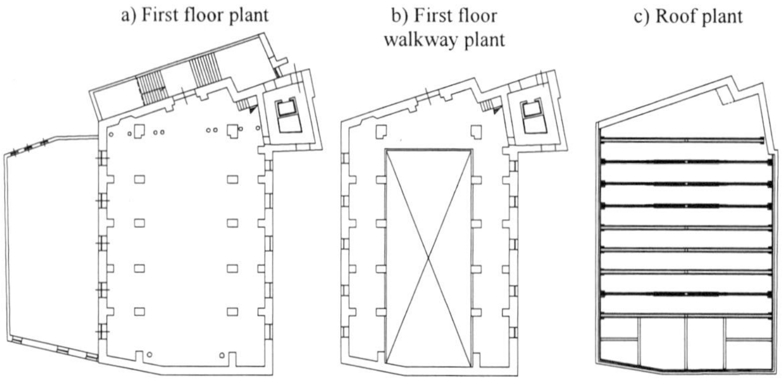

Figure 4. Plants of the building at different levels.

According to the in site inspections the floors of the chapel are made of steel joists, I beams with 0.12m height, and brick hollow flat blocks covered with a thick of 0.04m not reinforced cement mortar. The total thickness of the floors, including screed, plaster and pavement, is 0.22m. They are supported by emerging steel beams aligned along both the main directions. The floors are connected to the perimeter walls and to ten masonry columns with a rectangular section whose size is 1.10x0.78 m, divided into two rows (see figure 4). All the columns are longways and horizontally connected by round arches with an aesthetic function. The walkway is supported also by twelve circular cross-section columns.

The perimeter walls are made of tuff blocks and cement mortar alternate with solid bricks. The columns are made of solid bricks and cement mortar. The wood roof is composed of two pitches and it is sustained by nine trusses (figure 4 c).

3. NUMERICAL MODEL

A 3D numerical finite element (FE) model of the structure (figure 5) was implemented using the software SAP2000 [7]. In this study, as the aim of numerical modelling is to identify the linear dynamic behaviour of the building, the macro-modelling approach was used and the masonry was modelled as an isotropic continuum material.

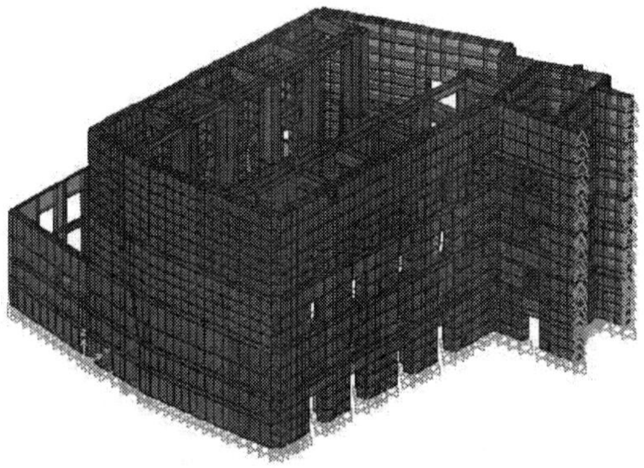

Figure 5. General view of the 3D numerical model.

The geometry was based on the results of a survey and the masonry walls and columns were modelled using shell elements taking care to reproduce their main geometric irregularities and all the openings of the building. The hypothesis of thick-shell elements has been considered for all the surface elements, defined using 4 nodes and 6 degrees of freedom for each node. Thickness between 0.3 m and 1.10 m has been considered to simulate the structural elements.

The elastic parameters like Young's modulus E, Poisson's coefficient ν, and weight per unit volume γ are reported in table 1 and should be considered as homogenous in the structure. These values were chosen on the basis of what suggested by the Italian Code [8,9] in Annex C8A.2, corresponding to tuff blocks or solid bricks with cement mortar.

The masses were directly associated with the structural elements according to the density and geometric dimensions; a uniform area mass was assigned to the floors according to their weight. Constant loads of 3.66 kN/m^2 and 1.86 kN/m^2 were applied respectively to the first and second floor whereas no live loads were applied, in accordance with the state of the structure during the dynamic test. Moreover, a diaphragm constraint at each floor was assumed. The connection between the soil and the structure has been considered rigid.

Table 1. Characteristics of the masonry.

	E [MPa]	ν [-]	γ [kN/m^3]
Tuff block and cement mortar	1260	0.4	16
Solid bricks with cement mortar	1800	0.4	18

In order to take into account the influence of the remaining part of the building on the modelled one, four different limit constraint conditions were considered at the intersection of the walls of part C (figure 3) with the other part of the aggregate (red building in figure 2):

- pinned walls (figure 5),
- full restrained walls,
- free walls,
- supported walls along their plane.

The main dynamic properties (frequencies and participating masses ratio) obtained for the different limit constraint conditions are shown in table 2 for the first three vibration modes of the structure.

Table 2. Dynamic properties.

Mode	Dynamic properties	Pinned walls	Restrained walls	Free walls
1	f [Hz]	6.17	6.22	5.16
	M_X [%]	13	16	7
	M_Y [%]	47	42	70
	M_{RZ} [%]	19	20	6
2	f [Hz]	7.65	7.94	5.64
	M_X [%]	36	34	68
	M_Y [%]	29	33	9
	M_{RZ} [%]	10	8	-
3	f [Hz]	10.96	11.28	6.63
	M_X [%]	-	-	-
	M_Y [%]	-	-	-
	M_{RZ} [%]	40	35	71

The results concerning the constraint condition "supported walls along their plane"" have not been reported since they are identical to those obtained for the condition "pinned walls".

Assuming as reference the constraint condition "pinned walls", it is worth to note that moving to the condition "restrained walls" the increase of frequency is less than 4%, on the contrary in the case of "free walls" the frequency of the first three vibration modes of the modelled structure significantly decreases of 17%, 26% and 39% respectively.

The constraint due to the adjacent structure has also a remarkable influence on the participating masses ratio and the mode shapes. In fact, the model with "free walls" gives high values of the participating masses ratio (70%, 68 % and 71%) and the mode shapes are mainly translational in Y direction, translational in X direction and torsional respectively. When the contact walls are constrained, the first three mode shapes become coupled, as shown by the comparison depicted in figure 6, and they are characterized by lower values of participating masses ratio.

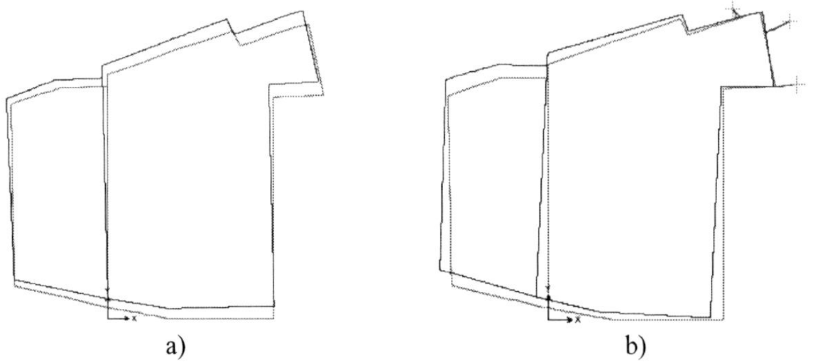

Figure 6. First mode shape: a) free walls, b) walls with supported constraint.

Therefore, the numerical analysis carried out highlighted that the influence of the aggregate on the investigated structure can be introduced with a constraint along the plane of the contact walls because the restraining of the other degrees of freedom are not influent.

4. DYNAMIC IDENTIFICATION

The dynamic response of the structure was studied through an ambient vibration test (AVT) performed in two setups. Five tri-axial MEMS piezoelectric accelerometers were fixed at the corner of the first and the roof floors according to the layout reported in figure 7.

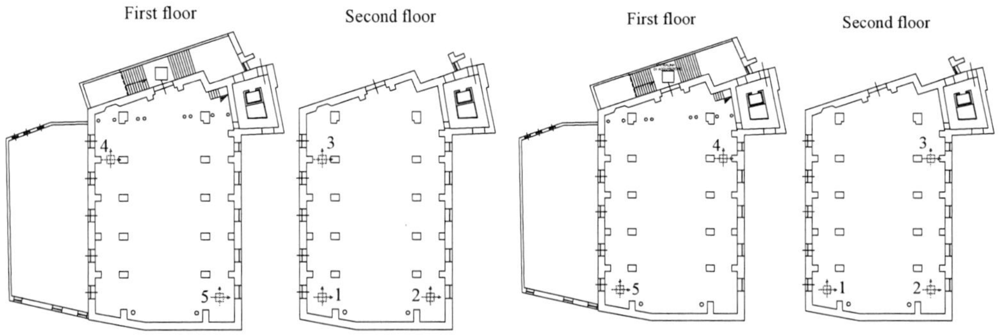

Figure 7. Setup of the experimental test.

Sensors 1 and 2 were chosen as reference sensors, the others were used as roving sensors. The goal of the two setups was to investigate more accurately the motion of the plan, influenced by the presence of the adjacent structure represented by the part C of the building (figure 3). All the instruments were placed with the axes parallel to the main directions of the structure.

During both the AVTs the accelerations were acquired at a sampling frequency of 1024 Hz for 1800s. According to the numerical model, the mode shapes of interest belong to the range of [0-25] Hz, therefore a factor of 16 decimated the accelerations collected before processing in order to have the final data of 64 samples per second. The modal parameters were identified by applying the Frequency Domain Decomposition (FDD) method [10] to the accelerations collected in each setup. In order to merge the mode shape pieces obtained from each setup, the technique proposed by Peeters was applied [11], assuming the accelerations collected by sensor 1 as reference measurements.

Figure 8 shows the identified frequencies and the corresponding mode shapes. The comparison between the mode shapes of the two floors suggests that the second floor is more deformable than the first one, which could be considered rigid. However, the higher deformability exhibited by the second floor makes the interpretation of the experimental results difficult. In fact, the mode shapes given by the few available experimental points could be representative of local modes of the floor instead of the global modes of the whole structure.

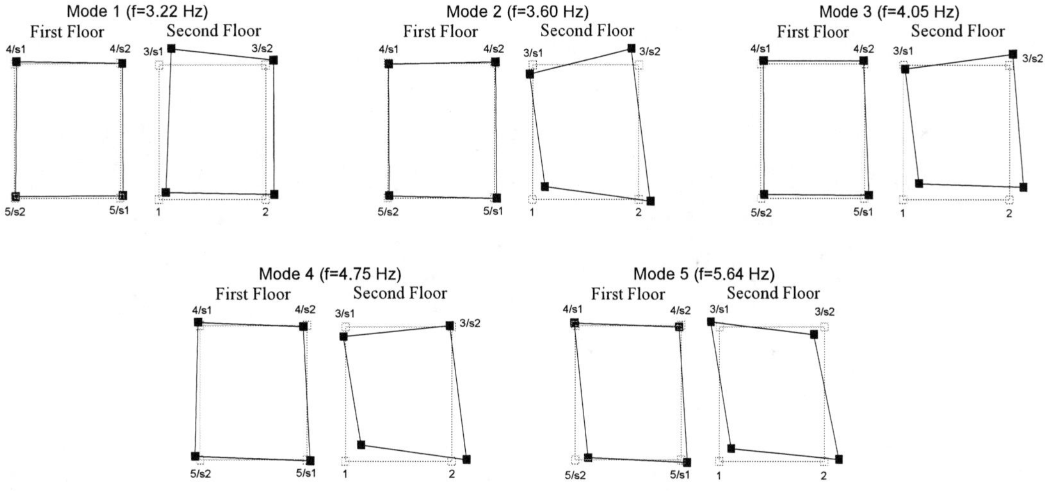

Figure 8. Experimental frequencies and mode shapes.

Anyway the experimental results were used to refine the numerical model presented in the previous section. In particular, in order to take into account the higher deformability of the second floor, it was remodelled introducing the steel I beams and removing the diaphragm, whereas the first floor was modelled using shell elements with a thickness of 0.04 m, that is the thickness of the concrete slab. The constraint along the plane of the contact walls was confirmed.

The modal analysis performed on the refined numerical model disclosed that most of the modes involved small participation masses and they were associated to local movements due to the lack of the rigid floor.

The overlap between the numerical mode shapes and the experimental ones is pictured in figure 9. It is clear that the second experimental mode is not identified by the numerical model, but a fairly good correspondence for the other four modes arises.

In order to compare the numerical frequencies with the experimental ones, a correlation analysis in terms of scattering between analytical and experimental values of frequencies, Eq. (1), was performed:

$$\Delta f[\%]=\left|\frac{f_i^e-f_i^n}{f_i^e}\right|\cdot 100 \tag{1}$$

where f_i^e is the experimental value and f_i^n is the numerical value of the natural frequency of the ith mode.

As reported in the last column of table 3, it is possible to observe that there is a quite small difference between the experimental and numerical frequencies, that is about 2% and 7% for the first and the fourth mode respectively. The third and fifth frequencies evince the main differences, which are about of 31% and -24% respectively.

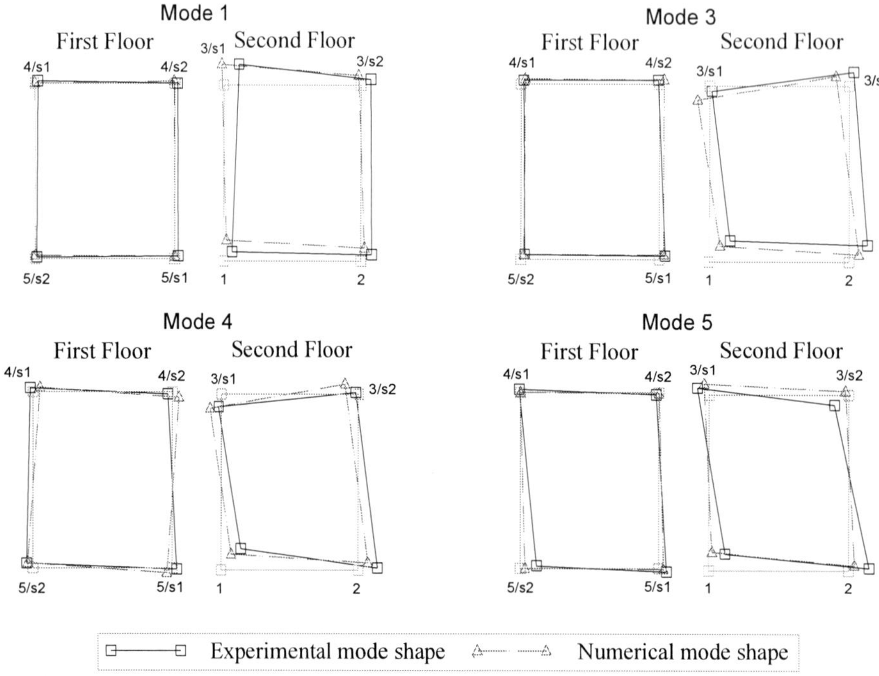

Figure 9. Overlapping of experimental and numerical mode shapes.

Table 3. Correlation Analysis.

Experimental mode shapes		Numerical mode shapes		Δf [%]
Mode	f [Hz]	Mode	f [Hz]	
1	3.22	66	3.30	2
2	3.6	-	-	-
3	4.05	131	5.30	31
4	4.75	126	5.1	7
5	5.64	101	4.3	-24

The analysis confirms the efficiency of the dynamic test and an acceptable reliability of the model, whose updating procedure was complicated by the flexiblity of the floor. In particular an increased number of instrumented points is necessary in this case.

5. CONCLUSIONS

In this work the structural identification of a masonry building in an aggregate construction was developed through the comparison between its experimental dynamic behaviour and a numerical model simulation. In this case study the procedure has pointed up that the deformability of the second floor activates local modes of vibration and it reduces the effect of the constraints exerted by the adjacent constructions. In fact, removing the hypothesis of rigid floor, the few experimental measures collected do not allow to identify the local modes. Anyway, the first five frequencies of the structure were estimated and their global character was analysed, achieving a good result for the first and the fourth modes. The research confirmed the efficiency of the dynamic test but it also highlighted the difficulties caused by the presence of flexible floors, which are usually typical of historical buildings.

REFERENCES

[1] De Stefano, A., Matta, E., Clemente, P. (2016). Structural health monitoring of historical heritage in Italy: some relevant experiences. *Journal of Civil Structural Health Monitoring*, 6, 83-106.

[2] Clemente, P., Rinaldis, D., Buffarini, G. (2007). Experimental seismic analysis of a historical building. *Journal of Intelligent Material Systems and Structures*, 18, 777-784.

[3] Gentile, C., Guidobaldi, M., Saisi, A. (2016). One-year dynamic monitoring of a historic tower: damage detection under changing environment. *Meccanica*, 51(11), 2873-2889.

[4] Torres, W., Almazan, J.L., Sandoval, C., Boroschek, R. (2017). Operational modal analysis and FE model updating of the Metropolitan Cathedral of Santiago, Chile. *Engineering Structures*, 143, 169-188.

[5] De Stefano, A., Ceravolo, R. (2007). Assessing the health state of ancient structures: the role of vibrational tests. *Journal of Intelligent Material Systems and Structures*, 18(8), 793-807.

[6] Ceravolo, R., Pistone, G., Zanotti Fragonara, L., Massetto, S., Abbiati, G. (2016). Vibration-based monitoring and diagnosis of cultural heritage: a methodological discussion in three examples. *International Journal of Architectural Heritage*, 10(4), 375-395.

[7] Computers and Structures (2016). SAP2000 version 18., Walnut Creek, CA.

[8] Ministro dei Lavori Pubblici e dei Trasporti (2008) DM 14/01/ 2008—Norme tecniche per le costruzioni (in Italian). Suppl. Ordin. Gazz. Uff. n. 29.

[9] Ministero dei Lavori Pubblici e dei Trasporti (2009) Circolare 2 febbraio 2009, n. 617—Istruzioni per l'applicazione delle ''Nuove Norme Tecniche per le Costruzioni'' di cui al Decreto Ministeriale del 14/01/2008 (in Italian).

[10] Brincker, R., Zhang, L., Andersen, P. (2001). Modal identification of output-only systems using frequency domain decomposition. *Smart Material and Structures*, 10, 441-445.

[11] Peeters, B. (2000). System identification and damage detection in civil engineering. *PhD Dissertation*, Department of Civil Engineering, University of British Columbia, Vancouver, BC, Canada.

IOMAC'19

8th International Operational Modal Analysis Conference

2019 May13-15 Copenhagen

STRUCTURAL UPDATING OF THE "JAVELIN" UAV USING OMA

Giuliano Coppotelli[1], *Federico Di Giandomenico*[2], *Pier Marzocca*[3], *Robert Carrese*[4], *Nishit Joseph*[5]

[1] *Associate Professor, University of Rome "La Sapienza", giuliano.coppotelli@uniroma1.it*

[2] *Engineer, University of Rome "La Sapienza", fede.digiando@gmail.com*

[3] *Professor, RMIT University, pier.marzocca@rmit.edu.au*

[4] *Research Fellow, RMIT University, robert.carrese@rmit.edu.au*

[5] *Ph.D. Student, RMIT University, nishit.joseph@student.rmit.edu.au*

ABSTRACT

The paper presents a novel technique to perform real-time system identification using output-only analysis. The modal parameters estimated with such methodology are then used in a numerical modal updating process. The fixed wing UAV employed to conduct the test campaign is the "Javelin," developed by RMIT University. The data collected during Flight Vibration Test are used to demonstrate the robustness of the real-time system identification procedure using OMA. Cornerstone of the developed methodology is the PLSCF estimator which represents clear stabilization diagram and is computationally efficient. The numerical model updating process is required whenever the correlation between numerical model and experimental data is not acceptable. Generally, a group of preselected variables are varied to minimize the error function between the numerical and experimental model. The estimated modal parameters are used in modal updating process to develop a numerical model which represents the dynamical behaviour of the "Javelin" during flight condition.

Keywords: Finite Element Model, Experimental Modal Analysis, Operational Modal Analysis

1. INTRODUCTION

The results of test campaign are employed to assess and eventually improve the numerical model because its accuracy is fundamental for an accurate design. The traditional Experimental Modal Analysis (EMA) is the research domain where system identification of vibrating structures is performed measuring both excitation and response of the system. From the input and output recordings it is possible to identify the modal model consisting in natural frequencies, damping ratios, mode shapes, and modal participation factors. On the other hand, Operational Modal Analysis (OMA) allows the modal parameter estimation with output-only measurements but it requests some hypothesis to be satisfied. First of all, the analysed system is considered linear. Secondly, the excitation has to be a normally distributed random (both in space and in time domain) characterized by a white noise amplitude distribution. Finally, the last limitation is that this kind of analysis works only for stationary conditions. Nevertheless, the OMA [1, 2, 3, 4] allows to avoid the artificial excitation and the ambient vibration is employed as input allowing modal parameter estimation with true boundary conditions, force field and vibration levels. Therefore, the perspective to achieve a reliable structural modal updating with output-only measurement and analysis holds significant interest. The OMA methods can be divided into two classes: time and frequency domains. In time domain, one of the most popular methods is the Stochastic Subspace Identification (SSI) in which the stochastic state space model is identified directly from the output correlations. On the other hand, in the frequency domain, Frequency Domain Decomposition (FDD) [2] and Maximum Likelihood (ML) are two of the mostly used methods. FDD, a non-parametric technique, is based on the Singular Value Decomposition (SVD) of the Power Spectral Density (PSD) matrix and it is able to detect mode-multiplicity. Additionally, in the frequency domain, the ML approach is based on the minimization of an error norm. A way to find the initial values for the ML technique was found in the Least-Squares Complex Frequency (LSCF) method that estimates a common-denominator transfer function model. Soon it was discovered that the initial values already presented a very accurate modal parameter estimation with a reduced computational effort. The Polyreference Least-Squares Complex Frequency (PLSCF), initially proposed for Frequency Response Functions (FRFs) to overcome the main drawbacks of LSCF, was extended to the operational case by Peeters et al [5]. Once the PSD matrix is calculated, the PLSCF estimator allows to build a stabilization diagram containing natural frequency, damping, and participation information. After the poles selection, the mode shapes are found with a Least-Squares Frequency Domain (LSFD) procedure. In this way, usage of SVD to decompose the residues can be avoided and also closely spaced or highly damped poles with large overlap can be separated. The algorithm presented in [6] is here employed for the modal parameter estimation. It is a real-time modal parameter estimation method using OMA. The employed estimator is the PLSCF whereas the automation is reached by means of a multi-stage clustering process [7]. It has been already tested on both numerical and experimental data. The modal base estimated with traditional EMA is compared with the one calculated by OMA in order to verify their agreement with the finite element model and, hence, to establish their compatibility for a modal updating. In fact, numerical models need to be improved to detect and take into account possible deviations from the linear elastic behaviour or to take into account details difficult to schematize from a numerical point of view. This is realizable following the correlation between the experimental and numerical models through specific coefficients. Finally, the F.E. model has been updated by tuning the initial numerical model and approach numerical modal parameters to the experimental ones. Yet, the selection of the structural parameters to be updated still represent a crucial choice that the analyst must face with.

2. THEORETICAL BACKGROUND

The theoretical background is strictly concentrated on the developed method for real-time modal parameter identification using output-only measurement. The reader could find details of experimental modal analysis and finite element analysis in literature.

2.1. Preprocessing

In the process of real-time system identification, data is continually acquired and automatically processed. A certain number of data samples must first be collected beforehand to be analysed. This generate an unavoidable delay between acquisition and outcome. There are two fundamental acquisition parameters, [6]. The Nyquist sampling theorem states that in order to avoid aliasing, the sampling frequency f_s must be at least twice the maximal measurable frequency f_{max} while the acquisition time T sets the frequency resolution $\triangle f$. Anyway, a zero-padding technique can be adopted to increase the frequency resolution. Once the data was acquired and preprocessed the PSD matrix was estimated. The PSD is the distribution of power per unit frequency and it is defined as the Fourier Transform of the correlation sequences. Anyway, noise levels must be reduced in order to diminish the bias on the measured parameters. The most popular non-parametric spectrum estimation is the Weighted Averaged Periodogram. In a first step the Fourier Transform of the signal is evaluated. In order to reduce the leakage effect, an appropriate window function is applied to the time signal. Then the unbiased spectrum of the weighted periodogram is calculated. The variance of the estimate is reduced by splitting the signal in overlapping segments and averaging the PSDs estimated

2.2. Polyreference Least-Squares Complex Frequency

For traditional Experimental modal analysis (EMA) the system identification of vibrating structures is performed measuring both excitation and response. From their relation, it is possible to identify the modal model consisting in natural frequencies, damping ratios, mode shapes, and modal participation factors. However, in some cases, it is rather difficult to measure forces or the actual operative conditions are important to ensure an adequate analysis. In this cases, OMA allows the modal parameter estimation just from output measurements. PLSCF is a frequency-domain OMA method and it requires the PSD matrix as primary data. The input spectra $S_{uu}(f) \in \mathbb{C}^{N_o \times N_i}$ and the output spectra $S_{yy}(f) \in \mathbb{C}^{N_o \times N_o}$ of a system represented by FRF $H(f) \in \mathbb{C}^{N_o \times N_i}$ are related as

$$S_{yy}(f) = H(f) S_{uu}(f) H(f)^H. \tag{1}$$

In case of OMA, the input spectra is considered frequency independent and the FRF can be represented as

$$H(f) = \sum_{i=1}^{n} \frac{\phi_i \, l_i^T}{j2\pi f - \lambda_i} + \frac{\phi_i^* \, l_i^H}{j2\pi f - \lambda_i^*} \tag{2}$$

where n is the number of modes, $\bullet^T$ is the transpose, $\bullet^*$ is the complex conjugate and $\bullet^H$ is the Hermitian. The vectors $\phi_i \in \mathbb{C}^{N_o}$ and $l_i \in \mathbb{C}^{N_i}$ are respectively the mode shapes and the modal participation factors while λ_i are the poles that, occurring in complex conjugate pairs, are related to natural frequencies f_n and damping ratios ζ as

$$\lambda_i, \lambda_i^* = -2\pi f_{ni} \zeta_i \pm j2\pi f_{ni} \sqrt{1 - \zeta_i^2}. \tag{3}$$

The modal decomposition of the output PSD matrix can be obtained from Eq. (1) and Eq. (2):

$$S_{yy}(f) = \sum_{i=1}^{n} \frac{\phi_i \, l_i^T}{j2\pi f - \lambda_i} + \frac{\phi_i^* \, l_i^H}{j2\pi f - \lambda_i^*} + \frac{l_i \, \phi_i^T}{-j2\pi f - \lambda_i} + \frac{l_i^* \, \phi_i^H}{-j2\pi f - \lambda_i^*} \tag{4}$$

where $l_i \in \mathbb{C}^l$ are the operational reference factors that are functions of modal parameters and input spectrum matrix. It is worthy to recall that the half-PSD is related to the full spectra as

$$S_{yy}(f) = S_{yy}^+(f) + S_{yy}^+(f)^H \tag{5}$$

and it can be parameterized in the same way of the FRF

$$S^+(f) = \sum_{i=1}^{n} \frac{\phi_i \, l_i^T}{j2\pi f - \lambda_i} + \frac{\phi_i^* \, l_i^H}{j2\pi f - \lambda_i^*}. \tag{6}$$

Therefore the PLSCF can be extended to OMA case. This approach starts considering the PSD matrix $S(f) \in \mathbb{C}^{N_o \times N_{ref}}$ generated by the total number N_o of available time histories and a reference number N_{ref} of them. The PSD matrix is decomposed by using a right matrix fraction description as

$$S(f) = B(f) \, A(f)^{-1} \tag{7}$$

where $B(f) \in \mathbb{C}^{N_o \times N_{ref}}$ is the numerator polynomial matrix and $A(f) \in \mathbb{C}^{N_{ref} \times N_{ref}}$ is the denominator polynomial matrix. Then, each rows is equal to

$$S_o(f) = B_o(f)\, A(f)^{-1} \quad \forall \quad o = 1, 2, ...N_o. \tag{8}$$

These quantities can be expressed as

$$B_o(f) = \sum_{r=0}^{p} \Omega^r(f)\, \beta_{or} \quad A(f) = \sum_{r=0}^{p} \Omega^r(f)\, \alpha_r \tag{9}$$

where $\Omega(f)$ are the polynomial basis functions and p is the polynomial order. Although, there are different ways to choose these polynomial functions, in order to obtain a model that is continuous or discrete in time. The discrete model is preferred, and the basis functions are expressed as

$$\Omega(f) = e^{j2\pi f t_s} \quad \forall \quad r = 0, 1, ...p. \tag{10}$$

The polynomial coefficients, that for simplicity are chosen to be real, are collected in the matrices β and α as

$$\beta_o = \begin{bmatrix} \beta_{o0} \\ \beta_{o1} \\ \cdots \\ \beta_{op} \end{bmatrix} \quad \in \mathbb{R}^{(p+1) \times N_{ref}} \quad \alpha = \begin{bmatrix} \alpha_0 \\ \alpha_1 \\ \cdots \\ \alpha_p \end{bmatrix} \quad \in \mathbb{R}^{(p+1)N_{ref} \times N_{ref}} \tag{11}$$

and finally assembled in θ:

$$\theta = \begin{bmatrix} \beta_1 \\ \beta_1 \\ \cdots \\ \beta_{N_o} \\ \alpha \end{bmatrix} \quad \in \mathbb{R}^{(p+1)(N_o+N_{ref}) \times N_{ref}}. \tag{12}$$

Therefore, the PSD matrix is now rewritten as function of the coefficients $S(f, \theta)$. These unknowns can be found by minimizing, in a non-linear least-squares way, the following error matrices

$$\epsilon_o^{NLS}(f_k, \theta) = w_o(f_k)(S_o(f_k, \theta) - \hat{S}_o(f_k)) \quad \forall \quad o = 1, 2, ...N_o \tag{13}$$

where $\hat{S}_o(f_k)$ is a measured quantity and $w_o(f_k)$ is a scalar weighting function. The equation errors for all the outputs and all the frequency lines are collected into a single scalar cost function

$$l^{NLS}(\theta) = \sum_{o=1}^{N_o} \sum_{k=1}^{N_f} tr\{\epsilon_o^{NLS}(f_k, \theta)^H \epsilon_o^{NLS}(f_k, \theta)\} \tag{14}$$

where $tr\{\bullet\}$ is the trace operator. The cost function is then minimized by setting all the derivative of $l^{NLS}(\theta)$, with respect to the unknown model coefficients θ, equal to zero. This operation conduces to non linear equations. However, it can be approximated to a linear least-squares one by right-multiplying equation Eq. (13) by the matrix A:

$$\epsilon_o^{LS}(f_k, \theta) = w_o(f_k) \sum_{r=0}^{p} (\Omega^r(f_k)\beta_{or} - \Omega^r(f_k)\hat{S}_o(f_k)\alpha_r). \tag{15}$$

The equation errors at each frequency line can be collected in a matrix $E_o^{LS}(\theta) \in \mathbb{C}^{N_f x N_{ref}}$ that can be decomposed as

$$E_o^{LS}(\theta) = \begin{bmatrix} \epsilon_o^{LS}(f_1, \theta) \\ \epsilon_o^{LS}(f_2, \theta) \\ \cdots \\ \epsilon_o^{LS}(f_k, \theta) \end{bmatrix} = \begin{bmatrix} X_o \; Y_o \end{bmatrix} \begin{bmatrix} \beta_o \\ \alpha \end{bmatrix}. \tag{16}$$

Indicating the Kronecker product with $\bigotimes$, the matrices $X_o \in \mathbb{C}^{N_f \times (p+1)}$ and $Y_o \in \mathbb{C}^{N_f \times (p+1)N_{ref}}$ can be expressed as

$$X_o = \begin{bmatrix} w_o(f_1)(\Omega^0(f_1) \dots \Omega^p(f_1)) \\ \dots \\ w_o(f_{N_f})(\Omega^o(f_{N_f}) \dots \Omega^p(f_{N_f})) \end{bmatrix} \quad Y_o = \begin{bmatrix} -w_o(f_1)(\Omega^o(f_1) \dots \Omega_p(f_1)) \bigotimes \hat{S}_o(f_1) \\ \dots \\ -w_o(f_{N_f})(\Omega^o(f_{N_f}) \dots \Omega^p(f_{N_f})) \bigotimes \hat{S}_o(f_{N_f}) \end{bmatrix}. \tag{17}$$

As done above it is possible to formulate a cost function based on the linearised equation errors

$$l^{LS}(\theta) = \sum_{o=1}^{N_o} \sum_{k=1}^{N_f} tr\{\epsilon_o^{LS}(f_k, \theta)^H \epsilon_o^{LS}(f_k, \theta)\}. \tag{18}$$

Minimizing this cost function a weighted linear least-squares problem is obtained:

$$l^{LS}(\theta) = \sum_{o=1}^{N_o} tr\{E_o^{LS}(\theta)^H E_o^{LS}(\theta)\} = \sum_{o=1}^{N_o} tr\{[\beta_o^T \alpha^T] \begin{bmatrix} X_o^H \\ Y_o^H \end{bmatrix} [X_o \, Y_o] \begin{bmatrix} \beta_o \\ \alpha \end{bmatrix}\} = tr\{\theta^T J^H J\theta)\} \tag{19}$$

where the Jacobian matrix is given by:

$$J = \begin{bmatrix} X_1 & 0 & \dots & 0 & Y_1 \\ 0 & X_2 & \dots & 0 & Y_2 \\ \dots & \dots & \dots & \dots & \dots \\ 0 & 0 & \dots & X_{N_o} & Y_{N_o} \end{bmatrix} \in \mathbb{C}^{N_o N_f \times (p+1)(N_o + N_{ref})}. \tag{20}$$

In case of real-valued coefficients θ, it can be shown that $J^H J$ can be replaced by $Re\{J^H J\}$; it follows that Eq. (19) can be replaced by the following one:

$$l^{LS}(\theta) = tr\{\theta^T Re\{J^H J\}\theta\} \tag{21}$$

where

$$Re\{J^H J\} = \begin{bmatrix} R_1 & 0 & \dots & 0 & S_1 \\ 0 & R_2 & \dots & 0 & S_2 \\ \dots & \dots & \dots & \dots & \dots \\ 0 & 0 & \dots & R_{N_o} & S_{N_o} \\ S_1^T & S_2^T & \dots & S_{N_o}^T & \sum_{o=1}^{N_o} T_o \end{bmatrix} \in \mathbb{R}^{(p+1)(N_o+N_{ref}) \times (p+1)(N_o+N_{ref})} \tag{22}$$

while the matrix $R_o \in \mathbb{R}^{(p+1)\times(p+1)}$, $S_o \in \mathbb{R}^{(p+1)\times(p+1)N_{ref}}$ and $T_o \in \mathbb{R}^{(p+1)N_{ref} \times (p+1)N_{ref}}$ can be expressed as

$$R_o = Re\{X_o^H X_o\} \quad S_o = Re\{X_o^H Y_o\} \quad T_o = Re\{Y_o^H Y_o\}. \tag{23}$$

The R_o, S_o and T_o submatrices have a Toeplitz structure enabling a fast construction using a FFT algorithm

$$R_{o,rs} = \sum_{k=1}^{N_f} |w_o(f_k)|^2 \Omega(f_k)^{s-r} \tag{24}$$

$$S_{o,rl} = -\sum_{f=1}^{N_f} |w_o(f_k)|^2 \hat{S}_o \Omega(f_k)^{s-r} \tag{25}$$

$$T_{o,kl} = \sum_{f=1}^{N_f} |w_o(f_k)|^2 \hat{S}_o \hat{S}_o^H \Omega(f_k)^{s-r} \tag{26}$$

with $k = [(r-1)N_{ref}+1 : rN_{ref}]$, $l = [(s-1)N_{ref}+1 : sN_{ref}]$ and $r, s = 1, 2, ...n+1$. The cost function in Eq. (21) is minimized by putting its derivatives with respect to the unknown polynomial coefficients θ equal to zero:

$$\frac{\partial l^{LS}(\theta)}{\partial \beta_o} = 2\big(R_o\beta_o + S_o\alpha\big) = 0 \quad \forall \quad o = 1, 2, \ldots, N_o, \tag{27}$$

$$\frac{\partial l^{LS}(\theta)}{\partial \alpha} = 2\sum_{o=1}^{N_o}\big(S_o^T\beta_o + RT_o\alpha\big) = 0. \tag{28}$$

Since only the denominator polynomial coefficients are necessary to build a stabilization diagram and compute modal participation factors, it is possible to use equation Eq. (27) to evaluate β_o and get the following equations

$$\begin{gathered}(2\sum_{o=1}^{l}(T_o - S_o^T R_o^{-1} S_o))\alpha = 0 \\ M\alpha = 0\end{gathered} \tag{29}$$

where $M \in \mathbb{R}^{(p+1)N_{ref}\times(p+1)N_{ref}}$ can be evaluated from the measured PSD matrix. The least-squares solution of Eq. (29) is found by fixing one of the denominator coefficients

$$\alpha = \begin{bmatrix} I_{N_{ref}} \\ -M(N_{ref}+1:(p+1)N_{ref}, N_{ref}+1:(p+1)N_{ref})^{-1} M(N_{ref}+1:(p+1)N_{ref}, 1:N_{ref}) \end{bmatrix} \tag{30}$$

The discrete time poles and the modal participation factor are obtained from the eigen problem of the companion matrix of α and a straightforward transformation can be applied to obtain results in the continuous time domain. In the modal parameter estimation process a good solution is represented by using a high modal order. It means that the PSDs are fitted with much more modes than is actually present in the experimental data. Once the poles are chosen, the mode shapes are found with the LSFD approach resolving:

$$S_{yy}(f) = \sum_{i=1}^{n} \frac{\phi_i\, l_i^T}{j2\pi f - \lambda_i} + \frac{\phi_i^*\, l_i^H}{j2\pi f - \lambda_i^*} + \frac{LR}{j2\pi f} + j2\pi f\, UR \tag{31}$$

in a least-squares sense. The unique unknown are the mode shapes ϕ_i, the lower residuals $LR \in \mathbb{R}^{N_o\times N_{ref}}$ and the upper residuals $UR \in \mathbb{R}^{N_o\times N_{ref}}$.

2.3. Clustering

Unsupervised learning is a type of machine learning algorithm. The most common unsupervised learning method is the cluster analysis that applies one or more clustering technique in order to find hidden patterns or groupings in a dataset. Therefore, the input dataset is divided within different cluster following a certain measure of similarity. The k-means clustering [8] is a partitioning methods and it divides data into distinct clusters based on distance to the centroid. On the other hand, the hierarchical clustering [9] builds a multilevel hierarchy of clusters. The automatic poles selection necessary for the mode shapes reconstruction is performed by means of a multi-stage clustering process that rests on the study carried out in [7]. It is important to define the relative difference between two samples of a generic scalar variable X as

$$dX_{ij} = \frac{|X_i - X_i|}{max(|X_i|, |X_j|)}. \tag{32}$$

In order to take into account the information relative to the operational reference factor the MAC is defined as

$$MAC_{ij} = \frac{|l_i^H \, l_j^*|^2}{(l_i^H l_i^*)\,(l_j^H l_j^*)} \tag{33}$$

and the relative difference in terms of operational reference factors is defined as

$$dMAC_{ij} = 1 - MAC_{ij}. \tag{34}$$

Stage 1

The first step takes in input the whole set of poles from PLSCF and automates the stabilization diagram generally obtained by setting preliminary parameters. A pole of a generic system order has a high probability of being a physical pole if a similar one is found in the previous order. The distance measured between two different poles is defined as:

$$dp_{ij} = d\lambda_{ij} + dMAC_{ij} \tag{35}$$

where $d\lambda$ and $dMAC$ are the poles and operational reference factor distances according respectively to Eq. (32) and Eq. (34). Therefore, for each pole, the nearest neighbor is found in the previous order and the single-mode validation criteria are evaluated. The feature vector is defined considering relative distances as:

$$p_i = [d\lambda_{ij} \; df_{ij} \; d\zeta_{ij} \; dMAC_{ij}] \tag{36}$$

A standard score normalization [10] is applied so that the clustering process is not dominated by features with large dispersion, specifically $d\zeta$:

$$\tilde{p}_i = \frac{p_i - \overline{p}_i}{\sigma(p_i)} \tag{37}$$

where $\overline{p}_i$ e $\sigma(p_i)$ are respectively the mean and standard deviation of the vectors p_i. At this point, a k-means clustering process is applied to group the poles with similar characteristic in one cluster. For this purpose, the number of clusters is two and the initial centroids of the probably physical ν_1 and certain numerical ν_2 poles are set equal to $-\sigma(p)$ e $+\sigma(p)$. In fact, after the standard score normalization the initial centroids are not anymore 0 and 1 respectively for physical and numerical clusters but their values is shifted. The k-means procedure minimizes the within-cluster sum squares in an iterative way:

$$\{C_1, C_2\} = arg \min_C \sum_{k=1}^{2} \sum_{p_i \in C_k} ||p_i - \nu_k||^2 \tag{38}$$

where ν_1 and ν_2 are the centroids of the sets C_1 and C_2. Finally, the cluster of certainly mathematical poles is discarded.

Stage 2

The second stage is the equivalent of operator visual inspection and it is performed by means of the agglomerative hierarchical clustering. Initially, each pole forms a cluster. Then, the mutual distance between all the different clusters is evaluated using Eq. (35) and considering the average distance between their elements. Then the two closest clusters are merged. The iterative process is repeated until the distance d_{ij} reaches the value of the 95th percentile of the set of distances in Stage 1. An additional constraint was introduced to avoid the pole splitting phenomena: each cluster cannot contain poles of the same order. The hierarchical clustering stage yields clusters containing poles with similar characteristics.

Stage 3

In the last stage, the clusters from the previous step are divided into two groups containing sets of physical and mathematical modes. In fact, the clusters of physical modes contain several elements whereas the cluster of mathematical ones only a few. Again, the k-means clustering approach is adopted. The considered parameter is the number of poles n_i of each cluster that was obtained from the previous stage. The centroids starting values are chosen equal to $max(n_i)$ and 0 respectively for physical and mathematical clusters. Therefore, the algorithm minimizes the following equation:

$$\{n_1, n_2\} = \min_{n} \sum_{k=1}^{2} \sum_{n_i \in n_{c,k}} ||n_i - n_{c,k}||^2 \tag{39}$$

where $n_{c,1}$ and $n_{c,2}$ are the centers of the sets n_1 and n_2. Finally, an iterative procedure is carried out to eliminate the outliers in each identified cluster and the poles with averaged damping value are selected.

3. GROUND VIBRATION TEST

The OMA approach presented in the previous section has been applied to estimate the modal properties of the fixed-wing UAV "Javelin". This electric engine propelled vehicle, Fig. 1, is developed by RMIT Unmanned Aerial Systems (UAS) research team. Its main characteristic are listed in Table 1. Several

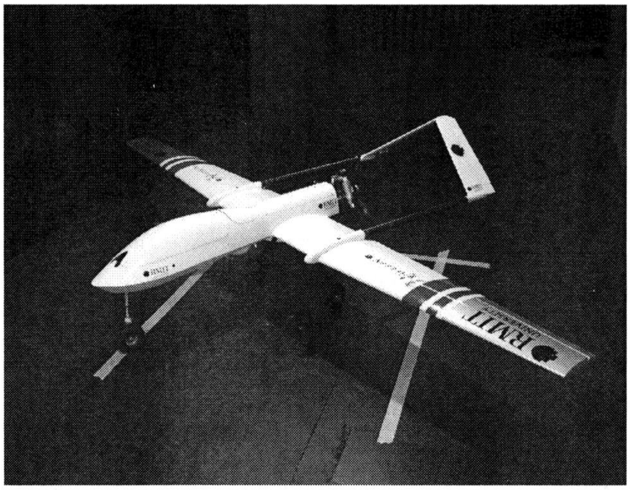

Figure 1: RMIT University's "Javelin"

Table 1: Main characteristics of the "Javelin"

Parameter	Value
Length	2000mm
Height	650mm
Wingspan	2800mm
Aspect Ratio	11
Empty Weight	8.7kg
MTOW	17kg
Endurance	2hours

test campaigns have been carried on such a "Javelin" structure. In this paper, focus will be given to the traditional Input/Output-based Ground Vibration Tests (GVTs) and to those tests where only responses were recorded to assess the developed OMA technique.

3.1. Experimental Modal Analysis

Two shakers were placed on the tips of the wings in an asymmetric position to excite bending and torsional modes of the wings. In order to have an accurate spatial representation of the dynamic behaviour of the vehicle, the roving accelerometers technique was carried out to acquire data on the wings, fuselage, booms, and tail. The chosen input was a white random noise with a sample rate of $256Hz$. The structure was hung from a supporting structure with an elastic rope to mimic the free-free boundary conditions, whereas the UAV mass configuration was chosen as close as possible to the actual flying condition. In order to asses possible effects of the support structure dynamics on the identification procedure, two GVTs were carried out. The first one aimed at the identification of the "Javelin" modal properties, whereas the second to the supporting structure alone. Indeed, for the second set of tests, a dummy mass, with the same weight of the "Javelin," was hung to simulate the same boundary conditions and the excitation was directly provided to the structure by means of modal hammer. As a result, modes at $4.84Hz$, $11.31Hz$, $17.89Hz$ and 42.54 were classified as external disturbances due to the support structure. The PSDs of the signals acquired are shown in Fig. 2. In the frequency range of interest

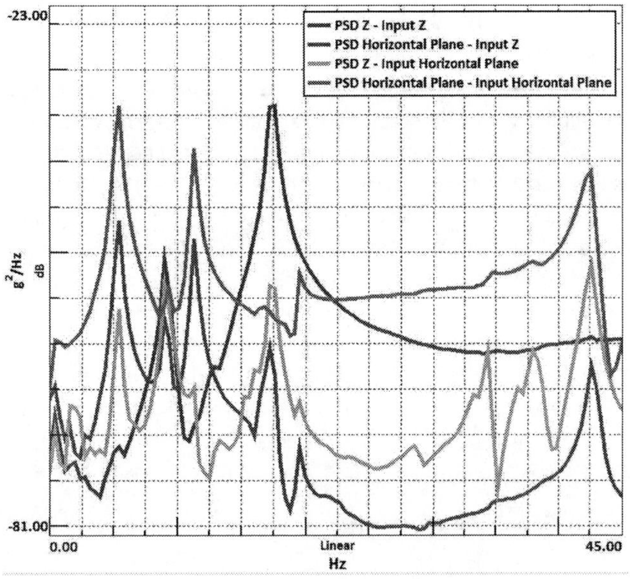

Figure 2: PSDs of the support structure

$5 - 50Hz$, 6 modes have been identified. In Table 2 natural frequencies and damping ratio are reported, whereas mode shapes are depicted in Fig. 3.

Table 2: Natural frequencies and damping ratios from EMA

Mode	f_n $[Hz]$	ζ $[\%]$
1	9.95	0.45
2	15.05	0.62
3	25.43	1.37
4	27.17	0.95
5	40.54	3.08
6	46.12	1.6

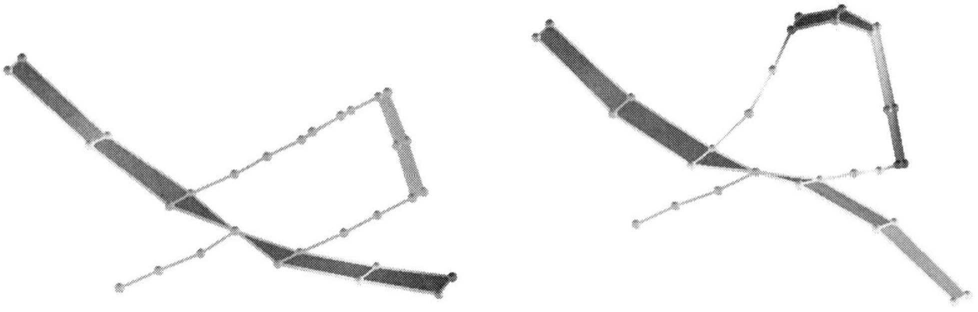

Figure 3: First and fifth mode shapes from GVT with EMA

3.2. Operational Modal Analysis

The second set of tests were performed to assess the developed OMA approach. The simple supported boundary condition was considered, whereas a finger tapping input was introduced to provide system the random excitation, both in space and in time. Differently from the previous case, only the accelerations were recorded on the wing at the same geometrical points considered for the EMA. It is worth remarking that such a boundary condition was chosen to have on-ground information about the "Javelin" modal properties to be compared with those estimated during flight tests. Therefore it is not possible to compare the modal parameters estimated from the EMA and OMA test activities. However, referring to the wing modes only and accepting a degree of change in the test configuration a good correlation between the first two wing bending modes has been achieved. Indeed, from Table 3, where the natural frequencies and damping ratios of the estimated modes are reported, such bending modes, Mode $\#2$ and Mode $\#6$, exhibit a good correlation with those of Tab. 2, Mode $\#2$ and Mode $\#5$, in terms of natural frequency shifts, being the corresponding mode shapes practically the same. The main differences are found to be at lower frequencies where an additional mode is found in the OMA and the natural frequencies are slight shifted. These facts are due to the strongly different boundary conditions rather than the type of analysis. In fact, in the first case the "Javelin" was hung by means of elastic rope whereas in the second GVT the simply supported condition was adopted. Thus, not only it is possible to confirm, as expected, that traditional modal analysis methods and OMA methods are giving the same modal picture of the structure, but also that the developed method worth further investigation because its capability to help the operator in estimating the modal parameters.

Table 3: Natural frequencies and damping ratios from OMA

Mode	f_n $[Hz]$	ζ $[\%]$
1	7.96	13.76
2	12.26	8.33
3	17.98	3.02
4	26.31	4.11
5	32.60	0.16
6	41.22	2.76
7	46.49	3.29

4. FINITE ELEMENT ANALYSIS

The preliminary finite element model of the "Javelin" wing structure was developed exclusively for the half-wing beyond the boom. This choice is motivated by the fact that flight test data will be used to update the finite element model in a near future. The model is composed by 43479 solid elements and the boundary conditions are obtained by means of clumping and spring actions in order to simulate as better as possible the real connection between the half-wing and the fuselage. Although such a boundary is not the actual one, it is generally recognized as a good representation of the wing/fuselage connection. The numerical modal analysis was carried out in the $0 - 100Hz$ frequency range. Only the modes vibrating in the direction orthogonal to the wing surface were considered. The evaluated natural frequencies are reported in Table 4, whereas the mode shapes are shown in Fig. 4.

Table 4: Natural frequencies and damping ratios from finite element analysis

Mode	f_n $[Hz]$
1	18.51
2	81.12

Figure 4: First and second mode shapes from finite element modal analysis

5. MODEL CORRELATION AND STRUCTURAL UPDATING

As a consequence of the analysis of the estimates of the UAV eigenproperties carried out in Section 3.2., both the EMA and OMA modal bases can be indifferently employed for the structural updating. For what concerns the finite element model, the first 2 mode shapes vibrating in the orthogonal direction to the wing surface, were identified in the $0 - 100$ Hz analysis frequency range. A visual inspection of the estimated mode shapes made possible the association of the first and second mode shapes of the finite element model with the first and sixth ones of the OMA. However, there was a strong difference in terms of natural frequencies as reported in Fig. 5. It is possible to notice how the ratio between the finite element natural frequencies and the experimental ones is about 2. This is due to the strong uncertainties in the elastic and material properties of the internal structure of the wing. Therefore, an updating of the finite element model was carried out by tuning the Young modulus of the components associated to the internal wing structure. Finally, the tuned finite element model presents really strong improvements. The updated natural frequencies are listed in Table 5 and the comparison with the experimental ones is shown in Fig. 6. The mode shapes are almost the same of that ones presented in Fig. 4.

Table 5: Natural frequencies and damping ratios from finite element analysis after updating

Mode	f_n $[Hz]$
1	9.64
2	41.23

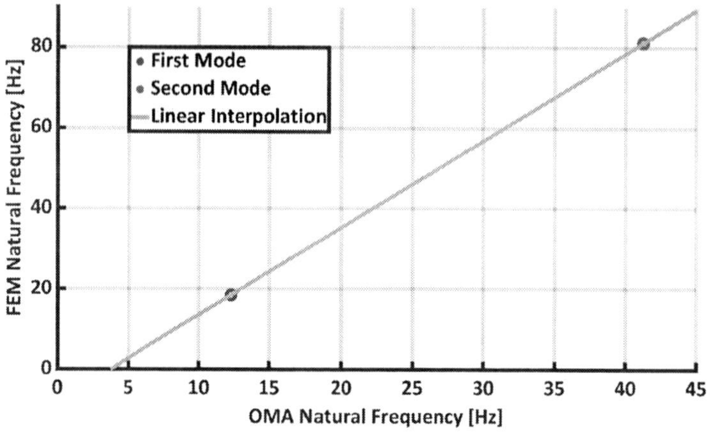

Figure 5: Comparison experimental and numerical natural frequencies before updating

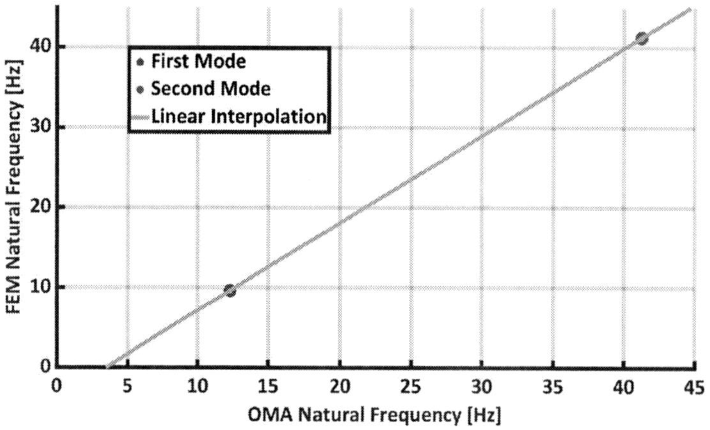

Figure 6: Comparison experimental and numerical natural frequencies after updating

6. CONCLUDING REMARKS

A novel technique for the estimate of the modal parameters in the framework of the operational modal analysis (OMA) has been presented. Such a method is based on the combined use of PLSCF estimator, which represents clear stabilization diagram and is computationally efficient, and the clustering algorithm that allows an easy tool to identify the mode shapes. The main advantage of such a technique is its numerical efficiency and its capability to automatically identify the modal parameters with practically no need of engineers judgment, as in almost all estimating techniques. Thus, among all the possible applications, a real-time system identification operating under actual working conditions is foreseen, such as flight test. The developed OMA technique has been applied to the fixed wing UAV "Javelin," developed by RMIT University. The estimated modal parameters are used in modal updating process to develop a numerical model which represents the dynamical behaviour of the Javelin during flight condition. Because of the very preliminary finite element model of the wing structure, and the high uncertainties associated to the material properties of the wing inner structure, only an initial structural updating has been carried out. By taking advantages of the modal properties estimated by using the developed approach, it was possible to update the internal mass and stiffness wing distribution to dramatically reduce the eigenfrequency shift to acceptable values, while keeping high the mode shape correlation.

ACKNOWLEDGEMENTS

This research has been supported by *"F.E. model updating of remotely piloted aircraft (RPA) using flight-test data"*, 2015, University of Rome "La Sapienza".

REFERENCES

[1] R. Brincker, L. Zhang, P. Andersen, Modal Identification from Ambient Responses Using Frequency Domain Decomposition, XVIII IMAC, S. Antonio, TX, (USA), (2000).

[2] R. Brincker, C. E. Ventura, P. Andersen, "Damping Estimation by Frequency Domain Decomposition", XIX IMAC, Kissimee, FL, (USA), (2001).

[3] A. Agneni, L. Balis Crema, G. Coppotelli, (2010) Output-Only Analysis of Structures with Closely Spaced Modes, Mechanical System and Signal Processing. Special Issue: Operational Modal Analysis, Vol 24, N. 5, July, pp. 1240-1249, ISSN: 0888-3270, doi: 10.1016/j.ymssp.2009.10.013.

[4] P. Van Overschee, B. De Moor, Subspace Identification for Linear Systems, Kluver Academic Publisher, (1996).

[5] Peeters, B., and Vander Auweraer, H., *"PolyMAX: A Revolution In Operational Modal Analysis"*, 1st International Operational Modal Analysis Conference, Vol.29, 205, pp. 228-250.

[6] Coppotelli, G., Di Giandomenico, F., Marzocca, P., and Marino, M., *"Real-Time System Identification for Fixed-Wing Aircraft"*, AIAA Scitech 2019 Forum, San Diego, California, 2019, (AIAA 2019-1533) https://doi.org/10.2514/6.2019-1533.

[7] Reynders, E., Houbrechts, J., and De Roeck, G., *"Fully Automated Operational Modal Analysis"*, Mechanical Systems and Signal Processing, Vol.29, No.228, 2012, pp. 15-34.

[8] Wu, J., *"Advances in K-means Clustering"*, Springer Theses, 2012.

[9] Mackay, D.J.C., *"Information Theory, Inference, and Learning Algorithm"*, Cambridge University Press, 2003.

[10] Neu, E., *"Vibration-Based Structural Health Monitoring of Cantilever-Like Structures Under Varying Wind Excitation"*, Master Dissertation, RMIT University, 2016.

IOMAC'19

8th International Operational Modal Analysis Conference

2019 May13-15 Copenhagen

TWO APPROACHES FOR DETERMINATION OF CONTACT LAYER STIFFNESS

Mikhail Kuts[1], and Vladimir Zhulev[2]

[1] PhD student, Bauman Moscow State Technical University, Moscow, Russia, kuts@bmstu.ru.

[2] PhD student, Bauman Moscow State Technical University, Moscow, Russia, vlzh92@gmail.com.

ABSTRACT

Joints contact zone has a major effect on the dynamic behaviour of structural systems. The approach of contact layer modelling as the third body with zero thickness is most common. In the paper two methods for determining of contact layer stiffness are presented: one is based on contact stiffness determination using a priori data about contact surfaces and contact pressure distribution; another is the method of finite element model updating and it is based on a calculation of sensitivity coefficient using experimental modal analysis. The second method is applied for determining of contact stiffness of fixed plate finite element model used for dynamic analysis. Results of the analysis were compared with results of experimental modal analysis of the plate. The first method has good convergence with experiment and can be used on the design stage. For more accurate simulations should use the second method.

Keywords: finite element models updating, finite element model verification, sensitivity coefficient, contact stiffness, contact dynamics.

1. INTRODUCTION

Due to a simulation of dynamic behaviour, such as simulation of the metal cutting process [1,2], errors occur, which leads to a significant difference between model and real construction behaviour. One of the reasons is the simplification of the contact zone between jointed parts [3]. The theory of elasticity, computational mathematics and modern numerical methods allows to estimate stiffness of parts with any configuration, but modelling of contact with real topography need a lot of computational resources and is not efficient. This is the reason why usually this area is ignored by combining adjacent nodes of the model, which leads to the simulation errors.

The better way is to replace the contact zone by elements with unknown equivalent parameters. The model, thus obtained, needs correction and determination right contact parameters. This correction can be made by using a methods of finite elements model (FE) refinement. There are two of them: the direct and the iterative. Direct methods change matrix components, that used in finite element simulation [4,5]. A disadvantage of these methods is that the parameters of the model can take a value beyond physically reasonable range after the refinement. Iterative methods do not have this disadvantage. Their main idea is that a target function is introduced, which is a measure of the discrepancy between calculated and experimental values of natural frequencies (NF), which can be minimized in several iterations by the methods of optimization theory. The method, based on the coefficient of sensitivity, calculation of which is described in work [6], is widespread. General equations are given in work [7].

However, there is another method, based on the calculation of contact stiffness. In works [8-10], devoted to the contact of rough surfaces, the relation between contact pressure and displacements was approximated by a power function. The limitation of this method is that it needs a huge count of empirical data for precise definition of contact layer pliability. In work [11,12] the method of calculation of contact stiffness, that takes into account materials of the contact parts, its surface roughness and contact pressure, was proposed. An advantage of this method is that it allows to define contact layer pliability on the design stage [13]. A disadvantage of this method is the scale effect caused by the increased influence of contact surface waviness.

In this paper, we review two approaches to determining the equivalent rigidity of the contact layer of assembled construction: by the method based on a priory data about contacted surfaces (1st method) and by the method of finite element model refinement based on calculation of the sensitivity coefficient using experimental modal analysis (2nd method). The aim of this work is to compare the results of both methods, that determine equivalent rigidity of elements in the contact layer of assembled construction by an example of the cantilever beam.

2. DESCRIPTION OF THE METHOD USED

2.1. Contact stiffness determination based on a priory data about contact surfaces (1st method)

2.1.1. Relation between contact stiffness, surface parameters and contact pressure

In the works [11,12] the relation between contact displacements and contact pressure was proposed:

$$\delta_n = Ra\, c_0 \varepsilon \sqrt{\frac{p}{E^*}}, \tag{1}$$

where Ra – arithmetical mean deviation of the assessed profile, c_0 - coefficient, which consider direction of contact surfaces roughness, ε - scale factor, which consider surface waviness and form error, $E^* = ((1-\mu_1)^2/E_1 + (1-\mu_2)^2/E_2)^{-1}$ – equivalent modulus of elasticity, in which E – Yang modulus and μ – Poisson's ratio of each of parts, p – contact pressure in the contact layer. Equation (1) can be linearized in the actual pressure p_0 domain:

$$\delta_n = k(p - p_0) + \delta_{n0},$$

where δ_{n0} – contact displacements from pressure p_0 and k_n – coefficient of contact pliability, which can be calculated by

$$k_n = \left.\frac{d\delta}{dp}\right|_{p=p_0} = \frac{Ra\, c_0^* \varepsilon}{2\sqrt{p_0 E}}. \tag{2}$$

According to the approach, the contact stiffness j_c can be determined by equations:

$$j_c = \frac{A}{k_n} \tag{3}$$

where A – a square of the contact surface. For precise simulation of contact layer behaviour, we need to know the distribution of contact pressure, caused by tightening. It can be obtained as result of finite element analysis (FEA), which was shown in work [14], where a zero thickness interface element, described in [15,16], was used for determination of contact pressure distribution. The pressure obtained by this method can be used for calculation of contact stiffness.

2.2. The method of FEM updating based on calculation of the sensitivity coefficient using experimental modal analysis (EMA)

2.2.1. Calculation of sensitivity coefficient

From the [17] it's known, that NF of model without damping can be calculated using Rayleigh relation:

$$\omega_i^2 = \frac{\boldsymbol{x}_i^T \boldsymbol{K} \boldsymbol{x}_i}{\boldsymbol{x}_i^T \boldsymbol{M} \boldsymbol{x}_i}, \tag{4}$$

where **K** – global stiffness matrix of system, **M** – global mass matrix of system, $\mathbf{x}_i$ – i^{th} mode of the model vibration, ω_i – i^{th} NF.

We can define the sensitivity coefficient natural frequency from changing the stiffness of a selected finite element by differentiating of equation (**4**) by its stiffness and performing some transformations:

$$\frac{\partial \omega_i}{\partial k_j} = \frac{\boldsymbol{x}_i^T \left(\boldsymbol{K}'^{k_j} - \omega_i^2 \boldsymbol{M}'^{k_j}\right) \boldsymbol{x}_i}{2\omega_i M_i} \approx \frac{\boldsymbol{x}_i^T \boldsymbol{K}_j' \boldsymbol{x}_i}{2\omega_i M_i k_j} = \frac{\Pi_{ij}}{\omega_i M_i k_j} \tag{5}$$

where $M_i = \boldsymbol{x}_i^T \boldsymbol{M} \boldsymbol{x}_i$ – i^{th} modal mass, k_j - stiffness of jth element, $\boldsymbol{K}'^{k_j}, \boldsymbol{M}'^{k_j}$- local derivative of global stiffness and mass matrices by stiffness of jth element, $\boldsymbol{K}_j'$- the stiffness matrix of jth element, supplemented by zeros till dimension of the global stiffness matrix, Π_{ij}- potential energy of deformation of jth element on the ith NF.

In the case when we need to tune the model on the N lower natural frequencies and stiffness variation is allowed in L finite elements, then it would be rational to combine sensitivity coefficients determined by equation (5) in a matrix with dimension $L \times N$, in which j^{th} row present sensitivity coefficients, considered in eigenmode for

$$\boldsymbol{T} = \begin{pmatrix} \frac{\partial \omega_1}{\partial k_1} & \frac{\partial \omega_2}{\partial k_1} & \cdots \\ \frac{\partial \omega_1}{\partial k_2} & \frac{\partial \omega_2}{\partial k_2} & \cdots \\ \vdots & \vdots & \ddots \end{pmatrix} \tag{6}$$

2.2.2. Algorithm of the stiffness refinement of the FE model

Vector of NF can be represented as a function of stiffness parameters of some elements and the Taylor expansion can be performed to it:

$$\boldsymbol{\omega}(\boldsymbol{k}) = \boldsymbol{\omega}(\boldsymbol{k}_0) + \frac{\boldsymbol{\omega}'(\boldsymbol{k})}{1!}(\boldsymbol{k} - \boldsymbol{k}_0) + \frac{\boldsymbol{\omega}''(\boldsymbol{k})}{2!}(\boldsymbol{k} - \boldsymbol{k}_0)^2 + \cdots + \frac{\boldsymbol{\omega}^{(n)}(\boldsymbol{k})}{n!}(\boldsymbol{k} - \boldsymbol{k}_0)^n. \tag{7}$$

Equation (7) linearization by stiffness vector $\boldsymbol{k}_0$ leads to recurrsive expression for unknown stiffness determination of the refinement model

$$\boldsymbol{k}_{i+1} = \boldsymbol{k}_i + (\boldsymbol{T}_i)^+ \cdot \left(\boldsymbol{\omega}(\boldsymbol{k}) - \boldsymbol{\omega}(\boldsymbol{k}_i)\right), \tag{8}$$

where i – number of iteration, $\boldsymbol{k}_{i+1}$ - stiffness vector be used on $(i+1)^{th}$ iteretion, $\boldsymbol{k}_i$- stiffness vector, used on i^{th} iteretion, $(\boldsymbol{T}_i)^+ = \boldsymbol{T}_i^T \left(\boldsymbol{T}_i^T \boldsymbol{T}_i^T\right)^{-1}$ – pseudoinverse matrix of sensitivity coefficients, $\boldsymbol{\omega}(\boldsymbol{k})$- vector of experimental values of the frequencies, $\boldsymbol{\omega}(\boldsymbol{k}_i)$ – vector of the frequencies, received on i^{th} iteretion of calculation.

2.2.3. *Algorithm of model updating*

For minimization of the disparity between natural frequency obtained in simulation, and natural frequency, obtained in modal testing, it is necessary to define equivalent stiffnesses of the model. For correct performing of this determination, the iterative algorithm of refinement is used.

If the disparity NF of the model and the real object is unacceptable, the sensitivity coefficients (5) are calculated, then the computation of stiffness of refinement elements is performed using equation (8). Then values of NF are calculated for the model with changed properties. The process is repeated till disparity reaches an acceptable value.

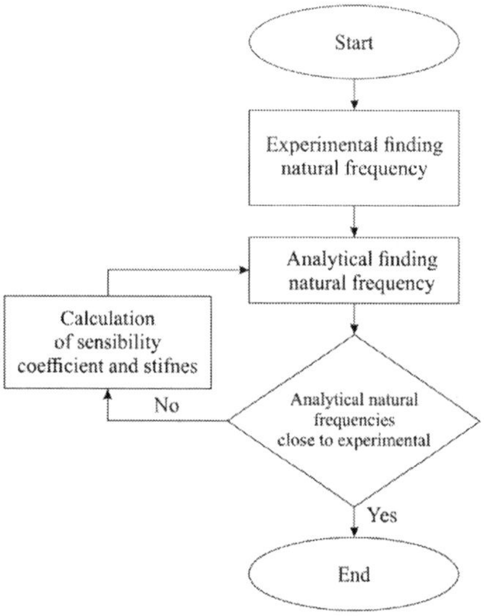

Figure 1. Flow chart of the finite element model updating algorithm based on calculating of the sensitivity coefficient.

3. DISCRIPTION OF THE INVESTIGATED OBJECT AND METHODS

3.1. Experimental apparatus

In this paper, the problem of contact stiffness identification of the steel plate, which is a turbine blade billet, is considered. The actual model of the billet with correct contact stiffness is needed for simulation of turbine blade cutting process. The scheme of the fixed plate and the photo of the experimental set for modal analysis is shown on fig. 2. The billet 1 is set on two steel backing pads 3 on the steel table 4 and fixed by two clamps 2. Clamps 2 are tightened by bolts 5, the tightening force was controlled by torque wrench (fig. 2-*b*). Contact surface of the backing pads is obtained by grinding and its roughness parameter Ra=0.8 mkm.

3.2. FE model description

The FE model was made in CAE system NX Nastran and represents parallelepiped with dimension $L\times W\times H$=300×120×15 mm, which was covered by a regular mesh of tetrahedral elements of the second order. All nodes, which are supposed to be in the contact area between billet and backing pads, and nodes in clamps domain are connected to CBUSH elements represented spring approximation. The constraints were made by fixing the second end of each spring. Each spring has unique rigidity, which was calculated by the 1st method and then specified by the 2nd method. The model representation is shown on fig. 3.

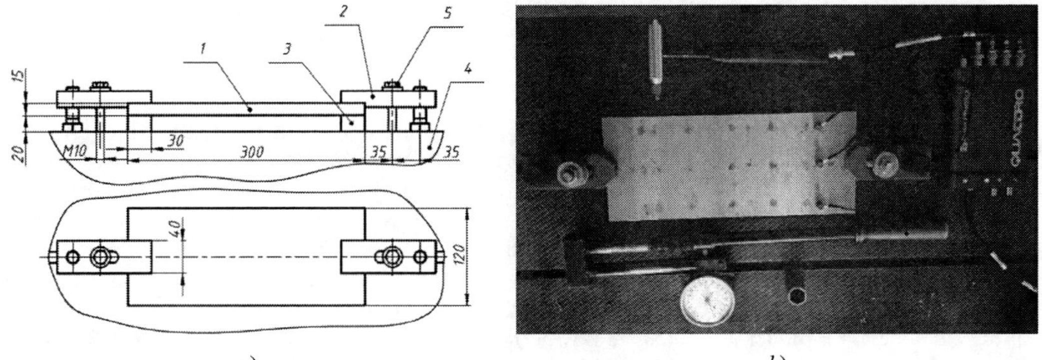

a) *b)*

Figure 2. Scheme (a) and photo (b) of experimental set: 1 – billet, 2 – clamps, 3 - backing pads, 4 – fundament table, 5 – tightening bolts

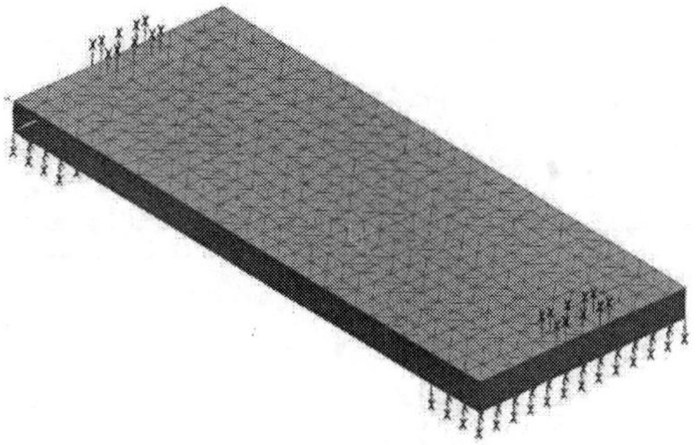

Figure 3. Representation of finite element model

3.3. Identification of modal characteristics using EMA

Identification of dynamic parameters was conducted on billet shown on fig. 2 using vibro-impulsive test. The vibroimpulsive impact was performed with KISTLER dynamometric hummer, and the data was measured by Brüel & Kjær accelerometers with further acquiring by ADC Quattro made by Data Physics (see fig. 2-*b*). The magnitude of obtained signal shown on the fig. 4. Identification of NF was performed in program ModalView, which is described in [18].

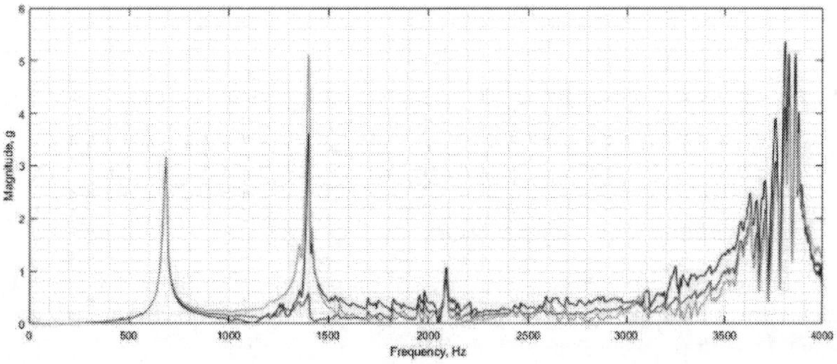

Figure 4. Magnitude spectrum of free vibration of billet with tightening force F_t=1700N

4. RESULTS OF INVESTIGATION

4.1. Tightening simulation for determination of contact pressure distribution

Contact pressure calculation was made in the FEA program written in the Python programming language. The contact layer was simulated by interface elements and nonlinear character of contact stiffness. In terms of the FE method, it presents material nonlinearity problem, which was counted by incremental force method with recalculation of the stiffness matrix on each iteration. Stiffness identification was performed for one support of the billet, caused by it symmetricity, allowing to consider the problem in terms of the flat problem of the theory of elasticity. Calculation scheme is shown on fig. 5-*a* and result of calculations are shown on fig. 5-*b*. The stiffness of each CBUSH springs in general FE model was calculated by performing equations (2) and (3) to the obtained stress distribution, where a square of spring neighbourhood was used as square A. Obtained distribution of contact pressure is shown on fig. 6.

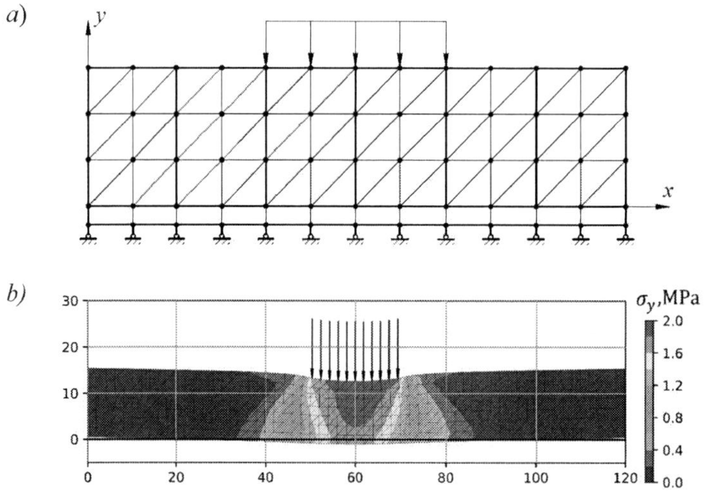

Figure 5. Calculation sheme (*a*) of considered problem and computation result (*b*)

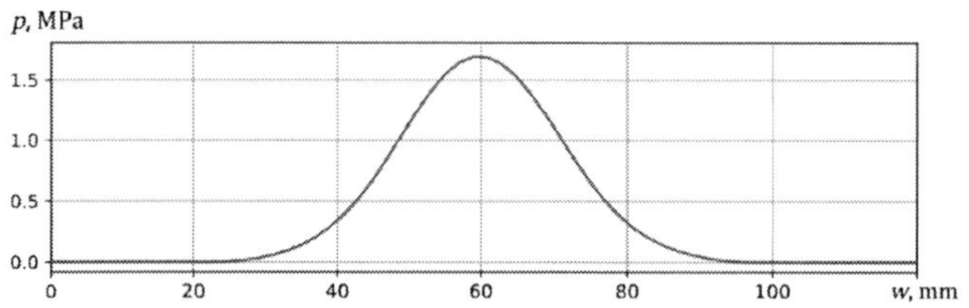

Figure 6. Pressure distribution and corresponding it springs stiffness

4.2. Numerical modal analysis and model updating

Numerical modal analysis (NMA) was performed to the model using obtained contact stiffness. The natural friquency values obtained in the experiment and in computation results are shown in table 1. Results of simulation with rigid constraints are shown for comparison.

Furthermore, the obtained values of contact stiffness were used as initial values for the algorithm of stiffness refinement. The algorithm of FE model stiffness identification, based on sensitivity coefficient calculation, was implemented using the programming language MATLAB. The CAE NX Nastran was used as FEM solver. Interpretation of obtained results was implemented in system WolframAlpha 9.0. Result and initial values of the contact stiffness are shown on the fig. 7.

Table 1. Value of calculated natural frequencies and its comparasion

Mode	Experimental NF [Hz]	NMA w/o contact modelling		NMA with contact stiffness modeling by 1st method		NMA after contact stiffness identification (2nd method)	
		NF [Hz]	Error [%]	NF [Hz]	Error [%]	NF [Hz]	Error [%]
1st	684.0	1318.1	92.7	693.3	1.3	684.0	0
2nd	1399.5	2114.9	51.1	1086.5	22.4	1399.5	0

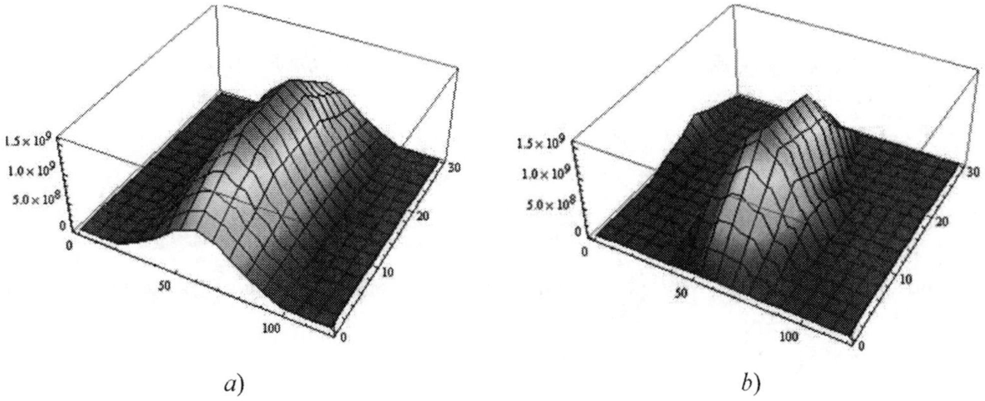

Figure 7. Initial (*a*) and result (*b*) contact stiffness distribution

5. CONCLUSION

Contact stiffness obtained by the first method allows simulating the dynamic behaviour accurately for frequencies not exceeding the first mode frequencies (the simulation error was ~1.5%). On the higher frequencies, it shows the worst results (the simulation error was ~22.4%) but can be used for preliminary estimation of the natural frequencies on the design stage. Accuracy can be increased by taking more contact parameters, such as waviness and contact hardness, into account.

The second method gives more accurate results, but it needs to conduct the experimental identification, meaning that it cannot be used without existing construction and it is preferable for precise simulation of the construction dynamic behaviour. Fast convergence can be obtained by usage of initial stiffness which is gained by the first method.

REFERENCES

[1] Voronov, S. A., Ivanov, I. I., & Kiselev, I. A. (2015). Investigation of the milling process based on a reduced dynamic model of cutting tool. *Journal of Machinery Manufacture and Reliability, 44*, 70-78.

[2] Voronov, S. A., Kiselev, I. A., & Ma, W. (2018). Influence of technological system's rigidity on the dynamics of grinding process of flexible parts. *MATEC Web of Conferences, 226*, 02002

[3] Zhulev, V., & Kuts, M. (2018). Contact models verification by the finite element model updating method based on the calculation of the sensitivity coefficient. *MATEC Web of Conferences, 226*, 02008

[4] Baruch, M., & Bar Itzhack, I. Y. (1979). Optimal weighted orthogonalization of measured modes. *AIAA Journal, 17*, 927-928.

[5] Berman, A., & Nagy, E. J. (1983). Improvement of a large analytical model using test data. *AIAA journal, 21*, 1168-1173.

[6] Géradin, M., & Rixen, D. J. (2014). *Mechanical vibrations: theory and application to structural dynamics*. John Wiley & Sons.

[7] Friswell, M., & Mottershead, J. E. (2013). *Finite element model updating in structural dynamics* (T. 38). Springer Science & Business Media.

[8] Levina, Z. M., & Reshetov, D. N. (1971). *Kontaktnaya dzheskost' mashin [Contact stiffness of machines]*. Moscow, Mashinostroenie.

[9] Demkin, N. B., & Ryzhov, E. V. (1981). *Kachestvo poverhnosti I kontakt detaley mashin [Surface quality and contact of machine parts]*. Moscow: Mashinostroenie.

[10] Ryzhov, E. V. (1966). *Kontaktnaya dzhestkost' detaley machin [Contact stiffness of the machine parts]*. Moscow, Mashinostroenie.

[11] Ivanov, A. S., & Murkin, S. V. (2016). Screw tightening in dynamically loaded threaded joints. *Russian Engineering Research, 36*, 809-810.

[12] Ivanov, A. S., & Murkin, S. V. (2016). Threaded joints in drives. *Russian Engineering Research, 36*, 611-619.

[13] Ermolaev, M. M. (2016). Taking account of the contact-layer pliability in end clip design. *36*(5), 355-359.

[14] Kuts M. S. (2019). Pressure Distribution in an Area of the Tightened Single Bolt Joint. *Izvestiya vysshikh uchebnykh zavedeniy. Mashinostroenie*, 3-10. doi:10.18698/0536-1044-2019-1-

[15] Beer, G. (1985). An isoparametric joint/interface element for finite element analysis. *International journal for numerical methods in engineering, 21*, 585-600.

[16] Sokolov, A. P., & Schetinin, V. N. (2018). Modeling of phases adhesion in composite materials based on spring finite element with zero length. *Key Engineering Materials*, *780*, 3-9.

[17] Biderman, V. L. (2017). *Teoriya mehanicheskih kolebaniy [Theory of mechanical vibrations]*. Moscow, Lenand.

[18] Kuts, V. A., Nikolaev, S. M., & Voronov, S. A. (2017). The procedure for subspace identification optimal parameters selection in application to the turbine blade modal analysis. *Procedia Engineering, 176*, 56-65.

IDENTIFICATION TECHNIQUES & RELATED TOPICS

IOMAC'19

8th International Operational Modal Analysis Conference
2019 May13-15 Copenhagen

APPLICATION OF A ROBUST MULTI-DATASET FREQUENCY DOMAIN DECOMPOSITION TO ESTIMATE THE GLOBAL MODAL PARAMETERS OF A HIGH-RISE BUILDING

Sandro D. R. Amador [1], *Niels J. Savnik* [2], *Evangelos I. Katsanos* [3], *Carlos E. Ventura* [4], *Rune Brincker* [5]

[1] Assistant Professor, Technical University of Denmark, Department of Civil Engineering, Brovej, Building 118, DK-2800 Kongens Lyngby, Denmark, sdio@byg.dtu.com.
[2] MSc. Civil Engineer, Read Jones Christoffersen Ltd., 1285 W Broadway suit 300, Vancouver, BC V6H 3X8, Canada, nsavnik@rjc.ca.
[3] Assistant Professor, Technical University of Denmark, Department of Civil Engineering, Brovej, Building 118, DK-2800 Kongens Lyngby, Denmark, vakat@byg.dtu.dk.
[4] Professor, The University of British Columbia, Department of Civil Engineering, 6250 Applied Science Lane, Vancouver BC V 6T 1Z4, Canada, ventura@civil.ubc.ca.
[5] Professor, Technical University of Denmark, Department of Civil Engineering, Brovej, Building 118, DK-2800 Kongens Lyngby, Denmark, runeb@byg.dtu.dk.

ABSTRACT

In multi-dataset identification with the classic Frequency Domain Decomposition (FDD) technique, the global mode shapes are obtained by identifying the mode shape parts of different patches separately. Then, the estimated mode shape parts are merged to form the global mode shapes by using the reference mode shape components. However, the presence of closely spaced or poorly excited modes can affect differently the estimation of the mode shape parts; hence, the resulting global mode shapes might not present well-defined modal configurations. This paper describes the application of a correlation spectrum based FDD technique to estimate the modal parameters of a high-rise building by identifying the global mode shape vectors in one step. This is expected to provide mode shape estimates with increased accuracy. To illustrate the performance of the correlation spectrum based FDD technique, the modal properties estimated with this technique is compared to those estimated with the classic FDD one.

Keywords: Modal Identification, Frequency Domain Decomposition, Multi-dataset Identification, Global Mode Shapes, High-rise Building

1. INTRODUCTION

The Frequency Domain Decomposition (FDD) technique is widely used in Operational Modal Analysis (OMA) to estimate the modal properties from vibration responses measured in output-only vibration tests. The classic FDD [1, 2] uses the data-driven spectra estimates - or the so-called *periodogram* or *Welch's* method [3], as it is known from scientific literature - as primary data to estimate the natural frequencies and their corresponding mode shapes. When dealing with vibration tests that involve multiple datasets, the FDD identification of the global mode shapes are carried out basically by identifying the modes shape parts from each dataset and merging the identified mode shape parts with aid of the reference mode shape components to form the estimated global mode shapes of the tested structure. A detailed description of the classic multi-dataset FDD can be found, for instance, in [4, 2].

It turns out that, in cases of non-stationary operating conditions, the tested structure tends to be excited differently over measured datasets, meaning that it is not always possible to identify the same physical modes in every measured dataset. Moreover, even in cases where the physical modes of the tested structure can be identified in all the datasets, the mode shape parts estimated from different datasets are influenced differently by the varying operating conditions, leading to not well defined global mode shape estimates. This problem is extensively discussed, for instance, in [5, 6]. In [7], an approach based on geometric projection of the individual mode shape parts is proposed to reduce the influence of non-stationary operating conditions on the estimates of the global mode shapes.

In this paper, novel approach is proposed to estimate the global mode shapes from multi-dataset output-only vibration data with FDD technique. The innovative aspects of such approach with regard to its classic FDD counterpart are related to the facts that: (i) rather than the classic *periodogram*, the correlation-driven spectral density estimates [3, 8] are used as primary data to identify the global mode shapes and the corresponding natural frequencies; and (ii) the identification of the global mode shapes is performed by taking the singular value decomposition of a global spectrum matrix which is assembled by stacking the spectrum matrix of the different datasets on the top of each other.

One of main differences of this approach with regard to the classic *periodogram*-driven FDD is that it forces the mode shape parts of the different datasets to be in the same subspace and, therefore, it is expected to provide clearer global mode shape estimates for closely spaced and/or poorly excited modes. The application of the proposed correlation spectrum based FDD is assessed and compared to the classic *periodogram*-driven FDD in the final part of the paper by means of a multi-dataset output-only vibration test of a high-rise building.

2. BACKGROUND THEORY

2.1. Correlation driven Spectrum Estimation

Rather than the *periodogram* spectrum (also known as "*Welch's*" spectrum), the multi-dataset FDD proposed in this paper uses the correlation spectrum (also known from literature as "*correlogram*" spectrum [3, 8]) as primary data. The non-parametric spectrum estimation from correlation function is accomplished by taking the discrete Fourier Transform of the correlation function

$$G_{yy}(\omega_f) = \sum_{k=-L}^{L} w_k R_k e^{-j\omega_f k\Delta t} \tag{1}$$

where $G_{yy}(\omega_f) \in \mathbb{C}^{N_o \times N_o}$ is the spectrum matrix computed at the discrete angular frequencies, ω_f, with N_o denoting the number of measured responses in the output-only vibration test; L is the maximum number of *time lags* at which the correlation matrices are estimated; w_k denotes a window function used to minimize the leakage and the statistical errors of the higher correlation *lags* on the resulting spectral matrix, Δt is the sampling interval and $j = \sqrt{-1}$ stands for the imaginary unit. The correlation-driven spectrum is widely used as primary data in parametric output-only modal identification, as seen, for instance, in [8], [9] and [10]. A detailed description of the non-parametric spectrum estimation technique based correlation functions can be found, for instance, in [3].

2.2. Proposed Multi-dataset FDD

In this section, a new approach is proposed to estimate the global mode shapes from test data recorded in multi-patch output-only vibration test with the FDD technique. This approach basically consists of: (1) estimating the spectral densities of each dataset from their corresponding correlation functions; (2) stacking all the estimated spectra on the top of each other without any prior scaling; (3) perform the identification; and (4) subsequently scale the mode shape parts to yield the global mode shape estimates for the tested structure. This merging strategy has been used in parametric mult-dataset modal identification [6] and [5]. In the following, however, a novel approach to post-scale the mode shape parts with the FDD technique is proposed. Underlying idea of this approach is to scale the singular vectors, rather than the mode shapes to yield the (scaled) global mode shapes of the tested structure. The first step to compute the scaled global mode shapes with this approach is to take the SVD of the global (unscaled) spectrum matrix, $G_u(\omega_f) \in \mathbb{C}^{N_s N_o \times N_{ref}}$, as

$$G_u(\omega_f) = \begin{bmatrix} G^1_{yy_{ref}}(\omega_f) \\ \vdots \\ G^{N_s}_{yy_{ref}}(\omega_f) \end{bmatrix} = U_{G_u}(\omega) S_{G_u}(\omega_f) V^H_{G_u}(\omega_f) \tag{2}$$

where $U_{G_u}(\omega_f) \in \mathbb{C}^{N_s N_o \times N_s N_o}$ is a matrix containing the singular vectors, $S_{G_u}(\omega_f) \in \mathbb{R}^{N_s N_o \times N_{ref}}$ a matrix containing the positive real valued singular values, and $V_{G_u} \in \mathbb{C}^{N_{ref} \times N_{ref}}$ a matrix containing unitary vectors, respectively, and $G^i_{yy_{ref}}(\omega_f) \in \mathbb{C}^{N_o \times N_{ref}}$ is the spectral matrix of the ith dataset; N_{ref} and N_s denote the number of responses used as reference in each dataset and the number of datasets acquired in the output-only vibration test, respectively; and $(\bullet)^H$ stands for the Hermitian (conjugate transpose of a complex matrix). The unscaled singular vectors, $U_{G_u}(\omega_f) \in \mathbb{C}^{N_{ref} \times N_s N_o}$, can be partitioned into the following block matrices

$$U_{G_u}(\omega_f) = \begin{bmatrix} U_{yy_{ref},1}(\omega_f) & U_{yy_{ref\sim},1}(\omega_f) \\ \vdots & \vdots \\ U_{yy_{ref},N_s}(\omega_f) & U_{yy_{ref\sim},N_s}(\omega_f) \end{bmatrix} = \begin{bmatrix} U_{y_{ref}y_{ref},1}(\omega_f) & U_{y_{ref}y_{ref\sim},1}(\omega_f) \\ U_{y_{mov}y_{ref},1}(\omega_f) & U_{y_{mov}y_{ref\sim},1}(\omega_f) \\ \vdots & \vdots \\ U_{y_{ref}y_{ref},N_s}(\omega_f) & U_{y_{ref}y_{ref\sim},N_s}(\omega_f) \\ U_{y_{mov}y_{ref},N_s}(\omega_f) & U_{y_{mov}y_{ref\sim},N_s}(\omega_f) \end{bmatrix} \tag{3}$$

where $U_{yy_{ref},i}(\omega_f) \in \mathbb{C}^{N_o \times N_{ref}}$, $U_{yy_{ref\sim},i}(\omega_f) \in \mathbb{C}^{N_o \times (N_s N_o - N_{ref})}$, $U_{y_{ref}y_{ref},i} \in \mathbb{C}^{N_{ref} \times N_{ref}}$, $U_{y_{mov}y_{ref},i}(\omega_f) \in \mathbb{C}^{N_m \times N_{ref}}$, $U_{y_{ref}y_{ref\sim},i}(\omega_f) \in \mathbb{C}^{N_{ref} \times (N_s N_o - N_{ref})}$, $U_{y_{mov}y_{ref\sim},i}(\omega_f) \in \mathbb{C}^{N_m \times (N_s N_o - N_{ref})}$ are sub-matrices of the global singular vectors, $U_{G_u}(\omega_f)$, that correspond to the ith patch; and the sub-matrices $U_{y_{ref}y_{ref},i}$ and $U_{y_{mov}y_{ref},i}(\omega_f)$ are sub-matrices of $U_{yy_{ref},i}(\omega_f)$ and $U_{yy_{ref\sim},i}(\omega_f)$, with N_m denoting the number of roving sensors. Once the global unscaled singular vectors are partitioned according to eqs. 3, the global (scaled) singular vectors can be computed as

$$U_{G_s}(\omega_f) = \begin{bmatrix} U_{y_{ref}y_{ref},R}(\omega_f) \\ U_{y_{mov}y_{ref},1}(\omega_f) U_{y_{ref}y_{ref},1}(\omega_f)^{-1} U_{y_{ref}y_{ref},R}(\omega_f) \\ \vdots \\ U_{y_{mov}y_{ref},N_s}(\omega_f) U_{y_{ref}y_{ref},N_s}(\omega_f)^{-1} U_{y_{ref}y_{ref},R}(\omega_f) \end{bmatrix} \tag{4}$$

where $U_{y_{ref}y_{ref},R}(\omega_f)$ is given by

$$U_{y_{ref}y_{ref},R}(\omega_f) = \frac{1}{N_s}\sum_{i=1}^{N_s} U_{y_{ref}y_{ref},i}(\omega_f) \tag{5}$$

From this point onwards, it is straightforward to estimate the global (scaled) mode shapes which is done just like as in the classic FDD approach, i.e., by picking the picks in the singular values plot and selecting the corresponding global mode shape vectors, Φ_{G_s}, from the scaled singular vectors, $U_{G_s}(\omega_f)$. The proposed procedure previously described to scale the global mode shapes after the identification with the **FDD** technique is summarized in Fig. 1.

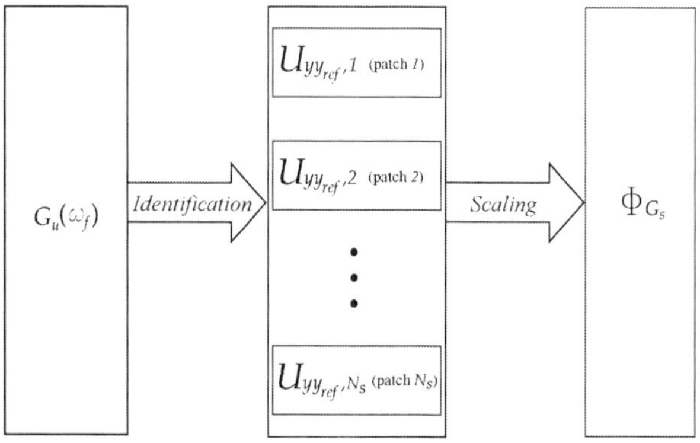

Figure 1 Identification flowchart of the scaling procedure with the proposed correlation spectrum based **FDD**

3. APPLICATION EXAMPLE

The application example consists of a multi-dataset vibration test performed on a Vancouver style high-rise building that normally resembles a podium-tower-shaped structure. This kind of structure is normally composed by a basement and low-rise buildings (2-3 storeys townhouses), and by a high-rise building that is often situated at the geometric centre of the basement. The tested Vancouver style building corresponds to the City Crest Tower depicted in Fig. 2, which is an 83.2 m tall RC building with a total of 32-storeys above the ground level. The high-rise building is located in Vancouver downtown (British Columbia, Canada), and was constructed from autumn 1992 to January 1994. The high-rise tower and the two-storey townhouses are connected structurally through the basement and two walkway bridges. The typical tower storey height is 2.6 m, except for the ground floor, where the height measures 4.0 m, in order to facilitate commercial activities.

Figure 2 The City Crest Tower, South-East (left) and South-West (right).

The City Crest Tower is situated in an earthquake-prone area with increased seismicity and its central concrete core has been designed to undertake the lateral forces induced by the earthquake excitations. The columns located in the perimeter of the slab is the essential part of the load-bearing gravity system. The columns are replaced by 204 mm thin walls from the 30th storey onwards. The construction method used for high-rise tower was the conventional in situ-cast of beams, columns, walls and slabs. The concrete core measures 10.3 m by 7.6 m (Fig. 3), and the wall thickness varies with the tower height, from 457 mm at the basement to 356 mm at the top floors. Figs. 2 and 3 illustrate how the floor plan layouts change significantly throughout the height of the tower. A detailed description of the City Crest Tower and its structural components can be found, for instance, in [11, 12] and the references cited therein.

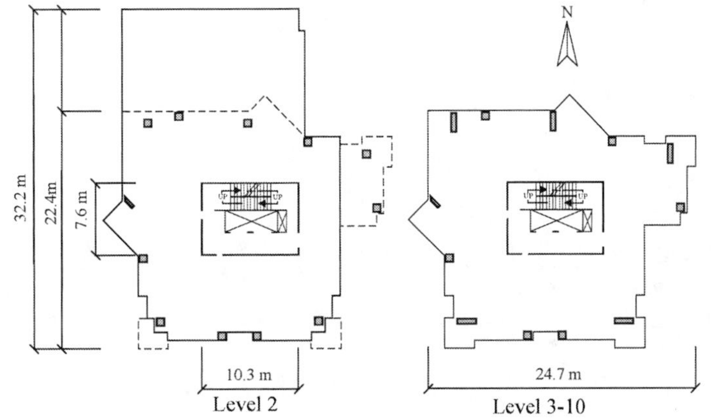

Figure 3 Level 2 (left) and level 3-10 (right) floor layout of the City Crest Tower.

3.1. Output-only Vibration Test

The vibration test campaign was performed over course of two days in the summer of 1993 with Kinematrix Inc. force balance accelerometers, each bolted to the concrete slab. The raw signals ware amplified, filtered and converted from analogue to digital on site.

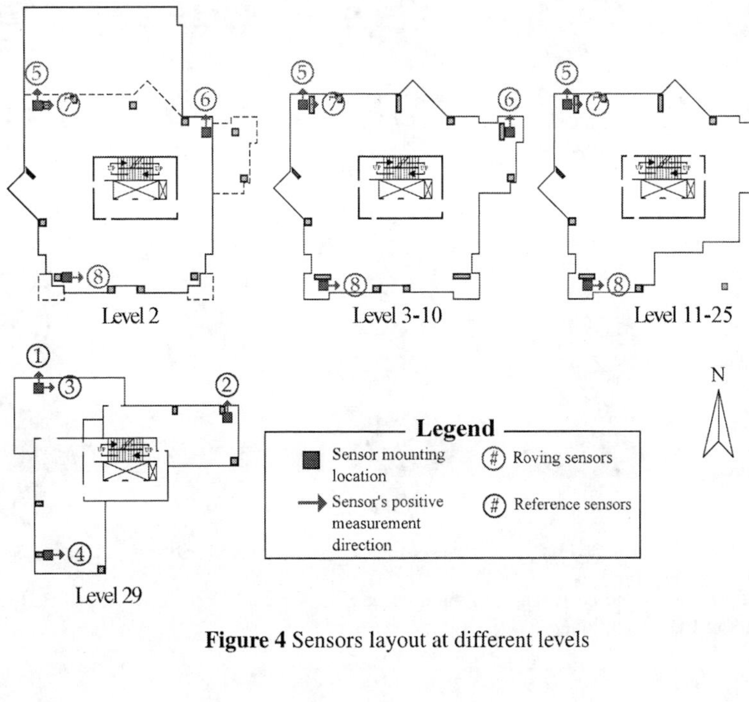

Figure 4 Sensors layout at different levels

Four roving and four reference sensors were included in the 19 different test setups adopted in the ambient vibration test, with the 29th floor being chosen as the reference floor. Fig. 4 illustrates the sensor locations throughout the 19 acquired datasets. The vibration responses in acceleration were acquired for 13 minutes and 39.2 seconds with a sampling rate of 40 Hz ensuring a Nyquist frequency of 20 Hz.

3.2. Identification with Classic FDD technique

The classic multi-dataset FDD technique [4] was applied to identify the modal properties of the City Crest Tower using the power spectral densities estimated with the *periodogram* approach from the measured acceleration responses. The identification was performed with the commercial software ARTeMIS Pro Modal (v4) [13], by making use of the geometrical model of the high-rise structure illustrated in Fig. 5a.

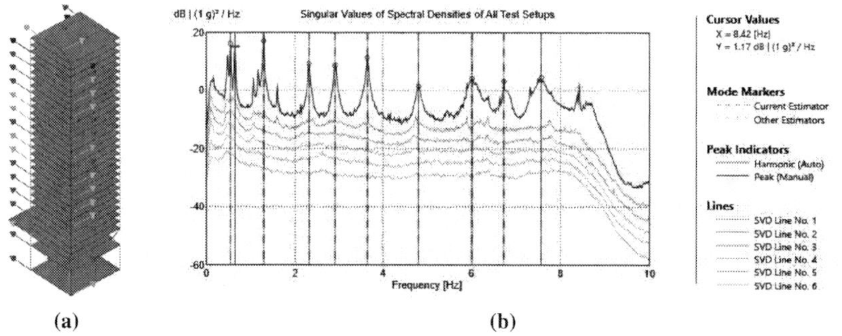

Figure 5 Geometry and measured DOFs in ARTeMIS software for the Operational Modal Analysis (a) and the FDD singular values of spectral densities (b)

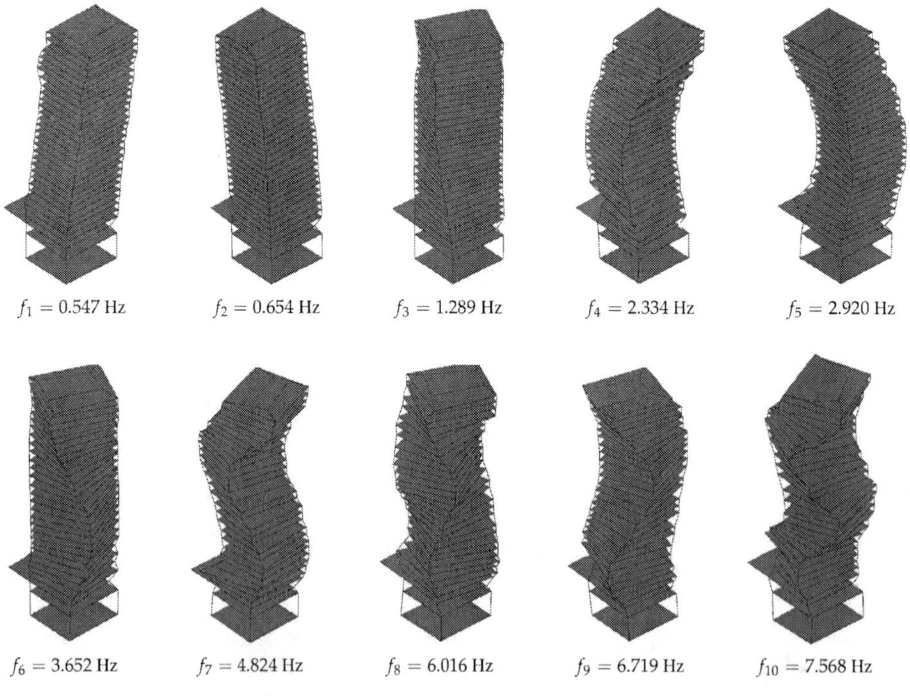

Figure 6 Natural frequencies and corresponding mode shapes of the City Crest Tower identified with the classic multi-dataset FDD technique

The vibration raw data signals of the 19 acquired datasets were filtered with a band pass filter defined by a bandpass frequency range of 0.1-10.0 Hz. Next, the power spectral densities were computed from the filtered data signals with a resolution of 2048 frequency lines. Once these all the spectra were computed, they were used as primary data by the FDD technique to identify the natural frequencies and the corresponding global mode shapes of the City Crest Tower.

The variations of the singular values computed from spectral densities of the reference sensors over frequency lines are shown in Fig. 5. From this plot, 10 vibration modes were clearly identified by simply picking the peaks in the singular values plot. The identification of the natural frequencies with classic FDD consists of determining the frequencies associated to each picked peak. The identification of the global mode shapes, on the other hand, is basically carried out in two steps: (1) by extracting the mode shape parts from the singular vectors of each dataset; and (2) by re-scaling the extracted mode shape parts using the reference mode shape components to yield the global mode shapes associated to the picked peaks. The identification results obtained with the classic multi-dataset FDD for City Crest Tower are summarized in Fig. 6.

3.3. Identification Results with Proposed FDD technique

The application of the correlation spectrum based FDD described in section 2.2. is illustrated by also using of the vibration data of the City Crest Tower. To this end, the correlation-driven spectrum of each dataset was estimated by means of eq. (1) and used as primary data in the identification with the FDD technique. These power spectral densities were estimated from the filtered data signals with a resolution of the 2048 frequency lines by making use of an exponential window with a decay constant of 99.9% to minimize the leakage.

Once the correlation-driven spectrum matrices of all the 19 acquired datasets were estimated, they were stacked on the top of each other to form the global spectrum matrix, $G_u(\omega)$. Afterwards, the singular value decomposition was applied to this matrix. The obtained singular values at the 2048 frequency lines are plotted in Fig. 7. Similarly to the classic *periodogram*-driven FDD, the natural frequencies were simply identified by picking the peaks in the singular values plot. The identification of the global mode shapes, however, was accomplished by following the strategy described in section 2.2., i.e., by scaling the singular vectors corresponding to each identified natural frequencies.

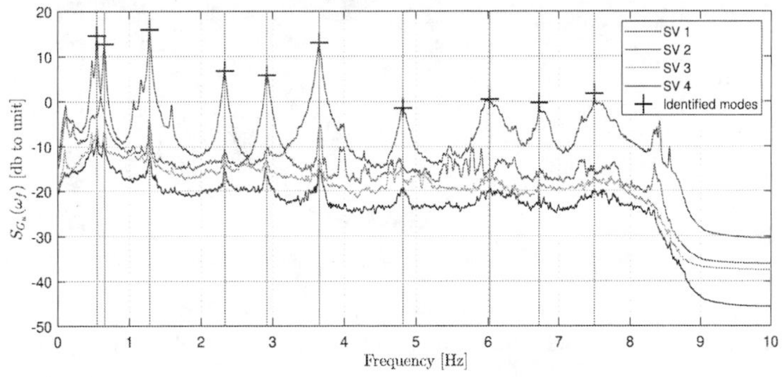

Figure 7 Singular values of the correlation-driven spectral densities

The results, in terms of natural frequencies and global mode shapes, obtained with the proposed multi-dataset FDD driven by correlation power spectrum densities is summarized in Figs. 8. Comparing these results to those shown in Fig. 6, one verifies that they are in very good agreement, both in terms of natural frequencies and global mode shapes, with the results obtained with classic multi-dataset FDD technique. The good agreement, in terms of global mode shapes, between the classic and proposed multi-dataset FDD approaches, is also corroborated by the Modal Assurance Criterion (MAC) values shown in Fig. 9.

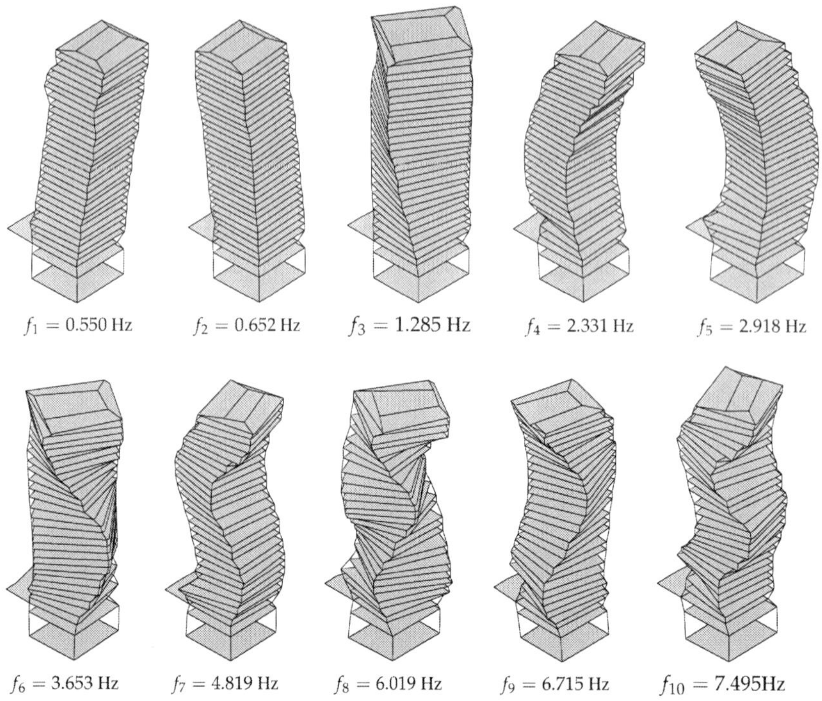

Figure 8 Natural frequencies and corresponding mode shapes of the City Crest Tower identified with the correlation spectrum FDD technique

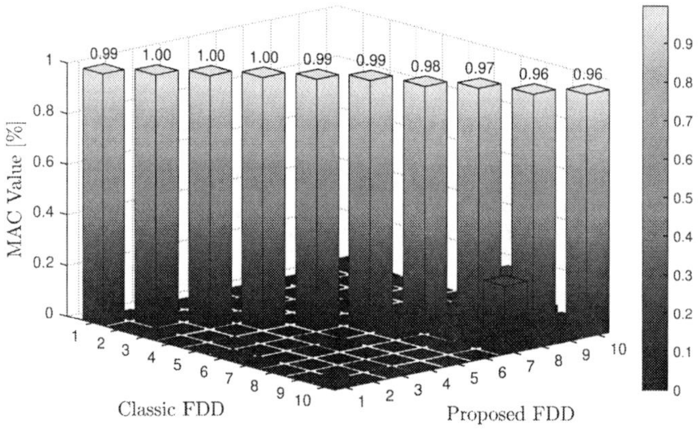

Figure 9 Modal Assurance Criterion (MAC) between the global mode shapes estimated with the classic multi-dataset FDD and those estimated with the proposed multi-dataset FDD driven by the correlation spectrum

4. CONCLUSIONS

In this paper, a novel multi-dataset FDD driven by correlation spectral densities is introduced. The underlying idea of this approach is to identify the natural frequencies and global mode shapes of vibration from a global spectral matrix containing the spectral matrices of all datasets stacked on the top of each other. In order to assess the robustness of proposed FDD, the technique was applied to the vibration data acquired in a multi-dataset output-only vibration test of a high rise building. By comparing the results obtained with such approach to those provided by the classic multi-dataset FDD for this particular application example, it was verified that the former are in very good agreement with the latter.

ACKNOWLEDGEMENTS

The authors acknowledge the funding received from Centre for Oil and Gas - DTU/Danish Hydrocarbon Research and Technology Centre (DHRTC).

REFERENCES

[1] Brincker, R. and Zhang, L. and Andersen, P. (2001) Modal identification of output-only systems using frequency domain decomposition. *Journal of Smart Materials and Structures*, 10, (pp. 441-445).

[2] Brincker, R. and Zhang, L. (2009) Frequency Domain Decomposition Revisited. *In proceedings of the the 5th International Operational Modal Analysis Conference (IOMAC)*, Portonovo, Italy.

[3] Mitra, S.K. (1998) Digital Signal Processing - A Computer-based Approach. *McGraw-Hill, New York, USA.*

[4] Brincker, R. and Ventura, C. (2015) Introduction To Operational Modal Analysis. *John Wiley and Sons*, 1st ed.

[5] Reynders, E., Magalhães, F., De-Roeck, G. and Cunha, A. (2009) Merging Strategies for Multi-Setup Operational Modal Analysis: Application to the Luiz I steel Arch Bridge. *In proceedings of the 27th International Modal Analysis Conference (IMACXXVII)*, 36(2), (pp. 115-127).

[6] Parloo, E., Guillaume, P. and Cauberghe, B. (2003) Maximum likelihood identification of non-stationary operational data. *Journal of Sound and Vibration*, 268(5) (pp. 971–991).

[7] Juul, M.Ø.Ø., Olsen, P., Balling, O., Amador, S.D.R. and Brincker, R. (2018) Comparison of two (geometric) algorithms for auto OMA. *In proceedings of International Modal Analysis Conference (IMAC) 2018*, Orlando, FL, USA.

[8] Peeters, B., Van-Der-Auweraera, H., Vanhollebeck, F. and Guillaume, P. (2007) Operational modal analysis for estimating the dynamic properties of a stadium structure during a football game. *Journal of Shock and Vibration*, 14(1), (pp. 283-303).

[9] Amador, S.D.R., Magalhães, F., Martins, N., Caetano, E. and Cunha, A. (2013) High Spatial Resolution Operational Modal Analysis of a Football Stadium Suspension Roof. *In proceedings of the the 5th International Operational Modal Analysis Conference (IOMAC)*, Guimarães, Portugal.

[10] Amador, S.D.R., Magalhães, F., Cunha, A. and Caetano, E. (2017) High spatial resolution modal identification of a stadium suspensionroof: Assessment of the estimates uncertainty and of modal contributions. *Journal of Engineering Structures*, 135, (pp 117-135).

[11] Pao, B. (1992) Structural drawings of the City Crest Tower. *Bogdonov Pao Associates Ltd.*

[12] Savnik, N.J., Katsanos, E.I., Amador, S.D.R., Ventura, C.E. and Brincker, R. (2018) Influence of diaphragm modelling on the dynamic performance of a reinforced concrete high-rise building. *In proceedings of the 28th International Conference on Noise and Vibration Engineering (ISMA)*, Leuven, Belgium.

[13] Structural Vibration Solutions A/S. (2017) ARTeMIS Pro Modal Version 4. Aalborg, Denmark, 2017. www.svibs.com.

IOMAC'19

8th International Operational Modal Analysis Conference

2019 May 13-15 Copenhagen

AUTOMATED OPTIMIZATION OF OUTPUT ONLY MODAL PARAMETER IDENTIFICATION

R. Volkmar[1], *K. Soal*[2], *L.H. Hughes*[3], *Y. Govers*[4], *M. Böswald*[5]

[1] Research Associate, Department of Structural Dynamics and System Identification, DLR - German Aerospace Center, Institute of Aeroelasticity, Göttingen, Germany, robin.volkmar@dlr.de.
[2] Research Associate, Department of Structural Dynamics and System Identification, DLR - German Aerospace Center, Institute of Aeroelasticity, Göttingen, Germany, keith.soal@dlr.de.
[3] Research Associate, Technical University of Munich (TUM), Munich, Germany, lloyd.hughes@tum.de.
[4] Team Leader Aeroelastic System Identification, Department of Structural Dynamics and System Identification, DLR - German Aerospace Center, Institute of Aeroelasticity, Göttingen, Germany, yves.govers@dlr.de
[5] Head of Department Structural Dynamics and System Identification, DLR - German Aerospace Center, Institute of Aeroelasticity, Göttingen, Germany, marc.boeswald@dlr.de.

ABSTRACT

The automation of modal parameter identification is important for processing big data with repeatability and without time consuming user interaction. This becomes even more important for complex structures whose modal parameters must be monitored in operation. During modal identification optimal poles have to be found out of many possibilities. For most real world examples with a huge amount of candidate poles the optimal solution cannot be calculated in reasonable time. This paper describes a method for the autonomous selection of optimal parameters within reasonable time constraints. The method modifies the idea of error propagation usually applied in training artificial neural networks. Poles are selected pseudo randomly and an error is calculated based on the difference between the synthesized and measured Cross Power Spectral Densities (CPSDs). This overall error is spread over the selected poles based on the poles influence on the error, i.e. the poles are assigned weights depending on their goodness. This random selection is repeated iteratively until the weights converge. The poles with best weights are selected as the final solution. The method was tested on simulated data and laboratory data from the DLR AIRcaft MODel (AIRMOD) structure and compared to other pole selection methods. The method provides equally good estimations of eigenfrequencies and better damping estimates than the other tested methods.

Keywords: automatic modal analysis, machine learning, fully automated modal analysis, online monitoring, ground vibration testing, flight vibration testing

1. INTRODUCTION

Structural health monitoring, flutter testing of aircraft prototypes and many other applications build upon the observation and tracking of modal parameters of the time variant structural behaviour. The automation of modal identification algorithms is important for repeatable processing of big data and without the need for time consuming user interaction. Furthermore, manual analysis outputs are user-dependent, i.e. on the one hand experts analyse data differently to unexperienced users and on the other hand even the same person will analyse data differently for the first and last data set of a structure or even between morning and evening. This becomes even more critical for complex structures in operation. During the last two decades the automation of modal parameter estimation has been of high interest in the modal analysis research community. So far, most approaches are based on the stabilization diagram. The first step is to find clusters of poles representing the same mode in the stabilization diagram and discriminate spurious clusters. Examples of those clustering algorithms can be found in [1-3].

These algorithms result in a stabilization diagram similar to that in Figure 2. The dataset shown in Figure 2 was obtained from a laboratory structure named AIRMOD (Figure 1) used at the German Aerospace Center (DLR) in Göttingen e.g. for the validation of dynamic testing methods [4-6]. The structure, a replica of the GARTEUR SM-AG19 model, is made of aluminium beams that represent the structural behaviour of an aircraft.

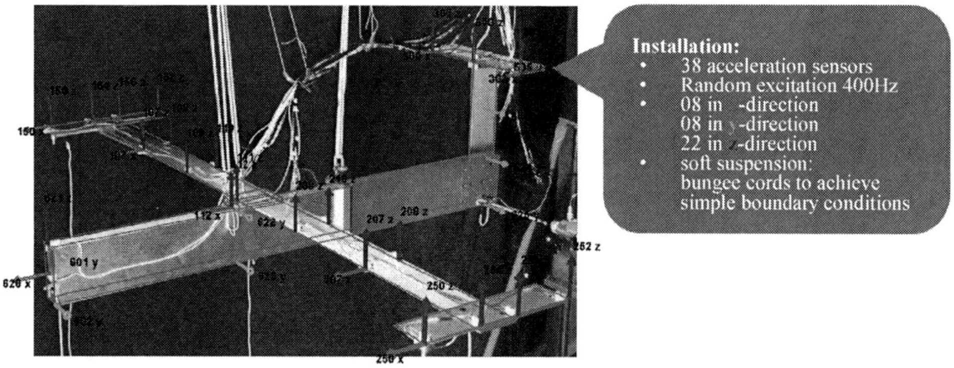

Figure 1. AIRMOD structure and test setup

Due to the symmetry of aircraft structure the model shows closely spaced poles throughout the whole frequency range.

Mode clusters in the stabilization diagram of Figure 2 are indicated by vertical pole groupings having the same colour. The key problem which remains and has not been addressed well in literature is: How to choose one pole out of each cluster which represents the underlying mode best? Many approaches order the poles of a cluster according to their damping values and select the pole that is median/mean in damping domain, e.g. [1]. Another approach is to search for consecutive model orders where the damping estimates change no more with increasing model order [5]. These assumptions are fast and straight forward to implement, but the accuracy of choosing the pole with the median damping of a cluster or within the region of stable damping requires further investigation. In this paper, a pole selection method is presented that automatically finds the best representatives of mode clusters by optimizing an error function.

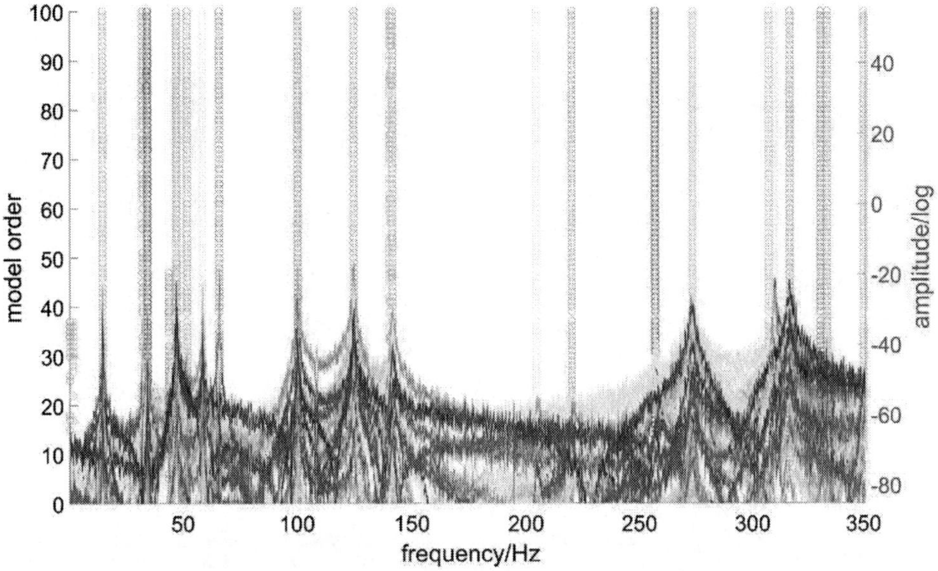

Figure 2. Stabilization diagram of laboratory structure AIRMOD

2. AUTOMATED POLE SELECTION

2.1. Error function

The proposed methodology selects a single from each mode cluster by optimizing an error function. The error function can be any measure that evaluates the final pole selection. As there is no ground truth of the model available in real applications, the available data closest to ground truth is used. Here, the measured Cross Power Spectral Densities (CPSDs) are used as the ground truth. Therefore, the error function is given by

$$E = \left(CPSDs_{meas} - CPSDs_{synth}\right)^2 \tag{1}$$

where E is the error, $CPSDs_{meas}$ are the measured CPSDs and $CPSDs_{synth}$ are the synthesized CPSDs calculated by using the final pole selection. This error is calculated for each channel separately and summed up afterwards. The error is illustrated in Figure 3. One should note that this error function could be substituted by any function that evaluates the pole selection.

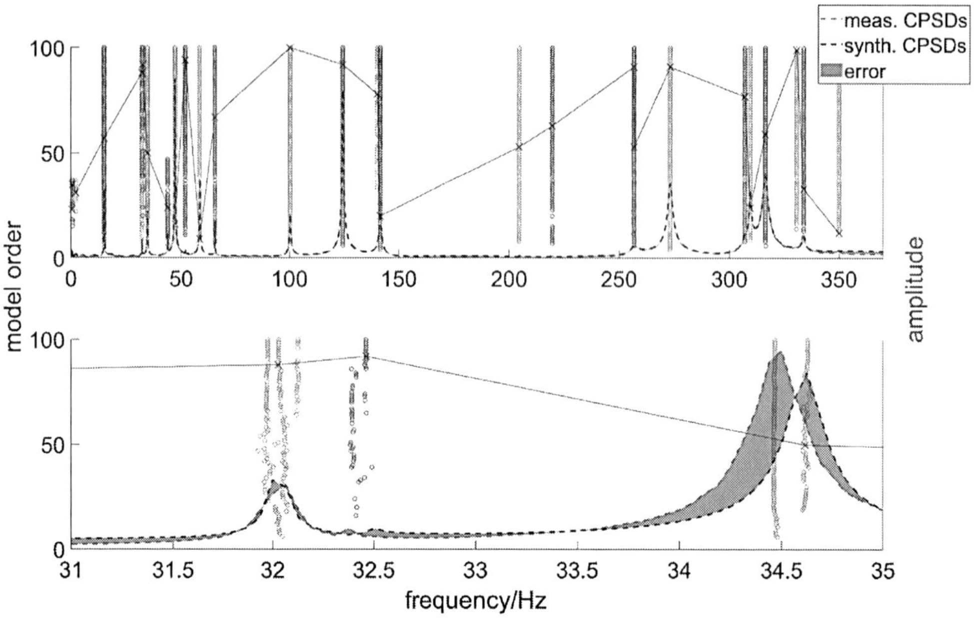

Figure 3. Example pole selection and the resulting error

Figure 3 shows an example pole selection. A random pole is chosen from each cluster. For simplicity, clusters are coloured alternating in light and dark grey. The amplitudes of CPSDs summed over all channels are plotted in green (measured) and blue (synthesized). The error is illustrated in red. Because of good clustering, the overall spectra fit well, as can be seen in the upper graph. In detail, one can see significant differences between the synthesized and measured spectra nearby the modes, see e.g. example modes in the lower graph zoomed between 31 and 35 Hz.

2.2. Optimization problem

In theory, all possible combinations of poles (one per cluster) have to be calculated to find the best selection (minimum error of synthesized spectra). Figure 4 illustrates the number of possible pole selections. Each line combination from the most left cluster to the most right cluster illustrates a possible pole selection. For better visibility only every tenth pole of each cluster is connected.

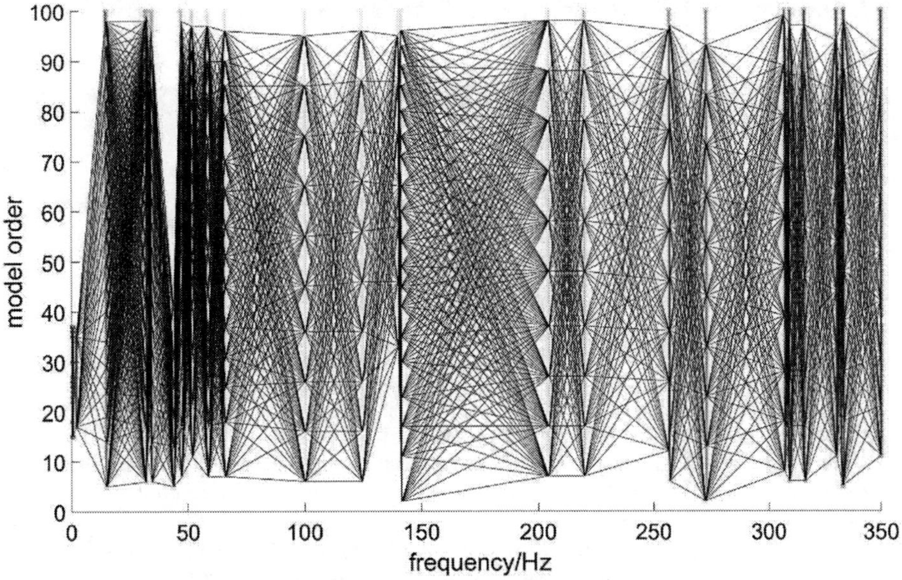

Figure 4. Possible pole selections

The number of possible pole selections can be calculated by

$$\prod_{c=1}^{C} noPoles_c \tag{2}$$

where $noPoles_c$ is the number of poles in cluster c and C is the total number of clusters. Needless to say that in most cases it is not possible to calculate all possible pole selections in reasonable time. The best pole selection needs to be estimated as efficiently as possible.

2.3. Learn best poles

The basic idea to solve the optimization problem stated in section 2.2 is to assign error weights to each pole so that the weights of all poles within the same cluster can be used to determine the cluster's best pole. In simple terms, a weight indicates the chance of the pole being part of a good solution. Therefore, the problem simplifies to determining weights that represent the goodness of poles. This problem of determining many weights based on an error function is a well-known task in training Artificial Neural Networks (ANN). It is in general solved by backpropagation [7]. Without going into further details, backpropagation adjusts a neuron's weight according to the neuron's participation in producing the error. This approach is now applied to the pole selection problem.

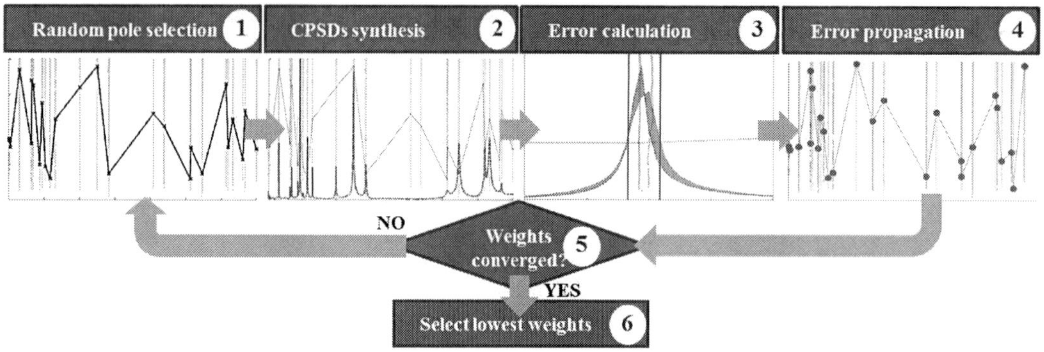

Figure 5. Process of learn best poles (LBP)

The overall process of learning the best poles selection (hereinafter referred to as LBP) is shown in Figure 5. In the first step, one pole from each cluster is chosen pseudo randomly, i.e. all poles of each cluster are chosen just as often. In this step rules can also be applied, for example: selecting poles of closely-spaced clusters in the same model order because of consistent damping estimates. In the second step, the selected poles are utilized to build a complete modal model and to synthesize CPSDs. Thirdly, the error (E) is calculated using the synthesized and measured CPSDs. The error propagation in the fourth step follows the rule that a mode impacts the spectra at frequencies nearby the eigenfrequency much stronger than it impacts the spectra at frequencies far apart from the eigenfrequency.

The conclusion is that the influence of a selected pole on the error is the spectra-error nearby the mode's eigenfrequency. A pole's error weight is therefore the spectral error nearby the eigenfrequency of the mode. By defining a frequency range that is used for the calculation of the poles weights (hereinafter referred to as local range) two objectives are possible: optimizing the whole spectra or optimizing the spectra in the vicinity of the modes only. If the whole spectra shall be optimized, the local ranges of two neighbouring modes border at the minimum of the measured sum of the CPSDs between their respective eigenfrequencies. In this way the best pole of each cluster optimizes the spectra between the two frequency minima surrounding a peak (see Figure 6 A). The spectra beyond these minima are subsequently optimized by the neighbouring mode clusters.

The disadvantage is that the important range for damping estimation (approximately the 3dB range) may not be optimal because of poor data between the two modes. In Figure 6 A one can see significant spectral error around 6Hz. A pole of the mode cluster at 15Hz would be chosen not only to optimize the spectral peak but also to optimize this arbitrary error at 6 Hz. Therefore, the second way of choosing the local range is introduced. The local range of a mode is set to be the 3dB range of the sum of the measured CPSDs (see Figure 6 B). The spectra between modes are not optimized directly anymore, but the spectral peaks close to eigenfrequencies are optimized more accurately.

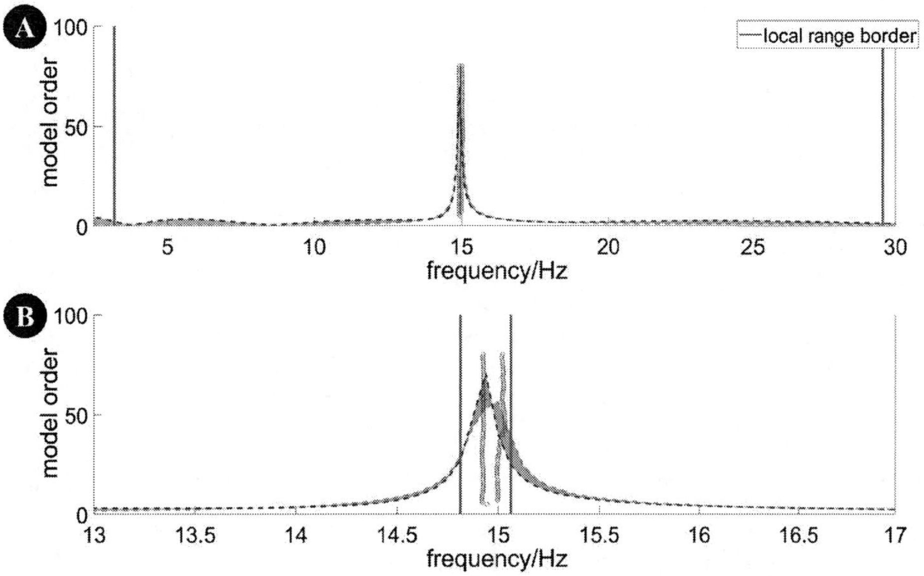

Figure 6. Frequency range for pole's weight calculation optimizing (A) Overall spectra; (B) 3dB-peaks

The errors within the local range for each pole (out of multiple selections) are averaged to give the weight of the pole. In the fifth step the weights of all poles of the cluster are compared to determine if the cluster converged. Convergence in this case means that after sorting all poles' weights within a cluster, the best pole does not change and the overall error of the best selection converges to within 1% range. Convergence is checked after all poles were selected at least five times each. After all clusters as well as the overall error converged, the poles with lowest weight in each cluster provide the best pole selection in the final step. Based on the eigenvalues of the best poles the eigenvectors are calculated using the Least Squares Frequency Domain (LSFD) method [8].

3. RESULTS

The methodology was tested on simulated data as well as measured data from AIRMOD structure. Two metrics are examined: required run time and accuracy. Both data sets are processed using operational Least Squares Complex Frequency (LSCF) [9]. Afterwards, a clustering technique similar to [1-3] is applied to obtain pole clusters. Four methods select one pole out of each cluster to build the modal model of the system. The pole selection methods consist of 1) manual pole selection by an expert; 2) LBP; 3) median damping selection; 4) stable damping selection. In 1) an experienced user selects one pole manually out of each cluster. The second method is introduced in section 2.3. In 3) the pole is chosen that is closest to the median damping of its cluster. In 4) the deviation of the damping with increasing model order is calculated. The region in which the damping varies least is the stable damping region. The first pole of the stable damping region is selected.

3.1. Data sets

The simulated data set is a 6 Degree-of-Freedom (DoF) Linear Time-Invariant (LTI) system with Gaussian distributed white noise of 70% times the signal mean added to the time data. The time data corresponds to a 10 minutes measurement. The laboratory data set is from the AIRMOD structure (see Figure 1 and Figure 2). AIRMOD was excited with a random signal up to 400Hz using an electro-magnetic shaker and the response was measured with 38 accelerometers for a duration of 160s [5]. The data sets are recorded with a sampling frequency of 125Hz (simulation) and 1024Hz (experiment).

3.2. Required run time

The required analysis time is measured after the pole clusters are built until the final poles are chosen (analysing the AIRMOD data set). The median damping selection and the stable damping selection run times are negligible (below one second). The manual pole selection depends on the analyst. In this case the expert knew the AIRMOD structure beforehand. The data set comprises 26 pole clusters. The required time to select all 26 poles manually took 10 minutes. The required time of LBP depends firstly on the time required for a single iteration (see steps 1-4 in Figure 5) but even more important on the number of iterations until the weights converge. The time required for a single iteration on a standard notebook (Dell Latitude with i7-6600U CPU 2.60GHz) is around 0.05 seconds. The number of required weight adjustments of each pole for the AIRMOD data set was in this case 25 until convergence. The overall required (average) time is the number of poles within the biggest cluster times 0.05 seconds. In the current AIRMOD example the biggest cluster contains 147 poles. Therefore, the required time is roughly 3 minutes (147*25*0.05 seconds) to process 26 mode clusters in the frequency range of 0-350Hz.

Table 1. Time required by pole selection methods for AIRMOD data set with 26 modes (0-350Hz)

Method	Manual selection	LBP	Median Damp	Stable Damp
Required time [min]	10	3	~0	~0

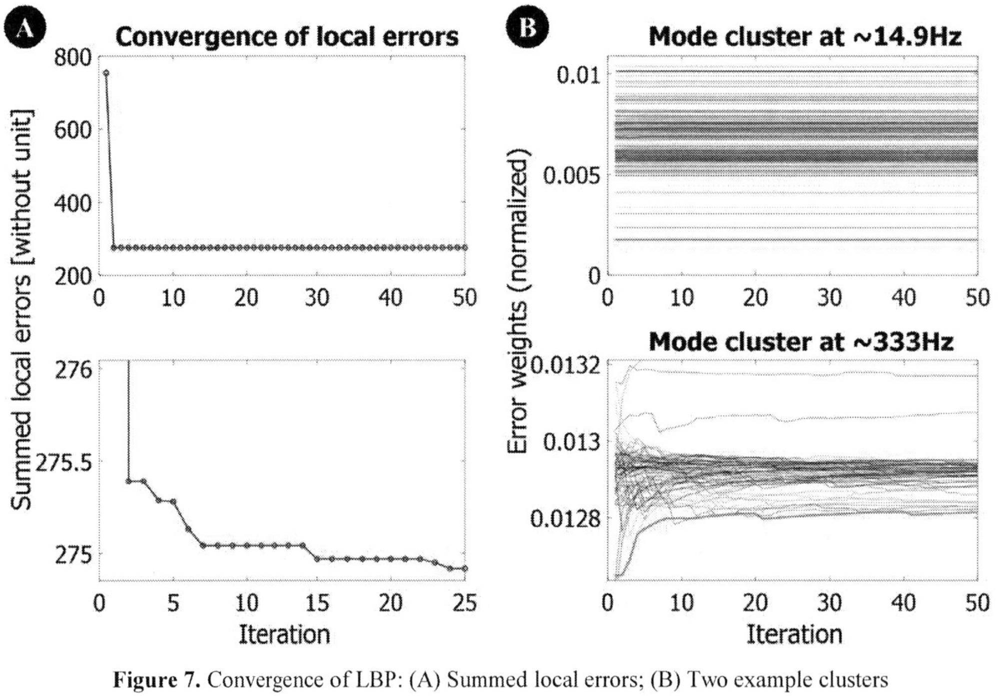

Figure 7. Convergence of LBP: (A) Summed local errors; (B) Two example clusters

The overall error and most of the pole clusters converge much faster as shown in Figure 7 A and upper graph of Figure 7 B. In Figure 7 B each line represents a weight of a pole. The best one is marked in bold green. Some clusters need more iteration, see e.g. lower graph of Figure 7 B. This happens in most cases if multiple poles result in almost the same synthesized spectra. The weights are therefore similar and the best pole of the cluster continues to change while the result stays the same. After about seven iterations the errors do not change significantly anymore. The time required reduces to 51 seconds.

The method can be classified as a perfectly parallel problem, because most iteration can run in parallel. As this work focusses the basic idea, the parallelization is not dealt with in this work, but can increase the performance drastically.

3.3. Accuracy

The accuracy of the pole selections can be quantified as the error of the identified eigenfrequencies and damping. In the case of testing the method with simulated data the error of each pole selection method can be calculated, since the analytical eigenfrequencies and damping are known. Additionally, the synthesized spectra around a mode's eigenfrequency contain information about the accuracy. Figure 8 shows the summed spectra of the simulated system and the summed synthesized spectra of pole selection methods for two example modes (left y-axis). Additionally, the selected poles are illustrated by squares that are located at the eigenfrequencies (x-axis) and damping (right y-axis). The analytical solution is illustrated by a green star. The spectra at the eigenfrequency of Mode 1 in the upper graph fit well to the simulated spectra. The damping values of the selected poles are also close to the analytical damping. In the lower graph the spectra at Mode 5 and 6 are shown. The poles selected by the methods differ in damping.

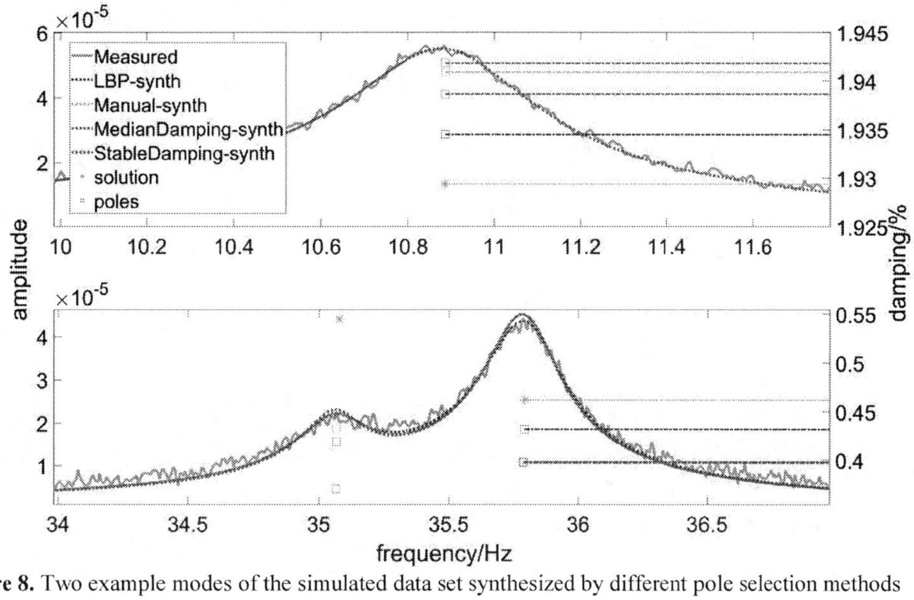

Figure 8. Two example modes of the simulated data set synthesized by different pole selection methods

Table 2 shows the errors of eigenfrequencies identified by the pole selection methods. The fields with lowest errors per mode are highlighted. The eigenfrequency errors of all four selection methods of all modes are below 0.05%. This result comes as no surprise because all poles within the pole clusters show very low variation. The damping errors are shown in Table 3. The identified damping of different selection methods vary more, this is expected because the deviation within clusters is higher than for eigenfrequencies. For some modes (e.g. 5) even the best pole of the cluster shows an error of ~20%. In accordance to [10] LSCF is prone to underestimate damping with increasing noise. LBP selects those poles provided by LSCF that have best damping values of all pole selection methods.

The methods were subsequently tested on the AIRMOD data set. The spectra comparison of two example modes is shown in Figure 9. In both examples one can see that the median damping and stable damping methods differ most from the measured spectra. The eigenfrequencies differ slightly, whereas the damping values differ significantly. An overview of all eigenfrequencies and damping values of both shown and a third example mode is given in Table 4 and Table 5, respectively. As the synthesized spectra of LBP fits best one can assume that LBP provides best damping estimations.

Table 2. Errors of identified eigenfrequencies of the simulated system

Mode	Frequency						
	Analytic [Hz]	Manual error [%]	LBP error [%]	Median Damp error [%]	Stable Damp error [%]	Cluster error range [%]	Cluster size [unit]
1	3.7023	0.0206	0.0034	0.0014	0.0028	[1.4e-05,0.0206]	69
2	10.885	0.0086	0.0043	0.0030	0.0029	[0.0015,0.0741]	68
3	16.647	0.0067	0.0002	0.0007	0.0004	[0.0002,0.0129]	69
4	27.592	0.0059	0.0042	0.0119	0.0042	[0.0009,0.0561]	53
5	35.079	0.0349	0.0349	0.0439	0.0331	[0.0097,0.0761]	21
6	35.791	0.0185	0.0045	0.0132	0.0201	[0.0031,2.3553]	64

Table 3. Errors in % of identified damping values of the simulated system's modes

Mode	Damping						
	Analytic [%]	Manual error [%]	LBP error [%]	Median Damp error [%]	Stable Damp error [%]	Cluster error range [%]	Cluster size [unit]
1	2.8856	0.7329	0.3523	0.4272	0.4382	[0.34308,0.78677]	69
2	1.9294	0.5968	0.2644	0.4804	0.6452	[0.16304,1.0919]	68
3	0.4141	1.6742	0.6175	0.7622	0.6563	[0.58159,2.4387]	69
4	0.8568	6.3516	4.8448	8.7882	4.8448	[4.8448,65.3788]	53
5	0.3920	20.6828	20.6828	32.0814	23.1541	[20.342,78.6944]	21
6	0.5448	13.8118	6.4790	13.8710	14.0632	[6.4412,67.53]	64

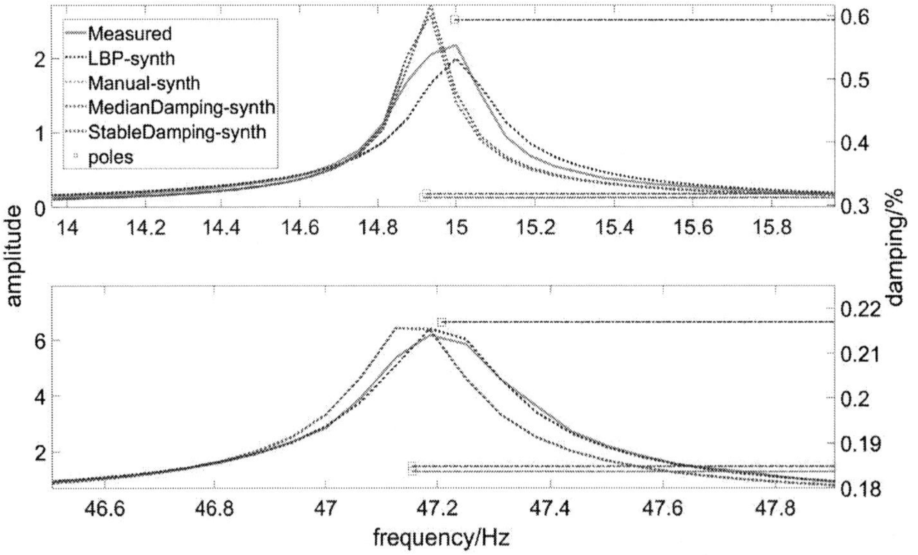

Figure 9. Measured and synthesized spectra of two example modes of AIRMOD.

Table 4. Comparison of example eigenfrequencies of AIRMOD pole selections

Mode	Eigenfrequency					
	Manually selected [Hz]	LBP [Hz]	Median Damp [Hz]	Stable Dam [Hz]	Cluster range [Hz]	Cluster size [unit]
1	14.918	14.997	14.918	14.927	[14.918,15.036]	146
2	47.155	47.208	47.155	47.155	[47.150,47.334]	104
3	316.258	316.256	316.252	316.251	[316.24,316.50]	74

Table 5. Comparison of damping of AIRMOD pole selections

Mode	Damping					
	Manually selected [%]	LBP [%]	Median Damp [%]	Stable Damp [%]	Cluster range [%]	Cluster size [unit]
1	0.3121	0.5937	0.3121	0.3182	[0.16746,0.59371]	146
2	0.1837	0.2169	0.1837	0.1848	[0.088199,0.27214]	104
3	0.3661	0.3597	0.3690	0.3690	[0.34759,0.37131]	74

4. CONCLUSIONS

This paper presents an automated pole selection method that addresses an important step of modal analysis automation. The method builds upon pole clusters that result from clustering poles of the stabilization diagram identified using LSCF. The method selects a single pole representing each cluster to build the complete modal model. The poles are chosen based on their probability (weight) to be part of the optimal solution, i.e. reproduces the measured CPSDs with minimal deviation. The poles' weights are trained similar to neurons in ANN using error propagation.

The results of the presented method are compared to three other pole selection methods: two based on poles' damping and one manual selection by an expert. The overall deviation of eigenfrequencies and damping is defined by the pole clusters. Nevertheless, the new method showed lowest errors in estimated damping selecting the final poles of a simulated system. Regarding the laboratory system the method reproduces the measured spectra best.

Computational time required for automatic pole selection is about 3 minutes for pole clusters with 147 poles (AIRMOD example). The time required can be reduced by shorten the learning phase. The results may become slightly less accurate, but still within an acceptable accuracy range. In the AIRMOD example a learning phase of about one minute already gives better results than the other methods. Additionally, in further work the required time can be reduced drastically by using parallelization. Because all iterations during learning phase are independent, many could run in parallel.

REFERENCES

[1] Reynders, E., & Houbrechts, J., & De Roeck, G. (2012). Fully automated (operational) modal analysis. *Mechanical Systems and Signal Processing*, 29, 228-250.

[2] Boroschek, R.L., & Bilbao, J. (2015) Evaluation of an automatic selection methodology of modal parameters from stability diagrams on a damaged building. In: *Proc. 6th International Operational Modal Analysis Conference*. Gijon, Spain.

[3] Marrongelli, G. & Magalhaes, F. & Cunha, A. (2017). Automated Operational Modal Analysis of an arch bridge considering the influence of the parametric methods inputs. In: *Proc. X Int. Conf. on Structural Dynamics*, EURODYN2017. Rome, Italy

[4] Govers, Y. & Böswald, M. & Göge, D. & Link, M. (2006). Analysis of Sources and Quantification of Uncertainty in Experimental Modal Data. In: *Int. Conf. on Noise and Vibration Engineering* (pp. 4161-4173), KU Leuven, Belgium.

[5] Govers, Y. (2012). Parameter identification of structural dynamic models by inverse statistical analysis, in Faculty of Civil and Environmental Engineering, 2012, University of Kassel, Cologne, Germany.

[6] Govers, Y. & Haddad Khodaparast, H. & Link, M. & Mottershead, J.E. (2015). A comparison of two stochastic model updating methods using the DLR AIRMOD test structure. *Mechanical Systems and Signal Processing*, 52–53(0), 105-114.

[7] Rumelhart, D.E. & Hinton, G.E. & Williams, R.J. (1986). Learning representations by back-propagating errors. *Nature*, 323, 533-536.

[8] Mergeay, M. (1983). Least squares complex exponential method and global system parameter estimation used by modal analysis. In: *Proc. of the 8th International Seminar on Modal Analysis*, Leuven, Belgium.

[9] Guillaume, P. & Verboven, P. & Vanlanduit, S. & Van der Auweraer, H. & Peeters, B. (2003). A polyreference implementation of the least-squares complex frequency-domain estimator, In: *Proc. of IMAC XXI,* Kissimmee, FL, USA.

[10] Böswald, M. (2016). Analysis of the bias in modal parameters obtained with frequency-domain rational fraction polynomial estimators, In: *Proc. of the International Conference of Noise and Vibration Engineering ISMA*, Leuven, Belgium.

IOMAC'19

8th International Operational Modal Analysis Conference
2019 May13-15 Copenhagen

BASIC CONCEPTS OF MODAL SCALING

M. Aenlle[1], and R. Brincker[2]

[1] Dr, Dept. of Construction and Manufacturing Engineering, University of Oviedo, aenlle@uniovi.es
[2] Prof., Department of Civil Engineering, Department of Civil Engineering, runeb@byg.dtu.dk

ABSTRACT

Mode shapes can be normalized in many different ways, the most common techniques being mass normalization, normalization to the unit length of the mode shape (length scaling) and normalization to a component (usually to the largest component) equal to unity (DOF scaling). For this reason, the modal mass of a mode shape is not unique but it depends on the normalization method used to define the mode shape. On one hand, the modal mass can be a mass or an inertia. On the other hand, the units of the modal mass depend on the scaling technique and its magnitude depends on the number of degree of freedoms (DOFs) used to discretize the model. In this paper, all these drawbacks are studied and a new and better definition of the modal mass is presented, which leads to a better engineering interpretation of this modal parameter

Keywords: Modal mass, Structural Dynamics, Modal Analysis

1. INTRODUCTION

When the modal model is used to define the dynamic behavior of a mechanical system, the modal parameters (natural frequencies, mode shapes and damping ratios) are needed [1,2,3,4]. Mass normalized mode shapes (hereafter denoted as $\boldsymbol{\phi}$), contain information of both the mode shape and the modal mass. A mode shape is defined un-scaled if it is not mass normalized. If un-scaled mode shapes, hereafter denoted as $\boldsymbol{\psi}$, are used, a new modal parameter for each mode, known as modal mass, is needed to define the dynamic behavior of a mechanical system. When classical modal analysis (CMA), also known as experimental modal analysis (EMA), is used to estimate the modal parameters of a system, mass normalized mode shapes are obtained in the estimation process [1,2,3]. On the contrary, in operational modal analysis (OMA) the force is not measured and only un-scaled mode shapes can be estimated [4].

The equation of motion of a structural dynamic system with no damping subjected to a force $\boldsymbol{p}$ is given by [4,5,6]:

$$\boldsymbol{K}\boldsymbol{u} + \boldsymbol{M}\ddot{\boldsymbol{u}} = \boldsymbol{p} \qquad (1)$$

Where $\boldsymbol{K}$ is the stiffness matrix, $\boldsymbol{M}$ the mass matrix and $\boldsymbol{u}$ and $\ddot{\boldsymbol{u}}$ are the displacement and the acceleration vector, respectively. Eq. (1) provides the eigenvalue equation:

$$(\boldsymbol{K} - \boldsymbol{M}\omega^2)\boldsymbol{\psi} = \boldsymbol{0} \tag{2}$$

Where $\boldsymbol{\psi}$ and ω are the unscaled mode shape and the natural frequency, respectively.

Mode shapes can be normalized in many different ways but when working with experimental mode shapes, the most common types of normalization are:

- Mass normalization (or normalization to the mass matrix of the system).
- Normalization to the unit length of the vector
- Normalization to a component equal to unity (usually the largest component).

On the other hand, numerical mode shapes are generally mass normalized or normalized to a component equal to unity.

The un-scaled ($\boldsymbol{\psi}$) and the scaled or mass normalized ($\boldsymbol{\phi}$) mode-shape vectors are related by the expression:

$$\boldsymbol{\phi} = \boldsymbol{\psi}\frac{1}{\sqrt{m}} \tag{3}$$

Where m is the modal mass and which can be obtained from the expression [4,5,6]:

$$m = \boldsymbol{\psi}^T\boldsymbol{M}\boldsymbol{\psi} \tag{4}$$

The length of a mode shape $\boldsymbol{\psi}$ (also denoted in algebra as Euclidean norm, Euclidean length or L^2norm) is given by:

$$L_\psi = \sqrt{\boldsymbol{\psi}^T \cdot \boldsymbol{\psi}} \tag{5}$$

A mode shape is said to be mass normalized if the modal mass is dimensionless unity, i..e:

$$m_\phi = \boldsymbol{\phi}^T\boldsymbol{M}\boldsymbol{\phi} = 1 \tag{6}$$

Mass normalized mode shapes $\boldsymbol{\phi}$ can be obtained from the unscaled mode shapes $\boldsymbol{\psi}$ by:

$$\{\boldsymbol{\phi}\} = \frac{\boldsymbol{\psi}}{\sqrt{\boldsymbol{\psi}^T\boldsymbol{M}\boldsymbol{\psi}}} \tag{7}$$

A mode shape $\{\boldsymbol{\psi}\}$ is normalized to the unit length, hereafter denoted $\boldsymbol{\psi}_L$, if its length is unity, and it can be obtained by:

$$\boldsymbol{\psi}_L = \frac{\boldsymbol{\psi}}{\sqrt{\boldsymbol{\psi}^T \cdot \boldsymbol{\psi}}} = \frac{\boldsymbol{\psi}}{L_\psi} \tag{8}$$

Where the length of the vector $\boldsymbol{\psi}_L$ is unity, i.e:

$$L_{\psi_L} = \sqrt{\boldsymbol{\psi}_L^T \cdot \boldsymbol{\psi}_L} = 1 \tag{9}$$

Another common type of normalization consists of assigning a magnitude equal to one to a component of the vector (usually to the largest component). A mode shape normalized in this way is hereafter denoted as $\boldsymbol{\psi}_U$. If the r-th DOF is chosen to be equal to unity, the mode shape $\boldsymbol{\psi}_U$ is related to $\boldsymbol{\psi}$ by:

$$\psi_U = \frac{\psi}{\psi_r} \tag{10}$$

Where ψ_r is an scalar corresponding to the r-th component of the vector $\boldsymbol{\psi}$.

If eq. (10) is particularized to mode shapes normalized to the unit length and to mode shapes normalized to a component equal to unity, it results in:

$$\boldsymbol{\phi} = \boldsymbol{\psi}_L \frac{\mathbf{1}}{\sqrt{m_{\psi_L}}} = \boldsymbol{\psi}_U \frac{\mathbf{1}}{\sqrt{m_{\psi_U}}} \tag{11}$$

Where m_{ψ_L} and m_{ψ_U} are the modal masses corresponding to the mode shapes $\boldsymbol{\psi}_L$ and $\boldsymbol{\psi}_U$, respectively.

Pre-multiplication of eq. (11) by $\boldsymbol{\phi}^T$, gives:

$$\frac{m_\phi = 1}{L_\phi^2} = \frac{m_{\psi_L}}{L_{\psi_L}^2 = 1} = \frac{m_{\psi_U}}{L_{\psi_U}^2} \tag{12}$$

2. UNITS

The modal mass m_ϕ corresponding to the mass normalized mode shape $\boldsymbol{\phi}$ is dimensionless unity. From eq. (6) it is easily inferred that the translational components $\boldsymbol{\phi}_T$ of the mode shape $\boldsymbol{\phi}$ have the units $\frac{1}{\sqrt{kg}}$ in the international system, whereas the units of the rotational components $\boldsymbol{\phi}_T$ are $\frac{1}{m\sqrt{kg}}$. On the other hand, the translational components of the mode shapes $\boldsymbol{\psi}_L$ and $\boldsymbol{\psi}_U$ are dimensionless and the modal masses m_{ψ_L} and m_{ψ_U} are given in kg. This has been summarized in Table 1.

Table 1. Units of modal parameters in the international system (SI). ----- indicates dimensionless.

Mass normalization		Normalization to unit length		Normalization to a component equal to unity	
Variable	Unit	Variable	Unit	Variable	unit
$\boldsymbol{\phi}_T$	$\frac{1}{\sqrt{kg}}$	$\boldsymbol{\psi}_{LT}$	-----	$\boldsymbol{\psi}_{UT}$	------
$\boldsymbol{\phi}_R$	$\frac{1}{m\sqrt{kg}}$	$\boldsymbol{\psi}_{LR}$	$\frac{1}{m}$	$\boldsymbol{\psi}_{UR}$	$\frac{1}{m}$
$m_\phi = 1$	-----	m_{ψ_L}	kg	m_{ψ_U}	kg
$L_\phi = \sqrt{\{\phi\}^T \cdot \{\phi\}}$	$\frac{1}{\sqrt{kg}}$	$L_{\psi_L} = 1$ $L_{\psi_L} = \sqrt{\{\psi_L\}^T \cdot \{\psi_L\}}$	-----	$L_{\psi_U} = \sqrt{\{\psi_U\}^T \cdot \{\psi_U\}}$	-----
q_ϕ	$m\sqrt{kg}$	q_{ψ_L}	m	q_{ψ_U}	m

With respect to the length of mode shapes, L_{ψ_L} and L_{ψ_U} are dimensionless whereas L_ϕ have units of $\frac{1}{\sqrt{kg}}$.

Experimental mode shapes usually only contain translational DOF's and they can be scaled with any of the methods presented in section 1. On the other hand, some numerical mode shapes only contain translational DOF's (3D models, 2D planar elasticity models), whereas beams, plates and shells contain both translational and rotational DOF's. When a mode shape contains both translational and rotational DOF's, it cannot be normalized to the unit length (the length cannot be calculated because the units are not consistent).

The modal mass can also be a modal inertia. If the mode shape $\boldsymbol{\psi} = \begin{Bmatrix} \boldsymbol{\psi}_T \\ \boldsymbol{\psi}_R \end{Bmatrix}$, containing both translational and rotational components, is normalized to a translational component equal to unity, the modal mass, is given in kg (see table 1). However, if we normalize the vector $\boldsymbol{\psi}$ to a rotational component equal to unity, the translational DOF's are given in meters and the rotational DOF's are dimensionless. The modal mass in this case is given in kgm^2,i.e. it is a modal inertia.

In analytical models both modal mass and modal inertia can be modal parameters of a mode shape. However, mass normalization and normalization to a component equal to unity (usually the largest translational component) are the normalization methods commonly available in numerical programs, i.e. the modal mass (kg) is the parameter normally consider in finite element programs.

If the vector of displacements $\boldsymbol{u}$ is decomposed in modal coordinates using mass-normalized mode shapes:

$$\boldsymbol{u} = \boldsymbol{\phi} \cdot \boldsymbol{q}_{\boldsymbol{\phi}} \tag{13}$$

the modal coordinates $\boldsymbol{q}_{\boldsymbol{\phi}}$ have the units $m\sqrt{kg}$.

If mode shapes $\boldsymbol{\psi}_L$ are used in the modal decomposition:

$$\boldsymbol{u} = \boldsymbol{\phi} \cdot \boldsymbol{q}_{\boldsymbol{\psi}_L} \tag{14}$$

the translational components of the mode shapes are dimensionless, and the units of the modal coordinates $\boldsymbol{q}_{\boldsymbol{\psi}_L}$coincide with the units of vector $\boldsymbol{u}$. The modal coordinates $\boldsymbol{q}_{\boldsymbol{\phi}}$and $\boldsymbol{q}_{\boldsymbol{\psi}_L}$are related by:

$$\boldsymbol{q}_{\boldsymbol{\phi}} = \boldsymbol{q}_{\boldsymbol{\psi}_L} \cdot \sqrt{m_{\psi_L}} \tag{15}$$

The same can be said for mode shapes $\boldsymbol{\psi}_U$.

3. EXPANSION AND REDUCTION OF MODELS

In structural dynamics model reduction means to reduce a finite element model to one with fewer degrees of freedom while the dynamic characteristics of the system are maintained [7]. In order that the reduced model have the same modal parameters as the full model, the modal masses must remain unchanged with all kinds of normalization, i.e.:

$$m_{\phi} = m_{\phi a} = 1, \qquad m_{\psi_L} = m_{\psi_{La}} \qquad m_{\psi_U} = m_{\psi_{Ua}} \tag{16}$$

Where the subindex 'a' indicates model with active DOF's.

However, the following properties are modified:

- The length of mode shapes $\boldsymbol{\phi}_a, \boldsymbol{\psi}_{L_a}$ ***and*** $\boldsymbol{\psi}_{U_a}$ are different to that of the corresponding full mode shapes (see table 2).
- the reduced mode shape $\boldsymbol{\psi}_{L_a}$ is no longer normalized to the unit length. If the reduced mode shape is normalized to the unit length($\boldsymbol{\psi}^*_{L_a}$ in table 2), the modal mass has to be modified accordingly.

- With mode shapes $\boldsymbol{\psi}_U$ and $\boldsymbol{\psi}_{U_a}$, the DOF with the component equal to unity must be the same in both the full and the reduced models. Otherwise, the modal mass has to be modified accordingly.

All the aforementioned properties are showed in table 2 by means an example.

Table 2. Example of mode shapes and modal masses in reduction

Mass normalization	Normalization to unit length	Normalization to a component equal to unity
$\boldsymbol{\phi} = \begin{Bmatrix} \boldsymbol{\phi}_a \\ \boldsymbol{\phi}_d \end{Bmatrix} = \begin{Bmatrix} \begin{Bmatrix} 0.9 \\ 0.72 \end{Bmatrix}_a \\ \{0.45\}_d \end{Bmatrix}$ $m_\phi = 1$ $L_\phi = 1.1597$	$\boldsymbol{\psi}_L = \begin{Bmatrix} \begin{Bmatrix} 0.7272 \\ 0.5818 \end{Bmatrix}_a \\ \{0.3636\}_d \end{Bmatrix}$ $m_{\psi_L} = 0.6535$ $L_{\psi_L}=1$	$\boldsymbol{\psi}_U = \begin{Bmatrix} \begin{Bmatrix} 1 \\ 0.8 \end{Bmatrix}_a \\ \{0.5\}_d \end{Bmatrix}$ $m_{\psi_U} = 1.234$ $L_{\psi_U} = 1.3748$

Reduction ⇓	*Reduction* ⇓		*Reduction* ⇓
$\boldsymbol{\phi}_a = \begin{Bmatrix} 0.9 \\ 0.72 \end{Bmatrix}$ $m_{\phi_a} = 1$ $L_{\phi a} = 1.0689$	$\boldsymbol{\psi}_{L_a} = \begin{Bmatrix} 0.7272 \\ 0.5818 \end{Bmatrix}$ $m_{\psi_{La}} = 0.6535$ $L_{\psi_{La}} = 0.9313$	$\boldsymbol{\psi}^*_{L_a} = \begin{Bmatrix} 0.7808 \\ 0.6247 \end{Bmatrix}$ $m^*_{\psi_{La}} = 0.7535$ $L^*_{\psi_{La}} = 1$	$\boldsymbol{\psi}_{U_a} = \begin{Bmatrix} 1 \\ 0.8 \end{Bmatrix}$ $m_{\psi_{Ua}} = 1.234$ $L_{\psi_{Ua}}=1.2806$

The modal masses m_{ψ_L} and $m^*_{\psi_{La}}$ are related by means of the equation:

$$m_{\psi_L} = m^*_{\psi_{La}} \cdot L^2_{\psi_{La}} \tag{17}$$

Where $L^2_{\psi_{La}}$ is the square length of the vector $\boldsymbol{\psi}_{L_a}$.

The same procedure must be followed with expansion of mode shapes.

4. MODAL ASSURANCE CRITERIA (MAC)

The modal assurance criteria (MAC) is the most used criteria to compare two mode shapes. We consider by convenience the mode shapes $\boldsymbol{\phi}_x$ and $\boldsymbol{\phi}_{FE}$, the subindices 'x' and'FE' denoting experimental and numerical models, respectively. The modal assurance criteria (MAC) is given as the square of the dot product between two vectors with unit length [1,2,3,4], i.e.:

$$MAC = \left|\boldsymbol{\psi}^T_{x_L} \cdot \boldsymbol{\psi}_{FE_L}\right|^2 = \cos^2\theta \tag{18}$$

From eq. (18) it is inferred that we cannot calculate the MAC between two vectors containing both translational and rotational DOF's, because these vectors cannot be normalized to the unit length.

In case of other kinds of normalization, the following expression must be used [1,2,3,4]:

$$MAC = \frac{\left|\boldsymbol{\phi}^T_x \cdot \boldsymbol{\phi}_{FE}\right|^2}{\left|\boldsymbol{\phi}^T_x \cdot \boldsymbol{\phi}_x\right|\left|\boldsymbol{\phi}^T_{FE} \cdot \boldsymbol{\phi}_{FE}\right|} = \frac{\left|\boldsymbol{\psi}^T_{x_U} \cdot \boldsymbol{\psi}_{FE_U}\right|^2}{\left|\boldsymbol{\psi}^T_{x_U} \cdot \boldsymbol{\psi}_{x_U}\right|\left|\boldsymbol{\psi}^T_{FE_U} \cdot \boldsymbol{\psi}_{FE_U}\right|} \tag{19}$$

5. COMPARISON OF MODAL MASSES

Let's consider two mode shapes $\boldsymbol{\psi}_{x_U}$ and $\boldsymbol{\psi}_{FE_U}$ with modal masses m_{x_U} and $m_{\psi_{FE_U}}$, respectively. The modal assurance criteria (MAC) can be used to compare both mode shapes and the MAC is unique because both mode shapes have to be normalized to the unit length of the vector. However, as it can be seen in the next example, if we compare the modal masses of two modes, the discrepancies are different depending on the normalization used for the mode shapes.

Example:

$$\boldsymbol{\phi}_x = \begin{Bmatrix} 0.32 \\ 0.56 \\ 0.27 \end{Bmatrix} \rightarrow \boldsymbol{\psi}_{x_L} = \begin{Bmatrix} 0.4577 \\ 0.8009 \\ 0.3861 \end{Bmatrix} \rightarrow \boldsymbol{\psi}_{x_U} = \begin{Bmatrix} 0.5714 \\ 1.0 \\ 0.4821 \end{Bmatrix}$$

$$m_{xL} = 2.045 \qquad m_{xU} = 3.189$$

$$\boldsymbol{\phi}_{FE} = \begin{Bmatrix} 0.30 \\ 0.59 \\ 0.30 \end{Bmatrix} \rightarrow \boldsymbol{\psi}_{FE_L} = \begin{Bmatrix} 0.4128 \\ 0.8119 \\ 0.4128 \end{Bmatrix} \rightarrow \boldsymbol{\psi}_{FE_U} = \begin{Bmatrix} 0.5085 \\ 1.0 \\ 0.5085 \end{Bmatrix}$$

$$m_{FE_L} = 1.894 \qquad m_{FE_U} = 2.873$$

$$\epsilon_L = 100 \cdot \left(1 - \frac{m_{FEL}}{m_{xL}}\right) = 7.38\% \quad \epsilon_U = 100 \cdot \left(1 - \frac{m_{FEU}}{m_{xL}}\right) = 9.909\%$$

We do not obtain the same error comparing the modal masses of mode shapes normalized to the length or comparing those corresponding to mode shapes normalized with the maximum component equal to unity. This is because the mode shapes $\boldsymbol{\psi}_{xU}$ and $\boldsymbol{\psi}_{FE_U}$ do not have the same length (figure 1).

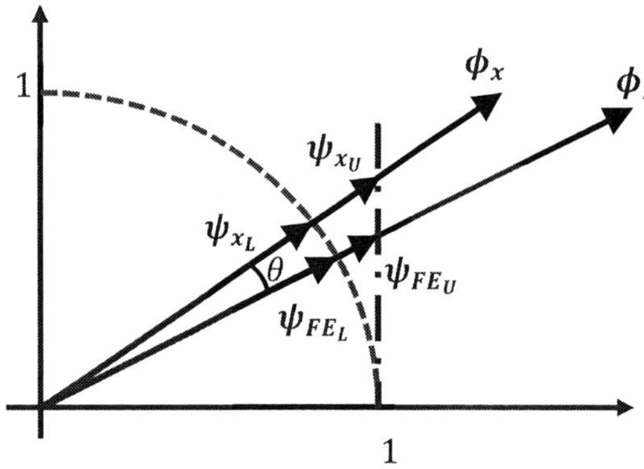

Figure 1. Representation of two-dimensional vectors with different kinds of normalization

In operational modal analysis, the force is not measured and the modal mass cannot be estimated [4]. Some authors [8] have proposed to normalize experimental un-scaled mode shapes using the modal masses of a finite element model. However, two aspects must be considered:

- Mode shapes $\boldsymbol{\psi}_{xU}$ and $\boldsymbol{\psi}_{FE_U}$ have different length (see figure 1), which means that the modal mass m_{FE_U} must not be used to scale $\boldsymbol{\psi}_{xU}$.
- The vector $\boldsymbol{\psi}_{FE_U}$ cannot be normalized to the unit length if both rotational and translational DOF's are present in the mode shape.

If the experimental mode shape only contains translational components (as it is common in modal analysis) the following procedure is recommended:

- The modal mass m_{FE_U} and the mode shape $\boldsymbol{\psi}_{FE_U}$ are known from the FE model.
- The mode shape $\boldsymbol{\psi}_{FE_U}$ is reduced to the active DOF's (vector $\boldsymbol{\psi}_{FE_{Ua}}$) whose modal mass is $m_{FEUa} = m_{FEU}$
- The modal mass $m_{FE_{La}}$ of the vector $\boldsymbol{\psi}_{FE_{La}}$ can be obtained by:

$$m_{FE_{La}} = \frac{m_{FE_{Ua}}}{L^2_{\psi_{FE_{Ua}}}} \quad (1)$$

- The experimental mode shape $\psi_{x_{La}}$ is normalized by:

$$\widehat{\phi}_{x_a} = \frac{\psi_{x_{La}}}{\sqrt{m_{FE_{La}}}} \quad (1)$$

Where '$\frown$' indicates approximation.

Example:

$$\psi_{x_{La}} = \begin{Bmatrix} 0.4577 \\ 0.8009 \\ \end{Bmatrix} \qquad \psi_{FE_U} = \begin{Bmatrix} 0.5085 \\ 1.0 \\ 0.5085 \end{Bmatrix} \rightarrow \psi_{FE_{Ua}} = \begin{Bmatrix} 0.5085 \\ 1.0 \\ \end{Bmatrix}$$

$$m_{FE_U} = 2.873 \qquad m_{FE_{Ua}} = 2.873$$

$$m_{FE_{La}} = \frac{m_{FE_{Ua}}}{L^2_{\psi_{FE_{Ua}}}} = \frac{2.873}{1.2586} = 2.287$$

$$\widehat{\phi}_{x_a} = \frac{\begin{Bmatrix} 0.4577 \\ 0.800 \end{Bmatrix}}{\sqrt{2.287}} = \begin{Bmatrix} 0.303 \\ 0.530 \end{Bmatrix} \qquad \phi_x = \begin{Bmatrix} 0.32 \\ 0.56 \\ 0.27 \end{Bmatrix}$$

6. CONCLUSIONS

Modal mass is one of the modal parameters needed to define the dynamic behavior of a structure. The values that the modal mass can take are dependent on the type of normalization. In this paper, the most common types of normalization have been considered: mass normalization, normalization to the unit length and normalization to the largest component equal to unit.

The units of the modal mass are also dependent on the normalization. The modal mass of mass normalized mode shape is dimensionless unity. If the modal masses of two modes are compared, the mode shapes have to be normalized to the unit length.

Although the length of a vector given by eq. (5) is usually considered in algebra and also in the field of structural dynamics and modal analysis, it presents two main inconveniences:

- Mode shapes with translational and rotational components cannot be normalized to length. As a result, the modal assurance criteria (MAC) cannot be calculated when a mode shape have both translational and rotational DOF's.
- The length of the mode shapes is dependent on the number of DOF's consider in the mode shape vector.

For the aforementioned reasons, mass normalization and normalization to a component equal to unity (usually the largest translational component) are the normalization methods commonly available in numerical programs.

Both modal mass and modal inertia can be modal parameters of a mode shape. The modal mass of a mode shape normalized to a displacement equal to unity, is given in kg. On the other hand, if the normalization is to a rotation equal to unity, then modal mass is given in kgm^2, i.e. it is a modal inertia. The same can be said for mode shapes normalized to the unit length: modal mass in kg for a mode shape with translational components and modal inertia in kgm^2 for mode shapes with rotational components.

ACKNOWLEDGEMENTS

The financing support given by Banco Santander through the Mobility Grants for Researchers of Professors of the University of Oviedo, is gratefully appreciated. The authors acknowledge the funding received from Centre for Oil and Gas - DTU/Danish Hydrocarbon Research and Technology Centre (DHRTC).

REFERENCES

[1] Ewins DJ (2000) *Modal Testing: Theory, Practice and Application*, Second Ed. London: Research Studies Press LTD

[2] Maia NMM. and Montalvao e Silva JM (2003) *Theoretical and Experimental Modal Analysis*. England: Research Studies Press LTD

[3] Heylen W, Lammens S and Sas P (2007) *Modal Analysis theory and testing*. Belgium: Katholieke Universiteit Leuven, Faculty of Engenieering

[4] Brincker R., Ventura C. (2015). *Introduction to Operational Modal Analysis*. Chichester : John Wiley & Sons Ltd.

[5] Clough RW and Penzien J (1993) *Dynamics of structures*, 2nd edition. New York: McGraw-Hill-

[6] Chopra AK (1995) *Dynamics of Structures*. New Jersey: Prentice Hall

[7] O'Callahan J.C., Avitabile P. and Riemer R. (1989). System Equivalent Reduction Expansion Process. *In: Proc. of the 7th Intl Modal Analysis Conference* (IMAC), (pp.29-37),Las vegas, USA.

[8] Schwarz B, Richardson M. (2006). Using FEA modes to scale experimental mode shapes. *In: International modal analysis conference* (IMAC XXIV), (paper 46), St Louis, USA.

IOMAC'19
8th International Operational Modal Analysis Conference
2019 May 13-15 Copenhagen

CONSISTENT REAL-VALUED AND ONE-SIDED SPECTRAL DENSITY FUNCTIONS

Yi Liu[1], Rune Brincker[2], John Macdonald[3]

[1] PhD student, Department of Civil Engineering, University of Bristol, yl15193@bristol.ac.uk.
[2] Professor, Department of Civil Engineering, Technical University of Denmark, runeb@byg.dtu.dk.
[3] Reader, Department of Civil Engineering, University of Bristol, John.Macdonald@bristol.ac.uk.

ABSTRACT

Due to the properties of the Fourier transform, the spectral density (SD) functions are not only defined over the Nyquist band, but over the double interval. Normally that includes negative frequencies and a corresponding SD matrix that is known to contain the same information as the SD matrix in the positive frequency band. In this paper, we will use the Parseval's theorem that expresses the equality between the sum over all SD matrices and the response covariance function as a basis to define a real-valued SD matrix that is only defined over all non-negative frequency bins. This new real and one-sided SD matrix fulfil the Parseval equation and we will also illustrate how it can be used successfully to perform identification in the operational modal analysis where modal parameters are to be identified from the operating response without any pre-knowledge about the excitation forces.

Keywords: Operational modal analysis, Parseval's theorem, spectral density, real-valued spectral density matrix.

1. INTRODUCTION

Normally in operational modal analysis (OMA) information is extracted from the random responses by calculating correlation functions and/or spectral density functions. If we consider a certain number of channels (sensors) N, then we would arrange the correlation functions in the correlation function (CF) matrix and the Spectral Density (SD) matrix. The CF and SD matrices are then $N \times N$ matrices, Brincker and Ventura [4].

It is well-known that the auto SD functions in the SD matrix (the diagonal elements) are real-valued functions, whereas the cross SD functions are complex valued functions. However, even though the cross-spectral density functions are in fact complex valued, the complex parts of these functions are normally relatively small compared to the real parts.

Further, when we add the SD functions matrices over the total frequency band to obtain the covariance matrix of the initial random responses based on the Parseval's theorem, this process will remove the imaginary parts of the SD matrix. It is because any imaginary part of the SD matrix contribution from the positive frequency band will be cancelled out due to the corresponding contribution from the negative frequency band.

As a result, it is natural to investigate a simple hypothesis stating: The imaginary parts of the SD matrix do not have any physical importance, and thus can be removed.

In this paper we will investigate this hypothesis based on a comparative simulation study. We will simulate random responses in the time domain, estimate the SD matrix using the classical Welch averaging technique, and then estimate the corresponding real-valued SD matrix simply by taking the real values of the classical SD matrix. Having done this, the so defined classical and real-valued SD matrices are then taken back to the time domain by using the inverse Fourier transform (iFT). The so obtained two versions of the correlation functions are then used to perform identification using the Polyreference technique [4], [5], and the accuracy of the two approaches are compared.

2. REAL-VALUE SD MATRIX

2.1. Parseval's theorem

In Fourier analysis, the Parseval's theorem is stating that the sum or integral of a function is equal to the sum or integral of the square of its transform, which is the result that the Fourier series or Fourier transform is unitary. Generally, there are two ways to approach the Parseval's theorem, the first one is derived from the correlation function [1] which is usually recognised in random process analysis, while the other one is proved based on convolution theorem [6] which is widely seen in digital signal processing.

Now suppose we have two real discrete time signals $x(n)$ and $y(n)$, each of which satisfies finite energy, which means the Fourier transforms of them exist. As we know that the cross-correlation of $x(n)$ and $y(n)$ is a sequence $r_{xy}(l)$, which is defined as [6]

$$r_{xy}(l) = \sum_{n=-\infty}^{\infty} x(n)y(n-l) \tag{1}$$

where $l = 0, \pm 1, \pm 2, \ldots$.

Specially, if both $x(n)$ and $y(n)$ are random signals, then $r_{xy}(l)$ will be a random sequence too, in which case, we will have to evaluate its statistical property. And if both of signals are second order ergodic, $r_{xy}(l)$ shall be given by [1], [8],

$$r_{xy}(l) = \mathrm{E}\left[x(n)y(n-l)\right] = \lim_{N\to 0}\frac{1}{N}\sum_{n=-N}^{N} x(n)y(n-l) \tag{2}$$

As usual, if we take the Fourier transform of $r_{xy}(l)$, we obtain the cross spectral density function $g(\omega)$.

$$g(\omega) = \sum_{l=-\infty}^{\infty}\sum_{n=-\infty}^{\infty} x(n)y(n-l)e^{-j\omega l} = \tilde{x}(\omega)\tilde{y}(-\omega) = \tilde{x}(\omega)\tilde{y}^*(\omega) \tag{3}$$

where $\tilde{x}(\omega)$

$$\tilde{x}(\omega) = \sum_{n=-\infty}^{\infty} x(n)e^{-j\omega n} \tag{4}$$

is the Fourier transform of $x(n)$, which is a continuous function of ω. While $\tilde{y}(\omega)$ represents the Fourier transform of $y(n)$. For real signals, we have $\tilde{y}(-\omega)=\tilde{y}^*(\omega)$.

In turn, we can find the inverse Fourier transform of $\tilde{x}(\omega)\tilde{y}(-\omega)$, which is

$$\frac{1}{2\pi}\int_{-\pi}^{\pi}\tilde{x}(\omega)\tilde{y}(-\omega)e^{j\omega l}\mathrm{d}\omega=\sum_{n=-\infty}^{\infty}x(n)y(n-l)=r_{xy}(l) \tag{5}$$

Now we consider the Fourier transform of the two signals, we have

$$\sum_{n=-\infty}^{\infty}x(n)y(n)e^{-j\Omega n}=\frac{1}{2\pi}\int_{-\pi}^{\pi}\tilde{x}(\omega)\tilde{y}(\Omega-\omega)\mathrm{d}\omega \tag{6}$$

Eq. (1) to Eq. (5) is the correlation analysis between two signals, while Eq. (6) is the convolution of the two signals. Here, when we look at the synthesis equation of the correlation of the two signals at $l=0$, and the analysis equation of the convolution of the two signals at the $\Omega=0$, it will lead us to the following relations,

$$\begin{cases}\sum_{n=-\infty}^{\infty}x(n)y(n)=\frac{1}{2\pi}\int_{-\pi}^{\pi}\tilde{x}(\omega)\tilde{y}(-\omega)\mathrm{d}\omega & l=0 \quad (a)\\ \sum_{n=-\infty}^{\infty}x(n)y(n)=\frac{1}{2\pi}\int_{-\pi}^{\pi}\tilde{x}(\omega)\tilde{y}(-\omega)\mathrm{d}\omega & \Omega=0 \quad (b)\end{cases} \tag{7}$$

We can see that the integrand $\tilde{x}(\omega)\tilde{y}(-\omega)$ is effectively given by Eq. (3), the cross-spectral density function. We can see that the two equations from This Eq. (7) are the same, but they have different meanings. To be specific, if we see $z(n)=x(n)y(n)$ as the new signal formed by two signals, then Eq. (7) (b) gives the Fourier transform of a signal at DC (direct current), while Eq. (7) (a)only means the value of the correlation function obtained at $l=0$, when $l\neq 0$, $r_{xy}(l)$ will be the distribution of $r_{xy}(0)$. Nevertheless, either way, Eq. (7) gives the general form of the Parseval's theorem for real discrete time signals.

For a special case, when $x(n)=y(n)$, Eq. (7) becomes [6]

$$\sum_{n=-\infty}^{\infty}|x(n)|^2=\frac{1}{2\pi}\int_{-\pi}^{\pi}|\tilde{x}(\omega)|^2\mathrm{d}\omega \tag{8}$$

which is the Parseval's theorem for signal $x(n)$.

On the other hand, the sum over all times of the signal squared in the time domain is defined as the energy of the signal. For instance, the energy of the signal $x(n)$ is defined as follows [6]

$$E=\sum_{n=-\infty}^{\infty}|x(n)|^2 \tag{9}$$

which is the term on the left hand side of Eq. (8). The energy of the signal at each time instant is equal to $|x(n)|^2$. For continuous time signals, the energy of a signal is given as [7]

$$E=\int_{-\infty}^{\infty}|x(t)|^2\mathrm{d}t \tag{10}$$

where $\left|x(t)\right|^2$ is the energy time density [7], then the signal's energy during a time interval of infinitesimal duration of $\mathrm{d}t$ centred on the time t is $\left|x(t)\right|^2 \mathrm{d}t$.

From Parseval's theorem, we know that the total energy of the signal can be calculated by summing power per sample across time or spectral power across frequency. Or in other words, the signal's energy is the same whether we look at it in the time domain or the frequency domain. Particularly, from Eq. (8) we can see that for a discrete time signal, the summation or integration of the signal squared over all time is equal to the energy of the signal calculated from a signal period $-\pi$ to π in frequency domain, since the Fourier transform of the discrete time signal is periodic with period 2π.

Accordingly, we can define the average power of the signal [6]

$$P = \lim_{N\to\infty} \frac{1}{N} \sum_{n=-\frac{N}{2}}^{\frac{N}{2}} \left|x(n)\right|^2 \tag{11}$$

which can also be interpreted as the variance of the signal σ_x^2. When the signal is periodic or have finite length, the limit shall be removed, and the duration of the summation of the signal squared is given in one period. In which case, σ_x^2 is given by

$$\sigma_x^2 = \frac{1}{N} \sum_{n=0}^{N-1} x^2(n) \tag{12}$$

The physical meaning of σ_x^2 represents the DC component of the signal, which is the mean amplitude of the waveform.

Due to the diversity of the unit choice, there are various definitions of the Fourier transform in application, the signal energy related by the Parseval's theorem will end up having different forms. But either way, the definition of the Power Spectral Density (PSD) should remain consistent. First, we shall look at the definition of the Energy Spectral Density (ESD). For instance,

$$\sum_{n=-\infty}^{\infty} \left|x(n)\right|^2 = \frac{1}{2\pi} \int_{-\pi}^{\pi} \left|\tilde{x}(\omega)\right|^2 \mathrm{d}\omega = \int_{-\frac{1}{2}}^{\frac{1}{2}} \left|\tilde{x}(f)\right|^2 \mathrm{d}f \tag{13}$$

where $\mathrm{d}f = \mathrm{d}\omega/2\pi$. Here, the meaning of $\left|\tilde{x}(f)\right|^2$ is the same as the $\left|\tilde{x}(\omega)\right|^2$ which is called as the ESD, the only difference is the examining scale, one is the angular frequency ω and the other is the ordinary frequency f. The name of the ESD is directly analogues to the energy time density $\left|x(t)\right|^2$ in the time domain. It should be pointed out that the ESD is usually used to describe the energy distribution with frequency for transients or pulse-like signals whose energy is concentrated around a finite time interval.

As we can see that many signals have spectral distributions that vary as time progresses. For such signals, we wish to know how much energy is in the frequency range around ω or f at times around n or t. Since the energy density in the time domain is the power, we can define the Power Spectral Density (PSD) in frequency domain. Based on Eq. (11) and Eq. (13), we will have

$$P = \lim_{N\to\infty} \frac{1}{2N} \sum_{n=-N}^{N} \left|x(n)\right|^2 = \int_{-\frac{1}{2}}^{\frac{1}{2}} \lim_{N\to\infty} \frac{1}{2N} \left|\tilde{x}(f)\right|^2 \mathrm{d}f \tag{14}$$

where

$$S(f) = \lim_{N\to\infty} \frac{1}{2N} \left|\tilde{x}(f)\right|^2 \tag{15}$$

is the PSD of the analysed signal.

The definition of the PSD is very useful for the describing of the energy distribution of the signal has infinite duration (continues over all time) or over a time period large enough that it could as well have been over an infinite time interval, for which it may have finite power but infinite energy, such as stationary process. Particularly, for a random signal, the PSD is given by

$$S(f) = \lim_{N\to\infty} \frac{1}{2N} \mathrm{E}\left[\left|\tilde{x}(f)\right|^2\right] \tag{16}$$

Now consider the periodic discrete time signals, the Fourier transform of which are discrete in the frequency domain. Therefore, if we suppose the discrete time periodic signal $x_p(n)$ with fundamental period N, then the energy of the signal within a single period is given by [6]

$$E_{pN} = \sum_{n=0}^{N-1} \left|x_p(n)\right|^2 = N \sum_{k=0}^{N-1} \left|\tilde{x}_p(k)\right|^2 \tag{17}$$

where

$$\tilde{x}_p(k) = \frac{1}{N} \sum_{n=0}^{N-1} x_p(n) e^{-j\frac{2\pi kn}{N}} \tag{18}$$

is the Fourier transform of $x_p(n)$, which is the discrete function, where $k = 0,1,2,\ldots,N-1$. Eq. (17) is the Parseval's theorem written in discrete time periodic signal in one period. Here the average power of the signal is given by

$$P_{pN} = \frac{1}{N} \sum_{n=0}^{N-1} \left|x_p(n)\right|^2 = \sum_{k=0}^{N-1} \left|\tilde{x}_p(k)\right|^2 \tag{19}$$

Here, $\left|\tilde{x}_p(k)\right|^2$ is the PSD of the signal at the k th frequency line.

However, for the aperiodic discrete time signals, the Fourier transform of which are continuous in the frequency domain, i.e., $\tilde{x}(\omega)$ or $\tilde{x}(f)$ is a continuous function of frequency, which is not computationally convenient. We normally need to sample the continuous spectrum of the signal, which leads to the Discrete Fourier Transform (DFT). As we can see, for discrete time periodic signal, the Parseval's theorem gives exact results in one period with N point.

In reality, we constantly need to truncate a continuing signal, which means, we will add a window to the signal. As a result, the signal we are dealing with is normally time limited with finite energy. For the discrete time periodic signal, when the analysing length of the signal for the DFT is the integral multiple of the fundamental period, then there will be no spectral leakage. In this case, the Parseval's theorem still gives exact results with this analysing length. However, when comes to the aperiodic signal with finite duration or the analysing length of the periodic signal does not satisfy the aforementioned assumption, it seems that if we sample the continuous spectrum $\tilde{x}(f)$ for a discrete time aperiodic signal it will result in energy loss, which means the Parseval's theorem does not stand. But this is not the case.

For a finite-duration aperiodic signal $x(n)$, we assume it is nonzero in the interval $0 \le n \le L-1$, and we observe it with N $(\ge L)$ points. The normal procedure of the DFT is to create a periodic repetition of $x(n)$ every N samples. This means the DFT convert the original aperiodic signal into a periodic signal with fundament period of N. Thus, based on our previous analysis of the discrete time periodic signal, the DFT version of Parseval's theorem for the aperiodic signal should also stand. However, the discretised form of the continuous spectral function of an aperiodic signal with N points is often expressed as

$$\tilde{x}(k)=\sum_{n=0}^{N-1}x(n)e^{-j\frac{2\pi kn}{N}} \tag{20}$$

While its inverse Fourier transform is

$$x(n)=\frac{1}{N}\sum_{k=0}^{N-1}\tilde{x}(k)e^{j\frac{2\pi kn}{N}} \tag{21}$$

Accordingly, the Parseval's theorem for the digital signal is given by (Stein, 2000)

$$\sum_{n=0}^{N-1}\left|x(n)\right|^{2}=\frac{1}{N}\sum_{k=0}^{N-1}\left|\tilde{x}(k)\right|^{2} \tag{22}$$

Now, $\left|\tilde{x}(k)\right|^{2}$ shall be interpreted as the ESD of the signal at the k th frequency line. While the coefficient $1/N$ is the sampling rate in the frequency domain. As ESD and PSD sometime can be very confusing to the readers, without differentiating them in the following context, we will call them Spectral Density (SD).

Practically, we normally deal with random measurements, so it is worth mentioning the Parseval's theorem for the random data. Assume we have two random measurements $x(n)$ and $y(n)$, then the Parseval's theorem written in DFT form is given by

$$\sum_{n=0}^{N-1}\mathrm{E}\left[x(n)y(n)\right]=\frac{1}{N}\sum_{k=0}^{N-1}\mathrm{E}\left[\tilde{x}(k)\tilde{y}^{*}(k)\right] \tag{23}$$

2.2. Covariance matrix and SD matrix

For a random response $\mathbf{y}(n)=\left(y_1(n),y_2(n),\cdots,y_{N_d}(n)\right)^{\mathrm{T}}$ with N_d measured degrees of freedom (DOF's), which is the also the same as the number of 1D sensors being used, the $N_d\times N_d$ covariance matrix $\mathbf{C}_y(n)$ for the random responses $\mathbf{y}(n)$ is classically defined as

$$\mathbf{C}_y(n)=\mathrm{E}\left[\mathbf{y}(n)\mathbf{y}^{\mathrm{T}}(n)\right] \tag{24}$$

Note that here we assume $\mathbf{y}(n)$ has zero mean. If $\mathbf{y}(n)$ is second order ergodic, then,

$$\mathbf{C}_y(n)=\mathrm{E}\left[\mathbf{y}(n)\mathbf{y}^{T}(n)\right]=\lim_{N\to 0}\frac{1}{N}\mathbf{Y}\mathbf{Y}^{\mathrm{T}} \tag{25}$$

where $\mathbf{Y}$ is a $N_d\times N$ matrix contains all the measurements from one sample. When our measurement has limited length with N, we can define the empirical covariance matrix then remove the limit in Eq. (25), which will be denoted as

$$\hat{\mathbf{C}}_y(n)=\frac{1}{N}\mathbf{Y}\mathbf{Y}^{\mathrm{T}} \tag{26}$$

Similarly, if we apply the Fourier transformation to $\mathbf{y}(n)$, then employ the same procedure to $\tilde{\mathbf{y}}(n)$ which is the Fourier transform of $\mathbf{y}(n)$, what we obtained is the SD matrix in frequency domain. At the k th frequency line, the SD matrix is given by

$$\mathbf{G}(k)=\mathrm{E}\left[\tilde{\mathbf{y}}^{*}(k)\tilde{\mathbf{y}}^{\mathrm{T}}(k)\right] \tag{27}$$

which is a $N_d \times N_d$ Hermitian matrix.

Now we can derive the matrix form of the Parseval's theorem for the limited length measurements by simply using Eq. (23),

$$\sum_{n=0}^{N-1} \mathrm{E}\left[\mathbf{y}(n)\mathbf{y}^T(n)\right] = \frac{1}{N}\sum_{k=0}^{N-1} \mathrm{E}\left[\tilde{\mathbf{y}}^*(k)\tilde{\mathbf{y}}^\mathrm{T}(k)\right] \tag{28}$$

When the data is second order ergodic, we can simplify the above equation to

$$N\hat{\mathbf{C}}_y(n) = \mathbf{Y}\mathbf{Y}^\mathrm{T} = \frac{1}{N}\sum_{k=0}^{N-1} \mathbf{G}(k) \tag{29}$$

In practice, if we have a piece of record of the time history, we would like to divide the total response time series into smaller data segments each containing N data points, and then perform the averaging over the number of segments N_e as prescribed using the Welch SD estimate [8]. One should note that in order to obtain full rank of the spectral density matrix when obtaining the Welch estimate, one should make sure that at least N_d number of averages is being used, i.e. $N_e \geq N_d$.

2.3. Define the real-value SD matrix

In order to formulate a meaningful real-valued spectral density, we shall take origin in the central equation from the previous section, the DFT form of the Parseval's theorem as given by Eq. (29).

Since in the DFT case, both the time function and the frequency domain function are periodic, we can choose the period as we want on both the time and the frequency axis. For the frequency axis, we will choose to follow normal practice having negative and positive frequencies, and where the maximum frequency is equal to the Nyquist frequency $f_v = 1/(2\Delta t)$, where Δt is the sampling time step. The period of the time function is then $T = N\Delta t$, and the frequency resolution is $\Delta f = 1/T$. This means that we have $N/2$ frequency steps from DC to the Nyquist frequency, thus we have $N/2+1$ frequency lines from DC to Nyquist, and then $N/2-1$ negative frequency lines, see Figure 1.(a), in which the classical discrete spectral density with 11 frequency lines from DC to Nyquist, and 9 negative frequency lines.

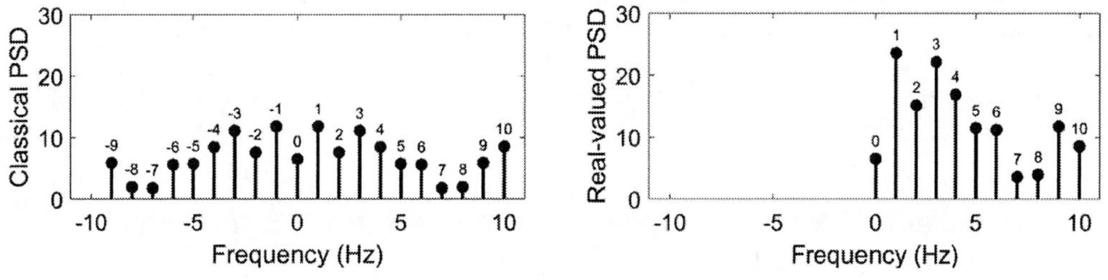

(a) The classical discrete spectral density (b) The real-valued and one-sided spectral density

Figure 1. Discrete spectral density

With this choice of frequency axis, the discrete frequencies are given by

$$f_k = k\Delta f\,; \quad k \in \left[-(N/2-1); N/2\,\right] \tag{30}$$

Performing the summation over the so defined frequency lines, the Parseval's theorem given by Eq. (29) is now expressed as

$$\hat{\mathbf{C}} = \frac{1}{N} \sum_{k=-(N/2-1)}^{N/2} \mathbf{G}_k \tag{31}$$

Where $\hat{\mathbf{C}} = \mathbf{Y}\mathbf{Y}^{\mathrm{T}}$.

As we know that with real measurements, the DC matrix $\mathbf{G}_0$ and the matrix $\mathbf{G}_{N/2}$ at Nyquist are always real. Noting that the remaining matrices are complex, but fulfil

$$\mathbf{G}_{-k} = \mathbf{G}_k^* \tag{32}$$

we can now write Eq. (31) as a sum over the non-negative frequency lines

$$\hat{\mathbf{C}} = \frac{1}{N}\left(\mathbf{G}_0 + \sum_{k=1}^{N/2-1} (\mathbf{G}_k + \mathbf{G}_k^*) + \mathbf{G}_{N/2}\right) \tag{33}$$

And we see that all terms are now real-valued. This leads us to define the meaningful real-valued and one-sided spectral density

$$\mathbf{S}_k = \begin{cases} \mathbf{G}_0; & k = 0 \\ \mathbf{G}_k + \mathbf{G}_k^*; & k \in [1; N/2-1]; \\ \mathbf{G}_{N/2}; & k = N/2 \end{cases} \tag{34}$$

See Figure 1.(b), it shows the real-valued and one-sided spectral density only having 11 non-negative frequency lines. The result is that we can express the Parseval theorem summing over the non-negative frequency lines

$$\hat{\mathbf{C}} = \frac{1}{N} \sum_{k=0}^{N/2} \mathbf{S}_k \tag{35}$$

Every SD matrix $\mathbf{S}_k$ can now be considered as the contribution to the covariance matrix from the frequency band $B_k = [f_k - \Delta f; f_k + \Delta f]$.

The defined real-valued SD matrix removed all the imaginary parts in the classical SD matrix, intuitively, it may seem that this procedure stripped off some information from the original data. However, the Parseval's theorem tells us that the imaginary parts in the SD matrix do not contribute to the overall signal energy. Moreover, Eq. (35) actually gives the real distribution of the signal energy along the frequency line. In order to eradicate our doubles, the subject of the next section will focus on verifying this real-valued SD via the Polyreference time domain method based on a numerical model with different frequency spacing.

3. MODAL PARAMETERS IDENTIFICATION BASED ON POLYREFERENCE TIME DOMAIN METHOD

3.1. Simulation case

In this section, a numerical model with two modes, one with a fixed frequency and one with a moving frequency is constructed. In other words, the spacing between the two frequencies is varied from closely spaced to reasonably separated modes. Ultimately, we want to evaluate the performance between the classical complex SD matrix and real-valued SD matrix, then to make a conclusion whether it is legitimate to through away the imaginary part of the SD matrix in the OMA. The comparison items will be the identified natural frequencies and the mode shapes. For the mode shapes, we will use the angle (the inverse of the MAC value) between the identified mode shape vector with the reference (actual) mode shape vector to assess the accuracy of the estimated mode shapes. Here is a brief introduction of the simulation case considered in this study.

The modal parameters are identified using the Polyreference technique [2][4]. The numerical modal model we consider in this study has four DOF's. Thus, using a Polyreference technique with two autoregressive matrices will have four modes, and as a result an identification with the two physical modes and two noise modes.

In the simulation, the first frequency f_1 is fixed, while the second frequency f_2 will be moving along the frequency line from close to f_1 to $0.75 f_{Ny}$. Table 1 gives a basic setting for the numerical simulation.

Table 1. Basic settings for the numerical simulation

Sample interval	$\Delta t = 0.323$
Data length for FFT	$\text{Nfft} = 512$
Number of segments.	$N_e = 32$
Total data points	$N = 1024 \times 32$
Frequency interval	$\Delta f = 1/(\text{Nfft} \times \Delta t) = 0.006\text{Hz}$
Number of runs	$N_r = 100$
Nyquist frequency	$f_{Ny} = 1/2\Delta t \approx 1.545\text{Hz}$
Noise level	1% of the maximum standard deviation of the 4 channels
Damping ratio	$\xi = 0.01$ for all four modes
Modal mass	Unity
First resonance frequency	$f_1 = 0.25 f_{Ny} \approx 0.386\text{Hz}$
Second frequency	$f_2 \in [0.404, 1.129]\text{Hz}$ which is ranging from f_1 to $0.75 f_{Ny}$.
Noise modes	Randomly generated with frequencies between $0.25 f_1$ to f_{Ny}.

Note that the initial vectors or actual modes we used to generate the responses are calculated in a random fashion, and between each vector a maximum 10% MAC value limit is given. This is needed to secure a lower linear correlation between each mode, since practically, the normal mode should be statistically independent with each other. Besides, all the initial vectors are real.

3.2. Identification results and discussion

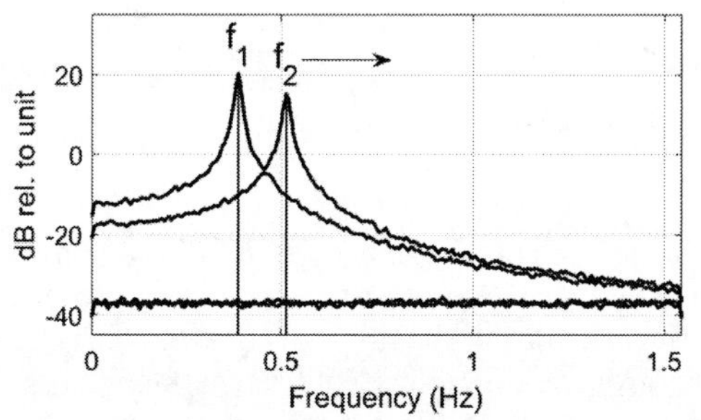

Figure 2. Singular values of spectral matrix

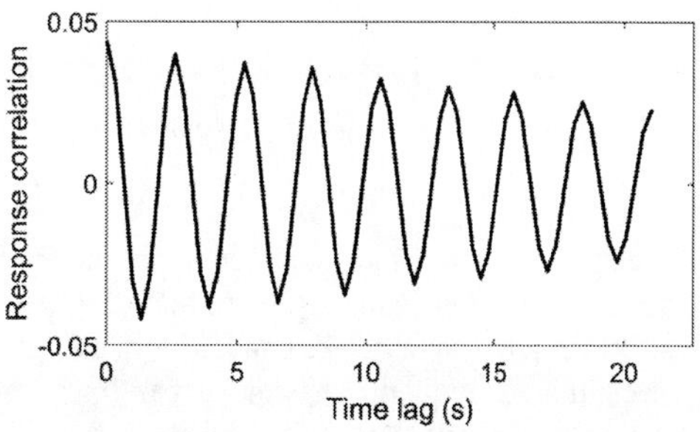

Figure 3. Response correlation of the system

The SD matrices of responses are estimated from the simulated responses via the Welch method. From here, the simulation will be split into two routes.

1. The first one keeps the classical SD matrices then take it back to the time domain by using inverse Fast Fourier transform (iFFT). What we obtained is the real-valued correlation matrices.
2. The other one will follow the idea given by Eq. (34), but we will not use it. Instead, we use the real value of the SD matrices from the whole positive axis. The reason being that we want to use traditional iFFT in which the negative axis is put equal to the values on the positive axis complex conjugate in order to secure a real-valued time domain function. Just like the one-sided SD according to Eq. (34) secures the right covariance matrix, also this iFFT gives the right covariance matrix.

The rest of the procedure will be the same. We apply the Polyreference method to the estimated correlation matrices we obtained from above procedure, but we take the transpose of all matrices in order to make sure that each column represents an unbiased free response as mentioned in Brincker and Ventura [4].

Figure 2 shows the singular value plot from one of the simulations based on the real-value SD. It should be pointed out that this plot is obtained by using the FDD (Frequency Domain Decomposition) method [4]. Figure 3 shows the response correlation of the system from one of the simulations based on the real-valued SD.

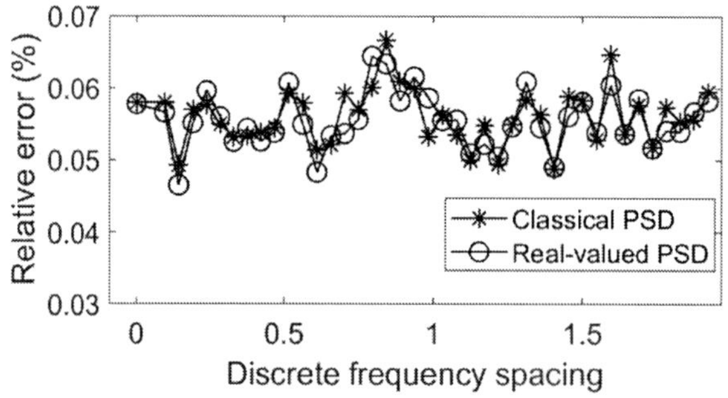

(a) Mode 1

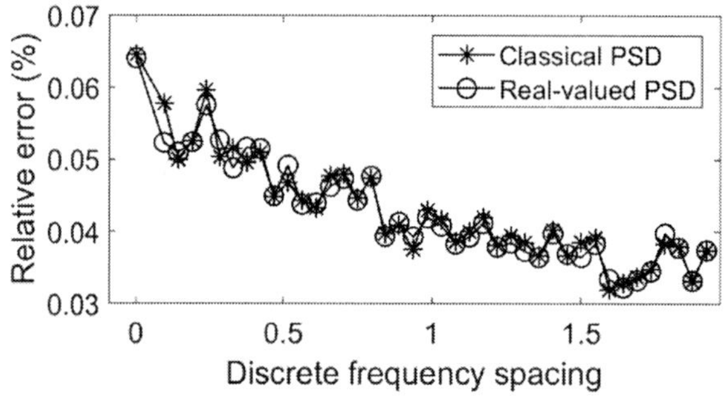

(b) Mode 2

Figure 4. Relative error (%) of the estimated frequencies

The relative errors of the estimated frequencies between the reference frequencies for the two physical modes are shown in Figure 4. Note that each point shown as a circle or an asterisk is an average of 100 runs. Extremely values were handled by setting the relative error threshold up to 0.2%. In other words, if the estimated frequency has more than 0.2% relative error, we deem the identification failed, then we discard that estimation. Besides, the abscissa of both plots shows the relative frequency spacing between f_2 and f_1, which is computed through the following fashion

$$r_f = \frac{f_2 - f_1}{f_1} \quad (36)$$

Since f_1 is fixed, there is no apparent trend to tell from Figure 4. (a) for the first mode. While for the second mode, the relative errors decrease with increasing frequency spacing. Furthermore, if we compare the relative errors between the two different procedure for these two modes, we cannot really tell the differences between the identified results, for the relative errors we obtained based on the classical SD are similar to the relative errors we obtained in terms of the real-valued SD. Additionally, the errors for both modes based on those two different procedures are all very low, they are both less than 0.07%. Overall, it means that the defined real-valued SD matrix makes sense, since the results in Figure. 4 tells us that the lack of the imaginary information of the SD matrix will not affect the identification of the natural frequency of the system.

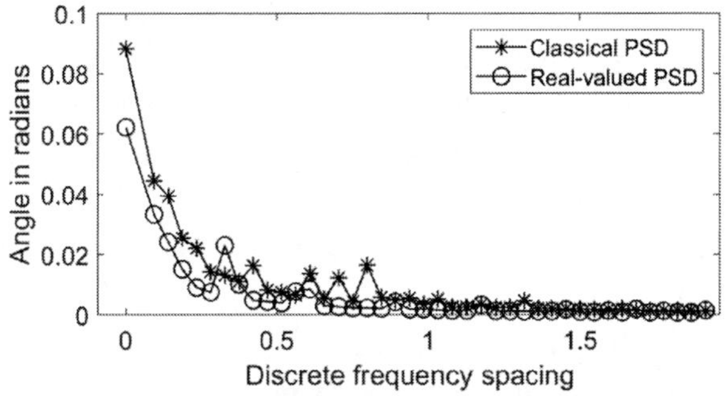

(a) Mode 1

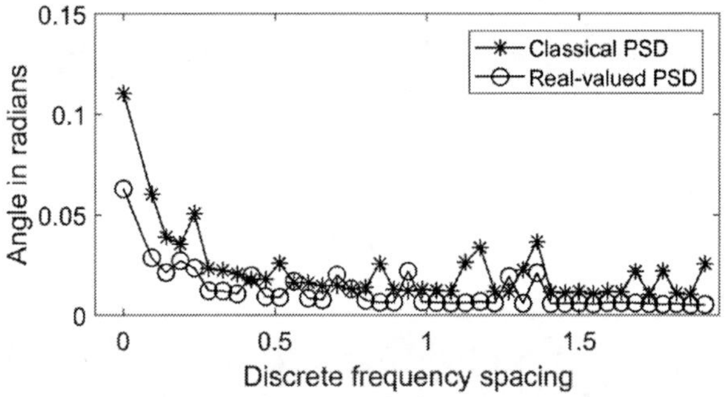

(b) Mode 2

Figure 5. Average angles between the identified mode shape and the refence mode shape

The results in Figure 5 further confirm this conclusion. From Figure 5 we see that, both modes show a decrease in error when the spacing gets larger, and we also see that the real-valued SD results in smaller errors on the mode shapes. It is well-known that when we get closer to the repeated pole case (when the frequency spacing approaches zero), then the two closely spaced mode will interact by rotating the two mode shapes in their common subspace, see Brincker and Aenlle [3]. However, we clearly see that the tendency is the same for the two approaches, and we also see that the angles by using the real-valued SD matrix decrease to about 30-50 % of the angles that we have used the classical complex valued SD.

4. CONCLUSIONS

In this paper, the new concept, real-valued one-sided SD matrix, which fulfils the Parseval's theorem, is verified by conducting a comparative simulation study with the classical complex-valued SD matrix. The simulation results clearly show that both approaches give the same level of accuracy for the frequencies. For the mode shapes the error measured as the MAC angles between the exact and the estimated mode shapes seem to be smaller when we use the real-valued SD matrix. Therefore, the results of the analysis support the initial hypothesis that we can remove the complex part of the SD matrix without losing quality in the identification process. However, whether the real-valued SD matrix is good for estimating the complex modes still needs to be investigated.

REFERENCES

[1] Bendat, J. S., & Piersol, A. G. (2010). *Random data: analysis and measurement procedures.*

[2] Brincker, R. (2014). Some Elements of Operational Modal Analysis. *Shock and Vibration*, 1–11.

[3] Brincker, R., & Lopez-Aenlle, M. (2015). Mode shape sensitivity of two closely spaced eigenvalues. *Journal of Sound and Vibration*, 334, 377–387.

[4] Brincker, R., & Ventura, C. E. (2015). *Introduction to Operational Modal Analysis. Introduction to Operational Modal Analysis*. Chichester, UK: John Wiley & Sons, Ltd.

[5] Maia, M. M., & Silva, M. . N. (1998). *Theoretical and Experimental Modal Analysis.* Research Studies Press.

[6] Proakis, J. G., & Manolakis, D. G. (2007). *Digital signal processing*. Pearson Prentice Hall.

[7] Stein, J. (Y). (2000). *Digital Signal Processing: A Computer Science Perspective.* New York, USA: John Wiley & Sons, Inc.

[8] Stoica, P., & Moses, R. L. (2005). *Spectral analysis of signals*. Pearson/Prentice Hall.

IOMAC'19

8th International Operational Modal Analysis Conference

2019 May13-15 Copenhagen

DETECTION OF NONLINEAR BEHAVIOR USING THE RANDOM DECREMENT TECHNIQUE

Karsten Krautwald Vesterholm[1], *Rune Brincker*[2], *Anders Brandt*[3]

[1] PhD student, Institute of Technology and Innovation, University of Southern Denmark (SDU), kav@iti.sdu.dk

[2] Professor, Department of Civil Engineering, Technical University of Denmark (DTU), runeb@byg.dtu.dk

[3] Associate Professor, Institute of Technology and Innovation, University of Southern Denmark (SDU), abra@sdu.dk

MOTIVATION/DESCRIPTION

Linearity is assumed in operational modal analysis (OMA), but this assumption is not always valid, and the detection method proposed here could help confirm or reject the assumption. This study investigates how the Random Decrement (RD) technique can be used as an output-only method of detecting nonlinear behavior. The RD technique involves identifying triggering points (TPs) in a response signal. For the detection method presented in this study, the RD technique is applied using the level crossing triggering condition. This means every time the response signal crosses some defined level, a triggering point is identified. The slope of the response signal at the identified TPs is random, and the slope is assumed to have no influence on the RD signature for linear systems. This assumption forms the basis of the procedure proposed in this study. n groups of TPs are defined based on the differentiated response signal. From each group of TPs, a RD signature is calculated. These are called group members. Grouping the TPs from the response of a system exhibiting nonlinear behavior in this way, causes the RD signatures calculated from the different groups of TPs to have different properties. For a linear system, the grouping does not cause a change in the RD signatures, thus allowing the detection of nonlinear behavior. The Shape Invariance Criteria (SIC) is used to compare RD signatures from different groups. SIC is the same calculation as the Modal Assurance Criteria (MAC), where instead of mode shapes, RD signatures are compared.

In Figure 1, the proposed steps to perform a detection of nonlinear behavior are presented. These steps are part of the analysis framework known as Nonlinearity Optimized Random Decrement (NORD), which is a framework for using RD to analyze various aspects of structural dynamical systems that are nonlinear.

RELEVANT RESULTS

The analysis procedure presented in Figure 1 is tested on two numerical SDOF systems, a linear case and a nonlinear case. The nonlinear case is a Duffing oscillator. The response of these two systems are simulated with a a zero mean Gaussian excitation force. The detection procedure is performed using 4 groups.

From a visual inspection of Figure 2 with analysis results of the linear system, the 4 RD signatures, one from each group, are overlapping almost entirely. This is confirmed by the SIC plot, where a value of

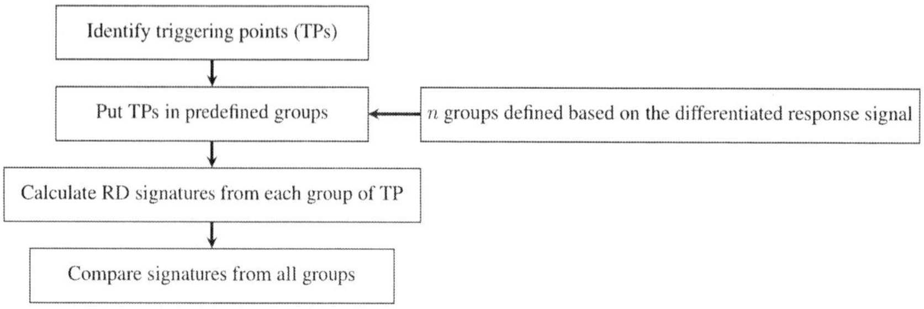

Figure 1: Block diagram of the steps of NORD, that has a focus on detecting nonlinear behavior

1 indicates that the signatures are equal. The lowest value is here 0.99, meaning the RD signatures are almost equal. When inspecting Figure 3 with results from the nonlinear system, the 4 RD signatures, are not overlapping. Here, the SIC plot again confirms this observation because many SIC values are significantly lower than 1, indicating that the signatures are different. Based on these two cases, nonlinear behavior can be differentiated from linear behavior in a qualitative way.

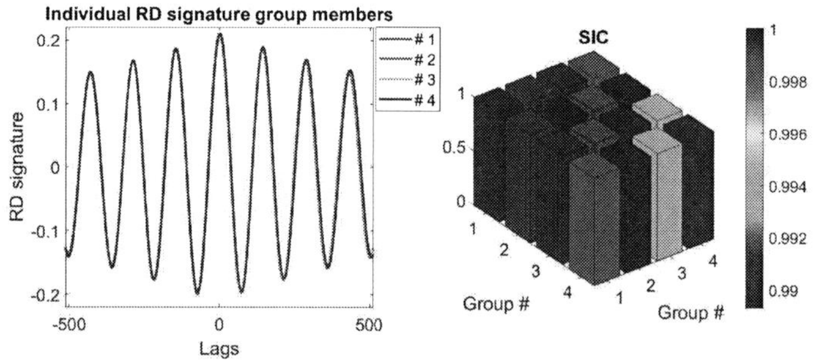

Figure 2: Linear SDOF system, left panel RD signatures calculated using the TPs from the 4 groups. Right panel illustrates the SIC when comparing all the groups

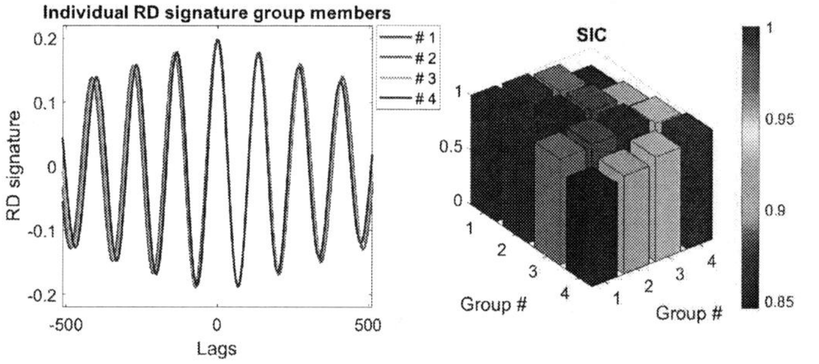

Figure 3: Nonlinear SDOF system a Duffing oscillator, left panel RD signatures calculated using the TPs from the 4 groups. Right panel illustrates the SIC when comparing all the groups

ACKNOWLEDGEMENTS

The authors acknowledge the funding received from Centre for Oil and Gas - DTU/Danish Hydrocarbon Research and Technology Centre (DHRTC).

CONCLUSIONS

The proposed method of detecting nonlinear behavior is investigated using two numerical cases of SDOF systems, a linear and a nonlinear. When comparing the random decrement signatures from different slope groups directly, and using the Shape Invariance Criteria, a difference between the linear and nonlinear system can be observed. This indicates that the proposed method can be used to confirm or reject the assumption of linearity in OMA. The method must be examined further to validate the assumption of the linear case being unaffected by grouping the triggering points.

IOMAC'19

8th International Operational Modal Analysis Conference
2019 May13-15 Copenhagen

ENABLING STRUCTURAL MODIFICATION THEORY FOR OMA

Joerg Bienert[1]

[1] Prof. Dr.-Ing., Technische Hochschule Ingolstadt THI, joerg.bienert@thi.de.

ABSTRACT

OMA has many practical advantages and has been established in the recent years. The disadvantage of unscaled mode shapes remained. Papers in the past have shown, that measurements with and without additional mass make it possible to find the scaling factor modal mass. The amount of additional mass can be optimized on the error estimations of the OMA data. Based on that classical FRFs can be synthesized and this paper show how structural modifications can be analysed on this FRF basis. Simple applications are mass, damping or stiffness modifications at single DOF. A more elaborate application is the structural coupling. Here also rotational DOF have to be considered. Other requirements are correct rigid body modes and no modal truncation. The theory is explained in detail and examples are shown for physical data.

Keywords: Comparison with Traditional Modal Analysis, Modal Scaling

1. INTRODUCTION

1.1. What is structural modification theory?

Structural modification theory is a well established method in structural dynamics. It is a consequent idea from the beginnings of FEM modelling and modal analysis as it reduces the effort for numerical simulation and testing as well.

1.1.1. Parametric type

The classical method is the parametric type with is based on the system matrices in analytical models.

$$\mathbf{M} \cdot \ddot{\mathbf{x}} + \mathbf{C} \cdot \dot{\mathbf{x}} + \mathbf{K} \cdot \mathbf{x} = 0 \tag{1}$$

Here the classical symbols for mass, damping and stiffness matrix are used, that are in the linear differential equation for the motion vector $\mathbf{x}$. By using the mode shape vector for a coordinate transformation

$$\mathbf{x} = \boldsymbol{\Theta} \cdot \mathbf{q} \tag{2}$$

the equation of motion can be made diagonal

$$\mathbf{M_0} \cdot \ddot{\mathbf{q}} + \mathbf{C_0} \cdot \dot{\mathbf{q}} + \mathbf{K_0} \cdot \mathbf{q} = \mathbf{0}. \tag{3}$$

The change of the structure by a mechanical modification would require a new setup of the system matrices and the analysis needs to be repeated without making profit of the former result. If the DOF do not change or only change slightly the former system can be modified by the changes in the system matrices $\boldsymbol{\Delta M}, \boldsymbol{\Delta C}, \boldsymbol{\Delta K}$ that yields in a modified system which is formulated in the modal coordinates of the former one

$$\left(\mathbf{M_0} + \Theta^{\mathrm{T}} \Delta \mathbf{M} \Theta\right) \cdot \ddot{\mathbf{q}} + \left(\mathbf{C_0} + \Theta^{\mathrm{T}} \Delta \mathbf{C}\, \Theta\right) \cdot \dot{\mathbf{q}} + \left(\mathbf{K_0} + \Theta^{\mathrm{T}} \Delta \mathbf{K}\, \Theta\right) \cdot \mathbf{q} = \mathbf{0}. \tag{4}$$

After the solution of the second, usually reduced size eigenvalue problem, the problem is solved and the motion of the physical DOF needs reverse modal transformation. This method can be applied also to experimental techniques. The mode shapes must be known at least at the modification DOF. Mode shapes are taken from the classical EMA as a scaling is necessary to setup the modal mass matrix $\mathbf{M_0}$. Additionally modal truncation errors may occur as the measured mode shapes do not represent the full system.

1.1.2. Non-parametric type

An improvement for the experimental approach is the non-parametric modification as the input is the measured transfer functions (FRFs) which does not suffer from modal truncation.

$$X_j = H_{jk} \cdot F_k \tag{5}$$

The question would be how the modifications $\Delta m, \Delta c, \Delta k$ or even rigid coupling $X_j = X_l$ can be introduced into the FRF. The desired FRF is the modified one which is formulated as the difference ΔH_{jk} to the unmodified system.

$$^{m}H_{jk} = H_{jk} + \Delta H_{jk} \tag{6}$$

To find this difference some basic mechanical constraints have to be introduced so that is yields in a algebraic formula for $\Delta \boldsymbol{H_{jk}}$.

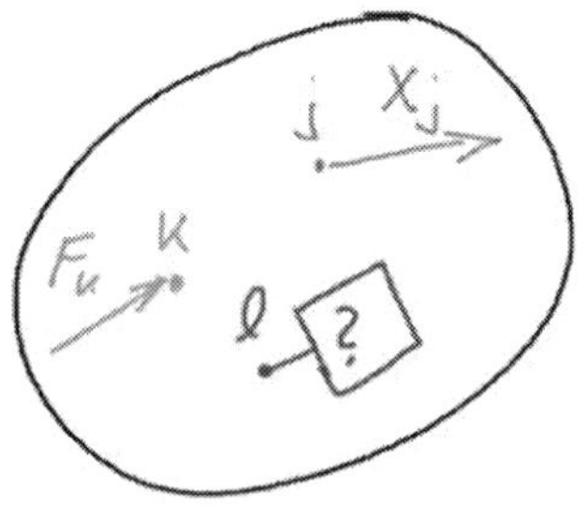

Figure 1. Data set used in the experiments.

Assume that we add a modification at the DOF named l. Then the modification introduces reaction forces $\mathbf{R_Z}$ that influence the transfer behavior between j and k.

$$\mathbf{X} = -\mathbf{H}_R \cdot \mathbf{R}_Z + \boldsymbol{H}_k \cdot F_k \tag{7}$$

The rearrangement of eq. (7) does not lead to a full rank system of equations

$$[\mathbf{I} \quad \mathbf{H}_R] \begin{bmatrix} \mathbf{X} \\ \mathbf{R}_Z \end{bmatrix} = \boldsymbol{H}_k \cdot F_k \tag{8}$$

as the constraints

$$\boldsymbol{Z}_R \begin{bmatrix} \boldsymbol{X} \\ \boldsymbol{R}_Z \end{bmatrix} = \mathbf{0} \tag{9}$$

have also to be considered. Combining both delivers a system with a low number of involved DOF that has to be solved algebraically:

$$\begin{bmatrix} \mathbf{I} & \mathbf{H}_R \\ \mathbf{Z}_R & \end{bmatrix} \begin{bmatrix} \mathbf{X} \\ \mathbf{R}_Z \end{bmatrix} = \boldsymbol{H}_k \cdot F_k \tag{10}$$

Resolving for the unknown ${}^{m}\boldsymbol{H}_{jk}$ a formula can be derived. T

$${}^{m}\boldsymbol{H}_{jk} = \mathbf{f}(\mathbf{H}_R, \boldsymbol{H}_k, \mathbf{Z}_R) \tag{11}$$

This is of course dependent of the type of constraint.

1.2. The lack of OMA and the basic idea

Although the OMA is an established method in structural dynamics the information of the data is less than in classical EMA. The reason is that the excitation forces are not known. The obtained modal data in terms of natural frequencies, damping and mode shapes may belong either to a small or a big real structure. If we are able to scale the eigenvectors to a preferred form of an identity matrix, $\mathbf{M}_0 = \boldsymbol{I}$, then the way for modification theory is open. The obvious way is parametric modification eq.(4). We would have to fill $\mathbf{C}_0$ with damping and $\mathbf{K}_0$ with natural frequency results of the modal analysis. For non-parametric modification the FRFs need to be rebuild from modal data. Also here the modal mass appears in the equation so that the problem of unscaled modes is the same.

To overcome this, the scaling of mode shapes is the target. This has been shown in literature by [1],[2],[3]. The idea is to measure a structure twice in different configurations. The change of frequency is then an indicator for the acting forces. The change between the two modifications must be known. Often an added mass is the simplest way to do that. This approach is also used in this paper. How the scaling works is shown in section 2.2.

2. THEORETICAL BACKGROUND OF STRUCTURAL MODIFICATION

In the following subsections the most important modifications are introduced and the result for the modification formula eq.(11) are given.

2.1. Some types of modifications

2.1.1. Added mass

One basic modification is an added mass on a DOF l. The resonance peaks are shifted to lower frequencies. On the other side the mass can also be negative. This could be used e.g. for the compensation of sensors on the structure.

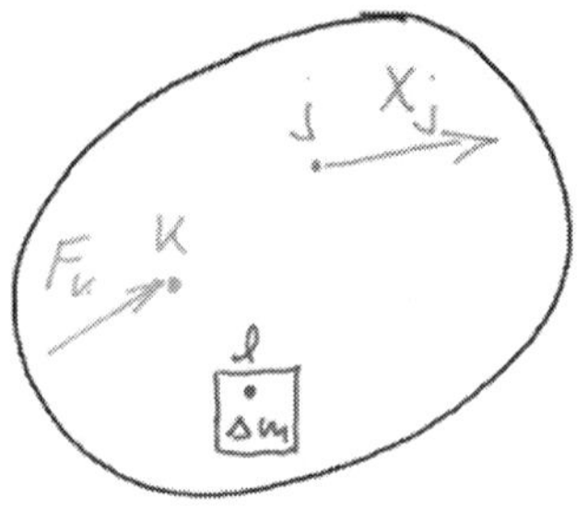

Figure 2. Modification by mass.

The related constraints and the modification formula are:

$$\begin{bmatrix} -H_{jl} & 1 & 0 \\ 1 & 0 & -\Delta m \cdot \Omega^2 \\ -H_{ll} & 0 & 1 \end{bmatrix} \begin{bmatrix} F_l \\ X_j \\ X_l \end{bmatrix} = \begin{bmatrix} H_{jk} \\ 0 \\ H_{lk} \end{bmatrix} \cdot F_k \tag{12}$$

$${}^{m}H_{jk} = H_{jk} - \frac{H_{jl}\, H_{lk}}{H_{ll}\Delta m \cdot \Omega^2 - 1} \tag{13}$$

2.1.2. *Added stiffness*

Stiffnesses can be applied versus the ground or versus other DOF. In Figure 3 the case versus ground is shown. Very similar results will be obtained for dampers.

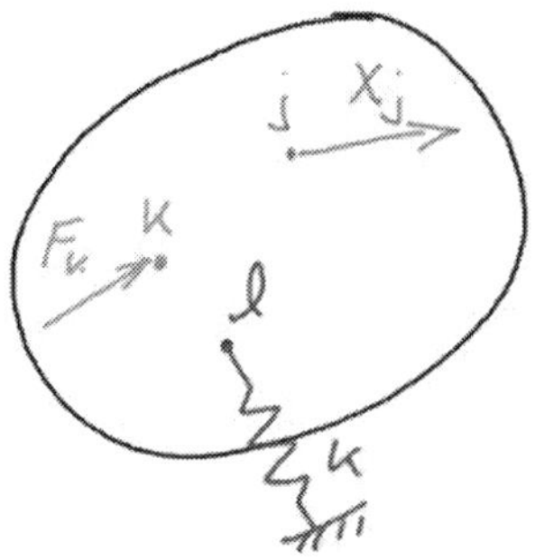

Figure 3. Modification by stiffness to the ground.

$$\begin{bmatrix} -H_{jl} & 1 & 0 \\ 1 & 0 & k \\ -H_{ll} & 0 & 1 \end{bmatrix} \begin{bmatrix} F_l \\ X_j \\ X_l \end{bmatrix} = \begin{bmatrix} H_{jk} \\ 0 \\ H_{lk} \end{bmatrix} \cdot F_k \tag{14}$$

$${}^{m}H_{jk} = H_{jk} - \frac{H_{jl}\, H_{lk}}{H_{ll} \cdot k + 1} \tag{15}$$

2.1.3. *DOF constraint*

DOF may be blocked so that the DOF is equal to zero.

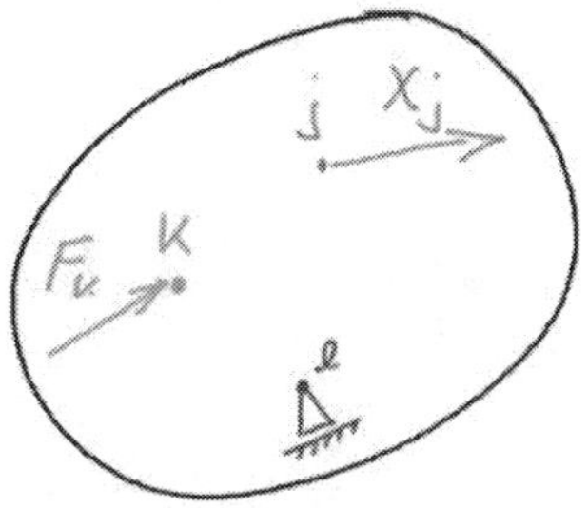

Figure 4. Modification by blocked DOF.

$$\begin{bmatrix} 1 & -H_{jl} \\ 0 & -H_{ll} \end{bmatrix} \begin{bmatrix} X_j \\ F_l \end{bmatrix} = \begin{bmatrix} H_{jk} \\ H_{ll} \end{bmatrix} \cdot F_k \tag{16}$$

$$^{m}H_{jk} = H_{jk} - \frac{H_{jl}\, H_{lk}}{H_{ll}} \tag{17}$$

2.1.4. *Tuned absorber*

The classical countermeasure to suppress a resonance is a tuned absorber. The split of the peak would be visible in the modified FRF.

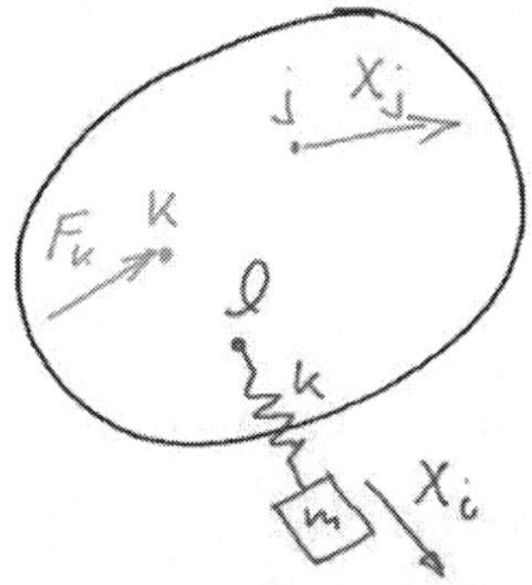

Figure 5. Modification by tuned absorber.

$$\begin{bmatrix} 1 & 0 & 0 & -H_{jl} \\ 0 & 1 & 0 & -H_{ll} \\ 0 & 0 & -m\,\Omega^2 & 1 \\ 0 & -k & +k & -1 \end{bmatrix} \begin{bmatrix} X_j \\ X_l \\ X_i \\ F_l \end{bmatrix} = \begin{bmatrix} H_{jk} \\ H_{lk} \\ 0 \\ 0 \end{bmatrix} \cdot F_k \tag{18}$$

$$^{m}H_{jk} = H_{jk} - \frac{H_{lk}\, H_{jl}\, k}{1 - \dfrac{k}{m\,\Omega^2} + k\, H_{ll}} \tag{19}$$

2.1.5. *Substructure coupling*

More complex is the connection of two DOF, because on each coupling point a force and a displacement is involved. The system of equations can nevertheless been solved. In this case it is not necessary, that the structures are uncoupled before. Also a coupling within a structure works with the same equations. The start with two uncoupled structures I and II looks like the matrix setup in eq.(20). If several DOFs have to be coupled then the modification can be done recursive. The matrix H_g will be updated step by step.

$$H_g = \begin{bmatrix} \boldsymbol{H}^I & \boldsymbol{0} \\ \boldsymbol{0} & \boldsymbol{H}^{II} \end{bmatrix} \tag{20}$$

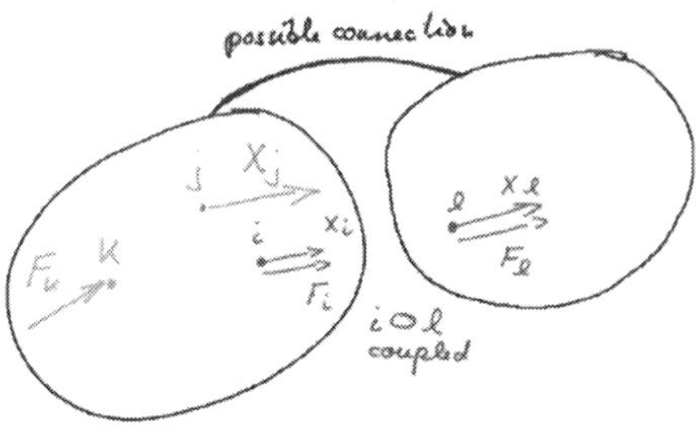

Figure 6. Substructure coupling.

$$\begin{bmatrix} 1 & 0 & 0 & -H_{ji} & -H_{jl} \\ 0 & 1 & 0 & -H_{ii} & -H_{il} \\ 0 & 0 & 1 & -H_{li} & -H_{ll} \\ 0 & 1 & -1 & 0 & 0 \\ 0 & 0 & 0 & 1 & 1 \end{bmatrix} \begin{bmatrix} X_j \\ X_i \\ X_l \\ F_i \\ F_l \end{bmatrix} = \begin{bmatrix} H_{jk} \\ H_{ik} \\ H_{lk} \\ 0 \\ 0 \end{bmatrix} \cdot F_k \tag{21}$$

$$^{m}H_{jk} = H_{jk} - \frac{(H_{ji} - H_{jl})(H_{ik} H_{lk})}{H_{ii} \underbrace{-H_{il} - H_{li}}_{H_{il}=H_{li}} H_{ll}} \tag{22}$$

2.1.6. *Further ideas*

The types of modification may have a lot of additional forms. Some sophisticated ones are e.g. for gyros [5]. This requires rotational DOF for the tilt movement. Then the modification theory can predict the FRF during a rotation with a certain rotational speed. Due to the gyro moments the system matrices get skew symmetric what has to be considered in the FRF matrix.

2.2. Eigenvector scaling by mass modification

As already mentioned the scaling of the mode shapes requires two measurement setups, where the decision was to add a mass for the separation of the cases. The OMA results are the unmodified natural circular frequencies ω_{0-no} for no added mass respectively ω_{0-with} with a single point mass or even a distribution of masses. With the assumption of changes in the frequencies but not in the mode shape a solution will be found. This requires either a small or equally distributed addition of mass. The modal masses are

$$m_{0-no} = \varphi^T \boldsymbol{M} \varphi; \qquad m_{0-with} = \varphi^T (\boldsymbol{M} + \boldsymbol{\Delta M}) \varphi \tag{23}$$

with $m_0 = \frac{k_0}{\omega_0^2}$ where k_0 keeps constant. From the ratio of the modified to the unmodified system

$$\frac{m_{0-with}}{m_{0-no}} = \frac{1}{\omega_{0-no}^2} \frac{\omega_{0-with}^2}{1} \tag{24}$$

one obtain the modal mass of the unmodified system:

$$m_{0-no} = \frac{\varphi^T \mathbf{\Delta M} \varphi}{\frac{\omega_{0-with}^2}{\omega_{0-no}^2} - 1} \tag{25}$$

The FRFs of the base structure can be built with a standard approach.

2.3. Some challenges

2.3.1. The right mass

The choice of the mass should be in accordance to the assumption that the mode shape vector does not change. This means, that a good result can be expected if the additional mass loading is proportional to the base mass of the structure. In most cases this will be difficult to apply.

A more simple way is the point mass at a certain DOF. This DOF should be outside a vibration node. To avoid significant changes the mass should be as small as possible. On the other side the frequency changes should be detected properly with consideration of the variance of the OMA frequency estimation. Table 1 shows an example of the frequency change by two different masses of 4.8 gr and 57.7 gr on a beam of 2.3kg and length of 1m.

Table 1. Frequency changes on a beam by mass loading at the end.

Frequencies from OMA [Hz]						
no mass	63,09	168,04	326,06	537,89	801,35	1118,56
4,76g	62,63	167,39	325,15	536,86	799,42	1114,97
57,7g	60,57	161,95	315,43	520,94	777,39	1085,40
Differences to "no mass loading" [Hz]						
4,76g	0,47	0,65	0,90	1,03	1,92	3,59
57,7g	2,52	6,09	10,63	16,95	23,96	33,16

2.3.2. Rotational DOF

Especially for structural coupling it is also necessary to consider rotational DOF. As already a simple example of a beam demonstrates the coupling of two beams by translational DOF only would result in a beam connected by a hinge. The typical approach to find slopes is the differential quotient. This can be applied be two neighbour DOF where again the difference of both must be outside the shape estimation variance. In many cases the polynomial fit of more than two DOF would improve the result.

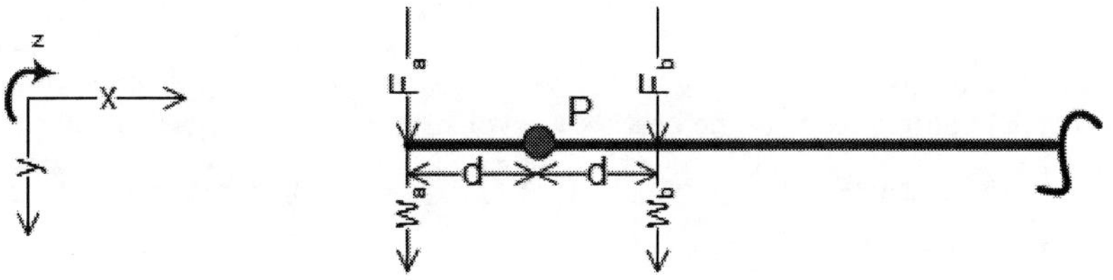

Figure 7. Substructure coupling with rotational DOF.

- $\varphi = \frac{1}{2\,d}(w_b - w_a)$
- $\frac{\varphi}{F_P} = \frac{1}{2\,d}(H_{bP} - H_{aP})$
- $\frac{y_P}{M} = \frac{1}{2\,d}(H_{bP} - H_{aP})$ (26)
- $\frac{\varphi}{M} = \frac{1}{(2\,d)^2}(H_{bb} - H_{ba} - H_{ab}b + H_{aa})$

3. DEMONSTRATION IN A LAB EXAMPLE

3.1. Test setup

To test new methods it is recommended that simple structures are used where the result is mostly known. In this case it is a homogeneous steel beam with rectangular cross section of the dimension 100x2,5x1,0 cm. The bearing condition is on soft foam, so that there are no distinct rigid body modes. As the rigid body modes are mandatory for the correct coupling they are obtained analytically. For more complex structures CAD would deliver the necessary mass distribution.

For the OMA excitation a small hammer with random distributed impacts was used. This leads to a very clear SVD diagram. The FRF reconstruction was based on 11 modes.

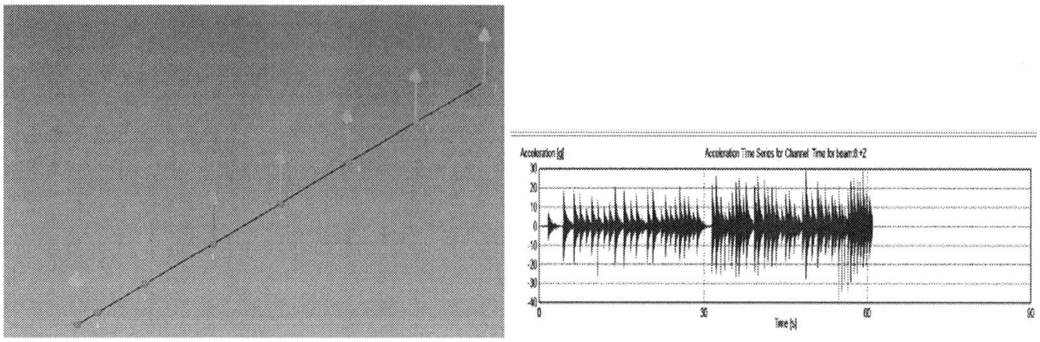

Figure 8. Beam with random impacts.

3.2. Application of modifications

All modifications could be applied successfully. As an example the result of added mass and tuned absorber are shown in fig. 9.

For the end point the driving point FRFs are plotted. The left diagram shows the FRF which is shifted to lower frequencies by the additional mass. This FRF meets the resonance peaks of the direct measurement with added mass. For the right diagram an absorber of 0,5% of the mass of the beam was tuned to the first natural frequency of the beam. The typical split of the frequency follows.

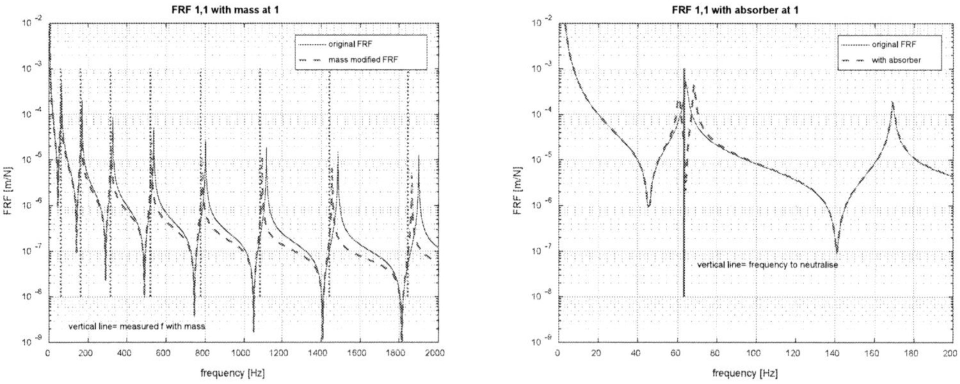

Figure 9. Added Mass (57gr - left); tuned absorber (tuning freq. = 1st nat. freq.).

3.3. MDOF rigid coupling

The coupling example is performed for the case that two equal beams of the former dimensions are coupled at one end. Beside the translational DOF 1 the rotational DOF has to be considered. This was realized by the differential quotient of DOF 1 and 8 that have a distance of 3 cm.

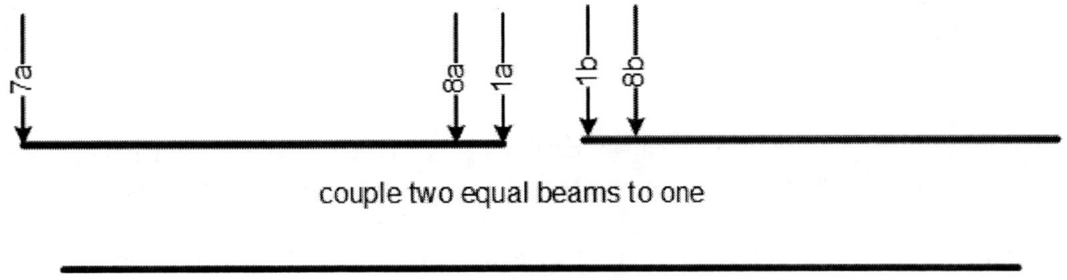

Figure 10. Beam coupling.

As the beams are equal it is known that the frequencies scale to ¼ due to $f \sim \frac{1}{L^2}$. Therefore the expected frequencies can be predicted by the vertical lines. The FRFs after the consecutive coupling of 2 DOF in fig. 11 show that the expected result is met. The result deteriorates a bit with higher frequencies as the modal truncation error comes into play. The second new mode has only a resonance peak for the FRF 7/7. The FRF 1/1 does not have the resonance here as after the coupling DOF 1 becomes a node in the middle of the beam.

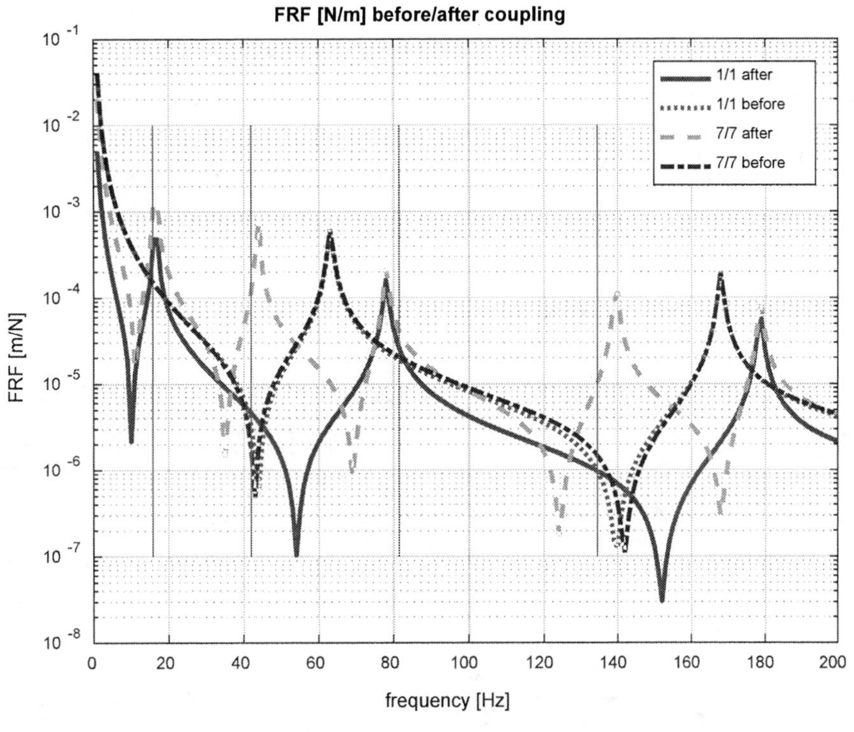

Figure 11. FRFs after substructure coupling.

4. SUMMARY AND OUTLOOK

The mode shape scaling is not a new idea but it is a necessary step to get FRFs in structural dynamics. The procedure has been explained theoretically and has been applied for a beam structure. After this a whole new field of applications is possible. The rigid coupling becomes the most challenging. This is not because of the theory behind. The very stiff coupling has a demand for very exact FRFs that have been rebuilt. This iterative coupling of several DOF exaggerates this.

REFERENCES

[1] Foltête, E. (2008): "Multiple operational mode shapes normalization from mass change". In: Proceedings of ISMA2008:2471–2480.

[2] Parloo, E. et al. (2002): "Sensitivity-Based Operational Mode Shape Normalization". In: Mechanical Systems and Signal Processing:757– 767

[3] Brincker, R. and P. Andersen (2003): "A Way of Getting Scaled Mode Shapes in Output Only Modal Testing". In: Proceedings of the 21st International Modal Analysis Conference (IMAC).

[4] Melnikov, A. et al (2017): "Determination of static stiffness from operational modal analysis", In: Proceedings of the 7th International Operational Modal Analysis Conference (IOMAC), THI Ingolstadt.

[5] Bienert, J. (1998): "Strukturmodifikation in der Modalanalyse am Beispiel der Kreiselwirkung von Rotoren"; VDI Fortschrittberichte, Reihe 11, Nr. 255, VDI Verlag, Düsseldorf.

IOMAC'19

8th International Operational Modal Analysis Conference
2019 May 13-15 Copenhagen

ENHANCED MODE SHAPE ESTIMATION IN MULTI-DATASET OMA USING FREQUENCY DOMAIN DECOMPOSITION

Sandro D. R. Amador [1] *and Rune Brincker* [2]

[1] Assistent Professor, Technical University of Denmark, Department of Civil Engineering, Brovej, Building 118, DK-2800 Kongens Lyngby, Denmark, sdio@byg.dtu.com.
[2] Full Professor, Technical University of Denmark, Department of Civil Engineering, Brovej, Building 118, DK-2800 Kongens Lyngby, Denmark, runeb@byg.dtu.dk.

ABSTRACT
The identification of the global mode shapes in multi-dataset vibration tests with the classic Frequency Domain Decomposition is carried out by identifying each dataset individually and by merging the individual mode shape parts with aid of the reference mode shape components. It turns out that, in case of closely spaced modes, the mode shape parts in the different datasets are computed from subspaces that are affected differently by the closest modes. In this circumstance, the global mode shape vectors formed by merging all the mode shape parts might not yield well-defined global shapes. In other to overpass this issue, another strategy is proposed in this paper to force the mode shape parts corresponding to each dataset to be in the same subspace, and thus, yield global mode shapes with clearer configuration. The efficiency of the proposed strategy is demonstrated using an application example in the final part of the paper.

Keywords: Modal Identification, Frequency Domain Decomposition, Multi-dataset Identification, Global Mode Shapes

1. INTRODUCTION

The classic FDD [1, 2] uses the data-driven spectra estimates - or the so-called *periodogram* or *Welch's* method [3], as it is known from scientific literature - as primary data to estimate the natural frequencies and their corresponding mode shapes. When dealing with multi-dataset vibration tests, the identification of the global mode shapes with classic FDD is carried out basically by identifying the modes shape parts from each dataset and by, subsequently, merging the identified mode shape parts with aid of the reference sensors to yield global mode shapes of the tested structure. A detailed description of the classic multi-dataset FDD can be found, for instance, in [4].

Under varying operating conditions, however, the measured datasets are excited differently by the operating/ambient conditions. In this circumstances, it is not always possible to extract the same physical modes from every measured dataset. In addition to these identification issues, the estimated global mode shapes might present unclear modal configuration if the modes are not well excited in all the measured datasets and/or if closely spaced are being estimated. In order overcome these issue, a new scaling approach based on geometric projection of the individual mode shape parts is described in [7]. In [5, 6, 9] this problem is addressed from the parametric modal identification perspective by merging the different datasets into a global data structure, which is subsequently used as primary data by the parametric modal identification techniques.

In this contribution, another approach is used to estimate the global mode shapes from multi-dataset output-only vibration data with FDD technique. The innovative aspects of this approach with regard to its classic FDD are related to the fact that: (i) rather than classic *periodogram*, the correlation-driven spectra [3, 8] are used as primary data to estimate the natural frequencies and global mode shapes; and (2) the identification of the global mode shapes is performed by taking the singular value decomposition of a global spectrum matrix which is assembled by stacking the spectrum matrix of the different datasets on the top of each other.

The application of the proposed correlation spectrum based FDD is assessed and compared to the classic *periodogram*-driven FDD in the final part of the paper by means of a multi-dataset output-only vibration test of a pedestrian bridge.

2. BACKGROUND THEORY

2.1. Correlation driven Spectrum Estimation

The multi-dataset FDD introduced in this paper uses the correlation spectra matrix (also known from literature as "*correlogram*" spectra [3, 8]) as primary data rather than the *periodogram* spectrum (also known as "*Welch's*" spectrum). The non-parametric spectrum estimation from correlation functions is accomplished by taking the discrete Fourier Transform of the correlation function, $R_k \in \mathbb{R}^{N_o \times N_o}$, as follows

$$G_{yy}(\omega_f) = \sum_{k=-L}^{L} w_k R_k e^{-j\omega_f k \Delta t} \tag{1}$$

where $G_{yy}(\omega_f) \in \mathbb{C}^{N_o \times N_o}$ is the spectrum matrix computed at the discrete angular frequencies, ω_f, with N_o denoting the number of measured sensors used in the output-only vibration test; L is the maximum number of *time lags* at which the correlation matrices are estimated; w_k denotes a window function used to minimize the leakage and the statistical errors of the higher correlation *lags* on the resulting spectral matrix, Δt is the sampling interval and $j = \sqrt{-1}$ stands for the imaginary unit. The correlation driven spectrum is widely used as primary data in parametric output-only modal identification, as seen, for instance, in [8], [10] and [11]. A detailed description of the non-parametric spectrum estimation technique based correlation functions can be found, for instance, in [3].

2.2. Pre-Scaled Global Mode Shapes

In classic *periodogram* spectrum based FDD, the identification of the global mode shapes are carried out by taking the **SVD** of the spectral densities corresponding to each patch individually and subsequently merging the obtained mode shape parts together with aid of the reference mode shape components that are common to all datasets. It turns out that, in presence of closely spaced or poorly excited modes, the accuracy of resulting global mode shapes obtained by merging all the mode shape parts can be compromised, leading to unclear global mode shape configurations. In this circumstances, the main advantages of using the correlation spectrum driven FDD in multi-dataset OMA with regard its *periodogram* spectrum driven counterpart is that, since the leakage on the spectrum estimates is minimized by making use of an exponential window, the spectral densities of each dataset can be stacked on the top each other to form a global spectral matrix. This merging strategy has been widely explored in parametric modal identification to yield the global mode shapes (as seen, for instance, in [6, 5, 11]), and is herein extended to the non-parametric modal parameter estimation with the correlation spectrum FDD. In order to construct this global spectral matrix, it is convenient to partition the spectra matrix of the ith patch, $G_{yy,i}$, as follows

$$G_{yy,i} = \begin{bmatrix} G_{yy_{ref},i} & G_{yy_{mov},i} \end{bmatrix} = \begin{bmatrix} G_{y_{ref}y_{ref},i} & G_{y_{ref}y_{mov},i} \\ G_{y_{mov}y_{ref},i} & G_{y_{mov}y_{mov},i} \end{bmatrix}, \forall i \in \{1, 2, \ldots, N_p\} \tag{2}$$

where $G_{yy_{ref},i} \in \mathbb{C}^{N_o \times N_{ref}}$ and $G_{yy_{mov},i} \in \mathbb{C}^{N_o \times N_{mov}}$ are the cross-spectra between all the responses and the reference responses, and cross-spectra between all the responses and the roving responses; $G_{y_{ref}y_{ref},i} \in \mathbb{C}^{N_{ref} \times N_{ref}}$, $G_{y_{mov}y_{ref},i} \in \mathbb{C}^{N_{mov} \times N_{ref}}$, $G_{y_{ref}y_{mov},i} \in \mathbb{C}^{N_{ref} \times N_{mov}}$ and $G_{y_{mov}y_{mov},i} \in \mathbb{C}^{N_{mov} \times N_{mov}}$ are the auto-spectra matrix of the reference responses, the cross-spectra matrix between the roving and reference responses, the cross-spectra matrix between the reference and roving responses and the auto-spectra matrix of the roving responses, with N_{ref} and N_{mov} standing for the number of reference and moving sensors, respectively, and the subscript i denoting the ith measured dataset; and N_p stands for the number patches used in the multi-patch output-only vibration test. Once the spectra matrix of each patch is partitioned according to eqs. (2), the global (scaled) spectrum matrix containing all the patches, $G_s(\omega) \in \mathbb{C}^{(N_{ref}+N_pN_{mov}) \times N_{ref}}$, can be computed for each frequency line, ω_f, as follows

$$G_s(\omega_f) = \begin{bmatrix} G_{y_{ref}y_{ref},R}(\omega_f) \\ G_{y_{mov}y_{ref},1}(\omega_f) G_{y_{ref}y_{ref},1}(\omega_f)^{-1} G_{y_{ref}y_{ref},R}(\omega_f) \\ \vdots \\ G_{y_{mov}y_{ref},N_p}(\omega_f) G_{y_{ref}y_{ref},N_p}(\omega_f)^{-1} G_{y_{ref}y_{ref},R}(\omega_f) \end{bmatrix} \tag{3}$$

where $G_{y_{ref}y_{ref},R} \in \mathbb{C}^{N_{ref} \times N_{ref}}$ is the reference spectra matrix used to scale the spectra matrix of each patch. In [6], it is proposed that this matrix should chosen as the average over the reference spectra matrices of the different patches, i.e

$$G_{y_{ref}y_{ref},R}(\omega_f) = \frac{1}{N_p} \sum_{i=1}^{N_p} G_{y_{ref}y_{ref},i}(\omega_f) \tag{4}$$

By following the merging strategy synthesized by eq. (3), one scales the spectra matrix of each patch before the identification takes place. This is illustrated by the identification flowchart depicted in Fig 1. This strategy has been widely applied to estimate the global mode shapes using parametric modal identification techniques, as verified, for instance, in [6, 5]. The underlying idea of this strategy is that, by stacking the pre-scaled spectra matrix of each patch on the top of each other, one forces the different mode shape parts to be in the same subspace. In this paper, this idea is extended to the non-parametric identification with FDD. In this case, the identification of the global mode shapes is carried out by simply taking the SVD of the formed (pre-scaled) global spectrum matrix, $G_s(\omega_f)$, as

$$G_s(\omega_f) = U_{G_s}(\omega_f) S_{G_s}(\omega_f) V_{G_s}^H(\omega_f) \tag{5}$$

where $U_{G_s}(\omega_f) \in \mathbb{C}^{(N_{ref}+N_pN_{mov}) \times (N_{ref}+N_pN_{mov})}$ is matrix containing the global singular vectors, $S_{G_s}(\omega_f) \in \mathbb{C}^{(N_{ref}+N_pN_{mov}) \times N_{ref}}$ is matrix containing the corresponding singular values and $V_{G_s}(\omega_f) \in \mathbb{C}^{N_{ref} \times N_{ref}}$ is a unit singular vectors matrix, with $(\bullet)^H$ denoting the Hermitian (conjugate transpose of a complex matrix). Once the singular value decomposition is computed, the global mode shapes, Φ_G, can be estimated from the singular vectors, $U_{G_s}(\omega_f)$, just like as in classic *periodogram*-driven FDD.

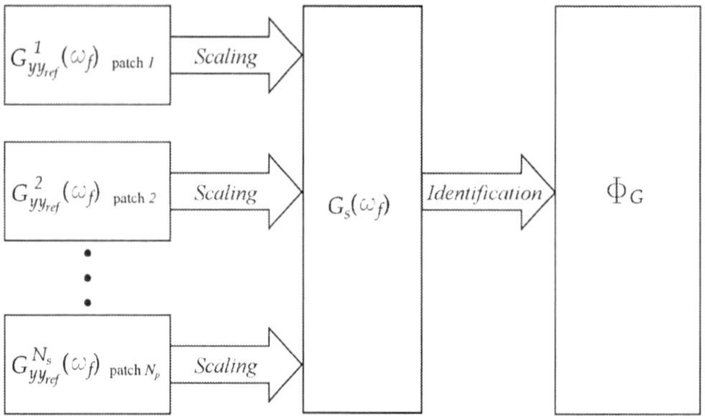

Figure 1 Identification flowchart with the proposed correlation spectrum driven FDD

3. APPLICATION EXAMPLE

The application example consists of a pedestrian footbridge located in Copenhagen area, Denmark. The "Grevestien" Footbridge, as it is known, was constructed to cross the Køge Bugt Motorway (E20/E47) right next to the exit 28. This 10 year old footbridge, which is owned by 'The Danish Road Directory', has a total of four spans and is basically composed by four concrete columns and a continuous pre-stressed concrete girder, as illustrated in Fig. 2.

Figure 2 Photo of the Grevestien Footbridge located in Copenhagen area, Denmark [15]

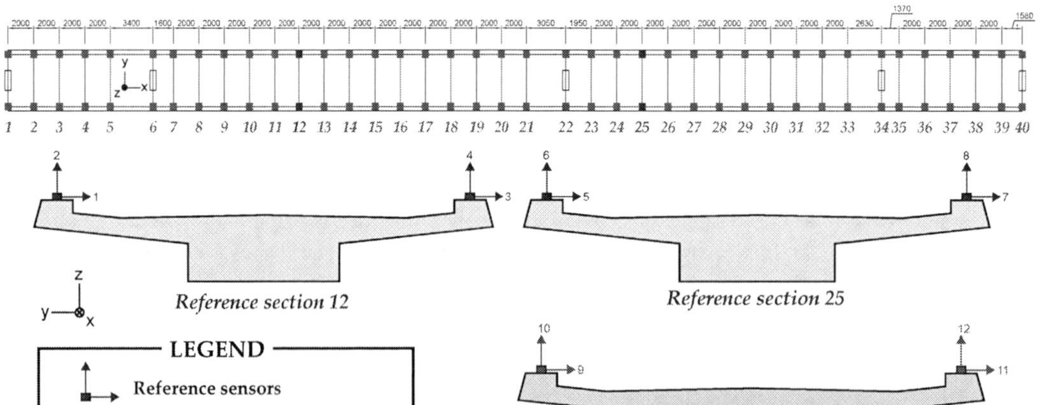

Figure 3 Locations and measurement directions of the reference (blue dots) and roving (red dots) sensors used in the multi-dataset vibration test of the "Grevestien" Footbridge [15]

The middle column was cast in-situ together with the concrete girder, whereas the rest of the marginal columns are simply supporting the main deck of the structure. Further details about the structural system and dimension of the "Grevestien" Footbridge can be found in [15] and references cited therein. The multi-dataset vibration test was carried out to assess the influence of the human-structure interaction on the dynamic performance of footbridges [15]. The ambient-induced responses of a total of 40 sections were measured along length of the structure by means of 38 different datasets to yield its global mode shapes with a high spatial resolution. A total of the 14 geophone sensors was used in each dataset to record the vibration responses of the footbridge in velocity. The sensors mounting locations and measurement directions adopted in the vibration test are indicated in Fig. 3. Each dataset was recorded with a sampling rate of 100 Hz for 10 mins.

3.1. Identification with Classic FDD technique

The classic multi-dataset FDD technique [4] was applied to identify the modal properties of the "Grevestien" Footbridge using the power spectral densities estimated with the *periodogram* approach from the measured velocity responses. The identification was performed with the commercial software ARTeMIS Pro Modal (v4) [14], by making use of the geometrical model of the foot-bridge created based on the dimensions shown in Fig. 3. The velocity vibration responses of the 38 acquired datasets were filtered with a band pass filter defined by a bandpass frequency range of 0.1-25.0 Hz. Afterwards, the power spectral densities were computed from the filtered data signals with a resolution of 2048 frequency lines.

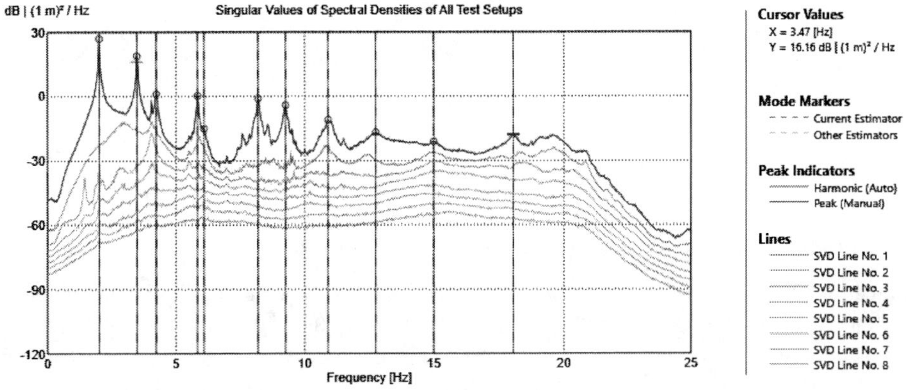

Figure 4 Vibration modes of the "Grevestien" Footbridge identified with the classic FDD technique

Next, the power spectral densities estimated from the filtered signals were used as primary data by the FDD technique to identify the natural frequencies and the corresponding global mode shapes of the "Grevestien" Footbridge. The variations of the singular values computed from the spectral densities of the reference sensors over frequency lines are shown in Fig. 4. A total of 11 vibration modes were clearly identified in the frequency range of 0-25 Hz by simply picking the peaks in the singular values plot. The identification of the natural frequencies with classic FDD consists of identifying the frequencies that correspond to each picked peak.

The identification of the global mode shapes, on the other hand, is basically carried out in two steps: (1) by extracting the mode shape parts from the singular vectors of each dataset; and (2) by re-scaling the extracted mode shape parts using the reference mode shape components to yield the global mode shapes associated to the picked peaks. The identification results obtained with the classic multi-dataset FDD for the "Grevestien" Footbridge are summarized in Fig. 5. By quickly inspecting the results shown in this figure, one verifies that, owing to the varying excitation levels over the different measured datasets, some of the global mode shapes do not present well defined modal configuration. This is the case of mode shapes 5, 8, 9 and 10.

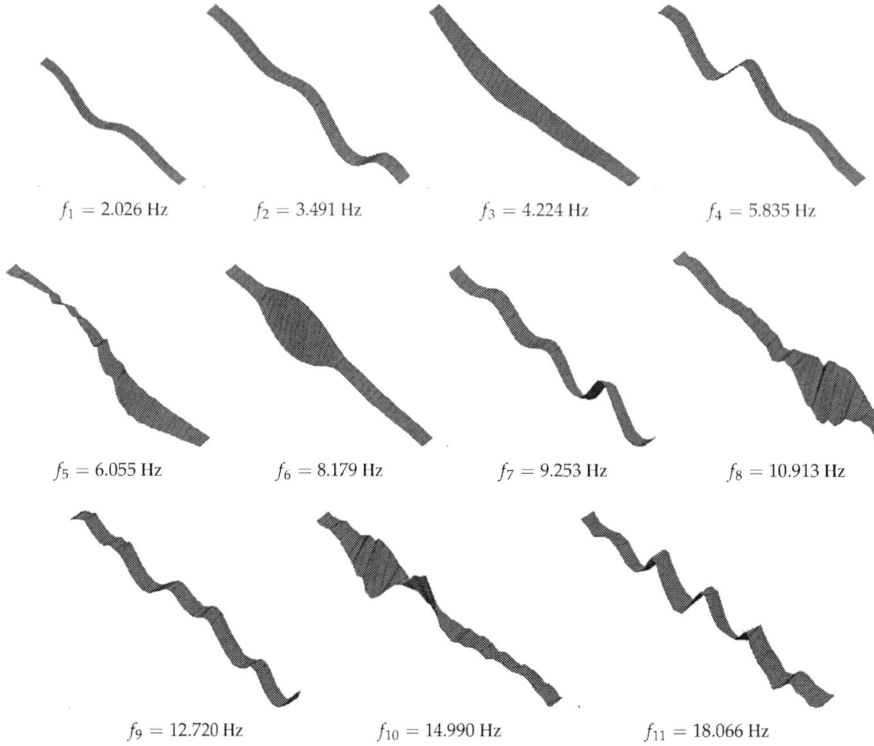

Figure 5 Modes shapes of the "Grevestien" footbridge identified with the classic FDD technique from the periodogram driven power spectral densities

3.2. Identification with Correlation Spectrum FDD technique

The application of the correlation spectrum based FDD described in section 2. is also illustrated by using of the vibration data of the "Grevestien" footbridge. To this end, the correlation-driven spectrum of each dataset was estimated by means of eq. (1) and used as primary data in the identification with the FDD technique. These power spectral densities were estimated from the filtered data signals with a resolution of the 2048 frequency lines by making use of an exponential window with a decay constant of 99.9% to minimize the leakage.

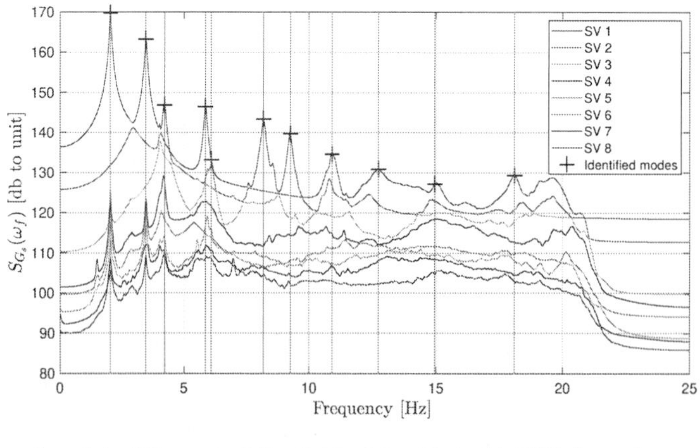

Figure 6 Vibration modes of the "Grevestien" Footbridge identified with FDD from the correlation based power spectrum

Once the correlation-driven spectrum matrices of all the 38 acquired datasets were estimated, they were stacked on the top of each other to form the global spectrum matrix, $G_s(\omega)$ according to equation (3). Afterwards, the singular value decomposition was applied to this matrix. The obtained singular values at the 2048 frequency lines are plotted in Fig. 6. Similarly to the classic *periodogram*-driven FDD, the natural frequencies were simply identified by picking the peaks in the singular values plot. The identification of the global mode shapes, however, was accomplished by following the strategy described in section 2.2., i.e., by selecting the corresponding vectors from the singular vector matrices, $U_s(\omega_f)$.

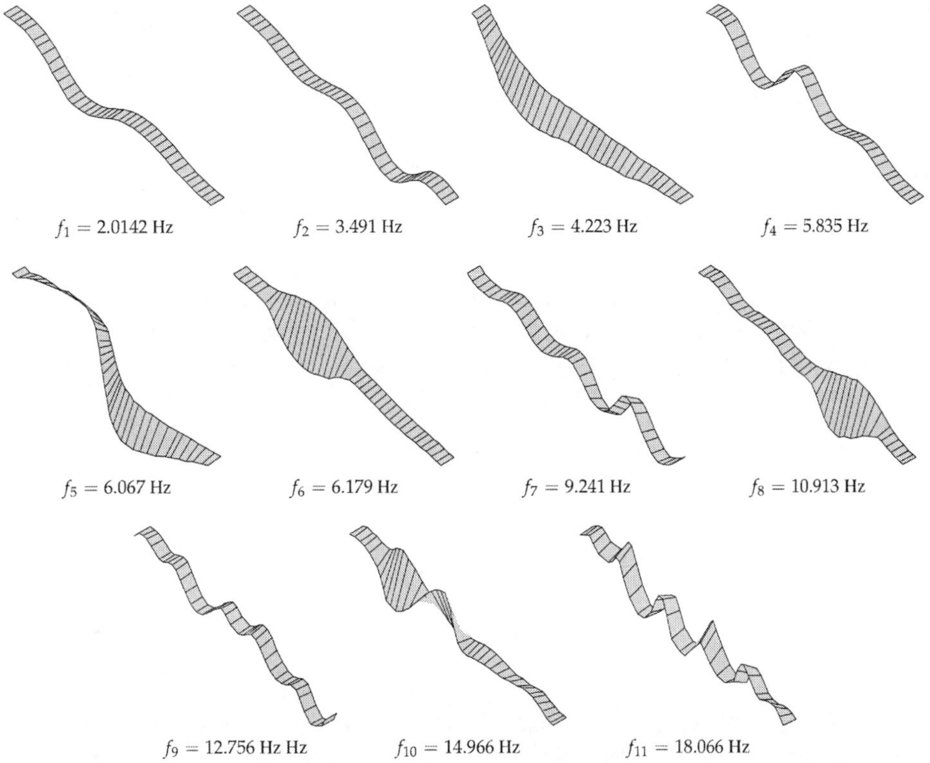

Figure 7 Modes shapes of the footbridge identified with the FDD technique from the correlation driven power spectral densities

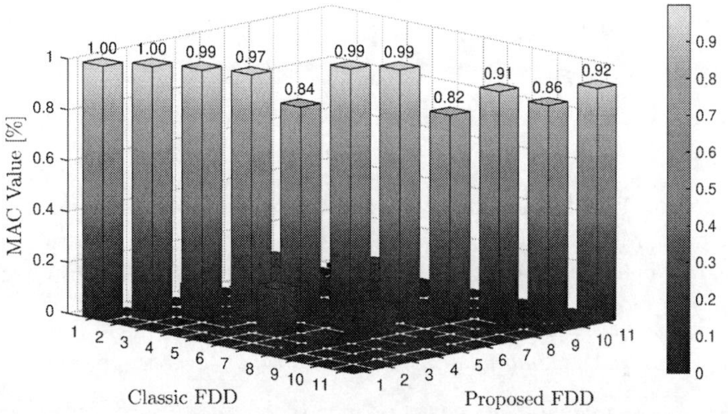

Figure 8 Modal Assurance Criterion (MAC) between the global mode shapes estimated with the classic multi-dataset FDD and those estimated with the proposed multi-dataset FDD driven by the correlation spectrum

The identification results obtained with the proposed multi-dataset FDD driven by correlation power spectrum densities is summarized in Figs. 7. Comparing these results to those shown in Fig. 5, its verified that they are in very good agreement, in terms of natural frequencies, with the results obtained with classic multi-dataset FDD technique. When comparing the global mode shapes, however, it is verified that the correlation spectrum driven multi-dataset FDD provided mode shapes with clearer modal configuration. The gain in accuracy of the global mode shape estimates provided obtained with correlation spectrum driven FDD becomes particularly more evident when the global shapes of modes 5, 8, 9, 10 and 11 are compared. This gain is also quantified by means of the Modal Assurance Criterion (MAC) values shown in Fig. 8.

4. CONCLUSIONS

In this paper, a novel multi-dataset FDD driven by correlation spectral densities is introduced. The underlying idea of this approach is to identify the natural frequencies and global mode shapes of vibration from a global spectral matrix containing pre-scaled spectral matrices of all datasets stacked on the top of each other. One of main advantages of this approach with regard to the classic *periodogram*-driven multi-dataset FDD is that it forces the mode shape parts of the different datasets to be in the same subspace and, therefore, tends to provide well-defined mode shape configurations. In order to assess the accuracy of the proposed multi-dataset FDD, the technique was applied to the vibration data acquired in a multi-dataset output-only vibration test of footbridge. By comparing the results obtained with such approach to those provided by the classic FDD, it was verified that the former provides global mode shape estimates with clearer modal configurations.

ACKNOWLEDGEMENTS

The authors acknowledge the funding received from Centre for Oil and Gas - DTU/Danish Hydrocarbon Research and Technology Centre (DHRTC).

REFERENCES

[1] Brincker, R. and Zhang, L. and Andersen, P. (2001) Modal identification of output-only systems using frequency domain decomposition. *Journal of Smart Materials and Structures*, 10, (pp. 441-445).

[2] Brincker, R. and Zhang, L. (2009) Frequency Domain Decomposition Revisited. *In proceedings of the the 5th International Operational Modal Analysis Conference (IOMAC)*, Portonovo, Italy.

[3] Mitra, S.K. (1998) Digital Signal Processing - A Computer-based Approach. *McGraw-Hill, New York, USA*.

[4] Brincker, R. and Ventura, C. (2015) Introduction To Operational Modal Analysis. *John Wiley and Sons*, 1st ed.

[5] Reynders, E., Magalhães, F., De-Roeck, G. and Cunha, A. (2009) Merging Strategies for Multi-Setup Operational Modal Analysis: Application to the Luiz I steel Arch Bridge. *In proceedings of the 27th International Modal Analysis Conference (IMACXXVII)*, 36(2), (pp. 115-127).

[6] Parloo, E., Guillaume, P. and Cauberghe, B. (2003) Maximum likelihood identification of non-stationary operational data. *Journal of Sound and Vibration*, 268(5) (pp. 971–991).

[7] Juul, M.Ø.Ø., Olsen, P., Balling, O., Amador, S.D.R. and Brincker, R. (2018) Comparison of two (geometric) algorithms for auto OMA. *In proceedings of International Modal Analysis Conference (IMAC) 2018*, Orlando, FL., USA.

[8] Peeters, B., Van-Der-Auweraera, H., Vanhollebeck, F. and Guillaume, P. (2007) Operational modal analysis for estimating the dynamic properties of a stadium structure during a football game. *Journal of Shock and Vibration*, 14(1), (pp. 283-303).

[9] Döhler1, M., Reynders, E.,Magalhães, F., Mevel, L., De-Roeck2, G. and Cunha, A. (2010) Pre- and Post-identification Merging for Multi-Setup OMA with Covariance-Driven SSI *In proceedings of International Modal Analysis Conference (IMAC) 2010*, Jacksonville, FL., USA.

[10] Amador, S.D.R., Magalhães, F., Martins, N., Caetano, E. and Cunha, A. (2013) High Spatial Resolution Operational Modal Analysis of a Football Stadium Suspension Roof. *In proceedings of the the 5th International Operational Modal Analysis Conference (IOMAC)*, Guimarães, Portugal.

[11] Amador, S.D.R., Magalhães, F., Cunha, A. and Caetano, E. (2017) High spatial resolution modal identification of a stadium suspensionroof: Assessment of the estimates uncertainty and of modal contributions. *Journal of Engineering Structures*, 135, (pp 117-135).

[12] Pao, B. (1992) Structural drawings of the City Crest Tower. *Bogdonov Pao Associates Ltd.*

[13] Savnik, N.J., Katsanos, E.I., Amador, S.D.R., Ventura, C.E. and Brincker, R. (2018) Influence of diaphragm modelling on the dynamic performance of a reinforced concrete high-rise building. *In proceedings of the 28th International Conference on Noise and Vibration Engineering (ISMA)*, Leuven, Belgium.

[14] Structural Vibration Solutions A/S. (2017) ARTeMIS Pro Modal Version 4. Aalborg, Denmark, 2017. www.svibs.com.

[15] Makkonen, N.H.B. and Salim, F. (2017) Evaluation of Human–Structure Interaction using Operational Modal Analysis". *Master's Report. Technical University of Denmark (DTU)*, Kgs. Lyngby, Denmark.

IOMAC'19

8th International Operational Modal Analysis Conference

2019 May13-15 Copenhagen

EVOLUTIONARY BASED APPROACH TO MODAL PARAMETER IDENTIFICATION

K. Soal[1], R. Volkmar[2], L.H. Hughes[3], Y. Govers[4] and M. Böswald[5]

[1] Research Associate, Department of Structural Dynamics and System Identification, German Aerospace Center (DLR), Institute of Aeroelasticity, Göttingen, Germany, keith.soal@dlr.de
[2] Research Associate, Department of Structural Dynamics and System Identification, German Aerospace Center (DLR), Institute of Aeroelasticity, Göttingen, Germany, robin.volkmar@dlr.de
[3] Research Associate, Technical University of Munich (TUM), München, Germany, lloyd.hughes@tum.de
[4] Team Leader, Department of Structural Dynamics and System Identification, German Aerospace Center (DLR), Institute of Aeroelasticity, Göttingen, Germany, yves.govers@dlr.de
[5] Head of Department, Department of Structural Dynamics and System Identification, German Aerospace Center (DLR), Institute of Aeroelasticity, Göttingen, Germany, marc.boeswald@dlr.de

ABSTRACT

An important task in modal analysis is the optimal selection of physical poles of a system. In this paper an Artificial Intelligence (AI) evolutionary algorithm is used to optimize the modal parameters from Output Only Modal Analysis (OMA). The evolutionary algorithm begins by generating a population selected randomly from mode clusters. The fitness of each individual is then evaluated based on the difference between the measured and synthesized spectra. The best individuals are then reproduced using a crossover strategy. A random mutation allows the exploration of the larger solution space in order to avoid convergence in local minima. The algorithm is tested on simulated data as well as the DLR AIRMOD laboratory structure, and is found to provide accurate and robust heuristic solutions to large and complex solution spaces.

Keywords: Artificial Intelligence, Automatic Modal Analysis, Genetic Algorithm

1. INTRODUCTION

Artificial Intelligence has seen a resurgence in recent years and is currently drawing much attention due to increasingly elegant solutions to complex problems. Various tools exist in the field of AI suited to solving different problems. These include logical programming, optimization techniques, probabilistic methods, classifiers and neural networks [1].

In the field of structural dynamics, experimental and operational modal analysis provide a set of parameters which characterize the dynamic behaviour of a structure. An important task in modal analysis is the optimal selection of physical poles of the system. In most cases this is performed by expert analysts who use previous experience, theoretical insight, and various indicators such as the

Modal Assurance Criterion (MAC), Mode Indicator Function (MIF), synthesised frequency spectra etc. to choose the most suitable parameters. This procedure is however, extremely time consuming and prone to human error. Furthermore, it is not possible to rely on user interaction for large data sets and short analysis duration as required by on-line monitoring.

Evolutionary algorithms are heuristic AI optimization techniques inspired by the process of biological evolution. Genetic Algorithms (GAs) are a class of evolutionary algorithms, which have been found to provide powerful tools for solving large and complicated optimization problems [2]. In the field of structural dynamics GAs have been successfully used to detect structural damage [2] [3], update Finite Element (FE) models [4], and optimize sensor placement [5].

In this paper a GA is investigated with regards to optimizing the modal parameters identified from vibration data. The GA is first introduced and discussed. The results from simulated data as well as a laboratory aircraft structure called AIRMOD are then presented, discussed and compared to results from experienced analysts.

2. THE GENETIC ALGORITHM

Genetic algorithms (GAs) are based on the concept of Darwin's theory of evolution [6]. GAs are capable of generating high quality solutions to complicated optimization problems using biological mechanisms such as reproduction (crossover), mutation and selection (survival of the fittest). They often perform well since they do not make assumptions about the underlying fitness landscape and do not rely on a good starting point [7].

The flow of a GA is illustrated in Figure 1. A population of solutions is first randomly initialized. Each population consists of a certain number of individuals which in turn consist of modal parameters (Eigenvalues and Eigenvectors). The number of individuals in the population is a user defined variable, and should be chosen large enough to ensure genetic diversity in the solution space, and small enough to enable desired computational time based on the hardware capacity available. The number of modal parameters that each individual consists of (genes) is determined by the number of mode clusters resulting from the modal identification algorithm, based on a Modal Assurance Criterion (MAC) threshold.

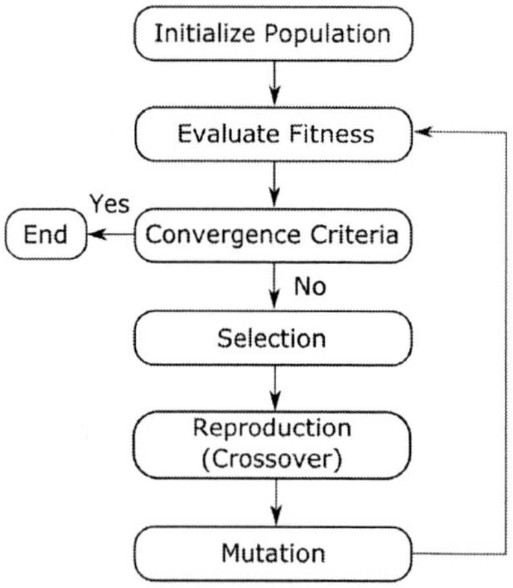

Figure 1. Flow of the Genetic Algorithm

In this paper results from the Least Squares Complex Frequency (LSCF) [8] algorithm are used, providing an over-determined set of candidate results from which the most likely solution should be identified. The GA can however, optimize modal parameters from any identification technique which produces mode clusters.

The fitness of each individual in the population is then evaluated based on an objective function. The objective function in this work is the difference between the measured and synthesised Power Spectral Density (PSD). The top performing N % of individuals are then selected for reproduction, together with a lucky few to maintain diversity. Different reproduction or crossover strategies can be used. The idea is to generate a new population from the pool of top performing (elite) and lucky individuals (selected randomly) in the previous generation. For each new solution (individual) a pair of parents is selected with a given probability of elite breeding, elite and middle class breeding and random breeding. The genes (modal parameters) of two selected parents are then randomly combined to create a child, and breeding continues until the new population or next generation of appropriate size is complete.

According to a user defined mutation probability, individuals of the new generation are finally mutated whereby a single gene is randomly interchanged from the original solution space. This provides further genetic diversity in order to find global minima and prevent the solution from becoming stuck in local minima. The algorithm then proceeds iteratively until a maximum number of generations have been produced or a satisfactory fitness level has been reached.

3. RESULTS

The GA was implemented using Object-Oriented Programming (OOP) in Matlab and integrated into the SASTools tool box of the department of Structural Dynamics and System Identification at DLR Göttingen. The results of the GA on simulated data as well as the AIRMOD laboratory structure are presented below.

3.1. Simulated Data

The GA was first tested on a 5 Degree Of Freedom (DOF) simulated dataset. The 5 DOF system was excited with Gaussian distributed white noise, sampled at 125 Hz for 10 minutes. Additionally, a high noise level of 0.7 times the signal mean was added to each signal to imitate the challenges of real data. The Cross Power Spectral Densities (CPSDs) of the signals were then calculated for use by the LSCF identification algorithm to estimate poles from model order 5 – 60 in the band 0 Hz – 45 Hz. The stabilisation diagram in Figure 2 shows the resulting 5 mode clusters with their respective Eigenfrequencies near the bottom, damping ratios near the top, and MIF values above the top line for the highest model orders . The fourth mode is seen to be poorly identified due to the high noise level. The aim is to now find an optimal system solution from each mode cluster.

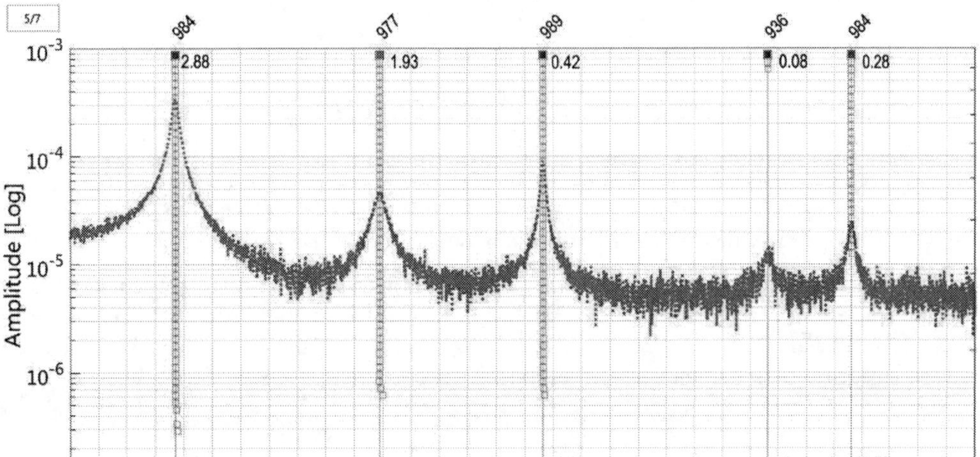

Figure 2. Stabilisation diagram of simulated data

The GA was run on the data with the following parameters:

- Population Size 100
- Elite Sample Size 20
- Lucky Sample Size 30
- Number of Generations 50
- Elite Breeding Probability 60 %
- Elite and Middle Class Breeding Probability 60 %
- Random Breeding 40 %
- Mutation Probability 40 %

From the resulting performance history in Figure 3 it can be seen that the first generation (individuals from 0 to 100) have a relatively large error due to their randomness. The average error is seen to improve in subsequent generations due to the retention of the elites (i.e. we don't kill the best parents). The large errors which subsequently occur are due to bad mutations. Mutation however, remains critically important to find global minima and bad mutants are discarded in the subsequent generation, therefore having no effect on the overall result.

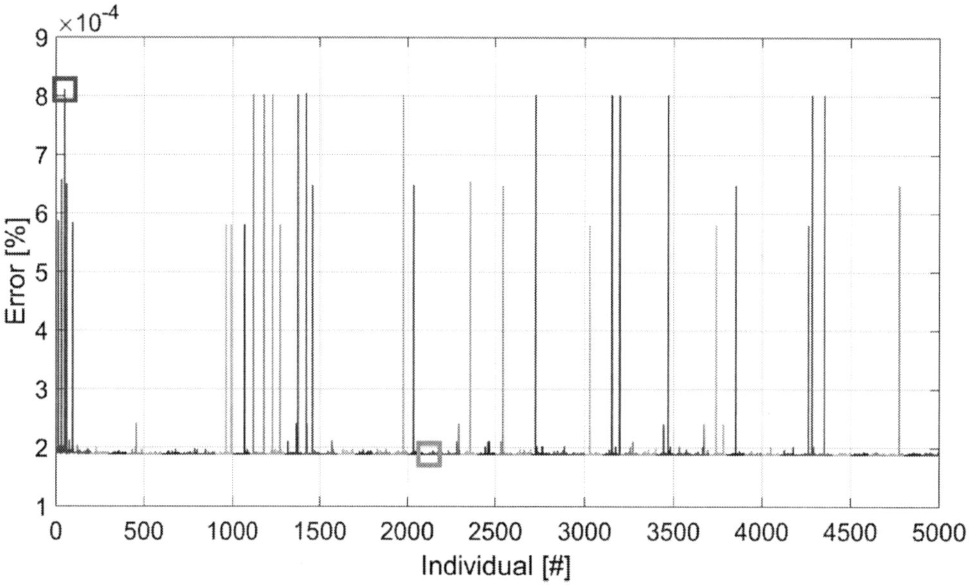

Figure 3. Performance history of all individuals

The best and worst results are indicated by the green and red squares respectively. Since the best solution occurs in the vicinity of the 2000 individual, this gives an indication that the result has converged. The worst individual results from random initialization rather than a mutation.

The performance of the best individual across the 50 generations is shown in Figure 4. The error is seen to converge after 20 generations. The magnitude of the error is small despite the high noise level. The goal of modal analysis is however, not the synthesised spectra but the resulting modal parameters, with particular focus on the damping which remains the most challenging parameter to estimate accurately.

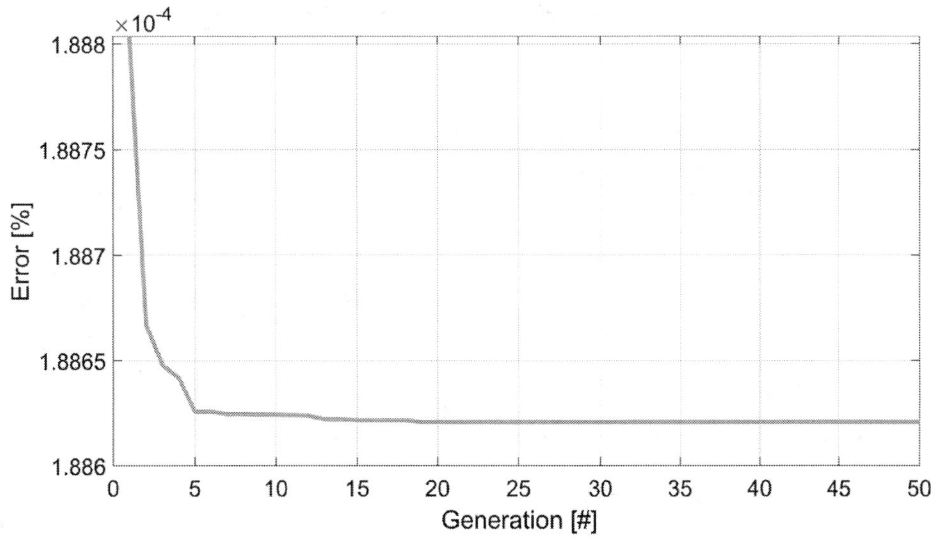

Figure 4. Performance history of the best individual in each generation.

A larger variation in the identified damping can be seen from the frequency vs damping plot in Figure 5. The GA optimized solution shown by the green dot is seen to successfully choose the pole closest to the analytical solution shown by the orange asterisk. The averaged synthesised spectra is seen to fit the averaged measured spectra with good quality around the peaks. The fourth mode clearly underestimates the damping, which is expected from observing the cluster (solution space) as well as a study by Böswald [9] which shows that LSCF is prone to underestimate damping in the presence of noise.

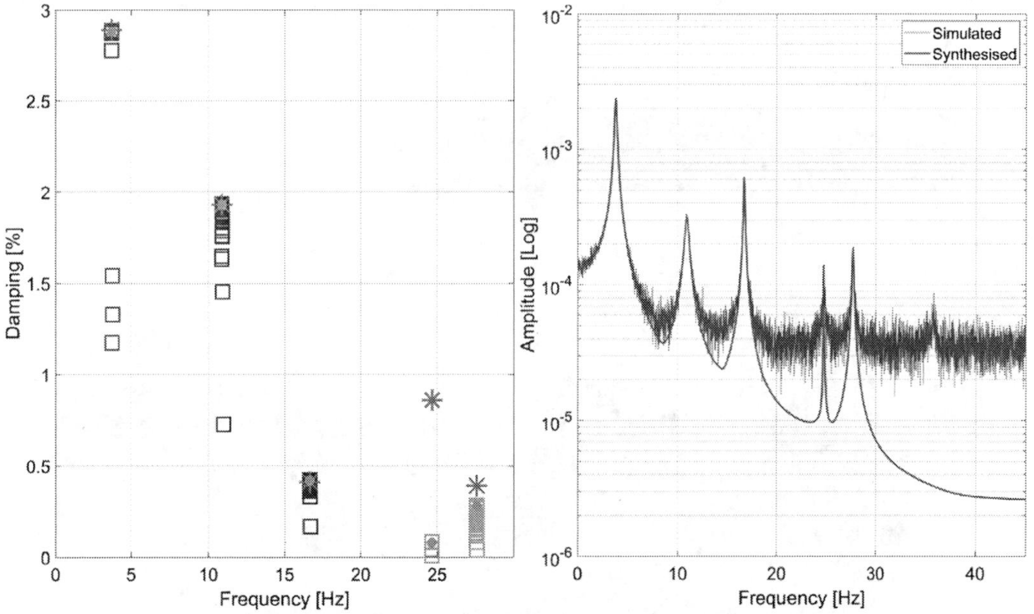

Figure 5. Frequency vs damping and synthesised spectra

A comparison between the experimental (identified) and numerical (simulated) results presented in Table 1 show less than 1 % error in frequency with less than 2 % damping error for the first three modes.

Table 1. Comparison between experimental and analytical results

Mode	Frequency			Damping		
	Experimental [Hz]	Analyitcal [Hz]	Error [%]	Experimental [%]	Analytical [%]	Error [%]
1	3.70	3.70	0.00	2.88	2.89	-0.26
2	10.89	10.89	0.04	1.94	1.93	0.29
3	16.65	16.65	0.00	0.42	0.41	1.76
4	24.64	24.66	-0.09	0.08	0.86	-90.20
5	27.59	27.59	-0.02	0.28	0.39	-27.70

3.2. Laboratory Data

The GA was then tested on measured data from the laboratory structure AIRMOD (AIRcraft MODel). AIRMOD is a replica of the GARTEUR SM-AG19 benchmark and was built at DLR Göttingen to study concepts for Ground Vibration Testing (GVT) by Govers [10] [11] [12]. The structure which is shown in Figure 6a is made of aluminium, has five bolted joints, a wing span of 2 m, fuselage length of 1.5 m, and a total weight of 44 Kg. Despite the simple appearance, the structural behaviour shows similarities to real aircraft which include symmetric and antisymmetric modes, closely spaced modes and non-linearities resulting from the bolted joints.

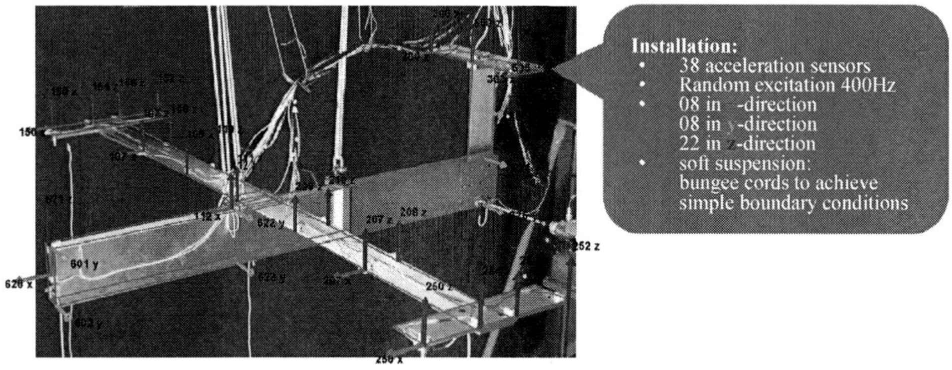

[a]

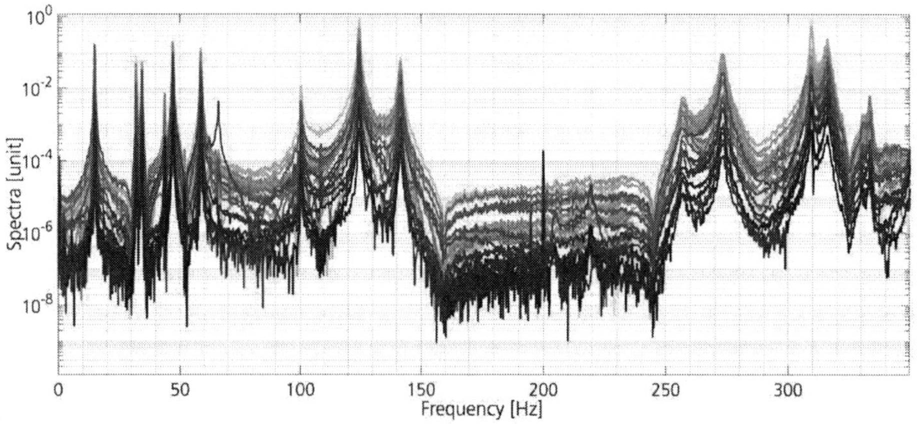

[b]

Figure 6. [a] AIRMOD structure and measurement setup [b] Cross Power Spectral Densities (CPSDs)

AIRMOD was instrumented with 38 piezo-resistive accelerometers as shown in Figure 6a, with measurement locations and directions based on the GARTEUR benchmark. It was tested under free-free boundary conditions using soft bungee cords with $f_{max}^{RBM} \approx 1/3 \cdot f_{min}^{elastic}$ separation between the highest Rigid Body Mode (RBM) and the lowest elastic mode. A 64 channel VXI data acquisition system controlled by DLR in-house software was used to record data at 1024 Hz as well as control an electrodynamic shaker.

The dataset used in this study was measured during the PhD research of Govers [10], and consists of 160 s of broadband random excitation from one shaker attached in the vertical direction at the wing tip. The spectra were computed using a Hanning window with 66 % overlap and a frequency resolution of 0.0063 Hz. The Cross Power Spectral Densities (CPSDs) for the band 0 Hz – 350 Hz with reference to an accelerometer in the vertical direction on the wing tip are shown in Figure 6b. Several distinct peaks are observed with varying steepness (damping).

The Least Squares Complex Frequency (LSCF) algorithm was used to identify the system poles from the CPSDs. The analysis was split into 11 bands from 0.1 Hz to 370 Hz and from model order 2 to 100. An in house learning algorithm was used to group the modes into physically meaningful clusters based on various mode quality indicators. The resulting stabilisation diagram showing the mode clusters as well as the sum of the CPSDs is shown inFigure 7.

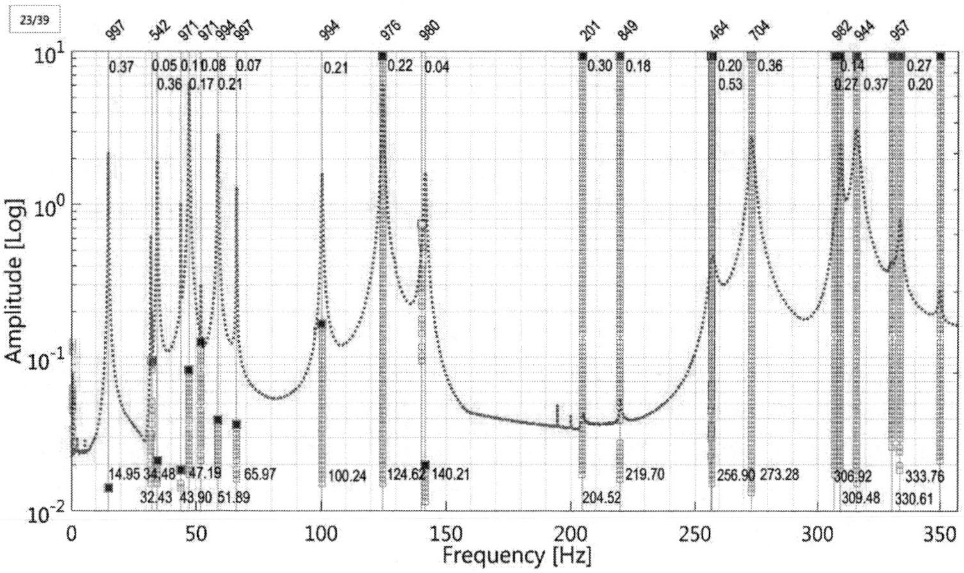

Figure 7. Stabilisation diagram of AIRMOD data

Firstly, it was observed that clusters were smaller at lower frequencies due to the smaller half-power bandwidths resulting at lower frequencies. Twenty seven unique clusters were identified, corresponding with peaks in the CPSDs. Once again the goal was to obtain the 'best' modes from these clusters which due to the size of the problem was not feasible to determine using brute force (i.e. computing every solution).

The GA was run on the data with the same parameters as the simulation case above, with the exception that the number of generations was increased to 200. Due to the larger channel count and higher computational load for calculating and synthesizing the spectra for each individual in each generation, the testing was performed on an Intel Xeon E5 CPU with 160 GB of RAM, which took 25 minutes to run.

This may seem like a long time but if we consider the size of the problem which has 2550 identified poles in 27 unique clusters then there exist 1.826 x 10^{51} possible unique combinations in the solution space which would be impossible to calculate. With only 20 000 solutions computed by the GA (100 individuals over 200 generations) the tradeoff between solution accuracy (which will be investigated next) and time must be decided in the context of the test requirements.

It should also be noted that the run time can be significantly sped up through the use of multi-threaded programming techniques as the computation and evaluation of each individual is largely self-standing. The efficient reduction of certain parameters such as the population size to 50 would reduce the time by half to 13 minutes, and should be investigated with regard to the structure and desired outcome of the test campaign.

The result of the GA performance history is shown in Figure 8. The error is initially large due to the random initialization, but converges quickly. The spikes are once again due to the mutation, and the best solution is found in the 152nd generation, indicated by the green square.

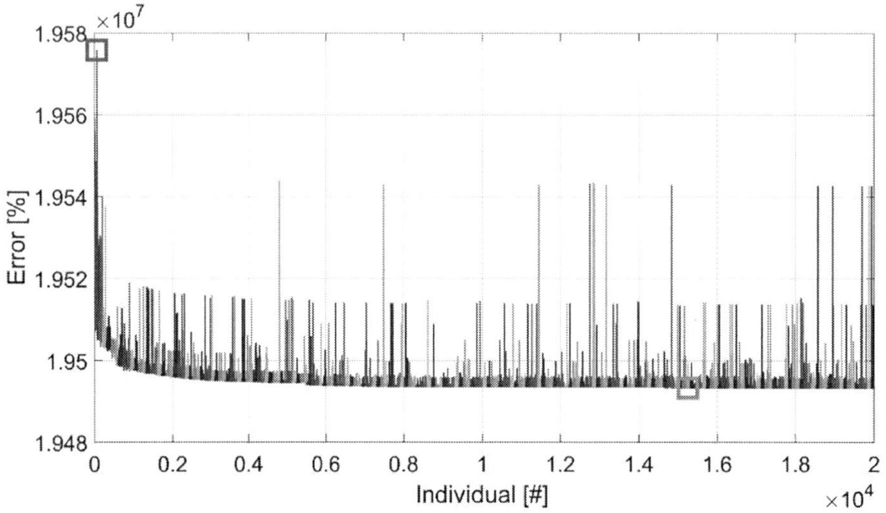

Figure 8. Performance history of all individuals

The perfromance history of the best indiviual is shown in Figure 9. The error shows signs of convergence after finding the best individual at generation 152.

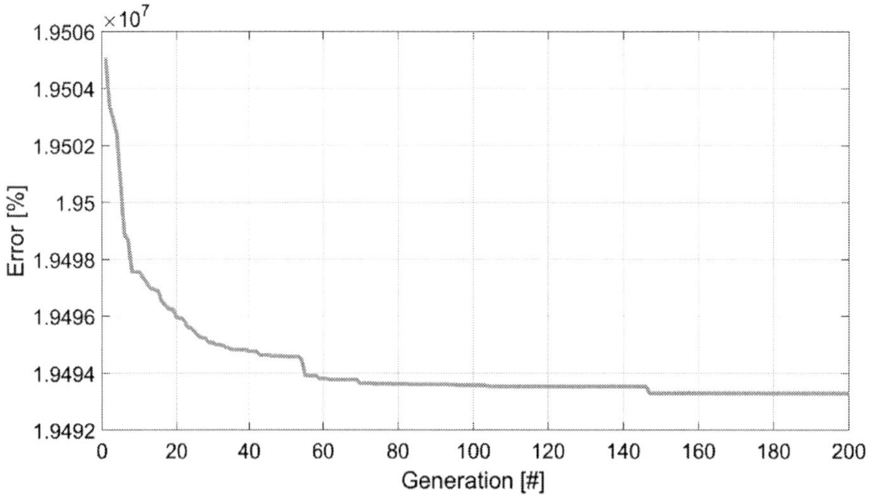

Figure 9. Performance history of the best individual

The variation in the damping can be observed from the frequency vs damping plots shown in Figure 10. The optimal solution from the GA is shown by the green dot. Despite no analytical solution, the synthesized spectra are seen to accurately fit the measured spectra, providing confidence in the results.

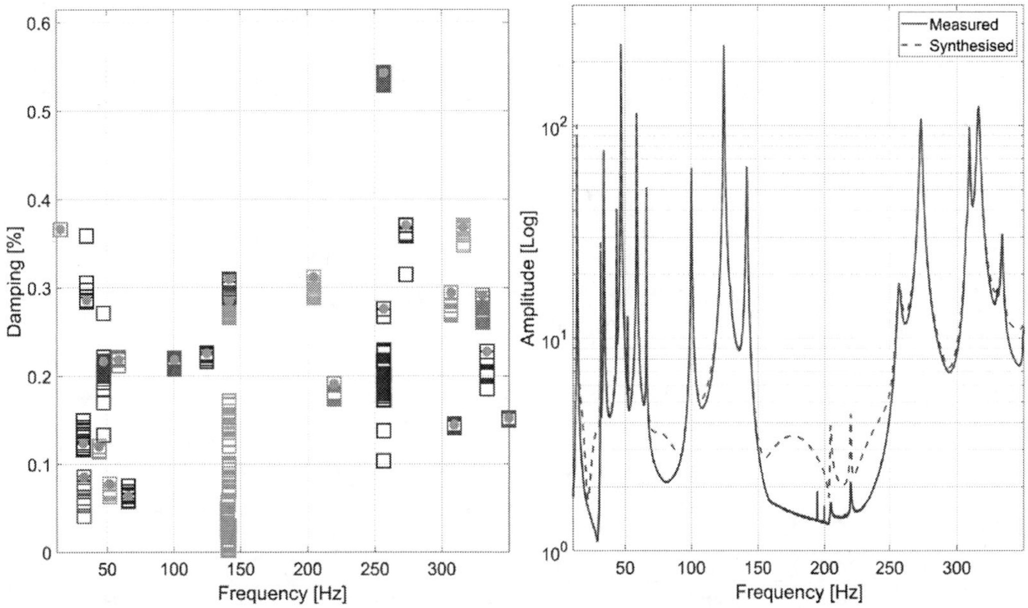

Figure 10. Frequency vs damping and synthesised spectra

The names, frequencies and damping of six elastic modes together with the difference between the GA solution and the results from experienced modal analysts are presented in Table 2. The frequencies are seen to agree to within 1 %. The damping shows a largest variation of 70 % and mean difference of 34 % which is in fact a small range considering other literature in this field [13] [14] [15].

Table 2. Comparison between GA results and experienced modal analyst (EA)

Mode	Name	Frequency			Damping		
		GA [Hz]	EA [Hz]	Diff [%]	GA [%]	EA [%]	Diff [%]
1	3n Wing Bending	14.95	14.91	0.27	0.37	0.63	70
2	Wing Torsion Antisymmetric	32.06	31.96	0.31	0.12	0.08	33
3	Wing Torsion Symmetric	32.41	32.33	0.25	0.08	0.06	25
4	4n Wing Bending	43.88	43.89	0.02	0.12	0.08	33
5	2n Wing Fore Aft Bending	51.89	51.88	0.02	0.07	0.05	28
6	VTP Torsion	65.98	65.93	0.08	0.06	0.05	16

The mode shapes of the six elastic modes are shown in Figure 11 and can be clearly identified as physical vibration modes of the structure.

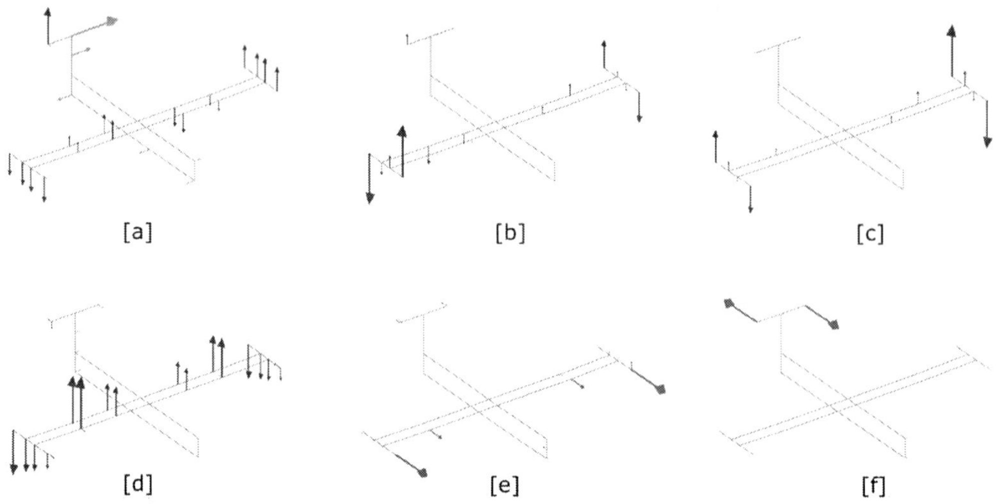

Figure 11. Mode shapes of six elastic modes

4. CONCLUSIONS

The ability to use AI in the form of a Genetic Algorithm to both optimize and automate modal parameter identification was realized and demonstrated. A GA was implemented, and the selection, reproduction (crossover) and mutation techniques were described in detail. The algorithm was first tested on a simulated data set where a key observation was that the objective function was found to deliver accurate modal parameters. The algorithm was then tested on data from the AIRMOD laboratory structure, where convergence of the error function was observed and where the synthesized spectra were seen to accurately fit the measured spectra. The comparison of the GA optimized modal parameters to those of experienced analysts (EA) showed less than 1 % difference in frequency, but an average of 34 % difference in damping. Whether the GA or EA damping estimates are more accurate is unknown, and will be investigated further in future research. Further investigations are also planned regarding a GA parametric study and the possibility of reducing computational time using GPU computing.

REFERENCES

[1] Russel, S. and Norvig, P. (2009). Artificial Intelligence: A Modern Approach, NJ, USA: Prentice Hall Press.

[2] Arya, B. and M. Sanayei, M. (2004). Structural Parameter Estimation Using Modal Responses and Utilizing Genetic Algorithm.

[3] Meruane, V. and Heylen, W. (2011). An hybrid real genetic algorithm to detect structural damage using modal properties, *Mechanical Systems and Signal Processing.*

[4] Larson, C.B. and Zimmeman, D.C. (1993). Structural Model Refinement Using a Genetic Algorithm Approach," in *11th International Modal Analysis Conference*.

[5] Jung, K., Cho, R. and B. Jeong, B. (2015). Sensor placement optimization for structural modal identification of flexible structures using genetic algorithm, in *Journal of Mechanical Science and Technology*.

[6] Goldberg, D.E. (1989). Genetic algorithms in search, optimization and machine learning, Addison-Wesley Publishing Company.

[7] Mitchell, M. (1998) An introduction to genetic algorithms, The MIT Press.

[8] Guillaume, P.P., Verboven, P., Vanlanduit, S., Van der Auweraer, H. and Peeters, B. (2003). A polyreference implementation of the least-squares complex frequency-domain estimator, in *IMAC XXI*, Kissimmee, FL.

[9] Böswald, M. (2016). Analysis of the bias in modal parameters obtained with frequency-domain rational fraction polynomial estimators, in *International Conference of Noise and Vibration Engineering ISMA*, Leuven.

[10] Govers, Y. (2012). *Parametric identification of structural dynamic models by inverse statistical analysis,* Cologne, Germany: Faculty of Civil and Environmental Engineering, University of Kassel.

[11] Govers, Y., Böswald, M., Göge, D. and Link, M. (2006). Analysis of sources and quantification of uncertainty in experimental modal data, in *International Conference on Noise and Vibration Engineering (ISMA)*, KU Leuven, Belgium.

[12] Govers, Y., Haddad Khodaparast, H., Link, M. and Mottershead, J.E. (2015). A comparison of two stochastic model updating methods using the DLR AIRMOD test structure, *Mechanical Systems and Signal Processing,* pp. 104-114.

[13] Orlowitz, E., and Brandt, A., (2001) Comparison of experimental and operational modal analysis on a laboratory test plate, *Measurement,* vol. 102, pp. 121-130.

[14] Gaul, L. and Nitsche, R. (2001). The Role of Friction in Mechanical Joints, *American Society of Mechanical Engineers (ASME),* vol. 54.

[15] Soal, K., Bienert, J. and Bekker, A. (2017). Inverse Joint Damping Parameter Estimation From Experimental Modal Analysis, in *International Conference on Structural Engineering Dynamics (ICEDyn)*, Ericeira, Portugal.

IOMAC'19

8th International Operational Modal Analysis Conference

2019May13-15 Copenhagen

EXPERIMENTALLY VALIDATED SPRURIOUS MODES REJECTION USING THE SMA ALGORITHM

Maher Abdelghani[1], and Dmitri Tcherniak[2]

[1] Associate Professor of Mech. Engr. University of Sousse-Tunisia. maher.abdelghani@gmail.com.

[2] Research engineer, Brüel & Kjær Sound & Vibration Measurement A/S, Denmark.

ABSTRACT

Recently a new In-Operation modal identification algorithm was proposed, namely the Stochastic Modal Appropriation algorithm (SMA) which identifies the natural frequencies and the damping ratios simultaneously, in a single step. The key idea behind the algorithm is to rotate parametrically the outputs correlation sequence so as it appears as the system impulse response. This work demonstrates the SMA's ability to automatically reject the harmonics and spurious/numerical modes leading to physical-only modes identification. After a mathematical proof, the method is validated on a simple experimental system subjected to simultaneous random and harmonic excitation.

Keywords: In-Operation modal analysis, harmonics, spurious modes, SMA

1. INTRODUCTION

Most of the conventional OMA algorithms assumes randomness of the excitation, both in time and space. If this assumption is violated, for example if some operating machines contribute to the excitation of the structure, the algorithm may lead to wrong results confusing the harmonics of the excitation with the structural modes. Different ways were suggested to avoid this, for example, by removing the harmonics from the response signals in a preprocessing step. In this case, different techniques could be employed, for example, time synchronous averaging, cepstrum-based filtering (liftering) and periodogram-based methods. A review and the example of the application of these techniques to operating wind turbine gearbox data can be found in [1]. If no harmonic cleansing steps are performed before loading the data to OMA, the harmonics can be detected manually based on the user knowledge and experience, and then excluded from the results. Some techniques, for example, based on band-pass filtering and kurtosis, are available to automate the harmonic detection process [2]. In contrast with the most of the state-of-the art OMA methods, Stochastic Modal Appropriation (SMA) algorithm has a built-in ability to reject harmonics and spurious/numerical modes [3]. The correlation sequence of the outputs of a structure under its operating conditions is a sum of decaying phased sinusoids. The phase shift is dependent on the damping ratio and has a particular mathematical expression, which is derived based on a physical background. Suppose there is a noise mode present in the correlation sequence (decaying phased sinusoid). The phase shift does not have the particular expression as for a physical mode. With the SMA algorithm, the correlation sequence is parametrically rotated until it hits a zero-phase shift. We get then a pure sinusoid (impulse response for a physical mode and just a pure sine for a noise mode). When the phase angle between the input and output is $\pm\pi/2$ the mode is isolated. This is a necessary condition. The noise mode may also be isolated. However, since the rotation annihilates the phase angle, which is related to the damping ratio, (the pole) the frequency and the damping ratio will be estimated simultaneously if and only if the mode is physical. This is a consequence of the particular structure of the phase angle in the correlation sequence. A noise mode will not satisfy this property.

In conclusion, a physical mode shall satisfy the following three conditions, which make it distinct:

1. Input/output phase angle $\pm\pi/2$;
2. Both the frequency and damping ratio can be estimated;
3. They can be estimated simultaneously.

As it is discussed and proven in the following, a pole that satisfies simultaneously these three conditions, is necessarily a physical mode. After elaborating the approach on a SDOF system, the algorithm is demonstrated on experimental data measured on a simple mechanical structure, which was simultaneously subjected to random and harmonic excitation. It is shown that the algorithm is able to automatically reject the excitation harmonics.

2. THE SMA ALGORITHM

Consider a SDOF system excited with unmeasured white noise. The impulse response of the system may be written as [4]:

$$h(t) = C_h e^{-\xi\omega_n t} sin(\omega_d t) \tag{1}$$

where ξ is the system damping ratio, ω_n is the system natural frequency and ω_d is the damped natural frequency.

The correlation sequence of the system output may be written as [5]:

$$R(t) = C_r e^{-\xi\omega_n t} sin(\omega_d t - \phi(\xi)) \tag{2}$$

where $\phi(\xi)$ is a phase shift that depends on the damping ratio. Both the impulse response and the correlation sequence can be considered as rotating vectors in the complex plane but with decaying amplitudes (spirals).

In the INOPMA algorithm [6], the correlation sequence was assumed to be an impulse response. This has led to the fact that the mode is isolated at a frequency $\omega^* = \omega_n\sqrt{1-4\xi^2}$ and not the natural frequency ω_n. This may be considered as a limitation of INOPMA. In this work we overcome this limitation and we show that it is still possible to isolate the mode at its natural frequency.

Let $\bar{R}(t,\alpha)$ be the image of $R(t)$ by a linear anti-symmetric function that depends on a certain design parameter α and consider the following sequence:

$$H(t,\alpha) = R(t) + \bar{R}(t,\alpha) \tag{3}$$

$H(t,\alpha)$ is then a rotation and stretching of the sequence $R(t)$. By varying α, it is possible to modify the phase shift as well as the amplitude of the correlation sequence and hence modify the damping ratio leading to a pure sinusoid. At this stage the mode is isolated.

In this work, we consider the following anti-symmetric function:

$$F(R(t),\alpha) = j\alpha R(t) \tag{4}$$

The SMA algorithm is similar to the INOPMA algorithm in the sense that one takes the convolution of the modified correlation sequence with a harmonic force with varying frequency.

In the frequency domain this means that the system transfer function (the Laplace transform of the correlation sequence) is multiplied by a complex factor $(1 + j\alpha)$. It can easily be shown that the transfer function phase angle is zero exactly at the following condition:

$$\begin{cases} \omega = \omega_n \\ \alpha = 2\xi \end{cases} \tag{5}$$

Geometrically this means that when the mode is isolated the vector representing the correlation sequence describes a circle meaning that the conservative part of the system is isolated. The non-conservative part follows immediately. Hence the system natural frequency as well as the damping ratio are identified at the same step.

3. HARMONICS REJECTION

In this section, it is proven that the SMA algorithm is robust against harmonics modeled as modes with zero damping.

Consider a SDOF system excited with unmeasured white noise. We show in the sequel that if the damping ratio is zero then the mode cannot be identified (the phase angle is never zero) and hence rejected.

The SMA algorithm is based on considering the following parametric correlation sequence:

$$H(t,\alpha) = (1 + j\alpha)R(t)$$

The Laplace Transform of this function can be shown to write as:

$$G(s) = (1 + j\alpha)\frac{s+2\xi\omega_n}{s^2+2\xi\omega_n s+\omega_n^2} \ .$$

The imaginary part of the Frequency Response is:

$$Im = (2\xi\alpha\omega_n + \omega)(\omega_n^2 - \omega^2) - (2\xi\omega_n - \alpha\omega)(2\xi\omega\omega_n),$$

and the real part is:

$$Re = (\omega_n^2 - \omega^2)(2\xi\omega_n - \alpha\omega) + 2\omega^2\xi\omega_n \ .$$

When the damping ratio is zero the tangent of the phase angle of the Frequency response reduces to:

$$tg = -\frac{\omega(\omega_n^2-\omega^2)}{\alpha\omega(\omega_n^2-\omega^2)} = -1/\alpha,$$

which is always different from zero. Consequently, for a harmonic, the angle between the input and the output is never zero meaning that the harmonic is never identified (no zero crossing).

4. SPURIOUS MODES REJECTION

We define in this section a spurious/numerical mode as a mode that is fitted to the system characteristic equation. This leads to a spurious frequency and damping that we still denote in the sequel as ω_n and ξ. The correlation sequence of the system output is given by [5]:

$$R(t) = e^{-\xi\omega_n t}\left[cos(\omega_d t) + \frac{\xi}{\sqrt{1-\xi^2}}sin(\omega_d t)\right] \tag{6}$$

The phase shift in this correlation sequence is given by:

$$tg(\theta) = \frac{\xi}{\sqrt{1-\xi^2}} \tag{7}$$

This particular expression of the phase shift is valid for physical modes only [3]. It is proposed to show in the sequel that if the phase shift of a correlation sequence enjoys this particular expression, then the mode is necessarily physical.

Consider the following correlation sequence:

$R_x(t) = e^{-\xi\omega_n t}[cos(\omega_d t) + x\, sin(\omega_d t)].$

The Laplace Transform of $(1 + j\alpha)R_x(t)$ is:

$G_x(s) = (1 + j\alpha)\frac{s+\omega_n(\xi+x\sqrt{1-\xi^2})}{s^2+2s\xi\omega_n+\omega_n{}^2}.$

The imaginary part of the numerator is:

$Im = -\,\omega^3 + \omega\omega_n^2 - \alpha\omega^2\omega_n(\xi + x\sqrt{1-\xi^2}) + \alpha\omega_n^3(\xi + x\sqrt{1-\xi^2}) + 2\xi\omega_n^2\omega(\xi + x\sqrt{1-\xi^2}) - 2\xi\omega^2\omega_n\alpha.$

With the isolating conditions

$\begin{cases}\omega = \omega_n \\ \alpha = 2\xi\end{cases},$

the above becomes $\omega_n^3(2\xi(\xi + x\sqrt{1-\xi^2}) - 4\xi^2) = 0$, leading to

$x = \frac{\xi}{\sqrt{1-\xi^2}}.$

This proves that under the SMA isolating conditions the mode is necessarily physical.

5. EXPERIMENTAL VALIDATION

The considered test object is a standard B&K demo plate (WA 0846), which is a rectangular aluminium plate with dimensions 290 x 250 x 8 mm^3; for the test, the plate was placed on a soft foam. A B&K demo motor WB 1471 with unbalanced rotor was attached to the plate; the motor was set to operate at 374 rps (Figure 1). For the experiment, the plate was excited by tapping its surface by the tip of a plastic pen. 16 monoaxial accelerometers B&K Type 4507 were mounted equidistantly on the plate on the grid points of a 4x4 grid, oriented to measure in the direction perpendicular to the plate surface. The data acquisition was performed by B&K LAN-Xi DAQ, the sampling frequency was set to 4096 Hz, and 60 seconds of the acceleration data were recorded, which was used as an input to both SMA and SSI algorithms.

To validate the results of SMA algorithm, commercial OMA software package PULSE Operational Modal Analysis 5.1.0.4 – x64 [7] was employed using the automatic identification mode, i.e. the default settings were applied, OMA-SSI-UPC method was employed.

The SMA algorithm was used with 256 correlation lags, using sensors 1 and 5 for the identification. The modes were identified as the angle crossings with zero. The comparison of the two methods is reported in Table 1.

Notice that the harmonics (374, 748, 1496 Hz) are clearly identifiable in the stabilization diagram (**Figure 2**) but rejected by both methods, though OMA-SSI-UPC declares the fundamental 374 Hz harmonic as a „noise mode" and automatically excludes it from the results. All the harmonics are automatically rejected by SMA.

Figure 1: The experimental setup

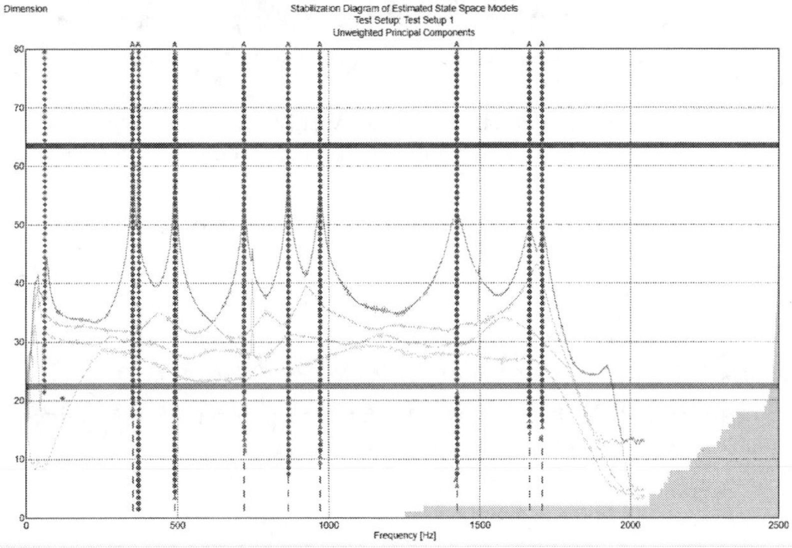

Figure 2: SSI-UPC stabilization diagram

Table 1: Experimental results comparing the SSI-UPC and SMA methods

OMA-SSI-UPC			SMA	
Comment	Frequency, Hz	Damping, %	Frequency, Hz	Damping, %
1st torsional mode (along Y axis)	353	0.57	353	0.6
The fundamental harmonic, automatically identified as a noise mode	372	0.05		
1st bending mode (along Y axis)	491	0.62	491	0.6
1st bending mode (along X axis)	720	0.98	719	0.75

2nd torsional mode (along Y axis)	867	0.47	864	0.75
2nd torsional mode (along X axis)	972	0.60	969	0.75
2nd bending mode (along Y axis)	1424	1.1	1420	1.3
2nd membrane mode	1663	0.69	1656	0.75
3rd torsional mode (along Y axis)	1706	0.67	1712	0.75

6. CONCLUSION

The paper briefly introduces the Stochastic Modal Appropriation algorithm (SMA), focusing on its unique ability to automatically reject erroneous "harmonic" and "spurious" modes, which otherwise could lead to incorrect dynamic identification of the structure under test. The method is demonstrated on the experimental data, and the results are compared with the results obtained using commercial OMA software.

REFERENCES

[1] T. Jacob, D. Tcherniak, R. Castiglione, "Harmonic Removal as a Pre-processing Step for Operational Modal Analysis: Application to Operating Gearbox Data", in Proceedings of *VDI Wissenforum*, Bremen, Germany, 2014.

[2] N.-J. Jacobsen, P. Andersen, "Operational Modal Analysis on Structures with Rotating Parts", in Proceedings of *Int. Modal Analysis Conference (IMAC)*, Orlando, FL, USA, 2008.

[3] M. Abdelghani, "Physical only modes identification using the stochastic modal appropriation algorithm (SMA)", Accepted *CMSM-March, Hammamet, Tunisia*, 2019.

[4] E. Balmès, C. Chapelier, P. Lubrina, P. Fargette, „An evaluation of modal testing results based on the force appropriation method", in Proceedings of *Int. Modal Analysis Conference (IMAC)*, Orlando, FL, USA, 1996.

[5] L. Meirovitch, "Elements of Vibration Analysis", *McGraw-Hill*, 1986.

[6] M. Abdelghani, M. I. Friswell, "Stochastic Modal Appropriation (SMA)", in Proceedings of *Int. Modal Analysis Conference (IMAC)*, Orlando, FL, USA, 2018.

[7] "PULSE Operational Modal Analysis Types 8760 – 8762," [Online]. Available: https://bksv.com/-/media/literature/Product-Data/bp2567.ashx.

IOMAC'19

8th International Operational Modal Analysis Conference

2019 May13-15 Copenhagen

FREQUENCY MONITORING IN A STRUCTURE ON SOFT SOIL BY MEANS OF N4SID IDENTIFICATION METHOD

Miguel Ángel García-Illescas[1], David Murià-Vila[2], Baruo Daniel Aldama[3] and Luis Alvarez-Icaza[4]

[1] Institute of Engineering, UNAM, Electrical and Computer Science Department. mgarciai@iingen.unam.mx.
[2] Institute of Engineering, UNAM, Structures and Materials Department. dmv@pumas.ii.unam.mx.
[3] Institute of Engineering, UNAM, Structures and Materials Department. BAldamaS@pumas.ii.unam.mx.
[4] Institute of Engineering, UNAM, Electrical and Computer Science Department. alvar@pumas.ii.unam.mx.

ABSTRACT

Frequencies are identified in a reinforced concrete structure composed by a building of 22-storey founded on soft soil, in Mexico City. This structure suffered damaged during the earthquake in 1985 being subsequently repaired. Since 2008 and by means of accelerometers, ambient vibration and seismic records have been registered. The objective of this paper is to analyze the use of N4SID subspace identification method to monitoring the frequencies of the building. To achieve this, ambient vibration records and moderate intensity earthquakes records are used in the identification process, where N4SID results are compared with those ones by using minimization modal method. Results are consistent in identifying the most representative vibration frequencies. The advantage by using N4SID subspace identification method is on a low-cost computer processing, its online implementation is feasible.

Keywords: Frequency monitoring, Recursive N4SID method, Modal minimization method

1. INTRODUCTION

Located in a zone of soft soil in Mexico City, the building consists of a tower of 22 stories and three low-rise structures with a basement in common. Since its construction in 1964, the building presented differential settlements and tilt movement in direction southwest. The 19 September 1985 earthquake caused damage in some coupling beams and columns. To cover these problems, the structure has been subjected to four underpinning in different years and the reinforcement of the tower between 2008 and 2009. Since 2008, the building has 28 high resolution uniaxial accelerometers located in different stories in the building and surrounding terrain, as it is shown in Figure 1.

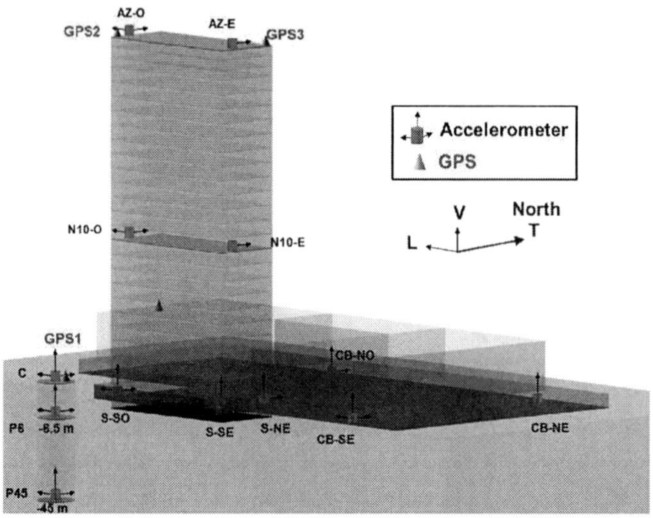

Figure 1. Schematic of the building and its instrumentation.

The structural health is monitored by a warning system called *AlertaE* [1] that estimates the state of the structure when seismic events take place. The system is based on two indicators of the seismic response site (peak ground acceleration PGA and Arias intensity I_{Arias}) and three indicators of structural performance (seismic coefficient Cs, inter-story drift SD and variation of fundamental translation frequencies VF). The possible structural condition of the building is established by weighting criterion developed by the five indicators, based on four colors: Green-slight damage, Yellow-intermediate dama, Orange-sever damage (urgent need to inspect the building) and Red is assigned when the inspection suggest evacuating the building. The efficiency of the *AlertaE* system has been tested by using ambient vibration tests and seismic events recorded from February 2011 [2].

The dynamic properties of the building are sensitive to the intensity of the movement of the ground. In order to study the time variation of the dynamic parameters of the building, seismic records are used in the estimation of three-dimensional simplified models by using modal minimization and N4SID subspace identification methods. MM method [3] minimizes the difference between the measured acceleration signals and those reproduced by a simplified modal superposition model. The MM method demands a high computational processing time and requires human intervention when it is tuned; making it difficult to monitor modal parameters in real time. On the other hand, subspace identification methods have been used in recent works both in tests on shaking tables and real buildings, see for example works [4-6]. These methods reported similar results in terms of accuracy when compared to other classical identification methods used in civil engineering based on frequency and time domains [7].

By contrasting their identification performance, in the presence of seismic events, this work is focused on analyzing the use of recursive N4SID subspace identification method when VF is monitored and the opportunity to be included in the *AlertaE* system, where the VF has been calculated using conventional spectral methods.

2. SUBSPACE IDENTIFICATION METHOD

The recursive N4SID subspace identification method [8] and its use methodology are described as follows. First, a discrete state space model is identified:

$$\boldsymbol{x}(k+1) = \boldsymbol{A}\boldsymbol{x}(k) + \boldsymbol{B}\boldsymbol{u}(k) \tag{1}$$

$$\boldsymbol{y}(k) \quad = \boldsymbol{C}\mathbf{x}(k) + \boldsymbol{D}\boldsymbol{u}(k) \tag{2}$$

where $\boldsymbol{x}(k)$ are the system states, displacements and velocities. Variables $\boldsymbol{u}(k)$ and $\boldsymbol{y}(k)$ are the system input and output, respectively. From a set of N input and output, the N4SID is used in the identification of the system matrices $(\boldsymbol{A}_N, \boldsymbol{C}_N)$ from witch the modal parameters can be calculated:

$$\omega_i = \frac{|ln\lambda_i|}{\Delta t}, \quad h_i = -\frac{ln|\lambda_j|}{|ln\lambda_j|}, \quad \boldsymbol{\phi} = \boldsymbol{C}_N\boldsymbol{\Phi} \tag{3}$$

where Δt is the sampling time and λ_i is the i-th eigenvalue of matrix $\boldsymbol{A}_N$. Mode shapes $(\boldsymbol{\phi})$ are the product of the matrix $\boldsymbol{C}_N$ and the eigenvector matrix $(\boldsymbol{\Phi})$ associated to $\boldsymbol{A}_N$. To achieve this, the N4SID method starts by sorting a set of input and output signals in Hankel matrices as follows:

$$\boldsymbol{U}_N = \begin{bmatrix} \boldsymbol{u}(1) & \boldsymbol{u}(2) & \cdots & \boldsymbol{u}(N-v+1) \\ \boldsymbol{u}(2) & \boldsymbol{u}(3) & \dots & \boldsymbol{u}(N-v+2) \\ \vdots & \vdots & \ddots & \vdots \\ \boldsymbol{u}(v) & \boldsymbol{u}(v+1) & \cdots & \boldsymbol{u}(N) \end{bmatrix}, \quad \boldsymbol{Y}_N = \begin{bmatrix} \boldsymbol{y}(1) & \boldsymbol{y}(2) & \cdots & \boldsymbol{y}(N-v+1) \\ \boldsymbol{y}(2) & \boldsymbol{y}(3) & \dots & \boldsymbol{y}(N-v+2) \\ \vdots & \vdots & \ddots & \vdots \\ \boldsymbol{y}(v) & \boldsymbol{y}(v+1) & \cdots & \boldsymbol{y}(N) \end{bmatrix}$$

where v corresponds to the number of blocks and N the data used in the identification process. After, both input and output are grouped in a condensed matrix:

$$\Xi_N = \boldsymbol{Y}_N \boldsymbol{\Pi}_{U_N}^T \boldsymbol{Y}_N^T \tag{4}$$

where $\boldsymbol{\Pi}_{U_N}^T = \boldsymbol{I} - \boldsymbol{U}_N^T\left(\boldsymbol{U}_N\boldsymbol{U}_N^T\right)^{-1}\boldsymbol{U}_N$ is a projection operator. The matrix is called condensed because its size remains constant as a new pair of input/output data is added, recursively. Applying a singular value decomposition to the condensed matrix, at each step k, the extended observability matrix is calculated, and by using a Moore-Penrose pseudoinverse (†), matrices $(\boldsymbol{A}_N, \boldsymbol{C}_N)$ are calculated as follows:

$$\boldsymbol{A}_N = \begin{bmatrix} \boldsymbol{C}_N \\ \vdots \\ \boldsymbol{C}_N\boldsymbol{A}_N \\ \boldsymbol{C}_N\boldsymbol{A}_N^{V-2} \end{bmatrix}^{\dagger} \begin{bmatrix} \boldsymbol{C}_N\boldsymbol{A}_N \\ \vdots \\ \boldsymbol{C}_N\boldsymbol{A}_N^2 \\ \boldsymbol{C}_N\boldsymbol{A}_N^{V-1} \end{bmatrix}$$

A common problem when using subspace identification methods is the presence of spurious modes that can be caused by nonlinearities, coupling effect or by measurements with poor signal-to-noise ratio [9]. To solve this problem, criteria based on check pair conjugated eigenvalues, damping within a threshold and mode shapes are used as follows. First, eigenvalues that are not complex conjugated pairs are removed. Next, modes whose damping values are out the range $(0, \zeta_M)$ eliminated; ζ_M was fixed to 25%. Then, modes are decoupled by analyzing the dominant direction of the corresponding modal shape. The previous step allows to separate the modes and perform a search for frequencies within thresholds and delete spurious modes using statistical tools as media and standard deviation values. Although these are simple criteria, most of the spurious modes are removed.

3. IDENTIFICATION RESULTS

To illustrate the identification process three of the most intense seismic events recorded are used: March 20, 2012 (event 12-1 – 7.4 Mw), April 18, 2014 (event 14-1 – 7.2 Mw) and September 07, 2017 (event 17-1 – 8.2 Mw). Detailed and complementary information is available in [2]. First, N4SID identification results are compared with those one available with MM method. In addition, the process was applied to an ambient vibration test recorded before the earthquakes.

The identification process was carried out using as input the acceleration signals at the base of the building in the transverse (T), longitudinal (L) and torsional (R) components. In a similar fashion, the output signals correspond to the acceleration signals registered on the roof of the building. Hankel matrices were constructed with 150 rows and 20,000 data; 20 s information windows. Three-dimensional models, from 12 to 140 with increments of 2, were identified in one second intervals. Finally, the spurious modes were removed following the steps previously mentioned. To illustrate the importance of removing the spurious modes, the Figure 2. shows the identification, component L, using the seismic event 12-1. It can be observed that the spurious modes appear from the beginning to the end of the seismic event. This figure shows two stabilization diagrams calculated in different instants of time: 150 and 500 s; before and after removing spurious modes. Meanwhile, the first mode can be estimated with acceptable accuracy, the second mode is less consistency and is surrounded by spurious modes. Clustering techniques can be used to improve results as has been shown in some works [10-11].

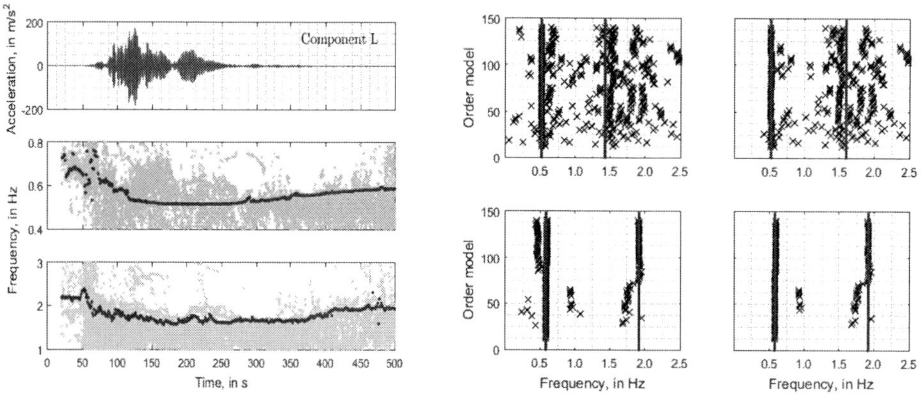

Figure 2. Identification with seismic event 12-1, component L, spurious modes (gray area). Stabilization diagram in instants of time 150 s (upper) and 500 s (lower), before and after removing spurious modes.

The identification process was carried out using Matlab software installed in a computer with Windows 10 OS, processor at 3.6 GHz and 16 GB memory RAM. Measuring the time between the start and end of each identification, including the process of removing spurious modes, this was 80% of the simulated time. For example, the seismic event 12-1 lasts 500 s and the processing time was about 400 s. The computational cost can be reduced either reducing the resolution with which the identification process is made or reducing the number of models identified. Then, the recursive N4SID method is feasible to be used on-line.

Seismic events 12-1 and 14-1 were used in the identification process with both MM and N4SID methods. Figure 3. shows the output acceleration signals in L, T, and R components together with the first two frequencies identified, case 12-1. In a similar fashion, Figure 4. shows the identification results for seismic event 14-1. In the N4SID case, the frequencies correspond the media value calculated in each iteration after removing the spurious. Average standard deviation values, included in the graphics, are below 0.1 Hz. The identification of the first mode is similar in L and T components using both identification methods. Although the values of the first mode, R component, are similar in magnitude, the variation increases in the MM method case. On the other hand, the identified second mode in both L, T and R components are different using both identification methods. This can be explained based on the participation factor reported in [2], comparing the system response based on the identified model and the one that was measured. So, the first mode has a participation factor between 80 and 90 % in both L and T directions. In the torsional direction R, the first mode has a contribution from 11 to 68% and the remainder of the system response depends on the first mode associated to L and T components. The second mode, in any component, has minimal participation, below 10%.

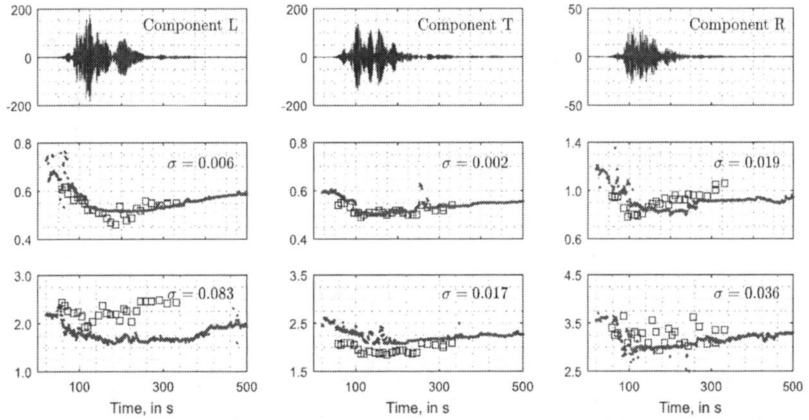

Figure 3. Seismic event 12-1 and identifies frequencies by using MM (square) and N4SID (dot) methods.

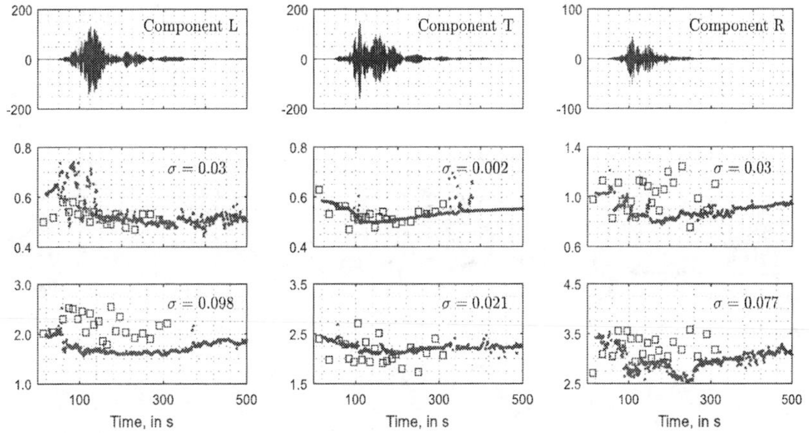

Figure 4. Seismic event 14-1 and identifies frequencies by using MM (square) and N4SID (dot) methods.

To analyze the consistency when the recursive N4SID method is used, the identification process was carried out using the seismic events previously mentioned. Then, the frequency values were calculated before (BE) and along the intense (IP) and final (FP) phases of the earthquakes, see Table 1. Additionally, an identification was performed for an ambient vibration test, registered in February 2012, before seismic event 12-1. First and second frequencies of modes, components L, T, and R, are as follows: 0.68 - 2.22, 0.60 - 2.42, and 1.12 - 3.62 Hz. These values differ until 5% to those reported in event 12-1 (BE) as can be observed in Table 1. On the other hand, frequency values show a higher level of reduction in the IP of the earthquakes, apparently related to the earthquake intensity.

Then, VF was calculated considering as reference the frequency values calculated BE for event 12-1. Subsequently, these values were compared with those reported at the FP of each one of the earthquakes. Starting with the first mode, it's clear there is a reduction in the frequency values. The first mode in components L and R shows a decrease around 16% and in component T of 7%. Results are similar in the second mode where the frequency values show an approximate reduction of 13%, 10% and 10% in L, T and R components, respectively. This suggests accumulative damage in the building.

Table 1. Identified frequencies for first and secon modes. VF estimated from ambient vibration test 2012.

	Component L				Component T				Component R			
Event	BE	IP	FP	VF%	BE	IP	FP	VF%	BE	IP	FP	VF %
Mode 1												
12-1	**0.685**	0.519	0.595	13	**0.595**	0.509	0.562	6	**1.153**	0.835	0.969	16
14-1	0.628	0.516	0.558	19	0.579	0.504	0.555	7	1.025	0.805	0.948	18
17-1	0.630	0.523	0.574	16	0.585	0.533	0.555	7	1.029	0.883	0.957	17
Mode 2												
12-1	**2.180**	1.627	1.954	10	**2.538**	2.121	2.312	9	**3.596**	2.984	3.317	8
14-1	1.994	1.625	1.886	13	2.387	2.133	2.273	10	3.369	2.881	3.246	10
17-1	2.139	1.757	1.903	13	2.391	2.120	2.256	11	3.483	2.835	3.244	10

About damping values, these are below 5% in the first mode using both identification methods, see Figure 5. Contrarily, the second mode has damping values between 5 and 10%, MM case, and about 3%, N4SID case. Standard deviation values are below 1.5% when N4SID is used and are lower compared with MM method case. This behavior confirms the second mode is difficult to estimate accurately. Additionally, the second mode shows a reduction in N4SID case, contrarily to MM case. Omitted for reason of space, damping values showed similar behavior in the identification with events 14-1 and 17-1.

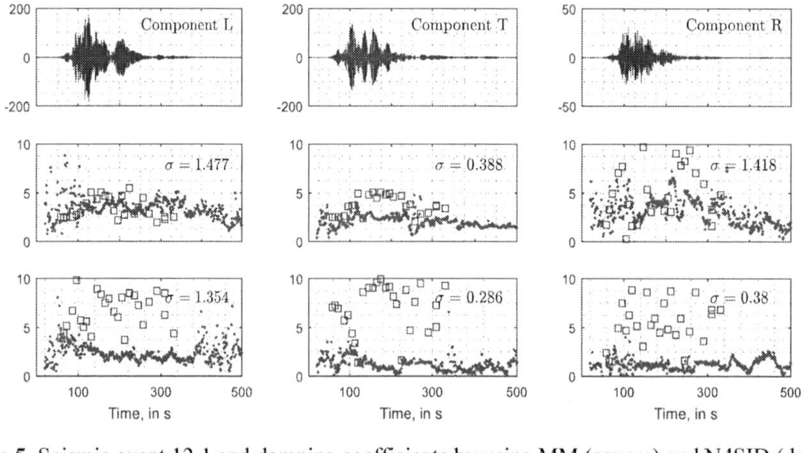

Figure 5. Seismic event 12-1 and damping coefficients by using MM (square) and N4SID (dot) methods.

4. CONCLUSIONS

Based on seismic events, two different identification methods were compared in monitoring the most representative frequencies for a building. Recursive N4SID method provides similar values when identifying the first mode in L, T, and R components, compared with MM method. Despite, second mode presents more variation using both methods, results are more consistent when using N4SID one. About damping values, despite higher variations using MM method, results are comparable in first mode, contrarily to second one. The difficulty to identify second mode can be related to its low participation factor. By analysing the VF, N4SID identification results are consistent, reporting a gradual reduction of the frequency values from an ambient vibration test registered before three moderate intensity earthquakes. This suggests an accumulative damage in the structure, as was reported by the warning system.

Finally, identification results based on N4SID method suggest that, despite the presence of spurious modes, this method can be used as an on-line monitoring system because of its low computational processing cost; identifying different order models with minimal time intervals, one second in this case. However, results can be improved either establishing criteria to perform the identification process in a more intelligent fashion or using, for instance, clustering techniques to remove spurious modes identifying modal parameters with lower errors.

ACKNOWLEDGEMENTS

The study was carried out with the financing provided by the Government of the Mexico City and the National Autonomous University of Mexico. The authors wish to thank the support of the UNAM. We thank J. Camargo, L.A. Aguilar, M. Ayala, M.A. Macías, D. Almora, L. Alcántara, J.M. Velasco, C. Pérez, A.L. Ruiz, R. Delgado, A. Mora, K. Pérez, H. Sandoval, M. Torres, G. Castro, M. Leonardo, R. Vázquez, I. Molina and L. Ramírez for the operation and maintenance of the instrumentation of the building, as well as for the collaboration in the pre-processing or analysis of the registers. The authors also thank the valuable comments and recommendations of S. Alcocer, S. Loera and R. Meli.

REFERENCES

[1] Murià-Vila, D., Aldama, B. D., & Loera, S. (2010). Structural warning for instrumented buildings. In: *Proc. 14th European conference on earthquake engineering*. Ohrid, Macedonia.

[2] Murià-Vila, D., Camargo, J., Rodríguez, F., & Aldama, B. D. (2017). Tilt and seismic response monitoring of a rehabilitated building. In: *Proc. 8th International Conference on Structural Health Monitoring of Intelligent Infrastructure* (pp. 1-10). Brisbane, Australia.

[3] Beck, J. L., & Jennings, P. C. (1980). Structural identification using linear models and earthquake records. *Earthquake Engineering & Structural Dynamics*, *8*(2), 145–160.

[4] Weng, J. H., & Loh, C. H. (2011). Recursive subspace identification for on-line tracking of structural modal parameter. *Mechanical Systems and Signal Processing*, *25*(8), 2923–2937.

[5] Boroschek, R., Aguilar, A., & León, P. (2014). Structural health monitoring using strong and weak earthquake motions. In *Proc., 10th National Conf. in Earthquake Engineering, Earthquake Engineering Research Institute*. Anchorage, AK.

[6] Chen, J.-D., & Loh, C.-H. (2017). Tracking modal parameters of building structures from experimental studies and earthquake response measurements. *Structural Health Monitoring*, 16(5). 551-567.

[7] Peeters, B., & Ventura, C. E. (2003). Comparative study of modal analysis techniques for bridge dynamic characteristics. *Mechanical Systems and Signal Processing*, 17(5), 965–988.

[8] Oku, H., & Kimura, H. (1999). A recursive 4SID from the input-output point of view. *Asian Journal of Control*, *1*(4), 258–269.

[9] Marchesiello, S., Fasana, A., & Garibaldi, L. (2016). Modal contributions and effects of spurious poles in nonlinear subspace identification. *Mechanical Systems and Signal Processing*, *74*, 111–132.

[10] Zonno, G., Aguilar, R., Boroschek, R., & Lourenço, P. B. (2018). Automated long-term dynamic monitoring using hierarchical clustering and adaptive modal tracking: validation and applications. *Journal of Civil Structural Health Monitoring*. *8*(5), 791-808.

[11] Boroschek, R. L., & Bilbao, J. A. (2019). Interpretation of stabilization diagrams using density-based clustring algorithm. *Engineering Structures*, *178*, 245–257.

IOMAC'19

8th International Operational Modal Analysis Conference

2019 May13-15 Copenhagen

MODAL MASS IN CLASSICAL AND OPERATIONAL MODAL ANALYSIS

M. Aenlle[1],F. Pelayo[1] and R. Brincker[2]

[1] Dr, Dept. of Construction and Manufacturing Engineering, University of Oviedo, aenlle@uniovi.es

[2] Prof., Department of Civil Engineering, Department of Civil Engineering, runeb@byg.dtu.dk

ABSTRACT

Mode shapes normalized to the mass matrix contain information of both the modal mass (magnitude of the vector) and the shape of the mode (deflection shape). In operational modal analysis (OMA), the forces are unknown and the modal masses cannot be estimated, i.e., only the un-scaled mode shapes can be identified for each mode. Several approaches have been proposed recently to determine the modal masses in OMA: to modify the dynamic behaviour of the structure (the mass change method), to combine the experimental mode shapes estimated by OMA and the mass matrix of a finite element model of the structure and to consider the experimental modal masses equal to those of a finite element model. It is also well known that a relatively high uncertainty is also expected in the modal masses when classical modal analysis (CMA) is applied. Nevertheless, only very few papers can be found in the literature related to the uncertainty in the modal scaling with CMA. In this paper, a methodology to determine the level of accuracy obtained in the estimation of the modal masses using OMA and CMA is proposed and validated by experimental tests carried out on lab-scaled structures.

Keywords: Modal mass, Modal analysis, Mode shapes

1. INTRODUCTION

When the modal model is used for structural response simulation, structural modification or health monitoring, all the modal parameters (natural frequencies, damping rations, mode shapes and modal masses) are needed [1,2,3,4]

In operational modal analysis (OMA) the forces are unknown and the mode shapes cannot be mass normalized, i.e., the modal masses cannot be estimated. Several approaches have been proposed recently based on modifying the dynamic behavior of the structure by changing the stiffness and/or the mass and then perform operational modal analysis on both the original and the modified structure [4,5], using the mass matrix of a finite element model [6] or considering for the experimental mode shapes the same modal masses as those of a finite element model [7].

With respect to classical modal analysis (CMA), mass normalized mode shapes are obtained in the estimation process. However, it is also well known that a relatively high uncertainty is expected in the modal masses. Nevertheless, only few papers can be found in the literature related to the uncertainty of modal masses with CMA. In [8] CMA was applied to determine the modal parameters a free-free beam, excited with an impulse hammer at 5 points and measuring the response with a scanning laser vibrometer. The modal masses for all of the modes were compared with those of an Euler Bernoulli beam, the error being less than 20%. Much of the discrepancy was attributed to the variation in the hammer blows and uncertainty in the damping estimates.

In [9] the modal masses of a simply supported concrete slab were estimated by both CMA and OMA, measuring the responses with 21 acceleration sensors. In CMA the slab was driven using uncorrelated random signals from two shakers with the same excitation. In OMA, the total mass change was in the range 5-10% of the total mass of the slab, locating different number of masses at different DOF's. The maximum discrepancies between the modal masses estimated by CMA and OMA were found to be less than 13%.

In [10] the modal mass corresponding to the first vertical mode of a footbridge was estimated with CMA and using two different excitations (random excitation and un-averaged chirp excitation) obtaining 53,188 kg and 48,763 kg, respectively, the difference being 8.32%.

In [11] the modal masses of a staircase and a helipad were estimated by CMA and operational modal analysis combined with mono-harmonic excitation (OMAH). The discrepancies in the modal estimates for the staircase were 8% and 40%, respectively, for the two modes considered in the investigation, whereas the differences in the modal estimates for the helipad were approx. 20% for the two modes.

In [10] it is mentioned that modal mass is the least reliable parameter when CMA is used to estimate modal parameters and also that it is very sensitive to response magnitude. On the other hand, the methods used in OMA to estimate the modal masses are also approximate and those based on experiments difficult to apply in big structures. Although the modal masses estimated with both OMA and CMA can be compared between them, the exact modal mass corresponding to each mode is, generally, not known and, consequently, it is not possible to quantify the error obtained with these techniques. In this paper, a methodology to determine the error obtained in the estimation of modal masses using OMA and CMA is presented and validated by experimental tests carried out on a steel cantilever beam and a steel T structure.

2. BASIC THEORY

In discrete systems, the mode shapes are vectors and the modal mass corresponding to an un-scaled mode shape ($\boldsymbol{\psi}$) can be calculated with the equation [1,2,3,4]:

$$m = \boldsymbol{\psi}^T \boldsymbol{M} \boldsymbol{\psi} \tag{1}$$

Where $\boldsymbol{M}$ is the mass matrix.

If the mass density ρ of the system is constant, eq. (1) can be expressed as:

$$m = \rho \boldsymbol{\psi}^T \boldsymbol{V} \boldsymbol{\psi} \tag{2}$$

Where $\boldsymbol{V}$ is a volume matrix.

If the total volume of the system is denoted as V_T, eq. (2) can also be formulated as:

$$m = M_T \frac{\boldsymbol{\psi}^T \boldsymbol{V} \boldsymbol{\psi}}{V_T} \tag{3}$$

Or:

$$m = M_T Z \tag{4}$$

Where the term Z is given by:

$$Z = \frac{\psi^T V \psi}{V_T} \tag{5}$$

And depends on the volume of the structure and the mode shapes:

If the mode shapes are normalized so that:

$$Z = \frac{\psi^T V \psi}{V_T} = 1 \tag{6}$$

the modal mass for all the modes is given by:

$$m = M_T \tag{7}$$

From eq. (7) it is inferred that if the mode shapes of a system with constant mass density are normalized using eq. (6), the modal mass is equal for all the modes and equal to the total mass of the system. With other normalization techniques, the modal mass is related to the total mass of the system by means of eq. (4).

Thus, the total mass of the system with constant mass density can be considered a reference and it can be used to determine the error obtained in the estimation of modal masses with OMA and CMA.

If a structure is discretized with many DOF's and they are uniformly distributed in the structure, eq. (5) can be accurately approximated by:

$$Z \cong \frac{\psi^T \psi}{N} \tag{8}$$

Where N is the number of nodes of the structure.

3. EXPERIMENTAL RESULTS

3.1. A steel cantilever beam

Operational modal testing was performed on a steel cantilever beam structure 1.75 m long and with a rectangular hollow section 100x40x4 mm. The total mass of the system was $M_T = 14.3\ kg$. The responses were recorded in 7 DOF's using 7 accelerometers with a sensitivity of 100 mV/g, located as is shown in Figure 1. The responses were recorded for a period of approximately 3 minutes at a sampling frequency of 2000 Hz and using a TEAC LX-120 data recorder. The structure was artificially excited applying repetitive hits random in time and space [4].

The modal masses were estimated by the mass change method [4,5]. The system was perturbed attaching lumped masses of 145 grams in seven points (same location as the sensors) with a total mass change of 1015 grams. With respect to the CMA, the same sensors and data acquisition system as those used in the OMA tests, where utilized in the modal testing, being the signals recorded at a sampling rate of 2000 Hz. An impact hammer with sensitivity 2.27 mV/N was used as excitation.

The modal parameters in OMA were identified with the Frequency Domain Decomposition (FDD) method [4]. As regards CMA, the modal parameters were identified from the frequency response functions (FRF's), using the Rational Fraction Polynomials (RFP) [1,2,3]. The estimated experimental natural frequencies with respect to the weak axes are shown in Table 1, from which it can be inferred that a good agreement exists between the results provided by CMA and OMA.

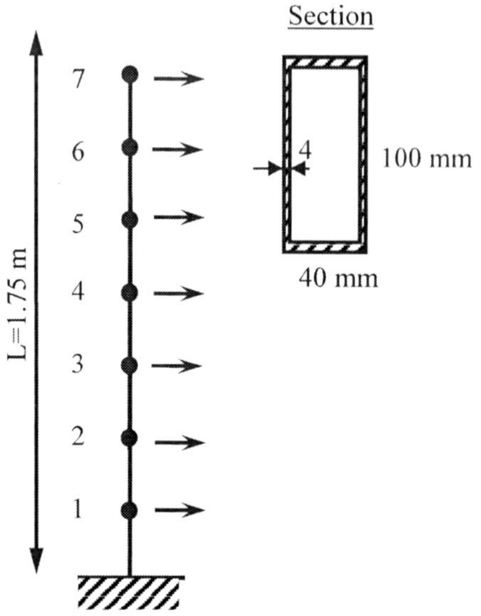

Figure 1. Test setup for the cantilever beam

A finite element model was also assembled in ABAQUS [14] using 28908 quadratic hexahedral elements of type C3D20R. The numerical natural frequencies corresponding to the first four modes are presented in table 1.

Table 1. Natural frequencies (Hz) for the cantilever beam.

Mode	OMA	CMA	FE
1	12.45	12.33	12.772
2	79.6	79.51	80.976
3	222.7	221.44	227.23
4	424.3	425.11	443.09

In this particular case, an analytical expression exists for the mode shapes and the exact values of Z (eq. (5)) can be determined, which are presented in Table 2 for mode shapes normalized to the largest component equal to unity. For the experimental models, the values of Z were calculated with eq. (5) using a lumped volume matrix. With respect to the numerical model, the values of Z were calculated with eq. (8). It can be observed in table 2 that the numerical model provides values of Z very close to the analytical ones. As regarding to the experimental models, the error increases with the order of the mode.

The analytical and the numerical modal masses, together with those estimated by modal testing (OMA and CMA) are presented in Table 3. It can be observed that the modal masses obtained with the numerical model approximates quite well the analytical values. With respect to the experimental modal masses obtained by OMA and CMA the error increases with the order of the mode when the mode shapes are normalized to the largest component equal to unity. However, the modal masses of two modes normalized to the largest component equal to unity must not be compared, because they have different values of Z [12,13].

Table 2. Values of Z for the cantilever beam. Mode shapes normalized to the largest component equal to unity. Experimental mode shapes normalized with a lumped volume matrix.

Mode	OMA	CMA	FE	Analytical
1	0.2948	0.2948	0.2569	0.25
2	0.3134	0.3134	0.2595	0.25
3	0.3537	0.3537	0.2597	0.25
4	0.3590	0.3590	0.2523	0.25

In order to compare modal masses, the mode shapes must be normalized to unit Z. In this case, the mass density of the structure is constant and the modal mass for all the modes have to be equal to the total mass of the structure $M_T = 14.3\ kg$. It can be observed in Table 3 that the maximum error between the exact value ($m = M_T = 14.3\ kg$) and the modal masses obtained from the experiments is 18.5% for CMA and 16.85% for OMA.

It is important to remark that the same mass normalized mode shape is obtained using the modal masses corresponding to mode shapes normalized to the largest component equal to unity or to unit Z. However, only the modal masses corresponding to mode shapes normalized to unit Z can be compared with the total mass $m = M_T = 14.3\ kg$. Nevertheless, this modal mass can only be calculated if the paramter Z is known, i.e. the accuracy obtained in the modal mass depends on the precision achieved in paramter Z.

Table 3. Modal masses (kg) estimated for the cantilever beam. Experimental mode shapes normalized with a lumped volume matrix. $\boldsymbol{M_T = 14.3\ kg}$

Mode	Normalization to the unit Z				Normalization to the largest component equal to unity			
	OMA	CMA	FE	Analytical	OMA	CMA	FE	Analytical
1	13.291	11.5003	14.2991	14.3	3.9181	3.3903	3.6728	3.575
2	12.587	11.6519	14.3009	14.3	3.9446	3.6517	3.7111	3.575
3	11.895	12.0294	14.3018	14.3	4.2078	4.2548	3.7139	3.575
4	13.362	14.6398	14.3104	14.3	4.7986	5.2557	3.6102	3.575

In order to obtain a good accuracy in the estimation of the modal mass, it is required that the parameter Z is calculated with a good accuracy. In this paper, parameter Z was calculated with a lumped volume matrix, but the accuracy can be significantly improved using a consistent volume matrix or expanding the experimental mode shapes to the un-measured DOF's. The results of parameter Z (eq. (8)) using expanded experimental mode shapes (expanded with the FE model using the local correspondence principle [4]) are presented in Table 4 and the modal masses in Table 5, where it can be observed that the modal masses have been estimated with a good accuracy, except for the 4th mode with both OMA and CMA.

Table 4. Values of Z for the cantilever beam. Expanded experimental mode shapes normalized to the largest component equal to unity.

Mode	OMA	CMA	FE	Analytical
1	0.2696	0.2696	0.2569	0.25
2	0.2759	0.2759	0.2595	0.25
3	0.2924	0.2924	0.2597	0.25
4	0.2945	0.2945	0.2523	0.25

Table 5. Modal masses (kg) estimated for the cantilever beam with expanded experimental mode shapes. Mode shapes normalized to unit Z. $\boldsymbol{M_T = 14.3\ kg}$

Mode	OMA	CMA	FE	Analytical
1	14.5447	12.5749	14.2991	14.3
2	14.2565	13.2370	14.3009	14.3
3	14.9518	14.5535	14.3018	14.3
4	16.2191	17.8446	14.3104	14.3

3.2. A steel T structure

The steel T structure consists of two welded 80x40x4 mm rectangular hollow section beams, being the vertical beam 1.5 m long and the horizontal one 1.2 m, respectively. The total mass of the system was $M_T = 19.35\ kg$ The operational modal testing was carried out measuring the responses in 24 DOF's and using 14 accelerometers with a sensitivity of 100 mv/g, located as shown in figure 2. Four reference accelerometers (in blue in figure 2) were used in each of the two data sets needed to cover all the DOF's. The data acquisition system was the same as that used in the cantilever beam. The responses were recorded for a period of approximately 3 minutes with a sampling frequency of 2000 Hz. The modal masses were estimated by the mass change method [4,5], and the system was perturbed attaching lumped masses of 145 grams in 8 points (same location as the sensors) which represents a total mass change of 1168 grams.

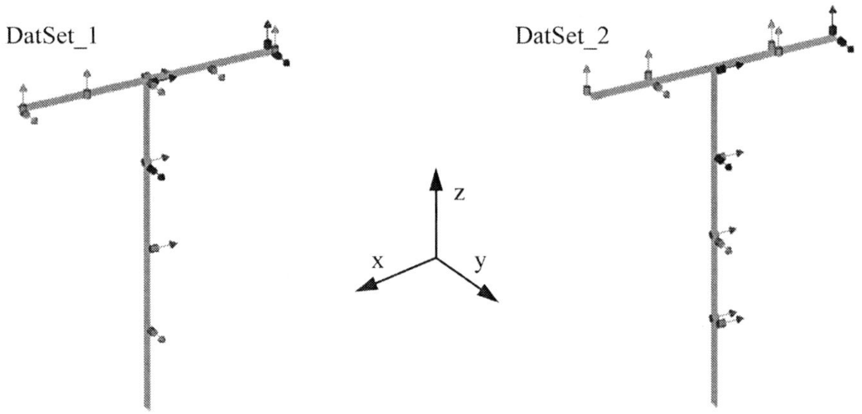

Figure 2. Test setup for the T structure

With respect to the CMA, the same sensors and data acquisition system as those used in the OMA tests, where utilized in the modal testing, being the signals recorded at a sampling rate of 2000 Hz. An impact hammer with sensitivity 2.27 mV/N was used as excitation.

The modal identification in OMA and CMA was performed with the same methods used for the cantilever beam. The natural frequencies of the eight modes considered in the investigation are shown in table 6 and the mode shapes in table 7, respectively. A finite element model was also assembled in ABAQUS [14] using 37800 quadratic hexahedral elements of type C3D20R, the numerical natural frequencies being shown in table 6.

For the experimental models, the values of Z were calculated with eq. (5) using a lumped volume matrix (see table 8), whereas the values of Z corresponding to the numerical model were calculated using eq. (8). The discrepancies between the experimenal and the numerical values of Z are significantly high, although the MAC between the numerial and the experimental mode shapes are higher than 0.98 for all the modes. Due to the fact that there are significant discrepancies between the values of Z corresponding to the experimental and the numerical mode shapes, large errors are expected in the modal masses for mode shapes normalized to unit Z. This highlights importance of obtaining a high degree of accuracy in the estimation of parameter Z.

Table 6. Natural frequencies (Hz) for the T structure.

Mode	OMA	CMA	FE
1	8.73	8.761	8.9636
2	16.35	16.426	16.441
3	27.00	27.059	25.631
4	42.36	42.52	45.082
5	150.2	150.8	150.56
6	299.9	304.22	302.83
7	319.6	320.35	316.53
8	530.2	532.25	507.29

Table 7. Mode shapes for the T structure.

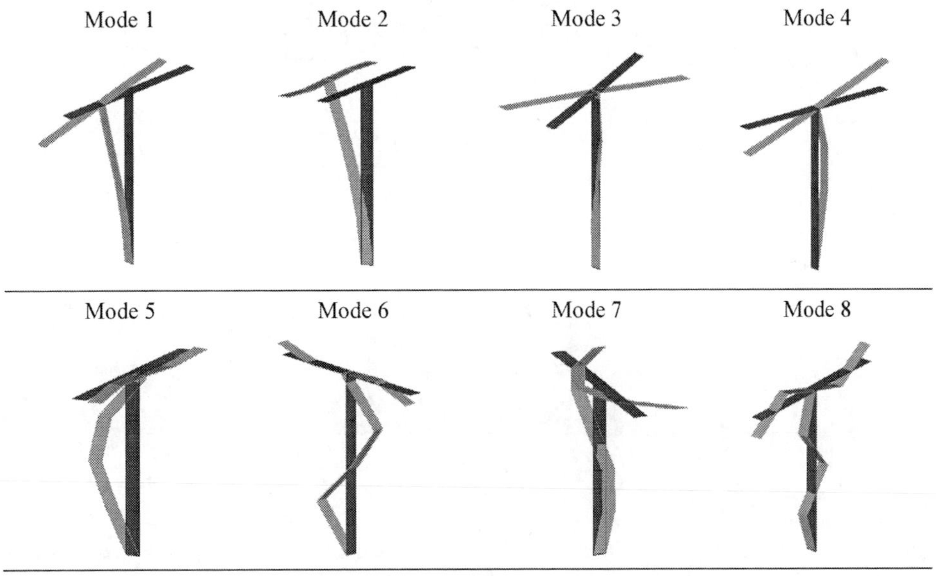

The analytical and the numerical modal masses, together with those estimated by modal testing (OMA and CMA) [15] are presented in Table 9. The numerical modal masses (mode shapes normalized to unit Z) are very close to the exact values given by eq. (7) $(m = M_T = 19.35\ kg)$. With respect to the experimental modal masses obtained by OMA and CMA, the error is significantly high due to the low precision achieved in the estimation of parameter Z.

The results of parameter Z (eq. (8)) using expanded experimental mode shapes are presented in Table 10 and the modal masses in Table 11 where it can be observed that the modal masses have been estimated with an error less than 20% for all the modes with both OMA and CMA, except for the 7th mode where the error was approximately 27%.

Table 8. Values of Z for the T structure. Mode shapes normalized to the largest component equal to unity. Experimental mode shapes normalized wiht a lumped volume matrix.

Mode	OMA	CMA	FE
1	0.6087	0.6087	0.6031
2	0.7281	0.7281	0.5474
3	0.2445	0.2445	0.1503
4	0.2711	0.2711	0.1796
5	0.2388	0.2388	0.2771
6	0.2240	0.2240	0.2589
7	0.2344	0.2344	0.1415
8	0.3528	0.3528	0.1958

Table 9. Modal masses estimated for the T structure. Experimental mode shapes normalized with a lumped volume matrix. $M_T = 19.35\ kg$

Mode	Normalization to unit Z			Normalization to the largest component equal to unity		
	OMA	CMA	FE	OMA	CMA	FE
1	16.0635	18.1328	19.3472	9.7778	11.0374	11.6087
2	12.9710	13.6245	19.3253	9.4442	9.9200	10.5141
3	10.9485	11.1851	19.2361	2.6769	2.7348	2.8825
4	11.9666	12.3011	19.2606	3.2442	3.3348	3.4549
5	24.0474	23.6042	19.3554	5.7425	5.6367	5.4083
6	21.6210	20.2872	19.3608	4.8431	4.5443	5.0772
7	12.6427	13.3548	19.2350	2.9634	3.1304	2.5421
8	9.3159	9.4456	19.2729	3.2866	3.3324	3.7529

4. CONCLUSIONS

A methodology to determine the accuracy obtained in the estimation of modal masses using OMA and CMA in systems with constant mass density, has been presented. It has been demonstrated and validated by experiments that the modal mass of a system with constant mass density is equal to the total mass of the system (for all the modes) when the mode shapes are normalized to the unit Z.

However, in order to obtain a good accuracy in the estimation of the modal mass, it is required that the parameter Z is calculated with a good accuracy. In this paper, parameter Z was calculated with a lumped volume matrix, which is a poor approximation if only few DOF's are considered to discretize the structures. The accuracy can be improved significantly using a consistent volume matrix or expanding the experimental mode shapes to the un-measured DOF's.

ACKNOWLEDGEMENTS

The financing support given by Banco Santander through the Mobility Grants for Researchers of Professors of the University of Oviedo, is gratefully appreciated. The authors acknowledge the funding received from Centre for Oil and Gas - DTU/Danish Hydrocarbon Research and Technology Centre (DHRTC).

Table 10. Values of Z for the T structure. Expanded experimental mode shapes normalized to the largest component equal to unity.

Mode	OMA	CMA	FE
1	0.6145	0.6145	0.6031
2	0.5483	0.5483	0.5474
3	0.1466	0.1466	0.1503
4	0.1860	0.1860	0.1796
5	0.2567	0.2567	0.2771
6	0.2503	0.2503	0.2589
7	0.1270	0.1270	0.1415
8	0.2015	0.2015	0.1958

Table 11. Modal masses (kg) estimated for the T structure with expanded experimental mode shapes. Mode shapes normalized to unit Z. $\boldsymbol{M_T = 19.35\ kg}$

Mode	OMA	CMA	FE
1	15.9118	17.9616	19.3472
2	17.2245	18.0923	19.3253
3	18.2599	18.6548	19.2361
4	17.4419	17.9290	19.2606
5	22.3705	21.9583	19.3554
6	19.3492	18.1554	19.3608
7	23.3339	24.6488	19.2350
8	16.3107	16.5380	19.2729

REFERENCES

[1] Ewins DJ (2000) *Modal Testing: Theory, Practice and Application*, Second Ed. London: Research Studies Press LTD

[2] Maia NMM. and Montalvao e Silva JM (2003) *Theoretical and Experimental Modal Analysis*. England: Research Studies Press LTD

[3] Heylen W, Lammens S and Sas P (2007) *Modal Analysis theory and testing*. Belgium: Katholieke Universiteit Leuven, Faculty of Engenieering

[4] Brincker R., Ventura C. (2015). *Introduction to Operational Modal Analysis*. Chichester : John Wiley & Sons Ltd.

[5] López-Aenlle, M., Brincker, R., Pelayo, F., and Canteli, A. (2012) On exact and approximated formulation for scaling-mode shapes in operational model analysis by mass and stiffness change. *Journal of sound and vibration*, **331**, 622–637.

[6] Aenlle M, Brincker R (2013). Modal Scaling in Operational Modal Analysis sing a Finite Element Model. *International Journal of Mechanical Sciences,* **76** ,86-101

[7] Schwarz B, Richardson M. (2006). Using FEA modes to scale experimental mode shapes. *In: International modal analysis conference* (IMAC XXIV), (paper 46), St Louis, USA.

[8] Allen MS, Sracic MW (2008), Mass normalized mode shapes using impact excitation and continuous-scan laser Doppler vibrometry, *International Conference on Vibration Measurements by Laser Techniques: Advances and Applications.* **7098**, 709804-709815.

[9] Fernández P, Reynolds P, López-Aenlle M, Canteli AF(2010), Experimental Evaluation of Mass Change Approaches for Scaling Factors Estimation. *IMAC XXVIII*. **4,** 109-118.

[10] Brandt A, Berardengo M, Manzonic M, Vanalib M, Cigada A (2019). Global scaling of operational modal analysis modes with the OMAH method. *Mechanical Systems and Signal Processing*. 117, 52-64.

[11] Zivanovic S, Pavic A, Reynolds P. (2006) Modal Testing and FE Model Tuning of a Lively Footbridge Structure, *Engineering Structures*, **28**, 857-868.

[12] Aenlle, M.L., Brincker R., Juul M.O.O. (2019), Modal Mass and Length of Mode Shapes in Structural Dynamics. Submitted to *Journal of Engineering Mechanics* (ASCE).

[13] Aenlle ML, Brincker R(2019), Basic Concepts of Modal Scaling . *In these Proceedings.*

[14] ABAQUS, Finite Element Analysis Software, Dassault Systemes, V́elizy-Villacoublay, France.

[15] Pelayo F, Aenlle ML, Brincker R (2014). Mass normalization of a 3D tubular structure combining operational modal analysis and a numerical model. *International Conference on Noise and Vibration Engineering (ISMA 2014)*, 3281-3291.

IOMAC'19

8th International Operational Modal Analysis Conference
2019 May13-15 Copenhagen

OPERATIONAL MODAL ANALYSIS BASED LINEAR SYSTEM IDENTIFICATION OF SYSTEMS WITH ELASTO-PERFECTLY-PLASTIC NONLINEAR BEHAVIOUR

T. Friis [1], *M. Tarpø* [2], *E. I. Katsanos* [3], *S. D. R. Amador* [4], *R. Brincker* [5]

[1] PhD stud., Technical University of Denmark, Denmark, tofri@byg.dtu.dk
[2] PhD stud., Aarhus University, Denmark, martar@eng.au.dk
[3] Assistant prof., Technical University of Denmark, Denmark, vakat@byg.dtu.dk
[4] Postdoc, Technical University of Denmark, Denmark, sdio@byg.dtu.dk
[5] Prof., Technical University of Denmark, Denmark, runeb@byg.dtu.dk

ABSTRACT
Operational Modal Analysis (OMA) is widely used to identify the modal properties of systems under ambient vibrations or normal operating conditions. The fundamental assumption of existing OMA methods is that the system is linear and time-invariant. Civil engineering structures, however, often violate this assumption, especially, when their dynamic behaviour is influenced by various sources of nonlinearity such as; the hysteretic behaviour of structural elements, friction between sliding surfaces and softening of the soil-foundation system. Along these lines, this paper assesses the linear frequency and damping estimation performance of two correlation driven OMA methods applied to a nonlinear system with bilinear (i.e., elasto-perfectly-plastic) behaviour. This assessment of the estimation performance compares the OMA based estimates to theoretical values of equivalent linear frequency and viscous damping and discusses the discrepancies. It is found that the OMA methods provide reliable results for the investigated simulation system with nonlinear damping and stiffness, though, with a bias in the related frequency and damping estimates arising in the correlation function estimation. The bias is, however, relatively small.

Keywords: Bilinear nonlinearity, stick-slip friction, hysteresis, equivalent linear stiffness and viscous damping, nonlinear dynamics, operational modal analysis, best linear approximation

1. INTRODUCTION

It is known from modal analysis of existing structures and mechanical systems that they often behave nonlinearly [1]. In many cases this complex behaviour might arise from phenomena such as geometrical nonlinearities, aerodynamics, hydrodynamics or hysteresis, e.g., internal friction in materials and friction between sliding surfaces in joints. Even so, in some cases it is undesirable, or impossible, to characterise and estimate the nonlinear parameters of the dynamic system. Instead the aim is to identify a linear system, which reliably describes the nonlinear system in relation to the associated conditions. Exemplary cases can be found among civil engineering structures, such as large bridges, highrise buildings and offshore structures. Within this engineering field, deterministic modal analysis is impractical and the application of stochastic modal analysis, known as Operational Modal Analysis (OMA), is often the preferred option. Consequently, the practitioner is left with a fit of linear models to a nonlinear system, due to the imperative assumption of linear and time-invariant systems in OMA.

In the literature, research has been focussed on modal analysis of nonlinear mechanical systems. Kerschen et al [2] reviewed the past and recent developments in system identification of nonlinear dynamical structures aimed for detection, characterisation and parameter estimation of nonlinear system in a deterministic setting. Schoukens et al [3] analysed, also in a deterministic setting, the impact of nonlinear distortions on the best linear approximated models of nonlinear responses. Both studies, however, did not account for the stochastic setting of OMA. Nevertheless, Zhang et al. [4] investigated the effect of quadratic stiffness together with cubic viscous damping and geometrical nonlinearity on OMA based estimation of modal characteristics. They found that the OMA methods extract most linear dynamic properties of nonlinear systems, though, with increased bias and statistical dispersion. The study did, however, not deal with systems exhibiting elasto-perfectly-plastic nonlinear behaviour. Thus, this particular nonlinearity, which can be interpreted as simplified hysteresis, is the focus of the present study. The elasto-perfectly-plastic nonlinearity is depicted in Fig. 1.

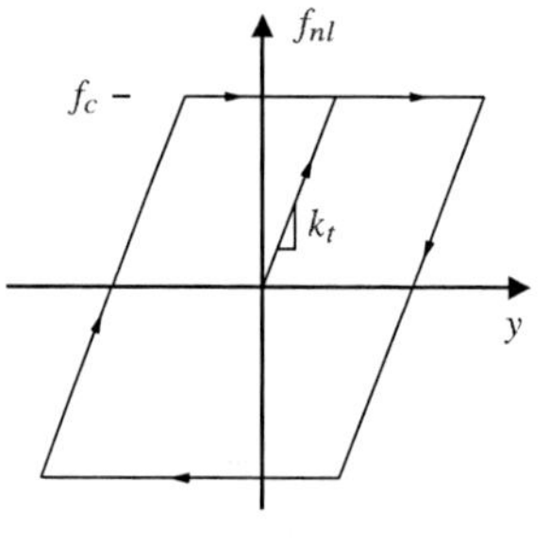

Figure 1: Depiction of the involved nonlinearity, denoted f_{nl}, over displacement y. k_t is the elastic stiffness and f_c is the perfectly plastic force level.

This article assesses the correlation driven OMA methods ability to linearly estimate the elasto-perfectly-plastic nonlinear system in an equivalent (best linear), or at least appropriate, manner. The assessment of the OMA based linear modal estimates of systems with elasto-perfectly-plastic nonlinear behaviour is carried out considering a simulated steel structure. By establishing the evaluation on a numerical test bed, the conditions of the assessment can be fully controlled ensuring an apparent interpretation of the findings.

The remainder of this paper is organised as Following. First, the paper describes a procedure for estimation of equivalent linear stiffness and viscous damping from the response of a nonlinear system. These parameters are used as the reference parameters for the OMA based linear estimation, since the former estimates constitute the linear system fitting the data most flawlessly. Subsequently, the employed OMA methods are presented with a successive description of the numerical case study and the involved simulation procedure. At last, estimation results of modal characteristics are given with a comparative assessment of the OMA based estimates with the theoretical reference values including an analysis discussion of the discrepancies.

2. ESTIMATION OF EQUIVALENT LINEAR STIFFNESS AND VISCOUS DAMPING (ELS)

The definition of equivalent linear stiffness and viscous damping employed herein is based on the method of equivalent linearisation introduced by Caughey [5]. The ideology of the approach is the formulation of a linear system, which is equivalent to the nonlinear one, in the sense that the difference between the two is minimal. In mathematical form, the definition can be described in the following manner:

$$\mathbf{M}\ddot{\mathbf{y}}_{nl}(t) + \mathbf{C}\dot{\mathbf{y}}_{nl}(t) + \mathbf{K}\mathbf{y}_{nl}(t) + \mathbf{f}_{nl}(\mathbf{y}_{nl}, \dot{\mathbf{y}}_{nl}, t) = \mathbf{x}(t) \tag{1}$$

$$\Rightarrow \quad \mathbf{M}\ddot{\mathbf{y}}_{nl}(t) + \mathbf{C}_{eq}\dot{\mathbf{y}}_{nl}(t) + \mathbf{K}_{eq}\mathbf{y}_{nl}(t) + \mathbf{e}(t)|_{min} = \mathbf{x}(t) \tag{2}$$

where $\mathbf{M}$, $\mathbf{C}$, and $\mathbf{K}$ are the mass, damping and stiffness matrices of the linear part of the system, respectively, $\mathbf{x}(t)$ is the external excitation, $\mathbf{y}(t)$ is response, $\{\dot{}\}$ denotes differentiation with respect to time t, and $\mathbf{e}(t)$ describes the difference between the nonlinear system and the equivalent linear system. The equivalent linear stiffness and viscous damping matrices, $\mathbf{C}_{eq}$ and $\mathbf{K}_{eq}$, describe the linear part of the system together with a linearisation of the nonlinear part.

The method employed herein for the task of estimating the equivalent linear parameters of the nonlinear system is based on a direct linear least squares fit of the physical parameters to the nonlinear response, e.g. least squares fit of $\mathbf{C}_{eq}$ and $\mathbf{K}_{eq}$. This approach is similar to a procedure by Mohammad et al [6], who estimated actual structural matrices of linear and nonlinear lumped parameter systems, thus exploited in a different manner and different formulation in the present context.

3. OMA METHODS FOR ESTIMATION OF LINEAR FREQUENCY AND VISCOUS DAMPING (OMA)

In the present study, two state-of-the-art OMA methods are employed. Especially, the Time-Domain Poly-Reference method (TDPR) is chosen together with the Poly-reference Least Squares Complex Frequency method (pLSCF). The TDPR method estimates the modal characteristics by a fitting of coefficients to correlation functions, while for the pLSCF method, coefficients are fitted to half spectral densities, thus, the estimates of modal characteristics are also based on correlation functions in the latter case. Both methods are described extensively in the literature, hence, only a short description of the actual implementation of the methods is provided in the following subsections along with relevant references.

3.1. Time-Domain Poly-Reference (TDPR)

The TDPR is one of the simplest methods based on correlation functions within the area of OMA and is extensively described in the literature. The reader is referred to Brincker and Ventura [7] and Vold [8]. The overall procedure of the method is to fit auto-regressive models in a poly-reference sense to correlation functions. The polynomial coefficients of the auto-regressive models are found by forming a least squared problem and solving it by the means of two block Hankel matrices. Successively, the modal parameters are computed by the eigenvalue decomposition of a companion matrix containing the polynomial coefficients. The present method offers the advantage of excluding time lags with statistical errors of the correlation functions. Therefore, the so-called noise tail is removed in an automated manner by the method proposed by Tarpø et al [9]. Lastly, the mathematical poles are excluded by removing poles with relatively unrealistic damping, i.e., modes with negative or high damping and conjungated pairs, leaving the physical poles.

3.2. Poly-reference Least Squares Complex Frequency (pLSCF)

The pLSCF method is an extended version of the Least Squares Complex Frequency method including poly-references and is described in the literature. The reader is referred to Peeters et al [10]. The overall principle of the method is to model the input-output relationship of the system by a right matrix-fraction model in the frequency domain. Analogous to the first method, the coefficients of this model are estimated from the half spectral densities by the means of an approximated linear least squared problem. Subsequently, a companion matrix is established from the coefficients and the poles and modal participation factors, and consequently the mode shapes, are obtained by computing its eigenvalue decomposition. The physical poles are sorted from the mathematical ones through a stability diagram. Herein, the selection procedure is running automatically by employing an agglomerative hierarchical clustering algorithm on the stable poles.

The pLSCF method is considered as a robust and efficient method that generates clear stabilisation diagrams. On the other, the method also has a tendency to underestimate the damping when the noise tail region of the correlation functions are included in the computation of the half spectral matrix. Traditionally and in the present study, this particular issue is handled by employing an exponential window on the correlation functions and subtracting the applied damping of the window after the estimation of the modal parameters.

4. NUMERICAL CASE STUDY

The comparative assessment of the related ELS and OMA based linear estimates of modal frequency and damping is performed on a finite element model of a simple T-shaped steel structure, see Fig. 2. The initial model was composed of three dimensional Timoschenko beam elements with 156 degrees-of-freedom (DOFs) in total, and subsequently reduced to ten DOFs by the system equivalent reduction and expansion process, proposed by O'Callahan [11]. The nonlinear, elasto-perfectly-plastic behaviour is modelled by including an elasto-perfectly-plastic element, a so-called Jenkins element, along DOF 3 with external support. The parameters of the Jenkins element were set to $f_c = 4$ N and $k_t = 12$ kN/m and a sequence of the force-displacement relationship of the element from one of the simulations can be found in Fig. 2. The sequence has a length of approximately eight periods of oscillation of the first two modes.
The simulation model was exposed to uncorrelated, normally distributed white noise in all ten DOFs, where the individual discrete time series of the excitation had a standard deviation of 15.9 N.

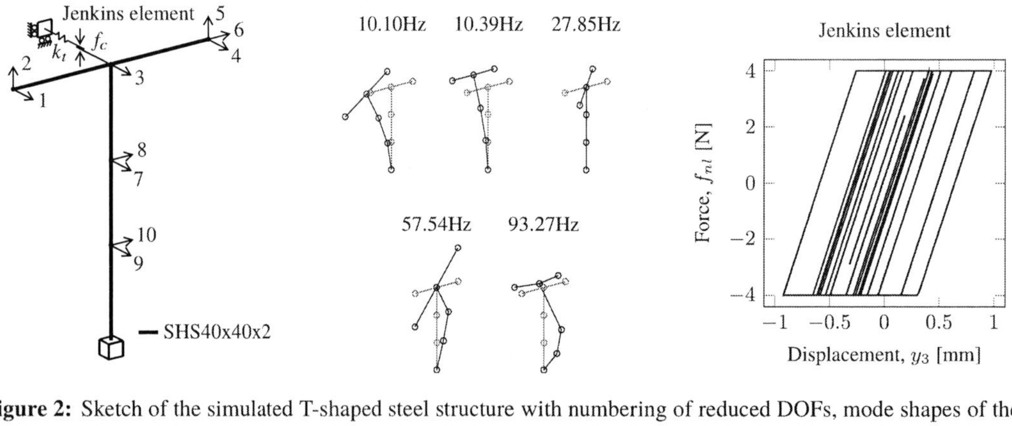

Figure 2: Sketch of the simulated T-shaped steel structure with numbering of reduced DOFs, mode shapes of the first five modes, and force-displacement plot of the Jenkins element for eight periods of oscillation of the simulation model.

The simulation study, involving the mentioned nonlinear finite element model, is carried out by first formulating the equation of motion in the conventional manner for the linear system. Successively, the nonlinear force of the Jenkins element is implemented through an additional term, $\mathbf{d}\, f_{nl}(\mathbf{y}(t), \dot{\mathbf{y}}(t))$. Thus, analogous to Eq. (1), the system of second order differential equations becomes:

$$\mathbf{M}\ddot{\mathbf{y}}(t) + \mathbf{C}\dot{\mathbf{y}}(t) + \mathbf{K}\mathbf{y}(t) + \mathbf{d} f_{nl}(\mathbf{y}(t), \dot{\mathbf{y}}(t)) = \mathbf{x}(t) \tag{3}$$

where $\mathbf{d}$ is a placement vector.

In the present study, the linear damping matrix is simply composed of the principles of proportional damping and the desired damping ratios of the linear system by:

$$\mathbf{C} = \sum_{j=1}^{J} (\mathbf{M}\mathbf{b}_j) \frac{c_j}{m_j^2} (\mathbf{M}\mathbf{b}_j)^T \tag{4}$$

where $\mathbf{b}_j$ is the mode shape of mode j, c_j is the modal dashpot coefficient and m_j is the modal mass. The first three modes of the T-shaped simulation model were assigned a damping ratio of 1% and the following two were assigned a damping ratio of 3%, not considering any effect of the Jenkins element. Before formulation the equation of motion in discrete form, compared to the continuous form, a transformation to state space is conducted:

$$\dot{\mathbf{z}}(t) = \mathbf{A}_c\mathbf{z}(t) + \mathbf{d}_c f_{nl}(\mathbf{y}(t), \dot{\mathbf{y}}(t)) + \mathbf{E}_c\mathbf{x}(t) \tag{5}$$

where

$$\mathbf{z}(t) = \begin{Bmatrix} \dot{\mathbf{y}}(t) \\ \mathbf{y}(t) \end{Bmatrix} \in \mathbb{R}^{2L\times1}, \quad \mathbf{A}_c = \begin{bmatrix} -\mathbf{M}^{-1}\mathbf{C} & -\mathbf{M}^{-1}\mathbf{K} \\ \mathbf{I} & \mathbf{0} \end{bmatrix} \in \mathbb{R}^{2L\times2L} \tag{6}$$

$$\mathbf{d}_c = \begin{Bmatrix} \mathbf{M}^{-1}\mathbf{d} \\ \mathbf{0} \end{Bmatrix} \in \mathbb{R}^{2L\times1}, \quad \mathbf{E}_c = \begin{bmatrix} \mathbf{M}^{-1} \\ \mathbf{0} \end{bmatrix} \in \mathbb{R}^{2L\times L} \tag{7}$$

and $\mathbf{I}$ is the identity matrix and L denotes the number of DOFs.
The simulations are carried out by time stepping the discrete version of Eq. (5) on the basis of the algorithm proposed by Lu et al [12], where the nonlinear force of the Jenkins element is iterated within each time step. The derivation of the discrete time stepping equation is conducted on the assumption of linear variation of the nonlinear forces and the external excitation between successive time steps, i.e., first order hold. The reader is referred to Lu et al [12] for a complete description of the numerical solution employed herein.

Naturally, when the study is dealing with random vibrations, the previously mentioned random generation of white noise excitation is implied together with the stochastic setting of OMA. These random generations entail different responses, which introduces slightly different equivalent linear parameters of the system between individual simulations. Along these lines, 500 Monte Carlo simulations were carried out with a simulation length of approximately 15,000 periods of the two lowest modes ($\approx$25min) of each simulation. The simulation length together with the amount of simulations should ensure a sufficient statistical support for the comparative assessment of the respective ELS and OMA based modal estimates.

5. RESULTS OF THE CASE STUDY

In the present section, the main results of the numerical case study is presented and discussed. With the given position of the Jenkins element, mainly the second mode is affected by the elasto-perfectly-plastic nonlinearity, and therefore, the presented results are mainly related to the parameters of the second mode. Furthermore, with the respective magnitude and position of the Jenkins element, the linear mode shape of the second is sustained in the nonlinear case, leaving the amplitude dependency of the modal parameters to only the natural frequency and the damping. The latter being quantified through the ratio of critical damping. Additionally, another Monte Carlo simulation study was conduction only on the linear system presented in the previous section to ensure correct implementation and handling of all modal parameter estimates. This particular study is not presented in the present paper and the reader is referred to Friis et al [13]. It should, however, be mentioned that no significant bias was observed among the OMA based modal parameter estimates in this Monte Carlo simulation study of the linear system.
The natural frequency and damping ratio estimates of mode 2, obtained by the respective ELS method and the two OMA methods, are found in Fig. 3. The main values are graphically illustrated in relation to the minimum and maximum values with the given displacement variation of the simulations together with stated mean values, $\{\bar{\cdot}\}$, and coefficients of variation, CV.

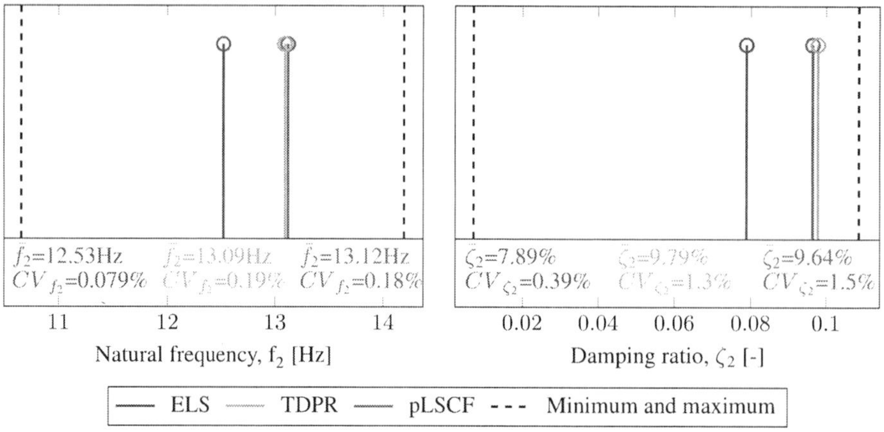

Figure 3: Results of frequency and damping estimation of mode 2 from the Monte Carlo simulation in terms of mean values and coefficients of determination. The dashed lines indicate the minimum and maximum frequency and damping of the second mode given the amplitude variation of the displacement throughout the simulations.

From the main results of natural frequency and damping ratio estimation in Fig. 3 it is observed that the two OMA methods provide almost identical results. On the other hand, the two OMA methods provide estimates of a higher value than the ELS method for both the natural frequency and the damping ratio. In order to assess the bias of the OMA methods in relation to the ELS estimates, one simulation was conducted with the same conditions as described in the previous section. This simulation is the foundation of two evaluations discussed in the following paragraphs. Furthermore for simplicity, mean values of the two OMA methods are used, which is considered acceptable due to their similarity.

The first evaluation of the ELS and OMA estimates is based on synthesisations of the acceleration, velocity and displacement response in the time domain. Two synthesisations are done; one based on the ELS modal estimates and one based on the OMA modal estimates. With the synthesisations, the error term of Eq. (2) is computed for the two cases, and subsequently used for quantification of the quality of the respective estimates. Initially, for the quantitative measure of the quality, each error function in vector format is transformed into a scalar function by calculating the euclidean norm for each time step, successively allowing the final transformation into a scalar value by using a mean value of the scalar function. Through this approach, the error of the ELS estimates is 0.70 N and the error of the OMA estimates is 0.76 N. Obviously, the ELS estimates are more accurate in relation to the definition in Eq. (2), but not much more accurate than the OMA estimates. Simply assuming linearity is causing the main magnitude of the error.

The second evaluation of the ELS and OMA estimates is based on synthesisations of the half spectra of the displacement response. A comparison of the amplitude and phase of the synthesised half spectra to the amplitude and phase the measured half spectra for DOF 1 and 3 can be found in Fig. 4. From the comparison it is observed that the synthesised amplitude and phase based on the ELS and OMA estimates, respectively, both fit perfectly for the linear mode 3, i.e., the peak and phase change at 27.85 Hz. However, only the synthesised amplitude and phase based on the OMA estimates fit perfectly with the nonlinearity affected mode 2 around 13 Hz. Based on this observation and the evaluation of the error term in the time domain, it is concluded that the averaging conducted in the estimation of the correlation functions is not compliant with the definition of a equivalent linear system in Eqs. (1) and (2). Thus, the two approaches do not unite in the same results. Nonetheless, keeping the amplitude variation of the frequency and damping in the simulations in mind together with the severity of assuming linearity, which was quantified by the evaluation of the error term, and the low statistical dispersion of the estimates, the OMA methods might have acceptable fidelity for most relevant cases. Moreover, the authors experienced proper workability of the OMA methods, when applied to the nonlinear responses.

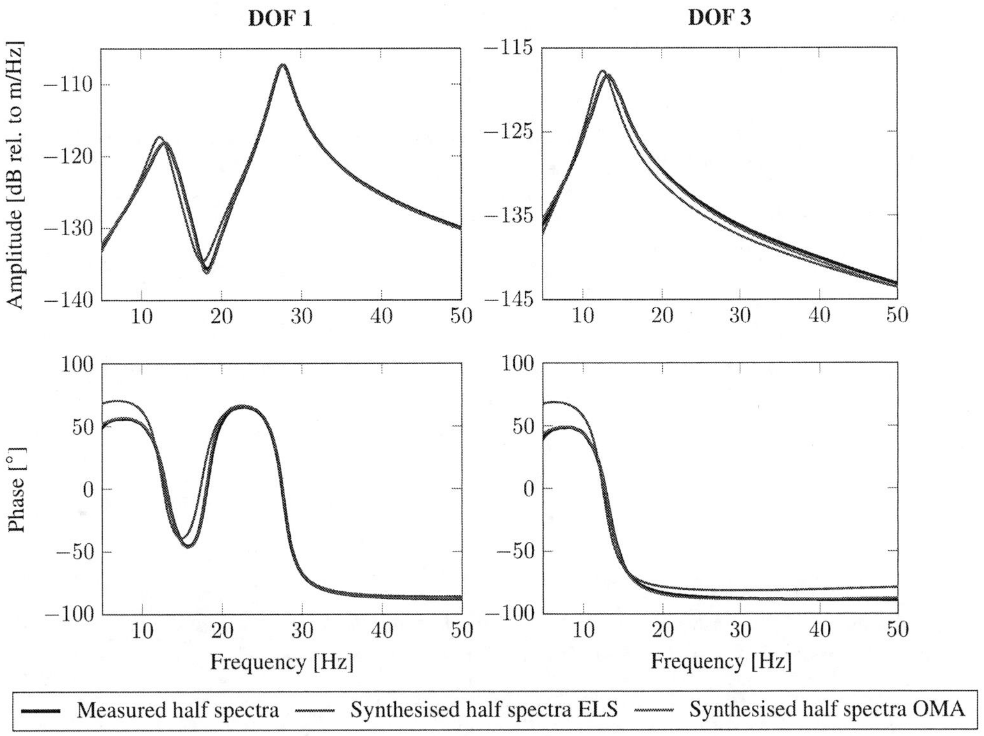

Figure 4: Comparison of synthesised auto half spectra based on the ELS and OMA estimates to actual half spectra of one nonlinear simulation.

6. CONCLUSION

The objective of the present study was to assess the linear stiffness and viscous damping estimation performance of correlation driven OMA methods on dynamic systems in random vibrations with elasto-perfectly-plastic nonlinear behaviour. A numerical test bed was appropriately established for the analysis by introducing a Jenkins element to the top of a finite element model of a simple T-shaped steel structure. The linear modal parameter estimation performance of two OMA based methods was comparatively assessed by comparing their outcome with theoretically derived estimates of an equivalent linear system. The evaluation was based on 500 Monte Carlo nonlinear numerical simulations of the system experiencing elasto-perfectly-plastic behaviour. It was found that the OMA methods provided reliable results for the investigated simulation system, though, with a bias in the related frequency and damping estimates. Based on an analysis of synthesised responses in both time and frequency domain, associated with the obtained theoretical and OMA based estimates, it was observed that the estimation of the correlation functions is not cultivating an estimation of the best fitting linear system. The discrepancy and bias is, however, relatively small, and the OMA based estimates might have acceptable fidelity for most relevant cases.

The findings of the present study calls for more research to fully map the bias in relation to the degree of the nonlinearity. In the present study, only one setting of the Jenkins element and only one excitation level were investigated. Furthermore, the effect averaging in the correlation function estimation should be further assessed to disclose which kind of equivalence it entails in relation to the obtained modal parameters.

ACKNOWLEDGEMENTS

The authors acknowledge the funding received from Centre for Oil and Gas - DTU/Danish Hydrocarbon Research and Technology Centre (DHRTC).

REFERENCES

[1] T. Friis, A. Orfanos, E. Katsanos, S. Amador, R. Brincker, *Effect of friction-induced nonlinearity on OMA-identified dynamic characteristics of offshore platform models*, Rotating Machinery, Vibro-Acoustics & Laser Vibrometry. Conference Proceedings of the Society for Experimental Mechanics (IMAC) Series 7 (15) (2018).

[2] G. Kerschen, K. Worden, A. F. Vakakis, J.-C. Golinval, *Past, present and future of nonlinear system identification in structural dynamics*, Mechanical Systems and Signal Processing 20 (3) (2006) 505 – 592.

[3] J. Schoukens, M. Vaes, R. Pintelon, *Linear System Identification in a Nonlinear Setting: Nonparametric Analysis of the Nonlinear Distortions and Their Impact on the Best Linear Approximation*, IEEE Control Systems Magazine 36 (3) (2016) 38–69.

[4] E. Zhang, R. Pintelon, P. Guillaume, *Modal Identification Using OMA Techniques: Nonlinearity Effect*, Shock and Vibration (2015).

[5] T. K. Caughey, *Equivalent Linearization Techniques*, Journal of the Acoustical Society of America 35 (11) (1963) 1706–1711.

[6] K. Mohammad, K. Worden, G. Tomlinson, *Direct parameter estimation for linear and non-linear structures*, Journal of Sound and Vibration 152 (3) (1992) 471 – 499.

[7] R. Brincker, C. Ventura, Introduction to Operational Modal Analysis, Wiley, 2015.

[8] H. Vold, *The Numerical Implementation of a Multi-Input Modal Estimation Method for Mini-Computers*, Proceedings of 1st International Modal Analysis Conference (1982).

[9] M. Tarpø, P. Olsen, S. Amador, M. Juul, R. Brincker, *On minimizing the influence of the noise tail of correlation functions in operational modal analysis*, Procedia Engineering 199 (2017) 1038–1043.

[10] B. Peeters, H. Van der Auweraer, P. Guillaume, J. Leuridan, *The PolyMAX frequency-domain method: a new standard for modal parameter estimation?*, Shock and Vibration 11 (3-4) (2004) 395–409.

[11] J. O'Callahan, P. Avitabile, R. Riemer, *System equivalent reduction and expansion process*, Proceedings of the 7th International Modal analysis conference, Society of Experimental Mechanics (1989) 29–37.

[12] L.-Y. Lu, L.-L. Chung, L.-Y. Wu, G.-L. Lin, *Dynamic analysis of structures with friction devices using discrete-time state-space formulation*, Computers & Structures 84 (15–16) (2006) 1049 – 1071.

[13] T. Friis, E. Katsanos, M. Tarpø, S. Amador, R. Brincker, *Output-only damping estimation of friction systems in ambient vibrations*, Proceedings of Noise and Vibration Engineering Conference (ISMA) (2018).

IOMAC'19

8th International Operational Modal Analysis Conference

2019 May13-15 Copenhagen

OPERATIONAL MODAL ANALYSIS USING THE STATE SPACE MODEL: ANALYZING THE EFFECT OF THE CORRELATION BETWEEN THE ERROR TERMS

Javier Cara[1]

[1] ETSI Industriales - Universidad Politécnica de Madrid, javier.cara@upm.es

ABSTRACT

Parametric Operational Modal Analysis consists on fitting a mathematical model to the vibration data, and in a second phase, to compute the modal parameters from the mathematical model applying closed formulas. One possibility is to use the state space model and the maximum likelihood method to estimate this model. But maximum likelihood method relies in maximizing the likelihood function, and this is in turn defined using the probabilistic distribution of the error terms. It is usual to admit that the error terms are uncorrelated, but taking into account the equation of vibrations these errors must be correlated. In this work, the effect of this correlation in the accuracy of the modal parameters is analyzed.

Keywords: Operational Modal Analysis, state space model, maximum likelihood estimation, EM algorithm

1. INTRODUCTION

Operational modal analysis can be performed in time domain and in frequency domain. In time domain, the most common model is the state space model:

$$x_{t+1} = Ax_t + w_t \tag{1}$$
$$y_t = Cx_t + v_t \tag{2}$$

In this model, matrices A and C are model parameters; y_t is the signal measured in the structural/mechanical system (mainly accelerations) at discrete time t; x_t is an internal and unobservable variable; w_t and v_t are random variables that model system and sensor uncertainties. The technique of operational modal analysis consists on:

1. Record the system accelerations, $\{y_1, y_2, \dots, y_t, \dots, y_N\}$.

2. Estimate model (1) from data y_t, $t = 1, \ldots, N$.
3. Compute the modal parameters from estimated matrices A and C (see [1] for details).

This work focuses on the second step. We are interested in estimate the state space model (1) using the maximum likelihood method. In this sense, we need to model w_t and v_t as multivariate random processes. We have two possibilities:

1. Uncorrelated normal processes:

$$\begin{bmatrix} w_t \\ v_t \end{bmatrix} \sim N\left(\begin{bmatrix} 0 \\ 0 \end{bmatrix}, \begin{bmatrix} Q & 0 \\ 0 & R \end{bmatrix}\right) \tag{3}$$

2. Correlated normal processes:

$$\begin{bmatrix} w_t \\ v_t \end{bmatrix} \sim N\left(\begin{bmatrix} 0 \\ 0 \end{bmatrix}, \begin{bmatrix} Q & S \\ S & R \end{bmatrix}\right) \tag{4}$$

Matrix S represents the correlation between the error terms w_t and v_t. From a theoretical point of view, model (4) is more correct than model (3) (see Section 2.), but from a mathematical point of view, model (3) is easiest to work with than model (4). In this work we analyze the influence of the matrix S in the quality of the modal parameters estimated.

2. THE STATE SPACE MODEL FOR MECHANICAL/STRUCTURAL SYSTEMS

The equation that model the dynamic behavior of a structural/mechanical system is:

$$M\ddot{q}(t) + G\dot{q}(t) + Kq(t) = F(t) \tag{5}$$

where $M \in \mathbb{R}^{n_d \times n_d}$, $G \in \mathbb{R}^{n_d \times n_d}$ and $K \in \mathbb{R}^{n_d \times n_d}$ are the mass, damping and stiffness matrices respectively; $F(t) \in \mathbb{R}^{n_d \times}$ is the force vector at time t; $q(t) \in \mathbb{R}^{n_d \times n_d}$ is the displacement vector at time t; dot means time derivative. We can write (5) as:

$$\ddot{q}(t) + M^{-1}G\dot{q}(t) + M^{-1}Kq(t) = M^{-1}F(t) \tag{6}$$

Using this equation, it is easy to follow:

$$\begin{bmatrix} \dot{q}(t) \\ \ddot{q}(t) \end{bmatrix} = \begin{bmatrix} 0 & I \\ -M^{-1}K & -M^{-1}G \end{bmatrix} \begin{bmatrix} q(t) \\ \dot{q}(t) \end{bmatrix} + \begin{bmatrix} 0 \\ M^{-1} \end{bmatrix} F(t) \tag{7}$$

$$\ddot{q}(t) = \begin{bmatrix} -M^{-1}K & -M^{-1}G \end{bmatrix} \begin{bmatrix} q(t) \\ \dot{q}(t) \end{bmatrix} + M^{-1}F(t) \tag{8}$$

Equations (7) and (8) form a state space model in continuous time:

$$\dot{x}(t) = A_c x(t) + B_c F(t) \tag{9}$$
$$y(t) = Cx(t) + DF(t) \tag{10}$$

where $x(t) = [q(t)\ \dot{q}(t)]^T$ is the state vector; $y(t)$ are the measurements (accelerations in this case);

$$A_c = \begin{bmatrix} 0 & I \\ -M^{-1}K & -M^{-1}G \end{bmatrix}, \quad B_c = \begin{bmatrix} 0 \\ M^{-1} \end{bmatrix}; \quad C = \begin{bmatrix} -M^{-1}K & -M^{-1}G \end{bmatrix}; \quad D = M^{-1}. \tag{11}$$

In discrete time (with time step equal to dt), model (9) becomes:

$$x_{t+1} = Ax_t + BF_t \tag{12}$$
$$y_t = Cx_t + DF_t \tag{13}$$

where

$$A = exp(Ac \cdot dt); \quad B = (A - I)A_c^{-1}B_c. \tag{14}$$

In Operational Modal Analysis the force vector is unknown, so it is modeled as a random process. We are going to consider $F_t \sim N(0, H)$, so calling $w_t = BF_t$ and $v_t = DF_t$ we have:

$$\begin{bmatrix} w_t \\ v_t \end{bmatrix} \sim N\left(\begin{bmatrix} 0 \\ 0 \end{bmatrix}, \begin{bmatrix} BHB^T & BHD^T \\ DHB^T & DHD^T \end{bmatrix}\right) = N\left(\begin{bmatrix} 0 \\ 0 \end{bmatrix}, \begin{bmatrix} Q & S \\ S & R \end{bmatrix}\right). \tag{15}$$

Therefore, from a theoretical point of view, the matrix S is different from zero in Operational Modal Analysis.

3. MAXIMUM LIKELIHOOD ESTIMATION OF THE STATE SPACE MODEL

Given the time series data

$$Y_N = \{y_1, y_2, \ldots, y_t, \ldots, y_N\}, \tag{16}$$

model (1) can be estimated using the maximum likelihood approach. The log-likelihood for this model can be written as:

$$\log L_{Y_N}(\theta) = -\frac{1}{2}\sum_{t=1}^{N} \log|\Sigma_t(\theta)| - \frac{1}{2}\sum_{t=1}^{N} \epsilon_t^T(\theta)\Sigma_t^{-1}(\theta)\epsilon_t(\theta), \tag{17}$$

where $\theta = \{A, C, Q, R, S\}$; ϵ_t are called the innovations, and are computed using the Kalman Filter (see [2]):

$$\epsilon_t = CVar(y_t|y_{t-1})C^T + R, \quad \epsilon_t \sim N(0, \Sigma_t). \tag{18}$$

We maximize Eq. (17) using the Expectation-Maximization algorithm. Consider we know both the observed outputs $Y_N = \{y_1, y_2, \ldots, y_N\}$ and the states $X_{N+1} = \{x_1, x_2, \ldots, x_{N+1}\}$. The density function is given by

$$f(X_{N+1}, Y_N) = f(x_0)\prod_{t=1}^{N} f(x_{t+1}, y_t|X_t, Y_{t-1}) \tag{19}$$

where

$$x_0 \sim N(\mu_0, P_0) \Rightarrow f(x_0) = \frac{1}{(2\pi)^{n_x/2}|P_0|^{1/2}} \exp\left(-\frac{1}{2}(x_0 - \mu_0)^T P_0^{-1}(x_0 - \mu_0)\right) \tag{20}$$

$$(x_{t+1}, y_t|X_t, Y_{t-1}) \sim N\left(\begin{bmatrix} Ax_t \\ Cx_t \end{bmatrix}, \begin{bmatrix} Q & S \\ S & R \end{bmatrix}\right) \tag{21}$$

Calling

$$V = \begin{bmatrix} Q & S \\ S & R \end{bmatrix}$$

$$\Rightarrow f(x_{t+1}, y_t|X_t, Y_{t-1}) = \frac{1}{(2\pi)^{(n_x+ny)/2}|V|^{1/2}} \cdot \exp\left(-\frac{1}{2}[(x_{t+1} - Ax_t)^T \quad (y_t - Cx_t)^T]V^{-1}\begin{bmatrix} x_{t+1} - Ax_t \\ y_t - Cx_t \end{bmatrix}\right) \tag{22}$$

The complete data likelihood is defined by $L(\theta) = f(X_{N+1}, Y_N)$. In practice the log-likelihood is used, so information is combined by addition. The objective therefore is to maximize $\log L(\theta)$. In this work we use a maximization procedure based on the Expectation Maximization algorithm (see [2]). The EM algorithm is simple to apply since at each iteration the optimal solution for the unknown parameters can be obtained from explicit formulas. It consists on two steps: the E-step and the M-step.

- **E-step (expectation step)**:

  Given the measured outputs Y_N and a value for the parameters θ_0, the log-likelihood $\log L(\theta)$ cannot be computed because the states X_{N+1} are unknown (in fact, the states are unobserved quantities). The method proposes to replace them with their expected values $\mathrm{E}[\log L_(\theta)|Y_N, \theta_0]$.

- **M-step (maximization step)**:

  Maximizing $\mathrm{E}[\log L(\theta)|Y_N, \theta_0]$ with respect to the parameters θ, constitutes the M-step. This is the strong point of the EM algorithm because the maximum values, obtained equating to zero the corresponding derivatives, are obtained from explicit formulas:

$$\frac{\partial}{\partial\theta}\mathrm{E}[\log L(\theta)|Y_N, \theta_0] = 0 \Rightarrow \boxed{\theta = \hat{\theta}} \tag{23}$$

A new E-step can be now performed considering $\theta_0 = \hat{\theta}$ what gives, applying the M-step, a new value for the parameters, $\hat{\theta}$. This leads to an iterative procedure in which the two steps, expectation and maximization, are repeated until the likelihood is maximized. This procedure is called the EM algorithm.

4. RESULTS

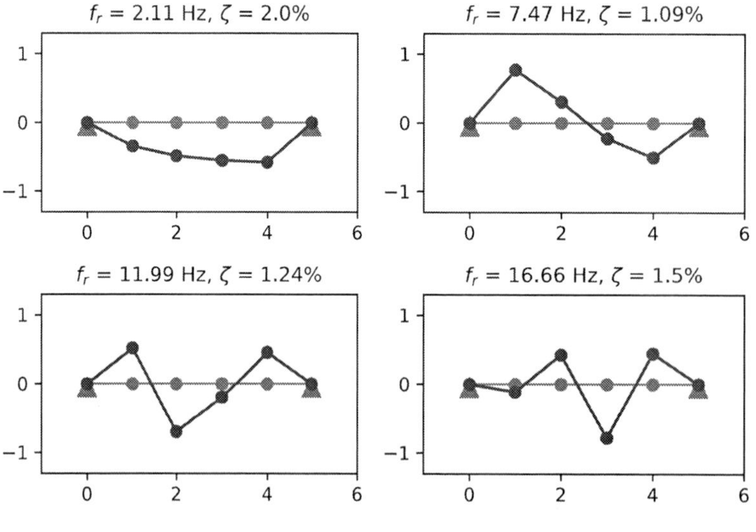

Figure 1: Theoretical modal parameters of the simulated system.

An four DOF mass-spring chain is used in this section to validate the proposed method:

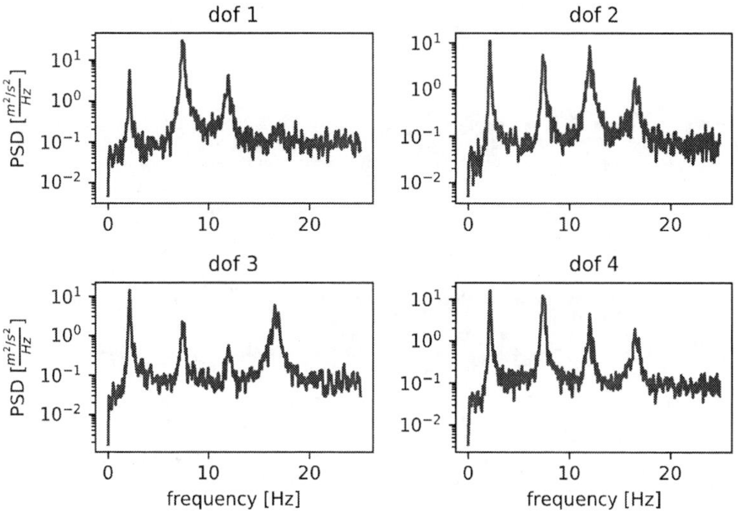

Figure 2: Power spectral density plot of one simulation.

- The mass matrix M is equal to the identity matrix with four rows and columns;
- Stiffness matrix:

$$K = \begin{bmatrix} 3000 & -2000 & 0 & 0 \\ -2000 & 5000 & -3000 & 0 \\ 0 & -3000 & 7000 & -4000 \\ 0 & 0 & -4000 & 4000 \end{bmatrix} \left(\frac{N}{m}\right); \tag{24}$$

- The damping matrix is built assuming Rayleigh damping by mean of

$$G = 0.488M + 2.421 \cdot 10^{-4}K \quad \left(\frac{N \cdot s}{m}\right). \tag{25}$$

- The inputs $u_t \in \mathbb{R}^{n_y \times 1}$ are modeled as a zero mean Gaussian white noise with variance matrix

$$\text{Var}(u_t) = \begin{bmatrix} 1.0 & 0.7 & 0.5 & 0.1 \\ 0.7 & 1.0 & 0.7 & 0.4 \\ 0.4 & 0.7 & 1.0 & 0.7 \\ 0.1 & 0.4 & 0.7 & 1.0 \end{bmatrix} \tag{26}$$

The modal parameters corresponding to this system are shown in Figure 1. We have simulated 500 different realizations for the system accelerations. Figure 2 shows the power spectral density plot of one of these simulations.

The natural frequencies estimated from these 500 simulations are included in Figure 3. We observe that if matrix S is included in the state space model, the bias of the estimates is reduced. This aspect is specially important in the first mode of vibration. However, the variance of the estimates does not change.

On the other hand, Figure 4 shows the damping ratios estimated. In this case, the results obtained are similar, whether the matrix S is considered or not.

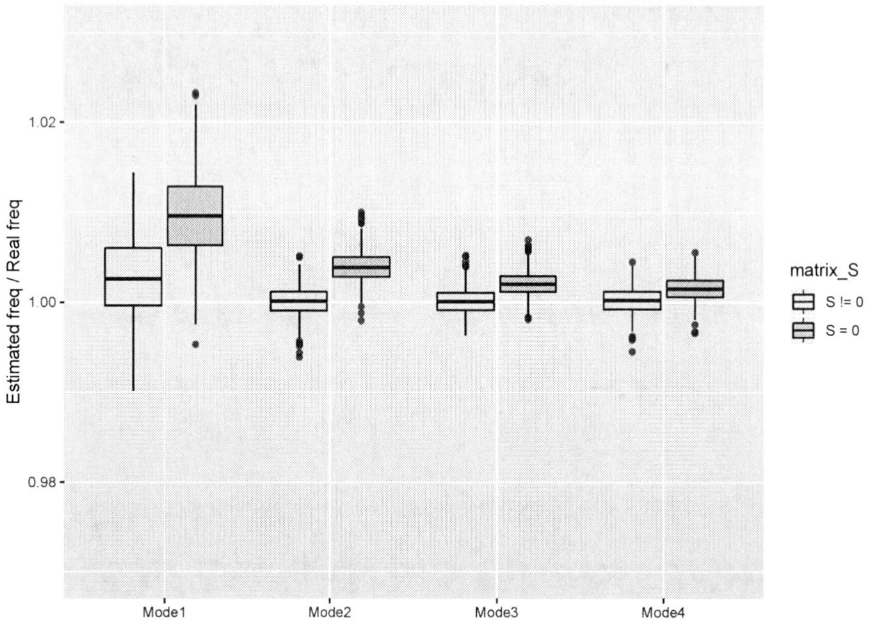

Figure 3: Data set used in the experiments.

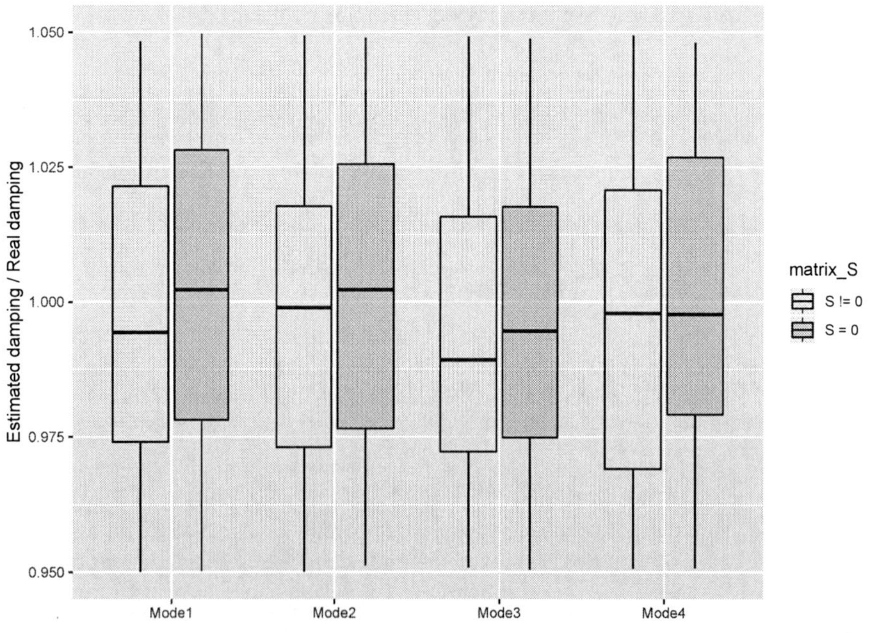

Figure 4: Data set used in the experiments.

5. CONCLUSIONS

We have analyzed the effect of the correlation between the error terms of the state space model in the quality of the modal parameters. We have found that including the correlation matrix improve the quality of the estimates, specially in natural frequencies. However, the differences are small.

In future work we want to study what happens with real data measured in large structures.

REFERENCES

[1] Cara, J. (2016) Computing the modal mass from the state space model in combined experimentaloperational modal analysis. *Journal of Sound and Vibration*, Volume 370, Pages 94-110, https://doi.org/10.1016/j.jsv.2016.01.043.

[2] Cara, F. J.; Carpio, J.; Juan, J.; Alarcón, E. (2012) An approach to Operational Modal Analysis using the Expectation Maximization Algorithm *Mechanical Systems and Signal Processing*, 31, 109-129.

IOMAC'19

8th International Operational Modal Analysis Conference

2019 May13-15 Copenhagen

THE USE OF LINE DETECTION TO IDENTIFY RANDOM IMPULSES IN LONG TIME HISTORIES

Anriette Bekker [1] *and Christof M. van Zijl* [1]

[1] A. Bekker, Sound and Vibration Research Group, Department of Mechanical and Mechatronic Engineering, Stellenbosch University, South Africa, annieb@sun.ac.za.

ABSTRACT

Impulsive transients occur in the occupational vibration of heavy mobile equipment operators, wave slamming on ship hulls and ice impacts on ship propellers. The investigation of such extreme load cases requires the automatic detection of random amplitude, non-periodic impulsive transients in acceleration measurements. It is well-known that impulsive events cause broad-band excitation of mechanical structures, which appear as line features in time-frequency representations, such as spectrograms and scalograms. It is proposed to use image processing and line-detection algorithms in compliment to existing signal processing techniques to increase the robust identification of impulsive transients in operational environments. A case study is presented whereby impulsive wave slamming on a vessel is determined through line detection on wavelet scalograms. In the present application of wave slamming the algorithm offers the benefit that the impulsive impact event can be distinguished from the high-amplitude oscillations (whipping) post the wave impact impact.

Keywords: Impulse detection, Wavelet transform, Wave slamming, Morlet

1. INTRODUCTION

Technologies such as vibration monitoring and digital twinning require long-term measurements on mechanical structures [1, 2]. Future trends increasingly call for a reduction in the analysis and processing time required to derive insight from such data.

The present work addresses the requirement to identify and quantify random impulsive events in measurements with long time histories. This need has arisen from measurements pertaining to human comfort in impulsive vibration environments, where much remains unclear about comfort and injury thresholds. As an example, impulsive wave slamming has proven problematic on a polar supply and research vessel as it disturbs work and sleep on board [8].

The present investigation offers a case study towards the automatic detection of wave slamming from acceleration measurements on a polar supply and research vessel for future correlation with human response measurements. Slamming is defined as the exposure of a vessel structure to large forces due to wave impacts for a short duration of time [3]. Often, slamming is followed by a global vibratory response known as whipping [4]. Stern slamming in combination with whipping induce vertical bending moments which influence the fatigue life and ultimate longitudinal strength of hull girders [4, 3, 5, 6].

The SA Agulhas II (SAAII), is a polar supply and research vessel (length, 134 m, width 22 m), which supports operations in Antarctica and the Southern Ocean. Bow slamming is expected in head seas for ships with ice-going hull shapes as a result of the increased bow flare angle required for effective ice-passage [3]. However, on the SAAII, stern slamming is problematic as it inhibits oceanographic research operations [7]. Omer and Bekker [7] found that, owing to its impulsive nature, wave slamming could be identified by the broadband excitation patterns in acceleration spectrograms close to the wave impact site. Slamming incidents concur with broadband vibration excitation, which result in line features on spectrograms. The authors highlighted that the segregation of bow and stern slams remains an importiant topic for future investigation. The authors [8] further found that human comfort is adversely affected if wave slamming increases in magnitude and if wave slamming occurs more frequently.

Against this backdrop, an automatic slamming detection algorithm is proposed to detect the time, magnitude and location of impulsive wave slamming on the hull of the SA Agulhas II polar supply and research vessel. It is envisioned that this algorithm will function within a full-scale monitoring system [9] which sets the requirement of computational efficiency towards real-time analysis.

2. METHODS

2.1. Vessel and full-scale measurements

Full-scale acceleration measurements were performed on a winter expedition to the Marginal Ice Zone (MIZ) South of Cape Town in July 2017. Wave slamming was encountered in open water as well as brash ice, comprising floes smaller than 3 m, and an average thickness of 40 to 60 cm.

Three operational case studies were selected for analysis and comprised 30 minutes of data. Case 1 and Case 2 reflect instances of severe slamming. The first case represents an open water storm, whereas the second is a rare occurance of wave slamming in brash ice. The final case represents ship responses in some of the mildest conditions experienced on this voyage in warmer open water.

Table 1: Data for three operational case studies on the 2017 Winter Cruise of the SA Agulhas II.

	Case 1 Open water storm	Case 2 Storm in MIZ	Case 3 Calm open water
Date	7 July	5 July 2017	12 July 2017
Time (UTC)	03:00 - 03:30 AM	01:00 - 1:30 AM	08:00 - 08:30 AM
Ship true heading [°]	0°	322°	307°
Swell height [m] and direction	3.5 WNW	6.0 WNW	2.0 SW
Ice conditions [-]	None (open water)	Brash ice (floes ¡ 3m)	None (open water)
Hull temperature [°C]	0.6°C	−1.8°C	18°C
Ship speed	27.8 - 29.0	11.4 - 15.0	13.9 - 25.6

Twelve vertical acceleration measurement channels, close to the waterline, were selected for analysis (see Fig.1). Measurements were performed continuously at a sample rate of 2048 Hz. The accelerometers included ICP type ($10\,\mathrm{mV/m.s^{-2}}$, $\pm 490\,\mathrm{m.s^{-2}}$ pk., Model: PCB333B32) and DC type ($20\,\mathrm{mV/m.s^{-2}}$, $98.1\,\mathrm{m.s^{-2}}$ pk., Model: PCB3711B111OG) accelerometers.

It was decided to capture vibration as closely as possible to the anticipated slamming locations in the bow and stern of the ship structure and place additional sensors at regular intervals along the vessel length as best is practically possible. At the stern, two sensors were placed on structural girders in the floor of

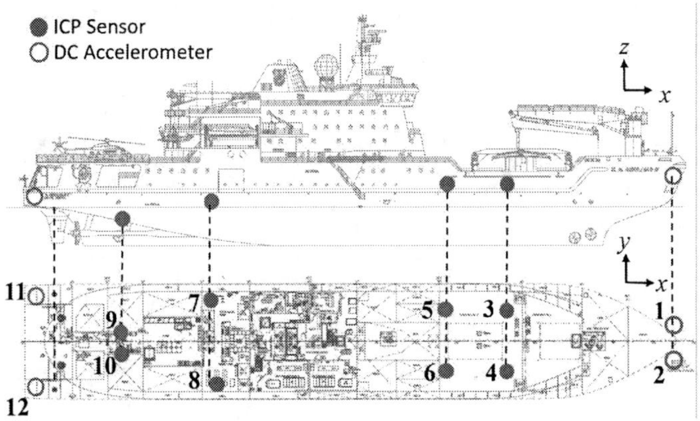

Figure 1: Layout of acceleration sensors used for slamming identification

Point reference	Channel	Axis	Deck	Side	Description	Type	Sensitivity [mV/m.s^{-2}]
1	9	Z+	4	Bow chain locker	Port side	DC	20.00
2	11	Z+	4	Bow chain locker	Starboard	DC	20.36
3	14	Z-	3	Cargo hold forward	Port side	ICP	9.96
4	15	Z-	3	Cargo hold forward	Starboard	ICP	10.05
5	16	Z-	3	Cargo hold aft	Port side	ICP	10.25
6	17	Z-	2	Cargo hold aft	Starboard	ICP	10.31
7	18	Z-	2	Fresh water room	Port side	ICP	10.44
8	19	Z+	2	Engine store	Starboard	ICP	10.36
9	20	Z+	2	Stern thruster	Port side	ICP	10.43
10	21	Z+	2	Stern thruster	Starboard	ICP	10.72
11	28	Z+	2	Steering gear aft	Port side	DC	20.13
12	29/25	Z+	2	Steering gear aft	Starboard	DC	20.25

Table 2: A summary of acceleration sensors used for slamming detection. The point reference numbers refer to the numbers indicated on the diagram in Fig. 1.

the flat transom of in the steering gear room Fig. 1. Towards the bow, two sensors each were placed at the stern thrusters and to the port-and starboard sides of the Central Measurement Unit (CMU) on Deck 3. A further four sensors measured acceleration in the corners of the Cargo hold towards the front of the super-structure on Deck 4. Finally, two sensors were placed in the Bow cargo space to capture vibration in close proximity to the bow wave impact site. Additional to the acceleration measurements, environmental parameters such as wave height and wind speed were recorded along with operational parameters of the vessel such as heading and ship speed.

2.2. Slamming detection algorithm

The proposed slamming detection algorithm is tasked to determine *the time instance and associated peak acceleration value* when waves slam into the hull structure. Over the course of a voyage these impulsive wave impacts occur at random and vary significantly in amplitude. The hypothesis is that the broadband excitation property of impulsive wave slamming will transpire as line features on scalogram images obtained using appropriate wavelet transforms. It is proposed to use line detection algorithms to determine the approximate timing of slamming incidences.

Conventional peak detection methodology requires an initial guess with respect to thresholding and a minimum time of recurrence. An example of this is shown in Fig.2 where acceleration peaks have been identified in a r.m.s. normalized acceleration signal, using the MATLAB function, `findpeaks`. For the purposes of this investigation a threshold was set, using the `('MinPeakHeight',6)` option in order to detect cases where the Crest Factor (CF) of the signal exceeds 6. This threshold is adopted from BS 6841 [10] which conservatively identifies a $CF > 6$ as an indicator that human vibration exposure is not well represented by r.m.s. metrics owing to transients with high peak values. In Fig.2 it can be seen that not only the impulsive wave impacts, but also the whipping response is identified (as expected).

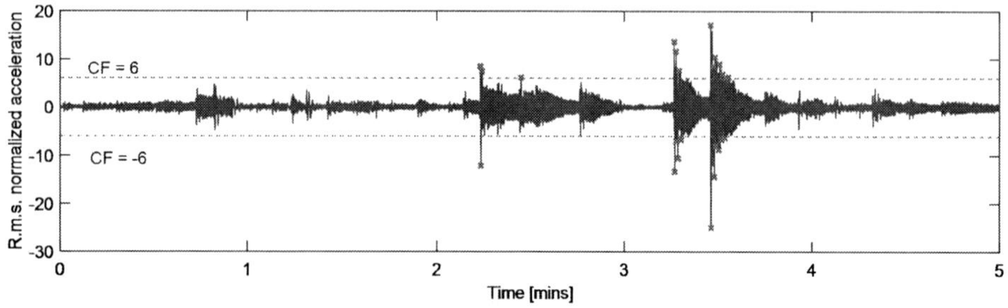

Figure 2: An normalized accelerometer measurement (with respect to r.m.s.) with peaks detected for $CF > 6$.

However, it could be desired to determine only the time and amplitude values of impulsive slamming events. Such information could be useful in evaluating how frequently the bow is impacted by waves in certain navigational conditions. Additionally, the wave impact site could possibly be identified from the impact timing in well-defined wave states. In turn, this would enable the segregation of bow slamming, which is expected, from stern slamming, which is deemed problematic. A step-wise description of the slamming detection algorithm is presented as follows:

- *Step 1: Measurement selection and signal conditioning:* In order to compare measurements from DC andd ICP sensors, signals were first detrended and then filtered to remove rigid body motion (high-pass filtering with a Butterworth filter, stopband of 0.5 Hz) and higer engine harmonics (Butterworth filter with a pass band below 20 Hz). The detrended signals were padded with ten seconds of zero data prior to filtering in order to eliminate filter settling artefacts in the time domain.

- *Step 2: Create a scalogram image using a continuous wavelet transform (Morlet):* The wavelet transform of a signal $x(t)$ is defined as:

$$\mathrm{WT}_x(a,b) = \langle \phi(a,b), x(t) \rangle = \frac{1}{\sqrt{a}} \int x(t) \psi^* \left(\frac{t-b}{a} \right) dt \tag{1}$$

$\mathrm{WT}_x(a,b)$ represents the wavelet transforming coefficient derived from a signal $x(t)$ when the scale is a and the time shifting parameter is b. In terms of notation, $\langle x, y \rangle$ indicates the inner product of two complex functions and an asterisk, *, denotes the complex conjugate (of a complex function, in this case). The mother wavelet is indicated by $\psi(t)$. Both $x(t)$ and $\psi(t)$ are assumed to be finite energy signals [11]. A function, $f(t)$, is a finite energy function when $\int_{-\infty}^{\infty} f(t)^2 dt < \infty$. The daughter wavelets $\psi_{(a,b)}(t)$ are scaled by a and translated by the shifting parameter, b. The factor, $\frac{1}{\sqrt{a}}$ is used to ensure energy preservation of the daughter wavelets as they are stretched over the scale, a. The Morlet wavelet has been cited [12] as being ideal for the detection of impulsive events in mechanical systems for the purposes of condition monitoring. This wavelet is described by the mathematical function:

$$\psi(t) = \frac{1}{2\pi} e^{(-\frac{t^2}{2}\beta^2)} [\cos \omega t + j \sin \omega t] = \frac{1}{2\pi} e^{(-\frac{t^2}{2}\beta^2)} e^{j\omega t} \tag{2}$$

The parameter, β, determines the geometric shape of the Morlet wavelet. When $\beta \leftarrow 0$, then $\frac{1}{2\pi} e^{(-\frac{t^2}{2}\beta^2)} e^{j\omega t}$ tends to a cosine function and the wavelet transfrom has a fine frequency resolution. If $\beta \leftarrow \infty$ then $\frac{1}{2\pi} e^{(-\frac{t^2}{2}\beta^2)} e^{j\omega t}$ tends to an impulse function and its time resolution will increase notably. It is expected that a Morlet wavelet with a larger β will be suitable to detect similarities with impulses in mechanical signals [12].

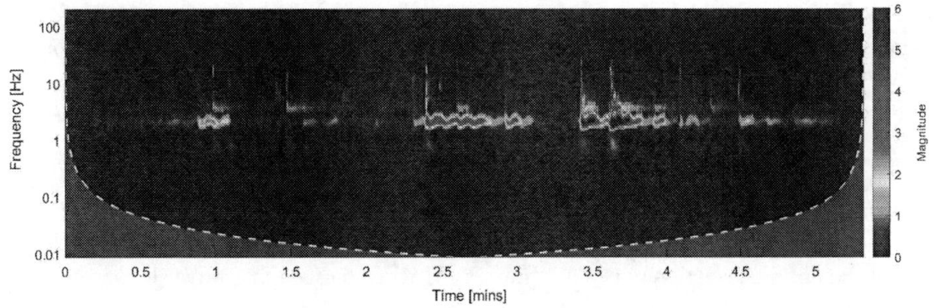

Figure 3: A continuous wavelet transform of an impulsive wave-slamming signal, using a Morlet wavelet.

- Step 3 & 4: Image selection and Canny edge detection. From Fig.3 it is observed that the feature-rich frequency range in slamming scalograms is found to be between 2 Hz and 24 Hz. Around 2 Hz, the harmonic content of the propeller fundamental frequency disturbs the line-like slamming features. Likewise, the fundamental bending modes around 1.9 Hz and 3.4 Hz [13]. For this reason a subspace of the scalogram images was selected between 4 Hz and 24 Hz. The scalogram colours were scaled to a grayscale image on which Canny edge detection was performed. Canny [14] proposed a computational approach whereby edges are marked at maxima in the gradient magnitude of a smoothed image which is obtained by using the derivative of the Gaussian filter. Canny [14] states that the success of this edge detection algorithm resides with the definition of a comprehensive set of goals, which include: 1.) Good detection, which implies a low probability of failing to mark true edge points. 2. Good localization, whereby edge pints should be as close as possible to the center of the true edge and 3.) finally, the multiple response requirement which specifies a single response per edge. A key strength of this method includes its ability to deal with varying signal-to-noise ratios through a noise estimation scheme and adaptive thresholding. Two thresholds are used to detect strong and weak edges, but retains weak edges only if they are connected to strong edges. The algorithm is more robust to noise and more likely to detect weak edges. In MATLAB, this method is utilized by calling the `edge` function and specifying the `'canny'` option. The output is a binary image with a value of 1 where an edge is present.

- *Step 5: Perform a Standard Hough Transform and line detection:* The Hough transform [15] is a non-linear mapping of points to sinusoidal lines. Hough [16] patented a methodology for the recognition of complex patterns from images. This method utilizes point-to-line mapping of the points, (x_i, y_i), of an image, I [17]. As an example, if a point in image I, had a value of 1, this point would be mapped to a line in a new image (in parameter space), J_i, with a value of 1 for each point on the line. A final image, J, is constructed from the sum of the J_i points that comprise the image. If n of the points are colinear in image I, the corresponding lines in image J are concurrent and have a value of n. This leads to the importiant conclusion that co-linear lines can be detected by searching for peaks in the line image J, where N co-linear lines intersect. Hough proposed the use of a point-to line mapping that maps colinear points to a set of parallel lines. Duda and Hart [15] later proposed a non-linear mapping, named the "Hough Transform", which mapped points to sinusoidal lines which are concurrent when the points in the original image are colinear. The advantage of this mapping is that co-linear points produce peaks in the Hough Transform, but within a bounded range which facilitates their detection. The sinusoidal lines are presented by the point-to-line mapping:

$$\rho = x\cos(\theta) + y\sin(\theta) \tag{3}$$

The variable ρ is the distance from the origin to the line along a vector perpendicular to the line and θ is the angle of the perpendicular projection from the origin to the line measured in degrees clockwise from the positive x-axis. The range of theta is $-90^\circ \leq \theta < 90^\circ$. The angle of the line itself is $\theta + 90^\circ$, also measured clockwise with respect to the positive x-axis. MATLAB facilitates the implimentation of line detection on a Standard Hough Transform of a binary image through the MATLAB function `hough.m`. Peaks are detected in the parameter space using the `houghpeaks` function. The associated lines through co-linear points are determined through the function `houghlines.m`. Hough line detection provides an option of additional input parameters `'FillGap'` and `'MinLength'` which could assist the analyst to detect more specific line attributes. Criticisms against the Hough transform include that it is computationally expensive. Davies [18] states that the principle computational cost is involved with calculating the parameter space, and not the detection of peaks. From Fig. 3 it can be seen that wave slamming concurs with an increase in the Morlet coefficients at multiple scales. For the present time scale of 5 minutes slamming appears as vertical lines, which narrows the angle of the line search in Hough parameter space. Critically the angle of the required line detection should concur with the cone of influence of the Morlet scalogram. The lines detected on the black and white Canny edge image, are presented in Fig. 4.

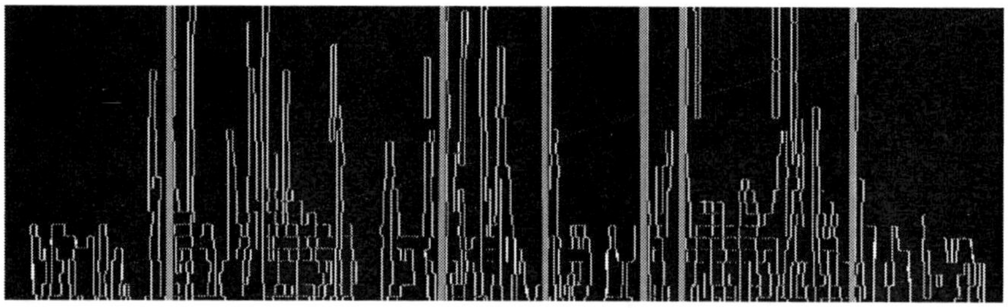

Figure 4: Line detection using the standard Hough transform on a black and white image.

- *Step 6 & 7: Map results from Hough parameter space to measurement time.* The peaks detected in the Hough transform are mapped to the pixel coordinates in the edge image (*Step 6*). The time resolution per pixel was $(792 - 112) = 680$ pixels on the x-axis of the plot area corresponds to the time scale (320 seconds) of the analyzed time signal (300 s measurements signal and 20 s zero-padding). The results were further interrogated against the scalograms as shown in Fig.5.

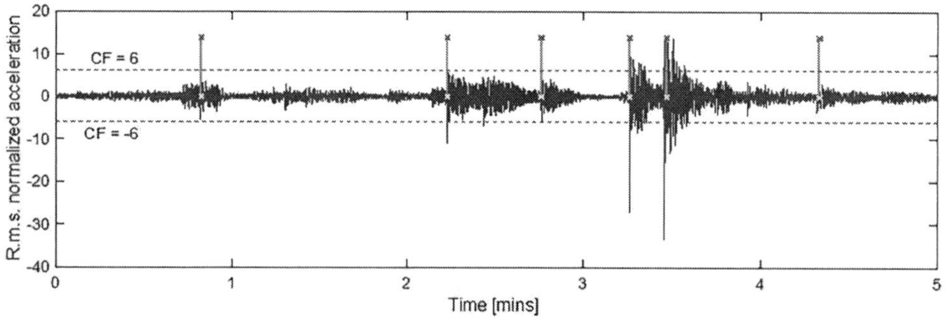

Figure 5: Line detection using the standard Hough transform on a black and white image.

- *Step 8: Peak search in measurement time history.* Line detection was used to determine the approximate timing of slamming incidents. In order to isolate problematic stern slamming, the wave impact location is to be determined. Omer and Bekker [7] showed that slamming incidence can be visualized using deflection shapes and that measurements closer to the impact location, peak first and are more impulsive. Based on this logic, the main deck measurement channels were interrogated around the approximate time instances determined from the line detection algorithm. A search length of 5 seconds was used, 2.5 seconds prior to the approximate time and 2.5 seconds after. The peak value and peak time were determined for each measurement within the indices specified by the searchlength. The crest factor for each slam was finally calculated from these values.

3. RESULTS

3.1. Conventional peak detection

The `findpeaks` MATLAB function was used to detect all peaks that exceed a $CF > 6$ (using the option `'MinPeakHeight'` in each of the twelve vertical hull measurements. A minimum peak distance of 0.5 a second was specified, using the `'MinPeakDistance'` option. As expected more high crest factor peaks are identified in cases where slamming is reported. In calmer water virtually no high crest factor peaks are identified. A greater number of high crest factor events are reported on the port side from which waves are approaching. More high crest factor acceleration peaks are detected at the front cargo hold sensor and rear steering gear sensors compared to other locations. This analysis shows a distribution of acceleration over the hull of the vessel which is useful to visualize potential fatigue effects. At this point not much information is portrayed about the likely incidence of wave slamming on the vessel hull as a peak value is determined every 0.5 s.

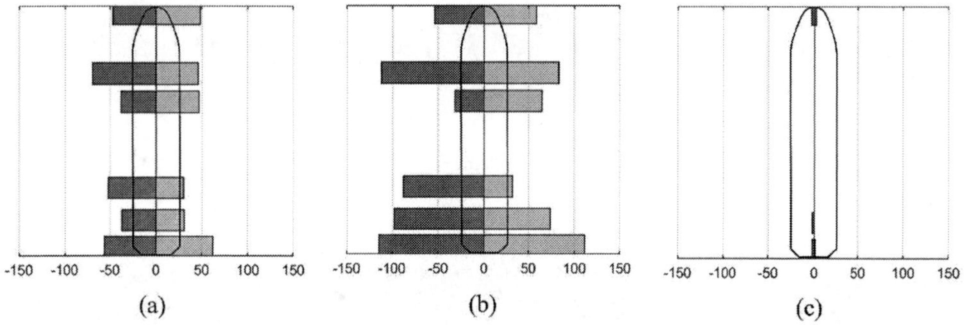

Figure 6: A summary of peaks detected along the vessel hull which exceed a crest factor of 6 for a (a) Open water storm, (b) MIZ storm and (c) Calm open water. Larger acceleration values with a $CF > 6$ are indicated by cyan bars on the starboard side and pink bars on the port side. The ship outline (top view) is indicated

3.2. Slamming localization

Based on the distributions of the peak acceleration and crest factors of the identified slamming events, it was decided to classify wave slams as stern slamming incidents if wave slams were first detected in the steering gear room and stern thruster sections of the vessel (Points 9, 10, 11 and 12). Bow slamming is identified is measurements peak first at sensors in the bow chain lockers and forward cargo hold (Points 1,2,3 and 4). Measured signals were interrogated in order to determine if slam timing, peak acceleration or crest factor would be the best identifier of the location where waves slam into the bow. This concept is illustrated in Fig. 7(a) and (b) which respectively reflect 100 seconds of data from the pairs of accelerometers in the stern and bow. As indicated by the $\star$ marker, there is a chance that closely spaced slams are not detected correctly and that the peaks from different slams are mismatched. A possible solution for this problem could include shortening the search length. However, it is unlikely that this challenge can be completely overcome in complex wave states where multiple waves might impact the hull simultaneously. Fig. 7(c) depicts the peak time in each of the measurement channels (y-axis) for every detected slam. Markers have been added to indicate the channel with the highest crest factor (○), highest peak acceleration (▲) and earliest peak time (●). The three greatest slams between 70 s and

90 s in Fig. 7(a) and (b) are interpreted as stern slams as the time signals peak prior to those in the bow. It is seen that the highest peak value and highest crest factor do not necessarily appear on the channel with the earliest peak time. A disadvantage is that the mis-identification of closely-spaced slams lead to the misinterpretation of the relative peak timing as the peak time no longer refers to the same slam. This aspect is to be further investigated to increase the robustness of algorithm in future.

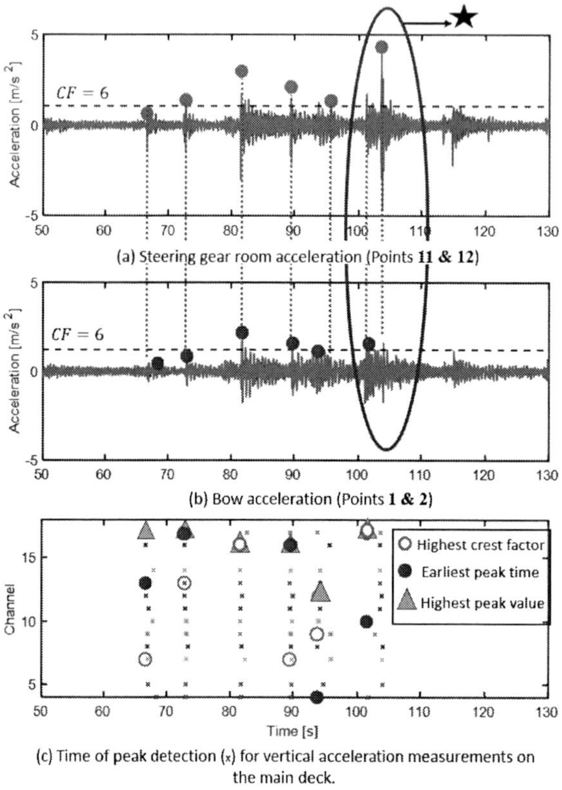

Figure 7: A diagram indicating the influence of using different acceleration metrics to determine wave impact site.

3.3. Slamming identification using line detection

The slamming detection algorithm, outlines in Section 2.2. is applied to the three case studies. Slamming incidents were identified, and then localized to determine the impact site of waves on the vessel hull. These slamming statistics are presented for the respective impact sites around the hull in Fig. 8. All detected impulsive events as well as significant slams ($CF > 6$) are presented. For Case 1 the vessel is cruising at full speed into 3.5 m waves. Structural excitation is dominated by bow slams, with more slams recorded at the starboard bow shoulder, although waves are approaching from the port side. Slamming for Case 2 is most frequent in the stern when the vessel is cruising at medium speed, almost directly into 6 m swell. Small slams frequently occur all around the vessel in oblique moderate seas, with no significant slams recorded. Interestingly, most measurements peak first on the starboard side of the ship even though the waves are approaching from the port side. Statistics such as these do provide some useful information asto the seakeeping performance of the vessel in different wave conditions. Additionally, the segregation of operational conditions, which evoke stern slamming can be determined. The frequency of wave impacts could further be extracted, prior to localization, in order to correlate these statistics with human response measurements for comfort and health. The algorithm is computionally more complicated and time consuming to implement than conventional peak-finding techniques.

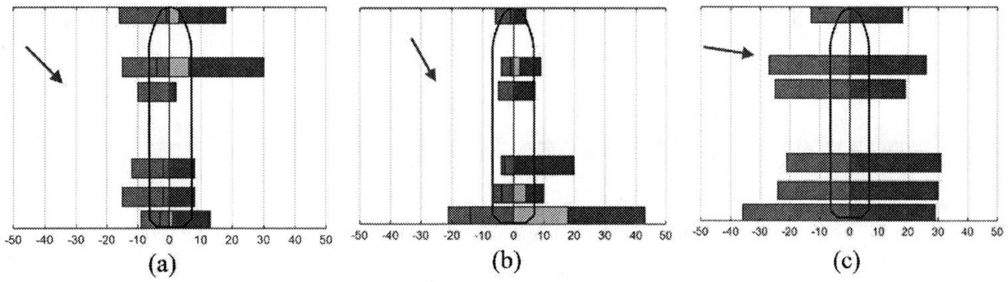

Figure 8: A summary of wave slamming impacts sites as recorded for the different case studies, (a) Open water storm, (b) MIZ storm and (c) Calm open water. The ship outline (top view) is indicated as well as the incident wave angle (blue arrow). The detected slamming counts are indicated by blue bars on the starboard side and red bars on the port side. Larger slams with a $CF > 6$ are indicated by cyan bars on the starboard side and pink bars on the port side.

4. CONCLUSIONS AND RECOMMENDATIONS

Random-amplitude, non-periodic wave slamming can be automatically extracted from long time histories using line detection on edge images of wavelet scalograms using the Morlet wavelet. Both, stern slamming and bow slamming produce high levels of peak acceleration. The present slamming detection algorithm is computationally expensive owing to the use of the continuous wavelet transform. Future work should focus on overcoming false impact localization information in complex wave states. Additionally, increased computational efficiency could be attained through alternatives to the continuous wavelet transform.

ACKNOWLEDGEMENTS

Funding from the National Research Foundation (NRF) through the South African National Antarctic Programme (SANAP Grant No.110737) is thankfully recognized. The authors further express thanks to the Department of Environmental Affairs and the Captain and Crew of the S.A. Agulhas II for their support and assistance during the Winter Cruise 2017.

REFERENCES

[1] Bekker, A., (2018) Exploring the blue skies potential of digital twin technology for a polar supply and research vessel. In: *International Marine Design Conference*, Helsinki, Finland.

[2] Erikstad, S. O. (2017) Merging physics, big data analytics and simulation for the next-generation digital twins In: Proceedings of the High Performance Marine Vehicles, Zewenwacht, South Africa.

[3] Kapsenberg, G. K. (2011) Slamming of ships: where are we now? *Philosophical Transactions of the Royal Society A: Mathematical, Physical and Engineering Sciences*, 369, 2892-2919.

[4] Dessi, D. (2014) Whipping-based criterion for the identification of slamming events *International Journal of Naval Architecture and Ocean Engineering*, 4, 1082-1095.

[5] Storhaug, G. (2014) Which sea states are dimensioning for container vessels when whipping is included? In: *International Conference on Ocean, Offshore and Arctic Engineering*. San Francisco, California.

[6] Bertram, V. (2011) *Practical ship hydrodynamics* Elsevier Science.

[7] Omer, H. and Bekker, A., (2016) Detection of wave slamming sites from ship deflections *Research and Development Journal of South Africa*, 32, 50-57.

[8] Omer H. and Bekker A., (2017) Human responses to wave slamming vibration on a polar supply and research vessel *Applied Ergonomics*, 67, 71-82.

[9] Bekker, A., Suominen, M., Kujala, P., De Waal, R. J. 0. and Soal, K. I. (2018) From data to insight for a polar supply and research vessel *Ship Technology Research*, 65, 1-17

[10] British Standards Institution, (1987) BS 6841 Guide to measurement and evaluation of human exposure to whole-body mechanical vibration and repeated shock

[11] Olhede, S. C. and Walden, A. T., (2002) Generalized Morse Wavelets *IEEE Transactions on Signal Processing*, 50(11), 2661-2670.

[12] Yang, W. X. and Ren, X. M. (2004) Detecting impulses in mechanical signals by wavelets *Eurasip Journal on Applied Signal Processing*, 8, 1156-1162.

[13] Soal, K., Bienert, J. and Bekker, A., (2015) Operational modal analysis on the polar supply and research vessel the S.A. Agulhas II In:*6th International Operational Modal Analysis Conference, IOMAC 2015*, Gijon, Spain.

[14] Canny, J. (1987) A Computational Approach to Edge Detection *IEEE Transactions on Signal Processing and Machine Intelligence*, 6, 679-698.

[15] Duda, R. O. and Hart, P. E., (1972) Use of the Hough transformation to detect lines and curves in pictures *Communications of the ACM*, 15(1), 11-15

[16] Hough, P. V. C. (1962) Method and means for recognizing complex patterns *United States Patent Office*, Patent US3069654, 1-3.

[17] Bhattacharya, P., Rosenfeld, A. and Weiss, I., (2002) Point-to-line mappings as Hough transforms. *Pattern Recognition Letters*, 23, 1705-1710.

[18] Davies, E. R (1993) Some methods for minimising computation with the Hough transform. *IEE Colloquium on Hough Transforms*, Institution of Electrical Engineers, London, United Kingdom, 2/1-2/6.

IOMAC'19
8th International Operational Modal Analysis Conference
2019 May13-15 Copenhagen

TIME DOMAIN MODAL PARAMETER ESTIMATION METHODS USED IN OMA: A COMPARISON

Silas Sverre Christensen [1], *and Anders Brandt* [2]

[1] Ph.D. candidate, Institute of Technology and Innovation, University of Southern Denmark, ssv@iti.sdu.dk.

[2] Associate Professor, Institute of Technology and Innovation, University of Southern Denmark, abra@iti.sdu.dk.

MOTIVATION

Within the field of Operational Modal Analysis (OMA) it is sought to estimate modal parameters that are consistent. Modal Parameter Estimation (MPE) methods that operate in the time domain have shown to perform well in OMA. However, it is not apparent whether MPE methods that adopt a low or high matrix polynomial order perform better over one another, or if they result in the same estimates of modal parameters. In this extended abstract, the modal parameter estimates computed from two such extremes are compared. The MPE methods used are the multi-reference Ibrahim Time Domain (MITD) method (similar to cov-SSI) and the Modified multi-reference Ibrahim Time Domain (MMITD) method (similar to PTD). To minimize inconsistency in decisions made from an operator, an Automated OMA algorithm is applied. Data from a research platform located in the North Sea (Fino3) have been processed and the results presented. The modal parameter estimates from the two MPE methods are discussed.

RELEVANT RESULTS

The data set processed corresponds to 3600 seconds of structural response measured from 24 accelerometers that were distributed on the platform. The lowest natural frequency was found to be $0.42\ Hz$, which allows approximately 1500 cycles of the first natural frequency in one data set. An unbiased estimator was used to compute the correlation functions using a block-size of 512 samples. In Figure 1 the (auto) correlation functions and (auto) power spectral density functions are shown. The (auto) correlation functions may be treated as free decay functions. The functions seem to decay after 250 time lag values. Furthermore the amplitude of some of the functions are significantly higher than others. By looking at the (auto) power spectral density plots it is quite obvious that there is a peak around $0.42\ Hz$ and a peak around $1.0\ Hz$ as well as a few peaks just below $2.0\ Hz$. Also, a few peaks are seen above $2.0\ Hz$. Only modes below $2.0\ Hz$ are considered in the following.

The (auto) correlation functions shown are used as input in the MPE methods, i.e. the MITD and the MMITD methods. The former produces mode shapes directly, while the latter yields modal participation factors that are used together with the poles and correlation functions, to estimate mode shapes using a time domain least squares fit. The two MPE methods require a user to select a maximum order as well as how many time lag values of the correlation function that should be used. The maximum model order is chosen to be 40 (80 poles), while the number of time lag is set to 50. It is common to plot the model order as a function of the natural frequency to reveal stable poles. This is known as a stabilization

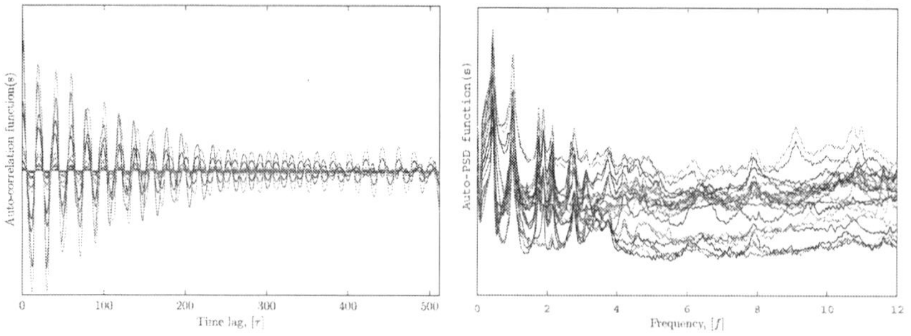

(**a**) (auto) correlation functions (**b**) (auto) power spectral density functions

Figure 1: (auto) correlation and power spectral density functions of the response data measured on Fino3

diagram, and is a useful tool to reveal physical poles. It is common to analyze such diagrams manually and select stable poles. However, this process is both time consuming and can be inconsistent. Therefore an automated algorithm for modal parameter estimation is used. The method was developed by the author and utilizes histogram analysis on the stabilization diagram to detect physical poles. This method also has a decision rule based on the modal assurance criterion (MAC) that ensures that poles in each bin are similar. The MITD method uses a low order matrix polynomial order, and the MMITD method uses a high matrix polynomial order. In the following we shall consider four scenarios, i.e. low order and high order normalization of the system equations for MITD and MMITD, respectively. See [1] for more details. A comparison of the mean frequency and mean damping ratio estimates can be seen in Table 1.

Table 1: Frequency and damping estimates using different Modal Parameter Estimation (MPE) methods and normalization of the system equations (Norm)

	MPE	Norm	Mode 1	Mode 2	Mode 3	Mode 4	Mode 5	Mode 6
Frequency [Hz]	MITD	Low	0.420	0.430	0.992	0.997	1.741	1.874
	MITD	High	0.420	0.431	0.992	0.998	1.742	1.874
	MMITD	Low	0.420	0.431	0.992	0.997	1.741	1.874
	MMITD	High	0.420	0.431	0.992	0.998	1.742	1.874
Damping [%]	MITD	Low	2.017	2.230	1.087	1.038	0.525	0.881
	MITD	High	1.952	2.276	1.108	1.209	0.497	0.844
	MMITD	Low	2.038	2.176	1.081	1.042	0.528	0.882
	MMITD	High	1.947	2.240	1.103	1.192	0.496	0.835

It appears that the frequency estimates are unaffected by the MPE method used as well as the normalization of the system equations. For the damping ratio estimates, the two MPE methods yield distinct estimates and it appears that the normalization of the system matrices has an effect on the damping ratio estimates. Furthermore, some modes seems to be more affected than others.

CONCLUSIONS

Response data measured on the Fino3 platform have been used to estimate modal parameters using two different MPE methods. For each method, either a low order or a high order normalization of the system equations were used. The frequency estimates were consistent for all four scenarios. The damping estimates seemed to be affected by the MPE method used, it showed some sensitivity whether a low order or a high order normalization of the system equations were used. The mean values were based on around 60-80 estimates having a relative error lower than 1.5 %. The MAC values of the estimates for each mode is above 0.99. Therefore, it can be concluded that for the current application and for the MPE methods used, a bias is introduced which depend on the normalization of the system equations. This should require further analysis. The work presented was supported by the INTERREG 5A Germany-Denmark program, with funding from the European Fund for Regional Development.

REFERENCES

[1] Allemang, R. J. and Brown D. L. (1998) A Unified Matrix Polynomial Approach to Modal Identification. *Journal of Sound and Vibration*, 221, 301-322.

IOMAC'19

8th International Operational Modal Analysis Conference
2019 May13-15 Copenhagen

TRACKING THE MODAL PARAMETERS OF TIME-VARYING STRUCTURES BY REGULARIZED NONPARAMETRIC ESTIMATION AND OPERATIONAL MODAL ANALYSIS

Péter Zoltán Csurcsia[1,2], Bart Peeters[1], Johan Schoukens[2]

[1] Siemens Industry Software, Interleuvenlaan 68, 3001 Leuven, Belgium, bart.peeters@siemens.com
[2] Vrije Universiteit Brussel, Department of Engineering Technology, Pleinlaan 2, B-1050 Elsene, Belgium

ABSTRACT

This paper presents an efficient nonparametric time-varying (TV) system identification method combined with mode tracking for Operational Modal Analysis (OMA). OMA is a special identification technique for estimating the modal properties of structures based on vibration data collected under real operating conditions and without having access to the excitation signals. The time-varying aspect refers to cases where the structural dynamic behavior changes as a function of time; e.g. due to changes in mass (fuel burn during launch; people filling a football stadium structure) or environmental conditions and interactions (temperature changes; aerodynamic forces causing flutter).

In this work a regularized time domain TV OMA method is presented to estimate the linear TV output autocorrelation function of the observed system. In a second step, parametric identification will be applied to track the modal parameters of the time-varying system. The method is illustrated using wind tunnel measurement on an airplane (component) model.

Keywords: Time-varying structures, Operational Modal Analysis, Flutter Testing

1. INTRODUCTION

The goal of this paper is to present the first results of a new estimation technique developed to deal with time-varying (TV) mechanical and civil structures measured in an Operational Modal Analysis (OMA) framework. OMA is a special identification technique for estimating the modal properties of structures based on vibration data collected when the structures are under real operating conditions without having access to the excitation signals. Such modal parameters are, for instance, the natural frequencies, mode shapes, damping ratios. The OMA framework can provide the engineers with useful information to understand the dynamic behavior of the underlying structure in real-life usage scenarios, and it can be used to validate and update the numerical models developed in the design phase [1] [2]. Methods for linear time-invariant (LTI) OMA have hence been developed and they are widely used also in the industrial environment, interested readers are referred to the detailed surveys [2] [3].

The dynamics of underlying systems may vary significantly when operating in real-life conditions. In this case, a TV modelling framework is needed because ignoring time variations might lead to instability and structural failures. A good example of a time-varying structure can be, for instance, an airplane. The time-varying behavior originates, for instance, from the decreasing weight due to the fuel consumption, and from different surface configurations during take-off, cruise and landing. Moreover, the resonance frequencies and damping ratios of an airplane vary as a function of the flight speed and altitude.

It is a common practice in system identification to use different types of short-time Fourier transform (SFT) techniques that describes slowly time-varying systems as a series of linear-time invariant (LTI) systems [4] [5] [6] [7] These SFT based models can describe the time-varying behavior quite well, when the time-variations are very smooth (i.e. the system varies very slowly). The drawback of these methods is that such an LTI model is not sufficient to describe the behavior of the underlying system, if the time variations are fast, or when a significant (sudden) variation occurs. A further issue is that in case of TV OMA, the applied system identification techniques must cope with a lack of knowledge of the excitation.

The proposed method is intended to overcome the issues with the classical SFT based methods, and it is based on the regularization methods that have been developed for nonparametric modelling of LTI systems [8] [9]. The main novelty of this work compared to the classical regularization framework is to formulate the regularization for the special case of the estimation of linear time-varying (LTV) systems in an industrial OMA framework. The proposed LTV OMA method is illustrated on a simulation example and on a wind tunnel testing measurement of a scaled aircraft model.

This paper is organized as follows: in Section 2 the basic concepts of this work are summarized, and the problem formulation is given. Section 3 provides the model structure and the cost function of the underlying problem. Section 4 summarizes the practical considerations of the regularization technique, the LTV OMA estimation method, and addresses the implementation procedure. Section 5 and 6 show a simulation and a measurement example where the results of the classical SFT framework are shown to compare to the results proposed method. Finally, the conclusions are provided in Section 7.

2. FUNDAMENTALS

In this section, a brief overview of the LTV OMA identification problem is presented from different aspects where we explain 1) the basic assumptions of our work, 2) the issues related to the nonparametric identification of LTV systems in general, and 3) the issues related to the OMA framework w.r.t. the classical identification framework.

2.1. Assumptions on the underlying system and measurement

In this paper a nonparametric description of (discrete) TV is considered. A causal LTV system can be characterized by its 2D impulse response function (IRF) $h[t,\tau]$. The steady-state output response to an arbitrary signal $u[t]$, measured with an $e[t]$ error, is given by [7] [10] [11] [12]:

$$y_m[t] = y[t] + e[t] = \sum_{\tau=0}^{+\infty} h[t,\tau]u[t-\tau] + e[t] \tag{1}$$

where the parameter t is the global time (the time when the system is measured) and τ is the system time (the direction of the impulse responses/lags). An illustration of a TV IRF is shown in Figure 1.a.

In the proposed estimation framework the following assumptions are imposed:

Assumption 1 The true output ($y[t]$) is measured with additive, i.i.d Gaussian noise ($e[t]$) with a zero mean and a finite variance (this assumption can be generalized to include colored noise).

Assumption 2 The TV IRF is smooth i.e. the spectral content of the LTV system is concentrated at the low frequencies. A detailed study on smoothness can be found [13].

Assumption 3 The considered LTV system is causal [7] and bounded-input, bounded-output stable [14].

Assumption 4 The length of the IRFs (L+1) is much shorter than the measurement length (N).

Assumption 5 In case of the OMA framework, the excitation signal $u[t]$ is not known, but in the frequency band of interest it is assumed to be (nearly) white noise with a finite variance [2].

2.2. Nonparametric identification of time-varying systems

2.2.1. Problem formulation

The challenge with nonparametric time-varying system identification is that the TV IRF is not uniquely determined from a single set of input and output signal– unlike LTI IRF case. Consider the model defined in (1). Imposing *Assumptions 1–4*, the following measured output $y_m[t]$ is given at time t:

$$y_m[t] = \sum_{\tau=0}^{L} h[t,\tau]u[t-\tau] + e[t] \tag{2}$$

where $t = 0 \dots N-1$.

2.2.2. Illustration

To illustrate the difficulties of (2) (i.e. LS problem), a steady state simulation example is shown in Figure 1. The underlying system is shown in Figure 1.a. The system is excited by white noise and no measurement (observation) noise has been added.

The simple LTI, the TV LS and the proposed regularized based estimates are shown in Figure 1.b–d. When the TV nature of the underlying system is ignored, one can obtain the LTI estimate shown in Figure 1.b. In this case the issue is that all the changes in the dynamics are completely lost. Figure 1.c. shows the TV LS solution which differs a lot from the true system and it does not correspond to our expectation: only few impulse responses are present, not all impulse responses are decaying, and the time variations are not smooth. The problem lies in the fact that there is a nonuniqeness issue. There are only N measured samples to estimate the nonparametric model containing NL samples. This underdetermined system of linear equations results in a situation where the nonparametric TV model that relates the input to the output is not unique. In order to achieve a more reliable and unique solution (see Figure 1.d. for the proposed method) some prior information shall be taken into account as well. This will be explained in the following sections.

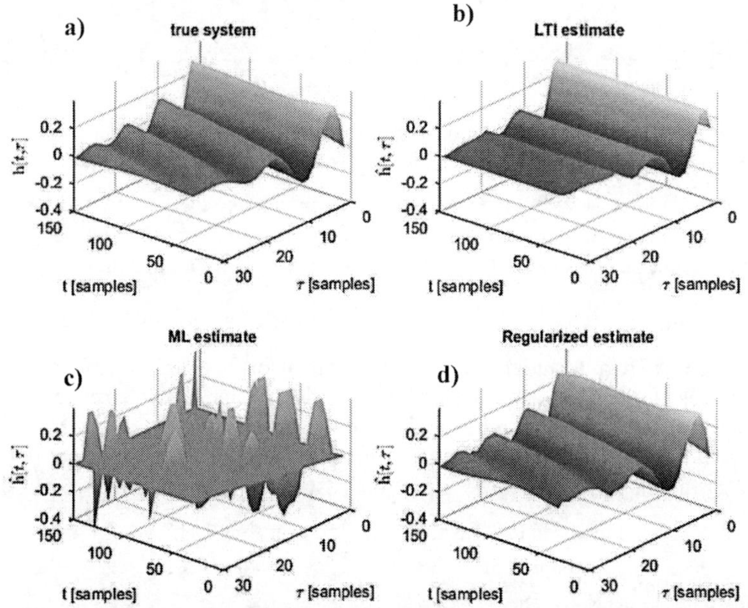

Figure 1 a) the TV IRF of the observed system b) the LTI estimate c) the ML estimate d) the regularized estimate. The system is excited by white noise. No observation noise is present.

2.3. Operational Modal Analysis Framework

In case of industrial measurements of large mechanical and civil structures (e.g. airplanes, bridges, wind turbines), the excitation signal is most of the time not measurable, or it would be too difficult and complex to measure [2] [3]. Because the excitation signal is not known (see *Assumption 5*) an impulse or frequency response function estimate cannot be directly obtained. Instead, the output autocorrelation function (ACF) and/or its Fourier transform are used in practice.

In this paper LTV systems are considered in the OMA setup (see Figure 2). The goal of this work is to nonparametrically identify the 2D TV ACF of the underlying system. In practice, after this stage, there is typically a parametric estimation procedure where the resonance frequencies and damping ratios are estimated, for instance, with the help of Polymax method [15].

For the sake of simplicity, the proposed methodology is explained on single output systems, but using advanced linear algebra it can be easily extended to systems with multiple outputs.

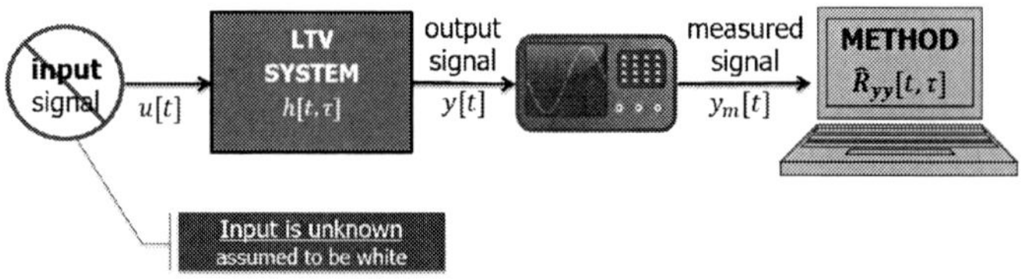

Figure 2 Schematic of the TV OMA. The excitation signal is not known but it is assumed to be (nearly) white in the frequency band of interest. The model obtained is based on the noisy output measurements of the underlying LTV system.

3. THE NONPARAMETRIC IDENTIFICATION METHOD

3.1. The model structure

In the OMA framework, the underlying TV systems are represented by their 2D ACF. When *Assumption 1–5* are satisfied, the 2D TV ACF centered around the measurement (global) time t, at time lag τ is estimated with the measured output signal y_m by smoothing over a window with a length of $L+1$:

$$\hat{R}_{y_m y_m}[t,\tau] = \frac{1}{L+1}\sum_{k=-\frac{L}{2}}^{\frac{L}{2}} y_m[t+\tau+k]y_m[t+k] \tag{3}$$

It is important to remark that depending upon the application and the measurement, different weightings of the ACF is possible, for more technical details see [16].

Next, the double time indices $[t,\tau]$ will be omitted in order to make the text more accessible. The key idea of this work is to extend the existing nonparametric regularization methods such that some advanced prior information – elaborated in Section 4 – can be taken into account.

3.2. The cost function

The basic idea of the LTI regularization technique is that by using some reasonable prior knowledge on the system dynamics (formalized later on), and by introducing some bias error (a systematic model error), the variance of the estimate can be significantly reduced such that a lower mean square error (MSE) error is achieved. In order to include the prior knowledge in the nonparametric representation, an augmented cost function (V) must be defined. This cost function consists of two parts.

The first part is the LS cost function (V_{LS}) which is defined for the 2D LTV ACF case as

$$V_{LS} = \left\| vect(R_{yy}) - vect(\hat{R}_{y_m y_m}) \right\|_2^2 \tag{4}$$

and the second part is the regularization cost function (V_r):

$$V_r = \sigma^2 vect(R_{yy}^T) P^{-1} vect(R_{yy}) \tag{5}$$

The new, combined cost function is given by:

$$V = V_{LS} + V_r \tag{6}$$

where P is a covariance matrix of the prior ACF, and σ^2 is the amount of regularization (prior) applied. By making a proper choice for P, smoothness and stability can be imposed on the estimated model (see Section 4). Minimizing (6) – with respect to R_{yy} – gives the 2D LTV ACF estimate:

$$vect(\hat{R}_{yy,reg}) = (I + \sigma^2 P^{-1})^{-1} vect(\hat{R}_{y_m y_m}) \tag{7}$$

where I denotes the identity matrix.

Note that σ^2 is usually (proportional to) the noise variance of the measurement.

4. REGULARIZATION

In the first part of this section the practical implementation of the inclusion of the prior knowledge into the covariance matrix is addressed and illustrated on the classical LTI impulse response estimation problem. In the second part the proposed method of LTV extension to ACFs is detailed. The last part of this section deals with the proposed parameter tuning technique.

4.1. Considered kernel functions

The covariance hypermatrix P is constructed by using kernel functions. P introduces the prior knowledge into the cost function as a prior correlation between the elements of the IRFs. The specific choice of the kernels, and the resulting covariance matrix has a major effect on the quality of the estimate. Next, the kernels that will be used in this paper are explained.

A Radial Basis Functions (RBF) is a function whose values depend only on the distance between different points. In this work this dependency is defined as follows) [17]:

$$P_{RBF}(i,j) = e^{-\frac{(i-j)^2}{\gamma}} \tag{8}$$

where $\gamma > 0$ is a parameter representing the length scale, and i, j are the two time points (sample indices). This type of RBF kernel is called Gaussian RBF kernel . By using this kernel, the smoothness assumption can be imposed on the system to be estimated. The larger the length scale γ, the smoother the resulting estimated function is. This kernel is illustrated in Figure 3 a–c.

In case of Diagonal Correlated (DC) kernels next to the smoothness assumption, exponentially decaying can be imposed and is defined as follows [9]:

$$P_{DC}(i,j) = e^{-\alpha|i-j|} e^{-\frac{\beta(i+j)}{2}} \tag{9}$$

where α gives a scaling to the correlation between neighboring IRF/ACF coefficients, β scales the exponential decaying, $\alpha, \beta \geq 0$.

In other words, α controls the smoothness: the smaller its value, the smoother the estimation is, and β controls the length of the IRF/ACF. This kernel function is illustrated in the Figure 3 f.

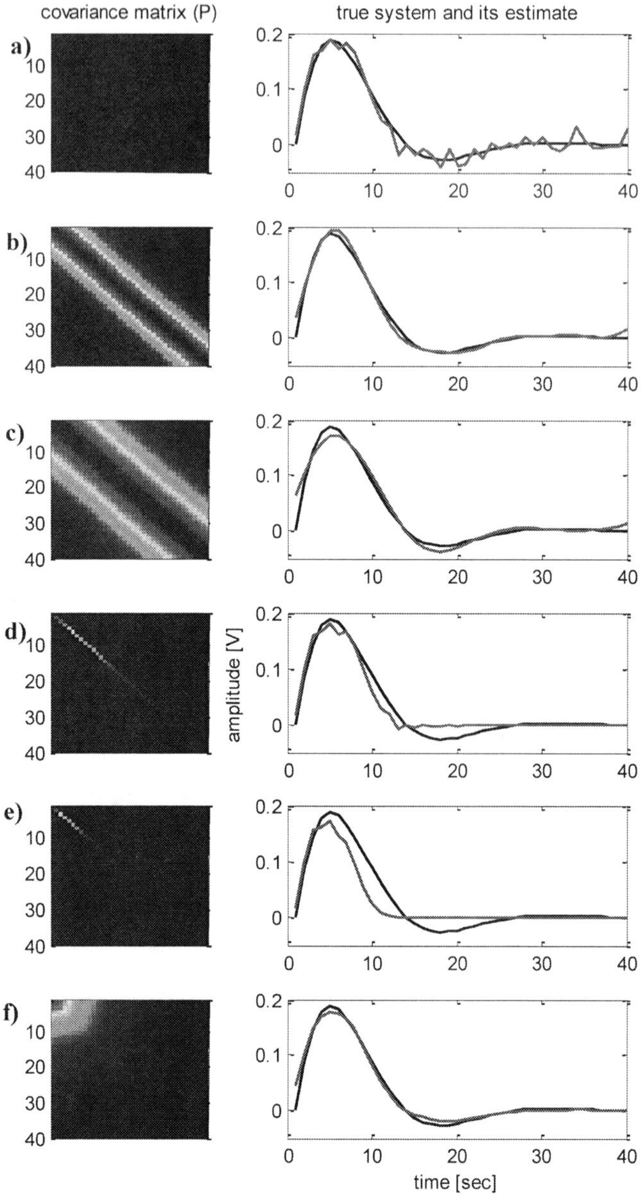

Figure 3 An example of different covariance matrices and regularized impulse response estimates. On the left different covariance matrices are shown. On the right, in black the true system and in gray its estimates are shown. The output is observed with an SNR of 20 **dB**. In figures (a)–(c) the smoothing is increased. In figures (d)–(e) the exponential decaying is increased. In figure (f) the optimal – w.r.t. MSE – smoothing and decaying is shown.

4.2. The LTV covariance matrix

In order to overview the properties of the TV ACF, an illustration is shown in Figure 4. This TV ACF correspond to the LTV system shown in Figure 1.a. By looking at this 2D ACF, several properties can be used to incorporate prior information to the TV covariance matrix – similarly to the concept of the classical 2D LTV IRF identification case [6] [7] with known input.

The first prior knowledge is that the considered ACFs are smooth. This smoothing is applied once over the system time τ which refers to "classical" evolution of IRF/ACF, and once over the global time t which gives a support to handle the time-varying behavior.

In addition to smoothing properties, another assumption can be imposed and incorporated in the covariance matrix by applying a more strict definition of stability: the IRFs and therefore the ACFs are exponentially decaying. Note, that most of the stable mechanical systems exploit this behaviour. When this is not the case other kernels might be used.

In the proposed approach, every point of the 2D ACF surface is connected to each other. It means that all the elements in the covariance matrix are non-zero, therefore the number of constraints is high, and the degrees of freedom of the system of linear equations (see Section 2.2) are significantly decreased resulting in a unique solution. The connections in the surface are defined for every possible pair of t and τ points, see Figure 4. The elements in the τ direction of the autocorrelations (horizontal blue direction) are linked by DC or TC kernels. Elements in the global time t direction (vertical red direction) are linked by RBF kernels. A graphical illustration is shown in Figure 4. The TV covariance matrix is then formulated as follows:

$$\mathrm{P}_{\{t_1,t_2\},\{\tau_1,\tau_2\}} = \mathrm{P}_{RBF}(t_1,t_2) \cdot \mathrm{P}_{DC}(\tau_1,\tau_2) \tag{10}$$

for every possible pair of t and τ.

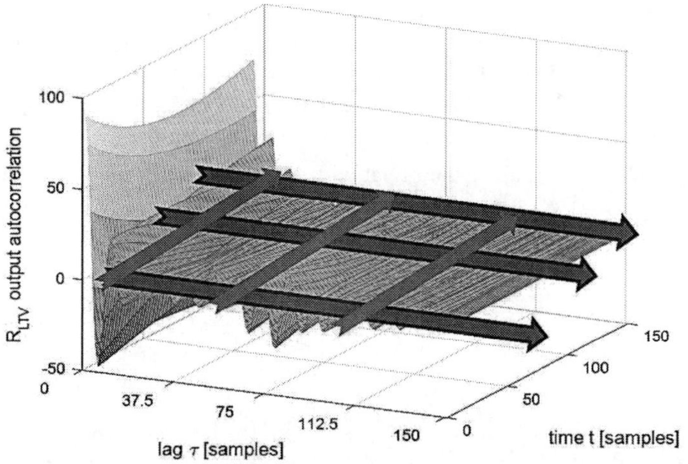

Figure 4 The TV output ACF of the system given in Figure 1.a. The arrows show the visualization of the possible regularization directions. The blue arrow refers to the $\boldsymbol{\tau}$ system time where decaying and smoothness of the adjacent elements can be imposed. The red arrow refers to the direction of time variations ($\boldsymbol{t}$ axis) where the smoothness of the adjacent autocorrelation functions can be imposed.

4.3. Tuning of the model complexity

$\gamma, \alpha, \beta, \sigma^2$ parameters in (7),(9)–(11) are the so called hyperparameters. The nonparametric system identification method presented in this work consists essentially of two steps: 1) optimization of the hyperparameters to tune the matrix P, and 2) computation of the model parameters using (7).

All the hyperparameters are tuned with the use of measured output data only. The hyperparameters are optimized in this case by maximizing the marginal likelihood of the observed output [18]. The interested reader can refer to [13], [6], [19] for more techniques for the tuning of the hyperparameters.

5. ILLUSTRATION ON A SIMULATION

5.1. The simulation setup

This section presents a simulation example of a second order time-varying system. The simulation time is 100 sec, the sampling frequency (f_s) is 128 Hz. The segmented window size ($L+1$) is 128 samples (which corresponds to 1 sec, 1 Hz resolution). The damping ratio varies linearly between 10% (at 0 sec) and 1% (at 100 sec). The resonance frequency (undamped natural frequency) varies between 10 (at 0 Hz) and 20 Hz (at 100 sec). The excitation signal is white noise, the output measurement is simulated with an SNR of 40 dB.

The simulation example is similar to the wind tunnel measurement elaborated in Section 6. In the latter one multiple modes are changing around the measurement time. In the simulation the first measurement mode is considered but in a shorter time with range larger changes in frequencies and damping ratios.

5.2. Results

In this section the parametric estimates of the resonance frequencies and damping ratios are compared, see Figure 5. The results of the traditional SFT approach (windowed correlogram estimates) [4] are compared to results of the proposed 2D regularization method. In case of SFT the output measurement is split into short subrecords, and each time the output ACF is calculated, and an additional exponential windowing is applied. This results in a series of ACFs which represents the classical TV ACF estimate. The power spectrum estimates are provided by the discrete Fourier transform of the ACFs. The resonance frequencies and damping ratios are estimated with the help of Polymax method. For the computational details and the application of Polymax we refer to [5] and [15].

The absolute estimation values and the relative errors are shown in Figure 5. Observe that the regularized estimate has significantly lower error levels in damping and the error levels are smooth trough the simulation. The major difference between the classical windowed and regularized estimate is the additional smoothing windowing applied over the measurement and autocorrelation time (see Figure 4).

Figure 6 shows the time-varying 2D autocorrelation function estimates for the windowed correlogram (SFT) case and the regularized correlogram methods. Observe that the regularized estimate is very smooth trough the simulation.

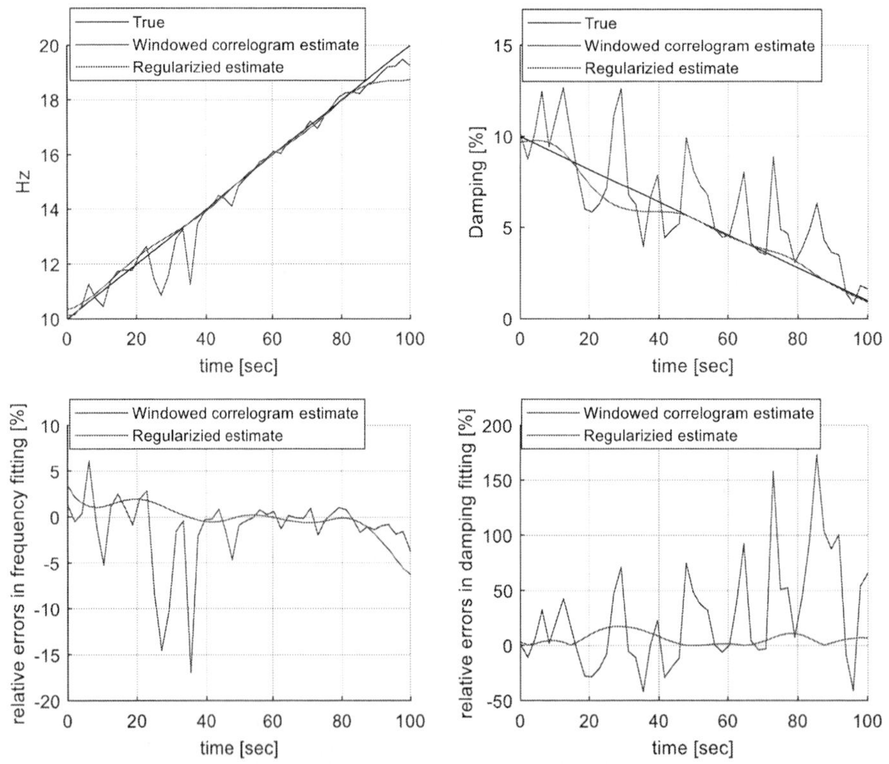

Figure 5 The time-varying frequency and damping ratio estimates of the simulation example are shown.

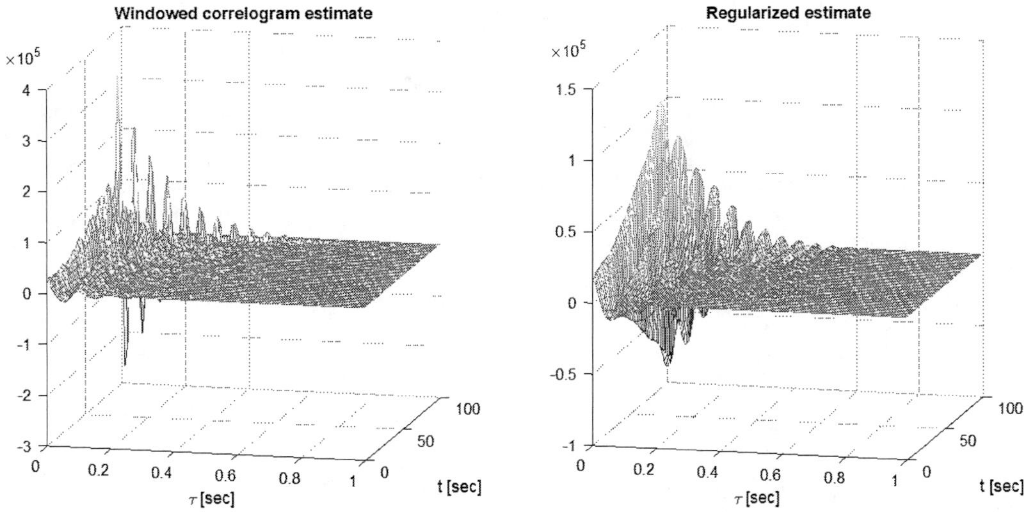

Figure 6 The time-varying output autocorrelation estimates of the simulated system are shown. On the left the classical windowed correlogram estimate (SFT) is shown. On the right the regularized estimate is shown.

6. RESULTS ON A WIND TUNNEL TESTING MEASUREMENT

6.1. The measurement setup

This section presents an industrial example of the flutter assessment of a scaled airplane model tested in a wind tunnel as detailed in [5]. The measurement time is $424\ \text{sec}$, the sampling frequency (f_s) is 500 Hz, the number of data samples (N) is 212000. The segmented window size ($L+1$) is 512 samples. The Mach number (ratio of airflow velocity to the sound speed) is varying between 0.07 and 0.79. An illustration of the measurement setup is given in Figure 7.

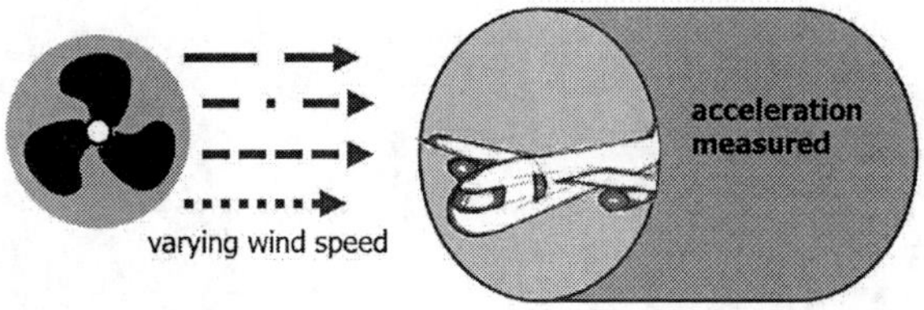

Figure 7 The measurement setup is shown. The airflow (wind speed) is varying while the airplane vibration is measured in the wind tunnel by means of accelerometers.

In this type of testing, it is desired to carefully verify and track the vibration behavior, since during flutter appearance, system destruction can occur. In this paper, wind tunnel data at various flow conditions are used to validate the approach for tracking the evolution of the resonance frequencies and damping ratios.

Further details on the measurement procedure can be found in [5]. Exact specifications on the airplane are omitted due to the confidentiality of the industrial project.

6.2. Results

In this section the time and frequency domain results of the traditional SFT approach [4] are compared to results of the proposed 2D regularization method.

Figure 8 shows the magnified time domain results of the classical SFT and regularization based TV ACF estimation. Observe that the SFT approach has issues with the decaying of ACFs (see between 300-400 secs), and the transitions between the adjacent ACFs are non-smooth. In case of regularized approach all the ACFs are interconnected resulting in 1) smooth transitions between the normalized adjacent ACFs 2) automatic decaying of ACFs.

Figure 9 shows the frequency domain results of the SFT and regularized approach. The most important part is the evolution the resonances and it can be best seen on the top view of the 2D power spectrum estimates. Observe that the traditional approach is very noisy where the regularized solution is smooth and more details can be captured.

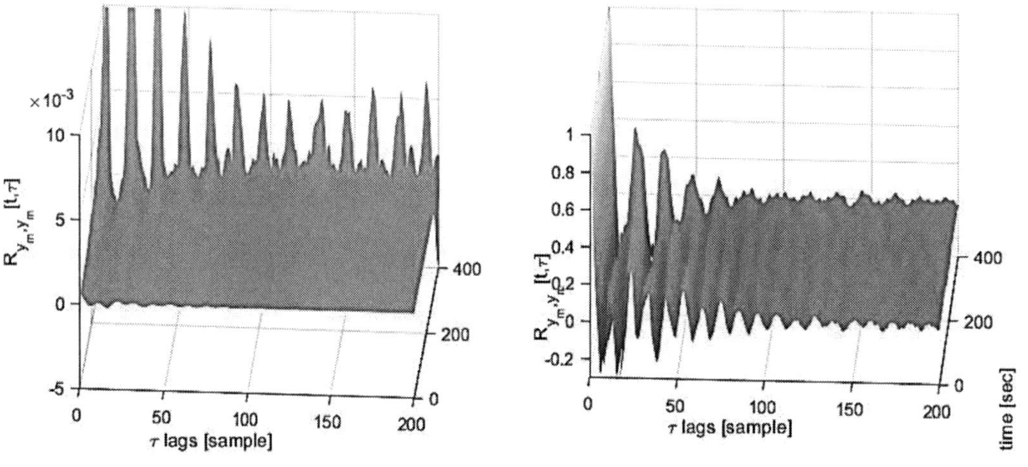

Figure 8 The time-varying output autocorrelation estimates of observed system are shown. On the left the estimate of classical SFT method is shown. On the right the proposed estimate is shown.

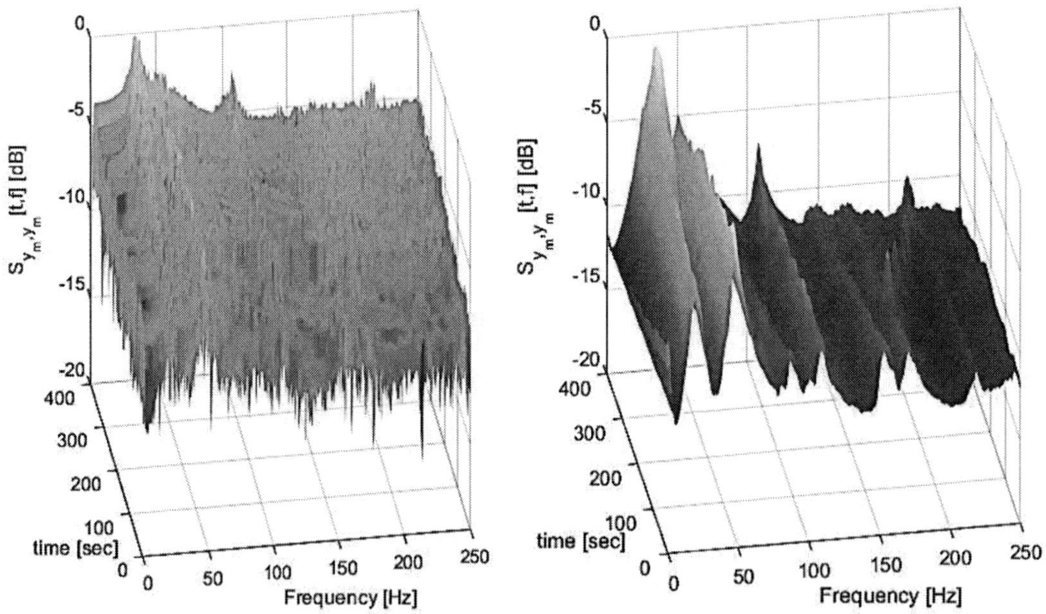

Figure 9 The time-varying output power spectrum estimates of observed system are shown. On the left the classical SFT estimate is shown. On the right the proposed method estimate is shown.

The Polymax modal parameter estimation method was applied in an automated way to the response spectra from all data segments. In the classical approach the spectra are obtained as the Fourier transform of the ACFs multiplied with an exponential window [5]. Polymax was also applied to the spectra obtained as the Fourier transform of the "regularized" ACFs (Figure 9 – Right). The results are shown in Figure 10. The time-varying character of the modes is clearly visible. The identified modes have been tracked and in Figure 11 shows, for instance, the eigenfrequency and damping ratio of the first mode as a function of time (and thus airspeed). From these figures, it can be concluded that the regularization approach yields more stable frequency and damping estimates when compared to the classical approach using an exponential window.

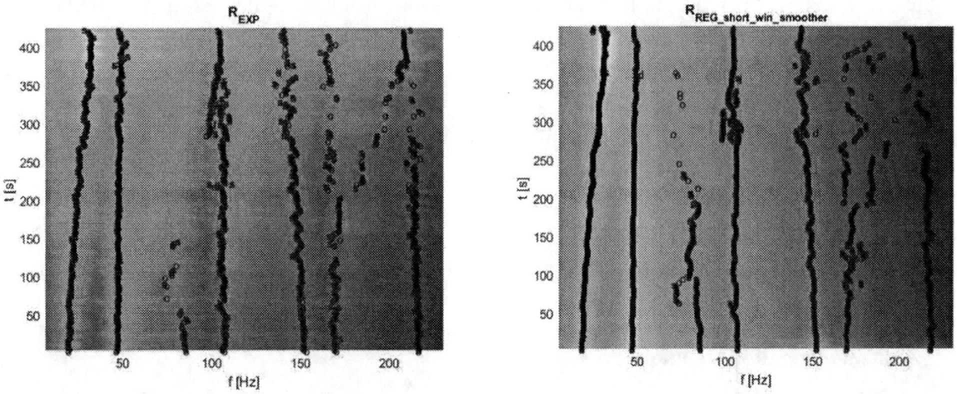

Figure 10 Automatic Polymax modal analysis results. Identified modes are represented by black symbols; the background picture represents the spectra. (Left) classical approach with exponential window; (Right) new regularisation approach.

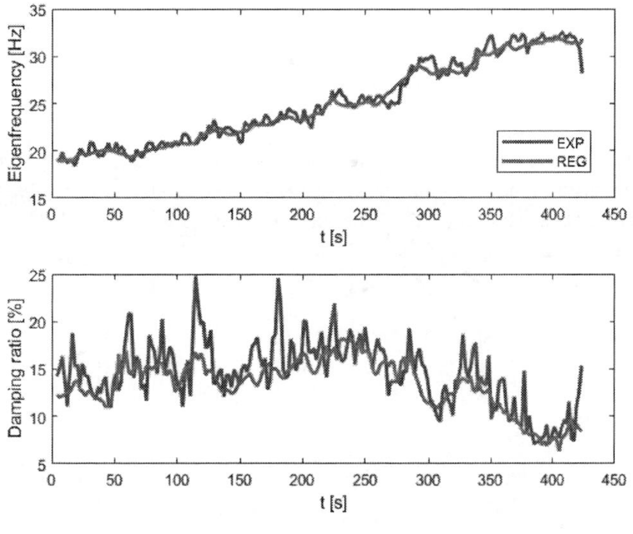

Figure 11 Continuous tracking results of eigenfrequencies (Top) and damping ratios (Bottom) of Mode around 20 Hz. The classical approach („EXP") is compared to the regularization approach („REG").

6.3. Computational complexity

At this point we comment on the computational complexity. The considered matrix sizes have a negative impact on the computational load which increases with total number of the parameters i.e.: 1) with number of measured points (window segments, N), and 2) with the resolution of the window ($L+1$).

In case of the classical SFT techniques, the memory needs and computational complexity are linear in terms of parameters ($O(N(L+1))$), whereas the regularization approach is more demanding, which is the main drawback of the technique.

In the proposed method, the 2D ACF is regularized, such that each point of the 2D ACF is connected. This results in a quadratic function of complexity ($O((N(L+1))^2)$).

In this particular measurement, the time and memory needed for a classical SFT solution are in the order of minutes/megabytes, whereas the regularized solution has a much higher computational time and memory needs in the magnitude of hours/gigabytes. There is an ongoing research how to decrease the resources necessary in order to use it for online tracking of modal parameters.

The exact computational time depends on many parameters such as the model complexity, the initial values of the hyperparameters and the technique used to tune the hyperparameters.

7. CONCLUSIONS

The main idea of the proposed time-varying regularized OMA framework is to provide more accurate and smoother estimates which are suitable for simulation, design and – indirectly – control. This will improve the overall quality and safety of products, and speed up the design process. Using the proposed advanced 2D regularization techniques it is possible:

- to reduce the noise influence such that the measurement quality will be significantly better
- to gain a better insight into the details of the time-variations

Further, a nonparametric TV OMA model can be used:

- to capture and to track the time-varying resonance frequencies and damping ratios
- to simulate and validate during the design phases

When it is necessary, the nonparametric TV OMA model can be used to estimate a parametric OMA model by cleaning up the data and allowing direct access to the mode shapes and making the control possible.

The drawback of the proposed method is that the computational load and memory need are significantly higher but this is negligible in the applications where 1) the preparation of the measurement setup takes days, and 2) the safety of the product and its intended users is concerned.

ACKNOWLEDGEMENTS

This work was funded by the Fund for Scientific Research (FWO-Vlaanderen), by the ERC advanced grant SNLSID, under contract 320378, and by the VLAIO Innovation Mandate project number HBC.2016.0235.

REFERENCES

[1] D. Edwins, Modal Testing: Theory, Practice and Applications (2nd edition), Research Studies Press L, 2000.

[2] B. Peeters and G. De Roeck, "Stochastic system identification for operational modal analysis: a review," *ASME Journal of Dynamic Systems, Measurement, and Control,* vol. 123, no. 4, pp. 659-667, 2001.

[3] E. Reynders, "System Identification Methods for (Operational) Modal Analysis: Review and Comparison," *Archives of Computational Methods in Engineering,* vol. 19, no. 1, pp. 51-124, 2012.

[4] Jont A. B., "Short Time Spectral Analysis, Synthesis, and Modification by Discrete Fourier Transform," *IEEE Transactions on Acoustics, Speech, and Signal Processing,* vol. 25, no. 3, pp. 235-238, 1977.

[5] B. Peeters, P. Karkle, M. Pronin and R. Van der Vorst, "Operational Modal Analysis for in-line flutter assessment during wind tunnel testing," in *15th International Forum on Aeroelasticity and Structural Dynamic*, 2011.

[6] P. Z. Csurcsia, Nonparametric identification of linear time-varying systems (Phd thesis), University Press, Zelzate, 2015.

[7] P. Z. Csurcsia and J. Lataire, "Nonparametric Estimation of Time-variant Systems Using 2D Regularization," *IEEE Transactions on Instrumentation & Measurement,* vol. 65, no. 5, pp. 1259-1270, 2016.

[8] G. Pillonetto, G. De Nicolao, "A new kernel-based approach for linear system identification," *Automatica,* vol. 46, no. 1, pp. 81-93, January 2010.

[9] G. Pillonetto, G. De Nicolao, "A new kernel-based approach for linear system identification," *Automatica,* vol. 46, no. 1, pp. 81-93, 2010.

[10] L. A. Zadeh, J. R. Ragazzini, "Frequency analysis of variable networks," *Proceedings of the IRE,* vol. 38, no. 3, pp. 291-299, 1950.

[11] L.A. Zadeh, "A general theory of linear signal transmission systems," *Journal of the Franklin Institute,* vol. 253, no. 4, p. 293–312, 1952.

[12] L. A. Zadeh, "Time-Varying Networks I," *Proceedings of the IRE,* vol. 49, no. 10, pp. 1488-1503, 1961.

[13] C. E. Rasmussen, C. K. I. Williams, Gaussian Processes for Machine Learning, The MIT Press, ISBN: 0-262-18253-X, 2006.

[14] R. Pintelon, J. Schoukens, System Identification: A Frequency Domain Approach, New Jersey: Wiley-IEEE Press, ISBN: 978-0470640371, 2012.

[15] B. Peeters, H. Van der Auweraer, P. Guillaume, J. Leuridan, "The PolyMAX Frequency-Domain Method: A New Standard for Modal Parameter Estimation?," *Shock and Vibration,* vol. 11, no. 3-4, pp. 359-409, 2004.

[16] R. Priemer, Introductory Signal Processing, World Scientific, ISBN: 9971509199, 1991.

[17] M. D. Buhmann, Radial Basis Functions: Theory and Implementations, New York\, ISBN: 9780521101332, 2009.

[18] G. Pillonetto, F. Dinuzzo, T. Chen , G. De Nicolao, L. Ljung, "Kernel methods in system identification, machine learning and function estimation: A survey," *Automatica,* vol. 50, no. 3, pp. 657-682, 2014.

[19] G. Birpoutsoukis, P. Z. Csurcsia, J. Schoukens, "Efficient Multidimensional Regularization for Volterra Series Estimation," *Mechanical Systems and Signal Processing,* vol. 104, pp. 896-914, 2017.

IOMAC'19
8th International Operational Modal Analysis Conference
2019 May13-15 Copenhagen

VARIANCE COMPUTATION OF MAC AND MPC FOR REAL-VALUED MODE SHAPES FROM THE STABILIZATION DIAGRAM

Szymon Gres[1], Michael Döhler [2], Palle Andersen[3], Laurent Mevel[2]

[1] Aalborg University, Department of Civil and Structural Engineering,
Thomas Manns Vej 23, 9000 Aalborg, Denmark

[2] Inria, Ifsttar, Univ. Rennes,
Campus de Beaulieu, 35042 Rennes, France

[3] Structural Vibration Solutions A/S,
NOVI Science Park, 9220 Aalborg, Denmark

ABSTRACT
Recent advances in efficient variance computation of modal parameter estimates from the output-only subspace-based identification algorithms make the modal parameter variance a practical modal indicator, indicating the accuracy of the estimation. A further modal indicator is the Modal Assurance Criterion (MAC), for which a recently developed uncertainty quantification scheme estimates the variance at a fixed model order. The Modal Phase Collinearity (MPC) is another popular indicator, for which an uncertainty scheme is currently missing. Unlike other modal parameters, which are Gaussian distributed, estimates of MAC and MPC are close to the border of their respective distribution support and cannot be approximated as a Gaussian random variable. This paper addresses the respective uncertainty quantification of MAC and MPC. The results are validated in the context of operational modal analysis (OMA) of a spring mass system.

Keywords: uncertainty quantification, operational modal analysis, Modal Assurance Criterion, Modal Phase Collinearity, stabilization diagram

1. INTRODUCTION

In Operational Modal Analysis (OMA) the modal parameters, namely natural frequencies, damping ratios and mode shapes, are estimated based on modeling of a linear system that is identified from measurements. It involves only the output data, such as accelerations, displacements, velocities or strains, recorded on the structure under some unknown, unmeasured, ambient excitation conditions. Estimates of the modal parameters are impaired with statistical uncertainties, since they are computed from data of finite length, which are usually also afflicted by noise. Hence, they are never equal to the true physical parameters of the structure, even if the assumed model is correct. Those uncertainties should be quantified or accounted for, which is often crucial in practice when interpreting the modal results.

In this context, first order perturbation theory is used to compute the variance of modal parameter estimates from the covariance-driven output-only stochastic subspace identification in [13], which is based on the developments of [11]. An efficient multi-order implementation of the latter scheme was derived in [4, 5]. This enabled the application of uncertainty quantification of the modal parameters in practical applications e.g. for computing the variance of natural frequencies, damping ratios and mode shapes estimated from bridge measurements [1, 2, 12]. The framework in [5] was extended to multi-setup subspace identification in [3]. Subsequently, the scheme for the uncertainty quantification of modal parameters was generalized to the family of input-output and output-only data-driven stochastic subspace identification methods in [9].

In the context of accounting for bias errors, the modal parameters can be clustered into so-called modal alignments by some practical criteria, like the relative difference between the parameters and the modal indicators. One modal alignment is a group of modal parameters that correspond to one theoretical mode and are estimated within a range of system orders. A group of modal alignments of some selected parameters, like the natural frequencies, is called a stabilization diagram. A strategy to compute the so called global modal parameters from the stabilization diagram was proposed in [1]. There, the global estimates of the modal parameters correspond to the means of the respective natural frequencies and the damping ratios at different modal orders, weighted with their statistical uncertainties. Like the estimates of the modal parameters computed at a single model order, the global estimates are stochastic variables thus their covariance and consequently the confidence bounds can be quantified, such as in [1].

The interpretation of the modal parameter estimates can be enhanced by the so-called modal indicators, which are quantities reflecting some physical aspects of the estimated mode shapes. Those indicators, Modal Assurance Criterion (MAC) and Modal Phase Collinearity (MPC), inherit the statistical uncertainties from the underlying mode shape estimates. While the statistical framework for modal parameters is well-known and developed in the context of subspace-based system identification methods, uncertainty quantification of modal indicators has not been carried out yet. In this paper we address the uncertainty quantification of MAC and MPC computed for estimates of real-valued mode shapes obtained from the stabilization diagram.

2. BACKGROUND

In this section the underlying mechanical model is recalled and the statistical parameters of interest are defined.

2.1. Vibration modeling

Motion behavior of a viscously damped, linear time-invariant (LTI) structural system can be represented by a discrete-time stochastic state-space model

$$\begin{cases} x_{k+1} = A_n x_k + w_k \\ y_k = C_n x_k + v_k \end{cases} \tag{1}$$

where $x_k \in \mathbb{R}^n$ are the states, and $A_n \in \mathbb{R}^{n \times n}$, $C_n \in \mathbb{R}^{r \times n}$ are the state transition and observation matrices estimated at a model order n. Vectors w_k with v_k denote the process and output noises. The eigenfrequencies f_i, damping ratios ζ_i and mode shapes φ_i of the underlying mechanical system are identified for $i = 1 \ldots n$ from the i-th eigenvalue λ_i and eigenvector Φ_i of A_n such that

$$f_i = \frac{|\lambda_{ci}|}{2\pi}, \; \zeta_i = \frac{-\Re(\lambda_{ci})}{|\lambda_{ci}|}, \; \varphi_i = C_n \Phi_i \tag{2}$$

where every eigenvalue of the continuous system λ_{ci} is computed with $e^{\lambda_{ci}\tau} = \lambda_i$. The $|(\cdot)|$ denotes the modulus operator and $\Re(\cdot)$ and $\Im(\cdot)$ express the real and imaginary parts of a complex variable.

2.2. MAC computation

Let $\hat{\varphi}$ and $\hat{\psi}$ be two mode shapes estimated on N samples. As N goes to infinity both mode shape estimates converge almost surely to their respective true values φ_* and ψ_*. The MAC formulation between two complex valued mode shapes vectors φ and ψ follows [6] and writes

$$\text{MAC} = \frac{|\varphi^H \psi|^2}{\varphi^H \varphi \psi^H \psi} = \frac{\varphi^H \psi \psi^H \varphi}{\varphi^H \varphi \psi^H \psi}. \tag{3}$$

A consistent estimate of the MAC can be obtained by using consistent estimates of the mode shape vectors φ and ψ. In this paper we will investigate the computation of MAC between two mode shape estimates of the same mode obtained from a modal alignment.

When assuming $\hat{\varphi} = \hat{\psi}$, meaning that the two mode shapes of interest are co-linear, the MAC yields 1, which is a constant value with no statistical uncertainty. On the other hand when the two modes shapes of interest are orthogonal $\hat{\varphi}^H \hat{\psi} = 0$ the MAC yields 0, which is also a constant value with no statistical uncertainty. Based on that, the MAC indicator is bounded between 0 and 1, which makes its uncertainty assessment difficult, especially when the estimates of MAC approach their theoretical bounds. That is what is investigated in this paper.

2.3. MPC computation

The complexity of a vector can be quantified by the Modal Phase Collinearity (MPC) [7, 10]. By definition the MPC is expressed as

$$\text{MPC}(\varphi) \triangleq \frac{(\lambda_1 - \lambda_2)^2}{(\lambda_1 + \lambda_2)^2} \tag{4}$$

where λ_1 and λ_2 are the eigenvalues of matrix $\begin{bmatrix} S_{xx} & S_{xy} \\ S_{yx} & S_{yy} \end{bmatrix} \in \mathbb{R}^{2\times 2}$, where $S_{xx} = \Re(\varphi)^T \Re(\varphi)$, $S_{yy} = \Im(\varphi)^T \Im(\varphi)$ and $S_{xy} = S_{yx} = \Re(\varphi)^T \Im(\varphi)$. The expression in (4) can be simplified to

$$\text{MPC}(\varphi) = \text{MAC}(\varphi, \overline{\varphi}) = \frac{(S_{xx} - S_{yy})^2 + 4(S_{xy})^2}{(S_{xx} + S_{yy})^2}, \tag{5}$$

which was established in [14]. Consequently, similar to the MAC, the MPC indicator computed from the data has some stochastic properties, that are functions of the stochastic properties of the mode shapes. Also, as well as the MAC, the MPC is bounded between 0 and 1, depending whether the mode shape of interest is respectively a purely imaginary or a purely real vector. The quantification of the statistical uncertainties of the estimates of the MPC is investigated in this paper.

2.4. Uncertainty quantification of modal parameters

Here we will set up some numerical simulation for which we will estimate the modal parameters and their underlying uncertainties. Consider a theoretical 6 DOF chain-like system that, for any consistent set of units, is modeled with a spring stiffness $k_1 = k_3 = k_5 = 100$ and $k_2 = k_4 = k_6 = 200$, mass $m_i = 1/20$ and a proportional modal damping matrix. The system is subjected to a white noise signal in all DOFs and sampled with a frequency of 50Hz for 2000 seconds. The responses are measured at DOFs 1, 2 and 5. White Gaussian noise with a standard deviation equal to 5% of the standard deviation of the output is added to the response at each channel. The computations are performed in a Monte Carlo setup with $m = 1000$ simulations. Both the output-only data driven subspace-based system identification (SSI-UPC) and the variance computation in the corresponding framework based on [5] are set up with time lags of 15 and 200 blocks for the covariance computation of the data Hankel matrix. To compute the modal alignments and the stabilization diagram, the considered system orders are in the range between 12 and 40. Six global modes are determined, with their respective modal parameters and their variances, in each simulation. The confidence intervals of the global modal parameters are computed after [1]. For the formation of each modal alignment the following criteria are used

- difference in two consecutive natural frequencies $\leq 1\%$,
- difference in two consecutive damping ratios $\leq 10\%$,
- MAC level between two consecutive mode shapes $\geq 99\%$,
- standard deviation of natural frequency computed with perturbation theory $\leq 1\%$.

The results presented first are established based on one realization of the Monte Carlo simulations. Figure 1 illustrates the estimates of the natural frequency with the corresponding 95% confidence intervals computed for model orders $12 - 40$ together with the estimates of the global natural frequency and its corresponding 95% confidence interval.

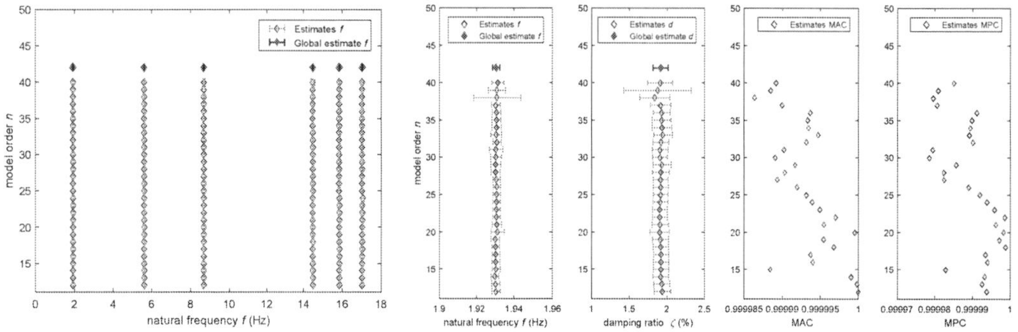

Figure 1: Stabilization diagram for natural frequencies with the corresponding 95% confidence intervals (left). Estimates of natural frequencies, damping ratios, MAC and MCF from the first modal alignment (right).

One can see that the natural frequency of each mode can be tracked along the system orders and the estimated variances are small, thus not visible in the scale presented on the Figure 1 (left). Subsequently, the dispersion of the natural frequencies, damping ratios and modal indicators is illustrated for the first modal alignment on Figure 1 (right). The fusion of the multi-order estimates of natural frequencies and damping ratios is reflected by the global estimates.

The variance of the modal parameter estimates computed with the Delta method based on one data set is reflected in the dispersion of the histogram of that parameter computed from the Monte Carlo simulations. This is illustrated in Figure 2 for the global estimates of the natural frequencies and damping ratios of the first mode and the estimates of the real and imaginary parts of the first DOF from the global mode shape corresponding to the first mode.

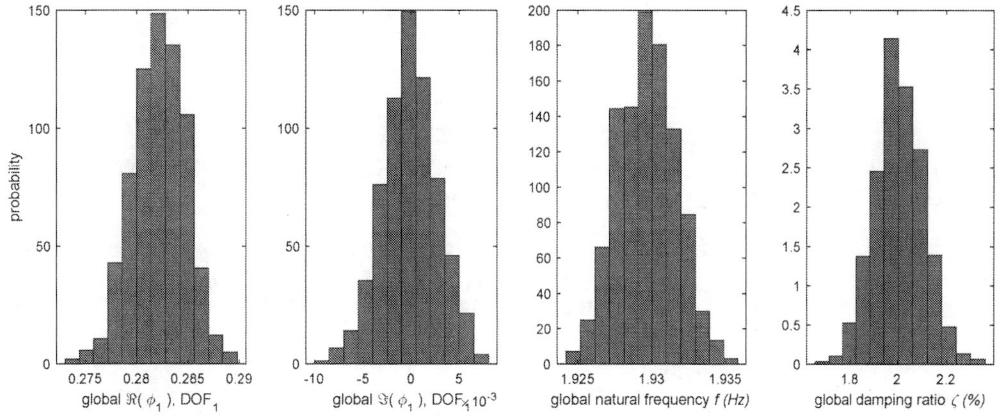

Figure 2: Histograms of the global estimates of modal parameters corresponding to the first mode based on Monte Carlo simulations. Respectively from the left: estimates of the real part of the global mode shape, the imaginary part of the global mode shape, global natural frequency and global damping ratio.

It can be observed that each histogram reflects some Gaussian distribution, which complies with the assumptions of the Delta method used in the Gaussian approximation of the modal parameter estimates. Additionally, confidence bounds of the global estimates of the natural frequency and damping ratio accurately encompass the area corresponding to the 95% quantile of the respective Monte Carlo histograms, which also validates the deployed theory.

2.5. Problem statement

Now we will illustrate how the distribution of the MAC and the MPC derived from the Monte Carlo histogram differs from the Gaussian distribution of the modal parameters when the considered mode shape estimates are asymptotically real-valued and selected from the same modal alignment. For that consider two cases of MAC and MPC, namely

1. MAC($\hat{\varphi}^{1,12}$, $\hat{\psi}^{1,14}$) is computed between the mode shapes from the first modal alignment at model orders 12 and 14, namely $\hat{\varphi}^{1,12}$ and $\hat{\psi}^{1,14}$,

2. MPC($\hat{\varphi}^{1,12}$) is computed for the mode shape corresponding to the first mode estimated at model order 12, namely $\hat{\varphi}^{1,12}$.

These distributions are illustrated on Figure 3.

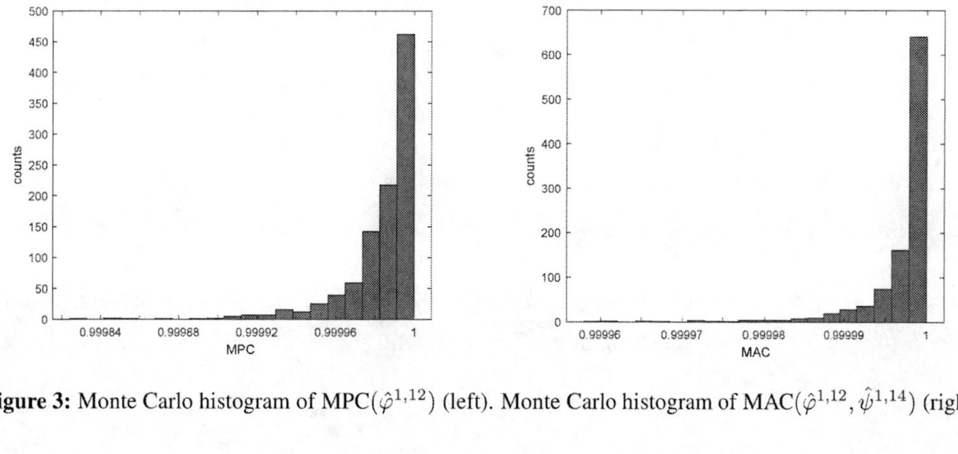

Figure 3: Monte Carlo histogram of MPC($\hat{\varphi}^{1,12}$) (left). Monte Carlo histogram of MAC($\hat{\varphi}^{1,12}$, $\hat{\psi}^{1,14}$) (right).

It can be observed that the histograms depicted in Figure 3 illustrate two non-Gaussian distributions of the considered MAC and MPC indicators. In the next section we will present a statistical framework that enables to quantify their variance and to approximate their distributions.

3. UNCERTAINTY QUANTIFICATION OF MAC AND MPC FOR THE REAL-VALUED MODE SHAPES FROM THE STABILIZATION DIAGRAM

Recall from (5) that $\text{MPC}(\varphi) = \text{MAC}(\varphi, \overline{\varphi})$. Based on that, define $g(\varphi, \psi)$ to be a function computing the MAC or MPC indicator evaluated for some given estimates of the mode shape vectors $\hat{\varphi}$ and $\hat{\psi}$. Note that $\psi = \overline{\varphi}$ for the computation of the MPC in $g(\varphi, \psi)$. The first order Taylor expansion of $g(\hat{\varphi}, \hat{\psi})$ writes as

$$g(\hat{\varphi}, \hat{\psi}) = g(\varphi_*, \psi_*) + \mathcal{J}^g_{\varphi_*,\psi_*} \hat{X} + o(||\hat{X}||) , \tag{6}$$

where $\hat{X} = \begin{bmatrix} \Re(\hat{\varphi} - \varphi_*)^T & \Im(\hat{\varphi} - \varphi_*)^T & \Re(\hat{\psi} - \psi_*)^T & \Im(\hat{\psi} - \psi_*)^T \end{bmatrix}^T$ and the Jacobian $\mathcal{J}^g_{\theta_*,\psi_*}$ is expressed as

$$\mathcal{J}^g_{\varphi_*,\psi_*} = \begin{bmatrix} \frac{\partial g}{\partial \text{vec}(\Re(\varphi))}(\varphi_*, \psi_*) & \frac{\partial g}{\partial \text{vec}(\Im(\varphi))}(\varphi_*, \psi_*) & \frac{\partial g}{\partial \text{vec}(\Re(\psi))}(\varphi_*, \psi_*) & \frac{\partial g}{\partial \text{vec}(\Im(\psi))}(\varphi_*, \psi_*) \end{bmatrix} .$$

A classical approach for the uncertainty quantification of $g(\hat{\varphi}, \hat{\psi})$ is to use a first order perturbation approach and use the first order Delta method to infer its distribution. The first order perturbation of $g(\hat{\varphi}, \hat{\psi})$ can be written as

$$\Delta g(\hat{\varphi}, \hat{\psi}) = \hat{\mathcal{J}}^g_{\hat{\varphi},\hat{\psi}} \hat{X} \approx \mathcal{J}^g_{\varphi_*,\psi_*} \hat{X} , \tag{7}$$

which assumes that $\mathcal{J}^g_{\varphi_*,\psi_*}$ is a non-zero matrix. Conditions for that are summarized in the following Lemma.

Lemma 1 *The necessary and sufficient conditions for* $\mathcal{J}^g_{\varphi_*,\psi_*} \neq 0$ *are*

$$\forall \varphi_*, \psi_* \in \mathbb{C}^r \; \mathcal{J}^g_{\varphi_*,\psi_*} \neq 0 \Leftrightarrow g(\varphi_*, \psi_*) \neq \{0, 1\} .$$

Hence, a first-order perturbation as in (7) is not sufficient to analyse the distribution of the function g for mode shapes that lead to MAC or MPC values of 0 or 1.

Now, consider the case of the MAC and the MPC for estimates of real-valued mode shapes selected from the model alignment a in the stabilization diagram. As such, it can be inferred from Section 2.2. and Section 2.3. that the true value of both indicators satisfies

1. $\text{MAC}(\varphi^a_*, \psi^a_*) = 1$, since both mode shapes correspond the the same mode,
2. $\text{MPC}(\varphi^a_*) = 1$, since the considered mode shape is asymptotically a real-valued vector.

That information, based on Lemma 1, suggests that $\mathcal{J}^g_{\varphi_*,\psi_*}$ is in fact a null matrix for these cases. The second order Taylor expansion of $g(\hat{\varphi}, \hat{\psi})$ can then be written as

$$g(\hat{\varphi}, \hat{\psi}) = g(\varphi_*, \psi_*) + \tfrac{1}{2}\hat{X}^T \text{H}^g_{\varphi_*,\psi_*} \hat{X} + o(||\hat{X}||^2) , \tag{8}$$

where $\text{H}^g_{\varphi_*,\psi_*}$ is the Hessian of function g. Recall that $\hat{X}_N = \sqrt{N}\hat{X}$ converges to a Gaussian variable $X_N \sim \mathcal{N}(0, \Sigma_{\varphi_*,\psi_*})$ when N goes to infinity. The asymptotic properties of $g(\hat{\varphi}, \hat{\psi})$ can be expressed as

$$N(g(\hat{\varphi}, \hat{\psi}) - g(\varphi_*, \psi_*)) \approx \tfrac{1}{2}\hat{X}_N^T \text{H}^g_{\varphi_*,\psi_*} \hat{X}_N \approx \tfrac{1}{2}X_N^T \text{H}^g_{\varphi_*,\psi_*} X_N , \tag{9}$$

which follows a distribution that can be approximated by a quadratic polynomial of the underlying mode shape vectors. This distribution is complex to determine, but it can be easily approximated. Rewrite (9) as a function $Q(\hat{X}_\mathcal{N})$ such that

$$Q(\hat{X}_\mathcal{N}) = \tfrac{1}{2}\hat{X}_\mathcal{N}^T \mathrm{H}^g_{\hat{\varphi},\hat{\psi}} \hat{X}_\mathcal{N} \approx \tfrac{1}{2}X_\mathcal{N}^T \mathrm{H}^g_{\varphi_*,\psi_*} X_\mathcal{N} \approx N\left(g(\hat{\varphi},\psi_*) - g(\varphi_*,\psi_*)\right) . \tag{10}$$

The distribution of $Q(\hat{X}_\mathcal{N})$ can be approximated with a scaled $\chi^2_{l_{PT}}$ distribution with l_{PT} degrees of freedom, after [8], as follows.

Lemma 2 *Assume that $\mathrm{H}^g_{\varphi_*,\psi_*}$ is a positive semi-definite matrix. The approximate probability distribution function of $Q(\hat{X}_\mathcal{N})$ writes*

$$f_Q(y) = \frac{1}{\alpha} f_{\chi^2_{l_{PT}}}\left(\frac{y-\beta}{\alpha}\right) \tag{11}$$

where $y \in [\beta, +\infty]$ and $f_Q(y) = 0$ for $y < \beta$. The respective scaling and shift parameters of the approximate distribution, α and β, are defined such that $\alpha = \sigma_Q/\sigma_{\chi^2}$ and $\beta = \mu_Q - (\mu_{\chi^2}\sigma_Q)/\sigma_{\chi^2}$. The mean μ_Q and standard deviation σ_Q of the quadratic form are computed using its first cumulants, c_1 and c_2, namely $\mu_Q = c_1$ and $\sigma_Q = \sqrt{2c_2}$, where the k-th asymptotic cumulant of $Q(\hat{X}_\mathcal{N})$ writes as

$$c_k = \mathrm{tr}\left((\tfrac{1}{2}\mathrm{H}^g_{\varphi_*,\psi_*}\Sigma_{\varphi_*,\psi_*})^k \right) . \tag{12}$$

The mean μ_{χ^2} and standard deviation σ_{χ^2} of the approximating $\chi^2_{l_{PT}}$ distribution are computed from its number of degrees of freedom l_{PT}, such that $\mu_{\chi^2} = l_{PT}$ and $\sigma_{\chi^2} = \sqrt{2l_{PT}}$, where $l_{PT} = c_2^3/c_3^2$.

The derivation of the expressions for the $\mathcal{J}^g_{\varphi_*,\psi_*}$, $\mathrm{H}^g_{\varphi_*,\psi_*}$ and necessary proofs for Lemma 1 and Lemma 2 are excluded from this paper due to the space limitation.

4. NUMERICAL VALIDATION

This section concludes the developments of this paper by presenting the results of the variance computation of the global MAC and MPC obtained from the stabilization diagram. The global estimates of MAC and MPC are computed for one realization among all the Monte Carlo simulations that corresponds to data set used to establish Figure 1 in Section 2.4.. Here the latter Figure is updated by the estimates of MAC and MPC and their corresponding 95% confidence bounds.

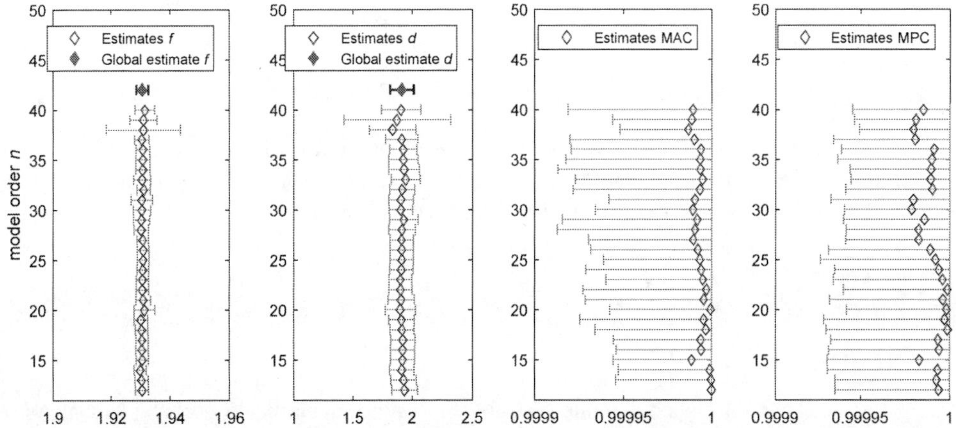

Figure 4: . Estimates of natural frequencies, damping ratios, MAC and MPC from the first modal alignment.

Despite both MAC and MPC being very close to their respective boundaries, their uncertainty can be quantified, as presented on Figure 4. Estimated uncertainties are small however, apart from illustrating the variances in the estimates of the MAC and MPC, the variances of both indicators reflect the underlying variances of the global mode shape estimates.

The quadratic fits to the Monte Carlo histogram from Figure 3 are compared to the classical Gaussian approximation of estimates of the MAC and the MPC based on the first order perturbation theory and Delta method, based on (7).

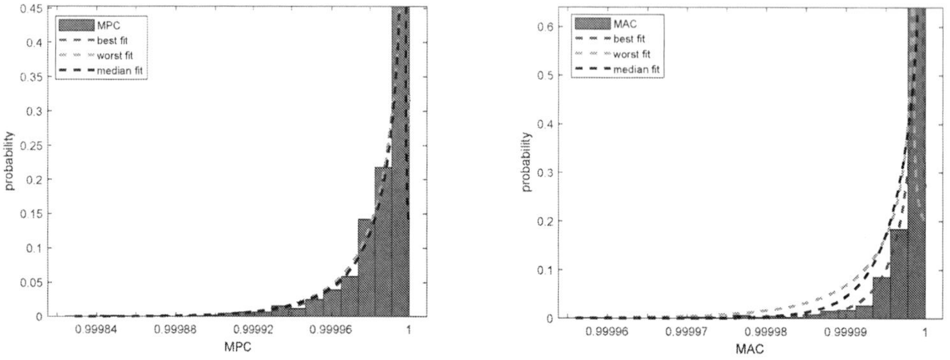

Figure 5: Monte Carlo histogram of MPC($\hat{\varphi}^{1,12}$) (left). Monte Carlo histogram of MAC($\hat{\varphi}^{1,12}, \hat{\psi}^{1,14}$) (right). Quadratic fits.

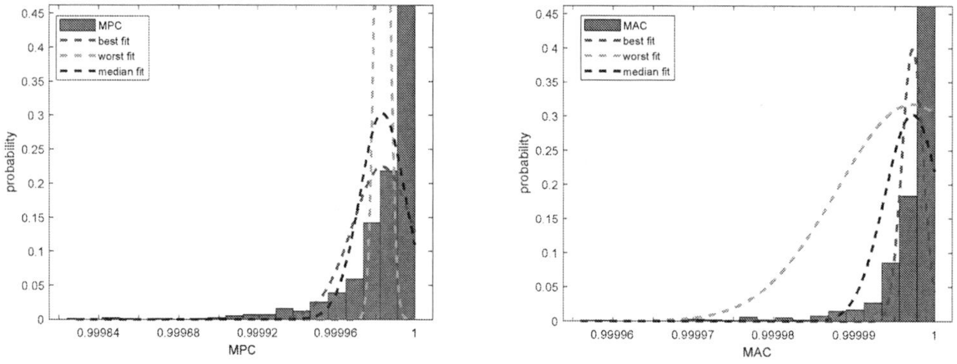

Figure 6: Monte Carlo histogram of MPC($\hat{\varphi}^{1,12}$) (left). Monte Carlo histogram of MAC($\hat{\varphi}^{1,12}, \hat{\psi}^{1,14}$) (right). Gaussian fits.

The Gaussian approximation for the distribution of the estimates of the MAC and the MPC obtained from the stabilization diagram is inadequate. Conversely, the quadratic approximation yields accurate fits, as expected. The best, the worst and the median fits presented on Figure 5 and Figure 6 are established based on the statistical properties of the respective distributions computed on one data set and evaluated thanks to a goodness of fit criterion.

5. CONCLUSIONS

In this paper, we have developed a framework for uncertainty quantification of the Modal Assurance Criterion (MAC) and Modal Phase Co-linearity (MPC) for the asymptotically real-valued mode shapes estimated through a stabilization diagram. The proposed scheme allows to accurately compute the variance and approximate the distribution of the aforementioned modal indicators using a quadratic approximation. The resultant framework is more adequate then the classical Gaussian approach for uncertainty quantification, which is illustrated based on numerical simulations.

REFERENCES

[1] M. Döhler, P. Andersen, and L. Mevel. Variance computation of modal parameter estimates from UPC subspace identification. In *IOMAC - 7th International Operational Modal Analysis Conference*, Ingolstadt, Germany, 2017.

[2] M. Döhler, F. Hille, L. Mevel, and W. Rücker. Structural health monitoring with statistical methods during progressive damage test of S101 bridge. *Engineering Structures*, 69:183 – 193, 06 2014.

[3] M. Döhler, X.-B. Lam, and L. Mevel. Uncertainty quantification for modal parameters from stochastic subspace identification on multi-setup measurements. *Mechanical Systems and Signal Processing*, 36:562–581, 04 2013.

[4] M. Döhler, X.-B. Lam, and L. Mevel. Multi-order covariance computation for estimates in stochastic subspace identification using QR decompositions. *IFAC Proceedings Volumes*, 47(3):9498 – 9503, 2014. 19th IFAC World Congress.

[5] M. Döhler and L. Mevel. Efficient multi-order uncertainty computation for stochastic subspace identification. *Mechanical Systems and Signal Processing*, 38(2):346–366, 2013.

[6] R. J. Allemang. The modal assurance criterion (MAC): Twenty years of use and abuse. *Journal of Sound and Vibration*, 37, 01 2003.

[7] J.-N. Juang and R. S. Pappa. An eigensystem realization algorithm for modal parameter identification and model reduction. *Journal of Guidance, Control, and Dynamics*, 8:620 – 627, 1985.

[8] H. Liu, Y. Tang, and H. H. Zhang. A new chi-square approximation to the distribution of non-negative definite quadratic forms in non-central normal variables. *Computational Statistics and Data Analysis*, 53(4):853 – 856, 2009.

[9] P. Mellinger, M. Döhler, and L. Mevel. Variance estimation of modal parameters from output-only and input/output subspace-based system identification. *Journal of Sound and Vibration*, 379(Supplement C):1 – 27, 2016.

[10] R. Pappa, K. B. Elliott, and A. Schenk. A consistent-mode indicator for the eigensystem realization algorithm. *Journal of Guidance Control and Dynamics*, 16, 09 1993.

[11] R. Pintelon, P. Guillaume, and J. Schoukens. Uncertainty calculation in (operational) modal analysis. *Mechanical Systems and Signal Processing*, 21(6):2359 – 2373, 2007.

[12] E. Reynders, K. Maes, G. Lombaert, and G. D. Roeck. Uncertainty quantification in operational modal analysis with stochastic subspace identification: Validation and applications. *Mechanical Systems and Signal Processing*, 66-67:13 – 30, 2016.

[13] E. Reynders, R. Pintelon, and G. D. Roeck. Uncertainty bounds on modal parameters obtained from stochastic subspace identification. *Mechanical Systems and Signal Processing*, 22(4):948 – 969, 2008. Special Issue: Crack Effects in Rotordynamics.

[14] P. Vacher, B. Jacquier, and A. Bucharles. Extensions of the mac criterion to complex modes. In *ISMA 2010 International Conference on Noise and Vibration Engineering*, 2010.

MEASUREMENT TECHNIQUES & VIRTUAL SENSING

IOMAC'19

8th International Operational Modal Analysis Conference
2019 May13-15 Copenhagen

BEST PRACTICES WHEN PERFORMING OPERATIONAL MODAL ANALYSIS – PART 1

Niels-Jørgen Jacobsen [1]

[1] Product Manager Structural Dynamics, Brüel & Kjær Sound & Vibration Measurements A/S, Niels-Jorgen.Jacobsen@bksv.com

ABSTRACT

When performing modal testing, attention must be paid to every step of the test to obtain the best possible results: from planning the measurement setup, to performing the measurements and carrying out the modal analysis and analysis validation. However, in contrast to classical modal analysis using controlled hammer or shaker excitation, operational modal analysis is typically performed in-situ with real-life unknown excitation forces from ambient or self-generated vibrations. Furthermore, operational modal analysis is often performed on large structures, where classical modal analysis can be impractical. Consequently, in addition to many of the best practices of modal testing also applying to operational modal analysis, specific ones apply.

This paper is the first in a series summarizing some of the best practices for performing operational modal analysis. It is aimed at the engineer who is new to operational modal analysis but probably also contains a few hints and tips for the more experienced engineer.

Keywords: Geometry creation, distributed data acquisition systems, dynamic operating range, transducer setup, accelerometer mounting check, measurement assumptions and procedure

1. INTRODUCTION

Performing operational modal analysis (OMA) has never been simpler due to the event of new, innovative and often automated techniques and tools that significantly improve the results, increase ease-of-use and productivity, and eliminate operator dependent results. However, common sense must always prevail. Thus, a proper understanding of the necessary steps and potential pitfalls in the various steps of a test campaign, combined with enough knowledge of the pros and cons of different techniques and tools is still essential to obtain the best possible results and avoid errors.

This paper is the first in a series of papers describing best practices when performing operational modal analysis. It focuses on test planning and the measurement setup and execution.

2. TEST PLANNING AND THE MEASUREMENT SETUP

Time used on test planning and test setup is often a significant part of the total test time and often where irreparable errors are made. To reduce test time, eliminate errors and perform the best possible measurements, the following can be recommended.

2.1. Create a proper test geometry

The test geometry represents the structure under test. Typically, it is a wireframe consisting of nodes connected by trace lines, and where triangular or quad elements might have been added between the nodes. The test geometry should be simple but detailed enough to properly identify and separate the different mode shapes.

Ideally, the test geometry should only include nodes where measurements are performed. The exception is non-measured nodes/DOFs, where the animation is easy to predict in the frequency range of interest, for example, fixed nodes; nodes on a rigid part of the structure, where only a single node then needs to be measured; or DOFs, where none or negligible vibration exist, for example in restrained nodes. Non-measured DOFs should be animated using nearest DOF interpolation or slave node equations to make the animations look undistorted.

However, a more refined test geometry is often advantageous to obtain smoother animations that help to better identify and understand the mode shapes, and is often requested for documentation purposes.

Powerful geometry creation techniques are essential to make good geometries in a short time. Basically, a test geometry can be created by decimating a Finite Element Model (FEM), meshing Computer Aided Design (CAD) models or building the geometry using nodes, trace lines and elements.

2.1.1. Decimating a Finite Element Model

By looking at the FEA results, you quickly obtain knowledge about the various mode shapes and which response DOFs are required to properly identify and separate the mode shapes. You can then rapidly create a reduced test geometry by clicking on the nodes to keep in the FEM and connecting them with trace lines and elements. You keep the size, orientation and optionally the node numbering of the FEM, which can be advantageous, if you later want to perform model correlation.

Figure 1. BK Connect Geometry Decimation. FE model left. Decimated test geometry right.

Another simple and efficient way to decimate a FEM is to select nodes on it and follow how the AutoMAC builds up for the reduced geometry consisting of the selected nodes. More automatic methods to define the response DOFs, and thereby the test nodes, also exist.

2.1.2. Meshing CAD models

Combining standard CAD curves (line, polyline, ellipse, hyperbolic, parabolic, spline, etc.), surfaces (triangle, rectangle, polygon, circle, ellipse, hyperbolic, parabolic, etc.), solids (box, cylinder, hemisphere, sphere, cone, etc.), and potentially arbitrary CAD models into compounds and subsequently meshing them into a test geometry is a very intuitive and fast top-down modelling approach for test geometry creation. With editor tools such as movable work planes, mirroring, copying, cutting planes, etc., advanced test geometries can be swiftly created.

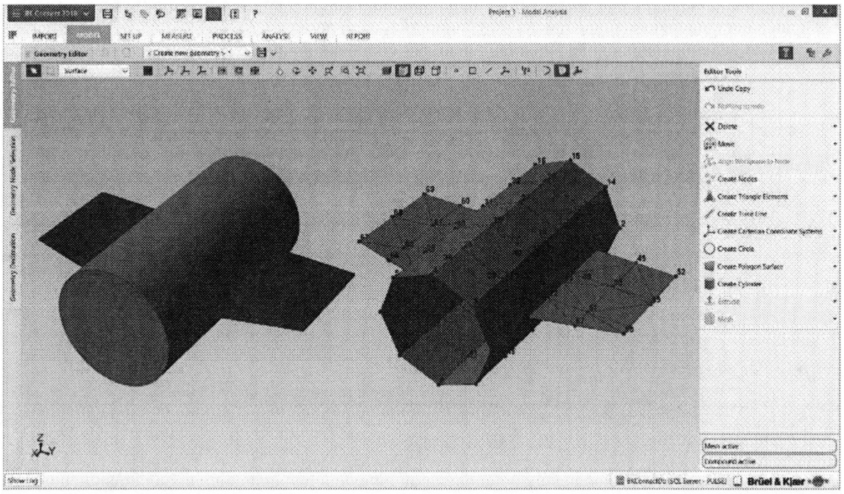

Figure 2. BK Connect Geometry Editor. CAD compound left. Meshed geometry right.

2.1.3. Building a geometry using nodes, trace lines and elements

Using nodes, trace lines and elements is the traditional way of creating geometry meshes and is suitable for simpler geometries. The geometry can be created by selecting nodes in a movable work plane and combining them by trace lines and elements. Editor tools, such as those mentioned above, can speed up the creation process. Alternatively, the geometry can be created by entering the information into tables.

It can often be advantageous to create the geometry in Excel® due to its many editing tools and then import the geometry into the measurement software.

2.2. Define data acquisition hardware configuration

For operational modal analysis measurements, two topics are of special concern regarding the hardware configuration. As the measurement objects are often large, the amount of cabling can be quite considerable if conventional hardware configuration with rack-mounted data acquisition modules are used. Using a distributed configuration can significantly reduce the cabling. Furthermore, operational modal analysis measurements are typically performed in-situ with real-life, unknown excitation forces from ambient or self-generated vibrations. Consequently, a high dynamic operating range is often needed.

2.2.1. Reducing the amount of cabling

Reducing the amount of cabling is one of the most important considerations in test preparation as it will provide faster setup and easier maintenance, minimize risk of setup and measurement errors, reduce noise and lower cable cost. Wireless transducers sound promising, but in many situations their size and mass loading are too high, their specifications inadequate and the price too high. A distributed data acquisition system is often the most optimal solution.

The combined use of the IEEE standards PTP (Precision Time Protocol) and PoE (Power over Ethernet) enables one-cable operation for data transfer and sample synchronization between the data acquisition modules and power supply [1], [2]. This makes it possible to drastically reduce the amount of cabling in distributed setups by placing the data acquisition modules close to the measurement object. The length of the transducer cables can be significantly reduced with only a single standard and inexpensive LAN cable from each data acquisition module connected to a LAN switch that, in turn, is connected to the measurement PC using a standard LAN cable.

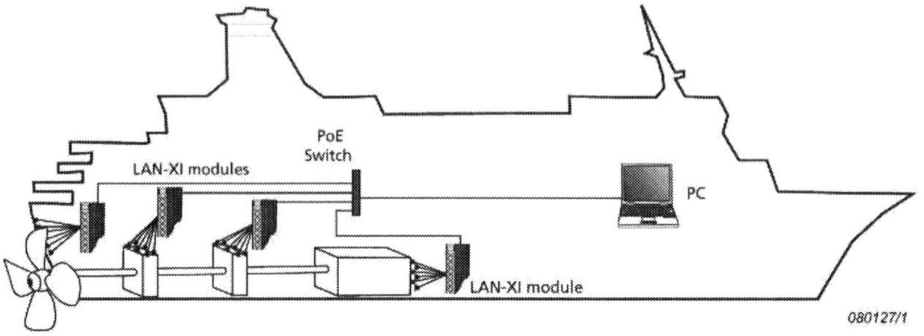

Figure 3. Using PTP and PoE, a distributed data acquisition hardware configuration can be made. This can drastically reduce the cabling for measurements on large structures.

2.2.2. Ensuring high dynamic operating range

With the introduction of the Dyn-X (Dynamics eXtreme) technology, data acquisition systems for the first time fully match or outperform the dynamic performance of high-quality transducers [3]. A Dyn-X input channel with a single input range has a useful analysis range of 125 dB narrowband and more than 160 dB broadband.

The Dyn-X technology utilizes a special analog input design to provide a very high dynamic range of the analog circuit, pre-conditioning the transducer signal before feeding it to the ADC. The Dyn-X input channels have no input attenuators, but a single input range from 0 to $10V_{peak}$.

The digitizing is performed synchronously in two specially selected, high-quality, 24-bit delta-sigma ADCs, and both data streams are fed to the DSP environment where dedicated algorithms in real-time merge the signals while obtaining an extremely high accuracy match in gain, offset and phase.

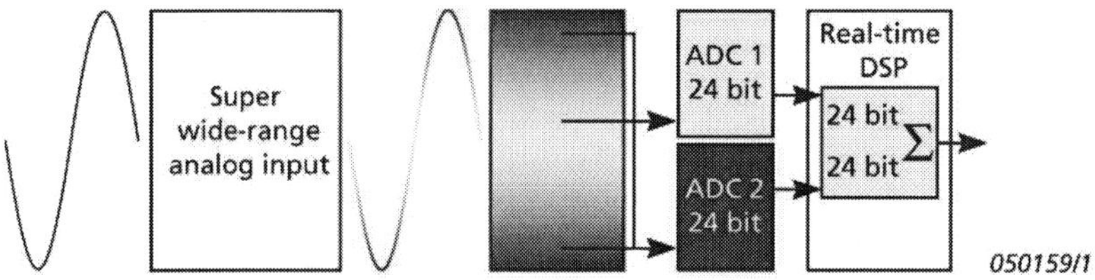

Figure 4. A simplified block diagram of the Dyn-X technology.

With no setting of input ranges, and with no need to be concerned about overloads, under-range measurements and the accuracy of the measurements done, the ease and safety of measuring are dramatically increased using Dyn-X technology. And with no need for trial runs to ensure correct input ranges for the various input channels, the certainty of getting the measurements right the first time is also significantly increased.

2.3. Transducer setup

Once the response DOFs have been defined and appropriate transducers, typically accelerometers, selected, they can be attached to the structure using various mounting techniques and the DOF and component information can be transferred to the measurement system. To avoid a manual, time-consuming and error-prone transfer, the Transducer Smart Setup app was introduced to make transducer setup as simple and automated as possible and, in addition, give the user instant access to specifications, documentation and calibration data [4], [5].

The Transducer Smart Setup app scans data matrix codes engraved on transducers containing information about the transducer type, serial number and the surface side of the transducer being scanned. Furthermore, when scanning the data matrix code, the app uses a patented algorithm to determine the orientation of the transducer relative to a predefined reference coordinate system.

In addition, you can scan customized 2D labels attached next to the transducers to read transducer position (component) and node ID. When all transducers and 2D labels in the test setup have been scanned, the information is seamlessly transferred to the BK Connect® measurement software for fast and safe setup. The transfer can take place using a cloud service such as iCloud, DropBox, Google Drive or OneDrive, using email or using a wired connection.

The link between the scanned information and the transducers connected to the hardware takes place through the transducers serial numbers. Using transducers with TEDS (Transducer Electronic Data Sheet), the serial numbers (plus information about the transducers' sensitivity, type number, manufacturer, calibration date, etc.), of the transducers connected to the LAN-XI data acquisition hardware are automatically detected and read into the BK Connect measurement software. This further reduces the setup time and eliminates typing errors compared to using non-TEDS transducers, where the information has to be entered manually. TEDS is specified in the IEEE 1451.4-2004 standard [6].

Moreover, the data matrix code contains a link giving you instant access to specifications, documentation and calibration data stored in the cloud.

Figure 5. Accelerometer with data matrix codes (left). Example of 2D label (right).

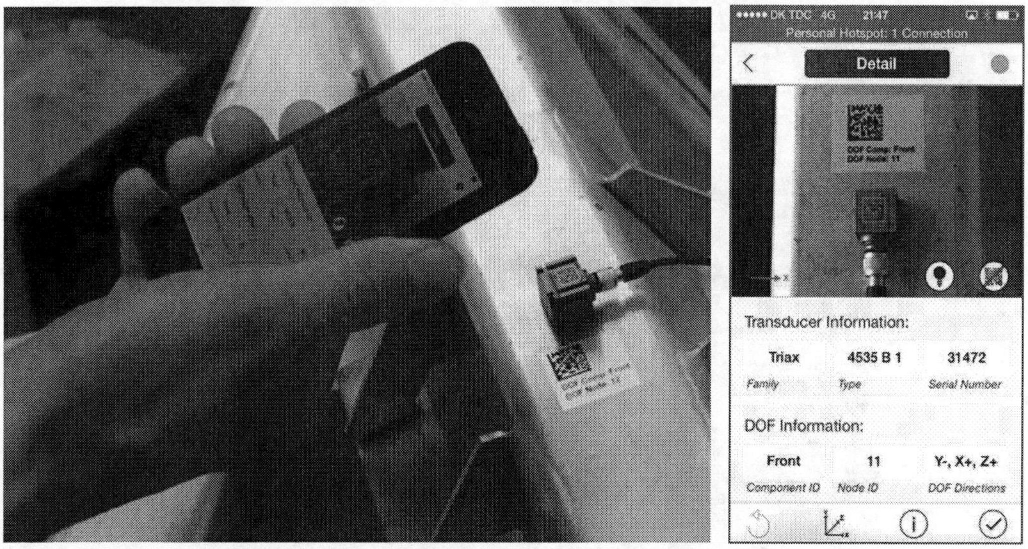

Figure 6. Scanning the data matrix code of an accelerometer and its associated 2D label provides the transducer and DOF information. If no 2D label is used, the Component ID and Node ID can be selected from a list of entries or can simply be typed in.

2.4. Accelerometer Mounting Check

Bad measurements due to improperly mounted accelerometers are, unfortunately, quite common. A non-optimal mounting technique might have been chosen resulting in bad measurements from the beginning, or the accelerometers might simply have become loose over time. In addition, changes to the cable connections might have materialized.

Often these imperfections are difficult to spot with the naked eye. Obviously, large-scale testing such as modal surveys with hundreds of mounted accelerometers, but also smaller-scale tests, can benefit greatly from a robust verification tool. The need obviously becomes even more apparent when the accelerometers are located in remote areas or areas with limited or no access.

The purpose of Accelerometer Mounting Check is to provide a simple and robust procedure to check changes in the mounting state of the attached accelerometers to ensure that they are properly mounted during the complete measurement. Accelerometer Mounting Check uses a classification algorithm with two features based on frequency response functions and coherence functions to divide the mounting states into two classes: Proper and Improper.

Accelerometer Mounting Check is a patented procedure implemented in Brüel & Kjær's measurement systems using LAN-XI hardware and BK Connect software. It works with all charge accelerometers and with newer Brüel & Kjær CCLD accelerometers with modified built-in preamplifiers.

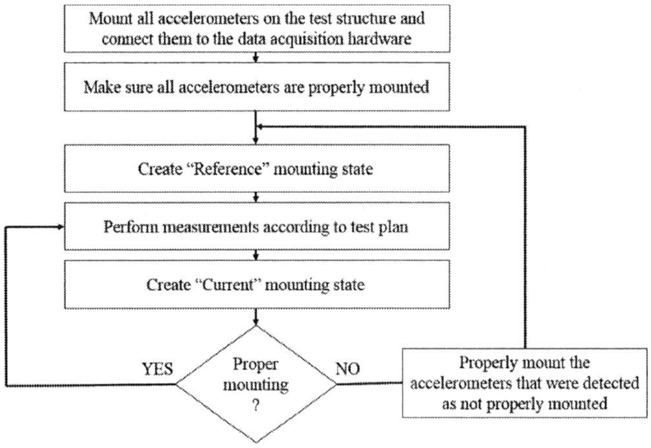

Figure 7. Accelerometer Mounting Check procedure.

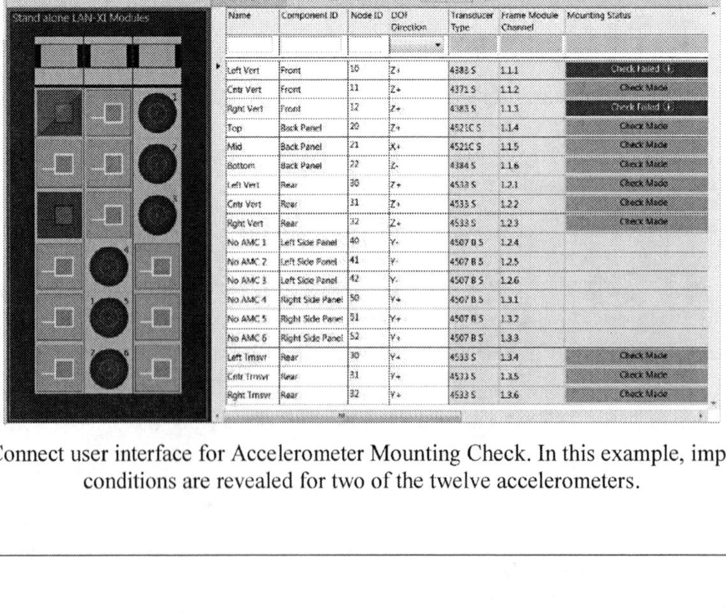

Figure 8. BK Connect user interface for Accelerometer Mounting Check. In this example, improper mounting conditions are revealed for two of the twelve accelerometers.

3. MEASUREMENT

Important topics to consider for obtaining the best possible measurements include measurement assumptions, measurement procedure and measurement time. Before performing the analysis, validation of the measurements should always be done as an integral part of the test.

3.1. Measurement assumptions

OMA is often confused with operating deflection shapes (ODS) analysis as, in both cases, the ambient or self-generated vibrations are used for excitation, only the responses are measured, and the measurement procedure is very similar. In ODS, no mathematical model of the structure under test is created. The responses are observed at a given operating condition and if that changes, new measurements must be performed. In OMA, however, a mathematical model is created to extract the modal parameters. In other words, ODS is signal analysis, whereas OMA is system analysis and therefore an assumption for OMA is that the structure is linear and time-invariant. Just as for classical modal analysis using hammer or shaker(s) excitation.

This assumption is never fully fulfilled, but by averaging the responses, a good linear approximation of a slightly non-linear system can be obtained. This is based on another assumption being fulfilled, that is the input signals are stationary and can be approximated by filtered, zero mean Gaussian noise, acting on the entire structure randomly in time and space. The more excitation points, the better.

If linearity studies have been performed on the structure, these results can be used to perform the measurements using the most optimal excitation conditions.

If strong deterministic signals such as harmonic components are present close to modes of interest, they should be significantly reduced to avoid affecting the extracted modal parameters. Time domain methods [7], [8] based on orthogonal projection and non-linear optimization are available as well as frequency domain methods based on kurtosis calculations [9], [10]. When strong deterministic signals are present, a measurement system with a high operating range should be used to allow the low-level stochastic content to be analysed after the deterministic content has been removed.

The best way to minimize time-invariance is to reduce the measurement time by measuring all DOFs simultaneously and not measure longer than required.

In classical modal analysis, the input level and spectrum are controlled, which is not the case in OMA. Hence, it must be ensured that the input level is sufficiently high and the spectrum broad-banded enough to excite all modes of interest. For weakly excited structures, it is often advantageous to add artificial excitation. For example, by using an impact hammer to excite the structure randomly in time and space without measuring the applied force.

Despite the assumption of stochastic input signals, OMA can also be successfully performed using a high degree of deterministic excitation. An example is run-up/down testing of engines. Several orders will be excited simultaneously, but also lower-level broad-banded stochastic responses. However, multiple runs must often be concatenated to get a sufficient long measurement time.

3.2. Measurement procedure

As previously mentioned, the measurement procedures for OMA and spectral ODS are very similar. Time recordings made for ODS can therefore be used for OMA and vice versa. Where spectral ODS always requires one reference for each frequency/order component analysed, OMA does not require any references if all DOFs are measured simultaneously, but one or more references, if measurements are made with roving transducers in order to extract repeated-roots and closely-coupled modes.

Reference DOFs should be selected, so they are well-excited for all modes of interest, which would typically be at corner points, free ends and along larger sections. Nodal lines (lines with no deformation for specific modes) should be avoided.

When roving measurements are performed, the measurement sequencing should be created in a way that facilitates quick and easy roving of the transducers. Mass loading should be minimized by selecting transducers with low weight compared to the dynamic mass of the structure, and the sequencing should take into consideration how to equalize the mass loading across the measurements by proper distribution of the transducers.

Geometry-guided measurements can simplify the test and reduce the risk of errors when roving measurements are performed. With geometry-guided measurements, the measurement software shows the positions of the transducers in the current measurement and where to position them in the next.

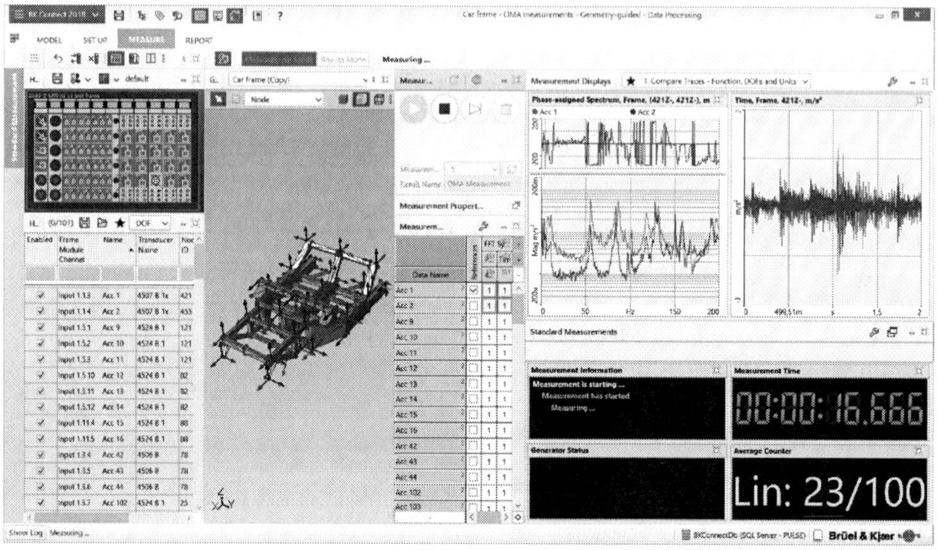

Figure 9. Example of geometry-guided measurements using BK Connect. The geometry with the DOFs currently measured is shown together with selected time and frequency functions for selected DOFs. Measurement status and progress is shown as well.

3.3. Measurement time

The measurement time depends on the period of the lowest mode of interest, the complexity of the structure and the type of excitation. As a rule of thumb, the measurement time should at least be one thousand times the period of the lowest mode of interest, Eq. (1). But if the structure exhibit non-linear behaviour, the mode density is high with several heavily damped modes, the excitation is weak and not continuously broad-banded and includes many dominant harmonic components, the measurement time should be significantly longer.

$$T \geq 1000 * \frac{1}{f_{min}} \tag{1}$$

In general, the longer the measurement time, the better the measurement quality. However, measurements should if possible only be performed, when the signal-to-noise ratio is good, the structure can be regarded as fairly invariant, and the environmental conditions fairly stable.

As will be described in the next paper, Singular Value Decomposition (SVD) plots is a robust tool for validating the measurement quality, including proper measurement time.

4. FUTURE WORK

Best practices for the subsequent measurement validation, analysis and analysis validation will follow in coming papers.

For measurement validation this includes topics such as:

- How Singular Value Decomposition (SVD) plots can reveal measurement quality in terms of properly excited modes and sufficient measurement time, poor signal quality due to, for example,

defective transducers and cable breaks, harmonic components, repeated-roots and closely coupled modes
- How Short Time Fourier Transform (STFT) contour plots can be used to separate structural modes from harmonic components

For analysis this includes topics such as:

- Techniques for removal/reduction of harmonic components
- Proper use of projection channels
- Pros and cons of different frequency and time domain modal parameter identification techniques
- Automatic mode estimation

The analysis validation will include topics such as:

- Uncertainty estimation of the modal parameters
- Response validation (synthesis)
- Comparison of results from different modal parameter identification techniques
- Mode shape comparison techniques and normalization
- Model correlation with FE models

5. CONCLUSION

When performing operational modal analysis, attention must be paid to every step of the test to obtain the best possible results: from planning the measurement setup, to performing the measurements and carrying out the analysis and analysis validation. As the first in a series of papers describing best practices, this paper dealt with the author's experience within test planning, measurement setup and measurement execution which typically constitutes a substantial part of the overall test time.

REFERENCES

[1] Jacobsen, N-J., Thorhauge, O. (2009). Data Acquisition Systems for Operational Modal Analysis. *3rd IOMAC Conference.* Portonovo, Italy.

[2] Jacobsen, N-J. (2009). A New Data Acquisition Concept for Sound and Vibration Measurements. *16th ICSV Conference.* Kraków, Poland.

[3] Jacobsen, N-J., Thorhauge, O. (2006). New Technology increases the Dynamic Ranges of Data Acquisition Systems. *24th IMAC Conference.* St. Louis, USA.

[4] Liu, B., Tcherniak, D., Jacobsen, N-J., Qvist Olsen, M. (2016). Smart Setup and Accelerometer Mounting Check for Vibration Measurements. *34th IMAC Conference,* Orlando, USA.

[5] Jacobsen, N-J. (2016). New techniques and tools for efficient test setup and system verification. *ISMA2016 Conference.* Leuven, Belgium.

[6] IEEE Standards Association (2004). Standard for a Smart Transducer Interface for Sensors and Actuators - Mixed-Mode Communication Protocols and Transducer Electronic Data Sheet (TEDS) Formats. *IEEE 1451.4-2004.*

[7] Gres, S., Andersen, P., Hoen, C., Damkilde, L. (2018). Orthogonal projection-based harmonic signal removal for operational modal analysis. *36th IMAC Conference.* Orlando, USA.

[8] Gres, S., Andersen, P., Damkilde, L. (2018). Operational Modal Analysis of Rotating Machinery. *36th IMAC Conference.* Orlando, USA.

[9] Jacobsen, N-J., Andersen, P., Brincker, R. (2007). Eliminating the Influence of Harmonic Components in Operational Modal Analysis. *25th IMAC Conference.* Orlando, USA.

[10] Jacobsen, N-J., Andersen, P. (2008). Operational Modal Analysis on Structures with Rotating Parts. *ISMA2008 Conference.* Leuven, Belgium.

IOMAC'19

8th International Operational Modal Analysis Conference
2019 May13-15 Copenhagen

ON THE POSSIBILITY OF UAV-MOUNTED LDVS FOR RESPONSE-ONLY DYNAMIC CHARACTERISATION OF REMOTE INFRASTRUCTURE

Ben Halkon[1]

[1] Dr, Centre for Audio, Acoustics & Vibration, University of Technology Sydney, Benjamin.Halkon@uts.edu.au.

ABSTRACT

Laser Doppler vibrometers are technically well suited to general application but they offer special benefits in a variety of challenging measurement scenarios which are now well documented and accepted. An interesting and potentially powerful example of such a challenging measurement scenario is one where the laser vibrometer is mounted on/in an unmanned aerial vehicle in order that autonomous measurement campaigns can be undertaken in remote and/or harsh environments. One important challenge to overcome in such a scenario is the measurement sensitivity to vibration of the instrument itself or indeed of any steering optics used to point the probe laser beam toward the target of interest. In this paper, recently reported means by which this measurement sensitivity can be rectified by simultaneously obtained correction measurements will be described. Specifically, this development opens up the possibility of laser Doppler vibrometry from unmanned aerial vehicles for response-only dynamic assessment of remote infrastructure, a measurement challenge of significant potential value.

Keywords: laser Doppler vibrometry; remote, non-contact vibration measurement;

1. INTRODUCTION

Laser Doppler vibrometers (LDVs) measure target surface vibration (in the direction of the incident laser beam) and are technically well-suited to general application with benefits over traditional contacting transducers in a range of challenging measurement scenarios [1]. A particular benefit of LDVs in the context of remote, response-only vibration measurements, for example for those from remote infrastructure such as bridges, towers, wind turbines, etc., is their non-contact nature. Indeed, with recent developments in commercially available systems, specifically the introduction of the 1550 nm, 10 mW laser, vibration measurement campaigns are now possible from up to '00s of m away from the location of interest [2].

Another particular advantage of LDVs over traditional equivalents is their wide, configurable dynamic and frequency ranges. Commercial systems typically offer sub-nanometre displacement resolution or peak velocity outputs up to '0s of m/s while down to DC or up to MHz are not uncommon associated settings. The choice of vibration measurement parameter between displacement and velocity yields a further advantage where extremes of vibration frequency preclude the reasonable use of one. Response-only measurements from remote infrastructure, where vibrations can naturally be expected to be at both the low frequency *and* amplitude end of what can be considered typical, might be expected to be especially relevant applications for LDVs.

One challenge in this respect, however, is the fundamental nature of the technique in terms of it being a *relative* vibration measurement of the target surface with respect to the instrument sensor head itself. Oftentimes the sensor head is tripod-mounted to minimise the influence of 'ambient vibration' but, particularly for such low-level vibrations as those expected in remote infrastructure testing, this may not always be sufficient. Preferable would be to realise an *absolute* vibration measurement device, equivalent in this sense to a more traditional contacting transducer such as an accelerometer. Only recently has this possibility started to become a reality through application of a comprehensive mathematical treatment of the of the velocity measured for arbitrary target and sensor head vibration and laser beam orientation [3].

In this paper a brief, practical review of the means by which an erroneous measurement of target vibration, adversely impacted by the vibration of the instrument sensor head, can now be 'fully' corrected, by using a single, carefully positioned 'correction' accelerometer [4]. Recent developments have included the use of a 'DC-response', variable capacitance accelerometer as the correction sensor with the *corrected* LDV measurement being compared to that of either a fixed, non-vibrating LDV [3] or to a lightweight piezoelectric accelerometer [4]. It has been shown theoretically and experimentally that, for typical real-world vibration levels, subtraction of the integrated accelerometer signal from that of the LDV yields error reductions between the uncorrected and corrected measurement on the order of '0s of dBs with phase agreement generally within '00s of mrad. To date, signal post-processing has been conveniently undertaken in the frequency domain where compensation for finite time delays due to differences between signal conditioning electronics between the LDV and correction accelerometer can also be readily completed. In order to progress towards the possibility of UAV-mounted LDVs for response-only dynamic characterisation of remote infrastructure, time domain processing [5] is needed.

2. TARGET AND INSTRUMENT ACCELEROMETER CALIBRATION

When embarking on a new LDV sensor head vibration correction measurement campaign, such as one where an LDV is mounted to a vibrating vehicle, the first step is to "calibrate" the *correction* transducer [3],[4]. Additionally, where a 'true' target vibration reference measurement is required (to confirm sensor head vibration correction validity), this also applies to the *target* transducer. Essentially, the relative sensitivity of the accelerometers must be determined. In traditional vibration measurement campaigns, this is readily achieved with an accelerometer calibrator at a single frequency, e.g. 159.2 Hz. Here, however, the LDV will be used as the vibration reference with the full measurement chain being calibrated; this accelerometer "relative (to the LDV) calibration" procedure is a two-part process. Sensitivity adjustment, in order to calibrate from an amplitude standpoint, then time delay adjustment, in order to rectify signal phase differences due to different accelerometer channel signal conditioning electronics versus that of the LDV, is completed.

As shown in Figure 1a, all accelerometers were stacked on top of one another and directly mounted to the shaker armature via a platform screwed into the central spigot; synthetic beeswax was used at the mating surfaces. The accelerometer sensitive axes were aligned with the shaker vibration direction. The reference laser vibrometer was rigidly mounted directly above accelerometers with the (highlighted) probe laser beam direction aligned with the accelerometer sensitive axes, the stand-off distance set to the 295 mm visibility maximum [6] and the laser spot focused on a small square of retroreflective tape stuck to the top surface of the uppermost accelerometer to maximise the optical signal level.

A broadband (white) noise vibration profile, generated in the data acquisition system (8 input, 4 output channel B&K Pulse LAN-XI 100 mainframe acquisition system fitted with a pair of Type 3160A 042 053 modules) for the frequency range of interest, 2.5 to 100 Hz. This source signal was amplified (B&K LDS LPA100) to drive an electrodynamic shaker (B&K LDS V201) to levels consistent with typical real-world vibration, i.e. c1-10 mm/s. All transducer signals were collected simultaneously in B&K Pulse LabShop as real and imaginary frequency spectra at fixed intervals in time without overlap to enable some averaging. As can be seen in Figure 1b, the target vibration level is reached between 10 and 100 Hz but below 10 Hz the level is amplifier is lower than anticipated, due to the limited low frequency capability of the amplifier and/or shaker.

The frequency domain-based, post-processing calibration procedure has been previously described in significant detail [3],[4] so will not be repeated here. Following calibration processing, the amplitude agreement between all the measured signals is, as expected excellent across the 10 to 100 Hz frequency range as shown in Figure 1b. In terms of the phase calibration, Figure 1c shows that there is a short time delay between the accelerometer and LDV signals, manifested as an underlying non-zero gradient in the phase difference plotted as a function of frequency. Before (dashed outline) and after (solid outline) finite time delay adjustment, this underlying gradient can be seen in the linear, zero-intercept trendline equation included for the "AccLDVR" signal only. While amplitude relative calibration is readily managed through the specification of the accelerometer(s) "actual sensitivity" within the acquisition system set-up, phase relative calibration cannot (currently) be realised similarly and must be applied subsequently in frequency domain post-processing concurrently with sensor head vibration correction.

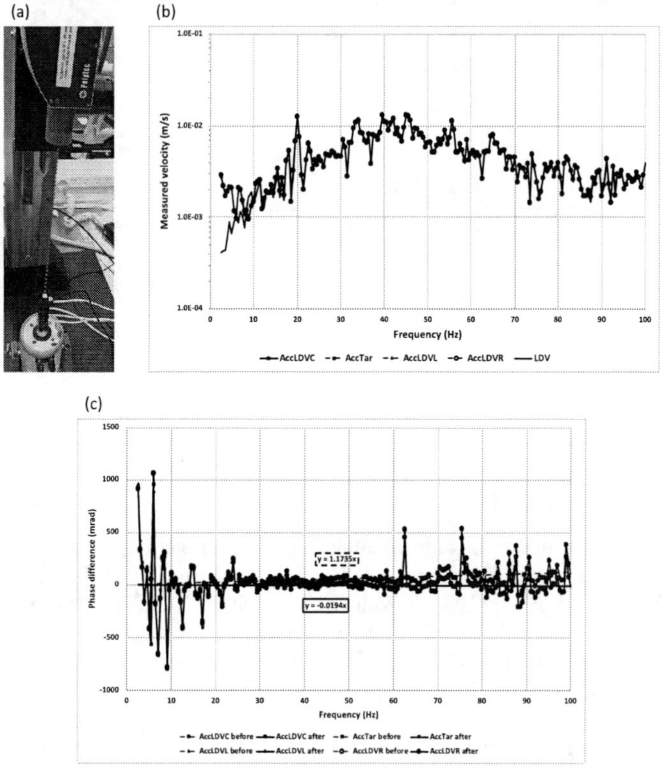

Figure 1. Accelerometer calibration; a) experimental set-up, b) amplitude and c) phase difference.

3. CORRECTION FOR LDV SENSOR HEAD VIBRATION

Sensitivity to instrument sensor head vibration can be readily confirmed in a straightforward experiment, such as that with an arrangement as set out in Figure 2. Here, the "Vibrating LDV" sensor head (Polytec NLV-2500 Compact Laser Vibrometer) was mounted, via a bespoke bracket, onto the central spigot of an electrodynamic shaker (LDS 455) and excited with a broadband signal amplified (LDS PA1000L) to yield a typical 'real-world' vibration level of c1-10 mm/s. The target of interest, a relatively lightweight and of small radius of curvature speaker cone, was fitted with a "teardrop" piezoelectric accelerometer (Dytran 3225F) to provide a 'true' "Vibrating target" reference measurement. With nominally zero target vibration, this is clearly reflective, as shown in Figure 3 (dotted curve), of the target vibration. Conversely, due to the 100% sensitivity of the LDV measurement (dashed curve) to vibration of the instrument sensor head itself, this signal is not representative of the actual target vibration. Unlike the accelerometer *absolute* target vibration measurement, the LDV measurement is of the target vibration *relative* to the LDV itself.

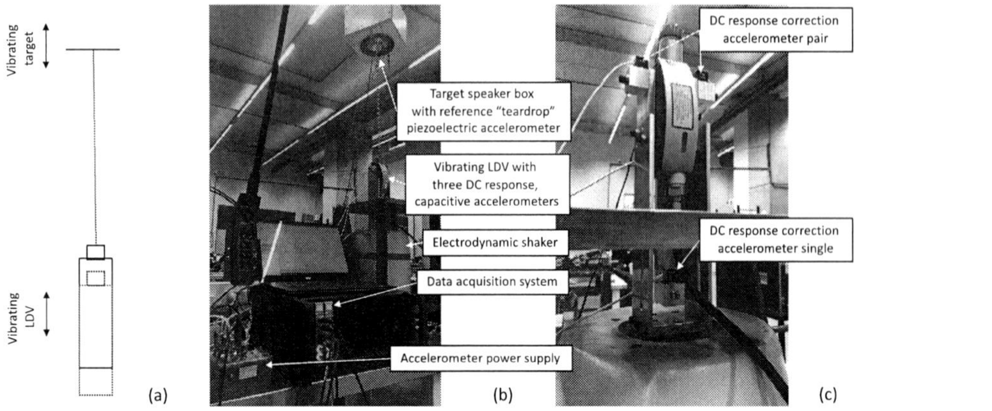

Figure 2. Experimental arrangement (a) schematic, (b) overall setup and (c) correction accelerometers.

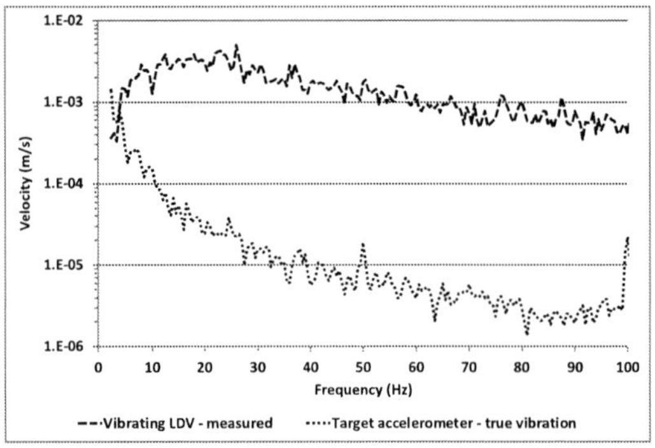

Figure 3. LDV measurement vs. true target vibration: sensor head vibration, no target vibration.

While the scenario described above is improbable to occur in practice, it might easily be the case that the vibration level of the instrument sensor head is *equivalent* to that of the target. Examples include measurement campaigns within noisy environments or within the cabins of automobiles or aircraft. Possibly the vibration frequencies of the vibrating instrument are not coincident with the target vibration frequencies of interest and their detrimental influence on the quality of the LDV measurement can thereby be neglected. Otherwise, it may be possible to vibration isolate the sensor head, for example using a tripod with rubber feet or some other anti-vibration mounting arrangement. If neither option exists, it would instead be more useful to be able to subtract the vibration of the LDV from the measured signal, thereby yielding an *absolute* rather than relative LDV vibration measurement.

Using the same experimental set-up previously described, but here with both sensor head *and* target undergoing typical vibration levels, Figure 4 again shows the erroneous LDV measurement (dashed curve) with the corresponding true vibration (dotted curve) also (just) observable. The error in the LDV measurement is particularly evident below 20 Hz, since it in this frequency range where the LDV vibration is concentrated (as a result of the frequency response of the shaker and amplifier combination). Making use of the signals, integrated and time-delay adjusted in the frequency domain as previously discussed, from the correction accelerometer location options shown in Figure 2c, the LDV measurement can be almost completely corrected. The two options for erroneous measurement correction presented here are i) to subtract the mean velocity signal from an accelerometer pair mounted equidistantly either side of the laser beam [3] or ii) subtract the velocity signal from a single accelerometer mounted directly on the laser beam axis to the rear of the sensor head [4]. As shown in Figure 4a, the two corrected LDV measurements are equivalent in both the accelerometer pair (solid line, + marker) and single accelerometer (solid line) cases. Furthermore, they are significantly improved estimates of the true vibration velocity, representing mean reductions in error of 17.5 dB in both cases.

Phase agreement between the two corrected LDV measurements and the true vibration, generally more challenging to achieve in any measurement scenario, particularly at low frequencies and/or vibration levels, is shown in Figure 4b in terms of the mean phase difference. Again, the curves from both options are indistinguishable and represent excellent correlation, particularly where the target vibration level is within the target, 'real-world relevant' range, i.e. above 1 mm/s.

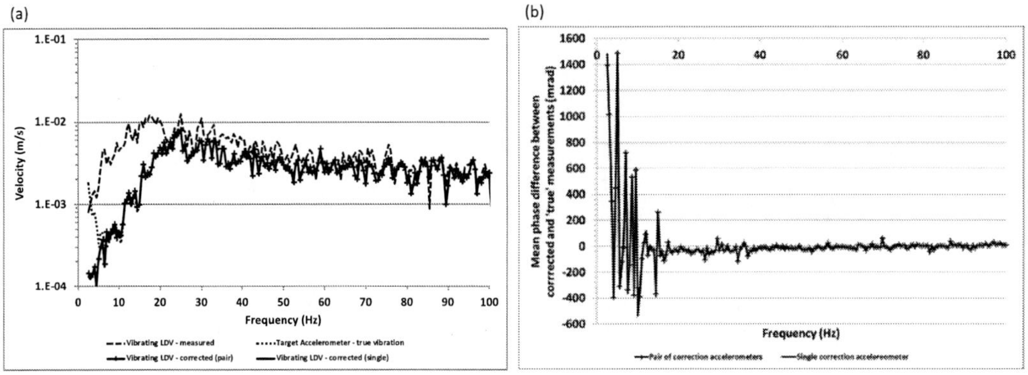

Figure 4. Measured and corrected LDV measurement vs. true target vibration: sensor head and target vibration.

4. CONCLUSIONS

To progress the possibility of UAV-mounted laser Doppler vibrometers for response-only dynamic characterisation of remote infrastructure, it has been necessary to validate the sensitivity of the instrument to vibration in the direction of the laser beam. With DC-response accelerometers and frequency domain processing techniques, the erroneous measurement can be almost completely corrected for stationary signals. For optimal outcomes, the correction sensor measurements must first be calibrated relative to the LDV both in amplitude and phase response terms. Furthermore, they must be carefully located on the instrument sensor head; a pair of accelerometers located equidistant about the laser beam axis or a single accelerometer mounted on the axis to the rear of the sensor head gave equivalent results. Future research will improve performance over a wider frequency range, particularly towards DC which is important for the intended application scenarios. Additionally, time domain processing will be necessary since operational vibrations are not stationary but transient in nature.

ACKNOWLEDGEMENTS

The authors wish to acknowledge the contributions of Mr Chris Chapman, Scientific Officer, and Workshop colleagues in the Faculty of Engineering and IT, University of Technology Sydney.

REFERENCES

[1] Rothberg, S. et al. (2017). An international review of laser Doppler vibrometry: making light work of vibration measurement. *Optics and Lasers in Engineering*, 99, 11–22.

[2] Polytec GmbH (2017). *RSV-150 Remote Sensing Vibrometer product brochure*. [Online] available: https://www.polytec.com/fileadmin/d/Vibrometrie/OM_DS_RSV-150_E_42319.pdf (27-2-19).

[3] Halkon B. and Rothberg S. (2017). Taking laser Doppler vibrometry off the tripod: correction of measurements affected by instrument vibration. *Optics and Lasers in Engineering*, 91, 16–23.

[4] Halkon B. and Rothberg S. (2018). Towards laser Doppler vibrometry from unmanned aerial vehicles. *Proceedings of the 13th Intl Conference on Vibration Measurements by Laser and Noncontact Techniques; Journal of Physics: Conference Series*, 1149, 012022.

[5] Halkon B. and Rothberg S. (2018). Taking laser Doppler vibrometry off the tripod. *Int. Cong. on Sound and Vib. (Hiroshima)* .

[6] Polytec GmbH (2016). *Compact Laser Vibrometer NLV-2500-5 Operating Instructions.*

IOMAC'19

8th International Operational Modal Analysis Conference
2019 May13-15 Copenhagen

THE EFFECT OF MODAL TRUNCATION AND SPATIAL DISTRIBUTION IN LOAD IDENTIFICATION

Michael Vigsø[1], *Rune Brincker*[2], *Christos Georgakis*[3]

[1] Ph.D. student, Dept. of Engineering, Aarhus University, Inge Lehmanns Gade 10, 8000 Aarhus C, Denmark, mvigso@eng.au.dk
[2] Professor, Dept. of Civil Engineering, Technical University of Denmark, Brovej, Building 118, 2800 Kgs. Lyngby, Denmark, runeb@byg.dtu.dk
[3] Professor, Dept. of Engineering, Aarhus University, Inge Lehmanns Gade 10, 8000 Aarhus C, Denmark, cg@eng.au.dk

ABSTRACT
Load identification in civil engineering application is a growing topic. This study aims to analyze the effect of the load spatial distribution and whether or not the spatial distribution is foreseen prior to the inverse computations. If the dynamic characteristics are based on operational modal analysis there might be errors (uncertainties) associated with the estimated modal parameters and although the variations might appear as insignificant, they potentially pose an enormous effect during the inverse calculations. Depending on the number of sensors and distribution inherently there will be a limit to the number of modes which can be identified. The consequences from these limitations together with assumptions on the load spatial distribution will be the scope for this study.

Keywords: Load identification, Modal truncation, Spatial distribution

1. INTRODUCTION

The beginning of load identification in structural dynamics is often said to begin with the review study by Stevens [1] who outlined the principles from the frequency domain. As the direct relation between the input and output of a dynamic system corresponds to a convolution in the time domain and hence a product in the frequency domain, the appealing first approach for load identification is often within this domain, e.g. as seen in [2–4]. Later studies, [5–11] cover more sophisticated ideas that by using a state space formulation of the dynamics. The real-time estimates are aided by the principles of a Kalman filter [12]. The Kalman filter merges the sensor information with the expected model behavior and though least squares obtains an optimal predicted system state. The state vector which typically includes the system displacement and velocities is expanded to include the load and hereafter referred to as the augmented Kalman filter. In order for the Kalman filter to work well, noise models (/error covariance models) must be defined. Deriving these may be difficult and are hence often based on experience. Neural networks are also starting to be used for load identification although we shall not dig into the history of this.

One of the driving items for load identification is the dynamic characteristics of the structure. These may be obtained through modal analysis. For this study let us assume that the modal parameters are obtained from an output-only approach. The principles of Operational Modal Analysis (OMA) can be applied for this purpose [13].

This study will focus on how well the load can be identified given natural uncertainties in the modal parameters. These include the modal parameters itself, but also the influence of missing modes. The performance will be examined from two different starting points: One where the load spatial distribution is unknown and another, where the spatial distribution is a known quantity and hence makes the identified load a scalar function of the distribution. Both approaches will be driven only by the structural response.

2. METHOD

Although the time domain approach may seem appealing due to the real-time application, this study will be seated in the frequency domain. For the general basic equation for the response of a linear multi degree of freedom system we have:

$$\underline{Y}(\omega) = \underline{\underline{H}}(\omega)\ \underline{X}(\omega) \tag{1}$$

These are the remains of the equivalent convolution integral in the time domain once the Fourier transformation is applied. Here, $\underline{Y}(\omega)$ is the frequency domain response of the system. $\underline{\underline{H}}(\omega)$ is the frequency response function and finally, $\underline{X}(\omega)$ is the loading in the frequency domain. Each of these are evaluated at the discrete angular frequency ω.

The frequency response function can be established from a sum of modal contributions. Here we assume that the modal parameters are available from the OMA while we ignore the fact that the mode shapes may be poorly scaled. The load identification process will be the reverse order of Eq. (1). The pseudo-inverse of the frequency response function will be premultiplied to the response vector and hence an estimate on the load is obtained. This is solved frequency by frequency. Although this can not be implemented in real-time, the estimates can be obtained by parallelization of the computations. The time domain load estimate is finally found from an inverse Fourier transformation.

In order not to overcomplicate the principles, we assume that the system has a finite number of degrees of freedom (DOFs). In addition to this, we assume all and every one of these DOFs are monitored through sensors. For instance, say we measure the displacements and rotations. Likewise, for the load, we assume that the spatial distribution must follow the discretization of the system such that loading will only act in the nodes (convenient assumption for the finite element formulation). Having a finite number of DOFs in the system also yields a finite number of modes of vibration.

The procedure described above allows for the identified load to be located in any DOF in the system. If the position of the load is known beforehand this can be included in the computations through a separation of variables. The load vector will then be separated into a spatial distribution vector and a scalar. Given that the distribution is not changing in time, it can be multiplied with the frequency response function prior to making the pseudo-inverse operation. Now, the estimated parameter will be the scalar function of the load while the distribution pattern is predefined.

3. SIMULATION

In order to demonstrate the value of a known load distribution, we have set up a simulated case study. A plane, five noded cantilever beam will be used for this study. The model has eight free degrees of freedom and hence eight modes of vibration. The beam model is shown on the left-hand side of Figure 1. Now, the beam is subjected to a loading history and the corresponding response is simulated using a Newmark scheme. The loading scenario is based on localized force acting at the second node from the top as indicated by $f(t)$ in Figure 1 and Figure 2. The load variation is composed of a square impulse followed by half a sine. This yields both dynamic and quasi-static response of the structure. The system is simulated at 10 kHz and then sampled at 1 kHz. Note that this puts the sampling frequency between the natural frequency of mode 6 and mode 7. A small amount of Gaussian noise is added to the sampled signal thus considered the "measured" response.

4. RESULTS AND DISCUSSION

We wish to use the measured response as a basis for the load identification and we hence apply the two different approaches mentioned in Section 2. That is one where the location of the load is known and one where the location is unknown. To grasp the performance of the of the two approaches we introduce errors into the frequency response function. Since the frequency response function is composed by a sum of modal contributions it is interesting to examine what happens to the load estimate once we truncate the modal space [14]. We will start out by including all eight modes in the identification process and then we will omit one mode and then two and so on. It will always be the mode with the highest frequency that will be omitted from the sum. When omitting modes from frequency response function it becomes rank deficient which emphasizes the need for the pseudo-inverse operation.

The preliminary effects of missing modes may be seen as the difference between columns in Figure 1 and Figure 2. We start from the left-hand side in Figure 1: The first column shows the load identification

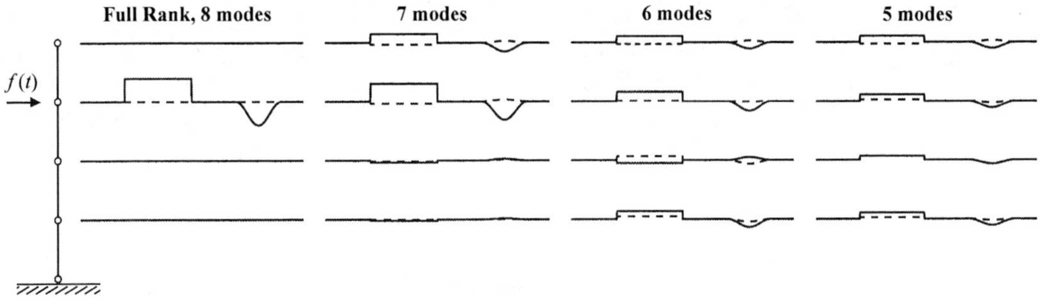

Figure 1: Load identification based on an *unknown* impact position. The figure shows the estimated load history given a different number of modes in the frequency response function. Each line corresponds to the input estimates for the given node. Solid line is the force estimates and dashed is the moment. The duration of the time history is ten seconds.

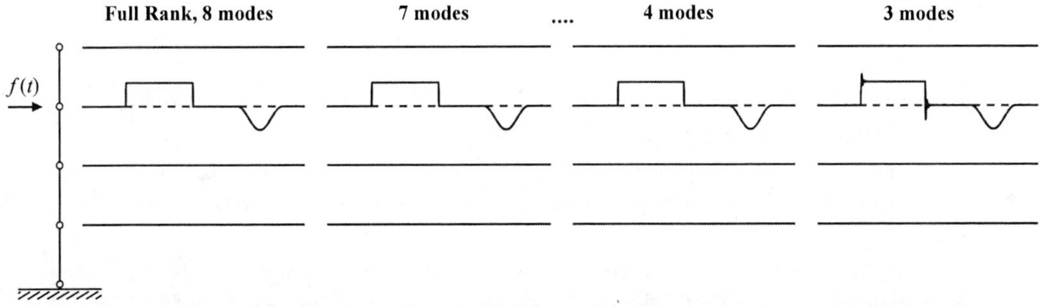

Figure 2: Load identification based on a *known* impact position. The figure shows the estimated load history given a different number of modes in the frequency response function. Each line corresponds to the input estimates for the given node. Solid line is the force estimates and dashed is the moment. The duration of the time history is ten seconds.

using all eight modes in the frequency response function, i.e. a full rank matrix. The identified load is shown as a time history for each of the respective nodes. The solid line indicates an identified force while the dashed line is an identified moment. A flat line corresponds to a zero load estimate. The second column similarly shows the identified load but based on a frequency response function build from only 7 modes. Column 3 and 4 are derived in a similar manner.

The estimated load from the full rank matrix yields a perfect estimate, with only minor scatter from the measurement noise (note that the modal parameters are at their true values). However, once modes are omitted from the frequency response function, the estimated load is smeared to all DOFs in the system and even in opposing directions.

If we look at the solution based on a known force location, the results are more appealing. In Figure 2 we see the results from a similar exercise. Once again the load is identified from a truncated frequency response function. Since the load is fixed to act in one DOF, only the remaining channels automatically obtain a zero load estimate i.e. a flat line. This yields a more consistent load identification. When only a few modes are included, we see that the estimates overshoot the impulse followed by ringing effect.

5. SUMMARY

The findings of the study prove that it is not in vain if we invest some effort into analyzing the spatial distribution of the load prior to estimating the load itself.

We have chosen a simple static system and the only source of error is the missing modes and some noise in the measurements. In real life applications, the error palette will be way more colorful. For instance, it is not hard to imagine that the identified modes may be subjected to some uncertainty, that is both the frequency, damping ratio and mode shape. This will fuel a more detailed study. This study is based on a contained system with finite degrees of freedom and "sensors" at any location and the load is composed of a single source and yet the estimates from unknown force location fail. If sensors are not located at the load source, expansion may be needed in order to predict the response at unmeasured locations.

Most methods seen in the literature conveniently assumes that the location of the load is a known parameter. This study has in a very simplified manner demonstrated why.

ACKNOWLEDGMENTS

The authors acknowledge the funding received from the Centre for Oil and Gas – DTU/Danish Hydrocarbon Research and Technology Centre (DHRTC).

REFERENCES

[1] K. Stevens. Force identification problems - an overview. *Proceedings of the SEM Spring Conference on Experimental Mechanics*, pages 838–844, 1987.

[2] Y. Liu and W. Shepard. Dynamic force identification based on enhanced least squares and total least-squares scheme in the frequency domain. *Journal of Sound and Vibration*, Vol: 282:37–60, 2005.

[3] M. Vigsø, M. Tarpø, J. Hansen, R. Brincker, and C. Georgakis. Scenario based approach for load identification. *Proceedings of the International Modal Analysis Conference, IMAC*, 2018.

[4] M. Aenlle, R. Brincker, P. Fernández, and A. Fernández. Load estimation from modal parameters. *Proceedings of the International Operational Modal Analysis Conference, iomac*, Vol. 1:pp 39–50, 2007.

[5] E. Lourens, E. Reynders, G. De Roeck, G Degrande, and G Lombaert. An argumented Kalman filter for force identification in structural dynamics. *Mechanical Systems and Signal Processing*, Vol. 27:pp 446–460, 2012.

[6] C. Ma and C. Ho. An inverse method for the estimation of input forces acting on non-linear structural systems. *Journal of Sound and Vibration*, pages 953–971, 2004.

[7] J. Liu, C. Ma, I. Kung, and D. Lin. Input force estimation of a cantilever plate by using a system identification technique. *Comput. Methods Appl. Mech. Engrg.*, pages 1309–1322, 2000.

[8] F. Naets, J. Cuadrado, and W. Desmet. Stable force identification in structural dynamics using Kalman filter and dummy-measurements. *Mechanical Systems and Signal Processing*, pages 235–248, 2015.

[9] K. Maes, K. van Nimmen, E. Lourens, A. Rezayat, P. Guillaume, and G. De Roeck. Verification of joint input-state estimation for force identification by means of in situ measurements on a footbridge. *Mechanical Systems and Signal Processing*, 2016.

[10] J. Wambacq, K. Maes, A. Rezayat, P. Guillaume, and G. Lombaert. Localization of dynamic forces on structures with an interior point method using group sparsity. *Mechanical Systems and Signal Processing*, 2018.

[11] E. Lourens, E. Reynders, G. De Roeck, G. Degrande, and G. Lombaert. An augmented Kalman filter for force identification in structural dynamics. *Mechanical Systems and Signal Processing*, 27:pp. 446–460, 2012.

[12] R. E. Kalman. A new approach to linear filtering and prediction problems. *Journal of Basic Engineering*, 82:35–45, 1960.

[13] R. Brincker and C. Ventura. *Introduction to Operational Modal Analysis*. John Wiley and Sons, Ltd, UK, 2015.

[14] M. Tarpø, M. Vigsø, and R. Brincker. Modal truncation in experimental modal analysis. *Proceedings of the International Modal Analysis Conference, IMAC*, 2018.

ROTATING MACHINERY & OMA

IOMAC'19

8th International Operational Modal Analysis Conference

2019 May 13-15 Copenhagen

A PARAMETRIC INVESTIGATION FOR OMA ON OPERATIONAL SHIP DATA

C.M. van Zijl[1], *and A. Bekker*[2]

[1] Masters Student, Sound and Vibration Research Group, Department of Mechanical and Mechatronic Engineering, Stellenbosch University, South Africa, 17534380@sun.ac.za.

[2] Associate Professor, Sound and Vibration Research Group, Department of Mechanical and Mechatronic Engineering, Stellenbosch University, South Africa, annieb@sun.ac.za.

ABSTRACT

A parametric investigation was conducted to obtain accurate SSI estimates of the modal parameters of a ship in its operational environment. The identified parameters will contribute towards a modal model which must predict full scale responses to environmental loading. The model may be used for autonomous modal tracking towards predictions of full-scale responses based on environmental parameters and inverse force estimation. The SSI-data algorithm relies on the specification of certain parameters namely the block length (number of samples in the data matrix), the block size and model order. The results of a modal identification are dependent on these parameters and it is therefore important to understand how these parameters affect the final solution. To this end, a parametric investigation was performed to recommend a suitable selection of these user parameters for the robust analysis of operational ship data.

Keywords: Operational modal analysis, Stochastic subspace identification, model order, block length, duration

1. INTRODUCTION

The Flotilla Foundation chartered the South African Polar Supply and Research Vessel, the SA Agulhas II in January 2019 to perform research in the Larsen B and C area and to search for Sir Ernest Shackleton's ship, Endurance under the sea ice in the Weddell Sea. The vessel was the first to navigate in these icy waters since an expedition by the Polarstern in 2002. The SA Agulhas II, classified as Polar Class PC-5, navigated through challenging Antarctic sea ice with the express goal of spending minimal time in transit. Full-scale measurements were performed on board whereby ice conditions, ice loads and structural vibration on the hull and propulsion system were recorded. In particular, the vessel was instrumented with an accelerometer network to determine full-scale dynamic responses of the operational ship structure. The measurements presented in the present work were recorded in January during the transit of the vessel from Penguin Bukta to the Western Weddell Sea as shown in Figure 1.

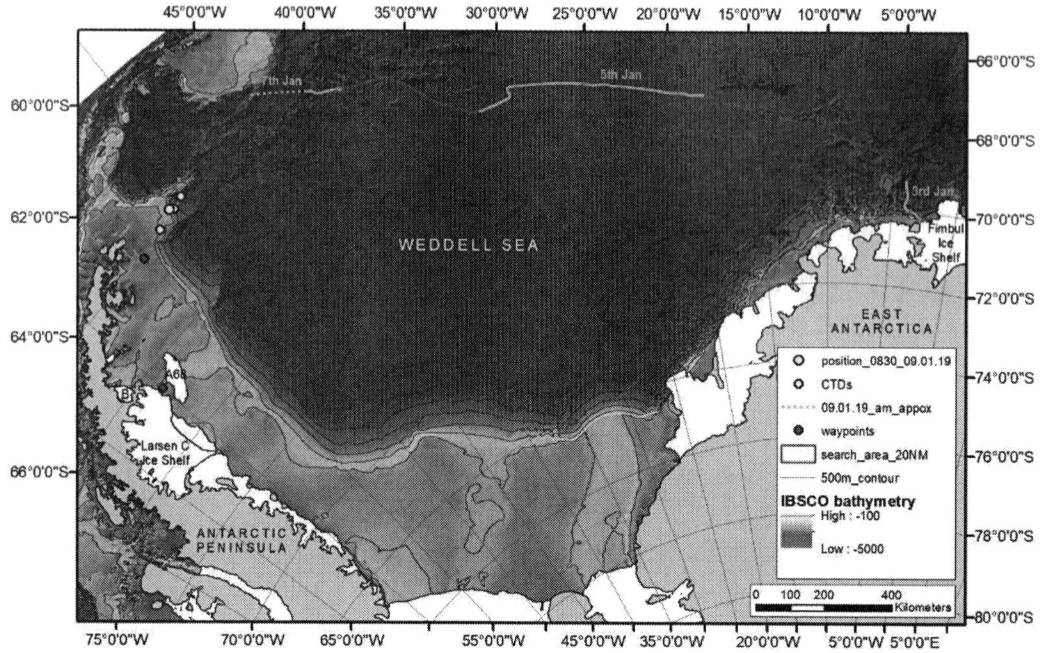

Figure 1. A map showing the transit of the SA Agulhas II Polar Supply and Research Vessel between Penguin Bukta and the Western Weddell Sea in January 2019.

Safe navigation in environments like the Weddell Sea and other Antarctic regions are challenging and depend largely on the knowledge and experience of navigational officers on the Bridge. It is envisioned that a network of full-scale vibration sensors have the potential to provide valuable insight into the responses of vessels in the operational environment and may be used to aid in navigational decision-making and long-term structural health monitoring. A potential means to extract useful information from large amounts of data is to build a modal model from output measurements using operational modal analysis (OMA). Tracking changes in modal parameters in relation to the operational and environmental conditions provides insight into the global vibration response of the structure which may be used to predict responses of the vessel based on forecasts of environmental conditions and estimating global loads acting on the vessel through inverse force estimation. In order to accomplish this goal accurate estimates of modal parameters are required. The data-driven Stochastic Subspace Identification (SSI-data) technique is explored through an investigation of the effect that user-specified parameters have on the identified modal model.

2. METHOD

2.1. Full-scale measurements

Measurements from 28 accelerometers were utilized in the present investigation. All measurements were sampled at 2048 Hz. Measurement locations are presented in Figure 2. Vertical acceleration was measured by six pairs of accelerometers on the port- and starboard sides of the vessel hull. Lateral motion of the ship is captured by two sensors, one on the starboard side at the stern and one on the vessel centre line in the bow chain locker. The remaining sensors monitored accelerations in the super-structure, closer to accommodation areas, recreational spaces and the bridge. The sensor network includes both DC and ICP accelerometers as summarized in Table 1. Data was acquired using an LMS SCADAS master-slave system and LMS.TurbineTesting data acquisition software.

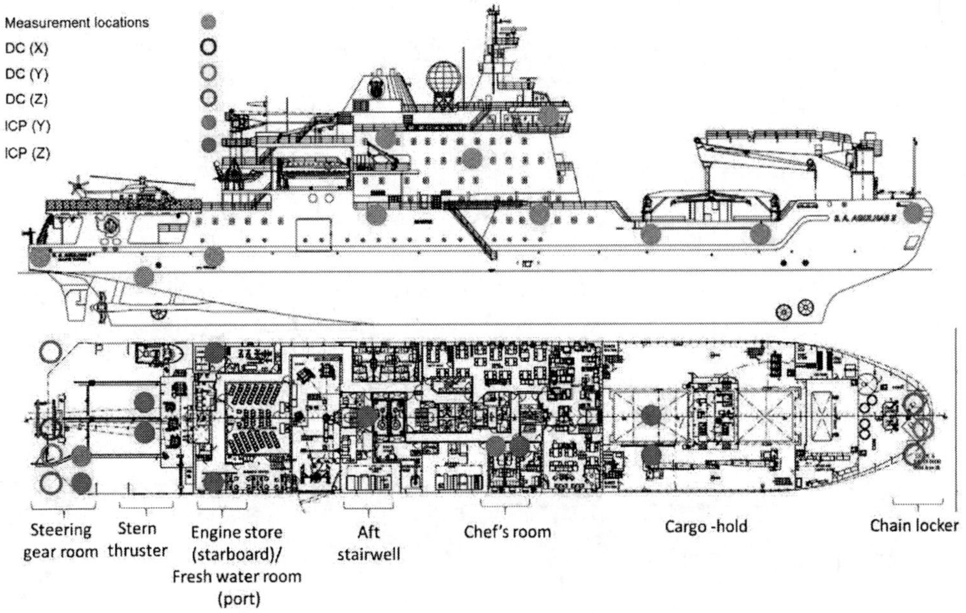

Figure 2 A diagram of the accelerometer network used for full-scale measurements on the SA Agulhas II.

Table 1. A list of sensor locations, sensors and measurement specifics for full-scale acceleration measurements.

Channel	Location	Side	Point ID	Deck	Axis	Type	Sensitivity [mV/m/s^2]
1	Bridge	Starboard	B01_S_X	9	X	DC	20.19
2	Bridge	Starboard	B01_S_Y	9	Y	DC	20.22
3	Bridge	Starboard	B01_S_Z	9	Z	DC	20.13
4	Bridge	Port	B02_P_Z	9	Z	ICP	10.18
5	Deck 8	Port	D801_P_Y	8	Y	ICP	10.2
6	Deck 8	Port	D801_P_Z	8	Z	ICP	10.06
7	Deck 7	Starboard	D701_S_Y	7	Y	ICP	10.03
8	Deck 7	Starboard	D701_S_Z	7	Z	ICP	10.13
9	Bow	Starboard	CL01_S_Z	4	Z	DC	20.24
10	Bow	Centre	CL02_0_Y	4	Y	DC	20.29
11	Bow	Port	CL03_P_Z	4	Z	DC	20.46
12	Chef's room	Starboard	CR01_S_Y	4	Y	ICP	10.13
13	Chef's room	Starboard	CR01_S_Z	4	Z	ICP	9.96
14	Aft stairwell	Centre	AS01_0_Z	4	Z	ICP	10.05
17	Cargo-hold	Starboard	CH01_S_Z	3	Z	ICP	9.7
18	Cargo-hold	Port	CH02_P_Z	3	Z	ICP	10.25
19	Cargo-hold	Starboard	CH03_S_Z	3	Z	ICP	10.23
20	Cargo-hold	Port	CH04_P_Z	3	Z	ICP	10.44
21	Engine store	Starboard	ES01_S_Z	2	Z	ICP	10.43
22	Fresh water	Port	FW01_P_Z	2	Z	ICP	10.42
23	Stern thruster	Starboard	ST01_S_Z	2	Z	ICP	10.34
24	Stern thruster	Port	ST02_P_Z	2	Z	ICP	10.36

25	Steering gear	Starboard	SG01_S_X	2	X	DC	20.23
26	Steering gear	Starboard	SG01_S_Y	2	Y	DC	20.23
27	Steering gear	Starboard	SG01_S_Z	2	Z	DC	20.29
28	Steering gear	Starboard	SG02_S_Y	2	Y	ICP	10.39
29	Steering gear	Starboard	SG02_S_Z	2	-Z	ICP	10.45
30	Steering gear	Port	SG03_P_Z	2	Z	DC	20.31

2.2. Case study and signal processing

A parametric investigation was performed on approxmately 120 minutes of data on the afternoon of 5 January 2019. This case study was selected as a result of the stationary operational conditions. The vessel was navigated at a constant speed of about 9 knots with a constant shaft speed of about 140 rpm. The heading remained constant and the wind speed varied by less than 5 knots.

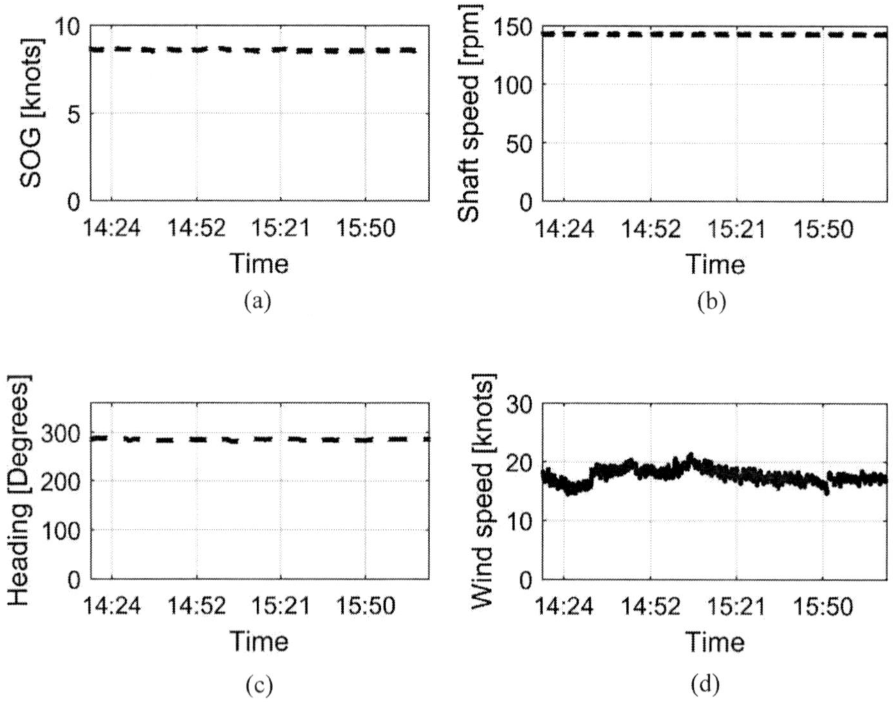

Figure 3 Operational paramaters of the SA Agulhas II on 5 January 2019. (a) Speed over ground (b) Shaft rpm (c) Heading and (d) Wind speed.

First signals from all accelerometers were detrended and decimated to 64 Hz. The time-series of a subset of reference sensors are presented in Figure 4. The selection of reference sensors are explained in Section 3. A noteworthy characteristic of the vibration signal is the relative stationarity of the time-series across all the measurement channels.

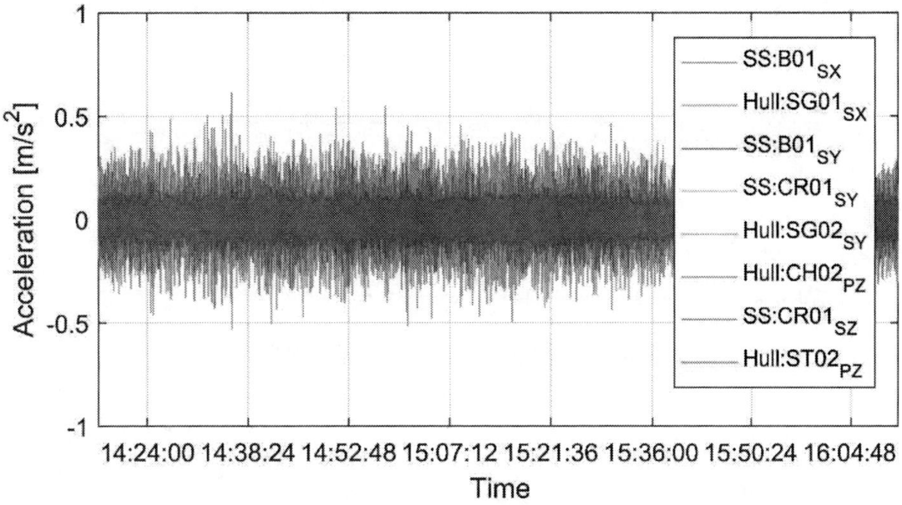

Figure 4 Decimated acceleration measurents for a 120 minute case study during navigation in the Weddell Sea.

Subsequently, power spectral densities (PSDs) were calculated from the decimated time-series signals. The PSDs of the reference channels are presented in Figure 5. Significant low frequency vibrations below 1 Hz are attributed to the rigid body motion of the vessel and wave period. In the frequency range between 1 to 9 Hz modal peaks may be identified that are present in most or all the reference channels measurements and are thought to represent the global modes of the vessel. Further modal peaks are identified that are only captured by one or a few of the subset of reference channels and may represent local modes of certain sub-structures on the vessel. All global and local structural modes that are identified from the PSDs in Figure 5 are listed in Table 2. Above 9 Hz the response measurements appear to be dominated by the harmonics of rotating components on-board the vessel. These harmonics are represented by sharp, narrow peaks.

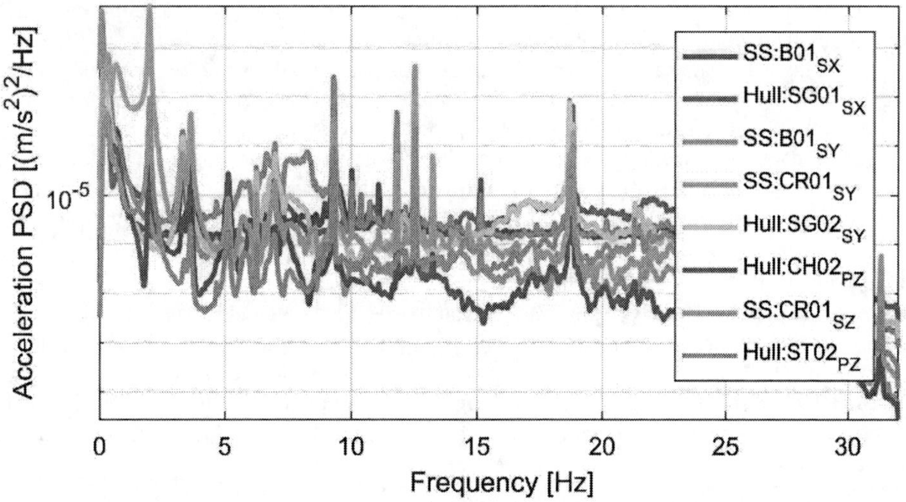

Figure 5 PSDs for a selection of reference channels (nfft = 2048, Hanning window, 50% overlap).

Table 2 Globl and local strucutral modes identified from PSDs of response measurements

Global structural modes	**Local structural modes**
Natural frequencies [Hz]	Natural frequencies [Hz]
1.97	3.38
3.31	5.09
3.63	6.97
5.16	
5.66	
5.97	
7.40	
8.30	
8.75	

Finally the raw time signal was filtered with a Type I Chebyshev bandpass filter, detrended and decimated to 64 Hz. The filter was constructed using the MATLAB Filter Designer toolbox and filter parameters were set to retain only frequency content in the bandwidth 1 to 9 Hz. The reasoning behind this is that most of the significant modal responses are thought to be captured in this bandwidth and that this processed signal would be most suitble for subsequent analyses.

2.3. Operational Modal Analysis

Operational modal analysis (OMA) was performed on the processed full-scale measurement set. In the present study the Frequency Domain Decomposition (FDD) technique and data-driven Stochastic Subspace Identification (SSI) techniques are used to perform operational modal analysis (OMA) on the SA Agulhas II. In-house MATLAB algorithms were developed from the companion code of an OMA textbook [1], the Abravibe signal processing and modal analysis toolbox [2] and an open source SSI toolbox available on Github called openSID [3].

2.3.1. Frequency domain decomposition

Theoretical background for FDD is covered in detail by [4]. In FDD a singular value decomposition (SVD) is calculated from the spectral density matrix of output-only response measurements at discrete frequency lines. The singular values at discrete frequencies contain information about the response of the structure at that frequency as well as measurement noise. If a mode is present near certain frequency lines there will be a peak in the singular values at these frequency lines. In a simple peak-picking version of FDD, natural frequencies may be determined by locating peaks in singular values and using the first singular vector that that frequency as an estimate of the mode shape. The singular vector corresponding to the singular value at this frequency is an estimate of the mode shape.Modifications of the FDD algorithm such as enhanced FDD (EFDD) [5] further makes it possible to estimate damping ratios.

2.3.2. Stochastic subspace identification

The reference-based SSI-data algorithm may be summarised by seven steps as illustrated in Figure 6. Much more detailed explanations are presented in [6] and[7]. First a data matrix is constructed directly from time-series acceleration measurements. At this stage the user must decide how many measurement samples to include in the data matrix (i.e. how long the measurement run must be). This is also referred to the block length of the data. The data matrix $Y \epsilon \mathbb{R}^{n_c \times n_s}$ consists of n_s data samples (columns) from n_c channels (rows):

$$[Y] = \begin{bmatrix} \boldsymbol{y}_{1:ns}^{1} \\ \boldsymbol{y}_{1:ns}^{2} \\ \vdots \\ \boldsymbol{y}_{1:ns}^{nc} \end{bmatrix} \tag{1}$$

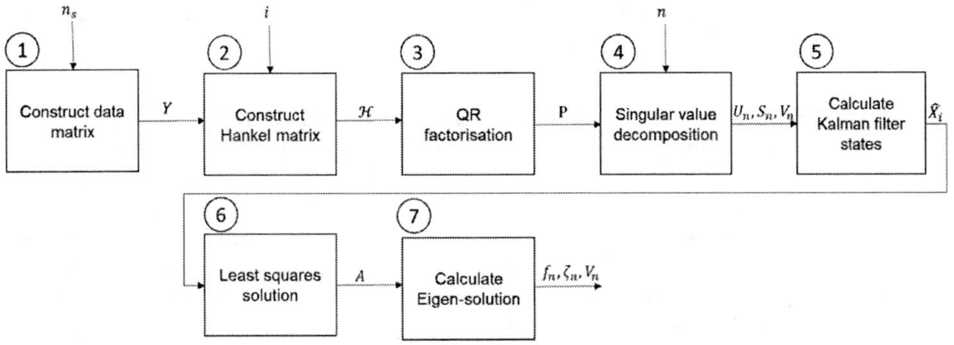

Figure 6 Data-driven stochastic subspace identification algorithm.

The second step is to build a Hankel matrix. In order to construct the Hankel matrix, the user must decide on a parameter referred to as the block size, i. Once the block length and block size are set, the Hankel matrix with $2i$ block rows is constructed by placing $j = n_s - 2i + 1$ samples in each block row. Each consecutive block row in the Hankel matrix is shifted by one measurement sample. The Hankel matrix may further be divided into two parts, a "past" and "future" part each having i block rows. In the reference-based version of SSI-data only a subset of reference channels are included in the "past" part of the Hankel matrix. The construction of the Hankel matrix is presented in Equation 2:

$$H = \frac{1}{\sqrt{j}} \begin{pmatrix} y_1^{ref} & y_2^{ref} & \cdots & y_j^{ref} \\ y_2^{ref} & y_3^{ref} & \cdots & y_{j+1}^{ref} \\ \vdots & \vdots & \ddots & \vdots \\ y_i^{ref} & y_{i+1}^{ref} & \cdots & y_{i+j-1}^{ref} \\ \hline y_{i+1} & y_{i+2} & \cdots & y_{i+j} \\ y_{i+2} & y_{i+3} & \cdots & y_{i+j+1} \\ \vdots & \vdots & \ddots & \vdots \\ y_{2i} & y_{2i+1} & \cdots & y_{2i+j-1} \end{pmatrix} = \left(\frac{H_p}{H_f} \right) \tag{2}$$

Third in the SSI-data algorithm is a QR factorisation of the block Hankel matrix. A part of the R factor from the QR factorisation is used to define a projection matrix that projects the "past" part of the Hankel matrix onto the "future" part. This projection matrix contains information for predicting future responses from past responses. The fourth step is to calculate singular value decomposition (SVD) of the projection matrix. A subspace of the factors of SVD matrices is then used to compute an observability matrix and Kalman filter state sequence in the fifth step of the algorithm. It is important to note that the dimensions of the subspace that is used to compute the observability matrix and Kalman filter states is another user defined parameter referred to as the model order. The observability matrix and Kalman filter states are well-defined in control engineering theory and for more details the reader is referred to [6], [7] and [8]. The relevance of the observability matrix and Kalman filter states in the present context is that the system matrix A can be obtained through solving a least squares problem, step six of the SSI-data algorithm. The system matrix is important as its Eigen-solution contain all the information necessary to characterise the dynamic behaviour of a physical structure. Therefore, step seven of the algorithm calculates the natural frequencies, damping ratios and mode shapes through an eigenvalue decomposition of the system matrix. The number of modes in the identified modal model is directly related to the model order selected by the user in Step 4.

3. PARAMETRIC INVESTIGATION

The SSI-data algorithm requires the specification of certain parameters namely the block length (number of samples in the data matrix), the block size and model order. The modal model that is identified using SSI is dependent on the selection of these parameters and it is therefore important to understand how these parameters affect the final solution. To this end, a parametric investigation was conducted.

A simple peak-picking version of the Frequency Domain Decomposition (FDD) technique was used to conduct a preliminary OMA analysis to determine estimates of the natural frequencies of the structure. Figure 7 presents the first eight singular values of the spectral density matrix of the processed signal. Most of the information relating to the physical structure are contained in the first three sets of singular values. This includes both peaks that represent modes of the structure and harmonics of rotating machinery. Harmonics are different from modal peaks in that they are sharper and narrower than modal peaks. The remaining singular values contain mostly information relating to measurement noise. Nine modal peaks may be identified from the first set of singular values as indicated in Figure 7. Additional peaks in the second and third set of singular values are identified in Figure 7 with dotted lines and may represent local modes of structural components on the ship.

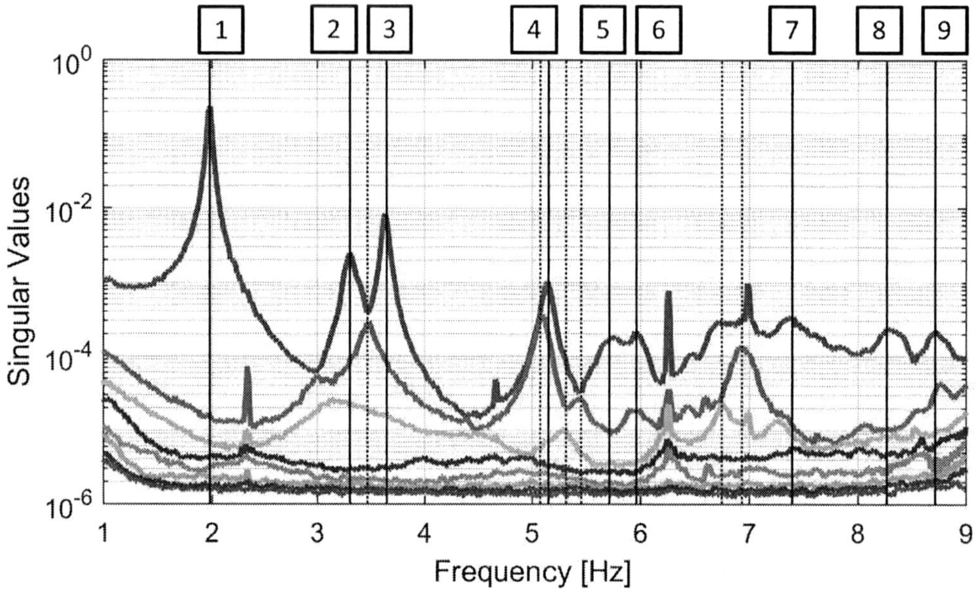

Figure 7 Singular value decomposition of spectral density matrix.

In the present study, only the first three modes identified in Figure 7 are explored in further detail. The reasoning behind selecting these modes is that they appear to be well-excited and are the dominating modes in a modal model of the ship and that a more in-depth study can be performed if fewer modes are considered. The natural frequencies of these modes are 1.97 Hz, 3.28 Hz and 3.63 Hz. Figure 8 (a) presents a simple discretised geometry of the hull (blue) and superstructure (red) of the SA Agulhas II. Figure 8 (b), (c) and (d) presents the mode shapes of the first three modes. Deformations of the hull are in green and the superstructure in orange. By inspection these modes appear to be the first vertical hull bending mode, the first lateral hull bending mode and second vertical hull bending mode. This agrees reasonably well with the modes determined using a finite element (FE) model of the ship [9] and previous studies by Soal [10].

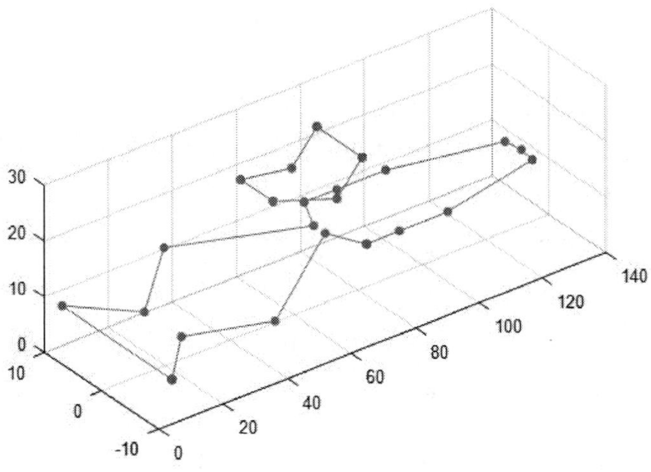
30
20
10
0
10
0
-10
0
20
40
60
80
100
120
140

(a)

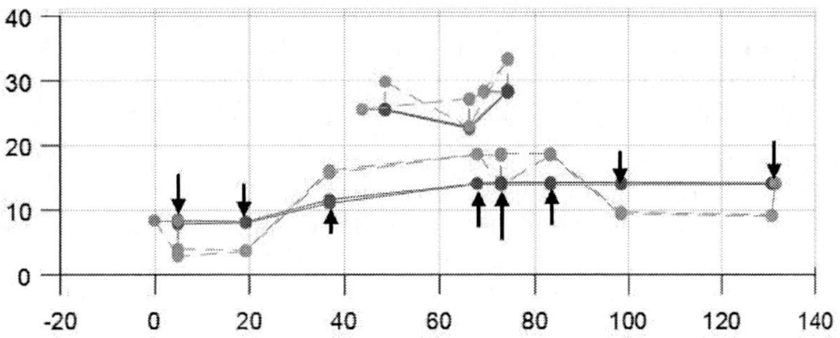
40
30
20
10
0
-20
0
20
40
60
80
100
120
140

(b)

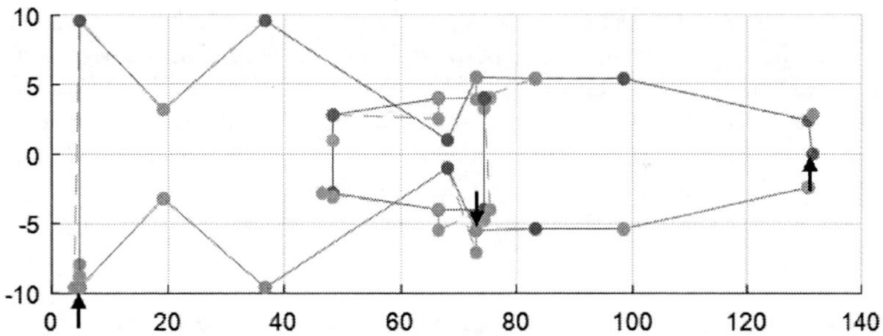
10
5
0
-5
-10
0
20
40
60
80
100
120
140

(c)

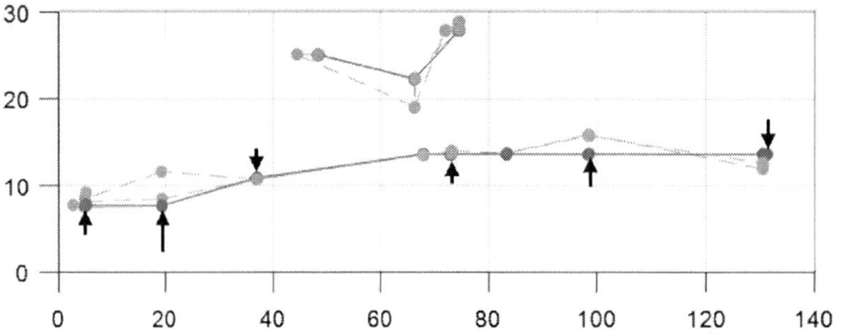

(d)

Figure 8 **(a)** Original discretised geometry of SA Agulhas II **(b)** First vertical bending **(c)** First lateral bending **(d)** Second vertical bending

A parametric investigation was conducted to explore the effect that certain user-specified parameters have on the modal estimates of the reference-based version data-driven SSI algorithm [7]. In particular, the effect of block length, block size and model order on SSI estimates of the first three modes are investigated. A subset of reference channels was selected by calculating the correlation between all measurement signals and selecting the channel that correlated most with the other measurement locations. Then channels that correlated least with the channel already in the reference set were added as references. Eight channels were selected as reference channels for this study.

The methodology of the parametric investigation was inspired by a previous OMA study of a high rise building in [11] and starts by initially only investigating the effect of block size and block length. Several modal identifications were performed with a combination of block sizes and block lengths. Ten block sizes ranging from 10 to 100 and eight block lengths that varied from 5 minutes to 40 minutes were used. Since modal estimates also vary depending on the model order, forty estimates for each mode at each combination of block length and block size were calculated. These forty estimates were obtained by allowing the model order to range from 2 to a maximum of 80. The maximum of 80 was motivated by the fact that for identification using eight reference channels with the minimum block size of 10, this is the highest achievable model order. Further, at a model order of 80 it is possible to identify forty modes which is far greater than the number of modes in the bandwidth of interest. Once the natural frequencies and damping at all model orders between 2 and 80 were identified for a given block size and block length the variance in frequency and damping were calculated. The variance in these modal parameters were then used as a metric to compare identifications at different block lengths and block sizes. Once a suitable block size and block length were selected, the effect of model order was investigated. Results of the parametric investigations are subsequently presented.

3.1. Block length and block size

3.1.1. Mode 1

The variance of frequency and damping estimates over model orders ranging from 2 to 80 for mode 1 is presented in Figure 9 (a) and (b). Variances are plotted as a function of block length for block sizes 10 to 100. Frequency variances are lower than 10^{-4} for all combinations of the user-selected parameters. Dramatic improvements in frequency variances are found for all block lengths greater than 5 minutes and for block sizes between 60 and 100. For these combinations of parameters, variance generally decreases with increasing block length and block size achieving a minimum at block size 100 and block length of 40 minutes. Block size 90 and 100 produce very similar frequency variances. Damping variances at extreme block lengths (5 minutes and 40 minutes) result in significant "spikes" at block sizes 30, 70 and 100. For block lengths from 10 to 35 minutes and all block sizes considered a more consistent trend is observed. In general, improved damping variances are found for higher block lengths. Block sizes 80 to 100 produce very similar damping variances, especially for higher block lengths (above 30 minutes). Although frequency variances are lowest for block size 100, damping variances are lower for block size 80.

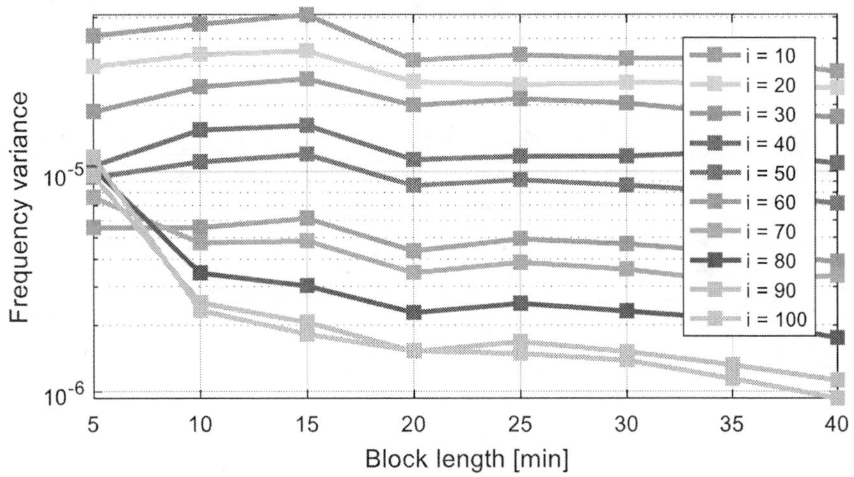

(a)

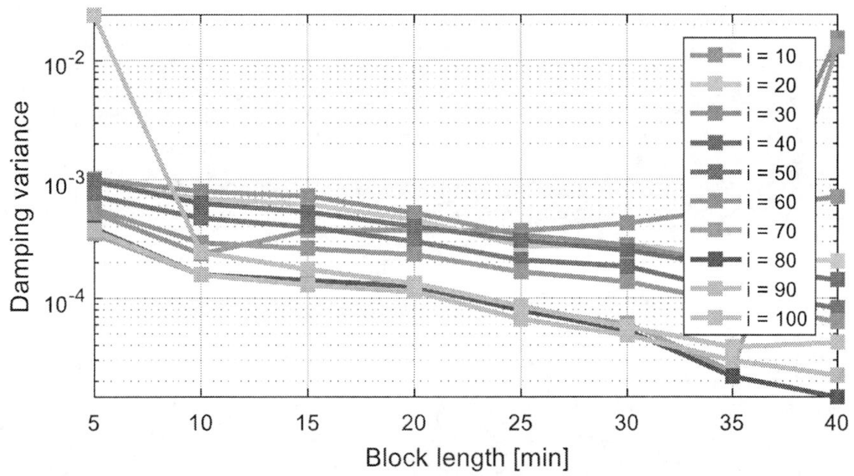

(b)

Figure 9. Results from a parametric investigation of the modal identification of Mode 1. The results show the variance of **(a)** frequency and **(b)** damping as a function of block length for different block sizes.

3.1.2. Mode 2

From the frequency and damping variances calculated for Mode 2 it is immediately obvious that remarkable improvements are found for block sizes above 10, see Figure 10 (a) and (b). Further improvement in both frequency and damping variances are found by increasing block size above 30 and using block lengths greater than 5 minutes. With these parameters, frequency variances generally tend to decrease as block size and block length increases. Considering damping variances for block sizes 40 to 100, it appears that there is significant advantage in selecting block lengths of at least 30 minutes. Similar frequency and damping variances are found for block sizes 90 and 100.

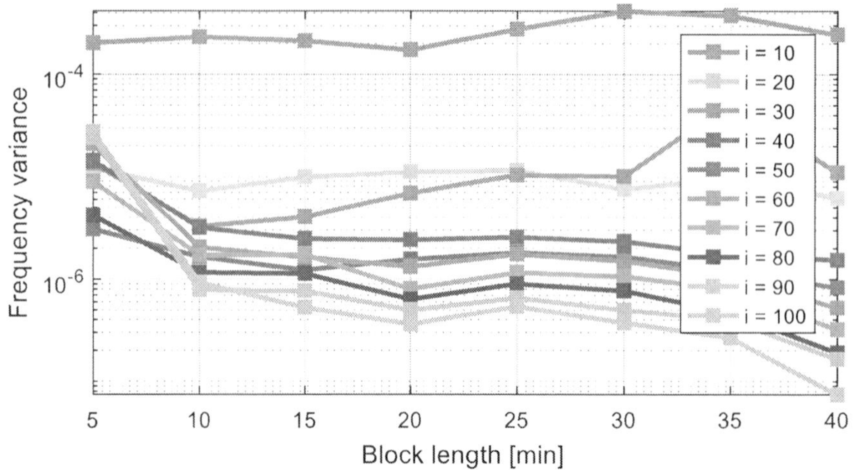

(a)

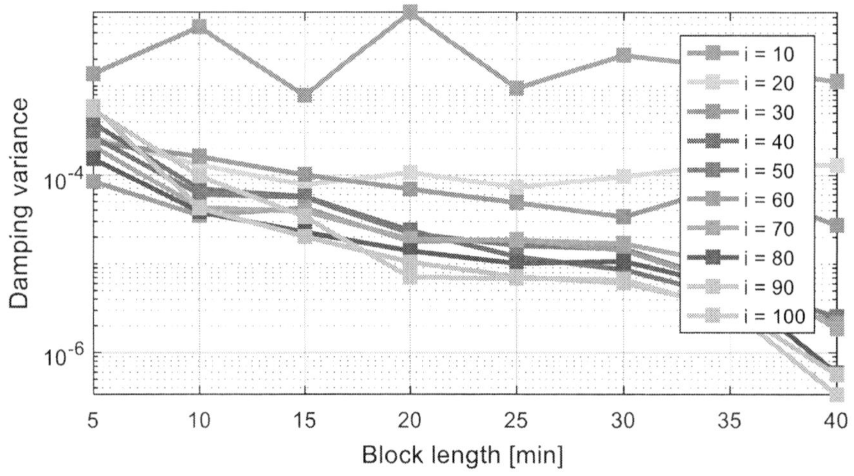

(b)

Figure 10. Results from a parametric investigation of the modal identification of Mode 2. The results show the variance of **(a)** frequency and **(b)** damping as a function of block length for different block sizes.

3.1.3. Mode 3

Both frequency and damping estimates are improved significantly by selecting a block size greater than 10, see Figure X (a) and (b). Generally, with increasing block size and block length frequency and damping variances tend to improve. Increasing block size above 30 yields a significant reduction of both frequency and damping variances, and damping variances improve significantly when block lengths are greater than 30 minutes. The lowest variances are found at block sizes greater than 60. An interesting observation is that at a "medium" block sizes of 50 or 60 relatively low frequency variances are achieved if a long enough block length is used. This indicates that it may be preferable to use longer block lengths and slightly lower block sizes.

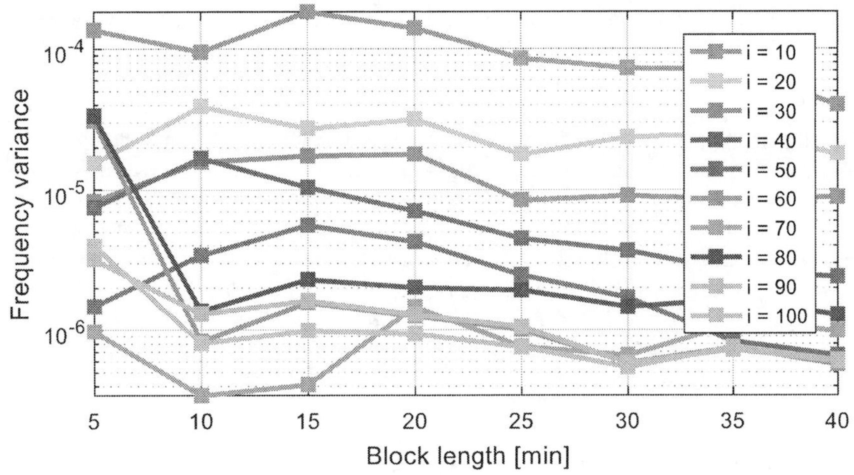

(a)

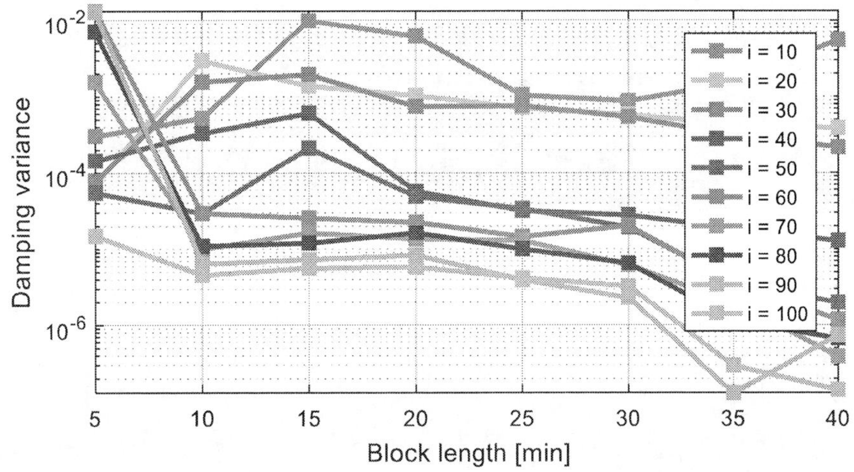

(b)

Figure 11. Results from a parametric investigation of the modal identification of Mode 3. The results show the variance of **(a)** frequency and **(b)** damping as a function of block length for different block sizes.

3.1.4. Summary

There a several combinations of parameters that yield similar results. In general, it is observed that increasing the block size and block length lowers variances in frequency and damping estimates. However, there are block sizes and block lengths above which the effect of increasing the parameters becomes less significant. Therefore, it is not worth the increased computational effort to select both high block sizes and block lengths. In terms of computational efficiency, slightly lower block sizes and higher block lengths are advisable. Suitable block sizes range from 60 to 100. A suitable block length is at least 20 minutes, but block lengths of 30 to 35 minutes are advised.

3.2. Model order

In SSI-data it is necessary to select the model order at which modal parameters are selected. The model order influences the maximum number of modes that can be contained in the modal model. It is often advised to over-specify the model order to capture all dynamic characteristics of the structure and simultaneously account for the effects of measurement and model noise and other model inaccuracies. However, at too high model orders over-fitting occurs which affects damping estimates in particular. Figure X illustrates how frequency and damping varies over model order for Mode 1 to 3 for a block size of 80 and block length of 35 minutes. The normalised change in frequency over model order is relatively low (less than 0.2 percent) and is significantly lower than the variation of damping over model order. Damping estimates spike sporadically at higher model orders due to overfitting (over 600%) at some model orders. At low model orders (less than 80) it appears that the model order is insufficient to capture all the relevant dynamics of the structure and that modal parameters are not yet completely stable to changes in model order. At too high model orders (over 140) overfitting causes spikes large spikes in damping estimates. In order to obtain a suitable modal model that contains information of the first three modes, a maximum model order of 100 is advised. However, a complete modal model would contain all the modes that were identified using FDD. It is recognised that it may be necessary to increase model orders if these modes are to be included in the modal model.

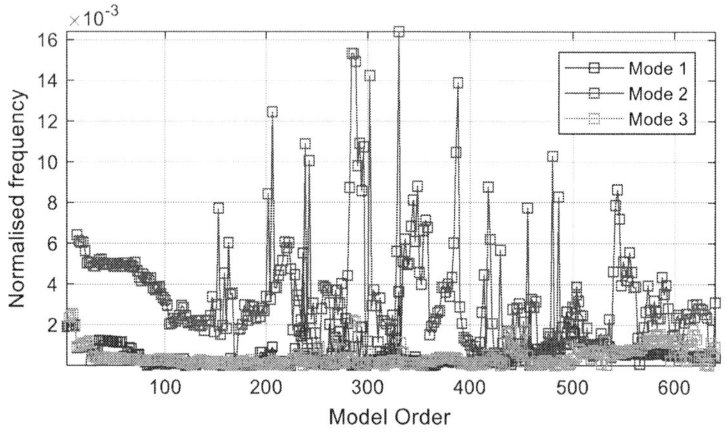

(a)

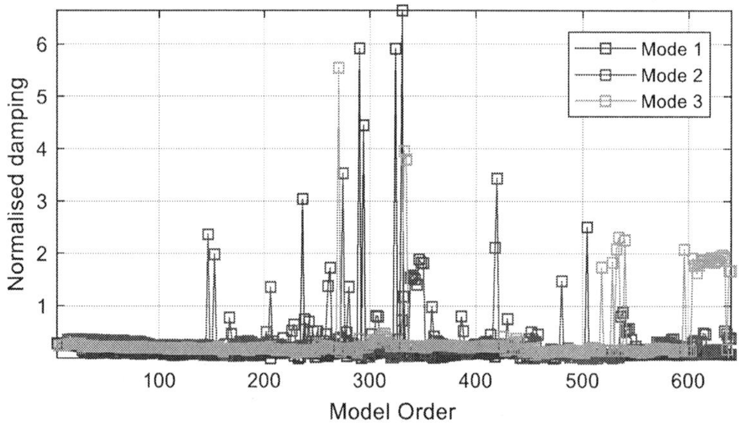

(b)

Figure 12. Normalised change in **(a)** frequency and **(b)** damping for Mode 1, 2 and 3 as model order changes.

4. CONCLUSIONS AND RECOMMENDATIONS

An operational modal analysis (OMA) was conducted on a polar supply and research vessel, the SA Agulhas II. A preliminary OMA using the Frequency Domain Decomposition (FDD) technique resulted in the identification of natural frequencies of several global structural modes. A parametric study was conducted to determine the effect of user-specified parameters on modal parameter estimates of three modes obtained using the data-driven Stochastic Subspace Identification (SSI-data) technique. In particular, the effect of block size, block length and model order were investigated. For the three modes high block lengths with duration above 30 minutes and block sizes between 60 and 100 were found to improve estimates in modal parameters. Model orders higher than 140 resulted in overfitting of the modal model and for the three modes under consideration a maximum model order of 100 is sufficient to capture all physical information and noise. It is recognised that the results of the parametric investigation may vary for non-stationary operating and environmental conditions and it is proposed that the study be extended to include such conditions. Further, the model order may be sufficient for the three modes under consideration but for modes that are not as well excited larger model orders may be required.

ACKNOWLEDGEMENTS

The Flotilla Foundation is acknowledged for funding the charter of the SA Agulhas II for the Weddell Sea Expedition, 2019. The authors express thanks to the Department of Environmental Affairs and Captain Knowledge Bengu and Crew of the S.A. Agulhas II for their support and assistance during the Weddell Sea Expedition 2019. Funding from the National Research Foundation (NRF) through the South African National Antarctic Programme (SANAP Grant No.110737) is thankfully recognized.

REFERENCES

[1] R. Brincker and C. Ventura, *Introduction to Operational Modal Analysis*, 1st ed. John Wiley & Sons, Ltd, 2015.

[2] A. Brandt, "The ABRAVIBE Toolbox for Teaching Vibration Analysis and Structural Dynamics," in *Conference Proceedings of the Society for Experimental Mechanics Series*, 2013, vol. 6, no. 203, pp. 131–141.

[3] K. I. Soal, *System identification and modal tracking on ship structures*. Stellenbosch : Stellenbosch University, 2018.

[4] R. Brincker, L. Zhang, and P. Andersen, "Modal Identification from Ambient Responses using Frequency Domain," in *Proceedings of the 18th International Modal Analysis Conference*, 2000.

[5] C. E. Ventura, R. Brincker, and P. Andersen, "Damping Estimation by Frequency Domain Decomposition," in *Proceedings of the International Modal Analysis Conference XIX*, 2001, pp. 698–703.

[6] B. van Overschee, P; de Moor, *Subspace Identification for Linear Systems: Theory - Implementation - Applications*. Dordrecht: Kluwer Academic Publishers, 1996.

[7] B. Peeters and G. de Roeck, "Reference-based Stochastic Subspace Identification for Output-only Modal Analysis," *Mech. Syst. Signal Process.*, vol. 13, pp. 855–878, 1999.

[8] B. Peeters and G. de Roeck, "Stochastic System Identification for Operational Modal Analysis: A Review," *J. Dyn. Syst. Meas. Control*, vol. 123, no. December, 2001.

[9] STX, *FINNSAP finite element analysis of the PSRV NB1368*. Rauma, Finland, 2010.

[10] K. I. Soal, *Vibration response of the polar supply and research vessel the S. A. Agulhas II in Antarctica and the Southern ocean*. Stellenbosch : Stellenbosch University, 2015.

[11] R. Sarlo, P. A. Tarazaga, and M. E. Kasarda, "High resolution operational modal analysis on a fi ve-story smart building under wind and human induced excitation," *Eng. Struct.*, vol. 176, no. July, pp. 279–292, 2018.

IOMAC'19

8th International Operational Modal Analysis Conference
2019 May13-15 Copenhagen

APPLICATION OF OMA TECHNIQUES TO LTP SYSTEMS

Massimiliano Deon [1], *Ilmar F. Santos* [2], *Giuliano Coppotelli* [3]

[1] Massimiliano Deon, Sapienza University of Rome, massimiliano.deon@gmail.com.
[2] Ilmar F. Santos, Technical University of Denmark, ifs@mek.dtu.dk.
[3] Giuliano Coppotelli, Sapienza University of Rome, giuliano.coppotelli@uniroma1.it

ABSTRACT
In this paper the results of the application of Operational Modal Analysis (OMA) techniques to rotating systems are shown. The system in study is a rotor-blade system, having time-varying parameters in the equations of motion when subject to rotation. The aim of this study is to show the results of the application of linear time invariant (LTI) OMA techniques to these kinds of systems, both numerically and experimentally, verifying the possibility of identifying both basis and parametric resonances.

Keywords: Conference, Operational, Modal, Analysis

1. INTRODUCTION

Operational Modal Analysis techniques allow the estimate of the modal parameters of a structures using only the output responses. In this way, the costs associated to test campaign are reduced and, in addition an increase of the accuracy of the modal signature is achieved due to the possibility to evaluate the behaviour of the system under the actual boundary conditions and excitation levels, both provided from the operating conditions [3]. Several techniques, both in frequency and in time domain, have been developed in recent years for linear time invariant systems, under the main common assumption that the excitation has to be stochastic with the same spectral characteristic of the white noise. Among the methods it is worth recalling here the Frequency Domain Decomposition (FDD, [4]), which is the one that has been used in this research. The OMA bases its algorithms on the experimental modal analysis, by substituting the Frequency Response Functions (FRF) (or the impulse response functions (IRF)), with the Power Spectral Density (PSD) functions (or the correlation functions (CF)). This substitution is possible due to the main assumption on the white noise behaviour of the excitation. In fact, thanks to this assumption, it is possible to develop the PSD functions in terms of modal parameters, in the same way of the frequency response functions [3].
The rotor-blade system in study, when rotating, cannot be modelled as a linear time invariant (LTI) system, because it posseses time-varying parameters, function of the angular position and of the angular velocity. If the angular velocity is constant, the system can be modelled as a linear time period (LTP)

system. An important consequence of the periodicity of the system's parameters is that the mode shapes of the system become time-periodic. This leads to the presence of unexpected resonances of the systems, called parametric resonances, at frequencies equal to the fundamental natural frequency $\pm$ the angular velocity. Mathematically, this system's behaviour can be demonstrated applying the principle of the harmonic balance to the time-varying eigenvalue problem, demonstrating mathematically that the parametric resonances of the system are the Fourier components of the Fourier series expansion of the time periodic mode shapes [2]. The application of Operational Modal Analysis to these kinds of systems necessitates of a further comment. The concept of Frequency Response Function is in fact not directly applicable to time-varying systems. Indeed, for a linear time periodic system, the steady state response to a complex exponential signal is not a complex exponential, but a complex exponential modulation of an harmonic signal [2]. The way of solving this issue is to consider as fundamental signal space for LTP systems not complex exponential signals, but exponentially modulated periodic (EMP) signals. These signals consist of a complex exponential modulation of a periodic signal of period the revolution period, such that input and output signal spaces are equal. Applying the principle of the harmonic balance to the equations of state, it is possible to introduce the operator Harmonic Transfer Function (HTF), that relates all the harmonics of the input to all the harmonics of the output. Using the HTF, under the assumption of white noise input, it is possible to obtain an expression for the power spectrum of a LTP system in terms of the modal parameters of the system, as in the case of LTI systems [5]. The power spectrum obtained in this way is called Harmonic Power Spectrum (HPS). Classical Operational Modal Analysis techniques can then be applied directly to the measured responses, or to an exponentially modulated version of the measured signals, with the aim of identifying fundamental and parametric resonances of the system.

2. OPERATIONAL MODAL ANALYSIS FOR LTP SYSTEMS

In the case of a linear time periodic (LTP) system, the definition of a transfer function between input and output is not straightforward, as in the case of LTI system. The reason is that the steady state response to the fundamental signal for LTI system, that is the complex exponential signal, is not a complex exponential, but it could contain in general an infinite number of harmonics of the angular velocity, all modulated by the input complex exponential [2].
The way of introducing a transfer function in case of LTP system is to consider another signal space as fundamental one, that is the exponentially modulated periodic signal space, which is a complex exponential modulation of all the harmonics of the rotation frequency. In the way, input and output signal spaces are equal and, through the application of the harmonic balance to the equations of state, it is possible to introduce the operator harmonic transfer function, which relates all the harmonics of the input to all the harmonics of the output in a systematic way [2]. This operator, in the same way as it is done with the LTI transfer function, may be expressed in terms of modal parameters [5]. Doing so, one obtains, in the frequency domain, what is shown in eq.(1).

$$\hat{\mathcal{H}}(\omega) = \sum_{r=1}^{N} \sum_{l=-\infty}^{\infty} \frac{\hat{\phi}_{r,l} \hat{L}_{r,l}}{j\omega - (\lambda_r - jl\omega_A)}$$

$$\hat{\phi}_{r,l} = [\cdots \phi_{r,-1-l}^T \, \phi_{r,-l}^T \, \phi_{r,1-l}^T \cdots]^T \tag{1}$$

$$\hat{L}_{r,l} = [\cdots l_{r,-1-l}^T \, l_{r,-l}^T \, l_{r,1-l}^T \cdots]$$

where the nth term in the vector $\hat{\phi}_{r,l}$ is $\phi_{r,n-l}$, the $(n-l)^{th}$ Fourier coefficient of the right eigenvector of the state matrix $\Phi_r(t)$ whereas $l_{r,l-m}^T$ is the $(l-m)^{th}$ Fourier coefficient of $L_r^T(t)B(t)$ where $L_r(t)$ is the r left eigenvector of the state matrix and $B(t)$ is the input matrix.
As it is possible to observe from eq.(1), the HTF has the same mathematical form as the expression of the FRF in terms of modal parameters for LTI systems. There is, however, a very important difference. Indeed, an LTP system of order N can potentially have an infinite number of peaks in his HTF, depending

on how many terms in $\hat{\phi}_{r,l}$ and $\hat{L}^T_{r,l}$ are non zero. Each peak will occur near the imaginary part of the base eigenvalue of the state matrix λ_r plus some integer multiple of the fundamental frequency ω_A.
Using this definition of the harmonic transfer function it is possible to give an expression of the power spectrum for LTP systems, which will be called *harmonic power spectrum*, in the case of white noise input. Experimentally, the harmonic power spectrum is built using an exponentially modulated version of the measured data such as it is given in eq.(2):

$$Y(\omega) = [\cdots\ y^T_{-2}(\omega)\ y^T_{-1}(\omega)\ y^T_0(\omega)\ y^T_{+1}(\omega)\ y^T_{+2}(\omega)\ \cdots]^T \tag{2}$$

where:

$$y_n(\omega) = \int_{-\infty}^{\infty} y(t)e^{(-j\omega - jn\omega_A)t}dt \tag{3}$$

If the input is reasonably flat, it is possible to obtain an expression for the harmonic power spectrum in terms of modal parameters.

$$\hat{S}_{yy}(\omega) = \sum_{r=1}^{2N}\sum_{l=-\infty}^{\infty} \frac{\hat{\phi}_{r,l}W(\omega)_{r,l}\hat{\phi}^H_{r,l}}{[j\omega - (\lambda_r - jl\omega_A)][j\omega - (\lambda_r - jl\omega_A)]^H} \tag{4}$$

where where $W(\omega)_{r,l} = \hat{L}_{r,l}G_{f,f}\hat{L}^H_{r,l}$ is a scalar term function of the input spectrum and of the characteristics of the system. If it is reasonably flat with respect to the frequency, then the harmonic power spectrum may be approximated as a sum of modal contributions. The harmonic power spectrum has the same mathematical form of the output power spectrum for a LTI system. There are, however, a few important differences, such as the fact that the expression in eq.(4) contains a summation both over the modes and over the harmonics. Moreover, the mode vectors are the Fourier coefficients of the time varying mode shapes of the LTP system.
Assuming underdamped modes, so that $\lambda_{r+N} = \lambda^*_r$, then the harmonic power spectrum, expressed as a modal contribution, has the form in eq.(5) [5].

$$\hat{S}_{yy}(\omega) = \sum_{r=1}^{N}\sum_{l=-\infty}^{\infty}\left(\frac{A_{1(r,l)}}{j\omega - (\lambda_n - jl\omega_A)} + \frac{A_{2(r,l)}}{-j\omega - (\lambda_n - jl\omega_A)} + C.C.\right) \tag{5}$$

where $A_{1,(r,l)}$ and $A_{s,(r,l)}$ are residue matrices built from the modal vectors of the LTP system, having as scalar scaling factors a parameter deriving from the scalar factor $W(\omega)$ and the system's properties, and $C.C.$ is indicating the complex conjugate terms.
Observing the expression in eq.(5), it is possible to make an important consideration. The residue matrices on the right-hand side of the equation are rank 1 matrices, and the matrix $\hat{S}_{yy}$ can be seen as a block matrix, where each block is the power spectrum matrix derived from two sets of data of the exponentially modulated output signals. This means that the harmonic power spectrum has the following form:

$$\hat{S}_{yy}(\omega) = \begin{bmatrix} \ddots & & & \\ & S_{-1,-1}(\omega) & S_{-1,0}(\omega) & S_{-1,1}(\omega) & \\ & S_{0,-1}(\omega) & S_{0,0}(\omega) & S_{0,1}(\omega) & \\ & S_{1,-1}(\omega) & S_{1,0}(\omega) & S_{1,1}(\omega) & \\ & & & & \ddots \end{bmatrix} \tag{6}$$

where $S_{i,j}$ is the power spectral density submatrix obtained from the $y_i(\omega)$ and $y_j(\omega)$ shifted output signals.
This means that, if the power spectrum is built directly from the output responses, the mode vectors found through the OMA techniques are the basis or parametric mode shapes at their respective frequency, since the corresponding terms in the residue matrix will be of the kind $\phi_{r,-l}\phi^H_{r,-l}$.

From what has been said it is evident that it is possible to apply directly the LTI techniques to the power spectrum built from the measured output responses. An important condition in order to obtain good estimates of the modal parameters is, however, that the harmonics of the periodic external force contributions, if present, have to be outside the frequency range of interest. If this is not the case, applying directly LTI OMA techniques to the measured responses could lead to highly inaccurate results, since the main hypothesis that the input be random would not be verified. In that case, it is necessary to remove these harmonic operating further on the measured output data [3, 6].
As a last comment, it is important to state that theoretically an infinite number of harmonics should be used to characterize the harmonic power spectrum, but practically most systems can be approximated by a finite, perhaps even small, number of harmonics.

2.1. Frequency Domain Decomposition-FDD

In this study the OMA LTI algorithm used is the Frequency Domain Decomposition method [4]. The Frequency Domain Decomposition method is an OMA method that deals directly with the Power Spectral Density. It gives the user a clear indication of the harmonic components in the response signal and it is able to distinguish efficiently close modes.
The estimate of the modal damping is not done immediately with the FDD algorithm. It is necessary to use a damping estimation technique. In this research the Logarithmic Decrement technique has been used. The way to apply this technique is first to choose a threshold MAC[1] value. Typical choices are MAC higher than 0.85. As long as the MAC value between a singular vector at a certain frequency line and the singular vector corresponding to the resonant frequency is higher than the threshold value, than the corresponding singular value belongs to the SDOF power spectral density function. If at a certain line none of the singular values has a singular vector with a MAC higher than the threshold the search is terminated. A region where this condition is verified is therefore identified and the Inverse Fast Fourier Transform (IFFT) is applied to the Power Spectrum, obtaining the correlation functions of the output. In this region the system is approximately an SDOF system and it is therefore possible to apply the Logarithmic Decrement technique.

3. DESCRIPTION OF THE TEST-RIG AND EXPERIMENTAL PROCEDURE

The rotating bladed system in study presents vibration coupling among rotor and blades. Rotor lateral motion is coupled to blade flexible motion. Fig.(1a) shows a schematic drawing of the mechanical model of such system. The system is composed of a rotating rigid disk onto which four equally distributed

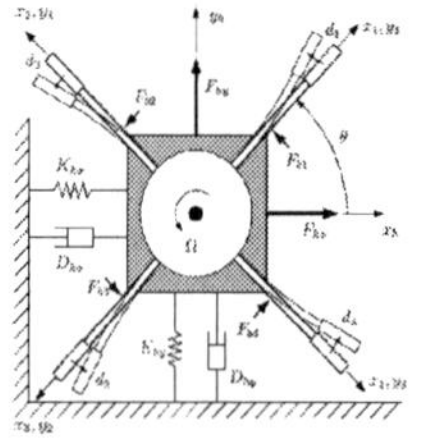

(a) Mechanical model of the coupled rotor-blade system

(b) Picture of the experimental test rig

Figure 1

flexible blades are radially clamped. At the tip end of each blade an additional mass is attached. Such tip masses emphasize the inertia of the blades and increase the vibration coupling among rotor and blades. The disk and shaft, onto which the disk is attached, are assumed to be rigid. They are supported in a flexible suspended rigid body performing only lateral planar movement in the x_h and y_h directions.

[1]The MAC value is a parameter used to indicate the similarity between two vectors. It is given by $MAC_{ij} = \frac{|\phi_i^T \phi_j|^2}{|\phi_i^T \phi_i||\phi_j^T \phi_j|}$

This rigid body supporting the disk and shaft will for convenience be referred to as the "hub" even though it is not rotating. Rotor angular movements and gyroscopic effects are assumed to be negligible. Such assumptions reduce complexity of the mathematical model describing the dynamics of the system. Moreover, the blades are attached non-twisted onto the disk, meaning that the flexible blade bending motion will be only in $x_h y_h$-plane. Coupling effects between blades flexible motion and rotor axial motion can therefore be neglected.

A total number of six sets of sensors and actuators are applied to the system in order to monitor the vibration levels and to apply input forces, such that the fundamental requirement for the application of the OMA techniques of input random both in time and in space may be respected. The locations of sensors and actuators are symbolized by arrows in fig.(1a). That means actuation forces F_{hx} and F_{hy} are applied acting onto the flexible suspended hub, and the four actuation forces F_{b1}, F_{b2}, F_{b3} and F_{b4} are applied to act orthogonally onto each one of the blades. Sensors are assumed to be placed at somewhat similar locations, measuring rotor lateral position and the blade deflections.

The dynamics of the rotor-blade system is described by the minimal number of coordinates x_h and y_h, denoting the absolute rotor lateral positions, and d_1, d_2, d_3 and d_4, denoting the blade tip point deflections. Fig.(1b) shows a picture of the experimental rig. As it possible to see, a small DC motor is built into the rig to drive the system. The torque is transmitted with the help of a pulley.

The sensors which have been used are eddy current sensors, one per blade, and two eddy current sensors to measure the rotor lateral movement. The signals from the blades eddy current sensors are sent from the rotating system to the non rotating reference system through a slip ring, and then all the signals are transmitted to the PC-based signal processor dSpace 1103.

The blade magnetic actuators are controlled from a personal computer connected to a Raspberry pi controller board built into the rig. The hub magnetic actuators are, in the same way, controlled from a personal computer connected to a Raspberry pi mounted outside of the rig.

The experimental testing procedure is to send random Voltages, according to a uniform distribution, from 0 to 20 V to the magnetic actuators, in order to excite the system randomly both in time and space with enough power. It can be demonstrated that the excitation band is sufficiently flat in the frequency range of interest (10 Hz-25 Hz) [1] so that the main requirements of OMA can be considered satisfied.

The tests have been performed, both in non-rotating and in rotating conditions, for long periods of time, from 20 to 40 minutes, in order to remove by time averaging procedures the noise effects and to have a high frequency resolution, and sampling at a sampling frequency of 250 Hz.

4. NUMERICAL VALIDATION OF THE APPLICATION OF LTI OMA TECHNIQUES ON LTP SYSTEMS

The first study performed is a numerical validation of the application of the FDD technique on the rotating system, in order to demonstrate its capacity of estimating both basis and parametric resonances.

The condition in study is that of angular velocity $\Omega = 2.5Hz$. The system's modal parameters are obtained theoretically through the hyper-eigenvalue problem, as briefly described in the theoretical part in sec.(2.). The hyper-eigenvalue problem gives modal vectors that contain all the Fourier components of the vector. It is important to say that not all of the parametric resonances of the system are going to be visible in the response of the system to a generic white noise input, such as the one that is being considered for the purpose of the research. Indeed, some of the Fourier components have negligible amplitude, with respect to the basis modes and to some of the parametric ones. For further comments on the subject see [1]. The estimate of the modal parameters of the system, that is done through the application of the FDD algorithm, is therefore done only for those basis and parametric modes that participate significantly to the system's response. The response of the system to a random input with zero mean and standard deviation approximately equal to 6N is then obtained using Matlab and Simulink. The response of the system was simulated for a period of 30 minutes and a sampling frequency of $250Hz$, and the solving algorithm used is a fixed step 4th order Runge Kutta. Fig.(2) shows the SVD obtained from the output simulated measurements, where both basis and parametric resonances have been identified.

	f1	f2	f3	f4	f5	f6	f1_1	$f1_{+1}$	$f2_{-1}$	$f2_{+1}$	$f5_{+1}$	$f6_{-1}$
th	12.20	14.16	17.67	17.67	18.15	18.36	9.70	14.70	11.66	16.66	20.65	15.86
est	12.24	14.21	17.74	17.74	18.16	18.64	9.72	14.71	11.67	16.66	20.83	15.63

Table 1: Comparison between the theoretical natural frequencies and the estimated ones. Basis natural frequencies on the left hand side, parametric natural frequencies on the right hand side. Angular velocity $2.5Hz$ (numerical simulations)

	$\zeta1$	$\zeta2$	$\zeta3$	$\zeta4$	$\zeta5$	$\zeta6$	$\zeta1_{-1}$	$\zeta1_{+1}$	$\zeta2_{-1}$	$\zeta2_{+1}$	$\zeta5_{+1}$	$\zeta6_{-1}$
th	0.17	0.68	2.23	2.23	2.20	1.71	0.21	0.14	0.83	0.58	1.93	1.98
est	0.33	0.72	1.05	1.05	1.26	1.38	0.40	0.25	0.89	0.62	2.32	2.75

Table 2: Comparison between the theoretical modal damping ratios and the estimated ones. Damping ratios of the basis modes on the left hand side, damping ratios of the parametric modes on the right hand side. Angular velocity $2.5Hz$ (numerical simulations)

As it possible to see from tab.(1) the estimates of the natural frequencies, both basis and parametric, are very accurate, with differences smaller than 1.5%. In fig.(3) is reported the comparison in terms of MAC number between numerical and estimated mode shapes. For the sake of brevity, the numerical values of the mode shapes have not been reported here. As it is possible to see from fig.(3), also the estimate of the mode shapes is very accurate, with MAC values near 1 for all the mode shapes.
The peak at $2.5Hz$ in fig.(2) comes from the harmonic contributions due to gravity and to the rotor eccentricity. As it is evident from the obtained results, this harmonic contribution, being outside the frequency range of interest, does not hinder the estimate of the modal parameters of the rotating system. From tab.(2) it is possible to see the comparison between the modal damping ratios of the basis and of the parametric resonances. It is evident that there are some difficulties in the estimation of the damping ratios of very close modes.

5. EXPERIMENTAL RESULTS

5.1. Standing still condition, no motor

The first test is performed with the free system and without the motor and sending a random voltage in all the electro-magnets. The angular position of the rotor is, according to the mechanical model in fig.(1a), $\theta = 0$. Fig.(4a) shows the singular value decomposition of the experimental power spectral density obtained from the experimentally measured responses. Tab.(3) and tab.(4) show the comparison between the numerical values and the experimental ones of the natural frequencies and the modal damping factors. As it it possible to see from tab.(3), the estimated natural frequencies to the numerical ones in this condition. Nevertheless, there is one important difference between the theoretical modes and the estimated experimental ones. The third mode, that may be seen to be a mode where the blades are all in phase, is found to be at higher frequency than expected. This is confirmed by fig.(4b), that shown the comparison between the mode shapes in terms of MAC values. For this comparison, the modes have been ordered for ascending order of natural frequency, and it is clear that experimentally the third numerical mode is found to be the sixth mode, so at higher frequency than expected. Looking at fig.(4a), it is possible to see how this mode is identified in the singular value plot as a very flat peak at $21.72Hz$, with a considerably lower amplitude (tens of dB) than the peaks corresponding to the other vibration modes, meaning that the power contribution of that mode to the response is lower with respect to the power contribution of the other modes. This is due to the fact that the rotor is not fixed, because it is free to rotate around its axis. Therefore, there is a transmission of power, of rotary motion, from the in-phase mode of all the blades to the whole system, so that the mode does not participate to the response as it would if the rotor was fixed.

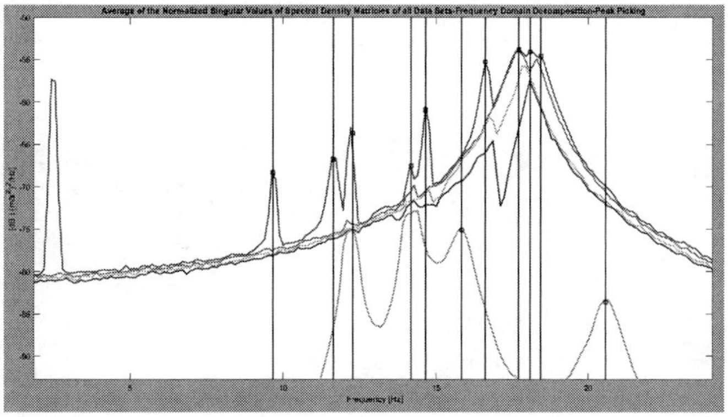

Figure 2: SVD of the PSD of the simulated output responses: standing still conditions

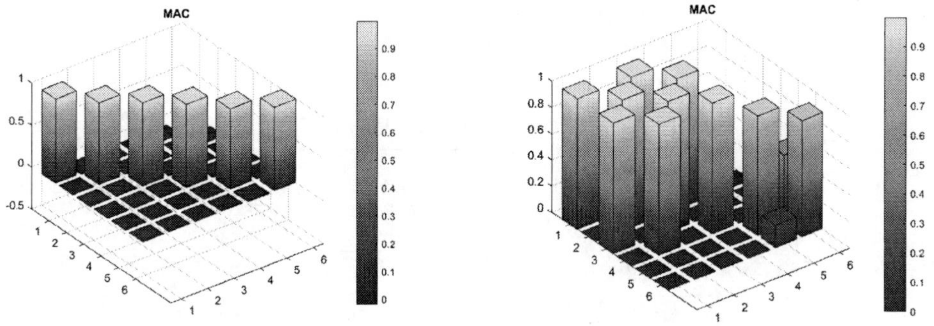

(**a**) MAC values basis mode shapes

(**b**) MAC values parametric mode shapes

Figure 3: MAC values numerical simulation

A demonstration of such a statement may be found in sec(5.3.).
From tab.(4) it is possible to see that the differences with respect to the damping ratios are higher than the differences with respect to the natural frequencies or the mode shapes.

5.2. Standing still condition, motor

The presence of the motor and the belt modifies partially the system, since the belt tends to act as a constraint in the belt direction itself. In fig.(5) it is shown the singular value decomposition obtained from measurements collected with this particular configuration, exciting randomly the electromagnets in the same way as in sec.(5.1.). Tab.(5) e tab.(6) show the comparison of natural frequencies and mode shapes between the original system and the new rotor-blade system + motor. From the experimental results it is possible to see how the main effect of presence of the belt is a change in the "rotor" modes of the system. In sec.(5.1.) it was shown that, with the free system, and without the presence of the motor, there are two modes at $13.30Hz$ and $13.75Hz$. The numerical values of the mode shapes were not reported in sec.(5.1.) for the sake of brevity, but it may be demonstrated that these two modes are fundamentally rotor modes, with the blades that vibrate following the rotor displacements, that are respectively in the x and y direction. In the case in study in this section, the presence of the belt causes a modification of the system: there is now only one rotor mode at $13.64Hz$, whose mode shape is a rotor displacement in a direction orthogonal to the belt. The belt constraints the system in its direction, and the amplitude of the vibrations in that direction is therefore sensibly lower with respect to the previous case. Looking at fig.(5) and tab.(5,6), is is possible to see how that mode appears, as an extremely flat peak in the singular value plot, at $21.16Hz$. The peak is flat and tens of dB lower than the peaks due to the other modes of the system, symptom of a low participation in the response, because of the belt constraint. The

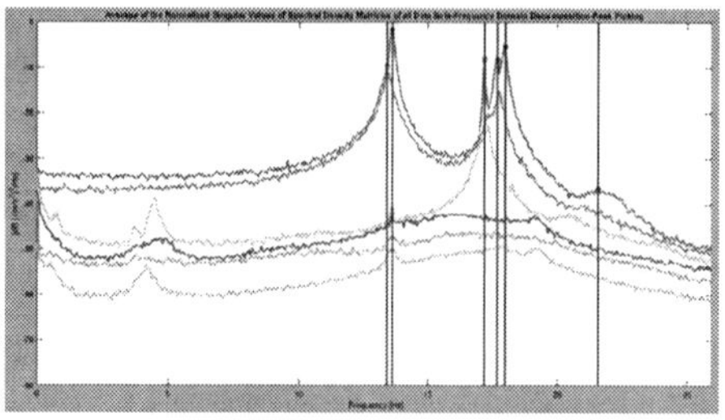

(a) Singular value decomposition (free system, no motor)

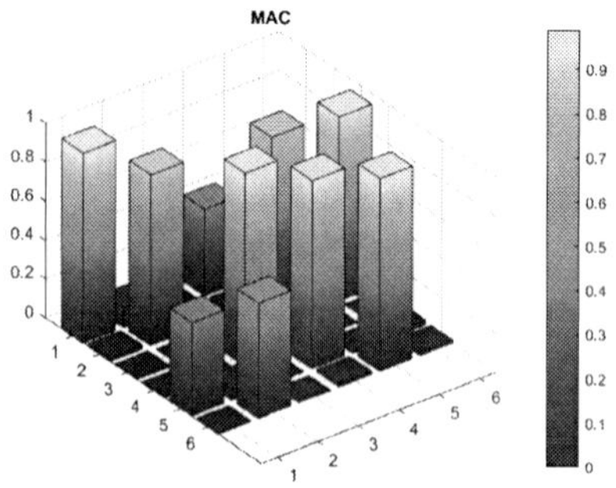

(b) MAC

Figure 4

	f1	f2	f3	f4	f5	f6
th	12.50	14.10	17.55	17.56	17.93	18.22
est	13.30	13.75	21.71	17.25	17.76	17.98

Table 3: Numerical natural frequencies of the system (up) and experimental natural frequencies (down) (Hz

	$\zeta 1$	$\zeta 2$	$\zeta 3$	$\zeta 4$	$\zeta 5$	$\zeta 6$
th	0.21	0.14	0.83	0.58	1.93	1.98
est	0.12	0.36	0.223	2.224	0.331	0.401

Table 4: Numerical percentage modal damping ratios of the system (up) and experimental ones (down) in the case of free rotor, without motor and belt

higher frequency instead is due to a stiffening effect due to the presence of the belt. The "blade" mode shapes, instead, are very similar to the testing condition of system without motor and therefore to the numerical ones.

5.3. Standing still system, fixed rotor, motor

In this section the results obtained by fixing the rotor and doing an OMA test will be presented. In particular, the comparison of the "blade" related mode shapes between the numerical ones and the experimental ones will be shown in terms of the MAC parameter, in order to determine the effect of the belt on the blade mode shapes. In fig.(6a) it is shown the SVD of the PSD matrix in this situation, where the "blade related" frequencies have been highlighted: as it is possible to see, a fourth peak appears in the SVD plot in the $16 - 17Hz$ frequency range. This peak was in fig.(5) at $22.33Hz$, indicated by the second singular value peaking at that frequency, with a low amplitude. This is the in-phase mode if all the blades, and in this way it has been demonstrated that the reason why in sec.(5.1.,5.2.) this mode participated less than the other modes to the system's response is that the rotor was tested in a non fixed configuration.

	f1	f2	f3	f4	f5	f6
th	12.50	14.10	17.55	17.56	17.93	18.22
exp	13.64	21.16	17.10	22.33	17.28	17.94

Table 5: Numerical natural frequencies of the system (up) and experimental natural frequencies (down), in the case of free rotor, with the presence of motor and belt

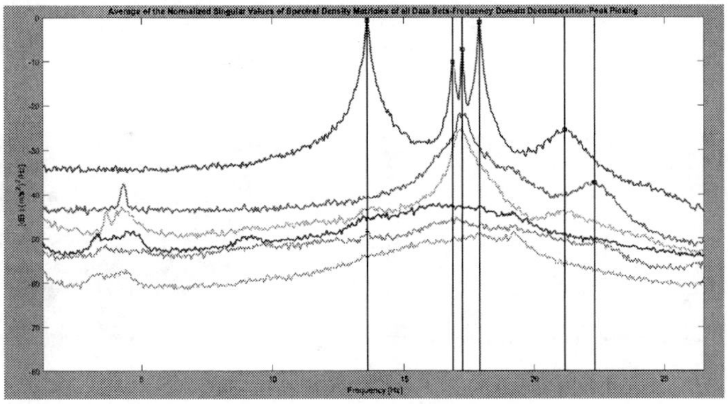

Figure 5: Singular value decomposition (free system, motor)

$_{th}$Mode1	$_{th}$Mode2	$_{th}$Mode3	$_{th}$Mode4	$_{th}$Mode5	$_{th}$Mode6
1	0	0.01	-0.01	-0.04	0
0	0.6	0	0	0	0.08
0	1	-1	1	0	-1
-0.80	0	1	1	-0.66	0
0	-1	-1	1	0	1
0.77	0	0.66	0.66	1	0
$_{exp}$Mode1	$_{exp}$Mode2	$_{exp}$Mode3	$_{exp}$Mode4	$_{exp}$Mode5	$_{exp}$Mode6
0.86	-0.96	-0.19	-0.11	0.06	0.02
1	1	0.18	0.17	0	0.27
0.51	0.39	-0.46	1	-0.98	-0.77
-0.26	0.57	1	0.95	0.75	0.55
-0.51	-0.51	-0.75	0.96	-0.74	1
0.32	-0.58	-0.81	0.99	1	-0.72

Table 6: Numerical eigenvectors of the system (up) and experimental eigenvectors (down) in the case of free rotor, with the presence of motor and belt

In fig.(6b), the MAC values are shown between the four numerical and the four experimental "blade" mode shapes. The estimated modes have been ordered in ascending order of estimated frequency. As it is possible see from fig.(6b), the MAC value is near to 1 for all the mode shapes, but an effect of the motor on the experimental modes is that the fourth mode (third in the picture) is experimentally the fifth (fourth in the picture) and vice versa. The natural frequencies and damping ratios of these modes have been omitted for the sake of brevity.

5.4. Rotating system

The operational modal analysis techniques have then been applied to the system rotating at several different angular velocities. For the sake of brevity, not all these studies are reported in this paper, but only the results obtained with the system rotating at the angular velocity $\Omega = 0.65Hz$. The presence of the belt introduces some differences with respect to the numerical model, as it was shown in sec.(5.2.). One of the modes, the "rotor" mode in the belt direction, has very low importance in the system's response, because the belt constraints the displacements in that direction. Therefore it is extremely difficult to identify such a vibrational component in rotating conditions, when both basis and parametric modes appear in the response. Therefore, since its participation in the response is low and it cannot be considered as a true mode of the system, because of the constraint of the belt, in these sections only the other five

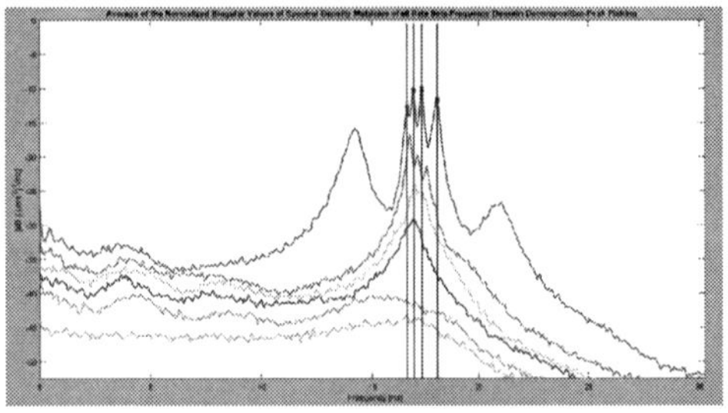

(**a**) SVD of the PSD: standing still conditions, motor, fixed system

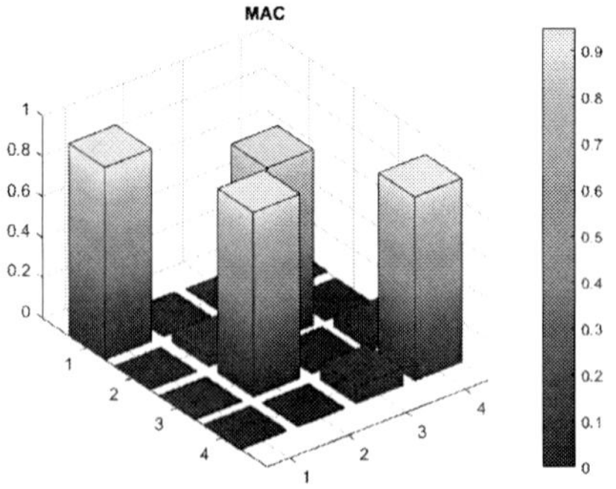

(**b**) MAC values between the "blade" mode shapes, i.e. modes 3,4,5,6

Figure 6

time-variant modes will be identified, both in their basis and parametric components, when possible.

5.4.1. $\Omega = 0.65Hz$

In this section the estimate of the modal parameters of the system rotating at $0.65Hz$ are shown. In fig.(7a) the singular value decomposition obtained from the PSD matrix of the output responses measured in this condition is shown. In fig(7a) the peaks related to basis and parametric modes are clearly visible.

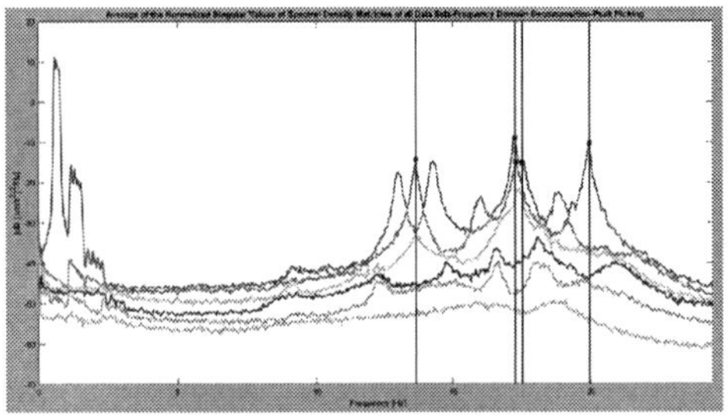

(**a**) Singular value decomposition ($\Omega = 0.65Hz$), basis resonances

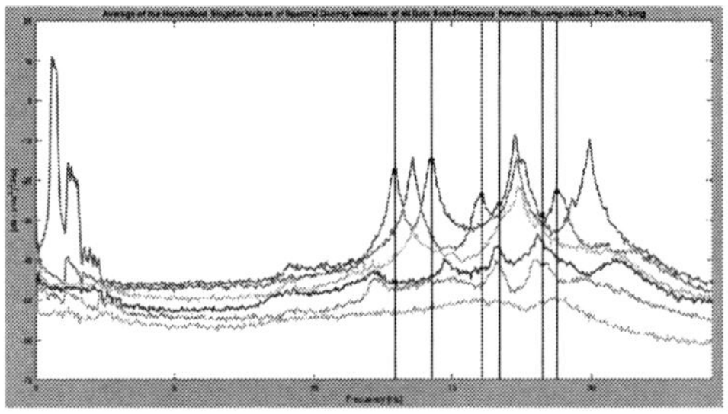

(**b**) Singular value decomposition ($\Omega = 0.65Hz$), parametric resonances

Figure 7

The highlighted peaks are the basis modes of the system at the system. The other peaks present in the response are the parametric resonances. The parametric resonances more evident are the ± 1 components of the first time-periodic mode of the system.
In tab.(7) the basis and parametric natural frequencies of the system are shown, as identified in the singular value decomposition of fig.(7a).

fb1	fb2	fb3	fb4	fb5	$fp1_{-1}$	$fp1_{+1}$	$fp4_{-2}$	$fp4_{-1}$	$fp3_{+1}$	$fp3_{+2}$
13.58	17.30	17.30	17.54	19.91	12.91	14.21	16.39	16.86	17.97	18.51

Table 7: Natural frequencies of the rotor-blade system. Basis natural frequencies on the left end side, parametric natural frequencies on the right end side ($\Omega = 0.65Hz$)

As it is evident from the comparison of the natural frequencies in tab.(3) and the natural frequencies of the system with the motor in tab.(5), there are very small differences with respect to all the natural frequencies but one. Indeed, one of the four "blade related" modes is now at almost $20Hz$. This is the

$\zeta 1$	$\zeta 2$	$\zeta 3$	$\zeta 4$	$\zeta 5$	$\zeta 1_{-1}$	$\zeta 1_{+1}$	$\zeta 4_{-2}$	$\zeta 4_{-1}$	$\zeta 3_{+1}$	$\zeta 3_{+2}$
0.67	0.27	0.27	0.43	0.55	0.75	0.54	0.46	0.16	0.25	0.35

Table 8: Damping ratios of the rotor-blade system. Damping ratios of the basis modes on the left end side, of the parametric modes on the right end side ($\Omega = 0.65Hz$)

in-phase mode of all the blades and such a difference is due to an influence of the belt on the system's dynamics under rotation. In tab.(9) the basis mode shapes, corresponding to the identified basis natural frequencies, are shown. In fig.(7b) the frequencies related to the parametric vibrations are highlighted.

Mode1	Mode2	Mode3	Mode4	Mode5
0.90	0	-0.01	0.01	0.01
1	0	0	-0.01	-0.02
-0.04	1	-0.54	0.87j	0.97
-0.04	-0.60	-0.21+0.97j	-0.72	0.91
-0.03	0.35	1	-0.93j	0.91
-0.03	-0.73	-0.38-0.92j	1	1

Table 9: Experimental basis mode shapes of the rotor-blade system

$Mode1_{-1}$	$Mode1_{+1}$	$Mode3_{-2}$	$Mode3_{-1}$	$Mode4_{+1}$	$Mode4_{+1}$
0.04	0.06	0.07	0.88+0.23j	0.41+0.84j	0.01
-0.02	0.03	0.02	-0.29+0.61j	1	-0.01
1	1	0.89j	0.60j	0.12+0.14j	1
0.97j	-0.92j	-0.89	1	0.21+0.20j	-0.95j
-0.89	-0.88	-0.72j	0.13-0.26j	0.18+0.08j	-0.91
-0.99j	0.97j	1	-0.58-0.37j	0.38-0.06j	0.97j

Table 10: Experimental parametric mode shapes of the rotor-blade system

As it is possible to see from fig.(7b), there are two parametric resonances of the order ± 1 originating from the first base mode at around $13Hz$, then there are four parametric resonances coming from the "blade" modes of the order $-2, -1, +1, +2$. Since the presence of the belt does not modify substantially the system in that frequency range, the conclusion is that the parametric modes of order $-2, -1$ are parametric resonances coming from the forth time-variant mode, whilst the parametric resonances of order $+1, +2$ are parametric resonances coming from the third time-variant mode. This is verified by looking at the frequencies where these modes occur.
The parametric natural frequencies are shown in tab.(7), whilst the damping ratios of basis and parametric resonance frequencies, respectively, are shown in tab.(8).
The parametric mode shapes are shown in tab.(10).
As a last comment, the values of the MAC parameters between the identified numerical basis "blade" mode shapes and the identified parametric mode shapes of the "blade" time-variant modes are shown in fig.(8). The estimated modes have been ordered for this analysis in ascending order of frequency.
As it is possible to see in fig.(8a), the estimated basis modes shapes are in good agreement with the numerical model. The only difference is that the in-phase mode of all the blades is experimentally the fourth "blade" mode, not the second, as it was expected from the numerical model. From fig.(8b), it is possible to see how the parametric modes of order ± 2 are in good agreement with the numerical model. This modes shapes are mainly "blade" modes, therefore only partially influenced by the presence of the belt. The parametric modes of order ± 1 instead are in very poor agreement with the numerical model. These two are "rotor" modes, therefore highly influenced by the presence of the belt.

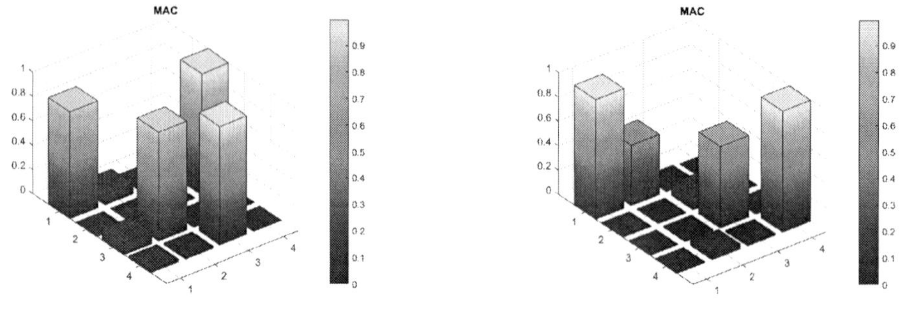

(a) MAC values basis mode shapes between estimated and numerical ones ($\Omega = 0.65Hz$)

(b) MAC values parametric mode shapes between estimated and numerical ones ($\Omega = 0.65Hz$)

Figure 8

6. BEHAVIOUR OF THE BASIS NATURAL FREQUENCY WITH THE ANGULAR VELOCITY

In this section it is shown how the basis natural frequencies of the system change with the angular velocity. In fig.(9) this behaviour is clearly represented, showing the basis natural frequency as a function of the angular velocity of the system. As it is possible to see from fig.(9), the four "blade" basis natural

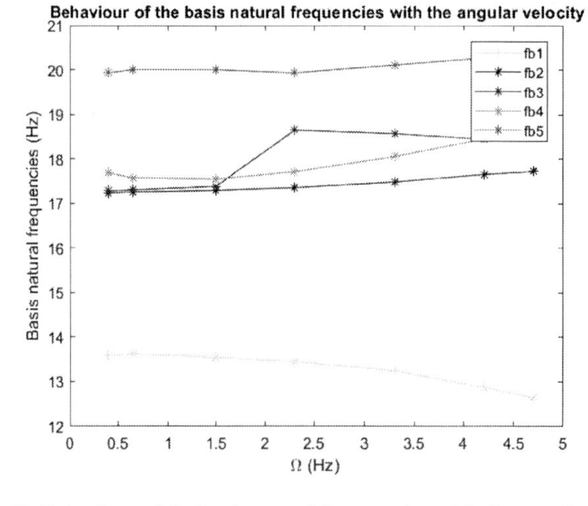

Figure 9: Behaviour of the basis natural frequencies with the angular velocity

frequencies tend to increase with the angular velocity, because of the centrifugal stiffening phenomenon of the blades.

The basis natural frequency at $13.Hz$, a "rotor" mode, seems instead to slightly decrease with increasing angular velocity.

7. CONCLUSIONS

In this research it has been demonstrated that LTI operational modal analysis techniques give the possibility to estimate the modal parameters of the system in rotating condition, both in their fundamental and parametric components. It has been shown in the different case studies how the basis "blade" natural frequencies increase due to centrifugal stiffening and how the parametric resonances appear in the response at frequencies equal to the the basis natural frequencies $\pm$ the angular velocity.

REFERENCES

[1] Ren Hardam Christensen. (2004) Active vibration control of rotor-blade systems. Phd thesis

[2] Norman L. Werely. (1991) Analysis and control of linear periodically time varying systems. Phd thesis

[3] Chiara Grappasonni. (2013) Development of modal analysis methodologies for the identification of aerospace structures in operating conditions. Phd thesis

[4] Brincker R., Ventura C. (2015) Introduction to Operational Modal Analysis. Wiley

[5] Allen, Chauan, Hansen. (2011) Advanced operation modal analysis method for linear time periodic system identification.

[6] Di Lorenzo. (2017) Operational Modal Analysis for rotating machines. Phd thesis

[7] Cauberghe B.. (2004) Applied frequency domain system identification in the field of experimental and operational modal analysis. Phd thesis

IOMAC'19

8th International Operational Modal Analysis Conference
2019 May13-15 Copenhagen

OPERATIONAL MODAL ANALYSIS OF MOVING AIRCRAFT LANDING GEAR DOORS IN FLIGHT

Jan Schwochow[1], *Julian Sinske*[1], *Ralf Buchbach*[1], *Yves Govers*[1], *Ramon Abarca-Lopez*[2]

[1] DLR – Institute of Aeroelasticity, Bunsenstraße10, 37073 Göttingen, Germany, jan.schwochow@dlr.de
[2] AIRBUS, Paseo de John Lenon s/n, 28906 Getafe, Madrid, Spain, ramon.abarca@airbus.com

ABSTRACT

The vibrations on the aircraft undercarriage triggered by unsteady aerodynamics forces are relevant for the design of these airframe components. Being generated by unsteady flow around itself or excited by vortices shed from other upstream components, e.g. the nose landing gear, these vibrations may occur on movable surfaces in the undercarriage area like the main landing gear doors, even though they are opened only for a short sequence while the landing gear is in transit.

The numerical simulation of the vibration level of the undercarriage is associated with uncertainties because of detached flow, vortex shedding and buffet, which needs experimental flight test results. Consequently, research activities comprises instrumented flight tests with a transport aircraft adapted for this purpose and operated by the German Aerospace Centre DLR. Different types of sensors were installed on the movable components of undercarriage, comprising accelerometers, strain gauges, travel and pressure sensors. To get detailed knowledge of the dynamic interaction of pressure loads and structural response on the nose and main landing gear doors, the simultaneous data acquisition of all signals was mandatory during deployment and retraction.

The flight test measurements are evaluated with output-only modal analysis based on the data-driven Stochastic Subspace Identification method (SSI). The vibration level results show trends for increasing flight velocity and different flight manoeuvre.

Keywords: Operational Modal Analysis, Aeroelasticity, Flight Vibration Test

1. INTRODUCTION

The vibrations on the aircraft undercarriage, especially the light-weight components like landing gear (LG) doors made out of composites, are relevant for the design. Being excited by vortices shed from other upstream components, e.g. the nose landing gear (NLG), these vibrations may occur on these movable surfaces in the aircraft undercarriage, even though they are open only for a short sequence while the MLGs are in transit during landing gear deployment and retraction. During the years, semi-empirical methods were used to anticipate towards flight tests.

Nowadays, high-precision computational fluid dynamics (CFD) simulation tools are becoming available that are capable for predicting unsteady aerodynamic phenomena as well as the dynamic response of the structure prior to flight testing. An example for numerical results from [1] to visualize the vorticity is shown in Figure 1, which may occur, when the landing gear is in transit (see Figure 2). These new capabilities allow the thorough prediction of potential transport aircraft undercarriage component vibrations and on the other hand the design of small aerodynamic devices, which impact the flow vorticity to mitigate the excitation levels of the structural response and prevent damages. Details can be found in [1], [2] and [3].

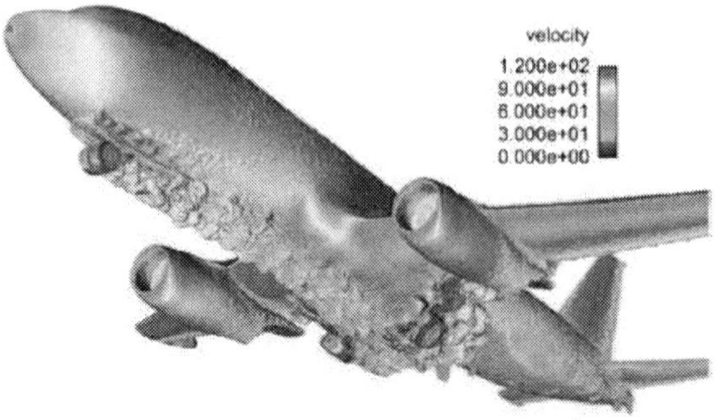

Figure 1. CFD-simulation of undercarriage vorticity [1]

Figure 2. Landing Gear in transit

The unsteady aerodynamic forces of the disturbed flow can randomly excite the extended gears with opened doors. The oscillating aircraft landing gear doors influence the kind of aerodynamic characteristics, which results in a coupled aerodynamic and structural interaction. Since the new multi-disciplinary simulation tools are still in the proving phase, there is a need for experimental flight test results to check their prediction capabilities. Consequently, the research activities within the AFLoNext project funded by the European Union comprises instrumented flight tests with a transport aircraft [4]. The test aircraft is originally a commercial transport aircraft, which was reconfigured to a research platform equipped with special data acquisition systems. To support the investigations on the aircraft undercarriage, a small rugged and customizable data acquisition system (DAQ) was installed outside of the aircraft cabin in the MLG bay containing the signal conditioning and A/D-converters of different type of sensors comprising accelerometers, pressure transducer, strain gauges, and travel sensors.

Due to the turbulent aerodynamic broadband excitation the modal identification process of the opened MLG door responses is predestined for the application of operational modal analysis OMA. The knowledge of the modal characteristics is an essential information for the dynamic loads analysis. Stochastic identification methods for systems with unknown input have been introduced decades ago, which are based on the Ho-Kalman algorithm [6]. Here, the block Hankel matrix formed by system responses is decomposed by singular value decomposition (SVD). The stochastic subspace identification method is one of the most robust and accurate system identification methods for output-only modal analysis of mechanical structures. Two types of implementation are available: the covariance-driven (SSI-cov) implementation and the data-driven (SSI-data) implementation [7]. The second type was applied for the output-only system identification of several aerolastic systems representing the full free-flying flexible aircraft or wind tunnel model as presented in [9] and [10].

In section 2 of this paper the flight test instrumentation is introduced in detail, followed by the discussion of the flight test results recorded for the sequence of deployment and retraction of the aircraft landing gear in section 3. In section 4 a short introduction of the theory behind the SSI-method is given, while the examples of the response signals measured on the MLG doors are analysed in section 5.

2. REQUIREMENTS FOR FLIGHT TEST INSTRUMENTATION

To fully understand the aircraft undercarriage phenomena, the measurement of the current position of NLG as vortex shedding generator, the deflection angle of MLG doors, unsteady aerodynamic loads on the MLG doors and the vibration level response were requested by the simulation experts for code validation. Supplementary, a camera with high frame rate has recorded the MLG and doors during transit. The final Flight Test Instrumentation FTI comprises the following installations:

- position measurement of the NLG leg via travel sensors (string potentiometer) to record the piston stroke at the NLG actuator (see Figure 3), which is a measure for NLG position,
- position measurement of both MLG doors via string potentiometer at hydraulic actuator,
- total load measurement of the applied load on each LG door via strain gauges at control rods of NLG + MLG doors (see Figure 4),
- vibration level measurement via accelerometers on MLG doors: 3x tri-axial, 1x bi-axial, 1x uni-axial sensors (see Figure 5),
- aerodynamic load measurement: via pressure transducers on in-/outboard surface of left-hand MLG door (see Figure 6).
- vibration level measurement via accelerometers on NLG doors: 4x uni-axial.

Figure 3. Travel sensor attached to NLG actuator

Figure 4. Strain gauge at MLG actuator

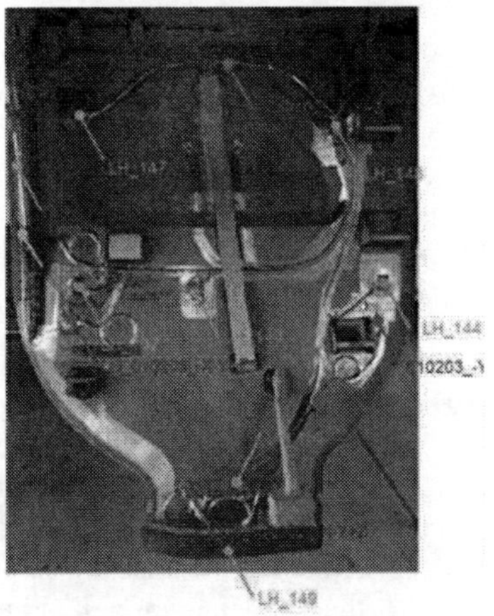

Figure 5. Accelerometers (red) and pressure transducers (blue) on left-hand MLG door inside

Figure 6. Pressure transducers (blue) on left-hand MLG door outside

All sensors were glued to the aircraft surface with two component epoxy adhesive, which is gap filling and durable down to low temperatures (-55°C). For simple removal of the parts the aircraft part surface was protected with aluminium foil tape. All outboard cables were glued to the aircraft surface with such tape.

2.1. Data Acquisition System

The signals of all different types of sensors must be acquired and logged simultaneously to computer hard disc to process the correlations between the aerodynamic vortex excitation and the acceleration response of the doors. Furthermore, the functionality of continuous online-monitoring of the acceleration response was mandatory to make sure that certain response levels are not exceeded during flight.

The available basic DAQ-system in the ATRA has capabilities to record a number of different types of data signals. Since it is installed in the cabin, such a configuration would mean, that all wiring must be routed from outside to the pressurized interior cabin. More than 100 wires would pass a sealed interface located in the fuselage bottom in the MLG bay. To avoid such an elaborate installation it was searched for an alternative, where the DAQ-system with signal conditioning and A/D-converters is installed outside of the cabin in the MLG bay. Using such a distributed setup, just the power supply and the network connection need to be routed into the cabin, where the system is controlled via a commercial mobile PC recording the data to hard disk. According to airworthiness specifications simplified verification can be applied for attachment of external masses in fuselage area if the total weight limit is below 10kg. The mounting of such device must bear a load factor of 10g, which results to 1kN limit load which might be introduced to the local airframe structure.

The distributed setup of the measurement units running outside the pressurized cabin required an especially robust system, reliably working at low temperatures < -50°C and low air pressure in high flight altitudes. The selected National Instruments CompactDAQ system, which is very compact and allows online access to the time data, is specified by the manufacturer only up to an altitude of 5000m and a temperature down to -40°C. This limited specification required an additional climatic chamber test in which the requirements of the flight profile were simulated, as it would occur during the targeted flight tests. During this chamber test, the measuring system together with the sensors was exposed to a pressure of less than 250 mbar, which simulated an altitude of approx. 11500 m and a temperature of below -50°C. The measurement system worked perfectly during this 3h test and showed no drifts in the measured signals, no errors or any failure.

The complete setup of the distributed measuring system shown in Figure 7 consists of two individual National Instruments chassis of type NI-cDAQ-9188XT. Each contains eight adaptable signal conditioning modules to support the need of the different sensor types. Both were covered by a rugged protective aluminum case box, which was attached on the keel beam of the aircraft in the MLG bay (see Figure 8). The total weight of this LoadDAQ-box is 9.5 kg, while the voltage power supply is 28V. This cabin outboard installation permits considerable shortening of the analog signal routing, which improves the signal to noise ratio and reduces the electromagnetic susceptibility from radio emission of the different communication antennas. A further request for the flight test qualification was a check of electromagnetic compatibility in an EMC chamber and later in the installed state on the entire aircraft.

The architecture of the DAQ-network consists of a central DAQ-PC, which is connected to the local aircraft network and records the data from the two NI-cDAQ chassis with sample rate of 2kHz and synchronously the flight condition parameters comprising flight speed, Mach number, flight altitude, static pressure, angle of attack, yaw angle and other made available by the basic aircraft DAQ-system. This main DAQ-PC distributes these data in the local network, so that further online evaluation and processing can be performed with additional PCs connected to the local network. In Figure 9 the architecture is depicted. The NI cDAQ-chassis are filled with the following conditioned I/O modules:

- 2x NI 9469 - synchronization of chassis,
- 8x NI 9234 – acceleration with IEPE-signal conditioning +/-5V, 4 channels per module,
- 3x NI 9234 – pressure transducer, +/-5V, IEPE disabled, 4 channels per module,

- 2x NI 9237 – +/-25mV/V full bridge analog input with 10V internal excitation,
- 1x NI 9239 – ±10 V simultaneous analog input for travel sensor, 4 channels per module.

Figure 10 shows the electrical block diagram of the FTI, where the three cable-line connection from MLG bay into cabin is indicated. The connection between MLG and NLG bay comprises several sensor cables.

Figure 7. LoadDAQ box equipped with two NI-cDAQ-9188XT

Figure 8. LoadDAQ box installed on the aircraft keel beam in the MLG bay.

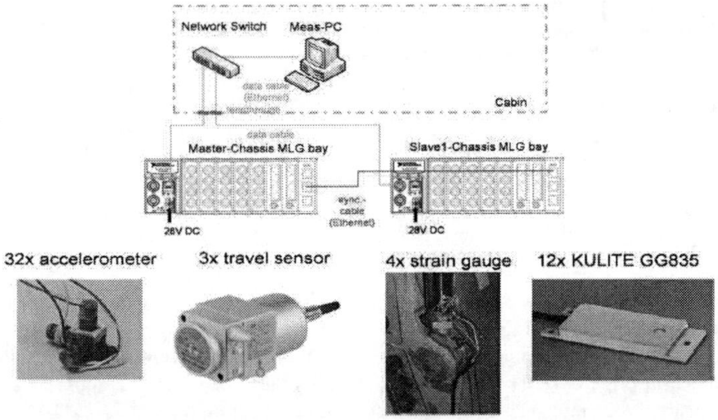

Figure 9. LoadDAQ-System with different sensor types.

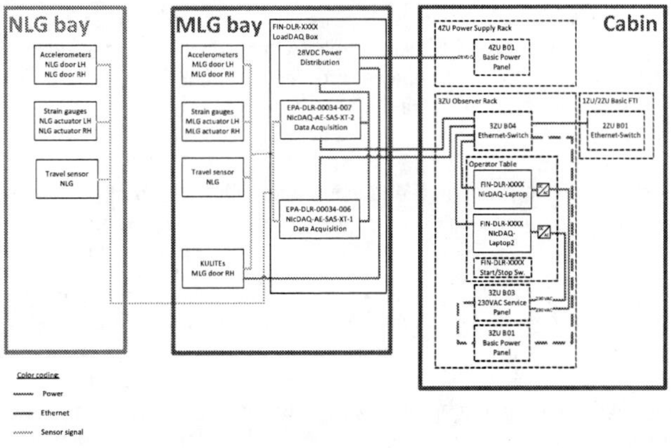

Figure 10. Electrical block diagram of distributed DAQ.

2.2. Data Acquisition Software

The software to control the measurement system and to acquire the signals is developed with NI LabVIEW 2016. Both NI-cDAQ chassis must be synchronized and all channels must be pre-defined with particular signal conditioning settings. Further, an infrastructure of network-streams is installed to continuously feed several analysis-computers connected to the network with live-data.

The basic data acquisition system of the aircraft supplies the current flight parameters via an additional network stream. These data are collected and stored synchronously with all measurements on the undercarriage.

2.3. Qualification for Flight Test

To guarantee a safe performance of the test flight, the German Aerospace Centre (DLR) operates an aero-technical Design Organisation (DO) to conduct research activities for customers. That comprises the development and supplemental type certification of interior and exterior test equipment / attachments or modifications in compliance with applicable airworthiness requirements CS-25 published by the European Aviation Safety Agency (EASA). The capabilities of the DO are the indispensable prerequisite for the efficient operation of the DLR aircraft fleet. In case of the actual FTI installation on the undercarriage the staff generated compliance reports for electrical structural and aerolastic substantiation. In so-called Special Instructions (SI) the installation procedure is written down step by step, so that the technical staff can follow the instructions and guarantee a qualified installation of the test equipment.

3. FLIGHT TEST RESULTS

The flight test matrix contains several test points at low and high flight speeds between 160kts and 250kts flying different angles of attack and yaw angles. Finally, a database was filled with experimental flight test results, which serves as the validation reference for the high-precision CFD-simulation tools to predict unsteady aerodynamic phenomena as well as the dynamic response of the aircraft undercarriage.

In Figure 11 flight test results are plotted for the deployment sequence of the landing gear at maximum speed of 250kts. The first diagram shows the deflection angles of NLG leg and left-hand MLG door and the total load applied on the door (blue curve) and measured via the strain gauge glued on the actuator rod (Figure 4). The second row contains the accelerations (Figure 5) and the bottom shows the measured pressures on outside and inside surface (Figure 6).

The course of the overall load measured by the actuator strain gauge needs some explanation. In the beginning, when the door is closed, the actuator pulls the door against the locking device. This avoids the dropping of the door caused by its own weight, when the locker is suddenly released. At this moment the pulling force is reduced to almost zero and the door opens first by its weight and later when there is gap between door and fuselage bottom by the aerodynamic lifting forces with tendency to open. When the door is fully deployed – sequence C –, the MLG starts to swing and passes the door. Due to the expulsion of the landing gear wheels additional aerodynamic loading is generated, which pulls the door into the stops. At half deflection angle the force is at its maximum – sequence E. Dynamic loads caused by the vibration occur on top of this static condition. At the end – sequence G – the door is closed, the actuator pulls against the locker again, while the landing gear is deployed.

Similarly, the impact of the NLG as vortex shedding generator can be observed from the comparison of the acceleration level at sequence C, when all doors are open but the NLG is still in the bay, and at sequence F, when the NLG is down. The same interrelation is observed in the retraction sequence between B and E in Figure 12. Here, the maximum speed is limited to 220kts due to the flight manual, which results in slightly lower maximum total loads in the actuator.

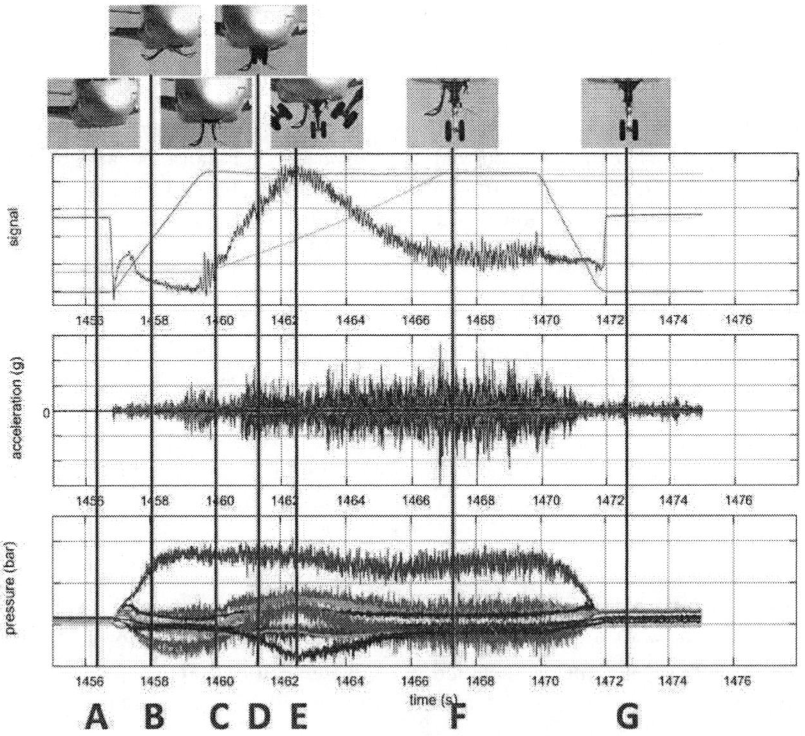

Figure 11. Deployment of LG, acceleration and pressures on left-hand MLG door at 250kts

Figure 12. Retraction of LG, acceleration and pressures on left-hand MLG door at 220kts

4. STOCHASTIC SUBSPACE IDENTIFICATION

The general mathematical modelling procedure linearizes the full nonlinear aeroelastic system about its operating point, which comprises current flight speed, flight altitude and trimmed condition including static deformation due to the lifting forces. The linearization routines can be used to develop both a first- and a second-order linearized representation. The complete nonlinear aeroelastic equations of motion can be written with following dependencies:

$$\left[M\left(\{q\},\{u\},t\right)\right]\{\ddot{q}\}+\left\{f\left(\{q\},\{\dot{q}\},\{u\},t\right)\right\}=0\,. \tag{1}$$

where $[M]$ is the mass matrix, $\{f\}$ is the nonlinear forcing function vector, $\{q\}$ is the vector of displacements, $\{u\}$ is the vector of control inputs, and t is time. Numerically, linearization perturbs all system variables about their respective operating point values. So, the displacement, velocity, and acceleration perturbation vectors are replaced with the first-order state vector and state derivative vector, in order to determine the first-order representation of the linear time-invariant (LTI)-system:

$$\{x\}=\begin{Bmatrix}\Delta q\\ \Delta\dot{q}\end{Bmatrix},\ \{\dot{x}\}=\begin{Bmatrix}\Delta\dot{q}\\ \Delta\ddot{q}\end{Bmatrix}\ \Rightarrow\ \begin{matrix}\{\dot{x}\}=[A_c]\{x\}+[B_c]\{\Delta u\}\\ \{y\}=[C]\{x\}+[D]\{\Delta u\}\end{matrix}\ . \tag{2}$$

If the time sampling step Δt is fixed, the continuous state-space model in Eq. (2) can be discretized in time, where k is the index of the time steps. While the inputs $\{u\}_k$ are unknown, the outputs $\{y\}_k$ can be measured, e.g. with accelerometers installed at adequate positions on the airframe. The LTI-system of Eq. (2) can now be converted from continuous-time to discrete-time domain by introducing the matrix exponential:

$$\begin{matrix}\{x\}_{k+1}=[A]\{x\}_k+\{w\},\quad with\ \ [A]=e^{[A_c](\Delta t)}\\ \{y\}_k=[C]\{x\}_k+\{v\}\end{matrix}\ . \tag{3}$$

The unknown exciting input terms $\{v\}$ and $\{w\}$ are assumed to be of stochastic type with discrete white noise nature and an expected value equal to zero. For application of the data-driven SSI, first the recorded output data samples are grouped in the so-called *Hankel*-matrix:

$$[Y]=\begin{bmatrix}[Y_p]\\ [Y_f]\end{bmatrix}=\begin{bmatrix}\{y\}_1 & \{y\}_2 & \{y\}_3 & \cdots & \{y\}_{N-2q}\\ \vdots & \vdots & \vdots & \ddots & \vdots\\ \{y\}_{2q} & \{y\}_{2q+1} & \{y\}_{2q+2} & \cdots & \{y\}_N\end{bmatrix}. \tag{4}$$

Each $\{y\}_k$ contains all acceleration repsonses at one certain point in time. The first subset with subscript p expresses the past information and f expresses the future, which has to be projected by the LTI-system in Eq. (3). The subscript q expresses the number of time increments to be used in the analysis, which needs to be pre-selected by the user. N represents the total number of acquired samples.

The first step is the orthogonal-triangular decomposition (QR-decomposition) of the Hankel-matrix. Then, the so-called system observability matrix is approximated by singular value decomposition (SVD) of the covariance submatrix between past and future. The dominating part determines the rank of the subspace representing the relevant dynamic system response, while the insignificant part contains the measurement noise. The observability matrix is truncated at the user-selected model order:

$$\begin{bmatrix}[Y_p]\\ [Y_f]\end{bmatrix}=\begin{bmatrix}[L_{11}] & 0\\ [L_{21}] & [L_{22}]\end{bmatrix}\begin{bmatrix}[Q_1]\\ [Q_2]\end{bmatrix}\ \Rightarrow\ [L_{21}]=\begin{bmatrix}[U_1] & [U_2]\end{bmatrix}\begin{bmatrix}[S_1] & \\ & [S_2]\end{bmatrix}\begin{bmatrix}[V_1]^T\\ [V_2]^T\end{bmatrix}\ \Rightarrow\ [O]=[U_1][S_1]^{1/2}. \tag{5}$$

The system matrix $[A]$ is now calculated via least-squares solution, while the output matrix $[C]$ is represented by the first block row of the observability matrix $[O]$:

$$[A]=[O_1]^{\dagger}[O_2],[O_1]=\begin{bmatrix}[C]\\ [C][A]\\ \vdots\\ [C][A]^{p-1}\end{bmatrix},[O_2]=\begin{bmatrix}[C][A]\\ [C][A]^2\\ \vdots\\ [C][A]^{p}\end{bmatrix}, \quad (6)$$

where † denotes the Moore–Penrose pseudo-inverse. The modal parameters of the system are found by performing eigenvalue decomposition of the identified system matrix $[A]$ from Eq. (6). This leads to the discrete-time system poles μ_i with corresponding eigenvectors $\{\psi\}_i$. The damped natural frequencies and damping ratios are calculated from the re-transferred continuous-time system poles:

$$f_i=\frac{\mathrm{Im}(\lambda_i)}{2\pi},\quad \zeta_i=-\frac{\mathrm{Re}(\lambda_i)}{|\lambda_i|},\quad \text{with}\quad \lambda_i=\frac{\ln(\mu_i)}{\Delta t},\quad \text{and}\quad \{\phi\}_i=[C]\{\psi\}_i. \quad (7)$$

All applied mathematical functions - QR-decomposition, SVD-decomposition and eigenvalue-decomposition - are standard matrix algebra routines, which are available from most mathematical software libraries. An introduction in signal processing and vibration analysis is given in [7].

There are a number of reasons why the SSI does not yield the exact system matrices $[A]$ and $[C]$, but only estimates :

- Due to the finite number of data samples N, the output covariance matrices cannot be calculated exactly, but only approximated by an estimate.
- The unmeasured inputs and the output measurement noise may not be white noise vectors.
- Due to the limited resolution of the A/D-conversion during the data acquisition, there might round-off errors in the recorded data samples.
- Because all real structures are to some extent nonlinear, nonlinear distortions that are not negligible might be present in the data.
- Since the system order must be chosen in advance, its value might be chosen too low or too high.

4.1. Stabilization Diagram

Traditionally, modal parameters are extracted for a series of increasing model orders up to an over-estimation of the system and the parameters obtained at each order are compared with the ones obtained at the previous order in the stabilization diagram. The model order is related to the number of retained singular values in the approximation of the subspace matrix in Eq. (5). In order to automatize this procedure is to evaluate the deviation of eigen frequencies, damping's and mode shapes over model order. The MACXP criteria, proposed by [12], expands the well-known Modal Assurance Criteria MAC by a pole-weighting, which takes the deviation of real and imaginary parts of the poles as additional weighting on the correlation of two compared mode shapes.

$$MACXP(\phi_i,\phi_j)=\frac{\left(\dfrac{|\phi_i^*\phi_j|}{|\overline{\lambda}_i+\lambda_j|}+\dfrac{|\phi_i^T\phi_j|}{|\lambda_i+\lambda_j|}\right)^2}{\left(\dfrac{\phi_i^*\phi_i}{2|\mathrm{Re}\,\lambda_i|}+\dfrac{|\phi_i^T\phi_i|}{2|\lambda_i|}\right)\left(\dfrac{\phi_j^*\phi_j}{2|\mathrm{Re}\,\lambda_j|}+\dfrac{|\phi_j^T\phi_j|}{2|\lambda_j|}\right)} \quad (8)$$

The MACXP can be interpreted in terms of the correlation function between the real decay responses associated to two modes.

In practice, the SSI procedure is applied for decreasing truncation order of the SVD in Eq. (5) starting from the user pre-selected maximum system order towards lower orders. The MACXP is evaluated for all identified poles and modes of two successive orders. If a correlation factor occurs higher than a given threshold, then both modes are tracked from the higher model order to the lower one. This procedure is repeated for several model orders to get a robust correlation of the physical poles and modes. Here, the Fast Multi-Order SSI Algorithm 2 procedure from reference [8] is exploited, where the LQ-decomposition and the SVD of Eq. (5) is performed only once for the highest model order. Then the least square problem of Eq. (6) can be solved for each model order.

5. OPERATIONAL MODAL ANALYSIS OF FLIGHT TEST RESULTS

For the identification of the modal parameters of the deployed MLG doors the acceleration measurements are evaluated. To ensure that the boundary conditions are constant, the time series to be analysed must limited to the sequence, where the maximum deflection angle is reached, which is measured via the travel sensors. The sequences can be identified from sequences between section C and F in Figure 11 and B and E in Figure 12, which offers the functionality for automatic evaluation. On the other hand the length of the sequence is only 10 seconds, which might introduce some uncertainty in the modal parameters.

As an example Figure 13 shows the window of time data to be analysed for a test point with door opening at flight speed V = 160kts, the resulting stabilization diagram of the identified poles and below the identified mode shapes. Some clear stabilized modes can be identified between 4-100 Hz, while there are also some spurious poles. In detail both left and right hand rigid body modes of the doors are found at f1 Hz and f2 Hz being f1~<f2 Hz, which have a slightly deviation in frequency that may be due to difference of the hydraulic actuators representing a non-linear spring stiffness and or very small aircraft yaw angle. Next there is in-plane bending at 2.65*f1 and 2.52*f2, respectively, and a torsion mode at 4.12*f1. The bending of the doors is identified at 5.69*f1 and 5.36*f2.

The results for flight speed V = 250kts are presented in Figure 14. Due to the increased dynamic pressure the vorticity and turbulence level is higher, which results in increased acceleration response levels on the doors. All basic mode shapes can be identified as in the 160kts case. For the rigid body mode the eigen frequencies are slightly increased caused by the unsteady aerodynamic loading at higher dynamic pressure. It is noticeable, that a new cluster of poles are identified between 7.1*f1-8.1*f1 Hz appears, which might be the result of a changed spectral contents of the vorticity exciting the doors. The assumption of white noise excitation seems not to be fully valid anymore.

6. CONCLUSIONS

The paper presents the preparation, execution and research scope of the AFLoNext flight test campaign dedicated to vibration measurements on the undercarriage of a transport aircraft, where the operational modal analysis is applied to identify the modal parameters of deployed Main Landing Gear Doors, which is an essential information for the dynamic loads analysis and for calibration of numerical simulation tools.

The suitability of the inexpensive NI-cDAQ measuring system for airborne test conditions has been successfully demonstrated during the flight test campaign under real conditions installed in the MLG bay, where the measuring system worked without any failure. The experimental flight test results will serve as a validation database for the upcoming new prediction numerical methods.

The operational modal analysis of the instrumented MLG doors is demonstrated with application of the Stochastic Subspace Identification method. In spite of the fact that the measuring time, while the doors are fully deployed, is very short, the identified modal parameters show reliable trends. On the other hand, output-only analysis might be the only chance to get modal results in the presented type of in-flight application.

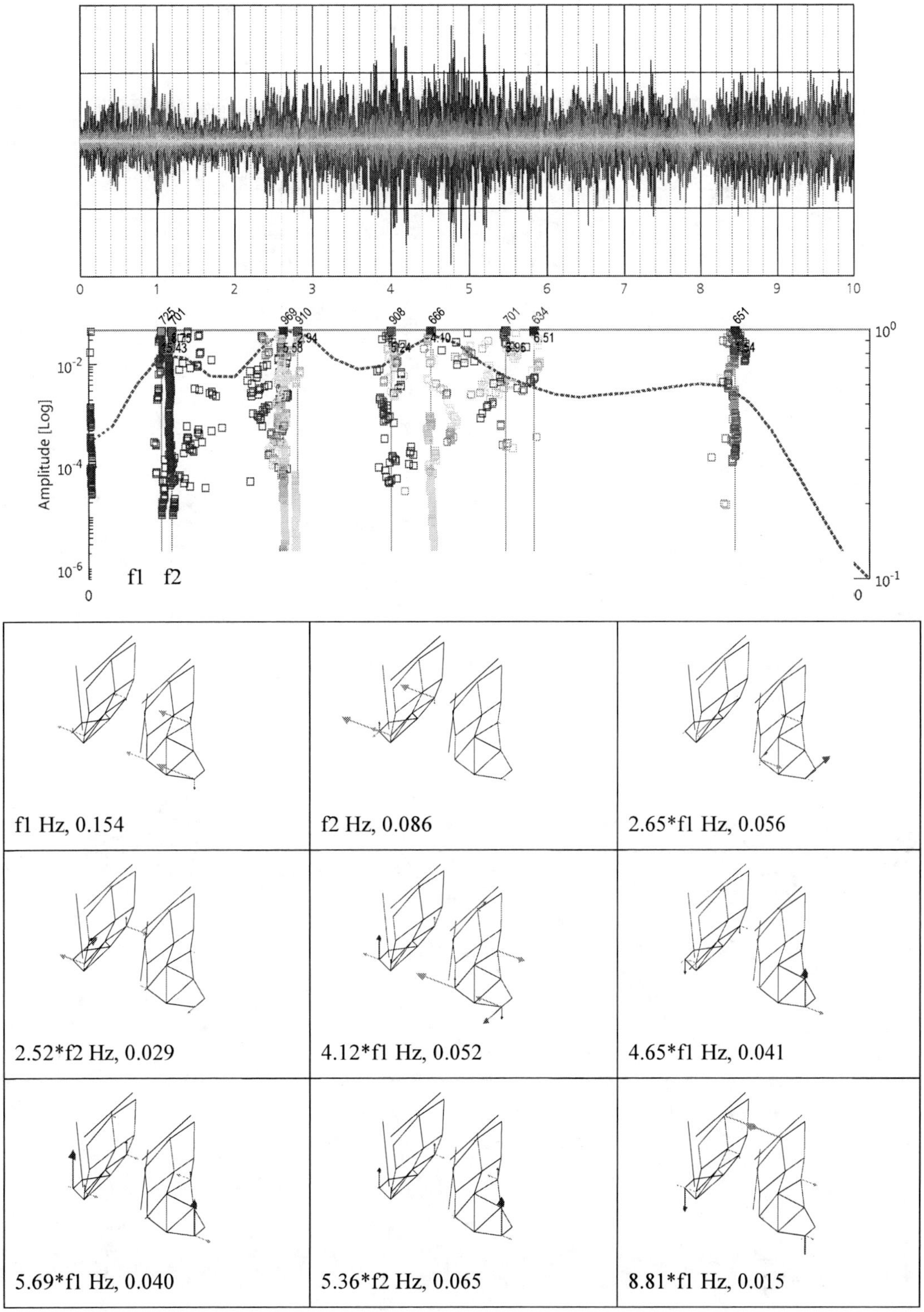

Figure 13. Door opening TP4 V=160kts, accelaration data, stabilzation diagram, and identified modes

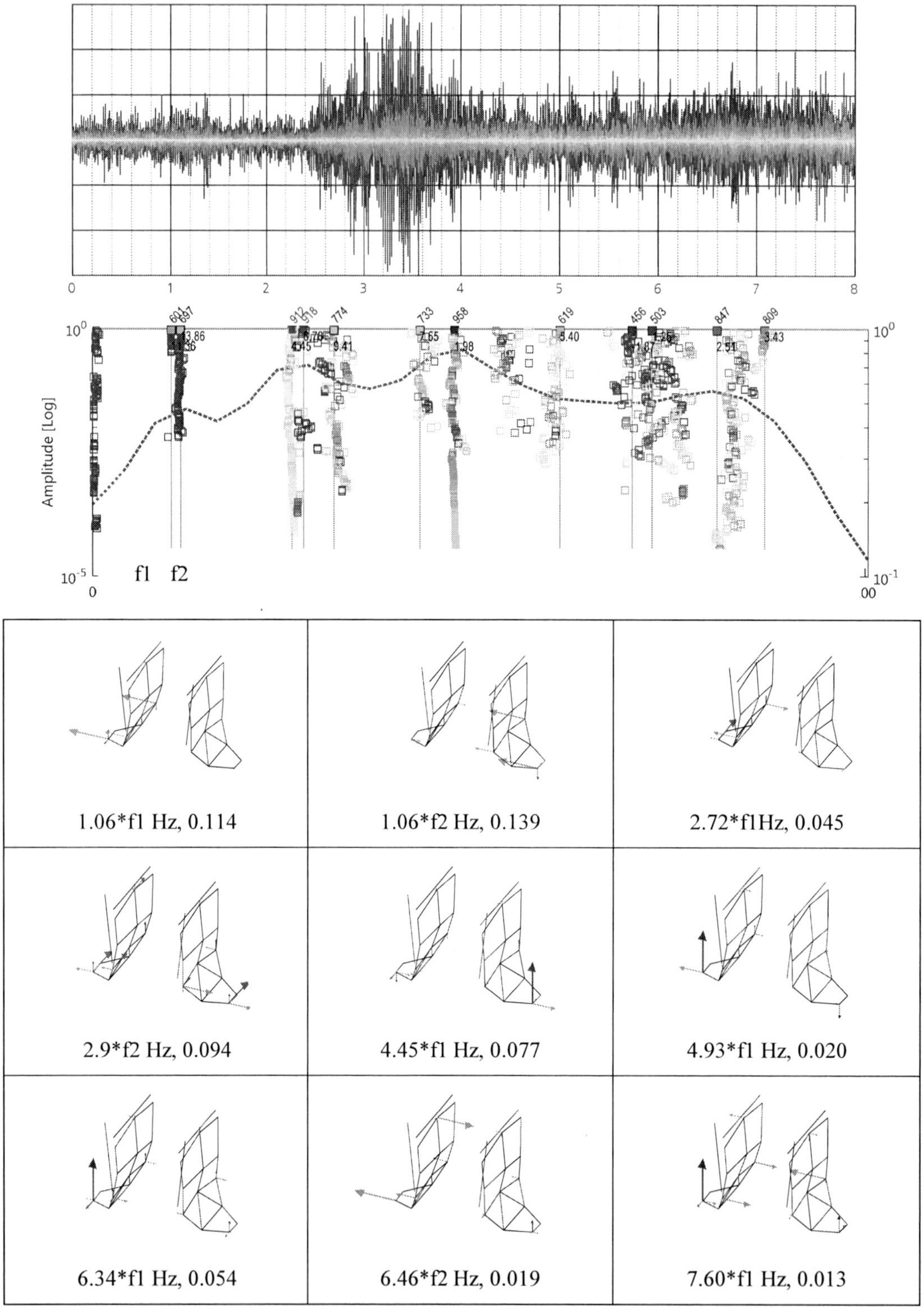

Figure 14. Door opening TP16 V=250kts, accelaration data, stabilzation diagram, and identified modes

ACKNOWLEDGMENTS

The authors would like to thank all partners involved in the AFLoNext Project and the DLR Flight Experiments Department in Braunschweig, Germany. Furthermore, the funding of the AFLoNext flight tests by the European Union within FP7 is gratefully acknowledged.

REFERENCES

[1] Shia-Hui Peng, Adam Jirasek, Mats Dalenbring, and Peter Eliasson (2016). Aerodynamic Excitation on MLG Door Exposed to Vortices Emanating from NLG of an Aircraft Model, 34th AIAA Applied Aerodynamics Conference, AIAA AVIATION Forum, (AIAA 2016-4043) https://doi.org/10.2514/6.2016-4043.

[2] Abarca-Lopez, R., Schwochow, J. (2018). Overview of AFLoNext flight testing on landing gear doors using vibration mitigation devices. AFLoNext final conference at ILA Berlin 2018, 26.-27.Apr. 2018, Berlin.

[3] Schwochow, J., Sinske, J., Buchbach, R. (2018). Inflight-Measurements of Aircraft Undercarriage Vibration during Deployment. In: ettc2018 - proceedings, Seite 54. AMA Service GmbH. ettc2018 - European Test and Telemetry Conference 2018, 26.-28.Jun. 2018, Nürnberg. ISBN 978-3-9816876-8-2.

[4] www.aflonext.eu

[5] http://www.dlr.de/fb/en/

[6] Ho, B.L., Kalman, R.E. (1966). Effective Construction of linear State-Variable Models from Input/Output functions. Regelungstechnik, vol. 14, no. 12, pp. 545-548.

[7] Van Overschee, P., De Moor, B. (1996), Subspace Identifcation for Linear Systems: Theory, Implementation and Applications, Kluwer Academic Publishers.

[8] Doehler, M., Mevel, L. (2010). Fast Multi-Order Stochastic Subspace Identification. INRIA Research Report RR-7429, 2010. <inria-00527484>.

[9] Schwochow, J., Jelicic, G (2015). Automatic Operational Modal Analysis for Aeroelastic Applications. 6th International Operational Modal Analysis Conference IOMAC, 12-14 May, Gijón, Spain.

[10] Böswald, M., Schwochow, J., Jelicic, G., Govers, Y. (2017). New Concepts for Ground and Flight Vibration Testing of Aircraft based on Output-Only Modal Analysis. 7th International Operational Modal Analysis Conference IOMAC, 10-12 May, Ingolstadt, Germany.

[11] http://www.ni.com/documentation/en/compactdaq-chassis/latest/cdaq-9188/specs/

[12] Vacher, P., Jacquier, A., Bucharles, A. (2010). Extensions of the MAC criterion to complex modes. In Proceedings of ISMA 2010.

IOMAC'19

8th International Operational Modal Analysis Conference
2019 May13-15 Copenhagen

OPERATIONAL MODAL ANALYSIS OF ULTRA-PRECISION MACHINE TOOL USING QUEFRENCY LIFTERING

Xingzhan Li[1], *and Xiaobin Yue*[2]

[1] Research engineer, Institute of Mechanical Manufacturing Technology, China Academy of Engineering Physics, 596 Yinhe RD, Chengdu, PR China, li_xingzhan@126.com.
[2] Research Professor, Institute of Mechanical Manufacturing Technology, China Academy of Engineering Physics, 64 Mianshan RD, Mianyang, PR China, yuexbin@sohu.com.

ABSTRACT

Dynamic properties of ultra-precision machine tool have a great influence to the cutting quality. Vibration of machine tool is transmitted to the machined surface during machining process. However, due to the complex structure and the dynamic effects of machining process, it is difficult to get enough modal parameters using experimental modal analysis. This paper adopts a quefrency liftering based method to identify the modal parameters of ultra-precision machine tool during machining process. First, quefrency liftering using real cepstrum is utilized to remove the harmonics caused by the spindle. Then, frequency spatial domain decomposition is applied to extract modal parameters using the filtered responses. The method is applied for operational modal analysis of an ultra-precision machine tool. The results of low frequency are compared with that of experimental modal analysis to validate the method. And, the results of high frequency are used to trace the source of machined surface waviness.

Keywords: Operational modal analysis, Machine tool, Quefrency liftering, FSDD, Surface waviness

1. INTRODUCTION

In the manufacturing industry, the dynamic properties of machine tool affect the surface quality and cutting stability. The classical technique used for estimating the modal properties of machine tool is experimental modal analysis (EMA). While, in the application of EMA, there are some problem for the structural health monitoring of ultra-precision machine tool. First, the dynamic properties may change with the working position and machine speed [1]. Since the input cannot always be recorded, EMA based on frequency response functions isn't suited for some scenarios. Second, the high order modal parameters are difficult to achieve for EMA method. The excitation of high order modal using impact hammer is hard. And, since the structure of machine tool is very complex, there are too many modes to identify exactly for high frequency band.

Operational modal analysis (OMA) has been applied to machine tool in the past 10 years [2, 3]. Based on the response during the machine process, the dynamic properties can be evaluated using different algorithms. The current study adopts the frequency spatial domain decomposition (FSDD) method [4] to identify the modal parameters of ultra-precision fly cutting machine tool. A quefrency liftering method using real cepstrum is utilized to remove the harmonics caused by the spindle and cutting force. And, the result of high order modes is used to trace the source of machined surface waviness.

2. THEORY AND APPLICATION

2.1. Quefrency liftering

To eliminate the influence of harmonic caused by spindle, quefrency liftering method using cepstrum is utilized. The complex cepstrum is defined as the inverse Fourier transform of the complex logarithm of the complex spectrum of a time signal

$$C(\tau) = \mathcal{F}^{-1}\{log(F(f))\} = \mathcal{F}^{-1}\{ln(A(f)) + j\phi(f)\} \tag{1}$$

where

$$F(f) = \mathcal{F}\{f(t)\} = A(f)e^{j\phi(f)} \tag{2}$$

is terms of the amplitude and phase of the spectrum.

Setting the phase term in Eq. (1) to zero, the real cepstrum can be obtained as

$$C_r(\tau) = \mathcal{F}^{-1}\{log(|F(f)|)\} = \mathcal{F}^{-1}\{ln(A(f))\} \tag{3}$$

The complex cepstrum contains the phase information from the spectrum allowing reconstruction of the signal in the time domain, while the real cepstrum allows only reconstruction of the power spectrum.

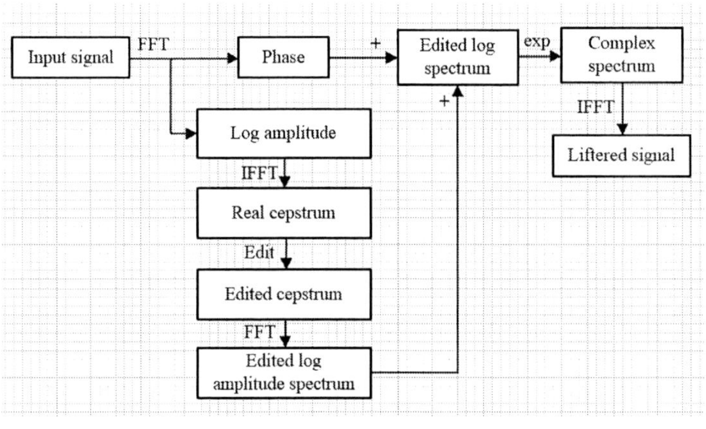

Figure 1. Flow chart of quefrency liftering using cepstrum [3].

The cepstrum can transform families of sidebands in the spectrum into several rahmonics of peaks in the quefrency domain. Therefore, by removing the rahmonics from the cepstrum, the families of peaks can be removed from the spectrum. Based on this idea, a method was proposed by Randall [3]. The flow chart of quefrency liftering using cepstrum is shown in Figure 1. First, keep the phase of the Fourier transform of original signal, and calculate the real cepstrum. Then, use the exponential window to lifter the real cepstrum in quefrency domain. Finally, the liftered time signal can be obtained by combining the original phase and edited log spectrum.

2.2. OMA of ultra-precision machine tool

Using the liftered time signal, the FSDD method is applied in the OMA of ultra-precision fly cutting machine tool. Figure 2 shows the test setup during the machine process. The accelerometers are used to record the responses on the work table. And the dynamometer under the workpiece is used to record the cutting force of three directions. Two cases are considered here. In the case 1, the workpiece is circular, while it is square in the case 2.

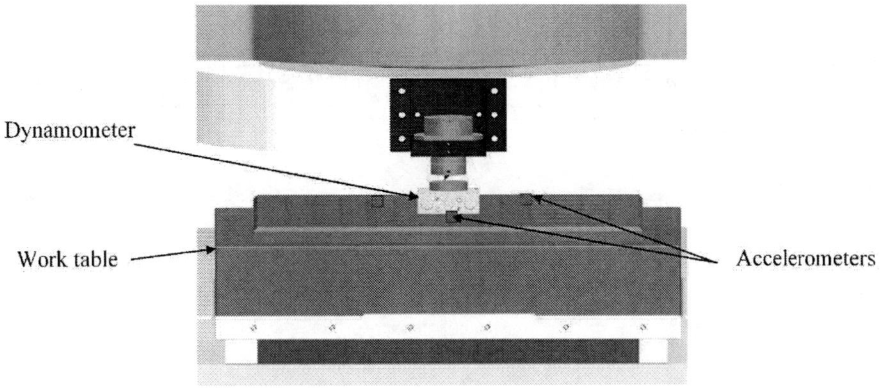

Figure 2. Test setup of ultra-precision machine tool during machine process.

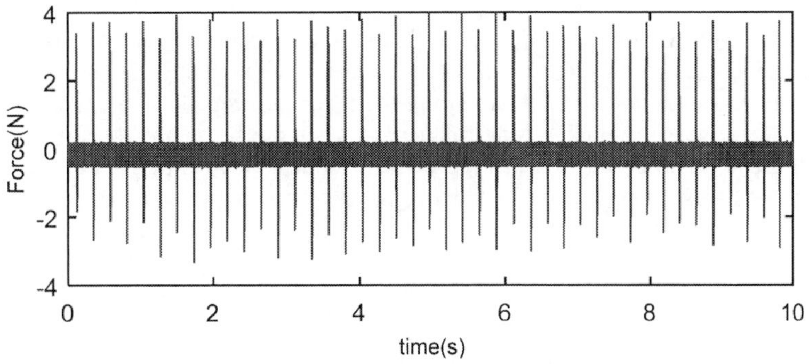

Figure 3. Cutting force of z direction.

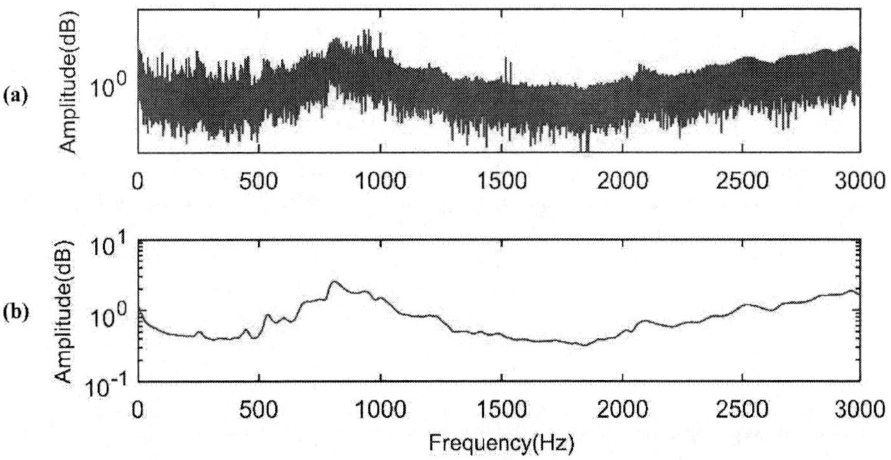

Figure 4. Spectrum of time domain signals: (a) Original signal, (b) Liftered signal.

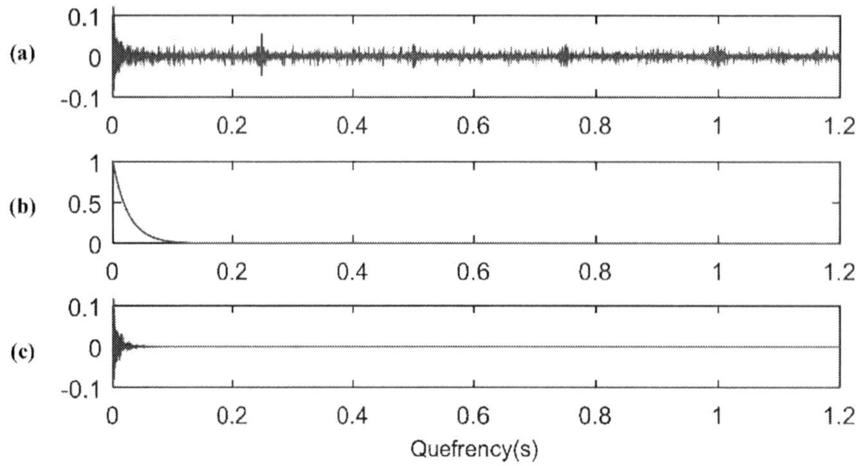

Figure 5. Cepstrum of time domain signals: (a) Original signal, (b) Exponential lifter, (c) Liftered signal.

Figure 3 shows the cutting force of Z direction. Due to the special interrupted cutting process of fly cutting machine tool, the cutting force has a same frequency with the spindle speed, which means the input of the machine tool is nonwhite noise during the machine process. Thus, in the Figure 4(a), the spectrum of original response signal has the frequency of spindle speed and its harmonic components. Liftering the original signal by method in Figure 1, the result is shown in Figure 4(b). It can be seen that the synchronous components of the original signal has been removed clearly. Figure 5 shows the process of the quefrency liftering. The original signal is transformed into cepstrum in Figure 5(a). There are several rahmonics of peaks in quefrency domain. Then, build an exponential window in Figure 5(b), and use this window to lifter the original cepstrum signal. The liftered signal in quefrency domain is shown in Figure 5(c). It can be seen that the rahmonics are removed. Transforming this signal back into the time domain, the liftered time signal can be obtained.

Table 1. Comparison between OMA and EMA results.

Mode	1	2	3	4	5	6	7	8	9
OMA results of case 1 (Hz)	10.78	74.53	259.5	342.8	448.9	534.4	680.3	795.8	917.2
OMA results of case 2 (Hz)	10.78	76.56	259.2	345.5	444.7	533.4	678.8	790.9	922.7
EMA results (Hz)	10.22	74.89	258.7	345.5	444.6	531.0	670.2	795.6	921.3

Based on these liftered time responses, the FSDD method is applied for the two cases. Table 1 shows the OMA results. Nine modal frequencies are identified during the 0-1000 Hz using OMA. For the case 1 and case 2, the result is very close. And, comparing with the results of EMA using impact hammer, it can be seen that the first nine modal frequencies are identified exactly using this OMA method. It should be pointed out that there are 27 modal frequencies during 0-1000 Hz from the EMA. Except the 9 frequencies shown in Table 1, the other modal frequencies are not excited during the machine process. In fact, in the structural health monitoring or dynamic analysis of machine tool, not all the modal frequencies can be excited, and the excited modes is more important than the other modes.

2.3. Source identification of surface waviness

Vibration of machine tool is transmitted to the machined surface during machining process. Thus, it is very important to identify the vibration source during the machine process. Considering the spatial frequency characteristic of the surface waviness, the dynamic properties of high frequency is needed. Follow the procedure of OMA above, identify the modal frequencies of work table during 1000-3000 Hz. Then, measure the surface topography of the finished surface. As shown in Figure 6, the section profile along the cutting direction is obtained from the 3D surface topography. Finally, analyse the characteristic frequency of profile and compared with the modal frequencies of the machine tool. The result shown in Figure 7 indicates that the maximum amplitude of surface waviness stems from one modal frequencies of cross beam of the fly cutting machine tool.

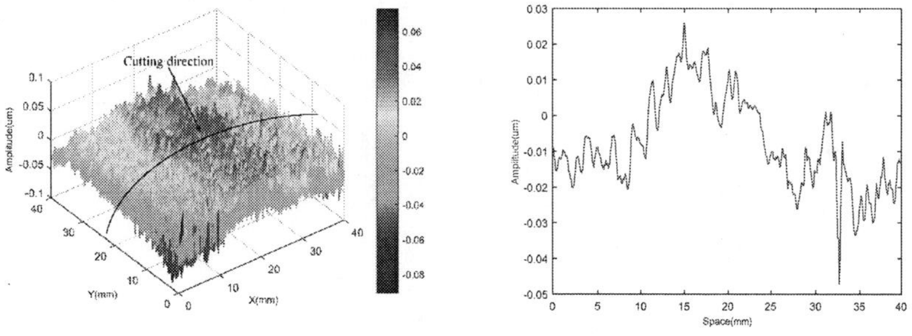

Figure 6. Test result: (left) 3D Surface topography, (right) Section profile along cutting direction.

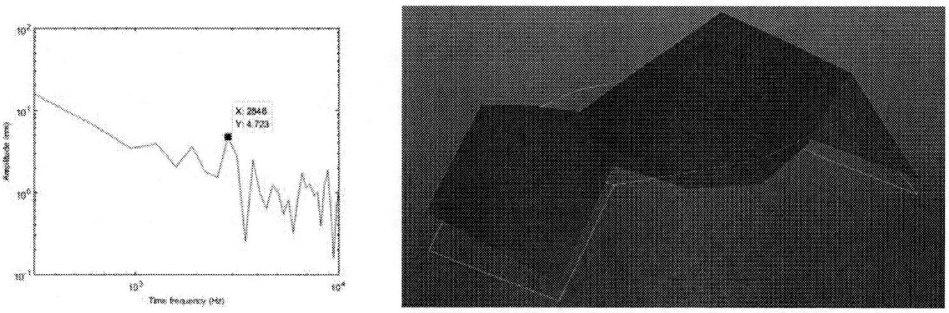

Figure 7. Comparison result: (left) Spatial frequency domain analysis of section profile, (right) Mode shape of cross beam at 2895 Hz.

3. CONCLUSIONS

The OMA method using quefrency liftering is applied in dynamic analysis and vibration source identification of ultra-precision fly cutting machine tool. The test result shows that the modal frequencies can be identified exactly and the vibration source can be confirmed.

ACKNOWLEDGEMENTS

This work was supported by Science Challenge Project (No. TZ2018006-0102), and National Natural Science Foundation of China (Grant No. 11802279).

REFERENCES

[1] Li, B. , Luo, B. , Mao, X. , Cai, H. , Peng, F. , & Liu, H. . (2013). A new approach to identifying the dynamic behavior of CNC machine tools with respect to different worktable feed speeds. *International Journal of Machine Tools and Manufacture*, 72(Complete), 73-84.

[2] Lamraoui, M., El Badaoui, M., & Guilleti, F. (2016). Chatter stability prediction for CNC machine tool in operating condition through operational modal analysis. *Mechanics & Industry*, 17(4), 402.

[3] Randall, R. B., Antoni, J., & Smith, W. A. (2019). A survey of the application of the cepstrum to structural modal analysis. *Mechanical Systems and Signal Processing*, 118, 716-741.

[4] Zhang, L., Wang, T., & Tamura, Y. (2010). A frequency-spatial domain decomposition (FSDD) method for operational modal analysis. *Mechanical systems and signal processing*, 24(5), 1227-1239.

SPECIAL APPLICATIONS

IOMAC'19

8th International Operational Modal Analysis Conference
2019 May13-15 Copenhagen

APPLICATIONS OF OPERATIONAL MODAL ANALYSIS TO THE ACOUSTIC OF MUSICAL INSTRUMENTS: SNARE DRUM AND CELLO

Natalia Fernández[1], Paula González[2], F. Pelayo[1], Rafael Claramunt[2], G. Ismael[1], M. López-Aenlle[1]*

[1] Department of Construction and Manufacturing Engineering. University of Oviedo. Gijón, Spain.
[2] Department of Mechanical Engineering, Polytechnic University of Madrid, Madrid, Spain.
[*] *fernandezpelayo@uniovi.es*

ABSTRACT

Sound waves are formed when the vibrations of musical instruments cause the medium (air) to vibrate. Although musical instruments are apparently something simple, they are actually complex systems where coupled motion between the air and the "structure" has a great influence in the acoustic of the instrument.

This is for example the case of bowed string instruments (violin or cello) where the top plate, the back plate and the enclosed air determine the resonance chamber where the vibration of the air is produced. In other cases, like drums, the interaction can be less relevant but not negligible. However, other parameters like the pre-stress applied to the membranes (drumhead) are more significant.

In this work, a vibration analysis of the top plate of a cello and the drumhead of a snare drum were carried out. Operational modal analysis (OMA) was applied to identify the modal parameters which are then used to improve the understanding of the acoustic properties of these musical instruments.

Keywords: Acoustic, Musical Instruments, Modal Analysis, Vibrations.

1. INTRODUCTION

Musical instruments are complex systems where, in general, coupled motion between air and the structure of the instrument is present. An instrument produces sound when a part of it vibrates creating motion in the air, i.e. sound waves which are sensed by the inner ear [1].

There are many types of musical instruments being mainly classified in string, wind or percussion instruments [2]. These families are, in turn, divided into different subfamilies, i.e. metal-reed, cane-reed, lip-driven or air-jet driven [3] for the wind family.

As musical instruments work under vibration conditions, modal analysis techniques have been used for improving the understanding of their acoustical properties [3, 4] as well as for a better design or manufacturing the instruments [5].

In this work, operational modal analysis is applied to identify the modal parameters of the top plate of a cello and the drumhead of a snare-drum.

2. TOP PLATE OF A CELLO

The first case presented is the OMA of a Cello. These instruments are part of the bowed string subfamily, like violins. Although the sound waves start when the strings vibrate, the final sound is greatly influenced by the chamber of the instrument. The top plate has significant influence in the whole chamber and the craft of making it defines the quality of the instrument. To finish the top plate, tapping techniques are used [3, 5]. These techniques allow to display the mode shapes of the plate using sand over the plate. Although this method is very effective, the tuning of the plate is made by carving and it can only be applied for wooden plates. However, when new materials, such as carbon fibber, want to be used, the final thicknesses of the plate must be known a priori. In this case, the modal parameters of a wooden top plate could be used for the design of cello top plates made of new materials.

2.1. Experimental program

A top plate of a cello (spruce wood) under free-free conditions, was tested using 16 acceleration channels, see Figure 1. The experimental responses were register with a Compact DAQ NI system at 2132 Hz and two PCB impact hammers with soft tips were used to apply small random hits [6] to the plate, random in time and space.

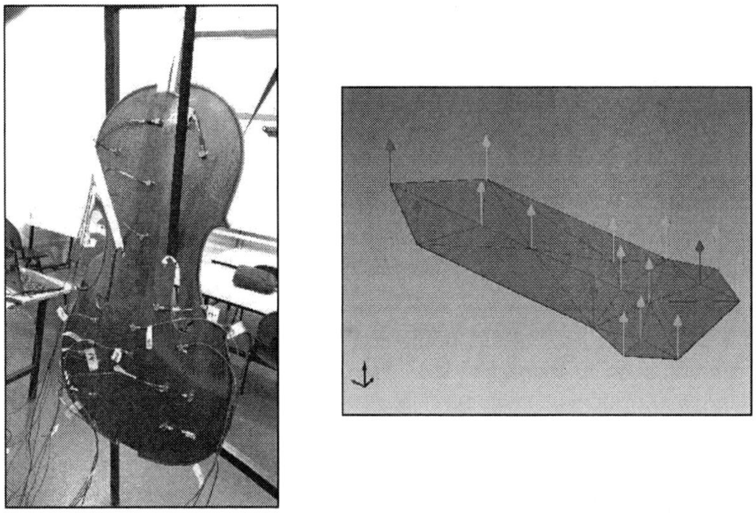

Figure 1. Cello top plate and measurements lay-out.

The modal parameters were estimated using the EFDD technique [7] implemented in the ArTeMis Modal software. Moreover, a simplified finite element (FE) model was assembled in ABAQUS and the mode shapes extracted to be compared with the experimental ones. Quadratic triangular elements of type STRI65 were used and typical spruce wood mechanical properties were considered.

2.2. Results

The singular value decomposition (SVD) and the modal parameters of the modes identified below 100 Hz are presented in Figure 2 and Table 1, respectively.

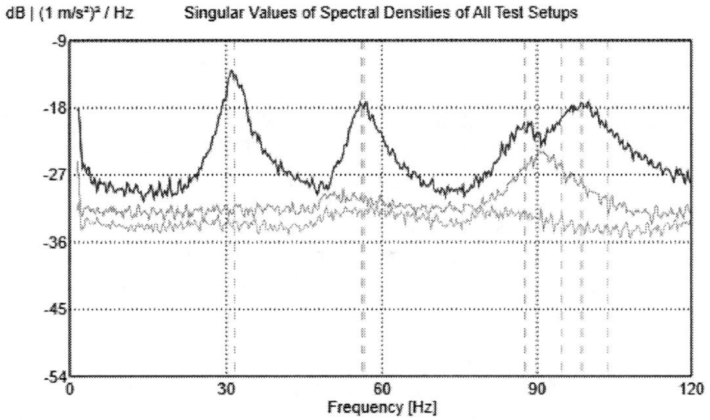

Figure 2. SVD of the measurements in the Cello top plate.

High damping ratios were estimated for the modes identified, see Table 1. This fact can be explained because of the properties (low density and soft wood) of the spruce wood. The experimental and the numerical mode shapes are presented in Figure 3.

Table 1. Experimental modal parameters of the cello top plate.

Mode	Experimental [Hz]	Damping [%]
1	31.644	5.838
2	56.518	4.772
3	87.724	5.136
4	98.781	3.856

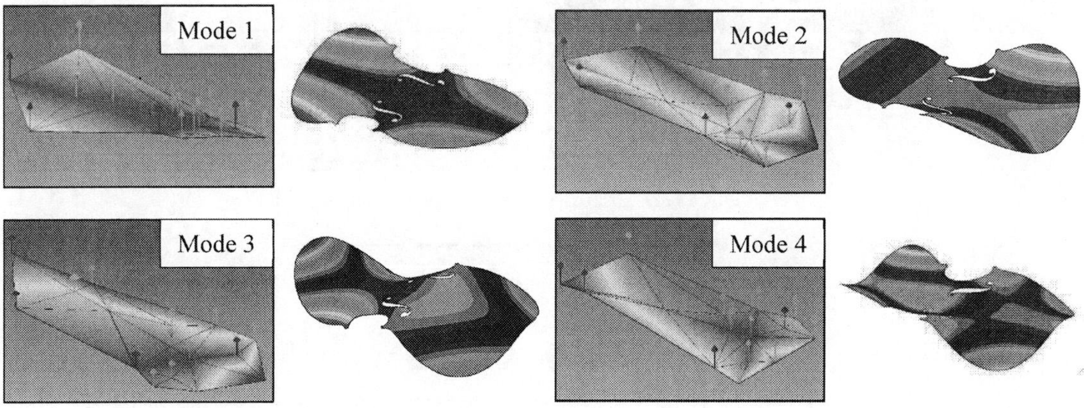

Figure 3. Mode shapes identified for the top plate of the cello in the range 0-100 Hz.

3. DRUMHEAD OF A SNARE DRUM

Snare drums are used in music bands, i.e. in the percussion corps. This percussion instrument consists mainly of three parts: the drumhead, the snare head and the body (cylindrical shell) which are joined with two rings (top and bottom). The rings are, in turn, joined with tension rods, which convert the drum in an overdeterminate system. Finally, the snare (a series of spiral metal strands) is attached and in contact with the bottom head (snare head), which produces the typical snare drum sound when the head vibrates.

Since the snare drum is an overdeterminate system, the pre-stress introduced in the head by means of the tension rods is a complex process where the ear of the musician is usually the most effective tool for the correct tuning of the instrument.

3.1. Experimental program

A Remo (Ambassador Coated) drumhead made from BOPET (biaxial oriented polyester film) was used in the experiments. The acceleration of 9 DOFs were measured with 6 low-mass PCB acceleration sensors using 2 Data Sets (see Figure 4). A sampling frequency of 2132 was used being the signals registered with a NI Compact DAQ system (see Figure 4). Artificial excitation [6] was applied to the drumhead using a drumstick. For comparison purposes a finite element (FE) model was assembled in ABAQUS where quadrilateral quadratic shell elements (S8R) were used.

The OMA was performed using the EFDD technique [7] implemented in the ARTEMIS MODAL software and the SVD of the OMA identification is presented in Figure 5.

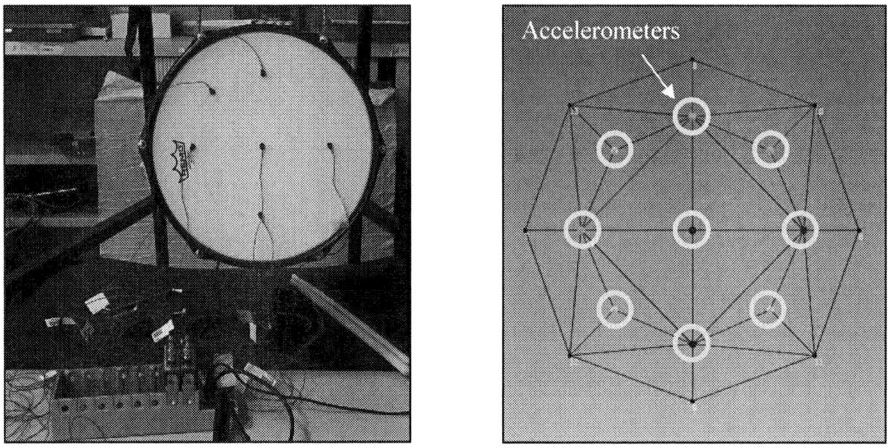

Figure 4. Data set 1 (left) and measurements lay-out.

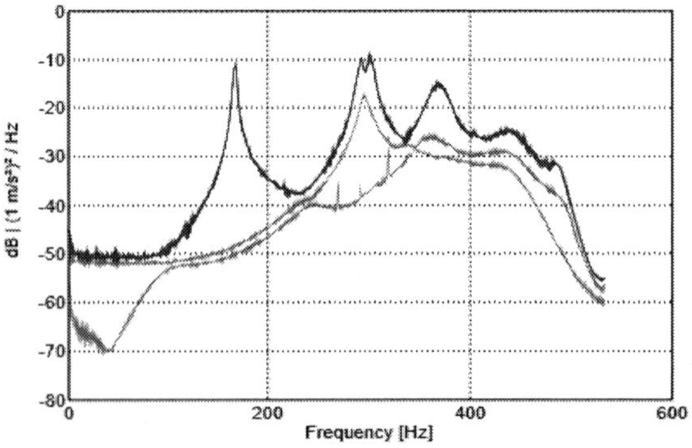

Figure 5. SVD for the OMA of the drumhead.

3.2. Results

The experimental natural frequencies and the mode shapes of the drumhead are presented in Table 2. Using analytical equations [8] and experimental results, an averaged value of approximately 6 MPa of pre-stress was obtained for the drumhead. This value was considered in the FE model and the numerical natural frequencies and the corresponding mode shapes are shown in Table 2. From the results, it can be inferred that a good agreement was obtained between the experimental and numerical results, being the maximum error 7.8% for the third mode. On the other hand, it is remarkable that modes 2 and 3 should be repeated modes [8]. This fact occurs in the numerical model, where the pre-stress over the drum head is perfect. However, in the SVD of the OMA, the corresponding peaks of the modes are close but not repeated (see Figure 5), which reveals that a non-uniform tension was applied to the tension rods during the experiments.

Table 2. Experimental modal parameters of the drumhead.

Mode	Frequency			Mode shapes	
	Experimental [Hz]	Numerical [Hz]	Error [%]	Experimental	Numerical
1	155.11	158.19	4.72	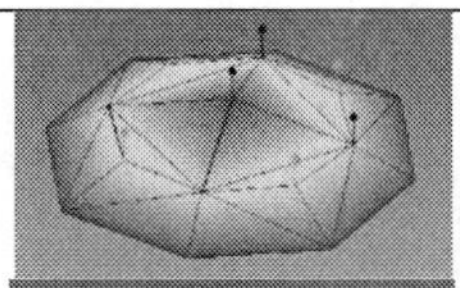	
2	267.54	258.91	3.22	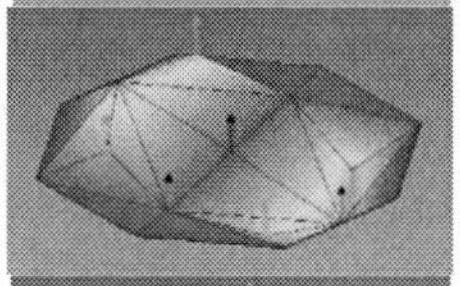	
3	281.07	258.91	7.88	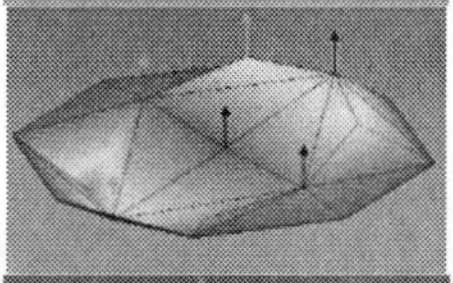	
4	350.82	346.88	1.57	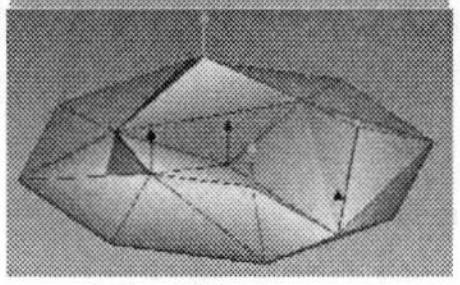	

4. CONCLUSIONS

Operational modal analysis is a useful tool that can be easily applied to study the dynamic behavior of musical instruments, which in turn have influence in its acoustical behavior.

The first natural frequencies, damping ratios and mode shapes of a wooden cello top plate were identified under free-free conditions. A higher damping is present in the identified modes, which can attributed to the nature of spruce wood.

On the other hand, OMA was applied to identify the natural frequencies and mode shapes of a snare drum. Although the drum looks like a simple system, its vibrations are directly conditioned by the pre-stress introduced in the drumhead. As the system is overdeterminate, it is not straightforward to apply the correct tension to the rods that allows the correct tuning of the instrument.

ACKNOWLEDGEMENTS

The financial support given by the University Institute of Industrial Technology of Asturias (IUTA) through the project SV-17-GIJÓN-1-21 is gratefully appreciated.

REFERENCES

[1] Helmholtz, H. (1885) *On the sensations of tone as a physiological basis for the theory of music*. Longmans, Green.

[2] Kartomi, M.J. (1990) *On concepts and classifications of musical instruments*. The University of Chicago Press.

[3] Fletcher, N.H. and Rossing, T. (1998) *The Physics of Musical Instruments*. Springer-Verlag, New York.

[4] Rossing, T. and Fletcher, N.H. (2004). *Principles of Vibration and Sound.* Springer-Verlag, New York.

[5] Chaigne, A. and Kergomard, J. (2016) *Acoustics of Musical Instruments.* Springer-Verlag, New York.

[6] Pelayo, F., López-Aenlle, M., Brincker, R. and Fernández-Canteli. (2009) A., Artificial Excitation in Operational Modal Analysis, *In Proc.* Of the 3th International Operational Modal Analysis Conference (IOMAC). Paper 223, Portonovo, Ancona.

[7] Brincker R, Zhang L-M and Anderson P. (2000) Modal Identification from Ambient Response Using Frequency Domain Decomposition. In: *Proceedings of the 18th IMAC*, pp. 625-630.

[8] Blevins, R. D. (2015). *Formulas for Dynamics, Acoustics and Vibratio*n. Wiley Series in Acoustics Noise and Vibration.

IOMAC'19

8th International Operational Modal Analysis Conference

2019 May13-15 Copenhagen

DYNAMIC STRESSES USING OMA AND A TIME DOMAIN EFFECTIVE YOUNG'S MODULUS FOR LAMINATED BEAMS WITH VISCOELASTIC CORE

F. Pelayo, G. Ismael and M. López Aenlle*

Department of Construction and Manufacturing Engineering, University of Oviedo, Campus de Gijón, Zona Oeste, Edificio 7, 33203, Gijón, Spain.

* fernandezpelayo@uniovi.es

ABSTRACT

The mechanical behavior of laminated beams with viscoelastic core such as sandwich glass beams, is frequency and temperature dependent. The response of these elements can be calculated using complicated analytical equations or very dense finite element models which are usually very high time-consuming, because many small 3D elements are needed to model accurately all the layers of the sandwich element. In order to simplify the analytical and the numerical calculations, simple analytical equations, based on the Effective Thickness concept, have been recently developed for estimating the static and the dynamic responses of these elements. In this paper, a novel approach to calculate time domain dynamic stresses in viscoelastic-core sandwich elements, which uses the experimental modal parameters estimated by OMA, is presented. The results obtained with the analytical equations are compared with those obtained in the experimental tests carried out on a simply supported laminated glass beam at different temperatures.

Keywords: Viscoelastic behaviour, dynamic stresses, operational modal analysis.

1. INTRODUCTION

1.1. Laminated glass

Laminated glass is a sandwich or layered material which consists of two or more plies of monolithic glass bonded with one or more interlayers of a polymeric material. The interlayers present viscoelastic behaviour, therefore the mechanical properties of the laminated glass are frequency (or time) and temperature dependent [1, 2].

In analytical and numerical models, glass mechanical behaviour is usually modelled as linear-elastic in the pre glass-breakage, whereas the polymeric interlayer is characterized as linear-viscoelastic [1]. Laminated glass is easy to assemble in a finite element models but a lot of small 3D elements are needed to mesh accurately because the thickness of the viscoelastic interlayer is usually very small compared with the dimension of the laminated glass element. Consequently, a lot of elements are needed to mesh correctly the interlayer and 3D models are very high time consuming if a full viscoelastic analysis is seldom performed.

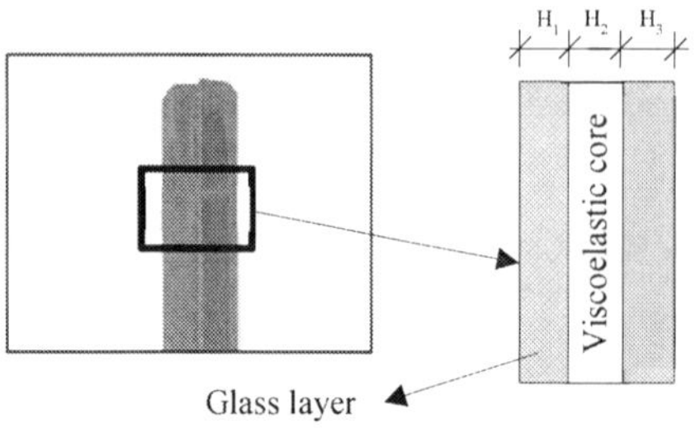

Figure 1: Laminated glass.

Several models were proposed in the 60's and 70's about the dynamic flexural vibration of sandwich beams with viscoelastic core [3, 4]. From these models, Aenlle and Pelayo [5]. derived an effective stiffness for the dynamic behavior of laminated glass beams from the RKU model [6]. With this technique, monolithic numerical models with an effective stiffness [5, 6, 7, 8, 9] can be used advantageously in place of layered models.

In this paper a methodology to estimate stresses in laminated glass beams in time domain is proposed, which combines the effective thickness concept and Operational Modal Analysis (OMA). The methodology has been validated by experimental tests carried out on a simply supported laminated glass beam at different temperatures.

2. STATE OF THE ART

2.1. Dynamic Effective Young's Modulus

The dynamic effective Young's modulus, $E_{eff}(\omega,T)$, is defined as the Young's modulus of a monolithic glass beam with constant thickness which provides the same stiffness as the laminated beam under same loading and boundary conditions. For a laminated sandwich beam (see Figure 1), the expression for the $E_{eff}(\omega,T)$ is given by [7]:

$$E_{eff}(\omega,T) = \frac{E}{1+Y}\left(1+\frac{Y}{1+\dfrac{EH_1H_2H_3\,k_l^2(\omega,T)}{G_2^*(\omega,T)(H_1+H_3)}}\right) \tag{1}$$

where the parameters of the expression are defined in Table 1.

Table 1. Parameters of the Equations [7].

ω	Frequency
T	Temperature
E	Young´s modulus of Glass
k_l	Wavenumer
H_1	Thickness of glass layer 1
H_2	Thickness of polymer interlayer
H_3	Thicks of glass layer 3
H_0	$H_2 + (H_1 + H_3)/2$
H_{TOT}	$H_1 + H_2 + H_3$
I_{TOT}	Second moment of área for H_{TOT}
Y	$\frac{H_0^2 E_1 H_1 E_3 H_3}{EI_T(E_1 H_1 + E_3 H_3)}$
I_T	$(H_1^3 + H_3^3)/12$
$G_2^*(\omega, T)$	Complex modulus of the Polymer interlayer
$EI^*(\omega, T)$	Effective stiffness (frequency domain)
$\eta_d(\omega, T)$	$\frac{1}{1 + \frac{E_1\, H_1\, H_2 E_3\, H_3\, k_l^2(\omega, T)}{G_2^*\,(\omega, T)(E_1 H_1 + E_3 H_3)(1 + Y)}}$

2.2. Stresses in Frequency Domain

Similarly to the previous section, a dynamic stress effective Young's modulus. $E_{i\sigma eff}(\omega, T)$ can also be defined for top (H_1) and bottom (H_2) layers [10], which are expresseed as:

$$E_{1\sigma eff}(\omega, T) = E\left[\eta_d(\omega, T) \cdot \frac{EI^*(\omega, T)}{EI_{TOT}} \frac{H_3 H_0}{H_1 + H_3} \cdot \frac{2}{H_1} + 1\right] \tag{2}$$

$$E_{3\sigma eff}(\omega, T) = E\left[\eta_d(\omega, T) \cdot \frac{EI^*(\omega, T)}{EI_{TOT}} \frac{H_1 H_0}{H_1 + H_3} \cdot \frac{2}{H_3} + 1\right] \tag{3}$$

Where the parameters of Eqs. (2) and (3) are presented in Table 1.

Finally, the stresses at layers 1 and 3 can be obtained using the expressions:

$$\sigma_1(x, \omega, T) = E_{1\sigma eff}(\omega, T) \cdot \frac{H_1}{2} \cdot w''(x, \omega, T) \tag{4}$$

$$\sigma_3(x, \omega, T) = E_{3\sigma eff}(\omega, T) \cdot \frac{H_3}{2} \cdot w''(x, \omega, T) \tag{5}$$

Where $w''(x, \omega, T)$ is the curvature of the beam and $E_{1\sigma eff}(\omega, T)$ and $E_{2\sigma eff}(\omega, T)$ are given by Eqs. (2) and (3), respectively.

3. MODAL EFFECTIVE YOUNG'S MODULUS TO CALCULATE STRESSES IN TIME DOMAIN

In structural dynamics it is often advantageous to express the responses of the system in terms of the mode shapes [11]. Due to the fact that the mode shapes possess orthogonality properties, the curvature of the beam can be obtained by the modal superposition method [11] ,i.e.

$$w''(x,\omega,T) = \sum_{i=1}^{Nmodes} \phi_i''(x) q_i(\omega,T) \tag{6}$$

Where $\phi_i''(x)$ and $q_i(\omega,T)$ are the second derivative of the i-th mode shape and the i-th modal coordinate, respectively. Substituting Eq. (6) in Eq. (4), the following expression for the stresses at the top of layer 1 is obtained:

$$\sigma_1(x,\omega,T) = E_{1\sigma eff}(\omega,T) \cdot \frac{H_1}{2} \cdot \sum_{i=1}^{Nmodes} \phi_i''(x)\, q_i(\omega,T) \tag{7}$$

A similar equation can be obtained for the bottom of layer 3 substituting expressión (6) in Eq. (5):

$$\sigma_3(x,\omega,T) = E_{3\sigma eff}(\omega,T) \cdot \frac{H_3}{2} \cdot \sum_{i=1}^{Nmodes} \phi_i''(x)\, q_i(\omega,T) \tag{8}$$

The stresses in time domain can be retrieved by inverse Fourier transform. However, an important simplification can be made in equations (7) and (8) if the effective Young's modulus $E_{\sigma eff}(\omega,T)$ is taken constant for each mode. With this assumption, the response can be estimated by modal superposition instead of using a convolution. In this work, it is proposed to consider for the i-th mode the effective Young's modulus $E_{1\sigma i}$ and $E_{3\sigma i}$ given by:

$$E_{1\sigma i}(T) = E_{1\sigma eff}(\omega_i,T) \tag{9}$$

And

$$E_{3\sigma i}(T) = E_{3\sigma eff}(\omega_i,T) \tag{10}$$

Now, introducing expressions (9) and (10) in Eqs. (7) and (8), respectively, and applying the inverse Fourier transform, the following expressions for estimating stressess in time domain are obtained:

$$\sigma_1(x,t,T) \cong \frac{H_1}{2} \cdot \sum_{i=1}^{Nmodes} E_{1\sigma i}(T) \cdot \phi_i''(x) \cdot q_i(t,T) \tag{11}$$

$$\sigma_3(x,t,T) = \frac{H_3}{2} \cdot \sum_{i=1}^{Nmodes} E_{3\sigma i}(T) \cdot \phi_i''(x) \cdot q_i(t,T) \tag{12}$$

The stress effective moduli $E_{1\sigma i}$ (T) and $E_{3\sigma i}$ (T) can be considered time domain modal stress effective Young's modulus for layers 1 and 3, respectively.

4. EXPERIMENTAL RESULTS

4.1. Experimental program and modal identification

In order to validate the technique proposed in this paper, the stresses of a laminated glass beam with annealed glass layers, PVB core and with the following geometrical data: $\mathrm{L} = 1$ m, $\mathrm{H}_1 = 3$mm, $\mathrm{H}_2 = 0.38$ mm, $\mathrm{H}_3 = 3$ mm, $\mathrm{b} = 0.1$ m, were predicted using Eqs. (9) and (10) and validated by experimental tests. The beam was supported in a steel testing frame with a distance between supports of 0.85m and tested at temperatures of 19 and 28 °C (see Fig. 2).

The responses were measured using seven uniformly distributed accelerometers with a sensitivity of 100 mV/g (see Figure 4) for approximately 4 minutes with a sampling frequency of 2132 Hz. A National Instruments Compact DAQ acquisition system equipped with NI9234 acceleration modules was used to record the signals.

The experimental modal parameters at 19 and 28 °C were identified with Operational Modal Analysis (OMA) using the Enhanced Frequency Domain Decomposition (EFDD) [12], implemented in the ARTEMIS MODAL software. The natural frequencies and the loss factors η (assuming that $\eta = 2\zeta$ [13]) are presented in Table 2.

Table 2. Natural frequencies and loss factors for the glass beam under simply supported boundary conditions.

	Temperature 19°C		Temperature 28°C	
Mode	Frequency [Hz]	Loss factor [%]	Frequency [Hz]	Loss factor [%]
1	30.16	4.28	29.00	6.04
2	92.70	1.73	88.93	3.19
3	186.50	2.35	182.14	3.98
4	313.42	2.76	303.92	4.15
5	465.53	2.89	450.34	4.65

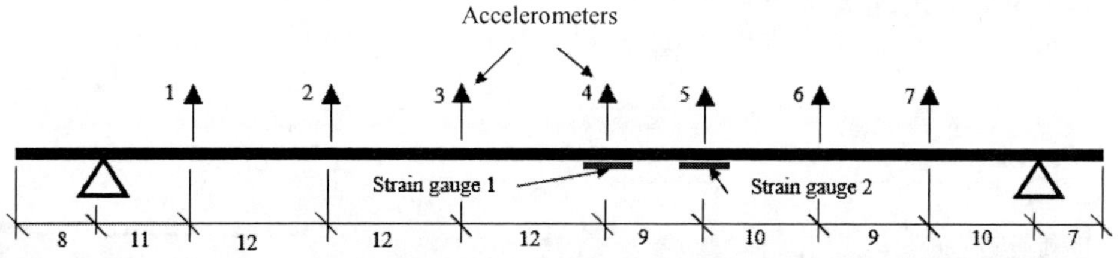

Figure 2. Test setup used in the experiments.

4.2 Experimental tests

To estimate stresses, the beam was excited with an impact hammer at several points of the structure. The responses were recorded with the same equipment used in OMA test and two strain gages HBM LY11-350 were attached at points 1 and 2 (see Figure 2).

The stresses at the points where the strain gages were attached (see Figure 2) were estimated using the methodology described in the previous sections. A Young's modulus of 72 GPa and a Poisson ratio $\nu = 0.22$, respectively, were considered for the glass layers, whereas the mechanical properties obtained with a DTMA in a previous work [15] were considered for the PVB.

Moreover, a monolithic finite element model was assembled in ABAQUS and the experimental mode shapes were expanded to the un-measured DOF's using the Local Correspondence Principle [15].

The frequency domain effective Young's modulus $E_{1\sigma eff}(\omega, T)$ was calculated using Eq. (2)*(2)* and the constant time stress effective Young's modulus, $E_{1\sigma}(T)$, using Eq. (9). The values for the different analyzed temperatures are shown in Table 3. In this case $E_{1\sigma eff}(T) = E_{3\sigma eff}(T)$ because $H_1 = H_3$.

The experimental modal coordinates were obtained from the experimental mode shapes and the experimental acceleration responses. The responses were divided in segments and the integration was performed in frequency domain using a high pass filter and a rectangular window with 50% overlap [12].

Table 3. time domain Effective Young's modulus $E_{1\sigma i}(T)$ used in the calculations.

Mode	Effective Young's modulus $E_{1\sigma i}$ x10^{11}[Pa]	
	T= 19 °C	T= 28 °C
1	1.44	1.36
2	1.40	1.29
3	1.35	1.21
4	1.29	1.13
5	1.25	1.07

4.2 Stress estimation

The time histories and the Power Spectral Densities (PSD) of the experimental stresses measured with a strain gage located at the midpoint of the beam (point 1 in Figure 2) and those predicted with Eqs. (11) and (12) at temperatures of 19 °C and 28 °C, respectively, are presented in Figure 3. Due to the fact that the strain gage is not located just in the middle of the span, all the modes contribute to the stress time histories. This fact is in agreement with the stresses recorded with the strain gage (see Figure 3).

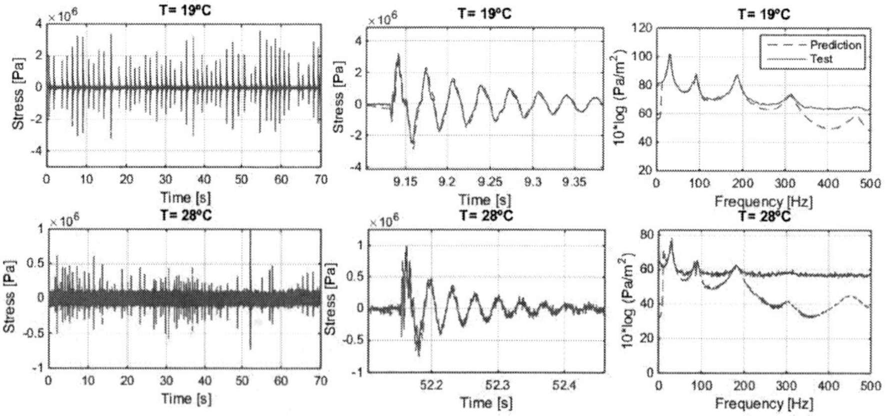

Figure 3. Predicted and experimental stresses at point 1 at 19°C and 28 °C (left: time history, center: detail of the time history, right: power spectral density).

From Figure 3 it is inferred that the stresses are predicted with a good accuracy at 19 °C and 28 °C; the error being less than 10% for the first natural frequency. The errors between the estimated and the experimental power spectral density of the stresses at the first natural frequency (peaks of the first mode) are presented in Table 4.

Table 4. Errors between the predicted and the experimental stress for the first mode at different temperatures in points 1 and 2.

Frequency [Hz]	Temperature [°C]	Error [%] Point 1	Point 2
30.16	19	6.26	7.82
29.00	28	8.80	9.11

It can be obeserved in Table 4 that the discrepancies increase with increasing temperature. This result is expected because the peaks at natural frequencies become wider with increasing temperature (higher damping) and the assumption of constant effective Young´s modulus for each natural frequency is less accurate as the width of the peak increases.

5. CONCLUSIONS

In practical calculations of laminated glass elements, as well as in preliminary designs, it is very useful to consider simplified methods. In the last years, several equations have been proposed to calculate displacements, internal forces, stresses, etc., in laminated glass beams and plates under static loading [2, 13, 22] and under dynamic loading [9, 11] using the effective thickness concept

In this paper a simple method to estimate the stresses in time domain, assuming a constant stress effective Young's modulus for each mode was proposed. This assumption allows to use the modal superposition principle to calculate stresses in time domain. The methodology is more accurate for lightly damped modes, i.e, for laminated glass the discrepancies increase with increasing temperature.

The proposed methodology was validated by experimental test carried out in a laminated glass beam at temperatures of 19 and 28 ^{o} C. It has been demonstrated that the proposed technique allows estimating stresses in laminated glass beams with a good accuracy, the errors being less than 8% at 19 °C and less that 10% at 28°C.

ACKNOWLEDGEMENTS

The financial support given by the Spanish Ministry of Education through the project BIA2014-53774-R is gratefully appreciated.

REFERENCES

[1] Ferry, J.D., (1980) *Viscoelastic Properties of Polymers*, Third ed., John Wiley & Sons, Ltd., New York.

[2] Benninson, S., M.HX, Q. and Davies, P., (2008) High-performance laminated glass for structurally efficient glazing. *Innovative Light-weight Structures and Sustainable Facades*, Hong Kong, May.

[3] Ross, D., Ungar, E.E., and Kerwin, E.M., (1959) Damping of Plate Flexural Vibrations by Means of Viscoelastic Laminate, *Structural Damping*, ASME, p. 49-88.

[4] DiTaranto, R.A., and McGraw, Jr, J.R., (1969) Vibratory Bending of Damped Laminated Plates, *J Eng Ind*, 91(4):1081-1090.

[5] López-Aenlle, M., Pelayo, F., 2013) Frequency Response of Laminated Glass Elements: Analytical Modelling and Effective Thickness, *Appl Mech Rev*, 65(2), 020802 (13 pages).

[6] Ungar, Eric E., Donald Ross, and JR Kerwin. (1959) Damping of flexural vibrations by alternate viscoelastic and elastic layers. No. AFCRL-TR-60-189. BOLT BERANEK AND NEWMAN INC CAMBRIDGE MA.

[7] M. López-Aenlle and Pelayo, F. (2014) Dynamic effective thickness in laminated-glass beams and plates, *Compos Part B-Eng*, 67:332-347.

[8] Calderone, I., Davies, P.S., and Benninson, S.J., (2009) Effective Laminate Thickness for the Design of Laminated Glass. In: *Glass Processing Days*, Tampere, Finland.

[9] Galuppi, L., and Royer-Carfagni, G.F. (2012) Effective Thickness of Laminated Glass Beams: New Expression via a Variational Approach, *J Struct Eng*, 38:53-67.

[10] Aenlle, Manuel L., F. Pelayo, and G. Ismael (2015) An effective thickness to estimate stresses in laminated glass beams under dynamic loadings. *Composites Part B: Engineering* 82: 1-12

[11] Clough Ray, W., and Penzien Joseph. (1995) *Dynamics of structures*. Computers & Structures, Inc.

[12] Brincker, Rune, and Carlos Ventura (2015). *Introduction to operational modal analysis*. John Wiley & Sons, 2015.

[13] Nashif, A.D., Jones, D.I.G., and Henderson, J.P., (1985) *Vibration Damping*. John Willey and Sons, New York.

[14] López-Aenlle, M. and Pelayo, F., (2013) The effective-thickness concept in laminated-glass elements under static loading. *Eng Struct*, 56:1092-1102.

[15] Rune Brincker, Anders Skafte, Manuel López-Aenlle, Aldo Sestieri, Walter D'Ambrogio, Alfonso Canteli, (2014) A local correspondence principle for mode shapes in structural dynamics, *Mech Syst Signal Pr*, 1(3):91-104.

IOMAC'19

8th International Operational Modal Analysis Conference
2019 May13-15 Copenhagen

RESEARCH AND DEVELOPMENT OF AN AIR-PUFF EXCITATION SYSTEM FOR LIGHTWEIGHT STRUCTURES

Ben Halkon[1], Andreas Rauter[2], Sebastian Oberst[3] and Steffen Marburg[4]

[1] Dr, Centre for Audio, Acoustics & Vibration, University of Technology Sydney, Benjamin.Halkon@uts.edu.au.
[2] Mr, Mechanical Engineering, Technical University of Munich, Andreas.Rauter@tum.de.
[3] Dr, Centre for Audio, Acoustics & Vibration, University of Technology Sydney, Sebastian.Oberst@uts.edu.au.
[4] Prof., Mechanical Engineering, Technical University of Munich, Steffen.Marburg@tum.de.

ABSTRACT

Lightweight, thin-walled structures appear in numerous engineering and natural structures. Due to their sensitivity, vibration excitation by, now traditional, contacting techniques, such as modally-tuned impact hammers or electrodynamic shakers, to investigate their dynamics is challenging since it typically adds substantial mass and/or stiffness at the excitation location. The research presented in this article, therefore, is intended to yield a system for the non-contact excitation of thin-walled structures through small, controlled blasts of air. An air-puff system, consisting of two fast-acting solenoid-controlled valves, a small air outlet nozzle and bespoke control software with a programmable valve control sequence, is researched and developed. The excitation impulse characteristics are investigated experimentally and described in detail for varying input control parameters. Ultimately, suitability of the system for the excitation of thin-walled structures is explored, for both a 3D-printed micro-satellite panel and a natural bee honeycomb, with promising results when compared to that of an impact hammer.

Keywords: lightweight structures, non-contact excitation, air-puff system, dynamic characterisation

1. INTRODUCTION

Since the advent of commercially viable personal computers in the late '70s and their development through the proceeding decades, engineers and scientists have been able to research and develop increasingly sophisticated mathematical and numerical computation and modelling techniques applicable to a myriad of applications that have without doubt revolutionized the increasingly man-made environment in which we live. One such example of a technology that has enable engineers to concur previously insurmountable feats is that of structural analysis, in particular finite element analysis. With the monumental increase in the performance of readily accessible processing capacity, digital simulations of simplified real-world systems have become increasingly complex with often millions of degrees-of-freedom now used to predict the static and dynamic behaviour of engineered systems for a variety of load cases and boundary conditions. Indeed, the modern era has moved towards clusters of processing nodes and 'cloud computing' whereby model complexity and/or solution speed can be further increased by distributing solve jobs for parallel completion. In order to yield maximum value from such increasingly complex models, however, experimental correlation and validation remains necessary.

Historically such validation has been undertaken with traditional contacting transducers, such as accelerometers and strain gauges, and excitation techniques, such as modally tuned impact hammers or electrodynamic shakers. Such techniques are typically only able to offer practical equivalent models with on the order of '0s to '00s of degrees-of-freedom, with validation/correlation of increasingly complex models therefore presenting a challenge. Furthermore, such contacting characterization techniques also potentially introduce significant mass/stiffness modifications to the structure under test simply due to the physical attachment of a transducer of some form. This is particularly true for the case of, increasingly of interest, lightweight structures, where such modification can lead to significant changes in dynamic performance. There are methodologies for the mathematical removal of such mass/stiffness modifications from experiment results and, of course, the numerical computational models to be validated can be adjusted to include estimates of the corresponding experimental modifications. It is, however, preferable to not have to manage these complications, especially when developing practically applicable techniques that can be readily adopted by the industrial vibration engineer/CAE analyst. Furthermore, such methodologies for correction are only validated for engineering systems and can generally not be applied to natural structures of heterogeneous material composition and nonlinear dynamic behaviour.

In parallel with developments in computational performance and associated numerical techniques, the research and development of non-contact vibratory response measurement techniques has been of significant interest, largely driven by the inherent ability with such techniques to be able to rapidly generate high spatial resolution or, indeed, 'whole-field' structural vibratory response surveys. Technologies such as laser Doppler vibrometry [1] in particular, but also, for example, dynamic electronic speckle pattern interferometry (ESPI) [2] and photogrammetry/high-speed digital image correlation (DIC) [2],[3]. Research and development of such non-contact response measurement techniques has accordingly been followed by the concomitant need for non-contact excitation techniques, for example using pressurized air pulses, [4]-[6], by focused speaker [7] or speaker arrays [6],[8] or, for example, by high-power lasers using ablation or shock waves which are focused on the structure itself [9] to generate ultrasonic surface acoustic waves which can be used to determine damage in e.g. composites or in geological structures. Such experimental dynamic characterisation techniques are especially valid for the excitation of lightweight structures such as micro-satellite [10], (live) biological samples or insect appendages [11]. Delicate samples cannot, however, sustain the local elevated temperatures associated with high-power lasers, which would denaturalise protein and cause damage. A very low level of excitation, with no significant temperature increase, is required and, therefore, this paper addresses the research and development of a system, which makes used of a short duration air jet for such excitation.

2. AIR-PUFF EXCITATION SYSTEM RESEARCH AND DEVELOPMENT

2.1. Theoretical basis for the design of the air-puff system

The over-arching intention of the research described in this paper is to make use of a short impulsive jet of air to induce an excitation force into a lightweight, thin-walled structure, in a similar manner to that in which a traditional, modally-tuned instrumented impact hammer might. An attempt to apply governing fluid dynamics principles and equations to the problem as, a first approximation, could be made but it is anticipated that, in the limit at least and not least given that air is a compressible fluid, these governing principles may display limited validity on the scale of the system and structures concerned. Instead, drawing similarities between an air-puff system and an impact hammer, it is simply initially the intention to be able to control two parameters: i) the mass flow rate, considered to be proportional to the force generated, of the fluid through the nozzle and ii) the duration of the impulse.

Drawing hypothetical similarities between the proposed non-contact excitation system and that of the more traditional, contacting technique, the duration of the impact for an instrumented hammer directly controls the frequency range over which the structure is excited. Indeed, for a perfect Dirac delta impulse, the frequency range is infinite; for finite duration impulses, the longer the impact duration, the narrower the frequency range over which the structural response is excited. In an instrumented hammer excitation scenario, the duration of the impact is a function of the local combined stiffness of the hammer tip and that of the structure under test; this is adjusted as required by changing the hammer tip stiffness. In the case of the air-puff system described here, the duration of the impulsive jet of air will be controlled by a pair of fast operating pneumatic solenoid valves as described in what follows.

2.2. Description of the physical arrangement of the air-puff system

Figure 1 shows the experimental arrangement of the proposed air-puff system developed during this study. Two solenoid valves (Festo MHJ9-QS-4-MF) are mounted in series, from the laboratory compressed air supply, on an aluminium board, which includes different mounting options for the air-puff system. Specifically, these options are a ¼"-20 UNC thread for a camera tripod mount and a clamp for standard laboratory rods of ½" (12.7 mm) in diameter allowing for convenient positioning of the device. An electronic power supply (Elektro-Automatik EA-PSI 9040-40 T 1000W DC), allowing valve voltage adjustment between 12 and 53 V, is used to drive the solenoid valve control electronics module.

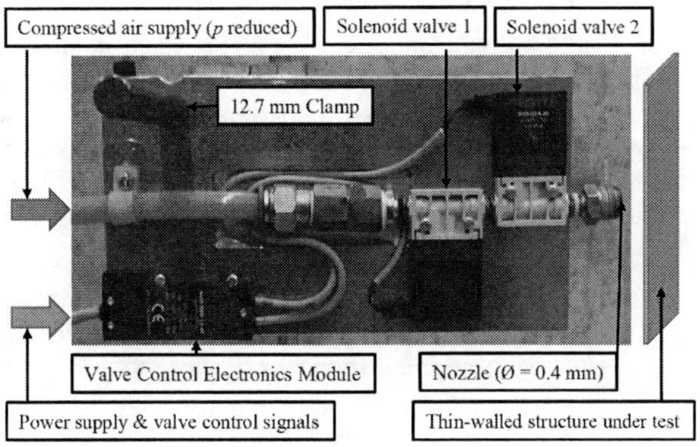

Figure 1. Experimental arrangement of the proposed air-puff system.

The reset mechanism utilized in the solenoid valves is that of an air spring for which the incoming pressurized air closes the valves when they are not activated by the solenoid. The pressurized air, adjustable between 0 and 7 bar, is assumed to be from an infinite volume source which maintains supply constant pressure during the operation of the air-puff system. Supply air pressure is adjusted using a pressure gauge, adjustable between 0.5 bar and 6 bar, upstream from the first valve. To achieve near point excitation and to excite small and sensitive structures, a small nozzle with an outlet diameter of 0.4 mm leads to an air jet at the front end of the air-puff system. A bespoke National Instruments LabVIEW-based control system was developed to enable control of the valve opening and closing.

2.3. Electromechanical characterisation of the air-puff system

2.3.1. Experimental methodology

In the GUI of the valve control software, the opening/closing sequence for the solenoid valves can be specified. Each valve is controllable individually by setting a sequence of up to eight open or close signals and the time duration for the segments. As can be seen in Figure 2, the typical sequence employed, so as to minimise the resulting impulse duration, is one whereby valve 2, that furthest downstream and thereby closest the structure under test, is open initially while valve 1 is initially closed. Shortly after opening valve 1, allowing the air to flow, valve 2 is closed, leading to a short duration puff of air. Sometime thereafter, and in advance of requiring a second pulse to excite the structure again, valve 1 can be closed and valve 2 opened. The entire cycle can then be repeated for a second "impact".

The first air-puff system control parameter, the overlap time duration, $\Delta t_{overlap}$, can thereby be specified with the second control parameter being the input pressure, p_{input}, set by adjusting the pressure gauge previously described. The air-puff system performance is described with reference to these two control parameters. To characterize the air-puff system excitation experimentally, the impulse peak force $F_{I,peak}$ and impulse duration Δt_I, defined graphically in Figure 3, were captured for varying input control paramcters. The experimental setup consisted of a piezoelectric force transducer (Dytran 1053V2) onto

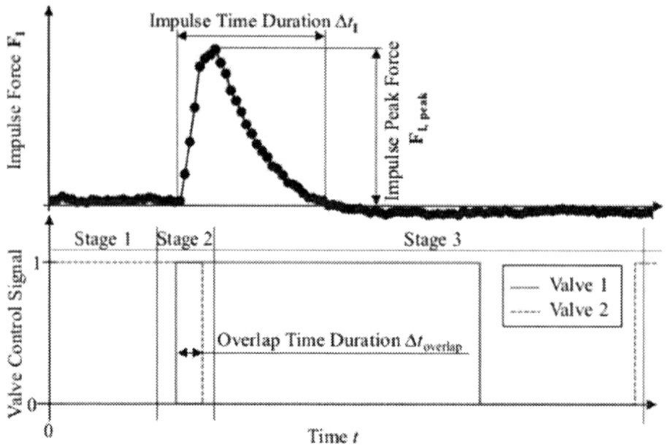

Figure 2. Typical valve control sequence showing control signals and example resulting force profile.

which the air puff was directed with the stand-off distance between the nozzle and the surface of the force transducer being adjustable. The force transducer was attached to a heavy, stiff steel block using a screw-on magnet mount plus a thin layer of synthetic beeswax, the latter preventing the magnetic connection from bouncing in high frequency vibration and therefore from parasitic frequency content potentially falsifying the measurements. Due to its weight, stiffness and boundary conditions, the steel block is assumed rigid and immune to the level of force generated by the air-puff system.

A Brüel & Kjær Type 3053-B-120 (12 channel, 25 kHz input module) data acquisition system was used to digitise the analogue force signal measured by the piezoelectric force transducer. The valve input control signals were measured in parallel enabling the definition of additional performance parameters for example including those relating to timing differences between the valve openings and the impulse peak force. Brüel & Kjær Pulse Reflex was utilised to set-up the acquisition parameters and perform signal analysis. The trigger threshold was set for the force sensor, with a 24 ms pre-trigger included to enable the entire impulsive force signal to be captured. Each measurement was recorded for 0.8 s, with a 2.56 kHz sample frequency, yielding a bandwidth of 1 kHz with 1.25 Hz resolution, i.e. 800 lines.

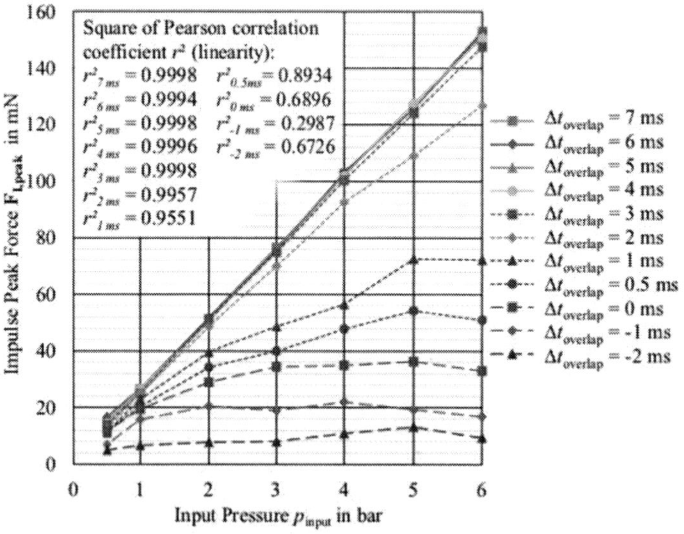

Figure 3. Impulse peak force vs. input pressure for varying valve opening overlap time duration.

2.3.2. Experimental observations

While the overlap time duration, $\Delta t_{overlap}$, and input pressure, p_{input}, were varied during the measurements, a valve control power supply of 50 V and a stand-off distance between the nozzle and the force transducer of 5 mm were specified and remained constant. Figure 3 shows the behaviour of $F_{I,peak}$ versus p_{input} for different $\Delta t_{overlap}$. A linear proportional relationship is visible for overlap time durations from 2 ms to 7 ms. To quantify the quality of the relationship, the square of the Pearson correlation coefficient (SPCC) r^2 is defined where $r^2 = 0$ means no correlation and $r^2 = 1$ confirms full linear correlation between the two parameters. For $\Delta t_{overlap}$ from 2 ms to 7 ms, the SPCC shows high values between 0.9957 and 0.9998. For $\Delta t_{overlap}$ from -2 ms to 1 ms, however, there is almost a step change in the performance characteristic with r^2 for a linear fit varying from 0.2987 to 0.9557. It is hypothesised that for valve behaviour for very short opening durations, loss effects within the system become significant with further investigation being required to fully confirm this behaviour.

As specified in Figure 2 previously, the second of the two air-puff parameters of interest in this application, the actual resulting impulse time duration, Δt_I, can also be determined and evaluated against the air-puff system input control parameters. Figure 4 shows this derived parameter against p_{input} and, again shows that, for $\Delta t_{overlap}$ from 2 to 7 ms, there appears to be a characteristic behaviour whereby Δt_I is at a minimum for p_{input} of 2 bar. Again, for $\Delta t_{overlap}$ of less than 2 ms, there is no apparent relationship.

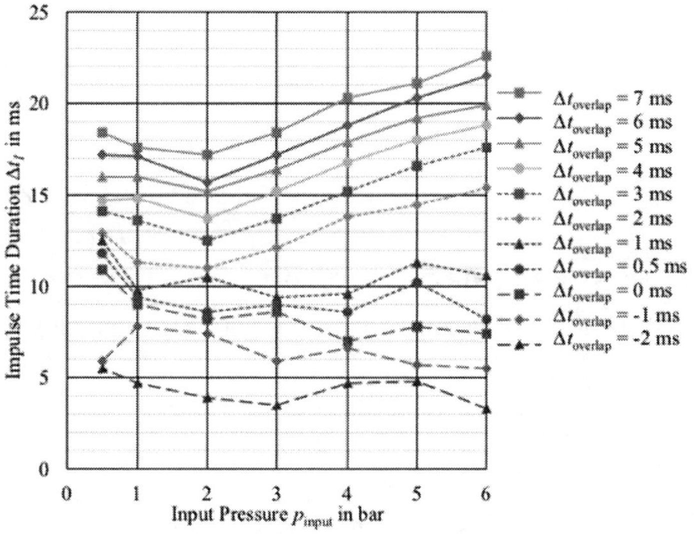

Figure 4. Actual impulse time duration vs. input pressure for varying valve opening overlap time duration.

The penultimate step of the benchtop characterisation of the air-puff system to be described is the example variation in $F_{I,peak}$ for varying the stand-off distance, $d_{stand\text{-}off}$ between the nozzle and the target; previously this was set to 5 mm. For this sub-investigation, p_{input} was set to 4 bar and $\Delta t_{overlap}$ to 1 ms. Figure 5 shows the interesting behaviour whereby, for the selected air-puff control system input parameters, $F_{I,peak}$ is a maximum at $d_{stand\text{-}off}$ 10 mm. The steep increase in $F_{I,peak}$ between 1 and 5 mm is evident. Further investigation is required to better characterise this behaviour for alternative air-puff system input control parameters; this will be the subject of future research and subsequent reporting.

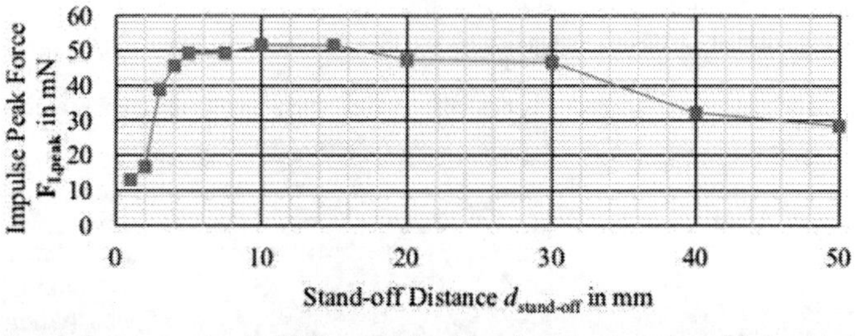

Figure 5. Impulse peak force vs. stand-off distance for 4 bar input pressure and 4 ms overlap time duration.

Lastly, a comparison of the impulsive force resulting excitation frequency spectrum achieved with a modally-tuned impact hammer (Brüel & Kjær Type 8204) with that of the air-puff system is presented in Figure 6. In this case, the air-puff system input parameters were again $p_{input} = 4$ bar, and $\Delta t_{overlap} = 1$ ms with $d_{stand\text{-}off}$ set to 5 mm. As shown in Figure 4, the resulting actual impulse force duration for these parameters is nominally 10 ms. The resulting frequency spectrum contains a "useful excitation range" (determined by a level of no less than one order magnitude lower than the peak) of up to c 233 Hz. In contrast, the impact hammer, complete with integral stainless steel tip, yielded an impact duration of 60 μs with the resulting excitation frequency spectrum being nominally flat across that range.

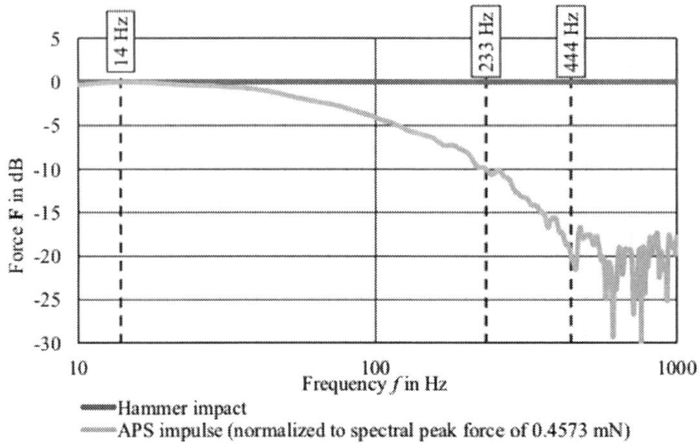

Figure 6. Comparison between impulse force for modally tuned impact hammer and air-puff system.

3. APPLICATION OF THE AIR-PUFF SYSTEM TO DYNAMIC CHARACTERISATION

To demonstrate the applicability of the air-puff system to structural dynamic characterisation, a pair of lightweight, thin-walled test specimens were evaluated. These were i) a 5 mm thickness, 100 x 100 mm ABS 3D-printed plate and ii) a bees' natural honeycomb structure. Comparisons between auto-power response only spectra for increasing numbers of averages are presented for excitation, either by modally tuned impact hammer (B&K Type 8204) or by the air-puff system. Both excitation, at a single point, and response accelerometer (Dytran 3225F), at an alternative single point, measurement locations were carefully chosen to attempt to excite the greatest number of structural resonances for comparison.

The first item under test described is a 3D-printed ABS plate weighing 51.7 g. It represents a multifunctional loadbearing panel from a cube micro-satellite and has a specific internal geometry intended to control the damping behaviour of the structure. Figure 7 shows the experimental arrangement. As can be observed therein, the ABS plate is "lightly suspended" on foam. This suspension arrangement enabled the collection of acceptable quality data for both excitation techniques with minimal change in the boundary conditions for each. For both excitation options, 0.64 s recordings were captured. For the air-puff system excitation, p_{input} = 6 bar, a $\Delta t_{overlap}$ = 1 ms (expected actual time impulse time duration approximately 10 ms based on Figure 4) and a $d_{stand\text{-}off}$ = 2 mm were arranged.

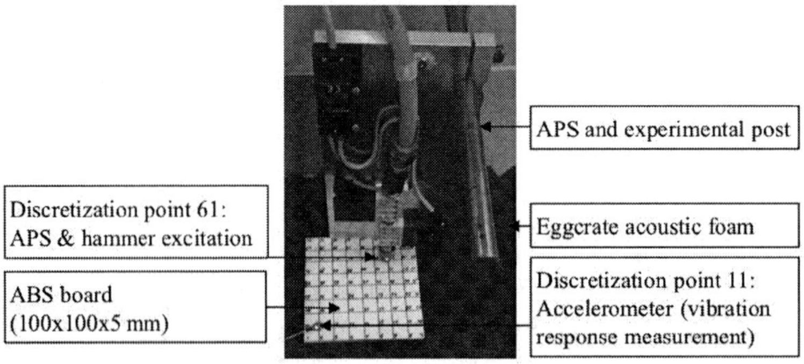

Figure 7. Experimental arrangement for ABS plate dynamic characterisation.

Figure 8 shows the correlation between the resulting auto-power spectra. Due to the relatively long impulse duration for the air-puff system vs. the impact hammer, it is expected that there is limited excitation energy above 250 Hz. Despite this, reasonable agreement between the resonant frequencies across the frequency can be observed. Indeed, at the lower frequencies and for data with multiple averages, the correlation is stronger. A future investigation would focus at the lower frequency range.

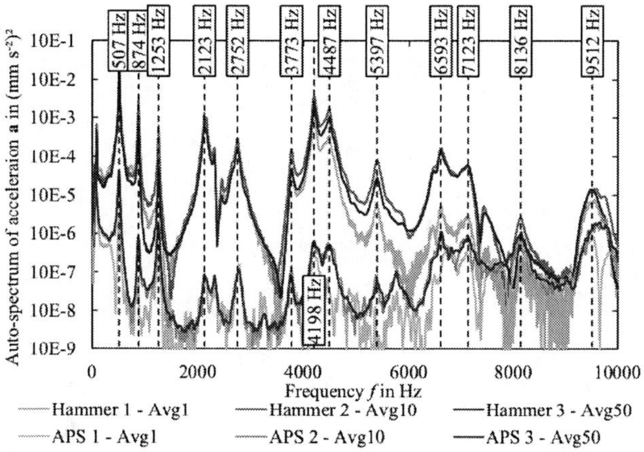

Figure 8. Comparison of response only auto-power spectra for ABS plate excitation.

The second item of interest under test is a natural bee honeycomb structure weighing only 1.2 g with approximate dimensions of 47 x 29 x 11 mm. Due to the very delicate nature of the item, the response measurement was made by a laser Doppler vibrometer orientated at 45 ° to the excitation direction in order to capture components of the response in two orthogonal directions. To minimise whole body motion of the structure, that would lead to significant challenges with making the response measurement due to the fixed probe laser beam orientation, the structure was mounted 'rigidly' to a block in a 'fixed-free' arrangement as shown in Figure 9. p_{input} = 6 bar, a $\Delta t_{overlap}$ = 0.5 ms (expected actual time impulse time duration 8 ms) and a $d_{stand\text{-}off}$ = 5 mm were arranged in this case for air-puff system excitation. Figure 10 shows the resulting auto-power spectra where agreement in the resonant frequencies of the structure is evident. There is particularly strong correlation between the techniques for 20 averages.

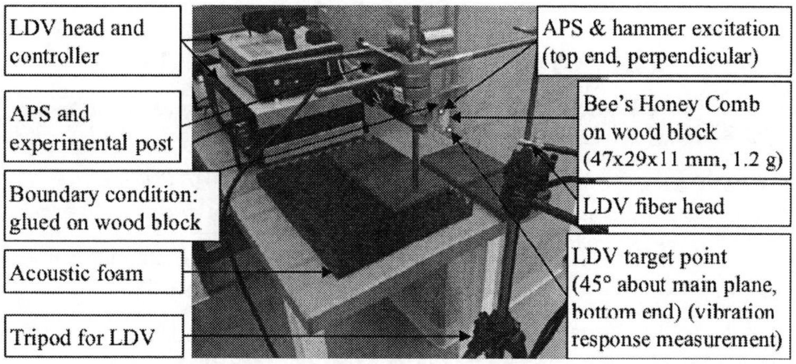

Figure 9. Experimental arrangement for bee honeycomb dynamic characterisation.

4. CONCLUSIONS

This paper has presented the research and development of a novel, fast-actuation pneumatic valve-based air-puff excitation system. The performance of the system for varying controllable parameters has been described and evaluated. Ultimately a comparison of the ability of the system to excited lightweight structures of interest has been presented with respect to a traditional, modally-tuned impact hammer equivalent technique with promising agreement observed, particularly at lower frequencies where the air-puff system is able to offer a reasonable level excitation. Future research will focus on the reduction of the pulse duration in order that a lower excitation level over a wider frequency range and a smaller excitation "spot" size might be realised. For this it is necessary to conduct a more comprehensive parameter and sensitivity study, to employ electro-magnetic values instead of mechanically opening solenoids and to explore tuning of the nozzle geometry. Whether filigree structures such as insect

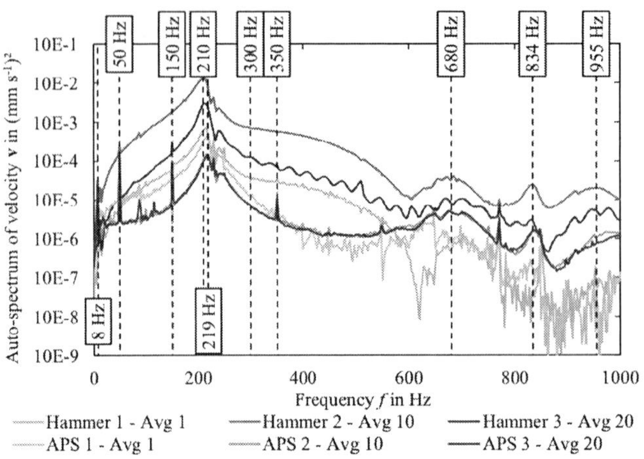

Figure 10. Example experimental arrangement of the air-puff system for dynamic characterisation.

appendages (legs, antennae, wings), expected to exhibit non-linear characteristics, can be sufficiently and carefully enough excited to determine their mechanical properties will be explored in the future.

ACKNOWLEDGMENTS

Andreas Rauter acknowledges the financial support provided by Sebastian Oberst through the UTS Centre for Audio, Acoustics and Vibration international visitor funds, enabling a visiting studentship to conduct the study. The authors wish to acknowledge the contribution made by Mr Chris Chapman, Scientific Officer, UTS to the development of the air-puff system hardware and software aspects.

REFERENCES

[1] Rothberg, S. et al. (2017). An international review of laser Doppler vibrometry: making light work of vibration measurement. *Optics and Lasers in Engineering*, 99, 11–22.

[2] Zanarini, A. (2019). Full field optical measurements in experimental modal analysis and model updating, *Journal of Sound and Vibration*, 442, 817-842.

[3] Baqersad, J., Poozesh, P., Niezrecki, C and Avitabile, P. (2017). Photogrammetry and optical methods in structural dynamics: A review, *Mechanical Systems and Signal Processing*, 86, 17-34.

[4] Vanlanduit, S., Daerden, F. and Guillaume, P. (2007). Experimental modal testing using pressurized air excitation. *Journal of Sound and Vibration*, 299, 83-98.

[5] Piraccini, M., Di Maio, D. and Di Sante, R. (2016). Nonlinear modal testing performed by pulsed-air jet excitation system. *Proceedings of the 34th IMAC, Vol.1*, 155-170.

[6] Farshidi, R., Trieu, D., Park, S.S. and Freiheit, T. (2010). Non-contact experimental modal analysis using air excitation and a microphone array. *Measurement*, 43, 755-765.

[7] Amraoui, Y.M. and Lieven, N.A.J. (2003). Noncontacting excitation and measurement of light structures. *Journal of Vibration and Acoustics*, 125, 114-119.

[8] Huber, T.M., Algren, M. and Raisbeck, C. (2016). Spatial distribution of acoustic radiation force for non-contact modal excitation. *Proceedings of the 34th IMAC, Vol.10,* 155–162.

[9] Hitchman, S., van Wijk, K. and Davidson, Z. (2016). Monitoring attenuation and the elastic properties of an apple with laser ultrasound. Postharvest Biology and Technology, 121, 71-77.

[10] Oberst, S. and Tuttle, S. (2018). Nonlinear dynamics of thin-walled elastic structures for applications in space, *Mechanical Systems and Signal Processing*, 110, 469-484.

[11] Oberst, S., Bann, G., Lai, J.C.S. and Evans, T.A. (2017). Cryptic termites avoid predatory ants by listening to their footsteps, *Ecology Letters*, 20, 212-22.

IOMAC'19

8th International Operational Modal Analysis Conference
2019 May 13-15 Copenhagen

OPERATIONAL MODAL ANALYSIS OF LOW FREQUENCY SURFACE WAVES IN LAKES AND RESERVOIRS

Zachariah Wynne [1], *Thomas Reynolds* [2], *Damien Bouffard* [3], *Geoffrey Schladow* [4], *Danielle Wain* [5]

[1] PhD Student, University of Edinburgh, UK, Z.Wynne@sms.ed.ac.uk.
[2] Chancellor's Fellow, University of Edinburgh, UK; Turing Fellow, The Alan Turing Institute, UK, T.Reynolds@ed.ac.uk.
[3] Researcher, Eawag, Swiss Federal Institute of Aquatic Science and Technology, Switzerland, Damien.Bouffard@eawag.ch.
[4] Professor, Tahoe Environmental Research Center, University of California Davis, USA, GSchladow@ucdavis.edu.
[5] Lake Science Director, 7 Lakes Alliance, USA, Danielle.Wain@7lakesalliance.org.

ABSTRACT

Wind driven oscillations of water surfaces (surface seiches) are a key driver of ecological fluxes, such as of oxygen and nutrients, within lakes and reservoirs. These seiches exhibit low frequency oscillations with periods typically in the range from minutes to days, closely-spaced modes and a low signal to noise ratio, which makes modal analysis by simple spectral techniques challenging. Time domain operational modal analysis, specifically the Random Decrement Technique, was applied to extract modal parameters for the dominant surface seiches of Lake Geneva, Switzerland, and Lake Tahoe, USA. The results obtained show good agreement with existing literature on the periods and damping ratios of the seiches, historically obtained in this field by visual selection of free-decay sections of the time series or half-power peak picking. These analyses illustrate the potential for the use of techniques developed for operational modal analysis in areas outside the realm of mechanical and civil structures dynamics.

Keywords: Random Decrement Technique, Low frequency oscillations, Novel applications

1. INTRODUCTION

When wind acts upon the surface of large bodies of water, such as lakes, reservoirs, lagoons, and semi-enclosed coastal bays, for an extended period of time and with a consistent direction, the stress of the wind on the water surface can lead to an upwelling of water at one end of the lake, as shown in Figure 1. Once the wind force undergoes a change of direction or reduction in magnitude, the water level seeks to find an equilibrium and an oscillation, known as a surface or barotropic seiche, is induced within the lake. The restoring force of this oscillation is gravity, with energy damped from the system through the friction between the body of water and the lake bed (water-sediment interface) and friction between water molecules [1]. The damping of surface seiches leads to a reduction in the amplitude of each subsequent oscillation and a slight increase of the period of oscillation in the absence of further forcing of the system [2, 3].

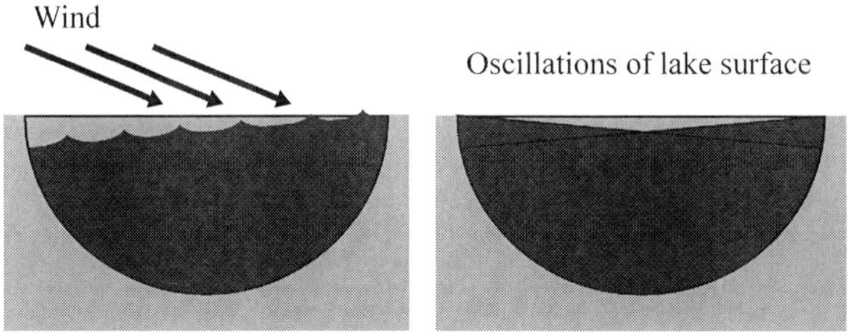

Figure 1: Surface seiche oscillation

Surface seiche motion can lead to flooding of areas around the perimeter of the lake and damage to boats and other structures within or close to it [4, 5, 6, 7]. They are of interest to ecologists as they provide a mechanism through which currents and nutrient fluxes are induced within the lake. Due to the introduction of additional nutrients into lakes from fertilizer run-off, this area of study is becoming increasingly important to prevent eutrophication, the build up of excessive nutrients within a water body, which may destroy fragile ecosystems and make the water unfit for human use or consumption due to algal and bacterial blooms [8].

There are a number of factors which make seiches difficult to analyse in practice, including the long period of the oscillation, which may range from minutes to days per cycle, the low signal to noise ratio and the excitation of multiple vibration modes within the lake, associated with different axis of oscillations. For lakes with multiple axes of similar lengths and bathymetry (underwater topography), these modes are close-modes of similar frequency.

The frequencies of surface seiches are well established for many lakes but few measurements of their associated damping behaviour were found in an extensive literature review. A widely cited [2, 9, 10, 11, 12, 13] but unverified study published in 1934 by A. Endrös [1], with the results reproduced in English in A. Defant's Physical Oceanography Volume II [2, Table 25. Pg. 187], used visual inspection of water elevation records for 35 lakes. Surface seiche periods and damping ratios were obtained through visual identification of 5 consecutive oscillations with decaying amplitudes which were deemed by Endrös to be free from further forcing.

The damping ratio of the lakes was expressed by Endrös through the logarithmic decrement, λ, and a damping constant or factor of friction, β. For the mth and nth peaks in each oscillation the logarithmic decrement is given by:

$$\lambda = \frac{\log(A_m) - \log(A_n)}{m-n} = \frac{\beta.T}{2} \tag{1}$$

Where T is the period of the oscillation in minutes and A is the amplitude of the peak. The amplitude of the nth wave is therefore given by:

$$A_n = A_1.e^{-\beta.\frac{n.T}{2}} \tag{2}$$

For the sake of clarity, in this paper, all damping is presented as a percentage of energy lost between oscillations, expressed by:

$$\text{Energy loss (\%)} = 100\left[1 - \frac{1}{e^{2\pi.\delta}}\right] \tag{3}$$

where δ is the damping ratio given by:

$$\delta = \frac{\beta}{2\pi/T} \tag{4}$$

Hence:

$$\text{Energy loss } (\%) = 100\left[1 - \frac{1}{e^{\beta/T}}\right] \tag{5}$$

Other studies of surface seiches have used frequency-domain spectral methods including power spectral density, coherence and least-squares harmonic analyses [14] to identify natural frequencies using spectral peaks. The associated damping ratios are often extracted using the peak-amplitude method, also known as the half-power or quality factor method [15]. These techniques are highly dependent on the filtering and windowing of the data during the frequency domain transformation and may struggle to extract accurate damping estimates for lakes with close-modes. A drawback of frequency domain techniques for use in the study of surface seiches is that they often appear intimidating to the user and there are numerous considerations in the selection of appropriate analysis parameters, improper selection of which may invalidate the modal parameters obtained.

In this paper we demonstrate the application of the random decrement method to extract the dominant seiches for Lake Geneva, Switzerland, and Lake Tahoe, USA. The results obtained for the frequencies of both seiches offer good agreement with previous measurements calculated through frequency domain analysis. The damping ratios obtained for Lake Geneva are of a similar magnitude to the results obtained by Endrös [1], while the damping ratio obtained for the Lake Tahoe dominant surface seiche is the first measurement of its kind. As this work represented the first application of the random decrement technique to the study of seiches, extensive sensitivity analyses were carried out on the input parameters for the random decrement method.

As there may be modes of vibration which are rarely excited but which result in lower frequencies of oscillation, the term 'dominant' seiche has been used throughout this paper to signify the lowest frequency seiche which is observable within the data analysed. The dominant seiche observed for both lakes within this study correlates with the lowest frequency surface seiche oscillation recorded within the literature. Due to the low frequency of seiche oscillations all results are presented as seiche periods in either cycles per hour or minutes as appropriate.

2. METHODOLOGY

2.1. Formation of the Random Decrement Model for Seiche Analysis

The random decrement model was formed of three components:

1. Data was filtered using a band-pass filter to remove low frequency oscillations from the dataset. These low frequency motions are associated with diurnal tides, the Coriolis effect and seasonal variations in water level. In all cases the periods of these motions are in excess of six hours and are easily filtered.

2. The data was analysed using a level-crossing Random Decrement Technique (RDT) [16, 17] with amplitude trigger levels specified as multiples of the standard deviation of the filtered dataset.

3. The Random Decrement Signature (RDS) obtained was analysed in the time domain using the Matrix-Pencil Method [18], a time-domain curve-fitting technique which uses the identification of response function poles as a solution to the generalised eigenvalue problem. The RDS is decomposed into a series of complex exponentials, from which the damping ratios and seiche periods are calculated.

MATLAB was used for the application of the Random Decrement model to both lakes. The use of the Matrix-Pencil Method is based on the assumption that the free-response of the lake oscillation is comprised exclusively of sinusoidal motion with a constant damping ratio, an assumption supported by prior observations [2, 19, 12, 7, 5].

3. CASE STUDIES

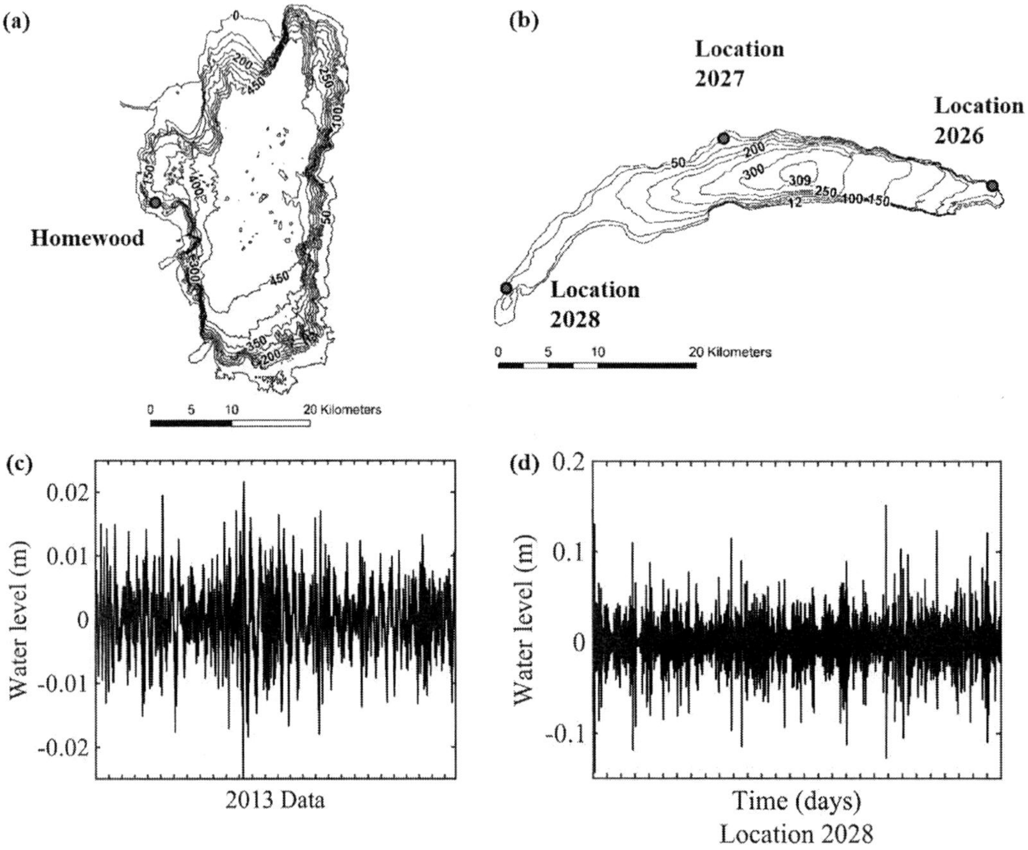

Figure 2: (a) Bathymetry of Lake Tahoe showing location of sampling site, (b) Bathymetry of Lake Geneva showing location of sampling sites, (c) Filtered 30-day sample of water level data for Lake Tahoe. (d) Filtered 30-day sample of water level data for Lake Geneva,

3.1. Study Site 1: Lake Geneva

Situated on the border of Switzerland and France, Lake Geneva is the largest freshwater lake in Western Europe with an average depth of 154m, a maximum depth of 309m and a surface area of 580km^2. The lake has a maximum width of 14km, with the crescent shape of the lake basin leading to northern and southern shorelines of length 95km and 72km respectively.

The dominant surface seiches in Lake Geneva both run along the east-west axis of the lake and have observed oscillation periods of 73.5 minutes (first dominant mode) and 36.7 minutes (second dominant mode). These seiches are associated with the prevailing north-easterly and south-westerly winds across the lake basin, with a small degree of seasonal variation observed in the dominant wind direction. At the shallower and narrower western end of the lake the mean seiche amplitude is 17.5cm for the first mode surface seiche, compared to a mean amplitude of 4cm at the eastern end of the basin [20].

Water elevation data was collected at ten minute intervals at three locations, referred to as locations 2026, 2027 and 2028 and shown on Figure 2b, between 00:00 on the 1st of January, 1974, and 23:50 on the 7th of January, 2013.

3.2. Study Site 2: Lake Tahoe

Lake Tahoe is the largest alpine lake in North America and is known for its exceptional water clarity. It has an average depth of 300m, a maximum recorded depth of 501m, a surface area of 490km^2 [8], and is situated on the border between Nevada and California in the western United States of America. The lake has an approximate length of 19km and 35km along its east-west and north-south axis respectively, as shown in Figure 2a. The prevailing south-westerly winds in the lake basin lead to four dominant seiche modes, with the first and second dominant surface seiche modes occurring along the north-south axis of the lake and the third and fourth dominant surface seiche modes occurring along the east-west axis. The mean surface seiche amplitude for the first dominant mode is between 2.5cm and 5cm at northern and southern extremities of the lake [21, pp 6.9.].

The water elevation datasets for Lake Tahoe were recorded at 30 second intervals at a thermistor chain located at Homewood, marked on Figure 2a, between 30 July 2013 00:00:00 and 6 December 2013 23:59:30, 1 January 2014 00:00:00 and 10 May 2014 23:59:30 and, 6 January 2015 00:00:00 and 15 May 2015 23:59:30. These datasets were analysed individually and as a combined dataset to allow for the validation of stationarity assumptions across the datasets.

3.3. Results of Random Decrement Technique Analysis

Where there are multiple channels of simultaneous data available to measure a system response there is benefit in the adoption of a linked-triggering approach for the RDT. The RDT is applied to a single channel of data referred to as the trigger channel, with the sampling of all other data channels occurring each time the triggering condition is met for the trigger channel [22]. For optimal identification of modal parameters, the trigger channel should have a high signal to noise ratio at the frequency of interest [23].

The power spectral densities for each of the three Lake Geneva datasets are provided in Figure 3. The dataset noise has been quantified based on the mean magnitude of the power spectral density at 1.85 cycles/hour and 0.79 cycles/hour, an area assessed through visual inspection of Figure 3 to fall outside the spectral peaks associated with the seiche oscillations. The ratios for the magnitude of the power spectral density at the first dominant seiche frequency and the mean noise levels is quantified in Table 1 for each of the datasets. Location 2028, presented in green, has the highest signal to noise ratio and has been used as the trigger channel for the linked-triggering RDT analysis.

Table 1: Comparison of signal to noise ratios for power spectral densities for Lake Geneva, Locations 2026 to 2028. Peak signal value corresponds to obtained dominant seiche frequency. Higher estimate of noise level based on noise level at 1.85 cycles per hour. Lower estimate of noise level based on noise level obtained at 0.79 cycles per hour.

Location	Background noise level		Peak value-Dominant Seiche Mode	Peak Signal: Noise ratio - Peak 1 - Mean
	Higher estimate	Lower estimate		
2026	1.65E-05	8.11E-06	5.65E-05	5.20
2027	1.04E-05	3.67E-06	3.39E-05	6.23
2028	3.65E-05	2.16E-05	4.51E-04	16.58

The results of the RDT analysis with a triggering value of 4 standard deviations of the location 2028 dataset is presented in Table 2 for each location. Consistent damping estimation for the seiche oscillation at locations 2026 and 2027 was not possible due to the smaller amplitude of the seiche and the greater levels of noise at these locations. The larger amplitude of the seiche oscillation at Location 2028 allowed consistent results for the energy loss associated with the dominant seiche to be obtained and are provided

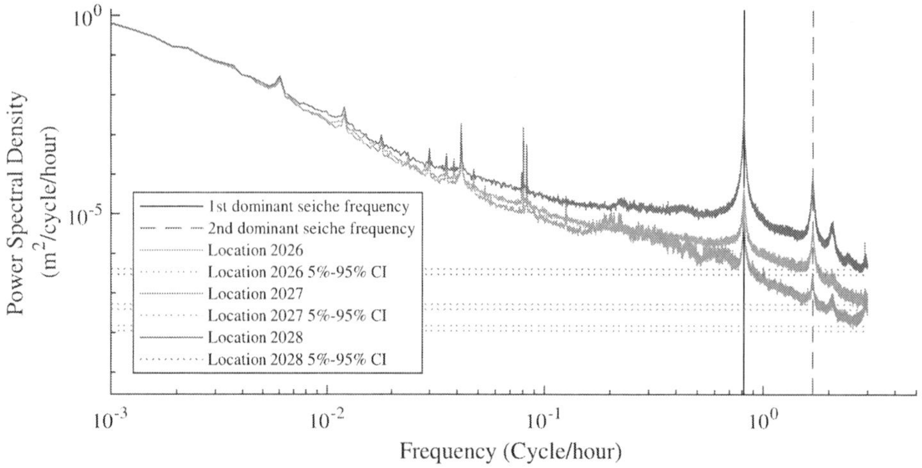

Figure 3: Power spectral density plot of filtered elevation data for Lake Geneva. Power spectra filtered through band-averaging of the power spectral density with a rectangular window of length 120 samples. Confidence intervals calculated using a Chi-square distribution with 120 degrees of freedom [24]

in Table 2. The seiche period obtained show strong agreement with the seiche period obtained through spectral methods by Graf [19] of 73.5 to 74.2 minutes and the 73.5 minute period obtained by Endrös [1] through visual inspection of unprocessed time-series data collected by Forel [25].

Endrös [1] reported an energy loss per oscillation of 2.96%, lower than the 4.72% obtained in this study but of a similar magnitude.

Table 2: Dominant seiche period obtained for Locations 2026 to 2028 on Lake Geneva through use of the linked triggering RDT analysis and energy loss for dominant seiche period for Location 2028. The triggering channel is defined as the channel for which when the triggering condition is met data sections are taken for all three locations (2026 to 2028) for the location specific RDSs. The triggering location used is Location 2028 with a triggering values of four standard deviations.

Triggering Channel = Location 2028				
Location 2026 Dominant Seiche - Period (Minutes)	Location 2027 - Dominant Seiche - Period (Minutes)	Location 2028 - Dominant Seiche - Period (Minutes)	Location 2028 - Location 2028 - Period (Minutes)	Number of Sections of data included in RDS per Location
73.63	73.80	73.78	4.72%	8,126

Presented in Figures 4a) and b) are the variation in the measured seiche period and energy loss respectively with varying level-crossing trigger values. In building vibration it has been suggested that this variation may be due to an amplitude dependant variation in the modal parameters [26, 27]. The variation in the parameters obtained at the lower levels of the triggering condition are likely due to triggering by measurement noise, at the higher levels of the triggering condition insufficient data sections are included within the RDS resulting in a poor estimation of the autocorrelation function. Based on Figure 4a) and b) a RDT trigger level of one standard deviation was found to be a reasonable lower bound for consistent modal parameter estimation for both lakes, with an upper bound set as when the number of data sections within the RDS fell below 2,000, a limit recommended by Tamura et al [28] for the use of the RDT with building vibration measurements. Within these limits the seiche period varied by between 0.01% and 0.21% of the mean period for the three locations across the trigger level range. The energy loss per oscillation for location 2028 varied between 4% and 4.9% across the trigger level range, suggesting a potential increase in energy dissipation with amplitude.

Presented in Figure 5 is the RDS for Locations 2028 with a triggering value of 4 standard deviations and with Location 2028 used as the triggering channel. In agreement with the observed increase in seiche amplitude at the shallower western end of the lake basin [20], the seiche amplitude obtained for Location 2028 through the linked-triggering RDT is an order of magnitude larger than that for locations 2026 and 2027, illustrated in Figure 7.

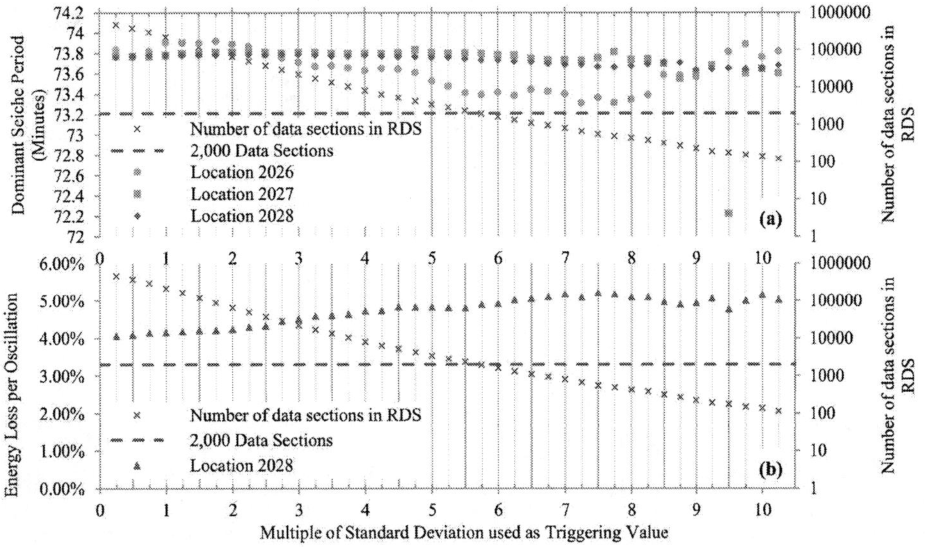

Figure 4: a) Variation in dominant seiche period and b) Variation in energy loss per seiche oscillation with varying triggering value for Location 2028. The resulting number of data sections averaged to produce the RDS is also plotted.

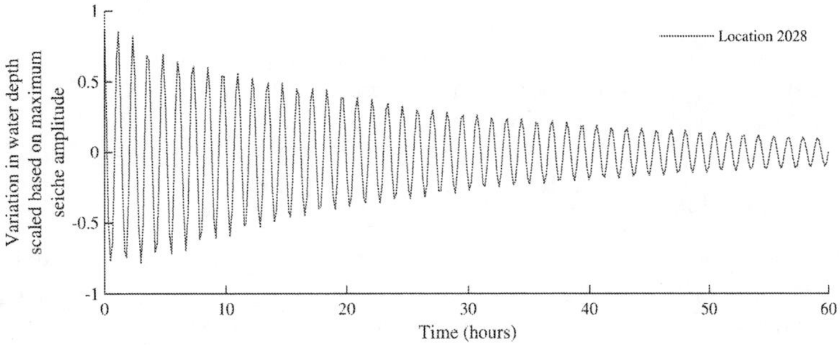

Figure 5: RDS for Location 2028, where Location 2028 is utilized as the triggering channel with a triggering value of four standard deviations. Amplitude scaled based on maximum seiche amplitude for Location 2028.

The seiche periods and damping ratio obtained for the dominant surface seiche at Lake Tahoe are provided in Table 3 alongside values obtained from the literature. No previous calculation of the damping ratio for this seiche was found in an extensive literature review. The variation in the seiche period obtained for various level crossing values of the RDT are presented in Figure 6. Consistent modal parameters were obtained for triggering values between one standard deviation of the dataset and when the number of sections in the RDS fell below 2,000. A slightly greater variation is observed in the energy loss per oscillation. Given the small magnitude of the seiche itself it seems unlikely that the physical damping mechanism would be greatly affected by even relatively large changes in amplitude. A percentage variation for the 2013 to 2015 combined dataset of 3.24% for the seiche period and 14.07% for the energy loss per oscillation is observed as the amplitude of the RDT triggering is varied from one standard deviation to when the number of segments within the RDS falls below 2,000.

Table 3: Dominant period and associated energy loss obtained through RDT analysis for Lake Tahoe for individual annual datasets (2013 to 2015) and for all data combined sequentially into a single dataset alongside values obtained from existing literature. The triggering value for the collection of data sections for the RDS was 1.5 standard deviations from the mean of the filtered data.

Source	Ichinose et al [30]	Tahoe Environmental Research Center [21, pp 6.9.]	RDT 2013	RDT 2014	RDT 2015	RDT 2013 - 2015
Period (Minutes)	11.22	11.7	11.22	11.21	11.22	11.21
Energy loss	N/A	N/A	1.09%	1.95%	1.79%	1.62%
Number of data sections included within RDS	N/A	N/A	3,250	5,210	5,152	15,104

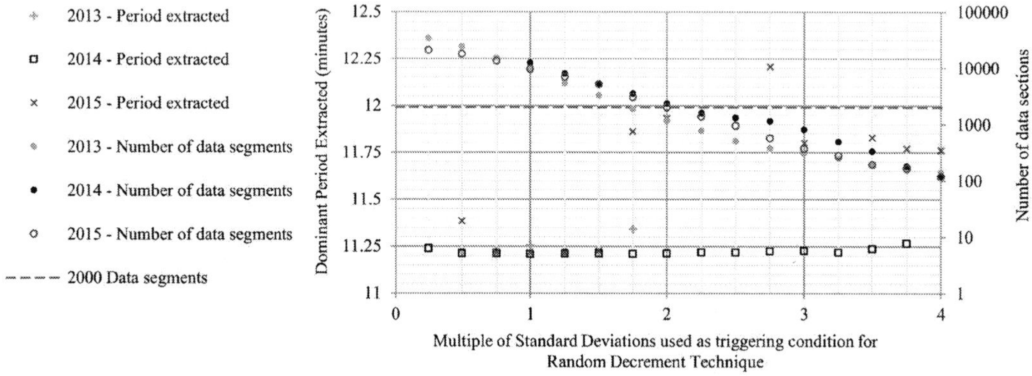

Figure 6: Comparison of seiche period (crosses and squares) extracted for Lake Tahoe, 2013 to 2015 water level data, using RDT, and number of data sections in the RDT analysis (circles) for varying trigger values. Dashed line corresponds to limit of 2,000 data sections proposed by Tamura et al [28] for the extraction of meaningful results. Once the number of data sections included within the RDS falls below 2,000, the obtained damping ratio begins to display random behaviour. Note: The following data points fall outside the plotted data range - 2013: 0.25 and 2 to 4 standard deviations used as trigger. 2014: 4 standard deviations used as trigger. 2015: 0.25, 2.25, 2.5 and 3.25 standard deviations used as trigger.

3.4. Lake Geneva mode shape

An advantage of the use of the linked triggering RDT for the Lake Geneva analysis is that the mode shape of the seiche can be approximated, illustrated in Figure 7. The phase difference and relative magnitude of the seiches is retained in the RDSs produced for all locations, as shown in Figure 8. At each time step a straight line is used to connect the surface elevation at each location, producing an estimate of the mode shape. This illustrates the greater seiche amplitude at the narrow, shallow western end of the lake basin, with a node located between location 2028 and 2027. As it is not expected that the mode shape is longitudinally symmetric, due to the variation of the lake bathymetry, this allows us to ascertain that the node location lies much closer to location 2027 than 2028, with locations 2026 and 2027 being in-phase with each other and in perfect anti-phase with location 2028.

4. DISCUSSION

4.1. Seiche Period

As the water level of Lake Geneva has been artificially maintained since 1885 [29] it would be expected that there would be little variation in seiche observations, as supported by the agreement in the seiche periods obtained in this study and in existing literature, presented in Table 2.

The seiche periods obtained in this study for the separate yearly data sets for Lake Tahoe give a mean pe-

STRUCTURE HEALTH MONITORING

IOMAC'19
8th International Operational Modal Analysis Conference
2019 May13-15 Copenhagen

A FIRST STEP IN QUANTIFYING THE VALUE OF OMA BASED FATIGUE STRESS ESTIMATION

Bruna Nabuco[1]*, Henning Brüske*[2]*, Michael Faber*[3]*, and Rune Brincker*[4]

[1] M.Sc., Denmark Technical University, brunan@dtu.dk.
[2] Ph.D., Aalborg University, heb@civil.aau.dk.
[3] Prof., Aalborg University, mfn@civil.aau.dk.
[4] Prof., Denmark Technical University, runeb@byg.dtu.dk.

ABSTRACT

To facilitate the modelling of the fatigue life of an offshore structure, a methodology based on the Operational Modal Analysis (OMA) is proposed. The idea is to utilize monitoring results as a means to reduce uncertainties associated with structural responses and to take benefit of this information to optimize assets integrity management. In the present work a scaled model of a structure is considered for which the displacements are measured under random excitation. The strains at any point of the model structure are estimated based on OMA and the accuracy is assessed and verified by comparing the estimates with strain gauge measurements. The obtained strains are used to evaluate the equivalent stress range, which is further used to compute fatigue failure probabilities as well as risk estimates. Obtaining information comes at a cost, which is quantified using value of information analysis. The value of information assessment is illustrated through a principal example.

Keywords: Value of Information, Fatigue stress, Offshore structure

1. INTRODUCTION

The engineering field that studies the modal properties of systems under ambient vibrations or normal operating conditions is denoted Operational Modal Analysis (OMA). OMA provides useful methods for modal analysis over several application domains of structural engineering [1]. Identification of modal properties of a structural system is the process of correlating the dynamic characteristics of a mathematical model with the physical properties of the structure of interest derived from experimental measurements. In OMA, measured data obtained under operational responses are utilized to estimate the parameters of models that describe the system behavior.

Assessments of fatigue damages of offshore structures are usually based on stresses derived from a finite element (FE) model of the structure subject to loads, which are modelled based on wave statistics. It is anticipated that the uncertainties associated with the assessed fatigue damage will be reduced when the FE model is updated according to OMA.

In the present paper, this approach is applied to a scaled model of typical tripod jacket platform. The objective is to validate the approach by comparing the strains obtained through OMA with strain gauge measurements.

The experiment data providing the basis for the validation are the same as those reported in a previous study [2].

Beyond the experimental case study, the application of fatigue reliability assessments and value of information analysis are illustrated on a principal example.

2. THEORY

Aiming to estimate the strains in any point of a structure using OMA, the first step is to measure the displacements in a few points of the structure using accelerometers. Then, a modal identification is undertaken to assess the dynamic properties of the structure, and on this basis the mode shape vectors are estimated, **A**.

The estimated modal coordinates, $\widehat{q}(t)$, are identified through a relation between the pseudo inverse of the mode shape matrix, $\mathbf{A}^{+}$, and the measured displacements, $\mathbf{y}(\mathrm{t})$:

$$\widehat{q}(t) = \mathbf{A}^{+}\,\mathbf{y}(\mathrm{t}) \tag{1}$$

In the present study, the mode shape matrix is smoothed by the use of the Local Correspondence (LC) principle [3] and expanded to the same number of degrees of freedom of the FE model (full matrix). Since the modal coordinates for strains and displacements are the same [4], the strain history, $\hat{\varepsilon}(t)$, is estimated as:

$$\hat{\varepsilon}(t) = \mathbf{A}_{\varepsilon}\,\widehat{q}(\mathrm{t}) \tag{2}$$

where $\mathbf{A}_{\varepsilon}$ is the full strain mode shape matrix from the FE model multiplied by a transformation matrix defined with the use of the LC principle.

3. CASE STUDY

Based on a typical tripod jacket, a scaled model 1:50 has been built in polymethyl methacrylate (PMMA) as presented in Figure 1. Reference [5] describes the model structure in more details.

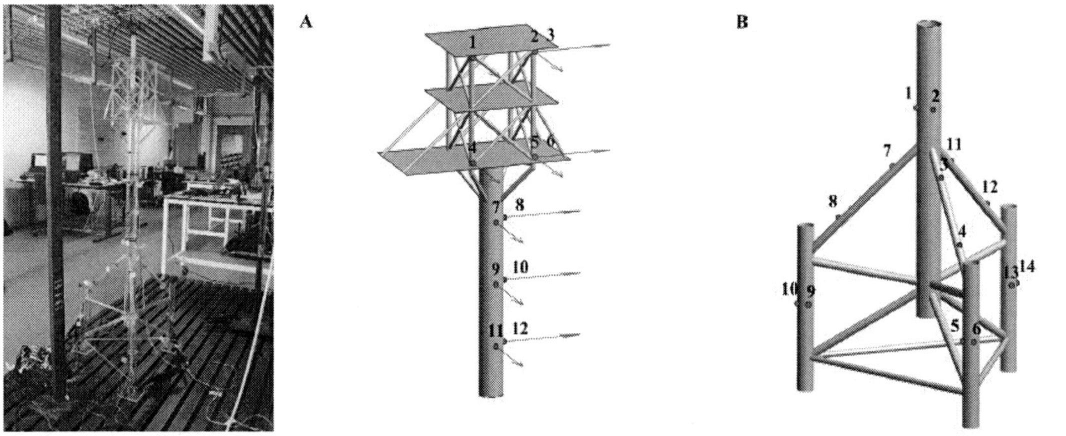

Figure 1. Photograph of the experimental model. A - Positions of the accelerometers. B - Positions of the strain gauges (SGl-SGl4).

The aim is to apply the OMA based stress estimation technique to assess the responses of the structure in areas not easily accessible – such as in the vicinity of joints below the sea-surface – from measurements obtained in easily accessible locations – e.g. along the topside. For this purpose, 12 uniaxial accelerometers are positioned on the upper part of the structure and 14 strain gauges are positioned on the lower part – see Figure 1.

Five data sets are established through simultaneous measurements of accelerations and strains induced by exciting the model structure with a nylon brush. Each data set has a duration of two minutes, which is equivalent to 32 minutes of measurements on a full-scale structure.

The data are acquired with a sampling frequency of 1651 Hz. A band pass filter is applied to filter both the acceleration and strain measurements with a cutoff at 5 Hz and 80 Hz in order to remove the noise at DC and only include the first five modes.

3.1. Modal Identification & FE model

A modal identification is performed to obtain the natural frequencies and mode shapes of the model structure using Frequency Domain Decomposition (FDD) [6], which is based on calculation of Spectral Density Matrices of the measured data series by discrete Fourier transformation. A segment size of 4096 is used for estimating the correlation function matrix and the spectral density matrix [1].

A FE model of the model structure is developed and its dynamic properties are compared with the modal identification results – see Table 1 and Figure 1.

Table 1. Comparison between experimental and numerical results.

	Mode 1	Mode 2	Mode 3	Mode 4	Mode 5
Experimental Frequency [Hz]	9.84	9.91	23.45	64.99	71.14
Numerical Frequency [Hz]	10.12	10.17	24.87	65.13	71.69
Error [%]	2.89	2.65	6.03	0.22	0.78
Modal Assurance Criterion (MAC)	0.983	0.984	0.9937	0.9788	0.9485

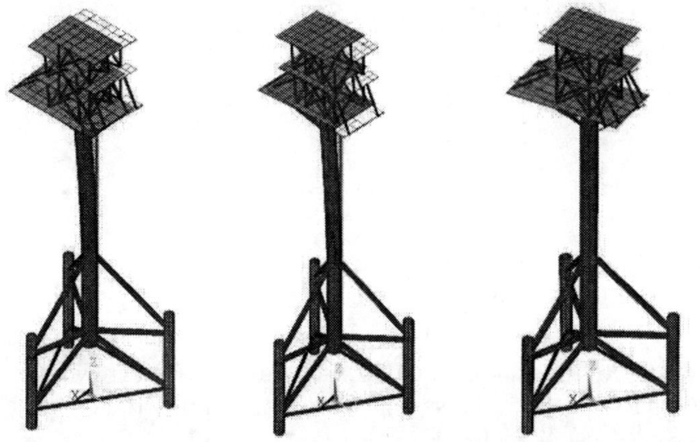

Figure 2. First three modes of the FE model.

3.2. Strain Responses and Quality Assurance

Using the FE model, the strains are estimated at the positions of each strain gauge (SG). Figure 3 (left) presents the estimated and measured strains at the position of SG2.

The accuracy of the estimated strains, $\hat{\boldsymbol{\varepsilon}}$, is verified by comparison with the measured strains, $\boldsymbol{\varepsilon}$. To this end the Time Response Assurance Criterion (TRAC) [7] is utilized according to Eq. (3). TRAC is a quality assurance quantitative measurement used to compare general shapes and tendencies in data series – see Figure 3 (right) for results.

$$TRAC = \frac{(\boldsymbol{\varepsilon}^T\,\hat{\boldsymbol{\varepsilon}})^2}{(\boldsymbol{\varepsilon}^T\,\boldsymbol{\varepsilon})(\hat{\boldsymbol{\varepsilon}}^T\,\hat{\boldsymbol{\varepsilon}})} \tag{3}$$

For the two strain gauges located on the main structure of the model, SG1 and SG2 (see Figure 1), the TRAC values are higher than 99.4%. The minimum TRAC value obtained was 97.6% at the position of SG14.

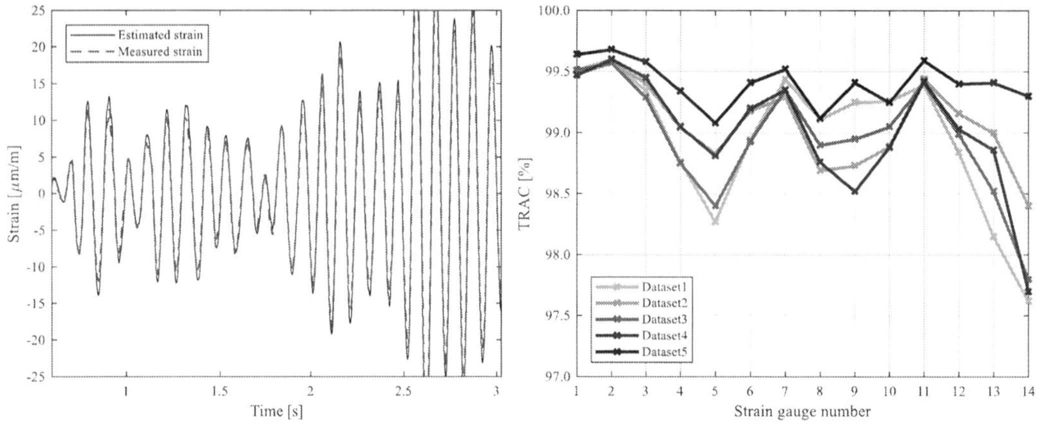

Figure 3. Strain history at channel 2 (left). TRAC results for SG1-SG14 (right).

4. FATIGUE ASSESSMENT

The fatigue life is modelled based on the S-N fatigue approach under the assumption of linear cumulative damage, D, as per Palmgren-Miner rule [8]:

$$D = \sum_{i=1}^{j} \frac{n_i}{N_i} = \frac{1}{a} \sum_{i=1}^{j} n_i \cdot S_i{}^{m} \tag{4}$$

where n is the number of stress cycles, N is the number of cycles to failure at constant stress range, S is the stress range at block i, m is the S-N slope parameter and a is the S-N curve intercept parameter.

The number of cycles of different stress ranges is assessed through the rainflow cycle counting algorithm [9] both for the estimated and the measured strain histories.

From fracture mechanics theory of fatigue, it is known that if the crack initiation phase is negligible, the slope parameter, m, of the SN-curve is identical to the exponent of the crack growth power law. This parameter depends mainly on the material property. For structural steels, as in offshore structures, most experimental data for crack growth give an exponent of 3 [10].

The S-N curve intercept parameter, a, depends on the geometry of the connection and type of weld. Since this is not a local fatigue assessment, the concept of equivalent stress range was introduced as a means to represent the spectral fatigue loading through only one equivalent stress range.

5. EQUIVALENT STRESS RANGE

There is a constant amplitude stress range that causes the same fatigue damage as the sequence of variable amplitude stress ranges it replaces for the same number of cycles [10]. This constant amplitude is known as the equivalent stress range.

This implies that the equivalent stress range, S_{eq}, is constant through the total number of cycles, N_t, and must give the same damage ratio as calculated using Eq. (4).

$$D = \frac{1}{a} N_t \left(S_{eq}\right)^{m} \tag{5}$$

where N_t is the total number of stress cycles, $N_t = \sum_i n_i$. By combining Eq. (4) and Eq. (5), the equivalent stress range can be expressed by:

$$S_{eq} = \left(\frac{1}{N_t} \sum_{i=1}^{j} n_i \cdot (S_i)^m \right)^{\frac{1}{m}} \tag{6}$$

It is observed that the equivalent stress range established through Eq. (6) does not depend on the S-N curve intercept parameter. Table 2 presents the results of equivalent stress range at the position of SG2, which exhibits more critical results in terms of stresses.

Table 2. Equivalent Stress Range at the position of SG 2 – without calibration.

Data set	σ_{eq} [MPa]		ε_{eq} [μ strains]		Difference
	Estimated	Measured	Estimated	Measured	[%]
1	17.11	18.04	85.53	90.20	**5.17%**
2	24.50	25.99	122.49	129.95	**5.74%**
3	18.84	19.92	94.18	99.61	**5.46%**
4	19.98	21.24	99.88	106.22	**5.97%**
5	46.02	49.33	230.10	246.65	**6.71%**

In case of applying this technique on a real structure, in addition to the measurements of the accelerometers, it would also be considered positioning a strain gauge at least in one location of the structure. In this way, the measurements of this strain gauge may be utilized to calibrate the values of strains estimated by OMA.

In the present study, this calibration is undertaken by first considering each strain gauge as the reference to calibrate all the others 13. However, since the strains at the different locations in the structure do not follow the same tendency, the calibrated values of the equivalent stress range are very close to the ones presented in Table 2.

SG1 and SG2 are both located at the main structure of the model, so it is expected that the measurements from these two strain gauges follow the same tendency. Therefore, Table 3 presents the equivalent stress range at SG2 after calibrating the strains only considering the measurements from SG1 as a reference.

Table 3. Equivalent Stress Range at the position of SG 2 – calibration according to SG1 measurements.

Data set	σ_{eq} [MPa]		ε_{eq} [μ strains]		Difference
	Estimated	Measured	Estimated	Measured	[%]
1	18.47	18.04	92.36	90.20	**-2.40%**
2	26.39	25.99	131.93	129.95	**-1.52%**
3	20.32	19.92	101.61	99.61	**-2.00%**
4	21.53	21.24	107.65	106.22	**-1.35%**
5	49.56	49.33	247.80	246.65	**-0.47%**

6. RELIABILITY ESTIMATION

The fatigue damage and resistance are both assumed to be lognormal distributed. The resistance is assumed to have an expected value equal to $\mu_R = 1$ and a coefficient of variation (CoV) equal to $\sigma_R^2 = 0.1$. The expected value and the CoV of D_t are assumed to be μ_D, and σ_D^2, respectively. For our simple example we consider μ_D to increase linearly from 0.0 to 1.0. Analogous, the damage standard deviation increases linear because the damage CoV is 0.25. The fatigue limit state equation may be written as:

$$L_{des} = R - D_t \tag{7}$$

The limit state equation for the case of OMA monitoring information is

$$L_{SHM} = R - D_t'' \tag{8}$$

Where D_t'' is a random variable with Bayesian posterior distribution obtained by Bayesian updating as:

$$D_t''(\theta|x) = \frac{D_t(x) \cdot D_{OMA_t}(x|\theta)}{\int_{-\infty}^{\infty} D_t(x) \cdot D_{OMA_t}(x|\theta) d\theta} \tag{9}$$

$D_{OMA_t}(x|\theta)$ is the likelihood, i.e. the distribution of the observation / measurement. Its parameters are θ, the conditioning variable, in our example it is the cov of the OMA results, and x is a prior parameter, the cov of prior distribution. The likelihood function D_{OMA} has the mean as D_t and θ is the sum of the strain gauge CoV (1%) and absolute mean of differences in Table 3. The resulting fatigue failure probability estimates ($P(L_{des})$ and $P(L_{SHM})$) are plotted in Figure 4. In the beginning of the considered time period the estimated failure probabilities differ only very little, but after about $t = 13$ the failure probability estimate based on OMA structural health monitoring information become significant smaller than the design estimate as shown by the graph of Δ, the difference of $P(L_{des})$ and $P(L_{SHM})$. According to [11] an annual fatigue failure probability of 10^{-2} is acceptable for unmanned platforms. The design model predicts in this case a service-life of $t = 28$ and with OMA information a service-life of $t = 35$. $1t$ may be understood as e.g. 1 year, although this can vary with respect to the reference period of the reliability criterion. In order to keep the focus on essential aspects of OMA and value of information, the reliability analysis is simplified by omitting information from previous fatigue failure-free service.

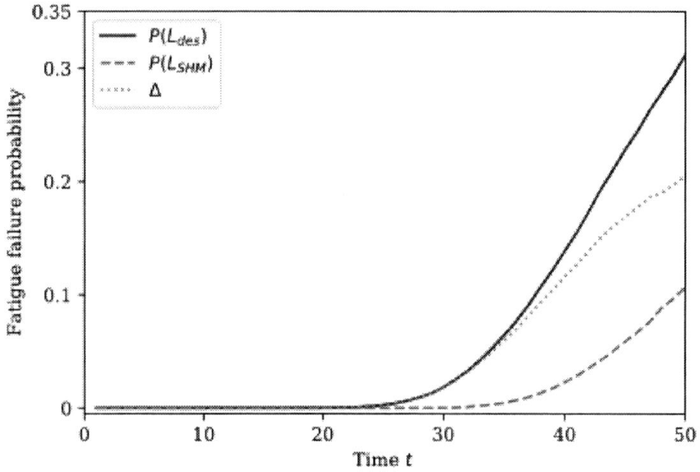

Figure 4: Annual fatigue failure probability estimates

7. VALUE OF INFORMATION

Value of information (VoI) is a concept in Bayesian decision theory. The VoI, V_I, compares the expected values of utilities obtained from a decision optimization based on prior information and pre-posterior information. Experiments yield sample information. Therefore, we base VoI on the expected value of sample information [12].

$$V_I = \min_{\boldsymbol{a}} E_{\boldsymbol{X}}\left[\boldsymbol{u}_{\text{prior}}(\boldsymbol{X},\boldsymbol{a})\right] - \min_{\boldsymbol{P},\boldsymbol{a}} E_{\boldsymbol{Z},\boldsymbol{X}}\left[\boldsymbol{u}_{\text{pre-post}}(\boldsymbol{Z},\boldsymbol{X},\boldsymbol{P},\boldsymbol{a})\right] \tag{10}$$

The maximum prior expected value of utility is determined by optimizing $\boldsymbol{u}_{\text{prior}}(\mathbf{X},\mathbf{a})$ depending on each of the states $\boldsymbol{X}$ and the action alternatives $\boldsymbol{a}$. The action alternatives are to extent the fatigue service-life based on OMA supported failure probability estimates or do not extent the service-life. In our example the utility is formulated as cost, thus the optimization will be a minimization. In order to choose the lowest expected value of the cost / utility, the vector $\boldsymbol{u}_{\text{pre-post}}(\boldsymbol{Z},\boldsymbol{X},\boldsymbol{P},\boldsymbol{a})$ must be minimized with respect to $\boldsymbol{a}$ and additionally to the choice of experiments $\boldsymbol{P}$. $\boldsymbol{Z}$ are random variables representing the unknown experiment (OMA) outcomes. A more detailed introduction of VoI can be found in [13].

By multiplying the cost of each year with the probability that it occurs, we get an expected value of the cost that can be objectively compared to the expected value of costs generated under different conditions. For simplicity of presentation, discounting is disregarded.

The fatigue life-cycle management is limited to the simplest case, in which no repairs or other remedial measures are considered. We analyze the effect of OMA information on the life-cycle performance. The OMA information is used in order to extend the fatigue-life. For simplicity only the fatigue failure consequences, e.g. loss of the structure's fitness for purpose 1,000,000 MU (monetary units), monitoring costs, and annual income of 10,000 MU are considered. Monitoring cost consist of annual SHM operation costs (1 MU) as well as the initial and decadal SHM system replacement costs (100 MU).

The operation, installation and replacement costs arise with probability = 1 at their time of occurrence. The probability of losing the structure to fatigue damage determines multiplied by the consequences of fatigue failure (above mentioned 1,000,000 MU) the expected failure costs. The expected income is the nominal income times the survival probability. Due to the low failure probabilities (see Figure 4), there is only little contribution to the expected value of costs before $t = 21$ when the cumulative expected cost of structure with OMA information exceed the expected cumulative costs of the monitored structure, see the failure probability influence also in Figure 5 (b). The graphs in Figure 5 (a) and (b) end at the estimated fatigue service-life of the monitored structure. The graph 'without OMA' in Figure 5 (a) does no longer change after the fatigue service-life of 28 t is reached, the monitored structure can still produce 7 t longer.

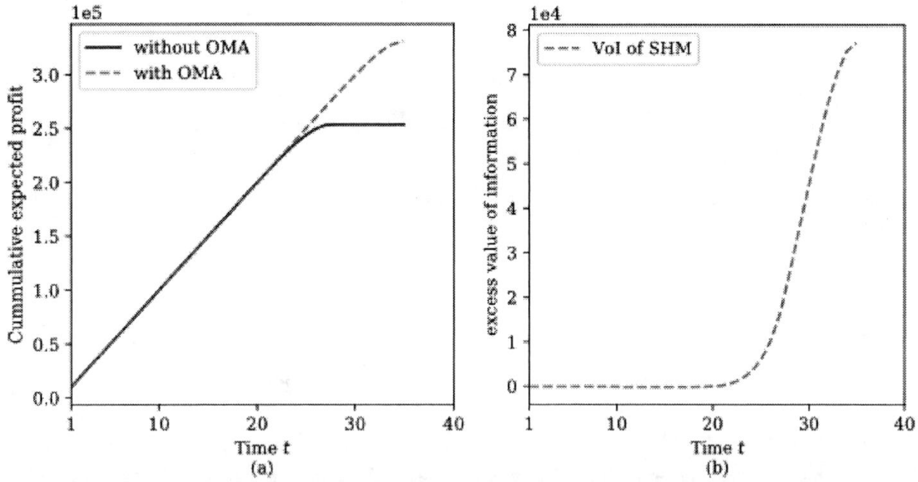

Figure 5: (a) Visualization to compare expected value of profits of the system utilizing OMA data vs. no additional information. (b) Excess VoI gained by the SHM system.

Figure 5 (b) shows the substantial value of information is generated by OMA due to the extended fatigue-life. The influence of the fatigue-life extension is apparent by the strong gradient at $t = 28$, where the service-life of the not monitored structure ends. The excess VoI becomes positive at $t = 21$, before reaching the predicted service-life.

8. CONCLUSIONS

OMA has been applied to a scaled model of a tripod jacket from which strains have been estimated with quality assurance, through Time Response Assurance Criterion, and used to calculate the equivalent stress range. A maximum difference of 6.71% was found when comparing the equivalent stress range based on the estimated strains with the one based on the measurements. This means it is possible to estimate the strains of a structure with good precision by performing structural health monitoring. Consequently, the fatigue assessment will be based on a more accurate value of stress and less uncertainties, which may allow for a fatigue life extension. It is important to note that in case the estimated strains are calibrated using one strain gauge as reference, the precision is increased – for this case study, we found a maximum difference of 2.40%.

In this example, we have obtained an extension of 7 t on the service-life by using OMA compared to the design fatigue life. However, it is important to note that this increase is only based on the standard deviation estimates.

It is expected to extend even more the fatigue life by taking the difference on the mean value into account assuming the design assumptions are conservative. This will be investigated in a further study.

Beyond a potential fatigue-life extension we also demonstrated in our principal example that the OMA information is of value, including costs it may produce, by reducing the expected costs stemming from fatigue failure before either, design or updated, fatigue-life is reached. The given examples for reliability and VoI analysis are very brief. They should be extended by considering other failure modes, better mechanical, consequence, cost, and income modelling, in order to provide a more comprehensive picture to understand the process.

ACKNOWLEDGEMENTS

The authors would like to thank Anders Skafte for sharing and providing input data from experiments in order to evaluate the results achieved in this paper.
The authors acknowledge the funding received from Centre for Oil and Gas – DTU/Danish Hydrocarbon Research and Technology Centre (DHRTC).

REFERENCES

[1] Brincker, R., & Ventura, C. (2015). Introduction to operational modal analysis. John Wiley and Sons, Inc., Chichester, West Sussex.

[2] Nabuco, B., Tarpø, M., Aïssani, A., & Brincker, R. (2017). Reliability Analysis of Offshore Structures Using OMA Based Fatigue Stresses. Proceedings of OMAE, paper 61730.

[3] Brincker, R., Skafte, A., López-Aenlle, M., Sestieri, A., D'Ambrogio, W., & Canteli, A. (2013). A local correspondence principle for mode shapes in structural dynamics. Mechanical Systems and Signal Processing 45, 91.

[4] Debao, L., Hongcheng, Z., & Bo, W. (1989). The principle and techniques of experimental strain modal analysis. Proceedings of 7th IMAC, 1285–1289.

[5] Skafte, A., Kristoffersen, J., Vestermark, J., Tygesen, U. T., & Brincker, R. (2017). Experimental study of strain prediction on wave induced structures using modal decomposition and quasi-static Ritz vectors. Engineering Structures 136, 261–276.

[6] Brincker, R., Zhang, L. & Andersen, P. (2001). Modal identification of output-only systems using frequency domain decomposition, Smart Materials and Structures 10 pp. 441–445.Christian.1939

[7] Avitabile, P., & Pingle, P. (2012). Prediction of full field dynamic strain from limited sets of measured data. Shock and Vibration 19, 765-785.

[8] Palmgren, A (1924). Die Lebensdauer von Kugellagern. VDI-Zeitschrift 68.

[9] ASTM E 1049-85 (Reapproved 1997), Standard practices for cycle counting in fatigue analysis, in: Annual Book of ASTM Standards, Vol. 03.01, Philadelphia 1999, pp. 710-718.

[10] Almar-Naess, A. (1985). Fatigue Handbook, Offshore Steel Structures. Tapir.

[11] DNVGL-RP-0005 (2014). Fatigue design of offshore steel structures.

[12] Raiffa, H., & Schlaifer, R. (1961). Applied statistical decision theory (3rd ed.). Havard University.

[13] Faber, M. H., & Thöns, S. (2013). On the Value of Structural Health Monitoring. In 22nd Annual Conference on European Safety and Reliability (pp. 2535–2544). London: Taylor & Francis Group.

IOMAC'19

8th International Operational Modal Analysis Conference
2019 May13-15 Copenhagen

ANALYSIS OF THE ENVIRONMENTAL INFLUENCE ON NATURAL FREQUENCIES OF A HOSPITAL BUILDING

Carlo Rainieri[1], Edwin Reynders[2], Giovanni Fabbrocino[3] and Guido De Roeck[4]

[1] Assistant Professor, University of Molise, carlo.rainieri@unimol.it.
[2] Assistant Professor, Katholieke Universiteit Leuven, edwin.reynders@kuleuven.be.
[3] Full Professor, University of Molise, giovanni.fabbrocino@unimol.it.
[4] Full Professor, Katholieke Universiteit Leuven, guido.deroeck@kuleuven.be.

ABSTRACT

Modal based Structural Health Monitoring (SHM) systems are often applied to detect structural ageing, degradation phenomena and damage due to hazardous events. However, the modal property estimates are also influenced by environmental and operational variables (EOVs) whose effects can hide damage. Direct modeling of the influence of EOVs on the modal characteristics of a structure is difficult, so black-box models are usually adopted as an alternative to map the changes of the modal properties with the EOVs. In particular, output-only techniques are particularly attractive when the set of measured EOVs is incomplete or the factors influencing the estimates cannot be clearly identified or measured. The present paper presents the results of some analyses aimed at identifying relevant EOVs and assessing their influence on the estimated natural frequencies of a hospital building through output-only techniques.

Keywords: Structural Health Monitoring, automated OMA, environmental effects, hospital.

1. INTRODUCTION

Hospitals play a fundamental role in post-earthquake emergency management, so they must be designed, built and maintained in a way able to ensure life safety to occupants and assistance to injured people. Nowadays, Structural Health Monitoring (SHM) technologies provide interesting opportunities for a near real-time assessment of the structural health after earthquakes. In this context, SHM systems provide contributions of paramount importance also in the field of structural management of existing healthcare facilities. In fact, high performance sensors in combination with the large computational power available today make possible the development of systems able to automatically process measurements of the structural response and to track global parameters representative of the health status of the structure.

Among the damage sensitive features that can be selected for damage detection, modal parameters extracted from the operational response of the structure are particularly attractive. They are frequently applied to develop SHM systems for the structural diagnosis of bridges and buildings [1]. In fact, modal based damage detection techniques have been widely investigated in the past and they are nowadays spreading in civil engineering also thanks to the development of reliable automated Operational Modal Analysis (OMA) procedures [2, 3]. The basic assumption of modal based damage detection is that damage affects the physical parameters (mass, stiffness and damping) of the structure, so that damage can be detected from the variations of the modal parameters.

Natural frequencies are often used as damage sensitive features because of the possibility of getting accurate estimates even in the presence of a few installed sensors. However, they are sensitive not only to damage but also to environmental and operational variables (EOVs). This represents a major drawback to the extensive application of modal based damage detection [4]. In fact, the changes in the natural frequency estimates due to EOVs can be of the same order of magnitude of those induced by damage. As a consequence, reliable and effective damage detection is possible only after the compensation of the environmental influence on the estimates, so that the resulting features are sensitive to damage, only [1].

Temperature is often responsible of large variations of natural frequency estimates over time. Compensating its effect requires a model able to reproduce the functional dependence of natural frequencies from the temperature. Regression models can be applied to this aim. However, the temperature distribution in actual structures is usually non-uniform and time dependent [5], so determining where the corresponding sensors should be placed is not trivial. This problem can be overcome by using output-only techniques so that measurements of the EOVs are not needed. This is particularly useful when the temperature is not the only parameter influencing the estimates, and the selection of the other EOVs to use in the development of the model is not straightforward. Statistical tools are often used for the sake of compensation of environmental effects on natural frequency estimates [6, 7]. Linear as well as non-linear procedures are available [8, 9].

In the present paper experimental data collected by the structural monitoring system installed on two adjacent buildings of the Cardarelli Hospital in Campobasso (Southern Italy) are analyzed in order to assess the influence of the temperature on the fundamental natural frequencies of the structure. After a short description of the monitoring system and the procedure for automated OMA, two procedures for compensation of environmental effects are reviewed and applied to the collected data. Results of compensations are finally discussed in view of SHM applications.

2. STRUCTURAL MONITORING OF THE CARDARELLI HOSPITAL

The main hospital - Cardarelli Hospital - in Campobasso (Southern Italy) consists of a number of reinforced concrete buildings designed and built according to out-dated seismic design codes. The vibration responses of two adjacent reinforced concrete structures hosting the inpatient wards are monitored since March 2016 [10]. The monitored structures have overall dimensions of about 78 m x 14 m in plan and 30 m in elevation. The two buildings are denoted as Block V and Block VI, respectively (Figure 1a), and a small structural joint separates them (Figure 1b).

Sixteen force-balance accelerometers (±0.5 g full scale range, 20 V/g sensitivity) have been installed at two upper levels along two orthogonal directions. Observability of translational as well as torsional modes is ensured by the installation of the sensors at opposite corners of the block plans. The accelerometers are wired to a centralized data acquisition system with 16 bit ADC. Data are sampled at 100 Hz and stored into a local MySQL database.

The collected data are continuously and automatically analyzed in order to track the evolution of the modal parameters over time. In particular, the monitoring system takes advantage of an original procedure to carry out automated OMA and continuously track the modal parameters of the monitored buildings [3]. The algorithm, called ARES® (acronym for Automated modal paRameter Extraction System), is able to provide accurate and precise modal parameter estimates without statically set thresholds and parameters. The key feature of the algorithm is, therefore, the absence of analysis parameters that have to be tuned at each new monitoring application. Reliability and accuracy of the algorithm have been demonstrated by a number of tests on simulated datasets, obtaining a success rate larger than 99% [3].

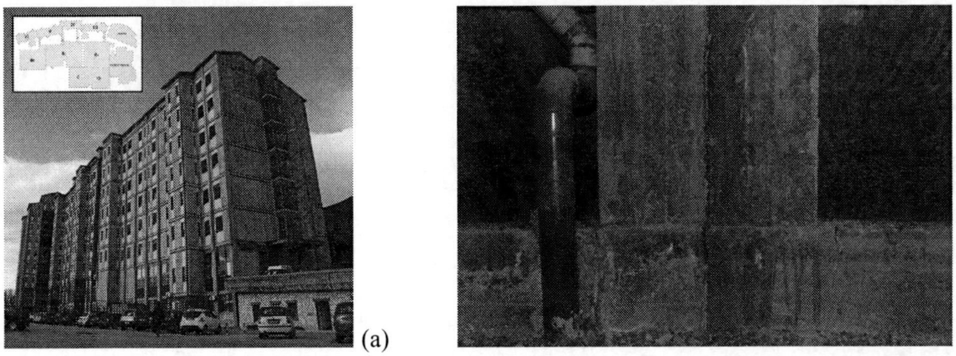

Figure 1. Monitored building blocks at the Cardarelli Hospital in Campobasso, Italy (a) and separation joint (b)

Sample results from continuous monitoring of the fundamental modal parameters are shown in Figure 2. The first four modes of the structure can be described as:

- global bending of the two blocks in the transverse direction;
- global bending of the two blocks in the longitudinal direction;
- global torsion involving the two blocks;
- torsion with counterrotating blocks.

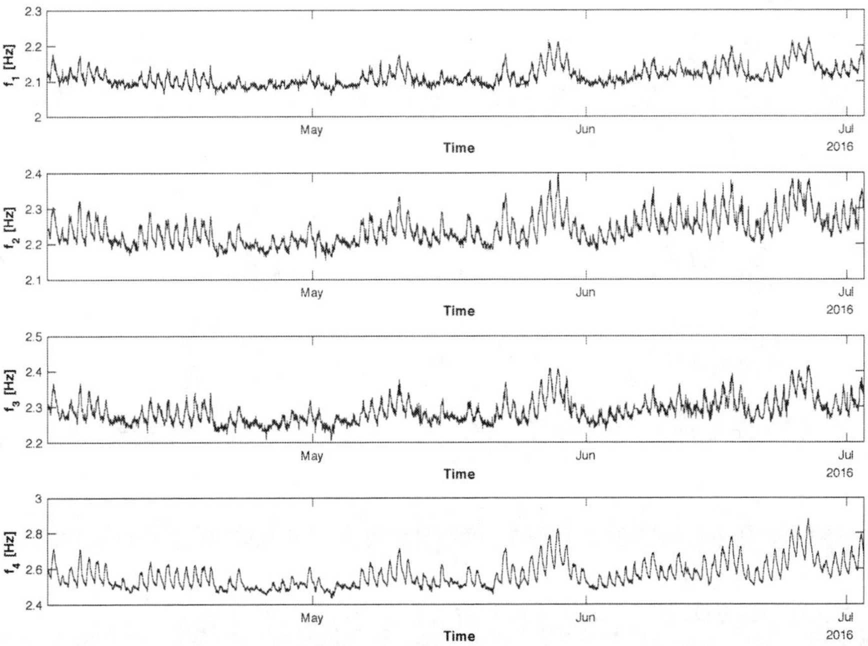

Figure 2. Fundamental natural frequency time series from April 1st to July 2nd, 2016

The plots in Figure 2 show that systematic swings occur every day, with a reduction of natural frequencies in the night and a gradual increase in the morning. The maximum value is usually reached in the early afternoon. Thus, temperature has a significant influence on the observed variations of the natural frequency estimates. The distribution of the estimates has been also assessed, as shown in Figure 3.

Time series and histograms of the fundamental frequencies can be explained taking into account that a very narrow joint divides the two blocks, and that direct sun radiation mainly affects the buildings along the predominant longitudinal extension. The thermal expansion affects the infill panels as well as the relative distance between the blocks; in particular, when the temperature increases, the distance between the two blocks decreases, and the interlocking yields some stiffness increase, which yields non-symmetric distributions of the estimates. In addition, a general increase of the fundamental frequencies with the temperature can be observed as a result of thermal expansion and interaction between structural and non-structural members.

Since the temperature affects the natural frequency estimates to a large extent, effective procedures for compensation of the environmental influence are needed in view of the development of effective SHM strategies.

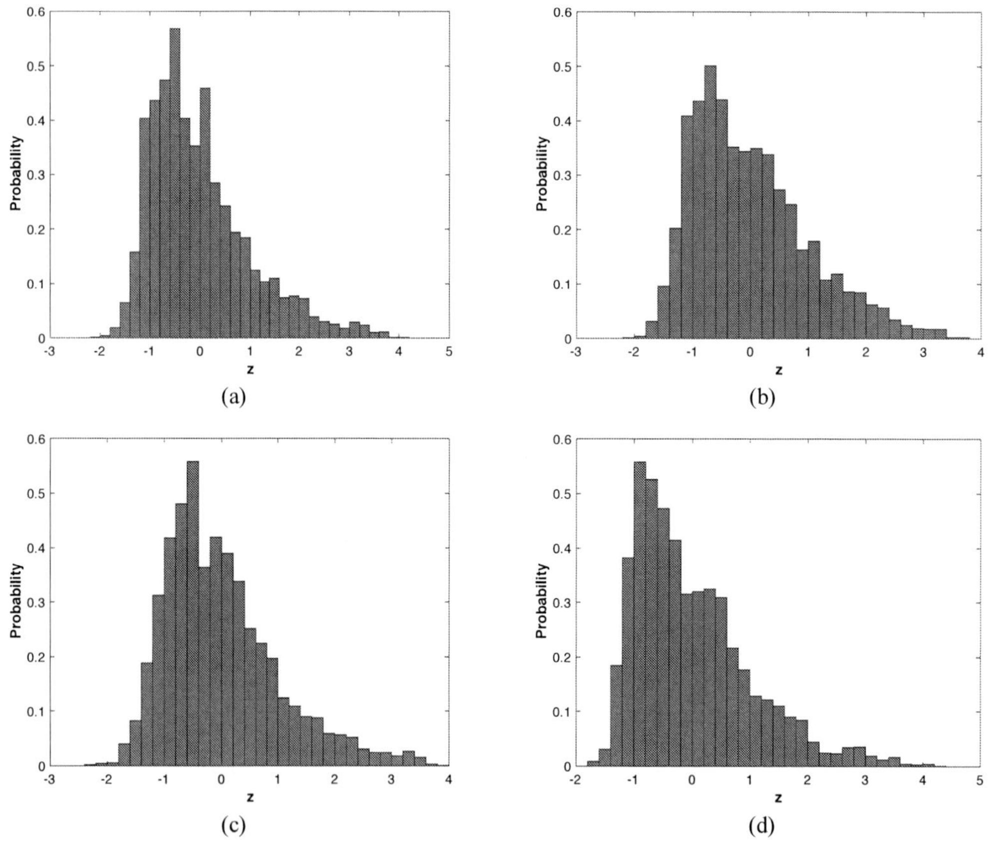

Figure 3. Histograms of natural frequencies: mode I (a), II (b), III (c), and IV (d)

3. COMPENSATION OF ENVIRONMENTAL EFFECTS

3.1. Output-only procedures for compensation of environmental influence

The difficulty in determining which EOVs should be measured and where the corresponding sensors should be placed is the reason why explicit measurements of EOVs are not carried out in the present application, and linear as well as non-linear output-only models are set in order to eliminate the environmental influence on the collected natural frequency estimates. Principal Component Analysis - (PCA) [7] is probably one of the most popular approaches for output-only compensation of environmental effects. The application of SOBI to assess the influence of EOVs on natural frequency estimates and to identify the patterns of relevant EOVs affecting the estimates has been also recently proposed [8]. When the Second Order Blind Identification (SOBI) is applied, the natural frequency time series **f** are modelled as a linear combination of sources **s** (the unknown environmental factors) through the mixing matrix **A**, plus the residue ε:

$$\mathbf{f} = \mathbf{A}\mathbf{s} + \varepsilon \tag{1}$$

Mixing matrix and sources are simultaneously estimated from the collected data.

When SOBI is applied in the context of SHM to model the influence of EOVs on the natural frequency estimates, the residue ε, obtained by subtracting the predicted natural frequencies to the corresponding experimental data, should be insensitive to the considered EOVs. Thus, its variations can be addressed to different factors, such as damage, and it can be profitably used as damage sensitive feature for vibration based SHM [1]. More details can be found elsewhere [8].

In addition to the linear model of Eq. (1), Kernel PCA (KPCA) is applied as a non-linear method for compensation of environmental effects [9]. The use of KPCA for compensation of the environmental influence on natural frequency estimates assumes that a non-linear relationship of the form:

$$\mathbf{\Phi}\left(\mathbf{y}_\mathbf{k}\right) = \mathbf{H}_0\mathbf{u}_\mathbf{k} + \mathbf{e}_\mathbf{k} \tag{2}$$

exists between the selected damage features $\mathbf{y}_\mathbf{k}$ (the natural frequency estimates in the present case) and the unknown EOVs $\mathbf{u}_\mathbf{k}$. In the following, the quantity $\mathbf{\Phi}(\mathbf{y}_\mathbf{k})$ is also referred to as Φ-image of the data sample $\mathbf{y}_\mathbf{k}$, where the operator $\mathbf{\Phi}$ denotes the nonlinear mapping of $\mathbf{y}_\mathbf{k}$ onto a high-dimensional feature space. The vector $\mathbf{e}_\mathbf{k}$ holds the information about the misfit between measured data and model predictions. Assuming that the misfit is small in the training phase, and taking advantage of the Mercer's theorem [11] so that the kernel function *k*:

$$k\left(\mathbf{y}_\mathrm{i},\mathbf{y}_\mathrm{j}\right) = \mathbf{\Phi}\left(\mathbf{y}_\mathrm{i}\right)^\mathrm{T}\mathbf{\Phi}\left(\mathbf{y}_\mathrm{j}\right) \tag{3}$$

can be specified instead of the nonlinear mapping $\mathbf{\Phi}$, the error norm in the feature space can be obtained as follows:

$$\left\|\mathbf{e}_\mathbf{k}\right\|^2 = \mathbf{K}_\mathbf{test}^\mathrm{T}\mathbf{A}_2\mathbf{A}_2^\mathrm{T}\mathbf{K}_\mathbf{test} \tag{4}$$

after solving the following eigenvalue problem:

$$\mathbf{KA} = \mathbf{A\Sigma} \tag{5}$$

and partitioning the matrix A as:

$$\mathbf{A} = \begin{bmatrix} \mathbf{A}_1 & \mathbf{A}_2 \end{bmatrix}, \qquad \mathbf{A}_2 \in \mathrm{R}^{n_t \times (n_t - n_u)} \tag{6}$$

K is the $n_t \times n_t$ kernel matrix computed on the training dataset, while $\mathbf{K}_\mathbf{test}$ is the $n_t \times n_s$ kernel matrix computed between the training samples and the entire dataset. The quantities n_t, n_s, and n_u denote the number of training samples, the total number of samples, and the dimension of the vector $\mathbf{u}_\mathbf{k}$, respectively. The superscript $^\mathrm{T}$ denotes transpose. In agreement with the procedure described in [9], the Gaussian Radial Basis Function (RBF) kernel is herein applied. It implicitly defines an infinite-dimensional mapped feature space by setting a single positive parameter σ:

$$k\left(\mathbf{y}_i,\mathbf{y}_j\right)=\exp\left(-\frac{\left\|\mathbf{y}_i-\mathbf{y}_j\right\|^2}{2\sigma^2}\right) \tag{7}$$

The misfit in the feature space can be computed once the parameters n_u and σ are set. The number of retained principal components n_u is set so that a given fraction of the normal variability is accounted for [9]; in particular, the ratio:

$$\mathrm{Fr}=\frac{\sum_{k=1}^{n_u} v_{kk}}{\sum_{k=1}^{n_t} v_{kk}} \geq \mathrm{TH} \tag{8}$$

is assumed to be equal to or larger than 0.99. In Eq. (8) v_{kk} is the k-th element of the eigenvalue matrix **Σ**. The optimal value of σ, on the other hand, is selected as the one maximizing the Shannon's information entropy [12].

3.2. Results and discussion

The collected data in terms of fundamental natural frequencies have been analyzed by SOBI, first. In particular, the method shows that one EOV is responsible for most of the variability of the estimates (Figure 4a) and that considering only the first eigenvalue of the zero-lag correlation matrix yields a fairly accurate model of the environmental variability of estimates (Figure 4b). However, some differences in the structural response arise in the testing period with respect to the training period, yielding residues that still show some patterns (Figure 5). In order to enhance the model of the environmental variations of natural frequencies, these have been also analyzed by KPCA.

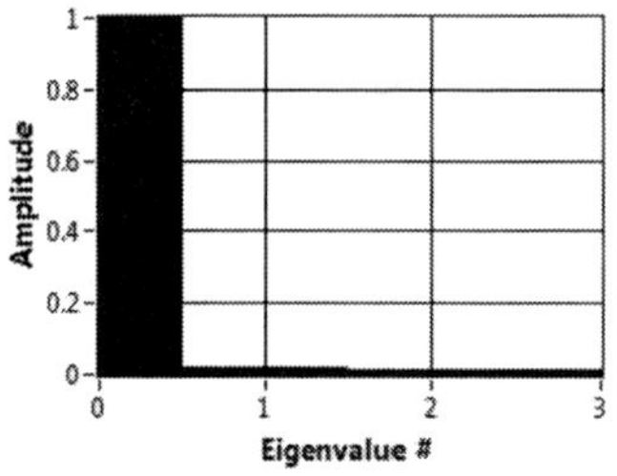

(a)

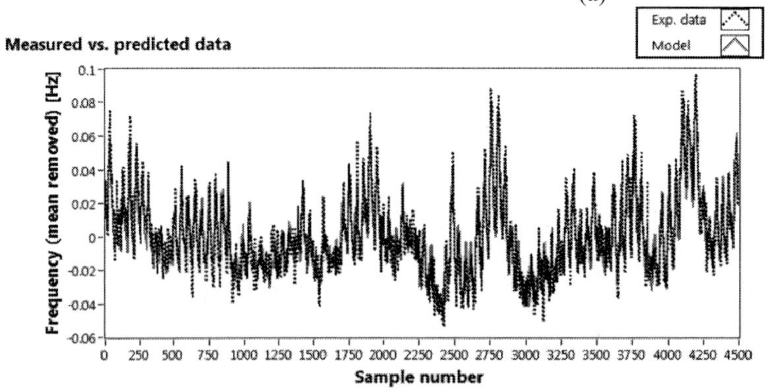

(b)

Figure 4. SOBI: estimation of number of sources (a) and sample comparison between data and predictions (b)

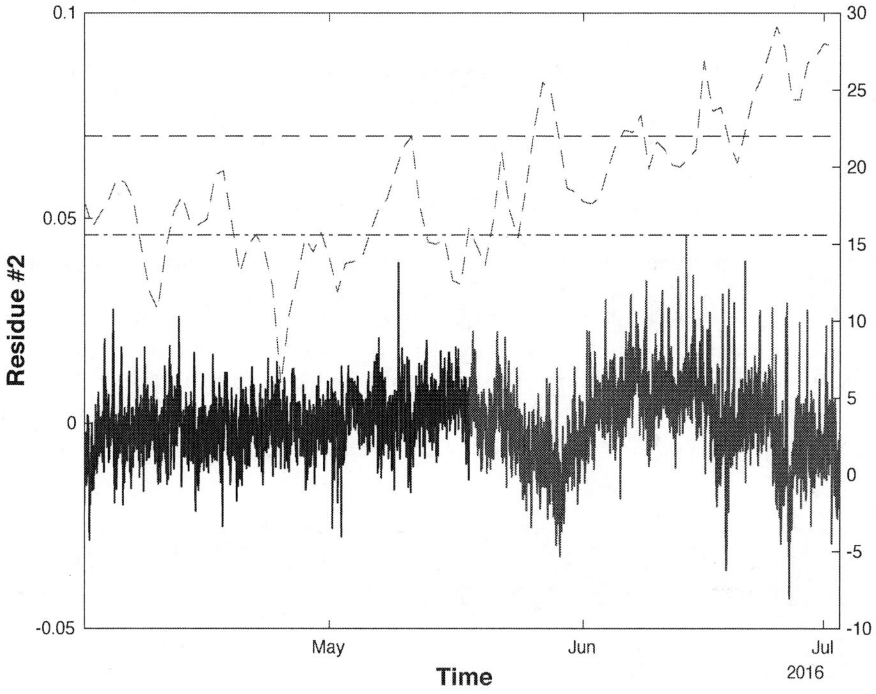

Figure 5. SOBI: sample residue time series (daily temperature in purple dashed line)

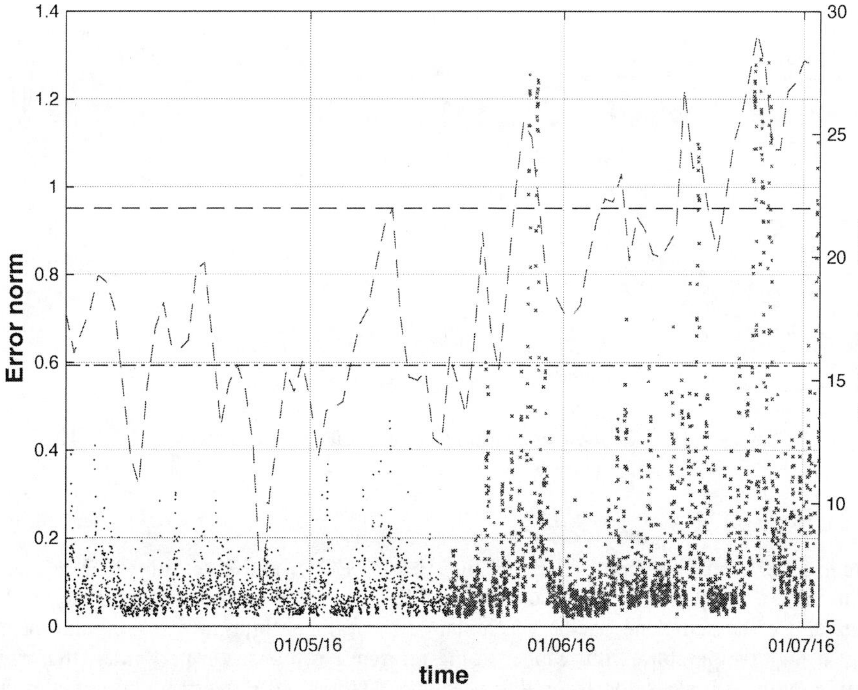

Figure 6. KPCA: misfit in the testing period from May 18th to July 2nd, 2016

Results of application of KPCA are shown in Figure 6 together with the evolution of the average local temperature in the period of interest. It is worth noting how the average daily temperature (purple dashed line in Figure 6) is in between 5°C and 22°C in the training period (from April 1st to May 17th, 2016) with a mean value of 15.6°C, and it increases up to 29°C in the testing period (from May 18th to July 2nd, 2016).

This is probably the reason behind the large values of the misfit occurring in the days characterized by very high average temperature. The discrete nature of the occurrence of large misfit values, on the other hand, seems to confirm the assumption that, when the temperature exceeds some threshold, the dynamic response of the structure changes as a result of the interlocking between the two buildings through the narrow separation joint. In order to confirm this result, the model trained on the same dataset has been applied to data referring to another monitoring period characterized by similar temperature conditions. In particular, data collected by the monitoring system from March 28th to May 2nd, 2017 are considered as second testing dataset. In this period the mean value of the average daily temperature was 12.9°C. Figure 7 shows that the misfit associated to this training dataset is of the same order of magnitude of the misfit in the training period, confirming the effectiveness of the model in compensating the influence of EOVs in similar conditions.

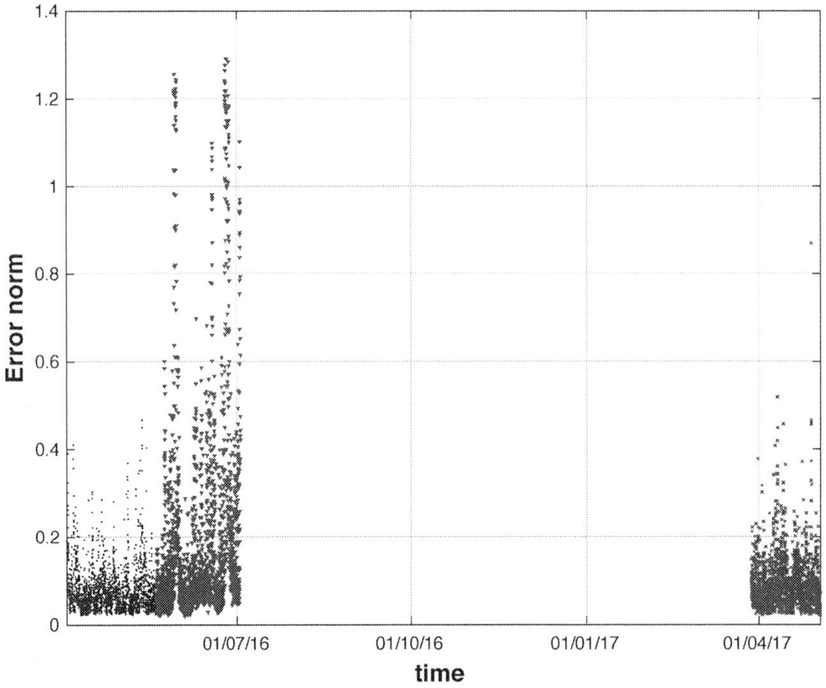

Figure 7. KPCA: misfit in the testing period from March 28th to May 2nd, 2017

4. CONCLUSIONS

The outcomes of a study aimed at identifying relevant EOVs and assessing their influence on the estimated natural frequencies of a hospital building through output-only techniques have been presented and discussed. Due to the particular structural configuration, a singular behavior was observed at high temperature with respect to the reference response. In particular, the presence of a few significant misfit values corresponding to days characterized by very high temperature seems to indicate an interaction between the two building blocks across the separation joint when the temperature exceeds some threshold. This phenomenon, only qualitatively outlined in this contribution, will be the object of further investigations in the future.

ACKNOWLEDGEMENTS

Supports to the research activities described in the present document from ASREM - Molise Region Health Authority, and the ReLuis-DPC Executive Project 2019-2021 - WP6 are gratefully acknowledged.

REFERENCES

[1] Farrar, C.R., & Worden, K. (2012). *Structural health monitoring: a machine learning perspective*, John Wiley and Sons Ltd., Chichester, UK.

[2] Magalhaes, F., Cunha, A., & Caetano, E. (2009). Online automatic identification of the modal parameters of a long span arch bridge. *Mechanical Systems and Signal Processing*, 23, 316-329.

[3] Rainieri, C., & Fabbrocino, G. (2015). Development and validation of an automated operational modal analysis algorithm for vibration-based monitoring and tensile load estimation. *Mechanical Systems and Signal Processing*, 60-61, 512-534.

[4] Peeters, B., & De Roeck, G. (2001). One-year monitoring of the Z24-Bridge: environmental effects versus damage events. *Earthquake Engineering and Structural Dynamics*, 30(2), 149-171.

[5] Nandan, H., & Singh, M.P. (2014). Effects of thermal environment on structural frequencies: Part I – A simulation study. *Engineering Structures*, 81, 480-490.

[6] Deraemaeker, A., Reynders, E., De Roeck, G., & Kullaa, J. (2008). Vibration-based structural health monitoring using output-only measurements under changing environment. *Mechanical Systems and Signal Processing*, 22, 34-56.

[7] Yan, A.-M., Kerschen, G., De Boe, P., & Golinval, J.-C. (2005). Structural damage diagnosis under varying environmental conditions – Part I: A linear analysis. *Mechanical Systems and Signal Processing*, 19, 847-864.

[8] Rainieri, C., Magalhaes, F., Gargaro, D., Fabbrocino, G., & Cunha, A. (2019). Predicting the variability of natural frequencies and its causes by Second-Order Blind Identification. *Structural Health Monitoring*, 18(2), 486-507.

[9] Reynders, E., Wursten, G., & De Roeck, G. (2014). Output-only structural health monitoring in changing environmental conditions by means of nonlinear system identification. *Structural Health Monitoring*, 13(1), 82-93.

[10] Rainieri, C., Gargaro, D., & Fabbrocino, G. (2018). Modal-based SHM of hospitals in earthquake prone regions. In: *Proc. 9th European Workshop on Structural Health Monitoring*. Manchester, United Kingdom.

[11] Mercer, J. (1909). Functions of positive and negative type, and their connection with the theory of integral equations. *Philosophical Transactions of the Royal Society A*, 209, 415-446.

[12] Shannon, C.E. (1948). A mathematical theory of communication. *The Bell System Technical Journal*, 27, 379-423.

IOMAC'19

8th *International Operational Modal Analysis Conference*
2019 May13-15 Copenhagen

AN INTEGRATED PERMANENT DYNAMIC MONITORING SYSTEM OF A TALL BULDING IN CENTRAL ITALY

Davide Arezzo[1], *Marco Regni*[2], *Sandro Carbonari*[3], *Fabrizio Gara*[4]

[1] PhD Student, Università Politecnica delle Marche, d.arezzo@pm.univpm.it.
[2] PhD Candidate, Università Politecnica delle Marche, m.regni@pm.univpm.it.
[3] Assistant Professor, Università Politecnica delle Marche, s.carbonari@staff.univpm.it.
[4] Associate Professor, Università Politecnica delle Marche, f.gara@staff.univpm.it.

ABSTRACT

This paper presents results of the dynamic monitoring of a 10-storey r.c. tower in central Italy, focusing on the effects of ambient conditions. The installed monitoring system consists of a set of three accelerometers located on the last floor of the tower, including a velocimeter located at the foundation level and an acquisition software that, through a specifically developed algorithm based on operational modal analysis techniques, automatically extracts the modal parameters of the building from the accelerometric recordings. Ambient registrations derive from a weather station installed on the roof of the tower. Effects of the ambient parameters on the dynamic properties of the building are presented and discussed. Moreover, the building response to low intensity seismic events registered during the monitoring period is compared with that obtained from a calibrated numerical model by applying at the base the input registered by the velocimeter.

Keywords: Continuous dynamic monitoring, dynamic identification, environmental conditions effects on modal properties, finite element model, Operational Modal Analysis

1. INTRODUCTION

In the last few years, the measurement of vibrations and the monitoring of the dynamic properties of a structure is emerging as the standard for obtaining information on structural health. This is due to the ease and reliability with which it is possible to identify, and therefore to monitor, a structure through operational modal analysis techniques. Over time, various output only dynamic identification techniques have been developed and successfully applied, which have become widely used, no longer only for research purposes. Moreover, these techniques are easy to be automated, being able to obtain real time information on the variation of the modal properties of the monitored structure [1-4].

The idea of detecting damage by monitoring changes in frequencies, modal shapes, and damping ratio, works in theory, but in practice still presents many issues. On the one hand, the installation of a monitoring system that can automatically and reliably identify frequencies, modal shapes and damping is still very costly for the typical structures of civil engineering as it would be necessary to use a large number of accelerometers in order to monitor a sufficient number of degrees of freedom and, moreover, it is often not possible to provide an accurate and reliable measurement of structural damping from ambient vibration measurements. On the other hand, it is possible to monitor the main vibration frequencies in a relatively simple way; in this case, variations in eigenfrequencies are often not enough to provide information about structural damage. In addition to the fact that even serious damage can have a limited effect on the overall dynamic response of the structure, one of the main drawbacks is the dependence of modal parameters on environmental conditions such as temperature [5-8], or the level of excitation to which the structure is subjected. In many cases, variations in environmental conditions can lead to variations in eigenfrequencies of the same order of magnitudes of those caused by damage [9].

This paper presents the results of the dynamic monitoring of a strategic structure in central Italy, the tower of the Engineering Faculty of the Università Politecnica delle Marche in Ancona (Figures 1a, 1b and Figure 2a). The tower has been selected as case study within a strategic research project funded by the University, which aims to develop low-cost wireless sensors for structural health monitoring purposes in order to reduce costs related to the installation of the monitoring systems. The research goals are achieved by performing conventional ambient vibration measurements on the tower to calibrate a finite element model to be used for the design of the permanent dynamic monitoring system exploiting low-noise high sensitivity piezoelectric accelerometers. Data from the monitoring system will be used as benchmark to validate the performance of the low-cost sensors, which are developed implementing MEMS accelerometers. Data from the monitoring system is also used to monitor the daily and seasonal fluctuations of the eigenfrequencies and the relative damping ratios, obtaining information on their dependency on the environmental conditions, registered by means of a meteorological station installed on the roof of the tower.

2. DESCRIPTION OF THE CASE STUDY

The Engineering Faculty of the Università Politecnica delle Marche was designed by architect Pietro Belluschi in 1976 and its construction ended in 1983. The building has a peculiarity: each floor takes its name depending on its altitude on the sea level (Figure 2b); thus, the tower of the Engineering faculty rises from 150 m above sea level (floor q150) to 195 m above sea level (q195). Each floor is characterised by an inter-storey height of 5 m. The structure is a r.c. frame, flanked by a staircase r.c. wall structure hosting the stairway and elevators, separated from the latter by a structural joint. The plan has a square regular shape, with 9 m equally spaced columns. The columns cross-sections taper with the height and at the upper floor are divided into 4 square sections connected to each other with a cross stiffening bracket. The beams have constant cross-sections at all floors. Finally, the roof is of flat type and the external infills are made up of prefabricated elements. The structure is founded on piles; in particular, 2x2 pile groups with piles of diameter 1 or 1.2 m is located beneath each column, excepting one edge column, founded on a 3 piles group.

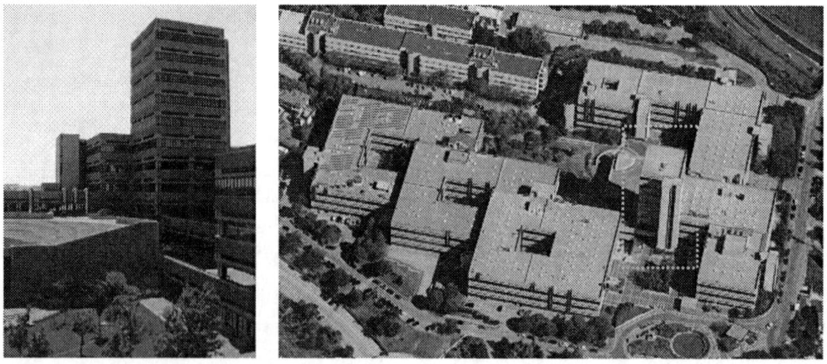

(a) (b)

Figure 1: view of the tower: (a) from north-west; (b) aerial view

3. AMBIENT VIBRATION TESTS AND MODEL UPDADITNG

Before the installation of the monitoring system, ambient vibration tests were carried out on the tower in order to identify the dynamics of the structure. To this purpose, three 393B31 PCB accelerometers were used for each floor, according to the configuration shown in Figure 2c, assuming the hypothesis of rigid floor. Accelerometers were connected to NI 9234 acquisition cards, mounted on the NI Cdaq-9178 chassis. The analog signals were sampled at 2048 Hz. During the post-processing, signals were resampled at 51,2 Hz in order to make files lighter. As usual, before resampling, signals were filtered with a low-pass filter at the Nyquist frequency to avoid aliasing. The covariance-driven Stochastic Subspace Identification method (SSI-COV) [10] was used to identify the dynamic properties of the tower from the recordings. The resulting first three mode shapes are shown in Figure 3 and the relevant eigen-frequencies are reported in Table 1.

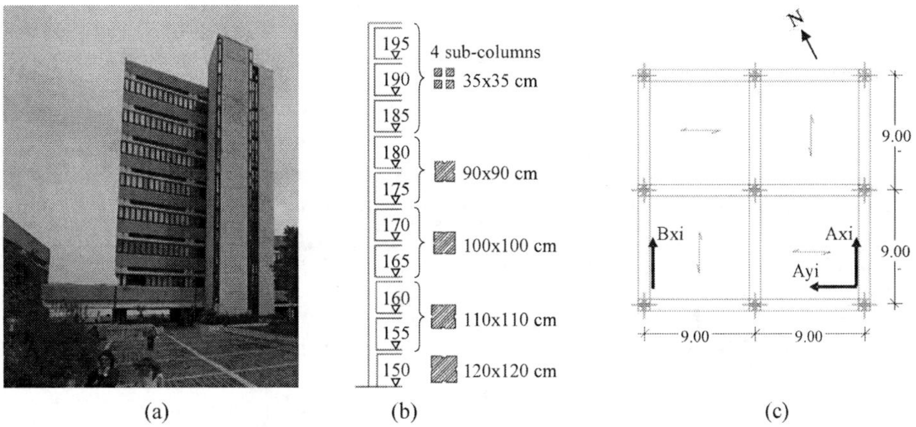

Figure 2: (a) view of the tower from south; (b) columns cross sections and altitude of the single floor; (c) typical floor plant and configuration of the sensors

Table 1. Comparison between experimental and numerical results.

Mode	Frequency			MAC
	Experimetal [Hz]	Numerical [Hz]	Error [%]	
1	1.07	1.05	1.87	0.96
2	1.21	1.18	2.48	0.91
3	1.51	1.49	1.32	0.98

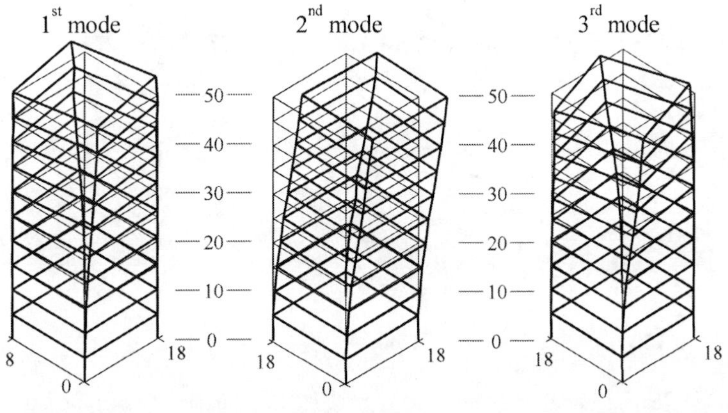

Figure 3: First three global mode shapes of the tower from AVTs

The results of ambient vibration tests are adopted to calibrate a Finite Element Model (FEM) of the tower, developed in the SAP2000 environment [11]. The model is designed to capture the tower's behaviour for operational conditions (i.e. subjected to ambient noise); beams and columns are modelled with frame elements and all non-structural components are schematised through shell elements. The fixed base assumption is considered, supported by the presence of deep foundations. Despite the presence of structural joints, experimental mode shapes clearly highlight the influence of adjacent buildings on the modal parameters. For this reason, the structure hosting the stairway is also modelled with shell elements and the mutual interaction is captured through elastic links of suitably calibrated stiffness. Comparison of results from the experimental tests with those obtained with the numerical model is shown in Figure 4 both in terms of mode shapes and MAC (Modal Assurance Criterion). Finally, Table 1 compares frequencies obtained from the FEM model and the experimental tests.

4. MONITORING SYSTEM AND FIRST RESULTS

The monitoring system was designed considering the cantilever-type behaviour of the whole structure and the results of the preliminary AVTs described in the previous section. Three sensors were installed at the last floor of the tower (q195), as shown in Figure 5d. The system is completely wired and consists of accelerometers PCB model 393B31 (Figure 5a), one data acquisition unit (DAQ), and one PC (Figure 5b). The monitoring system has been also equipped with a velocimeter installed at the foundation level (Figure 5b). In addition, in June 2018, the monitoring system was integrated with a davis vantage pro2 weather station (Figure 5c).

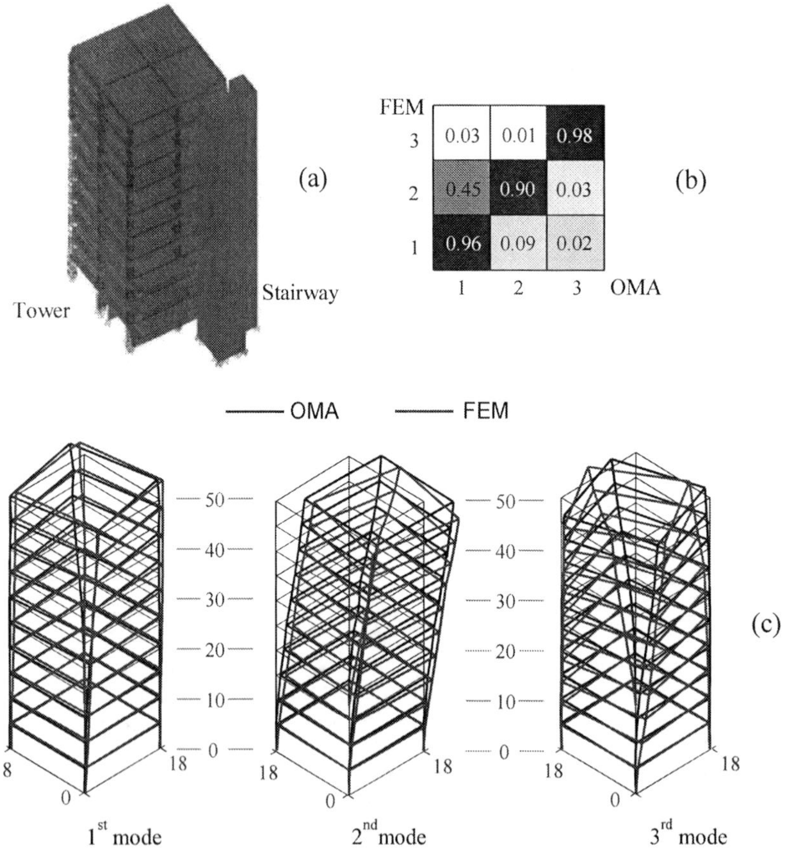

Figure 4: (a) 3D finite element model of the tower; (b) MAC; (c) Comparison of experimental and numerical mode shape

The PC is equipped with an ad hoc acquisition software, developed in LabVIEW environment [12], that manage 30 minutes recordings for 24 times per day. The acquisitions are saved on a server and processed real time through an algorithm running in parallel with the acquisition software, which carry out the SSI-COV algorithm. The algorithm provides the frequencies and damping ratios associated with the first three modes of the tower; the latter values are automatically associated the simultaneous temperature and wind speed acquisitions recorded by the weather station and, finally, results and the accelerometric records are saved on the server. A typical plot of the results of the monitoring system is shown in Figures 6a and 6b for two different periods of the year. Figure 6a shows results from 10/07/18 to 18/07/18, while in Figure 6b the reference period goes from 29/12/18 to 6/01/19.

Figure 5: (a) accelerometrs at the last floor; (b) acquisition station; (c) meteo station; (d) configuration of the monitoring system

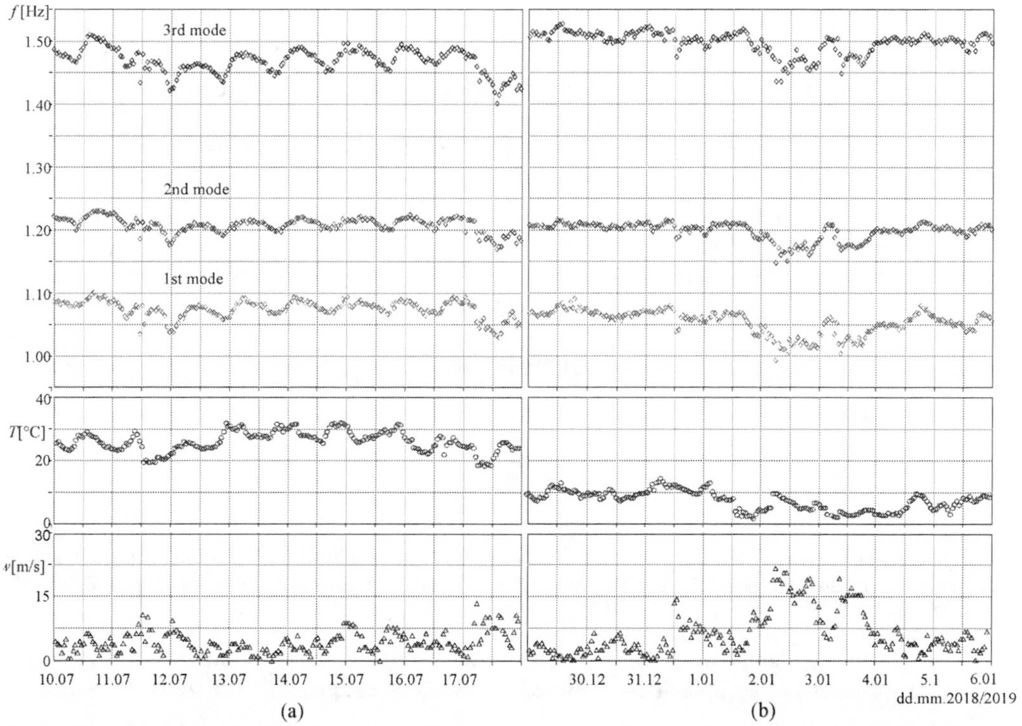

Figure 6: evolution of the air temperature and wind velocity during the monitoring period and histories of identified fundamental frequencies: (a) from 10/07/18 to 18/07/18; (b) from 29/08/18 to 6/01/19

It is worth noting an evident dependency of the vibration frequencies from temperature during summer. On the contrary, during winter, where the highest wind speeds have been recorded, a more pronounced dependency of the vibration frequencies from the wind speed is observed. In particular, a significant drop in the vibration frequencies can be observed by increasing the wind speed, particularly for the highest values, for which frequencies 9% lower than the mean ones were measured.

Even if data requires a more detailed statistical analysis, it can be concluded that the variation of the frequencies with the wind speed indicates a nonlinear tower response. This behaviour can be explained considering the presence of small nonlinear effects or frictions between structural and non-structural elements, with sliding surfaces that are activated only after certain intensity values of the applied external action are overcome [13, 14].

Thanks to the presence of the velocimeter at the foundation level and a trigger implemented within the acquisition routine, during the monitoring period it was possible to record the response of the structure to some low and medium intensity seismic events. In particular, referring to the earthquake occurred on 31/08/2018 (magnitude 3.5, 68 km distant from the tower) on the coast near the city of Pesaro (Figure 7a), it was possible to compare, through time history analysis, the real response of the structure with the response of the FEM model. Figure 7b shows the time histories recorded by the accelerometer at position $A_{198}X$ (Figure 5d) with the results of the analysis carried out on the FEM model. The numerical model reproduces quite well the tower response even if a model upgrading appears necessary to improve the matching of the measured and predicted response.

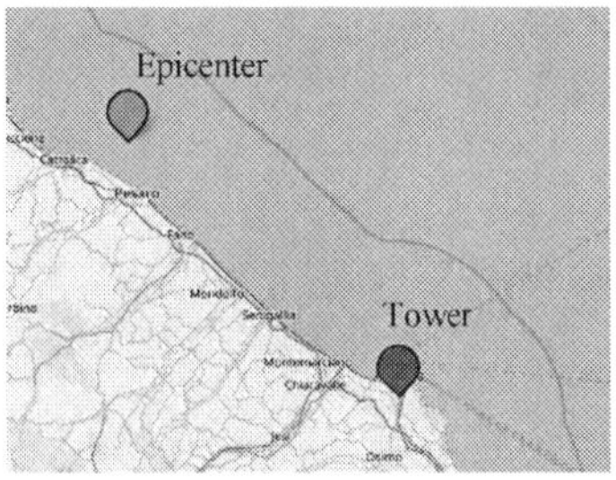

(a)

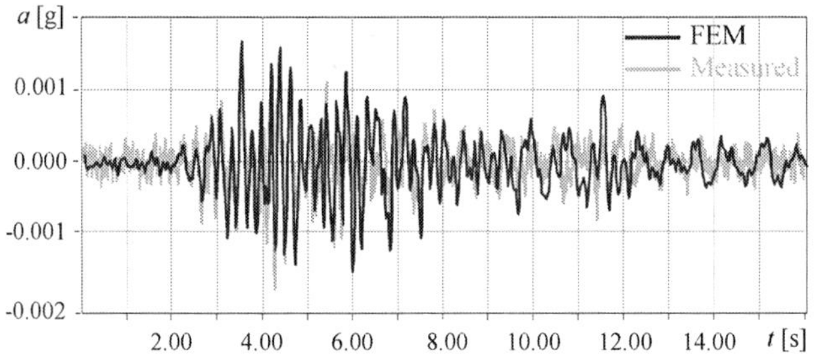

(b)

Figura 7: (a) epicenter of the registerd earthquake; (b) results of the time history analysis

5. CONCLUSIONS

Results from the dynamic monitoring of a strategic structure in central Italy, i.e. the tower of the Engineering Faculty of the Università Politecnica delle Marche in Ancona, has been presented. The developed monitoring system is firstly designed, starting from information obtained from the dynamic structural identification of the tower through conventional ambient vibration tests. Data from the monitoring system will be used as benchmark to validate the performance of the low-cost sensors and to study the daily and seasonal fluctuations of the eigenfrequencies and the relative damping ratios due to ambient conditions (mainly temperature and wind speed).

REFERENCES

[1] F. Magalhes, A. Cunha, E. Caetano, "Vibration based structural health monitoring of an arch bridge: from automated OMA to damage detection", Mech. Syst. Signal Process. Vol. 28, pp. 212–228, 2012.

[2] F.Magalhães, A. Cunha, E. Caetano, "Online automatic identification of the modal parameters of a long span arch bridge", Mech. Syst. Signal Process. Vol. 23, pp. 316–329, 2009.

[3] C. Rainieri, G. Fabbrocino, "Automated output-only dynamic identification of civil engineering structures", Mech. Syst. Signal Process. Vol. 24, pp. 678–695, 2010.

[4] F. Ubertini, C. Gentile, A. Materazzi, "Automated modal identification in operational conditions and its application to bridges", Eng. Struct. Vol. 46, pp 264–278, 2013.

[5] H. Sohn, "Effects of environmental and operational variability on structural health monitoring". Philos. Trans. R. Soc., Series A: Mathematical, Physical and Engineering Sciences, 365:539-560, 2007.

[6] A. Deraemaeker, E. Reynders, G. DeRoeck, J. Kullaa,"Vibration-based structural health monitoring using output-only measurements under changing environment", Mech. Syst. Signal Process. Vol. 22, pp. 34–56, 2008.

[7] F. Ubertini, G. Comanducci, N. Cavalagli et al., "Environmental effects on the San Pietro bell tower in Perugia, Italy, and their removal for structural performance assessment", Mech. Syst. Signal Process. Vol. 82, pp 307–322, 2017.

[8] Y. Xia, B. Chen, S. Weng, Y. Q. Ni, Y. L. Xu, "Temperature effect on vibration properties of civil structures: a literature review and case studies", Journal of Civil Structural Health Monitoring, Vol. 2, No. 1, pp. 29-46, 2012.

[9] C. Ranieri, D. Gargano, G. Fabbrocino, "On the use of second order blind identification for the characterization of the environmental influence on modal parameter estimates", EWSHM, Spain, Bilbao, 2016.

[10] Van Overschee, P., De Moor, B. "Subspace identification for linear systems", Kluwer Academic Publishers, Leuven, Belgio, 1996

[11] SAP2000 advanced (v14.1.0) "Static and dynamic finite element analysis of structures", Berkeley, CSI Computer & Structures, Inc., 2009.F. Ubertini, G. Comanducci, N. Cavalagli et al., "Environmental effects on the San Pietro bell tower in Perugia, Italy, and their removal for structural performance assessment", Mech. Syst. Signal Process. Vol. 82, pp 307–322, 2017.

[12] National Instruments. LabVIEW Signal Processing Course Manual. National Instruments Corporate Headquarters, 1997

[13] D. Arezzo, M. Regni, S. Carbonari, F. Gara, "Effects of environmental conditions on the dynamic properties of a 10-storey r.c. square tower", EESMS, Italy, Salerno, 2018.

[14] M. Regni, D. Arezzo, S. Carbonari, F. Gara, D. Zonta, "Effects of environmental conditions on the modal response of a 10-story reinforced concrete tower", Shock and Vibration, 18, articole ID 9476146, 2018.

IOMAC'19

8th International Operational Modal Analysis Conference
2019 May13-15 Copenhagen

OMA-BASED STRUCTURAL HEALTH MONITORING OF HISTORIC STRUCTURES

Carmelo Gentile[1], *and Antonella Saisi*[2]

[1] Professor, Department ABC, Politecnico di Milano, Milan, Italy, carmelo.gentile@polimi.it
[2] Assistant Professor, Department ABC, Politecnico di Milano, Milan, Italy, antonella.saisi@polimi.it

ABSTRACT

Structural Health Monitoring (SHM) is generally defined as a multi-disciplinary process involving: (a) the repeated or continuous measurement of the response of a structural system through arrays of appropriate sensors; (b) the extraction from measured data of features, which are representative of the health condition and (c) the statistical analysis of these features to detect any novelty or abnormal change in the investigated system. Among the different SHM strategies, the fully non-destructive nature and the minimum impact of the vibration monitoring makes the OMA-based approach especially suitable to address the preservation of Cultural Heritage structures and also to avoid, in some cases, inappropriate strengthening interventions. In the paper, the main ideas of OMA-based SHM of historic structures are presented and exemplified through the application to both relatively simple and very complex buildings, such as towers and cathedrals.

Keywords: Automated OMA, Environmental effects, Historic structures, Masonry towers, SHM

1. INTRODUCTION

In recent years, the Structural Health Monitoring (SHM) methodology based on continuous dynamic monitoring of structures and output-only modal identification has received increasing attention and the installation of dynamic monitoring systems, especially on bridges [1-3], has become more common. Among the many motivations for the raising scientific interest on dynamic monitoring, the most relevant are: (a) the ageing of existing structures (often accompanied by poor maintenance and harsh environmental conditions) as well as the increasing complexity of new constructions; (b) the technological advances, allowing more economical installation of monitoring systems and fully computer-based operation, with efficient transmission and processing of the collected data; (c) the possibility of performing the health condition assessment of a structure from the analysis of its dynamic response to ambient and/or operational excitation, with no need for artificial inputs.

Although the minimum impact of the vibration monitoring makes this technology especially suitable to the context of preservation of Cultural Heritage structures, the practical applications in this field are still quite limited [4-19]. A large part of published studies [4-9], [11], [14-17] focuses on the ancient towers, that represent a significant part of the existing Cultural Heritage buildings, as these historic structures were built over the centuries with different characteristics and functions: bell towers, lookout or defensive towers, chimneys and minarets.

The idea of performing cost-effective OMA-based SHM of ancient towers has been taking shape recently [4-9], [11], [14-17] as those structures are generally sensitive to ambient excitation and exhibit a cantilever-like behavior, so that the successful monitoring of the dynamic characteristics can be obtained by permanently installing a few high-sensitivity accelerometers (or seismometers) in the upper part of the building. In addition, masonry towers often exhibit high vulnerability to seismic actions, so that the possibility of using a limited number of sensors to provide an effective condition monitoring is of utmost importance to promote extensive and sustainable assessment programs. On the other hand, the availability of a limited number of sensors imposes the choice of resonant frequencies as features to be assumed as representative of the structural condition. Since resonant frequencies are also sensitive to factors other than structural changes, a vibration-based strategy for the preventive conservation of masonry towers should include:

1. Dynamic tests in operational conditions, carried out using an appropriate number of sensors in order to identify the dynamic characteristics of the tower and to highlight the most meaningful positions (among the possible ones) to be permanently instrumented;
2. Continuous monitoring and SHM, based on the installation of a limited number of sensors in the structure (at least 3 accelerometers and 1 temperature sensor). Data should be collected periodically [4] or continuously [6-8], [11], [14-17] and (automated) operational modal analysis (OMA) should be carried out to track the evolution in time of resonant frequencies, understand the environmental effects and detect the occurrence of any structural performance anomaly [7-8, 14-17];
3. After the SHM has revealed a significant deterioration of the structural condition, local assessment of damage should be carried out through detailed visual inspection and complementary non-destructive tests in order to plan strengthening interventions with more confidence, only if and where the interventions are really necessary.

The paper firstly exemplifies the application of the previous tasks (1) and (2) to three historic masonry towers, with the main objectives of understanding the possible "normal" changes of natural frequencies associated to environmental effects. The three investigated towers are the *Gabbia tower* in Mantua [7-8], the *San Vittore bell-tower* in Arcisate, Varese [14] and the *Santa Maria del Carrobiolo bell-tower* in Monza [17]. In all cases, the installation of the monitoring devices was preceded by historic and documentary research, visual inspection, topographic survey, non-destructive and minor-destructive tests of materials on site.

In the last part of the paper, the focus is moved to the vibration monitoring of complex Cultural Heritage buildings, requiring the installation of a large number of sensors and SHM strategies conceivably involving all the available modal parameters [20]. The main expectations are exemplified by using data collected in the continuous monitoring of the Milan Cathedral [18].

2. SHM OF ANCIENT TOWERS USING FEW ACCELEROMETERS

As previously pointed out, the application of OMA-based SHM is exemplified to three historic masonry towers [7-8], [14], [17]; in all the presented case studies, continuous dynamic monitoring systems, including few accelerometers and temperature sensors, were installed in the upper part of the buildings and automatic modal identification was performed. The identified natural frequencies clearly show a time evolution over the monitoring period due to the changing environment.

The dynamic monitoring systems were composed by: (a) one 4-channels data acquisition system (24-bit resolution and 102 dB dynamic range); (b) 3-4 high-sensitivity accelerometers; (c) at least one temperature sensor and (d) one industrial PC on site, for system management and data storage. Binary files, containing the acceleration time series and the temperature data, are created every hour, stored in the local PC and transmitted to Politecnico di Milano for being processed. The sampling frequency was 200 Hz, which is much higher than that required for the investigated structures; consequently, low pass filtering and decimation were applied to the data before the use of the modal identification tools.

The data files received from the monitoring systems are managed in LabVIEW, where the following tasks are automatically performed [21]: (a) creation of a database with the original data; (b) preliminary pre-processing (i.e. de-trending, automatic recognition and extraction of the time series corresponding to swinging of bells or possible seismic events); (c) evaluation of hourly-averaged acceleration amplitudes and temperature; (d) low-pass filtering and decimation of each dataset; (e) creation of a second database, with essential data records, to be used for automated OMA. Finally, the modal parameters of the towers are extracted from the measured acceleration data using an automated procedure [22], based on the covariance-driven Stochastic Subspace Identification (SSI-Cov) algorithm (see e.g. [23]).

2.1. Detecting damage under changing environment: the *Gabbia* Tower

The *Gabbia* tower [7-8] (Fig. 1), with its 54.0 m height, is the tallest tower in Mantua. The tower dates back to the 13th century and the structure is built in solid brick masonry, with the load-bearing walls being about 2.4 m thick, except in the upper levels, where the walls thickness decreases to about 0.7 m. As shown in Fig. 1, the tower is nowadays part of an important palace, whose load-bearing walls seem to be not effectively connected to the tower; nevertheless, several vaults and floors of the palace are directly supported by the tower. While the main part of the building – below the height of about 46.0 m from the ground level – did not exhibit any evident structural damage (with the materials being only affected by superficial decay), the upper part of the tower is in a poor state of preservation. In more details, at a distance of about 8.0 m from the top, the brick surface workmanship changes and the masonry quality significantly decreases (as it was confirmed by pulse sonic tests); furthermore, the presence of several structural discontinuities and the lack of mechanical connection between subsequent addings determined concerns on the seismic behavior of the upper part of the tower.

After preliminary ambient vibration tests (November 2012, Fig. 2), a simple dynamic monitoring system was installed in the tower on December 17th, 2012 (and removed at the beginning of July 2015). The sensing devices consisted of: (i) three piezoelectric accelerometers (WR model 731A, 10 V/g sensitivity and ±0.50 g peak), mounted on the cross-section at the crowning level of the tower (Fig. 2a), and (ii) one temperature sensor, installed on the S-W front and measuring the outdoor wall temperature.

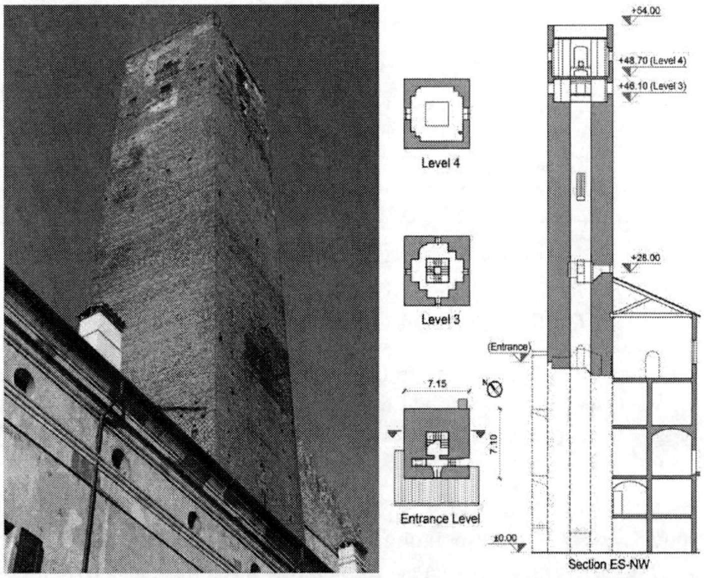

Figure 1. View of the *Gabbia* tower in Mantua, Italy and sections of the tower (dimensions in m).

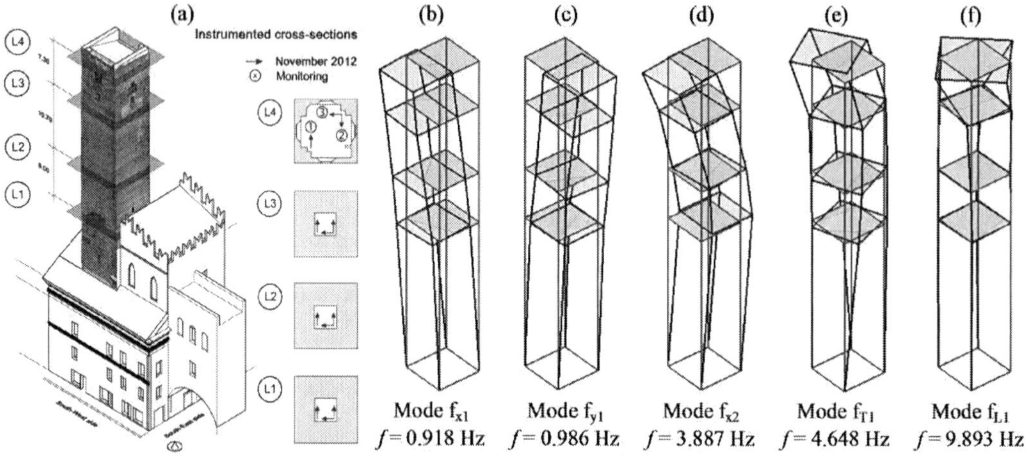

Figure 2. (a) Instrumented cross-sections and layout of the accelerometers during the preliminary tests (November 2012) and the continuous dynamic monitoring; (b)-(f) Identified modes of vibration.

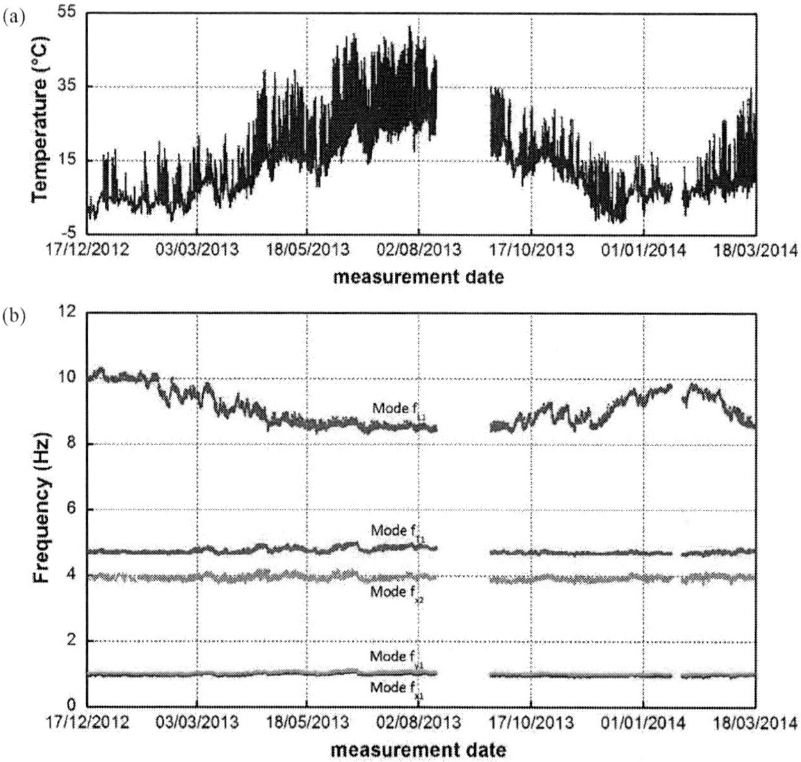

Figure 3. Time evolution (from 17/12/2012 to 17/03/2014) of: (a) the temperature measured on the S-W front of the tower; (b) the automatically identified natural frequencies.

Five vibration modes were identified in the preliminary ambient vibration tests and the corresponding natural frequencies were successfully tracked during the monitoring period. As shown in Fig. 2, the identified modes correspond to three bending modes (Figs. 2b-d), one torsion mode (Fig. 2e) and one local mode involving the upper part of the structure (Fig. 2f).

It should be noticed that, until June 2013, the tower's response to different far-field earthquakes was recorded. The strongest event – corresponding to an earthquake occurred in the Garfagnana region (Tuscany) on June 21st, 2013 – was characterized by a measured peak acceleration of about 20 cm/s^2, exceeding about 50 times the highest amplitude of normally observed ambient vibrations.

Figure 3 reports the time evolution of the outdoor temperature (S-W front, Fig. 3a) and of the automatically identified modal frequencies (Fig. 3b) for a period of about 15 months, from 17/12/2012 to 17/03/2014.

The temperature tracking reveals large fluctuations, between −2°C and +45°C, with significant daily variations on sunny days. A closer inspection of Fig. 3b highlights that the natural frequencies of global modes (f_{x1}, f_{y1}, f_{x2} and f_{T1}, Fig. 2) vary accordingly with the outdoor temperature. This correlation can be better investigated by plotting each modal frequency with respect to the recorded temperature. Figs. 4a-c show the results obtained for modes f_{x1}, f_{y1} and f_{T1} along with the best fit lines and the coefficient of determination R^2: the three plots refer to the time period from 17/12/2012 to 20/06/2013 and confirm that the frequency of global modes tends to increase with increased temperature. This behavior, observed in all studies of masonry towers can be explained by the closure of superficial cracks, minor masonry discontinuities or mortar gaps induced by the thermal expansion of materials [7].

The frequency-temperature relationships obtained after the Garfagnana earthquake (21/06/2013) are shown in Figs. 4d-f. The comparison with the results referred to the first six months of monitoring (Figs. 4a-c) reveals significant differences: the frequency dependence on temperature still remains roughly linear but the regression lines of all modes exhibit remarkable variations after the earthquake, with the temperature range being almost unchanged. This trend is also confirmed by the general decrease of the statistics of the natural frequencies (mean value, standard deviation, extreme values) summarized in Table 1 and highlights the occurrence of abnormal structural changes.

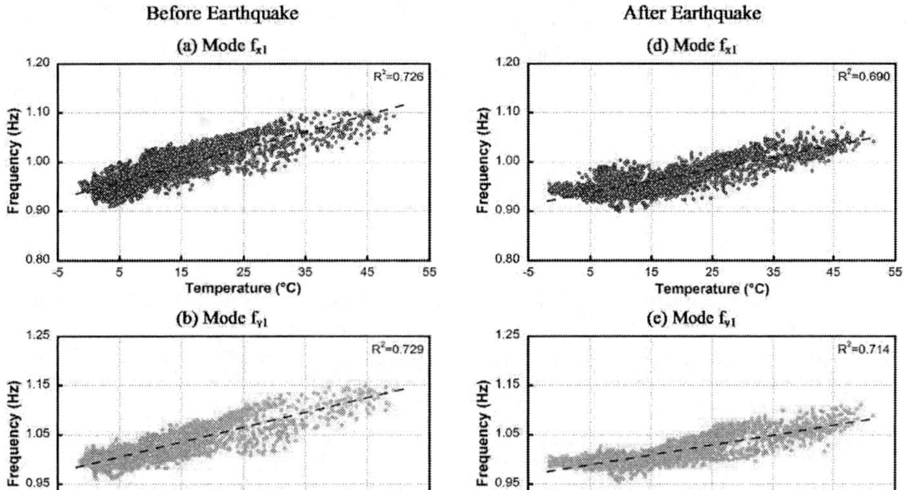

Figure 4. Natural frequency of modes f_{x1}, f_{y1} and f_{T1} plotted versus the outdoor temperature: (a)-(c) from 17/12/2012 to 20/06/2013; (d)-(f) after 21/06/2013.

Table 1. *Gabbia* tower : Statistics of the natural frequencies identified before and after the seismic event of 21/06/2013.

Mode	f_{ave} (Hz)		σ_f(Hz)		f_{min} (Hz)		f_{max} (Hz)	
	Before	After	Before	After	Before	After	Before	After
f_{x1}	0.985	0.968	0.038	0.031	0.910	0.897	1.102	1.070
f_{y1}	1.024	1.012	0.032	0.025	0.961	0.953	1.148	1.110
f_{x2}	3.941	3.929	0.075	0.063	3.758	3.742	4.194	4.137
f_{T1}	4.754	4.727	0.077	0.066	4.621	4.600	5.010	4.982
f_{L1}	9.222	8.937	0.554	0.433	8.385	8.332	10.327	9.862

It worth mentioning that very similar results have been more recently obtained during the seismic monitoring of the *San Pietro* bell-tower in Perugia [19] during the seismic sequence of Central Italy occurred in 2016. In both studies, clear permanent drops of natural frequencies have been observed after the seismic events and the frequency shifts were remarked by changes of the frequency-temperature relationships. In addition, even if the experimental data clearly reveal the occurrence of slight permanent changes [7-8], [19], the damage on the structures was not detectable through visual inspections.

In order to complete the discussion of the results of the *Gabbia* tower's monitoring with the local mode f_{L1}, Fig. 3b shows that frequency evolution of f_{L1} looks very different from the others and is characterized by significant frequency variations (approximately in the range 10.33-8.33 Hz); similarly, Table 1 confirms that high values of the standard deviation are especially observed for this mode. The observed behavior suggests the progress of a possible damage mechanism, conceivably related to the thrust exerted by the inclined wooden roof with increased temperature, and confirms the poor structural condition and the high vulnerability of the upper part of the tower. This conclusion seems to be confirmed by the frequency loss of the local mode detected after one year of monitoring (and after the earthquake), with the natural frequency being unable to reach the maximum values identified one year before in a similar temperature conditions (Fig. 3b).

2.2. Dynamic monitoring of the *San Vittore* bell-tower

The *San Vittore* bell tower [14] is located in the small town of Arcisate (northern Italy) and is connected to the neighboring church *Chiesa Collegiata di San Vittore* (11th century) on the east side and partly on the south side (Fig. 5). The tower, built in stonework masonry, is about 37.0 m high and has a square plan (5.8 m × 5.8 m); the thickness of the load-bearing walls progressively decreases from 135 cm at the ground level to 65 cm at the top.

The *San Vittore* bell tower has been studied by Politecnico di Milano since 2007: early studies included direct survey and testing of materials as well as ambient vibration tests and FE modeling [14]. Subsequently, a static monitoring system was installed in the tower; this system, aimed at collecting information on the evolution of crack patterns, included 15 extensometers and 8 temperature sensors, that measured internal and external temperature at different levels of the tower.

Two ambient vibration tests were conducted on June 2007 and June 2008. In both tests, the response of the tower was measured in 15 selected points (Fig. 6a) and datasets of 3600 s were collected adopting a sampling frequency of 200 Hz. Five vibration modes were identified in the frequency range 0-6 Hz (Fig. 6b-f). As expected, the identified modes can be classified as bending and torsion: dominant bending modes were identified at 1.22 (f_1, Fig. 6b), 1.28 (f_2, Fig. 6c), 4.01 (f_4, Fig. 6e) and 4.16 Hz (f_5, Fig. 6f) while only one torsion mode (f_3, Fig. 6d) was identified at 3.60 Hz. It is worth noting that the dominant bending modes of the tower (Figs. 6b-c and 6e-f) involve flexure practically along the diagonals.

In June 2009, a continuous dynamic monitoring system was installed in the bell tower, with the sensing devices consisting of 3 uni-axial Dytran 3191A1 piezoelectric accelerometers (10 V/g sensitivity and ±0.50 g peak). Logistical motivations and the results of the preliminary tests allowed to identify the level at 22.78 m (Fig. 6a) as the one to be instrumented in order to detect all the previously observed modes.

The continuous dynamic monitoring was carried out for 8 months (from June 2009 to February 2010), during which the monitoring system had to be stopped several times because of both normal maintenance and the installation of a new electrical system in the tower. It is worth mentioning that during the investigated time span, the static monitoring system installed in the tower not only provided temperature data to complement the dynamic monitoring but also indicated that no abnormal changes of the structural condition occurred.

Automated modal identification was performed using time windows of 2500 s [5], [14] which were obtained from each 1-hour recorded dataset after detection and removal of the time series corresponding to the ringing/swinging of bells. Hourly averaged temperature data were also recorded by a previously installed static monitoring system. Among the 8 available temperature measurements, correlation studies [5] indicated that the temperature recorded indoor on the East-side (T_{E1int}) and outdoor on the North-side (T_{N3ext}) are the most representative of the internal and external thermal condition of the tower, respectively. Hence, the temperature data T_{E1int} and T_{N3ext} were selected to investigate the correlation with the automatically identified natural frequencies.

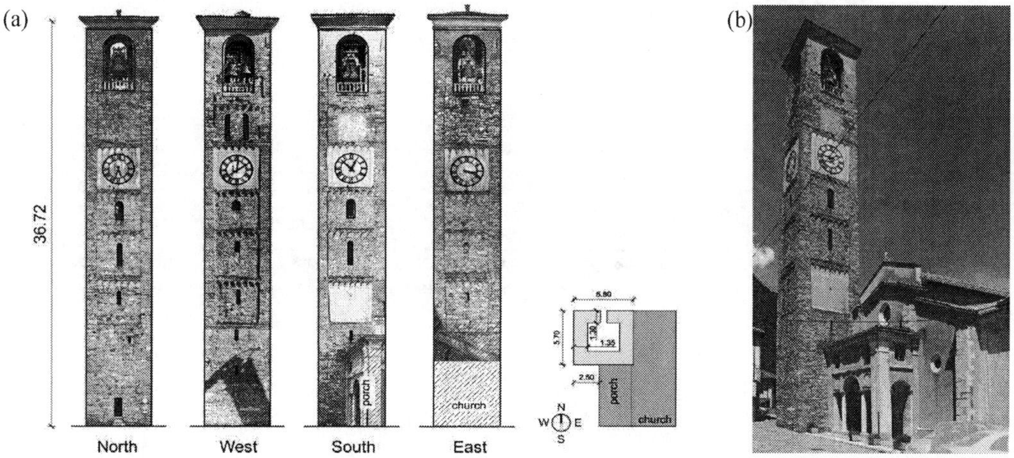

Figure 5. (a) Fronts and cross-section (dimensions in m) of the *San Vittore bell-tower*; (b) View of the tower.

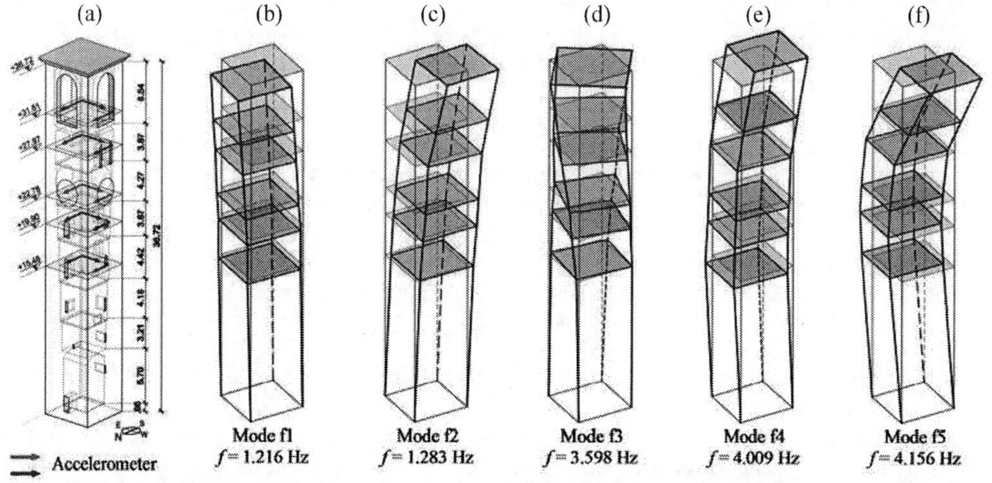

Figure 6. (a) Instrumented cross-sections and layout of accelerometers during the dynamic tests (blue and red arrows) and the continuous monitoring (red arrows); (b) Vibration modes identified from ambient responses.

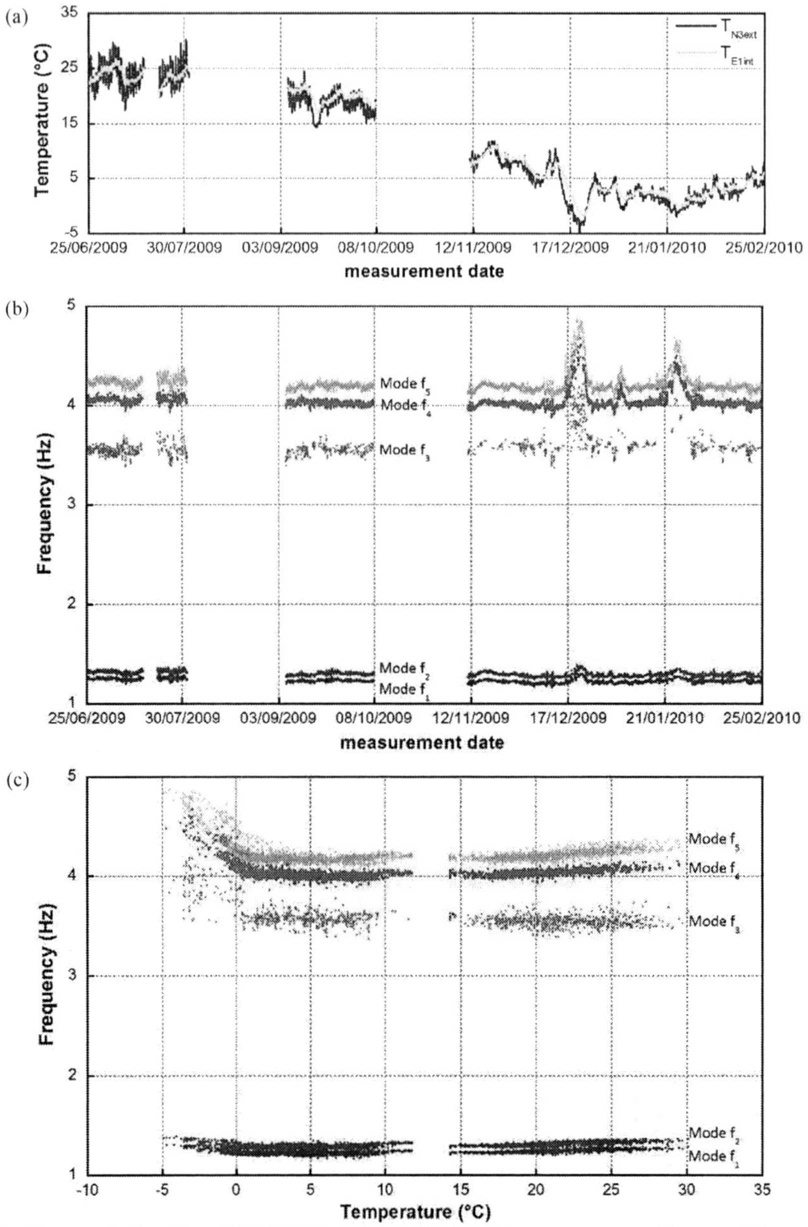

Figure 7. Time evolution (from 25/06/2009 to 24/02/2010) of the temperatures T_{N3ext} and T_{E1int}; (b) Time evolution (from 25/06/2009 to 24/02/2010) of the automatically identified natural frequencies; (c) Natural frequencies plotted with respect to the outdoor temperature (from 25/06/2009 and 24/02/2010).

Figure 7 shows the time evolution of temperatures (Fig. 7a) and natural frequencies (Fig. 7b) as well as the correlation between modal frequencies and the outdoor temperature T_{N3ext} (Fig. 7c). The statistics (mean value, standard deviation, minimum and maximum value) of the natural frequencies identified during the monitoring are reported in Table 2.

The inspection of Figs. 7a-c allows the following comments: (a) the bending modes are more frequently identified than the torsion mode, probably as a consequence of the low level of ambient excitation characterizing the tower; (b) similarly to the global modes of the *Gabbia* tower, the modal frequencies follow almost linearly the daily temperature variation, as their value increases with the increased temperature; (c) corresponding to below zero temperatures, the natural frequencies rapidly and significantly increase with decreased temperature. This last behavior, also observed in [11], is conceivably related to the freezing of the structural system (including its foundation) and to the presence of ice, which fills and closes the cracks, causing a temporary stiffening of the structure.

It is worth mentioning that, although the temperature effects on natural frequencies turned out to be quite complex for the *San Vittore* bell-tower, the well-known principal component analysis (PCA, see e.g. [16]) algorithm does provide a robust tool to remove the environmental effects and to develop effective prediction models of the identified frequencies for SHM purposes [14].

Table 2. *San Vittore* bell-tower: Statistics of the natural frequencies identified from 25/06/2009 and 24/02/2010.

Mode	f_{ave} (Hz)	σ_f(Hz)	f_{min} (Hz)	f_{max} (Hz)
f_1	1.228	0.019	1.162	1.290
f_2	1.297	0.021	1.240	1.367
f_3	3.552	0.056	3.371	3.774
f_4	4.023	0.033	3.880	4.184
f_5	4.196	0.042	4.043	4.372

2.3. Dynamic monitoring of the *Santa Maria del Carrobiolo* bell-tower

The last investigated tower belongs to the historic religious complex of *Santa Maria del Carrobiolo* [17] in Monza (Italy). The religious complex includes a church, a bell-tower, a monastery, an oratory and other minor buildings, which were erected at different times. The tower (Fig. 8a), about 33.7 m high, is built in solid brick masonry and has nearly square plan (5.93 m × 5.70 m); the thickness of the load bearing walls slightly decreases from 70 cm at the ground level to 58 cm at the top.

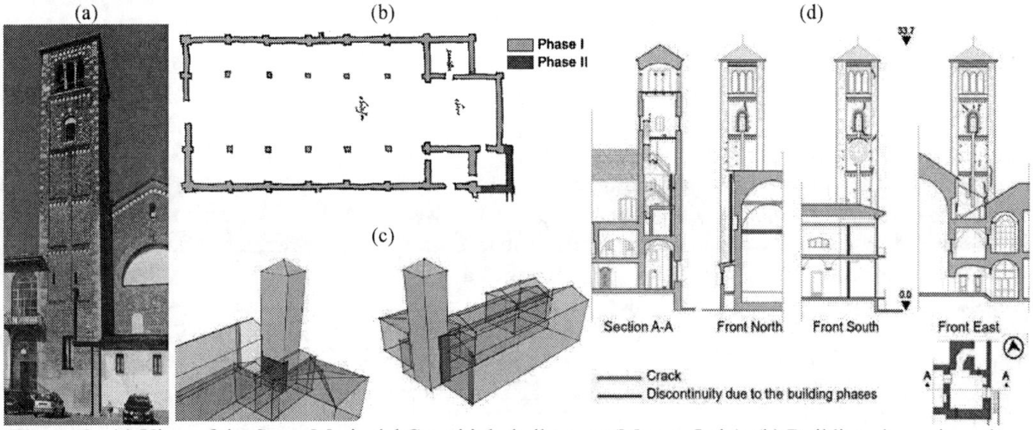

Figure 8. (a) View of the Santa Maria del Carrobiolo bell-tower (Monza, Italy); (b) Building phases in a plan dating back to 1572; (c) Schematic representation of the interaction between the bell-tower and the church apse; (d) Section and fronts of the bell-tower.

Historical documents testify that the construction of the church and monastery dates to the 13th century, whereas the bell-tower was completed in 1339 (Fig. 8b). The sequence of the construction stages has been confirmed by visual inspection of the masonry discontinuities: (a) the North and West sides of the tower are directly supported by the load-bearing walls of the apse and the right aisle of the church; (b) the Southern and Eastern load-bearing walls of the tower are continuous from the ground to the roof but do not exhibit any mechanical connections with the walls of the church (Figs. 8c and 8d). Moreover, several cracks cut the entire wall thickness, mainly at the level below the belfry (Fig. 8d), and a metallic tie-rod opposes to the opening of a deep crack on the Western wall of the bell-tower.

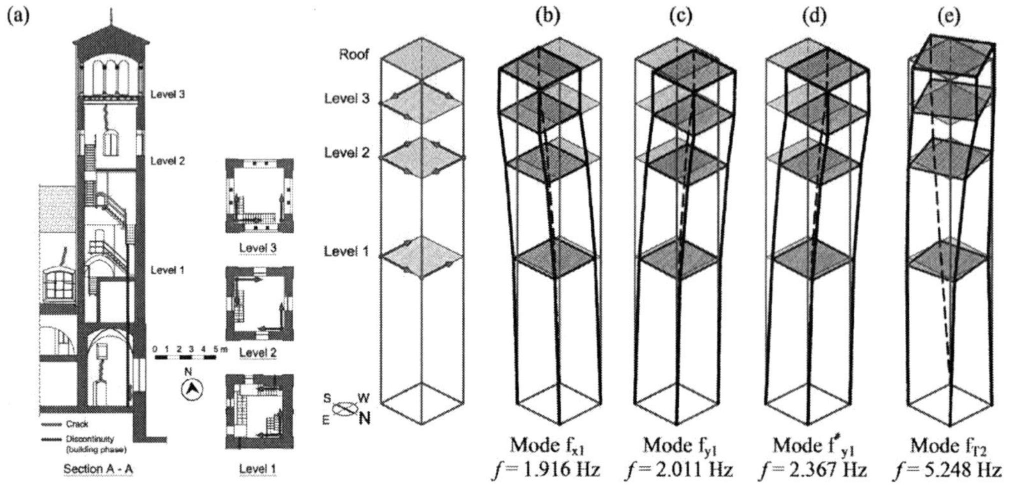

Figure 9. (a) Schematic of accelerometers layout and (b)-(e) selected vibration modes identified from ambient vibration tests.

The construction sequence adopted for the tower, not identified before, raised obvious concern about the performance of the structure under wind and seismic actions. Therefore, a wide research program was planned to assess the structural condition of the building and is currently in progress. In more details, the research consists of the following steps [14]: (a) prompt on-site investigation, including geometric survey and visual inspections; (b) static monitoring of the main cracks through the installation of 10 displacement transducers (as well as 5 temperature sensors) at different levels of the tower; (c) ambient vibration testing and identification of the dynamic characteristics of the tower; (d) installation of a simple dynamic monitoring system in the tower.

Ambient vibration tests were carried out on 23 September 2015 [14] and mainly aimed at evaluating the baseline dynamic characteristics of the tower before the installation of a continuous dynamic monitoring system in the building. Selected mode shapes identified by applying the SSI-Cov method are presented in Fig. 9 and reveal very peculiar dynamic characteristics of the tower, that are conceivably related to the structural arrangement and construction sequence of the building. In more details, closely spaced modes with similar mode shapes were clearly identified, so that the sequence of identified modes turns out to be very different from the expected regular series of two bending modes (one for each principal plane of the structure) and one torsion mode (see e.g., the *San Vittore* bell-tower). As shown in Fig. 9, the identified sequence of vibration modes (Fig. 9) includes: (a) the fundamental mode (f_{x1} = 1.92 Hz, Fig. 9b), involving dominant bending in the E-W direction; (b) two bending modes in the N-S direction, that are characterized by closely spaced natural frequencies (f_{y1} = 2.01 Hz and f^{*}_{y1} = 2.37 Hz) and very similar mode shapes (Figs. 9c and 9d).

The continuous dynamic monitoring system (Fig. 10a) installed in the tower since 22 October 2015 includes 4 MEMS accelerometers (Kistler model 8330A3, 1.2 V/g sensitivity, ± 3.00 g peak acceleration, 1.3 μg resolution and 0.4 μg/√Hz r.m.s. noise density), one Ethernet carrier with NI 9234 data acquisition module and one local PC for the management of the continuous acquisition and the data storage. In addition, 5 temperature sensors – denoted as T_{0N}, T_{1E}, T_{2E}, T_{2W} and T_S in Fig. 10a – were available, and measured both the indoor temperature at different levels of the tower and the outdoor temperature on the South side of the structure; hence, a relatively dense representation of the temperature conditions of the tower is achieved.

Figures 10b-c show the hourly averaged value of the measured temperatures in the monitoring period from 22 October 2015 to 21 October 2016. Table 3 summarizes the correlation coefficients between the environmental data during the same period. Figures 10b-c and Table 3 indicate that a large degree of correlation exists between all temperature data, with the measurements T_{1E}, T_{2E}, and T_{2W} being almost perfectly correlated and characterized by correlation coefficients very close to unity.

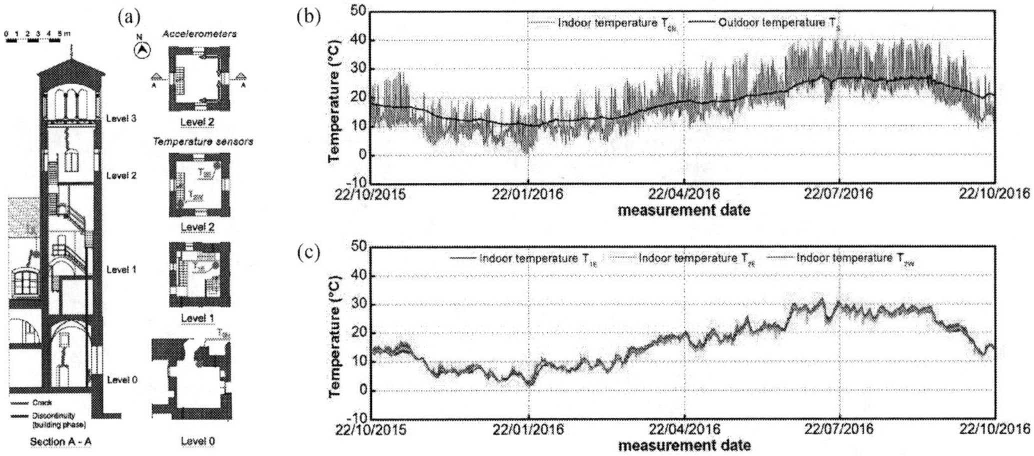

Figure 10. (a) Accelerometers and temperature sensors installed in the tower; (b) Variation in time of the measured temperatures T_{0N} and T_S; (c) Variation in time of the measured temperatures T_{1E}, T_{2E} and T_{2W}.

Table 3. Correlation coefficients between the measured temperatures (from 22/10/2015 to 21/10/2016).

	T_{0N}	T_{1E}	T_{2E}	T_{2W}	T_S
T_{0N}	1.000	0.967	0.957	0.960	0.837
T_{1E}		1.000	0.995	0.997	0.873
T_{2E}			1.000	0.998	0.900
T_{2W}				1.000	0.885
T_S					1.000

Figure 11 presents the evolution of the automatically identified modal frequencies in the first year of continuous dynamic monitoring (i.e., from 22/10/2015 to 21/10/2016), whereas the relevant statistics are summarized in Table 4 through the mean value (f_{ave}), the standard deviation (σ_f), and the extreme values (f_{min}, f_{max}) of each natural frequency. The results summarized in Fig. 11 and Table 4 allow the following comments:

1. Notwithstanding the low level of the ambient excitation, 4 normal modes were identified with high occurrence and accuracy;
2. The natural frequency of modes f_{x1} and f_{T2} exhibits significant increase in Spring and Summer period. This trend suggests that these modal frequencies are strongly affected by the temperature and – similarly to *Gabbia* tower and *San Vittore* bell-tower – increase with increased temperature;
3. On the contrary, the natural frequency of modes f_{y1} and f^*_{y1} exhibits very limited variation, with the standard deviation being equal to 0.009 and 0.015 Hz, respectively. For those modes, the frequency trend increase with increased temperature is conceivably balanced by the loss of tension in the metallic tie-rod placed on the West side and connecting the North and South load-bearing walls of the tower;
4. As shown in Fig. 11a, the natural frequencies of the two lower modes f_{x1} and f_{y1} exhibit crossing in Summer months. To the best of the authors' knowledge, this behavior has not been observed before on masonry towers and conceivably depends on the different effect exerted by the temperature on the natural frequencies of the two modes. Furthermore, the mode shape of both modes f_{x1} and f_{y1} tends to hybridize when crossing occurs: in other words, the two modes tend to involve biaxial bending in both the main E-W and N-S directions when the natural frequencies become very close to each other. It is further noticed that this hybridization, suggesting the occurrence of something similar to mode veering (see e.g. [24]), is more significantly detected for mode f_{y1}.

It is further noticed that ongoing numerical investigation indicates that the PCA-based regression turned out to be an effective tool to mitigate the environmental effects on automatically identified frequencies, in spite of the relatively small number of monitored frequencies.

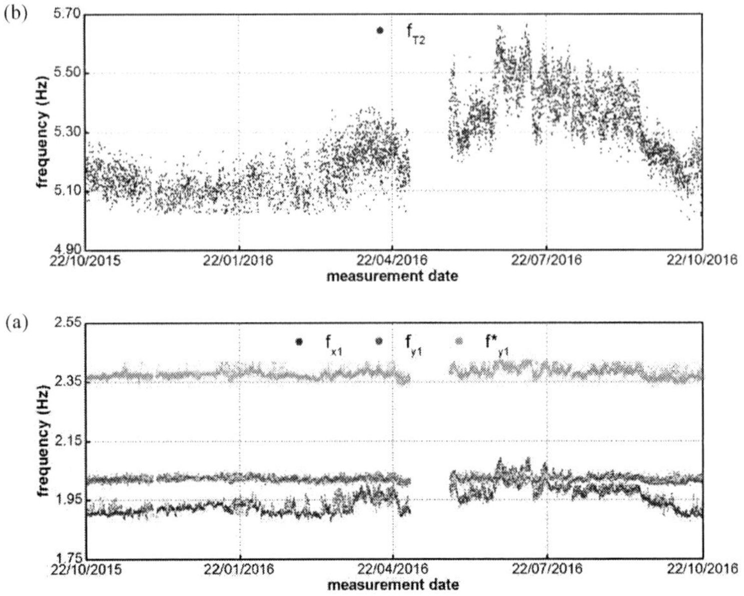

Figure 11. Time evolution of the automatically identified natural frequencies during the first year of monitoring (from 22/10/2015 to 21/10/2016): (a) modes f_{x1}, f_{y1} and f^*_{y1}; (b) mode f_{T2}.

Table 4. *Santa Maria del Carrobiolo* bell-tower: Statistics of the natural frequencies identified from 22/10/2015 to 21/10/2016.

Mode	f_{ave} (Hz)	σ_f (Hz)	f_{min} (Hz)	f_{max} (Hz)
f_{x1}	1.946	0.041	1.876	2.094
f_{y1}	2.020	0.009	1.990	2.053
f^*_{y1}	2.379	0.015	2.333	2.423
f_{T2}	5.265	0.141	5.001	5.663

3. CONTINUOUS MONITORING AND SHM OF COMPLEX HISTORIC BUILDINGS: THE CATHEDRAL OF MILAN

The Milan Cathedral (Figs. 12-13), erected between 1386 and 1813, is one of the largest masonry monuments ever built. The church exhibits the tallest main nave among Gothic Cathedrals, with the height of the vault intrados of the main nave being at about 45 m from the ground. The overall dimensions of the Latin cross-shaped plan are about 66 m × 158 m (Fig. 14), with the aisles and the central naves spanning 9.6 m and 19.2 m, respectively.

When compared with other Gothic cathedrals, the Milan Cathedral exhibits a peculiar structural system, with metallic tie-rods being permanently installed under each vault (Fig. 12b) and designed to exert an active part in resisting the lateral thrusts. Historical documents, dating back to year 1400, testify that the tension bars in the Milan Cathedral were permanently installed on the top of the piers during the construction with the aim of reducing the horizontal thrust on the lateral buttresses, as those buttresses were judged too slender by the French architect Jean Mignot. A total of 122 metallic tie-rods (Fig. 12b) is nowadays present in the Milan Cathedral and most of them are the original elements dating back to the age of construction.

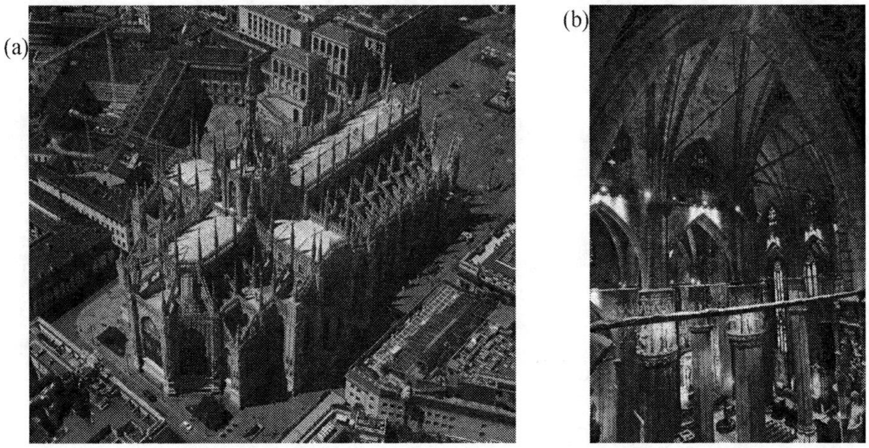

Figure 12. Milan Cathedral: (a) Aerial view (courtesy of Veneranda Fabbrica del Duomo di Milano); (b) Inside view of arches, vaults and iron tie-rods.

Figure 13. Longitudinal section of the Milan Cathedral (dimensions in m). (courtesy of Veneranda Fabbrica del Duomo di Milano)

Within the traditional collaboration between Politecnico di Milano and *Veneranda Fabbrica del Duomo di Milano* – the historic Institution established in 1387 and responsible for the preservation and development of the Cathedral – a structural monitoring system was recently designed and implemented with the two-fold objective of assisting the condition-based structural maintenance of the Cathedral and creating a large archive of experimental data useful to improve the knowledge of the monument.

The new monitoring system, fully computer based and with efficient transmission of the collected data, includes quasi-static and dynamic measurements [18]. The static monitoring system consists of: (a) bi-axial tilt-meters installed at the top of selected piers and at 3 levels of the Main Spire; (b) vibrating wire extensometers mounted on the iron tie-rods which are characterized by the higher tensile stress; (c) temperature and humidity sensors for the measurement of internal and external environmental parameters. The dynamic monitoring is performed through seismometers (electro-dynamic velocity sensors) installed at the top of 14 selected piers and at 3 levels of the Main Spire.

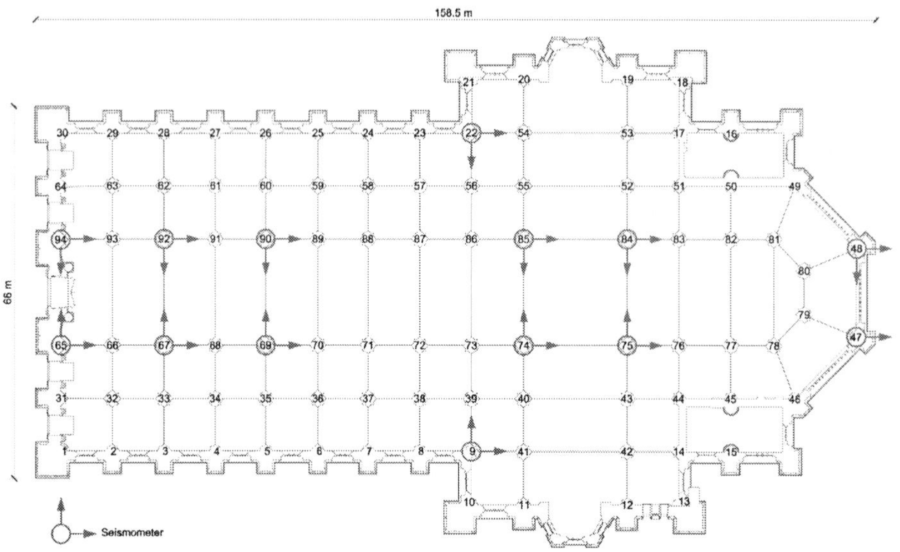

Figure 14. Map of the seismometers permanently installed inside the Milan Cathedral (dimensions in m).

3.1. The dynamic monitoring system

The dynamic monitoring system installed in the Cathedral of Milan is entirely based on SARA SS45 seismometers (electro-dynamic velocity transducers) [25]. The seismometer choice is motivated by: (a) the high sensitivity (78 V/[m/s]) and the excellent performance of electro-dynamic transducers in the low frequency range ($f \leq 100$ Hz); (b) the un-necessity of powering the sensors; (c) the possibility of obtaining a good estimate of the displacement time series by integrating the velocity records.

13 bi-axial seismometers and 1 mono-axial seismometer were installed at mounted at the top of selected piers (Fig. 14) and are continuously measuring the velocity in the two orthogonal N-S (transversal) and E-W (longitudinal) directions. The sensors installed on piers (94, 92, 90), (65, 67, 69), (22, 85, 84), (9, 74, 75) and (47, 48) are grouped and wired to five 24-bit digitizers SARA SL06 [25] and equipped with UMTS modems for data transfer. In addition, 9 seismometers are installed at 3 different levels of the Main Spire.

Preliminary dynamic tests were performed in the Milan Cathedral, by installing conventional accelerometers: (i) on the top of piers 22, 54 and 55 (6 channels of data, with 3+3 accelerometers oriented along N-S and S-W directions, respectively); (b) on the top of piers 9 and 39 (4 channels of data, with 2+2 sensors oriented along N-S and S-W directions, respectively). The results of these tests allowed to clearly identify 3 global modes of the Cathedral [18]. The lower vibration modes involve global motion of the Cathedral in the direction N-S (1.39 Hz) and E-W (1.70 Hz), whereas a certain classification of third mode (2.65 Hz) was not possible.

3.2. Dynamic characteristics of the church and SHM strategy

The dynamic monitoring system has been active since 16/10/2018. The automated OMA allows to identify 8 normal modes in frequency range 0-5 Hz. Figure 15 shows the lower 6 modes, as identified at the beginning of the monitoring (17/10/2018, h 11:00-12:00). It should be noticed that: (a) the lower two modes, as expected, are global sway modes of the Cathedral along the transverse (N-S, 1.39 Hz, Fig. 15a) and longitudinal (E-W, 1.70 Hz, Fig. 15b) direction; (b) the subsequent two modes (1.96 and 2.48 Hz, Figs. 15c and 15d) involve dominant motion in the N-S direction and bending of the naves; (c) the 5th mode involves out-of-phase bending of the North and South naves (2.64 Hz, Fig. 15e); (d) the 6th mode involves out-of-phase motion of the façade and apse in the E-W direction (2.76 Hz, Fig. 15f); (d) the damping ratios of all modes are quite high and range between 1.91% and 5.58%; (f) the longitudinal modes (E-W, Figs. 15b and 15f) seem to exhibit higher damping ratios.

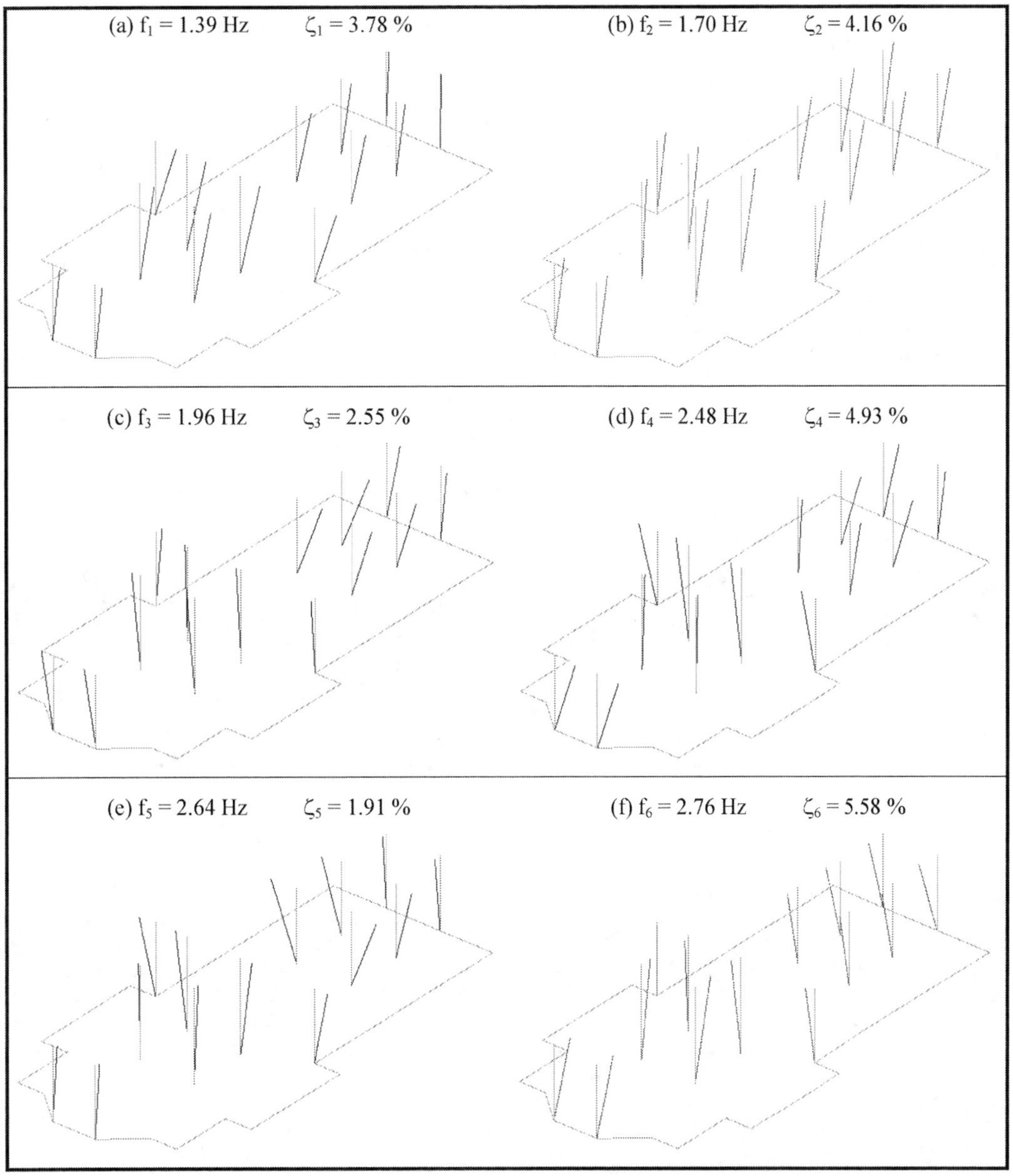

Figure 15. Selected vibration modes of the Milan Cathedral.
(The blue and red color highlights N-S and E-W dominant motion, respectively)

Figure 16a shows the evolution in time of the average indoor temperature during the first 4 months of monitoring. The corresponding variation of the modal frequencies versus time is illustrated in Fig. 16b. Even if the monitoring period is still quite limited, the dependence of resonant frequencies on (both indoor and outdoor) temperature seems to be very different from the one observed in masonry towers or in other masonry curches [10], [12-13]: the natural frequencies tend to increase with decreased temperature. Hence, during Winter time, the dependence of frequencies on temperature is conceivably driven by the iron tie-rods installed in the Cathedral (Fig. 12b).

It should be noticed that – unlike previous monitoring of churches [4], [10], [12-13] and palaces [19], where a limited number of quasi-static and dynamic sensors were permanently available – the Cathedral of Milan has been instrumented with a relatively large number of sensors [18] and also the environmental parameters are extensively monitored.

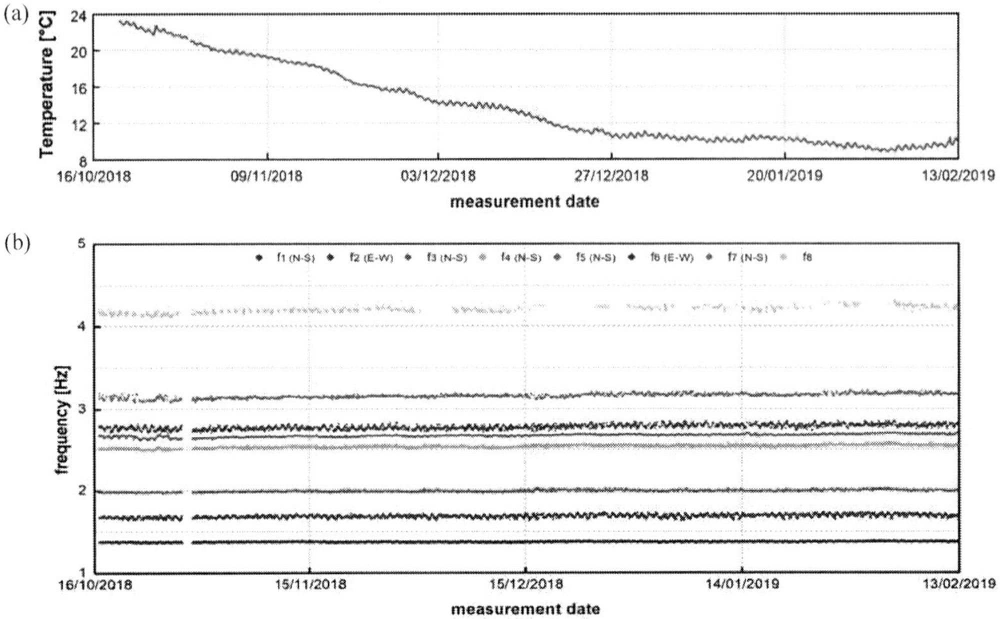

Figure 16. Time evolution (from 16/10/2018 to 12/02/2019) of: (a) the average temperature inside the Cathedral (b) the automatically identified natural frequencies..

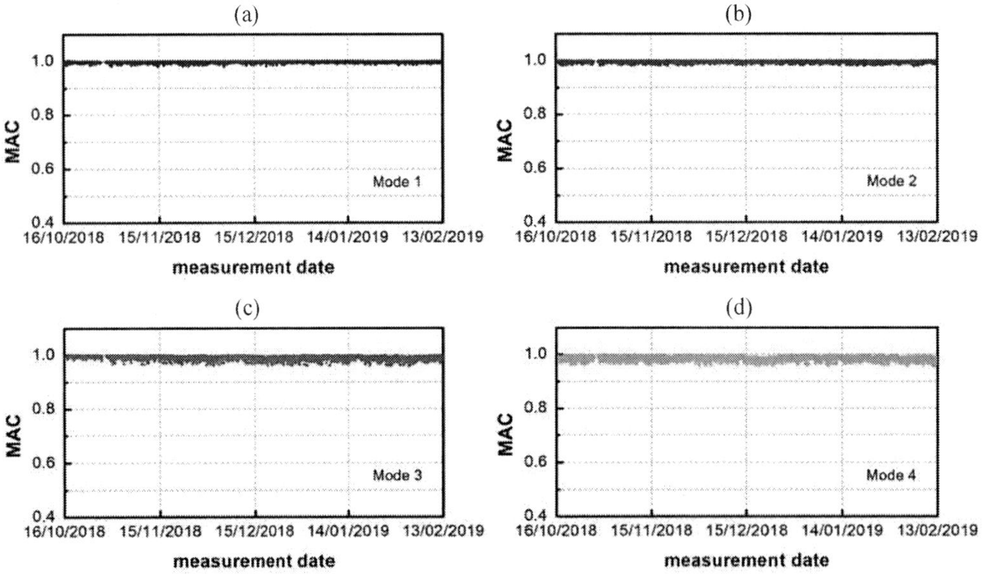

Figure 17. Time evolution (from 16/10/2018 to 12/02/2019) of the MAC of selected modes (with respect to the beginning of the dynamic monitoring).

Consequentlly, the SHM of the historic monument will be performed not only using the resonant frequencies but also checking the invariance of the mode shapes (Fig. 17) and related modal complexity [20]. In addition, the availability of quasi-static measurement of structural responses (such as the tilt of selected piers and the strain on a certain number of tie-rods) might contribute – directly or through the fusion with the data coming from OMA-based monitoring – to check the structural health condition of the Cathedral.

4. CONCLUSIONS

Selected results of the continuous dynamic monitoring of three historic towers have been reported in the first part of paper with the objectives of: (a) demonstrating that the successful monitoring of the dynamic characteristics can be obtained by permanently installing a few high-sensitivity accelerometers (or seismometers) in the upper part of the building; (b) better understanding the effects of changing temperature on the time evolution of continuously identified modal frequencies and (c) highlighting that the occurrence of slight damage under changing environment can be identified even installing a limited number of sensors in the structure.

Different temperature-driven effects on frequency changes have been observed in the investigated towers: (1) the increase of natural frequencies with increased temperature, due to the closure of superficial cracks and minor masonry discontinuities induced by the thermal expansion of materials; (2) the quick and significant increase of the modal frequencies with decreased temperature around the freezing condition (conceivably induced by the presence of ice, which fills and closes the cracks and causes a temporary stiffening of the structure); (3) the effects of the increased temperature at the local level, such as the increase of thrust exerted by inclined structural elements or the slackening of metallic ties.

In the second part of the paper, the focus is moved to the vibration monitoring of complex Cultural Heritage buildings, such as the Cathedral of Milan, where a relatively large monitoring system has been recently designed and implemented. In such instances, the possibility of adopting a SHM strategy which involves all the available modal parameters (i.e., resonant frequencies, mode shapes and modal complexity) has been discussed.

ACKNOWLEDGEMENTS

The support of the *Veneranda Fabbrica del Duomo di Milano* and the precious co-operation of F. Canali is gratefully acknowledged. Sincere thanks are due to F. Aquilano (*Veneranda Fabbrica del Duomo di Milano*) for the operational support on-site during the installation of the monitoring system in the Cathedral of Milan and to A. Ruccolo (PhD_ABC, Politecnico di Milano) for the support in the analysis of the data collected in the same Cathedral.

REFERENCES

[1] Wenzel, H. (2009). *Health monitoring of bridges*. John Wiley & Sons.

[2] Magalhães, F., Cunha, Á., & Caetano, E. (2012). Vibration based structural health monitoring of an arch bridge: from automated OMA to damage detection. *Mechanical Systems and Signal Processing* 28, 212-228.

[3] Cross, E.J., Koo, K.Y., Brownjohn, J.M.W., & Worden, K. (2013). Long-term monitoring and data analysis of the Tamar Bridge, *Mechanical Systems and Signal Processing* 35, 16-34.

[4] Ramos, L.F., Aguilar, R., Lourenco, P.B., & Moreira, S. (2013). Dynamic structural health monitoring of Saint Torcato Church, *Mechanical Systems and Signal Processing* 35, 1-15.

[5] Cabboi, A. (2013). *Automatic operational modal analysis: challenges and application to historic structures and infrastructures*. Ph.D. Thesis, University of Cagliari, Italy.

[6] Cantieni, R (2014) One-year monitoring of a historic bell tower. In: *Proceedings of the 9th international conference on structural dynamics, EURODYN 2014* (pp. 1493-1500). University of Porto.

[7] Saisi. A., Gentile, C., & Guidobaldi, M. (2015). Post-earthquake continuous dynamic monitoring of the Gabbia Tower in Mantua, Italy, *Construction and Building Materials* 81, 101-112.

[8] Gentile, C., Guidobaldi, M., & Saisi, A. (2016). One year of monitoring of historic tower: damage detection under changing environment, *Meccanica* 51, 2873-2889.

[9] Guidobaldi, M. (2016). *Vibration-based structural health monitoring for historic masonry towers*. Ph.D. Thesis, Politecnico di Milano, Italy.

[10] Masciotta, M.G., Roque, J.C.A., Ramos, L.F., & Lourenço, P.B. (2016). A multidisciplinary approach to assess the health state of heritage structures: The case study of the Church of Monastery of Jerónimos in Lisbon, *Construction and Building Materials* 116, 169-187.

[11] Ubertini, F., Comanducci, G., Cavalagli, N., Pisello, A.L., Materazzi, A.L., & Cotana, F. (2017). Environmental effects on natural frequencies of the San Pietro bell tower in Perugia, Italy, and their removal for structural performance assessment, *Mechanical Systems and Signal Processing* 82, 307-322.

[12] Elyamani, A., Caselles, O., Roca, P., & Clapes, J. (2017). Dynamic investigation of large historical cathedral, *Structural Control and Health Monitoring* 24(3), 1-25.

[13] Masciotta, M.G., Ramos, L.F., & Lourenço, P.B. (2017). The importance of structural monitoring as a diagnosis and control tool in the restoration process of heritage structures: A case study in Portugal, *Journal of Cultural Heritage* 27, 36-47.

[14] Cabboi, A., Gentile, C., & Saisi, A. (2017). From continuous vibration monitoring to FEM-based damage assessment: Application on a stone-masonry tower, *Construction and Building Materials* 156, 252–265.

[15] Ubertini, F., Cavalagli, N., Kita, A., & Comanducci, G. (2018). Assessment of a monumental masonry bell-tower after 2016 Central Italy seismic sequence by long-term SHM, *Bulletin of Earthquake Engineering* 16(2), 775-801.

[16] Azzara, R.M., De Roeck, G., Girardi, M., Padovani, C., Pellegrini, D., & Reynders, E. (2018). The influence of environmental parameters on the dynamic behaviour of the San Frediano bell tower in Lucca, *Engineering Structures* 156, 175-187.

[17] Saisi. A., Gentile, C., & Ruccolo, A. (2018). Continuous monitoring of a challenging heritage tower in Monza, Italy, *Journal of Civil Structural Health Monitoring* 8, 77-90.

[18] Canali, C., & Gentile, C. (2018). Continuous monitoring the Cathedral of Milan: documentary and preliminary investigations. In: *Proceedings of the 10th International Masonry Conference, 10th IMC* (pp. 2061-2072). International Masonry Society.

[19] Kita, A., Cavalagli, N., & Ubertini, F. (2019). Temperature effects on static and dynamic behavior of Consoli Palace in Gubbio, Italy, *Mechanical Systems and Signal Processing* 120, 180-202.

[20] Cabboi, A., Gentile, C., & Saisi, A. (2014). Vibration-based SHM of a centenary bridge: a comparative study between two different automated OMA techniques. In *Proceedings of the 9th international conference on structural dynamics, EURODYN 2014* (pp. 1461-1468). University of Porto.

[21] Busatta, F. (2012). *Dynamic monitoring and automated modal analysis of large structures: methodological aspects and application to a historic iron bridge*. PhD Thesis, Politecnico di Milano, Italy.

[22] Cabboi, A., Magalhães, F., Gentile, C., & Cunha, Á. (2017). Automated modal identification and tracking: application to an iron arch bridge, *Structural Control and Health Monitoring* 24(1), e1854.

[23] Peeters, B., & De Roeck, G. (1999). Reference-based Stochastic Subspace Identification for output-only modal analysis, *Mechanical Systems and Signal Processing* 13, 855-878.

[24] Benedettini, F., Zulli, D., & Alaggio, R. (2009). Frequency-veering and mode hybridization in arch bridges. In: *Proceedings of the 27th International Modal Analysis Conference IMAC-XXVII*. Orlando, USA.

[25] www.sara.pg.it/en. Available online: URL (accessed on 15 April 2018).

IOMAC'19

8th International Operational Modal Analysis Conference
2019 May 13-15 Copenhagen

STATISTICAL SUBSPACE BASED DAMAGE LOCALIZATION ON SAINT-NAZAIRE BRIDGE MOCK-UP

Md Delwar Hossain Bhuyan[1], *Michael Döhler*[2], *Yann Lecieux*[3], *Cyril Lupi*[3], *Jean-Christophe Thomas*[3], *Franck Schoefs*[3], *Falk Hille*[1], *Laurent Mevel*[2]

[1] BAM Federal Institute of Materials Research and Testing, Berlin, Germany, {md-delwar-hossain.bhuyan, falk.hille}@bam.de
[2] Univ. Rennes, Inria, Ifsttar COSYS/SII, Campus de Beaulieu, 35042 Rennes, France, {michael.doehler, laurent.mevel}@inria.fr
[3] GeM, University of Nantes, Nantes, France, {yann.lecieux, cyril.lupi, jean-christophe.thomas,franck.schoefs}@uni-nantes.fr

ABSTRACT

The subject of damage localization is an important issue for Structural Health Monitoring (SHM) particularly in mechanical or civil structures under ambient excitation. In this paper, the statistical subspace-based damage localization method has been applied on a benchmark application, namely a 1/200 scale model of the Saint-Nazaire Bridge, which is a cable-stayed bridge located on the Loire River near the river's mouth. The employed damage localization method combines data-driven features with physical parameter information from a finite element model in statistical tests, avoiding typical ill-conditioning problems of FE model updating. Damage is introduced in the mockup for cable failures on some of the 72 cables. The purpose of the experiment is to assess the capability of damage assessment methods to find a cable failure.

Keywords: damage localization, cable-stayed bridge, cable failure, structural health monitoring.

1. INTRODUCTION

Vibration-based structural health monitoring has become an important issue during the last decades [1–3], especially for bridges, buildings or offshore structures. We consider the case of output-only vibration measurements of a benchmark structure subject to ambient excitation.

Methods for damage detection are widely developed since they can operate purely data-based and do not require a finite element (FE) model of the monitored structure. Automated methods for damage localization are more sophisticated since a link between the measurement data and the physical properties of the structure is required, which is often given by a FE model. Experimental works on complex structures are required to validate the methods. Experimental works are usually focused on the study of two categories of structures: models tested in the laboratory, or real structures damaged and tested before destruction.

A lab benchmark that has been evaluated by several research groups is e.g. the ASCE Benchmark Test Frame at the University of British Columbia in Vancouver, Canada, which was established in 2002 [4]. Recent ambient vibration tests have been performed on the structure in 2017 [5].

In previous work [6], a benchmark for damage diagnosis on a cable-stayed bridge structure was proposed using output-only vibration data. The experimental work was carried out in the lab on a model scale 1/200 of the bridge of Saint-Nazaire in France, equipped with 10 accelerometers. The introduced damage is the rupture of one or two of the cables supporting the deck (see some examples in [7]). In [6], the statistical stochastic damage locating vector approach (S-SDDLV) was successfully applied to localize the damage. In this paper, the statistical subspace based residual approach [8, 9] is applied for damage localization. It operates on a data-driven residual vector that is statistically evaluated using information from a FE model, combining both data-driven and model-based methodologies.

This paper is organized as follows. In Section 2., the modeling of the structure is recalled. In Section 3., the damage localization framework is detailed and finally, applied on the bridge mockup in Section 4..

2. MODELING OF THE STRUCTURE

The behavior of a mechanical structure is assumed to be described by a linear time-invariant (LTI) dynamic system

$$M\ddot{\mathcal{X}}(t) + C\dot{\mathcal{X}}(t) + K\mathcal{X}(t) = f(t) \tag{1}$$

where M, C, $K \in \mathbb{R}^{d\times d}$ are the mass, damping and stiffness matrices, respectively, t indicates continuous time and $\mathcal{X} \in \mathbb{R}^d$ denotes the displacements at the d degrees of freedom (DOF) of the structure. The external force $f(t)$ is not measurable and modeled as white noise. Let the dynamic system (1) be observed at r coordinates. Defining the state vector $x = [\mathcal{X}\ \ \dot{\mathcal{X}}]^T$ and sampling at time steps $t = k\tau$ yields the discrete-time state-space model

$$\begin{cases} x_{k+1} = Ax_k + w_k \\ \quad\ y_k = Cx_k + v_k \end{cases}, \tag{2}$$

with state vector $x_k \in \mathbb{R}^n$, output vector $y_k \in \mathbb{R}^r$, the state transition matrix $A \in \mathbb{R}^{n\times n}$ and output matrix $C \in \mathbb{R}^{r\times n}$, where $n = 2d$ is the system order and r is the number of outputs.

3. DAMAGE LOCALIZATION FRAMEWORK

Let $\theta \in \mathbb{R}^l$ be a parameter vector that describes the monitored system in the current state, and $\theta_0 \in \mathbb{R}^l$ its value in the healthy reference system. We assume that damage is linked to stiffness changes, thus θ is the collection of stiffness parameters of the elements of the structure, where θ_0 is obtained from a finite element model in the reference state. For example, the components of θ can be the stiffnesses of a system, Young modulus of beam elements or it can be basically any quantity linked to damage-sensitive properties of the system.

In [8], a statistical framework has been set up for Gaussian residual vectors parametrized by θ with the purpose to decide which parts of θ have changed for damage localization. The Gaussian residual vector $\zeta \in \mathbb{R}^h$ is computed from the measurements of the system and needs to satisfy

$$\zeta \sim \begin{cases} \mathcal{N}(0, \Sigma) & \text{in reference state} \\ \mathcal{N}(\mathcal{J}\delta, \Sigma) & \text{in damaged state,} \end{cases} \tag{3}$$

with $\delta = \sqrt{N}(\theta - \theta_0) \in \mathbb{R}^l$ is the unknown change in parameter vector, N is the data length used for the computation of ζ, the sensitivity matrix $\mathcal{J} \in \mathbb{R}^{h\times l}$ has full column rank and the residual covariance matrix $\Sigma \in \mathbb{R}^{h\times h}$ is positive definite.

3.1. Subspace-based residual

In previous works on damage detection and localization [8, 10], the subspace-based residual function

$$\zeta^s \overset{\text{def}}{=} \sqrt{N}\,\text{vec}(S^T \widehat{\mathcal{H}}) \tag{4}$$

has been introduced, where $\widehat{\mathcal{H}}$ is an estimate of the block Hankel matrix of the output covariances of the current system (2)

$$\mathcal{H} \overset{\text{def}}{=} \begin{bmatrix} R_1 & R_2 & \dots & R_q \\ R_2 & R_3 & \dots & R_{q+1} \\ \vdots & \vdots & \ddots & \vdots \\ R_{p+1} & R_{p+2} & \dots & R_{p+q} \end{bmatrix}, \quad R_i = \mathbf{E}(y_k y_{k-i}^T), \quad \hat{R}_i = \frac{1}{N}\sum_{k=1}^{N} y_k y_{k-i}^T$$

and S is the left null space of $\mathcal{H}$ from the reference system. It can be obtained from a Hankel matrix $\mathcal{H}_0$ in the reference state through a singular value decomposition

$$\mathcal{H}_0 = \begin{bmatrix} U_1 & U_2 \end{bmatrix} \begin{bmatrix} D_1 & 0 \\ 0 & D_2 \approx 0 \end{bmatrix} \begin{bmatrix} V_1^T \\ V_2^T \end{bmatrix}$$

as $S = U_2$. When the system is in the reference state, the expected value of the product $S^T\widehat{\mathcal{H}}$ is zero, and when the system is damaged the product deviates from zero. The residual in (4) satisfies relation (3) asymptotically, and its sensitivity and covariance are given in detail in [10].

In the following, the statistical tests for damage localization are recalled.

3.2. Damage localization tests

For damage localization it has to be decided which parts of vector δ in (3) are non-zero, i.e. which parts of the parameter vector are changed. The structural elements corresponding to the changed parameters are thus damaged. To this end, each component of δ will be tested one after another. Denote the component to be tested by δ_a, and the remaining components by δ_b, such that

$$\delta = \begin{bmatrix} \delta_a \\ \delta_b \end{bmatrix}. \tag{5}$$

Then, $\delta_a = 0$ is tested against $\delta_a \neq 0$. Following (5), the sensitivity matrix $\mathcal{J}$ and the Fisher information matrix $F = \mathcal{J}^T\Sigma^{-1}\mathcal{J}$ are analogously arranged as

$$\mathcal{J} = \begin{bmatrix} \mathcal{J}_a\; \mathcal{J}_b \end{bmatrix}, F = \begin{bmatrix} F_{aa} & F_{ab} \\ F_{ba} & F_{bb} \end{bmatrix} = \begin{bmatrix} \mathcal{J}_a^T\Sigma^{-1}\mathcal{J}_a & \mathcal{J}_a^T\Sigma^{-1}\mathcal{J}_b \\ \mathcal{J}_b^T\Sigma^{-1}\mathcal{J}_a & \mathcal{J}_b^T\Sigma^{-1}\mathcal{J}_b \end{bmatrix}. \tag{6}$$

Direct tests Assuming that $\delta_b = 0$ for testing $\delta_a = 0$ against $\delta_a \neq 0$, the generalized likelihood ratio (GLR) test follows as

$$t_{dir} = \zeta^T\Sigma^{-1}\mathcal{J}_a^T(\mathcal{J}_a^T\Sigma^{-1}\mathcal{J}_a)^{-1}\mathcal{J}_a^T\Sigma^{-1}\zeta, \tag{7}$$

which is called direct test. The test statistic t_{dir} is χ^2 distributed with non-centrality parameter $\delta_a^T F_{aa}\delta_a$. For making decision about the damage location, the test variable is compared to a threshold. Note that the simplifying assumption $\delta_b = 0$ in this test that may lead to false alarms when testing an undamaged element while another element is actually damaged.

Minmax tests Instead of assuming the components of $\delta_b = 0$, the variable δ_b is substituted by its least favorable value for making a decision about δ_a, which leads to the minmax test as follows. Define the partial residuals

$$\zeta_a = \mathcal{J}_a^T\Sigma^{-1}\zeta \tag{8a}$$

$$\zeta_b = \mathcal{J}_b^T\Sigma^{-1}\zeta, \tag{8b}$$

and the robust residual

$$\zeta_a^* = \zeta_a - F_{aa}F_{bb}^{-1}\zeta_b,$$

whose mean is sensitive to changes δ_a but not to δ_b. Testing $\delta_a = 0$ against $\delta_a \neq 0$ with the GLR test yields

$$t_{mm} = \zeta_a^* F_a^{*-1} \zeta_a^*, \tag{9}$$

where $F_a^* = F_{aa} - F_{ab}F_{bb}^{-1}F_{ba}$. The test statistic t_{mm} is χ^2 distributed with non-centrality parameter $\delta_a^T F_a^* \delta_a$.

A prerequisite for the localization approach with the minmax tests is the independence of the parameterization in the sense that matrix (6) needs be full rank. This can be ensured through clustering the vectors of the normalized sensitivity matrix $\Sigma^{-1/2}\mathcal{J}$ and defining $\mathcal{J}_b$ as the cluster centers of the clusters not containing the currently tested element a. An adequate clustering approach for this problem has been shown to be complete-linkage clustering [9, 11].

4. APPLICATION: SAINT-NAZAIRE BRIDGE MOCK-UP

In this application, the statistical subspace method for damage localization is applied to the Saint-Nazaire bridge mockup. In previous work [6], the details of the experiment were presented and are shortly recalled here.

4.1. The real structure

The Saint-Nazaire Bridge is a cable-stayed bridge located in the Loire River near the river's mouth in the west of France. The bridge includes two access viaducts supported by pile foundations (Figure 1a). The northern viaduct (1115 m long) and the southern one (1521 m long) are made of pre-stressed concrete. The pile foundations of the central part are also made of concrete. The main structure (in blue on Figure 1a) is composed of a 720 m long cable-stayed metallic frame. The bridge deck, the cables, and the triangular bridge pylons are made of steel.

Some keys features are listed below to describe the structure:

- 72 cables
- 56 concrete piles
- Total length: 3356 meters
- Central structure: 720 meters
- Central span: 404 meters
- Height of deck of central bridge: 68 meters
- Height of the two central pylons: 130 meters
- Air draft of 61 meters

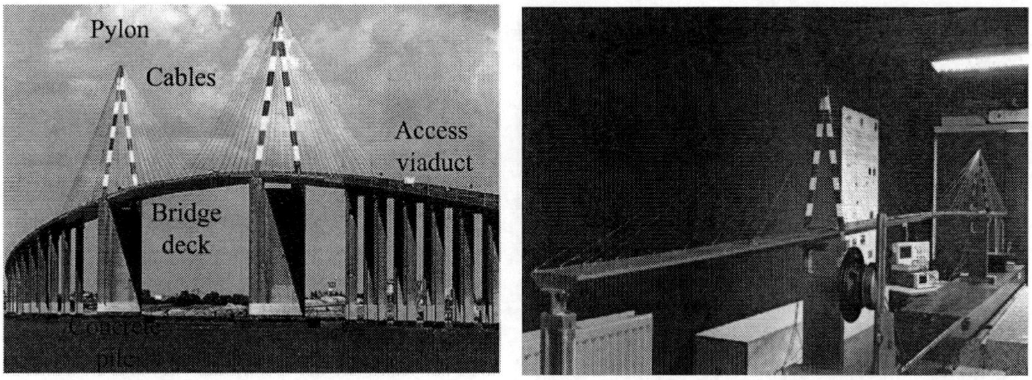

(a) View of the real structure

(b) Mockup of the central structure

Figure 1: Saint Nazaire bridge.

4.2. The mock-up and acquisition system

For the dynamic analysis of the structure, only the central bridge (metallic part) was considered. The study presented here was carried out on a 1/200 scale model of the structure, i.e. a 3.6 m long mockup positioned on two surface plates (Figure 1b). To obtain the geometrical and mechanical characteristics of the model, the length of the real structure is multiplied by a scale factor of 1/200. In order to preserve the scale factor for the masses, it was chosen to use building materials for the model with density similar or close to those used for the construction of the real bridge.

On the bridge model, there are 10 miniature piezoelectric accelerometers (0.8 gm) of sensitivity 100 mV/g (PCB of reference ICP) capable of measuring vertical accelerations. All the signals are collected on a data-logger (HBM reference MX16101) at the acquisition frequency of 4800 Hz. The excitation is provided by an audio boomer (see Figure 2a) which acts as a shaker. It is powered by the signal of a white noise generator (+/- 5V peak to peak, manufactured by Tektronix, reference AFG), amplified by a stereo amplifier. The signal is controlled with an oscilloscope. The devices of the signal acquisition chain and the shaker are visible in Figure 2a.

In the damaged and healthy states, acceleration data containing 581,118 and 588,620 samples are recorded, respectively.

4.3. Damage to structure

The damage to assess is a failure of a cable supporting the deck. It is introduced by removing the fastener connecting the cable and the deck. Thus, only the stiffness of the structure is modified and not its mass. Two damages are tested, the rupture of a cable, and the rupture of two cables symmetrical with respect to the pylon. These two elements located in the middle of the bridge are visible in Figure 2b.

4.4. The Saint Nazaire bridge mock-up finite element model and parameterization

The FE model has been built (see Figure 2b) with the student version of the ABAQUS software. The model consists of 180 beam elements and 72 truss elements for a total of 1062 degrees of freedom. The damaged elements are numbered 37 and 38.

The system parameter θ is defined as the collection of cable stiffnesses of each of the 72 cables, since it is the goal to localize the damage in these cables. Using a finite difference method, the sensitivity of the mode shapes and natural frequencies with respect to each cable stiffness is computed for the first 15 vertical modes obtained from the FE model. To analyze the impact of modal truncation in the residual sensitivity on the localization approach, 10 and 15 modes are used in its computation, respectively.

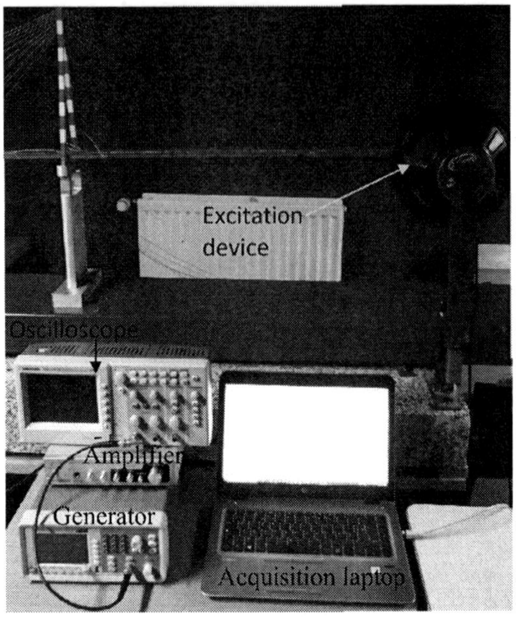

(**a**) Acquisition and excitation devices

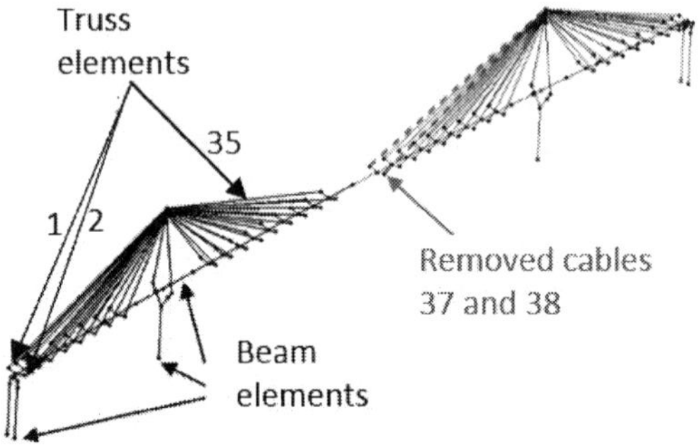

(**b**) Finite element model

Figure 2: Saint Nazaire bridge mockup.

The first four vertical mode shapes are shown in Figures 3. The cluster dendrogram is shown in Figure 4, visualizing the cluster construction based on a statistical distance measure between the sensitivities of the different cables that will be tested for damage. This distance corresponds to the cosine of the angle between the sensitivities, varying between 0 and 1. If the sensitivities of two elements are close, they are put into the same cluster, and only the cluster center is used in the minmax test as detailed in Section 3.2.. A threshold of 0.15 is set for close elements to be in the same cluster, indicated by the same colors in Figure 4.

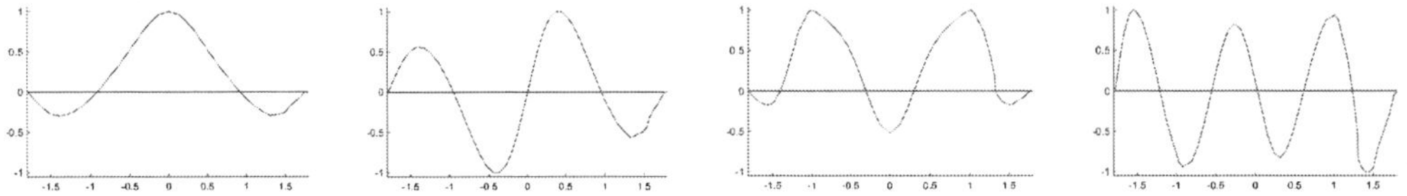

(**a**) 1st mode at 35.9 Hz (**b**) 2nd mode at 61.1 Hz (**c**) 3rd mode at 88.6 Hz (**d**) 4th mode at 121.5 Hz

Figure 3: Modeshapes (vertical) from FE model in the healthy state.

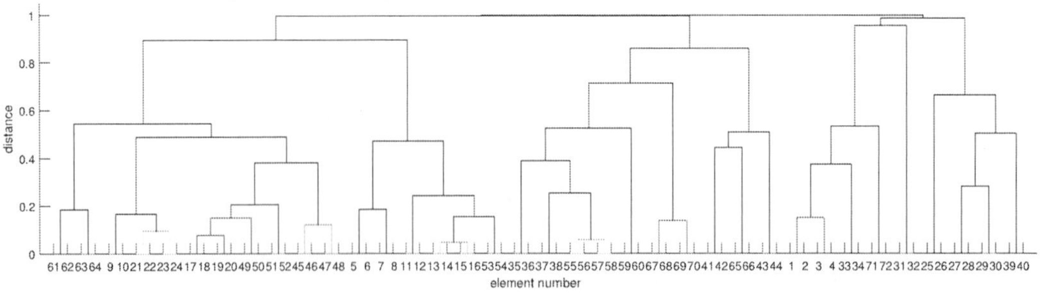

Figure 4: Dendrogram for clustering using 15 modes.

4.5. Localization results

The localization test statistics are computed for all 72 elements, which are corresponding to the cable stiffness (see Figure 2b), using a dataset in both damaged and healthy states. Note that damage was introduced by removing first cable number 37, and then cables 37 and 38 at the middle of the structure. The highest value of the test statistic indicates the most likely damage localization. The results are shown in Figures 5 - 6 and 7 - 8 using 10 and 15 vertical modes computed from the FE model, respectively, for both the direct and minmax tests, and the damage cases with one and two damaged cables.

Using 10 vertical modes in the sensitivity computation, it can be seen that the damage is not correctly localized in the direct and minmax tests for the respective test cases in Figures 5 and 6. However, the direct and minmax tests have the highest test values for the neighboring cable of the damaged elements. While the test statistic for other elements also react strongly in the direct test, this is much less the case in the minmax test. The performance for the tests for one and two damaged cables in Figures 5 and 6 is comparable.

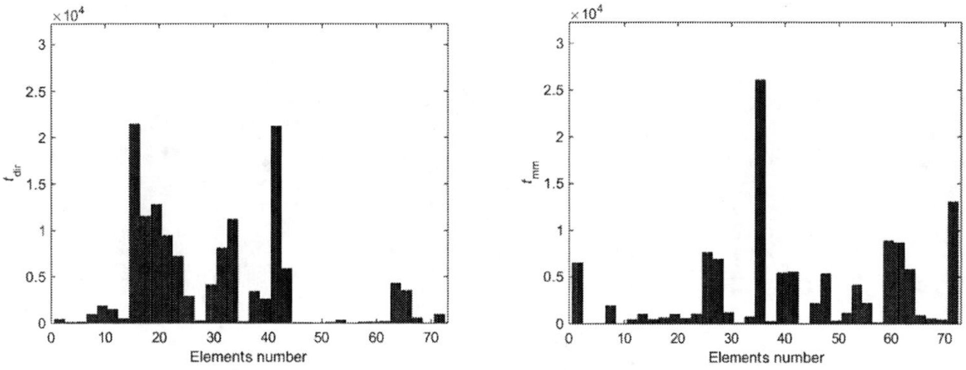

(a) Direct tests **(b)** Minmax tests

Figure 5: Test case 1: Localization for damaged cable 37, using 10 modes.

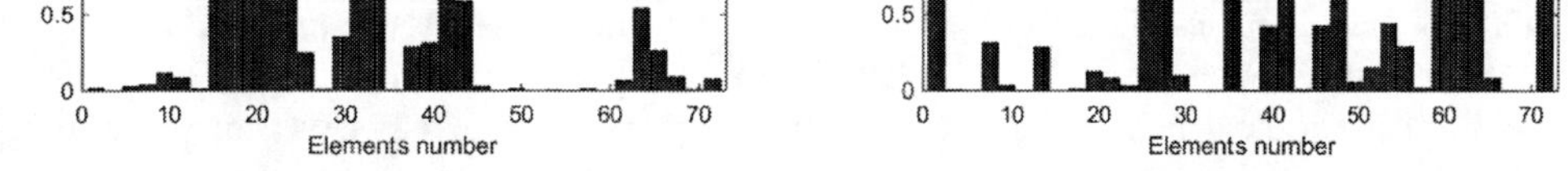

(c) Direct tests **(d)** Minmax tests

Figure 6: Test case 2: Localization for damaged cables 37 and 38, using 10 modes.

Considering 15 vertical modes instead of 10 in the sensitivity computation, it can be seen in Figures 7 and 8 that the highest value of the direct and minmax tests is correctly located in the damaged elements, which may be due to less modal truncation in the sensitivity computation. Note that the test for both elements 37 and 38 react in the same way, even if just one of them is damaged, since they cannot be distinguished by their sensitivities (see Figure 4). The direct test in Figures 7a and 7c reacts also at undamaged elements due to the violation of the assumptions in the test (see Section 3.2.), which clearly leads to false positive results in this case. In the minmax tests in Figures 7b and 7d, only the actual damaged elements show a strong test reaction, separating the damaged elements clearly from the undamaged ones.

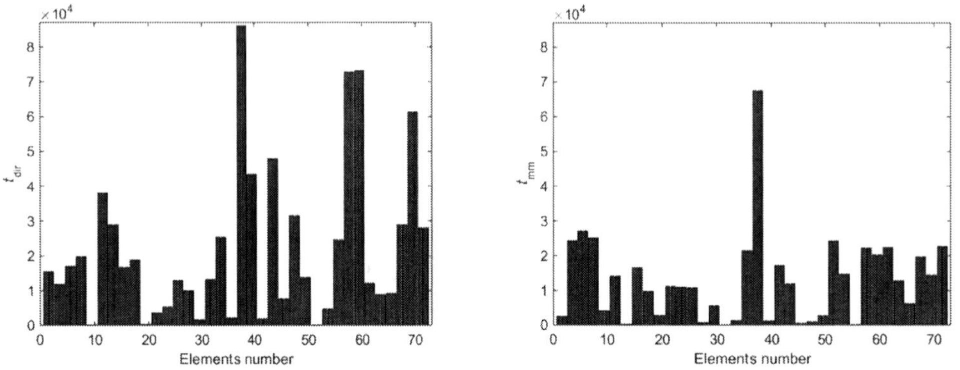

(a) Direct tests (b) Minmax tests

Figure 7: Test case 1: Localization for damaged cable 37, using 15 modes.

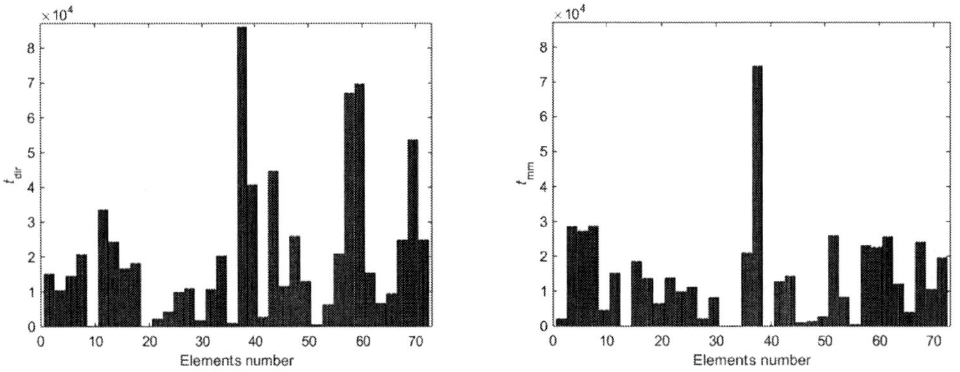

(c) Direct tests (d) Minmax tests

Figure 8: Test case 2: Localization for damaged cables 37 and 38, using 15 modes.

5. CONCLUSIONS

In this paper, the statistical subspace based damage localization method has been applied on output-only vibration measurements of a benchmark structure, the Saint-Nazaire bridge mockup. Here, two test cases were considered with one and two cable failures. In both test cases, the introduced damage was correctly localized at the damaged elements when the number of considered modes computed from the FE model was sufficiently high. It is noted that the FE model was not updated, and the conditions on its precision with the used method are rather light. Future work should include damage quantification using this approach.

ACKNOWLEDGEMENTS

The authors thank the physics department of the University of Nantes for providing the reduced scale bridge and the acquisition system. The support from DAAD/German Federal Ministry of Education and Research and the French Ministries of Foreign Affairs (MAEDI) and Education (MENESR) in the PROCOPE program is gratefully acknowledged.

REFERENCES

[1] C.R. Farrar, S.W. Doebling, and D.A. Nix. Vibration-based structural damage identification. *Philosophical Transactions of the Royal Society A: Mathematical, Physical and Engineering Science*, 359(1778):131–149, 2001.

[2] E.P. Carden and P. Fanning. Vibration based condition monitoring: a review. *Structural Health Monitoring*, 3(4):355–377, 2004.

[3] W. Fan and P. Qiao. Vibration-based damage identification methods: a review and comparative study. *Structural Health Monitoring*, 10(1):83–111, 2011.

[4] Ventura C.E., Lord J.F., Turek M., Serci A.M., Radulescu D., and Radulescu C. Experimental studies and remote monitoring of iasc-asce benchmark test frame. In *XXI International Modal Analysis Conference(pp. 3-6)*, 2003.

[5] S. Allahdadian, M. Döhler, C. Ventura, and L. Mevel. Damage localization of a real structure using the statistical subspace damage localization method. In *Proc. 11th International Workshop on Structural Health Monitoring (IWSHM)*, Stanford, CA, USA, 2017.

[6] M.D.H. Bhuyan, Y. Lecieux, J-C. Thomas, C. Lupi, F. Schoefs, M. Döhler, and L. Mevel. Statistical vibration-based damage localization on saint-nazaire bridge mockup. In *40th IABSE Symposium*, 19-21 September 2018, Nantes, France.

[7] N.T. Nghia and Samec V. Cable stay bridges investigation of cable rupture. *Journal of Civil Engineering and Architecture*, 10:270–279, 2016.

[8] M. Döhler, L. Mevel, and Q. Zhang. Fault detection, isolation and quantification from gaussian residuals with application to structural damage diagnosis. *Annual Reviews in Control*, 42:244–256, 2016.

[9] S. Allahdadian, M. Döhler, C. Ventura, and L. Mevel. Statistical sensitivity-based damage localization. 2019. Submitted to Mechanical Systems and Signal Processing.

[10] É. Balmès, M. Basseville, L. Mevel, H. Nasser, and W. Zhou. Statistical model-based damage localization: a combined subspace-based and substructuring approach. *Structural Control and Health Monitoring*, 15(6):857–875, 2008.

[11] S. Allahdadian. *Robust Statistical Subspace-Based Damage Assessment.* PhD thesis, University of British Columbia, Vancouver, Canada, 2017.

IOMAC'19

8th International Operational Modal Analysis Conference

2019 May 13-15 Copenhagen

THE EFFECT OF OPERATIONAL MODAL ANALYSIS IN STRAIN ESTIMATION USING THE MODAL EXPANSION

Marius Tarpø[1], *Bruna Nabuco*[2], *Christos Georgakis*[3], *Rune Brincker*[4]

[1] PhD student, Dept. of Engineering, Aarhus University, Inge Lehmanns Gade 10, 8000 Aarhus C, Denmark, martar@eng.au.dk
[2] PhD student, Dept. of Civil engineering, Technical University of Denmark, Brovej, Building 118, 2800 Kgs. Lyngby, Denmark, brunan@byg.dtu.dk
[3] Professor, Dept. of Engineering, Aarhus University, Inge Lehmanns Gade 10, 8000 Aarhus C, Denmark, cg@eng.au.dk
[4] Professor, Structural dynamics, Dept. of Civil engineering, Technical University of Denmark, Brovej, Building 118, 2800 Kgs. Lyngby, Denmark, runeb@byg.dtu.dk

ABSTRACT

The stress history of a structure in operation is important for the remaining fatigue lifetime. The fatigue critical locations are, however, often inaccessible or placed at damaging spots where sensors are easily corrupted. Virtual sensing techniques can be applied to estimate strain in unmeasured points. The Modal Expansion/Modal Decomposition is one of these techniques. This technique uses the mode shape of the structure to decorrelate a measured spatial limited response so it can expand this decorrelated response with the strain mode shape to estimate the strain response of the entire structure. These mode shapes come from either an updated Finite Element Model or a modal analysis. The experimental mode shapes use an expansion procedure - like the Local Correspondence Principle. This paper studies the effect of using experimental mode shapes in strain estimation using the Modal Expansion and the Local Correspondence Principle.

Keywords: Stress Estimation, Mode Shape Expansion, Virtual Sensing, Remote Sensing, Structural Health Monitoring

1. INTRODUCTION

Structural Health Monitoring is the process of monitoring the current state and condition of structures in operation by analysing the spatially limited data from a monitoring system. This monitoring system enables the owner to make decisions regarding the service of the structure to ensure safety. For structures prone to fatigue failure, the stress history is crucial for the assessment of the remaining service life. Thus, a fatigue assessment of an existing structure calls for the stress history in all fatigue critical locations. These locations are, however, often inaccessible or damaging for the sensors. Therefore, Virtual Sensing

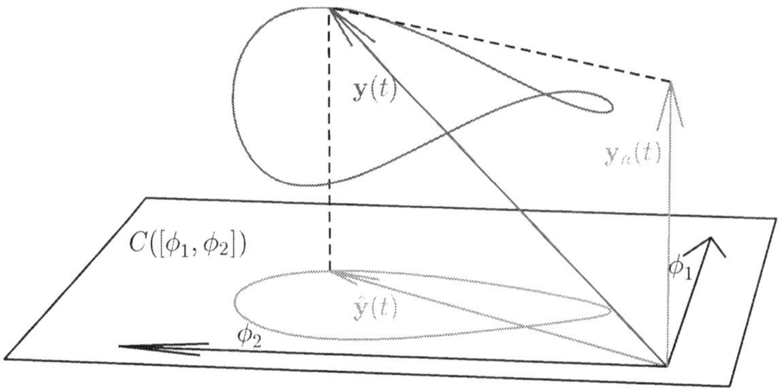

Figure 1: Illustration of Modal Expansion in $\mathbb{R}^3$ with a two-dimensional subspace: The response, $\mathbf{y}(t)$, is projected onto the subspace spanned by two mode shapes, ϕ_1 and ϕ_2, and this results in the truncated response, $\hat{\mathbf{y}}(t)$, where all response outside this subspace, $\mathbf{y}_n(t)$, is removed

is often applied to expand measurements from a few physical sensors to unmeasured locations using some process model [1].

In the literature for stress estimation, there exist multiple process models but we will focus on the Modal Expansion [2–6]. For modal expansion, there are two approaches: applying finite element mode shapes [4, 5, 7] or expanded experimental mode shapes [2, 3, 6]. The hypothesis of expanding experimental mode shape is that these mode shapes are more representable of the actual structure than the finite element model. The problematic of mode shape expansion is, however, case dependent. It depends on the spatial distribution of the sensors, the modelling errors on the finite element model, the identification error on the experimental mode shapes, and the measurement errors on the sensors.

This paper studies the effect of expanding experimental mode shapes in modal expansion for strain estimation. Based on a case study, expansion of mode shapes improves strain estimation since these experimental mode shapes form a better basis than the finite element mode shapes. Mode shapes expansion is, however, a fitting procedure so it introduces potential fitting errors. Hence, mode shape expansion of experimental modes are able to reduce errors in strain estimation but we must watch out for fitting errors in the expansion.

2. MODAL EXPANSION FOR STRAIN ESTIMATION

Modal Expansion is a least square regression technique that creates virtual sensors. This technique projects the response onto the linear subspace spanned by the applied mode shapes, as illustrated in Figure 1. It is based on the modal superposition/modal decorrelation that states: the response of a linear structure is a linear combination of its mode shapes [8].

$$\mathbf{y}(t) = \mathbf{\Phi}\mathbf{q}(t) \tag{1}$$

where $\mathbf{y}(t)$ is the response, $\mathbf{\Phi}$ is the modal matrix with mode shapes as column vectors, $\mathbf{\Phi} = [\phi_1, \ldots, \phi_N]$, and $\mathbf{q}(t)$ is the modal coordinates (or the linear combination of the mode shapes).

In practice, we have a truncated modal matrix from a finite element with modelling errors, $\tilde{\mathbf{\Phi}} = [\tilde{\phi}_1, \ldots, \tilde{\phi}_K]$, and a response measured in a few degrees-of-freedom with measurement errors, $\tilde{\mathbf{y}}_a(t) = \mathbf{y}_a(t) + \mathbf{n}_a(t)$.

$$\tilde{\mathbf{\Phi}} = \begin{bmatrix} \tilde{\mathbf{\Phi}}_a \\ \tilde{\mathbf{\Phi}}_d \end{bmatrix} \tag{2}$$

where the subscripts a and d denote the active and inactive degrees-of-freedom, respectfully.

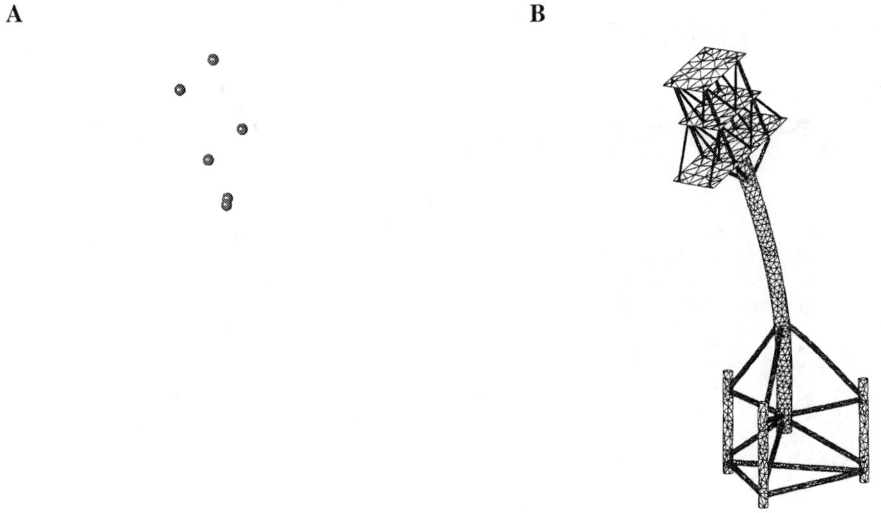

Figure 2: Illustration of mode shape expansion: A) the experimental mode shape and B) the expanded experimental mode shape using a finite element model

We estimate the modal coordinates by transforming the measured response.

$$\hat{\mathbf{q}}(t) \quad = \quad \tilde{\mathbf{\Phi}}_a^{\dagger}\tilde{\mathbf{y}}_a(t) \tag{3}$$

Now we transform and extend the estimated modal coordinates into the physical domain - similarly to an estimated subspace project of the measured response onto $C(\tilde{\mathbf{\Phi}})$.

$$\hat{\mathbf{y}}(t) \quad = \quad \tilde{\mathbf{\Phi}}\hat{\mathbf{q}}(t) \quad = \quad \tilde{\mathbf{\Phi}}\tilde{\mathbf{\Phi}}_a^{\dagger}\mathbf{y}_a(t) \tag{4}$$

The modal expansion reduces the subspace of the measured response while it extends the response to all degrees-of-freedom of interest. To optimise the response estimation, the applied modal matrix should provide a span very close to the column space of the system, $C(\tilde{\mathbf{\Phi}}) \approx C(\mathbf{\Phi})$.

Since the modal coordinates for strain and displacement are the same [9], we use the estimated modal coordinates, Eq. (3), and the strain mode shapes, $\tilde{\mathbf{\Phi}}_{\varepsilon}$, to estimate the strain response of the structure.

$$\hat{\varepsilon}(t) \quad = \quad \tilde{\mathbf{\Phi}}_{\varepsilon}\hat{\mathbf{q}}(t) \tag{5}$$

where $\hat{\varepsilon}(t)$ is the estimated strain response of the entire structure.

3. MODE SHAPES EXPANSION

The quality of strain estimation relies on the applied mode shapes and their ability to span the column space of the actual structure. Therefore, modelling errors in the finite element model transfer to the strain estimation. The hypothesis, behind expanding experimental mode shapes, is that the experimental mode shapes are more representable of the actual structure than the finite element model. This builds on the assumption, the estimation error on the experimental mode shapes from the operational modal analysis are lower than the modelling errors on the finite element model.

Mode Shape Expansion assumes, a linear relationship exists between the experimental mode shapes, $\mathbf{\Phi}_{exp}$, and the finite element mode shapes, $\mathbf{\Phi}_{FE}$.

$$\begin{aligned} \mathbf{\Phi}_{exp} &= \mathbf{\Phi}_{FE}\mathbf{T}_1 \\ &= \mathbf{T}_2\mathbf{\Phi}_{FE} \end{aligned} \tag{6}$$

Figure 3: Scale model of offshore platform

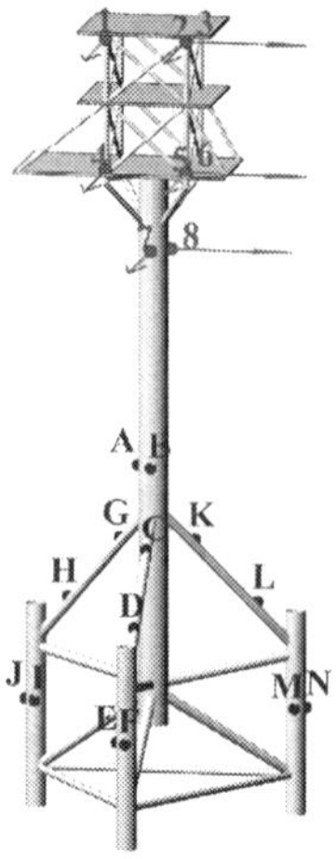

Figure 4: Position of sensors, red arrows illustrate uniaxial accelerometers and blue dots illustrate strain gauges

Thus, mode shape expansion is a linear transformation that updates the finite element model in a single step. Figure 2 illustrates the expansion of an experimental mode shape to the same degrees-of-freedom as a finite element model. The quality of the expansion depends on the fitting errors from setting up the transformation matrix. For more on mode shape expansion see [10].

Different techniques exist for calculating the transformation matrices, $\mathbf{T}_1$ or $\mathbf{T}_2$. In this paper, we focus on the Local Correspondence Principle [11] and a new implementation of the algorithm, which is under development at the time of writing.

4. CASE STUDY

We will study the effect of mode shape expansion in strain estimation using a new implementation of the Local Correspondence Principle. For this study, we will use an acrylic 1:50 scale model of an offshore platform, see Figure 3 and we created a corresponding finite element model. 8 uniaxial accelerometers are on the topside while 14 strain gauges are on the lower part of the model, see Figure 4. We sample the data with a frequency of 1651 Hz and we apply a bandpass filter that allows frequencies to pass above 7 Hz and below 80 Hz. To generate white Gaussian excitation, the model is excited by brushing the topside with a nylon brush.

4.1. Quality Measurement

We use the coefficient of determination, R_i^2, [12] as a quality measurement to check the quality of the strain estimation.

$$R_i^2 = 1 - \frac{\sum_{k=1}^{N} \left(\varepsilon_i(t_k) - \hat{\varepsilon}_i(t_k)\right)^2}{\sum_{k=1}^{N} \left(\varepsilon_i(t_k) - \mathrm{E}\left[\varepsilon_i(t)\right]\right)^2} \tag{7}$$

where $\mathrm{E}[X]$ is the expected value of X. When the coefficient of determination equals one, it indicates a perfect correlation and similar amplitudes.

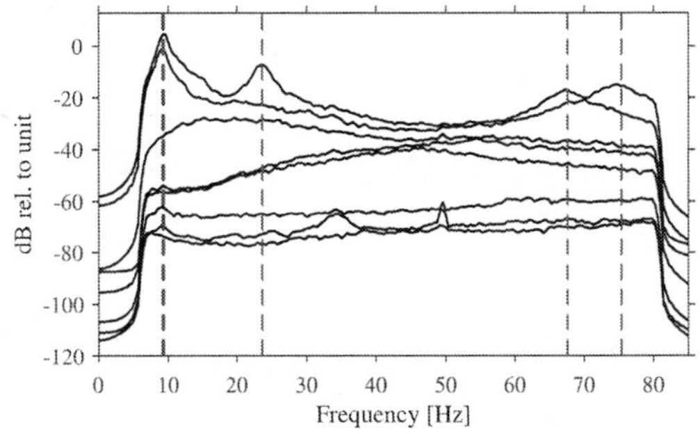

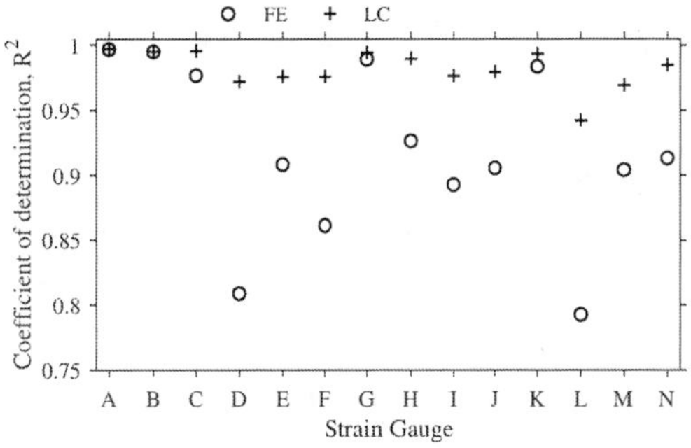

Figure 5: Singular values of spectral density matrix from scale model and the identified modes from an operational modal analysis using the Eigensystem Realization Algorithm (ERA) [14]

Figure 6: The quality measurement of strain estimation, the coefficient of determination, R_i^2

4.2. Operational Modal Analysis

To identify the experimental mode shapes, we apply Operational Modal Analysis [13]. For the signal processing of the data, we decimate with a factor of 8 and obtain a new sampling frequency of 206 Hz and we compute the correlation function matrix with 512 discrete time lags. We identify the modal parameter with the Eigensystem Realization Algorithm (ERA) [14] using 5 singular values and 4 block rows in the Hankel matrix. The identified modal parameters are displayed in Table 1 and Figure 5.

Table 1: Modal Parameters

Mode		1	2	3	4	5
Finite Element Model	Frequency [Hz]	10.1	10.2	24.9	65.1	71.7
Operational Modal Analysis	Frequency [Hz]	9.17	9.38	23.6	67.6	75.4
Modal Assurance Criterion	MAC [-]	0.986	0.997	0.998	0.996	0.991

4.3. Strain Estimation

To estimate the strain response as explained in section 2., we need the displacement and not the acceleration of the model. Therefore, the data from the accelerometers is integrated twice to get the displacement using the Fourier transform [13]. Then we estimate the strain response in all points with strain gauges using both finite element and expanded experimental mode shapes. Figure 6 displays the coefficient of determination for the strain estimation using finite element mode shapes and expanded experimental mode shapes. Strain gauge A is plotted in figures 7 and 8 for time and frequency domain respectfully. Figures 9 and 10 display time and frequency domain, respectfully, for strain gauge D.

For this case study, the values from the coefficient of determination indicate, expanded experimental mode shapes provide a better basis for strain estimation. Generally, the strain estimation based on expanded mode shape has the same or higher coefficient of determination values. Figures 9 and 10 support this statement where strain estimation based on finite element mode shapes results in too big amplitudes.

5. CONCLUSION

In this paper, we find, expanding experimental mode shapes can benefit strain estimation using the Modal Expansion. The expansion of experimental mode shapes can reduce the modelling errors of the finite element model if the experimental mode shapes are closer to the actual structure. Hence, it requires a good identification of the modal parameter. The expansion is, however, a fitting process, which introduces potential fitting errors. Thus, mode shape expansion should be used carefully.

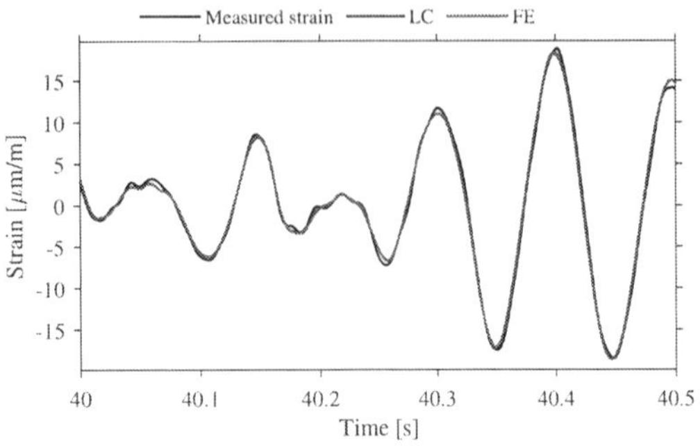

Figure 7: Time Domain, strain history for strain gauge A

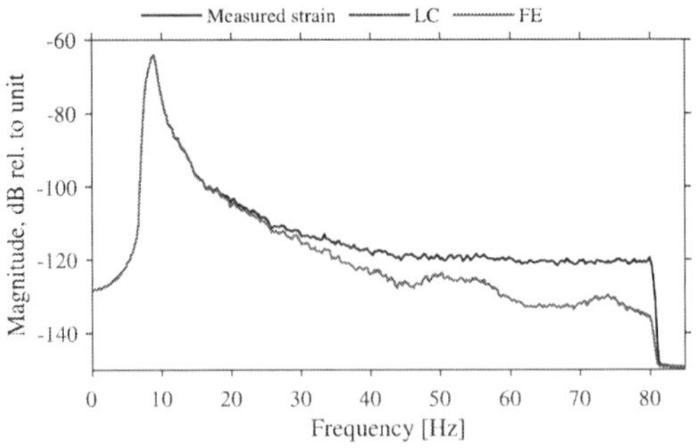

Figure 8: Frequency Domain, spectral density of strain gauge A

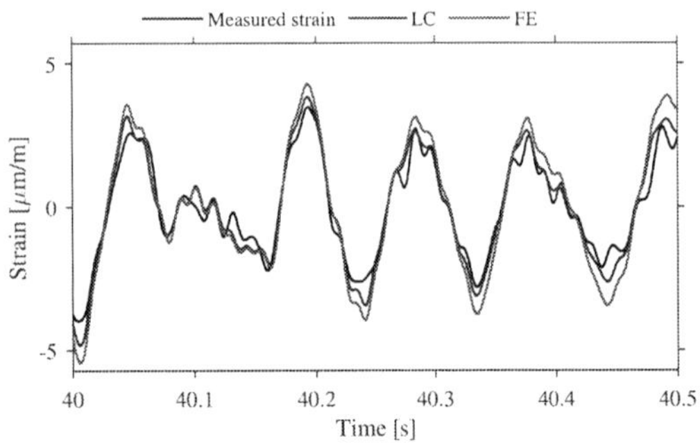

Figure 9: Time Domain, strain history for strain gauge D

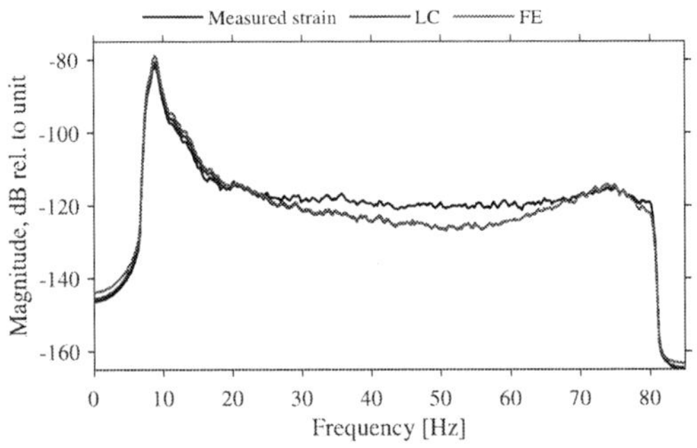

Figure 10: Frequency Domain, spectral density of strain gauge D

ACKNOWLEDGEMENTS

The authors acknowledge the funding received from the Centre for Oil and Gas - DTU/Danish Hydrocarbon Research and Technology Centre (DHRTC).

REFERENCES

[1] L. Liu, S. M. Kuo, and M. Zhou. Virtual sensing techniques and their applications. In *2009 International Conference on Networking, Sensing and Control*, pages 31–36, March 2009. doi: 10.1109/ICNSC.2009.4919241.

[2] A. Skafte, J. Kristoffersen, J. Vestermark, U. T. Tygesen, and R. Brincker. Experimental study of strain prediction on wave induced structures using modal decomposition and quasi static ritz vectors. *Engineering Structures*, 136:261–276, 4/1 2017.

[3] M. Tarpø, B. Nabuco, A. Skafte, J. Kristoffersen, J. Vestermark, S. Amador, and R. Brincker. Operational modal analysis based prediction of actual stress in an offshore structural model. *Procedia Engineering, X International Conference on Structural Dynamics EURODYN 2017*, 199:2262–2267, 2017.

[4] P. Avitabile and P. Pingle. Prediction of full field dynamic strain from limited sets of measured data. *Shock and Vibration*, 19(5):765–785, 2012.

[5] A. Iliopoulos, W. Weijtjens, D. Van Hemelrijck, and C. Devriendt. Fatigue assessment of offshore wind turbines on monopile foundations using multi-band modal expansion. *Wind Energy*, 20(8): 1463–1479, 2017. doi: 10.1002/we.2104.

[6] M. Tarpø, T. Friis, Bruna Nabuco, S Amador, E. Katsanos, and R. Brincker. Operational modal analysis based stress estimation in friction systems. In Gaetan Kerschen, editor, *Nonlinear Dynamics, Volume 1*, pages 143–153, Cham, 2019. Springer International Publishing. ISBN 978-3-319-74280-9.

[7] K. Maes, A. Iliopoulos, W. Weijtjens, C. Devriendt, and G. Lombaert. Dynamic strain estimation for fatigue assessment of an offshore monopile wind turbine using filtering and modal expansion algorithms. *Mechanical Systems and Signal Processing*, 76-77:592–611, 2016.

[8] R. W. Clough and J. Penzien. *Dynamics of structures*. CSI Computers & Structures, Inc., Berkeley, Calif., 2nd revised edition, 2003. ISBN 0070113947.

[9] L. Debao, Z. Hongcheng, and W. Bo. The principle and techniques of experimental strain modal analysis. *Proceedings of 7th IMAC*, pages 1285–1289, 1989.

[10] A. Skafte. *Applications of Expansion Techniques in Operational Modal Analysis*. PhD thesis, Aarhus University, DK, 2016.

[11] R. Brincker, A. Skafte, M. López-Aenlle, A. Sestieri, W. D'Ambrogio, and A. Canteli. A local correspondence principle for mode shapes in structural dynamics. *Mechanical Systems and Signal Processing*, 45(1):91–104, 2013.

[12] P.C Hansen, V. Pereyra, and G. Scherer. *Least squares data fitting with applications*. Johns Hopkins University Press, Baltimore, MD, USA, 2013. ISBN 9781421408583; 1421408589; 9781421407869; 1421407868.

[13] R. Brincker and C. Ventura. *Introduction to operational modal analysis*. John Wiley and Sons, Inc., Chichester, West Sussex,UK, 2015. ISBN 9781119963158.

[14] J. N. Juang and R. S. Pappa. An eigensystem realization algorithm for modal parameter identification and model reduction. *Journal of Guidance*, 8(5):620–627, 1985.

TEST & MONITORING OF WIND TURBINES

IOMAC'19
8th International Operational Modal Analysis Conference
2019 May13-15 Copenhagen

AUTOMATED OMA FOR MONITORING WIND TURBINE BLADE MODES FROM THE TOWER DURING OPERATION

W.Weijtjens [1], *C.Devriendt* [2]

[1] Dr.Ir., Offshore Wind Infrastructure Lab Vrije Universiteit Brussel, wout.weijtjens@owi-lab.be.
[2] Prof.Dr.Ir., Offshore Wind Infrastructure Lab Vrije Universiteit Brussel, christof.devriendt@owi-lab.be.

ABSTRACT
For wind turbines installed in the built environment, the risk of ice throw is a concern to operators. Large pieces of ice being thrown from the blades poses a severe risk for damage on infrastructure and, worse, personal safety. In industry several solutions do exist to detect the build-up of icing using operational modal parameters obtained from sensors on the blades.
In this research project an alternative strategy to detect icing is investigated. Using a sensor on the tower, to detect variations in the frequency of so-called rotor whirling modes as an indicator for ice. Previous results on parked turbines proof the concept of this method. In this follow-up research the possibility to estimate and track the rpm-dependent whirling modes from measurements on the tower is investigated. The paper primarily aims to detect and quantify the uncertainty in the estimation of the whirling modes' frequencies during operation of a wind turbine.

Keywords: Wind turbine, Ice detection, Wind turbine blades, Rotor modes

1. INTRODUCTION

The use of operational modal analysis for wind turbines has become a very active topic in both the operational modal analysisánd the structural health monitoring community and examples are widespread e.g. to list a few [1, 2, 3, 4, 5, 6]. There are several motivations to perform a continuous evaluation of the resonance frequencies of both the turbine substructure as well as the turbine blades. Ranging from the detection of scour on offshore wind turbines [7, 8] or the defects in the foundation of onshore foundations [9] over detecting issues in the blades [9, 2].
One of the more interesting applications of OMA for monitoring wind turbines is icing detection. The key idea is that the resonance frequency of the blades will decrease when the total mass of the blade increase as ice is developing on the blade. Detecting a decrease of the resonance frequencies of the blades can

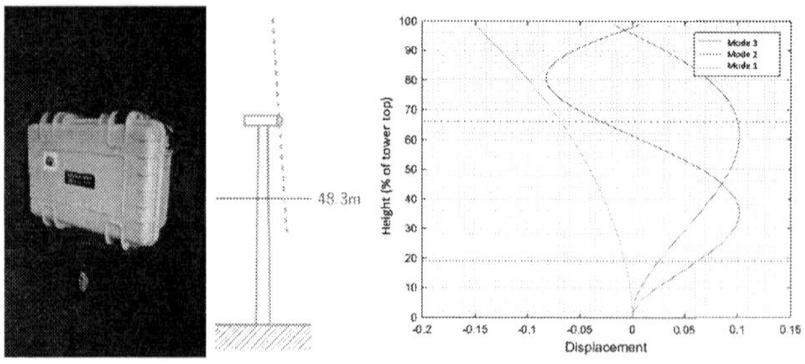

(a) Mobile monitoring system (b) Monitoring system placement (c) Expected mode shapes

Figure 1: (a) The mobile monitoring system, here shown during testing at the VUB. (b) The monitoring system was installed at 48m above the ground level, approximately at 2/3 of the tower height. (c) Typical mode shapes for an onshore wind turbine, results from a simple simulation.

thus be used to detect ice on the blades. To obtain a reliable estimate for the resonance frequencies of the blades, sensors are typically installed on the blades of the wind turbine and continuously processed to estimate the resonance frequencies. This concept already is commercially developed[10].
In the presented research an alternative strategy to detect icing is investigated. Rather to instrument the blades, the possibility to instrument the substructure with a single accelerometer is investigated. Initial simulated results shown in[11] reveal that the whirling frequencies, i.e. the rotor modes as observed from the tower, will decrease when icing occurs. Further research in [12] showed that during parked conditions (i.e. the turbine is not rotating) there were good signs that icing indeed could be detected. However, to achieve a full icing solution the rotor modes have to be reliably estimated during all operational conditions. A particular challenge is that the frequencies of the rotor modes, as observed from the tower, will depend on the rotor speed. This paper will investigate the reliability of the estimates of the rotor whirling modes using measurements from a short-term monitoring campaign on an onshore wind turbine.

2. MEASUREMENT CAMPAIGN AND METHODOLOGY

During the summer and fall of 2018 a short monitoring campaign was conducted by OWI-lab/VUB in collaboration with ENGIE Green and ENGIE Laborelec on a single onshore wind turbine. The main project motivation was to compare results from the tower measurements with results obtained from a fiber-optic strain measurement system in the blades of the turbines. This paper will only consider the data from the monitoring system installed by OWI-lab and focus on the question of detecting the rotor whirling modes.

2.1. Investigated structure

The instrumented turbine is a Senvion MM82, a 2.05MW wind turbine with a rotor diameter of 82m and is operated by ENGIE Green. The investigated structure had a total tower height of 76m. During the considered period the wind turbine was subjected to wind speeds of up to 17 m/s. The data-set contains periods below cut-in wind speed periods of variable rpm, periods of rated rotational speed as well as periods of rated output power. Data-sets beyond cut-out wind speed as well as data-sets during parked conditions beyond cut-in were not available from this campaign.
For the duration of the campaign the turbine SCADA data was made available by the turbine operator. The available SCADA data contained (a.o) wind speed, turbine yaw angle and the rotor speed (rpm).

2.2. Monitoring system

The monitoring system used is a 24SEA mobile system, integrated in a small suitcase, Figure. 1.(a). It contains a tri-axial ICP accelerometer and can sample at up to 1kHz. However, the key motivation to use this system is that it is *plug and play*. The system is fully self-contained and only requires a power-outlet, which are typically available at all service platforms in a wind turbine. The system records the accelerations, performs initial post-processing and transmits data to a server at the VUB. In case the transmission of data fails, the system can also save several months of measurements locally.
The sensors were installed at a height of 48m above the ground Figure. 1.(b), around 2/3 of the total tower height. This position is chosen as the optimal position of a single sensor setup. At 2/3 of the tower height, indicated as a green line in Figure. 1.(c), the first three modes are all present. A sensor installed at the top will have a worse sensitivity w.r.t. modes 2 and 3, although a better sensitivity is achieved for the first mode. A sensor installed at the bottom, red line in Figure. 1.(b) is more practical for installation, but does not offer good sensitivity to all modes. The position at 2/3 of the tower sacrifices a bit on sensitivity for the first mode, but guarantees a good sensitivity for all other modes. This assessment based on the simulated results in Figure. 1 is confirmed by the experimental mode shapes presented in [3].

2.3. Automated Operational Modal Analysis

The tri-axial measurements are down-sampled on site to a sampling frequency of 12.5Hz with an anti-aliasing filter starting at 5Hz. The records are then transmitted over the mobile telephone network to the VUB were the data is further processed.
As the objective of the campaign is an assessment of the modal behavior of the turbine the data is processed using the VUB **DYNA***wind* toolbox. As a first step all recorded signals are translated to the frame of reference of the nacelle using a yaw transformation based on the yaw-angle in the SCADA and the documented position of the monitoring system. As a result the vibrations are found in the Fore-Aft (FA), i.e. the direction of the nacelle and the wind, and the Side-Side (SS) directions, i.e. the cross-wind vibrations. The toolbox also includes an automated scheme for modal parameter estimation and tracking based on the research performed at OWI-lab [13] and the development of the pLSCF modal parameter estimator [14]. The following steps were applied to both the FA and SS vibration signals.

1. Calculation of the Correlogram spectrum
2. Curve fit of the correlogram spectrum with polynomial models of increasing model order
3. Calculation of the modal parameters for each of the curve-fitted models of different model orders . Visualized as a stabilization chart.
4. Automatic aggregation of the estimated modal parameters into clusters
5. Tracking of the resonance frequencies

These steps are also visualized in Figure. 2. For the current setup, with only a single accelerometer, it was not possible to identify the mode shapes of the turbine. As a consequence it was not possible to use the mode shapes for tracking the modes of the wind turbine. Instead a mode was tracked solely based on the expected resonance frequency (and optionally the damping ratio).

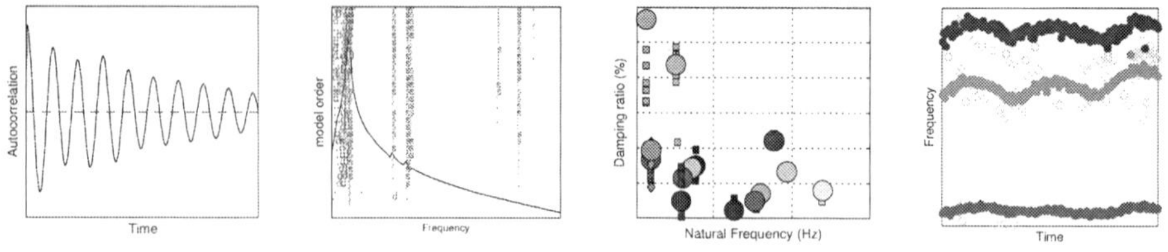

(a) Calculated autocorrelation of one output (b) The p-LSCF curve fitter gives a stabilization chart (c) The stabilization chart is condensed into a cluster plot (d) Tracking results

Figure 2: (a-c) Illustration of the three steps of the automated OMA approach for a parked turbine (d) Example of the tracking.[13]

3. RESULTS

3.1. Dynamic behavior

In Figure. 3 the identified modal parameters are plotted versus the rotational speed (rpm). This Campbell diagram serves to illustrate the modal behavior during operational conditions. Relevant modes as well as rotor harmonics are tracked tentatively to generate a clearer image of the behavior. As expected the rotor harmonics are clearly visible throughout the rpm range. However, the first and second order tower modes are still clearly visible in both FA and SS direction. The whirling modes, which show a rpm-dependent behavior, are also clearly visible (highlighted in Blue and Orange). These rotor whirling are of interest to this project as they are the projections of the rotor/blade modes to an observer on the tower (hence the rpm-dependent behavior). If icing is to be identified it will be made possible using these modes. Already from the results in Figure. 3 it can be observed that the likelihood of detecting the whirling modes is greater in the SS direction, with significant gaps in the detection of both forward and backward whirling modes in the FA direction.

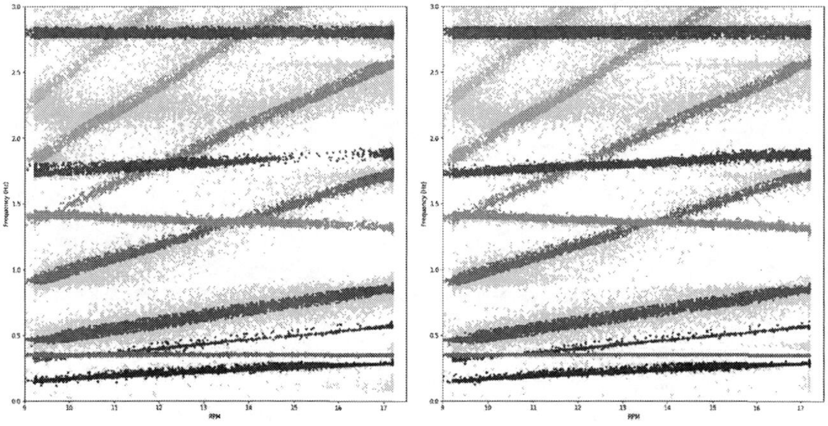

(a) FA (b) SS

Figure 3: FA and SS Campbell diagrams of the detected modes after modal parameter estimation with indicative tracking. In green the first order mode, in blue the forward whirling mode, in orange the backward whirling mode and in red the 2nd order mode. Modal parameters associated with rotor harmonics are plotted in shades of gray.

3.2. Whirling mode assessment

As shown Figure. 3 the whirling modes are clearly present in the Campbell diagrams. Both in FA and SS the whirling modes can be detected, but early results seem to indicate that the whirling modes are less observable in the FA direction.
To track the rpm-dependent rotor whirling modes following equations are used:

$$f_{SS,FW} = f_{root} + \Delta f(rpm) = 1.60Hz + rpm/60 \quad (1)$$

$$f_{SS,BW} = f_{root} - \Delta f(rpm) = 1.60Hz - rpm/60 \quad (2)$$

In a first assessment it was opted to assume the theoretical behavior of the whirling modes, e.g. as discussed in [15]. Hence both the Forward Whirling (FW) and the Backward Whirlng (BW) mode use the same *root* frequency of 1.6Hz. Note that when a sensor would be installed on the blades, it would identify this *root* frequency independent of the rotor speed. For now the variation of the frequency w.r.t. the rotor speed is also kept to the theoretical behavior of *rpm*/60, rather than using curve-fitted coefficients to the rotor speed. Later we will use a uni-variate model to improve on these results.
To evaluate the observability of rotor whirling modes all datasets in operational conditions, i.e. $rpm > 9$, are considered. A total of 8356 ten minute datasets were evaluated to quantify the observability of the whirling modes. A mode is considered as not observed when it is outside the original tracking frequency, as defined by (1) and (2), by $0.05Hz$. The resulting success rates are summarized in Table. 1. The results confirm the earlier observation that it is far more reliable to estimate the whirling modes from the SS direction than from the FA direction. This difference between the FA and SS observability has a physical cause. Most likely the most dominant rotor mode during operation is the so-called edgewise mode, i.e. a mode in the same direction as the rotating blade. This vibration mode does not leave the rotor plane and does not generate vibrations in the Fore-Aft direction. The flap-wise mode, which should be better visible in the Fore-Aft direction, is likely highly damped due to the air flow over the blade and not sufficiently excited to be detected. The results in Table. 1 align well with the results in presented in [3] who performed a similar study and also recorded success-rates close to 90% during the similar operational regime 4 using a set-up with multiple sensors. These results confirm that for the currently intended purposes the single sensor set-up is sufficient.
Based on the results in Table. 1 it is decided to proceed only with the SS whirling modes in rotating conditions. In Fig. 4 a detailed picture is given on the tracked whirling modes in SS. One can nicely see how the 6P and 9P harmonic pass through the area. Aside from the two whirling modes also the

	FA	SS
FW	38.4%	89.9%
BW	56.9%	90.1%

Table 1: Success rate for the detection of the whirling modes using either the FA or the SS signals.

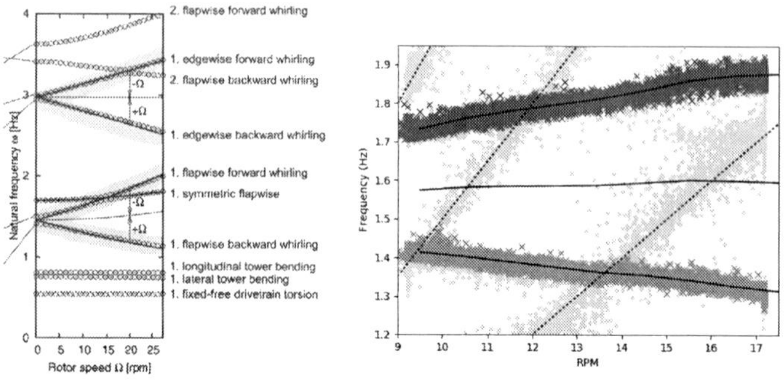

(a) Theoretical behavior

(b) Measurements

Figure 4: (a) Expected behavior of the whirling modes, figure modified from [15](b) Zoomed view on the whirling modes identified from operational modal analysis. The expected frequency of rotor harmonics are indicated with black dashed lines. Mainly the 6P and 9P modes pass through the considered frequency band. The black lines indicate the mean values per rpm bin.

aggregated means and the central *root* frequency are indicated. Interesting the root frequency has a *very slight* upward trend for increasing rotor speeds, which could be linked to the stiffening of the composite blade under the increasing centrifugal force. Note that this is not fully consistent with Fig. 4.(a) where only the flapwise mode sees this increase in frequency with rpm, while the considered whirling modes are expected to be related with the edgewise modes.

In Figure. 5 the histogram of the error between the actual recorded frequency of the whirling modes in the SS-direction and the frequency predicted by (1) and (2) is presented. One can clearly see that the found histogram does not correspond to a Gaussian distribution. A simple univariate model, considering only rpm, is introduced on top of the expressions (1) and (2), i.e. allow to deviate from the theoretical behavior. The error of this model is also included in Figure. 5.

The results reveal that after inclusion of a simple uni-variate model a standard deviation of less than 1%

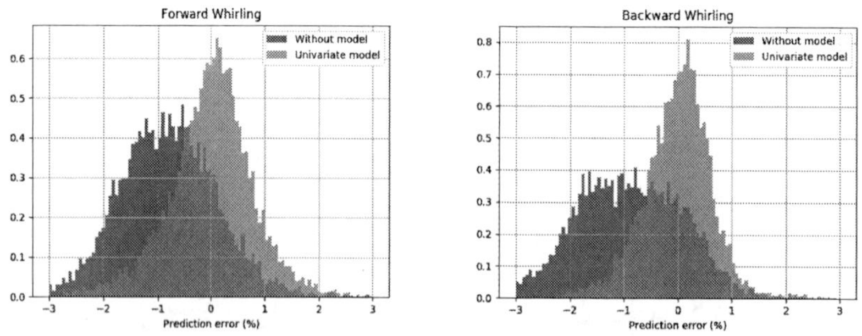

(a) Forward whirling

(b) Backward whirling

Figure 5: Relative error between the predicted frequency of the whirling mode and the detected frequencies. (Blue) When the theoretical model ((1) and (2)) is followed. (Orange) when a simple univariate (rpm) model is used.

is achieved.

4. CONCLUSION

Operational modal analysis has become a popular technique in the field of monitoring both onshore and offshore wind turbines. It has been successfully applied by different researchers in different turbine makes and models. In this paper the question whether the rotor whirling modes can reliably be estimated using a single sensor on the tower was investigated. During a short monitoring campaign on a 2MW onshore wind turbine acceleration measurements were recorded with a mobile monitoring system and modal parameters were estimated using the in-house **DYNA***wind* toolbox.
The results reveal that a 90% success rate is feasible for whirling modes when data from the SS direction is used and the turbine SCADA (in particular yaw and rpm) data is available. A standard deviation of less than 1% is feasible when a simple uni-variate model is used to predict the expected frequency of the whirling mode.

ACKNOWLEDGEMENTS

The authors like to acknowledge that this research was done in close collaboration with ENGIE Green and ENGIE Laborelec and appreciate their kind support throughout this project.
Wout Weijtjens is a postdoctoral fellow of the Research Foundation Flanders (FWO), Belgium. The financial support by FWO is gratefully acknowledged.

REFERENCES

[1] Hu, W.-H., Thöns, S., Rohrmann, R. G., Said, S., and Rücker, W. (2015). Vibration-based structural health monitoring of a wind turbine system part ii: Environmental/operational effects on dynamic properties. *Engineering Structures*, 89:273–290.

[2] Tcherniak, D. and Larsen, G. C. (2013). Application of oma to an operating wind turbine: now including vibration data from the blades. In *5th International Operational Modal Analysis Conference.*

[3] Oliveira, G., Magalhães, F., Cunha, Á., and Caetano, E. (2018a). Continuous dynamic monitoring of an onshore wind turbine. *Engineering Structures*, 164:22–39.

[4] Häckell, M. and Rolfes, R. (2013). Monitoring a 5mw offshore wind energy converter—condition parameters and triangulation based extraction of modal parameters. *Mechanical Systems and Signal Processing*, 40(1):322–343.

[5] Zierath, J., Rachholz, R., Rosenow, S.-E., Bockhahn, R., Schulze, A., and Woernle, C. (2018). Experimental identification of modal parameters of an industrial 2-mw wind turbine. *Wind Energy*, 21(5):338–356.

[6] Botz, M., Oberlaender, S., Raith, M., and Grosse, C. U. (2016). Monitoring of wind turbine structures with concrete-steel hybrid-tower design. In *EWSHM-8th European Workshop on Structural Health Monitoring. Bilbao, Spain.*

[7] Weijtjens, W., Verbelen, T., De Sitter, G., and Devriendt, C. (2014). Data normalization for foundation shm of an offshore wind turbine: A real-life case study. In *EWSHM-7th European Workshop on Structural Health Monitoring.*

[8] Weinert, J., Smolka, U., Schümann, B., and Chen, P. W. (2015). Detecting critical scour developments at monopile foundations under operating conditions. *Scientific Proceedings EWEA 2015.*

[9] Oliveira, G., Magalhães, F., Cunha, Á., and Caetano, E. (2018b). Vibration-based damage detection in a wind turbine using 1 year of data. *Structural Control and Health Monitoring*, 25(11):e2238.

[10] Kraemer, P., Friedmann, H., and Ebert, C. (2015). Vibration-based ice detection of rotor blades in wind turbines - the industrial realization of an shm-system. *Structural Health Monitoring 2015*.

[11] Weijtjens, W., Verbelen, T., Capello, E., and Devriendt, C. (2017). Vibration based structural health monitoring of the substructures of five offshore wind turbines. *Procedia Engineering*, 199:2294–2299.

[12] Weijtjens, W., Avendao-Valencia, L. D., Devriendt, C., and Chatzi, E. (20118). Cost-effective vibration based detection of wind turbine blade icing from sensors mounted on the tower. In *Proceedings of EWSHM 2018*.

[13] Devriendt, C., Magalhães, F., Weijtjens, W., De Sitter, G., Cunha, Á., and Guillaume, P. (2014). Structural health monitoring of offshore wind turbines using automated operational modal analysis. *Structural Health Monitoring*, 13(6):644–659.

[14] Peeters, B. and Van der Auweraer, H. (2005). Polymax: a revolution in operational modal analysis. In *Proceedings of the 1st International Operational Modal Analysis Conference, Copenhagen, Denmark*.

[15] Hansen, M. (2007). Aeroelastic instability problems for wind turbines. *Wind Energy*, 10(6):551–577.

IOMAC'19

8th International Operational Modal Analysis Conference
2019 May13-15 Copenhagen

MODAL ANALYSIS OF OPERATING WIND TURBINE ROTORS: TWO OMA METHODS TO DEAL WITH PERIODIC SYSTEMS

Dmitri Tcherniak[1]

[1] Brüel & Kjær Sound and Vibration Measurement A/S, dmitri.tcherniak@bksv.com

ABSTRACT

Two techniques, multiblade coordinate transformation and harmonic operational modal analysis, allow application of OMA to systems with bladed rotors, such as wind turbines. The latter can be considered as a linear periodic time variant system, and their experimental dynamic characterization is not a straightforward task. The paper presents the two techniques and demonstrates how they can help understanding the complex dynamic behavior of operating wind turbines.

Keywords: *wind turbine, rotor, operational, modal, analysis*

1. INTRODUCTION

Generally, modal analysis of operating wind turbines is not valid. Indeed, the main assumption of modal expansion is that the test object is time invariant, i.e. its stiffness, damping and mass properties do not change in time. This is not the case for operating wind turbines. However, if the rotor speed is constant or almost constant, the stiffness, damping (gyroscopic) and mass matrices used to model a wind turbine, become periodic, and the entire system can be considered as a linear periodic time variant (LPTV) system. From theoretical viewpoint, such systems are well-known in mechanics, however their experimental identification is a relatively new field of the research.

Straightforward application of OMA to an operating wind turbine, ignoring its time-periodicity, leads to odd results, and this approach should be avoided. However, there are two simple techniques to take time-periodicity into account: multiblade coordinate transformation and a technique based on harmonic power spectra. Both techniques function as a pre- and post-processing to the standard OMA algorithms. The presented paper summarizes the outcome of the previous works authored or co-authored by the author ([1], [2], [3], [4], [5], [6], [7], [8], [9], [10], [11], [12]), briefly explains the two methods, demonstrates what dynamic phenomena can be expected from operating wind turbines, and how the two methods can explain them.

1.1. Theoretical background

When deriving the equations of motion of a structure with a rotating rotor, one arrives to a second order differential equation with coefficients depending on the rotor position, often described by the rotor azimuth angle θ. The example of a system consisting of a stator and a solid disk rotor can be found in [13]; the derivation of the equations of motion for a system with a bladed rotor (such as a wind turbine) is given in [14]. For understanding the dynamics of a system with a bladed rotor, sometimes it is convenient to use a simplified lumped mass and stiffness model, as presented in [15]. Generally, the equation of motion has a form

$$\mathbf{M}(\theta(t))\ddot{\mathbf{y}}(t) + \mathbf{G}(\theta(t))\dot{\mathbf{y}}(t) + \mathbf{K}(\theta(t))\mathbf{y}(t) = \mathbf{0}, \tag{1}$$

where $\mathbf{M}, \mathbf{C}, \mathbf{K} \in \mathbb{R}^{R\times R}$ are the mass, damping and stiffness matrices respectively and vector $\mathbf{y}(t) \in \mathbb{R}^R$ is the displacements of system's R degrees of freedom over time t. Under the assumption that the rotor angular speed $\Omega = const$, thus $\theta(t) = \Omega t$, the matrices become time-periodic $\mathbf{M}(t+T) = \mathbf{M}(t), \mathbf{G}(t+T) = \mathbf{G}(t), \mathbf{K}(t+T) = \mathbf{K}(t)$ with period $T = 2\pi/\Omega$. Such systems are often referred as linear periodic time-variant (LPTV) or linear time-periodic (LTP) systems.

Classical modal analysis deals with linear time invariant (LTI) systems, described by the equation of motion with time-invariant coefficients:

$$\mathbf{M}\,\ddot{\mathbf{y}}(t) + \mathbf{C}\,\dot{\mathbf{y}}(t) + \mathbf{K}\,\mathbf{y}(t) = \mathbf{0}, \tag{2}$$

and modal analysis presents the non-trivial solution to (2) as a modal decomposition:

$$\mathbf{y}(t) = \sum_{r=1}^{R} b_r\, \boldsymbol{\phi}_r e^{\lambda_r t}, \tag{3}$$

where the mode shape $\boldsymbol{\phi}_r \in \mathbb{C}^R$ and the eigenvalue $\lambda_r \in \mathbb{C}$ constitute the modal parameters for the rth mode of the system, and $b_r \in \mathbb{C}$ is the mode participation factor, which depends on the system initial conditions. If the equations of motion are not known, the modal parameters can be derived from the observed dynamics of the system via the methods of Experimental and/or Operational Modal Analysis (EMA and OMA).

Generally, the classical modal analysis cannot be applied to time-variant systems. To briefly demonstrate it, let us recall the simplest and well-known example of an LPTV system, the Mathieu oscillator $m\,\ddot{y} + k(1 + \alpha\cos(\Omega t))\,y = 0$, where the stiffness is changing periodically. It is obvious that the natural frequency, as it is interpreted it in the frame of the classical modal analysis, is not an adequate descriptor of the much more complex dynamics of such a system.

Floquet theory suggests a solution to the problem. It proves that it is possible to present solution to (1) as a sum, similar to (3) but with periodic modes shapes $\mathbf{u}_r(t)$:

$$\mathbf{y}(t) = \sum_{r=1}^{R} b_r\, \mathbf{u}_r(t) e^{\lambda_r t}. \tag{4}$$

The mode shapes are complex T-periodic functions: $\mathbf{u}_r(t+T) = \mathbf{u}_r(t)$. The functions can be expanded into Fourier series as

$$\mathbf{u}_r(t) = \sum_{n=-\infty}^{+\infty} \mathbf{c}_{r,n} e^{jn\Omega t}, \tag{5}$$

and finally, the solution to (1) can be written as:

$$\mathbf{y}(t) = \sum_{r=1}^{R} b_r \sum_{n=-\infty}^{+\infty} \mathbf{c}_{r,n} e^{(\lambda_r + jn\Omega)t}. \tag{6}$$

There are clear similarities between (6) and (4): the solution to the equation of motion is sought as a superposition of R modes, but if in the case of the LTI system the mode is a time-invariant vector oscillating at frequency $Im(\lambda_r)$, in the LPTV case, the mode is a superposition of mode shape components. Each component is a static vector $\mathbf{C}_{r,n} \in \mathbb{C}^R$ oscillating at frequency $Im(\lambda_r) + jn\Omega$. In both cases, the damping is characterized by $Re(\lambda_r)$.

Thus, modal analysis of an LPTV system is the process of finding its Floquet exponents $\lambda_r \in \mathbb{C}$ and the Fourier coefficients $\mathbf{C}_{r,n}$. According to (6), there are infinitely many Fourier components in the expansion. However, in practice, only few are necessary to describe the modal dynamics with sufficient precision,

$$\mathbf{u}_r(t) \approx \sum_{n=-N}^{N} \mathbf{C}_{r,n} e^{jn\Omega t}. \tag{7}$$

It will be shown in the next section, that for an isotropic rotor with three blades, in the absence of gravity, three Fourier components ($N = 1$) are enough for the exact representation of the modes. With increasing rotor anisotropy, more components are needed, however for slightly anisotropic rotors (which is the typical case in real life), five or seven components ($N = 2, 3$, respectively) are sufficient.

In the engineering practice, it is often convenient to visualize mode shapes. To illustrate a periodic mode shape, it is necessary to visualize the shape of each of the $2N + 1$ components, together with their relative magnitude. In contrast to LTI systems, where the mode shapes are nearly real, the complexity of some Fourier components can be very high; in the next section it will be shown that the motion of one blade can lag the other by $2\pi/3$ radians even for systems with proportional damping. Therefore, to illustrate the Fourier components $\mathbf{C}_{r,n}$, it is useful to provide both magnitude and phase. For example, one of the four modes of the simple system depicted in **Figure 1a** can be visualized as shown in **Figure 1b**, as suggested in [16]. The common horizontal axis is the frequency axis, the top plot shows the phase and the bottom one shows the magnitude of the Fourier components $\mathbf{C}_{r,n}$. The presented mode consists of five components with significant magnitudes; there are more but their magnitudes are neglectable. The symbols denote each of the four degrees-of-freedom, the horizontal displacement of the "stator" x_C and the angles ϕ_1, ϕ_2 and ϕ_3, representing the inclinations of the blades from their undisturbed positions. Note, the degrees-of-freedom have different units, so the direct comparison of the magnitudes of x_C and ϕ_i is not valid. To explain the graphical representation, let's consider the components of the mode. The first one at 0.72 Hz mainly consists of the stator motion with some minor contributions from the three blades. The blades motion is collective, which is indicated by the zero phase on the top graph. The second component at 0.88 Hz is separated from the first one by the rotor speed $\Omega = 0.16\ Hz$. The component consists of the blades motion, the blades oscillate with the same magnitudes, the second blade lags the first one by 120^0, and the third blade lags the second one by 120^0, which can be seen from

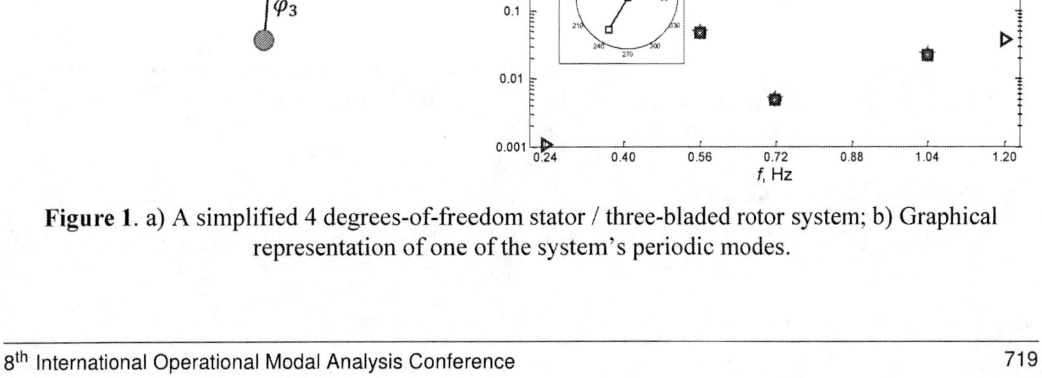

Figure 1. a) A simplified 4 degrees-of-freedom stator / three-bladed rotor system; b) Graphical representation of one of the system's periodic modes.

the phase plot and from the inset. Thus, this is a rotor backward whirling component. The component at 0.56 Hz is a forward whirling of the rotor, all three blades have the same magnitude though it is much smaller than the magnitude of the backward whirling component. The component at 1.20 Hz is the horizontal stator motion, whose magnitude is almost two decades smaller than the magnitude of the component at 0.72 Hz.

If the equations of motion are known, the Floquet exponents and Fourier coefficients can be found via *Floquet analysis* (for small number of DOFs) or *implicit Floquet analysis* (for great DOFs number), see [16], table 3.1; these methods are outside the scope of the paper. The paper is focusing on two methods for *experimental characterization* of LPTV systems; both methods rely on the ambient excitation of the system, thus can be considered as an extension of OMA to LPTV systems. The first method is based on the multiblade coordinate (MBC) transformation, and the second one utilizes the idea of harmonic transfer function.

2. MULTIBLADE COORDINATE TRANSFORMATION (MBC)

MBC transformation in application to wind turbines was introduced by Hansen, and its detailed description can be found in [14]. Later, the method was adopted to experimental characterization of wind turbines, [2].

The idea of the method lies in a special coordinate transformation known as a *multiblade coordinate transformation* or *Coleman* transformation. For a three-bladed rotor, the MBC transformation is

$$\begin{aligned} a_{0,k}(t) &= \frac{1}{3}\sum_{l=1}^{3} q_{l,k}(t), \\ a_{1,k}(t) &= \frac{2}{3}\sum_{l=1}^{3} q_{l,k}(t)\cos\big(\theta_l(t)\big), \\ b_{1,k}(t) &= \frac{2}{3}\sum_{l=1}^{3} q_{l,k}(t)\sin\big(\theta_l(t)\big). \end{aligned} \tag{8}$$

Here the three coordinates $q_{l,k}$ measured on the *rotor*, on the blade no. $l = 1 \dots 3$, at the position k, are converted to a set of three *multiblade coordinates* $a_{0,k}$, $a_{1,k}$ and $b_{1,k}$. The transformation uses the azimuth of the l-th blade $\theta_l(t)$. The coordinates s_p, $p = 1 \dots P$, measured on the not rotating parts of the system are not transformed. Thus, the vector $\mathbf{y}(t)$ in (1) is a combination of $3K$ rotor coordinates and P stator coordinates:

$$\mathbf{y}(t) = \{s_1, \dots, s_P, q_{1,1}, q_{2,1}, q_{3,1}, \dots, q_{1,K}, q_{2,K}, q_{3,K}\}^T. \tag{9}$$

The MBC transformation converts this vector into a new vector

$$\mathbf{w}(t) = \{s_1, \dots, s_P, a_{0,1}, a_{1,1}, b_{1,1}, \dots, a_{0,K}, a_{1,K}, b_{1,K}\}^T, \tag{10}$$

where the stator coordinates stay the same, whilst the rotor coordinates transform according to (8). The transformation can be written as

$$\mathbf{y}(t) = \mathbf{D}(t)\mathbf{w}(t), \tag{11}$$

where the transformation matrix $\mathbf{D}(t)$ can be readily derived from (8)**Error! Reference source not found.**. It has the following properties [14]: $\mathbf{D}(t)^{-1} = \mathbf{\Gamma}\mathbf{D}(t)^T$, $\dot{\mathbf{D}}(t) = \mathbf{D}(t)\mathbf{R}$ and $\ddot{\mathbf{D}}(t) = \mathbf{D}(t)\mathbf{R}^2$. The matrices $\mathbf{\Gamma}$ and $\mathbf{R}$ can be easily obtained, and they are time-invariant. Applying the transformation to (1), using the above-mentioned properties and pre-multiplying by $\mathbf{D}(t)^{-1}$ yield the equation of motion in multiblade coordinates:

$$\mathbf{M}_D(t)\ddot{\mathbf{w}}(t) + \big(2\mathbf{M}_D(t)\mathbf{R} + \mathbf{G}_D(t)\big)\dot{\mathbf{w}}(t) + \big(\mathbf{M}_D(t)\mathbf{R}^2 + \mathbf{G}_D(t)\mathbf{R} + \mathbf{K}_D(t)\big)\mathbf{w}(t) = \mathbf{0}, \tag{12}$$

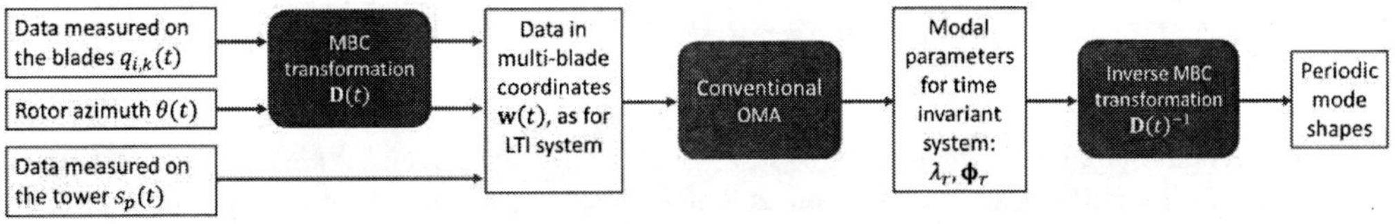

Figure 2. Application of MBC transformation to OMA, [2].

where $\mathbf{M}_D(t) = \boldsymbol{\Gamma}\mathbf{D}(t)^T\mathbf{M}(t)\mathbf{D}(t)$, $\mathbf{G}_D(t) = \boldsymbol{\Gamma}\mathbf{D}(t)^T\mathbf{G}(t)\mathbf{D}(t)$ and $\mathbf{K}_D(t) = \boldsymbol{\Gamma}\mathbf{D}(t)^T\mathbf{K}(t)\mathbf{D}(t)$. The important property of the MBC transformation is that *for isotropic rotors*, the mass and gyroscopic matrices are *time-invariant*: $\mathbf{M}_D(t) = \mathbf{M}_D$ and $\mathbf{G}_D(t) = \mathbf{G}_D$; the stiffness matrix is time-invariant in the absence of gravity, $\mathbf{K}_D(t) = \mathbf{K}_D$. In the presence of gravity, the latter becomes time-periodic with period $T/3$. Thus, for isotropic rotors, if the influence of gravity is neglected, the transformation converts the time-periodic EoM (1) into the time-invariant one:

$$\mathbf{M}_D\ddot{\mathbf{w}}(t) + (2\mathbf{M}_D\mathbf{R} + \mathbf{G}_D)\dot{\mathbf{w}}(t) + (\mathbf{M}_D\mathbf{R}^2 + \mathbf{G}_D\mathbf{R} + \mathbf{K}_D)\mathbf{w}(t) = \mathbf{0}, \tag{13}$$

and thus, allows application of classical modal analysis tools.

In case of OMA, the application of MBC transformation is shown in **Figure 2**. The time histories from the sensors located on the blades are converted to multiblade coordinates using (8); when installing the blade sensors, it is important to mount them as symmetric as possible, i.e. to place them on the same position and keep the same sensor orientation for each rotor blade. Another prerequisite untypical for classical modal analysis, is the need to measure the rotor azimuth $\theta(t)$. After MBC transformation, the resulting time histories $\mathbf{w}(t)$ become the input to a conventional OMA algorithm, which produces the modal parameters (for the discussion of the OMA assumptions in application to operating wind turbines, especially regarding to the wind excitation, refer to [1]).

OMA produces the modal parameters of the LTI system, with the mode shapes in multiblade coordinates. To convert them to blade coordinates, we apply the inverse MBC transformation

$$q_{l,k}(t) = a_{0,k}(t) + a_{1,k}(t)\cos(\theta_l(t)) + b_{1,k}(t)\sin(\theta_l(t)). \tag{14}$$

Let us consider an r-th mode shape $\boldsymbol{\phi}_r = \{S_{r,1}, \dots, S_{r,P}, A_{r,0,1}, A_{r,1,1}, B_{r,1,1}, \dots, A_{r,0,K}, A_{r,1,K}, B_{r,1,K}\}^T \in \mathbb{C}^{P+3K}$, where the capital letters denote the (complex) magnitude of the corresponding multiblade coordinates. According to (3), the mode will contribute to the overall dynamics of the structure as $\boldsymbol{\phi}_r e^{\lambda_r t}$. For the point k, located on the rotor, the modal magnitudes in the multiblade coordinates are $A_{r,0,k}, A_{r,1,k}, B_{r,1,k}$. Then, using (14) and employing the expression for the azimuth of the l-th blade $\theta_l(t) = \Omega t + 2\pi/3\,(l-1)$, the modal contribution in the *blade* coordinates is

$$\begin{aligned} u_{r,l,k}(t) = A_{r,0,k}\, e^{j\omega_r t}e^{-\sigma_r t} + A_{r,BW,k}e^{j(\omega_r-\Omega)t - j\frac{2\pi}{3}(l-1)}e^{-\sigma_r t} \\ + A_{r,FW,k}e^{j(\omega_r+\Omega)t + j\frac{2\pi}{3}(l-1)}e^{-\sigma_r t}, \end{aligned} \tag{15}$$

where $\lambda_r = j\omega_r - \sigma_r$, and the real positive ω_r and σ_r are the natural frequency and damping of the r-th mode, respectively. The complex magnitudes are $A_{r,BW,k} = \frac{1}{2}\left(A_{r,1,k} - jB_{r,1,k}\right)$ and $A_{r,FW,k} = \frac{1}{2}\left(A_{r,1,k} + jB_{r,1,k}\right)$.

For the point p located on the stator, the contribution of the r-th mode is

$$u_{r,p}(t) = S_{r,p}e^{j\omega_r t}e^{-\sigma_r t}. \tag{16}$$

Analyzing (15) and (16), we see that:

1. For the points on the rotor, the method produces time periodic mode shapes, which always consist of three components.

2. The three components oscillate at frequencies ω_r, $\omega_r - \Omega$ and $\omega_r + \Omega$, and they are called collective, backward- and forward whirling components.
3. All three blades have identical oscillation magnitudes.
4. The phase between the blades is 0 for the first component (therefore it is called *collective*), -120^0 for the second (*backward whirling*) and $+120^0$ for the third (*forward whirling*).
   The last two properties can be described as a mode shape *symmetry*. That is, MBC transformation *always* produces modes with symmetric mode shapes.
5. The coordinates measured on the not rotating parts always have only a single component, at frequency ω_r.

Drawing the analogy with the Floquet theory, one can notice that (15) and (16) are truncated versions of (5); for the point belonging to the rotor, $n = -1,0,+1$; λ_r and $\lambda_r \pm j\Omega$ are the three Floquet exponents, and $A_{r,0,k}$, $A_{r,BW,k}$ and $A_{r,FW,k}$ are the corresponding Fourier coefficients. For the points on the stator, $n = 0$, the only Floquet exponent is λ_r and the corresponding Fourier coefficient is $S_{r,p}$.

The abovementioned observations are valid for the systems under the assumption of rotor isotropy and neglectable gravity. The latter assumption can be accepted for out-of-plane rotor motion, where the vector of gravity is (almost) perpendicular to the blade motion. However, for the in-plane rotor motion, the gravity cannot be neglected. When the assumptions are not fulfilled, the application of the MBC transformation can lead to erroneous results, as not symmetrical effects of the rotor anisotropy will be smeared out and redistributed among all blades. The demonstration of this can be found in [8].

From the practical view, the application of MBC transformation sets tough requirements on the installation of sensors (accelerometers) on the blades: as the readings of the sensors are combined, cf. (8), a special attention shall be payed to mounting the sensor symmetrically on all three blades, which is a difficult task, especially for big rotors. To facilitate symmetric sensors mounting, in study [3], the rotor was taken down from the wind turbine, and a special mechanical fixture was employed to ensure the symmetric sensors placement. Apparently such a procedure is not feasible for modern huge wind turbines.

The application of MBC transformation-based OMA to simulated and measured data can be found in [4] and [8].

3. HARMONIC OMA

The MBC transformation is rather intuitive and simple, and this method could be recommended as a first step in understanding complex dynamics of systems with bladed rotors. However, any kind of asymmetry in the system, either in the form of gravity or the rotor anisotropy, enriches the dynamics with the features that the MBC transformation can not catch. In [17], Allen et al. suggested a framework that does not possess the limitations of the MBC transformation, and though the theoretical background behind the framework is rather complex, its practical implementation is quite straightforward. The framework is based on the Floquet theory [18] and on the concept of harmonic transfer functions introduced by Wereley [19].

In application to OMA, the framework can be either implemented in frequency domain (referred as H-OMA-FD), which is explained in detail in [17] or in time domain (H-OMA-TD), introduced in [10]. In this paper, only the practical implementation of H-OMA-TD is provided.

The flow of H-OMA-TD is given in **Figure 3**.

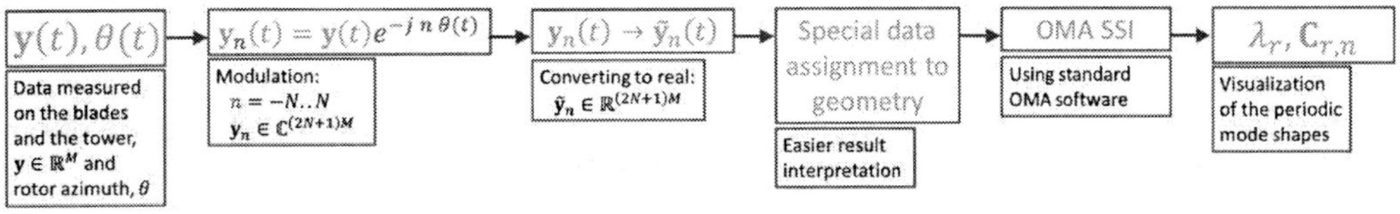

Figure 3. Flow of H-OMA-TD, [10].

The input to H-OMA-TD is M acceleration signals measured on the rotating and not rotating parts of the structure, $\mathbf{y}(t) \in \mathbb{R}^M$ and the rotor azimuth $\theta(t)$. The method assumes roughly constant rotor speed Ω, thus a special care shall be taken when selecting datasets for the analysis. Then one needs to select the value of N, *cf.* (7), following the abovementioned recommendations. After that, all acceleration signals are modulated by the phasor $e^{-jn\theta(t)}$ with $n = -N \ldots N$:

$$\mathbf{y}_n(t) = \mathbf{y}(t)e^{-jn\theta(t)}, \tag{17}$$

which results in $(2N+1)M$ complex time histories, $\mathbf{y}_n(t) \in \mathbb{C}^{(2N+1)M}$. As typical OMA algorithms (and commercially available software), do not accept complex input, the complex time histories shall be converted to the real ones. Study [6] provides some consideration on how such a conversion could be done, below a simple approach is outlined:

1. For the given exponentially modulated signals $\mathbf{y}_n(t)$ compute their periodogram $\mathcal{F}(\mathbf{y}_n(t))$ using a fast Fourier transform. The periodogram of complex $\mathbf{y}_n(t)$ is not a Hermitian function, i.e. its negative frequencies half is not a complex conjugate of the positive frequencies half;
2. Replace the negative frequencies part of the periodogram by the complex conjugate of the positive part: $\mathcal{F}(\mathbf{y}_n(t)) \to \tilde{\mathcal{F}}(\mathbf{y}_n(t))$, so the new periodogrm is a Hermetian function;
3. Using inverse FFT, generate the new time signals $\tilde{\mathbf{y}}_n(t) = \mathcal{F}^{-1}(\tilde{\mathcal{F}}(\mathbf{y}_n(t)))$.

The new time histories are real, and the positive half of their frequency spectra coincide with positive half of the spectra of the original signals. The obtained signals can be input to an OMA algorithm/software. In order to visualize mode shapes, commercial OMA software (for example, ARTeMIS [20] and B&K Type 8760-8762 [21]) provides a tool for assigning measured data to the test object geometry. As after the modulation (17), the number of signals $(2N+1)M$ exceeds the number of measurement points M, the H-OMA-TD method suggests adding $2N$ "clones" to the original geometry of the test object and assigning the time histories computed for a particular value of n to the corresponding "clone", **Figure 4**.

After running the selected OMA algorithm, the result interpretation (given in details in [6]) is rather straightforward: for each mode selected for animation, the "clones" will animate the corresponding Fourier component; the oscillation frequency of the "clone" shall be recalculated from the frequency of

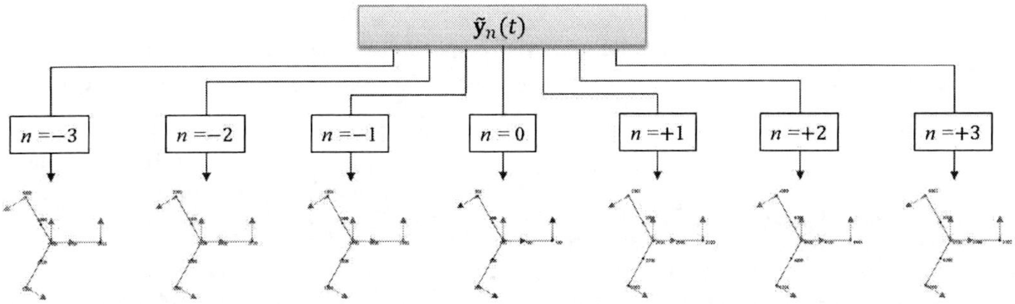

Figure 4. Assignment of the modulated time histories to the nodes of the extended test object geometry, [10].

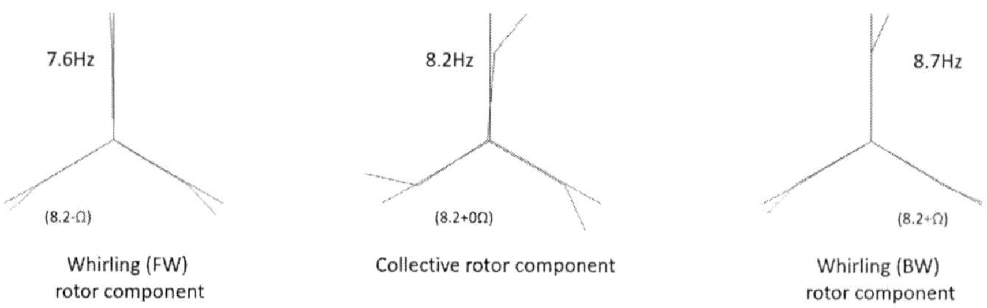

Figure 5. Assignment of the modulated time histories to the nodes of the extended test object geometry, [10].

the mode as $Im(\lambda_r) + n\,\Omega$. As an example, three components of the 1st in-plane collective rotor mode of Vestas V27 wind turbine operating at 32 rpm, are shown in **Figure 5**.

The application of H-OMA-TD to simulated and measured data can be found in [6], [7] and [10]. As the rotor anisotropy can indicate damage of one of the blades, H-OMA-TD can be considered as a useful analysis tool for such occasions, as it was demonstrated in [9] and [12].

From the practical viewpoint, the harmonic OMA method does not require very accurate sensor placing on the blades if compared with the MBC transformation. It worth to note that harmonic OMA can still be useful even in the cases when the acceleration data from the rotor is not available; due to modulation (17), more information can be extracted from the tower and nacelle signals, and the knowledge about the primary component of the periodic modes can be enriched by the awareness about the secondary components. Thus, the accurate measurement of the rotor azimuth (or at least rotor speed) is always recommended.

4. CONCLUSIONS

The paper addresses two experimental techniques, which allow extending OMA to LPTV systems such as operating wind turbines. The first technique, based on multiblade coordinate transformation, is intuitively simpler but its technical implementation is more demanding, and the method fails on systems with anisotropic rotors. The second technique, based on harmonic OMA, is more difficult to understand but from a practical viewpoint, it is quite straightforward. The technique is less demanding from the instrumentation perspective and can be applied to anisotropic rotors. Both techniques require the knowledge of rotor azimuth or at the least the rotor speed.

REFERENCES

[1] D. Tcherniak, S. Chauhan and M. H. Hansen, "Applicability limits of operational modal analysis to operational wind turbines," in *International Modal Analysis Conference (IMAC)*, Orlando, FL. USA, 2010.

[2] D. Tcherniak, S. Chauhan, M. Rossetti, I. Font, J. Basurko and O. Salgado, "Output-only modal analysis on operating wind turbines: Application to simulated data," in *European Wind Energy Conference*, Warsaw, Poland, 2010.

[3] D. Tcherniak and G. C. Larsen, "Application of OMA to an operating wind turbine: now including vibration data from the blade," in *International Operational Modal Analysis Conference (IOMAC)*, Guimarães, Portugal, 2013.

[4] S. Yang, D. Tcherniak and M. S. Allen, "Modal analysis of rotating wind turbine using multi-blade coordinate transformation and harmonic power spectrum," in *Int. Modal Analysis Conference (IMAC)*, Orlando, FL, USA, 2014.

[5] G. C. Larsen, P. Berring, D. Tcherniak, P. H. Nielsen and K. Branner, "Effect of damage to modal parameters of a wind turbine blade," in *European Workshop on Structural Health Monitoring*, Nantes, France, 2014.

[6] D. Tcherniak, S. Yang and M. S. Allen, "Experimental characterization of operating bladed rotor using harmonic power spectra and stochastic subspace identification," in *International Conference on Noise and Vibration Engineering (ISMA)*, Leuven, Belgium, 2014.

[7] D. Tcherniak and M. S. Allen, "Experimental characterization of an operating Vestas V27 wind turbine using harmonic power spectra and OMA SSI," in *International Operational Modal Analysis Conference (IOMAC)*, Gijón, Spain, 2015.

[8] O. R. Requesón, D. Tcherniak and G. C. Larsen, "Comparative study of OMA applied to experimental and simulated data from an operating Vestas V27 wind turbine," in *Operational Modal Analysis Conference (IOMAC)*, Gijón, Spain, 2015.

[9] D. Tcherniak, "Rotor anisotropy as a blade damage indicator for wind turbine structural health monitoring systems," *Mechanical Systems and Signal Processing,* vol. 74, pp. 183-198, 2016.

[10] D. Tcherniak and M. Allen, "Experimental dynamic characterization of operating wind turbines with anisotropic rotor," in *Int. Modal Analysis Conference (IMAC)*, Orlando (FL), USA, 2016.

[11] D. Tcherniak, "Detection and identification of a damaged blade without stopping the wind turbine," in *European Workshop on Structural Health Monitoring (EWSHM)*, Bilbao, Spain, 2016.

[12] D. Tcherniak, "Detection and identification of a damaged blade using only a tower sensor, without stopping the wind turbine," in *International Conference on Noise and Vibration Engineering (ISMA)*, Leuven, Belgium, 2016.

[13] D. J. Ewins, Modal Testing, Theory, Practice, and Application, Baldock, UK: Research Study Press Ltd., 2000.

[14] M. H. Hansen, "Improved modal dynamics of wind turbines to avoid stall-induced vibrations," *Wind Energy,* vol. 6, pp. 179-195, 2003.

[15] D. Tcherniak, "Loss of rotor isotropy as a blade damage indicator for wind turbine structure health monitoring systems," in *European Workshop on Structure Health Monitoring (EWSHM)*, Nantes, France, 2014.

[16] P. F. Skjoldan, "Aeroelastic modal dynamics of wind turbines including anisotropic effects," PhD Dissertation, Roskilde, Denmark, 2011.

[17] M. S. Allen, M. W. Sracic, S. Chauhan and M. H. Hansen, "Output-only modal analysis of linear time-periodic systems with application to wind turbine simulation data," *Mechanical Systems and Signal Proecessing,* vol. 25, pp. 1174-1191, 2011.

[18] W.-C. Xie, Dynamic Stability of Structures, New York: Cambridge University Press, 2006.

[19] N. M. Wereley, "Analysis and Control of Linear Periodically Time Varying Systems," PhD Dissertation, Department of Aeronautics and Astronautics, Massachusetts Institute of Technology, Cambridge, 1991.

[20] "Technical Specifications for the ARTeMIS Modal 5," 13 Jul 2018. [Online]. Available: http://www.svibs.com/Documents/ARTeMIS_Modal_Technical_Specs_ver5.pdf.

[21] "PULSE Operational Modal Analysis Types 8760 – 8762," [Online]. Available: https://bksv.com/-/media/literature/Product-Data/bp2567.ashx.

IOMAC'19
8th International Operational Modal Analysis Conference
2019 May13-15 Copenhagen

MODAL TESTING ON A 2 MW WIND TURBINE ROTOR BLADE

A. Schulze [1], *J. Luthe* [1], *J. Zierath* [2], *S.-E. Rosenow* [2], *R. Bockhahn* [2], *R. Rachholz* [1] *and C. Woernle* [1]

[1] Chair of Technical Mechanics/Dynamics, University of Rostock,
{andreas.schulze4, johannes.luthe, roman.rachholz, woernle}@uni-rostock.de.
[2] W2E Wind to Energy GmbH, {jzierath, serosenow, rbockhahn}@wind-to-energy.de.

ABSTRACT

This contribution describes the application of Operational Modal Analysis (OMA) to a 2 MW wind turbine rotor. The rotor spans a total diameter of 100 m and is lying on the ground for the measurement campaign. Due to a limited time span and for accessibility reasons modal testing of the rotor is performed on one blade only. Overall 13 PCB accelerometers are positioned along the blade in flapwise and edgewise directions, and the measurement duration is set to one hour. Furthermore, a multibody model of the rotor configuration is built up to support the interpretation of the OMA results from the blade with respect to the overall rotor system. The modal quantities identified by OMA are then compared to calculated values by Multibody Simulation (MBS) to investigate the quality of the modelling approach of the blades used in MBS. Findings from this investigation then allow conclusions to be drawn about the quality of existing turbine models with the same rotor model.

Keywords: Operational Modal Analysis, Wind Turbine Rotor Blade, Multibody Simulation

1. INTRODUCTION

Understanding the complex dynamic behaviour of wind turbine systems is a prerequisite in the design process of modern wind turbines in order to compete on the growing market for renewable energies. Here the development of detailed multibody models of the turbines is state of the art during the design process. However, as wind turbine systems comprise complex structural components, often manufactured by changing manufacturers, precise numerical modelling of the turbine system is often very costly or even unfeasible due to limited information about the structural turbine components. Of particular importance are the composite blades of the turbine rotor, which require a lot of manual work during the manufacturing process. This leads to uncertainties concerning mass, stiffness and damping distribution of the underlying model and a necessity for modal testing on the structure arises. Furthermore, additional errors are introduced by the modelling approach of the blades used in Multibody Simulation (MBS).

(a) (b)

Figure 1: (a) 2 MW wind turbine with rotor supported on the ground, (b) Sensor application via lifting platform

This contribution describes the application of Operational Modal Analysis (OMA) to a rotor blade of an industrial 2 MW wind turbine designed by W2E Wind to Energy. In Section 2 the test environment is described and prerequisites on the measurement process are emphasized. Furthermore the measurement equipment is briefly introduced, and an overview of the measurement grid chosen for modal testing on the blade is given. In Section 3 the build up of a detailed multibody model of the rotor configuration is motivated. Special interest is given to the blade modelling process and assumptions are made to account for the influence of the support condition on the dynamic behaviour of the rotor system. The results obtained from OMA and MBS are described and compared in detail in Section 4. Finally, concluding remarks on the results achieved within this contribution are given in Section 5.

2. MODAL TESTING ON THE ROTOR BLADE

The measurements were carried out on a rotor blade of the W2E-100/2.0 prototype wind turbine, developed and manufactured by W2E Wind to Energy. The rated power of the turbine is 2.05 MW. The hub height of the turbine is 100 m and the rotor spans a diameter of 100 m with a total blade length of 48.8 m.

2.1. Test environment and conditions

A basic problem in modal testing on a wind turbine rotor is the accessibility of measurement positions on the blades when the rotor is mounted to the turbine. In principle, it is possible to place the sensors on the surface of the blades via a crane system, which would result in considerable time and cost expense. In [1], a sensor set was attached to the rotor prior to its installation to the turbine hub. Here, long-term measurement campaigns were carried out on a wind turbine in operation with correspondingly high demands on the measurement system due to the harsh environmental conditions. An alternative approach is described in [2] where each blade is parked horizontally one at a time so that sensors can be attached to the blade interior by entering the blade through the turbine hub. A drawback of this approach is the limited range of measuring positions due to the decreasing cross-section over the blade length. For example, measurement locations at the blade tip, where the largest deflections are expected, cannot be utilized for modal testing.

Figure 2: Support structure for the turbine rotor

In this contribution modal testing on the rotor is carried out during turbine erection while the rotor is lying on ground, see Figure 1. This allows a more straightforward application of sensors due to a better accessibility of the rotor blades, making modal testing of the rotor comparatively cost and time efficient. On the other hand, new conditions arise for the measurement process, which also affect the analysis process of the data. These conditions are:

- Since the measurements are conducted during turbine erection, only a limited time window of approx. 5 hours is available without delaying the erection process.
- The rotor is mounted on the ground via a purpose-built support structure fixed to the rotor hub, see Figure 2.
- The measurements are conducted on one blade only, partly due to the limited time frame and partly due to only one blade being accessible via the driveway whereas the other blades protrude over an open field, see Figure 1
- The measured blade is pitched to opposite feathered position (270°), the other blades are in feathered position (90°).

2.2. Measurements

The measurement grid chosen for the modal testing on the blade is shown in Figure 3. Overall 13 measurement positions along the rotor blade are utilized for modal testing. The measurement positions S 1-5 allow the measurement of out-of-plane rotor vibrations (edgewise blade vibration respectively). The positions S 6-10 along the neutral line of the blade are chosen to measure in-plane rotor vibration (flapwise blade vibration respectively). Furthermore the positions S 11-13 are added to the measurement grid to account for blade torsion and in-plane rotor vibration.

The modal testing is conducted using the data acquisition system Dyn-X from BRUEL&KJAER with 2×24-bit AD-converter (dynamic range 160 dB) in combination with seismic accelerometers (piezo-electric, sensitivity: 10 V/g) from PCB (PCB Synotech GmbH, Germany), see Figure 4. As shown in Figure 1 a mobile lifting platform was available for the positioning of the sensors on the rotor blade. The measurement series had a duration of 1 hour exploiting the ambient wind conditions on ground only.

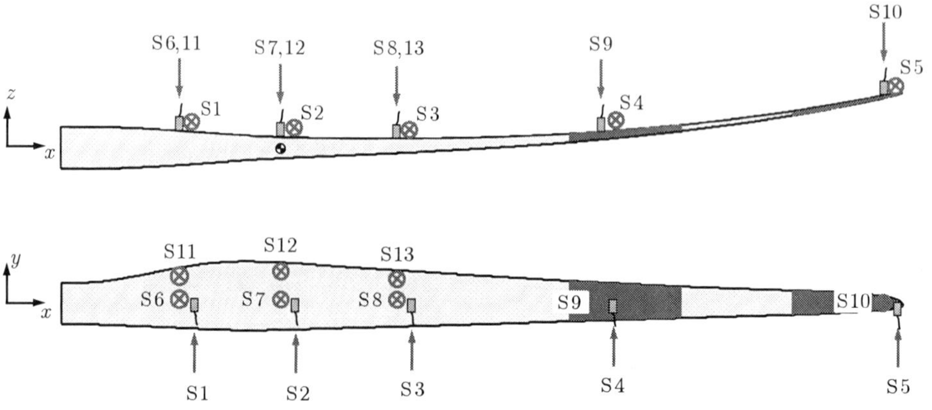

Figure 3: Measurement positions along the rotor blade.

(a) (b)

Figure 4: Measurement equipment: (a) BRUEL&KJAER Dyn-X data acquisition system, (b) PCB piezoelectric accelerometers at the blade tip (S 10, S 5).

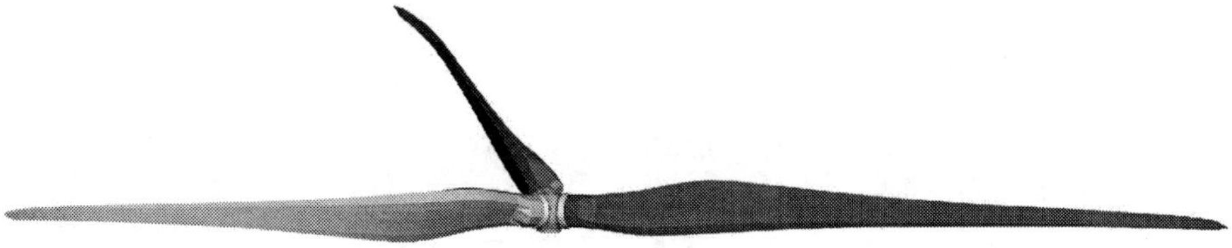

Figure 5: Multibody model of the rotor: Rotor hub (blue), Blades in feathered position (grey, not tested), Blade pitched to 270° (red, tested)

3. MULTIBODY MODEL

A multibody model of the plant rotor in measurement configuration was developed in the multibody software SIMPACK. Two objectives are pursued with this model. The main focus is to investigate the quality of the modelling approach, especially the quality of the blade modelling, by comparing numerical and experimental results. Findings from this investigation then allow conclusions to be drawn about the quality of existing turbine models with the same rotor model. Another objective of the model relates to the evaluation of the OMA results. Due to the limited time window, modal testing was performed on one rotor blade only. This implies that the dynamic behaviour of the entire rotor structure was observed on one part of the structure only, namely the rotor blade. However, the dynamic behaviour of a rotor is characterized by a complex interaction of coupling effects of all three blades [3]. An evaluation of the modal quantities of the entire rotor structure identified with OMA might therefore be very difficult on this basis. Here, the multibody model of the turbine rotor serves for an improved understanding of the OMA results. It should be noted that this approach requires a multibody model that already exhibits the basic dynamic properties of the real physical system.

The multibody model consists of the partial bodies of the three blade structures and the rotor hub which are coupled to each other via kinematic constraints, see Figure 5. In the model, the blade on which the modal testing was performed is highlighted in red. The dynamic behaviour of the rotor is strongly influenced by the dynamics of the individual blades and their coupling interaction in the rotor assembly. Therefore, the model quality of the rotor blades is decisive for the quality of the overall rotor model. For the model in Figure 5, the rotor blades were built up as flexible multibody models. Here the standard approach for the implementation of flexible bodies is followed comprising a preceding built up of a FE model of the blade, followed by model order reduction via component mode synthesis and implementation into the MBS environment through Floating Frame of Reference [4]. The FE blade model is based on simple mass and stiffness values at predefined cross-sections along the blade, and the first 10 eigen modes of the FE model are used for component mode synthesis. Furthermore, each blade is modelled using identical stiffness and mass distribution. As the hub is comparatively stiff compared to the rotor blades, it is implemented as a rigid body.

A further significant influence on the dynamic behaviour of the rotor model lies in the modelling of the support conditions of the rotor, see Figure 2. Especially the dynamic coupling between the blade bodies is determined by the flexible rotor support. Naturally, a detailed modelling of the support structure and especially the real ground conditions on the testing site exceeds the scope of this contribution. Instead, simplified modelling assumptions were applied to take the basic properties of the support conditions into account without excessive modelling effort. First, the rotor model is coupled to global frame through a spherical joint. This implies rigid behaviour of the support structure in the translational degrees of freedom of the rotor. In a second step, the three rotational degrees of freedom are coupled using torsional springs at the spherical joint. The equivalent stiffness values for the torsional springs are calculated based on a FE model of the support structure and by a assuming a simple Winkler foundation model to account for soil behaviour [5]. This approach much depends on the actual soil stiffness. As no soil samples

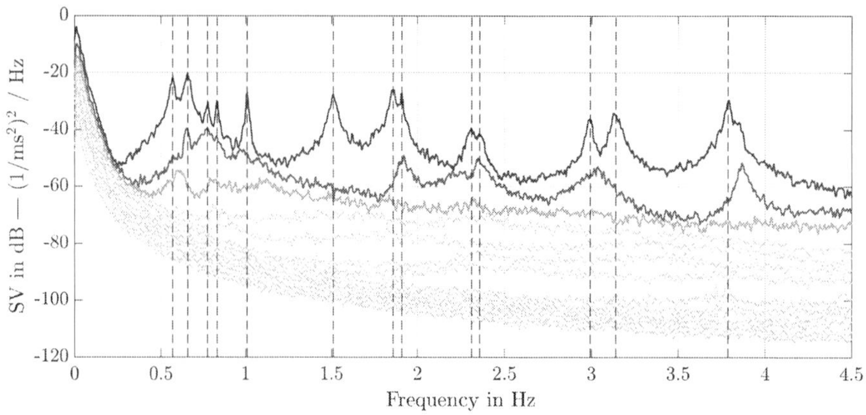

Figure 6: Singular values and identified natural frequencies using EFFD

were taken from the test site, the modulus was approximated on the basis of literature values [6]. The inaccuracies resulting from the modelling approach, especially with respect to the soil properties, allow only a limited conclusion about the real system behaviour. Therefore, two multibody simulations of the rotor were conducted, one with, according to the modelling approach, minimum equivalent rotational stiffness properties of the rotor support and one with maximum equivalent rotational stiffness properties.

4. MODAL IDENTIFICATION

The measured data of the test campaign on the rotor is analysed using the ARTeMIS software environment. For the extraction of modal parameters from the measurement the Enhanced Frequency Domain Decomposition (EFDD) method [7] was chosen. The corresponding singular values and identified natural frequencies (indicated via dotted lines) within a frequency band of 0 Hz to 4.5 Hz are given in Figure 6. Overall 13 distinct modes of the rotor are identified by EFFD within this frequency range.

A comparison of the results obtained by operational modal analysis and the modal parameters of the multibody model, including the double poles at 0.65 Hz and at 3.78 Hz, is given in Table 1 and Figure 7. The values MBS_{min} and MBS_{max} in Table 1 indicate results of the multibody simulation with maximum and minimum stiffness of the support structure, respectively. Furthermore, the absolute error between MBS and OMA results and the identified damping values are listed in the table. Figure 7 shows the rotor mode shapes 1 to 13 identified by OMA EFFD for the single blade as well the corresponding mode shapes of the rotor model. As can be observed in the figure, it might be very difficult to interpret the rotor modes identified on the individual blade. Only by comparison with the numerical model the measured modes can be uniquely assigned to the corresponding rotor modes.

Due to the symmetric construction of the rotor and the almost symmetric rotor blade positions (the measured rotor blade is rotated by 180° relative to the other blades), double poles for the modes 2/3, 8/9, 14/15 are obtained from the multibody model. These modes are characterized by an out-of-phase, in-plane (flapwise) oscillation of the rotor blades, see Figure 7. Additionally the double poles 4/5 and 10/11 arise due to the symmetric support condition. The mode shapes corresponding to these poles are characterized by a tilting motion of the rotor about the spherical joint.

The model-based double poles can also be identified in the measured singular value curves in Figure 6. Here however, the expected poles 4/5 (at around 0.8 Hz), 8/9 (at around 1.9 Hz) and 10/11 (at around 2.3 Hz) are instead characterized by closely spaced peaks. The main reason for the small separation of these peaks stems from unavoidable asymmetries both in the rotor structure and in the rotor support.

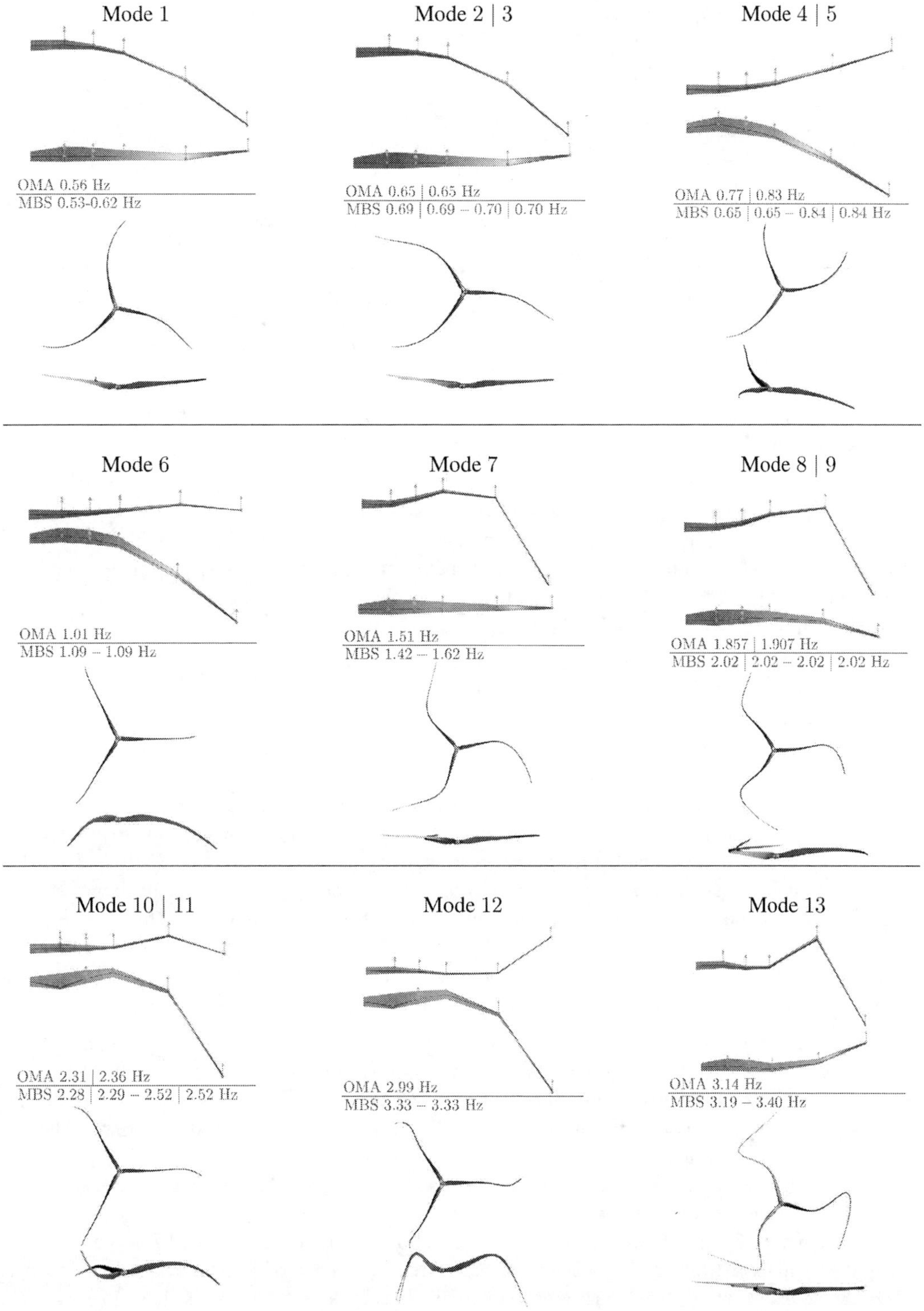

Figure 7: Mode shapes 1 to 13 and natural frequencies of the rotor marked by: OMA EFDD (upper half for each mode) and MBS (lower half for each mode). Mode numbers and natural frequencies belonging to double poles are separated by | . Mode numbers and natural frequencies from MBS results with minimum and maximum support stiffness are separated by –.

Table 1: Comparison between experimental and numerical results.

Mode Nr.	Natural Frequencies [Hz]			Error [Hz]		Damping [%]
	OMA EFDD	MBS_{min}	MBS_{max}	MBS_{min}	MBS_{max}	OMA EFFD
1	0.567	0.532	0.618	-0.035	+0.051	2.759
2	0.655	0.696	0.701	+0.041	+0.046	1.426
3	0.655	0.696	0.701	+0.041	+0.046	1.426
4	0.772	0.650	0.839	-0.122	+0.067	1.362
5	0.831	0.652	0.843	-0.179	+0.012	0.982
6	1.008	1.090	1.092	+0.082	+0.084	0.508
7	1.510	1.422	1.622	-0.088	+0.112	1.089
8	1.857	2.017	2.020	+0.160	+0.163	0.811
9	1.907	2.022	2.023	+0.115	+0.116	0.435
10	2.311	2.284	2.516	-0.027	+0.205	0.847
11	2.356	2.294	2.519	-0.062	+0.163	0.426
12	2.991	3.331	3.330	+0.340	+0.339	0.469
13	3.139	3.109	3.399	-0.030	+0.260	0.749
14	3.785	4.235	4.228	+0.450	+0.443	0.331
15	3.785	4.235	4.228	+0.450	+0.443	0.331

The identified mode shapes of the turbine rotor can be classified as in-plane rotor modes (modes 1, 2/3, 7, 8/9, 13, 14/15), dominated by flapwise bending of the blades, out-of-plane modes (modes 6, 12), dominated by edgewise blade bending, and as modes characterized by coupled in- and out-of-plane oscillations of the blades (modes 4/5, 10/11).

As can be observed in Figure 7, the coupled modes 4/5, 10/11 involve comparably large tilting motion of the rotor hub relative to the spherical joint. This implies a strong sensitivity of the corresponding natural frequencies to the support conditions of the rotor system, which is further confirmed by the MBS frequency values for minimum and maximum equivalent stiffness of the support The same effect can be observed for the in-plane modes 1, 7, 13. Here in-phase, in-plane blade bending (flapwise) is coupled to a simultaneous rotation of the rotor hub about the axis perpendicular to the rotor plane. The absolute errors between the natural frequencies of the model and the real structure, corresponding to the modes 1, 4/5, 7, 10/11, 13 that are strongly affected by the support stiffness, range from -0.18 Hz to $+0.26$ Hz. Considering the very simplified assumptions regarding the support properties, a relatively good agreement between the model and the real structure can thus be achieved with the natural frequencies of the real structure located in-between the upper and lower boundaries of the natural frequencies from MBS. However, a statement on the quality of the blade model cannot be derived from this analysis due to the strong influence of the support properties.

The in-plane and out-of-plane rotor modes 2/3, 6, 8/9, 12, 14/15 on the other hand appear to be insensitive with respect to the support stiffness. The out-of-plane modes 6, 12 of the rotor show in-phase edgewise bending of all three blades with the support assumed to be rigid in this direction. For the first out-of-plane mode 6 this assumption proves to be valid with an absolute error $+0.08$ Hz between the simulation model and the tested structure. As this mode is hardly affected by stiffness of the support, a good agreement can be observed between the blade model and the real rotor blades for this particular mode. For the next higher harmonic 12, however, an increase of the absolute error to $+0.34$ Hz is observed. A possible reason for this effect might lie in the modal reduction process of the FE blade model for integration into the MBS software. When using an insufficient number of shape functions (mode shapes of the single blade in this case) higher frequency oscillations of the assembled system (rotor) cannot be approximated sufficiently by by a superposition of the shape functions. This leads to a stiffening effect at higher frequencies which is observed for the out-of-plane rotor mode 12. Similar effects can be observed for the in-plane modes 2/3, 8/9, 14/15. Here two blades oscillate in-phase and one out-of-phase in flapwise (in-plane) direction for each mode accompanied by little to no motion of the hub. Analogous to the out-of-plane modes, the absolute error increases with higher natural frequencies from $+0.041/0.046$ Hz for the mode pair $2/3$ to $+0.450/0.450$ Hz. This effect further supports the assumption of insufficient set of shape functions in the blade modelling approach.

5. CONCLUSION

The modal properties of a turbine rotor lying on the ground were identified within a frequency band of 0 Hz to 4.5 Hz by the methods of Operational Modal Analysis and Enhanced Frequency Domain Decomposition. Utilizing a multibody model and approximating the properties of the rotor support, the modes of the entire rotor were uniquely identified from measurements on one blade only. Overall, a satisfactory agreement was found between the natural frequencies and mode shapes from the multibody model and from the measurements on the physical rotor. The out-of-plane rotor mode shapes and the in-plane mode shapes with phase flapwise bending of two blades and out-of-phase flapwise bending of the remaining blade are shown to be insensitive to a change of the rotor support stiffness. These modes in particular allow a deeper insight into the quality of the multibody modelling approach of the rotor blades which is also applied in the same way to models of entire wind energy turbines. Of special interest is the observed stiffening of the rotor blade model at higher natural frequencies. This effect indicates the use of an insufficient set of shape function in the model reduction process during blade modelling. The modal parameters of the rotor identified by OMA will be the basis for further investigations regarding the sensitivity of the multibody model dynamics to different sets of shape functions.

REFERENCES

[1] Tcherniak, D. and Larsen, G. C. (2013) Application of OMA to an Operating Wind Turbine: now including Vibration Data from the Blades. In: *Proc. 5th International Operational Modal Analysis Conference (IOMAC'13), Guimarães, Portugal.*

[2] Zierath, J., Bockhahn, R., Rachholz, R., Rosenow, S.-E., Schulze, A., Luthe, J. and Woernle, C. (2018) A Measurement and Signal Processing Concept for the Dynamic Analysis of Operating Wind Turbines. In: *Proc. 5th Joint International Conference on Multibody System Dynamics, Lisbon, Portugal.*

[3] Hansen, M. H. (2007) Aeroelastic instability problems for wind turbines. In: *Wind Energy, Vol. 10, No. 6, 2007, p. 551-577.*

[4] Shabana, A. A. (2014) Dynamics of multibody systems. In: *Cambridge University Press, Cambridge.*

[5] Johnson, K. L. (1992) Contact Mechanics. In: *Cambridge University Press, Cambridge.*

[6] Hahn, J. (1970) Durchlaufträger, Rahmen, Platten und Balken auf elastischer Bettung. In *Werner Verlag, 10., neubearb. und erw. Aufl., Düsseldorf.*

[7] Brincker, R., Ventura, C. E. and Andersen, P. (2001) Damping Estimation by Frequency Domain Decomposition. In: *Proc. of the 19th International Modal Analysis Conference (IMAC), Kissimmee, Florida, p. 698-703.*

IOMAC'19

8th International Operational Modal Analysis Conference

2019 May13-15 Copenhagen

MONITORING CAMPAIGN IN AN ONSHORE WIND FARM: INSTALLATION DESCRIPTION AND PRELIMINARY RESULTS

F. Magalhães[1], J. Pacheco[1], C. Moutinho[1], S. Guimarães[2], L. Noites[3], A. Cunha[1], M. Marques[2], J. Carlos Matos[2]

[1] CONSTRUCT- VIBEST, Faculty of Engineering, University of Porto, Portugal.
[2] INEGI, Porto, Portugal.
[3] Faculty of Engineering, University of Porto, Portugal.

ABSTRACT

In the context of the WindFarmSHM project a quite extensive experimental campaign is being performed in Tocha wind farm, an onshore wind farm located in Portugal. This includes the instrumentation of at least two wind turbines aiming the development, validation and optimization of monitoring strategies at the level of the wind farm for damage detection and fatigue analysis, using the response to operation loads measured by strain gages and accelerometers distributed in the tower and blades. The paper presents the experimental layout, introduces the processing tools under development and shows some initial results. At this preliminary stage, it will be evaluated the ability of the different monitoring components to track the modal parameters of the system composed by the tower and the rotor.

Keywords: Wind Turbine, Dynamic Monitoring, Operational Modal Analysis

1. INTRODUCTION

Portugal's electricity demand is covered in approximately 25% by wind energy, which is produced by more than 2500 wind turbines. Several European countries present equivalent figures. The management of this asset can strongly benefit from the development of cost effective monitoring strategies.

Furthermore, it is crucial to prepare the scientific community and the industry for several challenges, such as the evaluation of the need of replacement of wind turbines components at the end of their design life (wind turbines were designed to operate 20 years and the installation in Portugal started 23 years ago) and the installation of offshore wind turbines in high deep waters (as it is the case of the Portuguese shore) using innovative floating solutions. The extension of the lifespan of the existing wind turbines, the possibility of the reducing insuring costs by reducing the operation risk through monitoring and the possibility of expanding the capabilities for extracting energy from offshore winds, will certainly contribute to increase the competitiveness of this energy source.

Considering this background, the main goal of the recently started WindFarmSHM research project is the development, validation and optimization of new methodologies to continuously assess the structural elements of wind turbines: tower, blades and foundation. The monitoring strategy will be designed to be applied in the context of a wind farm, adequate for onshore and floating solutions, using optimized instrumentation layouts at a subgroup of wind turbines, and taking profit from the data provided by the acquisition systems already available in all wind turbines (SCADA), for the use of extrapolation techniques to assess all the wind turbines of the same wind farm (see Figure 1).

The research project will include the monitoring of at least two wind turbines of an onshore wind farm, comprehending accelerometers, strain gages and clinometers and the development of numerical models for the generation of artificial experimental data to validate the monitoring strategy in floating wind turbines.

The data processing will be based on the continuous evaluation of the parameters that drive the structure dynamic behaviour (vibration frequencies and damping) estimated from the structure response to ambient excitation (wind, waves, currents, soil vibrations) and advanced statistical modelling, having in mind two main goals: detection of stiffness reductions motivated by the appearance of damage and evaluation of the remaining fatigue life of the main structural components (see Figure 1).

In the project a very extensive instrumentation will be deployed in order evaluate different monitoring layout alternatives, but the final goal it to propose a minimal optimized monitoring layout based on a few number of easy to install sensors.

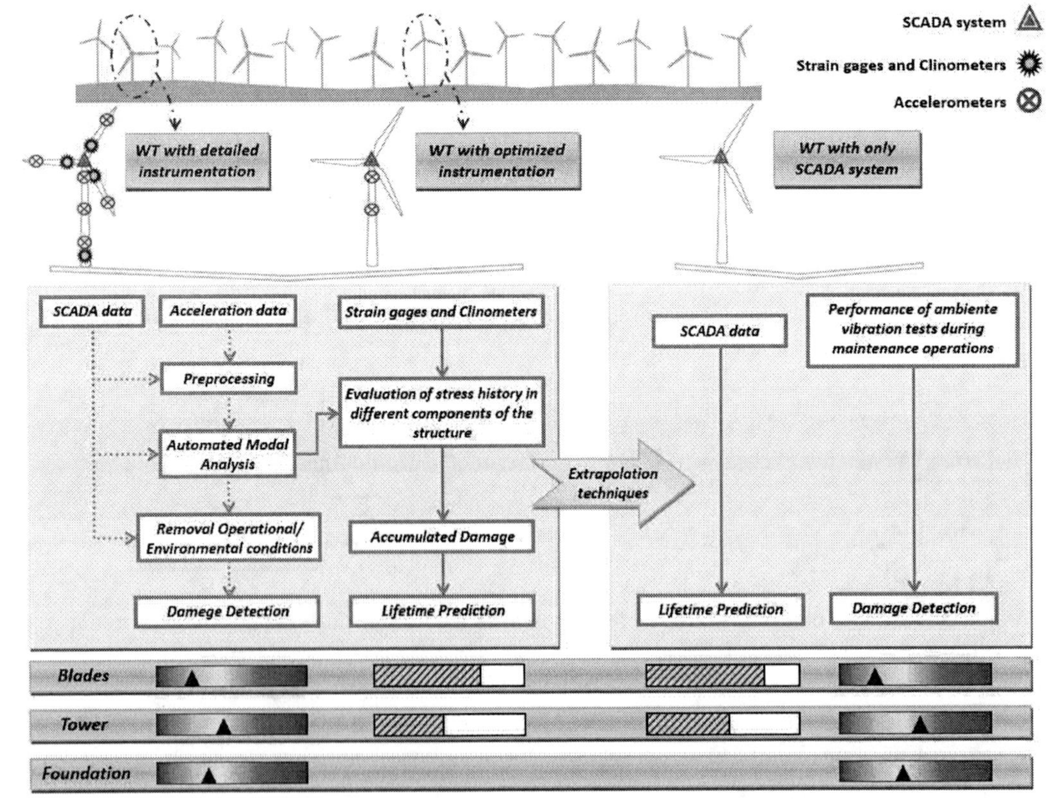

Figure 1. Monitoring Strategy.

2. TOCHA WIND FARM

The Tocha wind farm is owned by EDP Renewables and started its operation in May 2012. It is located in the central region of Portugal, approximately 3 km from the coast line. It consists of five Vestas wind turbines, model V100-1.8 MW (rotor diameter of 100m and 1.8MW of rated power). It is a variable speed, 3 blades rotor with individual pitch control for each blade. The hub is placed at a height of 95m and is supported by a steel tower. Since the soil is sand, the steel tower is connected to a 14by14m concrete slab supported by sixteen concrete piles with 1m diameter. The wind turbines operate for wind speeds between 4 and 20m/s and achieve the rated power for wind speeds of about 12m/s (Figure 2).

Figure 3 presents the geographic location of the wind farm and the distribution of the 5 wind turbines, identified with the numbers that will be used throughout this work.

As it is clear from Figure 4, the main wind direction is approximately North. So, considering the very soft orography of the terrain, wind turbines 1 and 2 are loaded by offshore winds with few perturbations, whereas the wind load of the other wind turbines may present additional turbulence motivated by wake effects.

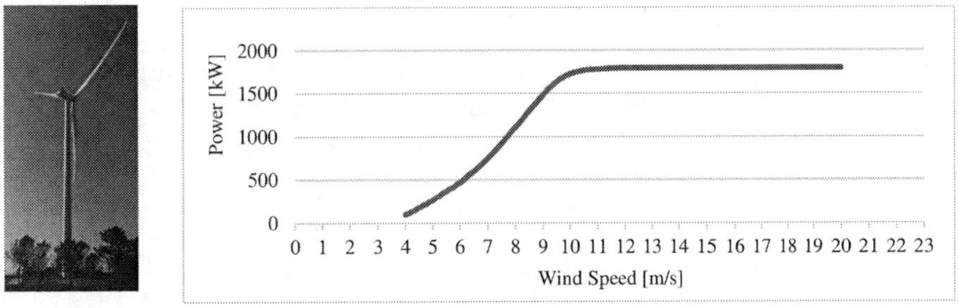

Figure 2. Photo of one wind turbine and power curve (https://en.wind-turbine-models.com).

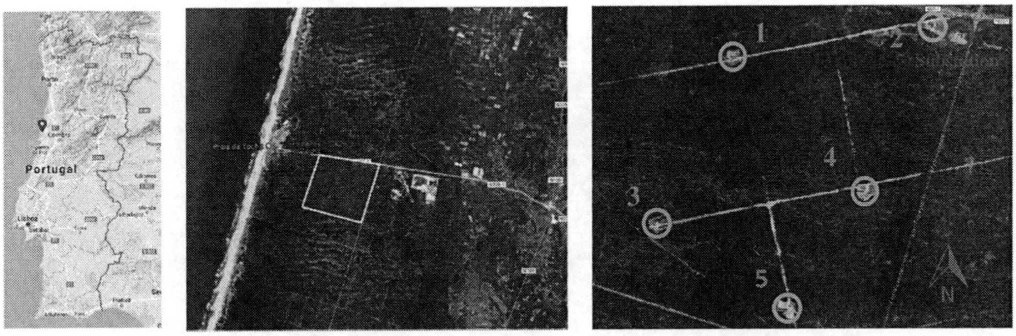

Figure 3. Location of Tocha Wind Farm with distribution of the 5 wind turbines.

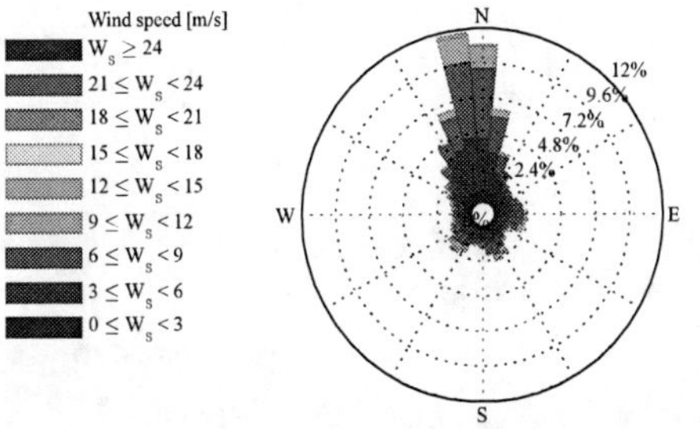

Figure 4. Characterization of the wind observed during 2017 (SCADA data)

2.1. Preliminary evaluation of the modal properties of the wind turbines

Before the installation of the monitoring systems a set of ambient vibration tests was performed in four of the 5 wind turbines in non-operating conditions (the rotor was stopped or idling).

The accelerations were measured with 4 standalone seismographs, with internal tri-axial force balance sensors that were placed in the horizontal platforms of the tower. The collected acceleration time series were first analysed in the frequency domain and then processed with Covariance driven Stochastic Subspace Identification method (SSI-COV) [1].

Figure 5 shows some of the results obtained for wind turbine 1. The top left plot shows two averaged normalized spectra: one for the for-aft direction, FA, (perpendicular to the rotor plane) and another for the side-side direction, SS, (parallel to the rotor plane). The natural frequencies associated with the first two pairs of tower bending modes stand out. In the stabilization diagram covering the full frequency range under analysis, the position of the first three pairs of tower bending modes is marked. The two zooms presented at the bottom of the figure show that with the SSI-COV method it is possible to separate the very close modes within the first two pairs of frequencies.

Figure 6 presents the identified mode shapes, which are compared to numerical results obtained from a preliminary simple numerical model (more advanced models are currently being developed in FAST [2]). Figure 7 compares the results obtained for the 4 tested wind turbines. All of them present quite similar natural frequencies, but wind turbine 5 seams to present a slightly different behaviour. For this reason and also because this is the wind turbine where higher turbulence is expected the monitoring camping will be focused on wind turbines 1 and 5.

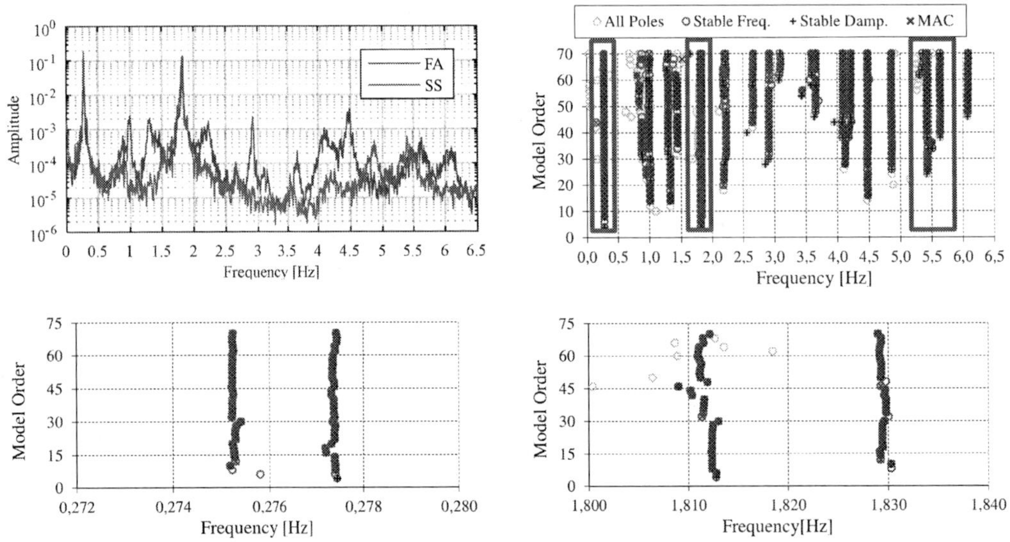

Figure 5. Ambient Vibration test results for wind turbine 1: average power spectra for FA and SS directions, stabilization diagram produced by the SSI-COV method and two zooms of this diagram.

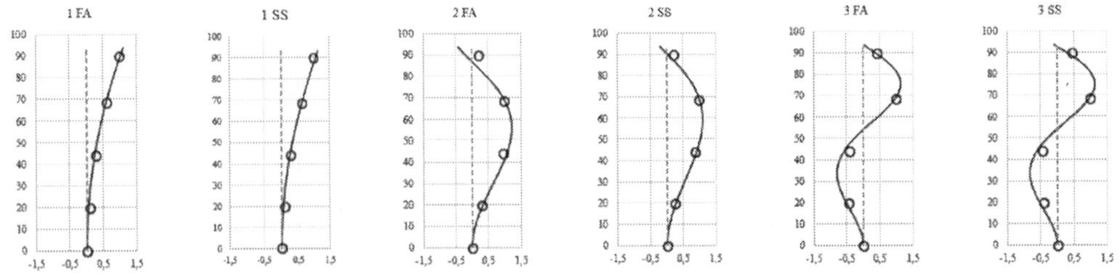

f = 0,275Hz   f = 0,277Hz   f = 1,829Hz   f = 1,812Hz   f = 5,635Hz   f = 5,426Hz

Figure 6. Mode shapes identified with the ambient vibration test of wind turbine 1

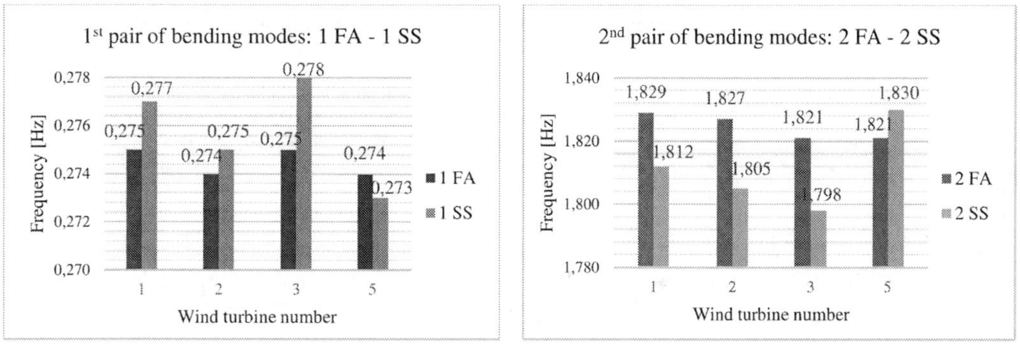

Figure 7. Comparison of the natural frequencies of 4 wind turbines

3. MONITORING SYSTEMS

The monitoring campaign foreseen in the project includes a very complete monitoring layout in one turbine, this is wind turbine 1, and intermediate layout in another one, this is wind turbine 5, and a simple monitoring layout in a third turbine.

At the present, only the instrumentation of wind turbine 1 is about to be finished. This already includes the following monitoring components:

- 2 alternative systems to characterize the accelerations at the tower: a commercial system based on a set of very low noise accelerometers and a customized low-cost system based on MEM accelerometers designed and assembled in FEUP;
- strain gages at the tower base to characterize the stresses during different operating conditions;
- a set of fiber optic strain gages to estimate bending moments at the blades roots;
- MEM accelerometers placed at the blades (10 meters from the root) to characterize their dynamics;

Complementary information about the wind characteristics and the turbine operation is provided by the SCADA system.

3.1. Tower Accelerometers

In order to obtain the best possible characterization of the tower accelerations a commercial system based on 6 force-balance accelerometers and a 24bits acquisition system was deployed. As depicted in Figure 8, this involved the instrumentation of 3 sections of the tower in two orthogonal horizontal directions. The sensors are connected by cables to a central acquisition system that continuously records acceleration time series. This data is accessible through an internet connection.

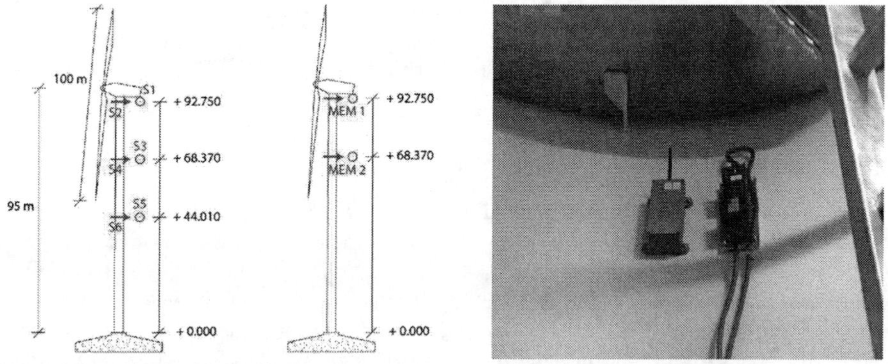

Figure 8. Sections instrumented with accelerometers: force balance (left), MEM (middle). Photos of the force balance sensors (connected to cables) and of the MEM based acquisition system (grey box with antenna).

The MEM based system is a standalone system developed at FEUP and integrates a tri-axial acceleration sensor (in this application just two directions are being recorded), a set of batteries that ensure 5 months of continuous operation, a memory card for data storage, high-precision clocks and a radio for data transmission. In the present application the data transmission is limited to state-of-health parameters to increase the system autonomy. Two of these devices were installed in the tower in the positions marked in Figure 8.

One of the project goals is the development and test of easy to deploy and cost effective systems for wind turbines testing and monitoring, so the evaluation of the performance of these devices designed and assembled in FEUP is very relevant.

3.2. Tower strains and rotations

This monitoring component is essential for fatigue assessment of the tower and is composed by 6 2D rosette strain gages (measurement of the strain in two orthogonal directions), 4 temperature sensors and 3 clinometers connected to digitizers and a field computer, installed in the tower base. Having in mind the evaluation of the static bending moments diagrams along the tower, the six strain gages are distributed in two tower sections: one with four sensors at 6.6m from the tower base and another section with 2 sensors at 7.8m from the tower base (see Figure 9). The temperature sensors and the measurement of the strain in the direction perpendicular to the tower axis are important to evaluate alternative procedures to minimize the temperature influence on the measured longitudinal strains.

The installation of the clinometers is still under preparation and aims to measure the rotation at the tower base and to alternatively estimate strains from two close rotation measurements. If effective, this alternative way of estimating the tower bending moments has the advantage of being less intrusive than the strain gages, whose installation implies the removal of tower painting.

The data acquisition of this monitoring component is assured by a LabView based program customized for this particular application.

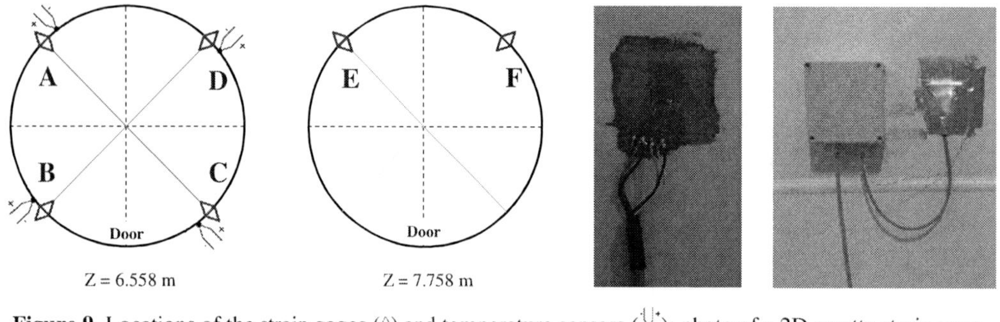

Figure 9. Locations of the strain gages (◊) and temperature sensors (V); photo of a 2D rosette strain gage before protection; and photo of the strain rosette and temperature sensor after protection and box for signal conditioning.

3.3. Blade Accelerometers

The same MEM based devices that were installed in the tower were also installed inside the blades, one in each blade, 10 meters from the blade root. The goal is the characterization of the rotor modes under different operation conditions. The analysis of the data collected during the ambient vibration tests showed the existence of several resonance frequencies that could not be attributed to tower fundamental modes. These are certainly rotor modes that it is important to characterize. Furthermore, the direct tracking of the modes might be beneficial for automatic identification of changes in the blades, which might be reductions in stiffness due to damages or additional masses due to icing.

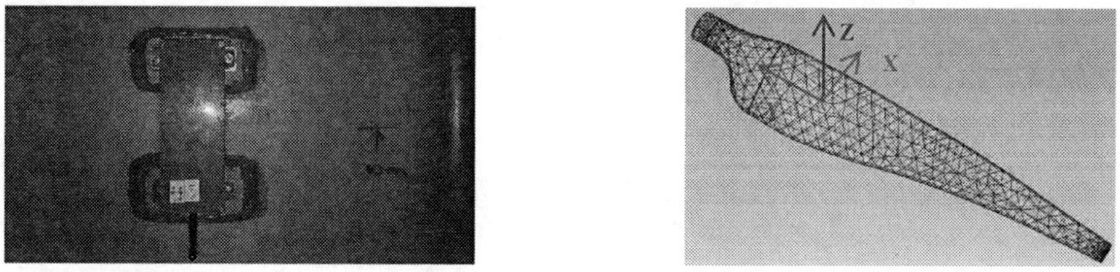

Figure 10. MEM based system installed inside one blade and direction of measurements (X approximately aligned with edgewise direction).

3.4. Blade Strains

The main goal of the blades strain monitoring is fatigue assessment of the blades and condition monitoring using automatically tracked modal parameters evolution. But the joint analysis of the blade loads and tower bending moments is also very interesting to understand the transmission of loads from the rotor to the tower.

The adopted solution is a commercial system provided by HBM/FiberSensing, called WindMeter. Each blade is instrumented with 4 fiber optic strain sensors and temperature sensors for compensation of the temperature effects. Each set of sensors is connected to a central acquisition system installed in the hub, which is then linked with a modem for remote access to the data (Figure 11).

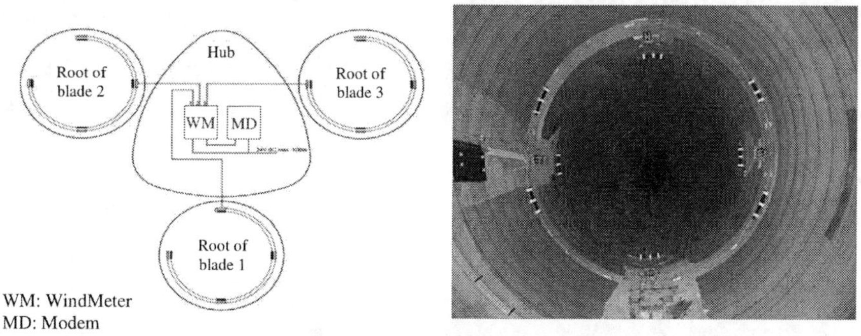

Figure 11. Strain measurement at the blades root: wiring and photo

4. PRELIMINARY MONITORING RESULTS

The installation of all the described components is still being tuned and the amount of collected data is still quite limited, so the presented results only intend to give a flavour of what is being measured and demonstrate the capabilities of this very extensive monitoring layout.

4.1. Tower Accelerometers

Figure 12 shows two examples of power spectra provided by the two alternative sensor types under test at the wind turbine tower. In non-operating conditions the pairs of peaks associated with the first two pairs of modes clearly stand out. In operating conditions additional peaks associated with 3Ω and 6Ω appear (Ω - frequency of rotor rotation), and the peaks associated with the second pair of modes become much more diffuse, which will make their tracking over time quite challenging.

The system designed and assembled at FEUP has demonstrated a performance comparable to the much more expensive and difficult to install commercial system.

Figure 13 presents colour maps constructed from singular value spectra calculated with the acceleration time series collected by the force balance sensors during one month, after their projection in the FA and SS directions. As expected, important variations of the frequency content are observed over time, due to the varying operating conditions, being still possible to visually track the time evolution of the natural frequencies associated with the first two pairs of tower modes.

Presently, the algorithms for modes tracking applied in reference [3] are being tuned for this particular application.

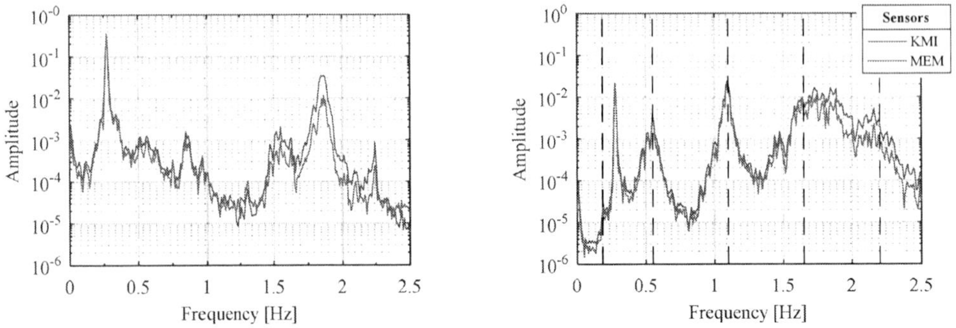

Pitch angle = 90°; Rotor speed = 0.0RPM; Wind speed = 2.9 m/s   Pitch angle = -1.7°; Rotor speed = 11.1RPM; Wind speed = 5.4 m/s

Figure 12. Power spectra from force balance (KMI) and MEM sensors (1Ω. 3Ω and 6Ω marked with dashed vertical lines)

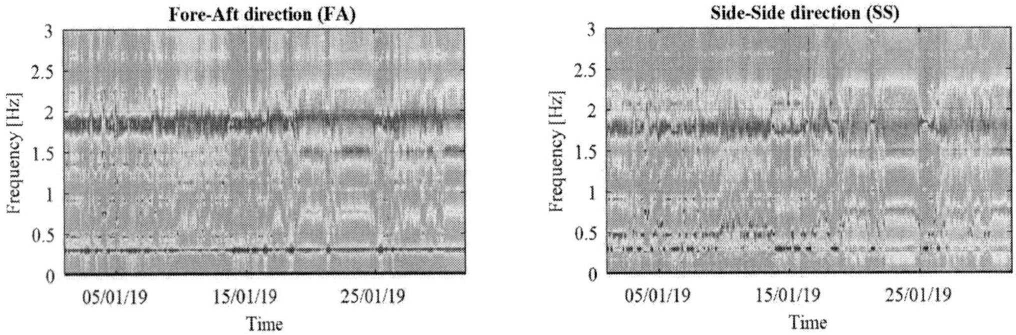

Figure 13. Colour maps with singular value spectra for the FA and SS directions during January/2019

4.2. Tower Strains

Figure 14 presents an example of recorded strain time series during a transition from operating to non-operating condition. This monitoring component was installed with the main goal of characterizing the static component of the response, but the figure shows that it has the capability to very accurately characterize the tower vibrations. This feature will be very relevant to test approaches for dynamic stresses estimation from acceleration measurements [4].

Operating Conditions

Time < 775 s:

- Pitch angle = -1.5°;
- Rotor speed = 8.9 rpm;
- Wind speed = 4.1 m/s;

Time > 800 s:

- Pitch angle = 90°;
- Rotor speed = 0.0 rpm;
- Wind speed = 4.3 m/s;

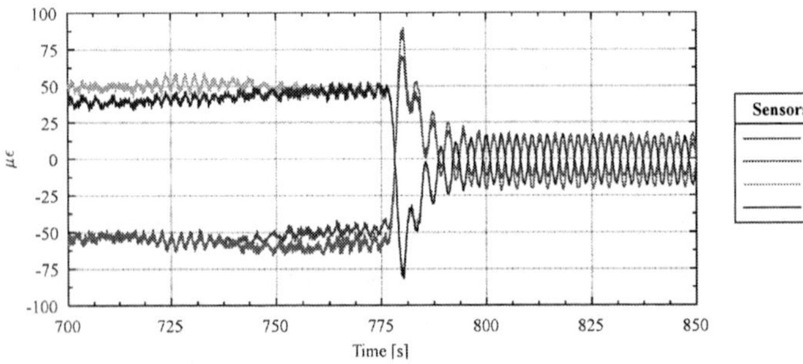

Figure 14. Example of strain time series (see sensor positions in Figure 9)

The power spectra presented in Figure 15 further validates the previous observation, it is possible to perform operational modal analysis using this data. Comparing these spectra with the ones presented in Figure 12 it seems that the tower modes are enhanced, so the strain measurements might be useful to help on the discrimination of the tower modes from the rotor modes observed in the tower.

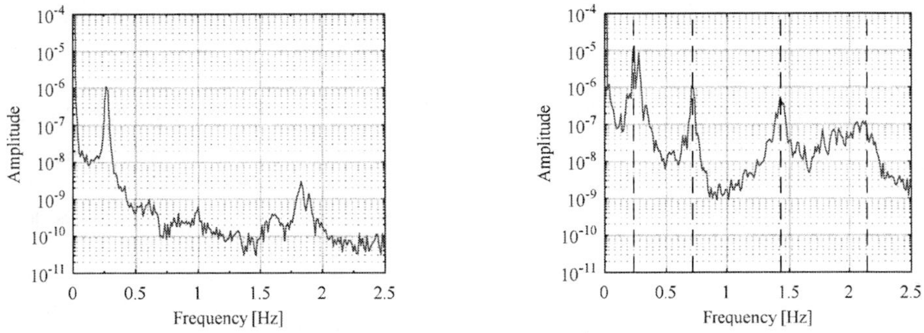

Pitch angle = 90°; Rotor speed = 0.0 rpm; Wind speed = 4.1 m/s

Pitch angle = -2.5°; Rotor speed = 14.4 rpm; Wind speed = 8.7 m/s

Figure 15. Averaged power spectra of the longitudinal strains A to D.

4.3. Blade Accelerometers

The simultaneous recording of acceleration time series in the blades will certainly permit the estimation of mode shapes using the procedure presented in [5], but at this preliminary stage only examples of time series (Figure 16) and spectra (Figure 17) are presented.

The spectrum derived from the acceleration time series recorded with the rotor stopped presents peaks at the tower main modes but also several other prominent resonance frequencies that are certainly associated with rotor modes.

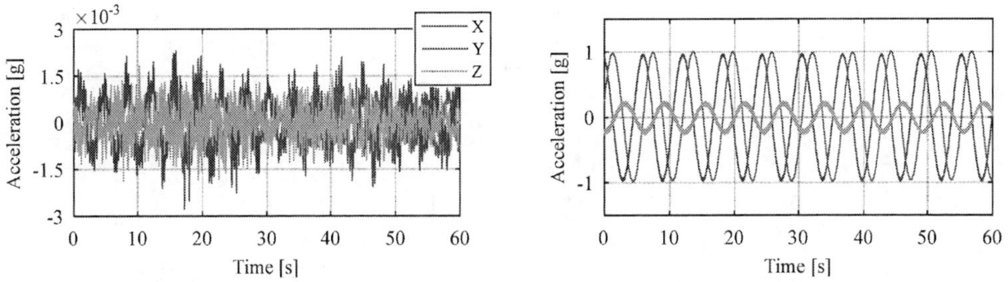

Pitch angle = 90°; Rotor speed = 0.0 rpm; Wind speed = 5.5 m/s

Pitch angle = 0°; Rotor speed = 10 rpm; Wind speed = 5.9 m/s

Figure 16. Example of acceleration time series and corresponding operation parameters (directions defined in Figure 10)

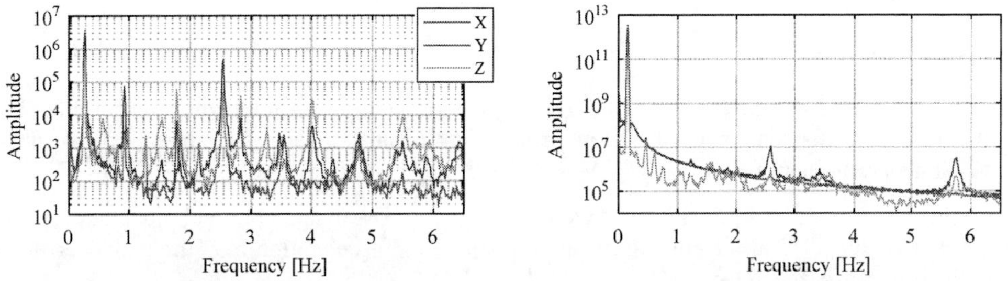

Figure 17. Power spectra of acceleration time series represented in Figure 16

Since the adopted sensors can measure the gravity, the accelerations collected during operation are dominated by the rotor rotation frequency, but still some other frequencies associated with flapwise (Z) and edgewise (X) vibrations can be observed.

4.4. Blade Strains

The blade strain monitoring main goal is the collection of stress stories to perform fatigue analyses of the blades, but the following results show that the collected data can be also used for operational modal analysis.

As opposition to the time series collected by the accelerometers installed in the blades, the strains are not so sensitive to the tower bending modes, since these produce movements of the blades but do not produce important bending. So, the peaks of the spectra presented in Figure 19 enhance the contribution of the blade modes. Plots presented in Figures 17 and 19 for parked condition show coincident peaks. In operation, the observed frequencies depend on the rotor rotating speed, so the peaks observed in the plots presented in the right side of Figures 17 and 19 do not coincide.

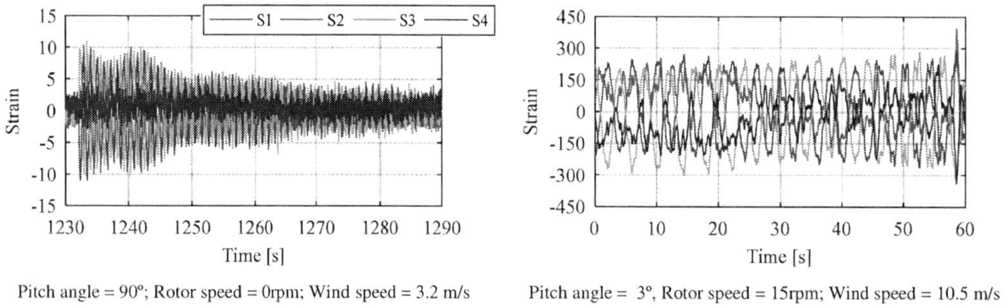

Figure 18. Example of detrended strain time series (static component was removed) and corresponding operation parameters (S1, S3 bending in the edgewise direction; S2, S4 bending in the flapwise direction)

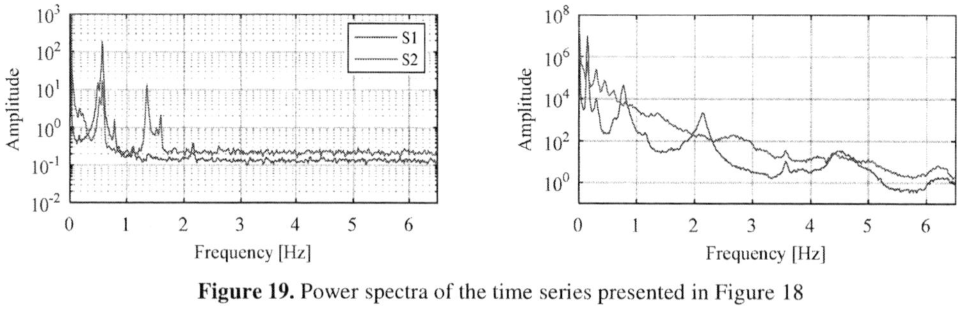

Figure 19. Power spectra of the time series presented in Figure 18

5. CONCLUSIONS

This paper presented the quite extensive monitoring camping that is being conducted in Tocha wind farm, described the installation of the monitoring components that are already in operation and presented some preliminary results.

The preliminary analyses performed in the frequency domain show that operational modal analysis has the potential to extract useful information from both strain and acceleration measurements performed either in the tower or in the blades.

A deeper processing of the data that is being continuously collected by all the monitoring components will certainly contribute to better understand the in-operation dynamic behavior of these quite complex structures, to devise processing procedures for effective evaluation of their structure health and to calculate accumulated damage due to fatigue.

ACKNOWLEDGEMENTS

The support of EDP Renewables and VESTAS in greatly acknowledged. The support of Fiber Sensing in the installation of the blades strains motoring system and of Nuno Pinto in the installation of the tower strains monitoring system is also deeply acknowledged.

This work was also financially supported by: WindFarmSHM Project (PTDC/ECI-EST/29558/2017), PhD Grant SFRH/BD/129688/2017, UID/ECI/04708/2019- CONSTRUCT - Instituto de I&D em Estruturas e Construções funded by national funds through the FCT/MCTES (PIDDAC).

REFERENCES

[1] Magalhães, F. & Cunha, A. (2011). Explaining Operational Modal Analysis with data from ana arch bridge. *Mechanical Systems and Signal Processing*, 25(5), 1431-1450.

[2] Sprague, M. & M. Jonkman, J. & Jonkman, B. (2015). FAST Modular Framework for Wind Turbine Simulation: New Algorithms and Numerical Examples. In: *Proc. 33rd Wind Energy Symposium*. Kissimmee, Florida.

[3] Oliveira, G. & Magalhães, F. & Cunha, A. & Caetano, E. (2018). Continuous dynamic monitoring of an onshore wind turbine, *Engineering Structures*, 164, 22-39.

[4] Maes, K. & Iliopoulos, A. & Weijtjens, W. & Devriendt, C. & Lombaert, G. (2016). Dynamic strain estimation for fatigue assessment of an offshore monopile wind turbine using filtering and modal expansion algorithms. *Mechanical Systems and Signal Processing*. 76.

[5] Tcherniak, D. & Chr Larsen, G. (2013). Application of OMA to an operating wind turbine: Now including vibration data from the blades. In: *Proc. 5th International Operational Modal Analysis Conference, IOMAC 2013*, Guimarães, Portugal.

IOMAC'19

8th International Operational Modal Analysis Conference

2019 May13-15 Copenhagen

LONG-TERM MODAL BEHAVIOUR ASSESSMENT OF WIND TURBINE DRIVETRAINS

P.J. Daems [1], *N. Gioia* [2], *C. Peeters* [3], *J. Helsen* [4], *P. Guillaume* [5]

[1] PhD Student, Vrije Universiteit Brussel, pieter-jan.daems@vub.be
[2] PhD Student, Vrije Universiteit Brussel, ngioia@vub.be
[3] PhD Student, Vrije Universiteit Brussel, cedric.peeters@vub.be
[4] Professor, Vrije Universiteit Brussel, jan.helsen@vub.be
[5] Professor, Vrije Universiteit Brussel, patrick.guillaume@vub.be

ABSTRACT

Over the last years Noise, Vibration and Harshness (NVH) problems have become important drivers in the design of wind turbine drivetrains. The knowledge of an accurate modal model is critical to tackle these issues. In this context, Operational Modal Analysis (OMA) is a commonly used method, as it allows to characterize the dynamic response behaviour of machines for their most important operating points. One of the most stringent limitations at present day is that processing vibration data classically requires user interaction. This paper investigates an automated OMA methodology. Long-term data of an offshore wind turbine will be processed to illustrate the developed automated algorithms. As vibration data of rotating machines is processed, there needs to be dealt with harmonic content. To this end, cepstral liftering and Order Based Modal Analysis (OBMA) will be used. After this pre-processing step, a p-LSCF algorithm will be used to perform the parameter estimation. Finally, the modal estimates will automatically be tracked to monitor their evolution in order to be able to deduce correlations between the operating regime of the turbine and the dynamic behaviour.

Keywords: Automatic Operational Modal Analysis, Wind turbine drivetrain, Harmonics, Machine learning, Noise Vibration and Harshness

1. INTRODUCTION

In recent years, the capacity of installed wind energy has rapidly been increasing. Especially the construction of offshore wind turbines is becoming increasingly popular, as the wind is steadier at sea than inland. A big challenge of these offshore farms however remains to reduce the Operation and Maintenance (O&M) costs. To this end, a so-called up-scaling trend is seen; the turbines are increased in size. This has as consequence that the produced power of the machine will increase, as the area swept by the blades will be bigger [1]. It is assumed that this decrease in number of machines per Mega-Watt results in a decrease of O&M costs of the wind farm [2]. This up-scaling trend however presents some additional design challenges, as it results in bigger (non quasi-static) loads on turbine components. This dynamic loading can significantly influence the machine lifetime and is moreover strongly related to the operating conditions of the machine [3]. The wide variability in these conditions makes it difficult to correctly model and predict the loading. Therefore, a design solely based on simulation models cannot be considered adequate. At present day, the models are validated by performing measurements either in field or in laboratory conditions. These aim to observe the prototypes over short periods in which specific operating conditions are captured. Within the context of the Internet of Things (IoT), a new design process is currently being developed, i.e. one where an updated model (digital twin) is obtained on the basis of the continuously incoming data stream of entire production fleets. This design process would have as added benefit that data will be acquired in all the different conditions at which the turbines operate. Moreover, it would allow to track the changes in dynamic behaviour machines experience in their lifetime. This new design process however requires that a set of smart algorithms is available that can process the incoming stream of (vibration) data completely autonomously.

In the context of continuously processing vibration data, Operational Modal Analysis (OMA) is a powerful methodology, as it allows to estimate the modal model of rotating machinery in their real operating conditions [4]. This experimental model can then be benchmarked with the simulation, which allows to update the model in case there are significant deviations. OMA is however based on the assumption that the input forces are white noise [5]. This is not the case in the field of rotating machinery . Several excitation sources can be present: known excitation forces (shaker, hammer), unknown stochastic forces (wind, waves, etc.) and unknown deterministic forces due to self-excitation of the structure. These deterministic forces result in erroneous modal estimates if the raw measurement data is not pre-processed to reduce the influence of the harmonic content [6]. OMA moreover also assumes time-invariance of the system, which is also violated as a wind turbine consists of different subsystems rotating with respect to one another. In this paper, a methodology will be discussed in order to tackle these challenges. The presented algorithms are automated in order to facilitate the autonomous processing of large data quantities.

2. METHODOLOGY AND THEORETICAL BACKGROUND

2.1. Dealing with the time-invariance of the system

Wind turbines are characterized by a wide variability in their operating conditions. This implies different loading on the machine components. A wind turbine moreover has several subsystems that allow to ensure that the turbine is directly facing the wind direction (yaw) and allow to control the amount of wind captured by the blades (pitch). This clearly demonstrates the time-variance of the system. The data therefore needs to be pre-processed in order to satisfy the fundamental assumptions of OMA. The approach used in this work makes use of machine learning methodologies in order to divide the data into blocks wherein the system can be considered time-invariant. This is done by observing different operating parameters, available from dedicated measurement systems (e.g. encoders, SCADA, etc.). The first step comprises of the automatic detection of certain events such as run-up and coast-down signals in time series data of the speed. This is done by using frequent pattern mining. In the initial learning phase of the algorithm, several events of interest are annotated manually. Afterwards, the patterns available in these are extracted to identify events that are sufficiently similar. From this new set of identified events, more frequent patterns can be extracted, allowing the algorithm to iteratively improve in identifying the different events. Once this is done on a sufficient amount of training data, the frequent patterns can be assumed to be representative for the different events. This means that transfer learning can then be used in order to identify events in different datasets without requiring to annotate reference events manually. A major challenge in this approach is the fact that there is significant variability in the different events due to the variable ambient conditions. This is taken into account in two different ways. First, the time series is binned. Second, the pattern recognition does not take place by requiring an exact match in pattern. It rather imposes that the distance between the reference patterns and the mined patterns is closer than a certain predefined threshold.

These results are exported into a no-SQL database in order to be able to assess the operating conditions for the different datasets (rotating, run-up, coast-down, standstill) automatically. Afterwards, more post-processing can be done in order to not only do the classification based on speed, but also on several more physical parameters (e.g. pitch, yaw, power).

2.2. Reduction of the harmonic influence

Now that there has been dealt with the time-variance of the system, there still needs to be dealt with the harmonic content in the signal. In this work, cepstral liftering is used for processing data from the machines operating at near constant speed, whereas Order Based Modal Analysis is used to process run-up or coast-down data. This shows the importance of being able to automatically assess the operating conditions of the rotating machine (Section 2.1.), as this determines the needed pre-processing.

2.2.1. *Cepstral liftering*

Cepstral liftering is a procedure that is based on transforming the signal from the time domain to the quefrency domain by means of a double application of the Fourier transform [7].

$$C_c(\tau) = \mathscr{F}^{-1} log(\mathscr{F}(X(t))) = \mathscr{F}^{-1}[ln(A(f)) + j\phi(f)] \tag{1}$$

In this equation, X(t) is the original signal in the time domain and A(f) and ϕ(f) are respectively the amplitude and the phase of the frequency domain signal. By setting the phase to zero in Equation (1), the formulation of the real cepstrum can be obtained (2):

$$C_r(\tau) = \mathscr{F}^{-1} ln(A(f)) \tag{2}$$

This ensures the possibility of going back to the time domain. The power of the cepstral lifter is based on the observation that the modal content is concentrated at low quefrencies, whereas the harmonic content is concentrated at higher quefrencies. By applying a low-pass lifter in this domain, the influence of the harmonic content is greatly reduced, allowing to perform OMA on the liftered signal [8].

2.2.2. *Order Based Modal Analysis (OBMA)*

OBMA uses run-up/coast-down data of rotary machinery in order to identify the physical poles of the system even in the presence of harmonics. During a run-up/coast-down, the measured response is mainly caused by rotational excitation. These considerations justify the idea to perform OMA on tracked orders rather than on the overall spectrum [9]. OBMA considers the run-up/coast-down as a multi-sine sweep excitation. In this algorithm, advanced order tracking techniques are combined with OMA. For rotating machinery, these orders are identified as the multiples or fractions of the rotational speed. The Order Tracking theory estimates the amplitude and the phase of the orders for varying rotational speed [10]. Two multi-sine signals are extracted when performing the order extraction. The first one is a frequency modulated sine wave signal with unitary amplitude. The frequency modulation is constructed to be synchronous with the excitation coming from the source. The second multi-sine is both amplitude and frequency modulated. These two signals are used respectively as an input signal and an output signal for the estimation of the FRF using an H_1 estimator.

2.3. Modal parameter estimation

A poly-reference least-square complex frequency-domain (p-LSCF) estimator is used in this work to perform the modal parameter estimation. An in-depth theoretical background on this algorithm can be found in [11]. This estimator is used as it generates a cleaner stabilisation diagram compared to other estimators such as stochastic subspace identification (SSI) or least-squares complex exponential (LSCE) methods. This makes automating the pole selection in the stabilisation diagram easier. The automated methodology is implemented based on different works in literature, such as ([12],[13]).

2.4. Modal tracking

After having performed the modal parameter estimation on different datasets, it is often of interest to be able to track the evolution of the modal parameters as a function of time and operating conditions. Classically, this is done by defining a so-called baseline of modes, i.e. a subset of modes of which the evolution has to be tracked. After this is done, the different poles are linked together using their match in frequency, damping and Modal Assurance Criterion (MAC) ([13],[14]). The MAC is defined as:

$$MAC(\phi_r, \phi_s) = \frac{|\phi_r^H \cdot \phi_s|^2}{(\phi_r^H \cdot \phi_s)(\phi_s^H \cdot \phi_r)} \quad (3)$$

In this equation, ϕ_r and ϕ_s are the two mode shapes associated with poles p_r and p_s and ^{H} is the Hermetian transpose. A problem with classical tracking algorithms is that the baseline is often pre-imposed, i.e. defined manually by having prior knowledge on the modal model (through previous measurement campaigns or simulation models). Moreover, they require the definition of a set of threshold parameters in frequency and MAC deviation in order to do the tracking. These parameters can significantly influence the tracking performance.

In this work, a fully automated tracking algorithm is implemented. First, a combination of clustering steps is used in order to define a baseline of modes to track in the different operating conditions of the machine under investigation. Due to the clustering routines, it is possible to define a set of statistical features for each cluster. Second, a classifier is used in order to classify the modes detected into the previously constructed baseline. In this step, the statistical boundaries are used to automatically define different threshold distances for the different modes. This allows to get an objective definition of these values such that these no longer influence the quality of the analysis. As the dynamic behaviour is expected to change depending on the operating conditions of the machine, a separate tracking procedure is done for each regime. Afterwards, a qualitative comparison can be made between the different results.

3. RESULTS

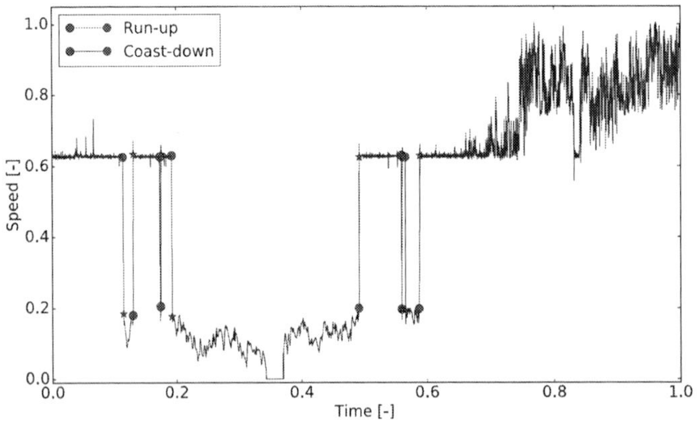

Figure 1: Speed profile of the wind turbine with automatically detected events. Axes values normalized for confidentiality reasons.

To illustrate the performance of the previously discussed algorithms, a stream of vibration data of a gearbox of a wind turbine will be processed automatically. This particular application is chosen for several reasons. First, the design of this component is crucial to avoid NVH problems. Second, the gearbox of a wind turbine consists of several gear stages, meaning that a significant amount of non-stationary harmonic content is present in the signals, allowing to showcase that the correct working of both the cepstral liftering and OBMA for a structure with significant complexity.

An example of a speed profile is shown in Figure 1. This is a subsignal of a multi-month measurement campaign which contains a significant amount of run-up and coast-down events, allowing to illustrate the entire processing chain. The first step is to detect these events in time series data, which will allow to process them using OBMA. The remaining (quasi) steady-state vibration data is grouped into three clusters, corresponding to the turbine operating at 1) idling, 2) intermediate speed and 3) nominal speed. For run-ups or coast-downs, the first and second harmonic of the intermediate speed shaft are tracked in order to be able to extract the modal parameters in frequency ranges that overlap with the one investigated with the OMA methodology with cepstral liftering.

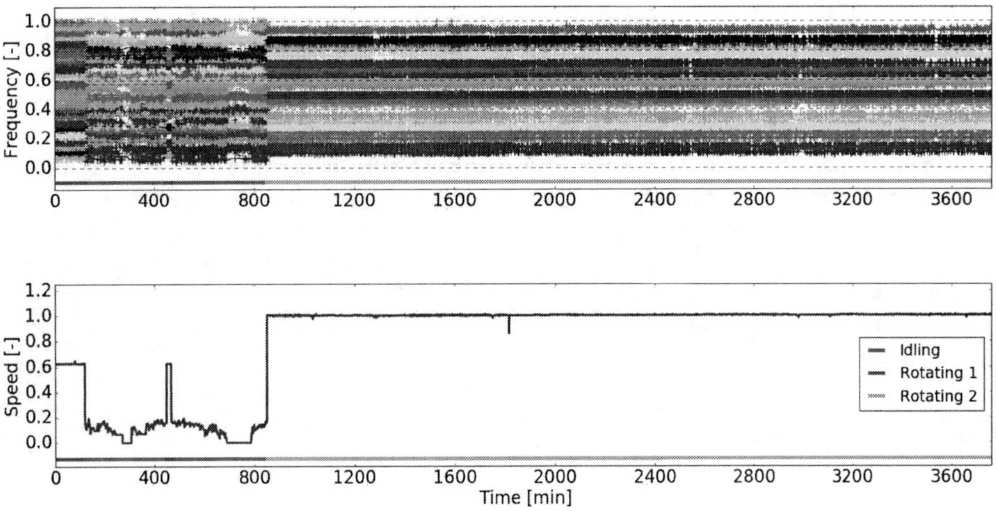

Figure 2: Results of the tracking algorithm for the different operating conditions. Axes values normalized for confidentiality reasons.

The performance of the tracking algorithm on the steady-state data can be seen in Figure 2. It can be seen that a high modal density is obtained in each of the operating regimes. It can also be noted that the tracking algorithm processes each operating regime separately, allowing to take the non-linear behavior of the turbine into account. Moreover, it should be noted that number of retrieved modes drops significantly when there was a rotor lock (zones at zero rpm), showing the benefit of testing in rotating or idling conditions.

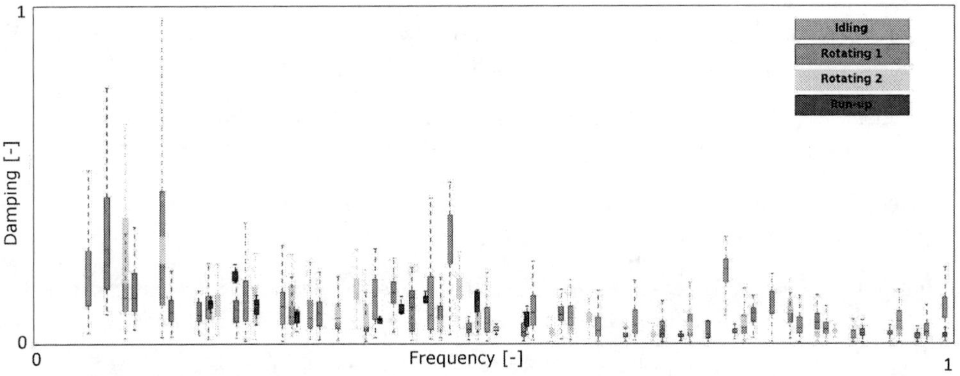

Figure 3: Comparison between the modal parameters obtained in the different operating regimes. Axes values normalized for confidentiality reasons.

A final summarizing plot between the values obtained in the four different investigated operating conditions can be seen in Figure 3. It can be noted that the estimated damping ratio is subject to a significant variability, even at the same operating speed. This is due to the fact that the damping will in reality not only be influenced by the operating speed of the turbine, but also by other operational parameters such as torque, pitch, yaw, etc. This shows the need of further coupling these results with SCADA and performing regression analyses in order to get an objective feeling on how the operating regime of the machine influences its dynamic behaviour.

4. CONCLUSIONS

This paper has presented a methodology for autonomously processing vibration data of rotating machinery. The implemented approach has been validated by processing vibration data of a wind turbine drivetrain. Special focus was given on how to automatically assess the operating condition of the machine and on how to deal with the harmonic content in the signal. To assess the operating conditions and to extract run-up and coast-down signals, a machine learning approach based on pattern mining and pattern recognition was implemented. Afterwards, two different methodologies to deal with the harmonic content in the vibration data were compared with one another. The entire processing chain shows promising results, as a good modal density is obtained for the different operating regimes. This fully automated approach can open the doors towards the processing of long-term vibration data, allowing smarter design approaches by obtaining additional design insights based on long-term field measurements for entire fleets of machines.

ACKNOWLEDGEMENTS

The authors would like to acknowledge the financial support of VLAIO (Flemish Agency for Innovation & Entrepreneurship) through the SBO project HYMOP and the SIM project MaSiWEC.

REFERENCES

[1] Wilson, C. (2012). "Up-scaling, formative phases, and learning in the historical diffusion of energy technologies." In *Energy Policy*, 50, 81-94.

[2] Helsen, J., Vanhollebeke, F., Vandepitte, D., & Desmet, W. (2012, September). Some trends and challenges in wind turbine upscaling. In *Proceedings of ISMA International Conference On Noise And Vibration 2012* (pp. ID-593).

[3] N. Gioia, P. Daems, C. Peeters, M. El-Kafafy, P. Guillaume, and J. Helsen, "Influence of the harmonics on the modal behavior of wind turbine drivetrains," In *Rotating Machinery, Vibro-Acoustics & Laser Vibrometry, Volume 7* (pp. 231-238). Springer, Cham.77

[4] Reynders, E. (2012). System identification methods for (operational) modal analysis: review and comparison. In *Archives of Computational Methods in Engineering*, 19(1), 51-124.

[5] Cauberghe, B. (2004). Applied frequency-domain system identification in the field of experimental and operational modal analysis. *PhD thesis*, VUB, Brussel.

[6] Pintelon, R., Peeters, B., & Guillaume, P. (2008). Continuous-time operational modal analysis in the presence of harmonic disturbances. In *Mechanical Systems and Signal Processing*, 22(5), 1017-1035.

[7] Randall, R. B., Sawalhi, N., & Coats, M. (2011). A comparison of methods for separation of deterministic and random signals. In *International Journal of Condition Monitoring*, 1(1), 11-19.

[8] Randall, R. B. (2017). A history of cepstrum analysis and its application to mechanical problems. In *Mechanical Systems and Signal Processing*, 97, 3-19.

[9] E. Di Lorenzo, S. Manzato, B. Peeters, F. Vanhollebeke, W. Desmet, and F. Marulo, "Order-based modal analysis: a modal parameter estimation technique for rotating machineries," In *6th International Operational Modal Analysis Conference Proceedings*, pp. 325–332, 2015.

[10] E. Di Lorenzo, S. Manzato, F. Vanhollebeke, S. Goris, B. Peeters, Bart, W. Desmet and M. Francesco, "Dynamic characterization of wind turbine gearboxes using Order-Based Modal Analysis", In *Proceedings of international conference on noise and vibration engineering (ISMA2014)*, pp. 4349-4362, 2014.

[11] Peeters, B., & Van der Auweraer, H. "PolyMAX: a revolution in operational modal analysis". In *1st International Operational Modal Analysis Conference*, Copenhagen, Denmark, 2005

[12] Chauhan, S., & Tcherniak, D. "Clustering approaches to automatic modal parameter estimation" In *Proceedings, International Modal Analysis Conference (IMAC).*

[13] Magalhaes, F., Cunha, A., & Caetano, E. "Online automatic identification of the modal parameters of a long span arch bridge". In *Mechanical Systems and Signal Processing*, 23(2), pp. 316-329, 2009

[14] El-Kafafy, M., Devriendt, C., Guillaume, P., & Helsen, J. (2017). "Automatic tracking of the modal parameters of an offshore wind turbine drivetrain system". In *Energies*, 10, 2017

IOMAC'19

8th International Operational Modal Analysis Conference
2019 May13-15 Copenhagen

STRAIN-BASED OPERATIONAL MODAL ANALYSIS FOR WIND TURBINE BLADES

E. Di Lorenzo [1], S. Manzato [2], M.M. Luczak [3], B. Peeters [4], and K. Branner [5]

[1] Senior Research Engineer, Siemens Industry Software NV, Interleuvenlaan 68, 3001, Leuven, Belgium, emilio.dilorenzo@siemens.com.
[2] Product Manager Structures, Siemens Industry Software NV, Interleuvenlaan 68, 3000, Leuven, Belgium
[3] Senior Researcher, DTU Wind Energy, Frederiksborgvej 399, 4000, Roskilde, Denmark.
[4] Product Line Manager Structures & Environmental, Siemens Industry Software NV, Interleuvenlaan 68, 3001, Leuven, Belgium.
[5] Senior Researcher, DTU Wind Energy, Frederiksborgvej 399, 4000, Roskilde, Denmark.

ABSTRACT

The aim of this paper is to explore alternative ways to determine the vibration characteristics of wind turbine blades to reduce the amount and duration of needed tests without compromising the quality of the retrieved information. Applied test setup configuration, test specimen mounting and measurement equipment are known to affect the test results. The investigation concerns the use of Operational Modal Analysis (OMA) method together with the existing instrumentation for fatigue and static testing. The wind turbine blade is clamped to the support structure and instrumented by means of many strain gauges. A so-called pull and release test can be performed, and the modal parameters can be obtained by analyzing the measured strains during this type of test. Numerical correlation can then be performed with respect to the validated FE model of the clamped blade allowing to enrich the acquired information.

Keywords: Operational Modal Analysis, Wind turbine blade, Strain measurements

1. INTRODUCTION

Wind turbine blades are subjected to highly irregular loading conditions during their lifetime. These are mainly due to the turbulent flow, gravity direction changing relative to the blades and inertia loading during accelerating or decelerating of the wind turbine. Both flapwise and edgewise directions of the blades are facing high loads during operation. The main source of flapwise loads is the aerodynamic force, whereas the edgewise loads are mainly due to the gravity. The flapwise loads are carried by the main spar (or girder) while edgewise loads are taken partially by spar and partially by reinforcement in the leading and trailing edges. The rest of the blade is usually constructed as sandwich panels with multi-axial laminates from glass fibre reinforced polymer (GFRP) as skins and a core from foam or balsa, ensuring low mass, resistance to torsion and buckling [1].

Currently wind turbine blade certification requires static and fatigue tests on the blade, to assess whether the blade can sustain the applied loads. Blade manufactures are required to carry out static and fatigue tests of full-scale blades prior to their deployment for commercial use according to international standards [2–4] and guidelines [5]. The static test applies the appropriate extreme load in all directions, i.e. leading edge, trailing edge, suction side and pressure side. The whole static test is then repeated after the fatigue test to ensure that the blade can handle extreme loads after it has been subjected to high cyclic loading. Dynamic tests are limited to the identification of the first and second flapwise natural frequencies, and of the first edgewise one. Tests aimed at damping and mode shapes estimation are only optional. However, a deeper understanding of the dynamic behavior of these structures is crucial to better analyze stability problems and failure modes, especially considering the continuing trend to further increase the size, complexity and flexibility of the blades.

Extensive measurement campaigns have been carried out at the DTU Wind Energy (former Risø National Laboratory) with different boundary conditions and instrumentation. In a first phase, the blade has been suspended in a so-called free-free condition and instrumented by using accelerometers to validate the Finite Element (FE) model in terms of modal parameters (e.g. natural frequencies, damping ratios and mode shapes). The results of the measurement campaign have been extensively described in [6, 7]. In a second phase, a nominally identical blade has been clamped to a rigid block through the circular interface plate in a flapwise configuration and instrumented by using strain gauges. A pull-release test has been performed and Operational Modal Analysis (OMA) technique has been applied to the strain measurements to retrieve the modal parameters. This is a first step towards OMA under a fatigue test in order to gain additional information about changes to the structure during the fatigue cycle. The acquired signals could be reused for enriching the available modal properties information and for improving the quality of the numerical models, as both cases yielded a comparably good correlation with the blade Finite Element model.

First of all, a brief description associated to the combination of OMA and strain measurements (the so-called Strain-based Operational Modal Analysis) will be provided. Afterwards the test setup and the instrumentation will be described and finally the results of the activity will be given.

2. STRAIN-BASED OPERATIONAL MODAL ANALYSIS

2.1. Strain-based modal analysis

Traditionally, modal analysis and testing has been associated with the use of classical sensors such as accelerometers or Laser Doppler Vibrometers that measure, respectively, the accelerations and the velocities on the object surface. In recent years the use of measured strains is gaining popularity and many authors [8, 9] investigated the use of strain measurements for estimating the modal parameters in several cases. The advantage of using strain gauges in our case is also related to the fact that a wind turbine blade to be used for certification test is instrumented by means of many strain sensors for static testing, fatigue testing and lifetime prediction. The fatigue testing verifies that the blade is able to withstand the operating loads for a full design life (about 20-30 years). Loads can be applied on one or two axes and the methods differs among different labs, while single axis fatigue test is currently in the standard.

In its first formulation, the Strain-based Modal Analysis was applied in cases in which the input force is well-known and Frequency Response Functions (FRFs) can be calculated. In this work the step further consists in applying the technique to an operational environment in which the input is unknown. This means moving from Experimental Modal Analysis (EMA) to Operational Modal Analysis (OMA).

In order to obtain the strain modal formulation, one can start with the fundamental theory of modal analysis. Modal theory states that the displacement on a given coordinate can be approximated by the summation of a n number of modes, as shown in Equation (1).

$$u(t) = \sum_{i=1}^{n} \phi_i q_i(t) \tag{1}$$

where $u(t)$ is the displacement response in x direction, ϕ_i is the ith displacement vibration mode and q_i is the generalized modal coordinate. For small displacements, given the theory of elasticity, the strain/displacement relationship is given by Equation (2).

$$\varepsilon_x = \frac{\partial}{\partial x} u \tag{2}$$

Similarly the same relationship exists between the strain vibration modes and the displacement modes (Equation (3)).

$$\psi_i = \frac{\partial}{\partial x} \phi_i \tag{3}$$

Taking into account the last two relationships, Equation (1) can be rewritten as Equation (4).

$$\varepsilon(t) = \sum_{i=1}^{n} \psi_i q_i(t) \tag{4}$$

Furthermore, the relationship between the generalized modal coordinate q and the input force F is explicated in Equation (5), where m_i, c_i and k_i are the ith modal mass, modal damping and modal stiffness and ω is the excitation frequency.
Substituting Equation (5) into Equation (4), the relationship between a force input and a strain output in terms of displacement and strain modes is represented in Equation (6).

$$q_i = \Lambda_i^{-1} \phi_i F \text{ , with } \Lambda_i = (-\omega^2 m_i + j\omega c_i + k_i) \tag{5}$$

$$\varepsilon_i = \sum_{i=1}^{n} \psi_i \Lambda_i^{-1} \phi_i F \tag{6}$$

Finally, Equation (7) represents the Strain Frequency Response Function (SFRF) in the matrix form.

$$[H^{\varepsilon}] = \sum_{i=1}^{n} \Lambda_i^{-1} \{\psi_i\}\{\phi_i\} = [\psi][\Lambda]^{-1}[\phi]^T \tag{7}$$

The matrix $[H^{\varepsilon}]$ has N_i columns which correspond to the number of excitation points (or the number of inputs) and N_o rows which are the number of strain gauge measurement points (or the number of output measurements).
Few considerations need to be taken into account with respect to the strain modal theory. In fact:

- The SFRF matrix is not symmetric and, as consequence, there is no reciprocity in strain modal analysis;
- Any column of the SFRF matrix contains all information about the strain modes, whereas any row contains information about the displacement mode;
- In order to obtain the strain mode shapes, a fixed excitation points needs to be used and the strain responses should be measured;
- By using roving impact hammer testing the displacement mode shapes can be obtained;

- The similarity of the strain modal formulation and the displacement modal formulation means that the same identification can be used for both techniques.

One of the main advantages of the use of strain gauges with respect to classical accelerometers-based modal analysis is related with the ability to obtain both strain mode shapes and displacement mode shapes with the same type of sensor. This is not achievable with the use of accelerometers. On the other hand several disadvantages needs also to be mentioned. It is, in fact, harder to instrument because the sensors need to be bonded to the structure surface and they are usually not reusable. Furthermore, when compared to accelerometers, a worse signal-to-noise ratio is achieved.

2.2. Operational Modal Analysis

In this work, the blade was pulled and then released to analyze its free vibrations. For this reason the load to which it was subjected could not be measured, and the Operational Modal Analysis, also known as output-only modal analysis, technique was used to estimate the modal parameters, more specifically, Operational Polymax was employed.
Several assumptions need to be fulfilled in order to apply successfully the technique: the system must be linear time invariant and the excitation forces have to be represented by a flat white noise spectrum in the frequency band of interest. The main difference with the classical modal analysis technique is due to the use of auto- and cross-correlations and auto- and cross-powers in place of impulse and frequency responses. Some reference signals need to be considered to perform the identification procedure. In the blade test case, the main hypothesis for applying OMA was respected as the data was acquired during the pull-release test in which the blade was free to oscillate.
The recording of the strain gauges was then used to calculate the strain auto- and cross-spectra that serve as input for the Operational Polymax algorithm.
The Polymax method, also known as the polyreference least-squares complex frequency-domain method, has been introduced as a new standard for modal parameter estimation by Peeters et al. [10]. It is a technique based on a weighted least-squares approach by using multiple-input-multiple-output frequency response functions as primary data. First a stabilisation diagram can be constructed and frequencies, damping and participation information can be extracted. Afterwards the mode shapes are found in a second least-squares step, based on the selection of the stable poles. The main advantage of such a method, if compared to other methods, is the very clear stabilisation diagram that can be obtained allowing simple stable poles identification.
The Polymax method has been extended for performing Operational Modal Analysis [11]. In this case it requires output spectra as primary data. Under the assumption of white noise excitation, output spectra can be modelled in a very similar way as Frequency Response Functions (FRFs).

3. RESULTS ANALYSIS

3.1. Test setup

The object of the study is a 14.3m long wind turbine blade made of glass fiber reinforced plastics. Multiple modal tests were carried out to identify the most reliable and time-efficient technique for estimating the modal parameters of the structure under test.

Initially the blade was suspended using two elastic chords for reproducing the free-free boundary conditions. The boundary conditions need to be known to validate the FE model. The results of the measurement campaign have been extensively described in [6, 7].

A second test on a nominally identical blade has been performed by using 76 strain gauges to instrument the blade. The deformation was measured at all these locations during a so-called pull and release test which is done by clamping the blade to a rigid steel-reinforced concrete block through the circular interface plate in a flapwise configuration and by pulling it towards the floor, as shown in Figure 1. The applied force and displacements were measured through a reel cable extensometer. Once the blade tip had reached the desired displacement, it was released, and the free vibration response recorded.

Afterwards, the measurements from the 76 strain gauges present on the blade were imported into Simcenter Testlab for further processing.

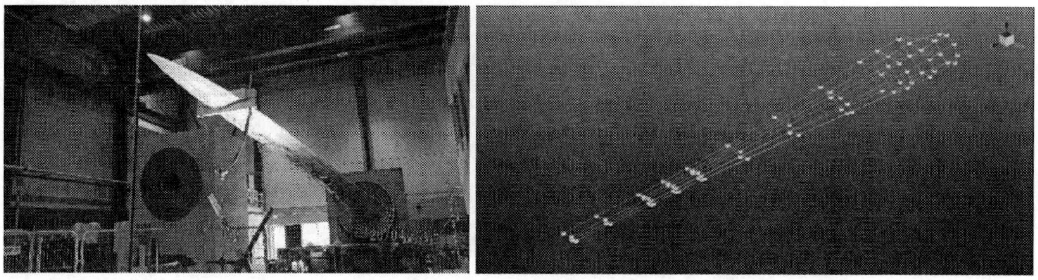

Figure 1. View of the wind turbine blade setup during the pull and release test instrumented with strain gauges (left); test geometry by using strain gauges in clamped conditions (right).

3.2. Test analysis

Four different tests were performed by changing the load at which the wind turbine blade was subjected: 1.50kN, 2.17kN, 2.65kN and 3.17kN. The loads were applied about 1m from the blade root. Twelve sections from the blade root to the blade tip were instrumented with 4 or 8 strain gauges per section. The test geometry and setup are shown in Figure 1.

Time data were acquired for about 2 minutes and with 200Hz sampling frequency and post-processed to be able to derive the strain mode shapes by using Operational Polymax. An exponential window with 10% exponent was applied to the strain gauge time histories to calculate their auto- and cross-spectra, with a frequency resolution of 0.195Hz. Figure 2 shows the acquired time histories for four different points (1, 3, 5, 7) at the same station (Sec12.0) along the blade. The difference in the static value measured by the strain gauges before and after the measurements can here be underlined.

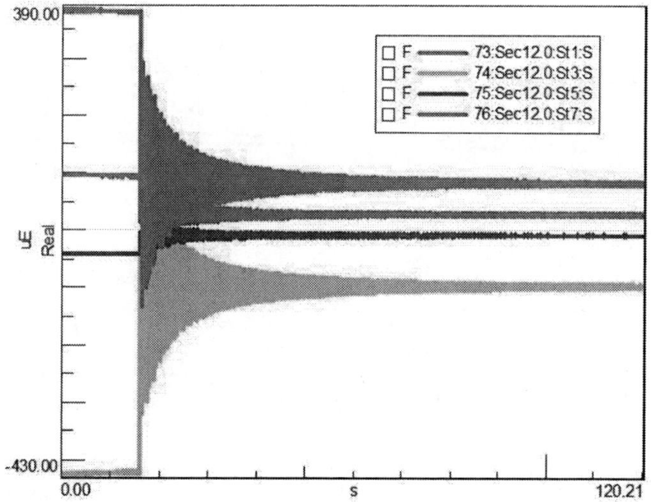

Figure 2. Strain gauges time histories for the points at the blade tip during pull-release test.

The calculated cross-power spectra for the same points are shown in Figure 3. Figure 4 illustrates the comparison of the calculated auto-power spectra for a single measured point at the four different force levels. It can be underlined that the wind turbine blade is quite linear in the analysed frequency range since there are no peak distortions by increasing the force levels.

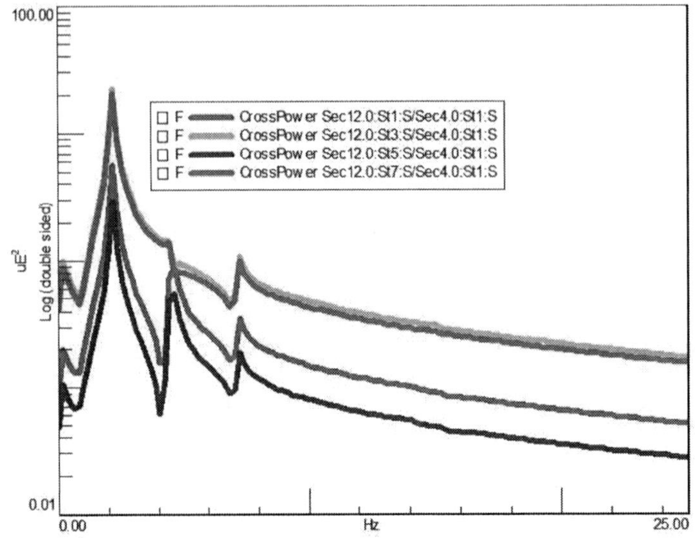

Figure 3. Calculated cross-powers for the points at the blade tip during pull-release test by using as reference the point at the Section 4.0.

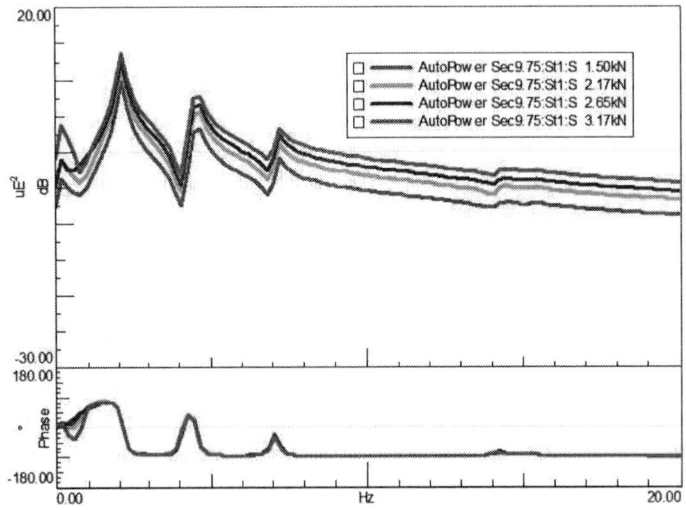

Figure 4. Auto-powers related to the point at 9.75m from the root section at different force levels (1.50kN, 2.17kN, 2.65kN and 3.17kN).

3.3. Test results

The main modes are clearly identified by the peaks in the frequency domain. Both natural frequencies and damping ratios can be identified by using the Operational Polymax modal parameters estimator. On the other hand, it is more complicated to compare directly the strain mode shapes with the Finite Element (FE) modelling results. In fact, this step requires further post-processing analysis.

Figure 5 shows the first four strain mode shapes and their description (flapwise or edgewise). Both natural frequencies and damping ratios are compared in Table 1 and Table 2 along the tests by gradually increasing the loading conditions. The frequencies are also compared with the ones obtained from the

FE model clamped at the root. The FE model was previously validated in free-free conditions. The match in terms of natural frequencies values is very good, as shown in Table 1.

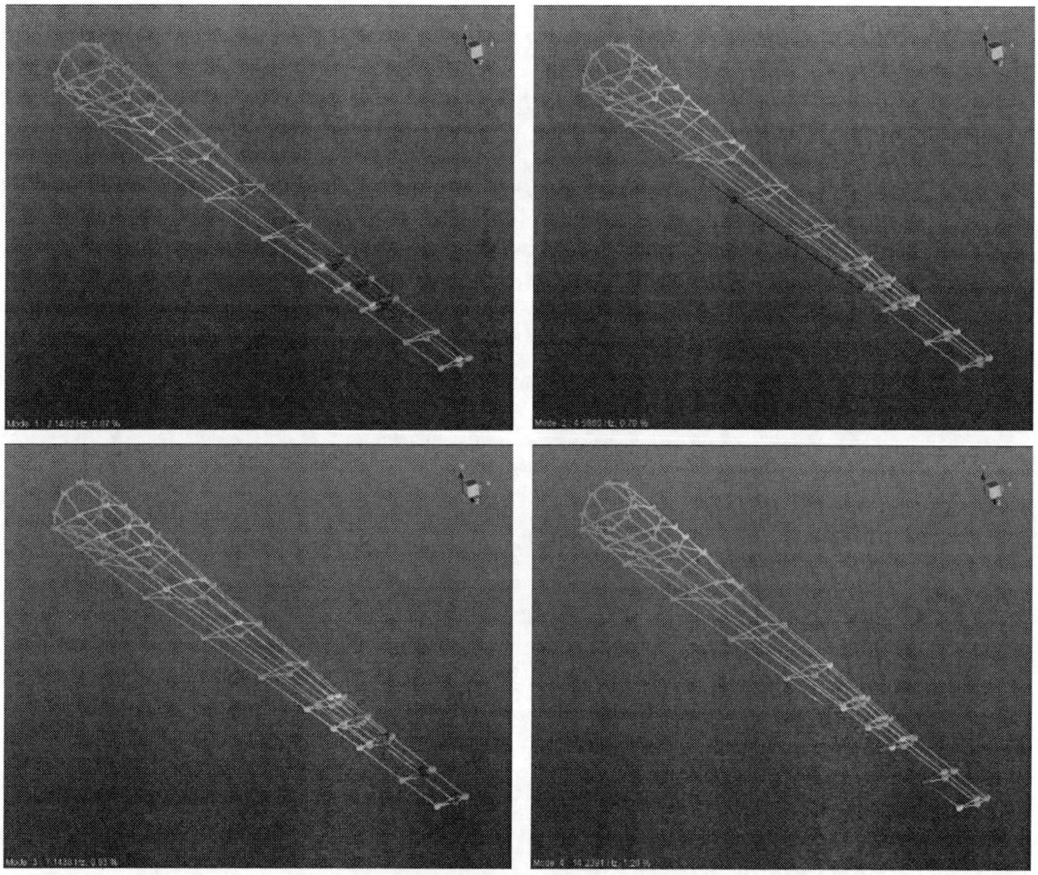

Figure 5. Strain mode shapes: 1st flapwise mode (top-left); 1st edgewise mode (top-right); 2nd flapwise mode (bottom-left); 2nd edgewise mode (bottom-right).

Table 1. Results of correlation analysis in terms of natural frequencies between tests at different loading conditions and simulation results in clamped conditions.

Mode	Natural frequencies				
	1.50kN [Hz]	2.17kN [Hz]	2.65kN [Hz]	3.17kN [Hz]	FE model [Hz]
1	2.15	2.15	2.15	2.14	2.38
2	4.56	4.56	4.56	4.56	4.20
3	7.14	7.14	7.14	7.14	7.35
4	14.23	14.24	14.24	14.25	12.59
5	15.33	15.33	15.32	15.24	14.37
6	25.19	25.24	25.30	25.70	22.69
7	33.41	33.35	33.29	33.54	29.42
8	37.02	37.06	37.07	37.21	31.58

IOMAC'19

8th International Operational Modal Analysis Conference
2019 May13-15 Copenhagen

VALIDATION OF VIRTUAL SENSING ON SUBSOIL STRAIN DATA OF AN OFFSHORE WIND TURBINE

M.Henkel [1], *W.Weijtjens* [2], *C.Devriendt* [3]

[1] M.Sc., Vrije Universiteit Brussel, maximilian.henkel@vub.be.

[2] Dr.Ir., Offshore Wind Infrastructure Lab Vrije Universiteit Brussel, wout.weijtjens@owi-lab.be.

[3] Prof.Dr.Ir., Offshore Wind Infrastructure Lab Vrije Universiteit Brussel, christof.devriendt@owi-lab.be.

ABSTRACT

Fatigue is the main design driver for offshore wind turbines on monopile foundations. With the first generation of farms reaching their design life structural reserves become apparent. Monitoring of the periodic strains at critical locations enables to assess the remaining useful lifetime. Typically, welded connections beneath the sea bed are determining the lifetime of the entire structure. Since no direct method e.g. visual inspection is feasible to analyze damage progress at these locations estimation methods are applied. Three turbines of the Belgian offshore wind farm Nobelwind were equipped with optical fiber strain gauges over the entire foundation length and with accelerometers on the turbine tower. In this contribution, a modal expansion algorithm is selected to reconstruct subsoil strain from accelerations measured on the tower. Within a short-term analysis strain estimations are validated against measurement data on submerged sensors and fatigue assessment is done on the validated data.

Keywords: Virtual Sensing, Fatigue Estimation, Measurement Data, Offshore Wind

1. INTRODUCTION

Offshore wind turbines (OWTs) are heavy dynamically loaded civil structures. The substructures experience the action of both wind and waves combined with the rotations of the wind turbine on top. The substructure design with the biggest market share for common water depths is so-called monopile foundation, which represents over 80% of all offshore wind turbines [1]. A monopile foundation is a single cylindrical steel pile with diameters ranging from 4 to 8 meter and lengths of up to 70 meter. These piles are considered to be relatively short with respect to their diameter, especially when compared to the piles typically found in offshore oil gas (OG). While industry usually still relies on engineering codes developed for OG industry in the 1970s[2][3] both the non-slender geometry of the monopile and the cyclic loads fall outside the original design codes. This limitation in design has led to an industry-wide mismatch between design expectations and the completed OWT. [4] reveals a common 10% underes-

timation of the first resonance frequency in a study on 400 offshore wind turbines. Resulting error in soil-pile response also influences the fatigue life of the turbine structure. The design of offshore wind turbines is driven by the fatigue of the substructure. Monopiles are designed in a way they can withstand 20 to 25 years of combined cyclic loading. In an optimized design, several welds are dimensioned to match this targeted lifetime. Generally, the most fatigue critical welds are found just below mudline. Since the monopile foundation has no structural redundancy the lifetime of the foundation is defined by the remaining life-time of the weld mostly damaged through fatigue. Rather than by relying on design expectations, updated information about this remaining life time is desired. Visual inspections on submerged welds are costly and below mudline unfeasible. Also the use of sensors to track fatigue progress is not common because of high costs of installation and maintenance combined with the risk to lose sensors while pile driving.
In this contribution, measurement data is used to learn about special characteristics of the strains on the submerged structure in order to emulate them. Precisely, measurement data of three monopiles from offshore wind equipped with strain gauges over their entire length is used to validate a method to estimate strains subsoil using a multi-band Modal decomposition and expansion algorithm. Within the subsequent fatigue assessment damage characteristics of submerged sensors are analyzed and the performance of the method is bench-marked.

2. MEASUREMENT SETUP

In the scope of the research project O&O Nobelwind three offshore wind turbines on monopile foundations were instrumented with a extensive monitoring system in the Nobelwind offshore wind farm.

2.1. Nobelwind

The Nobelwind offshore wind farm is situated in the Belgian North Sea consisting of fifty Vestas V112-3.3 MW turbines on monopile foundations. Generating power between 3 and 25 m/s wind speed these machines reach the rated output power at 13 m/s. For the Nobelwind measurement campaign three turbines were selected in the farm. The three turbines were chosen to reflect the dynamic and soil conditions of the entire farm. Among the selected turbines is the turbine at the lowest water depth and the deepest turbine in the farm. While two of the turbines were chosen at the opposite edges of the farm one is situated at one corner. The set of three turbines thus covers the expected range of frequencies as well as wind conditions.

2.2. Measurement setup

All three instrumented turbines received the same basic monitoring concept seen in 2(a) [5]. On the tower accelerometers (ACC) are mounted in three levels, the transition piece (TP) is equipped with two levels of resistive strain gauges and the monopile (MP) received optical strain gauges on several levels. The sensor levels on the monopiles differ between the three turbines to accommodate for differences in the design of the monopiles and different soil conditions. The monopiles were instrumented during monopile fabrication with 4 optical fiber lines. Each line is imprinted with 8 Bragg gratings. These Bragg gratings (FBGs) act as 8 localized strain sensors on a single optical fiber line and are positioned above and below the mud-line of the monopile foundation. Using FBG technology a total of 32 sensors was achieved with a minimal of required wiring. Note that the sensors had to be installed prior to the actual pile-driving of the turbine. To assure the sensors survived this process the subsoil sensors were covered with protective sheeting and a driving shoe. During installation some sensors failed during the pile-driving. However, the majority of fibers survived and all three monopiles have a functional monitoring set-up which is operational since August 2017.

Figure 1: (Left) The Nobelwind offshore wind farm, (Right) The finished monopile with 4 optical fibers.

2.3. Data Acquisition and Processing

The monitoring system sends a measurement file to an onshore server every ten minutes where it is paired with SCADA data. Before the data can be used for research purposes different pre-processing stages are applied. All strain gauge measurements contain offsets which can change over time. These offsets are removed using an in-house developed scheme for strain gauge calibration. Additionally, the strain sensors above water level have to be compensated for solar radiation. While the Bragg gratings allow to record strains at a sampling rate of $100Hz$ only low frequent strains are considered important for the fatigue analysis of the substructure. Thus, FBG data is sampled down to $12.5Hz$ after a filtering step to reduce high-frequent noise. The low pass filtering is performed by an eighth-order Butterworth filter with an upper frequency band of $4Hz$. The monitoring setup contains three separate systems: One for tower accelerometer and upper TP strain sensor $SGLAT017$, one for the lower strain gauge on the TP $SGLAT005$ and one for all fiber Bragg sensors e.g. $FBGLATmin017$. As a result these systems are not guaranteed to be synchronous. In fact, a slight drift between the clocks is discovered see Fig.2(b). This time dependent lag of the lower systems relative to the tower system was removed by correlating all strain gauges with the top strain gauge $SGLAT017$ for every data frame.

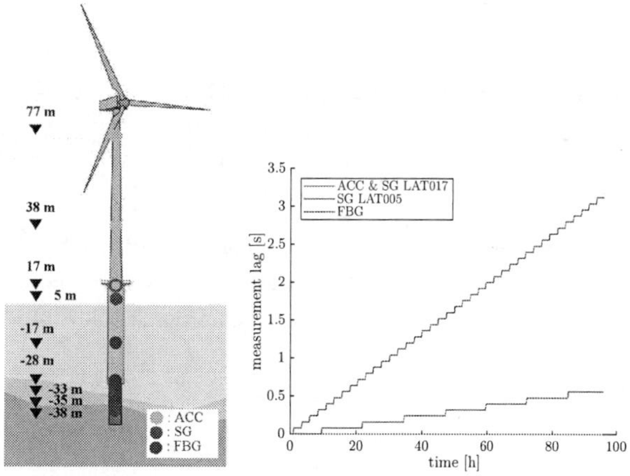

Figure 2: (Left) Schematic of the sensor setup at Nobelwind. (Right) Evolution of measurement lag of resistive strain gauges(brown) and FBGs(blue) over four days.

3. VIRTUAL SENSING

Virtual sensing is a generic term meaning a multitude of techniques which predict loads without direct measurements. For offshore wind different methods are further developed to estimate structural response by extrapolating measurement data of sensors in easily accessible locations. Response estimation algorithms predict stresses based on the dynamic modes and natural frequencies obtained from a linearized structural model. So-called joint input-state estimation (JISE), initially proposed in [6] and further developed in [7], estimates forces and corresponding states of the structural model based on filtering. Similarly, the Kalman filter estimates states based on a limited number of response measurements. JISE and Kalman filtering techniques are formulated in the state space, which allows to include damping and measurement uncertainties. Alternatively, the Modal Decomposition and Expansion (MDE) method assumes the structural response as a linear combination of the mode shape vectors and does not account for noise. Vibrations or strains are estimated without requiring knowledge of the natural frequencies and damping ratios [8, 9, 10, 11]. Modal expansion can be used both in a time domain or frequency domain representation. In a comparative study, Kalman filter, JISE and MDE were benchmarked [12] based on measurement data of an offshore wind turbine on monopile. [12] concludes on an acceptable performance in the prediction of acceleration responses despite use of the simplified linear modal model.

3.1. Modal decomposition and expansion

Modal decomposition defines the structural response as a linear combination of eigenvectors or mode shapes:

$$\vec{a}_m(t) = \sum_{i=1}^{n} \vec{\phi}_{i,m} q_i(t), \tag{1}$$

where $\vec{a}_m(t) \in \mathbb{R}^{n_m \times 1}$ is a vector that contains the n_m measured accelerations for each time instance t, n is the number of considered modes, $q_i(t) \in \mathbb{R}$ is the modal coordinate component of mode i, and $\vec{\phi}_{i,m} \in \mathbb{R}^{n_m \times 1}$ is the vector with the components of mode shape i at measurement locations m. These mode shapes can be derived either from numerical models or by operational modal analysis [8]. From Eq. (1), the modal coordinates quantifying the contribution of each mode are identified based on measured accelerations and the mode shape components at these locations. It follows:

$$\vec{q}(t) = \left(\mathbf{\Phi}_m^T \mathbf{\Phi}_m\right)^{-1} \mathbf{\Phi}_m^T \vec{a}_m(t) = \mathbf{\Phi}_m^\dagger \vec{a}_m(t), \tag{2}$$

where $\vec{q}(t) = \{q_1(t), q_2(t), \ldots, q_n(t)\}^T$ and $\mathbf{\Phi}_m = [\vec{\phi}_{1,m}, \vec{\phi}_{2,m}, \ldots, \vec{\phi}_{n,m}]$ combine the n considered mode shapes at the n_m measured degrees of freedom (DOFs). $\bullet^\dagger$ is the pseudo-inverse operator. It is pointed out that only for the number of measurements n_m, being equal or exceeding the number of considered modes n, Eq. (2) can be solved. For practical applications, this implies that the number of considered modes is always limited by the number of sensors installed to the structure.

Estimated modal coordinates derived from Eq. (2) are assumed to apply to the entire structure. Thus, Eq. (2) can be expanded to predict the accelerations and dynamic strains at any point as long as contained in the mode shape vectors obtained from a numerical model. The modal expansion at virtual sensor location p uses the following expression [8]:

$$\vec{\epsilon}^{\,p}_{dyn}(t) = \mathbf{\Phi}_{\epsilon p} \mathcal{L}^{-1} \left\{ \frac{1}{s^2} \mathcal{L} \left\{ \vec{q}(t) \right\} \right\}, \tag{3}$$

where $\mathbf{\Phi}_{\epsilon,p}$ comprises the mode shapes and strain mode shapes, respectively, of the n considered modes at the n_p DOFs, which coincide with the virtual sensor locations p. $\mathcal{L}\{\bullet\}$ and $\mathcal{L}^{-1}\{\bullet\}$ are the Laplace transformation and the inverse Laplace transformation, respectively.

In addition, the estimation of strains from acceleration measurements requires the double integration of accelerations to displacements. This double integration is performed on the estimated modal coordinates in the Laplace domain, resulting in the $1/s^2$ operation in Eq. (3).
However, during the double integration there is a considerable risk of blowing up frequency noise when approaching $0Hz$, resulting in erroneous predictions of displacement. As such [12] proposes to use a lower bound f_l for the acceleration data. The lower bound f_l is situated well below the first structural mode, while sufficiently high to avoid exaggerated low frequency contributions. From the high-pass

filtered acceleration data, the dynamic contribution of the strain extrapolation $\vec{\epsilon}^{p}_{dyn}$ is obtained through Eq. (3).
In [8] the band below f_l is then added using a static strain extrapolation. Instead of accelerometers, a single strain gauge level is used to extrapolate the quasi-static strain to all virtual sensors. The quasi-static estimation step is basically scaling the measured strain signal ϵ^{m}_{qs} with a deflection shape of the substructure $\vec{\phi}_{qs}$. This $\vec{\phi}_{qs}$ is derived from the low-pass filtered strain distribution on the monopile caused by a rotor top load where the upper filter bound is set to f_l.

$$\vec{\epsilon}^{p}_{qs}(t) = \vec{\phi}_{qs}\epsilon^{m}_{qs}(t) \tag{4}$$

The estimated strain with this dual-band MDE approach is thus calculated using following expression:

$$\vec{\epsilon}^{p}(t) = \vec{\epsilon}^{p}_{qs}(t) + \vec{\epsilon}^{p}_{dyn}(t) \tag{5}$$

3.2. Quality indicators

Reconstructed time series are evaluated using the Time Response Assurance Criterion (TRAC) and Frequency Response Assurance Criterion (FRAC). The TRAC checks the correlation between time domain signals, here predicted and measured stress $\vec{\sigma}^{p}(t)$ and $\vec{\sigma}(t)$ [13]. The TRAC returns single values for every virtual sensor location i ranging from 0 to 1, where values close to 1 imply a good agreement. The TRAC does not account for scaling errors between two signals but is suitable to detect phase shifts.

$$TRAC = \frac{[\vec{\sigma}(t)^{T}\vec{\sigma}^{p}(t)]^{2}}{[\vec{\sigma}(t)^{T}\vec{\sigma}(t)][\vec{\sigma}^{p}(t)^{T}\vec{\sigma}^{p}(t)]}, \tag{6}$$

where $\bullet^{T}$ denotes the transpose of the vector. In order to assess the estimated signal in the frequency-domain the FRAC is introduced. Similar to the TRAC, it returns the correlation between two signals but here transformed into frequency domain. With the FRAC the match between measurement and estimation can be assessed for a frequency band of interest. While the TRAC is unable to detect scaling errors an additional check with FRAC spots these because of different spectral densities.

$$FRAC = \frac{[\vec{\sigma}(f)^{H}\vec{\sigma}^{p}(f)]^{2}}{[\vec{\sigma}(f)^{H}\vec{\sigma}(t)][\vec{\sigma}^{p}(f)^{H}\vec{\sigma}^{p}(f)]}, \tag{7}$$

where $\bullet^{H}$ denotes the conjugate transpose of the complex frequency domain vector.
For fatigue assessment short-term damages($10min$) are calculated. First, sensor stresses are transformed into stresses in rotor plane (SS) and perpendicular (FA) using linear bending theory. Secondly, stress cycles are counted via Rainflow counting, followed by the linear damage accumulation as in Eq. (8). $n_{k,i}$ refers to the number of oscillations of frequency k on the virtual sensor location i for all time instances and $N_{k,i}$ is the assigned number of cycles to failure for stress range $\Delta\sigma_{k,i}$. Note, that no safety factors and stress concentration factors were applied. Rather than the total damage, the damage equivalent stress range $\Delta\sigma_{del,i}$, Eq. (10), is used as a quality indicator. It returns a single stress range that over $n_{del,i} = 10^{7}$ cycles will produce equal damage to the actual fatigue spectrum (9) [14]:

$$D_i = \sum_{k} \frac{n_{k,i}}{N_k} = \frac{1}{\bar{a}} \sum_{k} n_{k,i}\Delta\sigma^{m}_{k,i} \leq 1, \tag{8}$$

$$D_i = \frac{n_{del,i}}{N_{del,i}} = \frac{1}{\bar{a}} n_{del,i}\Delta\sigma^{m}_{del,i} \leq 1, \tag{9}$$

$$\Delta\sigma_{del,i} = \left(\frac{n_{del,i}}{\bar{a}D_i}\right)^{-\frac{1}{m}}, \tag{10}$$

where m is the negative inverse slope and $\bar{a}$ the intercept of S-N curve with N axis according to [15]. S-N curve D, $m = 3$, $\log \bar{a} = 11.687$, for free corrosion as defined in DNV GL RP-C203 [15] is applied to all welds for the sake of simplicity.

4. RESULTS

For this short-term validation of MDE measurement data of one turbine over a period of four days is used. The period is chosen in such a way that most operational conditions and a wide range of wind speeds would are present. This contribution uses a basic scheme of MDE as it would be used for strain predictions above water level.

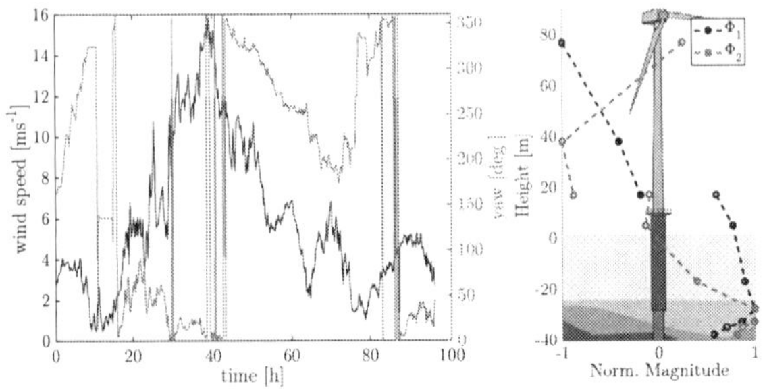

Figure 3: (Left) Wind speed(blue) versus time and yawing of turbine(orange) from ten minute SCADA data. (Right) Shapes of the first two structural modes as obtained from OMA.

4.1. Mode shape analysis

MDE requires the structural modes of the turbine. Since only the lowest frequent structural modes contribute considerably to fatigue the first two mode shapes are of most interest. In order to estimate stress MDE demands a mode shape component for every virtual sensor location. Thus, if no data of the estimation locations is available e.g. location is inaccessible mode shapes need to be obtained via finite element model. Within this contribution mode shapes are not retrieved from a numerical model but obtained via operational modal analysis (OMA) directly from operational strain data of the wind turbines. The operational modal analysis was performed on a combination of tower acceleration and substructure strain measurements using PolyMAX [16] technique. PolyMAX means poly-reference least squares frequency domain estimator for modal parameters and performs well in distinguishing physical modes from the numerical modes inherent to modal parameter estimation making it very suitable for automation. While a stationary FE-model returns a single set of mode shapes, results from operational data can change over time. Considering the short time period one set of mode shapes was calculated to fit all experienced environmental and operational conditons. Therefore, mode shapes were separately calculated for every 10 min data frame and averaged subsequently.
The dual-band approach of MDE uses a quasi-static pseudo mode shape instead of the dynamic modes for frequencies up to a frequency limit f_{lim}. This frequency was set to $0.15\ Hz$ because earlier analysis revealed considerable wave action between $0.15\ Hz$ and $0.25\ Hz$ [5]. The so-called static deflection shape is obtained from mean strain values of all strain sensors on TP and MP over a ten minute data frame.

4.2. Short-term subsoil strain estimation

Fig. 4 shows an example of the two staged stress estimation in MDE. First, the quasi-static stress is estimated by scaling the low-pass filtered stress of the top TP strain gauge $SGLAT017$ on the static deflection shape (also see Sec. 3.1.). The dynamic contribution based on tower acceleration measurements is added in a second step. Over four days stresses of 576 10 min data frames are predicted. In a first step TRAC values of the estimations are analyzed see Fig.6. Values worse 0.98 only occur at low wind speed i.e. below cut-in of the turbine. A closer look into time domain data Fig.5(a),(b),(c) shows generally good agreement between measurement and prediction. However, also three distinct error characteristics are visible: First, a phase lag between measurement and estimation occurs, especially pronounced on

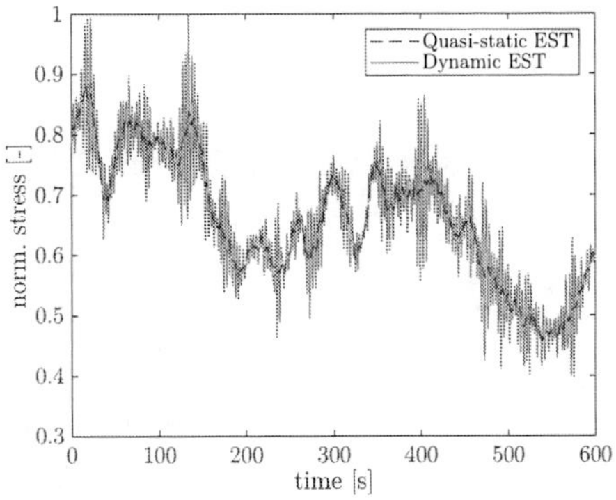

Figure 4: Estimation steps of MDE: Quasi-static(blue) and dynamic(orange) contribution.

lower sensors. Second, a small set of estimations contains a poor quasi-static fit, visible in FRAC values obtained for the quasi-static band Fig.6. Finally, estimated stress cycles often show a smaller amplitude than measured stresses. In these cases spectral plots show deviations in intensity of the natural frequencies, which is caused by imprecise mode shapes. Note, that these scaling effects in time domain data will not influence TRAC values, meaning the TRAC does not indicate this error characteristic. Additionally obtained FRAC values of solely the quasi-static frequency band show a high accuracy of the q-s prediction and only a small number of poor estimations in Fig.6 (b). Interestingly, MDE was able to reconstruct stresses which were not detected by the FBG. Fig.5(c) shows capabilities of MDE below the noise floor of the strain gauge. Since the method uses the modal coordinates of tower acceleration measurements, this phenomenon is explained by the better properties of accelerometers for high frequent vibrations.

4.3. Fatigue assessment

With the reconstructed time domain signal, fatigue assessment is done by obtaining damage equivalent stress ranges(DEL) of measurement and prediction. Fig.7(a) shows DELs of over all analyzed time frames. High DEL values are found in data frames with high wind speed thus an accurate prediction in these data frames is very important. However, as seen in Fig.7(b) precisely those data frames with high wind speed return highest relative errors on fatigue damage i.e. up to 60%. The error cause is easily determined because of the three error characteristics found in Sec.4.2. two only apply to low wind speed. Thus, the mainly underestimated spectral density of the two considered modes influences the fatigue estimates to deviate the most. MDE performs better for intermediate wind speeds between 4 and $9\ m/s$. Depending on sensor location the mean relative error on fatigue ranges from $-3\%(SGLAT005)$ to $-25\%(FBGLATmin33)$.

5. FUTURE WORK

This validation of a basic MDE scheme showed different challenges to work on. The phase lag found for locations below mud-line is likely to be caused by local damping. The used time-domain implementation of MDE is ad hoc not capable to learn damping since every time step is estimated independently. A frequency-domain implementation can help to solve this issue. Especially fatigue estimations showed offsets because of an erroneous spectral density at the first structural mode. The mode shapes in this contribution are defined as mean values of OMA estimations over all data frames. Even if these mode shapes offer the best fit over examined time in average that is not necessarily true for a single data frame. For a longer measurement period a definition of mode shapes dependent on environmental and operational condition is suggested. Finally, a bench marking of different response estimation methods is envisioned. Such a comparison should feature a sufficient time scale e.g. 6 months.

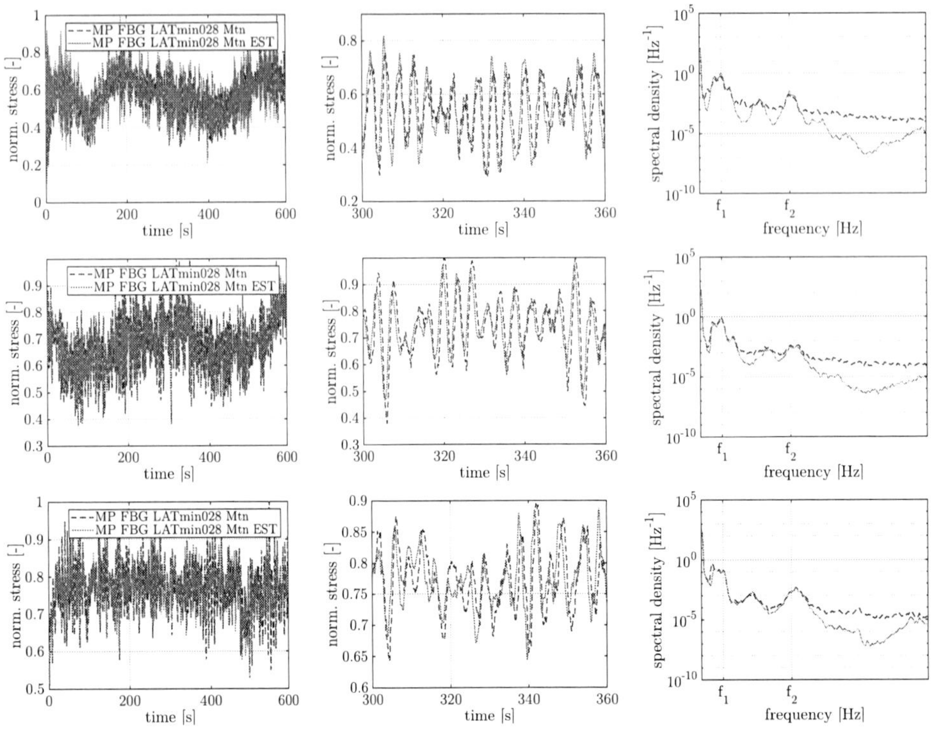

Figure 5: From left to right: Ten-minute time history, detail time history and power spectral density of measured (blue dashed) and predicted signal(orange) [Top: Data frame with 3.1 m/s wind speed, Middle:6.1 m/s Bottom: 12.0 m/s].

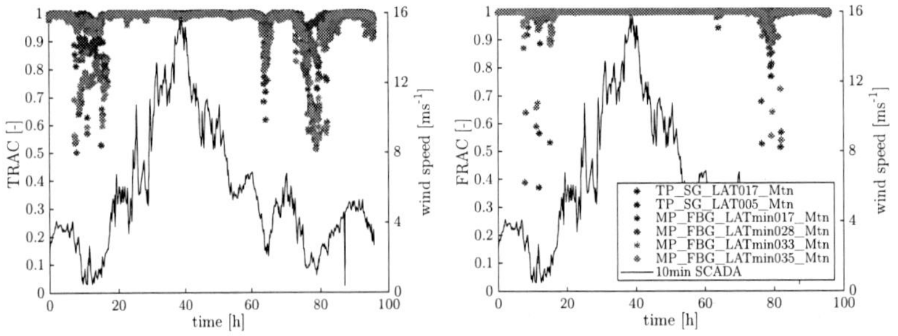

Figure 6: (Left) TRAC values for all data frames. (Right) FRAC values for quasi-static frequency band.

6. CONCLUSIONS

The dual-band scheme of modal decomposition and expansion technique showed capabilities to reconstruct stress time domain data with good accuracy especially for wind velocities between 4 and 9 m/s. TRAC calculations confirm proper fit between measurement and estimation for locations above and below mud-line. The additional used FRAC proves the high accuracy of the low frequent estimation. However, this short-term validation also showed different shortcomings when dealing with subsoil data. First, increased deviations of the reconstructed stress signal were found for wind speeds below cut-in. Partly an erroneous estimation of quasi-static stresses was causing this but mostly a phase lag was accountable for the poor result. This phase lag especially found on sensors sub soil is seen likely to be caused by the high local damping on this part of the structure. Fatigue calculations of the estimated stresses showed another shortcoming to be more severe. The spectral intensity of the first structural mode was underestimated especially for high wind speed causing stress cycle amplitudes to be down scaled. The resulting error on

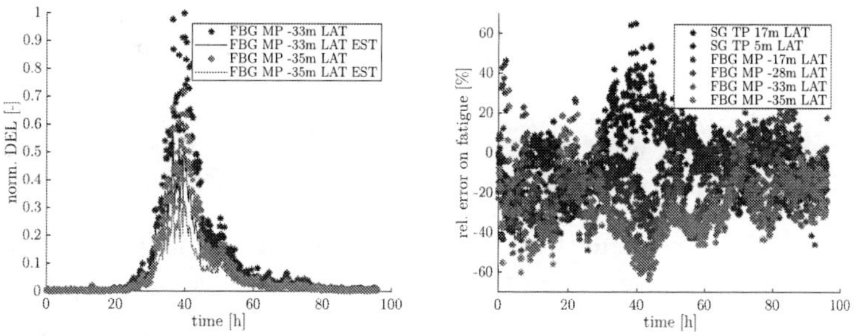

Figure 7: (Left) Damage equivalent load(DEL) of strain measurements and estimations. (Right) Relative error on DEL in strain estimation.

10 min. DEL values was in average 20 % but reached 60 % for single data frames. Overall this work could pinpoint challenges of the basic MDE scheme when dealing with subsoil data allowing to tune the method for this application.

ACKNOWLEDGEMENTS

The authors would like to thank the people at Nobelwind and Parkwind for their kind support during this project. O&O Nobelwind is a Flemish research project with support from VLAIO. Wout Weijtjens is a post-doctoral Fellow at the research foundation Flanders (FWO), their support is kindly acknowledged.

REFERENCES

[1] Ho, A., Mbistrova, A. (2017) The european offshore wind industry: key trends and statistics 2016 In: *https://windeurope.org/.*

[2] Cox, W., Reese, L., Grubbs, B. (1974) Field testing of laterally loaded piles in sand In: *Offshore Technology Conference.*

[3] Doherty, P., Gavin, K. (2011) Laterally loaded monopile design for offshore wind farms In: *Proceedings of the Institution of Civil Engineers - Energy*, 165, 7-17.

[4] Kallehave, D., Byrne, B., Thilsted, C., Mikkelsen, K. (2015) Optimization of monopiles for offshore wind turbines In: *Phil. Trans. R.Soc.A*, 373, 20140100.

[5] Henkel, M., Noppe, N., Weijtjens, W., Devriendt, C. (2018) Sub-soil strain measurements on an operational wind turbine for design validation and fatigue assessment In: *IOP Conf. Series: Journal of Physics*, 1037, 052032.

[6] Gillijns, S., De Moor, B. (2007) Unbiased minimum-variance input and state estimation for linear discrete-time systems with direct feedthrough In: *Automatica*, 43, 934-937.

[7] Lourens, E., Papadimitriou, C., Gillijns, S., Reynders, E., De Roeck, G., Lombaert, G. (2012) Joint input-response estimation for structural systems based on reduced-order models and vibration data from a limited number of sensors In: *Mechanical Systems and Signal Processing*, 29, 310-327.

[8] Iliopoulos, A., Weijtjens, W., Van Hemelrijck, D. and Devriendt, C. (2017) Fatigue assessment of offshore wind turbines on monopile foundations using virtual sensing. In: *Wind Energy*, 20, 1463-1479.

[9] Skafte, A., Tygesen, U., Brincker, R. (2014) Expansion of mode shapes and responses on the offshore platform valdemar In: *Dynamics of Civil Structures*, 4, 35-41.

[10] Hjelm, H., Brincker, R., Graugaard-Jensen, J., Munch, K. (2005) Determination of stress histories in structures by natural input modal analysis In: *Proceedings of IMAC XXIII.*

[11] Baqersad, J., Niezrecki, C., Avitabile, P. (2015) Extracting full-field dynamic strain on a wind turbine rotor subjected to arbitrary excitations using 3D point tracking and a modal expansion technique In: *Journal of Sound and Vibrationn*, 352, 16-29.

[12] Maes, K., Iliopoulos, A., Weijtjens, W., Devriendt, C., Lombaert, G. (2016) Dynamic strain estimation for fatigue assessment of an offshore monopile wind turbine using filtering and modal expansion algorithms In: *Mechanical Systems and Signal Processing*, 76-77, 592-611.

[13] Avitabile, P., Pingle, P. (2012) Prediction of full field dynamic strain from limited sets of measurement data In: *Shock and Vibration*, 19, 765-785.

[14] Berglind, J., Wisniewski, R. (2014) Fatigue estimation methods comparison for wind turbine control In: *arXiv*, 1411.3925.

[15] Det Norske Veritas AS (2015) RP-C203 Fatigue design of offshore steel structures.

[16] Peeters, B., Van der Auweraer, H. (2005) POLYMAX: a revolution in operational modal analysis In: *Proceedings of the 1st International Operational Modal Analysis Conference.*

INDEX OF AUTHORS

INDEX OF AUTHORS

L

M

N

O

P

R

S

T

U

V

W

Y

Z

iomac

International Operational
Modal Analysis Conference

DTU

Technical
University of
Denmark

DTU Civil Engineering
Department of Civil Engineering

IOMAC 2019

This conference is a review of recent theoretical and experimental research on Operational Modal Analysis, presented under the following topics:

- Applications in Civil Structures
- Damage Detection Under Changing Operational Conditions
- FEM Updating Using Operating Responses
- Identification Techniques & Related Topics
- Measurement Techniques & Virtual Sensing
- Rotating Machinery & OMA
- Special Applications
- Structural Health Monitoring
- Testing and Monitoring of Wind Turbines

IOMAC is the first conference on the subject of Operational Modal Analysis. The idea of IOMAC is to be the natural meeting place for everybody in the field - the scientist, the applicant, the vendor and the student, and also those who would like to get introduced to the field.

iomac

International Operational Modal Analysis Conference

DTU Technical University of Denmark

DTU Civil Engineering
Department of Civil Engineering